The
U.S. Intelligence
Community Law
Sourcebook

2019 Edition

116th U.S. Congress

A Compendium of National Security Related
Laws and Policy Documents

THE ABA STANDING COMMITTEE ON LAW AND NATIONAL SECURITY

THE
U.S. INTELLIGENCE
COMMUNITY LAW
SOURCEBOOK

2019 EDITION

116TH U.S. CONGRESS

A Compendium of National Security Related Laws and Policy Documents

ANDREW BORENE, ADAM PEARLMAN,
AND HARVEY RISHIKOF, EDITORS

WITH FOREWORD BY FORMER LEGAL ADVISER TO THE NATIONAL SECURITY COUNCIL, JUDGE JAMES E. BAKER, RET.

AMERICAN BAR ASSOCIATION
Defending Liberty
Pursuing Justice

Cover design by ABA Design

The materials contained herein represent the opinions and views of the authors and/or the editors, and should not be construed to be the views or opinions of the law firms or companies with whom such persons are in partnership with, associated with, or employed by, nor of the Standing Committee on Law and National Security or the American Bar Association, unless adopted pursuant to the bylaws of the Association.

Nothing contained in this book is to be considered as the rendering of legal advice for specific cases, and readers are responsible for obtaining such advice from their own legal counsel. This book and any forms and agreements herein are intended for educational and informational purposes only.

23 22 21 20 19   5 4 3 2 1

Cataloging-in-Publication Data is on file with the Library of Congress

ISBN: 978-1-64105-393-8

Discounts are available for books ordered in bulk. Special consideration is given to state bars, CLE programs, and other bar-related organizations. Inquire at Book Publishing, ABA Publishing, American Bar Association, 321 North Clark Street, Chicago, Illinois 60654.

www.ShopABA.org

U.S. Intelligence Community Law Sourcebook (7th Edition, Covering the 116th Congress) 2019–2020

A Compendium of National Security Related Laws and Policy Documents

Editors: Andrew Borene, Adam Pearlman, and Harvey Rishikof

TABLE OF CONTENTS

---

1. As reproduced on the House Legislative Counsel website, last visited Aug. 19, 2018.
2. *Id.*
3. *Id.*
4. *Id.*
5. *Id.*
6. The original, entire public law is reproduced in earlier editions of this Sourcebook. Because the provisions in Titles I-VI relate to the Foreign Intelligence Surveillance Act and are incorporated into that Act as reproduced earlier in this Sourcebook as amended and currently in-force, those titles are omitted here.
7. As reproduced on the Office of the Law Revision Counsel website, last visited Aug. 22, 2018.
8. As reproduced by the *ODNI Intelligence Community Legal Reference Book,* 2016.

---

9. For the entire Act, *see* the 2012 edition of *The U.S. Intelligence Community Law Sourcebook.*

10. As reproduced on the House Legislative Counsel website, last visited Aug. 19, 2018.

11. For full coverage of previous years' intelligence authorization acts, please refer to prior editions of *The U.S. Intelligence Community Law Sourcebook.*

12. As reproduced by the *ODNI Intelligence Community Legal Reference Book,* 2016.

13. *Id.*

14. *Id.*

DEDICATION

This publication is dedicated to all of our national security professionals, both civilians and those in uniform.

We work and rest more safely because you stand watch. Thank you for your service to our great Republic.

INTRODUCTION

National security related issues dominate the news in current times, and national security related law and policies are often key components of the discussion. The text of law and key policies provides a solid foundation for analysis, discussion, and understanding. My guiding tenet is "Know the Law, Find the Way." Whatever your role in the national security field—legal practitioner (government, corporate, private), judge, journalist, academia, legislator, or general public—this updated compendium of national security related laws and policy documents presents you with an excellent primary source to review the legal landscape.

This source book is unique in the national security related field and is prepared and sponsored by the American Bar Association Standing Committee on Law and National Security. Educating people on national security related legal topics—through speakers, podcasts, speakers, conferences, and publications—is a vital purpose of SCOLNS. Accordingly, members of this committee are experienced in the various aspects of national security law and lend their expertise to make this desktop reference thorough and current.

I am honored to be the new Chair of this standing committee, after recently retiring from federal government service where I practiced law for more than 30 years. Early in my career, I ventured into intelligence community activities and national security related law when this area of law was practiced by a few, not taught or available in any but a couple law schools, and case law was scant. It was excellent intelligence practitioners who guided and mentored me through the gray world, and who invited me to attend this committee's events. These events, particularly the annual conference on the review of national security law, were invaluable to building my knowledge and understanding in this field of law, as well as developing a network of expert practitioners. I wish this source book had been available 30 years ago! It would have made knowing the law and finding the way much easier and faster. May this book be useful to your practice and other endeavors in national security law and policy.

Cynthia R. Ryan
Chair, ABA Standing Committee on Law and National Security

ABOUT THE AMERICAN BAR ASSOCIATION'S STANDING COMMITTEE ON LAW AND NATIONAL SECURITY

The Standing Committee on Law and National Security is the oldest Committee in the ABA. Since 1962, the Committee has sustained an unwavering commitment to educating the Bar and the public on the importance of the rule of law in preserving the freedoms of democracy and our national security. Founded by then-ABA President and later Supreme Court Justice Lewis J. Powell, the Committee focuses on legal aspects of national security with particular attention to issues raised by legal responses to terrorist events. The Committee conducts studies, sponsors programs and administers working groups on law and national security-related issues to serve members and the profession. The Committee's website is www.americanbar.org/natsecurity. The Standing Committee is proud to include in its ranks, members who have served as Senators and Representatives, Director of Central Intelligence, Secretary of the Army, Deputy Secretary of Labor, ambassadors, legal advisers to the Department of State and National Security Council, general counsels to the Department of Defense, Central Intelligence Agency, National Security Agency, several military services, and key congressional committees; and a diverse range of prominent scholars from the nation's preeminent law schools.

The Standing Committee provides research and advice on a variety of subjects including: the restructuring of the intelligence community; cybersecurity; the legal system's ability to cope with transnational terrorism; economic threats, espionage, and organized crime in a borderless world; the role of the intelligence community in law enforcement; operational international law in the conduct of the military; and the role of law in preventing the proliferation of weapons of mass destruction.

From its inception, the Standing Committee has pursued its objectives through a diverse program of scholarship, conferences, workshops, and publications. One measure of the Committee's effectiveness is the rapid growth of national security law courses in recent years of the field it pioneered. Today, almost all of the nation's accredited law schools have one or more offerings in this field. The Committee also sponsors an Annual Review of National Security Law Conference each fall, a Student Writing Competition, Women in National Security programs, Teacher Training Workshops and several careers in national security law events held throughout the year.

The Standing Committee is a founding member of the ABA's Cybersecurity Legal Task Force. Please visit the ABA Cybersecurity Legal Task Force website— www.ambar.org/cyber—for details on the many ABA cyber initiatives.

ACKNOWLEDGMENTS

As the editors, we must give credit to many others for their time, assistance, and advice. As always, any value this sourcebook provides results from the input of an extended group of colleagues, friends, organizations, and willing experts who help us to varying degrees with feedback, criticism, and support. Many current and past members, advisors, and counselors associated with the ABA's Standing Committee on Law and National Security provided advice on shaping this and future editions.

Holly McMahon, the Staff Director of the ABA Standing Committee on Law & National Security, is the heart and soul of the committee and deserves special thanks – not only for this publication's seven editions, but for her contributions to the nation, the American legal community, and our extended committee family with her tireless efforts.

This year, a special thanks must go to the law firm of Fluet Huber + Hoang PLLC in Virginia, and especially to FH+H partner Francis Hoang (fhoang@fhhfirm.com) and Marlena Ewald (mewald@fhhfirm.com), a Senior Associate who provided excellent research support. Additional thanks is due to FH+H for their generous volunteer contributors to this project including resources, office space and especially their valuable time.

Credit must go to the organizational supporters of this work, the American Bar Association, the ABA's Standing Committee on Law & National Security, and ABA Publishing. As always, if any readers or reviewers have ideas for improvement in future editions, please do not hesitate to contact us through ABA Publishing or through the committee's website at www.americanbar.org/natsecurity.

Andrew Borene
Adam Pearlman
Harvey Rishikof

ABOUT THE EDITORS

Andrew M. Borene
Editor-in-Chief, U.S. Intelligence Community Law Sourcebook

Andrew Borene, JD, CISSP, is Director for the Homeland at George Mason University Law School's National Security Institute. Previously, he was a contractor Senior Advisor to the Intelligence Advanced Research Projects Activity (IARPA) within ODNI. He has been an Associate Deputy General Counsel at the Pentagon and served in the Middle East as a U.S. Marine Officer. He has senior executive experience at IBM and has led teams at Deloitte, Booz Allen Hamilton, LexisNexis, and Wells Fargo & Co. He has advised high-tech start-ups in robotics, analytics, special operations support and cybersecurity. Mr. Borene is a recipient of the FBI Director's Award for Exceptional Public Service and member of the Council on Foreign Relations. He holds a J.D. from the University of Minnesota, a B.A. in Economics from Macalester College, and completed executive education in international finance at Harvard University.

Adam Pearlman
Co-Editor, U.S. Intelligence Community Law Sourcebook

Adam R. Pearlman is a former Associate Deputy General Counsel of the United States Department of Defense. Mr. Pearlman previously held several positions in the U.S. Department of Justice, was a Law Clerk to the Honorable Royce C. Lamberth of the U.S. District Court for the District of Columbia, and during law school interned in the White House Counsel's Office under President George W. Bush. He is currently a Visiting Fellow at George Mason University's National Security Institute, and a National Security Fellow at the Foundation for Defense of Democracies. Mr. Pearlman earned his J.D., with honors, from The George Washington University Law School. He also holds a Master of Science of Strategic Intelligence from DIA's National Intelligence University.

Harvey Rishikof
Co-Editor, U.S. Intelligence Community Law Sourcebook

Harvey Rishikof is a visiting professor of law at Temple Law School for 2018-19. He is the former Director Military Commissions and Convening Authority at DoD, a former senior counsel at Crowell & Moring, and served as senior policy advisor to the Director of National Counterintelligence at the Office of the Director of National Intelligence. Mr. Rishikof was also legal counsel to the deputy director of the Federal Bureau of Investigation and Administrative Assistant to the Chief Justice of the Supreme Court. He was dean of faculty and a professor of law and national security studies at the National War College, and held a joint appointment at Drexel University in the law school and the iSchool, College of Information Science and Technology. Mr. Rishikof holds a J.D. from New York University School of Law, and an M.A. from Brandeis University.

I. Context and Commentary

Statement for the Record, Worldwide Threat Assessment of the U.S. Intelligence Community

By Daniel R. Coats, Director of National Intelligence

Senate Select Committee on Intelligence Washington D.C.

February 13, 2018

FOREWORD

Competition among countries will increase in the coming year as major powers and regional aggressors exploit complex global trends while adjusting to new priorities in US foreign policy. The risk of interstate conflict, including among great powers, is higher than at any time since the end of the Cold War. The most immediate threats of regional interstate conflict in the next year come from North Korea and from Saudi-Iranian use of proxies in their rivalry. At the same time, the threat of state and nonstate use of weapons of mass destruction will continue to grow.

- Adversaries and malign actors will use all instruments of national power—including information and cyber means—to shape societies and markets, international rules and institutions, and international hot spots to their advantage.

- China and Russia will seek spheres of influence and to check US appeal and influence in their regions. Meanwhile, US allies' and partners' uncertainty about the willingness and capability of the United States to maintain its international commitments may drive them to consider reorienting their policies, particularly regarding trade, away from Washington.

- Forces for geopolitical order and stability will continue to fray, as will the rules-based international order. New alignments and informal networks—outside traditional power blocs and national governments—will increasingly strain international cooperation.

Tension within many countries will rise, and the threat from Sunni violent extremist groups will evolve as they recoup after battlefield losses in the Middle East.

- Slow economic growth and technology-induced disruptions in job markets are fueling populism within advanced industrial countries and the very nationalism that contributes to tension among countries.

- Developing countries in Latin America and Sub-Saharan Africa face economic challenges, and many states struggle with reforms to tamp down corruption. Terrorists and criminal groups will continue to exploit weak state capacity in Africa, the Middle East, and Asia.

- Challenges from urbanization and migration will persist, while the effects of air pollution, inadequate water, and climate change on human health and livelihood will become more noticeable. Domestic policy responses to such issues will become more difficult—especially for democracies—as publics become less trusting of authoritative information sources.

GLOBAL THREATS

CYBER THREATS

The potential for surprise in the cyber realm will increase in the next year and beyond as billions more digital devices are connected—with relatively little built-in security—and both nation states and malign actors become more emboldened and better equipped in the use of increasingly widespread cyber toolkits.

The risk is growing that some adversaries will conduct cyber attacks—such as data deletion or localized and temporary disruptions of critical infrastructure—against the United States in a crisis short of war.

- In 2016 and 2017, state-sponsored cyber attacks against Ukraine and Saudi Arabia targeted multiple sectors across critical infrastructure, government, and commercial networks.

- Ransomware and malware attacks have spread globally, disrupting global shipping and production lines of US companies. The availability of criminal and commercial malware is creating opportunities for new actors to launch cyber operations.

- We assess that concerns about US retaliation and still developing adversary capabilities will mitigate the probability of attacks aimed at causing major disruptions of US critical infrastructure, but we remain concerned by the increasingly damaging effects of cyber operations and the apparent acceptance by adversaries of collateral damage.

Adversaries and Malign Actors Poised for Aggression

Russia, China, Iran, and North Korea will pose the greatest cyber threats to the United States during the next year.

These states are using cyber operations as a low-cost tool of statecraft, and we assess that they will work to use cyber operations to achieve strategic objectives unless they face clear repercussions for their cyber operations. Nonstate actors will continue to use cyber operations for financial crime and to enable propaganda and messaging.

- The use of cyber attacks as a foreign policy tool outside of military conflict has been mostly limited to sporadic lower-level attacks. Russia, Iran, and North Korea, however, are testing more aggressive cyber attacks that pose growing threats to the United States and US partners.

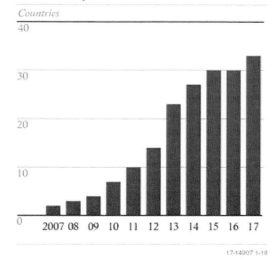

Countries With Cyber Attack Capabilities

Russia

We expect that Russia will conduct bolder and more disruptive cyber operations during the next year, most likely using new capabilities against Ukraine. The Russian Government is likely to build on the wide range of operations it is already conducting, including disruption of Ukrainian energy-distribution networks, hack-and-leak influence operations, distributed denial-of-service attacks, and false flag operations. In the next year, Russian intelligence and security services will continue to probe US and allied critical infrastructures, as well as target the United States, NATO, and allies for insights into US policy.

China

China will continue to use cyber espionage and bolster cyber attack capabilities to support national security priorities. The IC and private-sector security experts continue to identify ongoing cyber activity from China, although at volumes significantly lower than before the bilateral US-China cyber commitments of September 2015. Most detected Chinese cyber operations against US private industry are focused on cleared defense contractors or IT and communications firms whose products and services support government and private sector networks worldwide. China since 2015 has been advancing its cyber attack capabilities by integrating its military cyber attack and espionage resources in the Strategic Support Force, which it established in 2015.

Iran

We assess that Iran will continue working to penetrate US and Allied networks for espionage and to position itself for potential future cyber attacks, although its intelligence services primarily focus on Middle Eastern adversaries—especially Saudi Arabia and Israel. Tehran probably views cyberattacks as a versatile tool to respond to perceived provocations, despite Iran's recent restraint from conducting cyber attacks on the United States or Western allies. Iran's cyber attacks against Saudi Arabia in late 2016 and early 2017 involved data deletion on dozens of networks across government and the private sector.

North Korea
We expect the heavily sanctioned North Korea to use cyber operations to raise funds and to gather intelligence or launch attacks on South Korea and the United States. Pyongyang probably has a number of techniques and tools it can use to achieve a range of offensive effects with little or no warning, including distributed denial of service attacks, data deletion, and deployment of ransomware.

- North Korean actors developed and launched the WannaCry ransomware in May 2017, judging from technical links to previously identified North Korean cyber tools, tradecraft, and operational infrastructure. We also assess that these actors conducted the cyber theft of $81 million from the Bank of Bangladesh in 2016.

Terrorists and Criminals. Terrorist groups will continue to use the Internet to organize, recruit, spread propaganda, raise funds, collect intelligence, inspire action by followers, and coordinate operations. Given their current capabilities, cyber operations by terrorist groups mostly likely would result in personally identifiable information (PII) disclosures, website defacements, and denial-of-service attacks against poorly protected networks. Transnational criminals will continue to conduct for-profit cyber-enabled crimes, such as theft and extortion against US networks. We expect the line between criminal and nation-state activity to become increasingly blurred as states view cyber criminal tools as a relatively inexpensive and deniable means to enable their operations.

WEAPONS OF MASS DESTRUCTION AND PROLIFERATION

State efforts to modernize, develop, or acquire weapons of mass destruction (WMD), their delivery systems, or their underlying technologies constitute a major threat to the security of the United States, its deployed troops, and its allies. Both state and nonstate actors have already demonstrated the use of chemical weapons in Iraq and Syria. Biological and chemical materials and technologies—almost always dual-use—move easily in the globalized economy, as do personnel with the scientific expertise to design and use them for legitimate and illegitimate purposes. Information about the latest discoveries in the life sciences also diffuses rapidly around the globe, widening the accessibility of knowledge and tools for beneficial purposes and for potentially nefarious applications.

Russia
Russia has developed a ground-launched cruise missile (GLCM) that the United States has declared is in violation of the Intermediate-Range Nuclear Forces (INF) Treaty. Despite Russia's ongoing development of other Treaty-compliant missiles with intermediate ranges, Moscow probably believes that the new GLCM provides sufficient military advantages to make it worth risking the political reper-

cussions of violating the INF Treaty. In 2013, a senior Russian administration official stated publicly that the world had changed since the INF Treaty was signed in 1987. Other Russian officials have made statements complaining that the Treaty prohibits Russia, but not some of its neighbors, from developing and possessing ground-launched missiles with ranges between 500 and 5,500 kilometers.

China

The Chinese People's Liberation Army (PLA) continues to modernize its nuclear missile force by adding more survivable road-mobile systems and enhancing its silo-based systems. This new generation of missiles is intended to ensure the viability of China's strategic deterrent by providing a second-strike capability. China also has tested a hypersonic glide vehicle. In addition, the PLA Navy continues to develop the JL-2 submarine-launched ballistic missile (SLBM) and might produce additional JIN-class nuclear-powered ballistic missile submarines. The JIN-class submarines— armed with JL-2 SLBMs—give the PLA Navy its first long-range, sea-based nuclear capability. The Chinese have also publicized their intent to form a triad by developing a nuclear-capable next-generation bomber.

Iran and the Joint Comprehensive Plan of Action

Tehran's public statements suggest that it wants to preserve the Joint Comprehensive Plan of Action because it views the JCPOA as a means to remove sanctions while preserving some nuclear capabilities. Iran recognizes that the US Administration has concerns about the deal but expects the other participants—China, the EU, France, Germany, Russia, and the United Kingdom—to honor their commitments. Iran's implementation of the JCPOA has extended the amount of time Iran would need to produce enough fissile material for a nuclear weapon from a few months to about one year, provided Iran continues to adhere to the deal's major provisions. The JCPOA has also enhanced the transparency of Iran's nuclear activities, mainly by fostering improved access to Iranian nuclear facilities for the IAEA and its investigative authorities under the Additional Protocol to its Comprehensive Safeguards Agreement.

Iran's ballistic missile programs give it the potential to hold targets at risk across the region, and Tehran already has the largest inventory of ballistic missiles in the Middle East. Tehran's desire to deter the United States might drive it to field an ICBM. Progress on Iran's space program, such as the launch of the Simorgh SLV in July 2017, could shorten a pathway to an ICBM because space launch vehicles use similar technologies.

North Korea

North Korea will be among the most volatile and confrontational WMD threats to the United States over the next year. North Korea's history of exporting ballistic missile technology to several countries, including Iran and Syria, and its assistance during Syria's construction of a nuclear reactor— destroyed in 2007—illustrate its willingness to proliferate dangerous technologies.

In 2017 North Korea, for the second straight year, conducted a large number of ballistic missile tests, including its first ICBM tests. Pyongyang is committed to developing a long-range, nuclear-armed missile that is capable of posing a direct threat to the United States. It also conducted its sixth and highest yield nuclear test to date.

We assess that North Korea has a longstanding BW capability and biotechnology infrastructure that could support a BW program. We also assess that North Korea has a CW program and probably could employ these agents by modifying conventional munitions or with unconventional, targeted methods.

Pakistan
Pakistan continues to produce nuclear weapons and develop new types of nuclear weapons, including short-range tactical weapons, sea-based cruise missiles, air-launched cruise missiles, and longer-range ballistic missiles. These new types of nuclear weapons will introduce new risks for escalation dynamics and security in the region.

Syria
We assess that the Syrian regime used the nerve agent sarin in an attack against the opposition in Khan Shaykhun on 4 April 2017, in what is probably the largest chemical weapons attack since August 2013. We continue to assess that Syria has not declared all the elements of its chemical weapons program to the Chemical Weapons Convention (CWC) and that it has the capability to conduct further attacks. Despite the creation of a specialized team and years of work by the Organization for the Prohibition of Chemical Weapons (OPCW) to address gaps and inconsistencies in Syria's declaration, numerous issues remain unresolved. The OPCW-UN Joint Investigative Mechanism (JIM) has attributed the 4 April 2017 sarin attack and three chlorine attacks in 2014 and 2015 to the Syrian regime. Even after the attack on Khan Shaykhun, we have continued to observe allegations that the regime has used chemicals against the opposition.

ISIS
We assess that ISIS is also using chemicals as a means of warfare. The OPCW-UN JIM concluded that ISIS used sulfur mustard in two attacks in 2015 and 2016, and we assess that it has used chemical weapons in numerous other attacks in Iraq and Syria.

TERRORISM

Sunni violent extremists—most notably ISIS and al-Qa'ida—pose continuing terrorist threats to US interests and partners worldwide, while US-based homegrown violent extremists (HVEs) will remain the most prevalent Sunni violent extremist threat in the United States. Iran and its strategic partner Lebanese Hizballah also pose a persistent threat to the United States and its partners worldwide.

Sunni Violent Extremism
Sunni violent extremists are still intent on attacking the US homeland and US interests overseas, but their attacks will be most frequent in or near conflict zones or against enemies that are more easily accessible.

- Sunni violent extremist groups are geographically diverse; they are likely to exploit conflict zones in the Middle East, Africa, and Asia, where they can co-mingle terrorism and insurgency.

- ISIS and al-Qa'ida and their respective networks will be persistent threats, as will groups not subordinate to them, such as the Haqqani Taliban Network.

Sunni Violent Extremists' Primary Operating Areas as of 2017

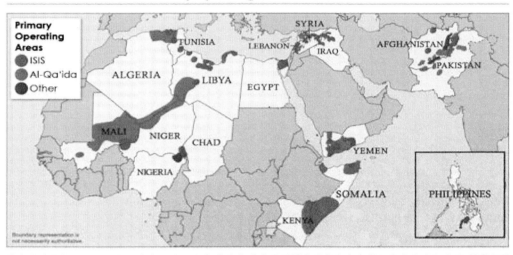

17-15890 12-17

ISIS

Over the next year, we expect that ISIS is likely to focus on regrouping in Iraq and Syria, enhancing its global presence, championing its cause, planning international attacks, and encouraging its members and sympathizers to attack in their home countries. ISIS's claim of having a functioning caliphate that governs populations is all but thwarted.

- ISIS core has started—and probably will maintain—a robust insurgency in Iraq and Syria as part of a long-term strategy to ultimately enable the reemergence of its so-called caliphate. This activity will challenge local CT efforts against the group and threaten US interests in the region.

- ISIS almost certainly will continue to give priority to transnational terrorist attacks. Its leadership probably assesses that, if ISIS-linked attacks continue to dominate public discourse, the group's narrative will be buoyed, it will be difficult for the counter-ISIS coalition to portray the group as defeated, and the coalition's will to fight will ultimately weaken.

- Outside Iraq and Syria, ISIS's goal of fostering interconnectivity and resiliency among its global branches and networks probably will result in local and, in some cases, regional attack plans.

Al-Qa'ida

Al-Qa'ida almost certainly will remain a major actor in global terrorism because of the combined staying power of its five affiliates. The primary threat to US and Western interests from al-Qa'ida's global network through 2018 will be in or near affiliates' operating areas. Not all affiliates will have the intent and capability to pursue or inspire attacks in the US homeland or elsewhere in the West.

- Al-Qa'ida's affiliates probably will continue to dedicate most of their resources to local activity, including participating in ongoing conflicts in Afghanistan, Somalia, Syria, and Yemen, as well as attacking regional actors and populations in other parts of Africa, Asia, and the Middle East.

- Al-Qa'ida leaders and affiliate media platforms almost certainly will call for followers to carry out attacks in the West, but their appeals probably will not create a spike in inspired attacks. The group's messaging since at least 2010 has produced few such attacks.

Homegrown Violent Extremists

Homegrown violent extremists (HVEs) will remain the most prevalent and difficult-to-detect Sunni terrorist threat at home, despite a drop in the number of attacks in 2017. HVE attacks are likely to continue to occur with little or no warning because the perpetrators often strike soft targets and use simple tactics that do not require advanced skills or outside training.

- HVEs almost certainly will continue to be inspired by a variety of sources, including terrorist propaganda as well as in response to perceived grievances related to US Government actions.

Iran and Lebanese Hizballah

Iran remains the most prominent state sponsor of terrorism, providing financial aid, advanced weapons and tactics, and direction to militant and terrorist groups across the Middle East and cultivating a network of operatives across the globe as a contingency to enable potential terrorist attacks.

Lebanese Hizballah has demonstrated its intent to foment regional instability by deploying thousands of fighters to Syria and by providing weapons, tactics, and direction to militant and terrorist groups. Hizballah probably also emphasizes its capability to attack US, Israeli, and Saudi Arabian interests.

COUNTERINTELLIGENCE AND FOREIGN DENIAL AND DECEPTION

The United States will face a complex global foreign intelligence threat environment in 2018. We assess that the leading state intelligence threats to US interests will continue to be Russia and China, based on their services' capabilities, intent, and broad operational scope. Other states in the Near East, South Asia, East Asia, and Latin America will pose local and regional intelligence threats to US interests. For example, Iranian and Cuban intelligence and security services continue to view the United States as a primary threat.

Penetrating the US national decisionmaking apparatus and the Intelligence Community will remain primary objectives for numerous foreign intelligence entities. Additionally, the targeting of national security information and proprietary information from US companies and research institutions involved with defense, energy, finance, dual-use technology, and other areas will remain a persistent threat to US interests.

Nonstate entities, including international terrorists and transnational organized crime groups, are likely to continue to employ and improve their intelligence capabilities, including human, technical, and cyber means. As with state intelligence services, these nonstate entities recruit sources and perform physical and technical surveillance to facilitate their illicit activities and to avoid detection and capture.

Trusted insiders who disclose sensitive or classified US Government information without authorization will remain a significant threat in 2018 and beyond. The sophistication and availability of information technology that increases the scope and impact of unauthorized disclosures exacerbate this threat.

Russia and Influence Campaigns

Influence operations, especially through cyber means, will remain a significant threat to US interests as they are low-cost, relatively low-risk, and deniable ways to retaliate against adversaries, to shape foreign perceptions, and to influence populations. Russia probably will be the most capable and aggressive source of this threat in 2018, although many countries and some nonstate actors are exploring ways to use influence operations, both domestically and abroad.

We assess that the Russian intelligence services will continue their efforts to disseminate false information via Russian state-controlled media and covert online personas about US activities to encourage anti-US political views. Moscow seeks to create wedges that reduce trust and confidence in democratic processes, degrade democratization efforts, weaken US partnerships with European allies, undermine Western sanctions, encourage anti-US political views, and counter efforts to bring Ukraine and other former Soviet states into European institutions.

- Foreign elections are critical inflection points that offer opportunities for Russia to advance its interests both overtly and covertly. The 2018 US mid-term elections are a potential target for Russian influence operations.

- At a minimum, we expect Russia to continue using propaganda, social media, false-flag personas, sympathetic spokespeople, and other means of influence to try to exacerbate social and political fissures in the United States.

EMERGING AND DISRUPTIVE TECHNOLOGY

New technologies and novel applications of existing technologies have the potential to disrupt labor markets and alter health, energy, and transportation systems.

We assess that technology developments—in the biotechnology and communications sectors, for example—are likely to outpace regulation, which could create international norms that are contrary to US interests and increase the likelihood of technology surprise. Emerging technology and new applications of existing technology will also allow our adversaries to more readily develop weapon systems that can strike farther, faster, and harder and challenge the United States in all warfare domains, including space.

- The widespread proliferation of artificial intelligence (AI)—the field of computer science encompassing systems that seek to imitate aspects of human cognition by learning and making decisions based on accumulated knowledge—is likely to prompt new national security concerns; existing machine learning technology, for example, could enable high degrees of automation in labor-intensive activities such as satellite imagery analysis and cyber defense. Increasingly capable AI tools, which are often enabled by large amounts of data, are also likely to present socioeconomic challenges, including impacts on employment and privacy.

- New biotechnologies are leading to improvements in agriculture, health care, and manufacturing. However, some applications of biotechnologies may lead to unintentional negative health effects, biological accidents, or deliberate misuse.

- The global shift to advanced information and communications technologies (ICT) will increasingly test US competitiveness because aspiring suppliers around the world will play a larger role in developing new technologies and products. These technologies include next-generation, or 5G, wireless technology; the internet of things; new financial technologies; and enabling AI and big data for predictive analysis. Differences in regulatory and policy approaches to ICT-related issues could impede growth and innovation globally and for US companies.

- Advanced materials could disrupt the economies of some commodities-dependent exporting countries while providing a competitive edge to developed and developing countries that create the capacity to produce and use the new materials. New materials, such as nanomaterials, are often developed faster than their health and environmental effects can be assessed. Advances in manufacturing, particularly the development of 3D printing, almost certainly will become even more accessible to a variety of state and nonstate actors and be used in ways contrary to our interests.

TECHNOLOGY ACQUISITIONS AND STRATEGIC ECONOMIC COMPETITION

Persistent trade imbalances, trade barriers, and a lack of market-friendly policies in some countries probably will continue to challenge US economic security. Some countries almost certainly will continue to acquire US intellectual property and propriety information illicitly to advance their own economic and national security objectives.

- China, for example, has acquired proprietary technology and early-stage ideas through cyber-enabled means. At the same time, some actors use largely legitimate, legal transfers and relationships to gain access to research fields, experts, and key enabling industrial processes that could, over time, erode America's long-term competitive advantages.

SPACE AND COUNTERSPACE

Continued global space industry expansion will further extend space-enabled capabilities and space situational awareness to nation-state, nonstate, and commercial space actors in the coming years, enabled by the increased availability of technology, private-sector investment, and growing international partnerships for shared production and operation. All actors will increasingly have access to space-derived information services, such as imagery, weather, communications, and positioning, navigation, and timing for intelligence, military, scientific, or business purposes. Foreign countries—particularly China and Russia—will continue to expand their space-based reconnaissance, communications, and navigation systems in terms of the numbers of satellites, the breadth of their capability, and the applications for use.

Both Russia and China continue to pursue antisatellite (ASAT) weapons as a means to reduce US and allied military effectiveness. Russia and China aim to have nondestructive and destructive counterspace weapons available for use during a potential future conflict. We assess that, if a future conflict were to occur involving Russia or China, either country would justify attacks against US and allied satellites as necessary to offset any perceived US military advantage derived from military, civil, or commercial space systems. Military reforms in both countries in the past few years indicate an increased focus on establishing operational forces designed to integrate attacks against space systems and services with military operations in other domains.

Russian and Chinese destructive ASAT weapons probably will reach initial operational capability in the next few years. China's PLA has formed military units and begun initial operational training with counterspace capabilities that it has been developing, such as ground-launched ASAT missiles. Russia probably has a similar class of system in development. Both countries are also advancing directed-energy weapons technologies for the purpose of fielding ASAT weapons that could blind or damage sensitive space-based optical sensors, such as those used for remote sensing or missile defense.

Of particular concern, Russia and China continue to launch "experimental" satellites that conduct sophisticated on-orbit activities, at least some of which are intended to advance counterspace capabilities. Some technologies with peaceful applications—such as satellite inspection, refueling, and repair—can also be used against adversary spacecraft.

Russia and China continue to publicly and diplomatically promote international agreements on the nonweaponization of space and "no first placement" of weapons in space. However, many classes of weapons would not be addressed by such proposals, allowing them to continue their pursuit of space warfare capabilities while publicly maintaining that space must be a peaceful domain.

TRANSNATIONAL ORGANIZED CRIME

Transnational organized criminal groups and networks will pose serious and growing threats to the security and health of US citizens, as well as to global human rights, ecological integrity, government revenues, and efforts to deal with adversaries and terrorists. In the most severe cases abroad, criminal enterprises will contribute to increased social violence, erode governments' authorities, undermine the integrity of international financial systems, and harm critical infrastructure.

Drug Trafficking

Transnational organized criminal groups supply the dominant share of illicit drugs consumed in the United States, fueling high mortality rates among US citizens.

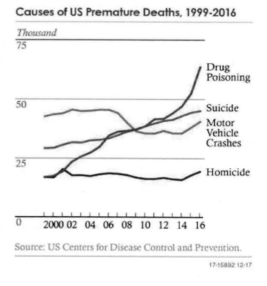

Causes of US Premature Deaths, 1999-2016

Source: US Centers for Disease Control and Prevention.

17-15892 12-17

- Americans in 2016 died in record numbers from drug overdoses, 21 percent more than in 2015.

- Worldwide production of cocaine, heroin, and methamphetamine is at record levels. US mortality from potent synthetic opioids doubled in 2016, and synthetic opioids have become a key cause of US drug deaths.

- Mexican criminal groups will continue to supply much of the heroin, methamphetamine, cocaine, and marijuana that cross the US-Mexico border, while China-based suppliers ship fentanyls and fentanyl precursors to Mexico-, Canada-, and US-based distributors or sell directly to consumers via the Internet.

Broader Threats from Transnational Crime

Transnational organized criminal groups, in addition to engaging in violence, will continue to traffic in human beings, deplete natural resources, and siphon money from governments and the global economy.

- Human trafficking will continue in virtually every country. International organizations estimate that about 25 million people are victims.

- The FBI assesses that US losses from cybercrime in 2016 exceeded $1.3 billion, and some industry experts predict such losses could cost the global economy $6 trillion by 2021.

- Criminal wildlife poaching, illegal fishing, illicit mining, and drug-crop production will continue to threaten economies, biodiversity, food supply security, and human health. For example, academic studies show that illicit mining alone adds some 650 to 1,000 tons of toxic mercury to the ecosystem each year.

- Transnational organized criminal groups probably will generate more revenue from illicit activity in the coming year, which the UN last estimated at $1.6-$2.2 trillion for 2014.

ECONOMICS AND ENERGY

Global growth in 2018—projected by the IMF to rise to 3.9 percent—is likely to become more broadly based, but growth remains weak in many countries, and inflation is below target in most advanced economies. The relatively favorable outlook for real economic growth suggests little near-term risk of unfavorable deficit-debt dynamics among the advanced economies. Supportive financial conditions and improving business sentiment will help to drive economic activity in advanced countries. China's growth may decelerate as the

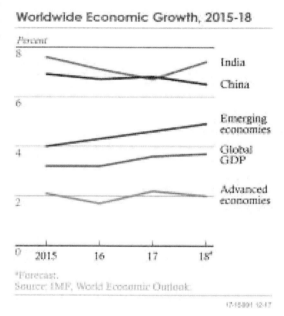

Worldwide Economic Growth, 2015-18

*Forecast.
Source: IMF, World Economic Outlook.

property sector cools and if Beijing accelerates economic reforms. India's economy is expected to rebound after headwinds from taxation changes and demonetization, and the continuing upswing in emerging and developing economies could be tempered by capital outflows from a stronger dollar and monetary policy normalization in the United States and Europe.

Oil-exporting countries continue to suffer from the late-2014 oil price drop, and their economic woes are likely to continue, with broader negative implications.

Subdued economic growth, combined with sharp increases in North American oil and gas production, probably will continue putting downward pressure on global energy prices, harming oil-exporting economies. The US Energy Information Administration forecasts that 2018 West Texas Intermediate and Brent prices will average $58 and $62 per barrel, respectively, far below the average annual prices of $98 and $109 in 2013.

- Low oil prices and production declines—along with poor economic policies—have pushed Venezuela and the state-owned oil company, Petroleos de Venezuela, to miss debt payments, putting them in selective default.

- Saudi Arabia and other Persian Gulf oil exporters have experienced sharp increases in budget deficits, forcing governments to issue debt and enact politically unpopular fiscal reforms, such as cuts to subsidies, social programs, and government jobs.

- In Africa, declining oil revenue, mismanagement, and inadequate policy responses to oil price shocks have contributed to Angolan and Nigerian fiscal problems, currency strains, and deteriorating foreign exchange reserves.

- OPEC member countries and select non-OPEC producers, including Russia, in early 2017 committed to cut oil production in order to lift prices, with compliance likely to be offset somewhat as Libya or Nigeria—both are exempt from the deal—are able to resume production.

HUMAN SECURITY

Governance shortfalls, violent conflict, environmental stresses, and increased potential for a global health crisis will create significant risks to human security, including high levels of human displacement and migration flows.

Governance and Political Turbulence

Domestic and foreign challenges to democracy and institutional capacity will test governance quality globally in 2018, especially as competitors manipulate social media to shape opinion. Freedom House reported the 11th consecutive year of decline in "global freedom" in 2017, and nearly one-quarter of the countries registering declines were in Europe.

- While the number of democracies has remained steady for the past decade, some scholars suggest the quality of democracy has declined.

- We note that more governments are using propaganda and misinformation in social media to influence foreign and domestic audiences.

- The number and sophistication of government efforts to shape domestic views of politics have increased dramatically in the past 10 years. In 2016, Freedom House identified 30 countries, including the Philippines, Turkey, and Venezuela, whose governments used social media to spread government views, to drive agendas, and to counter criticism of the government online.

Poor governance, weak national political institutions, economic inequality, and the rise of violent nonstate actors all undermine states' abilities to project authority and elevate the risk of violent—even regime-threatening—instability and mass atrocities.

Environment and Climate Change

The impacts of the long-term trends toward a warming climate, more air pollution, biodiversity loss, and water scarcity are likely to fuel economic and social discontent—and possibly upheaval—through 2018.

- The past 115 years have been the warmest period in the history of modern civilization, and the past few years have been the warmest years on record. Extreme weather events in a warmer world have the potential for greater impacts and can compound with other drivers to raise the risk of humanitarian disasters, conflict, water and food shortages, population migration, labor shortfalls, price shocks, and power outages. Research has not identified indicators of tipping points in climate-linked earth systems, suggesting a possibility of abrupt climate change.

- Worsening air pollution from forest burning, agricultural waste incineration, urbanization, and rapid industrialization—with increasing public awareness—might drive protests against authorities, such as those recently in China, India, and Iran.

- Accelerating biodiversity and species loss—driven by pollution, warming, unsustainable fishing, and acidifying oceans—will jeopardize vital ecosystems that support critical human systems. Recent estimates suggest that the current extinction rate is 100 to 1,000 times the natural extinction rate.

- Water scarcity, compounded by gaps in cooperative management agreements for nearly half of the world's international river basins, and new unilateral dam development are likely to heighten tension between countries.

Human Displacement

Global displacement almost certainly will remain near record highs during the next year, raising the risk of disease outbreaks, recruitment by armed groups, political upheaval, and reduced economic productivity.

Conflicts will keep many of the world's refugees and internally displaced persons from returning home.

Health

The increase in frequency and diversity of reported disease outbreaks—such as dengue and Zika—probably will continue through 2018, including the potential for a severe global health emergency that could lead to major economic and societal disruptions, strain governmental and international resources, and increase calls on the United States for support. A novel strain of a virulent microbe that is easily transmissible between humans continues to be a major threat, with pathogens such as H5N1 and H7N9 influenza and Middle East Respiratory Syndrome Coronavirus having pandemic potential if they were to acquire efficient human-to-human transmissibility.

- The frequency and diversity of disease outbreaks have increased at a steady rate since 1980, probably fueled by population growth, travel and trade patterns, and rapid urbanization. Ongoing global epidemics of HIV/AIDS, malaria, and tuberculosis continue to kill millions of people annually.

- Increasing antimicrobial resistance, the ability of pathogens—including viruses, fungi, and bacteria—to resist drug treatment, is likely to outpace the development of new antimicrobial drugs, leading to infections that are no longer treatable.

- The areas affected by vector-borne diseases, including dengue, are likely to expand, especially as changes in climatological patterns increase the reach of the mosquito.

- The World Bank has estimated that a severe global influenza pandemic could cost the equivalent of 4.8 percent of global GDP—more than $3 trillion—and cause more than 100 million deaths.

REGIONAL THREATS

EAST ASIA

China
China will continue to pursue an active foreign policy—especially in the Asia Pacific region—highlighted by a firm stance on its sovereignty claims in the East China Sea (ECS) and South China Sea (SCS), its relations with Taiwan, and its pursuit of economic engagement across the region. Regional tension will persist due to North Korea's nuclear and missile programs and simmering tension over territorial and maritime disputes in the ECS and SCS. China will also pursue efforts aimed at fulfilling its ambitious Belt and Road Initiative to expand China's economic reach and political influence across Eurasia, Africa, and the Pacific through infrastructure projects.

North Korea
North Korea's weapons of mass destruction program, public threats, defiance of the international community, confrontational military posturing, cyber activities,

and potential for internal instability pose a complex and increasing threat to US national security and interests.

In the wake of accelerated missile testing since 2016, North Korea is likely to press ahead with more tests in 2018, and its Foreign Minister said that Kim may be considering conducting an atmospheric nuclear test over the Pacific Ocean. Pyongyang's commitment to possessing nuclear weapons and fielding capable long-range missiles, all while repeatedly stating that nuclear weapons are the basis for its survival, suggests that the regime does not intend to negotiate them away.

Ongoing, modest improvements to North Korea's conventional capabilities continue to pose a serious and growing threat to South Korea and Japan. Despite the North Korean military's many internal challenges and shortcomings, Kim Jong Un continues to expand the regime's conventional strike options with more realistic training, artillery upgrades, and close-range ballistic missiles that improve North Korea's ability to strike regional US and allied targets with little warning.

Southeast Asia
Democracy and human rights in many Southeast Asian countries will remain fragile in 2018 as autocratic tendencies deepen in some regimes and rampant corruption and cronyism undermine democratic values.

Countries in the region will struggle to preserve foreign policy autonomy in the face of Chinese economic and diplomatic coercion.

- Cambodian leader Hun Sen will repress democratic institutions and civil society, manipulate government and judicial institutions, and use patronage and political violence to guarantee his rule beyond the 2018 national election. Having alienated Western partners, Hun Sen will rely on Beijing's political and financial support, drawing Cambodia closer to China as a result.

- The crisis resulting from the exodus of more than 600,000 Rohingyas from Burma to Bangladesh will threaten Burma's fledgling democracy, increase the risk of violent extremism, and provide openings for Beijing to expand its influence.

- *In the Philippines, President Duterte will continue to wage his signature campaign against drugs, corruption, and crime.* Duterte has suggested he could suspend the Constitution, declare a "revolutionary government," and impose nationwide martial law. His declaration of martial law in Mindanao, responding to the ISIS-inspired siege of Marawi City, has been extended through the end of 2018.

- *Thailand's leaders have pledged to hold elections in late 2018, but the new Constitution will institutionalize the military's influence.*

MIDDLE EAST AND NORTH AFRICA

Iran

Iran will seek to expand its influence in Iraq, Syria, and Yemen, where it sees conflicts generally trending in Tehran's favor, and it will exploit the fight against ISIS to solidify partnerships and translate its battlefield gains into political, security, and economic agreements.

- Iran's support for the Popular Mobilization Committee (PMC) and Shia militants remains the primary threat to US personnel in Iraq. We assess that this threat will increase as the threat from ISIS recedes, especially given calls from some Iranian-backed groups for the United States to withdraw and growing tension between Iran and the United States.

- In Syria, Iran is working to consolidate its influence while trying to prevent US forces from gaining a foothold. Iranian-backed forces are seizing routes and border crossings to secure the Iraq-Syria border and deploying proregime elements and Iraqi allies to the area. Iran's retaliatory missile strikes on ISIS targets in Syria following ISIS attacks in Tehran in June were probably intended in part to send a message to the United States and its allies about Iran's improving military capabilities. Iran is pursuing permanent military bases in Syria and probably wants to maintain a network of Shia foreign fighters in Syria to counter future threats to Iran. Iran also seeks economic deals with Damascus, including deals on telecommunications, mining, and electric power repairs.

- In Yemen, Iran's support to the Huthis further escalates the conflict and poses a serious threat to US partners and interests in the region. Iran continues to provide support that enables Huthi attacks against shipping near the Bab al Mandeb Strait and land-based targets deep inside Saudi Arabia and the UAE, such as the 4 November and 19 December ballistic missile attacks on Riyadh and an attempted 3 December cruise missile attack on an unfinished nuclear reactor in Abu Dhabi.

Iran will develop military capabilities that threaten US forces and US allies in the region, and its unsafe and unprofessional interactions will pose a risk to US Navy operations in the Persian Gulf.

Iran continues to develop and improve a range of new military capabilities to target US and allied military assets in the region, including armed UAVs, ballistic missiles, advanced naval mines, unmanned explosive boats, submarines and advanced torpedoes, and antishipand land-attack cruise missiles. Iran has the largest ballistic missile force in the Middle East and can strike targets up to 2,000 kilometers from Iran's borders. Russia's delivery of the SA-20c SAM system in 2016 has provided Iran with its most advanced long-range air defense system.

- Islamic Revolutionary Guard Corps (IRGC) Navy forces operating aggressively in the Persian Gulf and Strait of Hormuz pose a risk to the US Navy. Most IRGC interactions with US ships are professional, but as of mid-October, the Navy had recorded 14 instances of what it describes as "unsafe and/or unprofessional" interactions with Iranian forces during 2017, the most recent interaction occurring last August, when an unarmed Iranian drone flew close to the aircraft carrier USS Nimitz as fighter jets landed at night. The Navy recorded 36 such incidents in 2016 and 22 in 2015. Most involved the IRGC Navy. We assess that these interactions, although less frequent, will continue and that they are probably intended to project an image of strength and, possibly, to gauge US responses.

Iranian centrist and hardline politicians increasingly will clash as they attempt to implement competing visions for Iran's future. This contest will be a key driver in determining whether Iran changes its behavior in ways favorable to US interests.

- Centrists led by President Hasan Ruhani will continue to advocate greater social progress, privatization, and more global integration, while hardliners will view this agenda as a threat to their political and economic interests and to Iran's revolutionary and Islamic character.

- Supreme Leader Ali Khamenei's views are closer to those of the hardliners, but he has supported some of Ruhani's efforts to engage Western countries and to promote economic growth. The Iranian economy's prospects—still driven heavily by petroleum revenue—will depend on reforms to attract investment, strengthen privatization, and grow nonoil industries, which Ruhani will continue pursuing, much to the dismay of hardliners. National protests over economic grievances in Iran earlier this year have drawn more attention to the need for major reforms, but Ruhani and his critics are likely to use the protests to advance their political agendas.

- Khamenei has experienced health problems in the past few years, and, in an effort to preserve his legacy, he probably opposes moving Iran toward greater political and economic openness. As their relationship has deteriorated since the presidential election last June, Ruhani has tried to mend relations with Khamenei as well as his allies, but, in doing so, he risks failing to make progress on reforms in the near-term.

Syria

The conflict has decisively shifted in the Syrian regime's favor, enabling Russia and Iran to further entrench themselves inside the country. Syria is likely to experience episodic conflict through 2018, even as Damascus recaptures most of the urban terrain and the overall level of violence decreases.

- *The Syrian opposition's seven-year insurgency is probably no longer capable of overthrowing President Bashar al-Asad or overcoming a growing military disadvantage.* Rebels probably retain the resources to sustain the conflict for at least the next year.

- ISIS is likely on a downward trajectory in Syria; yet, despite territorial losses, it probably possesses sufficient resources, and a clandestine network in Syria, to sustain insurgency operations through 2018.

- Moscow probably cannot force President Asad to agree to a political settlement that he believes significantly weakens him, unless Moscow is willing to remove Asad by force. While Asad may engage in peace talks, he is unlikely to negotiate himself from power or offer meaningful concessions to the opposition.

- Russia and Iran are planning for a long-term presence, securing military basing rights and contracts for reconstruction and oil and gas exploitation. Iran is also seeking to establish a land corridor from Iran through Syria to Lebanon. The Kurdish People's Protection Unit—the Syrian militia of the Kurdistan Workers' Party (PKK)—probably will seek some form of autonomy but will face resistance from Russia, Iran, and Turkey.

- As of October 2017, there were more than 5 million Syrian refugees in neighboring countries, and an estimated 6.3 million internally displaced. Reconstruction could cost at least $100 billion and take at least 10 years to complete. Asad's battered economy will likely continue to require significant subsidies from Iran and Russia to meet basic expenses.

Iraq

Iraq is likely to face a lengthy period of political turmoil and conflict as it struggles to rebuild, reconstitute the Iraqi state, maintain pressure on ISIS, and rein in the Iranian-backed Shia militias that pose an enduring threat to US personnel.

- The Iraqi Government, which has accrued $120 billion in debt, requires substantial external assistance to cover hundreds of millions of dollars in humanitarian-aid shortfalls and a World Bank estimated $88.2 billion to restore heavily damaged infrastructure, industry, and service sectors in areas retaken from ISIS.

- Prime Minister Haydar al-Abadi's forceful reassertion of Baghdad's authority after the Kurdistan Regional Government's (KRG) independence referendum in September illustrates the divisions among Iraqi leaders over the future of the state. The move to curb Kurdish autonomy was popular among many Arab Shia and Sunnis and may prompt Iraqi leaders to be uncompromising in political reconciliation discussions in order to consolidate votes in the run-up to elections planned for next spring.

- ISIS will remain a terrorist and insurgent threat, and the group will seek to exploit Sunni discontent to conduct attacks and try to regain Iraqi territory. Baghdad will struggle to reorient the Iraqi Security Forces (ISF) from conventional warfare to counterinsurgency and counterterrorism against ISIS while consolidating state control of territory and integrating the Iranian-backed and Shia-dominated Popular Mobilization Committee (PMC).

- There is an increasing risk that some Shia militants will seek to attack US targets in Iraq because they believe that the US security presence is no longer needed, want to reassert Iraqi sovereignty, and support Iran's goal of reducing US influence in Iraq.

Baghdad will have to contend with longstanding and war-hardened ethnosectarian divisions between Shia, Sunnis, and Kurds that were kept in check by the threat from ISIS. Despite ISIS's loss of territory, the social and political challenges that gave rise to the group remain and threaten the cohesion of the Iraqi state.

Yemen

The war in Yemen is likely to continue for the foreseeable future because the Iranian-backed Huthis and the Saudi-led coalition remain far apart on terms for ending the conflict. The death of former Yemeni President Ali Abdallah Salih is only likely to further complicate the conflict as the Huthis and others scramble to win over those who previously backed Salih. We assess that the Huthis will continue to pursue their goals militarily and that, as a result, US allies and interests on the Arabian Peninsula will remain at risk of Huthi missile attacks until the conflict is resolved.

- Continued fighting almost certainly will worsen the vast humanitarian crisis, which has left more than 70 percent of the population—or about 20 million people—in need of assistance and aggravated a cholera outbreak that has reached nearly 1 million confirmed cases. Relief operations are hindered by security and bureaucratic constraints established by both the Huthi-Salih alliance and the Saudi-led coalition and by international funding shortages.

SOUTH ASIA

Afghanistan

The overall situation in Afghanistan probably will deteriorate modestly this year in the face of persistent political instability, sustained attacks by the Taliban-led insurgency, unsteady Afghan National Security Forces (ANSF) performance, and chronic financial shortfalls. The National Unity Government probably will struggle to hold long-delayed parliamentary elections, currently scheduled for July 2018, and to prepare for a presidential election in 2019. The ANSF probably will maintain control of most major population centers with coalition force support, but the intensity and geographic scope of Taliban activities will put those centers under continued strain. Afghanistan's economic growth will stagnate at around 2.5 percent per year, and Kabul will remain reliant on international donors for the great majority of its funding well beyond 2018.

Pakistan

Pakistan will continue to threaten US interests by deploying new nuclear weapons capabilities, maintaining its ties to militants, restricting counterterrorism cooperation, and drawing closer to China. Militant groups supported by Islamabad will continue to take advantage of their safe haven in Pakistan to plan and conduct attacks in India and Afghanistan, including against US interests.

Pakistan's perception of its eroding position relative to India, reinforced by endemic economic weakness and domestic security issues, almost certainly will exacerbate long-held fears of isolation and drive Islamabad's pursuit of actions that run counter to US goals for the region.

South Asian Threats Challenge
US Security Interests in 2018

- Deteriorating Political/Security Situation
- Militant Support
- India-Pakistan Tensions
- India-China Tensions
- Rohingya Refugee Crisis

India-Pakistan Tension

Relations between India and Pakistan are likely to remain tense, with continued violence on the Line of Control and the risk of escalation if there is another high-profile terrorist attack in India or an uptick in violence on the Line of Control.

India-China Tension

We expect relations between India and China to remain tense and possibly to deteriorate further, despite the negotiated settlement to their three-month border standoff in August, elevating the risk of unintentional escalation.

Bangladesh-Burma Rohingya Crisis

The turmoil resulting from more than 600,000 Rohingyas fleeing from Burma to Bangladesh increases regional tension and may expand opportunities for terrorist recruitment in South and Southeast Asia.

Further operations by Burmese security forces against Rohingya insurgents or sustained violence by ethnic Rakhine militias probably would make it difficult to repatriate Burmese from Bangladesh.

RUSSIA AND EURASIA

Russia

In his probable next term in office, President Vladimir Putin will rely on assertive and opportunistic foreign policies to shape outcomes beyond Russia's borders. He will also resort to more authoritarian tactics to maintain control amid challenges to his rule.

Moscow will seek cooperation with the United States in areas that advance its interests. Simultaneously, Moscow will employ a variety of aggressive tactics to bolster its standing as a great power, secure a "sphere of influence" in the post-Soviet space, weaken the United States, and undermine Euro-Atlantic unity. The highly personalized nature of the Russian political system will enable Putin to act decisively to defend Russian interests or to pursue opportunities he views as enhancing Russian prestige and power abroad.

Russia will compete with the United States most aggressively in Europe and Eurasia, while applying less intense pressure in "outer areas" and cultivating partnerships with US rivals and adversaries—as well as with traditional US partners—to constrain US power and accelerate a shift toward a "multipolar" world. Moscow will use a range of relatively low-cost tools to advance its foreign policy objectives, including influence campaigns, economic coercion, cyber operations, multilateral forums, and measured

Economic and Military Affiliations in Russia's Neighborhood

military force. Russia's slow economic growth is unlikely to constrain Russian foreign policy or by itself trigger concessions from Moscow in Ukraine, Syria, or elsewhere in the next year.

President Putin is likely to increase his use of repression and intimidation to contend with domestic discontent over corruption, poor social services, and a sluggish economy with structural deficiencies. He will continue to manipulate the media, distribute perks to maintain elite support, and elevate younger officials to convey an image of renewal. He is also likely to expand the government's legal basis for repression and to enhance his capacity to intimidate and monitor political threats, perhaps using the threat of "extremism" or the 2018 World Cup to justify his actions.

In 2018, Russia will continue to modernize, develop, and field a wide range of advanced nuclear, conventional, and asymmetric capabilities to balance its perception of a strategic military inferiority vis-a-vis the United States.

Ukraine
Ukraine remains at risk of domestic turmoil, which Russia could exploit to undermine Kyiv's pro-West orientation. These factors will threaten Ukraine's nascent economic recovery and potentially lead to changes in its foreign policy that further inflame tension between Russia and the West.

- Popular frustrations with the pace of reforms, depressed standards of living, perceptions of worsening corruption, and political polarization ahead of scheduled presidential and legislative elections in 2019 could prompt early elections.

- Opposition leaders will seek to capitalize on popular discontent to weaken President Petro Poroshenko and the ruling coalition ahead of elections in 2019.

The conflict in eastern Ukraine is likely to remain stalemated and marked by fluctuating levels of violence. A major offensive by either side is unlikely in 2018, although each side's calculus could change if it sees the other as seriously challenging the status quo. Russia will continue its military, political, and economic destabilization campaign against Ukraine to stymie and, where possible, reverse Kyiv's efforts to integrate with the EU and strengthen ties to NATO. Kyiv will strongly resist concessions to Moscow but almost certainly will not regain control of Russian-controlled areas of eastern Ukraine in 2018. Russia will modulate levels of violence to pressure Kyiv and shape negotiations in Moscow's favor.

- Russia will work to erode Western unity on sanctions and support for Kyiv, but the Kremlin is coping with sanctions at existing levels.

Belarus, the Caucasus, Central Asia, Moldova
The Kremlin will seek to maintain and, where possible, expand its influence throughout the former Soviet countries that it asserts are in its self-described sphere of influence.

Russia views Belarus as a critical buffer between itself and NATO and will seek to spoil any potential warming between Minsk and the West. Belarus President Aleksandr Lukashenko will continue close security cooperation with Moscow but will continue to aim for normalized relations with the West as a check on Russia's influence.

Russia's continued occupation of 20 percent of Georgia's territory and efforts to undermine its Western integration will remain the primary sources of Tbilisi's insecurity. The ruling Georgian Dream party is likely to seek to stymie the opposition and reduce institutional constraints on its power.

Tension over the disputed region of Nagorno-Karabakh could devolve into a large-scale military conflict between Armenia and Azerbaijan, which could draw in Russia to support its regional ally.

Both sides' reluctance to compromise, mounting domestic pressures, Azerbaijan's steady military modernization, and Armenia's acquisition of new Russian equipment sustain the risk of large-scale hostilities in 2018.

Russia will pressure Central Asia's leaders to reduce engagement with Washington and support Russian-led economic and security initiatives, while concerns about ISIS in Afghanistan will push Moscow to strengthen its security posture in the region. Poor governance and weak economies raise the risk of radicalization—especially among the many Central Asians who travel to Russia or other countries for work—presenting a threat to Central Asia, Russia, and Western societies. China will probably continue to expand outreach to Central Asia—while deferring to Russia on security and political matters—because of concern that regional instability could undermine China's economic interests and create a permissive environment for extremists, which, in Beijing's view, could enable Uighur militant attacks in China.

Moldova's ostensibly pro-European ruling coalition—unless it is defeated in elections planned for November—probably will seek to curb Russian influence and maintain a veneer of European reform while avoiding changes that would damage the coalition's grip on power. The current Moldovan Government probably will move forward on implementing Moldova's EU Association Agreement against the will of openly pro-Russian and Russian-backed President Igor Dodon. Settlement talks over the breakaway region of Transnistria will continue, but progress likely will be limited to small issues.

EUROPE

The European Union and European national governments will struggle to develop common approaches to counter a variety of security challenges, including instability on their periphery, irregular migration to their region, heightened terrorist threats, and Russian influence campaigns, undercutting Western cohesion.

- These concerns are spurring many countries to increase defense spending and enhance capabilities.

- European governments will need to strengthen their counterterrorism regimes to deal with a diverse threat, including ISIS aspirants and returning foreign fighters.

Turkey's counterterrorism cooperation with the United States against ISIS is likely to continue, but thwarting Kurdish regional ambitions will be a foreign policy priority. President Recep Tayyip Erdogan is likely to employ polarizing rhetoric, straining bilateral relations and cooperation on shared regional goals.

AFRICA

Nigeria—the continent's largest economy—will face a security threat from Boko Haram and ISIS West Africa (ISIS-WA) while battling internal challenges from criminal, militant, and secessionist groups.

ISIS-WA and Boko Haram are regional menaces, conducting cross-border attacks in Nigeria, Cameroon, Chad, and Niger and posing a threat to Western interests. Meanwhile, militant and secessionist groups in in the southern and central areas of Nigeria are capitalizing on longstanding social and economic grievances as the country nears the 2019 presidential election.

Politically fragile governments in Africa's Sahel region will remain vulnerable to terror attacks in 2018, despite efforts to coordinate their counterterror operations. ISIS and al-Qa'ida–allied groups, along with other violent extremists, will attempt to target Western and local government interests in the region, and a stalled peace process is likely to undercut the presidential election in Mali.

The Ethiopian and Kenyan Governments are likely to face opposition from publics agitating for redress of political grievances. Somalia's recently elected government probably will struggle to project its authority and implement security reforms amid the drawdown of African Union forces in 2018, while al-Shabaab— the most potent terrorist threat to US interests in East Africa—probably will increase attacks.

Clashes between the South Sudanese Government and armed opposition groups will continue, raising the risk of additional mass atrocities as both sides use ethnic militias and hate speech and the government continues its crackdown on ethnic minorities. The South Sudanese are the world's fastest growing refugee population, and the significant humanitarian challenges stemming from the conflict, including severe food insecurity, will strain the resources of neighboring countries hosting refugees.

Sudan is likely to continue some aspects of its constructive engagement with the United States following the suspension of sanctions because it has given priority to shedding its international pariah status and reviving its economy. Khartoum probably will acquiesce to some US requests, such as increasing counterterrorism cooperation and improving humanitarian access, but will be reluctant to take any steps that it perceives jeopardize its national security interests.

Political unrest and security threats across the region are likely to intensify as the Presidents of Burundi and the Democratic Republic of the Congo (DRC) face public and armed opposition to their rule and the Central African Republic (CAR) struggles to cope with a nationwide surge in conflict. Over-stretched UN missions in CAR and DRC are unlikely to stem the rising challenges from their concurrent humanitarian and security crises.

THE WESTERN HEMISPHERE

A key feature of the 2018 political environment in Latin America almost certainly will be popular frustration with low economic growth, corruption scandals, and the specter of endemic criminal activity in some countries. Larger and increasingly sophisticated middle classes—with greater access to social media—are demanding more accountability from their governments. Presidential elections, including those in Mexico and Colombia, will occur at a time when support for political parties and governing institutions is at record lows and could bolster the appeal of outsider candidates.

Mexico

Mexicans are focused on presidential and legislative elections scheduled for July 2018, in which corruption, high violence, and a tepid economy will be key issues. The Mexican Government has made slow progress implementing rule-of-law reforms and will continue to rely on the military to lead counternarcotics efforts. Mexico's $1.1 trillion economy benefits from strong economic fundamentals, but uncertainty over trade relationships and higher-than-expected inflation could further slow economic growth. President Enrique Pena Nieto is focusing on domestic priorities, including recovery from the September 2017 earthquakes and managing impacts from potential US policy shifts ahead of the elections. In recent years, Mexican US-bound migration has been net negative but might increase if economic opportunity at home declined.

Central America

Insecurity and lack of economic opportunities likely will remain the principal drivers of irregular migration from the Northern Triangle countries of El Salvador, Guatemala, and Honduras. Homicide rates in these countries remain high, and gang-related violence is still prompting Central Americans to flee.

Venezuela

Economic woes and international diplomatic pressure probably will put political pressure on the Venezuelan Government in 2018. Living standards have declined and shortages of basic goods are driving the increase in Venezuelans seeking asylum in the United States and the region. Venezuela's negotiations with creditors probably will lead to messy legal battles. Venezuela almost certainly will seek to minimize further disruptions to oil production and exports to maintain its critical oil export earnings. Oil prices have increased slightly this year, but crude oil production continues to decline.

Colombia

President Juan Manuel Santos will seek to cement implementation of the Revolutionary Armed Forces of Colombia (FARC) peace accord, as campaigning intensifies for the May 2018 presidential election. The FARC's new political-party status and the uncertainty around the transitional justice reforms will be a factor in the political environment ahead of elections. Substantial budget constraints will slow major programs or policy changes. The influx of FARC dissidents, drug traffickers, and other illegal actors into remote areas will challenge security forces during the next 12 months. Cocaine production in Colombia is at an all-time high, and crop substitution and eradication programs are facing stiff local resistance.

Cuba

Havana will seek to manage President Raul Castro's planned retirement in April 2018. Castro's successor will inherit a stagnant economy and a stalled economic reform process.

Haiti

As President Jovenel Moise begins his second year in office, he will confront competing interests within his government, a vocal opposition, and a fragile economy. Crime and protest activity will test the Haitian National Police following the departure of the UN Stabilization Mission in October 2017 and the transition to a police-only UN mission.

Statement for the Record, Confirmation Hearing

By Gina Haspel, to be Director of the Central Intelligence Agency

Senate Select Committee on Intelligence Washington D.C.

May 8, 2018

Chairman Burr, Vice Chairman Warner, members of the committee: Thank you for the opportunity to appear before you today. I am here because I have been nominated to lead the extraordinary men and women at the Central Intelligence Agency – men and women who are our country's silent warriors. These dedicated professionals spend much of their careers in difficult, far-flung outposts of the globe, striving to make our fellow Americans more secure at home. It has been the privilege of my professional life to be one of those CIA officers.

Now, I have been asked by President Trump to lead this workforce and to continue the work that Mike Pompeo and I began a little more than a year ago: ensuring that CIA is postured to meet the complex challenges our nation faces. Those challenges include a changing but still lethal threat from terrorist groups; a nuclear threat against the continental United States from a rogue state; destabilizing Iranian adventurism; an aggressive and sometimes brutal Russia; and the long-term implications of China's ambitions on the global stage.

While these challenges are daunting and offer few easy answers, I am confident the United States and the American people have the resolve to meet them head on. If I am confirmed as Director, you have my solemn commitment that I will position this Agency to provide the intelligence support our country needs to meet the challenges of today, and those of the future.

I welcome the opportunity to introduce myself to the American people for the first time—it is a new experience for me as I spent over 30 years under cover and in the shadows. I don't have any social media accounts, but otherwise I think you will find me to be a typical middle class American—one with a strong sense of right and wrong and one who loves this country.

I was born in Kentucky, and while my family has deep roots there, I was an Air Force "brat" and followed my father to postings all over the world. My childhood overseas instilled in me an appreciation for foreign languages and cultures, but also a deep understanding of the vital role of American leadership in confronting aggression abroad.

I joined the CIA in 1985 as an operations officer in the Clandestine Service. From my first days in training, I had a knack for the nuts and bolts of my profession. I excelled in finding and acquiring secret information that I obtained in brush passes, dead drops, or in meetings in dusty back allies of third world capitals. I recall my first foreign agent meeting was on a dark, moonless night with an agent I'd never met before. When I picked him up, he passed me the intelligence and I passed him extra money for the men he led. It was the beginning of an adventure I had only dreamed of.

The men who ran CIA in those days leaned forward in giving me the right opportunities to succeed or fail. When a very tough, old school leader announced that I was his pick to be Chief of Station in a small but important frontier post, a few competitors complained to me directly *"why would they send you?"* I owe that leader much for believing in me at a time when few women were given these opportunities. While I could have done without the long nights, sleeping on the floor of my station, I was proud of the work we did there including the successful capture of two major terrorists, a counterproliferation operation that went our way, and the dismantlement of a local terrorist cell.

Altogether, I have served seven tours in the field—four as Chief of Station— including hardship assignments in distant posts and, more recently, in the capital of a major US ally.

By any standard, my life at the Agency – and it has been my life – has exceeded all of my expectations, from that January day when I took my oath to today. There were few senior women leading at CIA in those days, and we are stronger now because that picture is changing. I did my part – quietly and through hard work – to break down those barriers. And I was proud to be the first woman to serve as the number-two in the Clandestine Service. It is not my way to trumpet the fact that I am a woman up for the top job, but I would be remiss in not remarking on it – not least because of the outpouring of support from young women at CIA who consider it a good sign for their own prospects.

My experience and success as an operations officer led to three leadership positions in the Clandestine Service, and one year ago, I was asked to serve as Deputy Director of CIA. The reaction of the workforce to a rare nomination of one of their own to be Director – someone who has been in the trenches with them – has been overwhelming. I am humbled by their confidence that I can successfully lead this Agency and inspired to work harder than ever to maintain that mutual trust.

They know that I don't need time to learn the business of what CIA does. I know CIA like the back of my hand. I know them, I know the threats we face, and I know what we need to be successful in our mission.

I have played a leading role this past year in setting us on the right path and I intend on continuing on that path if I am confirmed as Director.

Our strategy starts with strengthening our core business: collecting intelligence to help policymakers protect our country and advance American interests around the globe. It includes raising our investment against the most difficult intelligence gaps, putting more officers in the foreign field where our adversaries are, and emphasizing foreign language excellence. And, finally, it involves investing in our partnerships – both within the US Government and around the globe.

We must do everything we can to follow through on these investments and to make CIA as effective as it can possibly be, because the American people deserve no less than CIA's best effort.

This is especially true when it comes to confronting threats from North Korea, Iran, Russia, and China. Today, CIA officers are deployed across the globe, sometimes at significant personal risk, collecting critical human and technical intelligence. I have spent my entire career driving operations and, if confirmed, I will be able to leverage that experience against these hard targets beginning on day one.

I knew that accepting the president's nomination would raise questions about CIA classified activities and my career at the Agency. I also understand that it is important for the American people to get to know me so they are able to judge my fitness for this position. So over the last few weeks, we have leaned forward to make more information about my professional record public. We have also shared details on every aspect of my career through classified channels with this Committee, as well as with the rest of the Senate.

I think it is important to recall the context of those challenging times immediately following 9/11. For me, I had just returned to Washington from an overseas posting and I reported for duty the morning of 9/11. I knew in my gut when I saw the video of the first plane hitting the Tower in Manhattan that it was Bin Ladin. I got up from my desk and, like many others, walked over to the Counterterrorism Center and volunteered to help. I didn't leave for three years. We worked seven days a week, and I even had friends who postponed weddings and having babies. The men and women of CIA were driven to prevent another attack. The first boots on the ground in Afghanistan were my colleagues. The first US casualty in Afghanistan was a CIA officer and it was CIA who identified and captured the mastermind of 9/11 in a brilliant operation. I am proud of our work during that time. The hard lessons we learned from that experience inform my leadership of CIA today.

In light of my counterterrorism experience, I understand that what many people around the country want to know about are my views on CIA's former detention and interrogation program. I have views on this issue, and I want to be clear. Having served in that tumultuous time, I can offer you my personal commitment, clearly and without reservation, that under my leadership CIA will not restart such a detention and interrogation program.

CIA has learned some tough lessons, especially when asked to tackle missions that fall outside our expertise. For me, there is no better example of implementing lessons learned than what the Agency took away from the detention and interrogation program. In retrospect it is clear, as the SSCI Majority Report concludes, that CIA was not prepared to conduct a detention and interrogation program.

Today, the US Government has a clear legal and policy framework that governs detentions and interrogations. Specifically, the law provides that no individual in US custody may be subjected to any interrogation technique or approach that is not authorized by and listed in the Army Field Manual. I fully support the standards for detainee treatment required by law, and just as importantly, I will keep CIA focused on our collection and analysis missions that can best leverage the expertise found at the Agency.

Like I said, we learned important lessons following 9/11. As both a career intelligence officer and an American citizen, I am a strong believer in the importance of oversight. Simply put, experience has taught us that CIA cannot be effective without the people's trust. And we cannot hope to earn that trust without the accountability that comes with Congressional oversight.

If we can't share aspects of our secret work with the public, we should do so with their elected representatives. For CIA, oversight is a vital link to the open society we defend. It's a defining feature of the US Intelligence Community, and one of the many things that distinguishes us from the hostile services we face in the field.

If confirmed as Director, I will uphold the Agency's obligations to Congress and ensure that oversight works on behalf of the American people.

Mr. Chairman, I want to thank you and the Committee for the hard work that is put into the oversight process, and for the vital support that you provide to my fellow officers.

CIA has given a lot to me over the past three decades—a calling in service to my country, some real-life adventures, and the profound satisfaction of serving with some of the most talented and honorable men and women anyone could ever meet.

If confirmed, I hope to repay the debt I owe to this remarkable Agency by drawing on my experience. I know what my fellow officers need from me and, I know what our nation needs from CIA—truth, integrity, and courage.

Again, thank you for allowing me the opportunity to sit before you today, and I look forward to your questions.

Statement for the Record, Confirmation Hearing

By William R. Evanina, to be Director of the National Counterintelligence
and Security Center

Senate Select Committee on Intelligence Washington D.C.

May 15, 2018

Chairman Burr, Vice Chairman Warner, and Members of the Committee.

It's an honor to appear before you today as you consider my nomination to be the
first Senate confirmed Director of the National Counterintelligence and Security
Center (NCSC). I am grateful that the Congress has considered the position I
currently hold to be sufficiently important to require Senate confirmation—an
acknowledgment of the significant, and growing, challenges being addressed by
NCSC to enhance our nation's security.

In my capacity as Director of NCSC over the last several years, I've often appeared before this, and other Congressional committees. I have great respect for
the importance of Congress' oversight role, and I have prided myself in keeping
Congress fully and currently informed about developments within my cognizance
in the counterintelligence and security field. If confirmed, I will continue this
important information sharing commitment to Congress.

I am also honored and grateful that the President and the Director of National
Intelligence have the trust and confidence in my ability to continue to serve our
nation's counterintelligence and security enterprise.

I would first like to express my gratitude to my family; my mother Barbara, father
John, brother Stephen, and sister Tanya – and particularly my wife JulieAnne,
and my sons Dominic and Will, who are present with me today. Their love and
support means everything to me.

I also want to thank the men and women of NCSC and ODNI, who lead and
support both the counterintelligence and security mission as we have made NCSC
the global leader in both mission areas.

I was born and raised in Peckville, Pennsylvania. There—through my family and
neighbors—I learned the value of integrity, hard work, duty, pride in country, and
service to others. One of those neighbors—who lived just a few blocks from my
family's house—had a particularly strong influence on me.

Gino Merli was a Private First Class in the U.S. Army during World War II. He
landed on Omaha Beach on D-Day, and later fought in the Battle of the Bulge.
Mr. Merli was awarded the Medal of Honor for blocking a German advance at a
U.S. Army outpost in Belgium.

When I was growing up, he advised my friends and me about the importance of character, citizenship, and service. I also learned from Mr. Merli that we should never take our freedom for granted.

Mr. Chairman, I am proud to be a career public servant. I believe that my past service has been solid preparation for the position I hold today, and for which I'm being considered for confirmation.

I've been in the federal service for over twenty-nine years—twenty-two of which were spent as a Special Agent with the Federal Bureau of Investigation (FBI). And as I've described in the Committee's questionnaire, I've held a wide spectrum of leadership roles at the FBI in the law enforcement and national security fields. I have also been the Chief of the CIA's Counterespionage Group, so I have served in the lead domestic and international CI agencies.

Mr. Chairman, I have led the organization that is now known as the National Counterintelligence and Security Center since June, 2014. If confirmed, I will continue to lead NCSC and serve as the head of counterintelligence for the U.S. Government, and as the principal counterintelligence and security advisor to the Director of National Intelligence.

The foreign intelligence threat is one of the most significant threats to our country. On February 13, Director of National Intelligence Dan Coats appeared before this Committee to provide the Intelligence Community's annual threat assessment.

I agree with DNI Coats' assessment that the United States faces a complex global foreign intelligence threat. The most prominent state intelligence threats to U.S. interests will continue to be Russia and China, based on their services' capabilities, intent, and broad operational scope.

As a nation we were not prepared for Russia's intent and action to interfere in U.S. democratic processes and institutions. I believe that the Russian intelligence services will continue their efforts to encourage anti-U.S. political views, create wedges that reduce trust and confidence in democratic processes, weaken U.S. partnerships with European allies, and undermine Western sanctions.

Until fairly recently, China's use of its intelligence services to advance its national development (thereby undermining the economic security of the U.S.) did not receive adequate attention. The U.S. must continue to respond to China's systematic theft of U.S. technology across broad swaths of the U.S. economy, which represents a critical national security threat. Our economic security IS our national security.

The most critical CI threats cut across these threat actors: influence operations, critical infrastructure, supply chain, and traditional as well as economic espionage. Regional actors such as Iran and North Korea, and non-state actors such as terrorist groups, transnational criminal organizations, and hackers/hacktivists are growing in intent and capability.

Advanced technology previously available mainly to leading nation-states is now increasingly available to a wide range of nation-state and non-state actors as well. For example, a growing set of threat actors are now capable of using cyber operations to remotely access traditional intelligence targets, as well as a broader set of U.S. targets including critical infrastructure and supply chain, often without attribution.

Insider threats—sometimes with the encouragement of external actors – are a pernicious intelligence threat to maintaining our secrets and our national security. Unauthorized disclosures also have a devastating impact on the men and women who serve every day to protect our secrets, our data, our systems, and our personnel.

If confirmed, I commit to the continual leadership of the Intelligence Community and the U.S. Government efforts to address these significant, and increasingly complex, global intelligence threats to the United States.

As the Director of NCSC, and as prescribed in your legislation which created my role, I am responsible for leading and supporting the counterintelligence and security activities of the U.S. Intelligence Community, the U.S. Government, and U.S. private sector entities at risk from intelligence collection by foreign adversaries.

And I would like to emphasize that NCSC safeguards privacy and civil liberties, and practices appropriate transparency in all counterintelligence and security programs to ensure accountability to Congress and the American people.

Mr. Chairman, as you, the Vice Chairman, and all Members of this Committee are keenly aware, our government's security clearance process is outdated and inefficient, and requires a comprehensive overhaul. Currently, there are 4 million Americans deployed around the globe – in over 100 agencies and departments – who possess a security clearance. We must develop and implement a business process that results in the expeditious onboarding of highly qualified citizens – both in the U.S. government and cleared industry – with agility and complete reciprocity. At the same time, we must not reduce the quality of the investigations to ensure we are hiring a highly trusted workforce that will protect our nation's secrets. If confirmed, as the executor of the DNI's role as the Security Executive Agent, I am committed to leading this important government-wide effort on behalf of the DNI.

Mr. Chairman, I'd like to conclude my remarks by sharing a story that illustrates the commitment to public service that I, along with my colleagues at the National Counterintelligence and Security Center share.

One year ago, NCSC staff traveled to the National Archives to renew our Oath of Office as federal employees. We assembled in the National Archives' Exhibit Hall where our nation's foundational documents—the Constitution, the Bill of

Rights, and the Declaration of Independence—are on display. To me, these are sacred documents, and this was the most fitting place to renew our Oath and commitment to the laws of this great nation.

As federal civil servants, we pledge our loyalty to the Constitution and the rule of law. Our service to the American people is defined by scrupulous adherence to the law and the ideas and ideals embodied in these important documents.

I am honored to lead the NCSC workforce. I am also humbled that, if confirmed, I would become the first Senate confirmed Director to specifically represent the men and women of that organization who have toiled behind the scenes in the global counterintelligence and security arenas for decades protecting our nation. Our success in protecting our nation's security is based on teamwork in a hard-working, respectful, collaborative, and professional work environment with our partners throughout the government and private sector.

Public service is a tremendous honor as well as an enormous public trust. And as intelligence professionals, we are custodians of our nation's secrets. We have a special responsibility to our fellow citizens. All of us are firmly committed to serving the American people and abiding by the Constitution and the rule of law. If confirmed, I will remain committed to these essential goals.

Chairman Burr, Vice Chairman Warner, and Members of the Committee, thank you for your consideration of my nomination. I look forward to your questions.

Report of the Attorney General's Cyber Digital Task Force, U.S. Department of Justice

By U.S. Department of Justice, Office of the Deputy Attorney General

Cyber-Digital Task Force, Washington D.C.

July 2, 2018

Table of Contents

ATTORNEY GENERAL'S CYBER-DIGITAL TASK FORCE

TASK FORCE MEMBERS

Sujit Raman, Chair
Associate Deputy Attorney General
Office of the Deputy Attorney General

John P. Cronan
Assistant Attorney General (Acting)
Criminal Division

John C. Demers
Assistant Attorney General
National Security Division

Carl Ghattas
Executive Assistant Director
Federal Bureau of Investigation

John M. Gore
Assistant Attorney General (Acting)
Civil Rights Division

Andrew E. Lelling
United States Attorney
District of Massachusetts

David T. Resch
Executive Assistant Director
Federal Bureau of Investigation

Beth A. Williams
Assistant Attorney General
Office of Legal Policy

Peter A. Winn
Chief Privacy & Civil Liberties Officer (Actin
Director, Office of Privacy & Civil Liberties

Task Force Contributors

Matthew J. Sheehan
Counsel to the Deputy Attorney General
Staff Director

Elizabeth Aloi
Leonard Bailey
Michael F. Buchwald
Mark Champoux
Thomas Dettore
Richard Downing
Benjamin Fitzpatrick
Lindsey Freeman
Tashina Gauhar
Josh Goldfoot
Bonnie Greenberg

Brendan Groves
Aarash Haghighat
William Hall
Christopher Hardee
Adam Hickey
Ray Hulser
Anitha Ibrahim
Matthew Kluge
John T. Lynch, Jr.
Katrina Mulligan
Sean Newell
Erica O'Neil

Richard Pilger
Jason Poole
Andrew Proia
Kimberley Raleigh
Peter Roman
Opher Shweiki
Michael Stawasz
AnnaLou Tirol
Andrew Warden
J. Brad Wiegmann
Cory Wilson

And representatives from:

Bureau of Alcohol, Tobacco, Firearms, and Explosives Office of Strategic
    Intelligence & Information
Drug Enforcement Administration Office of Investigative Technology
Federal Bureau of Investigation Counterintelligence Division
Federal Bureau of Investigation Counterterrorism Division
Federal Bureau of Investigation Criminal Investigative Division
Federal Bureau of Investigation Cyber Division
Federal Bureau of Investigation Digital Transformation Office
Federal Bureau of Investigation Information Technology Branch
Federal Bureau of Investigation Office of Private Sector
Federal Bureau of Investigation Office of the Chief Information Officer
Federal Bureau of Investigation Office of the Director
Federal Bureau of Investigation Office of the General Counsel
Federal Bureau of Investigation Operational Technology Division
INTERPOL Washington, the U.S. National Central Bureau
Justice Management Division Office of the Chief Information Officer/
    Cybersecurity Services Staff
United States Marshals Service Investigative Operations Division
United States Marshals Service Judicial Security Division

INTRODUCTION

Cyber-enabled attacks are exacting an enormous toll on American businesses, government agencies, and families. Computer intrusions, cybercrime schemes, and the covert misuse of digital infrastructure have bankrupted firms, destroyed billions of dollars in investments, and helped hostile foreign governments launch influence operations designed to undermine fundamental American institutions.

The Department of Justice's primary mission is to keep the American people safe. We play a critical role in the federal government's shared effort to combat malicious, cyber-enabled threats.

In February 2018, the Attorney General established a Cyber-Digital Task Force within the Department and directed the Task Force to answer two basic, foundational questions: How is the Department responding to cyber threats? And how can federal law enforcement more effectively accomplish its mission in this important and rapidly evolving area?

This report addresses the first question. It begins by focusing on one of the most pressing cyber-enabled threats our Nation faces: the threat posed by malign foreign influence operations. Chapter 1 explains what foreign influence operations are, and how hostile foreign actors have used these operations to target our Nation's democratic processes, including our elections. This chapter concludes by describing the Department's protective efforts with respect to the upcoming 2018 midterm elections, and announces a new Department policy—grounded in our longstanding principles of political neutrality, adherence to the rule of law, and safeguarding the public trust—that governs the disclosure of foreign influence operations.

Chapters 2 and 3 discuss other cyber-enabled threats our Nation faces, particularly those connected with cybercrimes. These chapters describe the resources the Department is deploying to confront those threats, and how our efforts further the rule of law in this country and around the world. Chapter 4 focuses on a critical aspect of the Department's mission, in which the Federal Bureau of Investigation plays a lead role: responding to cyber incidents. Chapter 5 then turns the lens inward, focusing on the Department's efforts to recruit and train our own personnel on cyber matters. Finally, the report concludes in Chapter 6 with thoughts and observations about certain priority policy matters, and charts a path for the Task Force's future work. Over the next few months, the Department will build upon this initial report's findings, and will provide recommendations to the Attorney General for how the Department can even more efficiently manage the growing global cyber challenge.

The Department's Cyber Mission

Computer intrusions and attacks are crimes, and the Department of Justice fights crime. That is true regardless of whether the criminal is a transnational organized crime group, a lone hacker, or an officer of a foreign military or intelligence organization. In addition, the Department has unique and indispensable cybersecurity roles in the realm of foreign intelligence and counterintelligence.

In fighting criminal computer intrusions and attacks, the Department identifies, dismantles, and disrupts cyber threats. In doing so, we provide justice to victims and deter others from committing similar offenses. To fulfill our mission, we deploy criminal justice and intelligence tools to find malicious hackers, arrest them, incarcerate them, and require them to pay restitution to their victims. We shut down the dark markets criminals depend upon to buy and sell stolen information. We deprive criminals of the tools and services they use to attack American families and businesses. Working with private sector partners, we seek to deny foreign governments the infrastructure they would use to conduct illegal influence operations. We seize or disable the servers, domain names, and other infrastructure that transnational criminals rely upon to penetrate our borders. We use legal authorities to take control of virtual infrastructure—such as networks of compromised computers called "botnets"—to prevent future victimization. We share information gathered during our investigations to help victims protect themselves. And we do all of these things to fight modern threats while remaining faithful to our Nation's respect for personal freedom, civil liberties, and the rule of law.

Where appropriate, we also work closely with our interagency partners to support financial, diplomatic, and military measures to bring all possible instruments of national power to bear against cyber threats. Other departments have the primary responsibility for helping victims recover from cyber-attacks; we have the primary responsibility for conducting the investigation into who is responsible. We do not have the federal government lead for assisting election officials in securing their systems, but we do have the primary responsibility for investigating our foreign adversaries' efforts to target election infrastructure.

Similarly, we do not have the government's lead role in protecting private or government networks, in designing security standards, or in regulating how the private sector must defend itself. Those are important functions for which other government departments take responsibility—often, with our support and assistance. Our mission is to enforce the law, to ensure public safety, and to seek just punishment.

INTRODUCTION

How We Succeed

By faithfully executing the Department's crime-fighting mission, we have produced tangible and positive results for the American people. These results are reflected by the caliber of criminals we have taken offline and taken off the streets; the millions of computers we have liberated from botnets that harness their processing power for fraud and theft; the web cameras that no longer spy on unwitting victims; the dark markets selling illicit drugs, weapons, and child pornography we have disrupted and shuttered; the virtual currency we have seized from criminals; and the malicious software that is no longer offered for sale.

These tangible results have a secondary effect: deterrence. Deterrence is one of the primary objectives of criminal law, and it is a key factor in improving our Nation's cybersecurity. An effective deterrence policy requires us to have a credible capability to enforce the law, and therefore to deter offenders. A credible capability to enforce the law, in turn, requires the Department to be able to credibly investigate cybercrime. Without evidence, there is no attribution. Without attribution, there will be no consequences for offenders, and thus no deterrence.

Yet, the reality is that identity-masking technologies and international investigative barriers pose unique challenges for deterring cyber threats. This report details the ways in which we approach those challenges. We depend upon legal authorities to investigate computer crimes; upon the cooperation of the public and of the private sector to report

crimes and to help identify cyber threats; and upon the assistance of international partners to gather foreign evidence, apprehend criminals, and extradite suspects. Often, those authorities are exclusive to the Department of Justice and other law enforcement agencies. For example, the Department has the authority to obtain the subpoenas, court orders, and search warrants that the law requires in order to compel online service providers to produce crucial records that can reveal criminal activity.

"Our mission is to enforce the law, to ensure public safety, and to seek just punishment."

Preserving these investigative authorities and capabilities, and using them responsibly and consistent with law, is therefore vital to the Nation's cybersecurity. It is also a Department priority. The Department's agents and prosecutors need the authority and tools to obtain evidence; the technical skill to understand it; and the ability to introduce that evidence at trial and explain what it means. Maintaining these capabilities is, in part, a question of making sure investigators retain the lawful authority to access evidence in a changing digital landscape. It is also a question of building and maintaining a talented and dedicated workforce.

The Department—along with the entire U.S. government—wants Americans to be able to use their devices and computers secure in the knowledge that their data is safe. Many government departments and agencies are working toward that cybersecurity goal. And while this report catalogs the many ways that the Department is at the cutting edge of keeping Americans safe from cyber threats, we are also keenly aware that our tools and authorities are not sufficient by themselves to accomplish that goal. Our work is critical to cybersecurity, but our work, alone, is not enough to secure the Nation.

As Americans have shifted much of our economy, our communications, our news media, and our daily lives to the Internet, we are now discovering how vulnerable that shift makes us. To defend against cyberattacks from nation states and from equally sophisticated criminals, the American public should be able to turn to the government for leadership. This report details how the Department of Justice is responding to that call.

– **Sujit Raman**, *Chair,*
Attorney General's Cyber-Digital Task Force

Attorney General Jeff Sessions announces law enforcement's July 2017 seizure of AlphaBay, what was then the world's largest "Dark Market." In addition to traditional criminal enforcement actions, disrupting and dismantling the illicit underworld's digital infrastructure is a major facet of the Department of Justice's broader fight against cybercrime.

CHAPTER 1
COUNTERING MALIGN FOREIGN INFLUENCE OPERATIONS

Hostile foreign actors have long sought to influence, and to subvert, our Nation's democratic institutions. Modern technology—including the Internet and social media platforms—has both empowered and emboldened foreign governments and their agents in their attempts to affect U.S. attitudes, behaviors, and decisions in new and troubling ways.

The Department of Justice plays an important role in protecting the Nation's democratic processes from malign foreign influence operations. While the States, under the Constitution, have primary jurisdiction over the administration of elections,[1] the Department for decades has enforced federal criminal laws involving certain forms of ballot fraud.[2] We will continue our traditional commitment to combating such frauds, including any that foreign governments or their agents may attempt to perpetrate. (*See* page 4).

Foreign cyber-enabled and other active efforts to influence our democratic processes, including our elections, demand an urgent response. In the following pages, we provide background on malign foreign influence operations generally; outline five distinct types of foreign influence operations aimed at our elections or at broader political issues in the United States; and describe the Department's protective efforts with respect to such operations, including efforts designed to protect the upcoming 2018 midterm elections. We also

announce a Department policy regarding the factors to be considered in disclosing malign foreign influence operations to victims, other affected individuals, and the public. This policy provides guideposts for Department action to expose and thereby counter foreign influence threats—consistent with the fundamental principle that we always must seek to act in ways that are politically neutral, compliant with the First Amendment, and designed to maintain the public trust.

Ultimately, one of the most effective ways to counter malign foreign influence operations is to shine a light on the activity and raise awareness of the threat. In order to prevail against our adversaries, all of society must work together: from government at all levels; to social media providers and others in the private sector; to political candidates and organizations; to, perhaps most significantly, an active and informed citizenry.

Malign Foreign Influence Operations

Foreign influence operations include covert actions by foreign governments intended to sow division in our society, undermine confidence in our democratic institutions, and otherwise affect political sentiment and public discourse to achieve strategic geopolitical objectives. Foreign influence operations can pose a threat to national security—and they can violate federal criminal law.[3] Operations aimed at the United States are not new. These efforts have taken many forms across the decades, from funding communist newspapers and financing ostensibly independent non-profit groups to promote favored policies, to more recent efforts at creating and operating false U.S. personas on Internet sites designed to attract U.S. audiences and spread divisive messages. The nature of the problem, however—and how the U.S. government must combat it—is changing, as advances in technology allow foreign actors to reach unprecedented numbers of Americans covertly and without setting foot on U.S. soil. Fabricated news stories and sensational headlines like those sometimes found on social media platforms are just the latest iteration of a practice foreign adversaries have long employed in an effort to discredit and undermine individuals and organizations in the United States. Although the tactics have evolved, the goals of these activities generally remain the same: to spread disinformation and to sow discord on a mass scale in order to weaken the U.S. democratic process, and ultimately to undermine the appeal of democracy itself.

Malign foreign influence operations need not favor one political figure, party, or point of view. Foreign adversaries can take advantage of social media platforms to send contrary (and sometimes false) messages simultaneously to different groups of users based on those users' political and demographic characteristics, with the goal of heightening tensions between different groups in our society. By exacerbating and inflaming existing divisions, foreign-promoted narratives seek to spread turmoil, mistrust, and acrimony. For example, Russian-affiliated social media activities have been detected promoting content on multiple sides of controversial issues including race relations and gun control.

As one component of this strategy, foreign influence operations have targeted U.S. elections. Elections are a particularly attractive target for foreign influence campaigns because they provide an opportunity to undermine confidence in a core element of our democracy: the process by which we select our leaders. As explained in a January 2017 Intelligence Community Assessment published by the Office of the Director of National Intelligence ("ODNI") addressing Russian interference in the 2016 U.S. presidential election, Russia has had a "longstanding desire to undermine the U.S.-led liberal democratic order," and that nation's recent election-focused "activities demonstrated a significant escalation in directness, level of activity, and scope of effort compared to previous operations."[4] Russia's foreign influence campaign, according to this assessment, "followed a longstanding Russian messaging strategy that blends covert intelligence operations—such as cyber activity—with overt efforts by Russian Government agencies, state-funded media, third-party intermediaries, and paid social media users or 'trolls.'"[5]

Malign foreign influence operations did not begin in 2016, but the Internet-facilitated operations in that year were unprecedented in scale. The threat such operations pose to our society is unlikely to diminish. As the Director of National Intelligence recently observed, "Influence operations, especially through cyber means, will remain a significant threat to U.S. interests as they are low-cost, relatively low-risk, and deniable ways to retaliate against adversaries, to shape foreign perceptions, and to influence populations."[6] "Russia probably will be the most capable and aggressive source of this threat in 2018, although many countries and some nonstate actors are exploring ways to use influence operations, both domestically and abroad."[7] These actions require a strong and sustained response.

Types of Foreign Influence Operations Targeting Democratic and Electoral Processes

In advance of the 2018 midterm elections, the Department is mindful of ODNI's assessment that "Moscow will apply lessons learned from its campaign aimed at the U.S. presidential election to future influence efforts in the United States and worldwide, including against U.S. allies and their election processes."[8] The Intelligence Community ("IC") has recently assessed that Russia views the 2018 midterm elections as a potential target for continued influence operations.[9] Rus-

sia's strategy for conducting foreign influence operations against the United States, which may well inspire other countries to pursue similar operations, includes a broad spectrum of activity targeting U.S. democratic and electoral processes. We categorize such activity as follows:

1. Cyber operations targeting election infrastructure. Cyber operations could seek to undermine the integrity or availability of election-related data. For example, adversaries could employ cyber-enabled or other means to target election-associated infrastructure, such as voter registration databases and voting machines, or to target the power grid or other critical infrastructure in order to impair an election. Operations aimed at removing otherwise eligible voters from the rolls or attempting to manipulate the results of an election (or even simply spreading disinformation suggesting that such manipulation has occurred) could undermine the integrity and legitimacy of our free and fair elections, as well as public confidence in elec-

Identifying Potential Targets of Election Interference

| Potential Targets Related to Voter Influence | Potential Targets Related to Campaigns | Potential Targets Related to Political Entities | Potential Targets Related to Elections Infrastructure |

Credit: Cyber Threat Intelligence Integration Center

Foreign adversaries could target these categories of potential targets—or others—to interfere in U.S. elections through cyber operations.

DEPARTMENT OF JUSTICE PROGRAM
FOR COMBATING BALLOT FRAUD

"Every voter in a federal . . . election, . . . whether he votes for a candidate with little chance of winning or for one with little chance of losing, has a right under the Constitution to have his vote fairly counted, without its being distorted by fraudulently cast votes." *Anderson v. United States*, 417 U.S. 211, 227 (1974). The Department has a longstanding program for predicating, investigating, and prosecuting ballot fraud schemes—which may overlap with a criminal or national security investigation into a foreign influence operation. The Department's ballot fraud program brings together several components, including the Federal Bureau of Investigation ("FBI"); the Criminal Division's Public Integrity Section ("PIN"); United States Attorney's Offices around the nation; the Civil Rights Division ("CRT"); and the Department of Homeland Security ("DHS"). (Each component's specific role in the program is described in the endnotes.[16])

In the weeks and months leading up to the 2018 midterm elections, these components will plan responses to election-related issues and identify lines of coordination and communication. On Election Day, they and a commissioner from the U.S. Election Assistance Commission will arrange regular secure video teleconferences with Department leadership and other agencies, including the National Security Council. Other PIN and CRT managers and personnel also will be available throughout the period to answer telephone calls about suspected ballot fraud activity and to respond to questions from federal prosecutors and law enforcement agents, who in turn will be in close communication with state and local partners.

tion results. To our knowledge, no foreign government has succeeded in perpetrating ballot fraud, but the risk is real.

2. Cyber operations targeting political organizations, campaigns, and public officials.
Cyber operations could also seek to compromise the confidentiality or integrity of targeted groups' or targeted individuals' private information. For example, adversaries could conduct cyber or other operations against U.S. political organizations and campaigns to steal confidential information and use that information, or alterations thereof,

to discredit or embarrass candidates, undermine political organizations, or impugn the integrity of public officials. The IC has assessed that, during the 2016 election cycle, "Russia's intelligence services conducted cyber operations against targets associated with the 2016 U.S. presidential election, including targets associated with both major U.S. political parties."[10]

3. Covert influence operations to assist or harm political organizations, campaigns, and public officials.
Adversaries could also conduct covert influence operations to pro-

COUNTERING MALIGN FOREIGN INFLUENCE OPERATIONS

vide assistance that is prohibited from foreign sources to American political organizations, campaigns, and government officials. These operations might involve covert offers of financial, logistical, or other campaign support to—or covert attempts to influence the policies, positions, or opinions of—unwitting politicians, party leaders, campaign officials, or the public. For example, a federal grand jury indictment in February 2018 of thirteen Russian nationals recounts, among other things, instances in which Russians allegedly provided covert assistance and financial support to unwitting U.S. persons, unwitting individuals associated with a presidential campaign, and other unwitting political activists seeking to coordinate political activities.[11] The indictment also alleges that the Russians sought to discourage some Americans from voting in the 2016 presidential election, and denigrated certain candidates while supporting others. Russian actors also allegedly staged political rallies inside the United States while posing as U.S. grassroots entities and organized rallies inside the United States *after* the presidential election, both in protest of the election results and in support of the results.[12] Such covert influence operations could be reinforced by the use of "bots," which are automated programs that can expand and amplify social media messaging and bolster desired narratives. These operations can also be amplified by stolen information illicitly acquired through illegal cyber operations targeting government institutions, media, and political organizations or campaigns. Foreign agents could then use this stolen information to reinforce divisive narratives through systematic, controlled leaks timed to maximize political damage.

4. Covert influence operations, including disinformation operations, to influence public opinion and sow division. Using false U.S. personas, adversaries could covertly create and operate social media pages and other forums designed to attract U.S. audiences and spread disinformation or divisive messages. This could happen in isolation or in combination with other operations, and could be intended to foster specific narratives that advance foreign political objectives, or could be intended simply to turn citizens against each other. These messages need not relate directly to political campaigns. They could seek to depress voter turnout among particular groups, encourage third-party voting, or convince the public of widespread voter fraud to undermine confidence in election results. These messages could target discrete U.S. populations based on their political and demographic characteristics. They may mobilize Americans to sign online petitions and join issue-related rallies and protests, or even to incite violence. For example, advertisements from at least 2015 to 2017 linked to a Russian organization called the Internet Research Agency focused on divisive issues, including illegal immigration and gun rights, among others, and targeted those messages to groups most likely to react.

5. Overt influence efforts, such as the use of lobbyists, foreign media outlets, and other organizations, to influence policymakers and the public. Finally, adversaries could use state-owned or state-influenced media outlets, or employ lobbyists or lobbying firms, to reach U.S. policymakers or the public. Foreign governments can disguise these efforts as independent while using them to promote divisive narratives and political positions helpful to foreign objectives. Overt influence efforts by foreign governments—including by our adversaries—may not be illegal, provided they comply with the Foreign Agents Registration Act ("FARA"),[13] and with Federal Communications Commission regulations. However, the American people should be fully aware of any foreign government source of information so they can evaluate that source's credibility and significance for themselves.

The Department of Justice's Role in Countering Malign Foreign Influence Operations

The Department of Justice has a significant role in investigating and disrupting foreign government activity in the United States that threatens U.S. national security. In particular, the Department has an important role in identifying and combating malign foreign influence operations, and in enforcing federal laws that foreign agents may violate when engaging in such operations.

Consistent with its longstanding mission, the Department has broad authorities in this area that encompass both its law enforcement and counterintelligence responsibilities:

• The FBI is the primary investigative agency of the federal government and is authorized to investigate all violations of federal laws that are not exclusively assigned to another federal agency. *See* 28 U.S.C. § 533. In addition, 28 C.F.R. § 0.85(d) designates the FBI to take charge of investigative work in matters relating to espionage, sabotage, subversive activities, and related matters.

• Various federal statutes authorize the FBI to conduct investigations of federal crimes, make seizures and arrests, and serve warrants, both under national security authorities (title 50 of the U.S. Code) and law enforcement authorities (title 18 of the U.S. Code). For example, the FBI has primary investigative authority for all computer network intrusions relating to threats to national security, including "cases involving espionage, foreign counterintelligence, [and] information protected against unauthorized disclosure for reasons of national defense or foreign relations . . ." 18 U.S.C. § 1030(d)(2).

• Executive Order ("E.O.") 12333, as amended, establishes the FBI as the lead counterintelligence agency within the United States, and authorizes the FBI to conduct counterintelligence activities, collect foreign intelligence, or support foreign intelligence collection requirements of other agencies within the IC, and produce and disseminate foreign intelligence and counterintelligence. *See* E.O. 12333, § 1.7(g).

• These lead responsibilities are also reflected in presidential policies, such as Presidential Policy Directive ("PPD")-41 and PPD-21.

Working closely with our IC partners, the Department uses these authorities to identify, analyze, and disrupt the most significant threats from foreign influence operations. As explained below, the Department can act against these threats in several ways, either using its own authorities or supporting the

COUNTERING MALIGN FOREIGN INFLUENCE OPERATIONS

actions of other agencies. The Department also uses its investigative authority to develop information that can inform private sector efforts to guard against or deter foreign influence operations.

First, the Department's investigations may reveal conduct that warrants criminal charges. Criminal charges not only are a tool the Department uses to pursue justice, but also can help deter similar conduct in the future. We will work with our international partners to obtain custody of foreign defendants whenever possible. Those who seek to avoid justice in U.S. courts will find their freedom of travel significantly restricted. Criminal charges also provide the public with information about the illegal activities of foreign actors we seek to hold accountable.

Second, in some cases, the Department's investigations can support other U.S. government agencies' actions, such as financial sanctions or diplomatic and intelligence efforts. After a federal grand jury indicted thirteen Russians in connection with their alleged influence activities, for example, the Secretary of the Treasury imposed financial sanctions against those individuals under an executive order that authorizes sanctions for malicious cyber-enabled activity. The Department of the Treasury's actions blocked all property and interests in property of the designated persons subject to U.S. jurisdiction, and prohibited U.S. persons from engaging in transactions with the sanctioned individuals. In addition, the State Department often uses information from our investigations and criminal indictments in diplomatic efforts to attribute malign conduct to foreign adversaries, to build consensus with other nations to condemn such activities, and to build coalitions to counter such activities. Likewise, we work closely with DHS to share information about foreign influence operations in furtherance of DHS's election security mission.

Third, the Department's investigations produce information about threats and vulnerabilities that we can share with State and local election officials, political organizations, and other potential victims. Because these entities lack the FBI's investigative resources and legal authorities, sharing investigative information about the nature of the threat posed by foreign influence operations can help these entities detect and prevent operations that target them.

Fourth, the Department maintains strategic relationships with social media providers that reflect the private sector's critical role in addressing this threat. Social media providers have unique insight into their own networks and bear the primary responsibility for securing their own products, platforms, and services. The FBI can assist the providers' voluntary efforts to identify foreign influence activity and to enforce terms of service that prohibit the use of their platforms for such activities. This approach is similar to the Department's recent approaches in working with providers to address terrorist use of social media, and more traditional collaboration to combat child pornography, botnets, Internet fraud, and other misuse of digital infrastructure. By providing information about potential threats, the Department can help social media providers respond to malign use of their platforms, identify foreign influence operations on those platforms, share information across diverse products and services, and better ensure their users are not exposed to unlawful foreign influence.

Finally, information developed in our investigations can be used—either by the Department or in coordination with the Intelligence Community and other government partners—to help protect the public by exposing the nature of the foreign influence threat. The Department may alert victims or targets about foreign influence operations consistent with its longstanding policies and practices. As discussed below, in certain circumstances, public disclosure and attribution can also be an important means of countering the threat and rendering those operations less effective.

The Department of Justice's Framework to Counter Malign Foreign Influence Operations

The Department is preparing ahead of the 2018 midterm elections to ensure that we address as effectively as possible the five distinct types of foreign influence operations described above. To underscore this priority, the FBI in November 2017 established the Foreign Influence Task Force ("FITF"), which serves as the central coordinating authority within the FBI for investigations concerning foreign influence operations. The FITF integrates the FBI's cyber, counterintelligence, counterterrorism, and criminal law enforcement resources to ensure that the Department better understands the threat presented by malign foreign influence operations. An important part of the FITF's responsibility is

coordinating the Department's counter-foreign influence efforts with other federal agencies, including DHS, the State Department, the National Security Agency, and the Central Intelligence Agency. The FBI is also responsible for developing strategic relationships with state and local authorities, international partners, and the private sector, including social media and other technology companies, as part of a comprehensive approach to combating the foreign influence problem.

Armed with a deeper understanding of our foreign adversaries' operational methods and committed to leveraging the full range of our authorities, the Department has developed a strategic framework for countering foreign influence operations. *See* **Fig. 1**. This framework seeks to employ the Department's longstanding authorities proactively to pursue aggressive countermeasures—using traditional law enforcement tools, sharing information with potential victims and the private sector where appropriate, and exposing and attributing foreign influence operations where doing so is in the national interest. The Department's strategy aims to increase the resilience of democratic and election processes against the foreign influence threat, while recognizing that we cannot expect to eliminate those activities unless the responsible foreign governments alter their behavior.

1. Cyber operations targeting election infrastructure. Although the States are responsible for administering elections, and DHS has the federal government lead for assisting election officials in securing their systems, the FBI has the primary responsibility for investigating our foreign adversaries'

COUNTERING MALIGN FOREIGN INFLUENCE OPERATIONS

Figure 1:

Department of Justice Framework to Counter Malign Foreign Influence Operations

Cyber operations targeting election infrastructure (integrity and availability of data)	Cyber operations targeting political parties, campaigns, and public officials (confidentiality of data)	Covert influence operations to assist or harm political organizations, campaigns and public officials	Covert influence operations to influence public opinion and sow division	Overt influence efforts to influence policymakers and the public
DOJ and FBI Actions • Identify threats and warn potential targets (state officials), with DHS. • Investigate and disrupt intrusions and attacks, alerting victims consistent with applicable guidance. • Prosecute where possible. • Respond to reports of election day crimes (e.g. voter suppression, computer intrusions).	**DOJ and FBI Actions** • Identify threats and warn potential targets, with DHS. • Investigate and disrupt intrusions and attacks, alerting victims consistent with applicable guidance. • Prosecute where possible. • Raise awareness about malicious cyber operations, mitigation, and maintaining "cyber hygiene."	**DOJ and FBI Actions** • Investigate and disrupt activity by unregistered foreign agents. • Brief potential targets, consistent with applicable guidance. • Prosecute where possible. • Raise awareness about malicious cyber operations, mitigation, and maintaining "cyber hygiene."	**DOJ and FBI Actions** • Investigate and, as appropriate, disrupt foreign influence operations. • Attribute and expose activity, consistent with applicable guidance. • Prosecute where possible. • Notify social media, other providers of foreign influence operations and other abuse of their platforms.	**DOJ and FBI Actions** • Investigate possible FARA violations. • Prosecute where possible. • Compel registration as appropriate.
Other Agencies and Their Activities • IC produces intelligence on malicious cyber operations. • DHS shares intelligence (warnings) and best practices with victims and assists with recovery efforts *after* an intrusion (if requested). • Possible diplomatic, financial, or operational responses.	**Other Agencies and Their Activities** • IC produces intelligence on malicious cyber operations. • DHS shares intelligence (warnings) and best practices with victims and assists with recovery efforts *after* an intrusion (if requested). • Possible diplomatic, financial, or operational responses.	**Other Agencies and Their Activities** • IC produces intelligence on foreign influence efforts, goals. • DHS and State Dept. conduct outreach on trends in influence operations to domestic and foreign audiences. • Possible diplomatic, financial, or operational responses.	**Other Agencies and Their Activities** • DHS and State Dept. conduct outreach on trends in influence operations to domestic and foreign audiences. • DHS provides tools to private industry to protect against malign influence. • Possible diplomatic, financial, or operational responses.	**Other Agencies and Their Activities** • DHS and State Dept. conduct outreach on trends in influence operations to domestic and foreign audiences. • State Dept. responds to violations of norms by foreign actors.
Key Considerations • States own the election systems and data and are responsible for their administration and security.	**Key Considerations** • Private parties own systems and data and are responsible for their security. • Limited ability to protect against misuse of stolen information.	**Key Considerations** • May require cooperation of affected individuals and organizations to counter the threat. • Many engagements with foreign governments are legitimate.	**Key Considerations** • Technology companies bear primary responsibility for securing their own products, platforms, and services.	**Key Considerations** • Open communications by registered foreign media may be lawful.

efforts to target election infrastructure. In the event of a known or suspected cyber incident, the FBI will investigate the intrusion and will alert targets of the intrusions where appropriate. Prosecutors will follow the *Principles of Federal Prosecution*[14] in determining whether federal criminal charges are appropriate. The FBI also may identify threats and vulnerabilities to election infrastructure in the course of other criminal or intelligence investigations. Consistent with the Department's disclosure policy (described below), it will attempt to warn State and local officials who operate election systems about attempts to penetrate their systems and to share appropriate information about vulnerabilities they should patch or mitigate. In this regard, the FBI works closely with DHS and with the U.S. Election Assistance Commission, which certifies voting systems and establishes voting system guidelines.

To that end, in February 2018, the FBI, together with DHS and the IC, provided classified briefings to election officials from all 50 States to help increase awareness of foreign adversary intent and capabilities against the States' election infrastructure, as well as actions State and local officials can undertake to mitigate those threats. Establishing close relationships with those officials, in partnership with DHS, is critical because the Department's ability to identify and disrupt cyber actors who target election infrastructure requires the officials who operate that infrastructure to promptly share threat information with the FBI. The Department has emphasized the need for State and local officials promptly to share threat information with the FBI's National Cyber Investigative Joint Task Force ("NCIJTF"). NCIJTF includes over 20 partnering agencies from across law enforcement, the IC, and the Department of Defense, with representatives who are co-located and work jointly to accomplish the organization's mission from a whole-of-government perspective.

Establishing close relationships with State and local officials is also important to enable the Department to respond quickly to a major cyber intrusion before or during an election. The Department works closely with DHS in connection with such incidents. The Department will continue to work with DHS and State and local officials to plan what they should do, whom they should contact, and what assistance they may seek in the event of a significant intrusion into their systems. The FBI's general incident response activities are described in greater detail in Chapter 4.

2. Cyber operations targeting political organizations, campaigns, and public officials. The FBI investigates computer intrusions and attacks against U.S. victims, using its broad investigative authority and leveraging its close relationship with other IC agencies that have the authority to collect foreign intelligence outside the United States. Federal prosecutors may then charge the perpetrators, as appropriate. The FBI also alerts victims where possible and helps them respond to intrusions, often working closely with DHS, and provides threat information when necessary to address a specific threat or incident.

The FBI is working with DHS to ensure that political organizations and individuals within such organizations whom foreign adversaries may target are aware of the specific cyber

COUNTERING MALIGN FOREIGN INFLUENCE OPERATIONS

DEPARTMENT OF JUSTICE POLICY REGARDING NON-INTERFERENCE WITH ELECTIONS

The Department of Justice has a strong interest in the prosecution of election-related crimes, such as those involving federal and State campaign finance laws, federal patronage laws, and corruption of the election process, and Department employees must safeguard the Department's reputation for fairness, neutrality, and non-partisanship.

Partisan political considersations must play no role in the decisions of federal investigators or prosecutors regarding any investigations or criminal charges. Law enforcement officers and prosecutors may never select the timing of investigative steps or criminal charges for the purpose of giving an advantage or disadvantage to any candidate or political party.

For further guidance, prosecutors and law enforcement officers may contact the Criminal Division's Public Integrity Section. More detailed guidance is also available in sections 1-4.000 and 9-85.000 of the United States Attorneys' Manual, and in a treatise published by the Department called FEDERAL PROSECUTION OF ELECTION OFFENSES (8th ed. 2017).[17]

---

threats and vulnerabilities we are monitoring. These efforts have included providing defensive briefings to major political organizations such as the Republican and Democratic National Committees.

3. Covert influence operations to assist or harm political organizations, campaigns, and government officials. The FBI counters the activities of foreign governments and their proxies by proactively investigating unregistered foreign agents in the United States, alerting these foreign agents' targets (or intended targets) where appropriate, and raising public awareness of foreign influence methods and effective countermeasures both through appropriate enforcement actions and through assistance to other federal agencies and State or local authorities with enforcement authority.

The Department will aggressively enforce federal laws that require foreign agents to register with the U.S. government and that prohibit foreign nationals from tricking unwitting Americans into participating in, or accepting support from, foreign influence efforts. Along those lines, the Department has stepped up enforcement efforts against individuals and entities that had not fulfilled their obligations under the Foreign Agents Registration Act ("FARA"), including by educating prosecutors and agents nationwide about the importance of the statute and how to investigate it; expanding our outreach to individuals and entities who may be required to register; and achieving the registrations of sophisticated individuals and entities that had not fulfilled their legal obligations, including the American agents of Russian state-funded media networks (RT and Sputnik). Going forward, we will increase FARA awareness and compliance through increased outreach, by making additional advisory opinions public, and by issuing guidance if appropriate under Department policy. In addition, we will investigate and prosecute criminal violations of FARA and other laws that restrict the activities of foreign agents acting within the United States.

The Department also will seek to increase understanding of the foreign intelligence threat in order to reduce the effectiveness of covert activities and efforts to obscure the true motivation and origin of foreign influence operations. The FBI can provide defensive counterintelligence briefings to political organizations and campaigns as necessary to protect against and improve awareness of the foreign influence threat. In addition, the FBI continues to pursue criminal and traditional counterintelligence investigations to address the range of potential covert operations targeting political organizations.

4. Covert influence operations, including disinformation operations, to influence public opinion and sow division. Depending on the facts, a foreign government's efforts to use the Internet as part of a hostile effort to multiply its propaganda's malign influence on the American public may violate a number of federal laws on which the Department may base criminal investigations and prosecutions. The Department is also considering whether new criminal statutes aimed more directly at this type of activity are needed.

The Department has crafted a strategy to counter each phase of the foreign malign influence campaign cycle. *See* **Fig. 2**. While the success of a foreign influence campaign via the Internet and social media depends heavily on the adversary's ability to obscure the true motivation and origin of its activities—something the Internet can facilitate—the infrastructure of online accounts required to carry out such a campaign also provides the Department with opportunities for identification and disruption. For example, the FBI and IC partners may be able to identify and track foreign agents as they establish their infrastructure and mature their online presence, in which case authorities can work with social media companies to illuminate and ultimately disrupt those agents' activities, including through voluntary removal of accounts that violate a company's terms of service.

In addition to these activities, in some circumstances, public exposure and attribution of foreign influence operations, and of foreign governments' goals and methods in conducting them, can be an important means of countering the threat and rendering those operations less effective. Of course, partisan politics must play no role in the decision whether to disclose the existence of a foreign influence operation, and such disclosures must not be made for the purpose of conferring any advantage or disadvantage on any political or social group. In addition, the Department must seek to protect intelligence sources and methods and operational equities, and attribution itself may present challenges. It is also important not to take actions that merely exacerbate the impact of a foreign influence operation, or that re-victimize its victims. Given the competing in-

Figure 2: The Malign Foreign Influence Campaign Cycle

terests sometimes at stake, the Department has established a formal policy on the disclosure of foreign influence operations to guide its actions in this critically important area. That policy is found at pages 16–17.

5. Overt influence efforts, such as the use of foreign media outlets to influence policymakers and the public. Overt foreign government efforts to influence the American public or policymakers may be lawful so long as the relevant government complies with U.S. laws requiring public disclosure, along with other applicable laws. When foreign media outlets or lobbyists act as agents of foreign governments, they may be required to register as foreign agents under FARA. Media outlets with links to China, Japan, Russia, and South Korea have done so. Apart from enforcing such laws, the Department—in concert with the U.S. government as a whole, as well as with American society more broadly—can help increase public understanding of foreign influence operations.

Conclusion

The nature of foreign influence operations will continue to change as technology and our foreign adversaries' tactics change. Our adversaries will persist in seeking to exploit the diversity of today's information space, and the tactics and technology they employ will continue to evolve.

The Department plays an important role in combating foreign efforts to interfere in our elections, but it cannot alone solve the problem. There are limits to the Department's role—and the role of the U.S. government—

in addressing foreign influence operations aimed at sowing discord and undermining our Nation's institutions. Combating foreign influence operations requires a whole-of-society approach that relies on coordinated actions by federal, State, and local government agencies; support from potential victims and the private sector; and the active engagement of an informed public.

Even so, investigating and prosecuting those who violate our laws, disrupting particular operations, and exposing covert foreign activities can be useful in defending against this threat. It is therefore critical that the Department consistently evaluate existing law and policy governing its actions, as well as its strategic approach to the problem. In the short term, the Department must use all current authorities to counter the foreign influence threat, working closely with the IC, DHS, State and local governments, and where appropriate, the private sector.

We also must ensure that we are sharing information about the threat with potential victims, other affected individuals, and the public, consistent with our policies and our national security interests. In the longer term, we must consider what additional authorities or policies would be useful and appropriate to enable us to respond as effectively as possible to the foreign influence threat.

*   *   *

The story is told that a woman named Elizabeth Powel approached Benjamin Franklin when he was walking home after the Constitutional Convention in the summer of 1787. Powel asked Franklin what type of govern-

COUNTERING MALIGN FOREIGN INFLUENCE OPERATIONS

ment the Founders had created. Franklin replied: "A republic, madam, if you can keep it." Powel's question illustrates that it was not inevitable that our Nation would begin as a democratic republic. Franklin's answer reminds us that it is not inevitable that we will remain a democratic republic.[15]

Our Nation's democratic processes are strong. But the Constitution comes with a condition: we need to keep it. We are all keepers of the republic, and it is incumbent upon all of us, as a society, to counter the foreign influence threat. The Department of Justice will certainly play its part.

DEPARTMENT OF JUSTICE POLICY ON DISCLOSURE OF FOREIGN INFLUENCE OPERATIONS

Foreign influence operations include covert actions by foreign governments intended to sow divisions in our society, undermine confidence in our democratic institutions, and otherwise affect political sentiment and public discourse to achieve strategic geopolitical objectives. Such operations are often empowered by modern technology that facilitates malicious cyber activity and covert or anonymous communications with U.S. audiences on a mass scale from abroad.

Our Nation's democratic processes and institutions are strong and must remain resilient in the face of this threat. It is the policy of the Department of Justice to investigate, disrupt, and prosecute the perpetrators of illegal foreign influence activities where feasible. It is also the Department's policy to alert the victims and unwitting targets of foreign influence activities, when appropriate and consistent with the Department's policies and practices, and with our national security interests.

It may not be possible or prudent to disclose foreign influence operations in certain contexts because of investigative or operational considerations, or other constraints. In some circumstances, however, public exposure and attribution of foreign influence operations can be an important means of countering the threat and rendering those operations less effective.

Information the Department of Justice collects concerning foreign influence operations may be disclosed as follows:

- To support arrests and charges for federal crimes arising out of foreign influence operations, such as hacking or malicious cyber activity, identity theft, and fraud.

- To alert victims of federal crimes arising out of foreign influence operations, consistent with Department guidelines on victim notification and assistance.[18]

- To alert unwitting recipients of foreign government-sponsored covert support, as necessary to assist in countering the threat.

- To alert technology companies or other private sector entities to foreign influence operations where their services are used to disseminate covert foreign government propaganda or disinformation, or to provide other covert support to political organizations or groups.

**DEPARTMENT OF JUSTICE POLICY ON DISCLOSURE
OF FOREIGN INFLUENCE OPERATIONS,** *Continued*

- To alert relevant Congressional committees to significant intelligence activities, consistent with statutory reporting requirements and Executive Branch policies.

- To alert the public or other affected individuals, where the federal or national interests in doing so outweigh any countervailing considerations.[19]

In performing these functions, the Department will be mindful of the following principles and policies:

- Partisan political considerations must play no role in efforts to alert victims, other affected individuals, or the American public to foreign influence operations against the United States. Such efforts must not be for the purpose of conferring any advantage or disadvantage on any political or social group or any individual or organization.

- In considering whether and how to disclose foreign influence operations, or the details thereof, the Department will seek to protect intelligence sources and methods, investigations, and other U.S. government operations.

- Foreign influence operations will be publicly identified as such only when the Department can attribute those activities to a foreign government with high confidence. Disinformation or other support or influence by unknown or domestic sources not acting on behalf of a foreign government is beyond the scope of this policy.

- Where a criminal or national security investigation during an election cycle is at issue, the Department must also be careful to adhere to longstanding policies regarding the timing of charges or taking overt investigative steps.[20]

The Department (including the FBI) will not necessarily be the appropriate entity to disclose information publicly concerning a foreign influence operation. Where a Department component is considering whether to alert the general public to a specific foreign influence operation, consultation with the National Security Division is required. Nothing in this policy is intended to impair information sharing undertaken by Department components for investigative or intelligence purposes.

NOTES

[1] *See* U.S. Const. art. I, § 4 (Congressional elections) & art. II, § 4 (Presidential elections).

[2] The term "ballot fraud" in this context includes fraud in the processes by which voters are registered or by which votes are cast or tabulated.

[3] Foreign influence operations, while not always illegal, can implicate several U.S. federal criminal statutes, including (but not limited to): 18 U.S.C. § 371 (conspiracy); 18 U.S.C. § 951 (acting in the United States as an agent of a foreign government without prior notification to the Attorney General); 18 U.S.C. § 1001 (false statements); 18 U.S.C. § 1028A (aggravated identity theft); 18 U.S.C. § 1030 (computer fraud and abuse); 18 U.S.C. §§ 1343, 1344 (wire fraud and bank fraud); 18 U.S.C. § 1519 (destruction of evidence); 18 U.S.C. § 1546 (visa fraud); 22 U.S.C. § 618 (Foreign Agents Registration Act); 52 U.S.C. §§ 30109, 30121 (soliciting or making foreign contributions to influence federal elections, or donations to influence State or local elections).

[4] OFFICE OF THE DIRECTOR OF NATIONAL INTELLIGENCE, BACKGROUND TO "ASSESSING RUSSIAN ACTIVITIES AND INTENTIONS IN RECENT U.S. ELECTIONS": THE ANALYTIC PROCESS AND CYBER INCIDENT ATTRIBUTION ii (Jan. 2017) ("ODNI Report"), available at: https://www.dni.gov/files/documents/ICA_2017_01.pdf (last accessed June 29, 2018).

[5] ODNI Report at 2; *see also* U.S. HOUSE OF REPRESENTATIVES PERMANENT SELECT COMMITTEE ON INTELLIGENCE, REPORT ON RUSSIAN ACTIVE MEASURES viii (March 2018) ("In 2015, Russia began engaging in a covert influence campaign aimed at the U.S. presidential election. The Russian government, at the direction of Vladimir Putin, sought to sow discord in American society and undermine our faith in the democratic process."), available at: https://intelligence.house.gov/uploadedfiles/final_russia_investigation_report.pdf (last accessed June 29, 2018); MINORITY MEMBERS OF THE HOUSE PERMANENT SELECT COMMITTEE ON INTELLIGENCE, REPORT ON RUSSIAN ACTIVE MEASURES 12 (March 2018), available at: https://democrats-intelligence.house.gov/uploadedfiles/20180411_-_final_-_hpsci_minority_views_on_majority_report.pdf (last accessed June 29, 2018) (summarizing Russian covert cyber efforts and other intelligence and social media operations during the 2016 elections); U.S. SENATE SELECT COMMITTEE ON INTELLIGENCE, RUSSIAN TARGETING OF ELECTION INFRASTRUCTURE DURING THE 2016 ELECTION: SUMMARY OF INITIAL FINDINGS AND RECOMMENDATIONS 1 (May 2018) ("In 2016, cyber actors affiliated with the Russian Government conducted an unprecedented, coordinated cyber campaign against state election infrastructure . . . This activity was part of a larger campaign to prepare to undermine confidence in the voting process. The Committee has not seen any evidence that vote tallies were manipulated or that voter registration information was deleted or modified."), available at: https://www.burr.senate.gov/imo/media/doc/RussRptInstlmt1-%20ElecSec%20Findings,Recs2.pdf (last accessed June 29, 2018).

[6] Daniel R. Coats, Dir. of National Intelligence, "Statement for the Record: Worldwide Threat Assessment of the U.S. Intelligence Community," at 11 (Feb. 13, 2018), available at: https://www.dni.gov/files/documents/Newsroom/Testimonies/2018-ATA---Unclassified-SSCI.pdf (last accessed June 29, 2018).

[7] *Id.*

[8] ODNI Report at 5.

[9] Daniel R. Coats, Dir. of National Intelligence,

COUNTERING MALIGN FOREIGN INFLUENCE OPERATIONS

"Annual Threat Assessment: Opening Statement," *Worldwide Threats: Hearing Before the Senate Select Comm. on Intelligence*, 115TH CONG. (Feb. 13, 2018), at 18, available at: https://www.dni.gov/files/documents/Newsroom/Testimonies/ATA2018-asprepared.pdf (last accessed June 29, 2018).

[10] ODNI Report at 2.

[11] Indictment in *United States v. Internet Research Agency*, et al., No. 18-cr-32-DLF (D.D.C. Feb. 16, 2018), available at: https://www.justice.gov/file/1035477/download (last accessed June 29, 2018).

[12] *Id.*

[13] 22 U.S.C. § 611 *et seq.*

[14] *See* "Principles of Federal Prosecution," U.S. ATTORNEYS' MANUAL, TITLE 9, SECTION 27.000, available at: https://www.justice.gov/usam/usam-9-27000-principles-federal-prosecution (last accessed June 29, 2018).

[15] This story and its associated lessons are recounted in Rod J. Rosenstein, Deputy Attorney General, "Constitution Day Address," National Constitution Center (Sept. 18, 2017), available at: https://www.justice.gov/opa/speech/deputy-attorney-general-rod-j-rosenstein-delivers-constitution-day-address (last accessed June 29, 2018).

[16] As part of the Department's ballot fraud program, the **FBI** must maintain an Election Crimes Coordinator ("ECC") in each of its Divisions. The ECCs are the Department's primary liaison with State and local police agencies, and election administrators, as well as with other federal agencies, in the field. They attend regular trainings, coordinate local task force communications with State and local counterparts during elections, and handle intake reporting of ballot fraud alle-

gations from non-government groups or individuals. The FBI then investigates properly-predicated ballot fraud cases, in coordination with a local **U.S. Attorney's Office ("USAO")**. The FBI and USAO are free to exercise their discretion to conduct a preliminary investigation after assessing the case and ensuring non-interference with the election process. They may pursue a full field and grand jury investigation, and seek charges, after consultation with the Criminal Division's **Public Integry Section ("PIN")**. However, the FBI and other federal law enforcement agencies may not conduct investigations that would infringe the Department's non-interference with elections policy (*see* page 11), or that would unlawfully result in an armed federal presence at a polling site. *See* 18 U.S.C. § 592. For almost forty years, PIN has provided the field with an Election Crimes Branch Director. Pursuant to the United States Attorneys' Manual, the Director, assisted as needed by other managers and staff at PIN, functions as a mandatory consultant for the USAOs on all ballot fraud matters that progress beyond a preliminary investigation, see U.S.A.M. § 9-85.210, and as a subject matter expert available to provide advice and assistance to USAOs and the FBI. The Director coordinates and conducts mandatory live training with designated field personnel of the USAOs and FBI. The Director also leads an Election Day Watch program during federal election seasons to monitor and coordinate responses to election events while the polls are open on each federal election day. The Election Day Watch program is the Department's mechanism for ensuring consistent and efficient communication and coordination between interagency representatives, federal prosecutors and investigators in the field, and State and local partners. Each USAO must maintain a District Election Officer ("DEO") among its cadre of Assistant United States Attorneys. The DEOs are the Department's primary liaison with State and local counterparts in the field. They attend regular trainings, and as part of the Election Day

CYBER-DIGITAL TASK FORCE REPORT

Watch program, coordinate local task force communications with State and local counterparts leading up to and during the elections. DEOs also coordinate press releases concerning election-day procedures to facilitate reporting to the federal government of ballot fraud allegations from non-government groups or individuals. The Voting Section and Criminal Section of the Department's **Civil Rights Division ("CRT")** coordinates regularly with PIN to ensure that ballot fraud allegations are routed to the best response entity. CRT maintains a hotline that operates all year, including throughout federal election days, to facilitate reporting of allegations of potential voting-related federal law violations. CRT's Voting Section also enforces the civil provisions of a wide range of federal statutes that protect the right to vote, including the Voting Rights Act; the National Voter Registration Act; the Uniformed and Overseas Citizens Absentee Voting Act; the Help America Vote Act; and the Civil Rights Act. CRT's Criminal Section enforces federal criminal statutes that prohibit voter intimidation and voter suppression based on race, color, national origin, or religion. Finally, the **Department of Homeland Security ("DHS")** recently has joined existing efforts to combat ballot fraud in the specific area of cyber threats. In particular, DHS provides advice and resources to State and local counterparts to assess the risks to their computer systems for voter registration, balloting, and tabulation. DHS also has certain resources for incident response, though the FBI has greater local resources and, under PPD-41, retains the lead on incident response.

[17] This treatise is available online at: https://www. justice.gov/criminal/file/1029066/download (last accessed June 29, 2018). The most relevant discussion can be found at pages 84-85: "The Justice Department's goals in the area of election crime are to prosecute those who violate federal criminal law and, through such prosecutions, deter corruption of future elections. The Department

does not have a role in determining which candidate won a particular election, or whether another election should be held because of the impact of the alleged fraud on the election . . . . In investigating an election fraud matter, federal law enforcement personnel should carefully evaluate whether an investigative step under consideration has the potential to affect the election itself. Starting a public criminal investigation of alleged election fraud before the election to which the allegations pertain has been concluded runs the obvious risk of chilling legitimate voting and campaign activities. It also runs the significant risk of interjecting the investigation itself as an issue, both in the campaign and in the adjudication of any ensuing election contest . . . . Accordingly, overt criminal investigative measures ordinarily should not be taken in matters involving alleged fraud in the manner in which votes were cast or counted until the election in question has been concluded, its results certified, and all recounts and election contests concluded. Not only does such investigative restraint avoid interjecting the federal government into election campaigns, the voting process, and the adjudication of ensuing recounts and election contest litigation, but it also ensures that evidence developed during any election litigation is available to investigators, thereby minimizing the need to duplicate investigative efforts. Many election fraud issues are developed to the standards of factual predication for a federal criminal investigation during post-election litigation."

[18] *See Attorney General Guidelines for Victim and Witness Assistance* (May 2012), available at: https://www.justice.gov/sites/default/files/olp/docs/ag_guidelines2012.pdf (last accessed June 29, 2018); *see also* 42 U.S.C. § 10607 (Victims' Rights and Restitution Act).

[19] For example, there may be an important federal or national interest in publicly disclosing a foreign influence operation that threatens to un-

dermine confidence in the government or public institutions; risks inciting violence or other illegal actions; or may cause substantial harm, alarm, or confusion if left unaddressed. On the other hand, in some cases, public disclosure of a foreign influence operation may be counterproductive because it may amplify or otherwise exacerbate the foreign government's messaging, or may re-victimize the victim.

[20] *See,* e.g., U.S. DEPT. OF JUSTICE, FEDERAL PROSECUTION OF ELECTION OFFENSES 8-9, 84-85 (8th ed. 2017), quoted in *supra* note 17.

CHAPTER 2
CATEGORIZING SOPHISTICATED CYBER SCHEMES

Malign foreign influence operations represent a significant cyber-enabled threat to American society and national security. But they are not the only one. Every day, criminals and other hackers within the United States and around the world seek to use computers, smart devices, and other chip-enabled technology—as well as the networks that connect them—to victimize American consumers and businesses, or to do our government harm.

In this chapter, we describe some of the most prevalent and dangerous types of cybercrime schemes our Nation currently faces. Various actors, with varying motivations, perpetrate these schemes, targeting various categories of victims. All of these schemes, however, rely on the malicious, unauthorized use of computers to penetrate into another person's computer or network. This technical baseline provides a set of common operational techniques across the range of complicated cybercriminal plots. Indeed, in a threat landscape that constantly evolves and features a diverse set of actors, motivations, and targets, the prevalence of certain key techniques is a significant and rare constant.

Cybercrime Schemes

In the current landscape, cyber-enabled schemes tend to fall into one or more of five basic categories: (1) damage to computer systems; (2) data theft; (3) fraud/carding schemes; (4) crimes threatening personal privacy; and (5) crimes threatening critical infrastructure.

1. Damage to computer systems

Many cyber threats directly target computer systems and networks, seeking to damage the integrity or availability of data and services housed on those systems. For example, a **Distributed Denial of Service ("DDoS") attack** involves the orchestrated transmission of communications engineered to overwhelm the victim network's connection to the Internet in order to impair or disrupt that network's ability to send or receive communications. Because they require the near simultaneous and sustained sending of communications against a discrete target, DDoS attacks usually are launched by a large network of hijacked computers called a botnet. (For further discussion of botnets, see page 41.) Common targets of DDoS attacks include websites that the criminals wish to disable and push off-line, either because they disagree with the content, or because they wish to drive traffic to sites they prefer.

DDoS attacks can have crippling, far-reaching effects. In October 2016, for example, a massive DDoS attack targeting a U.S.-based company that controls much of the Internet's domain name system infrastructure brought down many of the world's best-known websites for several hours, including sites belonging to Twitter, Pinterest, CNN, Fox News, and Netflix. The botnet used to launch this attack was originally created a few years before. The Department recently convicted the botnet's creators after the leader of the group admitted that he and his conspirators developed it in part to initiate powerful DDoS attacks "against business competitors and others against whom [they] held grudges."[1]   They also used the botnet—which, in an alarming new twist, enlisted everyday so-called "Internet of Things" devices into its network of hijacked machines, thereby amplifying its strength by orders of magnitude[2]—to provide a source of revenue, either by renting it out to third-parties in exchange for payment, or by employing it to "extort hosting companies and others into paying protection money in order to avoid being targeted" by DDoS attacks.[3]

Hostile governments, too, may employ DDoS attacks to advance their geopolitical goals and undermine our national security. In March 2016, for example, a federal grand jury in New York indicted seven Iranian hackers belonging to two companies that worked for Iran's Islamic Revolutionary Guard Corps for their role in DDoS attacks targeting the public-facing websites of nearly fifty U.S. banks.[4] These DDoS attacks against the U.S. financial sector began in approximately December 2011, and occurred sporadically until September 2012, at which point they escalated in frequency to a near-weekly basis. On certain days during the DDoS campaign, victim computer servers were hit with massive amounts of traffic, which cut off hundreds of thousands of customers from online access to their bank accounts. These attacks collectively cost the banks tens of millions of dollars to remediate

as they worked to neutralize and mitigate the attacks on their servers. In 2017, the Department of the Treasury added the seven hackers to the Office of Foreign Assets Control ("OFAC") Specially Designated National and Blocked Persons List.[5]

Malign actors also use **ransomware** to inflict damage to a victim's computer systems. Ransomware is malicious computer code (or "malware") that blocks a victim's access to data on its systems, typically by encrypting the data and demanding that the victim pay a ransom, often in the form of a difficult-to-trace virtual currency, to restore the data. See **Fig. 1**.

Ransomware can be delivered in a variety of ways, including through fraudulent e-mails. Such e-mails can be drafted to look like they are from trustworthy senders, containing malicious attachments or links that, once opened or clicked, activate the ransomware. Some variants also try, once they have gained a foothold in a victim's network, to spread laterally across the network to encrypt files on other computers or servers to which the victim's device has access. A second common method involves planting ransomware in hacked websites, which infect the computers of visitors to the sites. In addition, it is not uncommon for criminals to use botnet infrastructure and code to facilitate the widespread delivery of ransomware.

Like DDoS attacks, ransomware attacks can impose immense costs. For example, in 2017, the "WannaCry" ransomware attack spread rapidly and indiscriminately around the world over a mere four days. This campaign—which ultimately was attributed to

CATEGORIZING SOPHISTICATED CYBER SCHEMES

Figure 1: The Anatomy of a Ransomware Attack

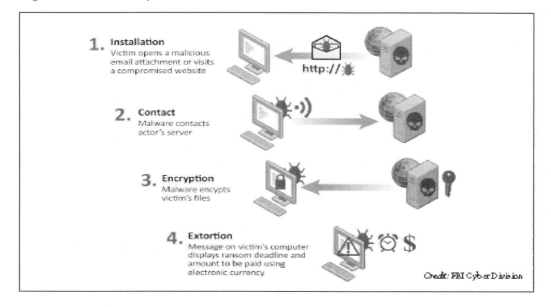

1. **Installation**
   Victim opens a malicious email attachment or visits a compromised website

2. **Contact**
   Malware contacts actor's server

3. **Encryption**
   Malware encrypts victim's files

4. **Extortion**
   Message on victim's computer displays ransom deadline and amount to be paid using electronic currency

Credit: FBI Cyber Division

the North Korean government—rendered useless "hundreds of thousands of computers in hospitals, schools, businesses, and homes in over 150 countries."[7] Total damages likely ran into the hundreds of millions of dollars. High-profile incidents such as the March 2018 attack that crippled Atlanta's city government make clear that ransomware schemes remain a threat.

Typically, cybercriminals run ransomware campaigns: the goal is to damage the victim's computer system in the short-term in order to get the victim to pay. If the scheme is to succeed, in other words, the victim needs to get their files back. By contrast, **destructive attacks**—another type of cyber threat that directly targets computer systems and networks—destroy the victim's data. For that reason, these attacks often are associated

with nation states and other entities that have broader motivations. To be sure, destructive attacks may come disguised as ransomware campaigns; the malware linked to the notorious "NotPetya" attack launched by the Russian military in June 2017, for example, locked up its victims' files and purported to demand a ransom. It soon became clear, however, that this cyberattack was "meant to paralyze, not profit," as victims who tried to pay found it almost impossible to do so.[9] This attack, which was "part of the Kremlin's ongoing effort to destabilize Ukraine," resulted in "the most destructive and costly cyberattack in history," "causing billions of dollars in damage across Europe, Asia, and the Americas."[10] Similarly, the "WannaCry" attack described above did not prove to be very lucrative to the attackers. Rather, it was a reckless attack that resulted in havoc and

CYBER-DIGITAL TASK FORCE REPORT

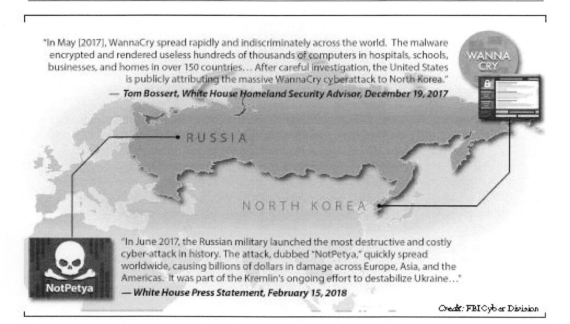

"In May [2017], WannaCry spread rapidly and indiscriminately across the world. The malware encrypted and rendered useless hundreds of thousands of computers in hospitals, schools, businesses, and homes in over 150 countries... After careful investigation, the United States is publicly attributing the massive WannaCry cyberattack to North Korea."
— *Tom Bossert, White House Homeland Security Advisor, December 19, 2017*

"In June 2017, the Russian military launched the most destructive and costly cyber-attack in history. The attack, dubbed "NotPetya," quickly spread worldwide, causing billions of dollars in damage across Europe, Asia, and the Americas. It was part of the Kremlin's ongoing effort to destabilize Ukraine..."
— *White House Press Statement, February 15, 2018*

Credit: FBI Cyber Division

destruction; any money that was raised was purely a side benefit.[11]

Perhaps the most notorious example of a destructive attack launched against a U.S. company was the November 2014 cyberattack by North Korea on Sony Pictures Entertainment ("SPE"). This attack destroyed much of SPE's computer systems, compromised private information, released valuable corporate data and intellectual property, and threatened employees, customers, and film distributers with violence. The attackers stole a large number of files—which included private correspondence, unreleased films, salary records, and social security numbers—and released much of the information to the public, imposing significant financial and other consequences. The attack forced SPE to take its company-wide computer network offline and left thousands of its computers inoperable.

In response to the cyberattack on SPE, the U.S. government publicly attributed the incident to the North Korean government, and then sanctioned a North Korean government agency, two trading companies, and ten North Korean individuals.[13]

2. Data Theft

As the world grows increasingly reliant on digital technology, and as companies store ever larger quantities of data about their customers and other individuals, criminals have sought to steal and profit from control over that data. The past decade has witnessed numerous publicly reported instances of criminals hacking into computer systems and stealing **personally identifying information ("PII")** about hundreds of millions of individuals.

CATEGORIZING SOPHISTICATED CYBER SCHEMES

According to one report, there were at least 686 data breaches reported in the first quarter of 2018, resulting in the theft of as many as 1.4 billion records.[14] Stolen PII can include dates of birth, social security numbers, credit card numbers, e-mail addresses, drivers' license numbers, payroll and tax information, and even answers to security questions used to log into systems—namely, everything needed to misappropriate victims' identities, make fraudulent purchases (including filing fraudulent claims for tax refunds), and craft phishing and other social engineering attacks on specific targets. Breaches of major retailers can reveal transaction information and expose these companies to massive financial losses, while imposing upon members of the public the risk that their identities will be used to commit other financial crimes, with all of the associated impacts. Crimes of this sort are tremendously costly to all involved. According to one estimate, the average total cost in 2017 to a victim company from a data breach was approximately $7.35 million.[15] The Internet Crime Complaint Center ("IC3"), the FBI unit that receives and tracks cybercrime complaints from victims, received a total of 3,785 complaints of corporate data breach in 2017, with reported losses exceeding $60 million.[16]

Government agencies face similar threats. As agencies try to use new information technologies to make it easier for individuals and entities to submit and obtain information necessary for paying taxes, obtaining benefits, or providing services, the avenues for potential breaches dramatically increase. Of course, government agencies collect and store sensitive information concerning not only the general public, but also their own employees. This fact makes them valuable targets. For example, the U.S. Office of Personnel Management announced in 2015 it had been victimized through two separate but related cyberattacks that resulted in the theft of highly sensitive background investigation records of current, former, and prospective federal employees and contractors, as well as the theft of personnel data of over 21 million people.[17] Data breaches like these degrade public trust in government agencies.

Sometimes, nation states facilitate the work of criminals who seek to steal and profit from user data. In March 2017, the Department announced criminal charges against two officers of the Russian Federal Security Service ("FSB") and two additional conspirators involving computer hacking, economic espionage, and other offenses in connection with a conspiracy to access Yahoo's network as well as information concerning millions of individual webmail accounts.[18] Those charges revealed that officers from the FSB unit that serves as the FBI's point of contact in Moscow on cybercrime matters were using criminal hackers—one of whom already had been publicly charged in two separate investigations in the United States—to target American webmail providers and technology companies, among others.

The public revelation that FSB officers for years had worked with a wanted cybercriminal, and had allowed him to further victimize his targets (for example, by searching compromised accounts for credit card and other information that could be monetized), laid bare for the public and international community the nexus between the Russian state apparatus and the Russian criminal underworld. These charges also demonstrated that the Russian government has not always been a responsible stakeholder in the fight against international cybercrime. One of the indicted hackers was arrested in Canada and brought to the United States; he pled guilty to eight criminal counts in U.S. federal court in November 2017, and was sentenced to a five-year prison term in May 2018.[19]   In December 2016, OFAC designated the FSB under a new executive order issued to expand the authority under E.O. 13694, which empowers the President to block the property of persons who engage in significant malicious cyber-enabled activities.[20]   On March 15, 2018, the Department of the Treasury also designated the FSB pursuant to section 224 of the Countering America's Adversaries Through Sanctions Act, which targets cyber actors operating on behalf of the Russian government in particular.

Malign actors can also use data thefts to further terrorist acts. In June 2015, an ISIL-linked hacker named Ardit Ferizi stole PII belonging to tens of thousands of customers of a U.S. company, including members of the military and other government personnel. Ferizi subsequently culled the PII belonging to 1,300 particular individuals employed by the U.S. government and provided that information to Junaid Hussain, a now-deceased ISIL recruiter and attack facilitator. In August 2015, Hussain posted the names on Twitter in the name of the Islamic State Hacking Division with a message saying, in part: "We are in your emails and computer systems, watching and recording your every move, we have your names and addresses, we are in your emails and social media accounts,

we are extracting confidential data and passing on your personal information to the soldiers of the khilafah, who soon with the permission of Allah will strike at your necks in your own lands!" Malaysian authorities detained Ferizi, who subsequently consented to extradition to the United States. He pleaded guilty and was sentenced to 20 years in prison for providing material support to ISIL, and for accessing a protected computer without authorization and obtaining information in order to provide material support to a designated foreign terrorist organization.[21]

THE COSTS OF INTELLECTUAL PROPERTY CRIME

Estimates vary regarding the size of economic loss that can be attributed to the theft of intellectual property and trade secrets. The Commission on the Theft of American Intellectual Property has estimated that the annual cost to the U.S. economy through the theft of trade secrets, and through counterfeit goods and pirated software, exceeds $225 billion and could be as high as $600 billion.[22] According to a cybersecurity industry report, the direct costs of cyber theft in 2014 for over 50 U.S.-based private and public sector organizations ranged from just under $2 million to $65 million each year per company, an increase of 82 percent over six years.[23] Pricewaterhouse Coopers estimated in 2014 that the United States lost between one and three percent of its gross domestic product each year due to trade secret theft.[24]

CATEGORIZING SOPHISTICATED CYBER SCHEMES

The **theft of intellectual property** represents another significant data theft problem. The two most notable types of cyber-enabled intellectual property crime are the infringement of copyrighted material over the Internet and the misappropriation of trade secrets stored in a digital format. Internet sites that profit from the unauthorized distribution of copyrighted movies, music, software, and other digital works can have a global reach, generate millions of dollars of illicit revenue for the operators, and cause extensive financial harm to the owners of the works being shared. While copyrighted works generally are intended to be accessible to the public under terms set by the copyright owner, trade secrets receive criminal protection specifically because they involve knowledge that is not known to the public and derive value from remaining secret.

Kim Dotcom, Finn Batato, Mathias Ortmann, Bram van der Kolk, and others are members of a worldwide criminal organization whose members allegedly engaged in criminal copyright infringement with estimated harm to copyright holders well in excess of $400 million, and which yielded over $175 million in illicit proceeds.[25] The conspirators operated a commercial website and service called Megaupload.com, which reproduced and distributed copies of popular copyrighted content without authorization and claimed at one time to account for four percent of total Internet traffic—including more than one billion total visits, 150 million registered users, and 50 million daily visitors. A federal grand jury charged members of the conspiracy with a number of conspiracy, racketeering, copyright infringement, money laundering, and fraud offenses. Dotcom

and the others were arrested in 2012 in New Zealand, but their extraditions to the United States still remain on appeal in that nation. Despite delays in the criminal case, the Department of Justice has prevailed in a civil forfeiture action in U.S. federal court to forfeit the proceeds of the criminal conspiracy.

Following the takedown of Megaupload.com, other online piracy sites grew in popularity. On July 20, 2016, Artem Vaulin of Ukraine was arrested in Poland based on U.S. federal charges for conspiracy to commit criminal copyright infringement, conspiracy to commit money laundering, and criminal copyright infringement.[26] Vaulin is alleged to have run one of the world's most visited illegal file-sharing websites, Kickass Torrents ("KAT"), which was seized as part of the operation. KAT enabled users to illegally reproduce and distribute hundreds of millions of copyrighted motion pictures, video games, television programs, musical recordings, and other electronic media. Initial investigation indicates that the copyrighted material was collectively valued at well over $1 billion, and that the site, which was in the top 100 most frequently visited sites on the Internet, received more than 50 million unique visitors each month.

On the trade secret front, the Department obtained a conviction in January 2018 in U.S. federal court against a China-based manufacturer and exporter of wind turbines that stole trade secrets from a U.S.-based company. The Chinese company, Sinovel Wind Group Co. Ltd., conspired with others to steal proprietary wind turbine technology from the American corporate victim in order to produce its own wind turbines and to retrofit

CYBER-DIGITAL TASK FORCE REPORT

existing wind turbines with stolen technology. These crimes cost the victim more than $1 billion in shareholder equity and almost 700 jobs—over half its global workforce.[27]

In addition, the Department has pursued charges not only against criminals seeking monetary gain, but also against nation-state actors engaged in economic espionage through cyber means. In May 2014, for example, a federal grand jury indicted five uniformed members of the Chinese military on charges of hacking and conducting economic espionage against large U.S. entities in the nuclear power, metal, and solar energy industries. The lengthy statement of charges described numerous specific instances where officers of the People's Liberation Army ("PLA") were alleged to have hacked into the computer systems of U.S. victims to steal

Figure 2: Chinese Military Officers Charged with Hacking and Economic Espionage

trade secrets and sensitive, internal communications for commercial advantage or private financial gain. *See* **Fig. 2**. Although the five charged PLA officers remain at large, this case illustrated how the Department's independent investigations and actions can play an important role as part of a broader, coordinated approach designed to support American companies, deter our adversaries, and otherwise change their behavior.

The indictment sent a clear message that the state-sponsored theft of trade secrets or other confidential business information, with the intent of providing competitive advantages to companies or commercial sectors, is unacceptable. This norm thereafter gained widespread acceptance, most notably in a bilateral agreement between the United States and China in September 2015,[28] and among the G20 at the Antalya Summit in Turkey in November 2015.[29] Although some U.S. cybersecurity firms indicate that computer intrusions by Chinese state-sponsored hackers targeting U.S. firms have decreased since then,[30] the U.S. government continues to monitor China's compliance with the norm, and with that nation's September 2015 commitment to cooperate on investigations of crimes emanating from its territory. To that end, in late 2017, the Department charged three Chinese nationals who worked for the purported Internet security firm known as Boyusec with stealing trade secrets and other confidential information from American firms until as recently as May 2017—long after the Chinese commitments of September 2015.[31] After the Department sought assistance from the Chinese authorities in investigating the allegations and "received

no meaningful response,"[32] the Department acknowledged as much and unsealed the indictment, providing insight into the status of China's adherence to norms it purportedly had embraced.

3. *Fraud/Carding Schemes*

At the core of fraud lies deceit. It can manifest in an intent to deceive by those one knows and trusts, or, as is often the case with cybercrime, by criminals defrauding victims by abusing the Internet's lack of a trusted and effective means to authenticate another's identity. Online systems with weak authentication and few indications for determining another's true identity have opened the door for fraudsters to commit numerous crimes by faking their online identities or fraudulently adopting the identities of others. Cyber fraud schemes take many forms, including Nigerian-letter scams in which fraudsters e-mail victims claiming to be Nigerian government officials in need of assistance in transferring stolen funds out of Nigeria. Recipients who respond are encouraged to cover upfront the supposed expenses for the transfers themselves, upon the fraudulent promise of later repayment, and to provide personal banking information and other identifying information—which is later used to drain victims' bank accounts.[33] Other forms include frauds that convince victims to donate to fake charities, especially after natural disasters, and fraudulent online transactions or exchanges in which no payment is made to, or no good or service is received by, the victim.[34]

Other schemes entice victims to purchase investment and financial instruments, often marketed with misleading claims of offering low-risk, high-reward guaranteed returns or overly consistent returns. Examples include Ponzi schemes, advance fee frauds, pyramid schemes, and market manipulation frauds. These schemes can target members of affinity groups, such as groups with a common religion or ethnicity, in order to exploit that supposed connection to build trust and operate the investment fraud against the victim.[35] Carding schemes are another major financial threat. These schemes involve criminals selling and purchasing hacked credit card information, typically through dark markets devoted to criminal activity, that is then used to commit fraudulent ATM transactions, purchase pre-paid gift cards, and buy goods that are then re-shipped to criminal organizations. In just one example, a group of Russian criminals hacked into systems at credit card processors, banks, retailers, and other companies, and stole over 160 million credit card numbers.[36]

4. Cyber-enabled crimes threatening personal privacy

Criminals regularly abuse the global reach, connectivity, and anonymity of information technology services to commit a wide range of crimes targeting specific individuals. Many of these behaviors represent reprehensible and often dangerous violations of the victim's privacy rights, and can have lasting, damaging impact. Examples of these crimes include sextortion and non-consensual pornography (sometimes colloquially called "revenge porn"), as well as cyber-enabled harassment and stalking of victims. Criminals are using online tactics—including computer hacking, phishing attacks, and social media manipulation—to gain access to sensitive, often sexually explicit information that they use to extort, harass, or stalk all types of people, including vulnerable youth and young adults.

Sextortion fact patterns vary, but some typical scenarios have emerged. A common fact pattern involves a perpetrator demanding something of value, typically sexually explicit images, from a victim. The perpetrator enforces these demands through threats to distribute material that the victim seeks to keep private, such as embarrassing or sexually explicit images involving the victim, or through threats to harm the victim's friends or family, for example by using stolen account information to bankrupt them. A primary tactic that sextortionists use is to lure the victim to share a compromising image or information, which, once obtained, the criminal can use to blackmail the victim into providing additional images or videos. Often, criminals use social engineering tactics to target victims. A common approach is to misrepresent themselves as peers—for example, using profile photos or avatars on social media websites bearing images close in age to the victim—to convince victims they are communicating with an age-appropriate individual who is actually interested in them. By fraudulently building a rapport using flattery, romance, and manipulation, criminals are able to befriend victims and entice them to share sensitive images or information. Other criminals have presented themselves as representatives from a modeling agency that is interested in representing the victim; still others have successfully impersonated the victim's partner in order to trick the victim. In addition,

CATEGORIZING SOPHISTICATED CYBER SCHEMES

criminals also obtain material from victims' online social media accounts, such as personal information and "friends lists," which the criminals exploit to present themselves as acquaintances or someone with similar interests. Finally, some criminals simply hack into a victim's computer and install malware that controls the device's cameras, thereby surreptitiously capturing compromising or personal video footage of the victim. As major consumers of social media, children and young adults are particularly vulnerable to these types of offenses.

Non-consensual pornography describes the distribution of nude or sexually explicit images and videos of an individual without the victim's consent. Images taken consensually during an intimate relationship are released once the relationship ends. Other times, perpetrators obtain consensually produced images by hacking into systems, or obtain non-consensually produced imagery through hidden cameras or by recording sexual assaults. The images may be posted online, often with identifying information and links to social media profiles, or may be sent directly to the victim's co-workers, friends, and family.[37] Non-consensual pornography sometimes overlaps with sextortion, particularly when the perpetrator threatens to distribute sexually explicit images of the victim unless the victim provides additional images or some other thing of value.

Cyber-enabled stalking and **harassment** are other particularly pernicious cyber threats against individuals. These terms cover similar criminal activity that threatens victims, though only cyberstalking is explicitly defined in federal criminal law.[38] Cyberstalking

includes any course of conduct or series of acts taken by the perpetrator that places the victim in reasonable fear of death or serious bodily injury, or causes, attempts to cause, or would reasonably be expected to cause substantial emotional distress to the victim or the victim's immediate family. Prohibited acts include repeated, unwanted, intrusive, and frightening communications from the perpetrator by phone, e-mail, or other forms of communication; harassment and threats communicated through the Internet, such as social media sites; and the posting of information or spreading rumors about the victim on the Internet. Cyber-enabled harassment, by contrast, involves more generalized threats to victims, and includes swatting and doxxing. **Swatting** involves deceiving emergency responders to dispatch a SWAT team or other police unit to the victim's home or location, purportedly because the victim has taken hostages or is otherwise armed and dangerous, which tragically has resulted in deadly outcomes. **Doxxing** involves broadcasting personal information about the victim on the Internet, exposing him or her to further harassment by others.

The Department vigorously pursues these acts when they rise to the level of federal crimes. As just one example, we prosecuted a Department of State employee at the U.S. Embassy in London for engaging in a widespread international computer hacking, cyberstalking, and sextortion campaign.[39] This defendant's scheme involved, among other steps, sending e-mails to thousands of potential victims pretending to be from his targets' e-mail provider. The defendant then used these e-mails to trick victims into revealing their account passwords, which he then used to hack into the accounts and search for sexually explicit photographs. Once the defendant located private photos, he searched for additional personal information about his victims, such as addresses and family member names. Using this information and the stolen explicit images, he then engaged in a cyberstalking campaign, threatening to release the photos if victims did not comply with his demands. This defendant ultimately was sentenced to 57 months in federal prison.[40]

5. *Cyber-enabled crimes threatening critical infrastructure*

Our Nation's critical infrastructure provides the essential services that underpin American society and serves as the backbone of our economy, security, and health systems.[41] Critical infrastructure includes the financial services sector, the electrical grid, dams, electoral systems, and over a dozen other sectors of society whose assets, systems, and networks are considered so vital to the United States that their incapacitation or destruction would have a debilitating effect on our national security, national economic security, national public health or safety, or any combination thereof.[42] These sectors are highly reliant on IT systems and networks. As such, threats targeting critical infrastructure deserve particular attention. For example, major energy systems, such as pipelines and refineries, operate using networked industrial control systems that permit remote operation of massive, geographically dispersed facilities and machines. These systems rely on sophisticated computer and communication networks that adversaries target by seeking to identify vulnerabilities

that can be used in the future to disrupt operations or to steal valuable proprietary information. In addition, perpetrators of ransomware schemes, as described above, have sought to exploit society's need for critical infrastructure to remain continuously operational by targeting (and extorting) hospitals, and other vital institutions, that cannot afford any downtime.

Increased connectivity has helped U.S. companies manage and monitor their businesses, but it also has made critical infrastructure vulnerable to cyberattack. Modernization has been a double-edged sword: while it has unlocked new potential for efficiency and performance, the resulting increased connectivity between devices and systems, and especially vital systems like the electrical grid and water treatment facilities, have also created new vulnerabilities and attack vectors that must be defended.[43] As a result, the industrial-control systems that manage and monitor many of our most important industrial facilities and systems are increasingly being targeted by adversaries intent on wreaking havoc.[44] This is not a hypothetical threat: one of the Iranian hackers indicted for the DDoS attacks against the U.S. financial sector is also alleged repeatedly to have gained access to the Supervisory Control and Data Acquisition ("SCADA") system of a dam in New York, allowing him to obtain information regarding the dam's status and operation. Had the system not been under maintenance at the time, the hacker would have been able to control the dam's sluice gate.[45]

Because private entities own and operate the vast majority of the Nation's critical infrastructure, the FBI works to make threat information available to affected sectors through briefings and widely distributed technical alerts developed jointly with DHS. In March 2018, for example, the FBI and DHS announced that for at least two years, Russian government cyber actors had "targeted government entities and multiple U.S. critical infrastructure sectors, including the energy, nuclear, commercial facilities, water, aviation, and critical manufacturing sectors."[46] This technical alert described a multistage Russian intrusion campaign that compromised small commercial facilities' networks and used them to stage malware and to conduct spear-phishing attacks, which allowed the Russians to gain remote access into energy sector networks. The Russian cyber actors then conducted network reconnaissance, before moving laterally across the network and collecting information pertaining to Industrial Control Systems. U.S. Treasury Secretary Steven Mnuchin referenced this activity when announcing that OFAC had sanctioned five Russian entities and nineteen Russian individuals.[47]

Likewise, in May 2018, the FBI and DHS issued a technical alert notifying the public about the FBI's high confidence that malicious North Korean government cyber actors have been using malware since at least 2009 "to target multiple victims globally and in the United States," across various sectors—including critical infrastructure sectors.[48]

*　　*　　*

This non-exhaustive list highlights the varied nature of the most serious cyber threats our Nation faces. To the extent the Department's most important responsibility is to keep Americans safe, it must continue combating these threats and aggressively monitoring how they evolve. One of the most important ways we can stay abreast (if not ahead) of cybercriminals is to fully understand the techniques they use to cause harm. The threats themselves will likely change, but the methods and tools these criminals use to commit computer intrusions and to steal from others have shown remarkable resilience.

Techniques Used to Facilitate Cyber Attacks

The availability of sophisticated technology allows criminals to commit crimes from distant locations, and to avoid detection by victims and law enforcement. Indeed, these technologies greatly expand our adversaries' reach and impact, permitting a small number of criminals to execute intrusions, schemes, and attacks that affect millions of victims. Four of the most common tools that criminals exploit to increase the scale of their attacks include social engineering, malicious software, botnets, and criminal infrastructure.

1. Social Engineering

Social engineering is a tactic criminals use to convince or trick targets into engaging in a specific activity, often by adopting a false identity online of someone the target knows or otherwise believes to be innocuous. Unfortunately, because it preys upon widespread trust that online identities are legitimate, social engineering is surprisingly effective and is a technique used in the vast majority of data breaches and online scams that the FBI investigates.[49]

In a **phishing** scam, for example, criminals impersonate a person or entity trusted by the victim in order to pressure the victim to engage in conduct that benefits the criminal. These schemes may involve sending fraudulent e-mails that appear to come from a legitimate source, such as a victim's bank or Internet Service Provider ("ISP"), requesting the recipient to click on a link to a website controlled by the criminals and to divulge personal account information, or seeking to get the victim to download malware under false pretenses.[50] Other fraudsters use intimidation and threats to entice the victim to act, such as by threatening to close an account, and often ask for usernames, passwords, dates of birth, Social Security numbers, bank numbers, PIN numbers, payment card numbers, or a mother's maiden name. The goal is to acquire PII that the fraudsters can then sell or use to commit other crimes, such as making fraudulent purchases, or to gain access to the victim's computer to steal information or install malware.

Business e-mail compromise ("BEC") scams are another variant of social engineering, where the goal is not to have the victim provide information, but rather to transfer money. Sometimes operating as part of sophisticated transnational criminal organizations, BEC scammers can send e-mails to employees with access to a company's financial system, tricking them into wiring payments to accounts controlled by the criminals. The e-mails often are designed to look as if they came directly from a senior execu-

tive, such as the company's Chief Executive Officer. In some cases, the scammers pick an address that does not belong to the executive but appears to be a real address for the executive, such as being off by one letter. In more sophisticated schemes, BEC fraudsters gain access to the victim company's e-mail system and send requests from the senior executive's actual e-mail account. In 2016, these schemes caused over $360 million of losses reported to the FBI—the largest of any category of cybercrime tracked by IC3.[52] In 2017, IC3 received over 15,000 BEC complaints with adjusted losses of over $675 million, which once again placed these schemes at the top of the loss list.[52]

2. *Malware*

Malware is malicious software that disrupts, damages, or otherwise compromises the integrity of computer systems and networks. It is frequently disseminated by fraudulently or otherwise unlawfully obtaining access to a victim's computer or system and then launching a malicious payload on the victim's system. Malware takes many different forms. Some versions are written to erase data or even render computers unusable, for example by overwriting critical information on their hard drives, thereby preventing the computers from starting. Other types of malware, such as ransomware programs (discussed above), render the data inaccessible by encrypting victims' systems and demanding a ransom with the promise of restoring the victims' data upon payment—a promise that is not always fulfilled. Spyware, including keyloggers, secretly record users' activities on computers, especially the entering of passwords, and transmit sensitive information back to criminals for further exploitation. Any of these actions may be performed by Trojans, which are programs disguised as legitimate software that, once uploaded onto victims' systems, launch hidden malicious software that operates in the background without the victims' knowledge.

3. Botnets

Botnets are vast networks of malware-infected computers and devices that criminals remotely control to conduct a wide range of cybercrime, including sending malware and spam against targets, launching DDoS attacks, and providing infrastructure for ransomware schemes. Botnets—a shortening of "ro**bot net**works"—operate as force multipliers for criminals, giving them control of hundreds, thousands, or even millions of computers to advance their schemes. Because of the relatively low cost of attempting to infect computers with malware, even a comparatively low infection rate can populate a botnet with a vast haul of compromised computers. Further, botnets help criminals cover their tracks from law enforcement by creating an intermediary layer of remotely controlled compromised systems between the criminals and investigators, making it even more challenging for law enforcement to determine who controls the botnet. Moreover, criminals running botnets often are located abroad, which further protects them due to the numerous challenges the Department faces in investigating foreign threats: limited access to digital evidence; delays caused by reliance on mutual legal assistance processes; and the possibility of safe haven from arrest or prosecution in their country of residence. The threat from botnets has in-

creased as individual hackers and organized criminal groups have used ever more sophisticated techniques to infect computers, encrypt communications, and avoid detection by investigators. Finally, as **Fig. 3** illustrates, the recent staggering growth in Internet-connected consumer devices—the so-called "Internet of Things"—has allowed malicious actors to build botnets from under-protected IoT devices to launch DDoS attacks.[53]

4. Criminal Infrastructure

Operating a criminal enterprise with some form of online presence requires a backend technical infrastructure that can be hidden from law enforcement. While some criminals may rely on their own computers and servers, more sophisticated operations lease services from "**bulletproof hosters**," that is, web hosting companies and data centers that purposefully are extremely lenient in what content they will host, make little to no effort to verify the true identity of their customers, and are designed to be unhelpful to law enforcement requests for information about their customers. Bulletproof hosters often are located in countries with less stringent cyber regulations and under-developed domestic cybercrime law enforcement capabilities, and are akin to digital safehouses where criminals can stash malware exploit kits, run botnets, and store PII stolen from hacked databases.

In addition to bulletproof hosters, cybercriminals regularly use the Dark Web, the collection of hidden sites and services that are only accessible to users of specific routing and anonymizing services and software. In recent years, criminals have launched so-

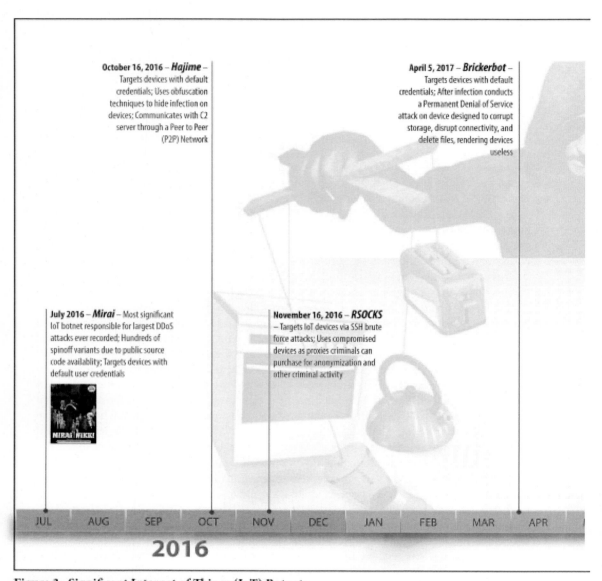

October 16, 2016 – *Hajime* – Targets devices with default credentials; Uses obfuscation techniques to hide infection on devices; Communicates with C2 server through a Peer to Peer (P2P) Network

April 5, 2017 – *Brickerbot* – Targets devices with default credentials; After infection conducts a Permanent Denial of Service attack on device designed to corrupt storage, disrupt connectivity, and delete files, rendering devices useless

July 2016 – *Mirai* – Most significant IoT botnet responsible for largest DDoS attacks ever recorded; Hundreds of spinoff variants due to public source code availablity; Targets devices with default user credentials

November 16, 2016 – *RSOCKS* – Targets IoT devices via SSH brute force attacks; Uses compromised devices as proxies criminals can purchase for anonymization and other criminal activity

| JUL | AUG | SEP | OCT | NOV | DEC | JAN | FEB | MAR | APR |

2016

Figure 3: Significant Internet of Things (IoT) Botnets

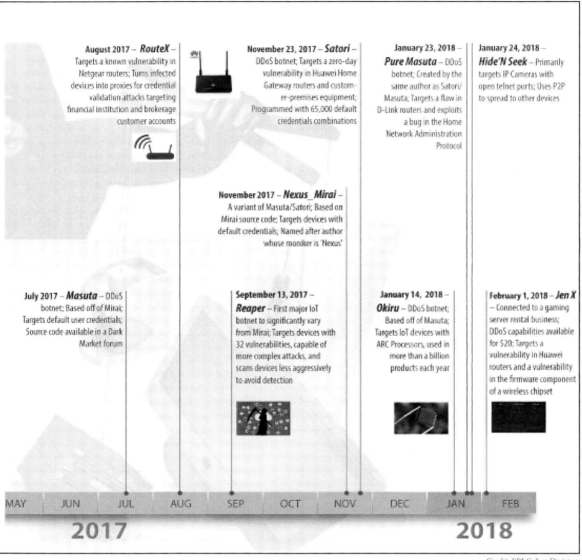

August 2017 – *RouteX* – Targets a known vulnerability in Netgear routers; Turns infected devices into proxies for credential validation attacks targeting financial institution and brokerage customer accounts

November 23, 2017 – *Satori* – DDoS botnet; Targets a zero-day vulnerability in Huawei Home Gateway routers and customer-premises equipment; Programmed with 65,000 default credentials combinations

January 23, 2018 – *Pure Masuta* – DDoS botnet; Created by the same author as Satori/Masuta; Targets a flaw in D-Link routers and exploits a bug in the Home Network Administration Protocol

January 24, 2018 – *Hide'N Seek* – Primarily targets IP Cameras with open telnet ports; Uses P2P to spread to other devices

November 2017 – *Nexus_Mirai* – A variant of Masuta/Satori; Based on Mirai source code; Targets devices with default credentials; Named after author whose moniker is 'Nexus'

July 2017 – *Masuta* – DDoS botnet; Based off of Mirai; Targets default user credentials; Source code available in a Dark Market forum

September 13, 2017 – *Reaper* – First major IoT botnet to significantly vary from Mirai; Targets devices with 32 vulnerabilities, capable of more complex attacks, and scans devices less aggressively to avoid detection

January 14, 2018 – *Okiru* – DDoS botnet; Based off of Masuta; Targets IoT devices with ARC Processors, used in more than a billion products each year

February 1, 2018 – *Jen X* – Connected to a gaming server rental business; DDoS capabilities available for $20; Targets a vulnerability in Huawei routers and a vulnerability in the firmware component of a wireless chipset

| MAY | JUN | JUL | AUG | SEP | OCT | NOV | DEC | JAN | FEB |

2017   **2018**

Credit: FBI Cyber Division

called dark markets, that is, websites hosted on the Dark Web in which vendors and buyers congregate to buy, sell, and trade illicit goods such as narcotics, credit card numbers, hacking tools, and stolen PII in an environment that protects the vendors' and buyer's anonymity. In the midst of an ongoing opioid crisis, the open availability of dark markets where fentanyl and other illicit narcotics are available for purchase and are delivered direct to consumers in the United States poses a significant public health threat.

Another persistent problem on the Dark Web are online child exploitation communities where like-minded sex offenders gather to promote the sexual abuse of children, provide an environment where such conduct seems "normal," educate each other about how to perpetrate child sex abuse without getting

caught, incentivize the production of images that document child sex abuse, and share images and videos depicting the sexual abuse and exploitation of children as young as infants and toddlers. Such communities are disturbingly commonplace, and frequently involve tens of thousands of members.

The growth and continued operation of these sites and communities is made possible by anonymizing technology that effectively hides the servers hosting the sites, as well as users, from normal law enforcement techniques. The best-known technology of this type is free software called The Onion Router ("Tor"). Tor transmits internet traffic through a global volunteer network of thousands of relays (i.e., proxy computers), using layers of encryption to obscure users' identities and geographical locations. Tor not only

---

THE ONION ROUTER (TOR)

Tor operates by routing encrypted communications through a series of relay computers. This obscures the route of the communications, thereby frustrating monitoring by third-parties, such as law enforcement. Communications sent from a computer using Tor are bounced through a series of intermediary servers, known as relays or nodes, chosen from among thousands of servers located throughout the world that individuals have volunteered to be part of the Tor network. Communications sent through these nodes—known as the Guard, Relay, and Exit nodes—are encrypted in a manner that conceals both the contents of the communication and the IP address of the computer that sent the communication. Each node knows only which other node gave it data, and which node is receiving data. None of the intermediate Tor nodes ever has access to both the sender's true IP address and the actual content of the communication.

CATEGORIZING SOPHISTICATED CYBER SCHEMES

anonymizes criminals' Internet traffic, but also allows them to host websites, called Hidden Services, on servers whose location is similarly masked using Tor. Criminals have exploited Hidden Services to facilitate numerous forms of illicit commercial and other criminal activity. Some of the most infamous Hidden Services are dark markets, including the now-shuttered Silk Road and AlphaBay, as well as notorious child exploitation communities. The Department's successes in shutting down these illicit marketplaces are described in further detail in Chapter 3.

Criminals' exploitation of increasingly sophisticated technologies to cover their tracks and avoid being caught represents a significant challenge to law enforcement. Criminals executing ransomware schemes often use anonymizing networks such as Tor to communicate with victims, even going so far as to set up Tor Hidden Services websites to answer victims' questions and to facilitate payment. In addition, the use of anonymizing proxy networks interferes with law enforcement's ability to trace these communications and identify the actors running the ransomware. Criminals also increasingly require payments to be made using virtual currencies or other mechanisms that complicate law enforcement efforts to track those payments. We discuss the impact of such anonymizing technologies on our investigations in Chapter 3. For now, suffice it to say that no discussion of the cyber threats our Nation confronts would be complete without the simple observation that as the Department continues to wage battle against cybercriminals, it will need to adequately meet the challenges posed by anonymizing technologies.

NOTES

[1] From the guilty plea materials in *United States v. Paras Jha,* No. 17-CRM-164 (D. Alaska, Dec. 5, 2017), available at: https://www.justice.gov/opa/press-release/file/1017546/download (last accessed June 29, 2018).

[2] *See* "Alert (TA16-288A): Heightened DDoS Threat Posed by Mirai and Other Botnets," UNITED STATES COMPUTER EMERGENCY READINESS TEAM, U.S. DEPT. OF HOMELAND SECURITY (last revised Oct. 17, 2017), available at: https://www.us-cert.gov/ncas/alerts/TA16-288A (last accessed June 29, 2018).

[3] *Jha* guilty plea, *supra* note 1.

[4] *See* Indictment in *United States v. Ahmad Fathi,* et al., No. 16-CRM-48 (S.D.N.Y., March 24, 2016), available at: https://www.justice.gov/opa/file/834996/download (last accessed June 29, 2018).

[5] *See* Press Release, "Treasury Targets Supporters of Iran's Islamic Revolutionary Guard Corps and Networks Responsible for Cyber-Attacks Against the United States," U.S. DEPT. OF TREASURY (Sept. 14, 2017), available at: https://www.treasury.gov/press-center/press-releases/Pages/sm0158.aspx (last accessed June 29, 2018).

[6] *See* Sujit Raman, "Petya or NotPetya? It All Just Makes You WannaCry!" RSA Conference 2018 (April 16, 2018) at 3, available at: https://published-prd.lanyonevents.com/published/rsaus18/sessionsFiles/8546/SEM-M03-Ransomware-and-Destructive-Attacks-Raman.pdf (last accessed June 29, 2018).

[7] "Press Briefing on the Attribution of the WannaCry Malware Attack to North Korea," THE WHITE HOUSE (Dec. 19, 2017), available at: https://www.whitehouse.gov/briefings-statements/press-briefing-on-the-attribution-of-the-wannacry-malware-attack-to-north-korea-121917/ (last accessed June 29, 2018).

[8] Andrew E. Kramer, "Ukraine Cyberattack Was Meant to Paralyze, not Profit, Evidence Shows," N. Y. TIMES (June 28, 2017), available at: https://www.nytimes.com/2017/06/28/world/europe/ukraine-ransomware-cyberbomb-accountants-russia.html (last accessed June 29, 2018).

[9] *See* the grugq, "Pnyetya: Yet Another Ransomware Outbreak," THE MEDIUM (June 27, 2017), available at: https://medium.com/@thegrugq/pnyetya-yet-another-ransomware-outbreak-59afd1ee89d4 (last accessed June 29, 2018) (contemporaneous reporting noting that "the worm . . . has an extremely poor payment pipeline," observing that "the pseudo-ransomware is in fact a wiper, with no potential for successfully recovering from an attack," and concluding: "[T]he real Petya was a criminal enterprise for making money. This is definitely not designed to make money. This is designed to spread fast and cause damage, with a plausibly deniable cover of 'ransomware.'").

[10] "Statement from the Press Secretary," THE WHITE HOUSE (Feb. 15, 2018), available at: https://www.whitehouse.gov/briefings-statements/statement-press-secretary-25/ (last accessed June 29, 2018).

[11] "Press Briefing on the Attribution of the WannaCry Malware Attack to North Korea," THE WHITE HOUSE (Dec. 19, 2017), available at: https://www.whitehouse.gov/briefings-statements/press-briefing-on-the-attribution-of-the-wannacry-malware-attack-to-north-korea-121917/ (last accessed June 29, 2018).

[12] *See* Keith Wagstaff, "Sony Hack Exposed 47,000 Social Security Numbers, Security Firm Says," NBC NEWS (Dec. 5, 2014), available at:

CATEGORIZING SOPHISTICATED CYBER SCHEMES

http://www.nbcnews.com/storyline/sony-hack/sony-hack-exposed-47-000-social-security-numbers-security-firm-n262711 (last accessed June 29, 2018).

[13] Press Release, "Treasury Imposes Sanctions Against the Government of The Democratic People's Republic Of Korea," U.S. DEPT. OF TREASURY (Jan. 2, 2015), available at: https://www.treasury.gov/press-center/press-releases/Pages/jl9733.aspx (last accessed June 29, 2018).

[14] Risk Placement Services, DATA BREACH QUICKVIEW REPORT, FIRST QUARTER 2018 2, 9 (2018), available at: https://www.rpsins.com/knowledge-center/items/data-breach-report-q1-2018/ (last accessed June 29, 2018).

[15] Ponemon Institute, 2017 COST OF DATA BREACH STUDY: UNITED STATES, p. 1, available at https://www.ponemon.org/library/2017-cost-of-data-breach-study-united-states (last accessed June 29, 2018).

[16] FEDERAL BUREAU OF INVESTIGATION, 2016 INTERNET CRIME Report 20, 21, available at: https://pdf.ic3.gov/2016_IC3Report.pdf (last accessed June 29, 2018).

[17] "What Happened," OFFICE OF PERSONNEL MANAGEMENT CYBERSECURITY RESOURCE CENTER (2015), available at: https://www.opm.gov/cybersecurity/cybersecurity-incidents/ (last accessed June 29, 2018).

[18] "U.S. Charges Russian FSB Officers and Their Criminal Conspirators for Hacking Yahoo and Millions of Email Accounts," U.S. DEPT. OF JUSTICE (March 15, 2017), available at: https://www.justice.gov/opa/pr/us-charges-russian-fsb-officers-and-their-criminal-conspirators-hacking-yahoo-and-millions (last accessed June 29, 2018).

[19] "Canadian Hacker Who Conspired With and Aided Russian FSB Officers Pleads Guilty," U.S. DEPT. OF JUSTICE (November 28, 2017), available at: https://www.justice.gov/opa/pr/canadian-hacker-who-conspired-and-aided-russian-fsb-officers-pleads-guilty (last accessed June 29, 2018).

[20] Executive Order 13757, "Taking Additional Steps to Address the National Emergency with respect to Significant Malicious Cyber-Enabled Activities," available at: https://www.treasury.gov/resource-center/sanctions/Programs/Documents/cyber2_eo.pdf (last accessed June 29, 2018). This order was later modified to permit U.S. persons shipping technology goods to Russia to obtain licenses from the FSB, as required by the Russian government. "General License No. 1, Authorizing Certain Transactions with the FSS," available at: https://www.treasury.gov/resource-center/sanctions/Programs/Documents/cyber_gl1.pdf (last accessed June 29, 2018).

[21] Press Release, "ISIL-Linked Kosovo Hacker Sentenced to 20 Years in Prison," U.S. DEPT. OF JUSTICE (Sept. 23, 2016), available at: https://www.justice.gov/opa/pr/isil-linked-kosovo-hacker-sentenced-20-years-prison (last accessed June 29, 2018).

[22] Commission on the Theft of American Intellectual Property, *Update to the IP Commission Report*, at 1 (2017), available at: http://www.ipcommission.org/report/IP_Commission_Report_Update_2017.pdf (last accessed June 29, 2018).

[23] National Counterintelligence and Security Center, *Evolving Cyber Tactics in Stealing U.S. Economic Secrets: Report to Congress on Foreign Economic Collection and Industrial Espionage in Cyberspace*, at 1 (Nov. 2016).

[24] Center *for* Responsible Enterprise And Trade & PricewaterhouseCoopers LLP, Economic Impact of Trade Secret Theft 3 (2014), available at: https://create.org/wp-content/uploads/2014/07/

CYBER-DIGITAL TASK FORCE REPORT

CREATe.org-PwC-Trade-Secret-Theft-FINAL-Feb-2014_01.pdf (last accessed June 29, 2018).

[25] Press Release, "Member Of Megaupload Conspiracy Pleads Guilty to Copyright Infringement Charges and is Sentenced to One Year in U.S. Prison," U.S. DEPT. OF JUSTICE (Feb. 13, 2015), available at: https://www.justice.gov/opa/pr/member-megaupload-conspiracy-pleads-guilty-copyright-infringement-charges-and-sentenced-one (last accessed June 29, 2018).

[26] Press Release, "U.S. Authorities Charge Owner of Most-Visited Illegal File-Sharing Website with Copyright Infringement," U.S. DEPT. OF JUSTICE (July 20, 2016), available at: https://www.justice.gov/opa/pr/us-authorities-charge-owner-most-visited-illegal-file-sharing-website-copyright-infringement (last accessed June 29, 2018).

[27] See Press Release, "Chinese Company Sinovel Wind Group Convicted of Theft of Trade Secrets," U.S. DEPT. OF JUSTICE (Jan. 24, 2018), available at: https://www.justice.gov/opa/pr/chinese-company-sinovel-wind-group-convicted-theft-trade-secrets (last accessed June 29, 2018).

[28] See Press Release, "FACT SHEET: President Xi Jinping's State Visit to the United States," THE WHITE HOUSE (Sept. 25, 2015), available at: https://obamawhitehouse.archives.gov/the-press-office/2015/09/25/fact-sheet-president-xi-jinpings-state-visit-united-states (last accessed June 29, 2018).

[29] See Press Release, "FACT SHEET: The 2015 G-20 Summit in Antalya, Turkey," THE WHITE HOUSE (Nov. 16, 2015), available at: https://obamawhitehouse.archives.gov/the-press-office/2015/11/16/fact-sheet-2015-g-20-summit-antalya-turkey (last accessed June 29, 2018).

[30] "Findings of the Investigation into China's Acts, Policies, and Practices related to Technology Transfer, Intellectual Property, and Innovation under Section 301 of the Trade Act of 1974," OFFICE OF THE UNITED STATES TRADE REPRESENTATIVE (March 22, 2018), at 169, available at: https://ustr.gov/sites/default/files/Section%20301%20FINAL.PDF (last accessed June 29, 2018) (citing reports).

[31] Press Release, "U.S. Charges Three Chinese Hackers Who Work at Internet Security Firm for Hacking Three Corporations for Commercial Advantage," U.S. DEPT. OF JUSTICE (Nov. 27, 2017), available at: https://www.justice.gov/opa/pr/us-charges-three-chinese-hackers-who-work-internet-security-firm-hacking-three-corporations (last accessed June 29, 2018).

[32] Elias Groll, "Feds Quietly Reveal Chinese State-Backed Hacking Operation," FOREIGN POLICY (Nov. 30, 2017), available at: http://foreignpolicy.com/2017/11/30/feds-quietly-reveal-chinese-state-backed-hacking-operation/ (last accessed June 29, 2018) (quoting Department spokesperson).

[33] FEDERAL BUREAU OF INVESTIGATION, "Nigerian Letter or '419' Fraud," available at: https://www.fbi.gov/scams-and-safety/common-fraud-schemes/nigerian-letter-or-419-fraud (last accessed June 29, 2018).

[34] FEDERAL BUREAU OF INVESTIGATION, "Business Fraud," available at https://www.fbi.gov/scams-and-safety/common-fraud-schemes/business-fraud (last accessed June 29, 2018).

[35] FEDERAL BUREAU OF INVESTIGATION, "Investment Fraud," available at https://www.fbi.gov/scams-and-safety/common-fraud-schemes/investment-fraud (last accessed June 29, 2018).

[36] Press Release, "Two Russian Nationals Sentenced to Prison for Massive Data Breach Conspiracy," U.S. DEPT. OF JUSTICE (Feb. 15, 2018),

CATEGORIZING SOPHISTICATED CYBER SCHEMES

available at: https://www.justice.gov/opa/pr/two-russian-nationals-sentenced-prison-massive-data-breach-conspiracy (last accessed June 29, 2018).

[37] *See* Joey L. Blanch & Wesley L. Hsu, "An Introduction to Violent Crime on the Internet," UNITED STATES ATTORNEYS' BULLETIN (May 2016), at 2.

[38] *See* 18 U.S.C. § 2261A.

[39] Press Release, "Former U.S. State Department Employee Sentenced to 57 Months in Extensive Computer Hacking, Cyberstalking and "Sextortion" Scheme," U.S. DEPT. OF JUSTICE (March 21, 2016), available at: https://www.justice.gov/opa/pr/former-us-state-department-employee-sentenced-57-months-extensive-computer-hacking (last accessed June 29, 2018).

[40] This report does not detail related crimes involving the sexual exploitation of children. For more detail on this criminal threat, *see* U.S. DEPT. OF JUSTICE, The National Strategy for Child Exploitation Prevention and Interdiction (Apr. 2016), available at: https://www.justice.gov/psc/file/842411/download (last accessed June 29, 2018).

[41] "Critical Infrastructure Security," U.S. DEPT. OF HOMELAND SECURITY, available at: https://www.dhs.gov/topic/critical-infrastructure-security (last accessed June 29, 2018).

[42] 42 U.S.C. § 5195c(e).

[43] *See* Richard J. Campbell, "Cybersecurity Issues for the Bulk Power System," CONG. RESEARCH SERV., 9R43989, at 9 (June 10, 2015), available at: https://www.fas.org/sgp/crs/misc/R43989.pdf ("Over time, modification of SCADA [Supervisory Control and Data Acquisition] systems has resulted in connection of many of these older, legacy systems to the Internet.") (last accessed June 29, 2018).

[44] *See id.*

[45] *See Fathi* indictment, *supra* note 4, at 14-16.

[46] Alert TA18-074A, "Russian Government Cyber Activity Targeting Energy and Other Critical Infrastructure," U.S. COMPUTER EMERGENCY READINESS TEAM, U.S. DEPT. OF HOMELAND SECURITY (March 15, 2018), available at: https://www.us-cert.gov/ncas/alerts/TA18-074A (last accessed June 29, 2018).

[47] Press Release, "Treasury Sanctions Russian Cyber Actors for Interference with the 2016 U.S. Elections and Malicious Cyber-Attacks," U.S. DEPT. OF TREASURY (Mar. 15, 2018), available at: https://home.treasury.gov/news/press-releases/sm0312 (last accessed June 29, 2018).

[48] Alert TA18-149A, "HIDDEN COBRA – Joanap Backdoor Trojan and Brambul Server Message Block Worm," U.S. COMPUTER EMERGENCY READINESS TEAM, U.S. DEPT. OF HOMELAND SECURITY (last revised May 31, 2018), available at: https://www.us-cert.gov/ncas/alerts/TA18-149A (last accessed June 29, 2018).

[49] *See generally* Mollie Halpern & Patrick Geahan, "FBI, This Week: Social Engineering," FEDERAL BUREAU OF INVESTIGATION (Oct. 14, 2016) (podcast transcript), available at: https://www.fbi.gov/audio-repository/ftw-podcast-social-engineering-101416.mp3/view (last accessed June 29, 2018).

[50] "Consumer Information: Phishing," FEDERAL TRADE COMMISSION (July 2017), available at: https://www.consumer.ftc.gov/articles/0003-phishing (last accessed June 29, 2018).

[51] FEDERAL BUREAU OF INVESTIGATION, 2016 Internet Crime Report 1, 9, available at: https://pdf.ic3.gov/2016_IC3Report.pdf (last accessed June 29, 2018).

[52] Federal Bureau of Investigation, 2017 Internet Crime Report 3, 12, available at: https://pdf.ic3.gov/2017_IC3Report.pdf (last accessed June 29, 2018).

[53] *See* "A Report to the President on Enhancing the Resilience of the Internet and Communications Ecosystem Against Botnets and Other Automated, Distributed Threats," U.S. Dept. of Commerce & U.S. Dept. of Homeland Security (May 22, 2018), available at: https://www.commerce.gov/sites/commerce.gov/files/media/files/2018/eo_13800_botnet_report_-_finalv2.pdf (last accessed June 29, 2018).

[54] Exploit kits are a type of malicious toolkit used to exploit security holes found in software applications for the purpose of spreading malware. These kits come with pre-written exploit code and target users running insecure or outdated software applications on their computers.

[55] Press Release, "Ross Ulbricht, The Creator And Owner Of The "Silk Road" Website, Found Guilty In Manhattan Federal Court On All Counts," U.S. Dept. of Justice (Feb. 5, 2015), available at: https://www.justice.gov/usao-sdny/pr/ross-ulbricht-creator-and-owner-silk-road-website-found-guilty-manhattan-federal-court (last accessed June 29, 2018).

[56] Press Release, "AlphaBay, the Largest Online 'Dark Market,' Shut Down," U.S. Dept. of Justice (July 20, 2017), available at: https://www.justice.gov/opa/pr/alphabay-largest-online-dark-market-shut-down (last accessed June 29, 2018).

[57] *See, e.g.,* Press Release, "Colorado and Illinois Men Sentenced to Prison for Engaging in Child Exploitation Enterprise," U.S. Dept. of Justice (Oct. 18, 2016), available at: https://www.justice.gov/opa/pr/colorado-and-illinois-men-sentenced-prison-engaging-child-exploitation-enterprise (last accessed June 29, 2018).

CHAPTER 3
DETECTING, DETERRING, AND DISRUPTING CYBER THREATS

The Department of Justice plays an essential role in detecting, deterring, and disrupting cyber threats. As the Nation's chief law enforcement officer, the Attorney General leads the Department's criminal and national security initiatives. Working with and through the Criminal Division, the National Security Division, and the 93 U.S. Attorney's Offices across the country, the Attorney General sets priorities for how those activities are conducted.[1]

Since the early 1990s, when the commercial Internet was in its infancy, the Department has combated computer crime. In the intervening years, the Department has expanded its focus to address burgeoning threats to public safety, economic security, and national security flowing from the widespread adoption of the Internet. Today, the Department deters and disrupts a broad spectrum of the Nation's cyber threats by enforcing federal laws through the array of legal tools and capabilities that its investigators and prosecutors have at their disposal.

In this chapter, we describe the key methods investigators and prosecutors use to gather evidence about cyber threats. We then explain the key legal authorities the Department applies to bring perpetrators to justice, or otherwise to disrupt and dismantle malicious cyber activity.

Key Investigative Techniques

To successfully bring malign cyber actors to justice, law enforcement first must gather evidence of their criminal activity and attribute that activity to particular individuals, organizations, or nation states. The key methods and sources of evidence for disrupting cyber threats include: gathering materials during incident response; reviewing open source data; conducting online reconnaissance; searching records from online providers; undertaking undercover investigations; engaging in authorized electronic surveillance; tracing financial transactions; searching storage media; and applying a variety of special techniques. Often, investigators also must work cooperatively with foreign partners to access evidence and disrupt transnational cyber threats.

1. Evidence Collection During Incident Response

Often the first evidence collected in an investigation concerning a cyber threat comes from the victim as part of the incident response. The Department encourages victims to contact law enforcement as soon as they believe they are the victim of a computer intrusion. Although many victims will simply provide consent to investigators collecting digital evidence on scene, subpoenas and search warrants can be obtained if the victim prefers. In either case, investigators are committed to working collaboratively with victims to minimize any disruption to business during an investigation.

After obtaining digital copies of any affected devices, investigators may then turn to other devices in the victim's architecture, including firewalls, log servers, and routers, to look for additional evidence of the perpetrator's presence. Investigators will also image these devices, as needed, and forensically examine them. Such devices often contain traces of a criminal's passage through the infrastructure on the way to the affected device. In particular, many devices maintain log files that show when, and from where, the device was accessed. In addition to preserving and copying digital evidence, investigators may interview employees (especially those tasked with responding to cyber threats or securing infrastructure), regular users of the affected systems, and management.

2. Online Data Review and Reconnaissance

After reviewing information obtained from a victim or other primary sources of information regarding a cyberattack, investigators frequently will review online data, which may be open source, to determine their next investigative steps. In undertaking these actions, as with all their actions, investigators are trained to act consistently with our Nation's rule of law principles, and with our society's foundational respect for civil rights and civil liberties.[2]

The first step in online reconnaissance often involves use of the Internet Corporation for Assigned Names and Numbers' WHOIS database.[3] WHOIS is a directory of all of the IP addresses and domains on the Internet. WHOIS records usually display the name and contact information of the registrar (the business that sold the IP address or domain). Investigators can use the contact information to send legal process to the registrar in order to discover more information about the registrant (the user of the IP address or domain). WHOIS often contains self-reported information about the registrant, as well. In addition, an investigator often can tell from WHOIS and related information where a website is being hosted or who is hosting the e-mail server for a website, either (or both) of which can provide additional avenues for investigation.

After consulting WHOIS, investigators often perform online reconnaissance of the identifiers they have collected. This reconnaissance includes web searches looking for whether the identifiers have been used elsewhere and searches of social media to determine whether the identifiers are related to any accounts.

3. Searching Records from Online Providers

Successful WHOIS searches and online reconnaissance often results in the identification of e-mail providers, social media companies, registrars, and web hosting and computer hosting companies that may control additional evidence about a subject or

DETECTING, DETERRING, AND DISRUPTING CYBER THREATS

target of an investigation. At this stage, an investigator will rely heavily on the provisions of the Electronic Communications Privacy Act ("ECPA"),[4] which specifically permits investigators to request evidence from providers of electronic communications and computer processing. Investigative teams may issue subpoenas to collect basic information about a subscriber to an identified account. Investigators also may use court orders issued under the authority of section 2703(d) of title 18, United States Code, which allows them to access additional non-content records for online accounts, such as log files or the e-mail addresses of others with whom the subscriber has corresponded.

Finally, with probable cause, investigators can seek a search warrant from a judge to obtain the contents of accounts, including copies of e-mails, photographs, text messages, and any other files stored with a provider up to and including the contents of an entire computer belonging to a target of the investigation and hosted with the provider.[5] Because cyber threat actors often communicate with each other using electronic communications to plan and execute their activities, these accounts can contain vast quantities of useful evidence. In addition, cyber threat actors sometimes keep other evidence in the contents of their accounts, such as records of their criminal activities, pictures that place them at the scene or with other members of the conspiracy, and other evidence that can help identify the actors and connect them to the illicit activity.

4. *Online Undercover Operations*

In order to investigate cyber threat activity, investigators may establish covert personas or consensually assume the accounts and identities of victims or cooperators to communicate online with the targets of the investigation. From such undercover operations, investigators gather inculpatory contents from communications, additional accounts, IP addresses, criminal proceeds, and records of criminal transactions such as the purchase of malware, botnets, or stolen credit cards.

5. *Electronic Surveillance*

Investigators may also need to conduct online surveillance on their targets. There are three federal statutes that authorize the collection of data on a real-time basis: the pen register and trap and trace ("PRTT") statute,[6] the wiretap statute,[7] and the Foreign Intelligence Surveillance Act ("FISA").[8] All three generally require investigators to obtain court authorization.

A PRTT allows investigators to obtain the dialing, routing, addressing, and signaling information of communications, including dialed calls, IP addresses, and e-mail headers. PRTTs can be obtained for cell phones, e-mail accounts, and other social media or messaging applications. Although a PRTT does not obtain the content of any communications, it can be useful in determining whether an account is still being used for criminal purposes, to help identify co-conspirators, or to locate a target.

CYBER-DIGITAL TASK FORCE REPORT

(NEW) RULE 41(b)(6)

Under Rule 41(b)(6) of the Federal Rules of Criminal Procedure, which went into effect in December 2016, "a magistrate judge with authority in any district where activities related to a crime may have occurred has authority to issue a warrant to use remote access to

FEDERAL RULES
OF
CRIMINAL PROCEDURE

DECEMBER 18, 2016

Printed for the use
of
THE COMMITTEE ON THE JUDICIARY
HOUSE OF REPRESENTATIVES

search electronic media and to seize or copy electronically stored information located within or outside that district if: (A) the district where the media or information is located has been concealed through technological means; or (B) in an investigation of a violation of 18 U.S.C. § 1030(a)(5), the media are protected computers that have been damaged without authorization and are located in five or more districts."

This provision makes two narrow, but important, changes in the law. First, where a suspect has hidden the location of his or her computer using technological means, the new Rule ensures that federal agents know which judge to go to in order to apply for a warrant. Second, where the crime involves the hacking of computers located in five or more different judicial districts, the new Rule ensures that federal agents may identify one judge to review an application for a search warrant rather than having to submit separate warrant applications in each judicial district across the nation—up to 94—where a computer is affected. In sum, Rule 41(b)(6) addresses the unique challenges created by botnet activity by clarifying that courts may issue warrants authorizing the search of multiple computers when the identified computers are located in multiple judicial districts.

Court-authorized wiretaps under the Wiretap Act or FISA permit investigators to listen to or observe the contents of communications in or near real time. For example, investigators can intercept wire and electronic communications over a target's cell phone or read the target's e-mail as it is sent, allowing them to locate targets, confirm relationships within a conspiracy, disrupt new criminal activity, and confirm previous activity. Every federal wiretap application must be approved by a senior Department official before it is submitted to a court. Federal courts, in turn, apply rigorous standards both in authorizing and supervising wiretaps.

DETECTING, DETERRING, AND DISRUPTING CYBER THREATS

6. *Special Techniques*

Cyber threat actors often try to hide their identities by disguising their IP address. A common way to do this is by using a proxy computer, which sits between the actor and his victim, to obfuscate the actor's IP address. As described in Chapter 2, threat actors also will often use The Onion Router ("Tor"), which is a particularly sophisticated network of relay computers, to hide their true IP address. To circumvent the challenges presented by threat actors' use of proxies and Tor, investigators can use **Network Investigative Techniques ("NITs")**. NITs include computer code that investigators can send covertly to a device that is hidden behind proxies. Once installed, a NIT can send law enforcement particular information, often including the device's true IP address—which investigators then can use to identify the subscriber and user of the device.

As described in Chapter 2, botnets pose unique challenges for law enforcement and so require special techniques to investigate and disrupt them. Identifying victim computers (or "bots") can be very difficult because the bots may be spread throughout the world. Criminal dark markets that rent or sell botnet access often obfuscate the location and other identifying information about individual bots. Until recently, this posed a significant jurisdictional hurdle, as an investigator had to know the location of a bot to get a search warrant for it. Now, thanks to a recent Department-led initiative to amend the Federal Rules of Criminal Procedure (see page 52), magistrate judges can authorize search warrants even if the location of the subject of the warrant is unknown. Bot-nets are controlled by command and control servers ("C2 servers"), which periodically issue orders to the bots. One way to disrupt a botnet is to seize control of the C2 server. Investigators can use criminal authorities to seize C2 servers; they can also use civil injunctive authority to seek the redirection of computers under the control of the botnet to a server controlled by the court, instead of by the threat actor's C2 server.

7. *Tracing Financial Transactions*

Pursuing illicit assets is an important part of any fraud investigation, and computer crime cases are no exception. To pursue traditional bank accounts, the United States has made extensive use of asset forfeiture authorities, including seizures involving correspondent bank accounts, as well as of sanctions programs, including the Global Magnitsky sanctions authority, to keep tainted funds out of the U.S. financial system. Yet, cybercriminals increasingly use **virtual currencies** to advance their activities and to conceal their assets. Because most virtual currencies lack any central authority, seizing them requires different approaches.

In recent years, the Department has relied on a variety of legal authorities to seize virtual currency that has been derived from illegal activity. These authorities include civil forfeiture orders, seizure warrants, and search warrants. Where, for instance, a target of an investigation stores virtual currency with a third-party service—typically, a virtual currency exchanger—investigators may seize that virtual currency by obtaining a seizure warrant for the user's account at that

CYBER-DIGITAL TASK FORCE REPORT

VIRTUAL CURRENCIES

"Virtual currencies" such as Bitcoin, Ether, and Monero are electronic assets that are circulated over the Internet as a form of value but are not backed by any government. Though virtual currencies have legitimate uses, they also often enable individuals to transfer money with high levels of anonymity to other users worldwide. Cyber criminals frequently transact in virtual currencies, and online criminal markets rely on virtual currencies to enable the purchase and sale of a wide variety of illegal goods and services. While law enforcement has made strides in its ability to trace virtual currency transactions, criminals often launder their virtual currency by mixing one user's money with multiple other users', or sending their virtual currency through a convoluted series of transactions, a process often called "mixing" or "tumbling."

---

third-party service. If the target stores the virtual currency locally (for example, on his own electronic devices, or on servers he controls), or even by printing the private keys onto a physical medium, investigators may seize the virtual currency through a traditional search warrant that allows the government to learn the private key. The seizure of virtual currency requires transferring the virtual currency to a government-controlled virtual currency wallet. If the virtual currency is stored with an overseas exchange, the Department will work with our foreign counterparts to effect the seizure.

Because of the risks that early conversion may pose, in most cases, virtual currency the government seizes is kept in the form it was seized and not liquidated (*i.e.*, converted to fiat currency or other virtual currency) until a final order of forfeiture is entered or an administrative forfeiture is final. [9] Agencies or prosecutors may, however, seek an order for the interlocutory sale of virtual currency at the request and/or consent of all parties with an ownership interest. Consultation with the Criminal Division's Money Laundering and Asset Recovery Section is required prior to any pre-forfeiture conversion, or seeking an order for interlocutory sale of virtual currency.

Any liquidation of virtual currency should be executed according to established written policies of the seizing agency and the U.S. Marshals Service. [10] The Department is developing guidance regarding disposition of alternative virtual currencies (*i.e.*, anonymity enhanced cryptocurrencies and ICO tokens) for which the Marshals Service does not yet have a process in place to take custody or liquidate via auction.

As detailed above, the Department in recent years has regularly used civil forfeiture authorities[11] and seizure warrants to seize virtual currency derived from malicious cyber activity associated with the Dark Web and botnets. More recently, in July 2017, the Department announced the indictment of a Russian national and an organization he allegedly operated, BTC-e, for facilitating transactions for international cybercriminals, and for receiving the criminal proceeds of numerous computer intrusions and hacking incidents, as well as of other crimes.[12] According to the indictment, BTC-e's virtual currency exchange allegedly did not require users to validate their identity, obscured and anonymized transactions and source of funds, and eschewed any anti-money laundering processes. Perhaps unsurprisingly, the exchange is alleged to have become popular with criminals. At the time of the indictment, the investigation revealed that BTC-e was alleged to have received more than $4 billion worth of virtual currency through its operation.

In parallel with the Department's actions, the Financial Crimes Enforcement Network ("FinCEN") assessed a $110 million civil money penalty against BTC-e for willfully violating U.S. anti-money laundering laws. The operator of the exchange was assessed a $12 million penalty for his role in the violations. FinCEN's announcement underscored the importance of the Department's partnerships with regulatory agencies in seeking to deter those who facilitate ransomware, dark net drug sales, and other illicit activity using virtual currency.

Just as virtual currencies have provided a new way for criminals to launder money, they also provide another avenue for **tax evasion**. In particular, evaders can abuse the anonymous and decentralized structure of virtual currencies in an attempt to conceal their income and assets. The relative lack of reporting requirements for virtual currency also contributes to its secrecy and thus to its usefulness in committing tax crimes. And with the increase in value of virtual currencies in recent years, this anonymity and secrecy may tempt individuals not to report as income their gains from the sale of virtual currency.

This is a particularly novel area for tax enforcement. But investigators pursuing tax investigations involving virtual currency can employ many of the techniques learned from money laundering investigations involving virtual currency. For instance, investigators can track the movement of funds across the public ledger of a virtual currency and identify when money moves into or out of virtual currency through exchanges and other parties. Moreover, the Internal Revenue Service ("IRS") Criminal Investigation division is making criminal tax evasion using virtual currencies a focus of its efforts, and the IRS is also pursuing civil and administrative remedies. Within the Department, the Tax Division is partnering with the IRS and U.S. Attorneys' Offices to investigate and prosecute tax crimes involving virtual currencies, and to litigate civil enforcement actions. Recently, the Tax Division, working with the IRS, issued and enforced the first virtual-currency-related "John Doe" summons to Coinbase, one of the largest virtual currency exchanges in the world.[13] As a result of this civil enforcement action, in March 2018, the exchange turned over to the IRS information regarding accounts "with at least the equivalent of $20,000 in any one transaction (buy, sell, send, or receive) in any one year during the 2013-2015 period."[14] This information should be useful in identifying particular individuals and transactions for further investigation.

In addition, Tax Division prosecutors are working with investigators and attorneys at IRS, as well as at the Department's Computer Crime and Intellectual Property section, to develop training and guidance for criminal tax cases involving virtual currencies. Because the tax treatment of virtual currencies is a new area, there are many uncertainties in the law that investigators and prosecutors will need to navigate. The Tax Division's trial attorneys also have worked with the FinCEN Intelligence, Cyber & Emerging Technology Section to identify appropriate techniques for civil tax investigations and litigation.

8. Traditional and Forensic Searches Involving Storage Media

Once a criminal is identified and arrested, investigators will seek electronic evidence from his personal storage media, including his laptops and phones. Such storage media often contain records that link the target to the evidence collected from providers or the victim, such as matching IP addresses, e-mail accounts, and photos and other personal identifiers. This evidence completes the connection between the criminal activity and the target. Such a search usually requires a traditional search warrant, based on probable cause. Investigators also will search

a target's residence, business, or automobile, looking for storage media that may contain evidence of the cyber threat. As with storage media collected during the initial incident response, investigators will image any electronic storage media before searching it, to preserve the contents for future searches and for use in court.

9. Cooperation with Foreign Governments

Cyber threats often emanate from international locations and use criminal networks that stretch across jurisdictions, many of which are not friendly to the rule of law or democratic values. At the same time, foreign sovereigns—including some of our closest allies—put limits on our government's ability to act on its own in every investigation where the targets, or evidence of their crimes, are located in another jurisdiction. Fortunately, the Department has built relationships with its counterparts around the world, that facilitate nimble information sharing in the event of an incident. This information sharing enables mitigation of the incident, and also promotes the preservation of evidence, even in situations where the evidence (or the perpetrators) are located outside the United States.

For more formal use of the information (e.g., to support charges and hold criminal actors accountable), the Department employs a vast network of international treaties and other relationships. The Criminal Division's Office of International Affairs ("OIA"), for example, leverages extradition treaties, mutual legal assistance treaties ("MLATs"), and other in-

DETECTING, DETERRING, AND DISRUPTING CYBER THREATS

The CLOUD Act

Due in part to the large volume of foreign government requests seeking electronic evidence in the custody or control of U.S.-based service providers, and the pressure those requests were placing on the smooth functioning of the MLAT process, the U.S. Congress, in March 2018, enacted, and the President signed into law, a statute called the Clarifying Lawful Overseas Use of Data (CLOUD) Act.

The CLOUD Act has two major effects. First, it clarifies that all warrants, subpoenas, and court orders issued pursuant to the Stored Communications Act, 18 U.S.C. § 2701 *et seq*—the law that governs the disclsoure of stored communicatons and transactional records held by third-party Internet service providers—apply to all data within a provider's possession, custody, or control, regardless of whether the data is stored inside or outside the United States. Second, it allows for bilateral treaties between the United States and foreign countries for the direct sharing of electronic evidence, without needing to use the MLAT process. The CLOUD Act incorporates safeguards to assure that such agreements are entered into only with countries with robust privacy and civil liberties protections, and that adhere to the rule of law.

The CLOUD Act represents a major commitment by the American government to continue the global fight against crime by ensuring that rights-respecting and privacy-protecting foreign governments gain access to the electronic evidence they need to pursue their own investigations of serious crime, even as the Act reduces pressure on the MLAT process generally, and encourages higher privacy and civil liberties standards around the world.

struments and available legal tools to support U.S. investigations and prosecutions of cybercriminals by returning fugitives to the United States to face trial, and by obtaining the evidence located overseas that is needed to build a case against them. OIA also facilitates the extradition of fugitives located in the United States and transfers evidence to foreign partners for those nations' criminal investigations.

When a criminal located overseas is wanted for prosecution or to serve a criminal sentence in the United States, OIA uses all the legal tools at its disposal—extradition, deportation, and other lawful measures—to ensure that the defendant will be transferred to the United States to stand trial in a U.S. court and be held accountable. The processes that must be followed to effectuate this result vary greatly in each case and depend on a range of factors, including, among others, the location of the criminal actor, his or her nationality, our law enforcement relationship with the host country, and the alleged criminal conduct at issue.

The United States currently has bilateral **extradition** treaties with over 100 countries.[15] These treaties, which establish reciprocal obligations to extradite persons charged with or convicted of certain crimes, contain varying features, including some that give the requested state the discretion to decline to extradite its nationals. Other common treaty provisions can affect the charges an individual may face after extradition. These include the statute of limitations, assurances against the imposition of a capital sentence, and the rule of specialty. Extradition requests that result in defendants facing trial in the United States or serving a U.S. criminal sentence generally require carefully prepared documentary submissions and extensive coordination between OIA, U.S. prosecutors, and law enforcement, including the FBI, U.S. Marshals Service, the State Department, and the foreign government.

The ease and speed with which fugitives can travel across jurisdictions highlight the importance of a treaty-based mechanism known as a provisional arrest. When the United States learns that a fugitive will be traveling to—or through—a country with which it has an extradition treaty, there often is not enough time to assemble and submit a formal request for extradition. Where time is of the essence, OIA can submit a provisional arrest request, which will enable the foreign partner to arrest and detain the fugitive for a short period of time until OIA submits the formal extradition request.

There are also countries with which the United States does not maintain an extradition treaty. In cases where the United States seeks the return of a fugitive from a non-treaty partner, OIA attempts to accomplish this through other legal means, including, where possible, securing extradition under the domestic law of the foreign country, and requests for deportation, expulsion, or other lawful transfer. The range of options available varies from case to case, including using lawful measures to ensure the wanted person's transit to a country from which the United States can secure his extradition.

DETECTING, DETERRING, AND DISRUPTING CYBER THREATS

EXTRADITIONS

Successfully prosecuting international computer crime cases has been notoriously difficult. Fortunately, the Department's international outreach has made it easier. In addition, the Department has relied on longstanding tools and processes, such as extradition treaties and alternatives to extradition, to ensure that some of the most notorious cybercriminals face justice in the United States.

In August 2016, for example, a U.S. federal court jury convicted **Roman Seleznev,** a Russian national, of various crimes associated with his theft and sale on the black market of tens of thousands of credit card numbers, which resulted in over $170 million in fraudulent purchases. A "pioneer" cybercriminal who became "one of the most revered point-of-sale hackers in the criminal underworld," Seleznev is the "highest profile long-term cybercriminal ever convicted by an American jury."[16] Seleznev was arrested in the Maldives in July 2014 and was subsequently expelled to the United States, where he is currently serving a 27-year federal sentence for his hacking crimes, concurrent to a 14-year federal sentence stemming from his involvement in a $50 million cyberfraud ring.[17]

More recently, in February 2018, the alleged creator of the Kelihos botnet (see Appendix 2), a Russian national named **Peter Levashov,** was extradited from Spain, and in March 2018, **Yevgeniy Nikulin,** of Moscow, made his initial appearance in U.S. federal court following his extradition from the Czech Republic to face allegations that he illegally accessed computers belonging to LinkedIn, Dropbox, and Formspring.

As these cases and others like them demonstrate, we have successfully dismantled international criminal rings and apprehended some of the most notorious international cybercriminals. At times, we have received valuable evidence from foreign authorities, including Russian law enforcement. But challenges remain, including an increased willingness by the Russian government to protect its nationals from extradition or other removal to the United States when its nationals are located in a third country. In such circumstances, Russia has applied pressure on the U.S. partner, seeking to thwart the U.S. extradition or other removal request. This practice is yet another factor that complicates our efforts to bring international cybercriminals to justice in the United States.

CYBER-DIGITAL TASK FORCE REPORT

In sum, cybercriminals should not be immune from justice simply because they operate outside of U.S. borders. Although there are state sovereignty principles that limit our ability to act unilaterally, OIA has a diverse toolkit that it can use to obtain foreign countries' cooperation and ensure that cybercriminals face justice in U.S. courts.

Investigating and prosecuting cyber criminals often also requires access to evidence located in foreign jurisdictions and assistance from foreign governments. This evidence and assistance may include electronic records, bank and business records, witness interviews, public records, investigative materials, and seizure of assets, to name a few examples. Each year, OIA receives thousands of such requests for mutual legal assistance from both domestic and foreign prosecutors seeking important evidence that may break open an investigative dead-end or secure a criminal conviction. Such requests for assistance to foreign governments are typically made pursuant to bilateral MLATs, regional instruments, or multilateral conventions, such as the international Convention on Cybercrime (known as the Budapest Convention). As the Central Authority for the United States under international instruments, OIA makes requests for assistance to treaty partners on behalf of U.S. prosecutors and executes requests it receives from abroad.

Many of the world's communications service providers are U.S. companies, and electronic records in their custody or control are often critical to cybercrime investigations, as well as other types of criminal and national security cases such as those targeting violent crime, terrorism, child exploitation, and criminal organizations using the Dark Web. As a result, OIA receives a high-volume of requests for electronic records in the custody or control of U.S. providers. OIA executes these requests—many of which concern cases involving foreign actors whose schemes have victimized U.S. citizens—as appropriate and pursuant to its treaty obligations. Doing so both increases the likelihood that foreign governments will be able to disrupt the illegal conduct and ensures their reciprocal cooperation when needed for the United States to obtain assistance from abroad.

Importantly, these cross-border requests for electronic evidence typically must meet the legal requirements of the requested state. In the United States, this means that for requests seeking the contents, say, of an e-mail account, a Department of Justice attorney—usually from OIA but sometimes from a partner U.S. Attorney's Office—must obtain a search warrant from a U.S. court on the foreign government's behalf. Probable cause is a distinctly American concept, and many countries struggle to articulate a sufficient basis in their requests to meet this legal standard. OIA works closely with requesting state partners to develop, where possible, the necessary basis to obtain a search warrant. Other U.S. legal requirements, including the "filtering" of any resulting productions, add to the complexity of this practice.

Because there are few rules governing most providers' retention of data in the normal course, it is important that electronic records associated with targeted accounts be "preserved" before they are deleted. Pursu-

DETECTING, DETERRING, AND DISRUPTING CYBER THREATS

THE BUDAPEST CONVENTION

The Budapest Convention (official name: the Council of Europe's Convention on Cybercrime) is a multilateral treaty that enhances international cooperation in cases involving computer-related crime. The treaty entered into force in 2004, requires Parties to have a basic level of domestic criminal law in the cyber field, and provides a platform for transnational law enforcement cooperation in investigations, evidence sharing, and extradition. The Convention also requires Parties to criminalize computer-related crimes such as computer hacking, fraud, and child sexual exploitation, and requires that Parties have the ability to effectively investigate computer-related crime through the collection and sharing of electronic evidence. Membership in the Convention is open to any nation. To date, nearly 60 countries spanning Europe, Asia, Australia, Africa, and North and South America have fully ratified the treaty, as illustrated below. The United States participated in the drafting of the Convention and became a Party to it in 2006.

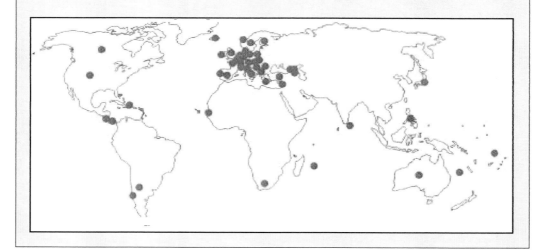

ant to U.S. law, U.S. investigators and prosecutors preserve targeted account data prior to obtaining a search warrant or other legal process for its disclosure. OIA and the Department's Computer Crime and Intellectual Property section routinely assist prosecutors and law enforcement around the world in performing this early, but important, investigative step.

10. *Joint or Parallel Investigations*

Law enforcement agencies from separate countries may wish to cooperatively investigate crimes having relevance and jurisdiction in both countries through joint or parallel investigations. Although these investigations may be established in the absence of a treaty, a number of existing treaties address the creation of joint investigative teams ("JITs"), thereby highlighting the potentially useful impact of such arrangements. These include, for example, global multilateral instruments like the 2000 United Nations Convention against Transnational Organized Crime,[18] and, in the case of the United States and the European Union, the 2003 Agreement on Mutual Legal Assistance between the United States of America and the European Union.[19] JITs can be useful tools to conduct joint operations, facilitate information sharing, and thwart criminal conduct. However, they are not perfect solutions for all cases with multi-jurisdictional dimensions. U.S. criminal law and practice differ in significant respects from that of foreign partners, and as a result, the prudent course is to assess opportunities for JITs on a case-by-case basis and to fashion cooperative efforts in a manner that works for all relevant participants.

Key Prosecution Tools

Once investigators have gathered evidence of cyber threat activity, the Department's prosecuting attorneys then determine whether that evidence is sufficient to bring charges under U.S. federal law. Cyber threat activity is a U.S. federal crime if it violates one or more of the following statutes, among others:

1. Computer Fraud and Abuse Act: 18 U.S.C. § 1030

The Computer Fraud and Abuse Act ("CFAA")[20] remains the U.S. government's principal tool for prosecuting computer crimes. In lay terms, the CFAA gives the owners of computers the right to control who may access their computers, take information from them, change how the computers work, or delete information on them. Just as the criminal laws against trespassing protect property rights in land, the CFAA protects property rights in computers. As such, the CFAA commits the United States to a cybersecurity policy that is founded on private property rights, and backed by enforcement of criminal law. The CFAA defines multiple crimes, and assigns each a different statutory maximum penalty.

Although a detailed description and analysis of each offense established by section 1030(a) is beyond the scope of this report,[21] below we provide a high-level overview of how the CFAA combats cyber threats.

Accessing a Computer and Obtaining Information: 18 U.S.C. § 1030(a)(2)

Section 1030(a)(2) protects the privacy of information stored on computers by criminalizing the act of accessing such information without authorization. The statute sets forth three distinct but overlapping crimes that collectively prohibit the unauthorized accessing of certain financial records stored on computers of financial institutions, of information from U.S. government computers, and of information from computers used in or affecting interstate or foreign commerce (for example, computers connected to the Internet). This provision applies both to outside hackers who gain access to victim computers without authorization from anywhere around the world, and to those who have

DETECTING, DETERRING, AND DISRUPTING CYBER THREATS

some authorization to access a computer, but who intentionally exceed that access.[22]

To violate section 1030(a)(2), a person must access, and thereby obtain, the prohibited information "intentionally." Mere mistake, inadvertence, or carelessness is insufficient.[23] Additionally, to be charged, the defendant must have understood that the access was unauthorized. Accordingly, federal prosecutions focus on hackers and insiders whose conduct evidences a clear intent to enter, without proper authorization, computer files or data belonging to another.

Damaging a Computer: 18 U.S.C. § 1030(a)(5)

Section 1030(a)(5) is a critical tool for prosecuting criminals who "damage" computers protected under the CFAA by causing computers to fail to operate as their owners intended. Section 1030(a)(5) is used to prosecute hackers or intruders who gain unauthorized access to a computer and commit criminal acts that, in any way, impair the integrity of data, a program, a system, or information, as well as change the way a computer is intended to operate. The statute extends to intruders who gain unauthorized access to a computer and send commands that delete files or shut the computer down. Subsection (a)(5) also may be used against cybercriminals who install malicious software that compromises a computer's integrity. Thus, installing remote access tools, bot code, and other attempts to persist on a victim's system are all chargeable under section 1030(a)(5). This provision is also an important tool for prosecuting criminals who cause intentional damage to computers by flooding an Internet connection with data during a distributed denial of service ("DDoS") attack.

Accessing a Computer to Defraud and Obtain Value: 18 U.S.C. § 1030(a)(4)

Section 1030(a)(4) establishes a felony offense that prosecutors use against hackers who access a protected computer without appropriate authorization in furtherance of a fraud to obtain something of value. The section bears similarities to the federal mail and wire fraud statutes (discussed below), but has a narrower jurisdictional scope by requiring that the cybercriminal victimize a protected computer without authorization or in excess of authorization.

Prosecutors use this provision against defendants who obtain information from a computer, and then later use that information to commit fraud. For example, section 1030(a)(4) was charged in a case involving a defendant who accessed a telephone company's computer without authorization, obtained calling card numbers, and then used those calling card numbers to make free long-distance telephone calls.[24] The provision also may be used to prosecute a defendant who alters or deletes records on a computer, and then receives something of value from an individual who relied on the accuracy of those altered or deleted records.[25]

Threatening to Damage a Computer: 18 U.S.C. § 1030(a)(7)

To deter high-tech attempts to commit old-fashioned extortion, section 1030(a)(7) criminalizes threats to interfere in any way with the normal operation of a protected computer or system, as well as threats to compromise the confidentiality or integrity of information contained therein. This provision encompasses threats by criminals to deny access to authorized users, erase or corrupt data or programs, or slow down or shutdown the operation of the computer system, such as via a DDoS attack. The provision also reaches threats to steal confidential data.

Charging Policies

The Department's decisions about when to open an investigation or charge a case under the CFAA are guided by the Intake and Charging Policy for Computer Crime Matters.[26] As the policy explains, prosecutors must consider a number of factors in order to ensure that charges are brought only in cases that serve a substantial federal interest.[27] The policy also requires prosecutors to conduct certain consultations to assure consistent practice across the Department. In particular, prosecutors must consult with the Department's Computer Crime and Intellectual Property section before bringing charges under the CFAA.

2.   Wire Fraud: 18 U.S.C. § 1343

The wire fraud statute is another particularly powerful and commonly applicable charge in computer crime cases involving fraud. Indeed, courts long have recognized that e-mails and other forms of Internet transmissions constitute "wire, radio, or television communication[s]" that may be pun-

ished under a wire fraud charge.[28] Section 1343 shares a number of common proof elements with section 1030(a)(4) of the CFAA, including the requirement that a defendant act with fraudulent intent; however, the wire fraud statute authorizes more punitive penalties that may be more commensurate to the harm suffered by victims in cases involving significant loss amounts. Section 1343 violations also can serve as a predicate for the Racketeer Influenced and Corrupt Organizations Act ("RICO") and money laundering charges, whereas most CFAA violations cannot.[29] Accordingly, the wire fraud statute is a particularly effective tool for prosecuting intricate networks of criminal hacker groups engaged in transnational organized crime.[30]

3.   Identity Theft: 18 U.S.C. §§ 1028(a)(7) and 1028A

Cybercriminals often commit computer intrusions to compromise and steal PII that may be sold on the black market, or directly used to commit other crimes, such as wire fraud. A criminal who misuses or traffics in stolen PII often violates a variety of identity theft statutes, including 18 U.S.C. §§ 1028(a)(7) and 1028A.

In relevant part, section 1028(a)(7) criminalizes the unauthorized transfer, possession, or use of a "means of identification of another person" with the intent to commit (or aid and abet) a violation of federal law, or any State or local felony. The term "means of identification," in turn, broadly refers to "any name or number that may be used, alone or in conjunction with any other information, to identify a specific individual."[31]

In computer intrusion cases, the Department also uses section 1028A (the "aggravated" identity theft statute) to prosecute individuals who engage in the unauthorized transfer, possession, or use of a "means of identification of another person" during and in relation to felony violations of certain enumerated federal offenses that are commonly associated with computer crime.[32] For example, "carders" who sell or trade stolen credit or debit card account information on online forums, or "phishers" who obtain the same type of information via fraudulent e-mails, often violate a predicate crime for a section 1028A violation. Similarly, defendants who violate the CFAA and obtain identity or account information may also violate this section. Although section 1028A is limited to a far narrower list of predicate offenses than section 1028(a)(7), it is an important and powerful tool in the Department's prosecutions of cybercriminals because those who are convicted of section 1028A are subject to a mandatory minimum two-year term of imprisonment.[33]

4. Economic Espionage and Theft of Trade Secrets: 18 U.S.C. §§ 1831-32

Trade secret law prohibits the unauthorized disclosure of confidential and proprietary information (for example, a formula or compilation of information) when that information possesses an independent economic value because it is secret, and the owner has taken reasonable measures to keep it secret.[34] Although the problem of trade secret theft predates the modern era of cybercrime, the increased digitalization of trade secrets, the rise of cyber espionage, and the global expansion of online marketplaces that traffic in intellectual property, have significantly magnified the threats that insiders, hackers, and nation states present to U.S. individuals and companies who maintain valuable trade secrets.[35] Indeed, in recent years, businesses across key sectors of the U.S. economy have suffered sophisticated and systematic cyber intrusions designed to steal sensitive commercial data from compromised networks, including research and design data, software source code, and plans for commercial and military systems.

The Department's principal tool for preventing and deterring serious instances of trade secret theft is the Economic Espionage Act ("EEA"). The EEA criminalizes two types of trade secret misappropriation: economic espionage under section 1831, and trade secret theft under section 1832. The economic espionage provision prohibits the theft of trade secrets for the benefit of a foreign government, instrumentality, or agent. The theft of trade secrets provision prohibits the commercial theft of trade secrets to benefit someone other than the owner. Although the provisions define separate offenses, they share a number of common proof elements. Notably, conviction under either statute requires the government to demonstrate beyond a reasonable doubt that: (1) the defendant misappropriated information; (2) the defendant knew or believed this information was proprietary and that he had no claim to it; and (3) the information was in fact a trade secret (unless the crime charged is a conspiracy or an attempt). Further, both provisions are subject to the EEA's broad definition of a "trade secret," which includes all types of information that the owner has taken reasonable measures to keep secret and that itself has independent economic value.[36] Both provisions also punish attempts and conspiracies to misappropriate trade secrets.[37] To promote enforcement, federal law provides special protections to victims in trade secret cases to ensure that the confidentiality of trade secret information is preserved during the course of criminal proceedings.[38]

5. Criminal Copyright: 17 U.S.C. § 506

Copyright law provides federal protection against infringement of certain exclusive rights, such as reproduction and distribution, of "original works of authorship," including computer software, literary works, musical works, and motion pictures.[39] As with trade secrets, the increased digitalization of copyrighted materials, as well as the global expansion of online marketplaces that traffic in intellectual property, have enhanced their attractiveness and, in turn, vulnerability to cybercriminals.

The Department's principal tool for preventing and deterring serious instances of copyright infringement is section 506(a) of title 17, United States Code, which criminalizes willful copyright infringement if committed "for purposes of commercial advantage or private financial gain," or "by the reproduction or distribution" of copyrighted works during a 180-day period that satisfies the statute's minimum retail value. Section 506(a)(1)(C) also makes it a crime to pre-re-

lease copyrighted materials, such as a commercial film, song, video game, or software, that are still "being prepared for commercial distribution," by making the material "available on a computer network accessible to members of the public."

6. Access Device Fraud:
18 U.S.C. § 1029

Section 1029 of title 18, United States Code, broadly prohibits the production, use, possession, or trafficking of unauthorized or counterfeit "access devices," such as PII, instrument identifiers, or other means of account access that may be used "to obtain money, goods, services, or any other thing of value, or that can be used to initiate a transfer of funds." Prosecutors commonly bring charges under section 1029 in "phishing" cases, in which a cybercriminal uses fraudulent e-mails to obtain bank account numbers and passwords. Section 1029 also is an effective tool in "carding" cases where a defendant purchases, sells, or transfers stolen bank account, credit card, or debit account information. Forfeiture is also available in many cases.[40]

7. Racketeer Influenced and Corrupt Organizations (RICO) Act:
18 U.S.C. §§ 1961–1968

Computer hacking conducted by transnational criminal groups poses a significant threat to American cybersecurity. Equipped with sizable funds, organized criminal groups operating abroad employ highly sophisticated malicious software, spear-phishing campaigns, and other hacking tools—some of which rival in sophistication those that nation states use—to hack into sensitive financial systems, conduct massive data breaches, spread ransomware, attack critical infrastructure, and steal critical intellectual property. For transnational cybercrime rings engaged in "racketeering" activity, such as identity theft, access device fraud, or wire fraud, a RICO charge may be a particularly effective tool for prosecuting individual members of the group. For instance, the RICO statute authorizes more severe penalties than the CFAA, including maximum sentences of 20 years or more depending on the nature of the predicate offense,[41] consecutive sentencing for RICO substantive and conspiracy convictions or violations of two substantive RICO subsections,[42] and forfeiture of all reasonably foreseeable proceeds of racketeering activity on a joint and several basis.[43] Section 1963(d)(2) of title 18, United States Code, also empowers prosecutors to obtain a pre-trial restraining order that preserves any assets that may be subject to forfeiture following conviction. In addition, a RICO conspiracy charge under section 1962(d) of title 18 allows prosecutors to hold one defendant responsible for the conduct of the enterprise.

8. *Wiretap Act: 18 U.S.C. § 2511*

The same surveillance statutes that empower law enforcement to collect evidence also protect the privacy of innocent Americans by criminalizing the unlawful collection of private communications. For example, the Wiretap Act shields private wire, oral, or electronic communications from illegal interception by another,[44] prohibits disclosure of any illegally intercepted communication,[45] and criminalizes unlawful use of that communication.[46] The Wiretap Act has proven to be an especially valuable tool for prosecuting cases involving spyware users and manufacturers, intruders using packet sniffers (i.e., tools that intercept data flowing in a network), persons improperly cloning e-mail accounts, and other cases involving the surreptitious collection of communications from a victim's computer.

To prosecute a defendant under this statute, however, federal courts have generally required that the "intercepted" communications be acquired "contemporaneously" or at approximately the same time as their transmission.[47] Accordingly, merely obtaining a copy of the contents of a recorded communication—for example, a year-old e-mail on a mail server—is not necessarily a criminal "intercept[ion]" of the communication under the Wiretap Act, though such an action may violate other provisions of law, including the Stored Communications Act, 18 U.S.C. § 2701.[48]

9. *Money Laundering: 18 U.S.C. §§ 1956, 1957*

Cybercrimes are often committed for financial gain. And as with other crimes, those committing cybercrimes will seek ways to conceal and spend their ill-gotten gains. Federal money laundering laws are thus an important tool for combatting cybercrime. These laws criminalize certain transactions undertaken with the proceeds of designated crimes, referred to as "specified unlawful activity" ("SUA").[49] Crimes classified as SUAs include many common charges brought in cybercrime cases, such as violations of the CFAA and wire fraud.

Section 1956 of title 18, United States Code, is the main money laundering charge. Among other things, this statute makes it a crime for a person to carry out a financial transaction involving SUA proceeds when the person knows the transaction involves illicit proceeds of some kind, and the transaction is designed to promote the carrying on of an SUA,[50] or to conceal "the nature, the location, the source, the ownership, or the control of the proceeds"[51] of the predicate crime. Section 1957 prohibits knowingly conducting certain monetary transactions involving SUA proceeds when the value is greater than $10,000.

Courts have broadly interpreted the scope of the transactions covered by the money laundering laws. In particular, courts have upheld the use of money laundering charges involving transactions in virtual currencies.[52]

10. Controlling the Assault of Non-Solicited Pornography and Marketing Act: 18 U.S.C. § 1037

The Controlling the Assault of Non-Solicited Pornography and Marketing ("CAN-SPAM") Act of 2003[53] provides a means for prosecuting those responsible for sending large amounts of unsolicited commercial e-mail messages (i.e., "spam"), including messages sent on social media sites. Al-though civil and regulatory provisions are the Act's primary enforcement mechanisms, it also created several new criminal offenses. Section 1037 addresses more egregious violations of the CAN-SPAM Act, particularly where the perpetrator has taken significant steps to hide his or her identity, or the source of the spam, from recipients, ISPs, or law enforcement agencies. Prosecutors have used this statute in the context of disrupting or dismantling botnets.

11. National Security Statutes

Some statutes that protect sensitive national security information are implicated in computer hacking investigations, when that information is targeted or stolen. For example, defense articles and services listed on the U.S. munitions list, 22 C.F.R. § 121.1, cannot be exported without a license without violating the Arms Export Control Act, 22 U.S.C. § 2778 ("AECA"). Other U.S.-origin items and related technology that have both commercial and military applications or otherwise warrant control are subject to the Export Administration Regulations ("EAR"), 15 C.F.R. pts. 730-74, and may require a license for export to certain countries or for certain uses. The statute that criminalizes violation of the EAR (among other regulations) is the International Emergency Economic Powers Act, 50 U.S.C. § 1705 ("IEEPA"). A Chinese aerospace engineer was recently convicted of violating AECA for helping hackers in the Chinese air force choose which defense contractors to target and which files related to military projects to steal;[54] and a network of Iranian computer hackers (one of whom was apprehended) was charged with violating AECA and Iranian sanctions under IEEPA for stealing specialized software from the networks of American software companies, which the defendants are alleged to have resold for profit to Iranian government entities.[55] Classified information and national defense information, too, are protected by a number of criminal statutes. The CFAA specifically prohibits obtaining certain restricted data and information protected against disclosure for reasons of national defense or foreign relations through unauthorized access to a computer, *see* 18 U.S.C. § 1030(a)(1), and espionage statutes prohibit the unauthorized retention of national defense information or its dissemination to an unauthorized person (whatever the means of doing so). *See* 18 U.S.C. §§ 793 & 794.

Finally, material support to terrorists is likewise prohibited, even if that support is provided online. *See* 18 U.S.C. §§ 2339A, 2339B. As discussed in Chapter 2, for example, Ardit Ferizi was an Islamic State of Iraq and the Levant ("ISIL")-linked hacker living in Malaysia who may never have met ISIL recruiters in Iraq. But when Ferizi broke into the networks of an American retailer, stole PII for thousands of U.S. persons, and culled that list down to approximately 1,300 military and other government personnel that he shared with ISIL for purposes of publishing a kill list and enabling ISIL to "hit them hard," he provided such support. Ferizi was apprehended, brought to the United States, and is now serving a 20-year sentence for providing material support to ISIL.[56]

Other Means of Dismantling, Disrupting, and Deterring Computer Crimes

While criminal prosecutions of malicious cyber activity (and seizing the ill-gotten gains of such activity) are an important aspect of the Department's approach to combating cybercrime, we recognize that the United States cannot simply prosecute its way out of the problem. Instead, the Department has embraced a comprehensive approach to deterring cyber threats that builds upon a broad array of criminal, civil, and national security authorities, tools, and capabilities. Indeed, the government as a whole relies on a range of civil and administrative tools to raise the costs associated with malicious cyber activity, and to disrupt ongoing activities in the cyber underworld.

To support this broader approach, we work to interdict cyber threats before they become actual incidents by denying malign actors access to infrastructure, tools, funds, and victims, as well as by working with international partners and members of the private sector, who often may be better positioned to prevent cybercrime.

Congress has given the Department the legal authority to disrupt, dismantle, and deter cyber threats through a blend of civil, criminal, and administrative powers beyond traditional prosecution. As a result, the Department has been a driving force behind the U.S. government's most notable and effective measures to disrupt online crime. As mentioned above, the Department often uses civil injunctions, as well as seizure and forfeiture authorities, to disrupt cybercriminal groups by seizing the computer servers and domain names those actors use to operate botnets. In cases where the actors cannot quickly be identified, such tools—exercised with proper judicial oversight—have helped the Department disrupt and dismantle ongoing criminal schemes, thereby protecting the public from further victimization. Finally, the Department, with the assistance of other U.S. government and international partners, also executes trade actions, and participates in various cyber operations designed to neutralize and eradicate international cyber threats.

1. Disrupting and Disabling International Botnets

In recent years, the Department has successfully disrupted and disabled a number of international botnets not only by arresting and prosecuting the criminals involved in their creation and administration, but also by leveraging other civil, criminal, and administrative authorities. For instance, the Department uses civil injunctive authority under section 1345 (injunctions against fraud) and section 2521 (injunctions against illegal interception) to authorize actions—such as seizing domains the botnet is using to communicate with command-and-control servers—to disrupt and disable a botnet's ongoing commission of fraud crimes or illegal wiretapping. Accompanying temporary restraining orders ("TROs") secured under Rule 65 of the Federal Rules of Civil Procedure also are important to disrupting

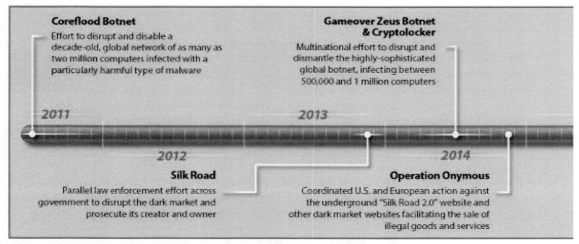

Figure 1: Recent Department efforts to dismantle botnets and dark markets.

DETECTING, DETERRING, AND DISRUPTING CYBER THREATS

a botnet, and taking immediate steps to prevent it from reconstituting.

Further, as discussed above, if law enforcement is able to take over the command-and-control structure of a botnet, the Department may now use the recently promulgated venue provision of criminal Rule 41(b)(6)(B) to issue commands to bots across a number of districts. For example, law enforcement may obtain identifying information from affected bot computers in order to contact owners and warn them of the infection. In addition, law enforcement might engage in an online operation designed to disrupt the botnet and restore full control over computers to their legal owners. Rule 41(b)(6)(B) allows the government to apply for warrants in a single judicial district to use these techniques.

Several successful examples of the Department's strategy for disrupting and disabling

botnets are illustrated in **Fig. 1,** and described in greater detail in Appendix 2.

2. *Dark Web Disruptions*

In recent years, the Dark Web's anonymity and low barriers to entry have attracted scores of criminals to Dark Web markets, including those trafficking in child pornography, illicit firearms, illegal drugs, murder-for-hire, and human trafficking. Sophisticated hackers also frequent Dark Web forums for the newest malware or stolen data, and might use the Tor network to host botnet command-and-control infrastructure that is more resistant to disruption and take-downs.

Despite the many challenges the Dark Web poses, law enforcement around the world have successfully disrupted criminals operating in the cyber underground by de-anonymizing users engaging in illegal activity;

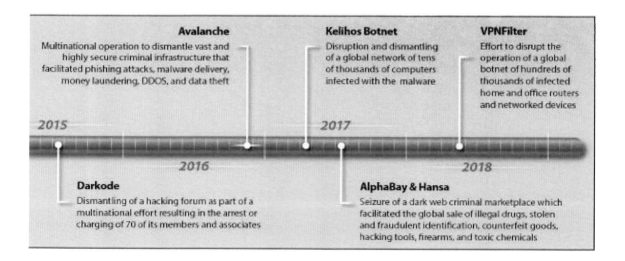

seizing their websites, domains, servers, and ill-gotten gains; and criminally prosecuting them. For instance, to pierce the Dark Web's anonymizing technology, the Department diligently pursues traditional investigative techniques, studies patterns of criminal activity, collaborates with international law enforcement partners, and develops human sources. Further, where anonymizing technologies make less intrusive investigative options ineffective, the Department also obtains warrants to perform remote searches using network investigative techniques under limited circumstances.[57] For example, appropriate scenarios for seeking a warrant to authorize a remote search include, but are not limited to: (1) obtaining stored content from a hidden provider by using a username and password; (2) identifying a criminal using a web-based e-mail account by sending a NIT to the criminal's e-mail account; and (3) identifying users of a hidden child pornography forum by sending a NIT to each computer used to log on to the website.

Once the cloak of anonymity has been pulled back, the Department leverages a range of civil and criminal tools, including civil and criminal forfeiture authorities, seizure warrants, and requests under mutual legal assistance agreements to dismantle the infrastructure undergirding the Dark Web systems and recover the proceeds of these illegal activities. Further, in many instances, individuals responsible for creating, operating, and using Dark Web forums and marketplaces are also criminally prosecuted. We describe in Appendix 3 some recent prominent examples of the Department's compre-

hensive strategy to combat malicious activity on the Dark Web.

3. Sanctions and Designations

To ensure that investigative information is used effectively to protect the Nation, the Department regularly interacts with the Departments of Commerce, Treasury, and State, as well as with other agencies and regulatory bodies, to support those departments' actions to identify and impose sanctions on malicious cyber actors.

Sanctions imposed by the Office of Foreign Assets Control at the Department of the Treasury can deprive subjects of their access to the U.S. financial system and their ability to do business with U.S. persons, and can be particularly effective in reaching foreign companies that benefit from stolen information. Since 2011, the Treasury Department has had the authority to block the property of transnational criminal organizations under Executive Order 13581 ("Blocking Property of Transnational Criminal Organizations"). Treasury also makes use of country-specific regimes to respond to nation-state behavior. As mentioned in Chapter 2, following North Korea's destructive malware attack on Sony Pictures Entertainment, the President in 2015 issued Executive Order 13687 ("Imposing Additional Sanctions with Respect to North Korea"). Using this new sanction authority, the Treasury Department designated three entities for being "controlled entities of the Government of North Korea" and ten

DETECTING, DETERRING, AND DISRUPTING CYBER THREATS

individuals for being "agencies or officials of the North Korean government."[58]

In 2015, the President also issued Executive Order 13694 ("Blocking the Property of Certain Persons Engaging in Significant Malicious Cyber-Enabled Activities"), which authorized the Secretary of the Treasury, in consultation with the Attorney General and the Secretary of State, to impose sanctions on individuals or entities that engage in malicious cyber-enabled activity that results in, or materially contributes to, a significant threat to the national security, foreign policy, or economic health or financial stability of the United States.[59] In December 2016, the President amended this executive order in "order to take additional steps to deal with the national emergency with respect to sig-

nificant malicious cyber-enabled activities . . . in view of the increasing use of such activities to undermine democratic processes or institutions."[60] The 2016 amendment expanded cyber-related sanctions and in an annex designated five Russian entities—including that nation's domestic and foreign intelligence services—and four Russian individuals who were determined to have interfered with or undermined U.S. election processes or institutions.[61] The list of designated parties was expanded again on March 15, 2018,[62] and yet again on June 11, 2018.[63]

Designations under E.O. 13694 are not limited to Russian actors. On March 23, 2018, in consultation with the Department, OFAC designated an Iranian entity, the Mabna Institute, and ten Iranian individuals who

Credit: Amy Mathers, U.S. Department of Justice

Deputy Attorney General Rod Rosenstein announces on March 23, 2018 the filing of criminal charges against nine Iranians alleged to have conducted a massive cyber theft campaign on behalf of the Islamic Revolutionary Guard Corps. The Treasury Department imposed sanctions the same day.

engaged in theft of valuable intellectual property and data from hundreds of U.S. and third-country universities and a media company for private financial gain.[64] (That same day, the Department unsealed criminal charges against the same entity and nine individuals.[65] *See* page 73.)

The Department will continue to support sanctions under such authorities by helping the Treasury Department draft sanction nomination packages based on the information gathered during our investigations. Where, for example, investigations identify hackers who victimize U.S. individuals or companies, or those who profit from criminal hacking by using stolen personal information or trade secrets, the Department works with the Treasury Department to craft appropriate sanctions against those responsible.

Similarly, the Commerce Department can place persons and companies on its Entity List if it finds that they are engaged in activities that are contrary to U.S. national security or foreign policy interests.[66] Persons and entities on the Entity List are subject to special licensing requirements for the export, re-export, and/or transfer (in-country) of items listed in the EAR. In 2014, for example, in addition to the Department of Justice's prosecution of a Chinese engineer for consulting with Chinese military hackers who stole aerospace technology, the Commerce Department placed his company on the Entity List, based on the FBI's nomination.[67] Such a listing can have dramatic consequences, cutting the firm off from U.S. exports and causing U.S. and foreign businesses to reconsider doing business with the designated entity.

4. *Trade Actions*

The Office of the United States Trade Representative ("USTR") can raise the issue of foreign cyber intrusions against American businesses in the context of its trade actions under various U.S. laws or trade agreements. As declared in a USTR report made public in April 2017, "The United States uses all trade tools available to ensure that its trading partners provide robust protection for trade secrets and enforce trade secrets laws."[68] The Department has worked closely with USTR to ensure that the Trade Representative is appropriately informed about cyber-enabled activity by nation states that may be actionable under U.S. trade laws.

Due in part to China's cyber-enabled theft of U.S. intellectual property and sensitive commercial information, the U.S. government in March 2018 announced various tariffs against China and various restrictions on Chinese investments.[69] The announcement came after USTR released a comprehensive public report as part of its investigation under section 301 of the Trade Act of 1974.[70] The USTR report establishes a clear record of China's cyber intrusions and cyber theft based on information provided by the Department, among other parts of the U.S. government. The report indicates that the Chinese government has used cyber intrusions to serve its strategic economic objectives and that "incidents of China's cyber intrusions against U.S. commercial entities align closely with China's industrial policy objectives."[71] For example, the PLA's theft of trade secrets from Westinghouse, Inc., as documented in an indictment brought by the Depart-

DETECTING, DETERRING, AND DISRUPTING CYBER THREATS

ment, illustrates how China uses cyber-enabled theft as one of multiple instruments to achieve its state-led technology development goals.[72] Likewise, the USTR report noted that "[i]n September 2017, the Department filed an indictment against three Chinese nationals who were owners, employees, and associates of the Guangzhou Bo Yu Information Technology Company Limited ("Boyusec"), a company that cybersecurity firms have linked to the Chinese government."[73] The USTR report contains other examples that illustrate how China uses cyber-enabled intrusions to further the commercial interests of Chinese state-owned enterprises, to the detriment of its foreign partners and competitors. Available evidence also indicates that China uses its cyber capabilities as an instrument to achieve its industrial policy and science and technology objectives. The Department has played an important role in bringing these threats to our national security to light.

5. *Cyber Operations*

Finally, the Department also assists other agencies in analyzing the legal and policy implications of operations conducted through cyberspace, and ensuring that these operations comply with the Constitution and applicable law. Where additional authority or injunctive relief is required to address conduct within the United States, the Department works with investigators and, as appropriate, the U.S. Attorney community, to pursue it. Intelligence gathered by the FBI using its national security investigative authorities may also assist agencies in planning or carrying out such operations.

NOTES

[1] The Department components responsible for this work are described in Chapter 5.

[2] For example, the FBI, as the federal government's primary investigative agency, must comply with *The Attorney General's Guidelines for Domestic FBI Operations*, available at: https://www.justice.gov/archive/opa/docs/guidelines.pdf (last accessed June 29, 2018), and the *FBI Domestic Investigations and Operations Guide*, available at: https://vault.fbi.gov/FBI%20Domestic%20Investigations%20and%20Operations%20Guide%20%28DIOG%29/fbi-domestic-investigations-and-operations-guide-diog-2013-version/FBI%20Domestic%20Investigations%20and%20Operations%20Guide%20%28DIOG%29%202013%20Version%20Part%2001%20of%201/view (last accessed June 29, 2018), which standardizes the FBI's criminal, national security, and foreign intelligence investigative activities. The *Attorney General's Guidelines* establish a set of basic principles that serve as the foundation for all FBI mission-related activities, and the professional identity of each FBI agent, including: (1) protecting the public includes protecting their rights and liberties; (2) investigating only for a proper and authorized law enforcement, national security, or foreign intelligence purpose; (3) ensuring that an independent, authorized law enforcement or national security purpose exists for initiating investigative activity—race, ethnicity, religion, or national origin alone can never constitute the sole basis for initiating investigative activity; (4) performing only authorized activities in pursuit of investigative activities; (5) employing the least intrusive means for investigation that do not otherwise compromise FBI operations; and (6) applying best judgment to the circumstances at hand to select the most appropriate investigative means to achieve the investigative goal.

[3] *See* ICANN WHOIS, available at: https://whois.icann.org/en (last accessed June 29, 2018).

[4] Pub. L. No. 99–508, 100 Stat. 1848 (1986) (codified at 18 U.S.C. § 2510 *et seq.*).

[5] *See* 18 U.S.C. § 2703.

[6] *Id.* § 3121 *et seq.*

[7] *Id.* § 2510 *et seq.*

[8] 50 U.S.C. § 1801 *et seq.*

Virtual currency seizures with a value of $500,000 or more must be forfeited judicially. The value is assessed on the date of agency seizure.

[10] *See, e.g.,* "For Sale Approximately 3,813.0481935 Bitcoins," U.S. MARSHALS SERVICE (Jan. 2018), available at: https://www.usmarshals.gov/assets/2018/bitcoinauction/ (last accessed June 29, 2018).

[11] 18 U.S.C. §§ 981-983.

[12] *See* Press Release, "Russian National And Bitcoin Exchange Charged In 21-Count Indictment For Operating Alleged International Money Laundering Scheme And Allegedly Laundering Funds From Hack Of Mt. Gox," U.S. DEPT. OF JUSTICE (July 26, 2017), available at: https://www.justice.gov/usao-ndca/pr/russian-national-and-bitcoin-exchange-charged-21-count-indictment-operating-alleged (last accessed June 29, 2018).

[13] A "John Doe" summons is an administrative summons that may be used, with court approval, to seek information about an ascertainable group or class of persons who may be involved in violating federal tax laws. *See* 26 U.S.C. § 7609(f) (2012).

DETECTING, DETERRING, AND DISRUPTING CYBER THREATS

[14] *United States* v. *Coinbase, Inc. et al.*, Order Regarding Petition to Enforce IRS Summons at 14 (Doc. 78), Case No. 3:17-cv-01431 (N.D. Cal.).

[15] *See* 18 U.S.C. § 3181 note (listing the countries with which the United States currently has a bilateral extradition agreement).

[16] Quoted from the United States's sentencing memorandum in *United States* v. *Roman Seleznev*, No. 11-CRM-007 (W.D. Wa., Apr. 14, 2017), available at: https://assets.documentcloud.org/documents/3673513/Seleznev-US-Atty-Sentencing-Memo.pdf (last accessed June 29, 2018).

[17] *See* Press Release, "Russian Cyber-Criminal Sentenced to 14 Years in Prison for Role in Organized Cybercrime Ring Responsible for $50 million in Online Identity Theft and $9 Million Bank Fraud Conspiracy," U.S. DEPT. OF JUSTICE (Nov. 30, 2017) (describing all of Seleznev's federal sentences), available at: https://www.justice.gov/opa/pr/russian-cyber-criminal-sentenced-14-years-prison-role-organized-cybercrime-ring-responsible (last accessed June 29, 2018).

[18] https://www.unodc.org/documents/middleeastandnorthafrica/organised-crime/UNITED NATIONS CONVENTION AGAINST TRANSNATIONAL ORGANIZED CRIME AND THE PROTOCOLS THERETO.pdf (Art. XIX) (last accessed June 29, 2018).

[19] https://www.state.gov/documents/organization/180815.pdf (Art. V) (last accessed June 29, 2018).

[20] Although the CFAA is primarily a criminal statute, individuals and companies may also bring private civil suits against CFAA violators. *See* 18 U.S.C. § 1030(g). This report does not address the civil provisions of the statute except as they may pertain to the criminal provisions.

[21] More specific guidance on the CFAA is available at: https://www.justice.gov/sites/default/files/criminal-ccips/legacy/2015/01/14/ccmanual.pdf (last accessed June 29, 2018).

[22] In the Second, Fourth, and Ninth Circuits, significant recent decisions have limited the definition of "exceeds authorized access" in 18 U.S.C. § 1030(e)(6) "to violations of restrictions on *access* to information, and not restrictions on its *use*." *See, e.g.*, *United States v. Nosal*, 676 F.3d 854, 863-64 (9th Cir. 2012). Other language in *Nosal* suggests that the Ninth Circuit's ultimate holding is broader: that an individual can "exceed[] authorized access" only by accessing data that he or she was never authorized to access, under any circumstances. Accordingly, in those circuits, the Department recommends against charging any case that relies on the definition of "exceeds authorized access" in 18 U.S.C. § 1030(e)(6), unless it can be proven that the computer user had *absolutely no authorization to access the relevant information.*

[23] *See, e.g.*, S. Rep. No. 432, 99th Cong., 2d Sess., *reprinted in* 1986 U.S.C.C.A.N. 2479, 2483.

[24] *See United States* v. *Lindsley*, 254 F.3d 71 (5th Cir. 2001).

[25] *See, e.g.*, *United States* v. *Butler*, 16 Fed. Appx. 99 (4th Cir. 2001) (unpublished).

[26] *See* Memorandum from Eric Holder, Attorney General, "Intake and Charging Policy for Computer Crime Matters," (Sept. 11, 2014), available at: https://www.justice.gov/criminal-ccips/file/904941/download (last accessed June 29, 2018).

[27] *See id.*

[28] *See, e.g.*, *United States* v. *Selby*, 557 F.3d 968, 978-79 (9th Cir. 2009) (finding defendant's act of

sending a single e-mail "sufficient to establish the element of the use of the wires in furtherance of the scheme"); *United States* v. *Drummond*, 255 Fed. Appx. 60, 64 (6th Cir. 2007) (unpublished) (affirming wire fraud conviction where defendant made airline reservation with stolen credit card over the Internet).

[29] As explained below, exceptions exist for terrorism-related violations of section 1030(a)(1) and 1030(a)(5)(A).

[30] The United States Attorneys' Manual provides further guidance regarding wire fraud charges, *see* U.S. DEPT. OF JUSTICE, UNITED STATES ATTORNEYS' MANUAL, § 9-43.000, as does the manual, IDENTITY THEFT AND SOCIAL SECURITY FRAUD (Office of Legal Education 2004).

[31] 18 U.S.C. § 1028(d)(7). Although there is little dispute about classifying a unique identifier, such as a social security number, as a "means of identification," some courts have questioned whether non-unique identifiers, such as names or birthdates, qualify as a "means of identification" when standing alone. *Compare United States v. Silva*, 554 F.3d 13, 23 n.4 (1st Cir. 2009) (finding doctor's signature constitutes a "means of identification"), *with United States v. Mitchell*, 518 F.3d 230, 232-36 (4th Cir. 2008) (requiring that non-unique identifiers be combined with additional information that permits the identification of a specific person).

[32] *E.g.*, 18 U.S.C. §§ 1028(a)(1)-(6), (8), 1029, 1030, 1037, 1343.

[33] 18 U.S.C. § 1028A(a)(1); *see also id.* § 1028A(a)(2) (providing a minimum five-year term for terrorism-related aggravated identity theft).

[34] *See* 18 U.S.C. §§ 1831, 1832.

[35] *Combating Economic Espionage and Trade Secret Theft, Hearing Before the S. Judiciary Comm.,*

Subcomm. on Crime and Terrorism of the S. Judiciary Comm., 113 Cong. 4 (2016) (statement of Randall C. Coleman, Assistant Dir., Counterintelligence Div. FBI), available at: https://www.govinfo.gov/content/pkg/CHRG-113shrg96009/pdf/CHRG-113shrg96009.pdf   (last accessed June 29, 2018).

[36] 18 U.S.C. § 1839(3).

[37] *See id.* §§ 1831(a)(4)-(5), 1832(a)(4)-(5). For an attempt, the defendant must (1) have the intent needed to commit one of the two crimes, and (2) perform an act amounting to a "substantial step" toward the commission of that crime. *United States* v. *Hsu*, 185 F.R.D. 192, 202 (E.D. Pa. 1999). For a conspiracy, the defendant must agree with one or more people to commit a violation, and one or more of the co-conspirators must commit an overt act to effect the object of the conspiracy. 18 U.S.C. §§ 1831(a)(5), 1832(a) (5).

[38] *See id.* § 1835.

[39] *See* 17 U.S.C. §§ 102(a), 106 (2012).

[40] *See* 18 U.S.C. § 1029(c)(1)(C), (c)(2).

[41] *Id.* § 1963(a).

[42] Organized Crime & Gang Section, U.S. DEPT. OF JUSTICE, CRIMINAL RICO: 18 U.S.C. §§1961-1968, A MANUAL FOR FEDERAL PROSECUTORS (May 2016), https://www.justice.gov/usam/file/870856/download (last visited June 29, 2018).

[43] *Id.* at 238-39.

[44] 18 U.S.C. § 2511(1)(a) & (b).

[45] *Id.* § 2511(1)(c) § (e).

[46] *Id.* § 2511(1)(d).

[47] *See, e.g., In re Pharmatrak, Inc. Privacy Litig.*, 329 F.3d 9, 21 (1st Cir. 2003).

DETECTING, DETERRING, AND DISRUPTING CYBER THREATS

48 Similarly, other surveillance statutes like the Pen Trap Act and FISA criminalize violations of their provisions. *See* 18 U.S.C. § 3121 (Pen Trap Act); 50 U.S.C. § 1809 (FISA).

49 18 U.S.C. § 1956(c)(7) (defining SUA).

50 *Id.* § 1956(a)(1)(A)(i).

51 *Id.* § 1956(a)(1)(B)(i).

52 *See United States* v. *Budovsky*, 2015 WL 5602853, at *12-13 (S.D.N.Y. Sept. 23, 2015) (holding that virtual currency created by Liberty Reserve constituted funds within the meaning of § 1956); *United States* v. *Ulbricht,* 31 F. Supp. 3d 540, 569-70 (S.D.N.Y. 2014) (holding that transactions involving Bitcoin were financial transactions within the scope of § 1956).

53 Pub. L. No. 108-187, 117 Stat. 2699 (2003).

54 Press Release, "Chinese National Who Conspired to Hack into U.S. Defense Contractors' Systems Sentenced to 46 Months in Federal Prison," U.S. Dept. of Justice (July 13, 2016), available at: https://www.justice.gov/opa/pr/chinese-national-who-conspired-hack-us-defense-contractors-systems-sentenced-46-months (last accessed June 15, 2018).

55 Press Release, "Two Iranian Nationals Charged in Hacking of Vermont Software Company," U.S. Dept. of Justice (July 17, 2017), available at: https://www.justice.gov/opa/pr/two-iranian-nationals-charged-hacking-vermont-software-company (last accessed June 15, 2018).

56 Press Release, "ISIL-Linked Kosovo Hacker Sentenced to 20 Years in Prison," U.S. Dept. of Justice (Sept. 23, 2016), available at: https://www.justice.gov/opa/pr/isil-linked-kosovo-hacker-sentenced-20-years-prison (last accessed June 15, 2018).

57 As with all investigative techniques, Department personnel are trained to use remote search tools appropriately and lawfully. Additionally, the FBI is required to adhere to the Attorney General's *Guidelines for Domestic FBI Operations* and the FBI's *Domestic Investigations and Operations Guide* in conducting remote searches and seizures; *see supra* note 2. These documents require the FBI to use the least intrusive method that is feasible when conducting a search. *See Guidelines for Domestic FBI Operations,* § 1(c)(2)(A); *Domestic Investigations and Operations Guide,* § 18.2.

58 Press Release, "Treasury Sanctions Additional North Korean Officials and Entities in Response to the Regime's Serious Human Rights Abuses and Censorship Activities," U.S. Dept. of the Treasury (Oct. 26, 2017), available at: https://www.treasury.gov/press-center/press-releases/Pages/sm0191.aspx (last accessed June 29, 2018).

59 Exec. Order No. 13694, 3 C.F.R. 297 (2016).

60 Exec. Order No. 13757, 3 C.F.R. 1 (2017).

61 *Id.*

62 Press Release, "Treasury Sanctions Russian Cyber Actors for Interference with the 2016 U.S. Elections and Malicious Cyber-Attacks," U.S. Dept. of Treasury (March 15, 2018), available at: https://home.treasury.gov/index.php/news/press-releases/sm0312 (last accessed June 29, 2018).

63 Press Release, "Treasury Sanctions Russian Federal Security Service Enablers," U.S. Dept. of Treasury (June 11, 2018), available at: https://home.treasury.gov/news/press-releases/sm0410 (last accessed June 29, 2018).

64 Press Release, "Treasury Sanctions Iranian Cyber Actors for Malicious Cyber-Enabled Activities Targeting Hundreds of Universities," U.S. Dept. of Treasury (March 23, 2018), available

at: https://home.treasury.gov/news/press-releases/sm0332 (last accessed June 29, 2018).

[65] Press Release, "Nine Iranians Charged With Conducting Massive Cyber Theft Campaign on Behalf of the Islamic Revolutionary Guard Corps," U.S. DEPT. OF JUSTICE (March 23, 2018), available at: https://www.justice.gov/opa/pr/nine-iranians-charged-conducting-massive-cyber-theft-campaign-behalf-islamic-revolutionary (last accessed June 29, 2018).

[66] Export Administration Regulations, Control Policy: End-User and End-Use Based, 15 C.F.R. §§ 744.1–.22 (2016), available at: https://www.gpo.gov/fdsys/pkg/CFR-2016-title15-vol2/xml/CFR-2016-title15-vol2-part744.xml (last accessed June 29, 2018).

[67] "Addition of Certain Persons to the Entity List," 79 Fed. Reg. 44680 (Aug. 1, 2014), available at: https://www.gpo.gov/fdsys/pkg/FR-2014-08-01/pdf/2014-17960.pdf (last accessed June 29, 2018) (adding PRC Lode Technology Corporation, a company owned by Su Bin, a Chinese national serving a prison term for conspiring with Chinese air force officers to exploit computer systems of U.S. companies and of DoD contractors to illicitly obtain and export information, including controlled technology, related to military projects).

[68] "2017 Special 301 Report," OFFICE OF THE UNITED STATES TRADE REPRESENTATIVE at 18 (April 2017), available at: https://ustr.gov/sites/default/files/301/2017%20Special%20301%20Report%20FINAL.PDF (last accessed June 29, 2018).

[69] See "Remarks by President Trump at Signing of a Presidential Memorandum Targeting China's Economic Aggression," THE WHITE HOUSE (March 22, 2018), available at: https://www.whitehouse.gov/briefings-statements/remarks-president-trump-signing-presidential-memorandum-targeting-chinas-economic-aggression/ (last accessed June 29, 2018).

[70] "Findings of the Investigation into China's Acts, Policies, and Practices related to Technology Transfer, Intellectual Property, and Innovation under Section 301 of the Trade Act of 1974," OFFICE OF THE UNITED STATES TRADE REPRESENTATIVE (March 22, 2018), available at: https://ustr.gov/sites/default/files/Section%20301%20FINAL.PDF (last accessed June 29, 2018).

[71] *Id.* at 153.

[72] *Id.* at 166.

[73] *Id.* at 168.

CHAPTER 4
RESPONDING TO CYBER INCIDENTS

As discussed in Chapter 3, the Department's role in disrupting and preventing cyber threats not only embraces the traditional model of criminal law enforcement—which involves arresting suspected criminals and imprisoning offenders after they have been convicted—but also extends beyond that model to the use of non-criminal authorities and remedies.

In this chapter, we discuss other non-criminal, yet critically important, aspects of the Department's overall cyber mission: responding to, preventing, and managing cyber incidents.

Building Relationships and Sharing Cyber Threat Information

When responding to cyber incidents, preparation is key. Preparation will help victims of cyber attacks speed their response, lessen the effects of exploitation, and hasten recovery. In order to best assist potential victims of cyber threats, the Department needs to prepare, too. Our preparation efforts involve relationship building, routine information sharing, and engaging with organizations and sectors that are at particular risk. And when incidents do occur, open lines of communication enable reporting and facilitate response efforts.

1. Operational Engagement

In building relationships with potential victims of cyberattacks, the FBI employs "operational engagement"—that is, tailored and targeted outreach. Building trust is fundamental to this approach, which initially may seem difficult to achieve, given concerns about privacy, legal privileges, and the protection of sensitive information. To address these concerns, the FBI as a first step seeks to share its own information with industry, through a variety of outreach initiatives and information sharing programs.

The FBI disseminates numerous reports geared directly to the private sector regarding cyber threats. *See* **Fig. 1.** Common FBI-issued reports include Private Industry Notifications ("PINs"), which provide contextual information about ongoing or emerging cyber threats, and FBI Liaison Alert System ("FLASH") reports, which provide technical indicators gleaned through investigations or intelligence. These communication methods facilitate information sharing with either a broad or sector-specific audience, and provide recipients with actionable intelligence to protect against cyber threats and to detect ongoing exploitation. The FBI also often collaborates with other government agencies, including DHS, to release joint products, such as Joint Analysis Reports ("JARs") and Joint Technical Advisories ("JTAs").

CYBER-DIGITAL TASK FORCE REPORT

Figure 1: FBI Product Lines

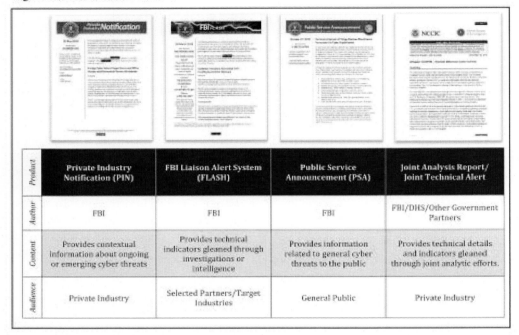

Product	Private Industry Notification (PIN)	FBI Liaison Alert System (FLASH)	Public Service Announcement (PSA)	Joint Analysis Report/ Joint Technical Alert
Author	FBI	FBI	FBI	FBI/DHS/Other Government Partners
Content	Provides contextual information about ongoing or emerging cyber threats	Provides technical indicators gleaned through investigations or intelligence	Provides information related to general cyber threats to the public	Provides technical details and indicators gleaned through joint analytic efforts.
Audience	Private Industry	Selected Partners/Target Industries	General Public	Private Industry

In certain circumstances, the FBI will join with sector-specific agencies[1] to execute an "action campaign" to quickly and efficiently advise a defined group of stakeholders of a particular cyber threat requiring their attention. *See* **Fig. 2.** These efforts serve a dual purpose of helping potentially targeted entities and advancing the FBI's cyber threat investigations.

The FBI also hosts targeted engagement events intended to bring together C-suite executives with government subject matter experts in order to build partnerships, encourage information sharing, and better understand the challenges the private sector faces in protecting against cyber threats.

In 2015, the FBI's Cyber Division began hosting a semi-annual Chief Information Security Officers ("CISO") Academy at the FBI Academy in Quantico, Virginia. The Academy seeks to enhance participants' understanding of the government and its functions by hosting approximately 30 CISOs representing key critical infrastructure sectors for a three-day training session. The event's sessions provide the latest information and intelligence on cyber threats, explain how the government interacts with private industry before, during, and after a cyberattack, explore investigative case studies, and engage participants in tabletop exercises. As of April 2018, the FBI had hosted four CISO Academies with over 120 total participants.

RESPONDING TO CYBER INCIDENTS

Figure 2: Recent FBI "action campaigns"

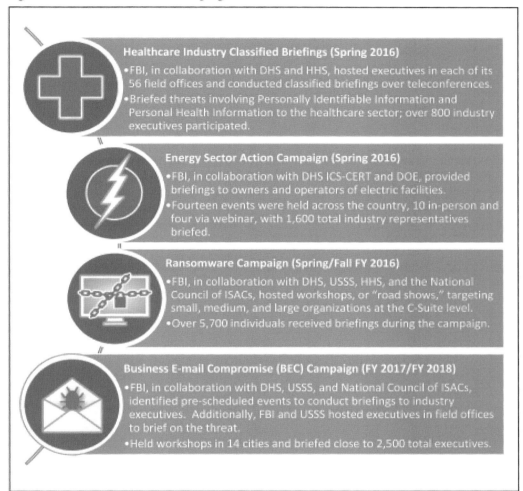

In addition, the FBI's Cyber Division, in collaboration with a host FBI field office and U.S. Attorney's Office, organizes one-day General Counsel Cyber Summits to bring corporate attorneys and CISOs together with Department personnel. At these summits, participants discuss how to overcome obstacles in information sharing and how best to work with the U.S. government when responding to a cyber incident. To date, the FBI has conducted four summits with over 500 total attendees.

2. Enduring Partnerships

The FBI has several established programs that enable connectivity, information sharing, and collaboration with the private sector on a range of hazards, including cyber threats. These programs include:

Domestic Security Alliance Council ("DSAC") was founded in 2006 as a national membership program to encourage public-private engagement between corporate chief security officers and the FBI on emerging threats facing the nation and economy. DHS was later added as a partner organization. With over 500 member companies, DSAC provides the FBI and DHS direct engagement with decision-makers in the U.S. economy's largest corporations and critical insight through the DSAC Executive Working Group.

InfraGard is a partnership between the FBI and members of the private sector for sharing information and promoting mutual learning relevant to the protection of the nation's critical infrastructure. In contrast to DSAC, InfraGard members join as individuals, not as corporations. There are over 50,000 vetted InfraGard members nationally, representing all critical infrastructure sectors, organized into 84 local chapters called "InfraGard Member Alliances." Each chapter is associated with its corresponding local FBI field office.

National Cyber-Forensics & Training Alliance ("NCFTA") was conceived in 1997 and the non-profit 501(c)(3) corporation was created in 2003. Headquartered in Pittsburgh, this organization has become an international model for joining law enforcement, private industry, and academia to build and share resources, strategic information, and cyber threat intelligence. Since its establishment, the NCFTA has evolved to keep up with the ever-changing cybercrime landscape. Today, the organization deals with threats from transnational criminal groups including spam, botnets, stock manipulation schemes, intellectual property theft, pharmaceutical fraud, telecommunication scams, and other financial fraud schemes that result in billions of dollars in losses to companies and consumers. The extensive knowledge base within the NCFTA has played a key role in some of the FBI's most significant cyber cases in the past several years.

RESPONDING TO CYBER INCIDENTS

National Domestic Communications Assistance Center ("NDCAC") is a national hub for technical knowledge management among law enforcement agencies that also strengthens law enforcement's relationships with the communications industry. Operated by the FBI's Operational Technology Division, the NDCAC leverages and shares law enforcement's collective technical knowledge and resources on issues involving real-time and stored communications to address challenges posed by advanced communications services and technologies. NDCAC develops and maintains relationships with industry to ensure law enforcement's understanding of new services and technologies, and it provides a venue to exchange information, streamline processes, and facilitate more efficient interaction between law enforcement and industry. NDCAC also educates industry on law enforcement's evidentiary processes and works with industry to verify that technical solutions work as expected.

Internet Crime Complaint Center ("IC3") provides the public with a reliable and convenient reporting mechanism to submit information to the FBI concerning suspected Internet-facilitated criminal activity and to develop effective alliances with law enforcement and industry partners. Since 2000, the IC3 has received complaints crossing the spectrum of cybercrime matters, to include online fraud in its many forms, including Intellectual Property Rights ("IPR") matters, computer intrusions, economic espionage, online extortion, identity theft and others. It is through this reporting that the program is able to analyze complaints for dissemination to the public, private industry, and for intelligence/investigative purposes for law enforcement.

3. Reporting Cyber Incidents and Notifying Targeted Entities

Through the numerous FBI and U.S. Attorneys' offices nationwide, the Department is uniquely positioned to interact with organizations that have experienced a cyber incident. The FBI has 56 field offices throughout the country, and has assisted victims of crime for over 100 years, including since the earliest days of computer crime. The FBI may learn through law enforcement or intelligence sources that a U.S. person or organization has suffered an incident or is the target of illicit cyber activity, and can proactively notify the targeted entity. Conversely, victims may be the first to detect the incident and then can notify the FBI. In either case, the Department stands ready to investigate the unauthorized activity and support victims.

Victim Notification

The Department identifies victims of cyber intrusion through a variety of means, such as from the FBI's ongoing contact with victims, from investigations of threat actors, from other members of the U.S. Intelligence Community, and from foreign partners. This information may be highly classified or may carry special handling or sharing restrictions based on the sensitivity of the source and the information provided. The FBI takes all reasonable steps to identify the targeted individual or entity, determine if there was an actual compromise, and assess if there is actionable information it may share.

Depending upon the circumstances, the FBI can undertake direct or indirect notice to victims or potential victims. "Direct" notification is typically handled in-person through established liaison contacts, such as by notifying the representatives of an institutional victim. Larger scale data breaches involving thousands or millions of affected customers are more complicated. In such circumstances, the FBI relies on victimized institutions to provide notification to affected individuals. In those cases, the victimized institution may be better situated to notify its customers or members of a large-scale data breach.

Reporting Intrusions to the FBI

While law enforcement and intelligence agencies can sometimes uncover malicious cyber activity before a victim detects it on their networks, in other cases a targeted organization will be the first to detect anomalous activity. It is critically important to report incidents to law enforcement, as each incident potentially involves the commission of a federal crime and may warrant investigation. The FBI is uniquely positioned to investigate and attri-

bute malicious cyber activity due to its dual criminal investigative and national security responsibilities.

While cyberattacks are typically conducted through technical means, behind the malicious activity is an actual individual or group perpetrating a crime. When the FBI is promptly notified, it can work to determine who caused the incident, link the incident to other incidents, maximize investigative opportunities, and potentially provide context regarding the actor, their tradecraft, and their motivations. Understanding who is targeting a victim's networks and for what purpose can inform defensive strategies and prevent future attacks. By notifying and assisting law enforcement, victims also help the FBI identify and pursue those responsible—which can help prevent future crimes against other victims. Such identification and pursuit is not limited to criminal response options. For example, attribution resulting from FBI investigative activities can support other U.S. government agencies' abilities to impose regulatory (e.g., sanctions), diplomatic, and technical costs upon those responsible for, or benefiting from, malicious cyber activities. Finally, notifying law enforcement may also place a victim company in a positive light with regulators, shareholders, and the public.

The Department encourages key organizations, particularly critical infrastructure owners and operators, to identify and form relationships with personnel in their local FBI field office, including through the partnerships detailed above, *before* an incident occurs. These pre-established relationships and open lines of communication will speed reporting and response efforts.

The White House's Council of Economic Advisors recently observed that most data breaches are not reported to the U.S. government.[2] This reluctance may be driven by a fear of regulatory action, of reputational harm, or of an interruption to business operations. The reluctance of organizations and businesses to disclose that they have been attacked constitutes a major challenge for the U.S. government in its battle against cyber-crime. Law enforcement cannot be effective without the cooperation of crime victims. A lack of cooperation may not only prevent discovery of evidence that could lead to identifying and holding the threat actors accountable, but also creates barriers to fully understanding the threat environment.

Responding to Cyber Incidents and Managing Crisis

1. Policy Framework

Presidential Policy Directive ("PPD")-41, titled "United States Cyber Incident Coordination," defines the term "cyber incident,"[3] and describes cyber incident response in terms of three concurrent and mutually beneficial lines of effort: **threat response** (investigation, attribution, and threat pursuit); **asset response** (remediation and recovery); and **intelligence support**. It also refers to a fourth, unnamed line of effort that is best described as **"business response"** (ensuring business continuity, addressing legal and regulatory issues, and external affairs). In the context of a nationally significant cyber incident, these activities are carried out in a coordinated way by the affected entity, by its third-party cybersecurity providers (if any), and by relevant federal agencies.

PPD-41 designates the Department of Justice, through the FBI and the National Cyber Investigative Joint Task Force ("NCIJTF"), as the lead federal agency for threat response activities in the context of a significant cyber incident. Through evidence collection, technical analysis, and related investigative tools, the FBI works to quickly identify the source of a cyber incident, connect that incident with related incidents, and determine attribution.

In addition to the cyber incident response framework laid out in PPD-41, the federal government also has adopted a Cyber Incident Severity Schema,[4] a rubric for describing an incident's significance and improving the federal government's response. An *incident of national significance* is rated as a Level 3 "High" (Orange), or greater. While the FBI does not allocate resources based exclusively on the schema rating, the rating serves as an enabler to various multi-agency coordination procedures and incident response efforts.

Both PPD-41 and the severity schema recognize that not all cyber incidents are "significant" from a national perspective. Thus, the scale and speed of a federal response will vary based on the facts and circumstances of particular cases. The FBI has capability, plans, and procedures to manage routine incidents. It also is prepared to react to circumstances requiring a more robust approach. Responses to both types of incidents are discussed below.

2. Routine Incident Response

The FBI's nationwide reach puts it in an optimal position to engage with potential victims. The FBI's field-centric model also allows it to respond quickly, and in-person, to cyber incidents—often in a matter of hours.

Each FBI field office houses a multi-agency Cyber Task Force ("CTF") modeled after the FBI's successful Joint Terrorism Task Force program. The task forces bring together cyber investigators, prosecutors, intelligence analysts, computer scientists, and digital forensic technicians from various federal, State, and local agencies present within the office's territory. The CTFs not only serve as a force multiplier, but also provide a forum for coordination amongst local partners for more effective incident response. This model also allows the FBI to draw on the relationships, expertise, authorities, and tools of the task force members.

In addition to these cyber-specific resources, the FBI has other technical assets it can use as needed to combat cyber threats. The FBI's Operational Technology Division develops and maintains a wide range of sophisticated equipment, capabilities, and tools to support investigations and to assist with technical operations. While every FBI field office has a computer forensics laboratory, certain field offices host a larger Regional Computer Forensic Laboratory. These resources can be leveraged throughout the FBI's response and investigative cycle to respond to cyber threats.

The FBI also has a strong international reach through a network of approximately 80 Legal Attaché offices throughout the world. It has supplemented 20 of these international offices with cyber-specific investigators to facilitate cooperation and information sharing to advance its cybercrime and national security investigations.

Because cyber threats and incidents occur around the clock, the FBI in 2014 established a steady-state, 24-hour watch capability called CyWatch. Housed at the NCIJTF, CyWatch is responsible for coordinating domestic law enforcement response to criminal and national security cyber intrusions, tracking victim notification, and partnering with the other federal cyber centers many times each day. CyWatch provides continuous connectivity to interagency partners to facilitate information sharing, and real-time incident management and tracking, as part of an effort to ensure that all relevant agencies are in communication.

3. Significant Incident Response

As directed by PPD-41, the FBI activates certain "enhanced coordination procedures" in the event of a "significant cyber incident."[5] These procedures include naming an accountable senior executive to manage the response and establishing a dedicated command center with a full array of communication capabilities.

Members of the local FBI Cyber Task Force will respond to the significant incident and a designated special agent will serve as the U.S. government's point of contact to the victim throughout the response. Nearby FBI field

RESPONDING TO CYBER INCIDENTS

Tips for Cooperative Cyber Incident Response

Preparation

- Develop a response plan that incorporates **notifying and collaborating with law enforcement.**
- **Establish a relationship with your local FBI Cyber Task Force and U.S. Attorney's Office** in advance of an incident; invite them to participate in exercises.
- Understand the threats and trends that may affect your organization and adjust defenses accordingly; FBI and DHS regularly publish relevant reports.

Discovery & Response

- **Notify the FBI* when you experience an incident**; your issue may be part of a larger adversary campaign.
- **Preserve key evidence** that will enable investigators to attribute the incident and pursue the actors (e.g., logs and artifacts, affected devices, analysis reports).
- Discuss options for leveraging **advice and other services** offered through other government agencies including DHS with the responding FBI team.

Recovery & Follow up

- **Share feedback on your experiences** with the local DOJ and FBI representatives. Consider conducting an after action review to discuss learnings to improve plans and performance in anticipation of future events.

Notify the FBI through the local Cyber Task Force or CyWatch (24/7) at 855-292-3937 or CyWatch@fbi.gov

---

offices can provide surge support and expertise as necessary, as each field office maintains personnel specifically trained on responding to incidents involving critical infrastructure and control systems. The response team may be further augmented by specialty support from FBI headquarters. For example, the FBI Cyber Action Team ("CAT") is the agency's elite rapid response force. On-call CAT members are prepared to deploy globally to bring their in-depth cyber intrusion expertise and specialized investigative skills to bear in response to significant cyber incidents. CAT's management and core team are based in the Washington, D.C. metro area and are supplemented by carefully selected and highly trained field personnel. The FBI also has technical analysis and operations units that directly support the response team through deep-dive malware analysis and digital forensics, and by implementing custom-built technical solutions to advance an investigation.

If a cyber incident generates physical impacts rising to the level of a crisis, the FBI has extensive crisis management capability. The FBI Crisis Management Unit coordinates the FBI's tactical and disaster relief efforts. The unit also provides the capability to activate command posts anywhere in the United States, and coordinates the FBI's vast investigative resources and infrastructure to support large-scale incidents regardless of type.

Finally, the FBI maintains a fleet of aircraft to support deployments when an immediate response is necessary, as well as command post vehicles to support on-scene operations.

Conclusion

The Department stands ready to assist victims of cyberattacks. By leveraging our field-centric model, investigative expertise, and partnerships at home and abroad, the Department works to pursue malicious cyber actors and to predict and prevent future attacks. We must continue to build trusting relationships and to work collaboratively to address the global cyber threat, and to impose costs on nation states, cybercriminals, and other malign cyber actors.

RESPONDING TO CYBER INCIDENTS

NOTES

[1] *See* "Sector Specific Agencies," U.S. Dept. of Homeland Security (July 11, 2017), available at: https://www.dhs.gov/sector-specific-agencies (last accessed June 29, 2018) (describing the "16 critical infrastructure sectors whose assets, systems, and networks, whether physical or virtual, are considered so vital to the United States that their incapacitation or destruction would have a debilitating effect on security, national economic security, national public health or safety, or any combination thereof," and listing the "Sector-Specific Agency" associated with each of these critical infrastructure sectors).

[2] "The Cost of Malicious Cyber Activity to the U.S. Economy," Council of Econ. Advisors, Exec. Office of the President, at 33 (Feb. 2018), available at: https://www.whitehouse.gov/wp-content/uploads/2018/02/The-Cost-of-Malicious-Cyber-Activity-to-the-U.S.-Economy.pdf (last accessed June 29, 2018).

[3] *See* "Presidential Policy Directive—United States Cyber Incident Coordination," The White House (July 26, 2016) ("PPD-41"), available at: https://obamawhitehouse.archives.gov/the-press-office/2016/07/26/presidential-policy-directive-united-states-cyber-incident (last accessed June 29, 2018) (defining a "cyber incident" as "[a]n event occurring on or conducted through a computer network that actually or imminently jeopardizes the integrity, confidentiality, or availability of computers, information or communications systems or networks, physical or virtual infrastructure controlled by computers or information systems, or information resident thereon. For purposes of [PPD-41], a cyber incident may include a vulnerability in an information system, system security procedures, internal controls, or implementation that could be exploited by a threat source.").

[4] *See* "NCCIC Cyber Incident Scoring System," U.S. Computer Emergency Readiness Team, available at: https://www.us-cert.gov/NCCIC-Cyber-Incident-Scoring-System (last accessed June 29, 2018).

[5] A "significant" cyber incident is one "that is likely to result in demonstrable harm to the national security interests, foreign relations, or economy of the United States or to the public confidence, civil liberties, or public health and safety of the American people." *See* PPD-41, *supra* note 3.

CHAPTER 5
TRAINING AND MANAGING OUR WORKFORCE

To appropriately identify, disrupt, dismantle, and deter computer intrusions and cyber-enabled crimes, the Department must develop and maintain a broad cadre of highly trained prosecutors, agents, and analysts. Whether identifying and locating cyber threat actors; collecting vital evidence through lawful process; or developing the latest tools to overcome sophisticated technologies criminals use to conceal their activities, Department personnel must understand how technology both facilitates criminal activity and can be used to detect, disrupt, and dismantle the same activity.

Investigators, for example, require advanced tools and resources to stay at least one step ahead of increasingly sophisticated anonymizing technologies that criminals and other adversaries exploit to avoid detection. Meanwhile, forensic analysts must possess the latest know-how to extract key evidence from sophisticated electronic media, such as encrypted cell phones and hard drives. Finally, prosecutors must tackle complex questions regarding legal authorities, jurisdiction, privacy, and other issues raised by investigating cybercrime and prosecuting those responsible for it.

The Department pursues two objectives in developing its workforce and specialized training initiatives. First, we seek to cultivate a multitude of attorneys who, in addition to superior legal skills, have the technologi-cal background and experience necessary to make appropriate decisions in technology cases. Second, we seek to retain a group of non-lawyer professionals whose primary expertise is technology. These computer scientists, engineers, and digital forensic investigators collaborate with attorneys and investigators, together forming a team with all necessary skills. Cultivating a workforce of technologically-savvy employees requires care in hiring and training, but also, crucially, requires that the Department make the right decisions about how it manages and organizes its employees.

How the Department internally organizes itself, and especially how it assigns cyber work, is a central part of the strategy to carry out its critical cyber mission and to recruit, train, and retain a technologically-expert workforce. In some respects, this challenge is not new. For example, prosecuting environmental crimes requires mastery both of a complex area of law and of relevant scientific facts; likewise, prosecuting antitrust and other complex business cases requires in-depth knowledge of how industries operate. The Department's solution to these challenges has been to build headquarters components and networks of attorneys and investigators that specialize in these technical areas of law enforcement. A similar strategy has worked well for cyber cases: the Department has concentrated its work of identifying, dismantling, disrupting, and deterring computer intrusions and other cyber-enabled crimes into a select number of headquarters components and into networks of specialized attorneys and investigators. This method of organization yields at least three benefits for recruitment, training, and retention—which, in turn, benefits the investigation and prosecution of cyber cases.

First, despite ever-increasing competition in the technology job market, the Department can attract skilled prospects who are inspired by our mission. The Department now has employees who, in addition to being excellent lawyers or investigators, also have deep experience in network defense, computer forensics, and software engineering. These employees very often came to work at the Department precisely because they wanted to work on cyber cases. Offering prospective employees the chance to work exclusively (or near-exclusively) in the rewarding and challenging field of computer crime is a significant recruiting advantage. But making that promise is credible only if the Department can offer employment in specialized units, where cyber work has been concentrated.

Second, training employees in cyber cases requires far more than classroom instruction or reading from textbooks. Every seasoned attorney and investigator knows that the bulk of his or her expertise came from practical, on-the-job experience. Because the Department's specialized cyber units both at headquarters and in the field expose attorneys and investigators to cyber investigations, and do so repeatedly, they build skills and human capital much more effectively

than if the work were dispersed indiscriminately around the Department.

Finally, the Department is constantly working to retain experienced attorneys and investigators in government employment. The skills of cyber investigators and attorneys are in heavy demand in the private sector, where salaries are much higher. The Department will lose this competition for talent if the only consideration is salary. Fortunately, that is not the only consideration for most employees. Only public service provides employees with so great an opportunity to protect and defend their country; in many ways, the work is itself a reward. To make maximum use of that reward, however, the Department's talented cyber workforce needs to be given regular opportunities to work on the cases and subject matter they feel most passionate about. Only an arrangement of specialized offices can offer that benefit.

In this spirit, the Department's criminal law enforcement entities, its United States Attorneys' Offices, and its relevant litigation divisions have dedicated workforce units and training initiatives that anchor the Department's broader strategy to recruit, train, and retain a technologically expert workforce in order to carry out its core cyber mission. These units and their specialized training initiatives are described below.

1. Federal Bureau of Investigation

As described in Chapter 4, the FBI is often a "first responder" to a cyber incident. With Cyber Task Forces located in each of its 56 field offices across the country, the FBI is prepared to respond to and investigate cyberattacks and intrusions wherever they may occur. Its agents serve both as investigators and high-tech specialists, capable of applying the most current technological know-how to collect evidence at the scene of a cyberattack or intrusion, analyze data forensically, and trace a cybercrime to its origins. Through its Cyber Division located at FBI headquarters in Washington, D.C., and the Operational Technology Division located at Quantico, Virginia, the FBI provides leadership to its global efforts to investigate cyber threats, whether they stem from criminal or national security actors. The Cyber Division has organized itself, both at headquarters and in FBI field offices, to focus its investigations and operations exclusively on computer intrusions and attacks, and related online threats.

The FBI is also responsible for the operation of the National Cyber Investigative Joint Task Force ("NCIJTF"), a multi-agency cyber center that serves as the national focal point for coordinating cyber investigations across government agencies. The NCIJTF is comprised of 30 plus partnering agencies from across law enforcement, the intelligence community, and the Department of Defense, with representatives who are co-located and work jointly to accomplish the organization's mission from a whole-of-government perspective. Members have access to and analyze data that provides a unique, comprehensive view of the Nation's cyber threat while working together in a collaborative environment in which they maintain the authorities and responsibilities of their

home agencies. The NCIJTF coordinates, integrates, and shares cyber threat information to support investigations and operations for the intelligence community, law enforcement, military, policy makers, and trusted foreign partners in the fight against cyber threats. The NCIJTF is responsible for coordinating whole-of-government cyber campaigns, integrating domestic cyber data, and sharing domestic cyber threat information.

The FBI Criminal Investigative Division has created the Hi-Tech Organized Crime Unit ("HTOCU") to launch a long term, proactive strategy to target transnational organized crime groups using advanced technology to conduct large scale computer-enabled and computer-facilitated crime. HTOCU works to bring traditional organized crime techniques, tradecraft, and strategies to bear on transnational criminal enterprises that use high technology to perpetrate criminal activity. HTOCU, in coordination with the FBI's Cyber Division and the Money Laundering Unit, has developed and implemented strategies to dismantle transnational criminal enterprises engaged in large-scale fraudulent activity. Furthermore, HTOCU works to identify new sources, technical vulnerabilities, collection opportunities, and emerging trends in cyber-enabled transnational organized criminal activity.

The Joint Criminal Opioid Darknet Enforcement ("J-CODE") Team is a new FBI initiative, announced by Attorney General Sessions in January 2018, to target drug trafficking—especially fentanyl and other opioids—on the Dark Web. Building on the work that began with the government's dismantling of Silk Road and AlphaBay, the FBI is bringing together agents, analysts, and professional staff with expertise in drugs, gangs, health care fraud and more, as well as federal, State, and local law enforcement partners from across the U.S. government, to focus on disrupting the sale of illegal drugs via the Dark Web and dismantling criminal enterprises that facilitate this trafficking. The J-CODE will create a formalized process to prioritize dark markets, vendors, and administrators for strategic targeting; to develop strategies to undermine confidence in the Dark Web; and to formulate de-confliction and operational requirements with other domestic and international partners.

In accordance with the requirements set forth in the Federal Cybersecurity Workforce Assessment Act of 2015, the Department, including the FBI, is identifying and coding federal positions that perform information technology, cybersecurity, and other cyber-related functions based on the work roles described in the National Initiative for Cybersecurity Education Framework.[1] This analysis will underpin an effort to prioritize areas of critical need within the workforce, and support possible recommendations for introducing new job roles that will improve the FBI's ability to respond to Internet-enabled crimes and technologically advanced threat actors.

With respect to training, the FBI has a number of programs to ensure its workforce possesses the key cyber skills and tools to succeed in their investigations, especially as

the technological landscape rapidly evolves. For instance, the FBI is implementing the "Cyber Certified" training and certification program for investigators, intelligence analysts, technical specialists, and attorneys, whether currently in the Cyber Program or working in other mission areas. These employees will be observed for future training and development activities.

In an attempt to rapidly increase the level of cyber knowledge shared throughout the organization, and in an effort to infuse cyber knowledge into traditionally non-cyber programs, the FBI has also created the Workforce Training Initiative ("WTI"). The WTI is designed to increase the number of employees who are capable of responding to, investigating, and analyzing a variety of cyber-related cross-programmatic matters, and its courses cover the breadth of cyber-related topics.

The On the Job Training ("OJT") initiative is a combination of classes and real world experiences encountered daily on a cyber squad. The OJT program takes place over a six-month period and requires a full-time commitment from participants. The participants are reassigned to a cyber squad and are expected to work cyber cases under the mentorship of cyber-skilled professionals. At the conclusion of the six-month program, participants return to their original squads with enhanced cyber skills to address cyber threats within that program and to share their knowledge. Upon completion of this program, participants will be designated Cyber Certified.

The FBI Digital Forensics program offers digital evidence related training and certifications to personnel dedicated to managing digital evidence challenges, and also offers technical training to the broader FBI workforce which familiarizes them with the challenges of properly preserving and handling digital evidence. The Forensic Examiner certification program includes over ten weeks of total training, practical exercises, mentorship, and a moot court which includes Department attorneys and senior examiners.

The FBI's Cyber Executive Certification Program provides high-level cyber training and prepares executives for their role in the cyber investigation process. Participants have the opportunity to obtain two industry standard certifications, in addition to the internal FBI certificate. Additionally, the digital evidence program offers advanced training to personnel supervisors of digital evidence workforce, preparing them to ensure the technical requirements of FBI investigation are met by the digital evidence staff.

Finally, FBI-led cyber training takes place at Cyber Academy campuses located at different points in the country, while digital evidence training occurs at Regional Computer Forensics Laboratories, and at FBI headquarters. Cyber training ranges from the Cyber Basic School, a two-week curriculum designed to instill cybersecurity fundamentals in all employees, to advanced training for seasoned cyber investigators. Digital evidence training includes guidance in analysis of Windows, Macintosh, UNIX, and mobile operating systems, Internet artifacts, secure device access, vehicle forensics, and Internet of Things related challenges.

2. The Criminal Division

Computer Crime and Intellectual Property Section

In 1996, the Department consolidated the Criminal Division's expertise in computer crime matters into a single office called the Computer Crime and Intellectual Property Section ("CCIPS"), with prosecutors devoted to pursuing computer crime prosecutions fulltime. Over the years, CCIPS's mission has grown beyond prosecution to include spearheading cyber policy and legislative initiatives, training and support, public outreach, and cybersecurity guidance. CCIPS consists of a team of specially trained attorneys dedicated to investigating and prosecuting high-tech crimes and violations of intellectual property laws, and to advising on legal issues concerning the lawful collection of electronic evidence.

Today, CCIPS is responsible for implementing the Department's national strategies to combat computer and intellectual property crimes worldwide by working with other Department components and government agencies, the private sector, academic institutions, and foreign counterparts, among others. Section attorneys work to improve the domestic and international legal, technological, and operational legal infrastructure to pursue network criminals most effectively. Working in support of and alongside the 94 U.S. Attorneys' Offices ("USAOs"), CCIPS prosecutes violations of federal law involving computer intrusions and attacks. CCIPS has also worked with the Treasury Department's Office of Foreign Asset Control to use new authorities under Executive Order 13694 to bring sanctions against foreign nationals for malicious cyber-enabled criminal activities. In conjunction with the Executive Office for United States Attorneys ("EOUSA"), described below, CCIPS conducts at least four multi-day in-person trainings and up to twelve webinars a year. It also maintains an internal website with information available to all Department components that is visited more than 90,000 times a year, and has a rotating daily duty-attorney system that responds to approximately 2,000 calls for advice a year.

In addition, the Criminal Division established the Computer Hacking and Intellectual Property ("CHIP") coordinator program in 1995 to ensure that each USAO and litigating division has at least one prosecutor who is specially trained on cyber threats, electronic evidence collection, and technological trends that criminals exploit. The CHIP network now includes approximately 270 prosecutors from USAOs and Main Justice, and aids in the coordination of multi-district prosecutions involving cyber threats. Specialized CHIP units exist in 25 designated USAOs. CHIP Assistant U.S. Attorneys (AUSAs) work with law enforcement partners from multiple law enforcement agencies at the outset of an investigation, often in consultation with CCIPS, to provide legal guidance, help craft an investigative plan, obtain

necessary search warrants and court orders, collect electronic evidence, and ultimately, build a criminal case. Pursuant to departmental regulation, U.S. Attorneys are responsible for ensuring that experienced and technically-qualified AUSAs serve as the district's CHIP prosecutors; ensuring that CHIP resources are dedicated to CHIP program objectives; ensuring that the USAO notifies, consults, and coordinates with CCIPS and other USAOs; and promoting and ensuring effective interaction with law enforcement, industry representatives, and the public in matters relating to computer and intellectual property crime.

Money Laundering and Asset Recovery Section

The Criminal Division's Money Laundering and Asset Recovery Section ("MLARS") leads the Department's asset forfeiture and anti-money laundering enforcement efforts. MLARS is responsible for, among other things, coordinating complex, sensitive, multi-district, and international money laundering and asset forfeiture investigations and cases; providing legal and policy assistance and training to federal, State, and local prosecutors and law enforcement personnel; and assisting Departmental and interagency policymakers by developing and reviewing legislative, regulatory, and policy initiatives.

With respect to cyber-enabled threats in particular, MLARS has established a Digital Currency Initiative that focuses on providing support and guidance to investigators, prosecutors, and other government agencies on cryptocurrency prosecutions and forfeitures. The Digital Currency Initiative will expand and implement cryptocurrency-related training to encourage and enable more investigators, prosecutors, and Department components to pursue such cases, while developing and disseminating policy guidance on various aspects of cryptocurrency, including seizure and forfeiture. Through the Initiative, MLARS will also advise AUSAs and federal agents on complex questions of law related to cryptocurrency to inform charging decisions and other prosecutorial strategies.

Office of Enforcement Operations, Electronic Surveillance Unit

Electronic surveillance is one of the most effective law enforcement tools for investigating many types of criminal enterprises, including cyber-based criminal enterprises that use electronic media and Internet-based technologies to perpetrate their crimes. The Electronic Surveillance Unit ("ESU") in the Criminal Division's Office of Enforcement Operations is responsible for reviewing all federal requests to conduct interceptions of wire, electronic, or oral communications pursuant to the Wiretap Act. ESU's specialized attorneys provide suggested revisions and offer guidance to ensure that electronic surveillance applications meet all constitutional, statutory, and Department policy requirements. Every federal wiretap application must be approved by a senior Department of Justice official before it is submitted to a court, and ESU makes recommendations to those officials based on its review. Additionally, ESU attorneys regularly conduct webinars and in-person trainings, and provide legal advice to federal prosecutors

and law enforcement agencies on the use of electronic surveillance. They also assist in developing Department policy on emerging technology and telecommunications issues.

Office of International Affairs

The Criminal Division's Office of International Affairs ("OIA") returns fugitives to face justice, and obtains essential evidence for criminal investigations and prosecutions worldwide by working with domestic partners and foreign counterparts to facilitate the cooperation necessary to enforce the law, advance public safety, and achieve justice. Drawing upon a vast network of international agreements and its expertise in extradition and mutual legal assistance, OIA in recent years has worked with domestic and foreign law enforcement to hold cybercriminals accountable in U.S. courts and obtain the evidence needed to untangle complex transnational cybercrime schemes.

In addition to its work supporting investigations and prosecutions of cybercriminals, OIA uses mutual legal assistance to obtain electronic evidence for foreign and domestic law enforcement personnel. As the need to obtain electronic evidence in virtually every type of criminal case has burgeoned, OIA has worked to modernize its practice in this area by creating a team of attorneys and support personnel specially trained in obtaining electronic evidence, and by implementing process efficiencies to ensure swift attention to requests from prosecutors and police. OIA is also actively engaged in the policy, legislative, and multilateral arenas in which topics concerning access to electronic evidence and law enforcement cooperation are discussed and debated to ensure that the Department's mission is advanced and that our law enforcement personnel get the tools they need to keep pace with ever-evolving threats. Consistent with these goals, OIA conducts regular training for U.S. prosecutors on the tools available to them to obtain evidence located overseas and to secure the return of fugitives. OIA also provides frequent regional and bilateral trainings to our foreign partners to bolster their ability to stop criminal activity before it reaches our shores.

3. *The National Security Division*

The investigation, disruption, and deterrence of national security cyber threats are among the highest priorities of the Department's National Security Division ("NSD"). These priorities come from a recognition that network defense alone is not enough to counter the threat. To the contrary, we must also impose costs on our adversaries using all of the U.S. government's lawfully available tools. This "all-tools" approach informs NSD's efforts to combat cyber threats to our national security, with the goal of deterring and disrupting cyber-based intrusions and attacks. In this context, national security cyber cases are those perpetrated by nation states, terrorists, or their agents or proxies, or cases involving the targeting of information that is controlled for national security purposes.

All NSD attorneys must take a cyber course within two years of joining the division. NSD also conducts annually a one-day cyber training in-house for all NSD employees, which is taught by NSD and CCIPS attorneys.

In addition, in 2012, NSD launched the National Security Cyber Specialist ("NSCS") network to equip USAOs around the Nation with prosecutors trained on national security cyber threats, such as nation-state cyber espionage activities and terrorists' use of technology to plot attacks. NSCS-Main is comprised of lawyers and other experts drawn from NSD's component sections and offices, as well as from CCIPS and ESU in the Criminal Division. NSCS-Main also coordinates as needed with other Department headquarters components, including the Civil Division, the Antitrust Division, the Office of Legal Policy, and the Office of Legal Counsel, and works closely with the Department's investigative components, including the FBI.

The NSCS Network also includes AUSAs in each of the USAOs; these AUSAs serve as their offices' primary points of entry for cases involving cyber threats to the national security and coordinate closely with NSCS-Main. NSD and CCIPS, in conjunction with EOUSA, provides annual training for NSCS members. The NSCS training covers a number of national security cyber topics to enhance the education of the prosecutors who handle these matters. In addition, through the National Security/Anti-Terrorism Advisory Council, there are approximately seven training courses conducted annually for national security prosecutors. Those trainings generally include a number of cyber-related sessions for national security prosecutors.

Finally, this year, for the first time, NSD is offering a Cyber Fellowship for those selected attorneys who applied to further their education on technology-related issues. Five attorneys were selected to participate in 2018 and have been attending a series of trainings offered by the FBI, the CIA, Carnegie Mellon University, and the SANS Institute. Those selected have also agreed to assist with training and other cyber initiatives at NSD.

4. United States Attorney's Offices / Executive Office for United States Attorneys

The United States Attorneys serve as the nation's principal litigators, under the direction of the Attorney General. There are 93 United States Attorneys stationed throughout the United States, Puerto Rico, the Virgin Islands, Guam, and the Northern Mariana Islands.[2] Each United States Attorney is the chief federal law enforcement officer of the United States within his or her particular jurisdiction. United States Attorneys conduct most of the trial work in which the United States is a party. Although the distribution of caseloads varies between districts, each USAO deals with every category of cases, including cybercrime prosecutions. As referenced above, the role of the CHIP AUSA was established to ensure that each USAO has personnel trained on cyber threats, electronic evidence collection, and technological trends exploited by criminals. Similarly, the NSCS program discussed above was designed to equip USAOs around the nation with prosecutors specially trained on national security cyber threats, such as nation state cyber espionage activities and terrorists' use

of technology to plan attacks. The USAOs also coordinate as needed with Department headquarters components, such as the Criminal and National Security Divisions, in a further effort to ensure the effectiveness of such cyber-oriented investigations and prosecutions.

EOUSA provides executive and administrative support for the 93 United States Attorneys. Such support includes legal education, administrative oversight, technical support, and the creation of uniform policies, among other responsibilities.

The National Advocacy Center, which EOUSA operates, provides numerous courses every year addressing a wide variety of cyber-related topics. These courses are attended by prosecutors from across the country and are tailored to address the training needs of attorneys with varying levels of experience handling cyber matters. Working with CCIPS and the National Security Division's Counterterrorism and Counterespionage sections, these cybercrime courses range from introductory to advanced level and have included training addressing the nature of computer forensics, the investigation of computer intrusions, and the use of electronic evidence, among other related topics. In short, each year, the Department trains hundreds of federal prosecutors in cybercrime and national security cyber matters.

In addition to these in-person training programs, EOUSA, through the Office of Legal and Victim Programs and the Office of Legal Education ("OLE"), sponsors additional cyber training, including webinars that are broadcast nationwide. These webinars allow the Department to provide supplemental cutting-edge training and allow prosecutors to view these presentations from their own offices, while still enabling them to remotely ask the presenters questions and download related materials. For example, EOUSA sponsored a webinar discussing new provisions of a Federal Rule of Evidence relating to electronic evidence, immediately after those provisions became effective. Almost 1,000 Department employees viewed that program. Working closely with CCIPS and OEO, additional notable webinars have included programs addressing legal standards for obtaining cell phone location information, searching and seizing computers and other digital devices, cryptocurrency, and social media and online investigations, to name just a few.

OLE, working with CCIPS, has also issued standalone written materials that prosecutors can use for training and law enforcement purposes.

5. *Drug Enforcement Administration*

The DEA enforces the Nation's controlled substance laws and regulations. Through its participation in J-CODE and beyond, DEA is developing its expertise in Dark Market investigations. DEA's Operational Support Unit ("STSO") serves as the point of contact between DEA offices and the technology and communications industry, in order to identify, address, and resolve subpoena and related compliance issues, as well as other legal and regulatory issues. STSO also dis-

seminates to the field guidance relating to these issues. STSO is attempting to bring DEA employees into a more advanced awareness of today's cyber world, so they can adapt to that environment while performing the daily tasks of Internet research and investigations.

6. *INTERPOL*

The mission of INTERPOL Washington (United States National Central Bureau), is to advance the law enforcement interests of the United States as the official representative to the International Criminal Police Organization (INTERPOL); to share criminal justice, humanitarian, and public safety information between our Nation's law enforcement community and its foreign counterparts; and to facilitate transnational investigative efforts that enhance the safety and security of our Nation.

INTERPOL Washington leverages a network of 192 countries connected by a secure communications platform to share information for the purpose of enhancing international cooperation in all areas of criminal investigation, including cybercrime investigations. INTERPOL Washington maintains an office dedicated to advancing the cybercrime investigations of U.S. law enforcement by establishing and maintaining relationships with the heads of cybercrime units of other countries; sharing information through the secure communications platform to assist cybercrime investigations conducted by the agencies of the Department of Justice and the Department of Homeland Security; and providing support to other federal, State, local, and tribal law enforcement agencies.

7. *Foreign Government Training Initiatives*

In addition to training its own personnel, the Department also provides training and technical assistance to foreign governments to ensure that they are equipped to address their own domestic cyber threats. As countries develop their own capacity to address cyber issues, they are also better equipped to assist the United States in investigations involving criminal conduct emanating from within their own borders. The Department has maintained a robust program for encouraging foreign governments to develop their criminal and procedural laws to address emerging cybercrime threats and capabilities, consistent with the Budapest Convention on Cybercrime. As discussed in Chapter 3, the Budapest Convention—which the United States ratified over ten years ago—provides a legal framework for criminalizing key types of cybercrime, developing the tools necessary to investigate such crime, and establishing the network for rapid international cooperation that must exist to investigate and prosecute cyber actors wherever they are located.

Using a balanced approach of frank policy discussions with countries that have technical capabilities similar to our own, combined with multilateral training initiatives aimed at countries whose legal infrastructure for addressing cyber threats is in earlier stages of development, the Department has continued to improve the capacity of other countries to address cyber threats around the world,

thereby also increasing our own capacity to thwart cyber threats.

8. *Department-Wide Cybersecurity Awareness Training*

In addition to the specialized units and training described above, the Department recognizes that cybersecurity effectiveness depends on everyone in the organization. Users are still one of the most attacked entities in the organization. Social engineering attacks (described in more detail in Chapter 2) come in many forms, are still effective, and can target anyone in the Department. As such, all Department employees must have a basic understanding of their responsibilities when handling the Department's information and accessing its information system, while being held accountable for abusing those responsibilities.

All Department personnel receive annual cybersecurity awareness training. In addition, all employees and contractors must sign the "Department of Justice Cybersecurity and Privacy Rules of Behavior (ROB) for General Users" agreement, which confirms that the employee or contractor completed the training and understands the applicable cybersecurity requirements and responsibilities. As the agreement makes clear, "each [Department] user is responsible for the security and privacy of [Department] information systems and their data."

Adequate training ensures that everyone within the Department has a basic understanding of the relevant threats, their role in protecting our information and information

TRAINING AND MANAGING OUR WORKFORCE

NOTES

[1] *See* National Institute for Standards and Technology, Special Publication 800-181, *National Initiative for Cybersecurity Education (NICE) Cybersecurity Workforce Framework* (Aug. 2017), available at: https://nvlpubs.nist.gov/nistpubs/SpecialPublications/NIST.SP.800-181.pdf (last accessed June 29, 2018).

[2] One United States Attorney is assigned to each of the 94 judicial districts, with the exception of Guam and the Northern Mariana Islands, where a single United States Attorney serves in both districts.

CHAPTER 6
LOOKING AHEAD

This report describes the most significant cyber threats our Nation faces, and catalogs the ways in which the Department confronts and combats those threats. As the discussion in previous chapters reveals, the Department has had many successes. At the same time, we face a number of challenges.

In this chapter, we further explore those challenges and identify specific areas for additional inquiry. We also outline eight key areas of future effort that will define the Department's work in the months ahead.

Specific Challenges

Each part of the Department's efforts to confront cyber threats—(1) preventing and responding to cyber incidents (Chapter 4); (2) investigating and prosecuting cyber-related crimes (Chapter 2); and (3) dismantling, disrupting, and detering malicious cyber threats (Chapter 3)—bears its own unique challenges.[1]

Here, we describe those challenges and, where applicable, discuss how the Department has begun addressing the challenge or what actions we may yet take to sharpen our efforts. Where appropriate, we also highlight issues that require further consideration and development due to the complex or evolving nature of the threat.

1. Challenges in Preventing and Responding to Cyber Incidents

Working with the Private Sector

Virtually every instance of cyber-related crime implicates the private sector in some way, whether the private sector is the target of malicious cyber activity, the provider of technology or services through which cybercrimes are committed or concealed, or the repository of evidence (such as communications) relating to cyber-enabled criminal activity. As such, the relationship that the Department, including the FBI, builds and maintains with the private sector is critical to our efforts to combat cybercrime. Fortunately, the Department and the private sector already have engaged in numerous formal and informal collaborations. Even so, the Department must deepen these relationships, particularly as technology evolves and the cast of service providers and technology manufacturers continues to change.

a. The Computer Security Research Community

The computer security research community—which is comprised of not only computer security companies but also individuals and organizations with expertise in computer security—has made valuable contributions to combating cyber threats by discovering significant exploitable vulnerabilities affecting, among other things, the confidentiality of data, the safety of Internet-connected devices, and the security of automobiles. Some security researchers have also been allies in law enforcement efforts to dismantle cyber threats. For example, assistance with malware analysis and mitigation techniques has helped law enforcement conduct operations against various cybercriminals, including through botnet takedowns.

Even so, some in the computer security research community harbor concerns that law enforcement may misconstrue as criminal activity their methods of searching for and analyzing vulnerabilities. Some researchers have even expressed anxiety that such concerns have chilled legitimate security research.

To ensure the Department maintains and fosters a positive, collaborative working relationship with computer security researchers, the Department should consider potential legal options to encourage and protect legitimate computer security research. For instance, a three-year exemption to the Digital Millennium Copyright Act ("DMCA")[2]—the result of rulemaking by the U.S. Copyright Office[3]—has allowed researchers to conduct vulnerability research on consumer products, including Internet of Things ("IoT") devices. IoT devices are prime targets of cybercriminals for use in illicit activities like distributed denial of service attacks. Finding and repairing vulnerabilities in consumer devices is important and will likely become

even more important as IoT devices proliferate, perform more household tasks, and collect more data capable of being monetized by criminals.

The Copyright Office has initiated its next rulemaking process to evaluate extending the DMCA exemptions. The Department has submitted input to the Copyright Office in support of extending and expanding the current security research exemption, with caveats intended to protect public safety and avoid confusion over legal research activities.[4] At the same time, the Department should continue evaluating existing laws and regulations to identify other opportunities to support and encourage legitimate computer security research. Finally, the Criminal Division's Cybersecurity Unit should conduct additional outreach to the computer security community. In doing so, the Unit should seek out opportunities to: (1) explain how the Department's policies and practices address concerns about unwarranted prosecutions for legitimate security research; and (2) better educate the computer security research community about the federal criminal laws implicated by computer security activities.

b. Encouraging Private Sector Reporting of Cyber Incidents

Another important component of the Department's collaboration with the private sector is the public-private work on information sharing and threat assessment. As discussed in Chapter 4, the FBI disseminates numerous reports directly to members of the private sector to inform them of cyber threats. This information sharing provides the private sector with actionable intelligence that enables them to take appropriate precautions.

Information sharing, however, is most effective when it flows two ways. When a private sector entity reports a breach or attempted intrusion, the Department gains valuable insights into threat activity that can help direct, in real time, law enforcement efforts to investigate and disrupt the malicious activity. Prompt reporting also provides information that officials can accumulate and share with other private sector entities to facilitate appropriate security measures. Indeed, efforts by the Department and FBI to help manage cyber incidents and, later, to bring perpetrators to justice through prosecution are best accomplished when the victim—who may be the first to discover an incident—reports the incident or intrusion in a timely manner.

Unfortunately, many cyber incidents in the United States are never reported to law enforcement. Victims—especially businesses—often decide not to report cyber incidents for a variety of reasons, including concerns about publicity and potential harm to the company's reputation or profits, and even concerns of retaliation by a nation state where they wish to do business. Some victims may simply not know how to report the incident to appropriate authorities. And still others, particularly larger companies, may try to act on their own to pursue, confront, or disrupt the perpetrator, though doing so may trig-

ger civil or even criminal liability, or may impact U.S. foreign relations. Regardless of the reason, lack of reporting is a significant impediment to the Department's efforts to thwart cybercriminals and to address threats to national security—particularly when new threats are emerging.

Encouraging reporting from private sector victims is thus critical to enhancing the Department's ability to prevent, deter, investigate, and prosecute (or otherwise disrupt) cybercrimes. To facilitate reporting, the Department should consider not only how to build deeper trust with the private sector, but also understand and address the private sector's needs and concerns related to reporting. This assessment should include understanding how best to incentivize reporting as well as how to eliminate obstacles or barriers. The Department should also continue its outreach to the private sector to identify additional areas for collaboration, especially with respect to reporting and information sharing. In the past, such outreach has resulted in industry-targeted guidance such as the Criminal Division Cybersecurity Unit's *Best Practices for Victim Reporting and Responding to Cyber Incidents.*[5]

The Department must also consider the role that DHS and other government agencies play in working with the private sector to ensure federal agencies' efforts are complementary and cooperative. In addition to DHS and other federal partners, the Department should continue to work with the agencies that regulate the private sector to evaluate expectations and encourage clear thresholds for reporting.

The Department's additional efforts on private sector reporting should also include attention to statutory data breach notification requirements. Currently, all 50 States have enacted separate notification laws setting standards governing notification by private entities when a data breach occurs, but there is no federal reporting requirement or standard. As such, companies must navigate and comply with the varying requirements in 50 State jurisdictions.[6] In the wake of recent high-profile data breaches exposing Americans' personal information, Congress has a revived interest in national notification requirements. A national data breach standard could increase federal law enforcement's effectiveness to pursue hackers and prevent data breaches.

c. Reviewing Guidance on Victim Notification

In 2012, the Attorney General issued General Guidelines for Victim and Witness Assistance ("AG Victim Guidelines" or "guidelines") that, among other things, discussed two statutes—the Victims' Rights and Restitution Act, 42 U.S.C. § 10607, and the Crime Victims' Rights Act, 18 U.S.C. § 3771—which accord certain rights to individuals who meet the statutory definition of "victim." The AG Victim Guidelines also address when FBI notification to victims and witnesses is appropriate and warranted. Given the evolving nature of cyber-enabled crimes—including the fact that it is not always easy to identify a cybercrime "victim" or the extent or nature

of the harm—the Department should review the AG Victim Guidelines to ensure, among other things, that the guidelines, and any related victim notification policies and practices, appropriately account for the unique and often nuanced nature of cybercrime.

Preventing Cyber-Related Vulnerabilities in Connection with Foreign Investment and Supply Chains

As part of its efforts to prevent cybercrime, the Department is concerned with mitigating vulnerabilities that threaten national security. Such areas concern foreign investment in domestic assets and foreign supply chains.

For example, a March 22, 2018 Presidential Memorandum observed that "China directs and facilitates the systematic investment in, and acquisition of, U.S. companies and assets by Chinese companies to obtain cutting-edge technologies and intellectual property and to generate large-scale technology transfer in industries deemed important by Chinese government industrial plans."[7] Under ambitious industrial policies, China aims to use foreign investment as a means of dominating cutting-edge technologies like advanced microchips, artificial intelligence, and electric cars, among others.

Currently, the Department responds to threats posed by foreign investment in the United States and the export of sensitive technology by enforcing U.S. export controls and through the Committee on Foreign Investment in the United States ("CFIUS"), a statutorily-established body that has authority to review transactions that could result in control of a U.S. business by a foreign person. As the March 22, 2018 Presidential Memorandum indicates, further coordination through CFIUS, enforcement of existing technology transfer controls, and other interagency efforts will be necessary to tackle risks from foreign investment in sensitive industries and technologies.

In addition to foreign investment, the Department is generally concerned with hardening supply chains. Technology supply chains are especially vulnerable, because the hardware components and software code that go into technology products often come from foreign sources, including developers in Russia and China.[8] To address these concerns, the Department coordinates with other government agencies and the private sector to effectively manage and mitigate cybersecurity risks in U.S. supply chains.

For example, the Department contributes to Team Telecom, an ad hoc interagency working group that considers the law enforcement, national security, and public safety implications of applications for licenses from the Federal Communications Commission involving a threshold percentage of foreign ownership or control. Moving forward, the Department should continue to engage with these and other interagency efforts to determine the best ways to strengthen defenses against national security risks.

2. Challenges in Investigating and Prosecuting Computer Crime

Accessing Data in the United States

Data not only is key to understanding the nature of cybercrime and the identity of perpetrators, but also is a primary source of evidence for prosecution. Unfortunately, the relevant data is often hard to reach, hidden on computers in different States or even in countries half a world away, lurking on dark markets, or protected by anonymized host servers or encryption. Recognizing that accessing data is the starting point and often the cornerstone of computer crime investigations and prosecutions, the Department has made concerted efforts to improve its ability to collect data related to criminal activity. However, several challenges to accessing data remain and require further collaboration with federal, State, and private sector partners.

One such challenge is the reality that cybercrime often does not take place in one identifiable, physical location. Sophisticated cybercriminals can control botnets spread throughout several States or countries and can hide their illegal activities on proxy networks. The rules governing law enforcement efforts, however, have largely not kept pace with these criminal realities. For this reason, the Department proactively engaged with the Federal Rules Committee and on December 1, 2016, an amended version of Rule 41 of the Federal Rules of Criminal Procedure went into effect. (That new Rule is discussed in detail in Chapter 3.)

The circumstances that the amendments to Rule 41 address are important, but they do not cover all instances where data related to criminal activity are stored in varying or unknown locations within the United States. The Department should identify any additional common or recurring circumstances where current legal authorities fall short of providing law enforcement with the tools necessary to access relevant data within the United States and determine whether changes similar to the recent Rule 41 amendments would be effective.

Accessing Data Abroad

The Department faces similar challenges in accessing data located outside the United States. As with the Rule 41 amendments in the domestic context, the Department recently engaged with partners to enhance our investigative authority in such circumstances. In particular, as the result of a joint effort between the private sector and the Department to bring clarity to investigative demands for data stored overseas, the Clarifying Lawful Overseas Use of Data Act ("CLOUD Act") became law on March 23, 2018. (The CLOUD Act is also discussed in Chapter 3.)

Passage of the CLOUD Act institutes a framework for technology companies to comply with investigative demands for data stored outside of the requesting country's territory, and creates processes to resolve thorny conflict of laws problems. The Act clarifies that the U.S. government's traditional authority in this area remains in force: communications service providers must disclose infor-

mation subject to a court order that is within their "possession, custody, or control," even if the electronic servers containing that information are located overseas. The CLOUD Act also authorizes our government to enter into formal agreements with other nations that remove legal barriers that would otherwise create conflict of laws problems where a provider is subject to a foreign court order to produce data stored in that other country. The Act requires both governments to "certify" that the laws and practices of the other country provide adequate protections for human rights and personal privacy. The agreements must also implement transparency measures and periodic reviews to ensure ongoing compliance. The Department is currently considering how it should implement such agreements.

Challenges remain, however, when investigating computer crimes that extend overseas, particularly because the CLOUD Act addresses only those instances where the relevant overseas data is possessed or controlled by an entity subject to U.S. jurisdiction. Many types of evidence fall outside those criteria, and traditional mutual legal assistance treaty ("MLAT") procedures may also fall short.

For those reasons, the Department continually aims to improve its international outreach efforts and to engage with international Internet governance bodies to encourage them not to apply rules that unreasonably restrict or interfere with valid investigations. For example, the Department is currently monitoring and assessing the impact of the European Union's sweeping General Data

Protection Regulation ("GDPR"), which went into effect on May 25, 2018.

Broadly speaking, the GDPR regulates how private companies and governments process, store, and transfer data concerning E.U. residents, including how such data and information is handled and transferred into and out of the E.U. Violators could be subject to fines up to 4% of their gross revenue worldwide or 20 million Euros, whichever is greater, creating a serious financial incentive for covered entities not to violate the new regulation. Exceptions written into the GDPR should ensure that it does not affect the ability of U.S. law enforcement to obtain evidence through MLATs. Also, law enforcement-to-law enforcement sharing is covered by a separate directive and is thus outside of the scope of the GDPR. Still, significant questions and uncertainties exist about the GDPR, which could negatively affect law enforcement, including by impeding information sharing.

For example, some interpret the GDPR to require that the publicly-available WHOIS system remove information about the registrants of Internet domain names from public access, thereby necessitating the building and maintenance of secured law enforcement portals to access that information. As described in Chapter 3, prosecutors and law enforcement agencies around the world use the WHOIS system thousands of times a day to investigate crimes ranging from botnets to online fraud. The registrant data in WHOIS can create crucial leads to targets' identities, locations, and other pieces of their criminal infrastructure. This data can also help identify additional victims. Due to the significant

risk associated with noncompliance with the GDPR, however, the private organization responsible for maintaining WHOIS has decided to remove much of the registrant data from the publicly-available segments of the system while the organization works with stakeholders, including the Department, to develop a GDPR-compliant system.

This is only one example of how the GDPR may be interpreted to impede the ability of law enforcement authorities to obtain data critical for their authorized criminal and civil law enforcement activities. Uncertainty about the GDPR also has placed in question not only voluntary disclosures of information about criminal activity—e.g., by their employees, contractors, or customers—to U.S. law enforcement agencies, but also may cause companies with a significant E.U. presence to become reluctant to comply even with disclosures required by legal process, such as warrants and subpoenas, for fear that such a disclosure would be in violation of the GDPR. Absent official guidance, companies with significant E.U. business may become reluctant to participate in mandatory data transfers to U.S. law enforcement and regulatory authorities, which would impede effective tax collection, limit the ability of agencies to stop anti-competitive business practices, impair the work of public health and safety agencies, and undermine the integrity of global banking, securities, and commodities markets. This could also undercut the Department's mitigation programs for businesses and individuals that wish to cooperate in areas such as fraud, bribery, money laundering, sanctions violations, and antitrust matters—programs that yield information that often results in criminal referrals, and thus relate to the Department's core mission.

In short, given the uncertainty that the GDPR presents in certain key areas, the Department (as well as the U.S. government as a whole) must continue to collaborate with European authorities and stakeholders to carefully monitor the GDPR's impacts.

The "Going Dark" Problem

One of the most significant challenges to the Department's ability to access investigative data is the "Going Dark" problem. "Going Dark" describes circumstances where the government is unable to obtain critical information in an intelligible and usable form (or at all), despite having a court order authorizing the government's access to that information. The problem impacts a range of issues, including data retention;[9] anonymization; provider compliance (or absence thereof); foreign-stored data; data localization laws; tool development and perishability; and other similar issues. The challenges posed by the Going Dark issue have achieved greatest prominence in the context of encryption.

These challenges have significantly grown in recent years as the sophistication of encryption has increased. In the past, only the most sophisticated criminals encrypted their communications and data storage; today the average consumer has access to better technology than sophisticated criminals had twenty years ago. Previously, providers used encryption of some sort but generally retained a way of accessing the unencrypted data if necessary or desired, including to comply with law enforcement search warrants or

wiretap orders. In the past several years, the Department has seen the proliferation of default encryption where the only person who can access the unencrypted information is the end user. The advent of such widespread and increasingly sophisticated encryption technologies that prevent lawful access poses a significant impediment to the investigation of most types of criminal activity, including violent crime, drug trafficking, child exploitation, cybercrime, money laundering (including through cryptocurrencies), and domestic and international terrorism.

Faced with the challenges posed by encrypted information, investigative agencies have sometimes looked to other sources of information and evidence, which can be costly to procure and maintain. While these efforts have occasionally been successful, evidence and information lost to encryption often cannot be replaced solely by pursuing other sources of evidence. For example, communications metadata, such as non-content information about who contacts whom in phone records, can be helpful in putting the pieces together, but it provides less information than the content of data and communications—a difference that can prove outcome-determinative in the context of a criminal investigation, where prosecutors must prove guilt beyond a reasonable doubt. Moreover, metadata is also often simply unavailable because there is no mandate for providers to be able to access it. Relatedly, in the context of a judicial order authorizing the real-time interception of communications, the court must find, by law, that alternate sources of data do not exist or are insufficient to meet the investigation's goals.

Going Dark

Warrant-proof encryption poses a serious challenge to effective law enforcement.

"To those of us charged with the protection of public safety and national security, encryption technology and its application…will become a matter of life and death which will directly impact our safety and freedoms."

— FBI Director Louis Freeh
July 9, 1997

"We have engaged the tech community aggressively to help solve this problem. You cannot take an absolutist view on this. So if your argument is strong encryption, no matter what, and we can and should, in fact, create black boxes, then that I think does not strike the kind of balance that we have lived with for 200, 300 years."

— President Barack Obama
March 11, 2016

"While convinced of the problem, I'm open to all constructive solutions, solutions that take the public safety issue seriously. We need a thoughtful and sensible approach, one that may vary across business models and technologies, but . . . we need to work fast."

— FBI Director Christopher Wray
March 7, 2018

1997

2016

2018

"To be very clear — the [U.K.] government supports strong encryption and has no intention of banning end-to-end encryption. But **the inability to gain access to encrypted data in specific and targeted instances is right now severely limiting our agencies' ability to stop terrorist attacks and bring criminals to justice.**"

– U.K. Home Secretary Amber Rudd
August 1, 2017

"Few issues have vexed law enforcement agencies more than this one. They can't get access to the data they need to stop crime and hold criminals to account. **95 per cent of [our intelligence organization's] most dangerous counter-terrorism targets actively use encrypted messages to conceal their communications.** We need access to digital networks and devices, and to the data on them, when there are reasonable grounds to do so. These powers must extend beyond traditional interception if our agencies are to remain effective and pre-empt and hold to account criminal activity. There will also need to be obligations on industry – telecommunications and technology service providers – to cooperate with agencies to get access to that data . . . . "

– Australian Minister for Law Enforcement & Cybersecurity Angus Taylor
June 6, 2018

Exploiting software vulnerabilities can be another way to access encrypted (or otherwise inaccessible) data on a phone or other

"Responsible encryption is achievable. Responsible encryption can involve effective, secure encryption that allows access only with judicial authorization. Such encryption already exists. Examples include the central management of security keys and operating system updates..."

—Deputy Attorney General Rod Rosenstein, October 10, 2017

device. The Department has, in some instances, lawfully exploited security flaws to access electronic data, including data stored on smartphones. This is a promising technique, and the Department should expand its use in criminal investigations. However, so-called "engineered access" is not a replacement for all the evidence, including evidence subject to a court order, that is lost. Moreover, expanding the government's exploitation of vulnerabilities for law enforce-

ment purposes will likely require significantly higher expenditures—and in the end it may not be a scalable solution. All vulnerabilities have a limited lifespan and may have a limited scope of applicability. Software developers may discover and fix vulnerabilities in the normal course of business, or the government's use of a vulnerability could alert developers to its existence. Finally, each vulnerability might have very limited applications—limited, for example, to a particular combination of phone model and operating system.

The challenges posed by the Going Dark problem are among law enforcement's most vexing. To address these challenges, the Department's efforts should include: (1) considering whether legislation to address encryption (and all related service provider access) challenges should be pursued; (2) coordinating with international law enforcement counterparts to better understand the international legal, operational, and technical challenges of encryption; (3) collecting accurate metrics and case examples that demonstrate the scope and impact of the problem; (4) working to use technical tools more robustly in criminal investigations; (5) insisting that providers comply with their legal obligations to produce all information in their possession called for by compulsory process, and holding them accountable when they do not; (6) working with State and local partners to understand the challenge from their perspective and to assist them technologically in significant cases; and (7) reaching out to academics, industry, and technologists to fully understand the implications and possibilities for lawful access solutions.

LOOKING AHEAD

Additional Investigative Authorities

The Department has identified at least two additional legal authorities it needs to support cyber-related investigations. First, exceptions to the court order requirements of the Pen Register statute, 18 U.S.C. § 3121, are unnecessarily narrow. That statute governs the real-time collection of non-content "dialing, routing, addressing, or signaling information" associated with wire or electronic communications. This information includes phone numbers dialed as well as the "to" and "from" fields of e-mail. In general, the statute requires a court order authorizing collection of such information on a prospective basis unless the collection falls within a statutory exception. The exceptions to the Pen Register statute, however, are not coextensive with the exceptions to the Wiretap Act, codified at 18 U.S.C. § 2511 *et seq*, which generally governs wiretaps to obtain the content of wire or electronic communications. This results in the illogical situation where non-content information associated with a communication is subject to more extensive protection than the content of the communication itself. Moreover, the Pen Register statute's consent provision could be clarified to allow users to provide direct, express consent for implementation of a pen/trap device by the government to facilitate cooperative investigation efforts. The Department stands ready to assist Congress in developing legislation to implement this needed improvement.

Second, the Department faces similar problems in obtaining electronic communication transactional records ("ECTRs")—the e-mail equivalent of toll billing records for telephone calls[10]—in national security investigations. ECTRs do not include the content of communications, but they can provide crucial evidence early in national security investigations, when investigators do not yet have a clear indication of a subject's network of contacts. Information obtained from ECTRs, such as e-mail addresses, can help establish the probable cause necessary to get a Foreign Intelligence Surveillance Act order or search warrant to allow the FBI to obtain the content of stored communications, identify a potential confidential human source who may be able to provide valuable intelligence, or help eliminate a subject from suspicion. As electronic networks increasingly have supplanted telephone networks as the means for terrorists and foreign agents to communicate, the ability to access these records efficiently has become even more important to the FBI's work.

Under 18 U.S.C. § 2709, electronic communication service providers are obliged to provide ECTRs in response to certain requests—sometimes called National Security Letters ("NSLs")—made in connection with qualifying national security investigations. Companies, however, have invoked an omission in section 2709 to refuse to provide ECTRs in response to NSLs. The statute states in paragraph (a) that wire or electronic communication service providers have a duty to provide ECTRs in response to a request made by the Director of the FBI under paragraph (b). But paragraph (b) fails expressly to include ECTRs in the categories of information the Director may request, even though paragraph (a) explicitly references ECTRs.

Clarifying the statutory authority would strengthen the Department's ability to conduct counterintelligence investigations and to identify and disrupt terrorist plots in the United States. Law enforcement has obtained equivalent telephone records with a simple subpoena for decades, and the courts have held that non-content metadata of this kind, held by third-party service providers, is not protected by the Fourth Amendment.[11] A proposal to clarify that the FBI may obtain ECTRs by issuing NSLs would reaffirm a similar type of authority to the equivalent type of electronic communications information.

Apprehending Criminals Located Abroad

Even when accessible data allows law enforcement to understand the nature of the crime, to identify potential perpetrators, and to build a case for prosecution, holding the guilty party or parties accountable can still be a challenge. While the Department has made several advances to enhance its ability to prosecute sophisticated cybercriminals, difficulties apprehending criminal suspects, as well as the need for additional prosecutorial authorities, continue to hinder our efforts to bring malicious cyber actors to justice.

For example, as with our successful effort to amend Rule 41, the Department worked with the Federal Rules Committee to tackle the problem of serving criminal defendants accused of committing computer crimes. Rule 4 governs the service of criminal process upon individuals and organizations—essentially the process by which prosecutors give notice of charges to, and initiate court proceedings against, a criminal defendant. Prior to the amendment, Rule 4 did not explicitly provide a method to serve process on an organization with no physical presence in the United States, an artifact of the pre-cyber era when organizations could hardly commit crimes in the United States without having a physical presence here. As discussed in Chapters 2 and 3, today, technology allows foreign actors to commit intellectual property and computer crimes in the United States from virtually anywhere in the world.

Rule 4, amended as of December 1, 2016, now provides prosecutors with a "non-exhaustive list of methods" for serving "an organization not within a judicial district of the United States." Most importantly, the amended Rule 4 allows the government to serve a foreign organization "by any . . . means that gives notice." For example, the government has relied on the amended Rule 4 to serve foreign organizations by mailing and e-mailing process to the foreign organization's U.S.-based defense counsel. The government has also served foreign organizations by mailing process to the registered agent for a recently dissolved U.S. subsidiary of the foreign organization or, in another case, by personally serving process on the president of a U.S. organization that shared a common "parent" organization with the subject of the summons. This change is particularly important in situations where a state-owned enterprise is charged with a crime but the foreign jurisdiction is unwilling to assist with efforts to serve process.

Service, however, is only one facet of the problem that the Department faces in attempting to hold sophisticated cybercriminals accountable. As noted throughout this report, attributing a cyber-incident to an individual or group of actors is difficult due to anonymizing technologies and encryption techniques that allow cybercriminals to remain hidden from law enforcement. Additionally, there are cybercriminals who, though identified, manage to remain beyond the reach of U.S. law enforcement, especially when they are located abroad. While the Department has several mechanisms to bring cybercriminals to the United States to face trial, including extradition treaties and collaborative relationships with other countries (*see* Chapter 3), these efforts are not always successful. Some foreign sovereigns choose not to cooperate or will do so only after imposing unreasonable limitations on law enforcement. Other countries may not punish perpetrators for the specific computer crime the United States is seeking to prosecute or may lack sophisticated domestic cybercrime law enforcement capabilities. In addition to continuing to build strong relationships with other countries and assisting their efforts to meet the requirements to join the Budapest Convention (also discussed in Chapter 3), the Department should continue to identify necessary additional authorities and potential mechanisms for bringing foreign-based cybercriminals to justice.

Additional Criminal Prohibitions

Once malicious cyber actors are identified, it is important for the Department to have the authorities necessary to prosecute those individuals for the illicit activity. Additional criminal prohibitions would help the De-

partment prosecute and deter malicious cyber activity.

a. Protecting Election Computers from Attack

The principal statute used to prosecute hackers—the Computer Fraud and Abuse Act ("CFAA")—currently does not prohibit the act of hacking a voting machine in many common situations. In general, the CFAA only prohibits hacking computers that are connected to the Internet (or that meet other narrow criteria for protection). In many conceivable situations, electronic voting machines will not meet those criteria, as they are typically kept off the Internet. Consequently, should hacking of a voting machine occur, the government would not, in many conceivable circumstances, be able to use the CFAA to prosecute the hackers. (The conduct could, however, potentially violate other criminal statutes.)

b. Insider Threat/Nosal Fix

Until recently, the Department regularly used the CFAA's prohibition on "exceeding authorized access" to prosecute insider threats—in particular, employees who abused permitted access to their employers' systems by stealing proprietary information or accessing information for their own illicit purposes and gain. The Department, for example, prosecuted police officers who sold their access to confidential criminal records databases, government employees who accessed private tax and passport records without authority, and bank employees who abused access to steal customers' identities. These employees had some right to access those computers, but their conduct was a crime under the CFAA because they intentionally exceeded their employer's computer use rules.

Decisions in the Second, Fourth, and Ninth Circuit Courts of Appeals, however, have limited the definition of "exceeds authorized access" in section 1030(e)(6) of the CFAA. In *United States* v. *Nosal*, 676 F.3d 854 (9th Cir. 2012) (en banc), the Ninth Circuit held that an indictment did not state a violation of the CFAA when it alleged that a former employee had asked current employees to access information in a proprietary database to aid him in starting a new firm. The company had computer policies that limited employee access to legitimate work purposes. Although the employees' efforts to access information for the benefit of the former employee's new firm violated the company's policies, the court held such an activity did not violate federal criminal law. According to the *Nosal* court, the definition of "exceeds authorized access" in section 1030(e)(6) "is limited to violations of restrictions on access to information, and not restrictions on its use." *Id.* at 863-64.[12]

Such decisions have caused grave damage to the government's ability to prosecute and protect against serious insider threats. If the CFAA can be used only against outsiders with no right at all to access computers, many insider threats—including those in the intelligence and law enforcement communities with access to extremely sensitive information—may go unpunished. Prosecutors should have adequate statutory authority to pursue insiders who abuse their computer

access for illicit means. Any such authority should also ensure appropriate consideration and treatment of legitimate privacy-related concerns.

c. CFAA as RICO Predicate

As discussed in Chapter 3, the Racketeer Influenced and Corrupt Organizations Act ("RICO") is an important prosecutorial tool for charging organizations engaged in a pattern of criminal activity because RICO violations carry substantial sentencing penalties as well as the ability for the government to seize assets of the criminal organization. RICO requires proof of, among other things, a pattern of "racketeering activity," which is defined as violations of two or more qualifying predicate criminal acts.

Currently, computer fraud under the CFAA does not qualify as a predicate act under the RICO statute, whereas similar conduct, such as wire fraud and mail fraud, does qualify. Adding the CFAA as a predicate offense for RICO purposes could increase our ability to fight cybercrime and take down criminal organizations engaged in such activities.

d. Combating Sextortion

"Sextortion" and related offenses are discussed in Chapter 2. Although such conduct may implicate certain existing criminal laws, there are no federal criminal statutes specifically addressing sextortion and non-consensual pornography. Additionally, while stalking, bullying, and harassment have more commonly been dealt with by local law enforcement or outside the criminal justice system, the use of computers and mobile networks has turned many such crimes into multi-jurisdictional and even multi-national offenses.[13] The increasingly expansive nature of these crimes, in addition to the use of new technologies, may merit a federal response. New federal criminal offenses specifically targeting sextortion and non-consensual pornography, as well as possible new sentencing enhancements for such offenses under existing authorities, could have merit.

3. Challenges in Connection with Other Legal Actions to Dismantling, Disrupting, and Deterring Malicious Cyber Conduct

As described in Chapter 3, in addition to traditional investigation and prosecution, the Department has an array of other techniques and tools to dismantle, disrupt, and deter cyber threats, including a blend of civil, criminal, and administrative powers. The Department has employed these tools to disable botnets, disrupt dark markets, and pursue sanctions against specified malicious actors. As with our investigation and prosecution activities, however, the Department needs additional tools and authorities to maximize effectiveness.

Tackling Tor/Dark Markets

The Department cannot disrupt cyber activity that it cannot find. This makes Tor and the existence of dark markets one of the greatest impediments to our efforts. As discussed in detail in Chapter 2, Tor provides anonymity in two ways—first, by anonymizing communications sent from computers running Tor, and second, by allowing individuals to operate websites on the Dark Web called Tor "Hidden Services" without divulging location information of the websites' servers.

While sometimes used for innocuous and even beneficial purposes, the anonymity afforded by Tor also poses a unique and significant threat to public safety. The anonymizing technology is effective, making it difficult to identify the physical location of dark market websites either to shut them down or to identify who is administering them. The result is that law enforcement investigators can observe and document the fact that disturbing criminal activity is occurring, but they cannot use the sort of investigative steps that ordinarily would allow them to determine who is perpetrating the crimes.

Combating criminals' abuse of Tor and their exploitation of dark markets requires a concerted effort. The Department should work with partners to develop new technological tools that will enable law enforcement to identify the true location of Hidden Services websites engaged in criminal activity. Effective development and use of these tools will enable law enforcement to locate and lawfully seize servers hosting such sites, and to identify the administrators, vendors, buyers, and participants who use them. In addition, the federal government should carefully evaluate its role in funding these anonymizing technologies, as currently the U.S. government is the primary source of funding for the Tor Project, the organization responsible for maintaining the Tor software.

Enhancing Our Ability to Disrupt Botnets

On May 22, 2018, DHS and the Department of Commerce released a joint report titled, "A Report to the President on Enhancing the Resilience of the Internet and Communications Ecosystem Against Botnets and Other Automated, Distributed Threats."[14] The report encourages collaboration between the government and private industry, recognizing that addressing the global botnet problem requires further discussions on market incentives and on securing products at all stages of their life cycle. The Department should play an active role in these efforts.

Despite being the principal law enforcement agency tasked with disrupting and dismantling botnets, the Department's current statutory authority is limited. As it stands today, the law gives federal courts the authority to issue injunctions to stop the ongoing commission of specified fraud crimes or illegal wiretapping through the use of botnets, by authorizing actions that prevent a continuing and substantial injury. The Department used this authority effectively in its successful disruption of the Coreflood botnet in 2011 and of the Gameover Zeus botnet in 2014. *See* Appendix 2. Because the criminals behind these particular botnets used them to intercept communications containing online financial account information and, with that information, committed fraud, the existing law allowed us to obtain court authority to disrupt the botnets by stopping the criminals' commands from reaching the infected computers.

Unfortunately, botnets can be and often are used for many other types of illegal activity beyond fraud or illegal wiretapping. As explained in Chapter 2, for example, malicious actors can employ botnets to steal sensitive corporate information, to harvest e-mail account addresses, to hack other computers, or to execute DDoS attacks against websites or other computers. When these crimes do not involve fraud or illegal wiretapping, courts may lack the statutory authority to issue an injunction to disrupt the botnet. The Department should evaluate the merits of creating a more comprehensive authority for courts to address all types of illegal botnets.

Advancing a CFAA Forfeiture Fix

As discussed in Chapter 3, the Department in recent years has regularly used civil forfeiture authorities to disrupt cybercriminal groups by seizing valuable assets such as computer servers and domain names used to operate botnets, as well as profits derived from illegal activity.[15] These actions are permissible even when it is not yet possible to arrest the offenders. Expanding forfeiture authority to CFAA offences could enhance the Department's capacity to dismantle, disrupt, and deter cyber threats by targeting the instruments of, and profits from, cybercrime.

Issues for Further Evaluation

In addition to helping facilitate action on the specific recommendations made above and elsewhere in this report, the Department should initiate a deeper evaluation of several key areas where strategic coordination is especially important. Some of these evaluations are already underway; others will be part of the Department's ongoing efforts to evaluate its authorities, practices, and resources.

The eight non-exclusive areas for deeper evaluation include:

1. Strengthening Our Own Defenses: Consistent with the President's May 2017 Executive Order on Strengthening the Cybersecurity of Federal Networks and Critical Infrastructure,[16] the Department is continually reassessing how best to defend its networks and reduce vulnerabilities. The Department should consider next steps and a longer-term strategy to maintain the security of its own defenses.

2. Enhancing Effective Collaboration with the Private Sector: The Department's ability to work collaboratively and effectively with the private sector will continue to be one of the most critical elements of our strategy to fight cybercrime. In the coming months, the Department should engage in a more extensive evaluation of our work with the private sector by seeking specific input from private sector participants. Where appropriate, we will make recommendations to enhance these collaborative efforts, including with regard to information-sharing, threat and incident notification, data breach notification standards, and frameworks for joint disruptive efforts, such as botnet takedowns.

3. Addressing Encryption and Anonymity (the Going Dark Array of Issues): Addressing the complex issues raised by the legal and technical barriers that prevent law enforcement from obtaining information in electronic form is another Department priority. As discussed above, it is critical that the Department maintain the ability to identify those who employ technology for illicit means and, with appropriate legal authority, to obtain evidence to bring criminals to justice. The Department should continue to develop a framework to ensure that these public safety and national security objectives can be met even as encryption and anonymizing technologies continue to evolve. In addition, the Department should explore and, as appropriate, adopt new investigative methods to replace the investigative opportunities that have been lost.

4. Addressing Malign Foreign Influence Operations: As discussed in Chapter 1, hostile foreign actors exploit the Internet and social media platforms to conduct influence operations against our Nation, including by spreading disinformation and propaganda online on a scale greater than has ever been observed before. In addition to implementing the disclosure policy discussed in Chapter 1, the Department should consider additional ways to improve our ability to respond to malign foreign influence operations, including whether new criminal statutes aimed directly at this threat are needed, and whether there are new ways we can work with the private sector in this area. Because this problem requires a whole-of-government solution, the Department should also consider how best to use existing or additional interagency coordination mechanisms to address the threat.

CYBER-DIGITAL TASK FORCE REPORT

5. *Addressing the Global Nature of Cyber-Enabled Crime:* A hallmark of technology-enabled crime is that it increasingly cuts across international boundaries, even when less sophisticated actors are behind the malicious activity. As discussed above, the global nature of cybercrime carries with it numerous impediments—both technological and arising out of foreign laws and international agreements—to the Department's ability to identify and locate malicious actors and bring them to justice. These impediments bear no easy solutions and may only grow as technology continues to evolve. The Department should continue evaluating this set of challenges and make additional recommendations to improve its global investigative and prosecutorial reach.

6. *Preparing for Emerging and Future Technology:* The technology behind current cyber-enabled threats will continue to evolve. The Department must ensure that its continued recalibration of efforts and resources not only aims at the major threats of today, but also prepares it for the emerging threats of tomorrow. The Department should continue to evaluate how its investigative and prosecutorial abilities can keep pace with, and even stay ahead of, the evolving technological threat. For example, the Department should continue evaluating the emerging threats posed by rapidly developing cryptocurrencies that malicious cyber actors often use, and autonomous vehicle technology, which has both ground and aerial applications (*e.g.*, unmanned aircraft systems).

7. *Sharpening Departmental and Interagency Organization of Efforts to Fight Cyber-Enabled Crime:* The Department's cyber-related mission requires effort and expertise from many components. Similarly, the Department's efforts make up just one part of the U.S. government's approach to cyber issues. As such, the Department must continuously review its internal coordination approach and resources, as well as how it interacts with its interagency partners, to determine if any improvements or adjustments are needed. Relatedly, the Department should continue evaluating how most effectively to recruit and retain attorneys, investigators, and professional staff with the necessary skills and mission-oriented mindset to ensure it has the human capital it needs to confront evolving cyber threats.

8. *Strengthening the Department's Tools and Authorities:* This report has described numerous additional recommendations to strengthen the Department's tools and authorities. Where such improvements are already known, the Department should seek ways to advance those improvements, including by seeking interagency approval to advocate for legislation, where appropriate.

In each of these key areas, the Department should not be merely reactive to known challenges and obstacles, but rather should pursue a strategic and forward-looking approach.

LOOKING AHEAD

NOTES

[1]   Challenges specific to foreign influence operations are discussed in detail in Chapter 1 and so are not repeated here.

[2]   The Digital Millennium Copyright Act, codified at 17 U.S.C. § 1201, prohibits the circumvention of technological controls, such as encryption and password protocols, that protect copyrighted works. Section 1201 also includes a rulemaking process that recognizes that, in some cases, exceptions to the general prohibition may be justified. Section 1201 requires the Copyright Office to conduct a rulemaking every three years to evaluate proposed exemptions proposed by the public to the anti-circumvention provision and to recommend appropriate proposals for adoption by the Librarian of Congress. The exemptions last only three years unless they are renewed in a subsequent proceeding.

[3]   The last rulemaking process conducted in 2016 resulted, *inter alia*, in a three-year exemption for "security research" conducted on particular categories of devices, including machines designed for use by individual consumers, motorized land vehicles, and certain medical devices. Security research included "good faith testing for and the identification, disclosure and correction of malfunctions, security flaws and vulnerabilities in computer programs." *See generally* U.S. COPYRIGHT OFFICE, "Section 1201 Rulemaking: Sixth Triennial Proceeding to Determine Exemptions to the Prohibition on Circumvention," (Oct. 2015), available at: https://www.copyright. gov/1201/2015/registers-recommendation.pdf (last accessed June 29, 2018).

[4]   *See* John T. Lynch, Jr., Chief, Department of Justice Computer Crime and Intellectual Property Section, to Regan Smith, General Counsel and Associate Register of Copyrights, Library of Congress (June 28, 2018), available at: https://www. justice.gov/criminal-ccips/page/file/1075496/ download (last accessed June 29, 2018). To date, the Department is unaware of any claims that the current security research exemption has thwarted or interfered with criminal investigations or prosecutions.

[5]   Available at: https://www.justice.gov/ sites/default/files/criminal-ccips/lega- cy/2015/04/30/04272015reporting-cyber-inci- dents-final.pdf (last accessed June 29, 2018).

[6]   *See* "Alabama Rolls with Tide as Last State to Adapt Breach Notification Law," Taft Stettinius & Hollister LLP (Apr. 30, 2018), available at: https://www.lexology.com/library/detail.aspx- ?g=cc0e9bb3-fe24-4211-b9dc-1fbfd350637f (last accessed June 29, 2018).

[7]   "Presidential Memorandum on the Actions by the United States Related to the Section 301 Investigation," THE WHITE HOUSE (March 22, 2018), available at: https://www.whitehouse. gov/presidential-actions/presidential-mem- orandum-actions-united-states-related-sec- tion-301-investigation/ (last accessed June 29, 2018).

[8]   For example, due to such concerns, DHS in September 2017 issued a directive requiring federal agencies to remove and discontinue use of antivirus software provided by Moscow-based Kaspersky Lab. Several months later, Congress enacted a government-wide ban on Kaspersky products and services that exceeded the scope of the DHS prohibition. Both measures came in response to growing national security concerns presented by the presence of Kaspersky products on U.S. information systems. Kaspersky challenged both measures in court, and both suits

CYBER-DIGITAL TASK FORCE REPORT

were dismissed at the pleading stage. Litigation continues in the court of appeals. Also in 2017, Congress amended 10 U.S.C. § 491 to restrict Department of Defense procurement of certain telecommunications equipment or services with particular Chinese or Russian origins.

9   Accessing data is further complicated in some circumstances by the lack of any uniform data retention standards or requirements for service providers. Without such requirements, data that is potentially critical to law enforcement investigations is simply not retained or in some cases is not retained long enough to be useful.

10   Telephone toll billing records include the originating phone number, the phone number called, and the date, time, and length of the call. ECTRs for e-mail show the sending e-mail address, the e-mail recipients, and the date, time, and size of the e-mail message.

11   *See, e.g., United States v. Forrester*, 512 F.3d 500, 510 (9th Cir. 2008) (holding that e-mail and Internet users have no reasonable expectation of privacy in to/from addresses of their messages or in IP addresses of websites visited).

12   *See also WEC Carolina Energy Solutions LLC v. Miller*, 687 F.3d 199, 207 (4th Cir. 2012) ("[W]e reject an interpretation of the CFAA that imposes liability on employees who violate a use policy[.]"); *United States v. Valle,* 807 F.3d 508 511 (2d Cir. 2015) (an individual "'exceeds authorized access' only when he obtains or alters information that he does not have authorization

to access for any purpose which is located on a computer that he is otherwise authorized to access").

13   For instance, a criminal in one State can easily disseminate graphic images and personally-identifying information of his victim in another State or around the world. He can store the images and information on servers in unfriendly foreign jurisdictions, using proxy technology to conceal his true location. He can threaten and extort the victim using end-to-end encrypted communication applications that store little or no information about subscribers. Without leaving home, the perpetrator can commit an elaborate and hard-to-trace scheme using technology easily accessible to anyone. Worse, someone with no technical sophistication at all can hire someone to do the harassment for him from a dark market online.

14   "A Report to the President on Enhancing the Resilience of the Internet and Communications Ecosystem Against Botnets and Other Automated, Distributed Threats," U.S. DEPT. OF COMMERCE & U.S. DEPT. OF HOMELAND SECURITY (May 22, 2018), available at: https://www.commerce.gov/sites/commerce.gov/files/media/files/2018/eo_13800_botnet_report_-_finalv2.pdf (last accessed June 29, 2018).

15   18 U.S.C. §§ 981-83.

16   Exec. Order No. 13,800, 82 Fed. Reg. 22391 (May 16, 2017).

APPENDIX 1

Office of the Attorney General
Washington, D. C. 20530
February 16, 2018

MEMORANDUM FOR HEADS OF DEPARTMENT COMPONENTS

FROM: THE ATTORNEY GENERAL

SUBJECT: Cyber-Digital Task Force

    The malicious use of technology poses an unprecedented threat against our nation. While computers, smart devices, and other chip-enabled machines—as well as the networks that connect them—have enriched our lives and have driven our economy, the malign use of these technologies harms our government, victimizes consumers and businesses, and endangers public safety and national security. Indeed, the scale of this cyber threat, and the range of actors that use cyber intrusions and attacks to achieve their objectives, have grown in alarming ways.

    The Department of Justice remains committed to confronting cyber threats by detecting, deterring, and disrupting malicious cyber activity through the enforcement of federal law. Therefore, today, I am establishing the Department's Cyber-Digital Task Force (the Task Force). This Task Force not only will canvass the many ways that the Department already combats the global cyber threat, but also will identify how federal law enforcement can more effectively accomplish its mission in this vital and evolving area.

    The Task Force shall be chaired by a senior Department official appointed by the Deputy Attorney General and shall consist of representatives from the Criminal Division; the National Security Division; the United States Attorney's Office community; the Office of Legal Policy; the Office of Privacy and Civil Liberties; the Office of the Chief Information Officer; the Bureau of Alcohol, Tobacco, Firearms and Explosives; the Drug Enforcement Administration; the Federal Bureau of Investigation; and the United States Marshals Service. The Deputy Attorney General may invite representatives from other Department components, and from other federal agencies, to participate in the Task Force as appropriate, and may establish subcommittees to focus the Task Force's efforts.

    Many of the most pressing cyber threats that our nation faces transcend easy categorization. These threats include: efforts to interfere with, or disable, our critical infrastructure; efforts to interfere with our elections; use of the Internet to spread violent ideologies and to recruit followers; theft of corporate, governmental, and private information on a mass scale; use of technology to avoid or frustrate law enforcement, or to mask criminal activity; and the mass exploitation of computers, along with the weaponizing of everyday consumer devices (as well as of the very architecture of the Internet itself) to launch attacks on American citizens and businesses. Evaluating these threats, and formulating a strategy to combat them, should be among the Task Force's highest priorities.

CYBER-DIGITAL TASK FORCE REPORT

Memorandum for Heads of Department Components
Subject: Cyber-Digital Task Force   Page 2

      I have asked for an initial report from the Task Force describing the Department's current cyber-related activities and offering initial recommendations by no later than June 30, 2018.

      The Internet has transformed our lives. We must ensure that Internet-based technologies remain sources of enrichment, rather than becoming forces of destruction and vectors of chaos. I look forward to our continued work together in support of a prosperous and safe America.

APPENDIX 2
RECENT SUCCESSFUL BOTNET DISRUPTIONS

VPNFilter

In May 2018, the Department took steps to disrupt the operation of a global botnet of hundreds of thousands of infected home and office ("SOHO") routers and other networked devices under the control of a group of actors known as the "Sofacy Group" (also known as "apt28," "sandworm," "x-agent," "pawn storm," "fancy bear" and "sednit").[1] The botnet, which the FBI and cybersecurity researchers called "VPNFilter," targets SOHO routers and network-access storage devices. In order to identify infected devices and facilitate their remediation, the U.S. Attorney's Office for the Western District of Pennsylvania applied for and obtained court orders authorizing the FBI to seize a domain that is part of the malware's command-and-control infrastructure. The FBI also put out a public service announcement urging individuals and organizations to reset their routers.[2]

The cumulative effect of these actions would be to purge parts of the malware from the routers that were reset, and to direct attempts by the remaining malware to reinfect the device to an FBI-controlled server, which captured the Internet Protocol ("IP") address of infected devices. A non-profit partner organization agreed to disseminate the IP addresses to those who can assist with remediating the botnet, including foreign CERTs and Internet service providers.

Although the devices would remain vulnerable to reinfection while connected to the Internet, these efforts maximized opportunities to identify and remediate the infection worldwide in the time available before Sofacy actors learned of the vulnerability in their command-and-control infrastructure.

Kelihos

On April 10, 2017, the Department announced an extensive effort to disrupt and dismantle the Kelihos botnet—a global network of tens of thousands of computers infected with the Kelihos malware.[3] Under the control of a cybercriminal, Peter Levashov, that botnet facilitated a range of malicious activities, including harvesting login credentials, distributing hundreds of millions of spam e-mails, and installing ransomware and other malicious software. The enormous volume of unsolicited spam e-mails sent by the botnet advertised counterfeit drugs, work-at-home scams, and a variety of other frauds, including deceptively promoted stocks in order to fraudulently increase their price (so-called "pump-and-dump" stock fraud schemes).

To liberate the victim computers from the botnet, the Department obtained civil and criminal court orders that authorized measures to neutralize the Kelihos botnet by (1) seizing domain names that the botnet used to communicate with the command-and-control servers, (2) establishing substitute servers that received the automated requests for instructions so that infected computers no longer communicated with the criminal operator, and (3) blocking any commands sent from the criminal operator attempting to regain control of the infected computers. As described in Chapter 3, Levashov was arrested in Spain and extradited to the U.S. to face justice.

Avalanche

On November 30, 2016, the Department, in coordination with German state and federal police, Europol, and various other countries and entities, conducted a takedown operation against the Avalanche malware infrastructure. This takedown led to the disabling of seven botnets that relied on this infrastructure and impacted approximately 10 different malware families that had utilized the Avalanche network.

The Avalanche network offered cybercriminals a secure infrastructure, designed to stand in the way of detection by law enforcement and cyber security experts, over which the criminals conducted malware campaigns as well as money laundering schemes known as "money mule" schemes. Access to the Avalanche network was offered to the cybercriminals through postings on exclusive underground online criminal forums. In these schemes, highly organized networks of "mules" purchased goods with stolen funds, enabling cybercriminals to launder the money they acquired through malware attacks or other illegal means.

The types of malware and money mule schemes operating over this network varied. Ransomware, such as Nymain, encrypted victims' computer files until the victim paid a ransom (typically in a form of electronic currency) to the cybercriminal. Other malware, such as GozNym, was designed to steal victims' sensitive banking credentials, which were directed through the intricate network of Avalanche servers to backend servers controlled by the cybercriminals and used to initiate fraudulent wire transfers.

The Avalanche network, which had been operating since at least 2010, was estimated to involve hundreds of thousands of infected computers worldwide. The monetary losses associated with malware attacks conducted over the Avalanche network were estimated to be in the hundreds of millions of dollars worldwide, although exact calculations are difficult due to the high number of malware families present on the network.

This operation required an unprecedented level of international coordination to seize, block, and sinkhole over 800,000 malicious domains associated with the Avalanche network. These domains had been used to send commands to infected devices, pass banking credentials to cyber criminals, and obfuscate efforts by law enforcement to investigate this conspiracy. The USAO for the Western District of Pennsylvania and the Computer Crime and Intellectual Property Section obtained a temporary restraining order which greatly assisted in this effort. The Department continues to build on the success of this operation, using information obtained through seized infrastructure to identify and arrest criminals responsible for the creation of the malware distributed via Avalanche.

Gameover Zeus & Cryptolocker

In 2014, the Department led a coalition of nearly a dozen foreign countries and a group of elite computer security firms to disrupt and dismantle the highly-sophisticated "Gameover Zeus botnet."[4] At its peak, that botnet consisted of a global network of between 500,000 and 1 million computers infected malware that used keystroke logging to collect online financial account information and, in turn, inflicted more than $100 million of losses to individuals in the United States. The Gameover Zeus network was also used to spread the Cryptolocker ransomware, which used cryptographic key pairs to encrypt the computer files of its victims and often left victims with no choice but to pay hundreds of dollars to obtain the decryption keys needed to unlock their files. As of April 2014, security researchers estimated that Cryptolocker had infected more than 234,000 computers and, according to one estimate, caused more than $27 million in ransom payments in its first two months in circulation.

To disrupt both the Gameover Zeus botnet and the Cryptolocker malware, the Department deployed a combination of criminal and civil tools available to law enforcement. As an initial matter, a federal grand jury indicated a key administrator of the botnet (Evgeniy Bogachev) with a 14-count indictment, and the Department filed a separate civil injunction against Bogachev as the leader of a tightly-knit gang of cyber criminals based in Russia and Ukraine responsible for both the Gameover Zeus and Cryptolocker schemes. Further, as in Kelihos, the Department obtained civil and criminal court orders authorizing measures to redirect requests for instructions by computers victimized by the two schemes away from the criminal operators to substitute servers established pursuant to court order. The FBI was also authorized to obtain the IP addresses of the victim computers reaching out to the substitute servers, and to provide that information to DHS's Computer Emergency Readiness Team (US-CERT) to help victims remove the Gameover Zeus malware from their computers.[5]

To identify servers as command-and-control hubs for the Gameover Zeus botnet and Cryptolocker malware, and to subsequently facilitate victims' efforts to remediate the damage to their computers, the Department also enlisted the assistance of numerous computer security firms and leading universities.

Coreflood

In 2011, the Department disrupted and disabled the decade-old "Coreflood" botnet through a civil complaint, search warrants, a criminal seizure warrant, and a temporary restraining order.[6]

This botnet was a global network of 100,000 computers infected with a particularly harmful type of malware named Coreflood, which could

be controlled remotely to steal private personal and financial information from unsuspecting computer users. The botnet's administrators, in turn, used the stolen information for a variety of criminal purposes, including stealing funds from the compromised accounts. In one example described in court filings, for instance, Coreflood leveraged information gleaned through illegal monitoring of Internet communications between a user and the user's bank to take over an online banking session and cause the fraudulent transfer of funds to a foreign account.

The Department employed a multi-prong enforcement strategy to dismantle the Coreflood botnet. It obtained search warrants to seize five command-and-control servers that remotely controlled hundreds of thousands of infected computers, and a seizure warrant to secure 29 domain names that the botnet used to communicate with the command-and-control servers. Federal authorities also obtained a temporary restraining order that authorized the government to replace the illegal command-and-control servers with substitute servers. To prevent the defendants from reconstituting the botnet through new servers, domains, and updated software, the TRO also authorized the government to respond to routine requests for direction from the infected computers in the United States with a command that temporarily stopped the Coreflood malware from running on the infected computers. By limiting the defendants' ability to control the botnet, computer security providers and victims were given the time and opportunity to remove the malware from infected computers. The Department also filed a civil complaint against 13 "John Doe" defendants associated with the botnet.

CYBER-DIGITAL TASK FORCE REPORT

NOTES

[1] Press Release, "Justice Department Announces Actions to Disrupt Advanced Persistent Threat 28 Botnet of Infected Routers and Network Storage Devices," U.S. Dept. of Justice (May 23, 2018), available at: https://www.justice.gov/opa/pr/justice-department-announces-actions-disrupt-advanced-persistent-threat-28-botnet-infected (last accessed June 29, 2018).

[2] Federal Bureau of Investigation, "Foreign Cyber Actors Target Home and Office Routers and Networked Devices Worldwide" (May 25, 2018), available at: https://www.ic3.gov/media/2018/180525.aspx (last accessed June 29, 2018).

[3] Press Release, "Justice Department Announces Actions to Dismantle Kelihos Botnet," U.S. Dept. of Justice (Apr. 10, 2017), available at: https://www.justice.gov/opa/pr/justice-department-announces-actions-dismantle-kelihos-botnet-0 (last accessed June 29, 2018).

[4] Press Release, "U.S. Leads Multi-National Action Against "Gameover Zeus" Botnet and "Cryptolocker" Ransomware, Charges Botnet Administrator," U.S. Dept. of Justice (June 2, 2014), available at: https://www.justice.gov/opa/pr/us-leads-multi-national-action-against-gameover-zeus-botnet-and-cryptolocker-ransomware (last accessed June 29, 2018).

[5] At no point during the operation did the FBI or law enforcement access the content of any of the victims' computers or electronic communications.

[6] Press Release, "Department of Justice Takes Action to Disable International Botnet," U.S. Dept. of Justice (Apr. 13, 2011), available at: https://www.justice.gov/opa/pr/department-justice-takes-action-disable-international-botnet (last accessed June 29, 2018).

APPENDIX 3
RECENT SUCCESSFUL DARK WEB DISRUPTIONS

AlphaBay & Hansa

On July 20, 2017, the Department announced the seizure of AlphaBay, an online criminal marketplace that had operated for over two years on the dark web and facilitated the sale throughout the world of deadly illegal drugs, stolen and fraudulent identification documents and access devices, counterfeit goods, malware and other computer hacking tools, firearms, and toxic chemicals. Around the time of its takedown, AlphaBay was the largest criminal marketplace on the Internet. Indeed, prior to the site's disruption, one AlphaBay staff member claimed that it serviced over 200,000 users and 40,000 vendors. AlphaBay operated as a hidden service on the "Tor" network, and used cryptocurrencies including Bitcoin, Monero, and Ethereum in order to hide the locations of its underlying servers and the identities of its administrators, moderators, and users. Based on law enforcement's investigation of AlphaBay, authorities believe the site was also used to launder hundreds of millions of dollars deriving from illegal transactions on the website.

The operation to seize the AlphaBay site coincided with efforts by Dutch law enforcement to investigate and take down the Hansa Market, another prominent dark web market. Like AlphaBay, Hansa Market was used to facilitate the sale of illegal drugs, toxic chemicals, malware, counterfeit identification documents, and illegal services. To maximize the disruptive impact of the joint takedowns, Dutch authorities took covert control over the Hansa Market during the period when AlphaBay was shutdown. That covert control not only allowed Dutch police to identify and disrupt the regular criminal activity on Hansa, but then also allowed the authorities to

sweep up all those new users who were displaced from AlphaBay and needed a new trading platform. The success of this joint operation stands out as yet another example of what international law enforcement can accomplish when working closely together to neutralize a cybercrime marketplace.

Silk Road

In late 2013, the Department joined with various law enforcement partners across the government to disrupt the hidden "Silk Road" website, and to prosecute its creator and owner, Ross Ulbricht.[1]

For the two years leading up to the Department's actions, Silk Road stood out as the most sophisticated and extensive criminal marketplace on the Internet, serving as a sprawling black-market bazaar where unlawful goods and services, including illegal drugs of virtually all varieties, were regularly bought and sold. At its height, several thousand drug dealers and other unlawful vendors used the site to distribute hundreds of kilograms of illegal drugs and other unlawful goods and services to well over 100,000 buyers, and to launder hundreds of millions of dollars deriving from these unlawful transactions.

To remain outside the reach of law enforcement, Silk Road's administrators anonymized the site's transactions by operating it on the Tor network and including a Bitcoin-based payment system designed to conceal its users' identities and locations. Despite these efforts, law enforcement ultimately pierced Silk Road's cloak of anonymity and seized control of the website, its domain, its servers, and 29,655 Bitcoins residing on those servers (worth approximately $28 million at the time of seizure). The creator and administrator of Silk Road, Ross Ulbricht, was also arrested and ultimately convicted of seven charges relating to money laundering and computer hacking, among others, and sentenced to life in federal prison. The government seized an additional 144,336 Bitcoins from Ulbricht's computer hard drive (worth approximately $130 million at the time of seizure).

Operation Onymous

Building on the success of the Silk Road takedown, in November 2014, U.S. and European authorities took joint action against the underground website known as "Silk Road 2.0," as well as dozens of additional dark market websites that were facilitating the sale of an astonishing range of illegal goods and services on hidden services within the Tor network, including weapons, drugs, murder-for-hire services, stolen identification data, money laundering, hacking services, and others.[2] Silk Road 2.0 was created in November 2013 to fill the void left by the government's seizure of the Silk Road website in October 2013. As with Silk Road, the Department used civil forfeiture authorities to seize control over 400 Tor website addresses known as ".onion" addresses, as well as the servers hosting them. Adminis-

trators associated with these Dark Web markets were criminally prosecuted.

Darkode

On July 15, 2015, the Department announced the dismantling of a computer hacking forum known as "Darkode" as part of a coordinated law enforcement action across 20 countries that led to the search, arrest, or charging of 70 Darkode members and associates.[3]

At the time of its takedown, the Darkode forum represented a uniquely grave threat to the integrity of data on computers because it provided a platform where highly-sophisticated cybercriminals congregated to buy, sell, and trade malware, botnets, and PII used to steal from U.S. citizens and individuals around the world. Before becoming a member of Darkode, prospective members were allegedly vetted through a process in which an existing member invited a prospective member to the forum for the purpose of presenting the skills or products that he or she could bring to the group. As part of Operation Shrouded Horizon, the FBI was able to disrupt and dismantle Darkode by infiltrating the forum's membership.

APPENDIX 3

NOTES

[1]   Press Release, "Manhattan U.S. Attorney Announces Seizure of Additional $28 Million Worth of Bitcoins Belonging to Ross William Ulbricht, Alleged Owner and Operator of "Silk Road" Website," FEDERAL BUREAU OF INVESTIGATION (Oct. 25, 2013), available at: https://archives.fbi.gov/archives/newyork/press-releases/2013/manhattan-u.s.-attorney-announces-seizure-of-additional-28-million-worth-of-bitcoins-belonging-to-ross-william-ulbricht-alleged-owner-and-operator-of-silk-road-website (last accessed June 29, 2018).

[2]   Press Release, "Dozens of Online 'Dark Markets' Seized Pursuant to Forfeiture Complaint Filed in Manhattan Federal Court in Conjunction with the Arrest of the Operator of Silk Road 2.0," FEDERAL BUREAU OF INVESTIGATION (Nov. 7, 2014), available at: https://www.fbi.gov/contact-us/field-offices/newyork/news/press-releases/dozens-of-online-dark-markets-seized-pursuant-to-forfeiture-complaint-filed-in-manhattan-federal-court-in-conjunction-with-the-arrest-of-the-operator-of-silk-road-2.0 (last accessed June 29, 2018).

[3]   Press Release, "Major Computing Hacking Forum Dismantled," U.S. DEPT. OF JUSTICE (July 15, 2015), available at: https://www.justice.gov/opa/pr/major-computer-hacking-forum-dismantled (last accessed June 29, 2018).

APPENDIX 4
GLOSSARY OF KEY TERMS

Acronym	Meaning
AECA	Arms Export Control Act
AUSA	Assistant United States Attorney
BEC	Business Email Compromise
Boyusec	Guangzhou Bo Yu Information Technology Company Limited
C&C	Command-and-Control
C.F.R.	Code of Federal Regulations
C2	Command and Control
CAATSA	Countering America's Adversaries Through Sanctions Act
CAN-SPAM	Controlling the Assault of Non Solicited Pornography and Marketing
CAT	Cyber Action Team
CCIPS	Computer Crime and Intellectual Property Section
CFAA	Computer Fraud and Abuse Act
CHIP	Computer Hacking and Intellectual Property
CFIUS	Committee on Foreign Investment in the United States
CISO	Chief Information Security Officer
CLOUD	Clarifying Lawful Overseas Use of Data
CNN	Cable News Network
CTF	Cyber Task Force, Federal Bureau of Investigation
DDoS	Distributed Denial of Service
DEA	Drug Enforcement Administration
DHS	Department of Homeland Security
DMCA	Digital Millennium Copyright Act
DOJ	Department of Justice
DSAC	Domestic Security Alliance Council

CYBER-DIGITAL TASK FORCE REPORT

Acronym	Meaning
EAR	Export Administration Regulations
ECPA	Electronic Communications Privacy Act
ECTR	Electronic Communication Transactional Record
EEA	Economic Espionage Act
EOUSA	Executive Office for United States Attorneys
ESU	Electronic Surveillance Unit
FBI	Federal Bureau of Investigation
FinCEN	Financial Crimes Enforcement Network
FISA	Foreign Intelligence Surveillance Act
FLASH	FBI Liaison Alert System
FSB	Russian Federal Security Service
GDPR	General Data Protection Regulation
HTOCU	Hi-Tech Organized Crime Unit
IC3	The Internet Crime Complaint Center
IEEPA	International Emergency Economic Powers Act
INTERPOL	International Criminal Police Organization
IoT	Internet of hings
IP (address)	Internet Protocol
IPR	Intellectual Property Rights
IRS	Internal Revenue Service
ISIL	Islamic State of Iraq and the Levant
ISP	Internet Service Provider
JAR	Joint Analysis Report
J-CODE	Joint Criminal Opioid Darknet Enforcement
JITs	Joint Investigative Teams
JTA	Joint Technical Advisory
KAT	Kickass orrents

APPENDIX 4

Acronym	Meaning
MLARS	Money Laundering and Asset Recovery Section, Criminal ivision
MLAT	Mutual Legal Assistance Treaty
MUCD	Military Unit Cover esignator
NCCIC	National Cybersecurity and Communications Integration Center
NCFTA	National Cyber-Forensics and Training Alliance
NCIJTF	National Cyber Investigative Joint Task Force
NDCAC	National Domestic Communications Assistance Center
NICE	National Initiative for Cybersecurity Education
NITs	Network Investigative Techniques
NSCS	National Security Cyber Specialists
NSD	National Security Division
NSL	National Security Letter
OFAC	Office of Foreign Assets Control
OIA	Office of International Affairs, Criminal ivision
OJT	On the Job Training
OLE	Office of Legal Education
P2P	Peer-to-Peer
PII	Personally Identifiable Information
PINs	Private Industry Notifications
PLA	People's Liberation Army
PPD	Presidential PolicyD irective
PRC	People's Republic of China
PRTT	Pen Register and Trap and Trace
PSA	Public Service Announcement
RICO	Racketeer Influenced and Corrupt Organizations Act
ROB	Rules of Behavior
SCADA	Supervisory Control and Data Acquisition

CYBER-DIGITAL TASK FORCE REPORT

Acronym	Meaning
SPE	Sony Pictures Entertainment
STSO	Operational Support Unit (Drug Enforcement Administration)
SUA	Specified Unlawful ctivity
Tor	The Onion Router
TRO	Temporary Restraining Order
USAO	United States ttorney's Office
USNCB	United States National Central Bureau (INTERPOL)
US-CERT	United States Computer Emergency Readiness Team
USTR	United States Trade Representative
RRA	Victims' Rights and Restitution ct
WTI	Workforce Training Initiative

Remarks as Prepared for Delivery, Aspen Security Forum

Aspen, Colorado, July 19, 2018
by Rod J. Rosenstein, Deputy Attorney General

It is a privilege to join you this afternoon at one of the world's premier security conferences.

We meet at a fraught moment. For too long, along with other nations, we enjoyed the extraordinary benefits of modern technology without adequately preparing for its considerable risks. Director of National Intelligence Dan Coats elevated the alarm last week, when he stated that "the digital infrastructure that serves this country is literally under attack." That is one of the rare instances when the word literally is used literally.

Our adversaries are developing cyber tools not only to steal our secrets and mislead our citizens, but also to disable our infrastructure by gaining control of computer networks.

Every day, malicious cyber actors infiltrate computers and accounts of individual citizens, businesses, the military, and all levels of government. Director Coats revealed that our adversaries "target[] government and businesses in the energy, nuclear, water, aviation and critical manufacturing sectors." They cause billions of dollars in losses, preposition cyber tools they could use for future attacks, and try to degrade our political system. So combating cybercrime and cyber-enabled threats to national security is a top priority of the Department of Justice.

Attorney General Jeff Sessions established a Cyber-Digital Task Force in February to consider two questions: What are we doing now to address cyber threats? And how can we do better?

Today, the Department of Justice is releasing a report that responds to the first question, providing a detailed assessment of the cyber threats confronting America and the Department's efforts to combat them.

The Task Force report addresses a wide range of issues, including how to define the multi-faceted challenges of cyber-enabled crime; develop strategies to detect, deter and disrupt threats; inform victims and the public about dangers; and maintain a skilled workforce.

The report describes six categories of cyber threats, and explains how the Department of Justice is working to combat them.

One serious type of threat involves direct damage to computer systems, such as Distributed Denial of Service attacks and ransomware schemes.

Another category is data theft, which includes stealing personally identifiable information and intellectual property.

The third category encompasses cyber-enabled fraud schemes.

A fourth category includes threats to personal privacy, such as sextortion and other forms of blackmail and harassment.

Attacks on critical infrastructure constitute the fifth category. They include infiltrating energy systems, transportation systems, and telecommunications networks.

Each of those complex and evolving threats is serious, and the report details the important work that the Department of Justice is doing to protect America from them.

I plan to focus today on a sixth category of cyber-enabled threats: malign foreign influence operations, described in chapter one of the task force report.

The term "malign foreign influence operations" refers to actions undertaken by a foreign government, often covertly, to influence people's opinions and advance the foreign nation's strategic objectives. The goals frequently include creating and exacerbating social divisions and undermining confidence in democratic institutions.

Influence operations are a form of information warfare. Covert propaganda and disinformation are among the primary weapons.

The Russian effort to influence the 2016 presidential election is just one tree in a growing forest. Focusing merely on a single election misses the point. As Director Coats made clear, "these actions are persistent, they are pervasive, and they are meant to undermine America's democracy on a daily basis, regardless of whether it is election time or not."

Russian intelligence officers did not stumble onto the ideas of hacking American computers and posting misleading messages because they had a free afternoon. It is what they do every day.

This is not a new phenomenon. Throughout the twentieth century, the Soviet Union used malign influence operations against the United States and many other countries. In 1963, for example, the KGB paid an American to distribute a book claiming that the FBI and the CIA assassinated President Kennedy.

In 1980, the KGB fabricated and distributed a fake document claiming that there was a National Security Council strategy to prevent black political activists from working with African leaders.

During the Reagan Administration, the KGB spread fake stories that the Pentagon developed the AIDS virus as part of a biological weapons research program.

As Jonathan Swift wrote in 1710, "Falsehood flies, and the Truth comes limping after it."

The Reagan Administration confronted the problem head on. It established an interagency committee called "the Active Measures Working Group" to counter Soviet disinformation. The group exposed Soviet forgeries and other propaganda.

Modern technology vastly expands the speed and effectiveness of disinformation campaigns. The Internet and social media platforms allow foreign agents to spread misleading political messages while masquerading as Americans.

Homeland Security Secretary Kirstjen Nielsen explained last weekend that our adversaries "us[e] social media, sympathetic spokespeople and other fronts to sow discord and divisiveness amongst the American people."

Elections provide an attractive opportunity for foreign influence campaigns to undermine our political processes. According to the intelligence community assessment, foreign interference in the 2016 election "demonstrated a significant escalation in directness, level of activity, and scope of effort compared to previous operations."

The Department's Cyber-Digital Task Force report contributes to our understanding by identifying five different types of malign foreign influence operations that target our political processes.

First, malicious cyber actors can target election infrastructure by trying to hack voter registration databases and vote-tallying systems. In 2016, foreign cyber intruders targeted election-related networks in as many as 21 states. There is no evidence that any foreign government ever succeeded in changing votes, but the risk is real. Moreover, even the possibility that manipulation may occur can cause citizens to question the integrity of elections.

Second, cyber operations can target political organizations, campaigns, and public officials. Foreign actors can steal private information through hacking, then publish it online to damage a candidate, campaign, or political party. They can even alter that stolen information to promote their desired narrative.

Russia's intelligence services conducted cyber operations against both major U.S. political parties in 2016, and the recent indictment of Russian intelligence officers alleges a systematic effort to leak stolen campaign information.

The third category of malign influence operations affecting elections involves offers to assist political campaigns or public officials by agents who conceal their connection to a foreign government. Such operations may entail financial and logistical support to unwitting Americans.

Fourth, adversaries covertly use disinformation and other propaganda to influence American public opinion. Foreign trolls spread false stories online about candidates and issues, amplify divisive political messages to make them appear more pervasive and credible, and try to pit groups against each other. They may also try to affect voter behavior by triggering protests or depressing voter turnout.

Finally, foreign governments use overt influence efforts, such as government-controlled media outlets and paid lobbyists. Those tactics may be employed lawfully if the foreign agents comply with registration requirements. But people should be aware when lobbyists or media outlets are working for a foreign government so they can evaluate the source's credibility. Particularly when respected figures argue in favor of foreign interests, it may matter to know that they are taking guidance from a foreign nation.

The election-interference charges filed in February demonstrate how easily human "trolls" distribute propaganda and disinformation. A Russian man recently admitted to a reporter that he worked with the trolls, in a separate department creating fake news for his own country. He "felt like a character in the book '1984' by George Orwell – a place where you have to write that white is black and black is white.... [Y]ou were in some kind of factory that turned lying ... into an industrial assembly line. The volumes were colossal – there were huge numbers of people, 300 to 400, and they were all writing absolute untruths."

When the man took a test for a promotion to the department working to fool Americans, he explained, "The main thing was showing that you are able to ... represent yourself as an American."

The former troll believes that Russian audiences pay no attention to fake internet comments. But he has a different opinion about Americans. He thinks that we can be deceived, because Americans "aren't used to this kind of trickery."

That remark is sort of a compliment. In repressive regimes, people always assume that the government controls media outlets. We live in a country that allows free speech, so people are accustomed to taking it seriously when other citizens express their opinions. But not everyone realizes that information posted on the Internet may not even come from citizens.

Moreover, Internet comments may not even come from human beings. Automated bots magnify the impact of propaganda. Using software to mimic actions by human users, bots can circulate messages automatically, creating the appearance that thousands of people are reading and forwarding information. Together, bots and networks of paid trolls operating multiple accounts allow foreign agents to quickly spread disinformation and create the false impression that it is widely accepted.

The United States is not alone in confronting malign foreign influence. Russia reportedly conducted a hack-and-release campaign against President Macron during last year's French elections, and instituted similar operations against political candidates in other European democracies. Other foreign nations also engage in malign influence activities.

So what can we do to defend our values in the face of foreign efforts to influence elections, weaken the social fabric, and turn Americans against each other? Like terrorism and other national security threats, the malign foreign influence threat requires a unified, strategic approach across all government agencies. The Departments of Justice, Homeland Security, State, Defense, Treasury, Intelligence agencies, and others play important roles.

Other sectors of society also need to do their part. State and local governments must secure their election infrastructure. Technology companies need to prevent misuse of their platforms. Public officials, campaigns, and other potential victims need to study the threats and protect themselves and their networks. And citizens need to understand the playing field.

The Department of Justice investigates and prosecutes malign foreign influence activity that violates federal criminal law. Some critics argue against prosecuting people who live in foreign nations that are unlikely to extradite their citizens. That is a shortsighted view.

For one thing, the defendants may someday face trial, if there is a change in their government or if they visit any nation that cooperates with America in enforcing the rule of law. Modern forms of travel and communication readily allow criminals to cross national boundaries. Do not underestimate the long arm of American law – or the persistence of American law enforcement. People who thought they were safely under the protection of foreign governments when they committed crimes against America sometimes later find themselves in federal prisons.

Second, public indictments achieve specific deterrence by impeding the defendants from traveling to rule-of-law nations and raising the risk they will be held accountable for future cybercrime. Wanted criminals are less attractive co-conspirators.

Third, demonstrating our ability to detect and publicly charge hackers will deter some others from engaging in similar conduct.

Fourth, federal indictments are taken seriously by the public and the international community, where respect for our criminal justice system – including an understanding of the presumption of innocence and the standard of proof beyond a reasonable doubt – means that our willingness to present evidence to a grand jury and ultimately at trial elicits a high degree of confidence in our allegations.

Fifth, victims deserve vindication, particularly when they are harmed by criminal acts that would be prosecuted if the perpetrator were located in the United States.

Sixth, federal criminal investigations support other penalties for malign foreign influence operations. For example, the Department of the Treasury can impose financial sanctions on defendants based on evidence exposed in indictments. Voters in foreign democracies, and influential citizens in autocratic regimes, can consider the allegations in making their own decisions about national leadership and foreign alliances.

The Department of the Treasury imposed sanctions on the individuals and entities identified in the February election-interference indictment, along with others engaged in malign activities. Nineteen individuals and five entities are subject to sanctions that freeze assets under American jurisdiction. Even if they are never brought to court, they will face consequences.

The sanctions forbid those individuals and entities from engaging in transactions with Americans and using the American financial system. The Administration followed up with similar financial sanctions for a broader range of malign activities against seven oligarchs, 12 companies, 17 Russian government officials, and two other entities.

Prosecutions are one useful tool to help deter modern criminals who remain beyond our shores. The same approach applies outside the context of crimes committed to influence elections. That is why our government regularly files charges against criminals who hide overseas, such as Iranian government hackers who broke into computer networks of a dam; Iranian hackers who infiltrated American universities, businesses and government agencies for the Islamic Revolutionary Guard Corps; an Iranian hacker who infiltrated and extorted a television network; Chinese government hackers who committed economic espionage; and Russian intelligence officers who stole data from an email service provider.

Intelligence assessments and criminal indictments are based on evidence. They do not reflect mere guesses. Intelligence assessments include analytical judgments based on classified information that cannot be disclosed because the evidence is from sources — people who will be unable to help in the future if they are identified and might be harmed in retaliation for helping America — and methods — techniques that would be worthless if our adversaries knew how we obtained the evidence. Indictments are based on credible evidence that the government must be prepared to introduce in court if necessary.

Some people may believe they can operate anonymously on the Internet, but cybercrime generally creates electronic trails that lead to the perpetrators.

Gathering intelligence about adversaries who threaten our way of life is a noble task. Outside the Department of Justice headquarters stands a statue of Nathan Hale. Hale was executed immediately, without a trial, after he was caught gathering intelligence for America during the Revolutionary War. His final words are recorded as follows: "I am so satisfied with the cause in which I have engaged, that my only regret is that I have but one life to offer in its service."

The days when foreign criminals could cause harm inside America from remote locations without fear of consequences are past. If hostile governments choose to give sanctuary to perpetrators of malicious cybercrimes after we identify them, those governments will need to take responsibility for the crimes, and individual perpetrators will need to consider the personal cost.

But criminal prosecutions and financial sanctions are not a complete solution. We need to take other steps to prevent malicious behavior.

To protect elections, the first priority is to harden our infrastructure. State governments run American elections and are responsible for maintaining cybersecurity, but they need federal help. The Department of Homeland Security takes the lead in helping to protect voting infrastructure, and the FBI leads federal investigations of intrusions.

The FBI works closely with DHS to inform election administrators about threats. DHS and the FBI provide briefings to election officials from all fifty states about our foreign adversaries' intentions and capabilities.

We also seek to protect political organizations, campaigns, candidates, and public officials. The FBI alerts potential victims about malicious cyber activities and helps them respond to intrusions. It shares detailed information about threats and vulnerabilities.

To combat covert foreign influence on public policy, we enforce federal laws that require foreign agents to register with the U.S. government. Those laws prohibit foreign nationals from tricking unwitting Americans while concealing that they are following orders from foreign government handlers. The Department of Justice is stepping up enforcement of the Foreign Agents Registration Act and related laws, and providing defensive counterintelligence briefings to local, state, and federal leaders and candidates.

Public attribution of foreign influence operations can help to counter and mitigate the harm caused by foreign government-sponsored disinformation. When people are aware of the true sponsor, they can make better-informed decisions.

We also help technology companies to counter covert foreign influence efforts. The FBI works with partners in the Intelligence Community to identify foreign agents as they establish their digital infrastructure and develop their online presence. The FBI helps technology companies disrupt foreign influence operations, by identifying foreign agents' activities so companies may consider the voluntary removal of accounts and content that violate terms of service and deceive customers.

Technology companies bear primary responsibility for securing their products, platforms, and services from misuse. Many are now taking greater responsibility for self-policing, including by removing fake accounts. We encourage them to make it a priority to combat efforts to use their facilities for illegal schemes.

Even as we enhance our efforts to combat existing forms of malign influence, the danger continues to grow. Advancing technology may enable adversaries to create propaganda in new and unforeseen ways. Our government must continue to identify and counter them.

Exposing schemes to the public is an important way to neutralize them. The American people have a right to know if foreign governments are targeting them with propaganda.

In some cases, our ability to expose foreign influence operations may be limited by our obligation to protect intelligence sources and methods, and defend the integrity of investigations.

Moreover, we should not publicly attribute activity to a source unless we possess high confidence that foreign agents are responsible. We also do not want to unduly amplify an adversary's messages, or impose additional harm on victims.

In all cases, partisan political considerations must play no role in our efforts. We cannot seek to benefit or harm any lawful group, individual or organization. Our government does not take any official position on what people should believe or how they should vote, but it can and should protect them from fraud and deception perpetrated by foreign agents.

Unfettered speech about political issues lies at the heart of our Constitution. It is not the government's job to determine whether political opinions are right or wrong.

But that does not leave the government powerless to address the national security danger when a foreign government engages in covert information warfare. The First Amendment does not preclude us from publicly identifying and countering foreign government-sponsored propaganda.

It is not always easy to balance the many competing concerns in deciding whether, when, and how the government should disclose information about deceptive foreign activities relevant to elections. The challenge calls for the application of neutral principles.

The Cyber-Digital Task Force Report identifies factors the Department of Justice should consider in determining whether to disclose foreign influence operations. The policy reflects an effort to articulate neutral principles so that when the issue the government confronted in 2016 arises again – as it surely will – there will be a framework to address it.

Meanwhile, the FBI's operational Foreign Influence Task Force coordinates investigations of foreign influence campaigns. That task force integrates the FBI's cyber, counterintelligence, counterterrorism, and criminal law enforcement resources to ensure that we understand threats and respond appropriately. The FBI task force works with other federal agencies, state and local authorities, international partners, and the private sector.

Before I conclude, I want to emphasize that covert propaganda disseminated by foreign adversaries is fundamentally different from domestic partisan wrangling. As Senator Margaret Chase Smith proclaimed in her 1950 declaration of conscience, we must address foreign national security threats "patriotically as Americans," and not "politically as Republicans and Democrats."

President Reagan's Under Secretary of State, Lawrence Eagleburger, wrote about Soviet active measures in 1983. He said that "it is as unwise to ignore the threat as it is to become obsessed with the myth of a super Soviet conspiracy manipulating our essential political processes." He maintained that free societies must expose disinformation on a "persistent and continuing" basis.

Over the past year, Congress passed three statutes encouraging the Executive Branch to investigate, expose, and counter malign foreign influence operations. Publicly exposing such activities has long been a feature of U.S. law. The Foreign Agents Registration Act, which Congress enacted in 1938 to deter Nazi propagandists, mandates that the American public know when foreign governments seek to influence them.

Knowledge is power. In 1910, Theodore Roosevelt delivered a timeless speech about the duties of citizenship. It is best known for the remark that "it is not the critic who counts." But Roosevelt's most insightful observation is that the success or failure of a republic depends on the character of the average citizen. It is up to individual citizens to consider the source and evaluate the credibility of information when they decide what to believe.

Heated debates and passionate disagreements about public policy and political leadership are essential to democracy. We resolve those disagreements at the ballot box, and then we keep moving forward to future elections that reflect the will of citizens. Foreign governments should not be secret participants, covertly spreading propaganda and fanning the flames of division.

The government plays a central role in combating malign foreign influence and other cyber threats. The Attorney General's Cyber-Digital Task Force report demonstrates that the Department of Justice is doing its part to faithfully execute our oath to preserve, protect, and defend America.

I regret that my time today is insufficient to describe the report in greater detail. It is available on the Department of Justice website. I hope you read it and find it a useful contribution to public discussion about one of the most momentous issues of our time.

In brief, the report explains that we must continually adapt criminal justice and intelligence tools to combat hackers and other cybercriminals. Traditional criminal justice is most often characterized by police chasing criminals and eyewitnesses pointing out perpetrators in courtrooms. Cybercrime requires additional tools and techniques.

We limit cybercrime damage by seizing or disabling servers, domain names, and other infrastructure that criminals use to facilitate attacks. We shut down the dark markets where criminals buy and sell stolen information. We restore control of compromised computers. We share information gathered during our investigations to help potential victims protect themselves. We seek restitution for victims. We pursue attribution and accountability for perpetrators. And we expose governments that defraud and deceive our citizens.

The Task Force report is just one aspect of our efforts. It is a detailed snapshot of how the Department of Justice assesses and addresses current cyber threats. The work continues, and not just within our Department.

Our government is doing more now than ever to combat malign foreign influence and other cyber threats. Trump Administration agency appointees and White House officials work with career professionals every day to prevent cybercrime and protect elections.

Our adversaries will never relent in their efforts to undermine America, so we must remain eternally vigilant in the defense of liberty, and the pursuit of justice. And we must approach each new threat united in our commitment to the principle reflected in the motto adopted at the founding of our Republic: e pluribus unum.

Thank you.

II. Statutes and Executive Orders

THE CONSTITUTION OF THE UNITED STATES OF AMERICA

Preamble

We the People of the United States, in Order to form a more perfect Union, establish Justice, insure domestic Tranquility, provide for the common defence, promote the general Welfare, and secure the Blessings of Liberty to ourselves and our Posterity, do ordain and establish this Constitution for the United States of America.

Article 1.

Section 1

All legislative Powers herein granted shall be vested in a Congress of the United States, which shall consist of a Senate and House of Representatives.

Section 2

The House of Representatives shall be composed of Members chosen every second Year by the People of the several States, and the Electors in each State shall have the Qualifications requisite for Electors of the most numerous Branch of the State Legislature.

No Person shall be a Representative who shall not have attained to the Age of twenty five Years, and been seven Years a Citizen of the United States, and who shall not, when elected, be an Inhabitant of that State in which he shall be chosen.

Representatives and direct Taxes shall be apportioned among the several States which may be included within this Union, according to their respective Numbers, which shall be determined by adding to the whole Number of free Persons, including those bound to Service for a Term of Years, and excluding Indians not taxed, three fifths of all other Persons.

The actual Enumeration shall be made within three Years after the first Meeting of the Congress of the United States, and within every subsequent Term of ten Years, in such Manner as they shall by Law direct. The Number of Representatives shall not exceed one for every thirty Thousand, but each State shall have at Least one Representative; and until such enumeration shall be made, the State of New Hampshire shall be entitled to choose three, Massachusetts eight, Rhode Island and Providence Plantations one, Connecticut five, New York six, New Jersey four, Pennsylvania eight, Delaware one, Maryland six, Virginia ten, North Carolina five, South Carolina five and Georgia three.

When vacancies happen in the Representation from any State, the Executive Authority thereof shall issue Writs of Election to fill such Vacancies.

The House of Representatives shall choose their Speaker and other Officers; and shall have the sole Power of Impeachment.

Section 3

The Senate of the United States shall be composed of two Senators from each State, chosen by the Legislature thereof, for six Years; and each Senator shall have one Vote.

Immediately after they shall be assembled in Consequence of the first Election, they shall be divided as equally as may be into three Classes. The Seats of the Senators of the first Class shall be vacated at the Expiration of the second Year, of the second Class at the Expiration of the fourth Year, and of the third Class at the Expiration of the sixth Year, so that one third may be chosen every second Year; and if Vacancies happen by Resignation, or otherwise, during the Recess of the Legislature of any State, the Executive thereof may make temporary Appointments until the next Meeting of the Legislature, which shall then fill such Vacancies.

No person shall be a Senator who shall not have attained to the Age of thirty Years, and been nine Years a Citizen of the United States, and who shall not, when elected, be an Inhabitant of that State for which he shall be chosen.

The Vice President of the United States shall be President of the Senate, but shall have no Vote, unless they be equally divided.

The Senate shall choose their other Officers, and also a President pro tempore, in the absence of the Vice President, or when he shall exercise the Office of President of the United States.

The Senate shall have the sole Power to try all Impeachments. When sitting for that Purpose, they shall be on Oath or Affirmation. When the President of the United States is tried, the Chief Justice shall preside: And no Person shall be convicted without the Concurrence of two thirds of the Members present.

Judgment in Cases of Impeachment shall not extend further than to removal from Office, and disqualification to hold and enjoy any Office of honor, Trust or Profit under the United States: but the Party convicted shall nevertheless be liable and subject to Indictment, Trial, Judgment and Punishment, according to Law.

Section 4

The Times, Places and Manner of holding Elections for Senators and Representatives, shall be prescribed in each State by the Legislature thereof; but the Congress may at any time by Law make or alter such Regulations, except as to the Place of Choosing Senators.

The Congress shall assemble at least once in every Year, and such Meeting shall be on the first Monday in December, unless they shall by Law appoint a different Day.

Section 5

Each House shall be the Judge of the Elections, Returns and Qualifications of its own Members, and a Majority of each shall constitute a Quorum to do Business; but a smaller number may adjourn from day to day, and may be authorized to compel the Attendance of absent Members, in such Manner, and under such Penalties as each House may provide.

Each House may determine the Rules of its Proceedings, punish its Members for disorderly Behavior, and, with the Concurrence of two-thirds, expel a Member.

Each House shall keep a Journal of its Proceedings, and from time to time publish the same, excepting such Parts as may in their Judgment require Secrecy; and the Yeas and Nays of the Members of either House on any question shall, at the Desire of one fifth of those Present, be entered on the Journal.

Neither House, during the Session of Congress, shall, without the Consent of the other, adjourn for more than three days, nor to any other Place than that in which the two Houses shall be sitting.

Section 6
The Senators and Representatives shall receive a Compensation for their Services, to be ascertained by Law, and paid out of the Treasury of the United States. They shall in all Cases, except Treason, Felony and Breach of the Peace, be privileged from Arrest during their Attendance at the Session of their respective Houses, and in going to and returning from the same; and for any Speech or Debate in either House, they shall not be questioned in any other Place.

No Senator or Representative shall, during the Time for which he was elected, be appointed to any civil Office under the Authority of the United States which shall have been created, or the Emoluments whereof shall have been increased during such time; and no Person holding any Office under the United States, shall be a Member of either House during his Continuance in Office.

Section 7
All bills for raising Revenue shall originate in the House of Representatives; but the Senate may propose or concur with Amendments as on other Bills.

Every Bill which shall have passed the House of Representatives and the Senate, shall, before it become a Law, be presented to the President of the United States; If he approve he shall sign it, but if not he shall return it, with his Objections to that House in which it shall have originated, who shall enter the Objections at large on their Journal, and proceed to reconsider it. If after such Reconsideration two thirds of that House shall agree to pass the Bill, it shall be sent, together with the Objections, to the other House, by which it shall likewise be reconsidered, and if approved by two thirds of that House, it shall become a Law. But in all such Cases the Votes of both Houses shall be determined by Yeas and Nays, and the Names of the Persons voting for and against the Bill shall be entered on the Journal of each House respectively. If any Bill shall not be returned by the President within ten Days (Sundays excepted) after it shall have been presented to him, the Same shall be a Law, in like Manner as if he had signed it, unless the Congress by their Adjournment prevent its Return, in which Case it shall not be a Law.

Every Order, Resolution, or Vote to which the Concurrence of the Senate and House of Representatives may be necessary (except on a question of Adjournment) shall be presented to the President of the United States; and before the Same shall take Effect, shall be approved by him, or being disapproved by him, shall be repassed by two thirds of the Senate and House of Representatives, according to the Rules and Limitations prescribed in the Case of a Bill.

Section 8
The Congress shall have Power To lay and collect Taxes, Duties, Imposts and Excises, to pay the Debts and provide for the common Defence and general Welfare of the United States; but all Duties, Imposts and Excises shall be uniform throughout the United States;

> To borrow money on the credit of the United States;

> To regulate Commerce with foreign Nations, and among the several States, and with the Indian Tribes;

> To establish an uniform Rule of Naturalization, and uniform Laws on the subject of Bankruptcies throughout the United States;

To coin Money, regulate the Value thereof, and of foreign Coin, and fix the Standard of Weights and Measures;

To provide for the Punishment of counterfeiting the Securities and current Coin of the United States;

To establish Post Offices and Post Roads;

To promote the Progress of Science and useful Arts, by securing for limited Times to Authors and Inventors the exclusive Right to their respective Writings and Discoveries;

To constitute Tribunals inferior to the supreme Court;

To define and punish Piracies and Felonies committed on the high Seas, and Offenses against the Law of Nations;

To declare War, grant Letters of Marque and Reprisal, and make Rules concerning Captures on Land and Water;

To raise and support Armies, but no Appropriation of Money to that Use shall be for a longer Term than two Years;

To provide and maintain a Navy;

To make Rules for the Government and Regulation of the land and naval Forces;

To provide for calling forth the Militia to execute the Laws of the Union, suppress Insurrections and repel Invasions;

To provide for organizing, arming, and disciplining the Militia, and for governing such Part of them as may be employed in the Service of the United States, reserving to the States respectively, the Appointment of the Officers, and the Authority of training the Militia according to the discipline prescribed by Congress;

To exercise exclusive Legislation in all Cases whatsoever, over such District (not exceeding ten Miles square) as may, by Cession of particular States, and the acceptance of Congress, become the Seat of the Government of the United States, and to exercise like Authority over all Places purchased by the Consent of the Legislature of the State in which the Same shall be, for the Erection of Forts, Magazines, Arsenals, dock-Yards, and other needful Buildings; And

To make all Laws which shall be necessary and proper for carrying into Execution the foregoing Powers, and all other Powers vested by this Constitution in the Government of the United States, or in any Department or Officer thereof.

Section 9

The Migration or Importation of such Persons as any of the States now existing shall think proper to admit, shall not be prohibited by the Congress prior to the Year one thousand eight hundred and eight, but a tax or duty may be imposed on such Importation, not exceeding ten dollars for each Person.

The privilege of the Writ of Habeas Corpus shall not be suspended, unless when in Cases of Rebellion or Invasion the public Safety may require it.

No Bill of Attainder or ex post facto Law shall be passed.

No capitation, or other direct, Tax shall be laid, unless in Proportion to the Census or Enumeration herein before directed to be taken.

No Tax or Duty shall be laid on Articles exported from any State.

No Preference shall be given by any Regulation of Commerce or Revenue to the Ports of one State over those of another: nor shall Vessels bound to, or from, one State, be obliged to enter, clear, or pay Duties in another.

No Money shall be drawn from the Treasury, but in Consequence of Appropriations made by Law; and a regular Statement and Account of the Receipts and Expenditures of all public Money shall be published from time to time.

No Title of Nobility shall be granted by the United States: And no Person holding any Office of Profit or Trust under them, shall, without the Consent of the Congress, accept of any present, Emolument, Office, or Title, of any kind whatever, from any King, Prince or foreign State.

Section 10

No State shall enter into any Treaty, Alliance, or Confederation; grant Letters of Marque and Reprisal; coin Money; emit Bills of Credit; make any Thing but gold and silver Coin a Tender in Payment of Debts; pass any Bill of Attainder, ex post facto Law, or Law impairing the Obligation of Contracts, or grant any Title of Nobility.

No State shall, without the Consent of the Congress, lay any Imposts or Duties on Imports or Exports, except what may be absolutely necessary for executing its inspection Laws: and the net Produce of all Duties and Imposts, laid by any State on Imports or Exports, shall be for the Use of the Treasury of the United States; and all such Laws shall be subject to the Revision and Control of the Congress.

No State shall, without the Consent of Congress, lay any duty of Tonnage, keep Troops, or Ships of War in time of Peace, enter into any Agreement or Compact with another State, or with a foreign Power, or engage in War, unless actually invaded, or in such imminent Danger as will not admit of delay.

Article 2.

Section 1

The executive Power shall be vested in a President of the United States of America. He shall hold his Office during the Term of four Years, and, together with the Vice-President chosen for the same Term, be elected, as follows:

Each State shall appoint, in such Manner as the Legislature thereof may direct, a Number of Electors, equal to the whole Number of Senators and Representatives to which the State may be entitled in the Congress: but no Senator or Representative, or Person holding an Office of Trust or Profit under the United States, shall be appointed an Elector.

The Electors shall meet in their respective States, and vote by Ballot for two persons, of whom one at least shall not lie an Inhabitant of the same State with themselves. And they shall make a List of all the Persons voted for, and of the Number of Votes for each; which List they shall sign and certify, and transmit sealed to the Seat of the Government of the United States, directed to the President of the Senate. The President of the Senate shall, in the Presence of the Senate and House of Representatives, open all the Certificates, and the Votes shall then be counted. The Person having the greatest Number of Votes shall be the President, if such Number be a Majority of the whole Number of Electors appointed; and if there be more than one who have such Majority, and have an equal Number of Votes, then the House of Representatives shall immediately choose by Ballot one of them for President; and if no Person have a Majority, then from the five highest on the List the said House shall in like Manner choose the President. But in choosing the President, the Votes shall be taken by States, the Representation from each State having one Vote; a quorum for this Purpose shall consist of a Member or Members from two-thirds of the States, and a Majority of all the States shall be necessary to a Choice. In every Case, after the Choice of the President, the Person having the greatest Number of Votes of the Electors shall be the Vice President. But if there should remain two or more who have equal Votes, the Senate shall choose from them by Ballot the Vice-President.

The Congress may determine the Time of choosing the Electors, and the Day on which they shall give their Votes; which Day shall be the same throughout the United States.

No person except a natural born Citizen, or a Citizen of the United States, at the time of the Adoption of this Constitution, shall be eligible to the Office of President; neither shall any Person be eligible to that Office who shall not have attained to the Age of thirty-five Years, and been fourteen Years a Resident within the United States.

In Case of the Removal of the President from Office, or of his Death, Resignation, or Inability to discharge the Powers and Duties of the said Office, the same shall devolve on the Vice President, and the Congress may by Law provide for the Case of Removal, Death, Resignation or Inability, both of the President and Vice President, declaring what Officer shall then act as President, and such Officer shall act accordingly, until the Disability be removed, or a President shall be elected.

The President shall, at stated Times, receive for his Services, a Compensation, which shall neither be increased nor diminished during the Period for which he shall have been elected, and he shall not receive within that Period any other Emolument from the United States, or any of them.

Before he enter on the Execution of his Office, he shall take the following Oath or Affirmation:

> "I do solemnly swear (or affirm) that I will faithfully execute the Office of President of the United States, and will to the best of my Ability, preserve, protect and defend the Constitution of the United States."

Section 2

The President shall be Commander in Chief of the Army and Navy of the United States, and of the Militia of the several States, when called into the actual Service of the United States; he may require the Opinion, in writing, of the principal Officer in each of the executive Departments, upon any subject relating to the Duties of their respective Offices, and he shall have Power to Grant Reprieves and Pardons for Offenses against the United States, except in Cases of Impeachment.

He shall have Power, by and with the Advice and Consent of the Senate, to make Treaties, provided two thirds of the Senators present concur; and he shall nominate, and by and with the Advice and Consent of the Senate, shall appoint Ambassadors, other public Ministers and Consuls, Judges of the supreme Court, and all other Officers of the United States, whose Appointments are not herein otherwise provided for, and which shall be established by Law: but the Congress may by Law vest the Appointment of such inferior Officers, as they think proper, in the President alone, in the Courts of Law, or in the Heads of Departments.

The President shall have Power to fill up all Vacancies that may happen during the Recess of the Senate, by granting Commissions which shall expire at the End of their next Session.

Section 3

He shall from time to time give to the Congress Information of the State of the Union, and recommend to their Consideration such Measures as he shall judge necessary and expedient; he may, on extraordinary Occasions, convene both Houses, or either of them, and in Case of Disagreement between them, with Respect to the Time of Adjournment, he may adjourn them to such Time as he shall think proper; he shall receive Ambassadors and other public Ministers; he shall take Care that the Laws be faithfully executed, and shall Commission all the Officers of the United States.

Section 4

The President, Vice President and all civil Officers of the United States, shall be removed from Office on Impeachment for, and Conviction of, Treason, Bribery, or other high Crimes and Misdemeanors.

Article 3.

Section 1

The judicial Power of the United States, shall be vested in one supreme Court, and in such inferior Courts as the Congress may from time to time ordain and establish. The Judges, both of the supreme and inferior Courts, shall hold their Offices during good Behavior, and shall, at stated Times, receive for their Services a Compensation which shall not be diminished during their Continuance in Office.

Section 2

The judicial Power shall extend to all Cases, in Law and Equity, arising under this Constitution, the Laws of the United States, and Treaties made, or which shall be made, under their Authority; to all Cases affecting Ambassadors, other public Ministers and Consuls; to all Cases of admiralty and maritime Jurisdiction; to Controversies to which the United States shall be a Party; to Controversies between two or more States; between a State and Citizens of another State; between Citizens of different States; between Citizens of the same State claiming Lands under Grants of different States, and between a State, or the Citizens thereof, and foreign States, Citizens or Subjects.

In all Cases affecting Ambassadors, other public Ministers and Consuls, and those in which a State shall be Party, the supreme Court shall have original Jurisdiction. In all the other Cases before mentioned, the supreme Court shall have appellate Jurisdiction, both as to Law and Fact, with such Exceptions, and under such Regulations as the Congress shall make.

The Trial of all Crimes, except in Cases of Impeachment, shall be by Jury; and such Trial shall be held in the State where the said Crimes shall have been committed; but when not committed within any State, the Trial shall be at such Place or Places as the Congress may by Law have directed.

Section 3

Treason against the United States, shall consist only in levying War against them, or in adhering to their Enemies, giving them Aid and Comfort. No Person shall be convicted of Treason unless on the Testimony of two Witnesses to the same overt Act, or on Confession in open Court.

The Congress shall have power to declare the Punishment of Treason, but no Attainder of Treason shall work Corruption of Blood, or Forfeiture except during the Life of the Person attainted.

Article 4.

Section 1

Full Faith and Credit shall be given in each State to the public Acts, Records, and judicial Proceedings of every other State. And the Congress may by general Laws prescribe the Manner in which such Acts, Records and Proceedings shall be proved, and the Effect thereof.

Section 2

The Citizens of each State shall be entitled to all Privileges and Immunities of Citizens in the several States.

A Person charged in any State with Treason, Felony, or other Crime, who shall flee from Justice, and be found in another State, shall on demand of the executive Authority of the State from which he fled, be delivered up, to be removed to the State having Jurisdiction of the Crime.

No Person held to Service or Labour in one State, under the Laws thereof, escaping into another, shall, in Consequence of any Law or Regulation therein, be discharged from such Service or Labour, But shall be delivered up on Claim of the Party to whom such Service or Labour may be due.

Section 3

New States may be admitted by the Congress into this Union; but no new States shall be formed or erected within the Jurisdiction of any other State; nor any State be formed by the Junction of two or more States, or parts of States, without the Consent of the Legislatures of the States concerned as well as of the Congress.

The Congress shall have Power to dispose of and make all needful Rules and Regulations respecting the Territory or other Property belonging to the United States; and nothing in this Constitution shall be so construed as to Prejudice any Claims of the United States, or of any particular State.

Section 4

The United States shall guarantee to every State in this Union a Republican Form of Government, and shall protect each of them against Invasion; and on Application of the Legislature, or of the Executive (when the Legislature cannot be convened) against domestic Violence.

Article 5.

The Congress, whenever two thirds of both Houses shall deem it necessary, shall propose Amendments to this Constitution, or, on the Application of the Legislatures of two thirds of the several States, shall call a Convention for proposing Amendments, which, in either Case, shall be valid to all Intents and Purposes, as part of this Constitution, when ratified by the Legislatures of three fourths of the several States, or by Conventions in three fourths thereof, as the one or the other Mode of Ratification may be proposed by the Congress; Provided that no Amendment which may be made prior to the Year One thousand eight hundred and eight shall in any Manner affect the first and fourth Clauses in the Ninth Section of the first Article; and that no State, without its Consent, shall be deprived of its equal Suffrage in the Senate.

Article 6.

All Debts contracted and Engagements entered into, before the Adoption of this Constitution, shall be as valid against the United States under this Constitution, as under the Confederation.

This Constitution, and the Laws of the United States which shall be made in Pursuance thereof; and all Treaties made, or which shall be made, under the Authority of the United States, shall be the supreme Law of the Land; and the Judges in every State shall be bound thereby, any Thing in the Constitution or Laws of any State to the Contrary notwithstanding.

The Senators and Representatives before mentioned, and the Members of the several State Legislatures, and all executive and judicial Officers, both of the United States and of the several States, shall be bound by Oath or Affirmation, to support this Constitution; but no religious Test shall ever be required as a Qualification to any Office or public Trust under the United States.

Article 7.

The Ratification of the Conventions of nine States, shall be sufficient for the Establishment of this Constitution between the States so ratifying the Same.

Done in Convention by the Unanimous Consent of the States present the Seventeenth Day of September in the Year of our Lord one thousand seven hundred and Eighty seven and of the Independence of the United States of America the Twelfth. In Witness whereof We have hereunto subscribed our Names.

George Washington—President and deputy from Virginia

New Hampshire—John Langdon, Nicholas Gilman

Massachusetts—Nathaniel Gorham, Rufus King

Connecticut—William Samuel Johnson, Roger Sherman

New York—Alexander Hamilton

New Jersey—William Livingston, David Brearley, William Paterson, Jonathan Dayton

Pennsylvania—Benjamin Franklin, Thomas Mifflin, Robert Morris, George Clymer, Thomas Fitzsimons, Jared Ingersoll, James Wilson, Gouvernour Morris

Delaware—George Read, Gunning Bedford Jr., John Dickinson, Richard Bassett, Jacob Broom

Maryland—James McHenry, Daniel of St Thomas Jenifer, Daniel Carroll

Virginia—John Blair, James Madison Jr.

North Carolina—William Blount, Richard Dobbs Spaight, Hugh Williamson

South Carolina—John Rutledge, Charles Cotesworth Pinckney, Charles Pinckney, Pierce Butler

Georgia—William Few, Abraham Baldwin

Attest: William Jackson, Secretary

Amendment 1

Congress shall make no law respecting an establishment of religion, or prohibiting the free exercise thereof; or abridging the freedom of speech, or of the press; or the right of the people peaceably to assemble, and to petition the Government for a redress of grievances.

Amendment 2

A well regulated Militia, being necessary to the security of a free State, the right of the people to keep and bear Arms, shall not be infringed.

Amendment 3

No Soldier shall, in time of peace be quartered in any house, without the consent of the Owner, nor in time of war, but in a manner to be prescribed by law.

Amendment 4

The right of the people to be secure in their persons, houses, papers, and effects, against unreasonable searches and seizures, shall not be violated, and no Warrants shall issue, but upon probable cause, supported by Oath or affirmation, and particularly describing the place to be searched, and the persons or things to be seized.

Amendment 5

No person shall be held to answer for a capital, or otherwise infamous crime, unless on a presentment or indictment of a Grand Jury, except in cases arising in the land or naval forces, or in the Militia, when in actual service in time of War or public danger; nor shall any person be subject for the same offense to be twice put in jeopardy of life or limb; nor shall be compelled in any criminal case to be a witness against himself, nor be deprived of life, liberty, or property, without due process of law; nor shall private property be taken for public use, without just compensation.

Amendment 6

In all criminal prosecutions, the accused shall enjoy the right to a speedy and public trial, by an impartial jury of the State and district wherein the crime shall have been committed, which district shall have been previously ascertained by law, and to be informed of the nature and cause of the accusation; to be confronted with the witnesses against him; to have compulsory process for obtaining witnesses in his favor, and to have the Assistance of Counsel for his defence.

Amendment 7

In Suits at common law, where the value in controversy shall exceed twenty dollars, the right of trial by jury shall be preserved, and no fact tried by a jury, shall be otherwise re-examined in any Court of the United States, than according to the rules of the common law.

Amendment 8

Excessive bail shall not be required, nor excessive fines imposed, nor cruel and unusual punishments inflicted.

Amendment 9

The enumeration in the Constitution, of certain rights, shall not be construed to deny or disparage others retained by the people.

Amendment 10

The powers not delegated to the United States by the Constitution, nor prohibited by it to the States, are reserved to the States respectively, or to the people.

Amendment 11

The Judicial power of the United States shall not be construed to extend to any suit in law or equity, commenced or prosecuted against one of the United States by Citizens of another State, or by Citizens or Subjects of any Foreign State.

Amendment 12

The Electors shall meet in their respective states, and vote by ballot for President and Vice-President, one of whom, at least, shall not be an inhabitant of the same state with themselves; they shall name in their ballots the person voted for as President, and in distinct ballots the person voted for as Vice-President, and they shall make distinct lists of all persons voted for as President, and of all persons voted for as Vice-President and of the number of votes for each, which lists they shall sign and certify, and transmit sealed to the seat of the government of the United States, directed to the President of the Senate;

The President of the Senate shall, in the presence of the Senate and House of Representatives, open all the certificates and the votes shall then be counted;

The person having the greatest Number of votes for President, shall be the President, if such number be a majority of the whole number of Electors appointed; and if no person have such majority, then from the persons having the highest numbers not exceeding three on the list of those voted for as President, the House of Representatives shall choose immediately, by ballot, the President. But in choosing the President, the votes shall be taken by states, the representation from each state having one vote; a quorum for this purpose shall consist of a member or members from two-thirds of the states, and a majority of all the states shall be necessary to a choice. And if the House of Representatives shall not choose a President whenever the right of choice shall devolve upon them, before the fourth day of March next following, then the Vice-President shall act as President, as in the case of the death or other constitutional disability of the President.

The person having the greatest number of votes as Vice-President, shall be the Vice-President, if such number be a majority of the whole number of Electors appointed, and if no person have a majority, then from the two highest numbers on the list, the Senate shall choose the Vice-President; a quorum for the purpose shall consist of two-thirds of the whole number of Senators, and a majority of the whole number shall be necessary to a choice. But no person constitutionally ineligible to the office of President shall be eligible to that of Vice-President of the United States.

Amendment 13

1. Neither slavery nor involuntary servitude, except as a punishment for crime whereof the party shall have been duly convicted, shall exist within the United States, or any place subject to their jurisdiction.
2. Congress shall have power to enforce this article by appropriate legislation.

Amendment 14

1. All persons born or naturalized in the United States, and subject to the jurisdiction thereof, are citizens of the United States and of the State wherein they reside. No State shall make or enforce any law which shall abridge the privileges or immunities of citizens of the United States; nor shall any State deprive any person of life, liberty, or property, without due process of law; nor deny to any person within its jurisdiction the equal protection of the laws.
2. Representatives shall be apportioned among the several States according to their respective numbers, counting the whole number of persons in each State, excluding Indians not taxed. But when the right to vote at any election for the choice of electors for President and Vice-President of the United States, Representatives in Congress, the Executive and Judicial officers of a State, or the members of the Legislature thereof, is denied to any of the male inhabitants of such State, being twenty-one years of age, and citizens of the United States, or in any way abridged, except for participation in rebellion, or other crime, the basis of representation therein shall be reduced in the proportion which the number of such male citizens shall bear to the whole number of male citizens twenty-one years of age in such State.
3. No person shall be a Senator or Representative in Congress, or elector of President and Vice-President, or hold any office, civil or military, under the United States, or under any

State, who, having previously taken an oath, as a member of Congress, or as an officer of the United States, or as a member of any State legislature, or as an executive or judicial officer of any State, to support the Constitution of the United States, shall have engaged in insurrection or rebellion against the same, or given aid or comfort to the enemies thereof. But Congress may by a vote of two-thirds of each House, remove such disability.

4. The validity of the public debt of the United States, authorized by law, including debts incurred for payment of pensions and bounties for services in suppressing insurrection or rebellion, shall not be questioned. But neither the United States nor any State shall assume or pay any debt or obligation incurred in aid of insurrection or rebellion against the United States, or any claim for the loss or emancipation of any slave; but all such debts, obligations and claims shall be held illegal and void.

5. The Congress shall have power to enforce, by appropriate legislation, the provisions of this article.

Amendment 15

1. The right of citizens of the United States to vote shall not be denied or abridged by the United States or by any State on account of race, color, or previous condition of servitude.

2. The Congress shall have power to enforce this article by appropriate legislation.

Amendment 16

The Congress shall have power to lay and collect taxes on incomes, from whatever source derived, without apportionment among the several States, and without regard to any census or enumeration.

Amendment 17

The Senate of the United States shall be composed of two Senators from each State, elected by the people thereof, for six years; and each Senator shall have one vote. The electors in each State shall have the qualifications requisite for electors of the most numerous branch of the State legislatures.

When vacancies happen in the representation of any State in the Senate, the executive authority of such State shall issue writs of election to fill such vacancies: Provided, That the legislature of any State may empower the executive thereof to make temporary appointments until the people fill the vacancies by election as the legislature may direct.

This amendment shall not be so construed as to affect the election or term of any Senator chosen before it becomes valid as part of the Constitution.

Amendment 18

1. After one year from the ratification of this article the manufacture, sale, or transportation of intoxicating liquors within, the importation thereof into, or the exportation thereof from the United States and all territory subject to the jurisdiction thereof for beverage purposes is hereby prohibited.

2. The Congress and the several States shall have concurrent power to enforce this article by appropriate legislation.

3. This article shall be inoperative unless it shall have been ratified as an amendment to the Constitution by the legislatures of the several States, as provided in the Constitution, within seven years from the date of the submission hereof to the States by the Congress.

Amendment 19

The right of citizens of the United States to vote shall not be denied or abridged by the United States or by any State on account of sex.

Congress shall have power to enforce this article by appropriate legislation.

Amendment 20

1. The terms of the President and Vice President shall end at noon on the 20th day of January, and the terms of Senators and Representatives at noon on the 3d day of January, of the years in which such terms would have ended if this article had not been ratified; and the terms of their successors shall then begin.
2. The Congress shall assemble at least once in every year, and such meeting shall begin at noon on the 3d day of January, unless they shall by law appoint a different day.
3. If, at the time fixed for the beginning of the term of the President, the President elect shall have died, the Vice President elect shall become President. If a President shall not have been chosen before the time fixed for the beginning of his term, or if the President elect shall have failed to qualify, then the Vice President elect shall act as President until a President shall have qualified; and the Congress may by law provide for the case wherein neither a President elect nor a Vice President elect shall have qualified, declaring who shall then act as President, or the manner in which one who is to act shall be selected, and such person shall act accordingly until a President or Vice President shall have qualified.
4. The Congress may by law provide for the case of the death of any of the persons from whom the House of Representatives may choose a President whenever the right of choice shall have devolved upon them, and for the case of the death of any of the persons from whom the Senate may choose a Vice President whenever the right of choice shall have devolved upon them.
5. Sections 1 and 2 shall take effect on the 15th day of October following the ratification of this article.
6. This article shall be inoperative unless it shall have been ratified as an amendment to the Constitution by the legislatures of three-fourths of the several States within seven years from the date of its submission.

Amendment 21

1. The eighteenth article of amendment to the Constitution of the United States is hereby repealed.
2. The transportation or importation into any State, Territory, or possession of the United States for delivery or use therein of intoxicating liquors, in violation of the laws thereof, is hereby prohibited.
3. The article shall be inoperative unless it shall have been ratified as an amendment to the Constitution by conventions in the several States, as provided in the Constitution, within seven years from the date of the submission hereof to the States by the Congress.

Amendment 22

1. No person shall be elected to the office of the President more than twice, and no person who has held the office of President, or acted as President, for more than two years of a term to which some other person was elected President shall be elected to the office of the President more than once. But this Article shall not apply to any person holding the office of President, when this Article was proposed by the Congress, and shall not prevent any person who may be holding the office of President, or acting as President, during the term

within which this Article becomes operative from holding the office of President or acting as President during the remainder of such term.

2. This article shall be inoperative unless it shall have been ratified as an amendment to the Constitution by the legislatures of three-fourths of the several States within seven years from the date of its submission to the States by the Congress.

Amendment 23

1. The District constituting the seat of Government of the United States shall appoint in such manner as the Congress may direct: A number of electors of President and Vice President equal to the whole number of Senators and Representatives in Congress to which the District would be entitled if it were a State, but in no event more than the least populous State; they shall be in addition to those appointed by the States, but they shall be considered, for the purposes of the election of President and Vice President, to be electors appointed by a State; and they shall meet in the District and perform such duties as provided by the twelfth article of amendment.

2. The Congress shall have power to enforce this article by appropriate legislation.

Amendment 24

1. The right of citizens of the United States to vote in any primary or other election for President or Vice President, for electors for President or Vice President, or for Senator or Representative in Congress, shall not be denied or abridged by the United States or any State by reason of failure to pay any poll tax or other tax.

2. The Congress shall have power to enforce this article by appropriate legislation.

Amendment 25

1. In case of the removal of the President from office or of his death or resignation, the Vice President shall become President.

2. Whenever there is a vacancy in the office of the Vice President, the President shall nominate a Vice President who shall take office upon confirmation by a majority vote of both Houses of Congress.

3. Whenever the President transmits to the President pro tempore of the Senate and the Speaker of the House of Representatives his written declaration that he is unable to discharge the powers and duties of his office, and until he transmits to them a written declaration to the contrary, such powers and duties shall be discharged by the Vice President as Acting President.

4. Whenever the Vice President and a majority of either the principal officers of the executive departments or of such other body as Congress may by law provide, transmit to the President pro tempore of the Senate and the Speaker of the House of Representatives their written declaration that the President is unable to discharge the powers and duties of his office, the Vice President shall immediately assume the powers and duties of the office as Acting President.

Thereafter, when the President transmits to the President pro tempore of the Senate and the Speaker of the House of Representatives his written declaration that no inability exists, he shall resume the powers and duties of his office unless the Vice President and a majority of either the principal officers of the executive department or of such other body as Congress may by law provide, transmit within four days to the President pro tempore of the Senate and the Speaker of the House of Representatives their written declaration that the President is unable to discharge the powers and duties of his office. Thereupon Congress shall decide the issue, assembling within forty eight hours for that purpose if not in session. If the Congress, within twenty one days after receipt of the latter written declaration, or, if Congress is not in session, within twenty one days after Congress is required to assemble, determines by two thirds vote of both Houses that the President is unable to discharge the powers and duties of his office, the Vice President shall continue to discharge the same as Acting President; otherwise, the President shall resume the powers and duties of his office.

Amendment 26

1. The right of citizens of the United States, who are eighteen years of age or older, to vote shall not be denied or abridged by the United States or by any State on account of age.
2. The Congress shall have power to enforce this article by appropriate legislation.

Amendment 27

No law, varying the compensation for the services of the Senators and Representatives, shall take effect, until an election of Representatives shall have intervened.

FEDERAL STATUTES

National Security Act of 1947

(Chapter 343; 61 Stat. 496; approved July 26, 1947)
[As Amended Through Jan. 19, 2018]

> AN ACT To promote the national security by providing for a Secretary of Defense; for a National Military Establishment; for a Department of the Army, a Department of the Navy, and a Department of the Air Force; and for the coordination of the activities of the National Military Establishment with other departments and agencies of the Government concerned with the national security.
>
> *Be it enacted by the Senate and House of Representatives of the United States of America in Congress assembled,*

SHORT TITLE

That this Act may be cited as the "National Security Act of 1947".

TABLE OF CONTENTS

---

1. Item editorially inserted.

---

2.   This section was redesignated as section 108 by section 705(a)(2) of P.L. 102–496, but this entry in the table of contents was not repealed.

3.   The item for section 109 was repealed by section 347(i)(1)(A) of Public Law 111–259.

4.   Section repealed without amending table of contents

---

5.   Item editorially inserted.

DECLARATION OF POLICY

SEC. 2. [50 U.S.C. §401] In enacting this legislation, it is the intent of Congress to provide a comprehensive program for the future security of the United States; to provide for the establishment of integrated policies and procedures for the departments, agencies, and functions of the Government relating to the national security; to provide a Department of Defense, including the three military Departments of the Army, the Navy (including naval aviation and the United States Marine Corps), and the Air Force under the direction, authority, and control of the Secretary of Defense; to provide that each military department shall be separately organized under its own Secretary and shall function under the direction, authority, and control of the Secretary of Defense; to provide for their unified direction under civilian control of the Secretary of Defense but not to merge these departments or services; to provide for the establishment of unified or specified combatant commands, and a clear and direct line of command to such commands; to eliminate unnecessary duplication in the Department of Defense, and particularly in the field of research and engineering by vesting its overall direction and control in the Secretary of Defense; to provide more effective, efficient, and economical administration in the Department of Defense; to provide for the unified strategic direction of the combatant forces, for their operation under unified command, and for their integration into an efficient team of land, naval, and air forces but not to establish a single Chief of Staff over the armed forces nor an overall armed forces general staff.

DEFINITIONS

SEC. 3. [50 U.S.C. §401a] As used in this Act:

(1) The term "intelligence" includes foreign intelligence and counterintelligence.

(2) The term "foreign intelligence" means information relating to the capabilities, intentions, or activities of foreign governments or elements thereof, foreign organizations, or foreign persons, or international terrorist activities.

(3) The term "counterintelligence" means information gathered and activities conducted to protect against espionage, other intelligence activities, sabotage, or assassinations conducted by or on behalf of foreign governments or elements thereof, foreign organizations, or foreign persons, or international terrorist activities.

(4) The term "intelligence community" includes the following:

(A) The Office of the Director of National Intelligence.

(B) The Central Intelligence Agency.

(C) The National Security Agency.

(D) The Defense Intelligence Agency.

(E) The National Geospatial-Intelligence Agency.

(F) The National Reconnaissance Office.

(G) Other offices within the Department of Defense for the collection of specialized national intelligence through reconnaissance programs.

(H) The intelligence elements of the Army, the Navy, the Air Force, the Marine Corps, the Federal Bureau of Investigation, and the Department of Energy.

(I) The Bureau of Intelligence and Research of the Department of State.

(J) The Office of Intelligence and Analysis of the Department of the Treasury.

(K) The elements of the Department of Homeland Security concerned with the analysis of intelligence information, including the Office of Intelligence of the Coast Guard.

(L) Such other elements of any other department or agency as may be designated by the President, or designated jointly by the Director of National Intelligence and the head of the department or agency concerned, as an element of the intelligence community.

(5) The terms "national intelligence" and "intelligence related to national security" refer to all intelligence, regardless of the source from which derived and including information gathered within or outside the United States, that—

(A) pertains, as determined consistent with any guidance issued by the President, to more than one United States Government agency; and

(B) that involves—

(i) threats to the United States, its people, property, or interests;

(ii) the development, proliferation, or use of weapons of mass destruction; or

(iii) any other matter bearing on United States national or homeland security.

(6) The term "National Intelligence Program" refers to all programs, projects, and activities of the intelligence community, as well as any other programs of the intelligence community designated jointly by the Director of National Intelligence and the head of a United States department or agency or by the President. Such term does not include programs, projects, or activities of the

military departments to acquire intelligence solely for the planning and conduct of tactical military operations by United States Armed Forces.

(7) The term "congressional intelligence committees" means—

    (A) the Select Committee on Intelligence of the Senate; and

    (B) the Permanent Select Committee on Intelligence of the House of Representatives.

TITLE I—COORDINATION FOR NATIONAL SECURITY

NATIONAL SECURITY COUNCIL

SEC. 101. [50 U.S.C. §402]

(a) There is here established a council to be known as the National Security Council (thereinafter in this section referred to as the "Council"). The President of the United States shall preside over meetings of the Council: *Provided,* That in his absence he may designate a member of the Council to preside in his place. The function of the Council shall be to advise the President with respect to the integration of domestic, foreign, and military policies relating to the national security so as to enable the military services and the other departments and agencies of the Government to cooperate more effectively in matters involving the national security.

The Council shall be composed of[1]—

(1) the President;

(2) the Vice President;

(3) the Secretary of State;

(4) the Secretary of Defense;

(5) the Director for Mutual Security;

(6) the Chairman of the National Security Resources Board; and

(7) the Secretaries and Under Secretaries of other executive departments and of the military departments, the Chairman of the Munitions Board, and the Chairman of the Research and Development Board, when appointed by the President by and with the advice and consent of the Senate, to serve at his pleasure.

(b) In addition to performing such other functions as the President may direct, for the purpose of more effectively coordinating the policies and functions of the departments and agencies of the Government relating to the national security, it shall, subject to the direction of the President, be the duty of the Council—

(1) to assess and appraise the objectives, commitments, and risks of the United States in relation to our actual and potential military power, in the interest of national security, for the purpose of making recommendations to the President in connection therewith; and

(2) to consider policies on matters of common interest to the departments and agencies of the Government concerned with the national security, and to make recommendations to the President in connection therewith.

(c) The Council shall have a staff to be headed by a civilian executive secretary who shall be appointed by the President and who shall receive a compensation of $10,000 a year.[1] The executive secretary, subject to the direction of the Council, is hereby authorized, subject to the civil-

---

1.   The positions of Director for Mutual Security, Chairman of the National Security ResourcesBoard, Chairman of the Munitions Board, and Chairman of the Research and DevelopmentBoard have been abolished by various Reorganiztion Plans. The statutory members of the National Security Council are the President, Vice President, Secretary of State, and Secretary ofDefense.

1.   The specification of the salary of the head of the National Security Council staff is obsoleteand has been superseded.

service laws and the Classification Act of 1923, as amended,[2] to appoint and fix the compensation of such personnel as may be necessary to perform such duties as may be prescribed by the Council in connection with the performance of its functions.

(d) The Council shall, from time to time, make such recommendations, and such other reports to the President as it deems appropriate or as the President may require.

(e) The Chairman (or in his absence the Vice Chairman) of the Joint Chiefs of Staff may, in his role as principal military adviser to the National Security Council and subject to the direction of the President, attend and participate in meetings of the National Security Council.

(f) The Director of National Drug Control Policy may, in the role of the Director as principal adviser to the National Security Council on national drug control policy, and subject to the direction of the President, attend and participate in meetings of the National Security Council.

(g) The President shall establish within the National Security Council a board to be known as the "Board for Low Intensity Conflict". The principal function of the board shall be to coordinate the policies of the United States for low intensity conflict.

(h)(1) There is established within the National Security Council a committee to be known as the Committee on Foreign Intelligence (in this subsection referred to as the "Committee").

(2) The Committee shall be composed of the following:

(A) The Director of National Intelligence.

(B) The Secretary of State.

(C) The Secretary of Defense.

(D) The Assistant to the President for National Security Affairs, who shall serve as the chairperson of the Committee.

(E) Such other members as the President may designate.

(3) The function of the Committee shall be to assist the Council in its activities by—

(A) identifying the intelligence required to address the national security interests of the United States as specified by the President;

(B) establishing priorities (including funding priorities) among the programs, projects, and activities that address such interests and requirements; and

(C) establishing policies relating to the conduct of intelligence activities of the United States, including appropriate roles and missions for the elements of the intelligence community and appropriate targets of intelligence collection activities.

(4) In carrying out its function, the Committee shall—

(A) conduct an annual review of the national security interests of the United States;

(B) identify on an annual basis, and at such other times as the Council may require, the intelligence required to meet such interests and establish an order of priority for the collection and analysis of such intelligence; and

(C) conduct an annual review of the elements of the intelligence community in order to determine the success of such elements in collecting, analyzing, and disseminating the intelligence identified under subparagraph (B).

(5) The Committee shall submit each year to the Council and to the Director of National Intelligence a comprehensive report on its activities during the preceding year, including its activities under paragraphs (3) and (4).

(i)(1) There is established within the National Security Council a committee to be known as the Committee on Transnational Threats (in this subsection referred to as the "Committee").

---

2.   The Classification Act of 1923 was repealed by the Classification Act of 1949. The Classifica-tion Act of 1949 was repealed by the law enacting title 5, United States Code (Public Law 89–544, Sept. 6, 1966, 80 Stat. 378), and its provisions were codified as chapter 51 and chapter53 of title 5. Section 7(b) of that Act (80 Stat. 631) provided: "A reference to a law replacedby sections 1–6 of this Act, including a reference in a regulation, order, or other law, is deemedto refer to the corresponding provision enacted by this Act."

(2) The Committee shall include the following members:

(A) The Director of National Intelligence.

(B) The Secretary of State.

(C) The Secretary of Defense.

(D) The Attorney General.

(E) The Assistant to the President for National Security Affairs, who shall serve as the chairperson of the Committee.

(F) Such other members as the President may designate.

(3) The function of the Committee shall be to coordinate and direct the activities of the United States Government relating to combating transnational threats.

(4) In carrying out its function, the Committee shall—

(A) identify transnational threats;

(B) develop strategies to enable the United States Government to respond to transnational threats identified under subparagraph (A);

(C) monitor implementation of such strategies;

(D) make recommendations as to appropriate responses to specific transnational threats;

(E) assist in the resolution of operational and policy differences among Federal departments and agencies in their responses to transnational threats;

(F) develop policies and procedures to ensure the effective sharing of information about transnational threats among Federal departments and agencies, including law enforcement agencies and the elements of the intelligence community; and

(G) develop guidelines to enhance and improve the coordination of activities of Federal law enforcement agencies and elements of the intelligence community outside the United States with respect to transnational threats.

(5) For purposes of this subsection, the term "transnational threat" means the following:

(A) Any transnational activity (including international terrorism, narcotics trafficking, the proliferation of weapons of mass destruction and the delivery systems for such weapons, and organized crime) that threatens the national security of the United States.

(B) Any individual or group that engages in an activity referred to in subparagraph (A).

(j) The Director of National Intelligence (or, in the Director's absence, the Principal Deputy Director of National Intelligence) may, in the performance of the Director's duties under this Act and subject to the direction of the President, attend and participate in meetings of the National Security Council.

(k) It is the sense of the Congress that there should be within the staff of the National Security Council a Special Adviser to the President on International Religious Freedom, whose position should be comparable to that of a director within the Executive Office of the President. The Special Adviser should serve as a resource for executive branch officials, compiling and maintaining information on the facts and circumstances of violations of religious freedom (as defined in section 3 of the International Religious Freedom Act of 1998), and making policy recommendations. The Special Adviser should serve as liaison with the Ambassador at Large for International Religious Freedom, the United States Commission on International Religious Freedom, Congress and, as advisable, religious nongovernmental organizations.

(l) PARTICIPATION OF COORDINATOR FOR THE PREVENTION OF WEAPONS OF MASS DESTRUCTION PROLIFERATION AND TERRORISM.—The United States Coordinator for the Prevention of Weapons of Mass Destruction Proliferation and Terrorism (or, in the Coordinator's absence, the Deputy United States Coordinator) may, in the performance of the Coordinator's duty as principal advisor to the President on all matters relating to the prevention of weapons of mass destruction proliferation and terrorism, and, subject to the direction of the President, attend and participate in meetings of the National Security Council and the Homeland Security Council.

JOINT INTELLIGENCE COMMUNITY COUNCIL

SEC. 101A. [50 U.S.C. §402-1]

(a) JOINT INTELLIGENCE COMMUNITY COUNCIL.—There is a Joint Intelligence Community Council.

(b) MEMBERSHIP.—The Joint Intelligence Community Council shall consist of the following:

(1) The Director of National Intelligence, who shall chair the Council.

(2) The Secretary of State.

(3) The Secretary of the Treasury.

(4) The Secretary of Defense.

(5) The Attorney General.

(6) The Secretary of Energy.

(7) The Secretary of Homeland Security.

(8) Such other officers of the United States Government as the President may designate from time to time.

(c) FUNCTIONS.—The Joint Intelligence Community Council shall assist the Director of National Intelligence in developing and implementing a joint, unified national intelligence effort to protect national security by—

(1) advising the Director on establishing requirements, developing budgets, financial management, and monitoring and evaluating the performance of the intelligence community, and on such other matters as the Director may request; and

(2) ensuring the timely execution of programs, policies, and directives established or developed by the Director.

(d) MEETINGS.—The Director of National Intelligence shall convene regular meetings of the Joint Intelligence Community Council.

(e) ADVICE AND OPINIONS OF MEMBERS OTHER THAN CHAIRMAN.—

(1) A member of the Joint Intelligence Community Council (other than the Chairman) may submit to the Chairman advice or an opinion in disagreement with, or advice or an opinion in addition to, the advice presented by the Director of National Intelligence to the President or the National Security Council, in the role of the Chairman as Chairman of the Joint Intelligence Community Council. If a member submits such advice or opinion, the Chairman shall present the advice or opinion of such member at the same time the Chairman presents the advice of the Chairman to the President or the National Security Council, as the case may be.

(2) The Chairman shall establish procedures to ensure that the presentation of the advice of the Chairman to the President or the National Security Council is not unduly delayed by reason of the submission of the individual advice or opinion of another member of the Council.

(f) RECOMMENDATIONS TO CONGRESS.—Any member of the Joint Intelligence Community Council may make such recommendations to Congress relating to the intelligence community as such member considers appropriate.

DIRECTOR OF NATIONAL INTELLIGENCE

SEC. 102. [50 U.S.C. §403]

(a) DIRECTOR OF NATIONAL INTELLIGENCE.—

(1) There is a Director of National Intelligence who shall be appointed by the President, by and with the advice and consent of the Senate. Any individual nominated for appointment as Director of National Intelligence shall have extensive national security expertise.

(2) The Director of National Intelligence shall not be located within the Executive Office of the President.

(b) PRINCIPAL RESPONSIBILITY.—Subject to the authority, direction, and control of the President, the Director of National Intelligence shall—

(1) serve as head of the intelligence community;

(2) act as the principal adviser to the President, to the National Security Council, and the Homeland Security Council for intelligence matters related to the national security; and

(3) consistent with section 1018 of the National Security Intelligence Reform Act of 2004, oversee and direct the implementation of the National Intelligence Program.

(c) PROHIBITION ON DUAL SERVICE.—The individual serving in the position of Director of National Intelligence shall not, while so serving, also serve as the Director of the Central Intelligence Agency or as the head of any other element of the intelligence community.

RESPONSIBILITIES AND AUTHORITIES OF THE DIRECTOR OF NATIONAL INTELLIGENCE

SEC. 102A. [50 U.S.C. §403-1]

(a) PROVISION OF INTELLIGENCE.—

(1) The Director of National Intelligence shall be responsible for ensuring that national intelligence is provided—

(A) to the President;

(B) to the heads of departments and agencies of the executive branch;

(C) to the Chairman of the Joint Chiefs of Staff and senior military commanders;

(D) to the Senate and House of Representatives and the committees thereof; and

(E) to such other persons as the Director of National Intelligence determines to be appropriate.

(2) Such national intelligence should be timely, objective, independent of political considerations, and based upon all sources available to the intelligence community and other appropriate entities.

(b) ACCESS TO INTELLIGENCE.—Unless otherwise directed by the President, the Director of National Intelligence shall have access to all national intelligence and intelligence related to the national security which is collected by any Federal department, agency, or other entity, except as otherwise provided by law or, as appropriate, under guidelines agreed upon by the Attorney General and the Director of National Intelligence.

(c) BUDGET AUTHORITIES.—

(1) With respect to budget requests and appropriations for the National Intelligence Program, the Director of National Intelligence shall—

(A) based on intelligence priorities set by the President, provide to the heads of departments containing agencies or organizations within the intelligence community, and to the heads of such agencies and organizations, guidance for developing the National Intelligence Program budget pertaining to such agencies and organizations;

(B) based on budget proposals provided to the Director of National Intelligence by the heads of agencies and organizations within the intelligence community and the heads of their respective departments and, as appropriate, after obtaining the advice of the Joint Intelligence Community Council, develop and determine an annual consolidated National Intelligence Program budget; and

(C) present such consolidated National Intelligence Program budget, together with any comments from the heads of departments containing agencies or organizations within the intelligence community, to the President for approval.

(2) In addition to the information provided under paragraph (1)(B), the heads of agencies and organizations within the intelligence community shall provide the Director of National Intelligence such other information as the Director shall request for the purpose of determining the annual consolidated National Intelligence Program budget under that paragraph.

(3)(A) The Director of National Intelligence shall participate in the development by the Secretary of Defense of the annual budgets for the Joint Military Intelligence Program and for Tactical Intelligence and Related Activities.

(B) The Director of National Intelligence shall provide guidance for the development of the annual budget for each element of the intelligence community that is not within the National Intelligence Program.

(4) The Director of National Intelligence shall ensure the effective execution of the annual budget for intelligence and intelligence-related activities.

(5)(A) The Director of National Intelligence shall be responsible for managing appropriations for the National Intelligence Program by directing the allotment or allocation of such appropriations through the heads of the departments containing agencies or organizations within the intelligence community and the Director of the Central Intelligence Agency, with prior notice (including the provision of appropriate supporting information) to the head of the department containing an agency or organization receiving any such allocation or allotment or the Director of the Central Intelligence Agency.

(B) Notwithstanding any other provision of law, pursuant to relevant appropriations Acts for the National Intelligence Program, the Director of the Office of Management and Budget shall exercise the authority of the Director of the Office of Management and Budget to apportion funds, at the exclusive direction of the Director of National Intelligence, for allocation to the elements of the intelligence community through the relevant host executive departments and the Central Intelligence Agency. Department comptrollers or appropriate budget execution officers shall allot, allocate, reprogram, or transfer funds appropriated for the National Intelligence Program in an expeditious manner.

(C) The Director of National Intelligence shall monitor the implementation and execution of the National Intelligence Program by the heads of the elements of the intelligence community that manage programs and activities that are part of the National Intelligence Program, which may include audits and evaluations.

(6) Apportionment and allotment of funds under this subsection shall be subject to chapter 13 and section 1517 of title 31, United States Code, and the Congressional Budget and Impoundment Control Act of 1974 (2 U.S.C. §621 et seq.).

(7)(A) The Director of National Intelligence shall provide a semi-annual report, beginning April 1, 2005, and ending April 1, 2007, to the President and the Congress regarding implementation of this section.

(B) The Director of National Intelligence shall report to the President and the Congress not later than 15 days after learning of any instance in which a departmental comptroller acts in a manner inconsistent with the law (including permanent statutes, authorization Acts, and appropriations Acts), or the direction of the Director of National Intelligence, in carrying out the National Intelligence Program.

(d) ROLE OF DIRECTOR OF NATIONAL INTELLIGENCE IN TRANSFER AND REPROGRAMMING OF FUNDS.—

(1)(A) No funds made available under the National Intelligence Program may be transferred or reprogrammed without the prior approval of the Director of National Intelligence, except in accordance with procedures prescribed by the Director of National Intelligence.

(B) The Secretary of Defense shall consult with the Director of National Intelligence before transferring or reprogramming funds made available under the Joint Military Intelligence Program.

(2) Subject to the succeeding provisions of this subsection, the Director of National Intelligence may transfer or reprogram funds appropriated for a program within the National Intelligence Program to another such program.

(3) The Director of National Intelligence may only transfer or reprogram funds referred to in subparagraph (A)—

    (A) with the approval of the Director of the Office of Management and Budget; and

    (B) after consultation with the heads of departments containing agencies or organizations within the intelligence community to the extent such agencies or organizations are affected, and, in the case of the Central Intelligence Agency, after consultation with the Director of the Central Intelligence Agency.

(4) The amounts available for transfer or reprogramming in the National Intelligence Program in any given fiscal year, and the terms and conditions governing such transfers and reprogrammings, are subject to the provisions of annual appropriations Acts and this subsection.

(5)(A) A transfer or reprogramming of funds or personnel may be made under this subsection only if—

    (i) the funds are being transferred to an activity that is a higher priority intelligence activity;

    (ii) the transfer or reprogramming supports an emergent need, improves program effectiveness, or increases efficiency;

    (iii) the transfer or reprogramming does not involve a transfer or reprogramming of funds to a Reserve for Contingencies of the Director of National Intelligence or the Reserve for Contingencies of the Central Intelligence Agency;

    (iv) the transfer or reprogramming results in a cumulative transfer or reprogramming of funds out of any department or agency, as appropriate, funded in the National Intelligence Program in a single fiscal year—

        (I) that is less than $150,000,000, and

        (II) that is less than 5 percent of amounts available to a department or agency under the National Intelligence Program; and

    (v) the transfer or reprogramming does not terminate an acquisition program.

    (B) A transfer or reprogramming may be made without regard to a limitation set forth in clause (iv) or (v) of subparagraph (A) if the transfer has the concurrence of the head of the department involved or the Director of the Central Intelligence Agency (in the case of the Central Intelligence Agency). The authority to provide such concurrence may only be delegated by the head of the department or agency involved to the deputy of such officer.

(6) Funds transferred or reprogrammed under this subsection shall remain available for the same period as the appropriations account to which transferred or reprogrammed.

(7) Any transfer or reprogramming of funds under this subsection shall be carried out in accordance with existing procedures applicable to reprogramming notifications for the appropriate congressional committees. Any proposed transfer or reprogramming for which notice is given to the appropriate congressional committees shall be accompanied by a report explaining the nature of the proposed transfer or reprogramming and how it satisfies the requirements of this subsection. In addition, the congressional intelligence committees shall be promptly notified of any transfer or reprogramming of funds made pursuant to this subsection in any case in which the transfer or reprogramming would not have otherwise required reprogramming notification under procedures in effect as of the date of the enactment of this subsection.

(e) TRANSFER OF PERSONNEL.—

    (1)(A) In addition to any other authorities available under law for such purposes, in the first twelve months after establishment of a new national intelligence center, the Director of National Intelligence, with the approval of the Director of the Office of Management and Budget and in consultation with the congressional committees of jurisdiction referred to in subparagraph (B), may transfer not more than 100 personnel authorized for elements of the intelligence community to such center.

(B) The Director of National Intelligence shall promptly provide notice of any transfer of personnel made pursuant to this paragraph to—

(i) the congressional intelligence committees;

(ii) the Committees on Appropriations of the Senate and the House of Representatives;

(iii) in the case of the transfer of personnel to or from the Department of Defense, the Committees on Armed Services of the Senate and the House of Representatives; and

(iv) in the case of the transfer of personnel to or from the Department of Justice, to the Committees on the Judiciary of the Senate and the House of Representatives.

(C) The Director shall include in any notice under subparagraph (B) an explanation of the nature of the transfer and how it satisfies the requirements of this subsection.

(2)(A) The Director of National Intelligence, with the approval of the Director of the Office of Management and Budget and in accordance with procedures to be developed by the Director of National Intelligence and the heads of the departments and agencies concerned, may transfer personnel authorized for an element of the intelligence community to another such element for a period of not more than 2 years.

(B) A transfer of personnel may be made under this paragraph only if—

(i) the personnel are being transferred to an activity that is a higher priority intelligence activity; and

(ii) the transfer supports an emergent need, improves program effectiveness, or increases efficiency.

(C) The Director of National Intelligence shall promptly provide notice of any transfer of personnel made pursuant to this paragraph to—

(i) the congressional intelligence committees;

(ii) in the case of the transfer of personnel to or from the Department of Defense, the Committees on Armed Services of the Senate and the House of Representatives; and

(iii) in the case of the transfer of personnel to or from the Department of Justice, to the Committees on the Judiciary of the Senate and the House of Representatives.

(D) The Director shall include in any notice under subparagraph (C) an explanation of the nature of the transfer and how it satisfies the requirements of this paragraph.

(3) It is the sense of Congress that—

(A) the nature of the national security threats facing the United States will continue to challenge the intelligence community to respond rapidly and flexibly to bring analytic resources to bear against emerging and unforeseen requirements;

(B) both the Office of the Director of National Intelligence and any analytic centers determined to be necessary should be fully and properly supported with appropriate levels of personnel resources and that the President's yearly budget requests adequately support those needs; and

(C) the President should utilize all legal and administrative discretion to ensure that the Director of National Intelligence and all other elements of the intelligence community have the necessary resources and procedures to respond promptly and effectively to emerging and unforeseen national security challenges.

(f) TASKING AND OTHER AUTHORITIES.—

(1)(A) The Director of National Intelligence shall—

(i) establish objectives, priorities, and guidance for the intelligence community to ensure timely and effective collection, processing, analysis, and dissemination (including access by users to collected data consistent with applicable law and, as appropriate, the guidelines referred to in subsection (b) and analytic products generated by or within the intelligence community) of national intelligence;

(ii) determine requirements and priorities for, and manage and direct the tasking of, collection, analysis, production, and dissemination of national intelligence by elements of the intelligence community, including—

(I) approving requirements (including those requirements responding to needs provided by consumers) for collection and analysis; and

(II) resolving conflicts in collection requirements and in the tasking of national collection assets of the elements of the intelligence community; and

(iii) provide advisory tasking to intelligence elements of those agencies and departments not within the National Intelligence Program.

(B) The authority of the Director of National Intelligence under subparagraph (A) shall not apply—

(i) insofar as the President so directs;

(ii) with respect to clause (ii) of subparagraph (A), insofar as the Secretary of Defense exercises tasking authority under plans or arrangements agreed upon by the Secretary of Defense and the Director of National Intelligence; or

(iii) to the direct dissemination of information to State government and local government officials and private sector entities pursuant to sections 201 and 892 of the Homeland Security Act of 2002 (6 U.S.C. §121, 482).

(2) The Director of National Intelligence shall oversee the National Counterterrorism Center and may establish such other national intelligence centers as the Director determines necessary. (3)(A) The Director of National Intelligence shall prescribe, in consultation with the heads of other agencies or elements of the intelligence community, and the heads of their respective departments, personnel policies and programs applicable to the intelligence community that—

(i) encourage and facilitate assignments and details of personnel to national intelligence centers, and between elements of the intelligence community;

(ii) set standards for education, training, and career development of personnel of the intelligence community;

(iii) encourage and facilitate the recruitment and retention by the intelligence community of highly qualified individuals for the effective conduct of intelligence activities;

(iv) ensure that the personnel of the intelligence community are sufficiently diverse for purposes of the collection and analysis of intelligence through the recruitment and training of women, minorities, and individuals with diverse ethnic, cultural, and linguistic backgrounds;

(v) make service in more than one element of the intelligence community a condition of promotion to such positions within the intelligence community as the Director shall specify; and

(vi) ensure the effective management of intelligence community personnel who are responsible for intelligence community-wide matters.

(B) Policies prescribed under subparagraph (A) shall not be inconsistent with the personnel policies otherwise applicable to members of the uniformed services.

(4) The Director of National Intelligence shall ensure compliance with the Constitution and laws of the United States by the Central Intelligence Agency and shall ensure such compliance by other elements of the intelligence community through the host executive departments that manage the programs and activities that are part of the National Intelligence Program.

(5) The Director of National Intelligence shall ensure the elimination of waste and unnecessary duplication within the intelligence community.

(6) The Director of National Intelligence shall establish requirements and priorities for foreign intelligence information to be collected under the Foreign Intelligence Surveillance Act of 1978 (50 U.S.C. §1801 et seq.), and provide assistance to the Attorney General to ensure that information derived from electronic surveillance or physical searches under that Act is disseminated so it may be used efficiently and effectively for national intelligence purposes, except that the Director shall have no authority to direct or undertake electronic surveillance or physical search operations pursuant to that Act unless authorized by statute or Executive order.

(7) The Director of National Intelligence shall perform such other functions as the President may direct.

(8) Nothing in this title shall be construed as affecting the role of the Department of Justice or the Attorney General under the Foreign Intelligence Surveillance Act of 1978.

(g) INTELLIGENCE INFORMATION SHARING.—

(1) The Director of National Intelligence shall have principal authority to ensure maximum availability of and access to intelligence information within the intelligence community consistent with national security requirements. The Director of National Intelligence shall—

(A) establish uniform security standards and procedures;

(B) establish common information technology standards, protocols, and interfaces;

(C) ensure development of information technology systems that include multi-level security and intelligence integration capabilities;

(D) establish policies and procedures to resolve conflicts between the need to share intelligence information and the need to protect intelligence sources and methods;

(E) develop an enterprise architecture for the intelligence community and ensure that elements of the intelligence community comply with such architecture; and

(F) have procurement approval authority over all enterprise architecture-related information technology items funded in the National Intelligence Program.

(2) The President shall ensure that the Director of National Intelligence has all necessary support and authorities to fully and effectively implement paragraph (1).

(3) Except as otherwise directed by the President or with the specific written agreement of the head of the department or agency in question, a Federal agency or official shall not be considered to have met any obligation to provide any information, report, assessment, or other material (including unevaluated intelligence information) to that department or agency solely by virtue of having provided that information, report, assessment, or other material to the Director of National Intelligence or the National Counterterrorism Center.

(4) Not later than February 1 of each year, the Director of National Intelligence shall submit to the President and to the Congress an annual report that identifies any statute, regulation, policy, or practice that the Director believes impedes the ability of the Director to fully and effectively implement paragraph (1).

(h) ANALYSIS.—To ensure the most accurate analysis of intelligence is derived from all sources to support national security needs, the Director of National Intelligence shall—

(1) implement policies and procedures—

(A) to encourage sound analytic methods and tradecraft throughout the elements of the intelligence community;

(B) to ensure that analysis is based upon all sources available; and

(C) to ensure that the elements of the intelligence community regularly conduct competitive analysis of analytic products, whether such products are produced by or disseminated to such elements;

(2) ensure that resource allocation for intelligence analysis is appropriately proportional to resource allocation for intelligence collection systems and operations in order to maximize analysis of all collected data;

(3) ensure that differences in analytic judgment are fully considered and brought to the attention of policymakers; and

(4) ensure that sufficient relationships are established between intelligence collectors and analysts to facilitate greater understanding of the needs of analysts.

(i) PROTECTION OF INTELLIGENCE SOURCES AND METHODS.—

(1) The Director of National Intelligence shall protect intelligence sources and methods from unauthorized disclosure.

(2) Consistent with paragraph (1), in order to maximize the dissemination of intelligence, the Director of National Intelligence shall establish and implement guidelines for the intelligence community for the following purposes:

(A) Classification of information under applicable law, Executive orders, or other Presidential directives.

(B) Access to and dissemination of intelligence, both in final form and in the form when initially gathered.

(C) Preparation of intelligence products in such a way that source information is removed to allow for dissemination at the lowest level of classification possible or in unclassified form to the extent practicable.

(3) The Director may only delegate a duty or authority given the Director under this subsection to the Principal Deputy Director of National Intelligence.

(j) UNIFORM PROCEDURES FOR SENSITIVE COMPARTMENTED INFORMATION.— The Director of National Intelligence, subject to the direction of the President, shall—

(1) establish uniform standards and procedures for the grant of access to sensitive compartmented information to any officer or employee of any agency or department of the United States and to employees of contractors of those agencies or departments;

(2) ensure the consistent implementation of those standards and procedures throughout such agencies and departments;

(3) ensure that security clearances granted by individual elements of the intelligence community are recognized by all elements of the intelligence community, and under contracts entered into by those agencies; and

(4) ensure that the process for investigation and adjudication of an application for access to sensitive compartmented information is performed in the most expeditious manner possible consistent with applicable standards for national security.

(k) COORDINATION WITH FOREIGN GOVERNMENTS.—Under the direction of the President and in a manner consistent with section 207 of the Foreign Service Act of 1980 (22 U.S.C. §3927), the Director of National Intelligence shall oversee the coordination of the relationships between elements of the intelligence community and the intelligence or security services of foreign governments or international organizations on all matters involving intelligence related to the national security or involving intelligence acquired through clandestine means.

(l) ENHANCED PERSONNEL MANAGEMENT.—

(1)(A) The Director of National Intelligence shall, under regulations prescribed by the Director, provide incentives for personnel of elements of the intelligence community to serve—

(i) on the staff of the Director of National Intelligence;

(ii) on the staff of the national intelligence centers;

(iii) on the staff of the National Counterterrorism Center; and

(iv) in other positions in support of the intelligence community management functions of the Director.

(B) Incentives under subparagraph (A) may include financial incentives, bonuses, and such other awards and incentives as the Director considers appropriate.

(2)(A) Notwithstanding any other provision of law, the personnel of an element of the intelligence community who are assigned or detailed under paragraph (1)(A) to service under the Director of National Intelligence shall be promoted at rates equivalent to or better than personnel of such element who are not so assigned or detailed.

(B) The Director may prescribe regulations to carry out this section.

(3)(A) The Director of National Intelligence shall prescribe mechanisms to facilitate the rotation of personnel of the intelligence community through various elements of the intelligence community in the course of their careers in order to facilitate the widest possible understanding by such personnel of the variety of intelligence requirements, methods, users, and capabilities.

(B) The mechanisms prescribed under subparagraph (A) may include the following:

(i) The establishment of special occupational categories involving service, over the course of a career, in more than one element of the intelligence community.

(ii) The provision of rewards for service in positions undertaking analysis and planning of operations involving two or more elements of the intelligence community.

(iii) The establishment of requirements for education, training, service, and evaluation for service involving more than one element of the intelligence community.

(C) It is the sense of Congress that the mechanisms prescribed under this subsection should, to the extent practical, seek to duplicate for civilian personnel within the intelligence community the joint officer management policies established by chapter 38 of title 10, United States Code, and the other amendments made by title IV of the Goldwater-Nichols Department of Defense Reorganization Act of 1986 (Public Law 99-433).

(4)(A) Except as provided in subparagraph (B) and subparagraph (D), this subsection shall not apply with respect to personnel of the elements of the intelligence community who are members of the uniformed services.

(B) Mechanisms that establish requirements for education and training pursuant to paragraph (3)(B)(iii) may apply with respect to members of the uniformed services who are assigned to an element of the intelligence community funded through the National Intelligence Program, but such mechanisms shall not be inconsistent with personnel policies and education and training requirements otherwise applicable to members of the uniformed services.

(C) The personnel policies and programs developed and implemented under this subsection with respect to law enforcement officers (as that term is defined in section 5541(3) of title 5, United States Code) shall not affect the ability of law enforcement entities to conduct operations or, through the applicable chain of command, to control the activities of such law enforcement officers.

(D) Assignment to the Office of the Director of National Intelligence of commissioned officers of the Armed Forces shall be considered a joint-duty assignment for purposes of the joint officer management policies prescribed by chapter 38 of title 10, United States Code, and other provisions of that title.

(m) ADDITIONAL AUTHORITY WITH RESPECT TO PERSONNEL.—

(1) In addition to the authorities under subsection (f)(3), the Director of National Intelligence may exercise with respect to the personnel of the Office of the Director of National Intelligence any authority of the Director of the Central Intelligence Agency with respect to the personnel of the Central Intelligence Agency under the Central Intelligence Agency Act of 1949 (50 U.S.C. §403a et seq.), and other applicable provisions of law, as of the date of the

enactment of this subsection to the same extent, and subject to the same conditions and limitations, that the Director of the Central Intelligence Agency may exercise such authority with respect to personnel of the Central Intelligence Agency.

(2) Employees and applicants for employment of the Office of the Director of National Intelligence shall have the same rights and protections under the Office of the Director of National Intelligence as employees of the Central Intelligence Agency have under the Central Intelligence Agency Act of 1949, and other applicable provisions of law, as of the date of the enactment of this subsection.

(n) ACQUISITION AUTHORITIES.—

(1) In carrying out the responsibilities and authorities under this section, the Director of National Intelligence may exercise the acquisition and appropriations authorities referred to in the Central Intelligence Agency Act of 1949 (50 U.S.C. §403a et seq.) other than the authorities referred to in section 8(b) of that Act (50 U.S.C. §403j(b)).

(2) For the purpose of the exercise of any authority referred to in paragraph (1), a reference to the head of an agency shall be deemed to be a reference to the Director of National Intelligence or the Principal Deputy Director of National Intelligence.

(3)(A) Any determination or decision to be made under an authority referred to in paragraph (1) by the head of an agency may be made with respect to individual purchases and contracts or with respect to classes of purchases or contracts, and shall be final.

(B) Except as provided in subparagraph (C), the Director of National Intelligence or the Principal Deputy Director of National Intelligence may, in such official's discretion, delegate to any officer or other official of the Office of the Director of National Intelligence any authority to make a determination or decision as the head of the agency under an authority referred to in paragraph (1).

(C) The limitations and conditions set forth in section 3(d) of the Central Intelligence Agency Act of 1949 (50 U.S.C. §403c(d)) shall apply to the exercise by the Director of National Intelligence of an authority referred to in paragraph (1).

(D) Each determination or decision required by an authority referred to in the second sentence of section 3(d) of the Central Intelligence Agency Act of 1949 shall be based upon written findings made by the official making such determination or decision, which findings shall be final and shall be available within the Office of the Director of National Intelligence for a period of at least six years following the date of such determination or decision.

(o) CONSIDERATION OF VIEWS OF ELEMENTS OF INTELLIGENCE COMMUNITY.— In carrying out the duties and responsibilities under this section, the Director of National Intelligence shall take into account the views of a head of a department containing an element of the intelligence community and of the Director of the Central Intelligence Agency.

(p) RESPONSIBILITY OF DIRECTOR OF NATIONAL INTELLIGENCE REGARDING NATIONAL INTELLIGENCE PROGRAM BUDGET CONCERNING THE DEPARTMENT OF DEFENSE.—Subject to the direction of the President, the Director of National Intelligence shall, after consultation with the Secretary of Defense, ensure that the National Intelligence Program budgets for the elements of the intelligence community that are within the Department of Defense are adequate to satisfy the national intelligence needs of the Department of Defense, including the needs of the Chairman of the Joint Chiefs of Staff and the commanders of the unified and specified commands, and wherever such elements are performing Government-wide functions, the needs of other Federal departments and agencies.

(q) ACQUISITIONS OF MAJOR SYSTEMS.—

(1) For each intelligence program within the National Intelligence Program for the acquisition of a major system, the Director of National Intelligence shall—

(A) require the development and implementation of a program management plan that includes cost, schedule, and performance goals and program milestone criteria, except that with respect to Department of Defense programs the Director shall consult with the Secretary of Defense;

(B) serve as exclusive milestone decision authority, except that with respect to Department of Defense programs the Director shall serve as milestone decision authority jointly with the Secretary of Defense or the designee of the Secretary; and

(C) periodically—

(i) review and assess the progress made toward the achievement of the goals and milestones established in such plan; and

(ii) submit to Congress a report on the results of such review and assessment.

(2) If the Director of National Intelligence and the Secretary of Defense are unable to reach an agreement on a milestone decision under paragraph (1)(B), the President shall resolve the conflict.

(3) Nothing in this subsection may be construed to limit the authority of the Director of National Intelligence to delegate to any other official any authority to perform the responsibilities of the Director under this subsection.

(4) In this subsection:

(A) The term "intelligence program", with respect to the acquisition of a major system, means a program that—

(i) is carried out to acquire such major system for an element of the intelligence community; and

(ii) is funded in whole out of amounts available for the National Intelligence Program.

(B) The term "major system" has the meaning given such term in section 4(9) of the Federal Property and Administrative Services Act of 1949 (41 U.S.C. §403(9)).

(r) PERFORMANCE OF COMMON SERVICES.—The Director of National Intelligence shall, in consultation with the heads of departments and agencies of the United States Government containing elements within the intelligence community and with the Director of the Central Intelligence Agency, coordinate the performance by the elements of the intelligence community within the National Intelligence Program of such services as are of common concern to the intelligence community, which services the Director of National Intelligence determines can be more efficiently accomplished in a consolidated manner.

OFFICE OF THE DIRECTOR OF NATIONAL INTELLIGENCE
SEC. 103. [50 U.S.C. §403-3]

(a) OFFICE OF DIRECTOR OF NATIONAL INTELLIGENCE.—There is an Office of the Director of National Intelligence.

(b) FUNCTION.—The function of the Office of the Director of National Intelligence is to assist the Director of National Intelligence in carrying out the duties and responsibilities of the Director under this Act, the National Security Act of 1947 (50 U.S.C. §401 et seq.), and other applicable provisions of law, and to carry out such other duties as may be prescribed by the President or by law.

(c) COMPOSITION.—The Office of the Director of National Intelligence is composed of the following:

(1) The Director of National Intelligence.

(2) The Principal Deputy Director of National Intelligence.

(3) Any Deputy Director of National Intelligence appointed under section 103A.

(4) The National Intelligence Council.

(5) The General Counsel.

(6) The Civil Liberties Protection Officer.

(7) The Director of Science and Technology.

(8) The National Counterintelligence Executive (including the Office of the National Counterintelligence Executive).

(9) Such other offices and officials as may be established by law or the Director may establish or designate in the Office, including national intelligence centers.

(d) STAFF.—

(1) To assist the Director of National Intelligence in fulfilling the duties and responsibilities of the Director, the Director shall employ and utilize in the Office of the Director of National Intelligence a professional staff having an expertise in matters relating to such duties and responsibilities, and may establish permanent positions and appropriate rates of pay with respect to that staff.

(2) The staff of the Office of the Director of National Intelligence under paragraph (1) shall include the staff of the Office of the Deputy Director of Central Intelligence for Community Management that is transferred to the Office of the Director of National Intelligence under section 1091 of the National Security Intelligence Reform Act of 2004.

(e) LIMITATION ON CO-LOCATION WITH OTHER ELEMENTS OF INTELLIGENCE COMMUNITY.—Commencing as of October 1, 2008, the Office of the Director of National Intelligence may not be co-located with any other element of the intelligence community.

DEPUTY DIRECTORS OF NATIONAL INTELLIGENCE
SEC. 103A. [50 U.S.C. §403-3a]

(a) PRINCIPAL DEPUTY DIRECTOR OF NATIONAL INTELLIGENCE.—

(1) There is a Principal Deputy Director of National Intelligence who shall be appointed by the President, by and with the advice and consent of the Senate.

(2) In the event of a vacancy in the position of Principal Deputy Director of National Intelligence, the Director of National Intelligence shall recommend to the President an individual for appointment as Principal Deputy Director of National Intelligence.

(3) Any individual nominated for appointment as Principal Deputy Director of National Intelligence shall have extensive national security experience and management expertise.

(4) The individual serving as Principal Deputy Director of National Intelligence shall not, while so serving, serve in any capacity in any other element of the intelligence community.

(5) The Principal Deputy Director of National Intelligence shall assist the Director of National Intelligence in carrying out the duties and responsibilities of the Director.

(6) The Principal Deputy Director of National Intelligence shall act for, and exercise the powers of, the Director of National Intelligence during the absence or disability of the Director of National Intelligence or during a vacancy in the position of Director of National Intelligence.

(b) DEPUTY DIRECTORS OF NATIONAL INTELLIGENCE.—

(1) There may be not more than four Deputy Directors of National Intelligence who shall be appointed by the Director of National Intelligence.

(2) Each Deputy Director of National Intelligence appointed under this subsection shall have such duties, responsibilities, and authorities as the Director of National Intelligence may assign or are specified by law.

(c) MILITARY STATUS OF DIRECTOR OF NATIONAL INTELLIGENCE AND PRINCIPAL DEPUTY DIRECTOR OF NATIONAL INTELLIGENCE.—

(1) Not more than one of the individuals serving in the positions specified in paragraph (2) may be a commissioned officer of the Armed Forces in active status.

(2) The positions referred to in this paragraph are the following:

(A) The Director of National Intelligence.

(B) The Principal Deputy Director of National Intelligence.

(3) It is the sense of Congress that, under ordinary circumstances, it is desirable that one of the individuals serving in the positions specified in paragraph (2)—

(A) be a commissioned officer of the Armed Forces, in active status; or

(B) have, by training or experience, an appreciation of military intelligence activities and requirements.

(4) A commissioned officer of the Armed Forces, while serving in a position specified in paragraph (2)—

(A) shall not be subject to supervision or control by the Secretary of Defense or by any officer or employee of the Department of Defense;

(B) shall not exercise, by reason of the officer's status as a commissioned officer, any supervision or control with respect to any of the military or civilian personnel of the Department of Defense except as otherwise authorized by law; and

(C) shall not be counted against the numbers and percentages of commissioned officers of the rank and grade of such officer authorized for the military department of that officer.

(5) Except as provided in subparagraph (A) or (B) of paragraph (4), the appointment of an officer of the Armed Forces to a position specified in paragraph (2) shall not affect the status, position, rank, or grade of such officer in the Armed Forces, or any emolument, perquisite, right, privilege, or benefit incident to or arising out of such status, position, rank, or grade.

(6) A commissioned officer of the Armed Forces on active duty who is appointed to a position specified in paragraph (2), while serving in such position and while remaining on active duty, shall continue to receive military pay and allowances and shall not receive the pay prescribed for such position. Funds from which such pay and allowances are paid shall be reimbursed from funds available to the Director of National Intelligence.

NATIONAL INTELLIGENCE COUNCIL
SEC. 103B. [50 U.S.C. §403-3b]

(a) NATIONAL INTELLIGENCE COUNCIL.—There is a National Intelligence Council.

(b) COMPOSITION.—

(1) The National Intelligence Council shall be composed of senior analysts within the intelligence community and substantive experts from the public and private sector, who shall be appointed by, report to, and serve at the pleasure of, the Director of National Intelligence.

(2) The Director shall prescribe appropriate security requirements for personnel appointed from the private sector as a condition of service on the Council, or as contractors of the Council or employees of such contractors, to ensure the protection of intelligence sources and methods while avoiding, wherever possible, unduly intrusive requirements which the Director considers to be unnecessary for this purpose.

(c) DUTIES AND RESPONSIBILITIES.—

(1) The National Intelligence Council shall—

(A) produce national intelligence estimates for the United States Government, including alternative views held by elements of the intelligence community and other information as specified in paragraph (2);

(B) evaluate community-wide collection and production of intelligence by the intelligence community and the requirements and resources of such collection and production; and

(C) otherwise assist the Director of National Intelligence in carrying out the responsibilities of the Director under section 102A.

(2) The Director of National Intelligence shall ensure that the Council satisfies the needs of policymakers and other consumers of intelligence.

(d) SERVICES AS SENIOR INTELLIGENCE ADVISERS.—Within their respective areas of expertise and under the direction of the Director of National Intelligence, the members of the National Intelligence Council shall constitute the senior intelligence advisers of the intelligence community for purposes of representing the views of the intelligence community within the United States Government.

(e) AUTHORITY TO CONTRACT.—Subject to the direction and control of the Director of National Intelligence, the National Intelligence Council may carry out its responsibilities under this section by contract, including contracts for substantive experts necessary to assist the Council with particular assessments under this section.

(f) STAFF.—The Director of National Intelligence shall make available to the National Intelligence Council such staff as may be necessary to permit the Council to carry out its responsibilities under this section.

(g) AVAILABILITY OF COUNCIL AND STAFF.—

(1) The Director of National Intelligence shall take appropriate measures to ensure that the National Intelligence Council and its staff satisfy the needs of policymaking officials and other consumers of intelligence.

(2) The Council shall be readily accessible to policymaking officials and other appropriate individuals not otherwise associated with the intelligence community.

(h) SUPPORT.—The heads of the elements of the intelligence community shall, as appropriate, furnish such support to the National Intelligence Council, including the preparation of intelligence analyses, as may be required by the Director of National Intelligence.

(i) NATIONAL INTELLIGENCE COUNCIL PRODUCT.—For purposes of this section, the term "National Intelligence Council product" includes a National Intelligence Estimate and any other intelligence community assessment that sets forth the judgment of the intelligence community as a whole on a matter covered by such product.

GENERAL COUNSEL
SEC. 103C. [50 U.S.C. §403-3c]

(a) GENERAL COUNSEL.—There is a General Counsel of the Office of the Director of National Intelligence who shall be appointed by the President, by and with the advice and consent of the Senate.

(b) PROHIBITION ON DUAL SERVICE AS GENERAL COUNSEL OF ANOTHER AGENCY.— The individual serving in the position of General Counsel may not, while so serving, also serve as the General Counsel of any other department, agency, or element of the United States Government.

(c) SCOPE OF POSITION.—The General Counsel is the chief legal officer of the Office of the Director of National Intelligence.

(d) FUNCTIONS.—The General Counsel shall perform such functions as the Director of National Intelligence may prescribe.

CIVIL LIBERTIES PROTECTION OFFICER
SEC. 103D. [50 U.S.C. §403-3d]

(a) CIVIL LIBERTIES PROTECTION OFFICER.—

(1) Within the Office of the Director of National Intelligence, there is a Civil Liberties Protection Officer who shall be appointed by the Director of National Intelligence.

(2) The Civil Liberties Protection Officer shall report directly to the Director of National Intelligence.

(b) DUTIES.—The Civil Liberties Protection Officer shall—

(1) ensure that the protection of civil liberties and privacy is appropriately incorporated in the policies and procedures developed for and implemented by the Office of the Director of National Intelligence and the elements of the intelligence community within the National Intelligence Program;

(2) oversee compliance by the Office and the Director of National Intelligence with requirements under the Constitution and all laws, regulations, Executive orders, and implementing guidelines relating to civil liberties and privacy;

(3) review and assess complaints and other information indicating possible abuses of civil liberties and privacy in the administration of the programs and operations of the Office and the Director of National Intelligence and, as appropriate, investigate any such complaint or information;

(4) ensure that the use of technologies sustain, and do not erode, privacy protections relating to the use, collection, and disclosure of personal information;

(5) ensure that personal information contained in a system of records subject to section 552a of title 5, United States Code (popularly referred to as the Privacy Act'), is handled in full compliance with fair information practices as set out in that section;

(6) conduct privacy impact assessments when appropriate or as required by law; and

(7) perform such other duties as may be prescribed by the Director of National Intelligence or specified by law.

(c) USE OF AGENCY INSPECTORS GENERAL.—When appropriate, the Civil Liberties Protection Officer may refer complaints to the Office of Inspector General having responsibility for the affected element of the department or agency of the intelligence community to conduct an investigation under paragraph (3) of subsection (b).

DIRECTOR OF SCIENCE AND TECHNOLOGY
SEC. 103E. [50 U.S.C. §403-3e]

(a) DIRECTOR OF SCIENCE AND TECHNOLOGY.—There is a Director of Science and Technology within the Office of the Director of National Intelligence who shall be appointed by the Director of National Intelligence.

(b) REQUIREMENT RELATING TO APPOINTMENT.—An individual appointed as Director of Science and Technology shall have a professional background and experience appropriate for the duties of the Director of Science and Technology.

(c) DUTIES.—The Director of Science and Technology shall—

(1) act as the chief representative of the Director of National Intelligence for science and technology;

(2) chair the Director of National Intelligence Science and Technology Committee under subsection (d);

(3) assist the Director in formulating a long-term strategy for scientific advances in the field of intelligence;

(4) assist the Director on the science and technology elements of the budget of the Office of the Director of National Intelligence; and

(5) perform other such duties as may be prescribed by the Director of National Intelligence or specified by law.

(d) DIRECTOR OF NATIONAL INTELLIGENCE SCIENCE AND TECHNOLOGY COMMITTEE.—

(1) There is within the Office of the Director of Science and Technology a Director of National Intelligence Science and Technology Committee.

(2) The Committee shall be composed of the principal science officers of the National Intelligence Program.

(3) The Committee shall—

(A) coordinate advances in research and development related to intelligence; and

(B) perform such other functions as the Director of Science and Technology shall prescribe.

NATIONAL COUNTERINTELLIGENCE EXECUTIVE
SEC. 103F. [50 U.S.C. §403-3f]

(a) NATIONAL COUNTERINTELLIGENCE EXECUTIVE.—The National Counterintelligence Executive under section 902 of the Counterintelligence Enhancement Act of 2002 (title IX of Public Law 107-306; 50 U.S.C. §402b et seq.) is a component of the Office of the Director of National Intelligence.

(b) DUTIES.—The National Counterintelligence Executive shall perform the duties provided in the Counterintelligence Enhancement Act of 2002 and such other duties as may be prescribed by the Director of National Intelligence or specified by law.

CHIEF INFORMATION OFFICER
SEC. 103G. [50 U.S.C. §403-3g]

(a) CHIEF INFORMATION OFFICER.—To assist the Director of National Intelligence in carrying out the responsibilities of the Director under this Act and other applicable provisions of law, there shall be within the Office of the Director of National Intelligence a Chief Information Officer who shall be appointed by the President, by and with the advice and consent of the Senate.

(b) CHIEF INFORMATION OFFICER OF INTELLIGENCE COMMUNITY.—The Chief Information Officer shall serve as the chief information officer of the intelligence community.

(c) DUTIES AND RESPONSIBILITIES.—Subject to the direction of the Director of National Intelligence, the Chief Information Officer shall—

(1) manage activities relating to the information technology infrastructure and enterprise architecture requirements of the intelligence community;

(2) have procurement approval authority over all information technology items related to the enterprise architectures of all intelligence community components;

(3) direct and manage all information technology-related procurement for the intelligence community; and

(4) ensure that all expenditures for information technology and research and development activities are consistent with the intelligence community enterprise architecture and the strategy of the Director for such architecture.

(d) PROHIBITION ON SIMULTANEOUS SERVICE AS OTHER CHIEF INFORMATION OFFICER.—An individual serving in the position of Chief Information Officer may not, while so serving, serve as the chief information officer of any other department or agency, or component thereof, of the United States Government.

INSPECTOR GENERAL OF THE INTELLIGENCE COMMUNITY
SEC. 103H. [50 U.S.C. 403–3h]

(a) OFFICE OF INSPECTOR GENERAL OF THE INTELLIGENCE COMMUNITY.—There is within the Office of the Director of National Intelligence an Office of the Inspector General of the Intelligence Community.

(b) PURPOSE.—The purpose of the Office of the Inspector General of the Intelligence Community is—

(1) to create an objective and effective office, appropriately accountable to Congress, to initiate and conduct independent investigations, inspections, audits, and reviews on pro-

grams and activities within the responsibility and authority of the Director of National Intelligence;

(2) to provide leadership and coordination and recommend policies for activities designed—

(A) to promote economy, efficiency, and effectiveness in the administration and implementation of such programs and activities; and

(B) to prevent and detect fraud and abuse in such programs and activities;

(3) to provide a means for keeping the Director of National Intelligence fully and currently informed about—

(A) problems and deficiencies relating to the administration of programs and activities within the responsibility and authority of the Director of National Intelligence; and

B) the necessity for, and the progress of, corrective actions; and

(4) in the manner prescribed by this section, to ensure that the congressional intelligence committees are kept similarly informed of—

(A) significant problems and deficiencies relating to programs and activities within the responsibility and authority of the Director of National Intelligence; and

(B) the necessity for, and the progress of, corrective actions.

(c) INSPECTOR GENERAL OF THE INTELLIGENCE COMMUNITY.—

(1) There is an Inspector General of the Intelligence Community, who shall be the head of the Office of the Inspector General of the Intelligence Community, who shall be appointed by the President, by and with the advice and consent of the Senate.

(2) The nomination of an individual for appointment as Inspector General shall be made—

(A) without regard to political affiliation;

(B) on the basis of integrity, compliance with security standards of the intelligence community, and prior experience in the field of intelligence or national security; and

(C) on the basis of demonstrated ability in accounting, financial analysis, law, management analysis, public administration, or investigations.

(3) The Inspector General shall report directly to and be under the general supervision of the Director of National Intelligence.

(4) The Inspector General may be removed from office only by the President. The President shall communicate in writing to the congressional intelligence committees the reasons for the removal not later than 30 days prior to the effective date of such removal. Nothing in this paragraph shall be construed to prohibit a personnel action otherwise authorized by law, other than transfer or removal.

(d) ASSISTANT INSPECTORS GENERAL.—Subject to the policies of the Director of National Intelligence, the Inspector General of the Intelligence Community shall—

(1) appoint an Assistant Inspector General for Audit who shall have the responsibility for supervising the performance of auditing activities relating to programs and activities within the responsibility and authority of the Director;

(2) appoint an Assistant Inspector General for Investigations who shall have the responsibility for supervising the performance of investigative activities relating to such programs and activities; and

(3) appoint other Assistant Inspectors General that, in the judgment of the Inspector General, are necessary to carry out the duties of the Inspector General.

(e) DUTIES AND RESPONSIBILITIES.—It shall be the duty and responsibility of the Inspector General of the Intelligence Community—

(1) to provide policy direction for, and to plan, conduct, supervise, and coordinate independently, the investigations, inspections, audits, and reviews relating to programs and activities within the responsibility and authority of the Director of National Intelligence;

(2) to keep the Director of National Intelligence fully and currently informed concerning violations of law and regulations, fraud, and other serious problems, abuses, and deficiencies relating to the programs and activities within the responsibility and authority of the Director, to recommend corrective action concerning such problems, and to report on the progress made in implementing such corrective action;

(3) to take due regard for the protection of intelligence sources and methods in the preparation of all reports issued by the Inspector General, and, to the extent consistent with the purpose and objective of such reports, take such measures as may be appropriate to minimize the disclosure of intelligence sources and methods described in such reports; and

(4) in the execution of the duties and responsibilities under this section, to comply with generally accepted government auditing.

(f) LIMITATIONS ON ACTIVITIES.—

(1) The Director of National Intelligence may prohibit the Inspector General of the Intelligence Community from initiating, carrying out, or completing any investigation, inspection, audit, or review if the Director determines that such prohibition is necessary to protect vital national security interests of the United States.

(2) Not later than seven days after the date on which the Director exercises the authority under paragraph (1), the Director shall submit to the congressional intelligence committees an appropriately classified statement of the reasons for the exercise of such authority.

(3) The Director shall advise the Inspector General at the time a statement under paragraph (2) is submitted, and, to the extent consistent with the protection of intelligence sources and methods, provide the Inspector General with a copy of such statement.

(4) The Inspector General may submit to the congressional intelligence committees any comments on the statement of which the Inspector General has notice under paragraph (3) that the Inspector General considers appropriate.

(g) AUTHORITIES.—

(1) The Inspector General of the Intelligence Community shall have direct and prompt access to the Director of National Intelligence when necessary for any purpose pertaining to the performance of the duties of the Inspector General.

(2)(A) The Inspector General shall, subject to the limitations in subsection (f), make such investigations and reports relating to the administration of the programs and activities within the authorities and responsibilities of the Director as are, in the judgment of the Inspector General, necessary or desirable.

(B) The Inspector General shall have access to any employee, or any employee of a contractor, of any element of the intelligence community needed for the performance of the duties of the Inspector General.

(C) The Inspector General shall have direct access to all records, reports, audits, reviews, documents, papers, recommendations, or other materials that relate to the programs and activities with respect to which the Inspector General has responsibilities under this section.

(D) The level of classification or compartmentation of information shall not, in and of itself, provide a sufficient rationale for denying the Inspector General access to any materials under subparagraph (C).

(E) The Director, or on the recommendation of the Director, another appropriate official of the intelligence community, shall take appropriate administrative actions against an employee, or an employee of a contractor, of an element of the intelligence community that fails to cooperate with the Inspector General. Such administrative action may include loss of employment or the termination of an existing contractual relationship.

(3) The Inspector General is authorized to receive and investigate, pursuant to subsection (h), complaints or information from any person concerning the existence of an activity within the authorities and responsibilities of the Director of National Intelligence constituting a violation of laws, rules, or regulations, or mismanagement, gross waste of funds, abuse of authority, or a substantial and specific danger to the public health and safety. Once such complaint or information has been received from an employee of the intelligence community—

(A) the Inspector General shall not disclose the identity of the employee without the consent of the employee, unless the Inspector General determines that such disclosure is unavoidable during the course of the investigation or the disclosure is made to an official of the Department of Justice responsible for determining whether a prosecution should be undertaken; and

(B) no action constituting a reprisal, or threat of reprisal, for making such complaint or disclosing such information to the Inspector General may be taken by any employee in a position to take such actions, unless the complaint was made or the information was disclosed with the knowledge that it was false or with willful disregard for its truth or falsity.

(4) The Inspector General shall have the authority to administer to or take from any person an oath, affirmation, or affidavit, whenever necessary in the performance of the duties of the Inspector General, which oath, affirmation, or affidavit when administered or taken by or before an employee of the Office of the Inspector General of the Intelligence Community designated by the Inspector General shall have the same force and effect as if administered or taken by, or before, an officer having a seal.

(5)(A) Except as provided in subparagraph (B), the Inspector General is authorized to require by subpoena the production of all information, documents, reports, answers, records, accounts, papers, and other data in any medium (including electronically stored information, as well as any tangible thing) and documentary evidence necessary in the performance of the duties and responsibilities of the Inspector General.

(B) In the case of departments, agencies, and other elements of the United States Government, the Inspector General shall obtain information, documents, reports, answers, records, accounts, papers, and other data and evidence for the purpose specified in subparagraph (A) using procedures other than by subpoenas.

(C) The Inspector General may not issue a subpoena for, or on behalf of, any component of the Office of the Director of National Intelligence or any element of the intelligence community, including the Office of the Director of National Intelligence.

(D) In the case of contumacy or refusal to obey a subpoena issued under this paragraph, the subpoena shall be enforceable by order of any appropriate district court of the United States.

(6) The Inspector General may obtain services as authorized by section 3109 of title 5, United States Code, at rates for individuals not to exceed the daily equivalent of the maximum annual rate of basic pay payable for grade GS–15 of the General Schedule under section 5332 of title 5, United States Code.

(7) The Inspector General may, to the extent and in such amounts as may be provided in appropriations, enter into contracts and other arrangements for audits, studies, analyses, and other services with public agencies and with private persons, and to make such payments as may be necessary to carry out the provisions of this section.

(h) COORDINATION AMONG INSPECTORS GENERAL.—

(1)(A) In the event of a matter within the jurisdiction of the Inspector General of the Intelligence Community that may be subject to an investigation, inspection, audit, or review by both the Inspector General of the Intelligence Community and an inspector general with oversight responsibility for an element of the intelligence community, the Inspector General of the Intelligence Community and such other inspector general shall expeditiously resolve the question of which inspector general shall conduct such investigation, inspection, audit, or review to avoid unnecessary duplication of the activities of the inspectors general.

    (B) In attempting to resolve a question under subparagraph (A), the inspectors general concerned may request the assistance of the Intelligence Community Inspectors General Forum established under paragraph (2). In the event of a dispute between an inspector general within a department or agency of the United States Government and the Inspector General of the Intelligence Community that has not been resolved with the assistance of such Forum, the inspectors general shall submit the question to the Director of National Intelligence and the head of the affected department or agency for resolution.

(2)(A) There is established the Intelligence Community Inspectors General Forum, which shall consist of all statutory or administrative inspectors general with oversight responsibility for an element of the intelligence community.

    (B) The Inspector General of the Intelligence Community shall serve as the Chair of the Forum established under subparagraph (A). The Forum shall have no administrative authority over any inspector general, but shall serve as a mechanism for informing its members of the work of individual members of the Forum that may be of common interest and discussing questions about jurisdiction or access to employees, employees of contract personnel, records, audits, reviews, documents, recommendations, or other materials that may involve or be of assistance to more than one of its members.

(3) The inspector general conducting an investigation, inspection, audit, or review covered by paragraph (1) shall submit the results of such investigation, inspection, audit, or review to any other inspector general, including the Inspector General of the Intelligence Community, with jurisdiction to conduct such investigation, inspection, audit, or review who did not conduct such investigation, inspection, audit, or review.

(i) COUNSEL TO THE INSPECTOR GENERAL.—

(1) The Inspector General of the Intelligence Community shall—

    (A) appoint a Counsel to the Inspector General who shall report to the Inspector General; or

    (B) obtain the services of a counsel appointed by and directly reporting to another inspector general or the Council of the Inspectors General on Integrity and Efficiency on a reimbursable basis.

(2) The counsel appointed or obtained under paragraph (1) shall perform such functions as the Inspector General may prescribe.

(j) STAFF AND OTHER SUPPORT.—

(1) The Director of National Intelligence shall provide the Inspector General of the Intelligence Community with appropriate and adequate office space at central and field office locations, together with such equipment, office supplies, maintenance services, and communications facilities and services as may be necessary for the operation of such offices.

(2)(A) Subject to applicable law and the policies of the Director of National Intelligence, the Inspector General shall select, appoint, and employ such officers and employees as may be necessary to carry out the functions, powers, and duties of the Inspector General. The Inspector General shall ensure that any officer or employee so selected, appointed, or employed has security clearances appropriate for the assigned duties of such officer or employee.

(B) In making selections under subparagraph (A), the Inspector General shall ensure that such officers and employees have the requisite training and experience to enable the Inspector General to carry out the duties of the Inspector General effectively.

(C) In meeting the requirements of this paragraph, the Inspector General shall create within the Office of the Inspector General of the Intelligence Community a career cadre of sufficient size to provide appropriate continuity and objectivity needed for the effective performance of the duties of the Inspector General.

(3) Consistent with budgetary and personnel resources allocated by the Director of National Intelligence, the Inspector General has final approval of—

(A) the selection of internal and external candidates for employment with the Office of the Inspector General; and

(B) all other personnel decisions concerning personnel permanently assigned to the Office of the Inspector General, including selection and appointment to the Senior Intelligence Service, but excluding all securitybased determinations that are not within the authority of a head of a component of the Office of the Director of National Intelligence.

(4)(A) Subject to the concurrence of the Director of National Intelligence, the Inspector General may request such information or assistance as may be necessary for carrying out the duties and responsibilities of the Inspector General from any department, agency, or other element of the United States Government.

(B) Upon request of the Inspector General for information or assistance under subparagraph (A), the head of the department, agency, or element concerned shall, insofar as is practicable and not in contravention of any existing statutory restriction or regulation of the department, agency, or element, furnish to the Inspector General, such information or assistance.

(C) The Inspector General of the Intelligence Community may, upon reasonable notice to the head of any element of the intelligence community and in coordination with that element's inspector general pursuant to subsection (h), conduct, as authorized by this section, an investigation, inspection, audit, or review of such element and may enter into any place occupied by such element for purposes of the performance of the duties of the Inspector General.

(k) REPORTS.—

(1)(A) The Inspector General of the Intelligence Community shall, not later than January 31 and July 31 of each year, prepare and submit to the Director of National Intelligence a classified, and, as appropriate, unclassified semiannual report summarizing the activities of the Office of the Inspector General of the Intelligence Community during the immediately preceding 6 month period ending December 31 (of the preceding year) and June 30, respectively. The Inspector General of the Intelligence Community shall provide any portion of the report involving a component of a department of the United States Government to the head of that department simultaneously with submission of the report to the Director of National Intelligence.

(B) Each report under this paragraph shall include, at a minimum, the following:

(i) A list of the title or subject of each investigation, inspection, audit, or review conducted during the period covered by such report.

(ii) A description of significant problems, abuses, and deficiencies relating to the administration of programs and activities of the intelligence community within the responsibility and authority of the Director of National Intelligence, and in the relationships between elements of the intelligence community, identified by the Inspector General during the period covered by such report.

(iii) A description of the recommendations for corrective action made by the

Inspector General during the period covered by such report with respect to significant problems, abuses, or deficiencies identified in clause (ii).

(iv) A statement of whether or not corrective action has been completed on each significant recommendation described in previous semiannual reports, and, in a case where corrective action has been completed, a description of such corrective action.

(v) A certification of whether or not the Inspector General has had full and direct access to all information relevant to the performance of the functions of the Inspector General.

(vi) A description of the exercise of the subpoena authority under subsection (g)(5) by the Inspector General during the period covered by such report.

(vii) Such recommendations as the Inspector General considers appropriate for legislation to promote economy, efficiency, and effectiveness in the administration and implementation of programs and activities within the responsibility and authority of the Director of National Intelligence, and to detect and eliminate fraud and abuse in such programs and activities.

(C) Not later than 30 days after the date of receipt of a report under subparagraph (A), the Director shall transmit the report to the congressional intelligence committees together with any comments the Director considers appropriate. The Director shall transmit to the committees of the Senate and of the House of Representatives with jurisdiction over a department of the United States Government any portion of the report involving a component of such department simultaneously with submission of the report to the congressional intelligence committees.

(2)(A) The Inspector General shall report immediately to the Director whenever the Inspector General becomes aware of particularly serious or flagrant problems, abuses, or deficiencies relating to programs and activities within the responsibility and authority of the Director of National Intelligence.

(B) The Director shall transmit to the congressional intelligence committees each report under subparagraph (A) within 7 calendar days of receipt of such report, together with such comments as the Director considers appropriate. The Director shall transmit to the committees of the Senate and of the House of Representatives with jurisdiction over a department of the United States Government any portion of each report under subparagraph (A) that involves a problem, abuse, or deficiency related to a component of such department simultaneously with transmission of the report to the congressional intelligence committees.

(3)(A) In the event that—

(i) the Inspector General is unable to resolve any differences with the Director affecting the execution of the duties or responsibilities of the Inspector General;

(ii) an investigation, inspection, audit, or review carried out by the Inspector General focuses on any current or former intelligence community official who—

(I) holds or held a position in an element of the intelligence community that is subject to appointment by the President, whether or not by and with the advice and consent of the Senate, including such a position held on an acting basis;

(II) holds or held a position in an element of the intelligence community, including a position held on an acting basis, that is appointed by the Director of National Intelligence; or

(III) holds or held a position as head of an element of the intelligence community or a position covered by subsection (b) or (c) of section 106;

(iii) a matter requires a report by the Inspector General to the Department of Justice on possible criminal conduct by a current or former official described in clause (ii);

(iv) the Inspector General receives notice from the Department of Justice declining or approving prosecution of possible criminal conduct of any current or former official described in clause (ii); or

(v) the Inspector General, after exhausting all possible alternatives, is unable to obtain significant documentary information in the course of an investigation, inspection, audit, or review, the Inspector General shall immediately notify, and submit a report to, the congressional intelligence committees on such matter.

(B) The Inspector General shall submit to the committees of the Senate and of the House of Representatives with jurisdiction over a department of the United States Government any portion of each report under subparagraph (A) that involves an investigation, inspection, audit, or review carried out by the Inspector General focused on any current or former official of a component of such department simultaneously with submission of the report to the congressional intelligence committees.

(4) The Director shall submit to the congressional intelligence committees any report or findings and recommendations of an investigation, inspection, audit, or review conducted by the office which has been requested by the Chairman or Vice Chairman or ranking minority member of either committee.

(5)(A) An employee of an element of the intelligence community, an employee assigned or detailed to an element of the intelligence community, or an employee of a contractor to the intelligence community who intends to report to Congress a complaint or information with respect to an urgent concern may report such complaint or information to the Inspector General.

(B) Not later than the end of the 14calendarday period beginning on the date of receipt from an employee of a complaint or information under subparagraph (A), the Inspector General shall determine whether the complaint or information appears credible. Upon making such a determination, the Inspector General shall transmit to the Director a notice of that determination, together with the complaint or information.

(C) Upon receipt of a transmittal from the Inspector General under subparagraph (B), the Director shall, within 7 calendar days of such receipt, forward such transmittal to the congressional intelligence committees, together with any comments the Director considers appropriate.

(D)(i) If the Inspector General does not find credible under subparagraph (B) a complaint or information submitted under subparagraph (A), or does not transmit the complaint or information to the Director in accurate form under subparagraph (B), the employee (subject to clause (ii)) may submit the complaint or information to Congress by contacting either or both of the congressional intelligence committees directly.

(ii) An employee may contact the congressional intelligence committees directly as described in clause (i) only if the employee—

(I) before making such a contact, furnishes to the Director, through the Inspector General, a statement of the employee's complaint or information and notice of the employee's intent to contact the congressional intelligence committees directly; and

(II) obtains and follows from the Director, through the Inspector General, direction on how to contact the congressional intelligence committees in accordance with appropriate security practices.

(iii) A member or employee of one of the congressional intelligence committees who receives a complaint or information under this subparagraph does so in that member or employee's official capacity as a member or employee of such committee.

(E) The Inspector General shall notify an employee who reports a complaint or information to the Inspector General under this paragraph of each action taken under this paragraph with respect to the complaint or information. Such notice shall be provided not later than 3 days after any such action is taken.

(F) An action taken by the Director or the Inspector General under this paragraph shall not be subject to judicial review.

(G) In this paragraph, the term "urgent concern" means any of the following:

(i) A serious or flagrant problem, abuse, violation of law or Executive order, or deficiency relating to the funding, administration, or operation of an intelligence activity within the responsibility and authority of the Director of National Intelligence involving classified information, but does not include differences of opinions concerning public policy matters.

(ii) A false statement to Congress, or a willful withholding from Congress, on an issue of material fact relating to the funding, administration, or operation of an intelligence activity.

(iii) An action, including a personnel action described in section 2302(a)(2)(A) of title 5, United States Code, constituting reprisal or threat of reprisal prohibited under subsection (g)(3)(B) of this section in response to an employee's reporting an urgent concern in accordance with this paragraph.

(H) Nothing in this section shall be construed to limit the protections afforded to an employee under section 17(d) of the Central Intelligence Agency Act of 1949 (50 U.S.C. 403q(d)) or section 8H of the Inspector General Act of 1978 (5 U.S.C. App.).

(6) In accordance with section 535 of title 28, United States Code, the Inspector General shall expeditiously report to the Attorney General any information, allegation, or complaint received by the Inspector General relating to violations of Federal criminal law that involves a program or operation of an element of the intelligence community, or in the relationships between the elements of the intelligence community, consistent with such guidelines as may be issued by the Attorney General pursuant to subsection (b)(2) of such section. A copy of each such report shall be furnished to the Director.

(l) CONSTRUCTION OF DUTIE SREGARDING ELEMENTS OFINTELLIGENCE COMMUNITY.—Except as resolved pursuant to subsection (h), the performance by the Inspector General of the Intelligence Community of any duty, responsibility, or function regarding an element of the intelligence community shall not be construed to modify or affect the duties and responsibilities of any other inspector general having duties and responsibilities relating to such element.

(m) SEPARATE BUDGET ACCOUNT.—The Director of National Intelligence shall, in accordance with procedures issued by the Director in consultation with the congressional intelligence committees, include in the National Intelligence Program budget a separate account for the Office of the Inspector General of the Intelligence Community.

(n) BUDGET.—(1) For each fiscal year, the Inspector General of the Intelligence Community shall transmit a budget estimate and request to the Director of National Intelligence that specifies for such fiscal year—

(A) the aggregate amount requested for the operations of the Inspector General;

(B) the amount requested for all training requirements of the Inspector General, including a certification from the Inspector General that the amount requested is sufficient to fund all training requirements for the Office of the Inspector General; and

(C) the amount requested to support the Council of the Inspectors General on Integrity and Efficiency, including a justification for such amount.

(2) In transmitting a proposed budget to the President for a fiscal year, the Director of National Intelligence shall include for such fiscal year—

(A) the aggregate amount requested for the Inspector General of the Intelligence Community;

(B) the amount requested for Inspector General training;

(C) the amount requested to support the Council of the Inspectors General on Integrity and Efficiency; and

(D) the comments of the Inspector General, if any, with respect to such proposed budget.

(3) The Director of National Intelligence shall submit to the congressional intelligence committees, the Committee on Appropriations of the Senate, and the Committee on Appropriations of the House of Representatives for each fiscal year—

(A) a separate statement of the budget estimate transmitted pursuant to paragraph (1);

(B) the amount requested by the Director for the Inspector General pursuant to paragraph (2)(A);

(C) the amount requested by the Director for the training of personnel of the Office of the Inspector General pursuant to paragraph (2)(B);

(D) the amount requested by the Director for support for the Council of the Inspectors General on Integrity and Efficiency pursuant to paragraph (2)(C); and

(E) the comments of the Inspector General under paragraph (2)(D), if any, on the amounts requested pursuant to paragraph (2), including whether such amounts would substantially inhibit the Inspector General from performing the duties of the Office of the Inspector General.

CHIEF FINANCIAL OFFICER OF THE INTELLIGENCE COMMUNITY
SEC. 103I. {50 U.S.C. 403–3i]

(a) CHIEF FINANCIAL OFFICER OF THE INTELLIGENCE COMMUNITY.—To assist the Director of National Intelligence in carrying out the responsibilities of the Director under this Act and other applicable provisions of law, there is within the Office of the Director of National Intelligence a Chief Financial Officer of the Intelligence Community who shall be appointed by the Director.

(b) DUTIES AND RESPONSIBILITIES.—Subject to the direction of the Director of National Intelligence, the Chief Financial Officer of the Intelligence Community shall—

(1) serve as the principal advisor to the Director of National Intelligence and the Principal Deputy Director of National Intelligence on the management and allocation of intelligence community budgetary resources;

(2) participate in overseeing a comprehensive and integrated strategic process for resource management within the intelligence community;

(3) ensure that the strategic plan of the Director of National Intelligence—

(A) is based on budgetary constraints as specified in the Future Year Intelligence Plans and Longterm Budget Projections required under section 506G; and

(B) contains specific goals and objectives to support a performancebased budget;

(4) prior to the obligation or expenditure of funds for the acquisition of any major system pursuant to a Milestone A or Milestone B decision, receive verification from appropriate authorities that the national requirements for meeting the strategic plan of the Director have been established, and that such requirements are prioritized based on budgetary constraints as specified in the Future Year Intelligence Plans and the Long term Budget Projections for such major system required under section 506G;

(5) ensure that the collection architectures of the Director are based on budgetary constraints as specified in the Future Year Intelligence Plans and the Longterm Budget Projections required under section 506G;

(6) coordinate or approve representations made to Congress by the intelligence community regarding National Intelligence Program budgetary resources;

(7) participate in key mission requirements, acquisitions, or architectural boards formed within or by the Office of the Director of National Intelligence; and

(8) perform such other duties as may be prescribed by the Director of National Intelligence.

(c) OTHER LAW.—The Chief Financial Officer of the Intelligence Community shall serve as the Chief Financial Officer of the intelligence community and, to the extent applicable, shall have the duties, responsibilities, and authorities specified in chapter 9 of title 31, United States Code.

(d) PROHIBITION ON SIMULTANEOUS SERVICE AS OTHER CHIEF FINANCIAL OFFICER.—An individual serving in the position of Chief Financial Officer of the Intelligence Community may not, while so serving, serve as the chief financial officer of any other department or agency, or component thereof, of the United States Government.

(e) DEFINITIONS.—In this section:

(1) The term "major system" has the meaning given that term in section 506A(e).

(2) The term "Milestone A" has the meaning given that term in section 506G(f).

(3) The term "Milestone B" has the meaning given that term in section 506C(e).

CENTRAL INTELLIGENCE AGENCY
SEC. 104. [50 U.S.C. §403-4]

(a) CENTRAL INTELLIGENCE AGENCY.—There is a Central Intelligence Agency.

(b) FUNCTION.—The function of the Central Intelligence Agency is to assist the Director of the Central Intelligence Agency in carrying out the responsibilities specified in section 104A(c).

DIRECTOR OF THE CENTRAL INTELLIGENCE AGENCY
SEC. 104A. [50 U.S.C. §403-4a]

(a) DIRECTOR OF CENTRAL INTELLIGENCE AGENCY.—There is a Director of the Central Intelligence Agency who shall be appointed by the President, by and with the advice and consent of the Senate.

(b) SUPERVISION.—The Director of the Central Intelligence Agency shall report to the Director of National Intelligence regarding the activities of the Central Intelligence Agency.

(c) DUTIES.—The Director of the Central Intelligence Agency shall—

(1) serve as the head of the Central Intelligence Agency; and

(2) carry out the responsibilities specified in subsection (d).

(d) RESPONSIBILITIES.—The Director of the Central Intelligence Agency shall—

(1) collect intelligence through human sources and by other appropriate means, except that the Director of the Central Intelligence Agency shall have no police, subpoena, or law enforcement powers or internal security functions;

(2) correlate and evaluate intelligence related to the national security and provide appropriate dissemination of such intelligence;

(3) provide overall direction for and coordination of the collection of national intelligence outside the United States through human sources by elements of the intelligence community authorized to undertake such collection and, in coordination with other departments, agencies, or elements of the United States Government which are authorized to undertake such collection, ensure that the most effective use is made of resources and that appropriate account is taken of the risks to the United States and those involved in such collection; and

(4) perform such other functions and duties related to intelligence affecting the national security as the President or the Director of National Intelligence may direct.

(e) TERMINATION OF EMPLOYMENT OF CIA EMPLOYEES.—

(1) Notwithstanding the provisions of any other law, the Director of the Central Intelligence Agency may, in the discretion of the Director, terminate the employment of any officer or employee of the Central Intelligence Agency whenever the Director deems the termination of employment of such officer or employee necessary or advisable in the interests of the United States.

(2) Any termination of employment of an officer or employee under paragraph (1) shall not affect the right of the officer or employee to seek or accept employment in any other department, agency, or element of the United States Government if declared eligible for such employment by the Office of Personnel Management.

(f) COORDINATION WITH FOREIGN GOVERNMENTS.—Under the direction of the Director of National Intelligence and in a manner consistent with section 207 of the Foreign Service Act of 1980 (22 U.S.C. §3927), the Director of the Central Intelligence Agency shall coordinate the relationships between elements of the intelligence community and the intelligence or security services of foreign governments or international organizations on all matters involving intelligence related to the national security or involving intelligence acquired through clandestine means.

(g) FOREIGN LANGUAGE PROFICIENCY FOR CERTAIN SENIOR LEVEL POSITIONS IN CENTRAL INTELLIGENCE AGENCY.—

(1) Except as provided pursuant to paragraph (2), an individual may not be appointed to a position in the Senior Intelligence Service in the Directorate of Intelligence or the Directorate of Operations of the Central Intelligence Agency unless the Director of the Central Intelligence Agency determines that the individual—

(A) has been certified as having a professional speaking and reading proficiency in a foreign language, such proficiency being at least level 3 on the Interagency Language Roundtable Language Skills Level or commensurate proficiency level using such other indicator of proficiency as the Director of the Central Intelligence Agency considers appropriate; and

(B) is able to effectively communicate the priorities of the United States and exercise influence in that foreign language.

(2) The Director of the Central Intelligence Agency may, in the discretion of the Director, waive the application of paragraph (1) to any position or category of positions otherwise covered by that paragraph if the Director determines that foreign language proficiency is not necessary for the successful performance of the duties and responsibilities of such position or category of positions.

DEPUTY DIRECTOR OF THE CENTRAL INTELLIGENCE AGENCY

SEC. 104B. {50 U.S.C. 403–4c}

(a) DEPUTY DIRECTOR OF THE CENTRAL INTELLIGENCE AGENCY.—There is a Deputy Director of the Central Intelligence Agency who shall be appointed by the President.

(b) DUTIES.—The Deputy Director of the Central Intelligence Agency shall—

(1) assist the Director of the Central Intelligence Agency in carrying out the duties and responsibilities of the Director of the Central Intelligence Agency; and

(2) during the absence or disability of the Director of the Central Intelligence Agency, or during a vacancy in the position of Director of the Central Intelligence Agency, act for and exercise the powers of the Director of the Central Intelligence Agency.

RESPONSIBILITIES OF THE SECRETARY OF DEFENSE PERTAINING TO THE NATIONAL INTELLIGENCE PROGRAM

SEC. 105. [50 U.S.C. §403–5]

(a) IN GENERAL.—Consistent with the sections 102 and 102A, the Secretary of Defense, in consultation with the Director of National Intelligence, shall—

(1) ensure that the budgets of the elements of the intelligence community within the Department of Defense are adequate to satisfy the overall intelligence needs of the Department of Defense, including the needs of the Chairman of the Joint Chiefs of Staff and the commanders of the unified and specified commands and, wherever such elements are performing government wide functions, the needs of other departments and agencies;

(2) ensure appropriate implementation of the policies and resource decisions of the Director by elements of the Department of Defense within the National Intelligence Program;

(3) ensure that the tactical intelligence activities of the Department of Defense complement and are compatible with intelligence activities under the National Intelligence Program;

(4) ensure that the elements of the intelligence community within the Department of Defense are responsive and timely with respect to satisfying the needs of operational military forces;

(5) eliminate waste and unnecessary duplication among the intelligence activities of the Department of Defense; and

(6) ensure that intelligence activities of the Department of Defense are conducted jointly where appropriate.

(b) RESPONSIBILITY FOR THE PERFORMANCE OF SPECIFIC FUNCTIONS.— Consistent with sections 102 and 102A of this Act, the Secretary of Defense shall ensure—

(1) through the National Security Agency (except as otherwise directed by the President or the National Security Council), the continued operation of an effective unified organization for the conduct of signals intelligence activities and shall ensure that the product is disseminated in a timely manner to authorized recipients;

(2) through the National Geospatial-Intelligence Agency (except as otherwise directed by the President or the National Security Council), with appropriate representation from the intelligence community, the continued operation of an effective unified organization within the Department of Defense—

(A) for carrying out tasking of imagery collection;

(B) for the coordination of imagery processing and exploitation activities;

(C) for ensuring the dissemination of imagery in a timely manner to authorized recipients; and

(D) notwithstanding any other provision of law, for—

(i) prescribing technical architecture and standards related to imagery intelligence and geospatial information and ensuring compliance with such architecture and standards; and

(ii) developing and fielding systems of common concern related to imagery intelligence and geospatial information;

(3) through the National Reconnaissance Office (except as otherwise directed by the President or the National Security Council), the continued operation of an effective unified organization for the research and development, acquisition, and operation of overhead reconnaissance systems necessary to satisfy the requirements of all elements of the intelligence community;

(4) through the Defense Intelligence Agency (except as otherwise directed by the President or the National Security Council), the continued operation of an effective unified system within the Department of Defense for the production of timely, objective military and military-related intelligence, based upon all sources available to the intelligence community,

and shall ensure the appropriate dissemination of such intelligence to authorized recipients;

(5) through the Defense Intelligence Agency (except as otherwise directed by the President or the National Security Council), effective management of Department of Defense human intelligence activities, including defense attaches; and

(6) that the military departments maintain sufficient capabilities to collect and produce intelligence to meet—

(A) the requirements of the Director of National Intelligence;

(B) the requirements of the Secretary of Defense or the Chairman of the Joint Chiefs of Staff;

(C) the requirements of the unified and specified combatant commands and of joint operations; and

(D) the specialized requirements of the military departments for intelligence necessary to support tactical commanders, military planners, the research and development process, the acquisition of military equipment, and training and doctrine.

(c) USE OF ELEMENTS OF DEPARTMENT OF DEFENSE.—The Secretary of Defense, in carrying out the functions described in this section, may use such elements of the Department of Defense as may be appropriate for the execution of those functions, in addition to, or in lieu of, the elements identified in this section.

ASSISTANCE TO UNITED STATES LAW ENFORCEMENT AGENCIES
SEC. 105A. [50 U.S.C. §403–5a]

(a) AUTHORITY TO PROVIDE ASSISTANCE.—Subject to subsection (b), elements of the intelligence community may, upon the request of a United States law enforcement agency, collect information outside the United States about individuals who are not United States persons. Such elements may collect such information notwithstanding that the law enforcement agency intends to use the information collected for purposes of a law enforcement investigation or counterintelligence investigation.

(b) LIMITATION ON ASSISTANCE BY ELEMENTS OF DEPARTMENT OF DEFENSE.—

(1) With respect to elements within the Department of Defense, the authority in subsection (a) applies only to the following:

(A) The National Security Agency.

(B) The National Reconnaissance Office.

(C) The National Geospatial-Intelligence Agency.

(D) The Defense Intelligence Agency.

(2) Assistance provided under this section by elements of the Department of Defense may not include the direct participation of a member of the Army, Navy, Air Force, or Marine Corps in an arrest or similar activity.

(3) Assistance may not be provided under this section by an element of the Department of Defense if the provision of such assistance will adversely affect the military preparedness of the United States.

(4) The Secretary of Defense shall prescribe regulations governing the exercise of authority under this section by elements of the Department of Defense, including regulations relating to the protection of sources and methods in the exercise of such authority.

(c) DEFINITIONS.—For purposes of subsection (a):

(1) The term "United States law enforcement agency" means any department or agency of the Federal Government that the Attorney General designates as law enforcement agency for purposes of this section.

(2) The term "United States person" means the following:

(A) A United States citizen.

(B) An alien known by the intelligence agency concerned to be a permanent resident alien.

(C) An unincorporated association substantially composed of United States citizens or permanent resident aliens.

(D) A corporation incorporated in the United States, except for a corporation directed and controlled by a foreign government or governments.

DISCLOSURE OF FOREIGN INTELLIGENCE ACQUIRED IN CRIMINAL INVESTIGATIONS; NOTICE OF CRIMINAL INVESTIGATIONS OF FOREIGN INTELLIGENCE SOURCES

SEC. 105B. [50 U.S.C. §403–5b]

(a) DISCLOSURE OF FOREIGN INTELLIGENCE.—

(1) Except as otherwise provided by law and subject to paragraph (2), the Attorney General, or the head of any other department or agency of the Federal Government with law enforcement responsibilities, shall expeditiously disclose to the Director of National Intelligence, pursuant to guidelines developed by the Attorney General in consultation with the Director, foreign intelligence acquired by an element of the Department of Justice or an element of such department or agency, as the case may be, in the course of a criminal investigation.

(2) The Attorney General by regulation and in consultation with the Director may provide for exceptions to the applicability of paragraph (1) for one or more classes of foreign intelligence, or foreign intelligence with respect to one or more targets or matters, if the Attorney General determines that disclosure of such foreign intelligence under that paragraph would jeopardize an ongoing law enforcement investigation or impair other significant law enforcement interests.

(b) PROCEDURES FOR NOTICE OF CRIMINAL INVESTIGATIONS.—Not later than 180 days after the date of enactment of this section, the Attorney General, in consultation with the Director of National Intelligence, shall develop guidelines to ensure that after receipt of a report from an element of the intelligence community of activity of a foreign intelligence source or potential foreign intelligence source that may warrant investigation as criminal activity, the Attorney General provides notice to the Director, within a reasonable period of time, of his intention to commence, or decline to commence, a criminal investigation of such activity.

(c) PROCEDURES.—The Attorney General shall develop procedures for the administration of this section, including the disclosure of foreign intelligence by elements of the Department of Justice, and elements of other departments and agencies of the Federal Government, under subsection (a) and the provision of notice with respect to criminal investigations under subsection (b).

APPOINTMENT OF OFFICIALS RESPONSIBLE FOR INTELLIGENCE RELATED ACTIVITIES

SEC. 106.¹ [50 U.S.C. §403–6]

(a) RECOMMENDATION OF DNI IN CERTAIN APPOINTMENTS.—

(1) In the event of a vacancy in a position referred to in paragraph (2), the Director of National Intelligence shall recommend to the President an individual for nomination to fill the vacancy.

(2) Paragraph (1) applies to the following positions:

---

1.   Section 1014 of the Intelligence Reform and Terrorism Prevention Act of 2004 (Public Law 108–458; 118 Stat. 3663) amended section 106 by striking all after the heading and inserting a new subsection (a). The section designation, while it no longer exists in the law, is shown above in order to reflect the probable intent of Congress.

(A) The Principal Deputy Director of National Intelligence.

(B) The Director of the Central Intelligence Agency.

(b) CONCURRENCE OF DNI IN APPOINTMENTS TO POSITIONS IN THE INTELLIGENCE COMMUNITY.—

(1) In the event of a vacancy in a position referred to in paragraph (2), the head of the department or agency having jurisdiction over the position shall obtain the concurrence of the Director of National Intelligence before appointing an individual to fill the vacancy or recommending to the President an individual to be nominated to fill the vacancy. If the Director does not concur in the recommendation, the head of the department or agency concerned may not fill the vacancy or make the recommendation to the President (as the case may be). In the case in which the Director does not concur in such a recommendation, the Director and the head of the department or agency concerned may advise the President directly of the intention to withhold concurrence or to make a recommendation, as the case may be.

(2) Paragraph (1) applies to the following positions:

(A) The Director of the National Security Agency.

(B) The Director of the National Reconnaissance Office.

(C) The Director of the National Geospatial-Intelligence Agency.

(D) The Assistant Secretary of State for Intelligence and Research.

(E) The Director of the Office of Intelligence of the Department of Energy.

(F) The Director of the Office of Counterintelligence of the Department of Energy.

(G) The Assistant Secretary for Intelligence and Analysis of the Department of the Treasury.

(H) The Executive Assistant Director for Intelligence of the Federal Bureau of Investigation or any successor to that position.

(I)[1] The Under Secretary of Homeland Security for Intelligence and Analysis.

(c) CONSULTATION WITH DNI IN CERTAIN POSITIONS.—

(1) In the event of a vacancy in a position referred to in paragraph (2), the head of the department or agency having jurisdiction over the position shall consult with the Director of National Intelligence before appointing an individual to fill the vacancy or recommending to the President an individual to be nominated to fill the vacancy.

(2) Paragraph (1) applies to the following positions:

(A) The Director of the Defense Intelligence Agency.

(B) The Assistant Commandant of the Coast Guard for Intelligence.

(C) Assistant Attorney General designated as the Assistant Attorney General for National Security under section 507A of title 28, United States Code.

NATIONAL SECURITY RESOURCES BOARD[2]
SEC. 107. [50 U.S.C. §404]

(a) The Director of the Office of Defense Mobilization,[3] subject to the direction of the President,

---

1.   Margin so in law.

2.   Section 107 deals with emergency preparedness. Section 50 of the Act of September 3, 1954(68 Stat. 1244), eliminated former subsection (a), relating to the establishment of the National Security Resources Board, and redesignated former subsections (b)–(d) as subsections (a)–(c).The section heading was not amended accordingly.

3.   The functions of the Director of the Office of Defense Mobilization under this section which previously were transferred to the President, were delegated to the Director of the Federal Emergency Management Agency by section 4–102 of Executive Order No. 12148 (July 20, 1979,44 F.R. 43239, 50 U.S.C. App. 2251 note).

is authorized, subject to the civil-service laws and the Classification Act of 1949,[4] to appoint and fix the compensation of such personnel as may be necessary to assist the Director in carrying out his functions.

(b) It shall be the function of the Director of the Office of Defense Mobilization to advise the President concerning the coordination of military, industrial, and civilian mobilization, including—

(1) policies concerning industrial and civilian mobilization in order to assure the most effective mobilization and maximum utilization of the Nation's manpower in the event of war.

(2) programs for the effective use in time of war of the Nation's natural and industrial resources for military and civilian needs, for the maintenance and stabilization of the civilian economy in time of war, and for the adjustment of such economy to war needs and conditions;

(3) policies for unifying, in time of war, the activities of Federal agencies and departments engaged in or concerned with production, procurement, distribution, or transportation of military or civilian supplies, materials, and products;

(4) the relationship between potential supplies of, and potential requirements for, manpower, resources, and productive facilities in time of war;

(5) policies for establishing adequate reserves of strategic and critical material, and for the conservation of these reserves;

(6) the strategic relocation of industries, services, government, and economic activities, the continuous operation of which is essential to the Nation's security.

(c) In performing his functions, the Director of the Office of Defense Mobilization shall utilize to the maximum extent the facilities and resources of the departments and agencies of the Government.

ANNUAL NATIONAL SECURITY STRATEGY REPORT
SEC. 108. [50 U.S.C. §404a]

(a)(1) The President shall transmit to Congress each year a comprehensive report on the national security strategy of the United States (hereinafter in this section referred to as a national security strategy report").

(2) The national security strategy report for any year shall be transmitted on the date on which the President submits to Congress the budget for the next fiscal year under section 1105 of title 31, United States Code.

(3) Not later than 150 days after the date on which a new President takes office, the President shall transmit to Congress a national security strategy report under this section. That report shall be in addition to the report for that year transmitted at the time specified in paragraph (2).

(b) Each national security strategy report shall set forth the national security strategy of the United States and shall include a comprehensive description and discussion of the following:

(1) The worldwide interests, goals, and objectives of the United States that are vital to the national security of the United States.

(2) The foreign policy, worldwide commitments, and national defense capabilities of the United States necessary to deter aggression and to implement the national security strategy of the United States.

---

4. The Classification Act of 1949 was repealed by the law enacting title 5, United States Code (Public Law 89–544, Sept. 6, 1966, 80 Stat. 378), and its provisions were codified as chapter51 and chapter 53 of that title.

(3) The proposed short-term and long-term uses of the political, economic, military, and other elements of the national power of the United States to protect or promote the interests and achieve the goals and objectives referred to in paragraph (1).

(4) The adequacy of the capabilities of the United States to carry out the national security strategy of the United States, including an evaluation of the balance among the capabilities of all elements of the national power of the United States to support the implementation of the national security strategy.

(5) Such other information as may be necessary to help inform Congress on matters relating to the national security strategy of the United States.

(c) Each national security strategy report shall be transmitted in both a classified and an unclassified form.

ANNUAL REPORT ON INTELLIGENCE
[Section 109 was repealed by section 347(a) of Public Law 111– 259.]

NATIONAL MISSION OF THE NATIONAL GEOSPATIAL-INTELLIGENCE AGENCY
SEC. 110. [50 U.S.C. §404e]

(a) IN GENERAL.—In addition to the Department of Defense missions set forth in section 442 of title 10, United States Code, the National Geospatial-Intelligence Agency shall support the imagery requirements of the Department of State and other departments and agencies of the United States outside the Department of Defense.

(b) REQUIREMENTS AND PRIORITIES.—The Director of National Intelligence shall establish requirements and priorities governing the collection of national intelligence by the National Geospatial-Intelligence Agency under subsection (a).

(c) CORRECTION OF DEFICIENCIES.—The Director of National Intelligence shall develop and implement such programs and policies as the Director and the Secretary of Defense jointly determine necessary to review and correct deficiencies identified in the capabilities of the National Geospatial-Intelligence Agency to accomplish assigned national missions, including support to the all-source analysis and production process. The Director shall consult with the Secretary of Defense on the development and implementation of such programs and policies. The Secretary shall obtain the advice of the Chairman of the Joint Chiefs of Staff regarding the matters on which the Director and the Secretary are to consult under the preceding sentence.

RESTRICTION ON INTELLIGENCE SHARING WITH THE UNITED NATIONS
SEC. 112. [50 U.S.C. §404g]

(a) PROVISION OF INTELLIGENCE INFORMATION TO THE UNITED NATIONS.—

(1) No United States intelligence information may be provided to the United Nations or any organization affiliated with the United Nations, or to any officials or employees thereof, unless the President certifies to the appropriate committees of Congress that the Director of National Intelligence, in consultation with the Secretary of State and the Secretary of Defense, has established and implemented procedures, and has worked with the United Nations to ensure implementation of procedures, for protecting from unauthorized disclosure United States intelligence sources and methods connected to such information.

(2) Paragraph (1) may be waived upon written certification by the President to the appropriate committees of Congress that providing such information to the United Nations or an organization affiliated with the United Nations, or to any officials or employees thereof, is in the national security interests of the United States.

(b) ANNUAL AND SPECIAL REPORTS.—

(1) The President shall report annually to the appropriate committees of Congress on the types and volume of intelligence provided to the United Nations and the purposes for which it was provided during the period covered by the report. The President shall also report to the appropriate committees of Congress within 15 days after it has become known to the United States Government that there has been an unauthorized disclosure of intelligence provided by the United States to the United Nations.

(2) The requirement for periodic reports under the first sentence of paragraph (1) shall not apply to the provision of intelligence that is provided only to, and for the use of, appropriately cleared United States Government personnel serving with the United Nations.

(3) In the case of the annual reports required to be submitted under the first sentence of paragraph (1) to the congressional intelligence committees, the submittal dates for such reports shall be as provided in section 507.

(c) DELEGATION OF DUTIES.—The President may not delegate or assign the duties of the President under this section.

(d) RELATIONSHIP TO EXISTING LAW.—Nothing in this section shall be construed to—

(1) impair or otherwise affect the authority of the Director of National Intelligence to protect intelligence sources and methods from unauthorized disclosure pursuant to section 103(c)(7) of this Act;[1] or

(2) supersede or otherwise affect the provisions of title V of this Act.

(e) DEFINITION.—As used in this section, the term "appropriate committees of Congress" means the Committee on Foreign Relations and the Select Committee on Intelligence of the Senate and the Committee on Foreign Relations and the Permanent Select Committee on Intelligence of the House of Representatives.

DETAIL OF INTELLIGENCE COMMUNITY PERSONNEL; INTELLIGENCE COMMUNITY ASSIGNMENT PROGRAM

SEC. 113. [50 U.S.C. §404h]

(a) DETAIL.—

(1) Notwithstanding any other provision of law, the head of a department with an element in the intelligence community or the head of an intelligence community agency or element may detail any employee within that department, agency, or element to serve in any position in the Intelligence Community Assignment Program on a reimbursable or a nonreimbursable basis.

(2) Nonreimbursable details may be for such periods as are agreed to between the heads of the parent and host agencies, up to a maximum of three years, except that such details may be extended for a period not to exceed one year when the heads of the parent and host agencies determine that such extension is in the public interest.

(b) BENEFITS, ALLOWANCES, TRAVEL, INCENTIVES.—

(1) An employee detailed under subsection (a) may be authorized any benefit, allowance, travel, or incentive otherwise provided to enhance staffing by the organization from which the employee is detailed.

(2) The head of an agency of an employee detailed under subsection (a) may pay a lodging allowance for the employee subject to the following conditions:

(A) The allowance shall be the lesser of the cost of the lodging or a maximum amount payable for the lodging as established jointly by the Director of National Intelligence and—

---

1. The amendment made by section 1072(a)(4) of Public Law 108–458 (118 Stat. 3692) to strike "section 103(c)(6) of this Act" and insert "section 102A(i) of this Act" could not be executed because the matter purported to be struck does not appear.

(i) with respect to detailed employees of the Department of Defense, the Secretary of Defense; and

(ii) with respect to detailed employees of other agencies and departments, the head of such agency or department.

(B) The detailed employee maintains a primary residence for the employee's immediate family in the local commuting area of the parent agency duty station from which the employee regularly commuted to such duty station before the detail.

(C) The lodging is within a reasonable proximity of the host agency duty station.

(D) The distance between the detailed employee's parent agency duty station and the host agency duty station is greater than 20 miles.

(E) The distance between the detailed employee's primary residence and the host agency duty station is 10 miles greater than the distance between such primary residence and the employee's parent duty station.

(F) The rate of pay applicable to the detailed employee does not exceed the rate of basic pay for grade GS–15 of the General Schedule.

DETAIL OF OTHER PERSONNEL
SEC. 113A. [50 U.S.C. 404h–1]

Except as provided in section 904(g)(2) of the Counterintelligence Enhancement Act of 2002 (50 U.S.C. 402c(g)(2)) and section 113 of this Act, and notwithstanding any other provision of law, an officer or employee of the United States or member of the Armed Forces may be detailed to the staff of an element of the intelligence community funded through the National Intelligence Program from another element of the intelligence community or from another element of the United States Government on a reimbursable or nonreimbursable basis, as jointly agreed to by the head of the receiving element and the head of the detailing element, for a period not to exceed 2 years.

ADDITIONAL ANNUAL REPORTS FROM THE DIRECTOR OF NATIONAL INTELLIGENCE
SEC. 114. [50 U.S.C. §404i]

(a) ANNUAL REPORT ON THE SAFETY AND SECURITY OF RUSSIAN NUCLEAR FACILITIES AND NUCLEAR MILITARY FORCES.—

(1) The Director of National Intelligence shall submit to the congressional leadership on an annual basis, and to the congressional intelligence committees on the date each year provided in section 507, an intelligence report assessing the safety and security of the nuclear facilities and nuclear military forces in Russia.

(2) Each such report shall include a discussion of the following:

(A) The ability of the Government of Russia to maintain its nuclear military forces.

(B) The security arrangements at civilian and military nuclear facilities in Russia.

(C) The reliability of controls and safety systems at civilian nuclear facilities in Russia.

(D) The reliability of command and control systems and procedures of the nuclear military forces in Russia.

(3) Each such report shall be submitted in unclassified form, but may contain a classified annex.

(b) ANNUAL REPORT ON HIRING AND RETENTION OF MINORITY EMPLOYEES.—

(1) The Director of National Intelligence shall, on an annual basis, submit to Congress a report on the employment of covered persons within each element of the intelligence community for the preceding fiscal year.

(2) Each such report shall include disaggregated data by category of covered person from each element of the intelligence community on the following:

(A) Of all individuals employed in the element during the fiscal year involved, the aggregate percentage of such individuals who are covered persons.

(B) Of all individuals employed in the element during the fiscal year involved at the levels referred to in clauses (i) and (ii), the percentage of covered persons employed at such levels:

(i) Positions at levels 1 through 15 of the General Schedule.

(ii) Positions at levels above GS–15.

(C) Of all individuals hired by the element involved during the fiscal year involved, the percentage of such individuals who are covered persons.

(3) Each such report shall be submitted in unclassified form, but may contain a classified annex.

(4) Nothing in this subsection shall be construed as providing for the substitution of any similar report required under another provision of law.

(5) In this subsection, the term "covered persons" means—

(A) racial and ethnic minorities;

(B) women; and

(C) individuals with disabilities.

(c) ANNUAL REPORT ON THREAT OF ATTACK ON THE UNITED STATES USING WEAPONS OF MASS DESTRUCTION.—

(1) Not later each year than the date provided in section 507, the Director of National Intelligence shall submit to the congressional committees specified in paragraph (3) a report assessing the following:

(A) The current threat of attack on the United States using ballistic missiles or cruise missiles.

(B) The current threat of attack on the United States using a chemical, biological, or nuclear weapon delivered by a system other than a ballistic missile or cruise missile.

(2) Each report under paragraph (1) shall be a national intelligence estimate, or have the formality of a national intelligence estimate.

(3) The congressional committees referred to in paragraph (1) are the following:

(A) The congressional intelligence committees.

(B) The Committees on Foreign Relations and Armed Services of the Senate.

(C) The Committees on International Relations and Armed Services of the House of Representatives.

(d) CONGRESSIONAL LEADERSHIP DEFINED.—In this section, the term "congressional leadership" means the Speaker and the minority leader of the House of Representatives and the majority leader and the minority leader of the Senate.

LIMITATION ON ESTABLISHMENT OR OPERATION OF DIPLOMATIC INTELLIGENCE SUPPORT CENTERS

SEC. 115. [50 U.S.C. 404j]

(a) IN GENERAL.—

(1) A diplomatic intelligence support center may not be established, operated, or maintained without the prior approval of the Director of National Intelligence.

(2) The Director may only approve the establishment, operation, or maintenance of a diplomatic intelligence support center if the Director determines that the establishment, operation, or maintenance of such center is required to provide necessary intelligence support in furtherance of the national security interests of the United States.

(b) PROHIBITION OF USE OF APPROPRIATIONS.—Amounts appropriated pursuant to authorizations by law for intelligence and intelligence-related activities may not be obligated or expended for the establishment, operation, or maintenance of a diplomatic intelligence support center that is not approved by the Director of National Intelligence.

(c) DEFINITIONS.—In this section:

(1) The term "diplomatic intelligence support center"means an entity to which employees of the various elements of the intelligence community (as defined in section 3(4)) are detailed for the purpose of providing analytical intelligence support that—

(A) consists of intelligence analyses on military or political matters and expertise to conduct limited assessments and dynamic taskings for a chief of mission; and

(B) is not intelligence support traditionally provided to a chief of mission by the Director of National Intelligence.

(2) The term "chief of mission" has the meaning given that term by section 102(3) of the Foreign Service Act of 1980 (22 U.S.C. 3902(3)), and includes ambassadors at large and ministers of diplomatic missions of the United States, or persons appointed to lead United States offices abroad designated by the Secretary of State as diplomatic in nature.

(d) TERMINATION.—This section shall cease to be effective onOctober 1, 2000.

TRAVEL ON ANY COMMON CARRIER FOR CERTAIN INTELLIGENCE COLLECTION PERSONNEL

SEC. 116. [50 U.S.C. §404k]

(a) IN GENERAL.—Notwithstanding any other provision of law, the Director of National Intelligence may authorize travel on any common carrier when such travel, in the discretion of the Director—

(1) is consistent with intelligence community mission requirements, or

(2) is required for cover purposes, operational needs, or other exceptional circumstances necessary for the successful performance of an intelligence community mission.

(b) AUTHORIZED DELEGATION OF DUTY.—The Director of National Intelligence may only delegate the authority granted by this section to the Principal Deputy Director of National Intelligence, or with respect to employees of the Central Intelligence Agency, to the Director of the Central Intelligence Agency.[1]

POW/MIA ANALYTIC CAPABILITY

SEC. 117. [50 U.S.C. §404l]

(a) REQUIREMENT.—

(1) The Director of National Intelligence shall, in consultation with the Secretary of Defense, establish and maintain in the intelligence community an analytic capability with responsibility for intelligence in support of the activities of the United States relating to individuals who, after December 31, 1990, are unaccounted for United States personnel.

(2) The analytic capability maintained under paragraph (1) shall be known as the "POW/MIA analytic capability of the intelligence community".

(b) UNACCOUNTED FOR UNITED STATES PERSONNEL.—In this section, the term "unaccounted for United States personnel" means the following:

(1) Any missing person (as that term is defined in section 1513(1) of title 10, United States Code).

(2) Any United States national who was killed while engaged in activities on behalf of the United States and whose remains have not been repatriated to the United States.

---

1. The amendment made by section 1072(a)(5) to strike "to the Deputy Director of Central Intelligence, or with respect to employees of the Central Intelligence Agency[,] the Director may delegate such authority to the Deputy Director for Operations" and insert "to the Principal Deputy Director of National Intelligence, or with respect to employees of the Central IntelligenceAgency, to the Director of the Central Intelligence Agency" was executed to reflect the probableintent of Congress. The comma after "Central Intelligence Agency" in the stricken matter doesnot appear.

SEMIANNUAL REPORT ON FINANCIAL INTELLIGENCE ON TERRORIST ASSETS
SEC. 118. [50 U.S.C. §404m]

(a) SEMIANNUAL REPORT.—On a semiannual basis, the Secretary of the Treasury (acting through the head of the Office of Intelligence Support) shall submit a report to the appropriate congressional committees that fully informs the committees concerning operations against terrorist financial networks. Each such report shall include with respect to the preceding six-month period—

(1) the total number of asset seizures, designations, and other actions against individuals or entities found to have engaged in financial support of terrorism;

(2) the total number of applications for asset seizure and designations of individuals or entities suspected of having engaged in financial support of terrorist activities that were granted, modified, or denied;

(3) the total number of physical searches of offices, residences, or financial records of individuals or entities suspected of having engaged in financial support for terrorist activity; and

(4) whether the financial intelligence information seized in these cases has been shared on a full and timely basis with the all departments, agencies, and other entities of the United States Government involved in intelligence activities participating in the Foreign Terrorist Asset Tracking Center.

(b) IMMEDIATE NOTIFICATION FOR EMERGENCY DESIGNATION.—In the case of a designation of an individual or entity, or the assets of an individual or entity, as having been found to have engaged in terrorist activities, the Secretary of the Treasury shall report such designation within 24 hours of such a designation to the appropriate congressional committees.

(c) SUBMITTAL DATE OF REPORTS TO CONGRESSIONAL INTELLIGENCE COMMITTEES.—In the case of the reports required to be submitted under subsection (a) to the congressional intelligence committees, the submittal dates for such reports shall be as provided in section 507.

(d) APPROPRIATE CONGRESSIONAL COMMITTEES DEFINED.—In this section, the term "appropriate congressional committees" means the following:

(1) The Permanent Select Committee on Intelligence, the Committee on Appropriations, and the Committee on Financial Services of the House of Representatives.

(2) The Select Committee on Intelligence, the Committee on Appropriations, and the Committee on Banking, Housing, and Urban Affairs of the Senate.

NATIONAL COUNTERTERRORISM CENTER
SEC. 119. [50 U.S.C. §404o]

(a) ESTABLISHMENT OF CENTER.—There is within the Office of the Director of National Intelligence a National Counterterrorism Center.

(b) DIRECTOR OF NATIONAL COUNTERTERRORISM CENTER.—

(1) There is a Director of the National Counterterrorism Center, who shall be the head of the National Counterterrorism Center, and who shall be appointed by the President, by and with the advice and consent of the Senate.

(2) The Director of the National Counterterrorism Center may not simultaneously serve in any other capacity in the executive branch.

(c) REPORTING.—

(1) The Director of the National Counterterrorism Center shall report to the Director of National Intelligence with respect to matters described in paragraph (2) and the President with respect to matters described in paragraph (3).

(2) The matters described in this paragraph are as follows:

(A) The budget and programs of the National Counterterrorism Center.

(B) The activities of the Directorate of Intelligence of the National Counterterrorism Center under subsection (h).

(C) The conduct of intelligence operations implemented by other elements of the intelligence community; and

(3) The matters described in this paragraph are the planning and progress of joint counterterrorism operations (other than intelligence operations).

(d) PRIMARY MISSIONS.—The primary missions of the National Counterterrorism Center shall be as follows:

(1) To serve as the primary organization in the United States Government for analyzing and integrating all intelligence possessed or acquired by the United States Government pertaining to terrorism and counterterrorism, excepting intelligence pertaining exclusively to domestic terrorists and domestic counterterrorism.

(2) To conduct strategic operational planning for counterterrorism activities, integrating all instruments of national power, including diplomatic, financial, military, intelligence, homeland security, and law enforcement activities within and among agencies.

(3) To assign roles and responsibilities as part of its strategic operational planning duties to lead Departments or agencies, as appropriate, for counterterrorism activities that are consistent with applicable law and that support counterterrorism strategic operational plans, but shall not direct the execution of any resulting operations.

(4) To ensure that agencies, as appropriate, have access to and receive all-source intelligence support needed to execute their counterterrorism plans or perform independent, alternative analysis.

(5) To ensure that such agencies have access to and receive intelligence needed to accomplish their assigned activities.

(6) To serve as the central and shared knowledge bank on known and suspected terrorists and international terror groups, as well as their goals, strategies, capabilities, and networks of contacts and support.

(e) DOMESTIC COUNTERTERRORISM INTELLIGENCE.—

(1) The Center may, consistent with applicable law, the direction of the President, and the guidelines referred to in section 102A(b), receive intelligence pertaining exclusively to domestic counterterrorism from any Federal, State, or local government or other source necessary to fulfill its responsibilities and retain and disseminate such intelligence.

(2) Any agency authorized to conduct counterterrorism activities may request information from the Center to assist it in its responsibilities, consistent with applicable law and the guidelines referred to in section 102A(b).

(f) DUTIES AND RESPONSIBILITIES OF DIRECTOR.—

(1) The Director of the National Counterterrorism Center shall—

(A) serve as the principal adviser to the Director of National Intelligence on intelligence operations relating to counterterrorism;

(B) provide strategic operational plans for the civilian and military counterterrorism efforts of the United States Government and for the effective integration of counterterrorism intelligence and operations across agency boundaries, both inside and outside the United States;

(C) advise the Director of National Intelligence on the extent to which the counterterrorism program recommendations and budget proposals of the departments, agencies, and elements of the United States Government conform to the priorities established by the President;

(D) disseminate terrorism information, including current terrorism threat analysis, to the President, the Vice President, the Secretaries of State, Defense, and Homeland Security, the Attorney General, the Director of the Central Intelligence Agency, and other officials of the executive branch as appropriate, and to the appropriate committees of Congress;

(E) support the Department of Justice and the Department of Homeland Security, and other appropriate agencies, in fulfillment of their responsibilities to disseminate terrorism information, consistent with applicable law, guidelines referred to in section 102A(b), Executive orders and other Presidential guidance, to State and local government officials, and other entities, and coordinate dissemination of terrorism information to foreign governments as approved by the Director of National Intelligence;

(F) develop a strategy for combining terrorist travel intelligence operations and law enforcement planning and operations into a cohesive effort to intercept terrorists, find terrorist travel facilitators, and constrain terrorist mobility;

(G) have primary responsibility within the United States Government for conducting net assessments of terrorist threats;

(H) consistent with priorities approved by the President, assist the Director of National Intelligence in establishing requirements for the intelligence community for the collection of terrorism information; and

(I) perform such other duties as the Director of National Intelligence may prescribe or are prescribed by law.

(2) Nothing in paragraph (1)(G) shall limit the authority of the departments and agencies of the United States to conduct net assessments.

(g) LIMITATION.—The Director of the National Counterterrorism Center may not direct the execution of counterterrorism operations.

(h) RESOLUTION OF DISPUTES.—The Director of National Intelligence shall resolve disagreements between the National Counterterrorism Center and the head of a department, agency, or element of the United States Government on designations, assignments, plans, or responsibilities under this section. The head of such a department, agency, or element may appeal the resolution of the disagreement by the Director of National Intelligence to the President.

(i) DIRECTORATE OF INTELLIGENCE.—The Director of the National Counterterrorism Center shall establish and maintain within the National Counterterrorism Center a Directorate of Intelligence which shall have primary responsibility within the United States Government for analysis of terrorism and terrorist organizations (except for purely domestic terrorism and domestic terrorist organizations) from all sources of intelligence, whether collected inside or outside the United States.

(j) DIRECTORATE OF STRATEGIC OPERATIONAL PLANNING.—

(1) The Director of the National Counterterrorism Center shall establish and maintain within the National Counterterrorism Center a Directorate of Strategic Operational Planning which shall provide strategic operational plans for counterterrorism operations conducted by the United States Government.

(2) Strategic operational planning shall include the mission, objectives to be achieved, tasks to be performed, interagency coordination of operational activities, and the assignment of roles and responsibilities.

(3) The Director of the National Counterterrorism Center shall monitor the implementation of strategic operational plans, and shall obtain information from each element of the intelligence community, and from each other department, agency, or element of the United States Government relevant for monitoring the progress of such entity in implementing such plans.

NATIONAL COUNTER PROLIFERATION CENTER
SEC. 119A. [50 U.S.C. §404o-1]

(a) ESTABLISHMENT.—Not later than 18 months after the date of the enactment of the National Security Intelligence Reform Act of 2004, the President shall establish a National Counter Proliferation Center, taking into account all appropriate government tools to prevent and halt the proliferation of weapons of mass destruction, their delivery systems, and related materials and technologies.

(b) MISSIONS AND OBJECTIVES.—In establishing the National Counter Proliferation Center, the President shall address the following missions and objectives to prevent and halt the proliferation of weapons of mass destruction, their delivery systems, and related materials and technologies:

(1) Establishing a primary organization within the United States Government for analyzing and integrating all intelligence possessed or acquired by the United States pertaining to proliferation.

(2) Ensuring that appropriate agencies have full access to and receive all-source intelligence support needed to execute their counter proliferation plans or activities, and perform independent, alternative analyses.

(3) Establishing a central repository on known and suspected proliferation activities, including the goals, strategies, capabilities, networks, and any individuals, groups, or entities engaged in proliferation.

(4) Disseminating proliferation information, including proliferation threats and analyses, to the President, to the appropriate departments and agencies, and to the appropriate committees of Congress.

(5) Conducting net assessments and warnings about the proliferation of weapons of mass destruction, their delivery systems, and related materials and technologies.

(6) Coordinating counter proliferation plans and activities of the various departments and agencies of the United States Government to prevent and halt the proliferation of weapons of mass destruction, their delivery systems, and related materials and technologies.

(7) Conducting strategic operational counter proliferation planning for the United States Government to prevent and halt the proliferation of weapons of mass destruction, their delivery systems, and related materials and technologies.

(c) NATIONAL SECURITY WAIVER.—The President may waive the requirements of this section, and any parts thereof, if the President determines that such requirements do not materially improve the ability of the United States Government to prevent and halt the proliferation of weapons of mass destruction, their delivery systems, and related materials and technologies. Such waiver shall be made in writing to Congress and shall include a description of how the missions and objectives in subsection (b) are being met.

(d) REPORT TO CONGRESS.—

(1) Not later than nine months after the implementation of this Act, the President shall submit to Congress, in classified form if necessary, the findings and recommendations of the President's Commission on Weapons of Mass Destruction established by Executive Order in February 2004, together with the views of the President regarding the establishment of a National Counter Proliferation Center.

(2) If the President decides not to exercise the waiver authority granted by subsection (c), the President shall submit to Congress from time to time updates and plans regarding the establishment of a National Counter Proliferation Center.

(e) SENSE OF CONGRESS.—It is the sense of Congress that a central feature of counter proliferation activities, consistent with the President's Proliferation Security Initiative, should include the physical interdiction, by air, sea, or land, of weapons of mass destruction, their delivery systems, and related materials and technologies, and enhanced law enforcement activities to identify and disrupt proliferation networks, activities, organizations, and persons.

NATIONAL INTELLIGENCE CENTERS
SEC. 119B. [50 U.S.C. §404o-2]

(a) AUTHORITY TO ESTABLISH.—The Director of National Intelligence may establish one or more national intelligence centers to address intelligence priorities, including, but not limited to, regional issues.

(b) RESOURCES OF DIRECTORS OF CENTERS.—

(1) The Director of National Intelligence shall ensure that the head of each national intelligence center under subsection (a) has appropriate authority, direction, and control of such center, and of the personnel assigned to such center, to carry out the assigned mission of such center.

(2) The Director of National Intelligence shall ensure that each national intelligence center has appropriate personnel to accomplish effectively the mission of such center.

(c) INFORMATION SHARING.—The Director of National Intelligence shall, to the extent appropriate and practicable, ensure that each national intelligence center under subsection (a) and the other elements of the intelligence community share information in order to facilitate the mission of such center.

(d) MISSION OF CENTERS.—Pursuant to the direction of the Director of National Intelligence, each national intelligence center under subsection (a) may, in the area of intelligence responsibility assigned to such center—

(1) have primary responsibility for providing all-source analysis of intelligence based upon intelligence gathered both domestically and abroad;

(2) have primary responsibility for identifying and proposing to the Director of National Intelligence intelligence collection and analysis and production requirements; and

(3) perform such other duties as the Director of National Intelligence shall specify.

(e) REVIEW AND MODIFICATION OF CENTERS.—The Director of National Intelligence shall determine on a regular basis whether—

(1) the area of intelligence responsibility assigned to each national intelligence center under subsection (a) continues to meet appropriate intelligence priorities; and

(2) the staffing and management of such center remains appropriate for the accomplishment of the mission of such center.

(f) TERMINATION.—The Director of National Intelligence may terminate any national intelligence center under subsection (a).

(g) SEPARATE BUDGET ACCOUNT.—The Director of National Intelligence shall, as appropriate, include in the National Intelligence Program budget a separate line item for each national intelligence center under subsection (a).

SEC. 119C. National Russian Threat Response Center.

(a) Establishment.—There is within the Office of the Director of National Intelligence a National Russian Threat Response Center (in this section referred to as the 'Center').

(b) Mission.—The primary missions of the Center shall be as follows:

(1) To serve as the primary organization in the United States Government for analyzing and integrating all intelligence possessed or acquired by the United States Government pertaining to threats posed by the Russian Federation to the national security, political sovereignty, and economic activity of the United States and its allies.

(2) To synchronize the efforts of the intelligence community with respect to countering efforts by Russia to undermine the national security, political sovereignty, and economic activity of the United States and its allies, including by—

(A) ensuring that each such element is aware of and coordinating on such efforts; and

(B) overseeing the development and implementation of comprehensive and integrated policy responses to such efforts.

(3) In coordination with the relevant elements of the Department of State, the Department of Defense, the intelligence community, and other departments and agencies of the United States—

(A) to develop policy recommendations for the President to detect, deter, and respond to the threats posed by Russia described in paragraph (1), including with respect to covert activities pursuant to section 503; and

(B) to monitor and assess efforts by Russia to carry out such threats.

(4) In coordination with the head of the Global Engagement Center established by section 1287 of the National Defense Authorization Act for Fiscal Year 2017 (Public Law 114–328), to examine current and emerging efforts by Russia to use propaganda and information operations relating to the threats posed by Russia described in paragraph (1).

(5) To identify and close gaps across the departments and agencies of the Federal Government with respect to expertise, readiness, and planning to address the threats posed by Russia described in paragraph (1).

(c) Director.—

(1) APPOINTMENT.—There is a Director of the Center, who shall be the head of the Center, and who shall be appointed by the Director of National Intelligence, with the concurrence of the Secretary of State. The Director may not simultaneously serve in any other capacity in the executive branch.

(2) REPORTING.—The Director of the Center shall directly report to the Director of National Intelligence.

(3) RESPONSIBILITIES.—The Director of the Center shall—

(A) ensure that the relevant departments and agencies of the Federal Government participate in the mission of the Center, including by recruiting detailees from such departments and agencies in accordance with subsection (e)(1); and

(B) have primary responsibility within the United States Government, in coordination with the Director of National Intelligence, for establishing requirements for the collection of intelligence related to, or regarding, the threats posed by Russia described in subsection (b)(1), in accordance with applicable provisions of law and Executive orders.

(d) Annual reports.—

(1) IN GENERAL.—At the direction of the Director of National Intelligence, but not less than once each year, the Director of the Center shall submit to the appropriate congressional committees a report on threats posed by Russia to the national security, political sovereignty, and economic activity of the United States and its allies.

(2) MATTERS INCLUDED.—Each report under paragraph (1) shall include, with respect to the period covered by the report, a discussion of the following:

(A) The nature of the threats described in such paragraph.

(B) The ability of the United States Government to address such threats.

(C) The progress of the Center in achieving its missions.

(D) Recommendations the Director determines necessary for legislative actions to improve the ability of the Center to achieve its missions.

(3) FORM.—Each report under paragraph (1) shall be submitted in unclassified form, but may include a classified annex.

(e) Employees.—

(1) DETAILEES.—Any Federal Government employee may be detailed to the Center on a reimbursable or nonreimbursable basis, and such detail shall be without interruption or loss of civil service status or privilege for a period of not more than 8 years.

(2) PERSONAL SERVICE CONTRACTORS.—The Director of National Intelligence, in consultation with the Secretary of State, may hire United States citizens or aliens as

personal services contractors for purposes of personnel resources of the Center, if—

(A) the Director of National Intelligence determines that existing personnel resources are insufficient;

(B) the period in which services are provided by a personal services contractor, including options, does not exceed 3 years, unless the Director of National Intelligence determines that exceptional circumstances justify an extension of up to 1 additional year;

(C) not more than 10 United States citizens or aliens are employed as personal services contractors under the authority of this paragraph at any time; and

(D) the authority of this paragraph is only used to obtain specialized skills or experience or to respond to urgent needs.

(3) SECURITY CLEARANCES.—Each employee detailed to the Center and contractor of the Center shall have the security clearance appropriate for the assigned duties of the employee or contractor.

(f) Board.—

(1) ESTABLISHMENT.—There is established a Board of the National Russian Threat Response Center (in this section referred to as the 'Board').

(2) FUNCTIONS.—The Board shall conduct oversight of the Center to ensure the Center is achieving the missions of the Center. In conducting such oversight, upon a majority vote of the members of the Board, the Board may recommend to the Director of National Intelligence that the Director of the Center should be removed for failing to achieve such missions.

(3) MEMBERSHIP.—

(A) APPOINTMENT.—The Board shall consist of 6 members. The head of each department or agency of the Federal Government specified in subparagraph (B) shall appoint a senior official from that department or agency, who shall be a member of the Senior Executive Service, as a member.

(B) DEPARTMENTS AND AGENCIES REPRESENTED.—The department or agency of the Federal Government specified in this subparagraph are the following:

(i) The Department of State.

(ii) The Department of Defense.

(iii) The Department of Justice.

(iv) The Department of the Treasury.

(v) The Department of Homeland Security.

(vi) The Central Intelligence Agency.

(4) MEETINGS.—The Board shall meet not less than biannually and shall be convened by the member appointed by the Secretary of State.

(g) International engagement.—The Director of the Center may convene biannual conferences to coordinate international efforts against threats posed by Russia described in subsection (b)(1).

(h) Termination.—The Center shall terminate on the date that is 8 years after the date of the enactment of this section.

(i) Appropriate congressional committees defined.—In this section, the term 'appropriate congressional committees' means—

(1) the congressional intelligence committees;

(2) the Committee on Foreign Affairs and the Committee on Armed Services of the House of Representatives; and

(3) the Committee on Foreign Relations and the Committee on Armed Services of the Senate.".

(b) Clerical amendment.—The table of contents at the beginning of such Act is amended by inserting after the item relating to section 119B the following new item:

TITLE II—THE DEPARTMENT OF DEFENSE

DEPARTMENT OF DEFENSE

SEC. 201. [50 U.S.C. §408] [Subsections (a) and (b) were repealed by section 307 of Public Law 87–651 (Act of September 7, 1962, 76 Stat. 526). Subsection (c) consisted of an amendment to another Act.]

(d) [50 U.S.C. 408] Except to the extent inconsistent with the provisions of this Act, the provisions of title IV of the Revised Statutes[1] as now of hereafter amended shall be applicable to the Department of Defense. [Sections 202–204 were repealed by section 307 of Public Law 87–651 (Act of September 7, 1962, 76 Stat. 526).]

DEPARTMENT OF THE ARMY

SEC. 205. [Subsections (a), (d), and (e) were repealed by the law enacting titles 10 and 32, United States Code (Act of August 10, 1956, 70A Stat. 676)].

(b) All laws, orders, regulations, and other actions relating to the Department of War or to any officer or activity whose title is changed under this section shall, insofar as they are not inconsistent with the provisions of this Act, be deemed to relate to the Department of the Army within the Department of Defense or to such officer or activity designated by his or its new title.

(c) [50 U.S.C. 409(a)] the term "Department of the Army" as used in this Act shall be construed to mean the Department of the Army at the seat of government and all field headquarters, forces, reserve components, installations, activities, and functions under the control or supervision of the Department of the Army.

DEPARTMENT OF THE NAVY

SEC. 206. (a) [50 U.S.C. 409(b)] The term "Department of the Navy" as used in this Act shall be construed to mean the Department of the Navy at the seat of government; the headquarters, United States Marine Corps; the entire operating forces of the United States Navy, including naval aviation, and of the United States Marine Corps, including the reserve components of such forces; all field activities, headquarters, forces, bases, installations, activities and functions under the control or supervision of the Department of the Navy; and the United States Coast Guard when operating as a part of the Navy pursuant to law.

[Subsections (b) and (c) were repealed by the law enacting titles 10 and 32, United States Code (Act of August 10, 1956, 70A Stat. 676)].

DEPARTMENT OF THE AIR FORCE

SEC. 207. [Subsections (a), (b), (d), (e), and (f) were repealed by the law enacting titles 10 and 32, United States Code (Act of Au-gust 10, 1956, 70A stat. 676)].

(c) [50 U.S.C. 409(c)] The term "Department of the Air Force" as used in this Act shall be construed to mean the Department of the Air Force at the seat of government and all field headquarters, forces, reserve components, installations, activities, and functions under the control or supervision of the Department of the Air Force.

---

1.   Title IV of the Revised Statutes consisted of sections 158–198 of the Revised Statutes. Sections 176 and 193 are codified as sections 492–1 and 492–2 of title 31, United States Code. The remainder of those sections have been repealed or replaced by provisions of title 5, United States Code, as enacted. See the "Tables" volume of the United States Code for the distribution of specific sections.

TITLE III—MISCELLANEOUS

NATIONAL SECURITY AGENCY VOLUNTARY SEPARATION

SEC. 301. 50 U.S.C. §409a

(a) SHORT TITLE.—This section may be cited as the "National Security Agency Voluntary Separation Act".

(b) DEFINITIONS.—For purposes of this section—

(1) the term "Director" means the Director of the National Security Agency; and

(2) the term "employee" means an employee of the National Security Agency, serving under an appointment without time limitation, who has been currently employed by the National Security Agency for a continuous period of at least 12 months prior to the effective date of the program established under subsection (c), except that such term does not include—

(A) a reemployed annuitant under subchapter III of chapter 83 or chapter 84 of title 5, United States Code, or another retirement system for employees of the Government; or

(B) an employee having a disability on the basis of which such employee is or would be eligible for disability retirement under any of the retirement systems referred to in subparagraph (A).

(c) ESTABLISHMENT OF PROGRAM.—Notwithstanding any other provision of law, the Director, in his sole discretion, may establish a program under which employees may, after October 1, 2000, be eligible for early retirement, offered separation pay to separate from service voluntarily, or both.

(d) EARLY RETIREMENT.—An employee who—

(1) is at least 50 years of age and has completed 20 years of service; or

(2) has at least 25 years of service, may, pursuant to regulations promulgated under this section, apply and be retired from the National Security Agency and receive benefits in accordance with chapter 83 or 84 of title 5, United States Code, if the employee has not less than 10 years of service with the National Security Agency.

(e) AMOUNT OF SEPARATION PAY AND TREATMENT FOR OTHER PURPOSES.—

(1) AMOUNT.—Separation pay shall be paid in a lump sum and shall be equal to the lesser of—

(A) an amount equal to the amount the employee would be entitled to receive under section 5595(c) of title 5, United States Code, if the employee were entitled to payment under such section; or

(B) $25,000.

(2) TREATMENT.—Separation pay shall not—

(A) be a basis for payment, and shall not be included in the computation, of any other type of Government benefit; and

(B) be taken into account for the purpose of determining the amount of any severance pay to which an individual may be entitled under section 5595 of title 5, United States Code, based on any other separation.

(f) REEMPLOYMENT RESTRICTIONS.—An employee who receives separation pay under such program may not be reemployed by the National Security Agency for the 12-month period beginning on the effective date of the employee's separation. An employee who receives separation pay under this section on the basis of a separation occurring on or after the date of the enactment of the Federal Workforce Restructuring Act of 1994 (Public Law 103–236; 108 Stat. 111) and accepts employment with the Government of the United States within 5 years after the date of the separation on which payment of the separation pay is based shall be required to repay the entire amount of the separation pay to the National Security Agency. If the employment is with an Executive agency (as defined by section 105 of title 5, United States Code), the Director of the Office of Personnel Management may, at the request of the head of the agency, waive the repayment if the individual involved possesses unique abilities and is the only qualified applicant available for the position. If the employment is with an entity in the legislative branch, the head of the entity or the appointing official may waive the repayment if the individual involved possesses unique abilities and is the only qualified applicant available for the position. If the employment is with the judicial branch, the Director of the Administrative Office of the United States Courts may waive the repayment if the individual involved possesses unique abilities and is the only qualified applicant available for the position.

(g) BAR ON CERTAIN EMPLOYMENT.—

(1) BAR.—An employee may not be separated from service under this section unless the employee agrees that the employee will not—

(A) act as agent or attorney for, or otherwise represent, any other person (except the United States) in any formal or informal appearance before, or, with the intent to influence, make any oral or written communication on behalf of any other person (except the United States) to the National Security Agency; or

(B) participate in any manner in the award, modification, or extension of any contract for property or services with the National Security Agency, during the 12-month period beginning on the effective date of the employee's separation from service.

(2) PENALTY.—An employee who violates an agreement under this subsection shall be liable to the United States in the amount of the separation pay paid to the employee pursuant to this section multiplied by the proportion of the 12-month period during which the employee was in violation of the agreement.

(h) LIMITATIONS.—Under this program, early retirement and separation pay may be offered only—

(1) with the prior approval of the Director;

(2) for the period specified by the Director; and

(3) to employees within such occupational groups or geographic locations, or subject to such other similar limitations or conditions, as the Director may require.

(i) REGULATIONS.—Before an employee may be eligible for early retirement, separation pay, or both, under this section, the Director shall prescribe such regulations as may be necessary to carry out this section.

(j) NOTIFICATION OF EXERCISE OF AUTHORITY.—The Director may[1] not make an offer of early retirement, separation pay, or both, pursuant to this section until 15 days after submitting to the congressional intelligence committees a report describing the occupational groups or geographic locations, or other similar limitations or conditions, required by the Director under subsection (h), and includes the proposed regulations issued pursuant to subsection (i).

(k) REMITTANCE OF FUNDS.—In addition to any other payment that is required to be made under subchapter III of chapter 83 or chapter 84 of title 5, United States Code, the National Security Agency shall remit to the Office of Personnel Management for deposit in the Treasury of the United States to the credit of the Civil Service Retirement and Disability Fund, an amount equal to 15 percent of the final basic pay of each employee to whom a voluntary separation payment has been or is to be paid under this section. The remittance required by this subsection shall be in lieu of any remittance required by section 4(a) of the Federal Workforce Restructuring Act of 1994 (5 U.S.C. §8331 note).

---

1. Section 941(b)(1) of the Intelligence Authorization Act for Fiscal Year 2003 (P.L. 107–306;116 Stat. 2431) amended this subsection by striking "'REPORTING REQUIRE-MENTS.—' and all that follows through 'The Director may' and inserting 'NOTIFICATION OF EXERCISE OF AUTHORITY.—The Director may'". There was no hyphen in law within the word "Requirements". The amendment has been executed to reflect the probable intent of Congress.

AUTHORITY OF FEDERAL BUREAU OF INVESTIGATION TO AWARD PERSONAL SERVICES CONTRACTS

SEC. 302. [50 U.S.C. §409b]

(a) IN GENERAL.—The Director of the Federal Bureau of Investigation may enter into personal services contracts if the personal services to be provided under such contracts directly support the intelligence or counterintelligence missions of the Federal Bureau of Investigation.

(b) INAPPLICABILITY OF CERTAIN REQUIREMENTS.—Contracts under subsection (a) shall not be subject to the annuity offset requirements of sections 8344 and 8468 of title 5, United States Code, the requirements of section 3109 of title 5, United States Code, or any law or regulation requiring competitive contracting.

(c) CONTRACT TO BE APPROPRIATE MEANS OF SECURING SERVICES.—The Chief Contracting Officer of the Federal Bureau of Investigation shall ensure that each personal services contract entered into by the Director under this section is the appropriate means of securing the services to be provided under such contract.

ADVISORY COMMITTEES AND PERSONNEL

SEC. 303. [50 U.S.C. §405]

(a) The Director of the Federal Emergency Management Agency, the Director of National Intelligence, and the National Security Council, acting through its Executive Secretary, are authorized to appoint such advisory committees and to employ, consistent with other provisions of this Act, such part-time advisory personnel as they may deem necessary in carrying out their respective functions and the functions of agencies under their control. Persons holding other offices or positions under the United States for which they receive compensation, while serving as members of such committees, shall receive no additional compensation for such service. Retired members of the uniformed services employed by the Director of National Intelligence who hold no other office or position under the United States for which they receive compensation, other members of such committees and other part-time advisory personnel so employed may serve without compensation or may receive compensation at a daily rate not to exceed the daily equivalent of the rate of pay in effect for grade GS–18 of the General Schedule established by section 5332 of title 5, United States Code, as determined by the appointing authority.

(b) Service of an individual as a member of any such advisory committee, or in any other part-time capacity for a department or agency hereunder, shall not be considered as service bringing such individual within the provisions of section 203, 205, or 207, of title 18, United States Code, unless the act of such individual, which by such section is made unlawful when performed by an individual referred to in such section, is with respect to any particular matter which directly involves a department or agency which such person is advising or in which such department or agency is directly interested.

AUTHORIZATION FOR APPROPRIATIONS

SEC. 307. [50 U.S.C. §411]

There are hereby authorized to be appropriated such sums as may be necessary and appropriate to carry out the provisions and purposes of this Act (other than the provisions and purposes of sections 102, 103, 104, 105 and titles V, VI, and VII).

DEFINITIONS

SEC. 308. [50 U.S.C. §410]

(a)[1] As used in this Act, the term "function" includes functions, powers, and duties.

---

1. Section 307 of Public Law 87–651 (Act of September 7, 1962, 76 Stat. 526) repealed section 308(a) less its applicability to sections 2, 101–103, and 303.

(b) As used in this Act, the term, "Department of Defense" shall be deemed to include the military departments of the Army, the Navy, and the Air Force, and all agencies created under title II of this Act.

SEVERABILITY
SEC. 309. [50 U.S.C. §401 note]

If any provision of this Act or the application thereof to any person or circumstances is held invalid, the validity of the remainder of the Act and of the application of such provision to other persons and circumstances shall not be affected thereby.

EFFECTIVE DATE
SEC. 310. [50 U.S.C. §401 note]

(a) The first sentence of section 202 (a) and sections 1, 2, 307, 308, 309, and 310 shall take effect immediately upon the enactment of this Act.

(b) Except as provided in subsection (a), the provisions of this Act shall take effect on whichever of the following days is the earlier: The day after the day upon which the Secretary of Defense first appointed takes office, or the sixtieth day after the date of the enactment of this Act.

REPEALING AND SAVING PROVISIONS
SEC. 411. [50 U.S.C. §412]

All laws, orders, and regulations inconsistent with the provisions of this title are repealed insofar as they are inconsistent with the powers, duties, and responsibilities enacted hereby: *Provided,* That the powers, duties, and responsibilities of the Secretary of Defense under this title shall be administered in conformance with the policy and requirements for administration of budgetary and fiscal matters in the Government generally, including accounting and financial reporting, and that nothing in this title shall be construed as eliminating or modifying the powers, duties, and responsibilities of any other department, agency, or officer of the Government in connection with such matters, but no such department, agency, or officer shall exercise any such powers, duties, or responsibilities in a manner that will render ineffective the provisions of this title.

TITLE V—ACCOUNTABILITY FOR INTELLIGENCE ACTIVITIES[1]

GENERAL CONGRESSIONAL OVERSIGHT PROVISIONS
SEC. 501. [50 U.S.C. §413]

(a)(1) The President shall ensure that the congressional intelligence committees are kept fully and currently informed of the intelligence activities of the United States, including any significant anticipated intelligence activity as required by this title.

(2) Nothing in this title shall be construed as requiring the approval of the congressional intelligence committees as a condition precedent to the initiation of any significant anticipated intelligence activity.

(b) The President shall ensure that any illegal intelligence activity is reported promptly to the congressional intelligence committees, as well as any corrective action that has been taken or is planned in connection with such illegal activity.

(c) The President and the congressional intelligence committees shall each establish such procedures as may be necessary to carry out the provisions of this title.

(d) The House of Representatives and the Senate shall each establish, by rule or resolution of such House, procedures to protect from unauthorized disclosure all classified information, and

---

1.   This title is also set out post at page 711 along with other materials relating to congressional oversight of intelligence activities.

all information relating to intelligence sources and methods, that is furnished to the congressional intelligence committees or to Members of Congress under this title. Such procedures shall be established in consultation with the Director of National Intelligence. In accordance with such procedures, each of the congressional intelligence committees shall promptly call to the attention of its respective House, or to any appropriate committee or committees of its respective House, any matter relating to intelligence activities requiring the attention of such House or such committee or committees.

(e) Nothing in this Act shall be construed as authority to withhold information from the congressional intelligence committees on the grounds that providing the information to the congressional intelligence committees would constitute the unauthorized disclosure of classified information or information relating to intelligence sources and methods.

(f) As used in this section, the term "intelligence activities" includes covert actions as defined in section 503(e), and includes financial intelligence activities.

REPORTING ON INTELLIGENCE ACTIVITIES OTHER THAN COVERT ACTIONS

SEC. 502. [50 U.S.C. §413a]

(a) IN GENERAL.—To the extent consistent with due regard for the protection from unauthorized disclosure of classified information relating to sensitive intelligence sources and methods or other exceptionally sensitive matters, the Director of National Intelligence and the heads of all departments, agencies, and other entities of the United States Government involved in intelligence activities shall—

(1) keep the congressional intelligence committees fully and currently informed of all intelligence activities, other than a covert action (as defined in section 503(e)), which are the responsibility of, are engaged in by, or are carried out for or on behalf of, any department, agency, or entity of the United States Government, including any significant anticipated intelligence activity and any significant intelligence failure; and

(2) furnish the congressional intelligence committees any information or material concerning intelligence activities, other than covert actions, which is within their custody or control, and which is requested by either of the congressional intelligence committees in order to carry out its authorized responsibilities.

(b) FORM AND CONTENTS OF CERTAIN REPORTS.—Any report relating to a significant anticipated intelligence activity or a significant intelligence failure that is submitted to the congressional intelligence committees for purposes of subsection (a)(1) shall be in writing, and shall contain the following:

(1) A concise statement of any facts pertinent to such report.

(2) An explanation of the significance of the intelligence activity or intelligence failure covered by such report.

(c) STANDARDS AND PROCEDURES FOR CERTAIN REPORTS.—The Director of National Intelligence, in consultation with the heads of the departments, agencies, and entities referred to in subsection (a), shall establish standards and procedures applicable to reports covered by subsection (b).

PRESIDENTIAL APPROVAL AND REPORTING OF COVERT ACTIONS
SEC. 503. [50 U.S.C. §413b]

(a) The President may not authorize the conduct of a covert action by departments, agencies, or entities of the United States Government unless the President determines such an action is necessary to support identifiable foreign policy objectives of the United States and is important to the national security of the United States, which determination shall be set forth in a finding that shall meet each of the following conditions:

(1) Each finding shall be in writing, unless immediate action by the United States is required and time does not permit the preparation of a written finding, in which case a written record of the President's decision shall be contemporaneously made and shall be reduced to a written finding as soon as possible but in no event more than 48 hours after the decision is made.

(2) Except as permitted by paragraph (1), a finding may not authorize or sanction a covert action, or any aspect of any such action, which already has occurred.

(3) Each finding shall specify each department, agency, or entity of the United States Government authorized to fund or otherwise participate in any significant way in such action. Any employee, contractor, or contract agent of a department, agency, or entity of the United States Government other than the Central Intelligence Agency directed to participate in any way in a covert action shall be subject either to the policies and regulations of the Central Intelligence Agency, or to written policies or regulations adopted by such department, agency, or entity, to govern such participation.

(4) Each finding shall specify whether it is contemplated that any third party which is not an element of, or a contractor or contract agent of, the United States Government, or is not otherwise subject to United States Government policies and regulations, will be used to fund or otherwise participate in any significant way in the covert action concerned, or be used to undertake the covert action concerned on behalf of the United States.

(5) A finding may not authorize any action that would violate the Constitution or any statute of the United States.

(b) To the extent consistent with due regard for the protection from unauthorized disclosure of classified information relating to sensitive intelligence sources and methods or other exceptionally sensitive matters, the Director of National Intelligence and the heads of all departments, agencies, and entities of the United States Government involved in a covert action—

(1) shall keep the congressional intelligence committees fully and currently informed of all covert actions which are the responsibility of, are engaged in by, or are carried out for or on behalf of, any department, agency, or entity of the United States Government, including significant failures; and

(2) shall furnish to the congressional intelligence committees any information or material concerning covert actions which is in the possession, custody, or control of any department, agency, or entity of the United States Government and which is requested by either of the congressional intelligence committees in order to carry out its authorized responsibilities.

(c)(1) The President shall ensure that any finding approved pursuant to subsection (a) shall be reported to the congressional intelligence committees as soon as possible after such approval and before the initiation of the covert action authorized by the finding, except as otherwise provided in paragraph (2) and paragraph (3).

(2) If the President determines that it is essential to limit access to the finding to meet extraordinary circumstances affecting vital interests of the United States, the finding may be reported to the chairmen and ranking minority members of the congressional intelligence committees, the Speaker and minority leader of the House of Representatives, the majority and minority leaders of the Senate, and such other member or members of the congressional leadership as may be included by the President.

(3) Whenever a finding is not reported pursuant to paragraph (1) or (2) of this section, the President shall fully inform the congressional intelligence committees in a timely fashion and shall provide a statement of the reasons for not giving prior notice.

(4) In a case under paragraph (1), (2), or (3), a copy of the finding, signed by the President, shall be provided to the chairman of each congressional intelligence committee. When access to a finding is limited to the Members of Congress specified in paragraph (2), a statement of the reasons for limiting such access shall also be provided.

(d) The President shall ensure that the congressional intelligence committees, or, if applicable, the Members of Congress specified in subsection (c)(2), are notified of any significant change in a previously approved covert action, or any significant undertaking pursuant to a previously approved finding, in the same manner as findings are reported pursuant to subsection (c).

(e) As used in this title, the term "covert action" means an activity or activities of the United States Government to influence political, economic, or military conditions abroad, where it is intended that the role of the United States Government will not be apparent or acknowledged publicly, but does not include—

(1) activities the primary purpose of which is to acquire intelligence, traditional counterintelligence activities, traditional activities to improve or maintain the operational security of United States Government programs, or administrative activities;

(2) traditional diplomatic or military activities or routine support to such activities;

(3) traditional law enforcement activities conducted by United States Government law enforcement agencies or routine support to such activities; or

(4) activities to provide routine support to the overt activities (other than activities described in paragraph (1), (2), or (3)) of other United States Government agencies abroad.

(f) No covert action may be conducted which is intended to influence United States political processes, public opinion, policies, or media.

FUNDING OF INTELLIGENCE ACTIVITIES
SEC. 504. [50 U.S.C. §414]

(a) Appropriated funds available to an intelligence agency may be obligated or expended for an intelligence or intelligence-related activity only if—

(1) those funds were specifically authorized by the Congress for use for such activities; or

(2) in the case of funds from the Reserve for Contingencies of the Central Intelligence Agency and consistent with the provisions of section 503 of this Act concerning any significant anticipated intelligence activity, the Director of the Central Intelligence Agency has notified the appropriate congressional committees of the intent to make such funds available for such activity; or

(3) in the case of funds specifically authorized by the Congress for a different activity—

(A) the activity to be funded is a higher priority intelligence or intelligence-related activity;

(B) the need for funds for such activity is based on unforeseen requirements; and

(C) the Director of National Intelligence, the Secretary of Defense, or the Attorney General, as appropriate, has notified the appropriate congressional committees of the intent to make such funds available for such activity;

(4) nothing in this subsection prohibits obligation or expenditure of funds available to an intelligence agency in accordance with sections 1535 and 1536 of title 31, United States Code.

(b) Funds available to an intelligence agency may not be made available for any intelligence or intelligence-related activity for which funds were denied by the Congress.

(c) No funds appropriated for, or otherwise available to, any department, agency, or entity of the United States Government may be expended, or may be directed to be expended, for any covert action, as defined in section 503(e), unless and until a Presidential finding required by subsection (a) of section 503 has been signed or otherwise issued in accordance with that subsection.

(d)(1) Except as otherwise specifically provided by law, funds available to an intelligence agency that are not appropriated funds may be obligated or expended for an intelligence or intelligence-related activity only if those funds are used for activities reported to the appropriate congressional committees pursuant to procedures which identify—

(A) the types of activities for which nonappropriated funds may be expended; and

(B) the circumstances under which an activity must be reported as a significant anticipated intelligence activity before such funds can be expended.

(2) Procedures for purposes of paragraph (1) shall be jointly agreed upon by the congressional intelligence committees and, as appropriate, the Director of National Intelligence or the Secretary of Defense.

(e) As used in this section—

(1) the term "intelligence agency" means any department, agency, or other entity of the United States involved in intelligence or intelligence-related activities;

(2) the term "appropriate congressional committees" means the Permanent Select Committee on Intelligence and the Committee on Appropriations of the House of Representatives and the Select Committee on Intelligence and the Committee on Appropriations of the Senate; and

(3) the term "specifically authorized by the Congress" means that—

(A) the activity and the amount of funds proposed to be used for that activity were identified in a formal budget request to the Congress, but funds shall be deemed to be specifically authorized for that activity only to the extent that the Congress both authorized the funds to be appropriated for that activity and appropriated the funds for that activity; or

(B) although the funds were not formally requested, the Congress both specifically authorized the appropriation of the funds for the activity and appropriated the funds for the activity.

NOTICE TO CONGRESS OF CERTAIN TRANSFERS OF DEFENSE ARTICLES AND DEFENSE SERVICES

SEC. 505. [50 U.S.C. §415]

(a)(1) The transfer of a defense article or defense service, or the anticipated transfer in any fiscal year of any aggregation of defense articles or defense services, exceeding $1,000,000 in value by an intelligence agency to a recipient outside that agency shall be considered a significant anticipated intelligence activity for the purpose of this title.

(2) Paragraph (1) does not apply if—

(A) the transfer is being made to a department, agency, or other entity of the United States (so long as there will not be a subsequent retransfer of the defense articles or defense services outside the United States Government in conjunction with an intelligence or intelligence-related activity); or

(B) the transfer—

(i) is being made pursuant to authorities contained in part II of the Foreign Assistance Act of 1961, the Arms Export Control Act, title 10 of the United States Code (including a law enacted pursuant to section 7307(a) of that title), or the Federal Property and Administrative Services Act of 1949, and

(ii) is not being made in conjunction with an intelligence or intelligence-related activity.

(3) An intelligence agency may not transfer any defense articles or defense services outside the agency in conjunction with any intelligence or intelligence-related activity for which funds were denied by the Congress.

(b) As used in this section—

(1) the term "intelligence agency" means any department, agency, or other entity of the United States involved in intelligence or intelligence-related activities;

(2) the terms "defense articles" and "defense services" mean the items on the United States Munitions List pursuant to section 38 of the Arms Export Control Act (22 CFR part 121);

(3) the term "transfer" means—

    (A) in the case of defense articles, the transfer of possession of those articles; and

    (B) in the case of defense services, the provision of those services; and

(4) the term "value" means—

    (A) in the case of defense articles, the greater of—

        (i) the original acquisition cost to the United States Government, plus the cost of improvements or other modifications made by or on behalf of the Government; or

        (ii) the replacement cost; and

    (B) in the case of defense services, the full cost to the Government of providing the services.

SPECIFICITY OF NATIONAL INTELLIGENCE PROGRAM BUDGET AMOUNTS FOR COUNTERTERRORISM, COUNTERPROLIFERATION, COUNTERNARCOTICS, AND COUNTERINTELLIGENCE

SEC. 506. [50 U.S.C. §415a]

(a) IN GENERAL.—The budget justification materials submitted to Congress in support of the budget of the President for a fiscal year that is submitted to Congress under section 1105(a) of title 31, United States Code, shall set forth separately the aggregate amount requested for that fiscal year for the National Intelligence Program for each of the following:

    (1) Counterterrorism.

    (2) Counterproliferation.

    (3) Counternarcotics.

    (4) Counterintelligence.

(b) ELECTION OF CLASSIFIED OR UNCLASSIFIED FORM.— Amounts set forth under subsection (a) may be set forth in unclassified form or classified form, at the election of the Director of National Intelligence.

BUDGET TREATMENT OF COSTS OF ACQUISITION OF MAJOR SYSTEMS BY THE INTELLIGENCE COMMUNITY

SEC. 506A. [50 U.S.C. §415a-1]

(a) INDEPENDENT COST ESTIMATES.—

    (1) The Director of National Intelligence shall, in consultation with the head of each element of the intelligence community concerned, prepare an independent cost estimate of the full life-cycle cost of development, procurement, and operation of each major system to be acquired by the intelligence community.

    (2) Each independent cost estimate for a major system shall, to the maximum extent practicable, specify the amount required to be appropriated and obligated to develop, procure, and operate the major system in each fiscal year of the proposed period of development, procurement, and operation of the major system.

    (3)(A) In the case of a program of the intelligence community that qualifies as a major system, an independent cost estimate shall be prepared before the submission to Congress of the budget of the President for the first fiscal year in which appropriated funds are anticipated to be obligated for the development or procurement of such major system.

        (B) In the case of a program of the intelligence community for which an independent cost estimate was not previously required to be prepared under this section, including a program for which development or procurement commenced before the date of the enactment of the Intelligence Authorization Act for Fiscal Year 2004, if the aggregate future costs of development or procurement (or any combination of such activities) of the program will exceed $500,000,000 (in current fiscal year dollars), the program shall qualify as a major system for purposes of this section, and an independent cost estimate for such major system shall be prepared before the submission to Congress of the budget of the President for the first fiscal year thereafter in which appropriated funds are anticipated to be obligated for such major system.

(4) The independent cost estimate for a major system shall be updated upon—

(A) the completion of any preliminary design review associated with the major system;

(B) any significant modification to the anticipated design of the major system; or

(C) any change in circumstances that renders the current independent cost estimate for the major system inaccurate.

(5) Any update of an independent cost estimate for a major system under paragraph (4) shall meet all requirements for independent cost estimates under this section, and shall be treated as the most current independent cost estimate for the major system until further updated under that paragraph.

(b) PREPARATION OF INDEPENDENT COST ESTIMATES.—

(1) The Director shall establish within the Office of the Director of National Intelligence an office which shall be responsible for preparing independent cost estimates, and any updates thereof, under subsection (a), unless a designation is made under paragraph (2).

(2) In the case of the acquisition of a major system for an element of the intelligence community within the Department of Defense, the Director and the Secretary of Defense shall provide that the independent cost estimate, and any updates thereof, under subsection (a) be prepared by an entity jointly designated by the Director and the Secretary in accordance with section 2434(b)(1)(A) of title 10, United States Code.

(c) UTILIZATION IN BUDGETS OF PRESIDENT.—

(1) If the budget of the President requests appropriations for any fiscal year for the development or procurement of a major system by the intelligence community, the President shall, subject to paragraph (2), request in such budget an amount of appropriations for the development or procurement, as the case may be, of the major system that is equivalent to the amount of appropriations identified in the most current independent cost estimate for the major system for obligation for each fiscal year for which appropriations are requested for the major system in such budget.

(2) If the amount of appropriations requested in the budget of the President for the development or procurement of a major system is less than the amount of appropriations identified in the most current independent cost estimate for the major system for obligation for each fiscal year for which appropriations are requested for the major system in such budget, the President shall include in the budget justification materials submitted to Congress in support of such budget—

(A) an explanation for the difference between the amount of appropriations requested and the amount of appropriations identified in the most current independent cost estimate;

(B) a description of the importance of the major system to the national security;

(C) an assessment of the consequences for the funding of all programs of the National Foreign Intelligence Program in future fiscal years if the most current independent cost estimate for the major system is accurate and additional appropriations are required in future fiscal years to ensure the continued development or procurement of the major system, including the consequences of such funding shortfalls on the major system and all other programs of the National Foreign Intelligence Program; and

(D) such other information on the funding of the major system as the President considers appropriate.

(d) INCLUSION OF ESTIMATES IN BUDGET JUSTIFICATION MATERIALS.—The budget justification materials submitted to Congress in support of the budget of the President shall include the most current independent cost estimate under this section for each major system for which appropriations are requested in such budget for any fiscal year.

(e) DEFINITIONS.—In this section:

(1) The term "budget of the President" means the budget of the President for a fiscal year as submitted to Congress under section 1105(a) of title 31, United States Code.

(2) The term "independent cost estimate" means a pragmatic and neutral analysis, assessment, and quantification of all costs and risks associated with the acquisition of a major system, which shall be based on programmatic and technical specifications provided by the office within the element of the intelligence community with primary responsibility for the development, procurement, or operation of the major system.

(3) The term "major system" means any significant program of an element of the intelligence community with projected total development and procurement costs exceeding $500,000,000 (in current fiscal year dollars), which costs shall include all end-to-end program costs, including costs associated with the development and procurement of the program and any other costs associated with the development and procurement of systems required to support or utilize the program.

ANNUAL PERSONNEL LEVEL ASSESSMENTS
FOR THE INTELLIGENCE COMMUNITY

SEC. 506B. [50 U.S.C. 415a–4]

(a) REQUIREMENTTOPROVIDE.—The Director of National Intelligence shall, in consultation with the head of each element of the intelligence community, prepare an annual personnel level assessment for such element that assesses the personnel levels for such element for the fiscal year following the fiscal year in which the assessment is submitted.

(b) SCHEDULE.—Each assessment required by subsection (a) shall be submitted to the congressional intelligence committees each year at the time that the President submits to Congress the budget for a fiscal year pursuant to section 1105 of title 31, United States Code.

(c) CONTENTS.—Each assessment required by subsection (a) submitted during a fiscal year shall contain the following information for the element of the intelligence community concerned:

(1) The budget submission for personnel costs for the upcoming fiscal year.

(2) The dollar and percentage increase or decrease of such costs as compared to the personnel costs of the current fiscal year.

(3) The dollar and percentage increase or decrease of such costs as compared to the personnel costs during the prior 5 fiscal years.

(4) The number of fulltime equivalent positions that is the basis for which personnel funds are requested for the upcoming fiscal year.

(5) The numerical and percentage increase or decrease of the number referred to in paragraph

(4) as compared to the number of fulltime equivalent positions of the current fiscal year.

(6) The numerical and percentage increase or decrease of the number referred to in paragraph

(4) as compared to the number of fulltime equivalent positions during the prior 5 fiscal years.

(7) The best estimate of the number and costs of core contract personnel to be funded by the element for the upcoming fiscal year.

(8) The numerical and percentage increase or decrease of such costs of core contract personnel as compared to the best estimate of the costs of core contract personnel of the current fiscal year.

(9) The numerical and percentage increase or decrease of such number and such costs of core contract personnel as compared to the number and cost of core contract personnel during the prior 5 fiscal years.

(10) A justification for the requested personnel and core contract personnel levels.

(11) The best estimate of the number of intelligence collectors and analysts employed or contracted by each element of the intelligence community.

(12) A statement by the Director of National Intelligence that, based on current and projected funding, the element concerned will have sufficient—

(A) internal infrastructure to support the requested personnel and core contract personnel levels;

(B) training resources to support the requested personnel levels; and

(C) funding to support the administrative and operational activities of the requested personnel levels.

VULNERABILITY ASSESSMENTS OF MAJOR SYSTEMS
SEC. 506C. [50 U.S.C. 415a–]

(a) INITIALVULNERABILITYASSESSMENTS.—

(1)(A) Except as provided in subparagraph (B), the Director of National Intelligence shall conduct and submit to the congressional intelligence committees an initial vulnerability assessment for each major system and its significant items of supply—

(i) except as provided in clause

(ii), prior to the completion of Milestone B or an equivalent acquisition decision for the major system; or

(ii) prior to the date that is 1 year after the date of the enactment of the Intelligence Authorization Act for Fiscal Year 2010 in the case of a major system for which Milestone B or an equivalent acquisition decision—

(I) was completed prior to such date of enactment; or

(II) is completed on a date during the 180day period following such date of enactment.

(B) The Director may submit to the congressional intelligence committees an initial vulnerability assessment required by clause (ii) of subparagraph (A) not later than 180 days after the date such assessment is required to be submitted under such clause if the Director notifies the congressional intelligence committees of the extension of the submission date under this subparagraph and provides a justification for such extension.

(C) The initial vulnerability assessment of a major system and its significant items of supply shall include use of an analysis based approach to—

(i) identify vulnerabilities;

(ii) define exploitation potential;

(iii) examine the system's potential effectiveness;

(iv) determine overall vulnerability; and

(v) make recommendations for risk reduction.

(2) If an initial vulnerability assessment for a major system is not submitted to the congressional intelligence committees as required by paragraph (1), funds appropriated for the acquisition of the major system may not be obligated for a major contract related to the major system. Such prohibition on the obligation of funds for the acquisition of the major system shall cease to apply on the date on which the congressional intelligence committees receive the initial vulnerability assessment.

(b) SUBSEQUENT VULNERABILITY ASSESSMENTS.—

(1) The Director of National Intelligence shall, periodically throughout the procurement of a major system or if the Director determines that a change in circumstances warrants the issuance of a subsequent vulnerability assessment, conduct a subsequent vulnerability

assessment of each major system and its significant items of supply within the National Intelligence Program.

(2) Upon the request of a congressional intelligence committee, the Director of National Intelligence may, if appropriate, recertify the previous vulnerability assessment or may conduct a subsequent vulnerability assessment of a particular major system and its significant items of supply within the National Intelligence Program.

(3) Any subsequent vulnerability assessment of a major system and its significant items of supply shall include use of an analysis based approach and, if applicable, a testingbased approach, to monitor the exploitation potential of such system and reexamine the factors described in clauses (i) through (v) of subsection (a)(1)(C).

(c) MAJOR SYSTEM MANAGEMENT.—The Director of National Intelligence shall give due consideration to the vulnerability assessments prepared for a given major system when developing and determining the National Intelligence Program budget.

(d) CONGRESSIONAL OVERSIGHT.—

(1) The Director of National Intelligence shall provide to the congressional intelligence committees a copy of each vulnerability assessment conducted under subsection (a) or (b) not later than 10 days after the date of the completion of such assessment.

(2) The Director of National Intelligence shall provide the congressional intelligence committees with a proposed schedule for subsequent periodic vulnerability assessments of a major system under subsection (b)(1) when providing such committees with the initial vulnerability assessment under subsection (a) of such system as required by paragraph (1).

(e) DEFINITIONS.—In this section:

(1) The term "item of supply" has the meaning given that term in section 4(10) of the Office of Federal Procurement Policy Act (41 U.S.C. 403(10)).

(2) The term "major contract" means each of the 6 largest prime, associate, or Governmentfurnished equipment contracts under a major system that is in excess of $40,000,000 and that is not a firm, fixed price contract.

(3) The term "major system" has the meaning given that term in section 506A(e).

(4) The term "Milestone B" means a decision to enter into major system development and demonstration pursuant to guidance prescribed by the Director of National Intelligence.

(5) The term "vulnerability assessment" means the process of identifying and quantifying vulnerabilities in a major system and its significant items of supply.

INTELLIGENCE COMMUNITY BUSINESS SYSTEM TRANSFORMATION
SEC. 506D. [50 U.S.C. 415a–6]

(a) LIMITATIONONOBLIGATION OFFUNDS.—

(1) Subject to paragraph (3), no funds appropriated to any element of the intelligence community may be obligated for an intelligence community business system transformation that will have a total cost in excess of $3,000,000 unless—

(A) the Director of the Office of Business Transformation of the Office of the Director of National Intelligence makes a certification described in paragraph (2) with respect to such intelligence community business system transformation; and

(B) such certification is approved by the board established under subsection (f).

(2) The certification described in this paragraph for an intelligence community business system transformation is a certification made by the Director of the Office of Business Transformation of the Office of the Director of National Intelligence that the intelligence community business system transformation—

(A) complies with the enterprise architecture under subsection (b) and such other policies and standards that the Director of National Intelligence considers appropriate; or

(B) is necessary—

(i) to achieve a critical national security capability or address a critical requirement; or

(ii) to prevent a significant adverse effect on a project that is needed to achieve an essential capability, taking into consideration any alternative solutions for preventing such adverse effect.

(3) With respect to a fiscal year after fiscal year 2010, the amount referred to in paragraph (1) in the matter preceding subparagraph (A) shall be equal to the sum of—

(A) the amount in effect under such paragraph (1) for the preceding fiscal year (determined after application of this paragraph), plus (B) such amount multiplied by the annual percentage increase in the consumer price index (all items; U.S. city average) as of September of the previous fiscal year.

(b) ENTERPRISE ARCHITECTURE FOR INTELLIGENCE COMMUNITY BUSINESS SYSTEMS.—

(1) The Director of National Intelligence shall, acting through the board established under subsection (f), develop and implement an enterprise architecture to cover all intelligence community business systems, and the functions and activities supported by such business systems. The enterprise architecture shall be sufficiently defined to effectively guide, constrain, and permit implementation of interoperable intelligence community business system solutions, consistent with applicable policies and procedures established by the Director of the Office of Management and Budget.

(2) The enterprise architecture under paragraph (1) shall include the following:

(A) An information infrastructure that will enable the intelligence community to—

(i) comply with all Federal accounting, financial management, and reporting requirements;

(ii) routinely produce timely, accurate, and reliable financial information for management purposes;

(iii) integrate budget, accounting, and program information and systems; and

(iv) provide for the measurement of performance, including the ability to produce timely, relevant, and reliable cost information.

(B) Policies, procedures, data standards, and system interface requirements that apply uniformly throughout the intelligence community.

(c) RESPONSIBILITIES FOR INTELLIGENCE COMMUNITY BUSINESS SYSTEM TRANSFORMATION.—The Director of National Intelligence shall be responsible for the entire life cycle of an intelligence community business system transformation, including review, approval, and oversight of the planning, design, acquisition, deployment, operation, and maintenance of the business system transformation.

(d) INTELLIGENCE COMMUNITY BUSINESS SYSTEM INVESTMENT REVIEW.—

(1) The Director of the Office of Business Transformation of the Office of the Director of National Intelligence shall establish and implement, not later than 60 days after the enactment of the Intelligence Authorization Act for Fiscal Year 2010, an investment review process for the intelligence community business systems for which the Director of the Office of Business Transformation is responsible.

(2) The investment review process under paragraph (1) shall—

(A) meet the requirements of section 11312 of title 40, United States Code; and

(B) specifically set forth the responsibilities of the Director of the Office of Business Transformation under such review process.

(3) The investment review process under paragraph (1) shall include the following elements:

(A) Review and approval by an investment review board (consisting of appropriate representatives of the intelligence community) of each intelligence community business system as an investment before the obligation of funds for such system.

(B) Periodic review, but not less often than annually, of every intelligence community business system investment.

(C) Thresholds for levels of review to ensure appropriate review of intelligence community business system investments depending on the scope, complexity, and cost of the system involved.

(D) Procedures for making certifications in accordance with the requirements of subsection (a)(2).

(e) BUDGET INFORMATION.—For each fiscal year after fiscal year 2011, the Director of National Intelligence shall include in the materials the Director submits to Congress in support of the budget for such fiscal year that is submitted to Congress under section 1105 of title 31, United States Code, the following information:

(1) An identification of each intelligence community business system for which funding is proposed in such budget.

(2) An identification of all funds, by appropriation, proposed in such budget for each such system, including—

(A) funds for current services to operate and maintain such system;

(B) funds for business systems modernization identified for each specific appropriation; and

(C) funds for associated business process improvement or reengineering efforts.

(3) The certification, if any, made under subsection (a)(2) with respect to each such system.

(f) INTELLIGENCE COMMUNITY BUSINESS SYSTEM TRANSFORMATION GOVERNANCE BOARD.—

(1) The Director of National Intelligence shall establish a board within the intelligence community business system transformation governance structure (in this subsection referred to as the "Board").

(2) The Board shall—

(A) recommend to the Director policies and procedures necessary to effectively integrate all business activities and any transformation, reform, reorganization, or process improvement initiatives undertaken within the intelligence community;

(B) review and approve any major update of—

(i) the enterprise architecture developed under subsection

(b); and

(ii) any plans for an intelligence community business systems modernization;

(C) manage crossdomain integration consistent with such enterprise architecture;

(D) coordinate initiatives for intelligence community business system transformation to maximize benefits and minimize costs for the intelligence community, and periodically report to the Director on the status of efforts to carry out an intelligence community business system transformation;

(E) ensure that funds are obligated for intelligence community business system transformation in a manner consistent with subsection

(a); and

(F) carry out such other duties as the Director shall specify.

(g) RELATION TO ANNUAL REGISTRATION REQUIREMENTS.— Nothing in this section shall be construed to alter the requirements of section 8083 of the Department of Defense Appropriations Act, 2005 (Public Law 108–287; 118 Stat. 989), with regard to information technology systems (as defined in subsection (d) of such section).

(h) RELATIONSHIP TO DEFENSE BUSINESS ENTERPRISE ARCHITECTURE.—Nothing in this section shall be construed to exempt funds authorized to be appropriated to the Department of Defense from the requirements of section 2222 of title 10, United States Code, to the extent that such requirements are otherwise applicable.

(i) RELATION TO CLINGER COHEN ACT.—

(1) Executive agency responsibilities in chapter 113 of title 40, United States Code, for any intelligence community business system transformation shall be exercised jointly by—

(A) the Director of National Intelligence and the Chief Information Officer of the Intelligence Community; and

(B) the head of the executive agency that contains the element of the intelligence community involved and the chief information officer of that executive agency.

(2) The Director of National Intelligence and the head of the executive agency referred to in paragraph (1)(B) shall enter into a Memorandum of Understanding to carry out the requirements of this section in a manner that best meets the needs of the intelligence community and the executive agency.

(j) REPORTS.—Not later than March 31 of each of the years 2011 through 2015, the Director of National Intelligence shall submit to the congressional intelligence committees a report on the compliance of the intelligence community with the requirements of this section. Each such report shall—

(1) describe actions taken and proposed for meeting the requirements of subsection (a), including—

(A) specific milestones and actual performance against specified performance measures, and any revision of such milestones and performance measures; and

(B) specific actions on the intelligence community business system transformations submitted for certification under such subsection;

(2) identify the number of intelligence community business system transformations that received a certification described in subsection (a)(2); and

(3) describe specific improvements in business operations and cost savings resulting from successful intelligence community business systems transformation efforts.

(k) DEFINITIONS.—In this section:

(1) The term "enterprise architecture" has the meaning given that term in section 3601(4) of title 44, United States Code.

(2) The terms "information system" and "information technology" have the meanings given those terms in section 11101 of title 40, United States Code.

(3) The term "intelligence community business system" means an information system, including a national security system, that is operated by, for, or on behalf of an element of the intelligence community, including a financial system, mixed system, financial data feeder system, and the business infrastructure capabilities shared by the systems of the business enterprise architecture, including people, process, and technology, that build upon the core infrastructure used to support business activities, such as acquisition, financial management, logistics, strategic planning and budgeting, installations and environment, and human resource management.

(4) The term "intelligence community business system transformation" means—

(A) the acquisition or development of a new intelligence community business system; or

(B) any significant modification or enhancement of an existing intelligence community business system (other than necessary to maintain current services).

(5) The term "national security system" has the meaning given that term in section 3542 of title 44, United States Code.

(6) The term "Office of Business Transformation of the Office of the Director of National Intelligence" includes any successor office that assumes the functions of the Office of Business Transformation of the Office of the Director of National Intelligence as carried out by the Office of Business Transformation on the date of the enactment of the Intelligence Authorization Act for Fiscal Year 2010.

REPORTS ON THE ACQUISITION OF MAJOR SYSTEMS
SEC. 506E. [50 U.S.C. 415a–7]

(a) DEFINITIONS.—In this section:

    (1) The term "cost estimate"—

        (A) means an assessment and quantification of all costs and risks associated with the acquisition of a major system based upon reasonably available information at the time the Director establishes the 2010 adjusted total acquisition cost for such system pursuant to subsection (h) or restructures such system pursuant to section 506F(c); and

        (B) does not mean an "independent cost estimate".

    (2) The term "critical cost growth threshold" means a percentage increase in the total acquisition cost for a major system of at least 25 percent over the total acquisition cost for the major system as shown in the current Baseline Estimate for the major system.

    (3)(A) The term "current Baseline Estimate" means the projected total acquisition cost of a major system that is—

        (i) approved by the Director, or a designee of the Director, at Milestone B or an equivalent acquisition decision for the development, procurement, and construction of such system;

        (ii) approved by the Director at the time such system is restructured pursuant to section 506F(c); or

        (iii) the 2010 adjusted total acquisition cost determined pursuant to subsection (h).

    (B) A current Baseline Estimate may be in the form of an independent cost estimate.

    (4) Except as otherwise specifically provided, the term "Director" means the Director of National Intelligence.

    (5) The term "independent cost estimate" has the meaning given that term in section 506A(e).

    (6) The term "major contract" means each of the 6 largest prime, associate, or Governmentfurnished equipment contracts under a major system that is in excess of $40,000,000 and that is not a firm, fixed price contract.

    (7) The term "major system" has the meaning given that term in section 506A(e).

    (8) The term "Milestone B" means a decision to enter into major system development and demonstration pursuant to guidance prescribed by the Director.

    (9) The term "program manager" means—

        (A) the head of the element of the intelligence community that is responsible for the budget, cost, schedule, and performance of a major system; or

        (B) in the case of a major system within the Office of the Director of National Intelligence, the deputy who is responsible for the budget, cost, schedule, and performance of the major system.

    (10) The term "significant cost growth threshold" means the percentage increase in the total acquisition cost for a major system of at least 15 percent over the total acquisition cost for such system as shown in the current Baseline Estimate for such system.

    (11) The term "total acquisition cost" means the amount equal to the total cost for development and procurement of, and systemspecific construction for, a major system.

(b) MAJOR SYSTEM COST REPORTS.—

(1) The program manager for a major system shall, on a quarterly basis, submit to the Director a major system cost report as described in paragraph (2).

(2) A major system cost report shall include the following information (as of the last day of the quarter for which the report is made):

(A) The total acquisition cost for the major system.

(B) Any cost variance or schedule variance in a major contract for the major system since the contract was entered into.

(C) Any changes from a major system schedule milestones or performances that are known, expected, or anticipated by the program manager.

(D) Any significant changes in the total acquisition cost for development and procurement of any software component of the major system, schedule milestones for such software component of the major system, or expected performance of such software component of the major system that are known, expected, or anticipated by the program manager.

(3) Each major system cost report required by paragraph (1) shall be submitted not more than 30 days after the end of the reporting quarter.

(c) REPORTS FOR BREACH OF SIGNIFICANT OR CRITICAL COST GROWTH THRESHOLDS.—If the program manager of a major system for which a report has previously been submitted under subsection (b) determines at any time during a quarter that there is reasonable cause to believe that the total acquisition cost for the major system has increased by a percentage equal to or greater than the significant cost growth threshold or critical cost growth threshold and if a report indicating an increase of such percentage or more has not previously been submitted to the Director, then the program manager shall immediately submit to the Director a major system cost report containing the information, determined as of the date of the report, required under subsection (b).

(d) NOTIFICATION TO CONGRESS OF COST GROWTH.—

(1) Whenever a major system cost report is submitted to the Director, the Director shall determine whether the current acquisition cost for the major system has increased by a percentage equal to or greater than the significant cost growth threshold or the critical cost growth threshold.

(2) If the Director determines that the current total acquisition cost has increased by a percentage equal to or greater than the significant cost growth threshold or critical cost growth threshold, the Director shall submit to Congress a Major System Congressional Report pursuant to subsection (e).

(e) REQUIREMENT FOR MAJOR SYSTEM CONGRESSIONAL REPORT.—

(1) Whenever the Director determines under subsection (d) that the total acquisition cost of a major system has increased by a percentage equal to or greater than the significant cost growth threshold for the major system, a Major System Congressional Report shall be submitted to Congress not later than 45 days after the date on which the Director receives the major system cost report for such major system.

(2) If the total acquisition cost of a major system (as determined by the Director under subsection (d)) increases by a percentage equal to or greater than the critical cost growth threshold for the program or subprogram, the Director shall take actions consistent with the requirements of section 506F.

(f) MAJOR SYSTEM CONGRESSIONAL REPOR TELEMENTS.—

(1) Except as provided in paragraph (2), each Major System Congressional Report shall include the following:

(A) The name of the major system.

(B) The date of the preparation of the report.

(C) The program phase of the major system as of the date of the preparation of the report.

(D) The estimate of the total acquisition cost for the major system expressed in constant baseyear dollars and in current dollars.

(E) The current Baseline Estimate for the major system in constant baseyear dollars and in current dollars.

(F) A statement of the reasons for any increase in total acquisition cost for the major system.

(G) The completion status of the major system—

(i) expressed as the percentage that the number of years for which funds have been appropriated for the major system is of the number of years for which it is planned that funds will be appropriated for the major system; and

(ii) expressed as the percentage that the amount of funds that have been appropriated for the major system is of the total amount of funds which it is planned will be appropriated for the major system.

(H) The fiscal year in which the major system was first authorized and in which funds for such system were first appropriated by Congress.

(I) The current change and the total change, in dollars and expressed as a percentage, in the total acquisition cost for the major system, stated both in constant baseyear dollars and in current dollars.

(J) The quantity of end items to be acquired under the major system and the current change and total change, if any, in that quantity.

(K) The identities of the officers responsible for management and cost control of the major system.

(L) The action taken and proposed to be taken to control future cost growth of the major system.

(M) Any changes made in the performance or schedule milestones of the major system and the extent to which such changes have contributed to the increase in total acquisition cost for the major system.

(N) The following contract performance assessment information with respect to each major contract under the major system:

(i) The name of the contractor.

(ii) The phase that the contract is in at the time of the preparation of the report.

(iii) The percentage of work under the contract that has been completed.

(iv) Any current change and the total change, in dollars and expressed as a percentage, in the contract cost.

(v) The percentage by which the contract is currently ahead of or behind schedule.

(vi) A narrative providing a summary explanation of the most significant occurrences, including cost and schedule variances under major contracts of the major system, contributing to the changes identified and a discussion of the effect these occurrences will have on the future costs and schedule of the major system.

(O) In any case in which one or more problems with a software component of the major system significantly contributed to the increase in costs of the major system, the action taken and proposed to be taken to solve such problems.

(2) A Major System Congressional Report prepared for a major system for which the increase in the total acquisition cost is due to termination or cancellation of the entire major system shall include only—

(A) the information described in subparagraphs (A) through (F) of paragraph (1); and

(B) the total percentage change in total acquisition cost for such system.

(g) PROHIBITION ON OBLIGATION OF FUNDS.—If a determination of an increase by a percentage equal to or greater than the significant cost growth threshold is made by the Director under subsection

(d) and a Major System Congressional Report containing the information described in subsection(f) is not submitted to Congress under subsection (e)(1), or if a determination of an increase by a percentage equal to or greater than the critical cost growth threshold is made by the Director under subsection (d) and the Major System Congressional Report containing the information described in subsection (f) and section 506F(b)(3) and the certification required by section 506F(b)(2) are not submitted to Congress under subsection (e)(2), funds appropriated for construction, research, development, test, evaluation, and procurement may not be obligated for a major contract under the major system. The prohibition on the obligation of funds for a major system shall cease to apply at the end of the 45day period that begins on the date—

(1) on which Congress receives the Major System Congressional Report under subsection (e)(1) with respect to that major system, in the case of a determination of an increase by a percentage equal to or greater than the significant cost growth threshold (as determined in subsection (d)); or

(2) on which Congress receives both the Major System Congressional Report under subsection (e)(2) and the certification of the Director under section 506F(b)(2) with respect to that major system, in the case of an increase by a percentage equal to or greater than the critical cost growth threshold (as determined under subsection (d)).

(h) TREATMENT OF COST INCREASES PRIOR TO ENACTMENT OF INTELLIGENCE AUTHORIZATION ACT FOR FISCAL YEAR 2010.—

(1) Not later than 180 days after the date of the enactment of the Intelligence Authorization Act for Fiscal Year 2010, the Director—

(A) shall, for each major system, determine if the total acquisition cost of such major system increased by a percentage equal to or greater than the significant cost growth threshold or the critical cost growth threshold prior to such date of enactment;

(B) shall establish for each major system for which the total acquisition cost has increased by a percentage equal to or greater than the significant cost growth threshold or the critical cost growth threshold prior to such date of enactment a revised current Baseline Estimate based upon an updated cost estimate;

(C) may, for a major system not described in subparagraph

(B), establish a revised current Baseline Estimate based upon an updated cost estimate; and

(D) shall submit to Congress a report describing—

(i) each determination made under subparagraph (A);

(ii) each revised current Baseline Estimate established for a major system under subparagraph (B); and

(iii) each revised current Baseline Estimate established for a major system under subparagraph (C), including the percentage increase of the total acquisition cost of such major system that occurred prior to the date of the enactment of such Act.

(2) The revised current Baseline Estimate established for a major system under subparagraph (B) or (C) of paragraph (1) shall be the 2010 adjusted total acquisition cost for the major system and may include the estimated cost of conducting any vulnerability assessments for such major system required under section 506C.

(i) REQUIREMENTS TO USE BASE YEAR DOLLARS.—Any determination of a percentage increase under this section shall be stated in terms of constant base year dollars.

(j) FORM OF REPORT.—Any report required to be submitted under this section may be submitted in a classified form.

CRITICAL COST GROWTH IN MAJOR SYSTEMS
SEC. 506F. [50 U.S.C. 415a–8]
(a) REASSESSMENT OF MAJOR SYSTEM.—If the Director of National Intelligence determines under section 506E(d) that the total acquisition cost of a major system has increased by a percentage equal to or greater than the critical cost growth threshold for the major system, the Director shall—

> (1) determine the root cause or causes of the critical cost growth, in accordance with applicable statutory requirements, policies, procedures, and guidance; and
> (2) carry out an assessment of—
>> (A) the projected cost of completing the major system if current requirements are not modified;
>> (B) the projected cost of completing the major system based on reasonable modification of such requirements;
>> (C) the rough order of magnitude of the costs of any reasonable alternative system or capability; and
>> (D) the need to reduce funding for other systems due to the growth in cost of the major system.

(b) PRESUMPTION OF TERMINATION.—

> (1) After conducting the reassessment required by subsection (a) with respect to a major system, the Director shall terminate the major system unless the Director submits to Congress a Major System Congressional Report containing a certification in accordance with paragraph (2) and the information described in paragraph (3). The Director shall submit such Major System Congressional Report and certification not later than 90 days after the date the Director receives the relevant major system cost report under subsection (b) or (c) of section 506E.
> (2) A certification described by this paragraph with respect to a major system is a written certification that—
>> (A) the continuation of the major system is essential to the national security;
>> (B) there are no alternatives to the major system that will provide acceptable capability to meet the intelligence requirement at less cost;
>> (C) the new estimates of the total acquisition cost have been determined by the Director to be reasonable;
>> (D) the major system is a higher priority than other systems whose funding must be reduced to accommodate the growth in cost of the major system; and
>> (E) the management structure for the major system is adequate to manage and control the total acquisition cost.
> (3) A Major System Congressional Report accompanying a written certification under paragraph (2) shall include, in addition to the requirements of section 506E(e), the root cause analysis and assessment carried out pursuant to subsection (a), the basis for each determination made in accordance with subparagraphs (A) through (E) of paragraph (2), and a description of all funding changes made as a result of the growth in the cost of the major system, including reductions made in funding for other systems to accommodate such cost growth, together with supporting documentation.

(c) ACTIONS IF MAJOR SYSTEM NOT TERMINATED.—If the Director elects not to terminate a major system pursuant to subsection (b), the Director shall—

> (1) restructure the major system in a manner that addresses the root cause or causes of the

critical cost growth, as identified pursuant to subsection (a), and ensures that the system has an appropriate management structure as set forth in the certification submitted pursuant to subsection (b)(2)(E);

(2) rescind the most recent Milestone approval for the major system;

(3) require a new Milestone approval for the major system before taking any action to enter a new contract, exercise an option under an existing contract, or otherwise extend the scope of an existing contract under the system, except to the extent determined necessary by the Milestone Decision Authority, on a nondelegable basis, to ensure that the system may be restructured as intended by the Director without unnecessarily wasting resources;

(4) establish a revised current Baseline Estimate for the major system based upon an updated cost estimate; and

(5) conduct regular reviews of the major system.

(d) ACTIONS IF MAJOR SYSTEM TERMINATED.—If a major system is terminated pursuant to subsection (b), the Director shall submit to Congress a written report setting forth—

(1) an explanation of the reasons for terminating the major system;

(2) the alternatives considered to address any problems in the major system; and

(3) the course the Director plans to pursue to meet any intelligence requirements otherwise intended to be met by the major system.

(e) FORM OF REPORT.—Any report or certification required to be submitted under this section may be submitted in a classified form.

(f) WAIVER.—(1) The Director may waive the requirements of subsections (d)(2), (e), and (g) of section 506E and subsections (a)(2), (b), (c), and (d) of this section with respect to a major system if the Director determines that at least 90 percent of the amount of the current Baseline Estimate for the major system has been expended.

(2)(A) If the Director grants a waiver under paragraph (1) with respect to a major system, the Director shall submit to the congressional intelligence committees written notice of the waiver that includes—

(i) the information described in section 506E(f); and

(ii) if the current total acquisition cost of the major system has increased by a percentage equal to or greater than the critical cost growth threshold—

(I) a determination of the root cause or causes of the critical cost growth, as described in subsection (a)(1); and

(II) a certification that includes the elements described in subparagraphs (A), (B), and (E) of subsection (b)(2).

(B) The Director shall submit the written notice required by subparagraph (A) not later than 90 days after the date that the Director receives a major system cost report under subsection (b) or (c) of section 506E that indicates that the total acquisition cost for the major system has increased by a percentage equal to or greater than the significant cost growth threshold or critical cost growth threshold.

(g) DEFINITIONS.—In this section, the terms "cost estimate", "critical cost growth threshold", "current Baseline Estimate", "major system", and "total acquisition cost" have the meaning given those terms in section 506E(a).

FUTURE BUDGET PROJECTIONS
SEC. 506G. [50 U.S.C. 415a–9]
(a) FUTURE YEAR INTELLIGENCE PLANS.—

(1) The Director of National Intelligence, with the concurrence of the Director of the Office of Management and Budget, shall provide to the congressional intelligence committees a Future Year Intelligence Plan, as described in paragraph (2), for—

(A) each expenditure center in the National Intelligence Program; and

(B) each major system in the National Intelligence Program.

(2)(A) A Future Year Intelligence Plan submitted under this subsection shall include the yearbyyear proposed funding for each center or system referred to in subparagraph (A) or (B) of paragraph (1), for the budget year for which the Plan is submitted and not less than the 4 subsequent fiscal years.

(B) A Future Year Intelligence Plan submitted under subparagraph (B) of paragraph (1) for a major system shall include—

(i) the estimated total lifecycle cost of such major system; and

(ii) major milestones that have significant resource implications for such major system.

(b) LONG TERM BUDGET PROJECTIONS.—

(1) The Director of National Intelligence, with the concurrence of the Director of the Office of Management and Budget, shall provide to the congressional intelligence committees a Longterm Budget Projection for each element of the intelligence community funded under the National Intelligence Program acquiring a major system that includes the budget for such element for the 5year period that begins on the day after the end of the last fiscal year for which yearbyyear pro posed funding is included in a Future Year Intelligence Plan for such major system in accordance with subsection (a)(2)(A).

(2) A Longterm Budget Projection submitted under paragraph (1) shall include—

(A) projections for the appropriate element of the intelligence community for—

(i) pay and benefits of officers and employees of such element;

(ii) other operating and support costs and minor acquisitions of such element;

(iii) research and technology required by such element;

(iv) current and planned major system acquisitions for such element;

(v) any future major system acquisitions for such element; and

(vi) any additional funding projections that the Director of National Intelligence considers appropriate;

(B) a budget projection based on effective cost and schedule execution of current or planned major system acquisitions and application of Office of Management and Budget inflation estimates to future major system acquisitions;

(C) any additional assumptions and projections that the Director of National Intelligence considers appropriate; and

(D) a description of whether, and to what extent, the total projection for each year exceeds the level that would result from applying the most recent Office of Management and Budget inflation estimate to the budget of that element of the intelligence community.

(c) SUBMISSION TO CONGRESS.—The Director of National Intelligence, with the concurrence of the Director of the Office of Management and Budget, shall submit to the congressional intelligence committees each Future Year Intelligence Plan or Longterm Budget Projection required under subsection (a) or (b) for a fiscal year at the time that the President submits to Congress the budget for such fiscal year pursuant section 1105 of title 31, United States Code.

(d) MAJOR SYSTEM AFFORDABILITY REPORT.—

(1) The Director of National Intelligence, with the concurrence of the Director of the Office of Management and Budget, shall prepare a report on the acquisition of a major system funded under the National Intelligence Program before the time that the President submits to Congress the budget for the first fiscal year in which appropriated funds are anticipated to be obligated for the development or procurement of such major system.

(2) The report on such major system shall include an assessment of whether, and to what

extent, such acquisition, if developed, procured, and operated, is projected to cause an increase in the most recent Future Year Intelligence Plan and Longterm Budget Projection submitted under section 506G for an element of the intelligence community.

(3) The Director of National Intelligence shall update the report whenever an independent cost estimate must be updated pursuant to section 506A(a)(4).

(4) The Director of National Intelligence shall submit each report required by this subsection at the time that the President submits to Congress the budget for a fiscal year pursuant to section 1105 of title 31, United States Code.

(e) DEFINITIONS.—In this section:

(1) BUDGET YEAR.—The term "budget year" means the next fiscal year for which the President is required to submit to Congress a budget pursuant to section 1105 of title 31, United States Code.

(2) INDEPENDENT COST ESTIMATE; MAJOR SYSTEM.—The terms "independent cost estimate" and "major system" have the meaning given those terms in section 506A(e).

REPORTS ON SECURITY CLEARANCES
SEC. 506H. [50 U.S.C. 415a–10]

(a) QUADRENNIAL AUDIT OF POSITION REQUIREMENTS.—

(1) The President shall every four years conduct an audit of the manner in which the executive branch determines whether a security clearance is required for a particular position in the United States Government.

(2) Not later than 30 days after the completion of an audit conducted under paragraph (1), the President shall submit to Congress the results of such audit.

(b) REPORT ON SECURITY CLEARANCE DETERMINATIONS.—

(1) Not later than February 1 of each year, the President shall submit to Congress a report on the security clearance process. Such report shall include, for each security clearance level—

(A) the number of employees of the United States Government who—

(i) held a security clearance at such level as of October 1 of the preceding year; and

(ii) were approved for a security clearance at such level during the preceding fiscal year;

(B) the number of contractors to the United States Government who—

(i) held a security clearance at such level as of October 1 of the preceding year; and

(ii) were approved for a security clearance at such level during the preceding fiscal year; and

(C) for each element of the intelligence community—

(i) the total amount of time it took to process the security clearance determination for such level that—

(I) was among the 80 percent of security clearance determinations made during the preceding fiscal year that took the shortest amount of time to complete; and

(II) took the longest amount of time to complete;

(ii) the total amount of time it took to process the security clearance determination for such level that—

(I) was among the 90 percent of security clearance determinations made during the preceding fiscal year that took the shortest amount of time to complete; and

(II) took the longest amount of time to complete;

(iii) the number of pending security clearance investigations for such level as of October 1 of the preceding year that have remained pending for—

(I) 4 months or less;

(II) between 4 months and 8 months;

(III) between 8 months and one year; and

(IV) more than one year;

(iv) the percentage of reviews during the preceding fiscal year that resulted in a denial or revocation of a security clearance;

(v) the percentage of investigations during the preceding fiscal year that resulted in incomplete information;

(vi) the percentage of investigations during the preceding fiscal year that did not result in enough information to make a decision on potentially adverse information; and

(vii) for security clearance determinations completed or pending during the preceding fiscal year that have taken longer than one year to complete—

(I) the number of security clearance determinations for positions as employees of the United States Government that required more than one year to complete;

(II) the number of security clearance determinations for contractors that required more than one year to complete;

(III) the agencies that investigated and adjudicated such determinations; and

(IV) the cause of significant delays in such determinations.

(2) For purposes of paragraph (1), the President may consider—

(A) security clearances at the level of confidential and secret as one security clearance level; and

(B) security clearances at the level of top secret or higher as one security clearance level.

(c) FORM.—The results required under subsection (a)(2) and the reports required under subsection (b)(1) shall be submitted in unclassified form, but may include a classified annex.

DATE OF SUBMITTAL OF VARIOUS ANNUAL AND SEMIANNUAL REPORTS TO THE CONGRESSIONAL INTELLIGENCE COMMITTEES

SEC. 507. [50 U.S.C. §415b]

(a) ANNUAL REPORTS.—

(1) The date for the submittal to the congressional intelligence committees of the following annual reports shall be the date each year provided in subsection (c)(1)(A):

(A) The annual report on intelligence required by section 109.

(B) The annual report on intelligence provided to the United Nations required by section 112(b)(1).

(C) The annual report on the protection of the identities of covert agents required by section 603.

(D) The annual report of the Inspectors Generals of the intelligence community on proposed resources and activities of their offices required by section 8H(g) of the Inspector General Act of 1978.

(E) The annual report on the acquisition of technology relating to weapons of mass destruction and advanced conventional munitions required by section 721 of the Intelligence Authorization Act for Fiscal Year 1997 (Public Law 104-293; 50 U.S.C. §2366).

(F) The annual report on commercial activities as security for intelligence collection required by section 437(c) of title 10, United States Code.

(G) The annual update on foreign industrial espionage required by section 809(b) of the Counterintelligence and Security Enhancements Act of 1994 (title VIII of Public Law 103–359; 50 U.S.C. App. §2170b(b)).

(H) The annual report on certifications for immunity in interdiction of aircraft engaged in illicit drug trafficking required by section 1012(c)(2) of the National Defense Authorization Act for Fiscal Year 1995 (22 U.S.C. §2291–4(c)(2)).

(I) The annual report on activities under the David L. Boren National Security Education Act of 1991 (title VIII of Public Law 102–183; 50 U.S.C. §1901 et seq.) required by section 806(a) of that Act (50 U.S.C. §1906(a)).

(J) The annual report on hiring and retention of minority employees in the intelligence community required by section 114(c).

(2) The date for the submittal to the congressional intelligence committees of the following annual reports shall be the date each year provided in subsection (c)(1)(B):

(A) The annual report on the safety and security of Russian nuclear facilities and nuclear military forces required by section 114(a).

(B) The annual report on the threat of attack on the United States from weapons of mass destruction required by section 114(c).

(C) The annual report on improvements of the financial statements of the intelligence community for auditing purposes required by section 114A.

(D) The annual report on counterdrug intelligence matters required by section 826 of the Intelligence Authorization Act for Fiscal Year 2003.

(b) SEMIANNUAL REPORTS.—The dates for the submittal to the congressional intelligence committees of the following semiannual reports shall be the dates each year provided in subsection (c)(2):

(1) The semiannual reports on the Office of the Inspector General of the Central Intelligence Agency required by section 17(d)(1) of the Central Intelligence Agency Act of 1949 (50 U.S.C. §403q(d)(1)).

(2) The semiannual reports on decisions not to prosecute certain violations of law under the Classified Information Procedures Act (18 U.S.C. App.) as required by section 13 of that Act.

(3) The semiannual reports on the activities of the Diplomatic Telecommunications Service Program Office (DTS–PO) required by section 322(a)(6)(D)(ii) of the Intelligence Authorization Act for Fiscal Year 2001 (22 U.S.C. §7302(a)(6)(D)(ii)).

(4) The semiannual reports on the disclosure of information and consumer reports to the Federal Bureau of Investigation for counterintelligence purposes required by section 624(h)(2) of the Fair Credit Reporting Act (15 U.S.C. §1681u(h)(2)).

(5) The semiannual provision of information on requests for financial information for foreign counterintelligence purposes required by section 1114(a)(5)(C) of the Right to Financial Privacy Act of 1978 (12 U.S.C. §3414(a)(5)(C)).

(6) The semiannual report on financial intelligence on terrorist assets required by section 118.

(c) SUBMITTAL DATES FOR REPORTS.—

(1)(A) Except as provided in subsection (d), each annual report listed in subsection (a)(1) shall be submitted not later than February 1.

(B) Except as provided in subsection (d), each annual report listed in subsection (a)(2) shall be submitted not later than December 1.

(2) Except as provided in subsection (d), each semiannual report listed in subsection (b) shall be submitted not later than February 1 and August 1.

(d) POSTPONEMENT OF SUBMITTAL.—

(1) Subject to paragraph (3), the date for the submittal of—

(A) an annual report listed in subsection (a)(1) may be postponed until March 1;

(B) an annual report listed in subsection (a)(2) may be postponed until January 1; and

(C) a semiannual report listed in subsection (b) may be postponed until March 1 or September 1, as the case may be, if the official required to submit such report submits to the congressional intelligence committees a written notification of such postponement.

(2)(A) Notwithstanding any other provision of law and subject to paragraph (3), the date for the submittal to the congressional intelligence committees of any report described in subparagraph (B) may be postponed by not more than 30 days from the date otherwise specified in the provision of law for the submittal of such report if the official required to submit such report submits to the congressional intelligence committees a written notification of such postponement.

(B) A report described in this subparagraph is any report on intelligence or intelligence-related activities of the United States Government that is submitted under a provision of law requiring the submittal of only a single report.

(3)(A) The date for the submittal of a report whose submittal is postponed under paragraph (1) or (2) may be postponed beyond the time provided for the submittal of such report under such paragraph if the official required to submit such report submits to the congressional intelligence committees a written certification that preparation and submittal of such report at such time will impede the work of officers or employees of the intelligence community in a manner that will be detrimental to the national security of the United States.

(B) A certification with respect to a report under subparagraph (A) shall include a proposed submittal date for such report, and such report shall be submitted not later than that date.

CERTIFICATION OF COMPLIANCE WITH OVERSIGHT REQUIREMENTS
SEC. 508. [50 U.S.C. 415d]

The head of each element of the intelligence community shall annually submit to the congressional intelligence committees—

(1) a certification that, to the best of the knowledge of the head of such element—

(A) the head of such element is in full compliance with the requirements of this title; and

(B) any information required to be submitted by the head of such element under this Act before the date of the submission of such certification has been properly submitted; or

(2) if the head of such element is unable to submit a certification under paragraph (1), a statement—

(A) of the reasons the head of such element is unable to submit such a certification;

(B) (B) describing any information required to be submitted by the head of such element under this Act before the date of the submission of such statement that has not been properly submitted; and

(C) (C) that the head of such element will submit such information as soon as possible after the submission of such statement.

TITLE VI—PROTECTION OF CERTAIN NATIONAL SECURITY INFORMATION

PROTECTION OF IDENTITIES OF CERTAIN UNITED STATES UNDERCOVER
INTELLIGENCE OFFICERS, AGENTS, INFORMANTS, AND SOURCES
SEC. 601. [50 U.S.C. §421]

(a) Whoever, having or having had authorized access to classified information that identifies a covert agent, intentionally discloses any information identifying such covert agent to any individual not authorized to receive classified information, knowing that the information disclosed so identifies such covert agent and that the United States is taking affirmative measures to conceal such covert agent's intelligence relationship to the United States, shall be fined under title 18, United States Code, or imprisoned not more than ten years, or both.

(b) Whoever, as a result of having authorized access to classified information, learns the identity of a covert agent and intentionally discloses any information identifying such covert agent to any individual not authorized to receive classified information, knowing that the information disclosed so identifies such covert agent and that the United States is taking affirmative measures to conceal such covert agent's intelligence relationship to the United States, shall be fined under title 18, United States Code, or imprisoned not more than five years, or both.

(c) Whoever, in the course of a pattern of activities intended to identify and expose covert agents and with reason to believe that such activities would impair or impede the foreign intelligence activities of the United States, discloses any information that identifies an individual as a covert agent to any individual not authorized to receive classified information, knowing that the information disclosed so identifies such individual and that the United States is taking affirmative measures to conceal such individual's classified intelligence relationship to the United States, shall be fined under title 18, United States Code, or imprisoned not more than three years, or both.

(d) A term of imprisonment imposed under this section shall be consecutive to any other sentence of imprisonment.

DEFENSES AND EXCEPTIONS
SEC. 602. [50 U.S.C. §422]

(a) It is a defense to a prosecution under section 601 that before the commission of the offense with which the defendant is charged, the United States had publicly acknowledged or revealed the intelligence relationship to the United States of the individual the disclosure of whose intelligence relationship to the United States is the basis for the prosecution.

(b)(1) Subject to paragraph (2), no person other than a person committing an offense under section 601 shall be subject to prosecution under such section by virtue of section 2 or 4 of title 18, United States Code, or shall be subject to prosecution for conspiracy to commit an offense under such section.

(2) Paragraph (1) shall not apply (A) in the case of a person who acted in the course of a pattern of activities intended to identify and expose covert agents and with reason to believe that such activities would impair or impede the foreign intelligence activities of the United States, or (B) in the case of a person who has authorized access to classified information.

(c) It shall not be an offense under section 601 to transmit information described in such section directly to either congressional intelligence committee.

(d) It shall not be an offense under section 601 for an individual to disclose information that solely identifies himself as a covert agent.

REPORT
SEC. 603. [50 U.S.C. §423]

(a) The President, after receiving information from the Director of National Intelligence, shall submit to the congressional intelligence committees an annual report on measures to protect the identities of covert agents, and on any other matter relevant to the protection of the identities of covert agents. The date for the submittal of the report shall be the date provided in section 507.

(b) The report described in subsection (a) shall be exempt from any requirement for publication or disclosure.

EXTRATERRITORIAL JURISDICTION
SEC. 604. [50 U.S.C. §424]

There is jurisdiction over an offense under section 601 committed outside the United States if the individual committing the offense is a citizen of the United States or an alien lawfully admitted to the United States for permanent residence (as defined in section 101(a)(20) of the Immigration and Nationality Act).

PROVIDING INFORMATION TO CONGRESS
SEC. 605. [50 U.S.C. §425]

Nothing in this title may be construed as authority to withhold information from the Congress or from a committee of either House of Congress.

DEFINITIONS
SEC. 606. [50 U.S.C. §426]

For the purposes of this title:

(1) The term "classified information" means information or material designated and clearly marked or clearly represented, pursuant to the provisions of a statute or Executive order (or a regulation or order issued pursuant to a statute or Executive order), as requiring a specific degree of protection against unauthorized disclosure for reasons of national security.

(2) The term "authorized", when used with respect to access to classified information, means having authority, right, or permission pursuant to the provisions of a statute, Executive order, directive of the head of any department or agency engaged in foreign intelligence or counterintelligence activities, order of any United States court, or provisions of any Rule of the House of Representatives or resolution of the Senate which assigns responsibility within the respective House of Congress for the oversight of intelligence activities.

(3) The term "disclose" means to communicate, provide, impart, transmit, transfer, convey, publish, or otherwise make available.

(4) The term "covert agent" means—

(A) a present or retired officer or employee of an intelligence agency or a present or retired member of the Armed Forces assigned to duty with an intelligence agency—

(i) whose identity as such an officer, employee, or member is classified information, and

(ii) who is serving outside the United States or has within the last five years served outside the United States; or

(B) a United States citizen whose intelligence relationship to the United States is classified information, and—

(i) who resides and acts outside the United States as an agent of, or informant or source of operational assistance to, an intelligence agency, or

(ii) who is at the time of the disclosure acting as an agent of, or informant to, the foreign counterintelligence or foreign counterterrorism components of the Federal Bureau of Investigation; or

(C) an individual, other than a United States citizen, whose past or present intelligence relationship to the United States is classified information and who is a present or former agent of, or a present or former informant or source of operational assistance to, an intelligence agency.

(5) The term "intelligence agency" means the Central Intelligence Agency, a foreign intelligence component of the Department of Defense, or the foreign counterintelligence or foreign counterterrorism components of the Federal Bureau of Investigation.

(6) The term "informant" means any individual who furnishes information to an intelligence

agency in the course of a confidential relationship protecting the identity of such individual from public disclosure.

(7) The terms "officer" and "employee" have the meanings given such terms by section 2104 and 2105, respectively, of title 5, United States Code.

(8) The term "Armed Forces" means the Army, Navy, Air Force, Marine Corps, and Coast Guard.

(9) The term "United States", when used in a geographic sense, means all areas under the territorial sovereignty of the United States and the Trust Territory of the Pacific Islands.

(10) The term "pattern of activities" requires a series of acts with a common purpose or objective.

TITLE VII—PROTECTION OF OPERATIONAL FILES

OPERATIONAL FILES OF THE CENTRAL INTELLIGENCE AGENCY
SEC. 701. [50 U.S.C. §431]

(a) The Director of the Central Intelligence Agency, with the coordination of the Director of National Intelligence, may exempt operational files of the Central Intelligence Agency from the provisions of section 552 of title 5, United States Code (Freedom of Information Act), which require publication or disclosure, or search or review in connection therewith.

(b) In this section, the term "operational files" means—

(1) files of the Directorate of Operations which document the conduct of foreign intelligence or counterintelligence operations or intelligence or security liaison arrangements or information exchanges with foreign governments or their intelligence or security services;

(2) files of the Directorate for Science and Technology which document the means by which foreign intelligence or counterintelligence is collected through scientific and technical systems; and

(3) files of the Office of Personnel Security which document investigations conducted to determine the suitability of potential foreign intelligence or counterintelligence sources; except that files which are the sole repository of disseminated intelligence are not operational files.

(c) Notwithstanding subsection (a) of this section, exempted operational files shall continue to be subject to search and review for information concerning—

(1) United States citizens or aliens lawfully admitted for permanent residence who have requested information on themselves pursuant to the provisions of section 552 of title 5, United States Code (Freedom of Information Act), or section 552a of title 5, United States Code (Privacy Act of 1974);

(2) any special activity the existence of which is not exempt from disclosure under the provisions of section 552 of title 5, United States Code (Freedom of Information Act); or

(3) the specific subject matter of an investigation by the congressional intelligence committees, the Intelligence Oversight Board, the Department of Justice, the Office of General Counsel of the Central Intelligence Agency, the Office of Inspector General of the Central Intelligence Agency, or the Office of the Director of National Intelligence for any impropriety, or violation of law, Executive order, or Presidential directive, in the conduct of an intelligence activity.

(d)(1) Files that are not exempted under subsection (a) of this section which contain information derived or disseminated from exempted operational files shall be subject to search and review.

(2) The inclusion of information from exempted operational files in files that are not exempted under subsection (a) of this section shall not affect the exemption under subsection (a) of this section of the originating operational files from search, review, publication, or disclosure.

(3) Records from exempted operational files which have been disseminated to and referenced in files that are not exempted under subsection (a) of this section and which have been returned to exempted operational files for sole retention shall be subject to search and review.

(e) The provisions of subsection (a) of this section shall not be superseded except by a provision of law which is enacted after the date of enactment of subsection (a), and which specifically cites and repeals or modifies its provisions.

(f) Whenever any person who has requested agency records under section 552 of title 5, United States Code (Freedom of Information Act), alleges that the Central Intelligence Agency has improperly withheld records because of failure to comply with any provision of this section, judicial review shall be available under the terms set forth in section 552(a)(4)(B) of title 5, United States Code, except that—

(1) in any case in which information specifically authorized under criteria established by an Executive order to be kept secret in the interest of national defense or foreign relations which is filed with, or produced for, the court by the Central Intelligence Agency, such information shall be examined ex parte, in camera by the court;

(2) the court shall, to the fullest extent practicable, determine issues of fact based on sworn written submissions of the parties;

(3) when a complainant alleges that requested records are improperly withheld because of improper placement solely in exempted operational files, the complainant shall support such allegation with a sworn written submission, based upon personal knowledge or otherwise admissible evidence;

(4)(A) when a complainant alleges that requested records were improperly withheld because of improper exemption of operational files, the Central Intelligence Agency shall meet its burden under section 552(a)(4)(B) of title 5, United States Code, by demonstrating to the court by sworn written submission that exempted operational files likely to contain responsive records currently perform the functions set forth in subsection (b) of this section; and

(B) the court may not order the Central Intelligence Agency to review the content of any exempted operational file or files in order to make the demonstration required under subparagraph (A) of this paragraph, unless the complainant disputes the Central Intelligence Agency's showing with a sworn written submission based on personal knowledge or otherwise admissible evidence;

(5) in proceedings under paragraphs (3) and (4) of this subsection, the parties shall not obtain discovery pursuant to rules 26 through 36 of the Federal Rules of Civil Procedure, except that requests for admission may be made pursuant to rules 26 and 36;

(6) if the court finds under this subsection that the Central Intelligence Agency has improperly withheld requested records because of failure to comply with any provision of this section, the court shall order the Central Intelligence Agency to search and review the appropriate exempted operational file or files for the requested records and make such records, or portions thereof, available in accordance with the provisions of section 552 of title 5, United States Code (Freedom of Information Act), and such order shall be the exclusive remedy for failure to comply with this section; and

(7) if at any time following the filing of a complaint pursuant to this subsection the Central Intelligence Agency agrees to search the appropriate exempted operational file or files for the requested records, the court shall dismiss the claim based upon such complaint.

(g) DECENNIAL REVIEW OF EXEMPTED OPERATIONAL FILES—

(1) Not less than once every ten years, the Director of the Central Intelligence Agency and the Director of National Intelligence shall review the exemptions in force under subsection (a) to determine whether such exemptions may be removed from any category of exempted files or any portion thereof.

(2) The review required by paragraph (1) shall include consideration of the historical value or other public interest in the subject matter of the particular category of files or portions thereof and the potential for declassifying a significant part of the information contained therein.

(3) A complainant who alleges that the Central Intelligence Agency has improperly withheld records because of failure to comply with this subsection may seek judicial review in the district court of the United States of the district in which any of the parties reside, or in the District of Columbia. In such a proceeding, the court's review shall be limited to determining the following:

(A) Whether the Central Intelligence Agency has conducted the review required by paragraph (1) before October 15, 1994, or before the expiration of the 10-year period beginning on the date of the most recent review.

(B) Whether the Central Intelligence Agency, in fact, considered the criteria set forth in paragraph (2) in conducting the required review.

OPERATIONAL FILES OF THE NATIONAL GEOSPATIAL-INTELLIGENCE AGENCY

SEC. 702. [50 U.S.C. §432]

(a) EXEMPTION OF CERTAIN OPERATIONAL FILES FROM SEARCH, REVIEW, PUBLICATION, OR DISCLOSURE.—

(1) The Director of the National Geospatial-Intelligence Agency, with the coordination of the Director of National Intelligence, may exempt operational files of the National Geospatial-Intelligence Agency from the provisions of section 552 of title 5, United States Code, which require publication, disclosure, search, or review in connection therewith.

(2)(A) Subject to subparagraph (B), for the purposes of this section, the term "operational files" means files of the National Geospatial-Intelligence Agency (hereafter in this section referred to as "NGA") concerning the activities of NGA that before the establishment of NGA were performed by the National Photographic Interpretation Center of the Central Intelligence Agency (NPIC), that document the means by which foreign intelligence or counterintelligence is collected through scientific and technical systems.

(B) Files which are the sole repository of disseminated intelligence are not operational files.

(3) Notwithstanding paragraph (1), exempted operational files shall continue to be subject to search and review for information concerning—

(A) United States citizens or aliens lawfully admitted for permanent residence who have requested information on themselves pursuant to the provisions of section 552 or 552a of title 5, United States Code;

(B) any special activity the existence of which is not exempt from disclosure under the provisions of section 552 of title 5, United States Code; or

(C) the specific subject matter of an investigation by any of the following for any impropriety, or violation of law, Executive order, or Presidential directive, in the conduct of an intelligence activity:

(i) The congressional intelligence committees.

(ii) The Intelligence Oversight Board.

(iii) The Department of Justice.

(iv) The Office of General Counsel of NGA.

(v) The Office of the Director of NGA.

(vi) The Office of the Inspector General of the National-Geospatial Intelligence Agency.

(4)(A) Files that are not exempted under paragraph (1) which contain information derived or disseminated from exempted operational files shall be subject to search and review.

(B) The inclusion of information from exempted operational files in files that are not exempted under paragraph (1) shall not affect the exemption under paragraph (1) of the originating operational files from search, review, publication, or disclosure.

(C) Records from exempted operational files which have been disseminated to and referenced in files that are not exempted under paragraph (1) and which have been returned to exempted operational files for sole retention shall be subject to search and review.

(5) The provisions of paragraph (1) may not be superseded except by a provision of law which is enacted after the date of the enactment of this section, and which specifically cites and repeals or modifies its provisions.

(6)(A) Except as provided in subparagraph (B), whenever any person who has requested agency records under section 552 of title 5, United States Code, alleges that NGA has withheld records improperly because of failure to comply with any provision of this section, judicial review shall be available under the terms set forth in section 552(a)(4)(B) of title 5, United States Code.

(B) Judicial review shall not be available in the manner provided for under subparagraph (A) as follows:

(i) In any case in which information specifically authorized under criteria established by an Executive order to be kept secret in the interests of national defense or foreign relations is filed with, or produced for, the court by NGA, such information shall be examined ex parte, in camera by the court.

(ii) The court shall, to the fullest extent practicable, determine the issues of fact based on sworn written submissions of the parties.

(iii) When a complainant alleges that requested records are improperly withheld because of improper placement solely in exempted operational files, the complainant shall support such allegation with a sworn written submission based upon personal knowledge or otherwise admissible evidence.

(iv)(I) When a complainant alleges that requested records were improperly withheld because of improper exemption of operational files, NGA shall meet its burden under section 552(a)(4)(B) of title 5, United States Code, by demonstrating to the court by sworn written submission that exempted operational files likely to contain responsive records currently perform the functions set forth in paragraph (2).

(II) The court may not order NGA to review the content of any exempted operational file or files in order to make the demonstration required under subclause (I), unless the complainant disputes NGA's showing with a sworn written submission based on personal knowledge or otherwise admissible evidence.

(v) In proceedings under clauses (iii) and (iv), the parties may not obtain discovery pursuant to rules 26 through 36 of the Federal Rules of Civil Procedure, except that requests for admissions may be made pursuant to rules 26 and 36.

(vi) If the court finds under this paragraph that NGA has improperly withheld requested records because of failure to comply with any provision of this subsection, the court shall order NGA to search and review the appropriate exempted operational file or files for the requested records and make such records, or portions thereof, available in accordance with the provisions of section 552 of title 5, United States Code, and such order shall be the exclusive remedy for failure to comply with this subsection.

(vii) If at any time following the filing of a complaint pursuant to this paragraph NGA agrees to search the appropriate exempted operational file or files for the requested records, the court shall dismiss the claim based upon such complaint.

(viii) Any information filed with, or produced for the court pursuant to clauses (i) and (iv) shall be coordinated with the Director of National Intelligence prior to submission to the court.

(b) DECENNIAL REVIEW OF EXEMPTED OPERATIONAL FILES.—

(1) Not less than once every 10 years, the Director of the National Geospatial-Intelligence Agency and the Director of National Intelligence shall review the exemptions in force under subsection (a)(1) to determine whether such exemptions may be removed from the category of exempted files or any portion thereof. The Director of National Intelligence must approve any determination to remove such exemptions.

(2) The review required by paragraph (1)[1] shall include consideration of the historical value or other public interest in the subject matter of the particular category of files or portions thereof and the potential for declassifying a significant part of the information contained therein.

(3) A complainant that alleges that NGA has improperly withheld records because of failure to comply with this subsection may seek judicial review in the district court of the United States of the district in which any of the parties reside, or in the District of Columbia. In such a proceeding, the court's review shall be limited to determining the following:

(A) Whether NGA has conducted the review required by paragraph (1) before the expiration of the 10-year period beginning on the date of the enactment of this section or before the expiration of the 10-year period beginning on the date of the most recent review.

(B) Whether NGA, in fact, considered the criteria set forth in paragraph (2) in conducting the required review.

OPERATIONAL FILES OF THE NATIONAL RECONNAISSANCE OFFICE

SEC. 703. [50 U.S.C. §432a]

(a) EXEMPTION OF CERTAIN OPERATIONAL FILES FROM SEARCH, REVIEW, PUBLICATION, OR DISCLOSURE.—

(1) The Director of the National Reconnaissance Office, with the coordination of the Director of National Intelligence, may exempt operational files of the National Reconnaissance Office from the provisions of section 552 of title 5, United States Code, which require publication, disclosure, search, or review in connection therewith.

(2)(A) Subject to subparagraph (B), for the purposes of this section, the term "operational files" means files of the National Reconnaissance Office (hereafter in this section referred to as "NRO") that document the means by which foreign intelligence or counterintelligence is collected through scientific and technical systems.

(B) Files which are the sole repository of disseminated intelligence are not operational files.

(3) Notwithstanding paragraph (1), exempted operational files shall continue to be subject to search and review for information concerning—

(A) United States citizens or aliens lawfully admitted for permanent residence who have requested information on themselves pursuant to the provisions of section 552 or 552a of title 5, United States Code;

---

1. In section 701(g)(2), the amendment to strike "of subsection (a) of this section" and insert "paragraph (1)" made by section 922(b)(2)(E) of the National Defense Authorization Act for Fiscal Year 2004 (Public Law 108–136; 117 Stat. 1537) was executed by striking "subsection (a)of this section" and inserting "paragraph (1)" in order to reflect the probable intent of Congress.

(B) any special activity the existence of which is not exempt from disclosure under the provisions of section 552 of title 5, United States Code; or

(C) the specific subject matter of an investigation by any of the following for any impropriety, or violation of law, Executive order, or Presidential directive, in the conduct of an intelligence activity:

(i) The Permanent Select Committee on Intelligence of the House of Representatives.

(ii) The Select Committee on Intelligence of the Senate.

(iii) The Intelligence Oversight Board.

(iv) The Department of Justice.

(v) The Office of General Counsel of NRO.

(vi) The Office of the Director of NRO.

(vii) The Office of the Inspector General of the NRO.

(4)(A) Files that are not exempted under paragraph (1) which contain information derived or disseminated from exempted operational files shall be subject to search and review.

(B) The inclusion of information from exempted operational files in files that are not exempted under paragraph (1) shall not affect the exemption under paragraph (1) of the originating operational files from search, review, publication, or disclosure.

(C) The declassification of some of the information contained in exempted operational files shall not affect the status of the operational file as being exempt from search, review, publication, or disclosure.

(D) Records from exempted operational files which have been disseminated to and referenced in files that are not exempted under paragraph (1) and which have been returned to exempted operational files for sole retention shall be subject to search and review.

(5) The provisions of paragraph (1) may not be superseded except by a provision of law which is enacted after the date of the enactment of this section, and which specifically cites and repeals or modifies its provisions.

(6)(A) Except as provided in subparagraph (B), whenever any person who has requested agency records under section 552 of title 5, United States Code, alleges that NRO has withheld records improperly because of failure to comply with any provision of this section, judicial review shall be available under the terms set forth in section 552(a)(4)(B) of title 5, United States Code.

(B) Judicial review shall not be available in the manner provided for under subparagraph (A) as follows:

(i) In any case in which information specifically authorized under criteria established by an Executive order to be kept secret in the interests of national defense or foreign relations is filed with, or produced for, the court by NRO, such information shall be examined ex parte, in camera by the court.

(ii) The court shall, to the fullest extent practicable, determine the issues of fact based on sworn written submissions of the parties.

(iii) When a complainant alleges that requested records are improperly withheld because of improper placement solely in exempted operational files, the complainant shall support such allegation with a sworn written submission based upon personal knowledge or otherwise admissible evidence.

(iv)(I) When a complainant alleges that requested records were improperly withheld because of improper exemption of operational files, NRO shall meet its burden under section 552(a)(4)(B) of title 5, United States Code, by demonstrating to the court by sworn written submission that exempted operational files likely to contain responsive records currently perform the functions set forth in paragraph (2).

(II) The court may not order NRO to review the content of any exempted operational file or files in order to make the demonstration required under subclause (I), unless the complainant disputes NRO's showing with a sworn written submission based on personal knowledge or otherwise admissible evidence.

(v) In proceedings under clauses (iii) and (iv), the parties may not obtain discovery pursuant to rules 26 through 36 of the Federal Rules of Civil Procedure, except that requests for admissions may be made pursuant to rules 26 and 36.

(vi) If the court finds under this paragraph that NRO has improperly withheld requested records because of failure to comply with any provision of this subsection, the court shall order NRO to search and review the appropriate exempted operational file or files for the requested records and make such records, or portions thereof, available in accordance with the provisions of section 552 of title 5, United States Code, and such order shall be the exclusive remedy for failure to comply with this subsection.

(vii) If at any time following the filing of a complaint pursuant to this paragraph NRO agrees to search the appropriate exempted operational file or files for the requested records, the court shall dismiss the claim based upon such complaint.

(viii) Any information filed with, or produced for the court pursuant to clauses (i) and (iv) shall be coordinated with the Director of National Intelligence prior to submission to the court.

(b) DECENNIAL REVIEW OF EXEMPTED OPERATIONAL FILES.—

(1) Not less than once every 10 years, the Director of the National Reconnaissance Office and the Director of National Intelligence shall review the exemptions in force under subsection (a)(1) to determine whether such exemptions may be removed from the category of exempted files or any portion thereof. The Director of National Intelligence must approve any determination to remove such exemptions.

(2) The review required by paragraph (1) shall include consideration of the historical value or other public interest in the subject matter of the particular category of files or portions thereof and the potential for declassifying a significant part of the information contained therein.

(3) A complainant that alleges that NRO has improperly withheld records because of failure to comply with this subsection may seek judicial review in the district court of the United States of the district in which any of the parties reside, or in the District of Columbia. In such a proceeding, the court's review shall be limited to determining the following:

(A) Whether NRO has conducted the review required by paragraph (1) before the expiration of the 10-year period beginning on the date of the enactment of this section or before the expiration of the 10-year period beginning on the date of the most recent review.

(B) Whether NRO, in fact, considered the criteria set forth in paragraph (2) in conducting the required review.

OPERATIONAL FILES OF THE NATIONAL SECURITY AGENCY
SEC. 704. [50 U.S.C. §432b]

(a) EXEMPTION OF CERTAIN OPERATIONAL FILES FROM SEARCH, REVIEW, PUBLICATION, OR DISCLOSURE.—The Director of the National Security Agency, in coordination with the Director of National Intelligence, may exempt operational files of the National Security

Agency from the provisions of section 552 of title 5, United States Code, which require publication, disclosure, search, or review in connection therewith.

(b) OPERATIONAL FILES DEFINED.—

(1) In this section, the term "operational files" means—

(A) files of the Signals Intelligence Directorate of the National Security Agency (and any successor organization of that directorate) that document the means by which foreign intelligence or counterintelligence is collected through technical systems; and

(B) files of the Research Associate Directorate of the National Security Agency (and any successor organization of that directorate) that document the means by which foreign intelligence or counterintelligence is collected through scientific and technical systems.

(2) Files that are the sole repository of disseminated intelligence, and files that have been accessioned into the National Security Agency Archives (or any successor organization) are not operational files.

(c) SEARCH AND REVIEW FOR INFORMATION.—Notwithstanding subsection (a), exempted operational files shall continue to be subject to search and review for information concerning any of the following:

(1) United States citizens or aliens lawfully admitted for permanent residence who have requested information on themselves pursuant to the provisions of section 552 or 552a of title 5, United States Code.

(2) Any special activity the existence of which is not exempt from disclosure under the provisions of section 552 of title 5, United States Code.

(3) The specific subject matter of an investigation by any of the following for any impropriety, or violation of law, Executive order, or Presidential directive, in the conduct of an intelligence activity:

(A) The Committee on Armed Services and the Permanent Select Committee on Intelligence of the House of Representatives.

(B) The Committee on Armed Services and the Select Committee on Intelligence of the Senate.

(C) The Intelligence Oversight Board.

(D) The Department of Justice.

(E) The Office of General Counsel of the National Security Agency.

(F) The Office of the Inspector General of the Department of Defense.

(G) The Office of the Director of the National Security Agency.

(H) The Office of the Inspector General of the National Security Agency.

(d) INFORMATION DERIVED OR DISSEMINATED FROM EXEMPTED OPERATIONAL FILES.—

(1) Files that are not exempted under subsection (a) that contain information derived or disseminated from exempted operational files shall be subject to search and review.

(2) The inclusion of information from exempted operational files in files that are not exempted under subsection (a) shall not affect the exemption under subsection (a) of the originating operational files from search, review, publication, or disclosure.

(3) The declassification of some of the information contained in exempted operational files shall not affect the status of the operational file as being exempt from search, review, publication, or disclosure.

(4) Records from exempted operational files that have been disseminated to and referenced in files that are not exempted under subsection (a) and that have been returned to exempted operational files for sole retention shall be subject to search and review.

(e) SUPERCEDURE OF OTHER LAWS.—The provisions of subsection (a) may not be superseded except by a provision of law that is enacted after the date of the enactment of this section and that specifically cites and repeals or modifies such provisions.

(f) ALLEGATION; IMPROPER WITHHOLDING OF RECORDS; JUDICIAL REVIEW.—

(1) Except as provided in paragraph (2), whenever any person who has requested agency records under section 552 of title 5, United States Code, alleges that the National Security Agency has withheld records improperly because of failure to comply with any provision of this section, judicial review shall be available under the terms set forth in section 552(a)(4)(B) of title 5, United States Code.

(2) Judicial review shall not be available in the manner provided for under paragraph (1) as follows:

(A) In any case in which information specifically authorized under criteria established by an Executive order to be kept secret in the interests of national defense or foreign relations is filed with, or produced for, the court by the National Security Agency, such information shall be examined ex parte, in camera by the court.

(B) The court shall determine, to the fullest extent practicable, the issues of fact based on sworn written submissions of the parties.

(C) When a complainant alleges that requested records are improperly withheld because of improper placement solely in exempted operational files, the complainant shall support such allegation with a sworn written submission based upon personal knowledge or otherwise admissible evidence. (D)(i) When a complainant alleges that requested records were improperly withheld because of improper exemption of operational files, the National Security Agency shall meet its burden under section 552(a)(4)(B) of title 5, United States Code, by demonstrating to the court by sworn written submission that exempted operational files likely to contain responsive records currently perform the functions set forth in subsection (b).

(ii) The court may not order the National Security Agency to review the content of any exempted operational file or files in order to make the demonstration required under clause (i), unless the complainant disputes the National Security Agency's showing with a sworn written submission based on personal knowledge or otherwise admissible evidence.

(E) In proceedings under subparagraphs (C) and (D), the parties may not obtain discovery pursuant to rules 26 through 36 of the Federal Rules of Civil Procedure, except that requests for admissions may be made pursuant to rules 26 and 36.

(F) If the court finds under this subsection that the National Security Agency has improperly withheld requested records because of failure to comply with any provision of this subsection, the court shall order the Agency to search and review the appropriate exempted operational file or files for the requested records and make such records, or portions thereof, available in accordance with the provisions of section 552 of title 5, United States Code, and such order shall be the exclusive remedy for failure to comply with this section (other than subsection (g)).

(G) If at any time following the filing of a complaint pursuant to this paragraph the National Security Agency agrees to search the appropriate exempted operational file or files for the requested records, the court shall dismiss the claim based upon such complaint.

(H) Any information filed with, or produced for the court pursuant to subparagraphs (A) and (D) shall be coordinated with the Director of National Intelligence before submission to the court.

(g) DECENNIAL REVIEW OF EXEMPTED OPERATIONAL FILES.—

(1) Not less than once every 10 years, the Director of the National Security Agency and the

Director of National Intelligence shall review the exemptions in force under subsection (a) to determine whether such exemptions may be removed from a category of exempted files or any portion thereof. The Director of National Intelligence must approve any determination to remove such exemptions.

(2) The review required by paragraph (1) shall include consideration of the historical value or other public interest in the subject matter of a particular category of files or portions thereof and the potential for declassifying a significant part of the information contained therein.

(3) A complainant that alleges that the National Security Agency has improperly withheld records because of failure to comply with this subsection may seek judicial review in the district court of the United States of the district in which any of the parties reside, or in the District of Columbia. In such a proceeding, the court's review shall be limited to determining the following:

> (A) Whether the National Security Agency has conducted the review required by paragraph (1) before the expiration of the 10-year period beginning on the date of the enactment of this section or before the expiration of the 10-year period beginning on the date of the most recent review.
>
> (B) Whether the National Security Agency, in fact, considered the criteria set forth in paragraph (2) in conducting the required review.

OPERATIONAL FILES OF THE DEFENSE INTELLIGENCE AGENCY
SEC. 705. [50 U.S.C. §432c]

(a) EXEMPTION OF OPERATIONAL FILES. —The Director of the Defense Intelligence Agency, in coordination with the Director of National Intelligence, may exempt operational files of the Defense Intelligence Agency from the provisions of section 552 of title 5, United States Code, which require publication, disclosure, search, or review in connection therewith.

(b) OPERATIONAL FILES DEFINED. —

> (1) In this section, the term "operational files" means—
>
> > (A) files of the Directorate of Human Intelligence of the Defense Intelligence Agency (and any successor organization of that directorate) that document the conduct of foreign intelligence or counterintelligence operations or intelligence or security liaison arrangements or information exchanges with foreign governments or their intelligence or security services; and
> >
> > (B) files of the Directorate of Technology of the Defense Intelligence Agency (and any successor organization of that directorate) that document the means by which foreign intelligence or counterintelligence is collected through technical systems.
>
> (2) Files that are the sole repository of disseminated intelligence are not operational files.

(c) SEARCH AND REVIEW FOR INFORMATION. —Notwithstanding subsection (a), exempted operational files shall continue to be subject to search and review for information concerning:

> (1) United States citizens or aliens lawfully admitted for permanent residence who have requested information on themselves pursuant to the provisions of section 552 or 552a of title 5, United States Code.
>
> (2) Any special activity the existence of which is not exempt from disclosure under the provisions of section 552 of title 5, United States Code.
>
> (3) The specific subject matter of an investigation by any of the following for any impropriety, or violation of law, Executive order, or Presidential directive, in the conduct of an intelligence activity:
>
> > (A) The Committee on Armed Services and the Permanent Select Committee on Intelligence of the House of Representatives.

(B) The Committee on Armed Services and the Select Committee on Intelligence of the Senate.

(C) The Intelligence Oversight Board.

(D) The Department of Justice.

(E) The Office of General Counsel of the Department of Defense or of the Defense Intelligence Agency.

(F) The Office of Inspector General of the Department of Defense or of the Defense Intelligence Agency.

(G) The Office of the Director of the Defense Intelligence Agency.

(d) INFORMATION DERIVED OR DISSEMINATED FROM EXEMPTED OPERATIONAL FILES.—

(1) Files that are not exempted under subsection (a) that contain information derived or disseminated from exempted operational files shall be subject to search and review.

(2) The inclusion of information from exempted operational files in files that are not exempted under subsection (a) shall not affect the exemption under subsection (a) of the originating operational files from search, review, publication, or disclosure.

(3) The declassification of some of the information contained in an exempted operational file shall not affect the status of the operational file as being exempt from search, review, publication, or disclosure.

(4) Records from exempted operational files that have been disseminated to and referenced in files that are not exempted under subsection (a) and that have been returned to exempted operational files for sole retention shall be subject to search and review.

(e) ALLEGATION; IMPROPER WITHHOLDING OF RECORDS; JUDICIAL REVIEW. —

(1) Except as provided in paragraph (2), whenever any person who has requested agency records under section 552 of title 5, United States Code, alleges that the Defense Intelligence Agency has withheld records improperly because of failure to comply with any provision of this section, judicial review shall be available under the terms set forth in section 552(a)(4)(B) of title 5, United States Code.

(2) Judicial review shall not be available in the manner provided under paragraph (1) as follows:

(A) In any case in which information specifically authorized under criteria established by an Executive order to be kept secret in the interest of national defense or foreign relations which is filed with, or produced for, the court by the Defense Intelligence Agency, such information shall be examined ex parte, in camera by the court.

(B) The court shall determine, to the fullest extent practicable, issues of fact based on sworn written submissions of the parties.

(C) When a complainant alleges that requested records were improperly withheld because of improper placement solely in exempted operational files, the complainant shall support such allegation with a sworn written submission based upon personal knowledge or otherwise admissible evidence.

(D)(i) When a complainant alleges that requested records were improperly withheld because of improper exemption of operational files, the Defense Intelligence Agency shall meet its burden under section 552(a)(4)(B) of title 5, United States Code, by demonstrating to the court by sworn written submission that exempted operational files likely to contain responsible records currently perform the functions set forth in subsection (b).

(ii) The court may not order the Defense Intelligence Agency to review the content of any exempted operational file or files in order to make the demonstration required under clause (i), unless the complainant disputes the Defense Intelligence

Agency's showing with a sworn written submission based on personal knowledge or otherwise admissible evidence.

(E) In proceedings under subparagraphs (C) and (D), the parties shall not obtain discovery pursuant to rules 26 through 36 of the Federal Rules of Civil Procedure, except that requests for admission may be made pursuant to rules 26 and 36.

(F) If the court finds under this subsection that the Defense Intelligence Agency has improperly withheld requested records because of failure to comply with any provision of this subsection, the court shall order the Defense Intelligence Agency to search and review the appropriate exempted operational file or files for the requested records and make such records, or portions thereof, available in accordance with the provisions of section 552 of title 5, United States Code, and such order shall be the exclusive remedy for failure to comply with this section (other than subsection (f)).

(G) If at any time following the filing of a complaint pursuant to this paragraph the Defense Intelligence Agency agrees to search the appropriate exempted operational file or files for the requested records, the court shall dismiss the claim based upon such complaint.

(H) Any information filed with, or produced for the court pursuant to subparagraphs (A) and (D) shall be coordinated with the Director of National Intelligence before submission to the court.

(f) DECENNIAL REVIEW OF EXEMPTED OPERATIONAL FILES. —

(1) Not less than once every 10 years, the Director of the Defense Intelligence Agency and the Director of National Intelligence shall review the exemptions in force under subsection (a) to determine whether such exemptions may be removed from a category of exempted files or any portion thereof. The Director of National Intelligence must approve any determinations to remove such exemptions.

(2) The review required by paragraph (1) shall include consideration of the historical value or other public interest in the subject matter of the particular category of files or portions thereof and the potential for declassifying a significant part of the information contained therein.

(3) A complainant that alleges that the Defense Intelligence Agency has improperly withheld records because of failure to comply with this subsection may seek judicial review in the district court of the United States of the district in which any of the parties reside, or in the District of Columbia. In such a proceeding, the court's review shall be limited to determining the following:

(A) Whether the Defense Intelligence Agency has conducted the review required by paragraph (1) before the expiration of the 10year period beginning on the date of the enactment of this section or before the expiration of the 10-year period beginning on the date of the most recent review.

(B) Whether the Defense Intelligence Agency, in fact, considered the criteria set forth in paragraph (2) in conducting the required review.

(g) TERMINATION.—This section shall cease to be effective on December 31, 2007.

PROTECTION OF CERTAIN FILES OF THE OFFICE OF THE DIRECTOR OF NATIONAL INTELLIGENCE

SEC. 706. [50 U.S.C. 432d]

(a) INAPPLICABILITY OF FOIA TO EXEMPTED OPERATIONAL FILES PROVIDED TO ODNI.—

(1) Subject to paragraph (2), the provisions of section 552 of title 5, United States Code, that require search, review, publication, or disclosure of a record shall not apply to a record

provided to the Office of the Director of National Intelligence by an element of the intelligence community from the exempted operational files of such element.

(2) Paragraph (1) shall not apply with respect to a record of the Office that—

(A) contains information derived or disseminated from an exempted operational file, unless such record is created by the Office for the sole purpose of organizing such exempted operational file for use by the Office;

(B) is disseminated by the Office to a person other than an officer, employee, or contractor of the Office; or

(C) is no longer designated as an exempted operational file in accordance with this title.

(b) EFFECT OF PROVIDING FILES TO ODNI.—Notwithstanding any other provision of this title, an exempted operational file that is provided to the Office by an element of the intelligence community shall not be subject to the provisions of section 552 of title 5, United States Code, that require search, review, publication, or disclosure of a record solely because such element provides such exempted operational file to the Office.

(c) SEARCH AND REVIEW FOR CERTAIN PURPOSES.—Notwithstanding subsection (a) or (b), an exempted operational file shall continue to be subject to search and review for information concerning any of the following:

(1) United States citizens or aliens lawfully admitted for permanent residence who have requested information on themselves pursuant to the provisions of section 552 or 552a of title 5, United States Code.

(2) Any special activity the existence of which is not exempt from disclosure under the provisions of section 552 of title 5, United States Code.

(3) The specific subject matter of an investigation for any impropriety or violation of law, Executive order, or Presidential directive, in the conduct of an intelligence activity by any of the following:

(A) The Select Committee on Intelligence of the Senate.

(B) The Permanent Select Committee on Intelligence of the House of Representatives.

(C) The Intelligence Oversight Board.

(D) The Department of Justice.

(E) The Office of the Director of National Intelligence.

(F) The Office of the Inspector General of the Intelligence Community.

(d) DECENNIAL REVIEW OF EXEMPTED OPERATIONAL FILES.—

(1) Not less than once every 10 years, the Director of National Intelligence shall review the exemptions in force under subsection (a) to determine whether such exemptions may be removed from any category of exempted files or any portion thereof.

(2) The review required by paragraph (1) shall include consideration of the historical value or other public interest in the subject matter of the particular category of files or portions thereof and the potential for declassifying a significant part of the information contained therein.

(3) A complainant that alleges that the Director of National Intelligence has improperly withheld records because of failure to comply with this subsection may seek judicial review in the district court of the United States of the district in which any of the parties reside, or in the District of Columbia. In such a proceeding, the court's review shall be limited to determining the following:

(A) Whether the Director has conducted the review required by paragraph (1) before the expiration of the 10year period beginning on the date of the enactment of the Intelligence Authorization Act for Fiscal Year 2010 or before the expiration of the

10year period beginning on the date of the most recent review.

(B) Whether the Director of National Intelligence, in fact, considered the criteria set forth in paragraph (2) in conducting the required review.

(e) SUPERSEDURE OF OTHER LAWS.—The provisions of this section may not be superseded except by a provision of law that is enacted after the date of the enactment of this section and that specifically cites and repeals or modifies such provisions.

(f) ALLEGATION; IMPROPER WITHHOLDING OF RECORDS; JUDICIAL REVIEW.—

(1) Except as provided in paragraph (2), whenever any person who has requested agency records under section 552 of title 5, United States Code, alleges that the Office has withheld records improperly because of failure to comply with any provision of this section, judicial review shall be available under the terms set forth in section 552(a)(4)(B) of title 5, United States Code.

(2) Judicial review shall not be available in the manner provided for under paragraph (1) as follows:

(A) In any case in which information specifically authorized under criteria established by an Executive order to be kept secret in the interests of national defense or foreign relations is filed with, or produced for, the court by the Office, such information shall be examined ex parte, in camera by the court.

(B) The court shall determine, to the fullest extent practicable, the issues of fact based on sworn written submissions of the parties.

(C)(i) When a complainant alleges that requested records were improperly withheld because of improper exemption of operational files, the Office may meet the burden of the Office under section 552(a)(4)(B) of title 5, United States Code, by demonstrating to the court by sworn written submission that exempted files likely to contain responsive records are records provided to the Office by an element of the intelligence community from the exempted operational files of such element.

(ii) The court may not order the Office to review the content of any exempted file in order to make the demonstration required under clause (i), unless the complainant disputes the Office's showing with a sworn written submission based on personal knowledge or otherwise admissible evidence.

(D) In proceedings under subparagraph (C), a party may not obtain discovery pursuant to rules 26 through 36 of the Federal Rules of Civil Procedure, except that requests for admissions may be made pursuant to rules 26 and 36 of the Federal Rules of Civil Procedure.

(E) If the court finds under this subsection that the Office has improperly withheld requested records because of failure to comply with any provision of this section, the court shall order the Office to search and review each appropriate exempted file for the requested records and make such records, or portions thereof, available in accordance with the provisions of section 552 of title 5, United States Code (commonly referred to as the Freedom of Information Act), and such order shall be the exclusive remedy for failure to comply with this section.

(F) If at any time following the filing of a complaint pursuant to this paragraph the Office agrees to search each appropriate exempted file for the requested records, the court shall dismiss the claim based upon such complaint.

(g) DEFINITIONS.—In this section:

(1) The term "exempted operational file" means a file of an element of the intelligence community that, in accordance with this title, is exempted from the provisions of section 552 of title 5, United States Code, that require search, review, publication, or disclosure of such file.

(2) Except as otherwise specifically provided, the term "Office" means the Office of the Director of National Intelligence.

TITLE VIII—ACCESS TO CLASSIFIED INFORMATION PROCEDURES

PROCEDURES

SEC. 801. [50 U.S.C 435]

(a) Not later than 180 days after the date of enactment of this title, the President shall, by Executive order or regulation, establish procedures to govern access to classified information which shall be binding upon all departments, agencies, and offices of the executive branch of Government. Such procedures shall, at a minimum—

(1) provide that, except as may be permitted by the President, no employee in the executive branch of Government may be given access to classified information by any department, agency, or office of the executive branch of Government unless, based upon an appropriate background investigation, such access is determined to be clearly consistent with the national security interests of the United States;

(2) establish uniform minimum requirements governing the scope and frequency of background investigations and reinvestigations for all employees in the executive branch of Government who require access to classified information as part of their official responsibilities;

(3) provide that all employees in the executive branch of Government who require access to classified information shall be required as a condition of such access to provide to the employing department or agency written consent which permits access by an authorized investigative agency to relevant financial records, other financial information, consumer reports, travel records, and computers used in the performance of Government duties, as determined by the President, in accordance with section 802 of this title, during the period of access to classified information and for a period of three years thereafter;

(4) provide that all employees in the executive branch of Government who require access to particularly sensitive classified information, as determined by the President, shall be required, as a condition of maintaining access to such information, to submit to the employing department or agency, during the period of such access, relevant information concerning their financial condition and foreign travel, as determined by the President, as may be necessary to ensure appropriate security; and

(5) establish uniform minimum standards to ensure that employees in the executive branch of Government whose access to classified information is being denied or terminated under this title are appropriately advised of the reasons for such denial or termination and are provided an adequate opportunity to respond to all adverse information which forms the basis for such denial or termination before final action by the department or agency concerned.

(b)(1) Subsection (a) shall not be deemed to limit or affect the responsibility and power of an agency head pursuant to other law or Executive order to deny or terminate access to classified information if the national security so requires. Such responsibility and power may be exercised only when the agency head determines that the procedures prescribed by subsection (a) cannot be invoked in a manner that is consistent with the national security.

(2) Upon the exercise of such responsibility, the agency head shall submit a report to the congressional intelligence committees.

REQUESTS BY AUTHORIZED INVESTIGATIVE AGENCIES

SEC. 802. [50 U.S.C. §436]

(a)(1) Any authorized investigative agency may request from any financial agency, financial institution, or holding company, or from any consumer reporting agency, such financial records, other financial information, and consumer reports as may be necessary in order to conduct any authorized law enforcement investigation, counterintelligence inquiry, or security determination. Any authorized investigative agency may also request records maintained by any commercial entity within the United States pertaining to travel by an employee in the executive branch of Government outside the United States.

(2) Requests may be made under this section where—

(A) the records sought pertain to a person who is or was an employee in the executive branch of Government required by the President in an Executive order or regulation, as a condition of access to classified information, to provide consent, during a background investigation and for such time as access to the information is maintained, and for a period of not more than three years thereafter, permitting access to financial records, other financial information, consumer reports, and travel records; and

(B)(i) there are reasonable grounds to believe, based on credible information, that the person is, or may be, disclosing classified information in an unauthorized manner to a foreign power or agent of a foreign power;

(ii) information the employing agency deems credible indicates the person has incurred excessive indebtedness or has acquired a level of affluence which cannot be explained by other information known to the agency; or

(iii) circumstances indicate the person had the capability and opportunity to disclose classified information which is known to have been lost or compromised to a foreign power or an agent of a foreign power.

(3) Each such request—

(A) shall be accompanied by a written certification signed by the department or agency head or deputy department or agency head concerned, or by a senior official designated for this purpose by the department or agency head concerned (whose rank shall be no lower than Assistant Secretary or Assistant Director), and shall certify that—

(i) the person concerned is or was an employee within the meaning of paragraph (2)(A);

(ii) the request is being made pursuant to an authorized inquiry or investigation and is authorized under this section; and

(iii) the records or information to be reviewed are records or information which the employee has previously agreed to make available to the authorized investigative agency for review;

(B) shall contain a copy of the agreement referred to in subparagraph (A)(iii);

(C) shall identify specifically or by category the records or information to be reviewed; and

(D) shall inform the recipient of the request of the prohibition described in subsection (b).

(b) Prohibition of Certain Disclosure—

(1) If an authorized investigative agency described in subsection (a) certifies that otherwise there may result a danger to the national security of the United States, interference with a criminal, counterterrorism, or counterintelligence investigation, interference with diplomatic relations, or danger to the life or physical safety of any person, no governmental or private entity, or officer, employee, or agent of such entity, may disclose to any person (other than those to whom such disclosure is necessary to comply with the request or an attorney to obtain legal advice or legal assistance with respect to the request) that such entity has received or satisfied a request made by an authorized investigative agency under this section.

(2) The request shall notify the person or entity to whom the request is directed of the nondisclosure requirement under paragraph (1).

(3) Any recipient disclosing to those persons necessary to comply with the request or to an attorney to obtain legal advice or legal assistance with respect to the request shall inform such persons of any applicable nondisclosure requirement. Any person who receives a disclosure under this subsection shall be subject to the same prohibitions on disclosure under paragraph (1).

(4) At the request of the authorized investigative agency, any person making or intending to make a disclosure under this section shall identify to the requesting official of the authorized investigative agency the person to whom such disclosure will be made or to whom such disclosure was made prior to the request, except that nothing in this section shall require a person to inform the requesting official of the identity of an attorney to whom disclosure was made or will be made to obtain legal advice or legal assistance with respect to the request under subsection (a).

(c)(1) Notwithstanding any other provision of law (other than section 6103 of the Internal Revenue Code of 1986), an entity receiving a request for records or information under subsection (a) shall, if the request satisfies the requirements of this section, make available such records or information within 30 days for inspection or copying, as may be appropriate, by the agency requesting such records or information.

(2) Any entity (including any officer, employee, or agent thereof) that discloses records or information for inspection or copying pursuant to this section in good faith reliance upon the certifications made by an agency pursuant to this section shall not be liable for any such disclosure to any person under this title, the constitution of any State, or any law or regulation of any State or any political subdivision of any State.

(d) Any agency requesting records or information under this section may, subject to the availability of appropriations, reimburse a private entity for any cost reasonably incurred by such entity in responding to such request, including the cost of identifying, reproducing, or transporting records or other data.

(e) An agency receiving records or information pursuant to a request under this section may disseminate the records or information obtained pursuant to such request outside the agency only—

(1) to the agency employing the employee who is the subject of the records or information;

(2) to the Department of Justice for law enforcement or counterintelligence purposes; or

(3) with respect to dissemination to an agency of the United States, if such information is clearly relevant to the authorized responsibilities of such agency.

(f) Nothing in this section may be construed to affect the authority of an investigative agency to obtain information pursuant to the Right to Financial Privacy Act (12 U.S.C. §3401 et seq.) or the Fair Credit Reporting Act (15 U.S.C. §1681 et seq.).

EXCEPTIONS

SEC. 803. [50 U.S.C. §437]

Except as otherwise specifically provided, the provisions of this title shall not apply to the President and Vice President, Members of the Congress, Justices of the Supreme Court, and Federal judges appointed by the President.

DEFINITIONS

SEC. 804. [50 U.S.C. §438]

For purposes of this title—

(1) the term "authorized investigative agency" means an agency authorized by law or regulation to conduct a counterintelligence investigation or investigations of persons who

are proposed for access to classified information to ascertain whether such persons satisfy the criteria for obtaining and retaining access to such information;

(2) the term "classified information" means any information that has been determined pursuant to Executive Order No. 12356 of April 2, 1982, or successor orders, or the Atomic Energy Act of 1954, to require protection against unauthorized disclosure and that is so designated;

(3) the term "consumer reporting agency" has the meaning given such term in section 603 of the Consumer Credit Protection Act (15 U.S.C. §1681a);

(4) the term "employee" includes any person who receives a salary or compensation of any kind from the United States Government, is a contractor of the United States Government or an employee thereof, is an unpaid consultant of the United States Government, or otherwise acts for or on behalf of the United States Government, except as otherwise determined by the President;

(5) the terms "financial agency" and "financial institution" have the meanings given to such terms in section 5312(a) of title 31, United States Code, and the term "holding company" has the meaning given to such term in section 1101(6) of the Right to Financial Privacy Act of 1978 (12 U.S.C. §3401);

(6) the terms "foreign power" and "agent of a foreign power" have the same meanings as set forth in sections 101 (a) and (b), respectively, of the Foreign Intelligence Surveillance Act of 1978 (50 U.S.C. §1801);

(7) the term "State" means each of the several States of the United States, the District of Columbia, the Commonwealth of Puerto Rico, the Commonwealth of the Northern Mariana Islands, the United States Virgin Islands, Guam, American Samoa, the Republic of the Marshall Islands, the Federated States of Micronesia, and the Republic of Palau, and any other possession of the United States; and

(8) the term "computer" means any electronic, magnetic, optical, electrochemical, or other high speed data processing device performing logical, arithmetic, or storage functions, and includes any data storage facility or communications facility directly related to or operating in conjunction with such device and any data or other information stored or contained in such device.

TITLE IX—APPLICATION OF SANCTIONS LAWS TO INTELLIGENCE ACTIVITIES

STAY OF SANCTIONS

SEC. 901. [50 U.S.C. §441]

Notwithstanding any provision of law identified in section 904, the President may stay the imposition of an economic, cultural, diplomatic, or other sanction or related action by the United States Government concerning a foreign country, organization, or person when the President determines and reports to Congress in accordance with section 903 that to proceed without delay would seriously risk the compromise of an ongoing criminal investigation directly related to the activities giving rise to the sanction or an intelligence source or method directly related to the activities giving rise to the sanction. Any such stay shall be effective for a period of time specified by the President, which period may not exceed 120 days, unless such period is extended in accordance with section 902.

EXTENSION OF STAY

SEC. 902. [50 U.S.C. §441a]

Whenever the President determines and reports to Congress in accordance with section 903 that a stay of sanctions or related actions pursuant to section 901 has not afforded sufficient time to obviate the risk to an ongoing criminal investigation or to an intelligence source or method that gave rise to the stay, he may extend such stay for a period of time specified by the President, which period may not exceed 120 days. The authority of this section may be used to extend the period of a stay pursuant to section 901 for successive periods of not more than 120 days each.

REPORTS

SEC. 903. [50 U.S.C. §441b]

Reports to Congress pursuant to sections 901 and 902 shall be submitted promptly upon determinations under this title. Such reports shall be submitted to the Committee on International Relations of the House of Representatives and the Committee on Foreign Relations of the Senate. With respect to determinations relating to intelligence sources and methods, reports shall also be submitted to the congressional intelligence committees. With respect to determinations relating to ongoing criminal investigations, reports shall also be submitted to the Committees on the Judiciary of the House of Representatives and the Senate.

LAWS SUBJECT TO STAY

SEC. 904. [50 U.S.C. §441c]

The President may use the authority of sections 901 and 902 to stay the imposition of an economic, cultural, diplomatic, or other sanction or related action by the United States Government related to the proliferation of weapons of mass destruction, their delivery systems, or advanced conventional weapons otherwise required to be imposed by the Chemical and Biological Weapons Control and Warfare Elimination Act of 1991 (title III of Public Law 102–182); the Nuclear Proliferation Prevention Act of 1994 (title VIII of Public Law 103– 236); title XVII of the National Defense Authorization Act for Fiscal Year 1991 (Public Law 101–510) (relating to the nonproliferation of missile technology); the Iran-Iraq Arms Nonproliferation Act of 1992 (title XVI of Public Law 102– 484); section 573 of the Foreign Operations, Export Financing Related Programs Appropriations Act, 1994 (Public Law 103–87); section 563 of the Foreign Operations, Export Financing Related Programs Appropriations Act, 1995 (Public Law 103–306); and comparable provisions.

TITLE X—EDUCATION IN SUPPORT OF NATIONAL INTELLIGENCE

SUBTITLE A—SCIENCE AND TECHNOLOGY

SCHOLARSHIPS AND WORK-STUDY FOR PURSUIT OF GRADUATE DEGREES IN SCIENCE AND TECHNOLOGY

SEC. 1001. [50 U.S.C. §441g]

(a) PROGRAM AUTHORIZED.—The Director of National Intelligence may carry out a program to provide scholarships and work-study for individuals who are pursuing graduate degrees in fields of study in science and technology that are identified by the Director as appropriate to meet the future needs of the intelligence community for qualified scientists and engineers.

(b) ADMINISTRATION.—If the Director of National Intelligence carries out the program under subsection (a), the Director shall administer the program through the Office of the Director of National Intelligence.

(c) IDENTIFICATION OF FIELDS OF STUDY.—If the Director of National Intelligence carries out the program under subsection (a), the Director shall identify fields of study under subsection (a) in consultation with the other heads of the elements of the intelligence community.

(d) ELIGIBILITY FOR PARTICIPATION.—An individual eligible to participate in the program is any individual who—

    (1) either—

        (A) is an employee of the intelligence community; or

        (B) meets criteria for eligibility for employment in the intelligence community that are established by the Director of National Intelligence;

(2) is accepted in a graduate degree program in a field of study in science or technology identified under subsection (a); and

(3) is eligible for a security clearance at the level of Secret or above.

(e) REGULATIONS.—If the Director of National Intelligence carries out the program under subsection (a), the Director shall prescribe regulations for purposes of the administration of this section.

FRAMEWORK FOR CROSS-DISCIPLINARY EDUCATION AND TRAINING

SEC. 1002. [50 U.S.C. §441g-1] The Director of National Intelligence shall establish an integrated framework that brings together the educational components of the intelligence community in order to promote a more effective and productive intelligence community through cross-disciplinary education and joint training.

SUBTITLE B – FOREIGN LANGUAGES PROGRAM

PROGRAM ON ADVANCEMENT OF FOREIGN LANGUAGES CRITICAL TO THE INTELLIGENCE COMMUNITY

SEC. 1011. [50 U.S.C. §441j]

(a) IN GENERAL.—The Secretary of Defense and the Director of National Intelligence may jointly carry out a program to advance skills in foreign languages that are critical to the capability of the intelligence community to carry out the national security activities of the United States (hereinafter in this subtitle referred to as the Foreign Languages Program').

(b) IDENTIFICATION OF REQUISITE ACTIONS.—In order to carry out the Foreign Languages Program, the Secretary of Defense and the Director of National Intelligence shall jointly identify actions required to improve the education of personnel in the intelligence community in foreign languages that are critical to the capability of the intelligence community to carry out the national security activities of the United States and to meet the long-term intelligence needs of the United States.

EDUCATION PARTNERSHIPS

SEC. 1012. [50 U.S.C. §441j-1]

(a) IN GENERAL.—In carrying out the Foreign Languages Program, the head of a covered element of the intelligence community may enter into one or more education partnership agreements with educational institutions in the United States in order to encourage and enhance the study in such educational institutions of foreign languages that are critical to the capability of the intelligence community to carry out the national security activities of the United States.

(b) ASSISTANCE PROVIDED UNDER EDUCATIONAL PARTNERSHIP AGREEMENTS.—Under an educational partnership agreement entered into with an educational institution pursuant to this section, the head of a covered element of the intelligence community may provide the following assistance to the educational institution:

(1) The loan of equipment and instructional materials of the element of the intelligence community to the educational institution for any purpose and duration that the head of the element considers appropriate.

(2) Notwithstanding any other provision of law relating to the transfer of surplus property, the transfer to the educational institution of any computer equipment, or other equipment, that is—

(A) commonly used by educational institutions;

(B) surplus to the needs of the element of the intelligence community; and

(C) determined by the head of the element to be appropriate for support of such agreement.

(3) The provision of dedicated personnel to the educational institution—

(A) to teach courses in foreign languages that are critical to the capability of the intelligence community to carry out the national security activities of the United States; or

(B) to assist in the development for the educational institution of courses and materials on such languages.

(4) The involvement of faculty and students of the educational institution in research projects of the element of the intelligence community.

(5) Cooperation with the educational institution in developing a program under which students receive academic credit at the educational institution for work on research projects of the element of the intelligence community.

(6) The provision of academic and career advice and assistance to students of the educational institution.

(7) The provision of cash awards and other items that the head of the element of the intelligence community considers appropriate.

VOLUNTARY SERVICES
SEC. 1013. [50 U.S.C. §441j-2]

(a) AUTHORITY TO ACCEPT SERVICES.—Notwithstanding section 1342 of title 31, United States Code, and subject to subsection (b), the Foreign Languages Program under section 1011 shall include authority for the head of a covered element of the intelligence community to accept from any dedicated personnel voluntary services in support of the activities authorized by this subtitle.

(b) REQUIREMENTS AND LIMITATIONS.—

(1) In accepting voluntary services from an individual under subsection (a), the head of a covered element of the intelligence community shall—

(A) supervise the individual to the same extent as the head of the element would supervise a compensated employee of that element providing similar services; and

(B) ensure that the individual is licensed, privileged, has appropriate educational or experiential credentials, or is otherwise qualified under applicable law or regulations to provide such services.

(2) In accepting voluntary services from an individual under subsection (a), the head of a covered element of the intelligence community may not—

(A) place the individual in a policymaking position, or other position performing inherently governmental functions; or

(B) compensate the individual for the provision of such services.

(c) AUTHORITY TO RECRUIT AND TRAIN INDIVIDUALS PROVIDING SERVICES.—The head of a covered element of the intelligence community may recruit and train individuals to provide voluntary services under subsection (a).

(d) STATUS OF INDIVIDUALS PROVIDING SERVICES.—

(1) Subject to paragraph (2), while providing voluntary services under subsection (a) or receiving training under subsection (c), an individual shall be considered to be an employee of the Federal Government only for purposes of the following provisions of law:

(A) Section 552a of title 5, United States Code (relating to maintenance of records on individuals).

(B) Chapter 11 of title 18, United States Code (relating to conflicts of interest).

(2)(A) With respect to voluntary services under paragraph (1) provided by an individual that are within the scope of the services accepted under that paragraph, the individual shall be deemed to be a volunteer of a governmental entity or nonprofit institution for purposes of the Volunteer Protection Act of 1997 (42 U.S.C. §14501 et seq.).

(B) In the case of any claim against such an individual with respect to the provision of such services, section 4(d) of such Act (42 U.S.C. §14503(d)) shall not apply.

(3) Acceptance of voluntary services under this section shall have no bearing on the issuance or renewal of a security clearance.

(e) REIMBURSEMENT OF INCIDENTAL EXPENSES.—

(1) The head of a covered element of the intelligence community may reimburse an individual for incidental expenses incurred by the individual in providing voluntary services under subsection (a). The head of a covered element of the intelligence community shall determine which expenses are eligible for reimbursement under this subsection.

(2) Reimbursement under paragraph (1) may be made from appropriated or nonappropriated funds.

(f) AUTHORITY TO INSTALL EQUIPMENT.—

(1) The head of a covered element of the intelligence community may install telephone lines and any necessary telecommunication equipment in the private residences of individuals who provide voluntary services under subsection (a).

(2) The head of a covered element of the intelligence community may pay the charges incurred for the use of equipment installed under paragraph (1) for authorized purposes.

(3) Notwithstanding section 1348 of title 31, United States Code, the head of a covered element of the intelligence community may use appropriated funds or nonappropriated funds of the element in carrying out this subsection.

REGULATIONS

SEC. 1014. [50 U.S.C. §441j-3]

(a) IN GENERAL.—The Secretary of Defense and the Director of National Intelligence shall jointly prescribe regulations to carry out the Foreign Languages Program.

(b) ELEMENTS OF THE INTELLIGENCE COMMUNITY.—The head of each covered element of the intelligence community shall prescribe regulations to carry out sections 1012 and 1013 with respect to that element including the following:

(1) Procedures to be utilized for the acceptance of voluntary services under section 1013.

(2) Procedures and requirements relating to the installation of equipment under section 1013(f).

DEFINITIONS

SEC. 1015. [50 U.S.C. §441j-4] In this subtitle:

(1) The term "covered element of the intelligence community" means an agency, office, bureau, or element referred to in subparagraphs (B) through (L) of section 3(4).

(2) The term "educational institution" means—

(A) a local educational agency (as that term is defined in section 9101(26) of the Elementary and Secondary Education Act of 1965 (20 U.S.C. §7801(26)));

(B) an institution of higher education (as defined in section 102 of the Higher Education Act of 1965 (20 U.S.C. §1002) other than institutions referred to in subsection (a)(1)(C) of such section); or

(C) any other nonprofit institution that provides instruction of foreign languages in languages that are critical to the capability of the intelligence community to carry out national security activities of the United States.

(3) The term "dedicated personnel" means employees of the intelligence community and private citizens (including former civilian employees of the Federal Government who have been voluntarily separated, and members of the United States Armed Forces who have been honorably discharged, honorably separated, or generally discharged under honorable circumstances and rehired on a voluntary basis specifically to perform the activities authorized under this subtitle).

SUBTITLE C—ADDITIONAL EDUCATION PROGRAMS

ASSIGNMENT OF INTELLIGENCE COMMUNITY PERSONNEL AS LANGUAGE STUDENTS

SEC. 1021. [50 U.S.C. §441m]

(a) IN GENERAL.—The Director of National Intelligence, acting through the heads of the elements of the intelligence community, may assign employees of such elements in analyst positions requiring foreign language expertise as students at accredited professional, technical, or other institutions of higher education for training at the graduate or undergraduate level in foreign languages required for the conduct of duties and responsibilities of such positions.

(b) AUTHORITY FOR REIMBURSEMENT OF COSTS OF TUITION AND TRAINING.—

(1) The Director of National Intelligence may reimburse an employee assigned under subsection (a) for the total cost of the training described in that subsection, including costs of educational and supplementary reading materials.

(2) The authority under paragraph (1) shall apply to employees who are assigned on a full-time or part-time basis.

(3) Reimbursement under paragraph (1) may be made from appropriated or nonappropriated funds.

(c) RELATIONSHIP TO COMPENSATION AS AN ANALYST.—Reimbursement under this section to an employee who is an analyst is in addition to any benefits, allowances, travel expenses, or other compensation the employee is entitled to by reason of serving in such an analyst position.

PROGRAM ON RECRUITMENT AND TRAINING

SEC. 1022. [50 U.S.C. 441n]

(a) PROGRAM.—

(1) The Director of National Intelligence shall carry out a program to ensure that selected students or former students are provided funds to continue academic training, or are reimbursed for academic training previously obtained, in areas of specialization that the Director, in consultation with the other heads of the elements of the intelligence community, identifies as areas in which the current capabilities of the intelligence community are deficient or in which fu ture capabilities of the intelligence community are likely to be deficient.

(2) A student or former student selected for participation in the program shall commit to employment with an element of the intelligence community, following completion of appropriate academic training, under such terms and conditions as the Director considers appropriate.

(3) The program shall be known as the Pat Roberts Intelligence Scholars Program.

(b) ELEMENTS.—In carrying out the program under subsection (a), the Director shall—

(1) establish such requirements relating to the academic training of participants as the Director considers appropriate to ensure that participants are prepared for employment as intelligence professionals; and

(2) periodically review the areas of specialization of the elements of the intelligence community to determine the areas in which such elements are, or are likely to be, deficient in capabilities.

(c) USE OF FUNDS.—Funds made available for the program under subsection (a) shall be used—

(1) to provide a monthly stipend for each month that a student is pursuing a course of study;

(2) to pay the full tuition of a student or former student for the completion of such course of study;

(3) to pay for books and materials that the student or former student requires or required to complete such course of study;

(4) to pay the expenses of the student or former student for travel requested by an element of the intelligence community in relation to such program; or

(5) for such other purposes the Director considers reasonably appropriate to carry out such program.

EDUCATIONAL SCHOLARSHIP PROGRAM
SEC. 1023. [50 U.S.C. 441o]

The head of a department or agency containing an element of the intelligence community may establish an undergraduate or graduate training program with respect to civilian employees and prospective civilian employees of such element similar in purpose, conditions, content, and administration to the program that the Secretary of Defense is authorized to establish under section 16 of the National Security Agency Act of 1959 (50 U.S.C. 402 note).

INTELLIGENCE OFFICER TRAINING PROGRAM
SEC. 1024. [50 U.S.C. 441p]

(a) PROGRAMS.—

(1) The Director of National Intelligence may carry out grant programs in accordance with subsection (b) to enhance the recruitment and retention of an ethnically and culturally diverse intelligence community workforce with capabilities critical to the national security interests of the United States.

(2) In carrying out paragraph (1), the Director shall identify the skills necessary to meet current or emergent needs of the intel ligence community and the educational disciplines that will provide individuals with such skills.

(b) INSTITUTIONAL GRANT PROGRAM.—

(1) The Director may provide grants to institutions of higher education to support the establishment or continued development of programs of study in educational disciplines identified under subsection (a)(2).

(2) A grant provided under paragraph (1) may, with respect to the educational disciplines identified under subsection (a)(2), be used for the following purposes:

(A) Curriculum or program development.

(B) Faculty development.

(C) Laboratory equipment or improvements.

(D) Faculty research.

(c) APPLICATION.—An institution of higher education seeking a grant under this section shall submit an application describing the proposed use of the grant at such time and in such manner as the Director may require.

(d) REPORTS.—An institution of higher education that receives a grant under this section shall submit to the Director regular reports regarding the use of such grant, including—

(1) a description of the benefits to students who participate in the course of study funded by such grant;

(2) a description of the results and accomplishments related to such course of study; and

(3) any other information that the Director may require.

(e) REGULATIONS.—The Director shall prescribe such regulations as may be necessary to carry out this section.

(f) DEFINITIONS.—In this section:

(1) The term "Director" means the Director of National Intelligence.

(2) The term "institution of higher education" has the meaning given the term in section 101 of the Higher Education Act of 1965 (20 U.S.C. 1001).

TITLE XI—ADDITIONAL MISCELLANEOUS PROVISIONS APPLICABILITY TO UNITED STATES INTELLIGENCE ACTIVITIES OF FEDERAL LAWS IMPLEMENTING INTERNATIONAL TREATIES AND AGREEMENTS

SEC. 1101. [50 U.S.C. 442]

(a) IN GENERAL.—No Federal law enacted on or after the date of the enactment of the Intelligence Authorization Act for Fiscal Year 2001 that implements a treaty or other international agreement shall be construed as making unlawful an otherwise lawful and authorized intelligence activity of the United States Government or its employees, or any other person to the extent such other person is carrying out such activity on behalf of, and at the direction of, the United States, unless such Federal law specifically addresses such intelligence activity.

(b) AUTHORIZED INTELLIGENCE ACTIVITIES.—An intelligence activity shall be treated as authorized for purposes of subsection (a) if the intelligence activity is authorized by an appropriate official of the United States Government, acting within the scope of the official duties of that official and in compliance with Federal law and any applicable Presidential directive.

COUNTERINTELLIGENCE INITIATIVES

SEC. 1102.

(a) INSPECTION PROCESS.—In order to protect intelligence sources and methods from unauthorized disclosure, the Director of National Intelligence shall establish and implement an inspection process for all agencies and departments of the United States that handle classified information relating to the national security of the United States intended to assure that those agencies and departments maintain effective operational security practices and programs directed against counterintelligence activities.

(b) ANNUAL REVIEW OF DISSEMINATION LISTS.—The Director of National Intelligence shall establish and implement a process for all elements of the intelligence community to review, on an annual basis, individuals included on distribution lists for access to classified information. Such process shall ensure that only individuals who have a particularized "need to know" (as determined by the Director) are continued on such distribution lists.

(c) COMPLETION OF FINANCIAL DISCLOSURE STATEMENTS REQUIRED FOR ACCESS TO CERTAIN CLASSIFIED INFORMATION.—The Director of National Intelligence shall establish and implement a process by which each head of an element of the intelligence community directs that all employees of that element, in order to be granted access to classified information referred to in subsection (a) of section 1.3 of Executive Order No. 12968 (August 2, 1995; 60 Fed. Reg. 40245; 50 U.S.C. 435 note), submit financial disclosure forms as required under subsection (b) of such section.

(d) ARRANGEMENTS TO HANDLE SENSITIVE INFORMATION.—The Director of National Intelligence shall establish, for all elements of the intelligence community, programs and procedures by which sensitive classified information relating to human intelligence is safeguarded against unauthorized disclosure by employees of those elements.

MISUSE OF THE OFFICE OF THE DIRECTOR OF NATIONAL INTELLIGENCE NAME, INITIALS, OR SEAL

SEC. 1103. [50 U.S.C. 442b]

(a) PROHIBITED ACTS.—No person may, except with the written permission of the Director of National Intelligence, or a designee of the Director, knowingly use the words "Office of the

Director of National Intelligence", the initials "ODNI", the seal of the Office of the Director of National Intelligence, or any colorable imitation of such words, initials, or seal in connection with any merchandise, impersonation, solicitation, or commercial activity in a manner reasonably calculated to convey the impression that such use is approved, endorsed, or authorized by the Director of National Intelligence.

(b) INJUNCTION.—Whenever it appears to the Attorney General that any person is engaged or is about to engage in an act or practice which constitutes or will constitute conduct prohibited by subsection (a), the Attorney General may initiate a civil proceeding in a district court of the United States to enjoin such act or practice. Such court shall proceed as soon as practicable to the hearing and determination of such action and may, at any time before final determination, enter such restraining orders or prohibitions, or take such other action as is warranted, to prevent injury to the United States or to any person or class of persons for whose protection the action is brought.

SEC. 1104. [50 U.S.C. 3234] PROHIBITED PERSONNEL PRACTICES IN THE INTELLIGENCE COMMUNITY.

(a) DEFINITIONS.—In this section:

(1) AGENCY.—The term "agency" means an executive department or independent establishment, as defined under sections 101 and 104 of title 5, United States Code, that contains an intelligence community element, except the Federal Bureau of Investigation.

(2) COVERED INTELLIGENCE COMMUNITY ELEMENT.—The term "covered intelligence community element"—

(A) means—

(i) the Central Intelligence Agency, the Defense Intelligence Agency, the National Geospatial-Intelligence Agency, the National Security Agency, the Office of the Director of National Intelligence, and the National Reconnaissance Office; and

(ii) any executive agency or unit thereof determined by the President under section 2302(a)(2)(C)(ii) of title 5, United States Code, to have as its principal function the conduct of foreign intelligence or counterintelligence activities; and

(B) does not include the Federal Bureau of Investigation.

(3) PERSONNEL ACTION.—The term "personnel action" means, with respect to an employee in a position in a covered intelligence community element (other than a position excepted from the competitive service due to its confidential, policy-determining, policymaking, or policy-advocating character)—

(A) an appointment;

(B) a promotion;

(C) a disciplinary or corrective action;

(D) a detail, transfer, or reassignment;

(E) a demotion, suspension, or termination;

(F) a reinstatement or restoration;

(G) a performance evaluation;

(H) a decision concerning pay, benefits, or awards;

(I) a decision concerning education or training if such education or training may reasonably be expected to lead to an appointment, promotion, or performance evaluation; or

(J) any other significant change in duties, responsibilities, or working conditions.

(b) IN GENERAL.—Any employee of an agency who has authority to take, direct others to take, recommend, or approve any personnel action, shall not, with respect to such authority, take or fail to take a personnel action with respect to any employee of a covered intelligence community element as a reprisal for a lawful disclosure of information by the employee to the Director of National Intelligence (or an employee designated by the Director of National Intelligence for such purpose), the Inspector General of the Intelligence Community, the head of the employing agency (or an employee designated by the head of that agency for such purpose), the appropriate inspector general of the employing agency, a congressional intelligence committee, or a member of a congressional intelligence committee, which the employee reasonably believes evidences—

(1) a violation of any Federal law, rule, or regulation; or

(2) mismanagement, a gross waste of funds, an abuse of authority, or a substantial and specific danger to public health or safety.

(c) ENFORCEMENT.—The President shall provide for the enforcement of this section.

(d) EXISTING RIGHTS PRESERVED.—Nothing in this section shall be construed to—

(1) preempt or preclude any employee, or applicant for employment, at the Federal Bureau of Investigation from exercising rights provided under any other law, rule, or regulation, including section 2303 of title 5, United States Code; or

(2) repeal section 2303 of title 5, United States Code.

CENTRAL INTELLIGENCE AGENCY ACT OF 1949

(Chapter 227; 63 Stat. 208; approved June 20, 1949)
[As Amended Through P.L. 112–87, Enacted January 3, 2012]

AN ACT To provide for the administration of the Central Intelligence Agency, established pursuant to section 102, National Security Act of 1947, and for other purposes.

Be it enacted by the Senate and House of Representatives of the United States of America in Congress assembled,

DEFINITIONS

SECTION 1. [50 U.S.C. 403a]
That when used in this Act, the term—

(1) "Agency" means the Central Intelligence Agency;

(2) "Director" means the Director of the Central Intelligence Agency; and

(3) "Government agency" means any executive department, commission, council, independent establishment, corporation wholly or partly owned by the United States which is an instrumentality of the United States, board, bureau, division, service, office, officer, authority, administration, or other establishment, in the executive branch of the Government.

SEAL OF OFFICE

SEC. 2. [50 U.S.C. 403b]
The Director shall cause a seal of office to be made for the Central Intelligence Agency, of such design as the President shall approve, and judicial notice shall be taken thereof.

PROCUREMENT AUTHORITIES

SEC. 3. [50 U.S.C. 403c]
(a) In the performance of its functions the Central Intelligence Agency is authorized to exercise the authorities contained in sections 2(c) (1), (2), (3), (4), (5), (6), (10), (12), (15), (17), and sections 3, 4, 5, 6, and 10 of the Armed Services Procurement Act of 1947[1] (Public Law 413, Eightieth Congress, second session).

(b) In the exercise of the authorities granted in subsection (a) of this section, the term "Agency head" shall mean the Director, the Deputy Director, or the Executive of the Agency.

(c) The determinations and decisions provided in subsection (a) of this section to be made by the Agency head may be made with respect to individual purchases and contracts or with respect to classes of purchases or contracts, and shall be final. Except as provided in subsection (d) of this section, the Agency head is authorized to delegate his powers provided in this section, including the making of such determinations and decisions, in his discretion and subject to his direction, to any other officer or officers or officials of the Agency.

---

1. The Armed Services Procurement Act of 1947 was repealed by the law enacting titles 10 and 32, United States Code (Act of August 10, 1956, 70A Stat. 1). The cited sections were replaced by sections 2304(a) (1)–(6), (10), (12), (15), and (17), 2305 (a)–(c). 2306, 2307, 2308, 2309, 2312, and 2313 of title 10. Section 49(b) of that Act provided: "References that other laws, regulations, and orders make to the replaced law shall be considered to be made to the corresponding provisions of [the sections enacting titles 10 and 32]."

(d) The power of the Agency head to make the determinations or decisions specified in paragraphs (12) and (15) of section 2(c) and section 5(a) of the Armed Services Procurement Act of 1947 [1] shall not be delegable. Each determination or decision required by paragraphs (12) and (15) of section 2(c), by section 4 or by section 5(a) of the Armed Services Procurement Act of 1947,[1] shall be based upon written findings made by the official making such determinations, which findings shall be final and shall be available within the Agency for a period of at least six years following the date of the determination.

[Original section 4 (50 U.S.C. 403d) was repealed by section 21(b)(2) of Public Law 85–507 (72 Stat. 337, July 7, 1958).]

TRAVEL, ALLOWANCES, AND RELATED EXPENSES
SEC. 4. [50 U.S.C. 403e]

(a) Under such regulations as the Director may prescribe, the Agency, with respect to its officers and employees assigned to duty stations outside the several States of the United States of America, excluding Alaska and Hawaii, but including the District of Columbia, shall—

(1)(A) pay the travel expenses of officers and employees of the Agency, including expenses incurred while traveling pursuant to authorized home leave;

(B) pay the travel expenses of members of the family of an officer or employee of the Agency when proceeding to or returning from his post of duty; accompanying him on authorized home leave; or otherwise traveling in accordance with authority granted pursuant to the terms of this or any other Act;

(C) pay the cost of transporting the furniture and household and personal effects of an officer or employee of the Agency to his successive posts of duty and, on the termination of his services, to his residence at time of appointment or to a point not more distant, or, upon retirement, to the place where he will reside;

(D) pay the cost of packing and unpacking, transporting to and from a place of storage, and storing the furniture and household and personal effects of an officer or employee of the Agency, when he is absent from his post of assignment under orders, or when he is assigned to a post to which he cannot take or at which he is unable to use such furniture and household and personal effects, or when it is in the public interest or more economical to authorize storage; but in no instance shall the weight or volume of the effects stored together with the weight or volume of the effects transported exceed the maximum limitations fixed by regulations, when not otherwise fixed by law;

(E) pay the cost of packing and unpacking, transporting to and from a place of storage, and storing the furniture and household and personal effects of an officer or employee of the Agency in connection with assignment or transfer to a new post, from the date of his departure from his last post or from the date of his departure from his place of residence in the case of a new officer or employee and for not to exceed three months after arrival at the new post, or until the establishment of residence quarters, whichever shall be shorter; and in connection with separation of an officer or employee of the Agency, the cost of packing and unpacking, transporting to and from a place of storage, and storing for a period not to exceed three months, his furniture and household and personal effects; but in no instance shall the weight or volume of the effects stored together with the

---

1.   See footnote on previous page. The cited provisions were replaced by paragraphs (12) and (15) of section 2304(a) and section 2307(a) of title 10.

weight or volume of the effects transported exceed the maximum limitations fixed by regulations, when not otherwise fixed by law. [1]

(F) pay the travel expenses and transportation costs incident to the removal of the members of the family of an officer or employee of the Agency and his furniture and household and personal effects, including automobiles, from a post at which, because of the prevalence of disturbed conditions, there is imminent danger to life and property, and the return of such persons, furniture, and effects to such post upon the cessation of such conditions; or to such other post as may in the meantime have become the post to which such officer or employee has been assigned.

(2) Charge expenses in connection with travel of personnel, their dependents, and transportation of their household goods and personal effects, involving a change of permanent station, to the appropriation for the fiscal year current when any part of either the travel or transportation pertaining to the transfer begins pursuant to previously issued travel and transfer orders, notwithstanding the fact that such travel or transportation may not all be effected during such fiscal year, or the travel and transfer orders may have been issued during the prior fiscal year.

(3)(A) Order to any of the several States of the United States of America (including the District of Columbia, the Commonwealth of Puerto Rico, and any territory or possession of the United States) on leave of absence each officer or employee of the Agency who was a resident of the United States (as described above) at time of employment, upon completion of two years' continuous service abroad, or as soon as possible thereafter.

(B) While in the United States (as described in paragraph (3)(A) of this section) on leave, the service of any officer or employee shall be available for work or duties in the Agency or elsewhere as the Director may prescribe; and the time of such work or duty shall not be counted as leave.

(C) Where an officer or employee on leave returns to the United States (as described in paragraph (3)(A) of this section), leave of absence granted shall be exclusive of the time actually and necessarily occupied in going to and from the United States (as so described) and such time as may be necessarily occupied in awaiting transportation.

(4) Notwithstanding the provisions of any other law, transport for or on behalf of an officer or employee of the Agency, a privately owned motor vehicle in any case in which it shall be determined that water, rail, or air transportation of the motor vehicle is necessary or expedient for all or any part of the distance between points of origin and destination, and pay the costs of such transportation. Not more than one motor vehicle of any officer or employee of the Agency may be transported under authority of this paragraph during any four-year period, except that, as replacement for such motor vehicle, one additional motor vehicle of any such officer or employee may be so transported during such period upon approval, in advance, by the Director and upon a determination, in advance, by the Director that such replacement is necessary for reasons beyond the control of the officer or employee and is in the interest of the Government. After the expiration of a period of four years following the date of transportation under authority of this paragraph of a privately owned motor vehicle of any officer or employee who has remained in continuous service outside the several States of the United States of America, excluding Alaska and Hawaii, but including the District of Columbia, during such period, the transportation of a replacement

---

1.   So in original. The period probably should be a semicolon.

for such motor vehicle for such officer or employee may be authorized by the Director in accordance with this paragraph.

(5)(A) In the event of illness or injury requiring the hospitalization of an officer or full time employee of the Agency, incurred while on assignment abroad, in a locality where there does not exist a suitable hospital or clinic, pay the travel expenses of such officer or employee by whatever means the Director deems appropriate and without regard to the Standardized Government Travel Regulations and section 5731 of title 5, United States Code, to the nearest locality where a suitable hospital or clinic exists and on the recovery of such officer or employee pay for the travel expenses of the return to the post of duty of such officer or employee of duty. If the officer or employee is too ill to travel unattended, the Director may also pay the travel expenses of an attendant;

> (B) Establish a first-aid station and provide for the services of a nurse at a post at which, in the opinion of the Director, sufficient personnel is employed to warrant such a station: *Provided,* That, in the opinion of the Director, it is not feasible to utilize an existing facility;

> (C) In the event of illness or injury requiring hospitalization of an officer or full time employee of the Agency incurred in the line of duty while such person is assigned abroad, pay for the cost of the treatment of such illness or injury at a suitable hospital or clinic;

> (D) Provide for the periodic physical examination of officers and employees of the Agency and for the cost of administering inoculations or vaccinations to such officers or employees.

> (6) Pay the costs of preparing and transporting the remains of an officer or employee of the Agency or a member of his family who may die while in travel status or abroad, to his home or official station, or to such other place as the Director may determine to be the appropriate place of interment, provided that in no case shall the expense payable be greater than the amount which would have been payable had the destination been the home or official station.

(7) Pay the costs of travel of new appointees and their dependents, and the transportation of their household goods and personal effects, from places of actual residence in foreign countries at time of appointment to places of employment and return to their actual residences at the time of appointment or a point not more distant: *Provided,* That such appointees agree in writing to remain with the United States Government for a period of not less than twelve months from the time of appointment.

Violation of such agreement for personal convenience of an employee or because of separation for misconduct will bar such return payments and, if determined by the Director or his designee to be in the best interests of the United States, any money expended by the United States on account of such travel and transportation shall be considered as a debt due by the individual concerned to the United States.

(b)(1) The Director may pay to officers and employees of the Agency, and to persons detailed or assigned to the Agency from other agencies of the Government or from the Armed Forces, allowances and benefits comparable to the allowances and benefits authorized to be paid to members of the Foreign Service under chapter 9 of title I of the Foreign Service Act of 1980 (22 U.S.C. 4081 et seq.) or any other provision of law.

(2) The Director may pay allowances and benefits related to officially authorized travel, personnel and physical security activities, operational activities, and cover-related activities (whether or not such allowances and benefits are otherwise authorized under this section or any other provision of law) when payment of such allow-

ances and benefits is necessary to meet the special requirements of work related to such activities. Payment of allowances and benefits under this paragraph shall be in accordance with regulations prescribed by the Director. Rates for allowances and benefits under this paragraph may not be set at rates in excess of those authorized by section 5724 and 5724a of title 5, United States Code, when reimbursement is provided for relocation attributable, in whole or in part, to relocation within the United States.

(3) Notwithstanding any other provision of this section or any other provision of law relating to the officially authorized travel of Government employees, the Director, in order to reflect Agency requirements not taken into account in the formulation of Government-wide travel procedures, may by regulation—

(A) authorize the travel of officers and employees of the Agency, and of persons detailed or assigned to the Agency from other agencies of the Government or from the Armed Forces who are engaged in the performance of intelligence functions, and

(B) provide for payment for such travel, in classes of cases, as determined by the Director, in which such travel is important to the performance of intelligence functions.

(4) Members of the Armed Forces may not receive benefits under both this section and title 37, United States Code, for the same purpose. The Director and Secretary of Defense shall prescribe joint regulations to carry out the preceding sentence.

(5) Regulations, other than regulations under paragraph (1), issued pursuant to this subsection shall be submitted to the Permanent Select Committee on Intelligence of the House of Representatives and the Select Committee on Intelligence of the Senate before such regulations take effect.

GENERAL AUTHORITIES

SEC. 5. [50 U.S.C. 403f]

(a) IN GENERAL.—

In the performance of its functions, the Central Intelligence Agency is authorized to—

(1) Transfer to and receive from other Government agencies such sums as may be approved by the Office of Management and Budget, for the performance of any of the functions or activities authorized under section 104A of the National Security Act of 1947 (50 U.S.C. 403–4a).[1], and any other Government agency is authorized to transfer to or receive from the Agency such sums without regard to any provisions of law limiting or prohibiting transfers between appropriations. Sums transferred to the Agency in accordance with this paragraph may be expended for the purposes and under the authority of this Act without regard to limitations of appropriations from which transferred;

(2) Exchange funds without regard to section 3651 Revised Statutes (31 U.S.C. 543);

(3) Reimburse other Government agencies for services of personnel assigned to the Agency, and such other Government agencies are hereby authorized, without regard to provisions of law to the contrary, so to assign or detail any officer or employee for duty with the Agency;

(4) Authorize personnel designated by the Director to carry firearms to the extent necessary for the performance of the Agency's authorized functions, except that, within the United States, such authority shall be limited to the purposes of protection of classified materials and information, the training of Agency personnel and other authorized persons in the use of firearms, the protection of Agency installations and property, the protection of current and former Agency personnel and their immediate families, defectors and their

---

1. So in law. See amendment made by section 802(1) of Public Law 111–259.

immediate families, and other persons in the United States under Agency auspices, and the protection of the Director of National Intelligence and such personnel of the Office of the Director of National Intelligence as the Director of National Intelligence may designate;

(5) Make alterations, improvements, and repairs on premises rented by the Agency, and pay rent therefor;

(6) Determine and fix the minimum and maximum limits of age within which an original appointment may be made to an operational position within the Agency, notwithstanding the provision of any other law, in accordance with such criteria as the Director, in his discretion, may prescribe; and

(7) Notwithstanding section 1341(a)(1) of title 31, United States Code, enter into multiyear leases for up to 15 years.

(b) SCOPE OF AUTHORITY FOR EXPENDITURE.—

(1) The authority to enter into a multiyear lease under subsection (a)(7) shall be subject to appropriations provided in advance for—

(A) the entire lease; or

(B) the first 12 months of the lease and the Government's estimated termination liability.

(2) In the case of any such lease entered into under subparagraph (B) of paragraph (1)—

(A) such lease shall include a clause that provides that the contract shall be terminated if budget authority (as defined by section 3(2) of the Congressional Budget and Impoundment Control Act of 1974 (2 U.S.C. 622(2))) is not provided specifically for that project in an appropriations Act in advance of an obligation of funds in respect thereto;

(B) notwithstanding section 1552 of title 31, United States Code, amounts obligated for paying termination costs with respect to such lease shall remain available until the costs associated with termination of such lease are paid;

(C) funds available for termination liability shall remain available to satisfy rental obligations with respect to such lease in subsequent fiscal years in the event such lease is not terminated early, but only to the extent those funds are in excess of the amount of termination liability at the time of their use to satisfy such rental obligations; and

(D) funds appropriated for a fiscal year may be used to make payments on such lease, for a maximum of 12 months, beginning any time during such fiscal year.

(c) TRANSFERS FOR ACQUISITION OF LAND.—

(1) Sums appropriated or otherwise made available to the Agency for the acquisition of land that are transferred to another department or agency for that purpose shall remain available for 3 years.

(2) The Director shall submit to the Select Committee on Intelligence of the Senate and the Permanent Select Committee on Intelligence of the House of Representatives a report on the transfer of sums described in paragraph (1) each time that authority is exercised.

SEC. 6. [50 U.S.C. 403g]

In the interests of the security of the foreign intelligence activities of the United States and in order further to implement section 102A(i) of the National Security Act of 1947 that the Director of National Intelligence shall be responsible for protecting intelligence sources and methods from unauthorized disclosure, the Agency shall be exempted from the provisions of sections 1 and 2, chapter 795 of the Act of August 28, 1935 [1] (49 Stat. 956, 957; 5 U.S.C. 654),

---

1.   The cited Act of August 28, 1935, was repealed by the Independent Offices Appropriation Act, 1961 (Public Law 86–626, 74 Stat. 427).

and the provisions of any other laws which require the publication or disclosure of the organization, functions, names, official titles, salaries, or numbers of personnel employed by the Agency: *Provided,* That in furtherance of this section, the Director of the Office of Management and Budget shall make no reports to the Congress in connection with the Agency under section 607, title VI, chapter 212 of the Act of June 30, 1945, as amended [1] (5 U.S.C. 947(b)).

SEC. 7. [50 U.S.C. 403h]

Whenever the Director, the Attorney General and the Commissioner of Immigration shall determine that the admission of a particular alien into the United States for permanent residence is in the interest of national security or essential to the furtherance of the national intelligence mission, such alien and his immediate family shall be admitted to the United States for permanent residence without regard to their inadmissibility under the immigration or any other laws and regulations, or to the failure to comply with such laws and regulations pertaining to admissibility: *Provided,* That the number of aliens and members of their immediate families admitted to the United States under the authority of this section shall in no case exceed one hundred persons in any one fiscal year.

APPROPRIATIONS

SEC. 8. [50 U.S.C. 403j]

(a) Notwithstanding any other provisions of law, sums made available to the Agency by appropriation or otherwise may be expended for purposes necessary to carry out its functions, including—

(1) personal services, including personal services without regard to limitations on types of persons to be employed, and rent at the seat of government and elsewhere; health-service program as authorized by law (5 U.S.C. 150); [2] rental of news-reporting services; purchase or rental and operation of photographic, reproduction, cryptographic, duplication and printing machines, equipment and devices, and radio-receiving and radio-sending equipment and devices, including telegraph and teletype equipment; purchase, maintenance, operation, repair, and hire of passenger motor vehicles, and aircraft, and vessels of all kinds; subject to policies established by the Director, transportation of officers and employees of the Agency in Government-owned automotive equipment between their domiciles and places of employment, where such personnel are engaged in work which makes such transportation necessary, and transportation in such equipment, to and from school, of children of Agency personnel who have quarters for themselves and their families at isolated stations outside the continental United States where adequate public or private transportation is not available; printing and binding; purchase, maintenance, and cleaning of firearms, including purchase, storage, and maintenance of ammunition; subject to policies established by the Director, expenses of travel in connection with, and expenses incident to attendance at meetings of professional, technical, scientific, and other similar organizations when such attendance would be a benefit in the conduct of the work of the Agency; association and library dues; payment of premiums or costs of surety bonds for officers or employees without regard to the provisions of 61 Stat. 646; 6 U.S.C. 14; [1] payment of claims pursuant to 28 U.S.C.; acquisition of necessary land and the

---

1.   Section 607 of the Act of June 30, 1945, was repealed by section 301(85) of the Budget and Accounting Procedures Act of 1950 (64 Stat. 843).

2.   The law codified to section 150 of title 5 before the enactment of that title was replaced by section 7901 of title 5 upon the enactment of that title by Public Law 89–544 (Sept. 6, 1966, 80 Stat. 378).

1.   Section 14 of title 6, United States Code, relating to the purchase of bonds to cover Government employees, was repealed by section 203(1) of Public Law 92–310 (Act of June 6, 1972, 86 Stat. 202).

clearing of such land; construction of buildings and facilities without regard to 36 Stat. 699; 40 U.S.C. 259, 267; [2] repair, rental, operation, and maintenance of buildings, utilities, facilities, and appurtenances; and

(2) supplies, equipment, and personnel and contractual services otherwise authorized by law and regulations, when approved by the Director.

(b) The sums made available to the Agency may be expended without regard to the provisions of law and regulations relating to the expenditure of Government funds; and for objects of a confidential, extraordinary, or emergency nature, such expenditures to be accounted for solely on the certificate of the Director and every such certificate shall be deemed a sufficient voucher for the amount therein certified.

[Original section 9 (50 U.S.C. 403i) was repealed by section 601(b) of Public Law 763, 68 Stat. 1115; September 1, 1954.]

SEPARABILITY OF PROVISIONS
SEC. 9. [50 U.S.C. 403a note]

If any provision of this Act, or the application of such provision to any person or circumstances, is held invalid, the remainder of this Act or the application of such provision to persons or circumstances other than these as to which it is held invalid, shall not be affected thereby.

SHORT TITLE
SEC. 10. [50 U.S.C. 401 note]

This Act may be cited as the "Central Intelligence Agency Act of 1949".

AUTHORITY TO PAY DEATH GRATUITIES
SEC. 11. [50 U.S.C. 403k]

(a)(1) The Director may pay a gratuity to the surviving dependents of any officer or employee of the Agency who dies as a result of injuries (other than from disease) sustained outside the United States and whose death—

(A) resulted from hostile or terrorist activities; or

(B) occurred in connection with an intelligence activity having a substantial element of risk.

(2) The provisions of this subsection shall apply with respect to deaths occurring after June 30, 1974.

(b) Any payment under subsection (a)—

(1) shall be in an amount equal to the amount of the annual salary of the officer or employee concerned at the time of death;

(2) shall be considered a gift and shall be in lieu of payment of any lesser death gratuity authorized by any other Federal law; and

(3) shall be made under the same conditions as apply to payments authorized by section 14 of the Act of August 1, 1956 (22 U.S.C. 2679a).[1]

---

2. Section 3734 of the Revised Statutes of the United States, formerly classified to sections 259 and 267 of title 40, was repealed by section 17(12) of the Public Buildings Act of 1959 (Public Law 86–249, 73 Stat. 485). That Act is shown in the United States Code as chapter 12 of title 40 (40 U.S.C. 601 et seq.).

1. Section 14 of the Act of August 1, 1956, was repealed effective February 15, 1981, by section 2205(10) of the Foreign Service Act of 1980 (Public Law 96–465, 94 Stat. 2160. The subject of death gratuities for Foreign Service employees is now covered by section 413 of that Act (22 U.S.C. 3973; 94 Stat. 2092). Section 2401(c) of that Act (94 Stat. 2168) provided: "References in law to provisions of the Foreign Service Act of 1946 or other law superseded by that Act shall be deemed to include reference to the corresponding provisions of this Act.".

AUTHORITY TO ACCEPT GIFTS, DEVISES, AND BEQUESTS

SEC. 12. [50 U.S.C. 403l]

(a)(1) Subject to the provisions of this section, the Director may accept, hold, administer, and use gifts of money, securities, or other property whenever the Director determines it would be in the interest of the United States to do so.

(2) Any gift accepted under this section (and any income produced by any such gift)—

(A) may be used only for—

(i) artistic display;

(ii) purposes relating to the general welfare, education, or recreation of employees or dependents of employees of the Agency or for similar purposes; or

(iii) purposes relating to the welfare, education, or recreation of an individual described in paragraph (3); and

(B) under no circumstances may such a gift (or any income produced by any such gift) be used for operational purposes.

(3) An individual described in this paragraph is an individual who—

(A) is an employee or a former employee of the Agency who suffered injury or illness while employed by the Agency that—

(i) resulted from hostile or terrorist activities;

(ii) occurred in connection with an intelligence activity having a significant element of risk; or

(iii) occurred under other circumstances determined by the Director to be analogous to the circumstances described in clause (i) or (ii);

(B) is a family member of such an employee or former employee; or

(C) is a surviving family member of an employee of the Agency who died in circumstances described in clause (i), (ii), or (iii) of subparagraph (A).

(4) The Director may not accept any gift under this section that is expressly conditioned upon any expenditure not to be met from the gift itself or from income produced by the gift unless such expenditure has been authorized by law.

(5) The Director may, in the Director's discretion, determine that an individual described in subparagraph (A) or (B) of paragraph (3) may accept a gift for the purposes described in paragraph (2)(A)(iii).

(b) Unless otherwise restricted by the terms of the gift, the Director may sell or exchange, or invest or reinvest, any property which is accepted under this section, but any such investment may only be in interest-bearing obligations of the United States or in obligations guaranteed as to both principal and interest by the United States.

(c) There is hereby created on the books of the Treasury of the United States a fund into which gifts of money, securities, and other intangible property accepted under the authority of this section, and the earnings and proceeds thereof, shall be deposited. The assets of such fund shall be disbursed upon the order of the Director for the purposes specified in subsection (a) or (b).

(d) For purposes of Federal income, estate, and gift taxes, gifts accepted by the Director under this section shall be considered to be to or for the use of the United States.

(e) For the purposes of this section, the term "gift" includes a bequest or devise.

(f) The Director, in consultation with the Director of the Office of Government Ethics, shall issue regulations to carry out the authority provided in this section. Such regulations shall ensure that such authority is exercised consistent with all relevant ethical constraints and principles, including—

(1) the avoidance of any prohibited conflict of interest or appearance of impropriety; and

(2) a prohibition against the acceptance of a gift from a foreign government or an agent of a foreign government.

MISUSE OF AGENCY NAME, INITIALS OR SEAL
SEC. 13. [50 U.S.C. 403m]

(a) No person may, except with the written permission of the Director, knowingly use the words "Central Intelligence Agency", the initials "CIA", the seal of the Central Intelligence Agency, or any colorable imitation of such words, initials, or seal in connection with any merchandise, impersonation, solicitation, or commercial activity in a manner reasonably calculated to convey the impression that such use is approved, endorsed, or authorized by the Central Intelligence Agency.

(b) Whenever it appears to the Attorney General that any person is engaged or is about to engage in an act or practice which constitutes or will constitute conduct prohibited by subsection (a), the Attorney General may initiate a civil proceeding in a district court of the United States to enjoin such act or practice. Such court shall proceed as soon as practicable to the hearing and determination of such action and may, at any time before final determination, enter such restraining orders or prohibitions, or take such other action as is warranted, to prevent injury to the United States or to any person or class of persons for whose protection the action is brought.

RETIREMENT EQUITY FOR SPOUSES OF CERTAIN EMPLOYEES
SEC. 14. [50 U.S.C. 403n]

(a) The provisions of sections 102, 221(b) (1)–(3), 221(f), 221(g), 221(h)(2), 221(i), 221(l), 222, 223, 224, 225, 232(b), 241(b), 241(d), and 264(b) of the Central Intelligence Agency Retirement Act (50 U.S.C. 403 note) establishing certain requirements, limitations, rights, entitlements, and benefits relating to retirement annuities, survivor benefits, and lump-sum payments for a spouse or former spouse of an Agency employee who is a participant in the Central Intelligence Agency Retirement and Disability System shall apply in the same manner and to the same extent in the case of an Agency employee who is a participant in the Civil Service Retirement and Disability System.

(b) The Director of the Office of Personnel Management, in consultation with the Director of the Central Intelligence Agency, shall prescribe such regulations as may be necessary to implement the provisions of this section.

SECURITY PERSONNEL AT AGENCY INSTALLATIONS
SEC. 15. [50 U.S.C. 403o]

(a)(1) The Director may authorize Agency personnel within the United States to perform the same functions as officers and agents of the Department of Homeland Security, as provided in section 1315(b)(2) of title 40, United States Code, with the powers set forth in that section, except that such personnel shall perform such functions and exercise such powers—

> (A) within the Agency Headquarters Compound and the property controlled and occupied by the Federal Highway Administration located immediately adjacent to such Compound;
>
> (B) in the streets, sidewalks, and the open areas within the zone beginning at the outside boundary of such Compound and property and extending outward 500 feet;
>
> (C) within any other Agency installation and protected property; and
>
> (D) in the streets, sidewalks, and open areas within the zone beginning at the outside boundary of any installation or property referred to in subparagraph (C) and extending outward 500 feet.

(2) The performance of functions and exercise of powers under subparagraph (B) or (D) of paragraph (1) shall be limited to those circumstances where such personnel can identify specific and articulable facts giving such personnel reason to believe that the performance of such functions and exercise of such powers is reasonable to protect against physical

damage or injury, or threats of physical damage or injury, to Agency installations, property, or employees.

(3) Nothing in this subsection shall be construed to preclude, or limit in any way, the authority of any Federal, State, or local law enforcement agency, or any other Federal police or Federal protective service.

(4) The rules and regulations enforced by such personnel shall be the rules and regulations prescribed by the Director and shall only be applicable to the areas referred to in subparagraph (A) or (C) of paragraph (1).

(b) The Director is authorized to establish penalties for violations of the rules or regulations promulgated by the Director under subsection (a) of this section. Such penalties shall not exceed those specified in section 1315(c)(2) of title 40, United States Code.

(c) Agency personnel designated by the Director under subsection (a) of this section shall be clearly identifiable as United States Government security personnel while engaged in the performance of the functions to which subsection (a) of this section refers.

(d)(1) Notwithstanding any other provision of law, any Agency personnel designated by the Director under subsection (a), or designated by the Director under section 5(a)(4) to carry firearms for the protection of current or former Agency personnel and their immediate families, defectors and their immediate families, and other persons in the United States under Agency auspices, shall be considered for purposes of chapter 171 of title 28, United States Code, or any other provision of law relating to tort liability, to be acting within the scope of their office or employment when such Agency personnel take reasonable action, which may include the use of force, to—

    (A) protect an individual in the presence of such Agency personnel from a crime of violence;

    (B) provide immediate assistance to an individual who has suffered or who is threatened with bodily harm; or

    (C) prevent the escape of any individual whom such Agency personnel reasonably believe to have committed a crime of violence in the presence of such Agency personnel.

(2) Paragraph (1) shall not affect the authorities of the Attorney General under section 2679 of title 28, United States Code.

(3) In this subsection, the term "crime of violence" has the meaning given that term in section 16 of title 18, United States Code.

HEALTH BENEFITS FOR CERTAIN FORMER SPOUSES
OF CENTRAL INTELLIGENCE AGENCY EMPLOYEES
SEC. 16. [50 U.S.C. 403p]

(a) Except as provided in subsection (e), any individual—

(1) formerly married to an employee or former employee of the Agency, whose marriage was dissolved by divorce or annulment before May 7, 1985;

(2) who, at any time during the eighteen-month period before the divorce or annulment became final, was covered under a health benefits plan as a member of the family of such employee or former employee; and

(3) who was married to such employee for not less than ten years during periods of service by such employee with the Agency, at least five years of which were spent outside the United States by both the employee and the former spouse, is eligible for coverage under a health benefits plan in accordance with the provisions of this section. (b)(1) Any individual eligible for coverage under subsection (a) may enroll in a health benefits plan for self alone or for self and family if, before the expiration of the six-month period beginning

on the effective date of this section, and in accordance with such procedures as the Director of the Office of Personnel Management shall by regulation prescribe, such individual—

(A) files an election for such enrollment; and

(B) arranges to pay currently into the Employees Health Benefits Fund under section 8909 of title 5, United States Code, an amount equal to the sum of the employee and agency contributions payable in the case of an employee enrolled under chapter 89 of such title in the same health benefits plan and with the same level of benefits.

(2) The Director of the Central Intelligence Agency shall, as soon as possible, take all steps practicable—

(A) to determine the identity and current address of each former spouse eligible for coverage under subsection (a); and

(B) to notify each such former spouse of that individual's rights under this section.

(3) The Director of the Office of Personnel Management, upon notification by the Director of the Central Intelligence Agency, shall waive the six-month limitation set forth in paragraph (1) in any case in which the Director of the Central Intelligence Agency determines that the circumstances so warrant.

(c) ELIGIBILITY OF FORMER WIVES OR HUSBANDS.—

(1) Notwithstanding subsections (a) and (b) and except as provided in subsections (d), (e), and (f), an individual—

(A) who was divorced on or before December 4, 1991, from a participant or retired participant in the Central Intelligence Agency Retirement and Disability System or the Federal Employees Retirement System Special Category;

(B) who was married to such participant for not less than ten years during the participant's creditable service, at least five years of which were spent by the participant during the participant's service as an employee of the Agency outside the United States, or otherwise in a position the duties of which qualified the participant for designation by the Director as a participant under section 203 of the Central Intelligence Agency Retirement Act (50 U.S.C. 2013); and

(C) who was enrolled in a health benefits plan as a family member at any time during the 18-month period before the date of dissolution of the marriage to such participant; is eligible for coverage under a health benefits plan.

(2) A former spouse eligible for coverage under paragraph (1) may enroll in a health benefits plan in accordance with subsection (b)(1), except that the election for such enrollment must be submitted within 60 days after the date on which the Director notifies the former spouse of such individual's eligibility for health insurance coverage under this subsection.

(d) CONTINUATION OF ELIGIBILITY.—Notwithstanding subsections (a), (b), and (c) and except as provided in subsections (e) and (f), an individual divorced on or before December 4, 1991, from a participant or retired participant in the Central Intelligence Agency Retirement and Disability System or Federal Employees' Retirement System Special Category who enrolled in a health benefits plan following the dissolution of the marriage to such participant may continue enrollment following the death of such participant notwithstanding the termination of the retirement annuity of such individual.

(e)(1) Any former spouse who remarries before age fifty-five is not eligible to make an election under subsection (b)(1).

(2) Any former spouse enrolled in a health benefits plan pursuant to an election under subsection (b)(1) or to subsection (d) may continue the enrollment under the conditions of eligibility which the Director of the Office of Personnel Management shall by regulation prescribe, except that any former spouse who remarries before age fifty-

five shall not be eligible for continued enrollment under this section after the end of the thirty-one-day period beginning on the date of remarriage.

(3)(A) A former spouse who is not eligible to enroll or to continue enrollment in a health benefits plan under this section solely because of remarriage before age fifty-five shall be restored to such eligibility on the date such remarriage is dissolved by death, annulment, or divorce.

(B) A former spouse whose eligibility is restored under subparagraph (A) may, under regulations which the Director of the Office of Personnel Management shall prescribe, enroll in a health benefits plan if such former spouse—

(i) was an individual referred to in paragraph (1) and was an individual covered under a benefits plan as a family member at any time during the 18-month period before the date of dissolution of the marriage to the Agency employee or annuitant; or

(ii) was an individual referred to in paragraph (2) and was an individual covered under a benefits plan immediately before the remarriage ended the enrollment.

(f) No individual may be covered by a health benefits plan under this section during any period in which such individual is enrolled in a health benefits plan under any other authority, nor may any individual be covered under more than one enrollment under this section.

(g) For purposes of this section the term "health benefits plan" means an approved health benefits plan under chapter 89 of title 5, United States Code.

SEC. 17. [50 U.S.C. 403q] INSPECTOR GENERAL FOR THE AGENCY.

(a) PURPOSE; ESTABLISHMENT.—In order to—

(1) create an objective and effective office, appropriately accountable to Congress, to initiate and conduct independently inspections, investigations, and audits relating to programs and operations of the Agency;

(2) provide leadership and recommend policies designed to promote economy, efficiency, and effectiveness in the administration of such programs and operations, and detect fraud and abuse in such programs and operations;

(3) provide a means for keeping the Director fully and currently informed about problems and deficiencies relating to the administration of such programs and operations, and the necessity for and the progress of corrective actions; and

(4) in the manner prescribed by this section, ensure that the Senate Select Committee on Intelligence and the House Permanent Select Committee on Intelligence (hereafter in this section referred to collectively as the "intelligence committees") are kept similarly informed of significant problems and deficiencies as well as the necessity for and the progress of corrective actions, there is hereby established in the Agency an Office of Inspector General (hereafter in this section referred to as the "Office").

(b) APPOINTMENT; SUPERVISION; REMOVAL.—

(1) There shall be at the head of the Office an Inspector General who shall be appointed by the President, by and with the advice and consent of the Senate. This appointment shall be made without regard to political affiliation and shall be on the basis of integrity and demonstrated ability in accounting, auditing, financial analysis, law, management analysis, public administration, or investigation. Such appointment shall also be made on the basis of compliance with the security standards of the Agency and prior experience in the field of foreign intelligence.

(2) The Inspector General shall report directly to and be under the general supervision of the Director.

(3) The Director may prohibit the Inspector General from initiating, carrying out, or completing any audit, inspection, or investigation if the Director determines that such prohibition is necessary to protect vital national security interests of the United States.

(4) If the Director exercises any power under paragraph (3), he shall submit an appropriately classified statement of the reasons for the exercise of such power within seven days to the intelligence committees. The Director shall advise the Inspector General at the time such report is submitted, and, to the extent consistent with the protection of intelligence sources and methods, provide the Inspector General with a copy of any such report. In such cases, the Inspector General may submit such comments to the intelligence committees that he considers appropriate.

(5) In accordance with section 535 of title 28, United States Code, the Inspector General shall report to the Attorney General any information, allegation, or complaint received by the Inspector General relating to violations of Federal criminal law that involve a program or operation of the Agency, consistent with such guidelines as may be issued by the Attorney General pursuant to subsection (b)(2) of such section. A copy of all such reports shall be furnished to the Director.

(6) The Inspector General may be removed from office only by the President. The President shall communicate in writing to the intelligence committees the reasons for any such removal not later than 30 days prior to the effective date of such removal. Nothing in this paragraph shall be construed to prohibit a personnel action otherwise authorized by law, other than transfer or removal.

(c) DUTIES AND RESPONSIBILITIES.—It shall be the duty and responsibility of the Inspector General appointed under this section—

(1) to provide policy direction for, and to plan, conduct, supervise, and coordinate independently, the inspections, investigations, and audits relating to the programs and operations of the Agency to ensure they are conducted efficiently and in accordance with applicable law and regulations;

(2) to keep the Director fully and currently informed concerning violations of law and regulations, fraud and other serious problems, abuses and deficiencies that may occur in such programs and operations, and to report the progress made in implementing corrective action;

(3) to take due regard for the protection of intelligence sources and methods in the preparation of all reports issued by the Office, and, to the extent consistent with the purpose and objective of such reports, take such measures as may be appropriate to minimize the disclosure of intelligence sources and methods described in such reports; and

(4) in the execution of his responsibilities, to comply with generally accepted government auditing standards.

(d) SEMIANNUAL REPORTS; IMMEDIATE REPORTS OF SERIOUS OR FLAGRANT PROBLEMS; REPORTS OF FUNCTIONAL PROBLEMS; REPORTS TO CONGRESS ON URGENT CONCERNS.—

(1) The Inspector General shall, not later than January 31 and July 31 of each year, prepare and submit to the Director a classified semiannual report summarizing the activities of the Office during the immediately preceding six-month periods ending December 31 (of the preceding year) and June 30, respectively. Not later than the dates each year provided for the transmittal of such reports in section 507 of the National Security Act of 1947, the Director shall transmit such reports to the intelligence committees with any comments he may deem appropriate. Such reports shall, at a minimum, include a list of the title or subject of each inspection, investigation, review, or audit conducted during the reporting period and—

(A) a description of significant problems, abuses, and deficiencies relating to the administration of programs and operations of the Agency identified by the Office during the reporting period;

(B) a description of the recommendations for corrective action made by the Office during the reporting period with respect to significant problems, abuses, or deficiencies identified in subparagraph (A);

(C) a statement of whether corrective action has been completed on each significant recommendation described in previous semiannual reports, and, in a case where corrective action has been completed, a description of such corrective action;

(D) a certification that the Inspector General has had full and direct access to all information relevant to the performance of his functions;

(E) a description of the exercise of the subpoena authority under subsection (e)(5) by the Inspector General during the reporting period; and

(F) such recommendations as the Inspector General may wish to make concerning legislation to promote economy and efficiency in the administration of programs and operations undertaken by the Agency, and to detect and eliminate fraud and abuse in such programs and operations.

(2) The Inspector General shall report immediately to the Director whenever he becomes aware of particularly serious or flagrant problems, abuses, or deficiencies relating to the administration of programs or operations. The Director shall transmit such report to the intelligence committees within seven calendar days, together with any comments he considers appropriate.

(3) In the event that—

(A) the Inspector General is unable to resolve any differences with the Director affecting the execution of the Inspector General's duties or responsibilities;

(B) an investigation, inspection, or audit carried out by the Inspector General should focus on any current or former Agency official who—

(i) holds or held a position in the Agency that is subject to appointment by the President, by and with the advice and consent of the Senate, including such a position held on an acting basis; or

(ii) holds or held the position in the Agency, including such a position held on an acting basis, of—

(I) Deputy Director;

(II) Associate Deputy Director;

(III) Director of the National Clandestine Service;

(IV) Director of Intelligence;

(V) Director of Support; or

(VI) Director of Science and Technology.

(C) a matter requires a report by the Inspector General to the Department of Justice on possible criminal conduct by a current or former Agency official described or referred to in subparagraph (B);

(D) the Inspector General receives notice from the Department of Justice declining or approving prosecution of possible criminal conduct of any of the officials described in subparagraph (B); or

(E) the Inspector General, after exhausting all possible alternatives, is unable to obtain significant documentary information in the course of an investigation, inspection, or audit, the Inspector General shall immediately notify and submit a report on such matter to the intelligence committees.

(4) Pursuant to Title V of the National Security Act of 1947, the Director shall submit to

the intelligence committees any report or findings and recommendations of an inspection, investigation, or audit conducted by the office which has been requested by the Chairman or Ranking Minority Member of either committee.

(5)(A) An employee of the Agency, or of a contractor to the Agency, who intends to report to Congress a complaint or information with respect to an urgent concern may report such complaint or information to the Inspector General.

(B) Not later than the end of the 14-calendar day period beginning on the date of receipt from an employee of a complaint or information under subparagraph (A), the Inspector General shall determine whether the complaint or information appears credible. Upon making such a determination, the Inspector General shall transmit to the Director notice of that determination, together with the complaint or information.

(C) Upon receipt of a transmittal from the Inspector General under subparagraph (B), the Director shall, within 7 calendar days of such receipt, forward such transmittal to the intelligence committees, together with any comments the Director considers appropriate.

(D)(i) If the Inspector General does not find credible under subparagraph (B) a complaint or information submitted under subparagraph (A), or does not transmit the complaint or information to the Director in accurate form under subparagraph (B), the employee (subject to clause (ii)) may submit the complaint or information to Congress by contacting either or both of the intelligence committees directly.

(ii) The employee may contact the intelligence committees directly as described in clause (i) only if the employee—

(I) before making such a contact, furnishes to the Director, through the Inspector General, a statement of the employee's complaint or information and notice of the employee's intent to contact the intelligence committees directly; and

(II) obtains and follows from the Director, through the Inspector General, direction on how to contact the intelligence committees in accordance with appropriate security practices.

(iii) A member or employee of one of the intelligence committees who receives a complaint or information under clause (i) does so in that member or employee's official capacity as a member or employee of that committee.

(E) The Inspector General shall notify an employee who reports a complaint or information to the Inspector General under this paragraph of each action taken under this paragraph with respect to the complaint or information. Such notice shall be provided not later than 3 days after any such action is taken.

(F) An action taken by the Director or the Inspector General under this paragraph shall not be subject to judicial review.

(G) In this paragraph:

(i) The term "urgent concern" means any of the following:

(I) A serious or flagrant problem, abuse, violation of law or Executive order, or deficiency relating to the funding, administration, or operations of an intelligence activity involving classified information, but does not include differences of opinions concerning public policy matters.

(II) A false statement to Congress, or a willful withholding from Congress, on an issue of material fact relating to the funding, administration, or operation of an intelligence activity.

(III) An action, including a personnel action described in section 2302(a)(2)(A) of title 5, United States Code, constituting reprisal or threat of reprisal prohibited under subsection (e)(3)(B) in response to an employee's reporting an urgent concern in accordance with this paragraph.

(ii) The term "intelligence committees" means the Permanent Select Committee on Intelligence of the House of Representatives and the Select Committee on Intelligence of the Senate.

(e) AUTHORITIES OF THE INSPECTOR GENERAL.—

(1) The Inspector General shall have direct and prompt access to the Director when necessary for any purpose pertaining to the performance of his duties.

(2) The Inspector General shall have access to any employee or any employee of a contractor of the Agency whose testimony is needed for the performance of his duties. In addition, he shall have direct access to all records, reports, audits, reviews, documents, papers, recommendations, or other material which relate to the programs and operations with respect to which the Inspector General has responsibilities under this section. Failure on the part of any employee or contractor to cooperate with the Inspector General shall be grounds for appropriate administrative actions by the Director, to include loss of employment or the termination of an existing contractual relationship.

(3) The Inspector General is authorized to receive and investigate complaints or information from any person concerning the existence of an activity constituting a violation of laws, rules, or regulations, or mismanagement, gross waste of funds, abuse of authority, or a substantial and specific danger to the public health and safety. Once such complaint or information has been received from an employee of the Agency—

(A) the Inspector General shall not disclose the identity of the employee without the consent of the employee, unless the Inspector General determines that such disclosure is unavoidable during the course of the investigation or the disclosure is made to an official of the Department of Justice responsible for determining whether a prosecution should be undertaken; and

(B) no action constituting a reprisal, or threat of reprisal, for making such complaint or providing such information may be taken by any employee of the Agency in a position to take such actions, unless the complaint was made or the information was disclosed with the knowledge that it was false or with willful disregard for its truth or falsity.

(4) The Inspector General shall have authority to administer to or take from any person an oath, affirmation, or affidavit, whenever necessary in the performance of his duties, which oath affirmation, or affidavit when administered or taken by or before an employee of the Office designated by the Inspector General shall have the same force and effect as if administered or taken by or before an officer having a seal.

(5)(A) Except as provided in subparagraph (B), the Inspector General is authorized to require by subpoena the production of all information, documents, reports, answers, records, accounts, papers, and other data in any medium (including electronically stored information or any tangible thing) and documentary evidence necessary in the performance of the duties and responsibilities of the Inspector General.

(B) In the case of Government agencies, the Inspector General shall obtain information, documents, reports, answers, records, accounts, papers, and other data and evidence for the purpose specified in subparagraph (A) using procedures other than by subpoenas.

(C) The Inspector General may not issue a subpoena for or on behalf of any other element or component of the Agency.

(D) In the case of contumacy or refusal to obey a subpoena issued under this paragraph, the subpoena shall be enforceable by order of any appropriate district court of the United States.

(6) The Inspector General shall be provided with appropriate and adequate office space at central and field office locations, together with such equipment, office supplies, maintenance services, and communications facilities and services as may be necessary for the operation of such offices.

(7) Subject to applicable law and the policies of the Director, the Inspector General shall select, appoint and employ such officers and employees as may be necessary to carry out his functions. In making such selections, the Inspector General shall ensure that such officers and employees have the requisite training and experience to enable him to carry out his duties effectively. In this regard, the Inspector General shall create within his organization a career cadre of sufficient size to provide appropriate continuity and objectivity needed for the effective performance of his duties.

(8)(A) The Inspector General shall—

(i) appoint a Counsel to the Inspector General who shall report to the Inspector General; or

(ii) obtain the services of a counsel appointed by and directly reporting to another Inspector General or the Council of the Inspectors General on Integrity and Efficiency on a reimbursable basis.

(B) The counsel appointed or obtained under subparagraph (A) shall perform such functions as the Inspector General may prescribe.

(9) The Inspector General may request such information or assistance as may be necessary for carrying out his duties and responsibilities from any Government agency. Upon request of the Inspector General for such information or assistance, the head of the Government agency involved shall, insofar as is practicable and not in contravention of any existing statutory restriction or regulation of the Government agency concerned, furnish to the Inspector General, or to an authorized designee, such information or assistance. Consistent with budgetary and personnel resources allocated by the Director, the Inspector General has final approval of—

(A) [1] the selection of internal and external candidates for employment with the Office of Inspector General; and

(B) [1] all other personnel decisions concerning personnel permanently assigned to the Office of Inspector General, including selection and appointment to the Senior Intelligence Service, but excluding all security-based determinations that are not within the authority of a head of other Central Intelligence Agency offices.

(f) SEPARATE BUDGET ACCOUNT.—

(1) Beginning with fiscal year 1991, and in accordance with procedures to be issued by the Director of National Intelligence in consultation with the intelligence committees, the Director of National Intelligence shall include in the National Intelligence Program budget a separate account for the Office of Inspector General established pursuant to this section.

(2) For each fiscal year, the Inspector General shall transmit a budget estimate and request through the Director to the Director of National Intelligence that specifies for such fiscal year—

(A) the aggregate amount requested for the operations of the Inspector General;

(B) the amount requested for all training requirements of the Inspector General, including a certification from the Inspector General that the amount requested is sufficient to fund all training requirements for the Office; and

(C) the amount requested to support the Council of the Inspectors General on Integrity and Efficiency, including a justification for such amount.

---

1.   Margin so in law.

(3) In transmitting a proposed budget to the President for a fiscal year, the Director of National Intelligence shall include for such fiscal year—

(A) the aggregate amount requested for the Inspector General of the Central Intelligence Agency;

(B) the amount requested for Inspector General training;

(C) the amount requested to support the Council of the Inspectors General on Integrity and Efficiency; and

(D) the comments of the Inspector General, if any, with respect to such proposed budget.

(4) The Director of National Intelligence shall submit to the Committee on Appropriations and the Select Committee on Intelligence of the Senate and the Committee on Appropriations and the Permanent Select Committee on Intelligence of the House of Representatives for each fiscal year—

(A) a separate statement of the budget estimate transmitted pursuant to paragraph (2);

(B) the amount requested by the Director of National Intelligence for the Inspector General pursuant to paragraph (3)(A);

(C) the amount requested by the Director of National Intelligence for training of personnel of the Office of the Inspector General pursuant to paragraph (3)(B);

(D) the amount requested by the Director of National Intelligence for support for the Council of the Inspectors General on Integrity and Efficiency pursuant to paragraph (3)(C); and

(E) the comments of the Inspector General under paragraph (3)(D), if any, on the amounts requested pursuant to paragraph (3), including whether such amounts would substantially inhibit the Inspector General from performing the duties of the Office.

(g) TRANSFER.—There shall be transferred to the Office the office of the Agency referred to as the "Office of Inspector General." The personnel, assets, liabilities, contracts, property, records, and unexpended balances of appropriations, authorizations, allocations, and other funds employed, held, used, arising from, or available to such "Office of Inspector General" are hereby transferred to the Office established pursuant to this section.

(h) INFORMATION ON WEBSITE.—

(1) The Director of the Central Intelligence Agency shall establish and maintain on the homepage of the Agency's publicly accessible website information relating to the Office of the Inspector General including methods to contact the Inspector General.

(2) The information referred to in paragraph (1) shall be obvious and facilitate accessibility to the information related to the Office of the Inspector General.

SPECIAL ANNUITY COMPUTATION RULES FOR CERTAIN EMPLOYEES' SERVICE ABROAD

SEC. 18. [50 U.S.C. 403r]

(a) Notwithstanding any provision of chapter 83 of title 5, United States Code, the annuity under subchapter III of such chapter of an officer or employee of the Central Intelligence Agency who retires on or after October 1, 1989, is not designated under section 203 of the Central Intelligence Agency Retirement Act, and has served abroad as an officer or employee of the Agency on or after January 1, 1987, shall be computed as provided in subsection (b).

(b)(1) The portion of the annuity relating to such service abroad that is actually performed at any time during the officer's or employee's first ten years of total service shall be computed at the rate and using the percent of average pay specified in section 8339(a)(3) of title 5, United States Code, that is normally applicable only to so much of an employee's total service as exceeds ten years.

(2) The portion of the annuity relating to service abroad as described in subsection (a) but that is actually performed at any time after the officer's or employee's first ten years of total service shall be computed as provided in section 8339(a)(3) of title 5, United States Code; but, in addition, the officer or employee shall be deemed for annuity computation purposes to have actually performed an equivalent period of service abroad during his or her first ten years of total service, and in calculating the portion of the officer's or employee's annuity for his or her first ten years of total service, the computation rate and percent of average pay specified in paragraph (1) shall also be applied to the period of such deemed or equivalent service abroad.

(3) The portion of the annuity relating to other service by an officer or employee as described in subsection (a) shall be computed as provided in the provisions of section 8339(a) of title 5, United States Code, that would otherwise be applicable to such service.

(4) For purposes of this subsection, the term "total service" has the meaning given such term under chapter 83 of title 5, United States Code.

(c) For purposes of subsections (f) through (m) of section 8339 of title 5, United States Code, an annuity computed under this section shall be deemed to be an annuity computed under subsections

(a) and (o) of section 8339 of title 5, United States Code.

(d) The provisions of subsection (a) of this section shall not apply to an officer or employee of the Central Intelligence Agency who would otherwise be entitled to a greater annuity computed under an otherwise applicable subsection of section 8339 of title 5, United States Code.

SPECIAL RULES FOR DISABILITY RETIREMENT AND DEATH-IN-SERVICE BENEFITS WITH RESPECT TO CERTAIN EMPLOYEES

SEC. 19. [50 U.S.C. 403s]

(a) OFFICERS AND EMPLOYEES TO WHOM CIARDS SECTION 231 RULES APPLY.—Notwithstanding any other provision of law, an officer or

(1) has five years of civilian service credit toward retirement under such subchapter III of chapter 83, title 5, United States Code;

(2) has not been designated under section 203 of the Central Intelligence Agency Retirement Act (50 U.S.C. 403 note), as a participant in the Central Intelligence Agency Retirement and Disability System;

(3) has become disabled during a period of assignment to the performance of duties that are qualifying toward such designation under such section 203; and

(4) satisfies the requirements for disability retirement

under section 8337 of title 5, United States Code— shall, upon his own application or upon order of the Director, be retired on an annuity computed in accordance with the rules prescribed in section 231 of such Act, in lieu of an annuity computed as provided by section 8337 of title 5, United States Code.

(b) SURVIVORS OF OFFICERS AND EMPLOYEES TO WHOM CIARDS SECTION 232 RULES APPLY.—Notwithstanding any other provision of law, in the case of an officer or employee of the Central Intelligence Agency subject to retirement system coverage under subchapter III of chapter 83, title 5, United States Code, who—

(1) has at least eighteen months of civilian service credit toward retirement under such subchapter III of chapter 83, title 5, United States Code;

(2) has not been designated under section 203 of the Central Intelligence Agency Retirement Act (50 U.S.C. 2013), as a participant in the Central Intelligence Agency Retirement and Disability System;

(3) prior to separation or retirement from the Agency, dies during a period of assignment to

the performance of duties that are qualifying toward such designation under such section 203; and

(4) is survived by a widow or widower, former spouse, and/ or a child or children as defined in section 204 and section 232 of the Central Intelligence Agency Retirement Act of 1964 for Certain Employees [1], who would otherwise be entitled to an annuity under section 8341 of title 5, United States Code—such surviving spouse, former spouse, or child of such officer or employee shall be entitled to an annuity computed in accordance with section 232 of such Act, in lieu of an annuity computed in accordance with section 8341 of title 5, United States Code.

(c) ANNUITIES UNDER THIS SECTION DEEMED ANNUITIES UNDER CSRS.—The annuities provided under subsections (a) and (b) of this section shall be deemed to be annuities under chapter 83 of title 5, United States Code, for purposes of the other provisions of such chapter and other laws (including the Internal Revenue Code of 1986) relating to such annuities, and shall be payable from the Central Intelligence Agency Retirement and Disability Fund maintained pursuant to section 202 of the Central Intelligence Agency Retirement Act.

GENERAL COUNSEL OF THE CENTRAL INTELLIGENCE AGENCY
SEC. 20. [50 U.S.C. 403t]

(a) There is a General Counsel of the Central Intelligence Agency, appointed from civilian life by the President, by and with the advice and consent of the Senate.

(b) The General Counsel is the chief legal officer of the Central Intelligence Agency.

(c) The General Counsel of the Central Intelligence Agency shall perform such functions as the Director may prescribe.

CENTRAL SERVICES PROGRAM
SEC. 21. [50 U.S.C. 403u]

(a) IN GENERAL.—The Director may carry out a program under which elements of the Agency provide items and services on a reimbursable basis to other elements of the Agency, nonappropriated fund entities or instrumentalities associated or affiliated with the Agency, and other Government agencies. The Director shall carry out the program in accordance with the provisions of this section.

(b) PARTICIPATION OF AGENCY ELEMENTS.—

(1) In order to carry out the program, the Director shall—

(A) designate the elements of the Agency that are to provide items or services under the program (in this section referred to as "central service providers");

(B) specify the items or services to be provided under the program by such providers; and

(C) assign to such providers for purposes of the program such inventories, equipment, and other assets (including equipment on order) as the Director determines necessary to permit such providers to provide items or services under the program.

(2) The designation of elements and the specification of items and services under paragraph (1) shall be subject to the approval of the Director of the Office of Management and Budget.

(c) CENTRAL SERVICES WORKING CAPITAL FUND.—

(1) There is established a fund to be known as the Central Services Working Capital Fund (in this section referred to as the "Fund"). The purpose of the Fund is to provide sums for activities under the program.

---

1. The amendment made by section 803(a)(3)(B)(iii) of P.L. 102–496 (106 Stat. 3252) was not executable. The amendment strikes "widow or widower, former spouse, and/or child or children as defined in section 204 and section 232 of such the Central Intelligence Agency Retirement Act of 1964 for Certain Employees" and inserts "surviving spouse, former spouse, or child as defined in section 102 of the Central Intelligence Agency Retirement Act".

(2) There shall be deposited in the Fund the following:

(A) Amounts appropriated to the Fund.

(B) Amounts credited to the Fund from payments received by central service providers under subsection (e).

(C) Fees imposed and collected under subsection (f)(1).

(D) Amounts received in payment for loss or damage to equipment or property of a central service provider as a result of activities under the program.

(E) Other receipts from the sale or exchange of equipment or property of a central service provider as a result of activities under the program.

(F) Receipts from individuals in reimbursement for utility services and meals provided under the program.

(G) Receipts from individuals for the rental of property and equipment under the program.

(H) Such other amounts as the Director is authorized to deposit in or transfer to the Fund.

(3) Amounts in the Fund shall be available, without fiscal year limitation, for the following purposes:

(A) To pay the costs of providing items or services under the program.

(B) To pay the costs of carrying out activities under subsection (f)(2).

(d) LIMITATION ON AMOUNT OF ORDERS.—The total value of all orders for items or services to be provided under the program in any fiscal year may not exceed an amount specified in advance by the Director of the Office of Management and Budget.

(e) PAYMENT FOR ITEMS AND SERVICES.—

(1) A Government agency provided items or services under the program shall pay the central service provider concerned for such items or services an amount equal to the costs incurred by the provider in providing such items or services plus any fee imposed under subsection (f). In calculating such costs, the Director shall take into account personnel costs (including costs associated with salaries, annual leave, and workers' compensation), plant and equipment costs (including depreciation of plant and equipment other than structures owned by the Agency), operation and maintenance expenses, amortized costs, and other expenses.

(2) Payment for items or services under paragraph (1) may take the form of an advanced payment by an agency from appropriations available to such agency for the procurement of such items or services.

(f) FEES.—

(1) The Director may permit a central service provider to impose and collect a fee with respect to the provision of an item or service under the program. The amount of the fee may not exceed an amount equal to four percent of the payment received by the provider for the item or service.

(2) The Director may obligate and expend amounts in the Fund that are attributable to the fees imposed and collected under paragraph (1) to acquire equipment or systems for, or to improve the equipment or systems of, central service providers and any elements of the Agency that are not designated for participation in the program in order to facilitate the designation of such elements for future participation in the program.

(g) TERMINATION.—

(1) Subject to paragraph (2), the Director of the Central Intelligence Agency and the Director of the Office of Management and Budget, acting jointly—

(A) may terminate the program under this section and the Fund at any time; and

(B) upon such termination, shall provide for the disposition of the personnel, assets, liabilities, grants, contracts, property, records, and unexpended balances of appropriations, authorizations, allocations, and other funds held, used, arising from, available to, or to be made available in connection with the program or the Fund.

(2) The Director of the Central Intelligence Agency and the Director of the Office of Management and Budget may not undertake any action under paragraph (1) until 60 days after the date on which the Directors jointly submit notice of such action to the Permanent Select Committee on Intelligence of the House of Representatives and the Select Committee on Intelligence of the Senate.

DETAIL OF EMPLOYEES

SEC. 22. [50 U.S.C. 403v]

The Director may—

(1) detail any personnel of the Agency on a reimbursable basis indefinitely to the National Reconnaissance Office without regard to any limitation under law on the duration of details of Federal Government personnel; and

(2) hire personnel for the purpose of any detail under paragraph (1).

INTELLIGENCE OPERATIONS AND COVER ENHANCEMENT AUTHORITY

SEC. 23. [50 U.S.C. 403w]

(a) DEFINITIONS.—In this section—

(1) the term "designated employee" means an employee designated by the Director of the Central Intelligence Agency under subsection (b); and

(2) the term "Federal retirement system" includes the Central Intelligence Agency Retirement and Disability System, and the Federal Employees' Retirement System (including the Thrift Savings Plan).

(b) IN GENERAL.—

(1) AUTHORITY.—Notwithstanding any other provision of law, the Director of the Central Intelligence Agency may exercise the authorities under this section in order to—

(A) protect from unauthorized disclosure—

(i) intelligence operations;

(ii) the identities of undercover intelligence officers;

(iii) intelligence sources and methods; or

(iv) intelligence cover mechanisms; or

(B) meet the special requirements of work related to collection of foreign intelligence or other authorized activities of the Agency.

(2) DESIGNATION OF EMPLOYEES.—The Director of the Central Intelligence Agency may designate any employee of the Agency who is under nonofficial cover to be an employee to whom this section applies. Such designation may be made with respect to any or all authorities exercised under this section.

(c) COMPENSATION.—The Director of the Central Intelligence Agency may pay a designated employee salary, allowances, and other benefits in an amount and in a manner consistent with the nonofficial cover of that employee, without regard to any limitation that is otherwise applicable to a Federal employee. A designated employee may accept, utilize, and, to the extent authorized by regulations prescribed under subsection (i), retain any salary, allowances, and other benefits provided under this section.

(d) RETIREMENT BENEFITS.—

(1) IN GENERAL.—The Director of the Central Intelligence Agency may establish and administer a nonofficial cover employee retirement system for designated employees (and the spouse, former spouses, and survivors of such designated employees). A desig-

nated employee may not participate in the retirement system established under this paragraph and another Federal retirement system at the same time.

(2) CONVERSION TO OTHER FEDERAL RETIREMENT SYSTEM.—

(A) IN GENERAL.—A designated employee participating in the retirement system established under paragraph (1) may convert to coverage under the Federal retirement system which would otherwise apply to that employee at any appropriate time determined by the Director of the Central Intelligence Agency (including at the time of separation of service by reason of retirement), if the Director of the Central Intelligence Agency determines that the employee's participation in the retirement system established under this subsection is no longer necessary to protect from unauthorized disclosure—

(i) intelligence operations;

(ii) the identities of undercover intelligence officers;

(iii) intelligence sources and methods; or

(iv) intelligence cover mechanisms.

(B) CONVERSION TREATMENT.—Upon a conversion under this paragraph—

(i) all periods of service under the retirement system established under this subsection shall be deemed periods of creditable service under the applicable Federal retirement system;

(ii) the Director of the Central Intelligence Agency shall transmit an amount for deposit in any applicable fund of that Federal retirement system that—

(I) is necessary to cover all employee and agency contributions including—

(aa) interest as determined by the head of the agency administering the Federal retirement system into which the employee is converting; or

(bb) in the case of an employee converting into the Federal Employees' Retirement System, interest as determined under section 8334(e) of title 5, United States Code; and

(II) ensures that such conversion does not result in any unfunded liability to that fund; and

(iii) in the case of a designated employee who participated in an employee investment retirement system established under paragraph (1) and is converted to coverage under subchapter III of chapter 84 of title 5, United States Code, the Director of the Central Intelligence Agency may transmit any or all amounts of that designated employee in that employee investment retirement system (or similar part of that retirement system) to the Thrift Savings Fund.

(C) TRANSMITTED AMOUNTS.—

(i) IN GENERAL.—Amounts described under subparagraph (B)(ii) shall be paid from the fund or appropriation used to pay the designated employee.

(ii) OFFSET.—The Director of the Central Intelligence Agency may use amounts contributed by the designated employee to a retirement system established under paragraph (1) to offset amounts paid under clause (i).

(D) RECORDS.—The Director of the Central Intelligence Agency shall transmit all necessary records relating to a designated employee who converts to a Federal retirement system under this paragraph (including records relating to periods of service which are deemed to be periods of creditable service under subparagraph (B)) to the head of the agency administering that Federal retirement system.

(e) HEALTH INSURANCE BENEFITS.—

(1) IN GENERAL.—The Director of the Central Intelligence Agency may establish and administer a nonofficial cover employee health insurance program for designated em-

ployees (and the family of such designated employees). A designated employee may not participate in the health insurance program established under this paragraph and the program under chapter 89 of title 5, United States Code, at the same time.

(2) CONVERSION TO FEDERAL EMPLOYEES HEALTH BENEFITS PROGRAM.—

(A) IN GENERAL.—A designated employee participating in the health insurance program established under paragraph (1) may convert to coverage under the program under chapter 89 of title 5, United States Code, at any appropriate time determined by the Director of the Central Intelligence Agency (including at the time of separation of service by reason of retirement), if the Director of the Central Intelligence Agency determines that the employee's participation in the health insurance program established under this subsection is no longer necessary to protect from unauthorized disclosure—

(i) intelligence operations;

(ii) the identities of undercover intelligence officers;

(iii) intelligence sources and methods; or

(iv) intelligence cover mechanisms.

(B) CONVERSION TREATMENT.—Upon a conversion under this paragraph—

(i) the employee (and family, if applicable) shall be entitled to immediate enrollment and coverage under chapter 89 of title 5, United States Code;

(ii) any requirement of prior enrollment in a health benefits plan under chapter 89 of that title for continuation of coverage purposes shall not apply;

(iii) the employee shall be deemed to have had coverage under chapter 89 of that title from the first opportunity to enroll for purposes of continuing coverage as an annuitant; and

(iv) the Director of the Central Intelligence Agency shall transmit an amount for deposit in the Employees' Health Benefits Fund that is necessary to cover any costs of such conversion.

(C) TRANSMITTED AMOUNTS.—Any amount described under subparagraph (B)(iv) shall be paid from the fund or appropriation used to pay the designated employee.

(f) LIFE INSURANCE BENEFITS.—

(1) IN GENERAL.—The Director of the Central Intelligence Agency may establish and administer a nonofficial cover employee life insurance program for designated employees (and the family of such designated employees). A designated employee may not participate in the life insurance program established under this paragraph and the program under chapter 87 of title 5, United States Code, at the same time.

(2) CONVERSION TO FEDERAL EMPLOYEES GROUP LIFE INSURANCE PROGRAM.—

(A) IN GENERAL.—A designated employee participating in the life insurance program established under paragraph (1) may convert to coverage under the program under chapter 87 of title 5, United States Code, at any appropriate time determined by the Director of the Central Intelligence Agency (including at the time of separation of service by reason of retirement), if the Director of the Central Intelligence Agency determines that the employee's participation in the life insurance program established under this subsection is no longer necessary to protect from unauthorized disclosure—

(i) intelligence operations;

(ii) the identities of undercover intelligence officers;

(iii) intelligence sources and methods; or

(iv) intelligence cover mechanisms.

(B) CONVERSION TREATMENT.—Upon a conversion under this paragraph—

(i) the employee (and family, if applicable) shall be entitled to immediate coverage under chapter 87 of title 5, United States Code;

(ii) any requirement of prior enrollment in a life insurance program under chapter 87 of that title for continuation of coverage purposes shall not apply;

(iii) the employee shall be deemed to have had coverage under chapter 87 of that title for the full period of service during which the employee would have been entitled to be insured for purposes of continuing coverage as an annuitant; and

(iv) the Director of the Central Intelligence Agency shall transmit an amount for deposit in the Employees' Life Insurance Fund that is necessary to cover any costs of such conversion.

(C) TRANSMITTED AMOUNTS.—Any amount described under subparagraph (B)(iv) shall be paid from the fund or appropriation used to pay the designated employee.

(g) EXEMPTION FROM CERTAIN REQUIREMENTS.—The Director of the Central Intelligence Agency may exempt a designated employee from mandatory compliance with any Federal regulation, rule, standardized administrative policy, process, or procedure that the Director of the Central Intelligence Agency determines—

(1) would be inconsistent with the nonofficial cover of that employee; and

(2) could expose that employee to detection as a Federal employee.

(h) TAXATION AND SOCIAL SECURITY.—

(1) IN GENERAL.—Notwithstanding any other provision of law, a designated employee—

(A) shall file a Federal or State tax return as if that employee is not a Federal employee and may claim and receive the benefit of any exclusion, deduction, tax credit, or other tax treatment that would otherwise apply if that employee was not a Federal employee, if the Director of the Central Intelligence Agency determines that taking any action under this paragraph is necessary to—

(i) protect from unauthorized disclosure—

(I) intelligence operations;

(II) the identities of undercover intelligence officers;

(III) intelligence sources and methods; or

(IV) intelligence cover mechanisms; and

(ii) meet the special requirements of work related to collection of foreign intelligence or other authorized activities of the Agency; and

(B) shall receive social security benefits based on the social security contributions made.

(2) INTERNAL REVENUE SERVICE REVIEW.—The Director of the Central Intelligence Agency shall establish procedures to carry out this subsection. The procedures shall be subject to periodic review by the Internal Revenue Service.

(i) REGULATIONS.—The Director of the Central Intelligence Agency shall prescribe regulations to carry out this section. The regulations shall ensure that the combination of salary, allowances, and benefits that an employee designated under this section may retain does not significantly exceed, except to the extent determined by the Director of the Central Intelligence Agency to be necessary to exercise the authority in subsection (b), the combination of salary, allowances, and benefits otherwise received by Federal employees not designated under this section.

(j) FINALITY OF DECISIONS.—Any determinations authorized by this section to be made by the Director of the Central Intelligence Agency or the Director's designee shall be final and conclusive and shall not be subject to review by any court.

(k) SUBSEQUENTLY ENACTED LAWS.—No law enacted after the effective date of this section shall affect the authorities and provisions of this section unless such law specifically refers to this section.

NATIONAL SECURITY AGENCY ACT OF 1959

[Public Law 86–36; 73 Stat. 63; approved May 29, 1959]
[As Amended Through P.L. 113–126, Enacted July 7, 2014]

> AN ACT To provide certain administrative authorities for the National Security Agency, and for other purposes.

Be it enacted by the Senate and House of Representatives of the United States of America in Congress assembled, That [50 U.S.C. 3601] this Act may be cited as the "National Security Agency Act of 1959".

SEC. 2. [50 U.S.C. 3602]

(a)(1) There is a Director of the National Security Agency.

(2) The Director of the National Security Agency shall be appointed by the President, by and with the advice and consent of the Senate.

(3) The Director of the National Security Agency shall be the head of the National Security Agency and shall discharge such functions and duties as are provided by this Act or otherwise by law or executive order.

(b) There is a Director of Compliance of the National Security Agency, who shall be appointed by the Director of the National Security Agency and who shall be responsible for the programs of compliance over mission activities of the National Security Agency.

SEC. 3. [Section 3 consisted of amendments to section 1581(a) of title 10, United States Code.]

SEC. 4. [Section 4 was repealed by section 1633(b)(1) of P.L. 104–201 (September 23, 1996, 110 Stat. 2751); 50 U.S.C. 3603.]

SEC. 5. [50 U.S.C. 3604]

Officers and employees of the National Security Agency who are citizens or nationals of the United States may be granted additional compensation, in accordance with regulations which shall be prescribed by the Secretary of Defense, not in excess of additional compensation authorized by section 207 of the Independent Offices Appropriation Act, 1949, as amended (5 U.S.C. 118h), [1] for employees whose rates of basic compensation are fixed by statute.

SEC. 6. [50 U.S.C. 3605]

(a) Except as provided in subsection (b) of this section, nothing in this Act or any other law (including, but not limited to, the first section and section 2 of the Act of August 28, 1935 (5 U.S.C. 654) [2]) shall be construed to require the disclosure of the organization or any function

---

1.   The Independent Offices Appropriation Act, 1949, was repealed by the law enacting title 5, United States Code (Public Law 89–554, Sept 6, 1966, 80 Stat. 378). Section 207 of that Act was codified as section 5941 of title 5, United States Code.

2.   Repealed by section 101 of Public Law 86–626 (July 12, 1960, 74 Stat. 427).

of the National Security Agency, of any information with respect to the activities thereof, or of the names, titles, salaries, or number of the persons employed by such agency.

(b) The reporting requirements of section 1582 of title 10, United States Code, shall apply to positions established in the National Security Agency in the manner provided by section 4 of this Act.

SEC. 7. [Section 7 was repealed by section 8(a) of Public Law 89–554 (September 6, 1966, 80 Stat. 660); 50 U.S.C. 3606.]

SEC. 8. [50 U.S.C. 3604 note]
The foregoing provisions of this Act shall take effect on the first day of the first pay period which begins later than the thirtieth day following the date of enactment of this Act.

SEC. 9. [50 U.S.C. 3607]
(a) Notwithstanding section 322 of the Act of June 30, 1932 (40 U.S.C. 278a), section 5536 of title 5, United States Code, and section 2675 of title 10, United States Code, the Director of the National Security Agency, on behalf of the Secretary of Defense, may lease real property outside the United States, for periods not exceeding ten years, for the use of the National Security Agency for special cryptologic activities and for housing for personnel assigned to such activities.

(b) The Director of the National Security Agency, on behalf of the Secretary of Defense, may provide to certain civilian and military personnel of the Department of Defense who are assigned to special cryptologic activities outside the United States and who are designated by the Secretary of Defense for the purposes of this subsection—

    (1) allowances and benefits—

        (A) comparable to those provided by the Secretary of State to members of the Foreign Service under chapter 9 of title I of the Foreign Service Act of 1980 (22 U.S.C. 4081 et seq.) or any other provision of law; and

        (B) in the case of selected personnel serving in circumstances similar to those in which personnel of the Central Intelligence Agency serve, comparable to those provided by the Director of Central Intelligence to personnel of the Central Intelligence Agency;

    (2) housing (including heat, light, and household equipment) without cost to such personnel, if the Director of the National Security Agency, on behalf of the Secretary of Defense determines that it would be in the public interest to provide such housing; and

    (3) special retirement accrual in the same manner provided in section 303 of the Central Intelligence Agency Retirement Act (50 U.S.C. 403 note) and in section 18 of the Central Intelligence Agency Act of 1949.

(c) The authority of the Director of the National Security Agency, on behalf of the Secretary of Defense, to make payments under subsections (a) and (b), and under contracts for leases entered into under subsection (a), is effective for any fiscal year only to the extent that appropriated funds are available for such purpose.

(d) Members of the Armed Forces may not receive benefits under both subsection (b)(1) and title 37, United States Code, for the same purpose. The Secretary of Defense shall prescribe such regulations as may be necessary to carry out this subsection.

(e) Regulations issued pursuant to subsection (b)(1) shall be submitted to the Permanent Select Committee on Intelligence of the House of Representatives and the Select Committee on Intelligence of the Senate before such regulations take effect.

SEC. 10. [50 U.S.C. 3608]

(a) The Director of the National Security Agency shall arrange for, and shall prescribe regulations concerning, language and language-related training programs for military and civilian cryptologic personnel. In establishing programs under this section for language and language-related training, the Director—

(1) may provide for the training and instruction to be furnished, including functional and geographic area specializations;

(2) may arrange for training and instruction through other Government agencies and, in any case in which appropriate training or instruction is unavailable through Government facilities, through nongovernmental facilities that furnish training and instruction useful in the fields of language and foreign affairs;

(3) may support programs that furnish necessary language and language-related skills, including, in any case in which appropriate programs are unavailable at Government facilities, support through contracts, grants, or cooperation with nongovernmental educational institutions; and

(4) may obtain by appointment or contract the services of individuals to serve as language instructors, linguists, or special language project personnel.

(b)(1) In order to maintain necessary capability in foreign language skills and related abilities needed by the National Security Agency, the Director, without regard to subchapter IV of chapter 55 of title 5, United States Code, may provide special monetary or other incentives to encourage civilian cryptologic personnel of the Agency to acquire or retain proficiency in foreign languages or special related abilities needed by the Agency.

(2) In order to provide linguistic training and support for cryptologic personnel, the Director—

(A) may pay all or part of the tuition and other expenses related to the training of personnel who are assigned or detailed for language and language-related training, orientation, or instruction; and

(B) may pay benefits and allowances to civilian personnel in accordance with chapters 57 and 59 of title 5, United States Code, and to military personnel in accordance with chapter 7 of title 37, United States Code, and applicable provisions of title 10, United States Code, when such personnel are assigned to training at sites away from their designated duty station.

(c)(1) To the extent not inconsistent, in the opinion of the Secretary of Defense, with the operation of military cryptologic reserve units and in order to maintain necessary capability in foreign language skills and related abilities needed by the National Security Agency, the Director may establish a cryptologic linguist reserve. The cryptologic linguist reserve may consist of former or retired civilian or military cryptologic personnel of the National Security Agency and of other qualified individuals, as determined by the Director of the Agency. Each member of the cryptologic linguist reserve shall agree that, during any period of emergency (as determined by the Director), the member shall return to active civilian status with the National Security Agency and shall perform such linguistic or linguistic-related duties as the Director may assign.

(2) In order to attract individuals to become members of the cryptologic linguist reserve, the Director, without regard to sub-chapter IV of chapter 55 of title 5, United States Code, may provide special monetary incentives to individuals eligible to become members of the cryptologic linguist reserve and to acquire or retain proficiency in foreign languages or special related abilities.

(3) In order to provide training and support for members of the cryptologic linguist reserve, the Director—

(A) may pay all or part of the tuition and other expenses related to the training of individuals in the cryptologic linguist reserve who are assigned or detailed for language and language-related training, orientation, or instruction; and
(B) may pay benefits and allowances in accordance with chapters 57 and 59 of title 5, United States Code, to individuals in the cryptologic linguist reserve who are assigned to training at sites away from their homes or regular places of business.

(d)(1) The Director, before providing training under this section to any individual, may obtain an agreement with that individual that—

(A) in the case of current employees, pertains to continuation of service of the employee, and repayment of the expenses of such training for failure to fulfill the agreement, consistent with the provisions of section 4108 of title 5, United States Code; and
(B) in the case of individuals accepted for membership in the cryptologic linguist reserve, pertains to return to service when requested, and repayment of the expenses of such training for failure to fulfill the agreement, consistent with the provisions of section 4108 of title 5, United States Code.

(2) The Director, under regulations prescribed under this section, may waive, in whole or in part, a right of recovery under an agreement made under this subsection if it is shown that the recovery would be against equity and good conscience or against the public interest.

(e)(1) Subject to paragraph (2), the Director may provide to family members of military and civilian cryptologic personnel assigned to representational duties outside the United States, in anticipation of the assignment of such personnel outside the United States or while outside the United States, appropriate orientation and language training that is directly related to the assignment abroad.

(2) Language training under paragraph (1) may not be provided to any individual through payment of the expenses of tuition or other cost of instruction at a non-Government educational institution unless appropriate instruction is not available at a Government facility.

(f) The Director may waive the applicability of any provision of chapter 41 of title 5, United States Code, to any provision of this section if he finds that such waiver is important to the performance of cryptologic functions.

(g) The authority of the Director to enter into contracts or to make grants under this section is effective for any fiscal year only to the extent that appropriated funds are available for such purpose.

(h) Regulations issued pursuant to this section shall be submitted to the Permanent Select Committee on Intelligence of the House of Representatives and the Select Committee on Intelligence of the Senate before such regulations take effect.

(i) The Director of the National Security Agency, on behalf of the Secretary of Defense, may, without regard to section 4109(a)(2)(B) of title 5, United States Code, pay travel, transportation, storage, and subsistence expenses under chapter 57 of such title to civilian and military personnel of the Department of Defense who are assigned to duty outside the United States for a period of one year or longer which involves cryptologic training, language training, or related disciplines.

SEC. 11. [50 U.S.C. 3609]

(a)(1) The Director of the National Security Agency may authorize agency personnel within the United States to perform the same functions as officers and agents of the Department of Homeland Security, as provided in section 1315(b)(2) of title 40, United States Code, with the powers set forth in that section, except that such personnel shall perform such functions and exercise such powers—

    (A) at the National Security Agency Headquarters complex and at any facilities and protected property which are solely under the administration and control of, or are used exclusively by, the National Security Agency; and

    (B) in the streets, sidewalks, and the open areas within the zone beginning at the outside boundary of such facilities or protected property and extending outward 500 feet.

(2) The performance of functions and exercise of powers under subparagraph (B) of paragraph (1) shall be limited to those circumstances where such personnel can identify specific and articulable facts giving such personnel reason to believe that the performance of such functions and exercise of such powers is reasonable to protect against physical damage or injury, or threats of physical damage or injury, to agency installations, property, or employees.

(3) Nothing in this subsection shall be construed to preclude, or limit in any way, the authority of any Federal, State, or local law enforcement agency, or any other Federal police or Federal protective service.

(4) The rules and regulations enforced by such personnel shall be the rules and regulations prescribed by the Director and shall only be applicable to the areas referred to in subparagraph (A) of paragraph (1).

(5) Agency personnel authorized by the Director under paragraph (1) may transport an individual apprehended under the authority of this section from the premises at which the individual was apprehended, as described in subparagraph (A) or (B) of paragraph (1), for the purpose of transferring such individual to the custody of law enforcement officials. Such transportation may be provided only to make a transfer of custody at a location within 30 miles of the premises described in subparagraphs (A) and (B) of paragraph (1).

(b) The Director of the National Security Agency is authorized to establish penalties for violations of the rules or regulations prescribed by the Director under subsection (a). Such penalties shall not exceed those specified in section 1315(c)(2) of title 40, United States Code.

(c) Agency personnel designated by the Director of the National Security Agency under subsection (a) shall be clearly identifiable as United States Government security personnel while engaged in the performance of the functions to which subsection (a) refers.

(d)(1) Notwithstanding any other provision of law, agency personnel designated by the Director of the National Security Agency under subsection (a) shall be considered for purposes of chapter 171 of title 28, United States Code, or any other provision of law relating to tort liability, to be acting within the scope of their office or employment when such agency personnel take reasonable action, which may include the use of force, to—

    (A) protect an individual in the presence of such agency personnel from a crime of violence;

    (B) provide immediate assistance to an individual who has suffered or who is threatened with bodily harm;

    (C) prevent the escape of any individual whom such agency personnel reasonably believe to have committed a crime of violence in the presence of such agency personnel; or

    (D) transport an individual pursuant to subsection (a)(2).

(2) Paragraph (1) shall not affect the authorities of the Attorney General under section 2679 of title 28, United States Code.

(3) In this subsection, the term "crime of violence" has the meaning given that term in section 16 of title 18, United States Code.

SEC. 12. [50 U.S.C. 3610]

(a)(1) The Secretary of Defense (or his designee) may by regulation establish a personnel system for senior civilian cryptologic personnel in the National Security Agency to be known as the Senior Cryptologic Executive Service. The regulations establishing the Senior Cryptologic Executive Service shall—

(A) meet the requirements set forth in section 3131 of title 5, United States Code, for the Senior Executive Service;

(B) provide that positions in the Senior Cryptologic Executive Service meet requirements that are consistent with the provisions of section 3132(a)(2) of such title;

(C) provide, without regard to section 2, rates of pay for the Senior Cryptologic Executive Service that are not in excess of the maximum rate or less than the minimum rate of basic pay established for the Senior Executive Service under section 5382 of such title, and that are adjusted at the same time and to the same extent as rates of basic pay for the Senior Executive Service are adjusted;

(D) provide a performance appraisal system for the Senior Cryptologic Executive Service that conforms to the provisions of subchapter II of chapter 43 of such title;

(E) provide for removal consistent with section 3592 of such title, and removal or suspension consistent with subsections (a), (b), and (c) of section 7543 of such title (except that any hearing or appeal to which a member of the Senior Cryptologic Executive Service is entitled shall be held or decided pursuant to procedures established by regulations of the Secretary of Defense or his designee);

(F) permit the payment of performance awards to members of the Senior Cryptologic Executive Service consistent with the provisions applicable to performance awards under section 5384 of such title;

(G) provide that members of the Senior Cryptologic Executive Service may be granted sabbatical leaves consistent with the provisions of section 3396(c) of such title. [1]

(H) provide for the recertification of members of the Senior Cryptologic Executive Service consistent with the provisions of section 3393a of such title.

(2) Except as otherwise provided in subsection (a), the Secretary of Defense (or his designee) may—

(A) make applicable to the Senior Cryptologic Executive Service any of the provisions of title 5, United States Code, applicable to applicants for or members of the Senior Executive Service; and

(B) appoint, promote, and assign individuals to positions established within the Senior Cryptologic Executive Service without regard to the provisions of title 5, United States Code, governing appointments and other personnel actions in the competitive service.

(3) The President, based on the recommendations of the Secretary of Defense, may award ranks to members of the Senior Cryptologic Executive Service in a manner consistent with the provisions of section 4507 of title 5, United States Code.

(4) Notwithstanding any other provision of this section, the Director of the National

---

1. Public Law 101–194, sec. 506(c)(2) (103 Stat. 1759) amended sec. 12(a)(1)(G) by inserting "and" after the semicolon at the end of (G). Because there was not a semicolon at the end of (G), the amendment was not executed. This amendment would have taken effect on January 1, 1991.

Security Agency may detail or assign any member of the Senior Cryptologic Executive Service to serve in a position outside the National Security Agency in which the member's expertise and experience may be of benefit to the National Security Agency or another Government agency. Any such member shall not by reason of such detail or assignment lose any entitlement or status associated with membership in the Senior Cryptologic Executive Service.

(b) The Secretary of Defense (or his designee) may by regulation establish a merit pay system for such employees of the National Security Agency as the Secretary of Defense (or his designee) considers appropriate. The merit pay system shall be designed to carry out purposes consistent with those set forth in section 5401(a) of title 5, United States Code.

(c) Nothing in this section shall be construed to allow the aggregate amount payable to a member of the Senior Cryptologic Executive Service under this section during any fiscal year to exceed the annual rate payable for positions at level I of the Executive Schedule in effect at the end of such year.

SEC. 13. [50 U.S.C. 3611]

(a) The Director of the National Security Agency may make grants to private individuals and institutions for the conduct of cryptologic research. An application for a grant under this section may not be approved unless the Director determines that the award of the grant would be clearly consistent with the national security.

(b) The grant program established by subsection (a) shall be conducted in accordance with the Federal Grant and Cooperative Agreement Act of 1977 (41 U.S.C. 501 et seq.) to the extent that such Act is consistent with and in accordance with section 6 of this Act.

(c) The authority of the Director to make grants under this section is effective for any fiscal year only to the extent that appropriated funds are available for such purpose.

SEC. 14. [50 U.S.C. 3612]

Funds appropriated to an entity of the Federal Government other than an element of the Department of Defense that have been specifically appropriated for the purchase of cryptologic equipment, materials, or services with respect to which the National Security Agency has been designated as the central source of procurement for the Government shall remain available for a period of three fiscal years.

SEC. 15. [50 U.S.C. 3613]

(a) No person may, except with the written permission of the Director of the National Security Agency, knowingly use the words "National Security Agency", the initials "NSA", the seal of the National Security Agency, or any colorable imitation of such words, initials, or seal in connection with any merchandise, impersonation, solicitation, or commercial activity in a manner reasonably calculated to convey the impression that such use is approved, endorsed, or authorized by the National Security Agency.

(b) Whenever it appears to the Attorney General that any person is engaged or is about to engage in an act or practice which constitutes or will constitute conduct prohibited by subsection (a), the Attorney General may initiate a civil proceeding in a district court of the United States to enjoin such act or practice. Such court shall proceed as soon as practicable to the hearing and determination of such action and may, at any time before final determination, enter such restraining orders or prohibitions, or take such other action as is warranted, to prevent injury to the United States or to any person or class of persons for whose protection the action is brought.

SEC. 16. [50 U.S.C. 3614]
(a) The purpose of this section is to establish an undergraduate and graduate training program, which may lead to a baccalaureate or graduate degree, to facilitate the recruitment of individuals, particularly minority high school students, with a demonstrated capability to develop skills critical to the mission of the National Security Agency, including mathematics, computer science, engineering, and foreign languages.

(b) The Secretary of Defense is authorized, in his discretion, to assign civilians who may or may not be employees of the National Security Agency as students at accredited professional, technical, and other institutions of higher learning for training at the undergraduate or graduate level in skills critical to effective performance of the mission of the Agency.

(c) The National Security Agency may pay, directly or by reimbursement to program participants, expenses incident to assignments under subsection (b), in any fiscal year only to the extent that appropriated funds are available for such purpose.

(d)(1) To be eligible for assignment under subsection (b), a program participant, [1] must agree in writing—

> (A) to continue in the service of the Agency for the period of the assignment and to complete the educational course of training for which the program participant is assigned;
>
> (B) to continue in the service of the Agency following completion of the assignment for a period of one-and-a-half years for each year of the assignment or part thereof;
>
> (C) to reimburse the United States for the total cost of education (excluding the program participant's pay and allowances) provided under this section to the program participant if, prior to the program participant's completing the educational course of training for which the program participant is assigned, the assignment or the program participant's employment with the Agency is terminated—
>
> > (i) by the Agency due to misconduct by the program participant;
> >
> > (ii) by the program participant voluntarily; or
> >
> > (iii) by the Agency for the failure of the program participant to maintain such level of academic standing in the educational course of training as the Director of the National Security Agency shall have specified in the agreement of the program participant under this subsection; and
>
> (D) to reimburse the United States if, after completing the educational course of training for which the program participant is assigned, the program participant's employment with the Agency is terminated either by the Agency due to misconduct by the program participant or by the program participant voluntarily, prior to the program participant's completion of the service obligation period described in subparagraph (B), in an amount that bears the same ratio to the total cost of the education (excluding the program participant's pay and allowances) provided to the program participant as the unserved portion of the service obligation period described in subparagraph (B) bears to the total period of the service obligation described in subparagraph (B).

(2) Subject to paragraph (3), the obligation to reimburse the United States under an agreement described in paragraph (1), including interest due on such obligation, is for all purposes a debt owing the United States.

---

1.   So in law, the comma following "program participant" probably should not appear. Also, the amendment by section 312(b)(2)(B)(i)(I) of Public Law 111–259 striking "an employee of the Agency," and inserting "a program participant," was carried out to reflect the probable intent of Congress. The comma at the end of the matter proposed to be struck did not appear in law.

(3)(A) A discharge in bankruptcy under title 11, United States Code, shall not release a person from an obligation to reimburse the United States required under an agreement described in paragraph (1) if the final decree of the discharge in bankruptcy is issued within five years after the last day of the combined period of service obligation described in subparagraphs (A) and (B) of paragraph (1).

(B) The Secretary of Defense may release a person, in whole or in part, from the obligation to reimburse the United States under an agreement described in paragraph (1) when, in his discretion, the Secretary determines that equity or the interests of the United States so require.

(C) The Secretary of Defense shall permit an program participant assigned under this section who, prior to commencing a second academic year of such assignment, voluntarily terminates the assignment or the program participant's employment with the Agency, to satisfy his obligation under an agreement described in paragraph (1) to reimburse the United States by reimbursement according to a schedule of monthly payments which results in completion of reimbursement by a date five years after the date of termination of the assignment or employment or earlier at the option of the program participant.

(e) Agency efforts to recruit individuals at educational institutions for participation in the undergraduate and graduate training program established by this section shall be made openly and according to the common practices of universities and employers recruiting at such institutions.

(f) Chapter 41 of title 5 and subsections (a) and (b) of section 3324 of title 31, United States Code, shall not apply with respect to this section.

(g) The Secretary of Defense may issue such regulations as may be necessary to implement this section.

(h) The undergraduate and graduate training program established under this section shall be known as the Louis Stokes Educational Scholarship Program.

SEC. 17. [Section 17 was repealed by section 806(b)(2) of P.L. 103–359 (October 14, 1994, 108 Stat. 3442); 50 U.S.C. 3615.]

SEC. 18. [50 U.S.C. 3616]

(a) The Secretary of Defense may pay the expenses referred to in section 5742(b) of title 5, United States Code, in the case of any employee of the National Security Agency who dies while on a rotational tour of duty within the United States or while in transit to or from such tour of duty.

(b) For the purposes of this section, the term "rotational tour of duty", with respect to an employee, means a permanent change of station involving the transfer of the employee from the National Security Agency headquarters to another post of duty for a fixed period established by regulation to be followed at the end of such period by a permanent change of station involving a transfer of the employee back to such headquarters.

SEC. 19. [50 U.S.C. 3617]

(a) There is established the National Security Agency Emerging Technologies Panel. The Panel is a standing panel of the National Security Agency. The Panel shall be appointed by, and shall report directly to, the Director of the National Security Agency.

(b) The Panel shall study and assess, and periodically advise the Director on, the research, development, and application of existing and emerging science and technology advances, advances in encryption, and other topics.

(c) The Federal Advisory Committee Act (5 U.S.C. App.) shall not apply with respect to the Panel.

SEC. 20. [50 U.S.C. 3618]
(a) The Director may collect charges for evaluating, certifying, or validating information assurance products under the National Information Assurance Program or successor program.
(b) The charges collected under subsection (a) shall be established through a public rulemaking process in accordance with Office of Management and Budget Circular No. A–25.
(c) Charges collected under subsection (a) shall not exceed the direct costs of the program referred to in that subsection.
(d) The appropriation or fund bearing the cost of the service for which charges are collected under the program referred to in subsection (a) may be reimbursed, or the Director may require advance payment subject to such adjustment on completion of the work as may be agreed upon.
(e) Amounts collected under this section shall be credited to the account or accounts from which costs associated with such amounts have been or will be incurred, to reimburse or offset the direct costs of the program referred to in subsection (a).

Authorization for Use of Military Force

Pub. L. No. 107-40, 115 Stat. 224 (2001)

JOINT RESOLUTION

To authorize the use of United States Armed Forces against those responsible for the recent attacks launched against the United States.

Whereas, on September 11, 2001, acts of treacherous violence were committed against the United States and its citizens; and

Whereas, such acts render it both necessary and appropriate that the United States exercise its rights to self-defense and to protect United States citizens both at home and abroad; and

Whereas, in light of the threat to the national security and foreign policy of the United States posed by these grave acts of violence; and

Whereas, such acts continue to pose an unusual and extraordinary threat to the national security and foreign policy of the United States; and

Whereas, the President has authority under the Constitution to take action to deter and prevent acts of international terrorism against the United States: Now, therefore, be it

Resolved by the Senate and House of Representatives of the United States of America in Congress assembled,

SECTION 1. SHORT TITLE.

This joint resolution may be cited as the 'Authorization for Use of Military Force'.

SECTION 2. AUTHORIZATION FOR USE OF UNITED STATES ARMED FORCES.

(a) IN GENERAL—That the President is authorized to use all necessary and appropriate force against those nations, organizations, or persons he determines planned, authorized, committed, or aided the terrorist attacks that occurred on September 11, 2001, or harbored such organizations or persons, in order to prevent any future acts of international terrorism against the United States by such nations, organizations or persons.

(b) War Powers Resolution Requirements—

   (1) SPECIFIC STATUTORY AUTHORIZATION- Consistent with section 8(a)(1) of the War Powers Resolution, the Congress declares that this section is intended to constitute specific statutory authorization within the meaning of section 5(b) of the War Powers Resolution.

   (2) APPLICABILITY OF OTHER REQUIREMENTS—Nothing in this resolution supersedes any requirement of the War Powers Resolution.

Approved September 18, 2001.

Intelligence Reform and Terrorism Prevention Act of 2004

(Pub. L. No. 108-458, 118 Stat. 3742, as amended through Jan. 19, 2018)

AN ACT To reform the intelligence community and the intelligence and intelligence-related activities of the United States Government, and for other purposes.

Be it enacted by the Senate and House of Representatives of the United States of America in Congress assembled,

SHORT TITLE; TABLE OF CONTENTS

SECTION 1.

(a) SHORT TITLE.—This Act may be cited as the "Intelligence Reform and Terrorism Prevention Act of 2004.

(b) TABLE OF CONTENTS.—The table of contents for this Act is as follows:

TITLE I—REFORM OF THE INTELLIGENCE COMMUNITY

SHORT TITLE

SEC. 1001. This title may be cited as the "National Security Intelligence Reform Act of 2004".

SUBTITLE A—ESTABLISHMENT OF DIRECTOR OF NATIONAL INTELLIGENCE REORGANIZATION AND IMPROVEMENT OF MANAGEMENT OF INTELLIGENCE COMMUNITY

SEC. 1011.

(a) IN GENERAL.—Title I of the National Security Act of 1947 (50 U.S.C. §402 et seq.) is amended by striking sections 102 through 104 and inserting the following new sections: [amendments omitted here—see the National Security Act of 1947 in this book]

(b) SENSE OF CONGRESS.—It is the sense of Congress that—

(1) the human intelligence officers of the intelligence community have performed admirably and honorably in the face of great personal dangers;

(2) during an extended period of unprecedented investment and improvements in technical collection means, the human intelligence capabilities of the United States have not received the necessary and commensurate priorities;

(3) human intelligence is becoming an increasingly important capability to provide information on the asymmetric threats to the national security of the United States;

(4) the continued development and improvement of a robust and empowered and flexible human intelligence work force is critical to identifying, understanding, and countering the plans and intentions of the adversaries of the United States; and

(5) an increased emphasis on, and resources applied to, enhancing the depth and breadth of human intelligence capabilities of the United States intelligence community must be among the top priorities of the Director of National Intelligence.

(c) TRANSFORMATION OF CENTRAL INTELLIGENCE AGENCY.—The Director of the Central Intelligence Agency shall, in accordance with standards developed by the Director in consultation with the Director of National Intelligence—

(1) enhance the analytic, human intelligence, and other capabilities of the Central Intelligence Agency;

(2) develop and maintain an effective language program within the Agency;

(3) emphasize the hiring of personnel of diverse backgrounds for purposes of improving the capabilities of the Agency;

(4) establish and maintain effective relationships between human intelligence and signals intelligence within the Agency at the operational level; and

(5) achieve a more effective balance within the Agency with respect to unilateral operations and liaison operations.

(d) REPORT.—

(1) Not later than 180 days after the date of the enactment of this Act, the Director of the Central Intelligence Agency shall submit to the Director of National Intelligence and the congressional intelligence committees a report setting forth the following:

(A) A strategy for improving the conduct of analysis (including strategic analysis) by the Central Intelligence Agency, and the progress of the Agency in implementing that strategy.

(B) A strategy for improving the human intelligence and other capabilities of the Agency, and the progress of the Agency in implementing that strategy.

(2)(A) The information in the report under paragraph (1) on the strategy referred to in paragraph (1)(B) shall—

(i) identify the number and types of personnel required to implement that strategy;

(ii) include a plan for the recruitment, training, equipping, and deployment of such personnel; and

(iii) set forth an estimate of the costs of such activities.

(B) If as of the date of the report under paragraph (1), a proper balance does not exist between unilateral operations and liaison operations, such report shall set forth the steps to be taken to achieve such balance.

REVISED DEFINITION OF NATIONAL INTELLIGENCE

SEC. 1012. Paragraph (5) of section 3 of the National Security Act of 1947 (50 U.S.C. §401a) is amended to read as follows:

"(5) The terms "national intelligence" and "intelligence related to national security" refer to all intelligence, regardless of the source from which derived and including information gathered within or outside the United States, that—

"(A) pertains, as determined consistent with any guidance issued by the President, to more than one United States Government agency; and "(B) that involves—

"(i) threats to the United States, its people, property, or interests; "(ii) the development, proliferation, or use of weapons of mass destruction; or

"(iii) any other matter bearing on United States national or homeland security.".

JOINT PROCEDURES FOR OPERATIONAL COORDINATION BETWEEN DEPARTMENT OF DEFENSE AND CENTRAL INTELLIGENCE AGENCY

SEC. 1013.

(a) Development of Procedures—The Director of National Intelligence, in consultation with the Secretary of Defense and the Director of the Central Intelligence Agency, shall develop joint procedures to be used by the Department of Defense and the Central Intelligence Agency to improve the coordination and deconfliction of operations that involve elements of both the Armed Forces and the Central Intelligence Agency consistent with national security and the protection of human intelligence sources and methods. Those procedures shall, at a minimum, provide the following:

(1) Methods by which the Director of the Central Intelligence Agency and the Secretary of Defense can improve communication and coordination in the planning, execution, and sustainment of operations, including, as a minimum—

(A) information exchange between senior officials of the Central Intelligence Agency and senior officers and officials of the Department of Defense when planning for such an operation commences by either organization; and

(B) exchange of information between the Secretary and the Director of the Central Intelligence Agency to ensure that senior operational officials in both the Department of Defense and the Central Intelligence Agency have knowledge of the existence of the ongoing operations of the other.

(2) When appropriate, in cases where the Department of Defense and the Central Intelligence Agency are conducting separate missions in the same geographical area, a mutual agreement on the tactical and strategic objectives for the region and a clear delineation of operational responsibilities to prevent conflict and duplication of effort.

(b) Implementation Report- Not later than 180 days after the date of the enactment of the Act, the Director of National Intelligence shall submit to the congressional defense committees (as defined in section 101 of title 10, United States Code) and the congressional intelligence committees (as defined in section 3(7) of the National Security Act of 1947 (50 U.S.C. §401a(7))) a report describing the procedures established pursuant to subsection (a) and the status of the implementation of those procedures.

ROLE OF DIRECTOR OF NATIONAL INTELLIGENCE IN APPOINTMENT OF CERTAIN OFFICIALS RESPONSIBLE FOR INTELLIGENCE-RELATED ACTIVITIES

SEC. 1014. Section 106 of the National Security Act of 1947 (50 U.S.C. §403-6) is amended by striking all after the heading and inserting the following:

[amendments omitted here—see the National Security Act of 1947 in this book]

EXECUTIVE SCHEDULE MATTERS

SEC. 1015.

(a) EXECUTIVE SCHEDULE LEVEL I.—Section 5312 of title 5, United States Code, is amended by adding at the end the following new item:

"Director of National Intelligence.".

(b) EXECUTIVE SCHEDULE LEVEL II.—Section 5313 of title 5, United States Code, is amended by adding at the end the following new items:

"Principal Deputy Director of National Intelligence. "Director of the National Counterterrorism Center. "Director of the National Counter Proliferation Center.".

(c) EXECUTIVE SCHEDULE LEVEL IV.—Section 5315 of title 5, United States Code, is amended—

(1) by striking the item relating to the Assistant Directors of Central Intelligence; and

(2) by adding at the end the following new item: "General Counsel of the Office of the National Intelligence Director.".

INFORMATION SHARING

SEC. 1016.

(a) DEFINITIONS.—In this section:

(1) HOMELAND SECURITY INFORMATION.—The term "homeland security information" has the meaning given that term in section 892(f) of the Homeland Security Act of 2002 (6 U.S.C. §482(f)).

(2) INFORMATION SHARING COUNCIL.—The term "Information Sharing Council" means the Information Systems Council established by Executive Order 13356, or any successor body designated by the President, and referred to under subsection (g).

(3) INFORMATION SHARING ENVIRONMENT.—The terms "information sharing environment" and "ISE" mean an approach that facilitates the sharing of terrorism and homeland security information, which may include any method determined necessary and appropriate for carrying out this section.

(4) PROGRAM MANAGER.—The term "program manager" means the program manager designated under subsection (f).

(5) TERRORISM INFORMATION.—The term "terrorism information"—

(A) means all information, whether collected, produced, or distributed by intelligence, law enforcement, military, homeland security, or other activities relating to—

(i) the existence, organization, capabilities, plans, intentions, vulnerabilities, means of finance or material support, or activities of foreign or international terrorist groups or individuals, or of domestic groups or individuals involved in transnational terrorism;

(ii) threats posed by such groups or individuals to the United States, United States persons, or United States interests, or to those of other nations;

(iii) communications of or by such groups or individuals; or

(iv) groups or individuals reasonably believed to be assisting or associated with such groups or individuals; and

(B) includes weapons of mass destruction information.

(6) WEAPONS OF MASS DESTRUCTION INFORMATION.—The term "weapons of mass destruction information" means information that could reasonably be expected to assist in the development, proliferation, or use of a weapon of mass destruction (including a chemical, biological, radiological, or nuclear weapon) that could be used by a terrorist organization against the United States, including information about the location of any stockpile of nuclear materials that could be exploited for use in such a weapon that could be used by a terrorist or a terrorist organization against the United States.

(b) INFORMATION SHARING ENVIRONMENT.—

(1) ESTABLISHMENT.—The President shall—

(A) create an information sharing environment for the sharing of terrorism information in a manner consistent with national security and with applicable legal standards relating to privacy and civil liberties;

(B) designate the organizational and management structures that will be used to operate and manage the ISE; and

(C) determine and enforce the policies, directives, and rules that will govern the content and usage of the ISE.

(2) ATTRIBUTES.—The President shall, through the structures described in subparagraphs (B) and (C) of paragraph (1), ensure that the ISE provides and facilitates the means for sharing terrorism information among all appropriate Federal, State, local, and tribal entities, and the private sector through the use of policy guidelines and technologies. The President shall, to the greatest extent practicable, ensure that the ISE provides the functional equivalent of, or otherwise supports, a decentralized, distributed, and coordinated environment that—

(A) connects existing systems, where appropriate, provides no single points of failure, and allows users to share information among agencies, between levels of government, and, as appropriate, with the private sector;

(B) ensures direct and continuous online electronic access to information;

(C) facilitates the availability of information in a form and manner that facilitates its use in analysis, investigations and operations;

(D) builds upon existing systems capabilities currently in use across the Government;

(E) employs an information access management approach that controls access to data rather than just systems and networks, without sacrificing security;

(F) facilitates the sharing of information at and across all levels of security;

(G) provides directory services, or the functional equivalent, for locating people and information;

(H) incorporates protections for individuals' privacy and civil liberties;

(I) incorporates strong mechanisms to enhance accountability and facilitate oversight, including audits, authentication, and access controls;

(J) integrates the information within the scope of the information sharing environment, including any such information in legacy technologies;

(K) integrates technologies, including all legacy technologies, through Internet-based services, consistent with appropriate security protocols and safeguards, to enable connectivity among required users at the Federal, State, and local levels;

(L) allows the full range of analytic and operational activities without the need to centralize information within the scope of the information sharing environment;

(M) permits analysts to collaborate both independently and in a group (commonly known as "collective and non-collective collaboration"), and across multiple levels of national security information and controlled classified information;

(N) provides a resolution process that enables changes by authorized officials regarding rules and policies for the use, and retention of information within the scope of the information sharing environment; and

(O) incorporates continuous, real-time, and immutable audit capabilities, to the maximum extent possible.

(c) PRELIMINARY REPORT.—Not later than 180 days after the date of the enactment of this Act, the program manager shall, in consultation with the Information Sharing Council—

(1) submit to the President and Congress a description of the technological, legal, and policy issues presented by the creation of the ISE, and the way in which these issues will be addressed;

(2) establish an initial capability to provide electronic directory services, or the functional equivalent, to assist in locating in the Federal Government intelligence and terrorism information and people with relevant knowledge about intelligence and terrorism information; and

(3) conduct a review of relevant current Federal agency capabilities, databases, and systems for sharing information.

(d) GUIDELINES AND REQUIREMENTS.—As soon as possible, but in no event later than 270 days after the date of the enactment of this Act, the President shall—

(1) leverage all ongoing efforts consistent with establishing the ISE and issue guidelines for acquiring, accessing, sharing, and using information, including guidelines to ensure that information is provided in its most shareable form, such as by using tearlines to separate out data from the sources and methods by which the data are obtained;

(2) in consultation with the Privacy and Civil Liberties Oversight Board established under section 1061, issue guidelines that—

(A) protect privacy and civil liberties in the development and use of the ISE; and

(B) shall be made public, unless nondisclosure is clearly necessary to protect national security; and

(3) require the heads of Federal departments and agencies to promote a culture of information sharing by—

(A) reducing disincentives to information sharing, including over-classification of information and unnecessary requirements for originator approval, consistent with applicable laws and regulations; and

(B) providing affirmative incentives for information sharing.

(e) IMPLEMENTATION PLAN REPORT.—Not later than one year after the date of the enactment of this Act, the President shall, with the assistance of the program manager, submit to Congress a report containing an implementation plan for the ISE. The report shall include the following:

(1) A description of the functions, capabilities, resources, and conceptual design of the ISE, including standards.

(2) A description of the impact on enterprise architectures of participating agencies.

(3) A budget estimate that identifies the incremental costs associated with designing, testing, integrating, deploying, and operating the ISE.

(4) A project plan for designing, testing, integrating, deploying, and operating the ISE.

(5) The policies and directives referred to in subsection (b)(1)(C), as well as the metrics and enforcement mechanisms that will be utilized.

(6) Objective, systemwide performance measures to enable the assessment of progress toward achieving the full implementation of the ISE.

(7) A description of the training requirements needed to ensure that the ISE will be adequately implemented and properly utilized.

(8) A description of the means by which privacy and civil liberties will be protected in the design and operation of the ISE.

(9) The recommendations of the program manager, in consultation with the Information Sharing Council, regarding whether, and under what conditions, the ISE should be expanded to include other intelligence information.

(10) A delineation of the roles of the Federal departments and agencies that will participate in the ISE, including an identification of the agencies that will deliver the infrastructure needed to operate and manage the ISE (as distinct from individual department or agency components that are part of the ISE), with such delineation of roles to be consistent with—

(A) the authority of the Director of National Intelligence under this title, and the amendments made by this title, to set standards for information sharing throughout the intelligence community; and

(B) the authority of the Secretary of Homeland Security and the Attorney General, and the role of the Department of Homeland Security and the Attorney General, in coordinating with State, local, and tribal officials and the private sector.

(11) The recommendations of the program manager, in consultation with the Information Sharing Council, for a future management structure for the ISE, including whether the position of program manager should continue to remain in existence.

(f) PROGRAM MANAGER.—

(1) DESIGNATION.—Not later than 120 days after the date of the enactment of this Act, with notification to Congress, the President shall designate an individual as the program manager responsible for information sharing across the Federal Government. The individual designated as the program manager shall serve as program manager until removed from service or replaced by the President (at the President's sole discretion). The program manager, in consultation with the head of any affected department or agency, shall have and exercise governmentwide authority over the sharing of information within the scope of the information sharing environment, including homeland security information, terrorism information, and weapons of mass destruction information, by all Federal departments, agencies, and components, irrespective of the Federal department, agency, or component in which the program manager may be administratively located, except as provided by law.

(2) DUTIES AND RESPONSIBILITIES.—

(A) IN GENERAL.—The program manager shall, in consultation with the Information Sharing Council—

(i) plan for and oversee the implementation of, and manage, the ISE;

(ii) assist in the development of policies, as appropriate, to foster the development and proper operation of the ISE;

(iii) consistent with the direction and policies issued by the President, the Director of National Intelligence, and the Director of the Office of Management and Budget, issue governmentwide procedures, guidelines, instructions, and functional standards, as appropriate, for the management, development, and proper operation of the ISE;

(iv) identify and resolve information sharing disputes between Federal departments, agencies, and components; and

(v) assist, monitor, and assess the implementation of the ISE by Federal departments and agencies to ensure adequate progress, technological consistency and policy compliance; and regularly report the findings to Congress.

(B) CONTENT OF POLICIES, PROCEDURES, GUIDELINES, RULES, AND STANDARDS.—The policies, procedures, guidelines, rules, and standards under subparagraph (A)(ii) shall—

(i) take into account the varying missions and security requirements of agencies participating in the ISE;

(ii) address development, implementation, and oversight of technical standards and requirements;

(iii) take into account ongoing and planned efforts that support development, implementation and management of the ISE;

(iv) address and facilitate information sharing between and among departments and agencies of the intelligence community, the Department of Defense, the homeland security community and the law enforcement community;

(v) address and facilitate information sharing between Federal departments and agencies and State, tribal, and local governments;

(vi) address and facilitate, as appropriate, information sharing between Federal departments and agencies and the private sector;

(vii) address and facilitate, as appropriate, information sharing between Federal departments and agencies with foreign partners and allies; and

(viii) ensure the protection of privacy and civil liberties.

(g) INFORMATION SHARING COUNCIL.—

(1) ESTABLISHMENT.—There is established an Information Sharing Council that shall assist the President and the program manager in their duties under this section. The Information Sharing Council shall serve until removed from service and replaced by the President (at the sole discretion of the President) with a successor body.

(2) SPECIFIC DUTIES.—In assisting the President and the program manager in their duties under this section, the Information Sharing Council shall—

(A) advise the President and the program manager in developing policies, procedures, guidelines, roles, and standards necessary to establish, implement, and maintain the ISE;

(B) work to ensure coordination among the Federal departments and agencies participating in the ISE in the establishment, implementation, and maintenance of the ISE;

(C) identify and, as appropriate, recommend the consolidation and elimination of current programs, systems, and processes used by Federal departments and agencies to share information, and recommend, as appropriate, the redirection of existing resources to support the ISE;

(D) identify gaps, if any, between existing technologies, programs and systems used by Federal departments and agencies to share information and the parameters of the proposed information sharing environment;

(E) recommend solutions to address any gaps identified under subparagraph (D);

(F) recommend means by which the ISE can be extended to allow interchange of information between Federal departments and agencies and appropriate authorities of State and local governments;

(G) assist the program manager in identifying and resolving information sharing disputes between Federal departments, agencies, and components;

(H) identify appropriate personnel for assignment to the program manager to support staffing needs identified by the program manager; and

(I) recommend whether or not, and by which means, the ISE should be expanded so as to allow future expansion encompassing other relevant categories of information.

(3) CONSULTATION.—In performing its duties, the Information Sharing Council shall consider input from persons and entities outside the Federal Government having significant experience and expertise in policy, technical matters, and operational matters relating to the ISE.

(4) INAPPLICABILITY OF FEDERAL ADVISORY COMMITTEE ACT.—The Information Sharing Council (including any subsidiary group of the Information Sharing Council) shall not be subject to the requirements of the Federal Advisory Committee Act (5 U.S.C. App.).

(5) DETAILEES.—Upon a request by the Director of National Intelligence, the departments and agencies represented on the Information Sharing Council shall detail to the program manager, on a reimbursable basis, appropriate personnel identified under paragraph (2)(H).

(h) PERFORMANCE MANAGEMENT REPORTS.—

(1) IN GENERAL.—Not later than two years after the date of the enactment of this Act, and not later than June 30 of each year thereafter, the President shall submit to Congress

a report on the state of the ISE and of information sharing across the Federal Government.

(2) CONTENT.—Each report under this subsection shall include—

(A) a progress report on the extent to which the ISE has been implemented, including how the ISE has fared on the performance measures and whether the performance goals set in the preceding year have been met;

(B) objective system-wide performance goals for the following year;

(C) an accounting of how much was spent on the ISE in the preceding year;

(D) actions taken to ensure that procurement of and investments in systems and technology are consistent with the implementation plan for the ISE;

(E) the extent to which all terrorism watch lists are available for combined searching in real time through the ISE and whether there are consistent standards for placing individuals on, and removing individuals from, the watch lists, including the availability of processes for correcting errors;

(F) the extent to which State, tribal, and local officials are participating in the ISE;

(G) the extent to which private sector data, including information from owners and operators of critical infrastructure, is incorporated in the ISE, and the extent to which individuals and entities outside the government are receiving information through the ISE;

(H) the measures taken by the Federal government to ensure the accuracy of information in the ISE, in particular the accuracy of information about individuals;

(I) an assessment of the privacy and civil liberties protections of the ISE, including actions taken in the preceding year to implement or enforce privacy and civil liberties protections; and

(J) an assessment of the security protections used in the ISE.

(i) AGENCY RESPONSIBILITIES.—The head of each department or agency that possesses or uses intelligence or terrorism information, operates a system in the ISE, or otherwise participates (or expects to participate) in the ISE shall—

(1) ensure full department or agency compliance with information sharing policies, procedures, guidelines, rules, and standards established under subsections (b) and (f);

(2) ensure the provision of adequate resources for systems and activities supporting operation of and participation in the ISE;

(3) ensure full department or agency cooperation in the development of the ISE to implement government-wide information sharing; and

(4) submit, at the request of the President or the program manager, any reports on the implementation of the requirements of the ISE within such department or agency.

(j) REPORT ON THE INFORMATION SHARING ENVIRONMENT.—

(1) IN GENERAL.—Not later than 180 days after the date of enactment of the Implementing Recommendations of the 9/11 Commission Act of 2007, the President shall report to the Committee on Homeland Security and Governmental Affairs of the Senate, the Select Committee on Intelligence of the Senate, the Committee on Homeland Security of the House of Representatives, and the Permanent Select Committee on Intelligence of the House of Representatives on the feasibility of—

(A) eliminating the use of any marking or process (including "Originator Control") intended to, or having the effect of, restricting the sharing of information within the scope of the information sharing environment, including homeland security information, terrorism information, and weapons of mass destruction information, between and among participants in the information sharing environment, unless the President has—

(i) specifically exempted categories of information from such elimination; and

(ii) reported that exemption to the committees of Congress described in the matter preceding this subparagraph; and

(B) continuing to use Federal agency standards in effect on such date of enactment for the collection, sharing, and access to information within the scope of the information sharing environment, including homeland security information, terrorism information, and weapons of mass destruction information, relating to citizens and lawful permanent residents;

(C) replacing the standards described in subparagraph (B) with a standard that would allow mission-based or threat-based permission to access or share information within the scope of the information sharing environment, including homeland security information, terrorism information, and weapons of mass destruction information, for a particular purpose that the Federal Government, through an appropriate process established in consultation with the Privacy and Civil Liberties Oversight Board established under section 1061, has determined to be lawfully permissible for a particular agency, component, or employee (commonly known as an "authorized use" standard); and

(D) the use of anonymized data by Federal departments, agencies, or components collecting, possessing, disseminating, or handling information within the scope of the information sharing environment, including homeland security information, terrorism information, and weapons of mass destruction information, in any cases in which—

(i) the use of such information is reasonably expected to produce results materially equivalent to the use of information that is transferred or stored in a nonanonymized form; and

(ii) such use is consistent with any mission of that department, agency, or component (including any mission under a Federal statute or directive of the President) that involves the storage, retention, sharing, or exchange of personally identifiable information.

(2) DEFINITION.—In this subsection, the term 'anonymized data' means data in which the individual to whom the data pertains is not identifiable with reasonable efforts, including information that has been encrypted or hidden through the use of other technology.

(k) ADDITIONAL POSITIONS.—The program manager is authorized to hire not more than 40 full-time employees to assist the program manager in—

(1) activities associated with the implementation of the information sharing environment, including—

(A) implementing the requirements under subsection (b)(2); and

(B) any additional implementation initiatives to enhance and expedite the creation of the information sharing environment; and

(2) identifying and resolving information sharing disputes between Federal departments, agencies, and components under subsection (f)(2)(A)(iv).

(l) AUTHORIZATION OF APPROPRIATIONS.—There is authorized to be appropriated to carry out this section $30,000,000 for each of fiscal years 2008 and 2009.

ALTERNATIVE ANALYSIS OF INTELLIGENCE
BY THE INTELLIGENCE COMMUNITY

SEC. 1017.

(a) IN GENERAL.—Not later than 180 days after the effective date of this Act, the Director of National Intelligence shall establish a process and assign an individual or entity the responsibility for ensuring that, as appropriate, elements of the intelligence community conduct alternative analysis (commonly referred to as "red-team analysis") of the information and conclusions in intelligence products.

(b) REPORT—Not later than 270 days after the effective date of this Act, the Director of National Intelligence shall provide a report to the Select Committee on Intelligence of the Senate and the Permanent Select Committee of the House of Representatives on the implementation of subsection (a).

PRESIDENTIAL GUIDELINES ON IMPLEMENTATION
AND PRESERVATION OF AUTHORITIES

SEC. 1018. The President shall issue guidelines to ensure the effective implementation and execution within the executive branch of the authorities granted to the Director of National Intelligence by this title and the amendments made by this title, in a manner that respects and does not abrogate the statutory responsibilities of the heads of the departments of the United States Government concerning such departments, including, but not limited to:

(1) the authority of the Director of the Office of Management and Budget; and

(2) the authority of the principal officers of the executive departments as heads of their respective departments, including, but not limited to, under—

(A) section 199 of the Revised Statutes (22 U.S.C. §2651);

(B) title II of the Department of Energy Organization Act (42 U.S.C. §7131 et seq.);

(C) the State Department Basic Authorities Act of 1956;

(D) section 102(a) of the Homeland Security Act of 2002 (6 U.S.C. §112(a)); and

(E) sections 301 of title 5, 113(b) and 162(b) of title 10, 503 of title 28, and 301(b) of title 31, United States Code.

ASSIGNMENT OF RESPONSIBILITIES
RELATING TO ANALYTIC INTEGRITY

SEC. 1019.

(a) ASSIGNMENT OF RESPONSIBILITIES.—For purposes of carrying out section 102A(h) of the National Security Act of 1947 (as added by section 1011(a)), the Director of National Intelligence shall, not later than 180 days after the date of the enactment of this Act, assign an individual or entity to be responsible for ensuring that finished intelligence products produced by any element or elements of the intelligence community are timely, objective, independent of political considerations, based upon all sources of available intelligence, and employ the standards of proper analytic tradecraft.

(b) RESPONSIBILITIES.—

(1) The individual or entity assigned responsibility under subsection (a)—

(A) may be responsible for general oversight and management of analysis and production, but may not be directly responsible for, or involved in, the specific production of any finished intelligence product;

(B) shall perform, on a regular basis, detailed reviews of finished intelligence product or other analytic products by an element or elements of the intelligence community covering a particular topic or subject matter;

(C) shall be responsible for identifying on an annual basis functional or topical areas of analysis for specific review under subparagraph (B); and

(D) upon completion of any review under subparagraph (B), may draft lessons learned, identify best practices, or make recommendations for improvement to the analytic tradecraft employed in the production of the reviewed product or products.

(2) Each review under paragraph (1)(B) should—

(A) include whether the product or products concerned were based on all sources of available intelligence, properly describe the quality and reliability of underlying sources, properly caveat and express uncertainties or confidence in analytic judgments, properly distinguish between underlying intelligence and the assumptions and judgments of analysts, and incorporate, where appropriate, alternative analyses; and

(B) ensure that the analytic methodologies, tradecraft, and practices used by the element or elements concerned in the production of the product or products concerned meet the standards set forth in subsection (a).

(3) Information drafted under paragraph (1)(D) should, as appropriate, be included in analysis teaching modules and case studies for use throughout the intelligence community.

(c) ANNUAL REPORTS.—Not later than December 1 each year, the Director of National Intelligence shall submit to the congressional intelligence committees, the heads of the relevant elements of the intelligence community, and the heads of analytic training departments a report containing a description, and the associated findings, of each review under subsection (b)(1)(B) during such year.

(d) CONGRESSIONAL INTELLIGENCE COMMITTEES DEFINED.—In this section, the term "congressional intelligence committees" means—

(1) the Select Committee on Intelligence of the Senate; and

(2) the Permanent Select Committee on Intelligence of the House of Representatives.

SAFEGUARD OF OBJECTIVITY IN INTELLIGENCE ANALYSIS
SEC. 1020.

(a) IN GENERAL.—Not later than 180 days after the effective date of this Act, the Director of National Intelligence shall identify an individual within the Office of the Director of National Intelligence who shall be available to analysts within the Office of the Director of National Intelligence to counsel, conduct arbitration, offer recommendations, and, as appropriate, initiate inquiries into real or perceived problems of analytic tradecraft or politicization, biased reporting, or lack of objectivity in intelligence analysis.

(b) REPORT. —Not later than 270 days after the effective date of this Act, the Director of National Intelligence shall provide a report to the Select Committee on Intelligence of the Senate and the Permanent Select Committee on Intelligence of the House of Representatives on the implementation of subsection (a).

SUBTITLE B—NATIONAL COUNTERTERRORISM CENTER, NATIONAL COUNTER PROLIFERATION CENTER, AND NATIONAL INTELLIGENCE CENTERS

NATIONAL COUNTERTERRORISM CENTER
SEC. 1021. Title I of the National Security Act of 1947 (50 U.S.C. §402 et seq.) is amended by adding at the end the following new section:

[amendments omitted here—see the National Security Act of 1947 in this book]

NATIONAL COUNTER PROLIFERATION CENTER
SEC. 1022. Title I of the National Security Act of 1947, as amended by section 1021 of this Act, is further amended by adding at the end the following new section:

[amendments omitted here—see the National Security Act of 1947 in this book]

NATIONAL INTELLIGENCE CENTERS
SEC. 1023. Title I of the National Security Act of 1947, as amended by section 1022 of this Act, is further amended by adding at the end the following new section:

[amendments omitted here—see the National Security Act of 1947 in this book]

SUBTITLE C—JOINT INTELLIGENCE COMMUNITY COUNCIL

JOINT INTELLIGENCE COMMUNITY COUNCIL

SEC. 1031. Title I of the National Security Act of 1947 (50 U.S.C. §402 et seq.) is amended by inserting after section 101 the following new section:

[amendments omitted here—see the National Security Act of 1947 in this book]

SUBTITLE D—IMPROVEMENT OF EDUCATION FOR THE INTELLIGENCE COMMUNITY

ADDITIONAL EDUCATION AND TRAINING REQUIREMENTS

SEC. 1041.

(a) FINDINGS.—Congress makes the following findings:

(1) Foreign language education is essential for the development of a highly-skilled workforce for the intelligence community.

(2) Since September 11, 2001, the need for language proficiency levels to meet required national security functions has been raised, and the ability to comprehend and articulate technical and scientific information in foreign languages has become critical.

(b) LINGUISTIC REQUIREMENTS.—

(1) The Director of National Intelligence shall—

(A) identify the linguistic requirements for the Office of the Director of National Intelligence;

(B) identify specific requirements for the range of linguistic skills necessary for the intelligence community, including proficiency in scientific and technical vocabularies of critical foreign languages; and

(C) develop a comprehensive plan for the Office to meet such requirements through the education, recruitment, and training of linguists.

(2) In carrying out activities under paragraph (1), the Director shall take into account education grant programs of the Department of Defense and the Department of Education that are in existence as of the date of the enactment of this Act.

(3) Not later than one year after the date of the enactment of this Act, and annually thereafter, the Director shall submit to Congress a report on the requirements identified under paragraph (1), including the success of the Office of the Director of National Intelligence in meeting such requirements. Each report shall notify Congress of any additional resources determined by the Director to be required to meet such requirements.

(4) Each report under paragraph (3) shall be in unclassified form, but may include a classified annex.

(c) PROFESSIONAL INTELLIGENCE TRAINING.—The Director of National Intelligence shall require the head of each element and component within the Office of the Director of National Intelligence who has responsibility for professional intelligence training to periodically review and revise the curriculum for the professional intelligence training of the senior and intermediate level personnel of such element or component in order to—

(1) strengthen the focus of such curriculum on the integration of intelligence collection and analysis throughout the Office; and

(2) prepare such personnel for duty with other departments, agencies, and elements of the intelligence community.

CROSS-DISCIPLINARY EDUCATION AND TRAINING.

SEC. 1042. Title X of the National Security Act of 1947 (50 U.S.C. §441g) is amended by adding at the end the following new section:
[amendments omitted here—see the National Security Act of 1947 in this book]
165 INTELLIGENCE REFORM AND TERRORISM PREVENTION ACT OF 2004

INTELLIGENCE COMMUNITY SCHOLARSHIP PROGRAM

SEC. 1043. Title X of the National Security Act of 1947, as amended by section 1042 of this Act, is further amended by adding at the end the following new section:
[amendments omitted here—see the National Security Act of 1947 in this book]

SUBTITLE E—ADDITIONAL IMPROVEMENTS OF INTELLIGENCE ACTIVITIES

SERVICE AND NATIONAL LABORATORIES AND THE INTELLIGENCE COMMUNITY

SEC. 1051. The Director of National Intelligence, in cooperation with the Secretary of Defense and the Secretary of Energy, should seek to ensure that each service laboratory of the Department of Defense and each national laboratory of the Department of Energy may, acting through the relevant Secretary and in a manner consistent with the missions and commitments of the laboratory—

(1) assist the Director of National Intelligence in all aspects of technical intelligence, including research, applied sciences, analysis, technology evaluation and assessment, and any other aspect that the relevant Secretary considers appropriate; and

(2) make available to the intelligence community, on a community-wide basis—

(A) the analysis and production services of the service and national laboratories, in a manner that maximizes the capacity and services of such laboratories; and

(B) the facilities and human resources of the service and national laboratories, in a manner that improves the technological capabilities of the intelligence community.

OPEN SOURCE INTELLIGENCE

SEC. 1052.

(a) SENSE OF CONGRESS—It is the sense of Congress that—

(1) the Director of National Intelligence should establish an intelligence center for the purpose of coordinating the collection, analysis, production, and dissemination of open-source intelligence to elements of the intelligence community;

(2) open-source intelligence is a valuable source that must be integrated into the intelligence cycle to ensure that United States policymakers are fully and completely informed; and

(3) the intelligence center should ensure that each element of the intelligence community uses open-source intelligence consistent with the mission of such element.

(b) REQUIREMENT FOR EFFICIENT USE BY INTELLIGENCE COMMUNITY OF OPENSOURCE INTELLIGENCE.—The Director of National Intelligence shall ensure that the intelligence community makes efficient and effective use of open-source information and analysis.

(c) REPORT—Not later than June 30, 2005, the Director of National Intelligence shall submit to the congressional intelligence committees a report containing the decision of the Director as to whether an open-source intelligence center will be established. If the Director decides not to establish an open-source intelligence center, such report shall also contain a description of how the intelligence community will use open-source intelligence and effectively integrate open-source intelligence into the national intelligence cycle.

(d) CONGRESSIONAL INTELLIGENCE COMMITTEES DEFINED.—In this section, the term "congressional intelligence committees' means—

    (1) the Select Committee on Intelligence of the Senate; and

    (2) the Permanent Select Committee on Intelligence of the House of Representatives.

NATIONAL INTELLIGENCE RESERVE CORPS

SEC. 1053.

(a) ESTABLISHMENT.—The Director of National Intelligence may provide for the establishment and training of a National Intelligence Reserve Corps (in this section referred to as "National Intelligence Reserve Corps") for the temporary reemployment on a voluntary basis of former employees of elements of the intelligence community during periods of emergency, as determined by the Director.

(b) ELIGIBLE INDIVIDUALS.—An individual may participate in the National Intelligence Reserve Corps only if the individual previously served as a full time employee of an element of the intelligence community.

(c) TERMS OF PARTICIPATION.—The Director of National Intelligence shall prescribe the terms and conditions under which eligible individuals may participate in the National Intelligence Reserve Corps.

(d) EXPENSES.—The Director of National Intelligence may provide members of the National Intelligence Reserve Corps transportation and per diem in lieu of subsistence for purposes of participating in any training that relates to service as a member of the Reserve Corps.

(e) TREATMENT OF ANNUITANTS.—

    (1) If an annuitant receiving an annuity from the Civil Service Retirement and Disability Fund becomes temporarily reemployed pursuant to this section, such annuity shall not be discontinued thereby.

    (2) An annuitant so reemployed shall not be considered an employee for the purposes of chapter 83 or 84 of title 5, United States Code.

(f) TREATMENT UNDER OFFICE OF DIRECTOR OF NATIONAL INTELLIGENCE PERSONNEL CEILING.—A member of the National Intelligence Reserve Corps who is reemployed on a temporary basis pursuant to this section shall not count against any personnel ceiling applicable to the Office of the Director of National Intelligence.

SUBTITLE F—PRIVACY AND CIVIL LIBERTIES

PRIVACY AND CIVIL LIBERTIES OVERSIGHT BOARD

SEC. 1061.

(a) IN GENERAL.—There is established as an independent agency within the executive branch a Privacy and Civil Liberties Oversight Board (referred to in this section as the 'Board').

(b) FINDINGS.—Consistent with the report of the National Commission on Terrorist Attacks Upon the United States, Congress makes the following findings:

    (1) In conducting the war on terrorism, the Government may need additional powers and may need to enhance the use of its existing powers.

    (2) This shift of power and authority to the Government calls for an enhanced system of checks and balances to protect the precious liberties that are vital to our way of life and to ensure that the Government uses its powers for the purposes for which the powers were given.

(3) The National Commission on Terrorist Attacks Upon the United States correctly concluded that 'The choice between security and liberty is a false choice, as nothing is more likely to endanger America's liberties than the success of a terrorist attack at home. Our history has shown us that insecurity threatens liberty. Yet, if our liberties are curtailed, we lose the values that we are struggling to defend.'.

(c) PURPOSE.—The Board shall—

(1) analyze and review actions the executive branch takes to protect the Nation from terrorism, ensuring that the need for such actions is balanced with the need to protect privacy and civil liberties; and

(2) ensure that liberty concerns are appropriately considered in the development and implementation of laws, regulations, and policies related to efforts to protect the Nation against terrorism.

(d) FUNCTIONS.—

(1) ADVICE AND COUNSEL ON POLICY DEVELOPMENT AND IMPLEMENTA-TION.—The Board shall—

(A) review proposed legislation, regulations, and policies related to efforts to protect the Nation from terrorism, including the development and adoption of information sharing guidelines under subsections (d) and (f) of section 1016;

(B) review the implementation of new and existing legislation, regulations, and policies related to efforts to protect the Nation from terrorism, including the implementation of information sharing guidelines under subsections (d) and (f) of section 1016;

(C) advise the President and the departments, agencies, and elements of the executive branch to ensure that privacy and civil liberties are appropriately considered in the development and implementation of such legislation, regulations, policies, and guidelines; and

(D) in providing advice on proposals to retain or enhance a particular governmental power, consider whether the department, agency, or element of the executive branch has established—

(i) that the need for the power is balanced with the need to protect privacy and civil liberties;

(ii) that there is adequate supervision of the use by the executive branch of the power to ensure protection of privacy and civil liberties; and

(iii) that there are adequate guidelines and oversight to properly confine its use.

(2) OVERSIGHT.—The Board shall continually review—

(A) the regulations, policies, and procedures, and the implementation of the regulations, policies, and procedures, of the departments, agencies, and elements of the executive branch relating to efforts to protect the Nation from terrorism to ensure that privacy and civil liberties are protected;

(B) the information sharing practices of the departments, agencies, and elements of the executive branch relating to efforts to protect the Nation from terrorism to determine whether they appropriately protect privacy and civil liberties and adhere to the information sharing guidelines issued or developed under subsections (d) and (f) of section 1016 and to other governing laws, regulations, and policies regarding privacy and civil liberties; and

(C) other actions by the executive branch relating to efforts to protect the Nation from terrorism to determine whether such actions—

(i) appropriately protect privacy and civil liberties; and

(ii) are consistent with governing laws, regulations, and policies regarding privacy and civil liberties.

(3) RELATIONSHIP WITH PRIVACY AND CIVIL LIBERTIES OFFICERS.— The Board shall—

(A) receive and review reports and other information from privacy officers and civil liberties officers under section 1062;

(B) when appropriate, make recommendations to such privacy officers and civil liberties officers regarding their activities; and

(C) when appropriate, coordinate the activities of such privacy officers and civil liberties officers on relevant interagency matters.

(4) TESTIMONY.—The members of the Board shall appear and testify before Congress upon request.

(e) REPORTS.—

(1) IN GENERAL.—The Board shall—

(A) receive and review reports from privacy officers and civil liberties officers under section 1062; and

(B) periodically submit, not less than semiannually, reports—

(i)(I) to the appropriate committees of Congress, including the Committee on the Judiciary of the Senate, the Committee on the Judiciary of the House of Representatives, the Committee on Homeland Security and Governmental Affairs of the Senate, the Committee on Homeland Security of the House of Representatives, the Committee on Oversight and Government Reform of the House of Representatives, the Select Committee on Intelligence of the Senate, and the Permanent Select Committee on Intelligence of the House of Representatives; and

(II) to the President; and

(ii) which shall be in unclassified form to the greatest extent possible, with a classified annex where necessary.

(2) CONTENTS.—Not less than 2 reports submitted each year under paragraph (1)(B) shall include—

(A) a description of the major activities of the Board during the preceding period;

(B) information on the findings, conclusions, and recommendations of the Board resulting from its advice and oversight functions under subsection (d);

(C) the minority views on any findings, conclusions, and recommendations of the Board resulting from its advice and oversight functions under subsection (d);

(D) each proposal reviewed by the Board under subsection (d)(1) that—

(i) the Board advised against implementation; and

(ii) notwithstanding such advice, actions were taken to implement; and

(E) for the preceding period, any requests submitted under subsection (g)(1)(D) for the issuance of subpoenas that were modified or denied by the Attorney General.

(f) INFORMING THE PUBLIC.—The Board shall—

(1) make its reports, including its reports to Congress, available to the public to the greatest extent that is consistent with the protection of classified information and applicable law; and

(2) hold public hearings and otherwise inform the public of its activities, as appropriate and in a manner consistent with the protection of classified information and applicable law.

(g) ACCESS TO INFORMATION.—

(1) AUTHORIZATION.—If determined by the Board to be necessary to carry out its responsibilities under this section, the Board is authorized to—

(A) have access from any department, agency, or element of the executive branch, or any Federal officer or employee of any such department, agency, or element, to all relevant records, reports, audits, reviews, documents, papers, recommendations, or other relevant material, including classified information consistent with applicable law;

(B) interview, take statements from, or take public testimony from personnel of any department, agency, or element of the executive branch, or any Federal officer or employee of any such department, agency, or element;

(C) request information or assistance from any State, tribal, or local government; and

(D) at the direction of a majority of the members of the Board, submit a written request to the Attorney General of the United States that the Attorney General require, by subpoena, persons (other than departments, agencies, and elements of the executive branch) to produce any relevant information, documents, reports, answers, records, accounts, papers, and other documentary or testimonial evidence.

(2) REVIEW OF SUBPOENA REQUEST.—

(A) IN GENERAL.—Not later than 30 days after the date of receipt of a request by the Board under paragraph (1)(D), the Attorney General shall—

(i) issue the subpoena as requested; or

(ii) provide the Board, in writing, with an explanation of the grounds on which the subpoena request has been modified or denied.

(B) NOTIFICATION.—If a subpoena request is modified or denied under subparagraph (A)(ii), the Attorney General shall, not later than 30 days after the date of that modification or denial, notify the Committee on the Judiciary of the Senate and the Committee on the Judiciary of the House of Representatives.

(3) ENFORCEMENT OF SUBPOENA.—In the case of contumacy or failure to obey a subpoena issued pursuant to paragraph (1)(D), the United States district court for the judicial district in which the subpoenaed person resides, is served, or may be found may issue an order requiring such person to produce the evidence required by such subpoena.

(4) AGENCY COOPERATION.—Whenever information or assistance requested under subparagraph (A) or (B) of paragraph (1) is, in the judgment of the Board, unreasonably refused or not provided, the Board shall report the circumstances to the head of the department, agency, or element concerned without delay. The head of the department, agency, or element concerned shall ensure that the Board is given access to the information, assistance, material, or personnel the Board determines to be necessary to carry out its functions.

(h) MEMBERSHIP.—

(1) MEMBERS.—The Board shall be composed of a fulltime chairman and 4 additional members, who shall be appointed by the President, by and with the advice and consent of the Senate.

(2) QUALIFICATIONS.—Members of the Board shall be selected solely on the basis of their professional qualifications, achievements, public stature, expertise in civil liberties and privacy, and relevant experience, and without regard to political affiliation, but in no event shall more than 3 members of the Board be members of the same political party. The President shall, before appointing an individual who is not a member of the same political party as the President, consult with the leadership of that party, if any, in the Senate and House of Representatives.

(3) INCOMPATIBLE OFFICE.—An individual appointed to the Board may not, while serving on the Board, be an elected official, officer, or employee of the Federal Government, other than in the capacity as a member of the Board.

(4) TERM.—Each member of the Board shall serve a term of 6 years, except that—

(A) a member appointed to a term of office after the commencement of such term may serve under such appointment only for the remainder of such term; and

(B) upon the expiration of the term of office of a member, the member shall continue to serve until the member's successor has been appointed and qualified, except that no member may serve under this subparagraph—

(i) for more than 60 days when Congress is in session unless a nomination to fill the vacancy shall have been submitted to the Senate; or

(ii) after the adjournment sine die of the session of the Senate in which such nomination is submitted.

(5) QUORUM AND MEETINGS.—The Board shall meet upon the call of the chairman or a majority of its members. Three members of the Board shall constitute a quorum.

(i) COMPENSATION AND TRAVEL EXPENSES.—

(1) COMPENSATION.—

(A) CHAIRMAN.—The chairman of the Board shall be compensated at the rate of pay payable for a position at level III of the Executive Schedule under section 5314 of title 5, United States Code.

(B) MEMBERS.—Each member of the Board shall be compensated at a rate of pay payable for a position at level IV of the Executive Schedule under section 5315 of title 5, United States Code, for each day during which that member is engaged in the actual performance of the duties of the Board.

(2) TRAVEL EXPENSES.—Members of the Board shall be allowed travel expenses, including per diem in lieu of subsistence, at rates authorized for persons employed intermittently by the Government under section 5703(b) of title 5, United States Code, while away from their homes or regular places of business in the performance of services for the Board.

(j) STAFF.—

(1) APPOINTMENT AND COMPENSATION.—The chairman of the Board, in accordance with rules agreed upon by the Board, shall appoint and fix the compensation of a full-time executive director and such other personnel as may be necessary to enable the Board to carry out its functions, without regard to the provisions of title 5, United States Code, governing appointments in the competitive service, and without regard to the provisions of chapter 51 and subchapter III of chapter 53 of such title relating to classification and General Schedule pay rates, except that no rate of pay fixed under this subsection may exceed the equivalent of that payable for a position at level V of the Executive Schedule under section 5316 of title 5, United States Code.

(2) DETAILEES.—Any Federal employee may be detailed to the Board without reimbursement from the Board, and such detailee shall retain the rights, status, and privileges of the detailee's regular employment without interruption.

(3) CONSULTANT SERVICES.—The Board may procure the temporary or intermittent services of experts and consultants in accordance with section 3109 of title 5, United States Code, at rates that do not exceed the daily rate paid a person occupying a position at level IV of the Executive Schedule under section 5315 of such title.

(k) SECURITY CLEARANCES.—

(1) IN GENERAL.—The appropriate departments, agencies, and elements of the executive branch shall cooperate with the Board to expeditiously provide the Board members

and staff with appropriate security clearances to the extent possible under existing procedures and requirements.

(2) RULES AND PROCEDURES.—After consultation with the Secretary of Defense, the Attorney General, and the Director of National Intelligence, the Board shall adopt rules and procedures of the Board for physical, communications, computer, document, personnel, and other security relating to carrying out the functions of the Board.

(l) TREATMENT AS AGENCY, NOT AS ADVISORY COMMITTEE.— The Board—

(1) is an agency (as defined in section 551(1) of title 5, United States Code); and

(2) is not an advisory committee (as defined in section 3(2) of the Federal Advisory Committee Act (5 U.S.C. App.)).

(m) AUTHORIZATION OF APPROPRIATIONS.—There are authorized to be appropriated to carry out this section amounts as follows:

(1) For fiscal year 2008, $5,000,000.

(2) For fiscal year 2009, $6,650,000.

(3) For fiscal year 2010, $8,300,000.

(4) For fiscal year 2011, $10,000,000.

(5) For fiscal year 2012 and each subsequent fiscal year, such sums as may be necessary.

SENSE OF CONGRESS ON DESIGNATION OF PRIVACY AND CIVIL LIBERTIES OFFICERS

SEC. 1062.

(a) DESIGNATION AND FUNCTIONS.—The Attorney General, the Secretary of Defense, the Secretary of State, the Secretary of the Treasury, the Secretary of Health and Human Services, the Secretary of Homeland Security, the Director of National Intelligence, the Director of the Central Intelligence Agency, and the head of any other department, agency, or element of the executive branch designated by the Privacy and Civil Liberties Oversight Board under section 1061 to be appropriate for coverage under this section shall designate not less than 1 senior officer to serve as the principal advisor to—

(1) assist the head of such department, agency, or element and other officials of such department, agency, or element in appropriately considering privacy and civil liberties concerns when such officials are proposing, developing, or implementing laws, regulations, policies, procedures, or guidelines related to efforts to protect the Nation against terrorism;

(2) periodically investigate and review department, agency, or element actions, policies, procedures, guidelines, and related laws and their implementation to ensure that such department, agency, or element is adequately considering privacy and civil liberties in its actions;

(3) ensure that such department, agency, or element has adequate procedures to receive, investigate, respond to, and redress complaints from individuals who allege such department, agency, or element has violated their privacy or civil liberties; and

(4) in providing advice on proposals to retain or enhance a particular governmental power the officer shall consider whether such department, agency, or element has established—

(A) that the need for the power is balanced with the need to protect privacy and civil liberties;

(B) that there is adequate supervision of the use by such department, agency, or element of the power to ensure protection of privacy and civil liberties; and

(C) that there are adequate guidelines and oversight to properly confine its use.

(b) EXCEPTION TO DESIGNATION AUTHORITY.—

(1) PRIVACY OFFICERS.—In any department, agency, or element referred to in subsection (a) or designated by the Privacy and Civil Liberties Oversight Board, which has a statutorily created privacy officer, such officer shall perform the functions specified in subsection
(a) with respect to privacy.

(2) CIVIL LIBERTIES OFFICERS.—In any department, agency, or element referred to in subsection (a) or designated by the Board, which has a statutorily created civil liberties officer, such officer shall perform the functions specified in subsection (a) with respect to civil liberties.

(c) SUPERVISION AND COORDINATION.—Each privacy officer or civil liberties officer described in subsection (a) or (b) shall—

(1) report directly to the head of the department, agency, or element concerned; and

(2) coordinate their activities with the Inspector General of such department, agency, or element to avoid duplication of effort.

(d) AGENCY COOPERATION.—The head of each department, agency, or element shall ensure that each privacy officer and civil liberties officer—

(1) has the information, material, and resources necessary to fulfill the functions of such officer;

(2) is advised of proposed policy changes;

(3) is consulted by decision makers; and

(4) is given access to material and personnel the officer determines to be necessary to carry out the functions of such officer.

(e) REPRISAL FOR MAKING COMPLAINT.—No action constituting a reprisal, or threat of reprisal, for making a complaint or for disclosing information to a privacy officer or civil liberties officer described in subsection (a) or (b), or to the Privacy and Civil Liberties Oversight Board, that indicates a possible violation of privacy protections or civil liberties in the administration of the programs and operations of the Federal Government relating to efforts to protect the Nation from terrorism shall be taken by any Federal employee in a position to take such action, unless the complaint was made or the information was disclosed with the knowledge that it was false or with willful disregard for its truth or falsity.

(f) PERIODIC REPORTS.—

(1) IN GENERAL.—The privacy officers and civil liberties officers of each department, agency, or element referred to or described in subsection (a) or (b) shall periodically, but not less than quarterly, submit a report on the activities of such officers—

(A)(i) to the appropriate committees of Congress, including the Committee on the Judiciary of the Senate, the Committee on the Judiciary of the House of Representatives, the Committee on Homeland Security and Governmental Affairs of the Senate, the Committee on Oversight and Government Reform of the House of Representatives, the Select Committee on Intelligence of the Senate, and the Permanent Select Committee on Intelligence of the House of Representatives;

(ii) to the head of such department, agency, or element; and

(iii) to the Privacy and Civil Liberties Oversight Board; and

(B) which shall be in unclassified form to the greatest extent possible, with a classified annex where necessary.

(2) CONTENTS.—Each report submitted under paragraph (1) shall include information on the discharge of each of the functions of the officer concerned, including—

(A) information on the number and types of reviews undertaken;

(B) the type of advice provided and the response given to such advice;

(C) the number and nature of the complaints received by the department, agency, or element concerned for alleged violations; and

(D) a summary of the disposition of such complaints, the reviews and inquiries conducted, and the impact of the activities of such officer.

(g) INFORMING THE PUBLIC.—Each privacy officer and civil liberties officer shall—

(1) make the reports of such officer, including reports to Congress, available to the public to the greatest extent that is consistent with the protection of classified information and applicable law; and

(2) otherwise inform the public of the activities of such officer, as appropriate and in a manner consistent with the protection of classified information and applicable law.

(h) SAVINGS CLAUSE.—Nothing in this section shall be construed to limit or otherwise supplant any other authorities or responsibilities provided by law to privacy officers or civil liberties officers.

SUBTITLE G—CONFORMING AND OTHER AMENDMENTS

CONFORMING AMENDMENTS RELATING TO ROLES OF DIRECTOR OF NATIONAL INTELLIGENCE AND DIRECTOR OF THE CENTRAL INTELLIGENCE AGENCY

SEC. 1071.

(a) NATIONAL SECURITY ACT OF 1947.—

(1) The National Security Act of 1947 (50 U.S.C. §401 et seq.) is amended by striking "Director of Central Intelligence" each place it appears in the following provisions and inserting "Director of National Intelligence":

(A) Section 101(h)(2)(A) (50 U.S.C. §402(h)(2)(A)).

(B) Section 101(h)(5) (50 U.S.C. §402(h)(5)).

(C) Section 101(i)(2)(A) (50 U.S.C. §402(i)(2)(A)).

(D) Section 101(j) (50 U.S.C. §402(j)).

(E) Section 105(a) (50 U.S.C. §403-5(a)).

(F) Section 105(b)(6)(A) (50 U.S.C. §403-5(b)(6)(A)).

(G) Section 105B(a)(1) (50 U.S.C. §403-5b(a)(1)).

(H) Section 105B(b) (50 U.S.C. §403-5b(b)), the first place it appears.

(I) Section 110(b) (50 U.S.C. §404e(b)).

(J) Section 110(c) (50 U.S.C. §404e(c)).

(K) Section 112(a)(1) (50 U.S.C. §404g(a)(1)).

(L) Section 112(d)(1) (50 U.S.C. §404g(d)(1)).

(M) Section 113(b)(2)(A) (50 U.S.C. §404h(b)(2)(A)).

(N) Section 114(a)(1) (50 U.S.C. §404i(a)(1)).

(O) Section 114(b)(1) (50 U.S.C. §404i(b)(1)).

(P) Section 115(a)(1) (50 U.S.C. §404j(a)(1)).

(Q) Section 115(b) (50 U.S.C. §404j(b)).

(R) Section 115(c)(1)(B) (50 U.S.C. §404j(c)(1)(B)).

(S) Section 116(a) (50 U.S.C. §404k(a)).

(T) Section 117(a)(1) (50 U.S.C. §404l(a)(1)).

(U) Section 303(a) (50 U.S.C. §405(a)), both places it appears.

(V) Section 501(d) (50 U.S.C. §413(d)).

(W) Section 502(a) (50 U.S.C. §413a(a)).

(X) Section 502(c) (50 U.S.C. §413a(c)).

(Y) Section 503(b) (50 U.S.C. §413b(b)).

(Z) Section 504(a)(3)(C) (50 U.S.C. §414(a)(3)(C)).

(AA) Section 504(d)(2) (50 U.S.C. §414(d)(2)).

(BB) Section 506A(a)(1) (50 U.S.C. §415a-1(a)(1)).

(CC) Section 603(a) (50 U.S.C. §423(a)).

(DD) Section 702(a)(1) (50 U.S.C. §432(a)(1)).

(EE) Section 702(a)(6)(B)(viii) (50 U.S.C. §432(a)(6)(B)(viii)).

(FF) Section 702(b)(1) (50 U.S.C. §432(b)(1)), both places it appears. (GG) Section 703(a)(1) (50 U.S.C. §432a(a)(1)).

(HH) Section 703(a)(6)(B)(viii) (50 U.S.C. §432a(a)(6)(B)(viii)).

(II) Section 703(b)(1) (50 U.S.C. §432a(b)(1)), both places it appears.

(JJ) Section 704(a)(1) (50 U.S.C. §432b(a)(1)).

(KK) Section 704(f)(2)(H) (50 U.S.C. §432b(f)(2)(H)).

(LL) Section 704(g)(1)) (50 U.S.C. §432b(g)(1)), both places it appears.

(MM) Section 1001(a) (50 U.S.C. §441g(a)).

(NN) Section 1102(a)(1) (50 U.S.C. §442a(a)(1)). (OO) Section 1102(b)(1) (50 U.S.C. §442a(b)(1)). (PP) Section 1102(c)(1) (50 U.S.C. §442a(c)(1)). (QQ) Section 1102(d) (50 U.S.C. §442a(d)).

(2) That Act is further amended by striking "of Central Intelligence" each place it appears in the following provisions:

(A) Section 105(a)(2) (50 U.S.C. §403-5(a)(2)).

(B) Section 105B(a)(2) (50 U.S.C. §403-5b(a)(2)).

(C) Section 105B(b) (50 U.S.C. §403-5b(b)), the second place it appears.

(3) That Act is further amended by striking "Director" each place it appears in the following provisions and inserting "Director of National Intelligence":

(A) Section 114(c) (50 U.S.C. §404i(c)).

(B) Section 116(b) (50 U.S.C. §404k(b)).

(C) Section 1001(b) (50 U.S.C. §441g(b)).

(D) Section 1001(c) (50 U.S.C. §441g(c)), the first place it appears.

(E) Section 1001(d)(1)(B) (50 U.S.C. §441g(d)(1)(B)).

(F) Section 1001(e) (50 U.S.C. §441g(e)), the first place it appears.

(4) Section 114A of that Act (50 U.S.C. §404i-1) is amended by striking "Director of Central Intelligence" and inserting "Director of National Intelligence, the Director of the Central Intelligence Agency"

(5) Section 504(a)(2) of that Act (50 U.S.C. §414(a)(2)) is amended by striking "Director of Central Intelligence" and inserting "Director of the Central Intelligence Agency".

(6) Section 701 of that Act (50 U.S.C. §431) is amended—

(A) in subsection (a), by striking "Operational files of the Central Intelligence Agency may be exempted by the Director of Central Intelligence" and inserting "The Director of the Central Intelligence Agency, with the coordination of the Director of National Intelligence, may exempt operational files of the Central Intelligence Agency"; and

(B) in subsection (g)(1), by striking "Director of Central Intelligence" and inserting "Director of the Central Intelligence Agency and the Director of National Intelligence".

(7) The heading for section 114 of that Act (50 U.S.C. §404i) is amended to read as follows:

"ADDITIONAL ANNUAL REPORTS FROM THE DIRECTOR OF NATIONAL INTELLIGENCE".

(b) CENTRAL INTELLIGENCE AGENCY ACT OF 1949.—

(1) The Central Intelligence Agency Act of 1949 (50 U.S.C. §403a et seq.) is amended by striking "Director of Central Intelligence" each place it appears in the following provisions and inserting "Director of National Intelligence":

    (A) Section 6 (50 U.S.C. §403g).

    (B) Section 17(f) (50 U.S.C. §403q(f)), both places it appears.

(2) That Act is further amended by striking "of Central Intelligence" in each of the following provisions:

    (A) Section 2 (50 U.S.C. §403b).

    (B) Section 16(c)(1)(B) (50 U.S.C. §403p(c)(1)(B)).

    (C) Section 17(d)(1) (50 U.S.C. §403q(d)(1)).

    (D) Section 20(c) (50 U.S.C. §403t(c)).

(3) That Act is further amended by striking "Director of Central Intelligence" each place it appears in the following provisions and inserting "Director of the Central Intelligence Agency":

    (A) Section 14(b) (50 U.S.C. §403n(b)).

    (B) Section 16(b)(2) (50 U.S.C. §403p(b)(2)).

    (C) Section 16(b)(3) (50 U.S.C. §403p(b)(3)), both places it appears.

    (D) Section 21(g)(1) (50 U.S.C. §403u(g)(1)).

    (E) Section 21(g)(2) (50 U.S.C. §403u(g)(2)).

(c) CENTRAL INTELLIGENCE AGENCY RETIREMENT ACT.—Section 101 of the Central Intelligence Agency Retirement Act (50 U.S.C. §2001) is amended by striking paragraph (2) and inserting the following new paragraph (2):

    "(2) DIRECTOR.—The term "Director" means the Director of the Central Intelligence Agency.".

(d) CIA VOLUNTARY SEPARATION PAY ACT.—Subsection (a)(1) of section 2 of the Central Intelligence Agency Voluntary Separation Pay Act (50 U.S.C. §2001 note) is amended to read as follows:

    "(1) the term "Director" means the Director of the Central Intelligence Agency;".

(e) FOREIGN INTELLIGENCE SURVEILLANCE ACT OF 1978.—(1) The Foreign Intelligence Surveillance Act of 1978 (50 U.S.C. §1801 et seq.) is amended by striking "Director of Central Intelligence" each place it appears and inserting "Director of National Intelligence".

(f) CLASSIFIED INFORMATION PROCEDURES ACT.—Section 9(a) of the Classified Information Procedures Act (5 U.S.C. App.) is amended by striking "Director of Central Intelligence" and inserting "Director of National Intelligence".

(g) INTELLIGENCE AUTHORIZATION ACTS.—

(1) PUBLIC LAW 103-359- Section 811(c)(6)(C) of the Counterintelligence and Security Enhancements Act of 1994 (title VIII of Public Law 103-359) is amended by striking "Director of Central Intelligence" and inserting "Director of National Intelligence".

(2) PUBLIC LAW 107-306-

    (A) The Intelligence Authorization Act for Fiscal Year 2003 (Public Law 107-306) is amended by striking "Director of Central Intelligence, acting as the head of the intelligence community," each place it appears in the following provisions and inserting "Director of National Intelligence":

        (i) Section 313(a) (50 U.S.C. §404n(a)).

        (ii) Section 343(a)(1) (50 U.S.C. §404n-2(a)(1))

    (B) That Act is further amended by striking "Director of Central Intelligence" each place it appears in the following provisions and inserting "Director of National Intelligence":

(i) Section 904(e)(4) (50 U.S.C. §402c(e)(4)).

(ii) Section 904(e)(5) (50 U.S.C. §402c(e)(5)).

(iii) Section 904(h) (50 U.S.C. §402c(h)), each place it appears.

(iv) Section 904(m) (50 U.S.C. §402c(m)).

(C) Section 341 of that Act (50 U.S.C. §404n-1) is amended by striking "Director of Central Intelligence, acting as the head of the intelligence community, shall establish in the Central Intelligence Agency" and inserting "Director of National Intelligence shall establish within the Central Intelligence Agency".

(D) Section 352(b) of that Act (50 U.S.C. §404-3 note) is amended by striking "Director" and inserting "Director of National Intelligence".

(3) PUBLIC LAW 108-177-

(A) The Intelligence Authorization Act for Fiscal Year 2004 (Public Law 108-177) is amended by striking "Director of Central Intelligence" each place it appears in the following provisions and inserting "Director of National Intelligence":

(i) Section 317(a) (50 U.S.C. §403-3 note).

(ii) Section 317(h)(1).

(iii) Section 318(a) (50 U.S.C. §441g note).

(iv) Section 319(b) (50 U.S.C. §403 note).

(v) Section 341(b) (28 U.S.C. §519 note).

(vi) Section 357(a) (50 U.S.C. §403 note).

(vii) Section 504(a) (117 Stat. 2634), both places it appears.

(B) Section 319(f)(2) of that Act (50 U.S.C. §403 note) is amended by striking "Director" the first place it appears and inserting "Director of National Intelligence".

(C) Section 404 of that Act (18 U.S.C. §4124 note) is amended by striking "Director of Central Intelligence" and inserting "Director of the Central Intelligence Agency".

OTHER CONFORMING AMENDMENTS

SEC. 1072.

(a) NATIONAL SECURITY ACT OF 1947.—

(1) Section 101(j) of the National Security Act of 1947 (50 U.S.C. §402(j)) is amended by striking "Deputy Director of Central Intelligence" and inserting "Principal Deputy Director of National Intelligence".

(2) Section 105(a) of that Act (50 U.S.C. §403-5(a)) is amended by striking "The Secretary" in the matter preceding paragraph (1) and inserting "Consistent with sections 102 and 102A, the Secretary".

(3) Section 105(b) of that Act (50 U.S.C. §403-5(b)) is amended by striking "103 and 104" in the matter preceding paragraph (1) and inserting "102 and 102A".

(4) Section 112(d)(1) of that Act (50 U.S.C. §404g(d)(1)) is amended by striking "section 103(c)(6) of this Act" and inserting "section 102A(i) of this Act".

(5) Section 116(b) of that Act (50 U.S.C. §404k(b)) is amended by striking "to the Deputy Director of Central Intelligence, or with respect to employees of the Central Intelligence Agency, the Director may delegate such authority to the Deputy Director for Operations" and inserting "to the Principal Deputy Director of National Intelligence, or with respect to employees of the Central Intelligence Agency, to the Director of the Central Intelligence Agency".

(6) Section 506A(b)(1) of that Act (50 U.S.C. §415a-1(b)(1)) is amended by striking "Office of the Deputy Director of Central Intelligence" and inserting "Office of the Director of National Intelligence".

(7) Section 701(c)(3) of that Act (50 U.S.C. §431(c)(3)) is amended by striking "Office of

the Director of Central Intelligence" and inserting "Office of the Director of National Intelligence".

(8) Section 1001(b) of that Act (50 U.S.C. §441g(b)) is amended by striking "Assistant Director of Central Intelligence for Administration" and inserting "Office of the Director of National Intelligence".

(b) CENTRAL INTELLIGENCE AGENCY ACT OF 1949.—Section 6 of the Central Intelligence Agency Act of 1949 (50 U.S.C. §403g) is amended by striking "section 103(c)(7) of the National Security Act of 1947 (50 U.S.C. §4033(c)(7))" and inserting "section 102A(i) of the National Security Act of 1947".

(c) CENTRAL INTELLIGENCE AGENCY RETIREMENT ACT.—Section 201(c) of the Central Intelligence Agency Retirement Act (50 U.S.C. §2011(c)) is amended by striking "paragraph (6) of section 103(c) of the National Security Act of 1947 (50 U.S.C. §403-3(c)) that the Director of Central Intelligence" and inserting "section 102A(i) of the National Security Act of 1947 (50 U.S.C. §403-3(c)(1)) that the Director of National Intelligence".

(d) INTELLIGENCE AUTHORIZATION ACTS.—

(1) PUBLIC LAW 107-306-

(A) Section 343(c) of the Intelligence Authorization Act for Fiscal Year 2003 (Public Law 107-306; 50 U.S.C. §404n-2(c)) is amended by striking "section 103(c)(6) of the National Security Act of 1947 (50 U.S.C. §403-3((c)(6))" and inserting "section 102A(i) of the National Security Act of 1947 (50 U.S.C. §403-3(c)(1))".

(B)(i) Section 902 of that Act (also known as the Counterintelligence Enhancements Act of 2002) (50 U.S.C. §402b) is amended by striking "President" each place it appears and inserting "Director of National Intelligence".

(ii) Section 902(a)(2) of that Act is amended by striking "Director of Central Intelligence" and inserting "Director of the Central Intelligence Agency".

(C) Section 904 of that Act (50 U.S.C. §402c) is amended—

(i) in subsection (c), by striking "Office of the Director of Central Intelligence" and inserting "Office of the Director of National Intelligence"; and

(ii) in subsection (l), by striking "Office of the Director of Central Intelligence" and inserting "Office of the Director of National Intelligence".

(2) PUBLIC LAW 108-177-

(A) Section 317 of the Intelligence Authorization Act for Fiscal Year 2004 (Public Law 108-177; 50 U.S.C. §403-3 note) is amended—

(i) in subsection (g), by striking "Assistant Director of Central Intelligence for Analysis and Production" and inserting "Deputy Director of National Intelligence"; and

(ii) in subsection (h)(2)(C), by striking "Assistant Director" and inserting "Deputy Director of National Intelligence".

(B) Section 318(e) of that Act (50 U.S.C. §441g note) is amended by striking "Assistant Director of Central Intelligence for Analysis and Production" and inserting "Deputy Director of National Intelligence".

ELEMENTS OF INTELLIGENCE COMMUNITY UNDER NATIONAL SECURITY ACT OF 1947

SEC. 1073. Paragraph (4) of section 3 of the National Security Act of 1947 (50 U.S.C. §401a) is amended to read as follows:

"(4) The term "intelligence community" includes the following: "(A) The Office of the Director of National Intelligence. "(B) The Central Intelligence Agency. "(C) The National Security Agency. "(D) The Defense Intelligence Agency. "(E) The National Geospatial-Intelligence Agency. "(F) The National Reconnaissance Office. "(G) Other offices within the Department of Defense for the collection of specialized national intelligence through reconnaissance programs. "(H) The intelligence elements of the Army, the Navy, the Air Force, the Marine Corps, the Federal Bureau of Investigation, and the Department of Energy. "(I) The Bureau of Intelligence and Research of the Department of State. "(J) The Office of Intelligence and Analysis of the Department of the Treasury. "(K) The elements of the Department of Homeland Security concerned with the analysis of intelligence information, including the Office of Intelligence of the Coast Guard. "(L) Such other elements of any other department or agency as may be designated by the President, or designated jointly by the Director of National Intelligence and the head of the department or agency concerned, as an element of the intelligence community.".

REDESIGNATION OF NATIONAL FOREIGN INTELLIGENCE PROGRAM AS NATIONAL INTELLIGENCE PROGRAM

SEC. 1074.
(a) REDESIGNATION.—Paragraph (6) of section 3 of the National Security Act of 1947 (50 U.S.C. §401a) is amended by striking "Foreign".
(b) CONFORMING AMENDMENTS.—
(1)(A) Section 506 of the National Security Act of 1947 (50 U.S.C. §415a) is amended—
(i) in subsection (a), by striking "National Foreign Intelligence Program" and inserting "National Intelligence Program"; and
(ii) in the section heading, by striking "FOREIGN".
(B) Section 105 of that Act (50 U.S.C. §403-5) is amended—
(i) in paragraphs (2) and (3) of subsection (a), by striking "National Foreign Intelligence Program" and inserting "National Intelligence Program"; and
(ii) in the section heading, by striking "FOREIGN".
(2) Section 17(f) of the Central Intelligence Agency Act of 1949 (50 U.S.C. §403q(f)) is amended by striking "National Foreign Intelligence Program" and inserting "National Intelligence Program".

REPEAL OF SUPERSEDED AUTHORITY
SEC. 1075. Section 111 of the National Security Act of 1947 (50 U.S.C. §404f) is repealed.

CLERICAL AMENDMENTS TO NATIONAL SECURITY ACT OF 1947
SEC. 1076. The table of contents in the first section of the National Security Act of 1947 is amended—
(1) by striking the items relating to sections 102 through 105 and inserting the following new items: "SEC. 101A. Joint Intelligence Community Council. "SEC. 102. Director of National Intelligence. "SEC. 102A. Responsibilities and authorities of the Director of National Intelligence. "SEC. 103. Office of the Director of National Intelligence. "SEC. 103A. Deputy Directors of National Intelligence. "SEC. 103B. National Intelligence Council. "SEC. 103C. General Counsel. "SEC. 103D. Civil Liberties Protection Officer. "SEC. 103E. Director of Science and Technology. "SEC. 103F. National Counterintelligence Executive. "SEC. 104. Central Intelligence Agency. "SEC. 104A. Director of the Central Intelligence Agency. "SEC. 105. Responsibilities of the Secretary of Defense pertaining to the National Intelligence Program.";
(2) by striking the item relating to section 111;
(3) by striking the item relating to section 114 and inserting the following new item: "SEC. 114. Additional annual reports from the Director of National Intelligence.";

(4) by inserting after the item relating to section 118 the following new items: "SEC. 119. National Counterterrorism Center. "SEC. 119A. National Counter Proliferation Center. "SEC. 119B. National intelligence centers.

(5) by striking the item relating to section 506 and inserting the following new item: "SEC. 506. Specificity of National Intelligence Program budget amounts for counterterrorism, counterproliferation, counternarcotics, and counterintelligence."; and

(6) by inserting after the item relating to section 1001 the following new items: "SEC. 1002. Framework for cross-disciplinary education and training. "SEC. 1003. Intelligence Community Scholarship Program.".

CONFORMING AMENDMENTS RELATING TO PROHIBITING DUAL SERVICE OF THE DIRECTOR OF THE CENTRAL INTELLIGENCE AGENCY

SEC. 1077. Section 1 of the Central Intelligence Agency Act of 1949 (50 U.S.C. §403a) is amended—

(1) by redesignating paragraphs (a), (b), and (c) as paragraphs (1), (2), and (3), respectively; and

(2) by striking paragraph (2), as so redesignated, and inserting the following new paragraph (2): "(2) "Director" means the Director of the Central Intelligence Agency; and".

AUTHORITY TO ESTABLISH INSPECTOR GENERAL FOR THE OFFICE OF THE DIRECTOR OF NATIONAL INTELLIGENCE

SEC. 1078. The Inspector General Act of 1978 (5 U.S.C. App.) is amended by inserting after section 8J the following new section: "AUTHORITY TO ESTABLISH INSPECTOR GENERAL OF THE OFFICE OF THE DIRECTOR OF NATIONAL INTELLIGENCE"

SEC. 8K. If the Director of National Intelligence determines that an Office of Inspector General would be beneficial to improving the operations and effectiveness of the Office of the Director of National Intelligence, the Director of National Intelligence is authorized to establish, with any of the duties, responsibilities, and authorities set forth in this Act, an Office of Inspector General.".

ETHICS MATTERS

SEC. 1079.

(a) POLITICAL SERVICE OR PERSONNEL.—Section 7323(b)(2)(B)(i) of title 5, United States Code, is amended—

(1) in subclause (XII), by striking "or" at the end; and

(2) by inserting after subclause (XIII) the following new subclause: "(XIV) the Office of the Director of National Intelligence; or".

(b) DELETION OF INFORMATION ABOUT FOREIGN GIFTS.—Section 7342(f)(4) of title 5, United States Code, is amended—

(1) by inserting "(A)" after "(4)";

(2) in subparagraph (A), as so designated, by striking "the Director of Central Intelligence" and inserting "the Director of the Central Intelligence Agency"; and

(3) by adding at the end the following new subparagraph: "(B) In transmitting such listings for the Office of the Director of National Intelligence, the Director of National Intelligence may delete the information described in subparagraphs (A) and (C) of paragraphs (2) and (3) if the Director certifies in writing to the Secretary of State that the publication of such information could adversely affect United States intelligence sources.".

(c) EXEMPTION FROM FINANCIAL DISCLOSURES.—Section 105(a)(1) of the Ethics in Government Act (5 U.S.C. App.) is amended by inserting "the Office of the Director of National Intelligence," before "the Central Intelligence Agency".

CONSTRUCTION OF AUTHORITY OF DIRECTOR OF NATIONAL INTELLIGENCE TO ACQUIRE AND MANAGE PROPERTY AND SERVICES

SEC. 1080. Section 113(e) of title 40, United States Code, is amended—
    (1) in paragraph (18), by striking "or" at the end;
    (2) in paragraph (19), by striking the period at the end and inserting "; or"; and
    (3) by adding at the end the following new paragraph: "(20) the Office of the Director of National Intelligence.".

GENERAL REFERENCES.

SEC. 1081.

(a) DIRECTOR OF CENTRAL INTELLIGENCE AS HEAD OF INTELLIGENCE COMMUNITY.—Any reference to the Director of Central Intelligence or the Director of the Central Intelligence Agency in the Director's capacity as the head of the intelligence community in any law, regulation, document, paper, or other record of the United States shall be deemed to be a reference to the Director of National Intelligence.

(b) DIRECTOR OF CENTRAL INTELLIGENCE AS HEAD OF CIA.—Any reference to the Director of Central Intelligence or the Director of the Central Intelligence Agency in the Director's capacity as the head of the Central Intelligence Agency in any law, regulation, document, paper, or other record of the United States shall be deemed to be a reference to the Director of the Central Intelligence Agency.

(c) COMMUNITY MANAGEMENT STAFF.—Any reference to the Community Management Staff in any law, regulation, document, paper, or other record of the United States shall be deemed to be a reference to the staff of the Office of the Director of National Intelligence.

SUBTITLE H—TRANSFER, TERMINATION, TRANSITION, AND OTHER PROVISIONS

TRANSFER OF COMMUNITY MANAGEMENT STAFF

SEC. 1091.

(a) TRANSFER.—There shall be transferred to the Office of the Director of National Intelligence such staff of the Community Management Staff as of the date of the enactment of this Act as the Director of National Intelligence determines to be appropriate, including all functions and activities discharged by the Community Management Staff as of that date.

(b) ADMINISTRATION.—The Director of National Intelligence shall administer the Community Management Staff after the date of the enactment of this Act as a component of the Office of the Director of National Intelligence under section 103 of the National Security Act of 1947, as amended by section 1011(a) of this Act.

TRANSFER OF TERRORIST THREAT INTEGRATION CENTER

SEC. 1092.

(a) TRANSFER.—There shall be transferred to the National Counterterrorism Center the Terrorist Threat Integration Center (TTIC) or its successor entity, including all functions and activities discharged by the Terrorist Threat Integration Center or its successor entity as of the date of the enactment of this Act.

(b) ADMINISTRATION.—The Director of the National Counterterrorism Center shall administer the Terrorist Threat Integration Center after the date of the enactment of this Act as a component of the Directorate of Intelligence of the National Counterterrorism Center under section 119(i) of the National Security Act of 1947, as added by section 1021(a) of this Act.

TERMINATION OF POSITIONS OF ASSISTANT DIRECTORS OF CENTRAL INTELLIGENCE

SEC. 1093.

(a) TERMINATION.—The positions referred to in subsection (b) are hereby abolished.

(b) COVERED POSITIONS.—The positions referred to in this subsection are as follows:

> (1) The Assistant Director of Central Intelligence for Collection.
>
> (2) The Assistant Director of Central Intelligence for Analysis and Production.
>
> (3) The Assistant Director of Central Intelligence for Administration.

IMPLEMENTATION PLAN

SEC. 1094. The President shall transmit to Congress a plan for the implementation of this title and the amendments made by this title. The plan shall address, at a minimum, the following:

> (1) The transfer of personnel, assets, and obligations to the Director of National Intelligence pursuant to this title.
>
> (2) Any consolidation, reorganization, or streamlining of activities transferred to the Director of National Intelligence pursuant to this title.
>
> (3) The establishment of offices within the Office of the Director of National Intelligence to implement the duties and responsibilities of the Director of National Intelligence as described in this title.
>
> (4) Specification of any proposed disposition of property, facilities, contracts, records, and other assets and obligations to be transferred to the Director of National Intelligence.
>
> (5) Recommendations for additional legislative or administrative action as the President considers appropriate.

DIRECTOR OF NATIONAL INTELLIGENCE REPORT ON IMPLEMENTATION OF INTELLIGENCE COMMUNITY REFORM

SEC. 1095.

(a) REPORT.—Not later than one year after the effective date of this Act, the Director of National Intelligence shall submit to the congressional intelligence committees a report on the progress made in the implementation of this title, including the amendments made by this title. The report shall include a comprehensive description of the progress made, and may include such recommendations for additional legislative or administrative action as the Director considers appropriate.

(b) CONGRESSIONAL INTELLIGENCE COMMITTEES DEFINED.—In this section, the term "congressional intelligence committees" means—

> (1) the Select Committee on Intelligence of the Senate; and
>
> (2) the Permanent Select Committee on Intelligence of the House of Representatives.

TRANSITIONAL AUTHORITIES

SEC. 1096.

(a) IN GENERAL.—Upon the request of the Director of National Intelligence, the head of any executive agency may, on a reimbursable basis, provide services or detail personnel to the Director of National Intelligence.

(b) TRANSFER OF PERSONNEL.—In addition to any other authorities available under law for such purposes, in the fiscal year after the effective date of this Act, the Director of National Intelligence—

> (1) is authorized within the Office of the Director of National Intelligence 500 new personnel billets; and

> (2) with the approval of the Director of the Office of Management and Budget, may detail not more than 150 personnel funded within the National Intelligence Program to the Office of the Director of National Intelligence for a period of not more than 2 years.

EFFECTIVE DATES

SEC. 1097.

(a) IN GENERAL.—Except as otherwise expressly provided in this Act, this title and the amendments made by this title shall take effect not later than six months after the date of the enactment of this Act.

(b) SPECIFIC EFFECTIVE DATES.—

> (1)(A) Not later than 60 days after the date of the appointment of the first Director of National Intelligence, the Director of National Intelligence shall first appoint individuals to positions within the Office of the Director of National Intelligence.

>> (B) Subparagraph (A) shall not apply with respect to the Principal Deputy Director of National Intelligence.

> (2) Not later than 180 days after the effective date of this Act, the President shall transmit to Congress the implementation plan required by section 1094.

> (3) Not later than one year after the date of the enactment of this Act, the Director of National Intelligence shall prescribe regulations, policies, procedures, standards, and guidelines required under section 102A of the National Security Act of 1947, as amended by section 1011(a) of this Act.

SUBTITLE I—OTHER MATTERS

STUDY OF PROMOTION AND PROFESSIONAL MILITARY EDUCATION SCHOOL SELECTION RATES FOR MILITARY INTELLIGENCE OFFICERS

SEC. 1101.

(a) STUDY.—The Secretary of Defense shall conduct a study of the promotion selection rates, and the selection rates for attendance at professional military education schools, of intelligence officers of the Armed Forces, particularly in comparison to the rates for other officers of the same Armed Force who are in the same grade and competitive category.

(b) REPORT.—The Secretary shall submit to the Committees on Armed Services of the Senate and House of Representatives a report providing the Secretary's findings resulting from the study under subsection (a) and the Secretary's recommendations (if any) for such changes in law as the Secretary considers needed to ensure that intelligence officers, as a group, are selected for promotion, and for attendance at professional military education schools, at rates not less than the rates for all line (or the equivalent) officers of the same Armed Force (both in the zone and below the zone) in the same grade. The report shall be submitted not later than April 1, 2005.

EXTENSION AND IMPROVEMENT OF AUTHORITIES OF PUBLIC INTEREST DECLASSIFICATION BOARD

SEC. 1102.

(a) DIRECTION.—Section 703(a) of the Public Interest Declassification Act of 2000 (title

VII of Public Law 106-567; 114 Stat. 2856; 50 U.S.C. §435 note) is amended—
    (1) by inserting "(1)" after "ESTABLISHMENT-"; and
    (2) by adding at the end the following new paragraph: "(2) The Board shall report directly to the President or, upon designation by the President, the Vice President, the Attorney General, or other designee of the President. The other designee of the President under this paragraph may not be an agency head or official authorized to classify information under Executive Order 12958, or any successor order.".
(b) PURPOSES.—Section 703(b) of that Act (114 Stat. 2856) is amended by
adding at the end the following new paragraph: "(5) To review and make recommendations to the President in a timely manner with respect to any congressional request, made by the committee of jurisdiction, to declassify certain records or to reconsider a declination to declassify specific records.".
(c) RECOMMENDATIONS ON SPECIAL SEARCHES.—Section 704(c)(2)(A) of that Act (114 Stat. 2860) is amended by inserting before the period the following: ", and also including specific requests for the declassification of certain records or for the reconsideration of declinations to declassify specific records'.
(d) DECLASSIFICATION REVIEWS.—Section 704 of that Act (114 Stat. 2859) is further amended by adding at the end the following new subsection: "(e) DECLASSIFICATION REVIEWS.—If requested by the President, the Board shall review in a timely manner certain records or declinations to declassify specific records, the declassification of which has been the subject of specific congressional request described in section 703(b)(5).".
(e) NOTIFICATION OF REVIEW.—Section 706 of that Act (114 Stat. 2861) is
amended by adding at the end the following new subsection: "(f) NOTIFICATION OF REVIEW.—In response to a specific congressional request for declassification review described in section 703(b)(5), the Board shall advise the originators of the request in a timely manner whether the Board intends to conduct such review.".
(f) EXTENSION.—Section 710(b) of that Act (114 Stat. 2864) is amended by striking "4 years" and inserting "8 years".

SEVERABILITY

SEC. 1103. If any provision of this Act, or an amendment made by this Act, or the application of such provision to any person or circumstance is held invalid, the remainder of this Act, or the application of such provision to persons or circumstances other those to which such provision is held invalid shall not be affected thereby.

TITLE III—SECURITY CLEARANCES SECURITY CLEARANCES; LIMITATIONS
SEC. 3002.
(a) DEFINITIONS.—In this section:
    (1) CONTROLLED SUBSTANCE.—The term 'controlled substance' has the meaning given that term in section 102 of the Controlled Substances Act (21 U.S.C. 802).
    (2) COVERED PERSON.—The term 'covered person' means—
        (A) an officer or employee of a Federal agency;
        (B) a member of the Army, Navy, Air Force, or Marine Corps who is on active duty or is in an active status; and
        (C) an officer or employee of a contractor of a Federal agency.
    (3) RESTRICTED DATA.—The term 'Restricted Data' has the meaning given that term in section 11 of the Atomic Energy Act of 1954 (42 U.S.C. 2014).

(4) SPECIAL ACCESS PROGRAM.—The term 'special access program' has the meaning given that term in section 4.1 of Executive Order No. 12958 (60 Fed. Reg. 19825).

(b) PROHIBITION.—After January 1, 2008, the head of a Federal agency may not grant or renew a security clearance for a covered person who is an unlawful user of a controlled substance or an addict (as defined in section 102(1) of the Controlled Substances Act (21 U.S.C. 802)).

(c) DISQUALIFICATION.—

(1) IN GENERAL.—After January 1, 2008, absent an express written waiver granted in accordance with paragraph (2), the head of a Federal agency may not grant or renew a security clearance described in paragraph (3) for a covered person who—

(A) has been convicted in any court of the United States of a crime, was sentenced to imprisonment for a term exceeding 1 year, and was incarcerated as a result of that sentence for not less than 1 year;

(B) has been discharged or dismissed from the Armed Forces under dishonorable conditions; or

(C) is mentally incompetent, as determined by an adjudicating authority, based on an evaluation by a duly qualified mental health professional employed by, or acceptable to and approved by, the United States Government and in accordance with the adjudicative guidelines required by subsection (d).

(2) WAIVER AUTHORITY.—In a meritorious case, an exception to the disqualification in this subsection may be authorized if there are mitigating factors. Any such waiver may be authorized only in accordance with—

(A) standards and procedures prescribed by, or under the authority of, an Executive order or other guidance issued by the President; or

(B) the adjudicative guidelines required by subsection (d).

(3) COVERED SECURITY CLEARANCES.—This subsection applies to security clearances that provide for access to—

(A) special access programs;

(B) Restricted Data; or

(C) any other information commonly referred to as 'sensitive compartmented information'.

(4) ANNUAL REPORT.—

(A) REQUIREMENT FOR REPORT.—Not later than February 1 of each year, the head of a Federal agency shall submit a report to the appropriate committees of Congress if such agency employs or employed a person for whom a waiver was granted in accordance with paragraph (2) during the preceding year. Such annual report shall not reveal the identity of such person, but shall include for each waiver issued the disqualifying factor under paragraph (1) and the reasons for the waiver of the disqualifying factor.

(B) DEFINITIONS.—In this paragraph:

(i) APPROPRIATE COMMITTEES OF CONGRESS.—The term 'appropriate committees of Congress' means, with respect to a report submitted under subparagraph (A) by the head of a Federal agency—

(I) the congressional defense committees;

(II) the congressional intelligence committees;

(III) the Committee on Homeland Security and Governmental Affairs of the Senate;

(IV) the Committee on Oversight and Government Reform of the House of Representatives; and

(V) each Committee of the Senate or the House of Representatives with oversight authority over such Federal agency.

(ii) CONGRESSIONAL DEFENSE COMMITTEES.—The term 'congressional defense committees' has the meaning given that term in section 101(a)(16) of title 10, United States Code.

(iii) CONGRESSIONAL INTELLIGENCE COMMITTEES.— The term 'congressional intelligence committees' has the meaning given that term in section 3 of the National Security Act of 1947 (50 U.S.C. 401a).

(d) ADJUDICATIVE GUIDELINES.—

(1) REQUIREMENT TO ESTABLISH.—The President shall establish adjudicative guidelines for determining eligibility for access to classified information.

(2) REQUIREMENTS RELATED TO MENTAL HEALTH.—The guidelines required by paragraph (1) shall—

(A) include procedures and standards under which a covered person is determined to be mentally incompetent and provide a means to appeal such a determination; and

(B) require that no negative inference concerning the standards in the guidelines may be raised solely on the basis of seeking mental health counseling.

Foreign Intelligence Surveillance Act of 1978

(Pub. L. 95–511 of October 25, 1978; 92 Stat. 1783, 50 U.S.C. ch.36 (1978), as amended (as reproduced by the ODNI Intelligence Community Legal Reference Book, 2012))

> AN ACT To authorize electronic surveillance to obtain foreign intelligence information.

Be it enacted by the Senate and House of Representatives of the United States of America in Congress assembled,

SHORT TITLE

That this Act may be cited as the "Foreign Intelligence Surveillance Act of 1978".

TABLE OF CONTENTS

TITLE I—ELECTRONIC SURVEILLANCE WITHIN THE UNITED STATES FOR FOREIGN INTELLIGENCE PURPOSES

DEFINITIONS

SECTION 101. [50 U.S.C. §1801] As used in this title:

(a) "Foreign power" means—

(1) a foreign government or any component, thereof, whether or not recognized by the United States;

(2) a faction of a foreign nation or nations, not substantially composed of United States persons;

(3) an entity that is openly acknowledged by a foreign government or governments to be directed and controlled by such foreign government or governments;

(4) a group engaged in international terrorism or activities in preparation therefor;

(5) a foreign-based political organization, not substantially composed of United States persons;

(6) an entity that is directed and controlled by a foreign government or governments; or

(7) an entity not substantially composed of United States persons that is engaged in the international proliferation of weapons of mass destruction.

(b) "Agent of a foreign power" means—

(1) any person other than a United States person, who—

(A) acts in the United States as an officer or employee of a foreign power, or as a member of a foreign power as defined in subsection (a)(4);

(B) acts for or on behalf of a foreign power which engages in clandestine intelligence activities in the United States contrary to the interests of the United States, when the circumstances of such person's presence in the United States indicate that such person may engage in such activities in the United States, or when such person knowingly aids or abets any person in the conduct of such activities or knowingly conspires with any person to engage in such activities;

(C) engages in international terrorism or activities in preparation therefore [sic];

(D) engages in the international proliferation of weapons of mass destruction, or activities in preparation therefor; or

(E) engages in the international proliferation of weapons of mass destruction, or activities in preparation therefor for or on behalf of a foreign power; or

(2) any person who—

(A) knowingly engages in clandestine intelligence gathering activities for or on behalf of a foreign power, which activities involve or may involve a violation of the criminal statutes of the United States;

(B) pursuant to the direction of an intelligence service or network of a foreign power, knowingly engages in any other clandestine intelligence activities for or on behalf of such foreign power, which activities involve or are about to involve a violation of the criminal statutes of the United States;

(C) knowingly engages in sabotage or international terrorism, or activities that are in preparation therefor, for or on behalf of a foreign power;

(D) knowingly enters the United States under a false or fraudulent identity for or on behalf of a foreign power or, while in the United States, knowingly assumes a false or fraudulent identity for or on behalf of a foreign power; or

(E) knowingly aids or abets any person in the conduct of activities described in subparagraph (A), (B), or (C) or knowingly conspires with any person to engage in activities described in subparagraph (A), (B), or (C).

(c) "International terrorism" means activities that—

(1) involve violent acts or acts dangerous to human life that are a violation of the criminal laws of the United States or of any State, or that would be a criminal violation if committed within the jurisdiction of the United States or any State;

(2) appear to be intended—

(A) to intimidate or coerce a civilian population;

(B) to influence the policy of a government by intimidation or coercion; or

(C) to affect the conduct of a government by assassination or kidnapping; and

(3) occur totally outside the United States, or transcend national boundaries in terms of the means by which they are accomplished, the persons they appear intended to coerce or intimidate, or the locale in which their perpetrators operate or seek asylum.

(d) "Sabotage" means activities that involve a violation of chapter 105 of title 18, United States Code, or that would involve such a violation if committed against the United States.

(e) "Foreign intelligence information" means—

(1) information that relates to, and if concerning a United States person is necessary to, the ability of the United States to protect against—

(A) actual or potential attack or other grave hostile acts of a foreign power or an agent of a foreign power;

(B) sabotage, international terrorism, or the international proliferation of weapons of mass destruction by a foreign power or an agent of a foreign power; or

(C) clandestine intelligence activities by an intelligence service or network of a foreign power or by an agent of a foreign power; or

(2) information with respect to a foreign power or foreign territory that relates to, and if concerning a United States person is necessary to—

(A) the national defense or the security of the United States; or

(B) the conduct of the foreign affairs of the United States.

(f) "Electronic surveillance" means—

(1) the acquisition by an electronic, mechanical, or other surveillance device of the contents of any wire or radio communications sent by or intended to be received by a particular, known United States person who is in the United States, if the contents are acquired by intentionally targeting that United States person, under circumstances in which a person has a reasonable expectation of privacy and a warrant would be required for law enforcement purposes;

(2) the acquisition by an electronic, mechanical, or other surveillance device of the contents of any wire communication to or from a person in the United States, without the consent of any party thereto, if such acquisition occurs in the United States, but does not include the acquisition of those communications of computer trespassers that would be permissible under section 2511(2)(i) of title 18, United States Code;

(3) the intentional acquisition by an electronic, mechanical, or other surveillance device of the contents of any radio communication, under circumstances in which a person has a reasonable expectation of privacy and a warrant would be required for law enforcement purposes, and if both the sender and all intended recipients are located within the United States; or

(4) the installation or use of an electronic, mechanical, or other surveillance device in the United States for monitoring to acquire information, other than from a wire or radio communication, under circumstances in which a person has a reasonable expectation of privacy and a warrant would be required for law enforcement purposes.

(g) "Attorney General" means the Attorney General of the United States (or Acting Attorney General), the Deputy Attorney General, or, upon, the designation of the Attorney General, the

Assistant Attorney General designated as the Assistant Attorney General for National Security under section 507A of title 28, United States Code.

(h) "Minimization procedures", with respect to electronic surveillance, means—

(1) specific procedures, which shall be adopted by the Attorney General, that are reasonably designed in light of the purpose and technique of the particular surveillance, to minimize the acquisition and retention, and prohibit the dissemination, of nonpublicly available information concerning unconsenting United States persons consistent with the need of the United States to obtain, produce, and disseminate foreign intelligence information;

(2) procedures that require that nonpublicly available information, which is not foreign intelligence information, as defined in subsection (c)(1), shall not be disseminated in a manner that identifies any United States person, without such person's consent, unless such person's identity is necessary to understand foreign intelligence information or assess its importance;

(3) notwithstanding paragraphs (1) and (2), procedures that allow for the retention and dissemination of information that is evidence of a crime which has been, is being, or is about to be committed and that is to be retained or disseminated for law enforcement purposes; and

(4) notwithstanding paragraphs (1), (2), and (3), with respect to any electronic surveillance approved pursuant to section 102(a), procedures that require that no contents of any communication to which a United States person is a party shall be disclosed, disseminated, or used for any purpose or retained for longer than 72 hours unless a court order under section 105 is obtained or unless the Attorney General determines that the information indicates a threat of death or serious bodily harm to any person.

(i) "United States person" means a citizen of the United States, an alien lawfully admitted for permanent residence (as defined in section 101(a)(20) of the Immigration and Nationality Act), an unincorporated association a substantial number of members of which are citizens of the United States or aliens lawfully admitted for permanent residence, or a corporation which is incorporated in the

United States, but does not include a corporation or an association which is a foreign power, as defined in subsection (a) (1), (2), or (3).

(j) "United States", when used in a geographic sense, means all areas under the territorial sovereignty of the United States and the Trust Territory of the Pacific Islands.

(k) "Aggrieved person" means a person who is the target of an electronic surveillance or any other person whose communications or activities were subject to electronic surveillance.

(l) "Wire communication" means any communications while it is being carried by a wire, cable, or other like connection furnished or operated by any person engaged as a common carrier in providing or operating such facilities for the transmission of interstate or foreign communications.

(m) "Person" means any individual, including any officer or employee of the Federal Government, or any group, entity, association, corporation, or foreign power.

(n) "Contents", when used with respect to a communication, includes any information concerning the identity of the parties to such communications or the existence, substance, purport, or meaning of that communication.

(o) "State" means any State of the United States, the District of Columbia, the Commonwealth of Puerto Rico, the Trust Territory of the Pacific Islands, an any territory or possession of the United States.

(p) 'Weapon of mass destruction' means—

(1) any explosive, incendiary, or poison gas device that is designed, intended, or has the capability to cause a mass casualty incident;

(2) any weapon that is designed, intended, or has the capability to cause death or serious bodily injury to a significant number of persons through the release, dissemination, or impact of toxic or poisonous chemicals or their precursors;

(3) any weapon involving a biological agent, toxin, or vector (as such terms are defined in section 178 of title 18, United States Code) that is designed, intended, or has the capability to cause death, illness, or serious bodily injury to a significant number of persons; or

(4) any weapon that is designed, intended, or has the capability to release radiation or radioactivity causing death, illness, or serious bodily injury to a significant number of persons.'.

AUTHORIZATION FOR ELECTRONIC SURVEILLANCE FOR FOREIGN INTELLIGENCE PURPOSES

SEC. 102. [50 U.S.C. §1802]

(a)(1) Notwithstanding any other law, the President, through the Attorney General, may authorize electronic surveillance without a court order under this title to acquire foreign intelligence information for periods of up to one year if the Attorney General certifies in writing under oath that—

    (A) the electronic surveillance is solely directed at—

        (i) the acquisition of the contents of communications transmitted by means of communications used exclusively between or among foreign powers, as defined in section 101(a) (1), (2), or (3); or

        (ii) the acquisition of technical intelligence, other than the spoken communications of individuals, from property or premises under the open and exclusive control of a foreign power, as defined in section 101(a) (1), (2), or (3);

    (B) there is no substantial likelihood that the surveillance will acquire the contents of any communications to which a United States person is a party; and

    (C) the proposed minimization procedures with respect to such surveillance meet the definition of minimization procedures under section 101(h); and if the Attorney General reports such minimization procedures and any changes thereto to the House Permanent Select Committee on Intelligence and the Senate Select Committee on Intelligence at least thirty days prior to their effective date, unless the Attorney General determines immediate action is required and notifies the committees immediately of such minimization procedures and the reason for their becoming effective immediately.

(2) An electronic surveillance authorized by this subsection may be conducted only in accordance with the Attorney General's certification and the minimization procedures adopted by him. The Attorney General shall assess compliance with such procedures and shall report such assessments to the House Permanent Select Committee on Intelligence and the Senate Select Committee on Intelligence under the provisions of section 108(a).

(3) The Attorney General shall immediately transmit under seal to the court established under section 103(a) a copy of his certification. Such certification shall be maintained under security measures established by the Chief Justice with the concurrence of the Attorney General, in consultation with the Director of National Intelligence, and shall remain sealed unless—

    (A) an application for a court order with respect to the surveillance is made under sections 101(h)(4) and 104; or

    (B) the certification is necessary to determine the legality of the surveillance under section 106(f).

(4) With respect to electronic surveillance authorized by this subsection, the Attorney General may direct a specified communication common carrier to—

(A) furnish all information, facilities, or technical assistance necessary to accomplish the electronic surveillance in such a manner as will protect its secrecy and produce a minimum of interference with the services that such carrier is providing its customers; and

(B) maintain under security procedures approved by the Attorney General and the Director of National Intelligence any records concerning the surveillance or the aid furnished which such carrier wishes to retain. The Government shall compensate, at the prevailing rate, such carrier for furnishing such aid.

(b) Applications for a court order under this title are authorized if the President has, by written authorization, empowered the Attormey General [sic] to approve applications to the court having jurisdiction under section 103, and a judge to whom an application is made may, notwithstanding any other law, grant an order, in conformity with section 105, approving electronic surveillance of a foreign power or an agent of a foreign power for the purpose of obtaining foreign intelligence information, except that the court shall not have jurisdiction to grant any order approving electronic surveillance directed solely as described in paragraph (1)(A) of subsection (a) unless such surveillance may involve the acquisition of communications of any United States person.

DESIGNATION OF JUDGES

SEC. 103. [50 U.S.C. §1803]

(a)(1) The Chief Justice of the United States shall publicly designate 11 district court judges from at least seven of the United States judicial circuits of whom no fewer than 3 shall reside within 20 miles of the District of Columbia who shall constitute a court which shall have jurisdiction to hear applications for and grant orders approving electronic surveillance anywhere within the United States under the procedures set forth in this Act, except that no judge designated under this subsection (except when sitting en banc under paragraph (2)) shall hear the same application for electronic surveillance under this Act which has been denied previously by another judge designated under this subsection. If any judge so designated denies an application for an order authorizing electronic surveillance under this Act, such judge shall provide immediately for the record a written statement of each reason for his decision and, on motion of the United States, the record shall be transmitted, under seal, to the court of review established in subsection (b).

(2)(A) The court established under this subsection may, on its own initiative, or upon the request of the Government in any proceeding or a party under section 501(f) or paragraph (4) or (5) of section 702(h), hold a hearing or rehearing, en banc, when ordered by a majority of the judges that constitute such court upon a determination that—

(i) en banc consideration is necessary to secure or maintain uniformity of the court's decisions; or

(ii) the proceeding involves a question of exceptional importance.

(B) Any authority granted by this Act to a judge of the court established under this subsection may be exercised by the court en banc. When exercising such authority, the court en banc shall comply with any requirements of this Act on the exercise of such authority.

(C) For purposes of this paragraph, the court en banc shall consist of all judges who constitute the court established under this subsection.

(b) The Chief Justice shall publicly designate three judges, one of whom shall be publicly designate as the presiding judge, from the United States district courts or courts of appeals who together shall comprise a court of review which shall have jurisdiction to review the denial of any application made under this Act. If such court determines that the application was properly denied, the court shall immediately provide for the record a written statement of each reason for its decision and, on petition of the United States for a writ of certiorari, the record shall be transmitted under seal to the Supreme Court, which shall have jurisdiction to review such decision.

(c) Proceedings under this Act shall be conducted as expeditiously as possible. The record of proceedings under this Act, including applications made and orders granted, shall be maintained under security measures established by the Chief Justice in consultation with the Attorney General and the Director of National Intelligence.

(d) Each judge designated under this section shall so serve for a maximum of seven years and shall not be eligible for redesignation, except that the judges first designated under subsection (a) shall be designated for terms of from one to seven years so that one term expires each year, and that judges first designated under subsection (b) shall be designated for terms of three, five, and seven years.

(e)(1) Three judges designated under subsection (a) who reside within 20 miles of the District of Columbia, or, if all of such judges are unavailable, other judges of the court established under subsection (a) as may be designated by the presiding judge of such court, shall comprise a petition review pool which shall have jurisdiction to review petitions filed pursuant to section 1861(f)(1) or 1881a(h)(4).

(2) Not later than 60 days after the date of the enactment of the USA PATRIOT Improvement and Reauthorization Act of 2005, the court established under subsection (a) shall adopt and, consistent with the protection of national security, publish procedures for the review of petitions filed pursuant to section 1861(f)(1) or 1881a(h)(4) by the panel established under paragraph (1). Such procedures shall provide that review of a petition shall be conducted in camera and shall also provide for the designation of an acting presiding judge.

(f)(1) A judge of the court established under subsection (a), the court established under subsection (b) or a judge of that court, or the Supreme Court of the United States or a justice of that court, may, in accordance with the rules of their respective courts, enter a stay of an order or an order modifying an order of the court established under subsection (a) or the court established under subsection (b) entered under any title of this Act, while the court established under subsection (a) conducts a rehearing, while an appeal is pending to the court established under subsection (b), or while a petition of certiorari is pending in the Supreme Court of the United States, or during the pendency of any review by that court.

(2) The authority described in paragraph (1) shall apply to an order entered under any provision of this Act.

(g)(1) The courts established pursuant to subsections (a) and (b) may establish such rules and procedures, and take such actions, as are reasonably necessary to administer their responsibilities under this Act.

(2) The rules and procedures established under paragraph (1), and any modifications of such rules and procedures, shall be recorded, and shall be transmitted to the following:

(A) All of the judges on the court established pursuant to subsection (a).

(B) All of the judges on the court of review established pursuant to subsection (b).

(C) The Chief Justice of the United States.

(D) The Committee on the Judiciary of the Senate.

(E) The Select Committee on Intelligence of the Senate.

(F) The Committee on the Judiciary of the House of Representatives.

(G) The Permanent Select Committee on Intelligence of the House of Representatives.

(3) The transmissions required by paragraph (2) shall be submitted in unclassified form, but may include a classified annex.

(i) Nothing in this Act shall be construed to reduce or contravene the inherent authority of the court established under subsection (a) to determine or enforce compliance with an order or a rule of such court or with a procedure approved by such court.

APPLICATION FOR AN ORDER

SEC. 104. [50 U.S.C. §1804]

(a) Each application for an order approving electronic surveillance under this title shall be made by a Federal officer in writing upon oath or affirmation to a judge having jurisdiction under section 103. Each application shall require the approval of the Attorney General based upon his finding that it satisfies the criteria and requirements of such application as set forth in this title. It shall include—

(1) the identity of the Federal officer making the application;

(2) the identity, if known, or a description of the specific target of the electronic surveillance;

(3) a statement of the facts and circumstances relied upon by the applicant to justify his belief that—

(A) the target of the electronic surveillance is a foreign power or an agent of a foreign power; and

(B) each of the facilities or places at which the electronic surveillance is directed is being used, or is about to be used, by a foreign power or an agent of a foreign power;

(4) a statement of the proposed minimization procedures;

(5) a description of the nature of the information sought and the type of communications or activities to be subjected to the surveillance;

(6) a certification or certifications by the Assistant to the President for National Security Affairs, an executive branch official or officials designated by the President from among those executive officers employed in the area of national security or defense and appointed by the President with the advice and consent of the Senate, or the Deputy Director of the Federal Bureau of Investigation, if designated by the President as a certifying official —

(A) that the certifying official deems the information sought to be foreign intelligence information;

(B) that a significant purpose of the surveillance is to obtain foreign intelligence information;

(C) that such information cannot reasonably be obtained by normal investigative techniques;

(D) that designates the type of foreign intelligence information being sought according to the categories described in section 101(e); and

(E) including a statement of the basis for the certification that—

(i) the information sought is the type of foreign intelligence information designated; and

(ii) such information cannot reasonably be obtained by normal investigative techniques;

(7) a summary statement of the means by which the surveillance will be effected and a statement whether physical entry is required to effect the surveillance;

(8) a statement of the facts concerning all previous applications that have been made to any judge under this title involving any of the persons, facilities, or places specified in the application, and the action taken on each previous application; and

(9) a statement of the period of time for which the electronic surveillance is required to be maintained, and if the nature of the intelligence gathering is such that the approval of the use of electronic surveillance under this title should not automatically terminate when

the described type of information has first been obtained, a description of facts supporting the belief that additional information of the same type will be obtained thereafter.

(b) The Attorney General may require any other affidavit or certification from any other officer in connection with the application.

(c) The judge may require the applicant to furnish such other information as may be necessary to make the determinations required by section 105.

(d) (1)(A) Upon written request of the Director of the Federal Bureau of Investigation, the Secretary of Defense, the Secretary of State, or the Director of National Intelligence, or the Director of the Central Intelligence Agency, the Attorney General shall personally review under subsection (a) an application under that subsection for a target described in section 101(b)(2).

> (B) Except when disabled or otherwise unavailable to make a request referred to in subparagraph (A), an official referred to in that subparagraph may not delegate the authority to make a request referred to in that subparagraph.
>
> (C) Each official referred to in subparagraph (A) with authority to make a request under that subparagraph shall take appropriate actions in advance to ensure that delegation of such authority is clearly established in the event such official is disabled or otherwise unavailable to make such request.

(2)(A) If as a result of a request under paragraph (1) the Attorney General determines not to approve an application under the second sentence of subsection (a) for purposes of making the application under this section, the Attorney General shall provide written notice of the determination to the official making the request for the review of the application under that paragraph. Except when disabled or otherwise unavailable to make a determination under the preceding sentence, the Attorney General may not delegate the responsibility to make a determination under that sentence. The Attorney General shall take appropriate actions in advance to ensure that delegation of such responsibility is clearly established in the event the Attorney General is disabled or otherwise unavailable to make such determination.

> (B) Notice with respect to an application under subparagraph (A) shall set forth the modifications, if any, of the application that are necessary in order for the Attorney General to approve the application under the second sentence of subsection (a) for purposes of making the application under this section.
>
> (C) Upon review of any modifications of an application set forth under subparagraph (B), the official notified of the modifications under this paragraph shall modify the application if such official determines that such modification is warranted. Such official shall supervise the making of any modification under this subparagraph. Except when disabled or otherwise unavailable to supervise the making of any modification under the preceding sentence, such official may not delegate the responsibility to supervise the making of any modification under that preceding sentence. Each such official shall take appropriate actions in advance to ensure that delegation of such responsibility is clearly established in the event such official is disabled or otherwise unavailable to supervise the making of such modification.

ISSUANCE OF AN ORDER
SEC. 105. [50 U.S.C. §1805]

(a) Upon an application made pursuant to section 104, the judge shall enter an ex parte order as requested or as modified approving the electronic surveillance if he finds that—

> (1) the application has been made by a Federal officer and approved by the Attorney General;

(2) on the basis of the facts submitted by the applicant there is probable cause to believe that—

(A) the target of the electronic surveillance is a foreign power or an agent of a foreign power: Provided, That no United States person may be considered a foreign power or an agent of a foreign power solely upon the basis of activities protected by the first amendment to the Constitution of the United States; and

(B) each of the facilities or places at which the electronic surveillance is directed is being used, or is about to be used, by a foreign power or an agent of a foreign power;

(3) the proposed minimization procedures meet the definition of minimization procedures under section 101(h); and

(4) the application which has been filed contains all statements and certifications required by section 104 and, if the target is a United States person, the certification or certifications are not clearly erroneous on the basis of the statement made under section 104(a)(7)(E) and any other information furnished under section 104(d).

(b) In determining whether or not probable cause exists for purposes of an order under subsection (a)(2), a judge may consider past activities of the target, as well as facts and circumstances relating to current or future activities of the target.

(c) (1) SPECIFICATIONS.—An order approving an electronic surveillance under this section shall specify—

(A) the identity, if known, or a description of the specific target of the electronic surveillance identified or described in the application pursuant to section 104(a)(3) of this Act;

(B) the nature and location of each of the facilities or places at which the electronic surveillance will be directed, if known;

(C) the type of information sought to be acquired and the type of communications or activities to be subjected to the surveillance;

(D) the means by which the electronic surveillance will be effected and whether physical entry will be used to effect the surveillance; and

(E) the period of time during which the electronic surveillance is approved.

(2) DIRECTIONS.—An order approving an electronic surveillance under this section shall direct—

(A) that the minimization procedures be followed;

(B) that, upon the request of the applicant, a specified communication or other common carrier, landlord, custodian, or other specified person, or in circumstances where the Court finds, based upon specific facts provided in the application, that the actions of the target of the application may have the effect of thwarting the identification of a specified person, such other persons, furnish the applicant forthwith all information, facilities, or technical assistance necessary to accomplish the electronic surveillance in such a manner as will protect its secrecy and produce a minimum of interference with the services that such carrier, landlord, custodian, or other person is providing that target of electronic surveillance;

(C) that such carrier, landlord, custodian, or other person maintain under security procedures approved by the Attorney General and the Director of National Intelligence any records concerning the surveillance or the aid furnished that such person wishes to retain; and

(D) that the applicant compensate, at the prevailing rate, such carrier, landlord, custodian, or other person for furnishing such aid.

(3) SPECIAL DIRECTIONS FOR CERTAIN ORDERS.—An order approving an electronic surveillance under this section in circumstances where the nature and location of each of

the facilities or places at which the surveillance will be directed is unknown shall direct the applicant to provide notice to the court within ten days after the date on which surveillance begins to be directed at any new facility or place, unless the court finds good cause to justify a longer period of up to 60 days, of—

   (A) the nature and location of each new facility or place at which the electronic surveillance is directed;

   (B) the facts and circumstances relied upon by the applicant to justify the applicant's belief that each new facility or place at which the electronic surveillance is directed is or was being used, or is about to be used, by the target of the surveillance;

   (C) a statement of any proposed minimization procedures that differ from those contained in the original application or order, that may be necessitated by a change in the facility or place at which the electronic surveillance is directed; and

   (D) the total number of electronic surveillances that have been or are being conducted under the authority of the order.

(d)(1) An order issued under this section may approve an electronic surveillance for the period necessary to achieve its purpose, or for ninety days, whichever is less, except that

   (A) 1 an order under this section shall approve an electronic surveillance targeted against a foreign power, as defined in section 101(a), (1), (2), or (3), for the period specified in the application or for one year, whichever is less, and

   (B) an order under this Act for a surveillance targeted against an agent of a foreign power, who is not a United States person may be for the period specified in the application or for 120 days, whichever is less.

(2) Extensions of an order issued under this title may be granted on the same basis as an original order upon an application for an extension and new findings made in the same manner as required for an original order, except that

   (A) an extension of an order under this Act for a surveillance targeted against a foreign power, a defined in paragraph (5), (6), or (7) of section 101(a), or against a foreign power as defined in section 101(a)(4) that is not a United States person, may be for a period not to exceed one year if the judge finds probable cause to believe that no communication of any individual United States person will be acquired during the period, and

   (B) an extension of an order under this Act for a surveillance targeted against an agent of a foreign power who is not a United States person may be for a period not to exceed 1 year.

(3) At or before the end of the period of time for which electronic surveillance is approved by an order or an extension, the judge may assess compliance with the minimization procedures by reviewing the circumstances under which information concerning United States persons was acquired, retained, or disseminated.

(e)(1) Notwithstanding any other provision of this title, the Attorney General may authorize the emergency employment of electronic surveillance if the Attorney General—

   (A) reasonably determines that an emergency situation exists with respect to the employment of electronic surveillance to obtain foreign intelligence information before an order authorizing such surveillance can with due diligence be obtained;

   (B) reasonably determines that the factual basis for the issuance of an order under this title to approve such electronic surveillance exists;

   (C) informs, either personally or through a designee, a judge having jurisdiction under section 103 at the time of such authorization that the decision has been made to employ emergency electronic surveillance; and

   (D) makes an application in accordance with this title to a judge having jurisdiction under section 103 as soon as practicable, but not later than 7 days after the Attorney General authorizes such surveillance.

(2) If the Attorney General authorizes the emergency employment of electronic surveillance under paragraph (1), the Attorney General shall require that the minimization procedures required by this title for the issuance of a judicial order be followed.

(3) In the absence of a judicial order approving such electronic surveillance, the surveillance shall terminate when the information sought is obtained, when the application for the order is denied, or after the expiration of 7 days from the time of authorization by the Attorney General, whichever is earliest.

(4) A denial of the application made under this subsection may be reviewed as provided in section 103.

(5) In the event that such application for approval is denied, or in any other case where the electronic surveillance is terminated and no order is issued approving the surveillance, no information obtained or evidence derived from such surveillance shall be received in evidence or otherwise disclosed in any trial, hearing, or other proceeding in or before any court, grand jury, department, office, agency, regulatory body, legislative committee, or other authority of the United States, a State, or political subdivision thereof, and no information concerning any United States person acquired from such surveillance shall subsequently be used or disclosed in any other manner by Federal officers or employees without the consent of such person, except with the approval of the Attorney General if the information indicates a threat of death or serious bodily harm to any person.

(6) The Attorney General shall assess compliance with the requirements of paragraph (5).

(f) Notwithstanding any other provision of this Act, officers, employees, or agents of the United States are authorized in the normal course of their official duties to conduct electronic surveillance not targeted against the communications of any particular person or persons, under procedures approved by the Attorney General, solely to—

(1) test the capability of electronic equipment, if—

(A) it is not reasonable to obtain the consent of the persons incidentally subjected to the surveillance;

(B) the test is limited in extent and duration to that necessary to determine to capability of the equipment;

(C) the contents of any communication acquired are retained and used only for the purpose of determining the capability of the equipment, are disclosed only to test personnel, and are destroyed before or immediately upon completion of the test; and

(D) Provided, That the test may exceed ninety days only with the prior approval of the Attorney General;

(2) determine the existence and capability of electronic surveillance equipment being used by persons not authorized to conduct electronic surveillance, if—

(A) it is not reasonable to obtain the consent of persons incidentally subjected to the surveillance;

(B) such electronic surveillance is limited in extent and duration to that necessary to determine the existence and capability of such equipment; and

(C) any information acquired by such surveillance is used only to enforce chapter 119 of title 18, United States Code, or section 705 of the Communications Act of 1934, or to protect information from unauthorized surveillance; or

(3) train intelligence personnel in the use of electronic surveillance equipment, if—

(A) it is not reasonable to—

(i) obtain the consent of the persons incidentally subjected to the surveillance;

(ii) train persons in the course of surveillances otherwise authorized by this title; or

    (iii) train persons in the use of such equipment without engaging in electronic surveillance;

   (B) such electronic surveillance is limited in extent and duration to that necessary to train the personnel in the use of the equipment; and

   (C) no contents of any communication acquired are retained or disseminated for any purpose, but are destroyed as soon as reasonably possible.

(g) Certifications made by the Attorney General pursuant to section 102(a) and applications made and orders granted under this title shall be retained for a period of at least ten years from the date of the certification or application.

(h) No cause of action shall lie in any court against any provider of a wire or electronic communication service, landlord, custodian, or other person (including any officer, employee, agent, or other specified person thereof) that furnishes any information, facilities, or technical assistance in accordance with a court order or request for emergency assistance under this Act for electronic surveillance or physical search.

(i) In any case in which the Government makes an application to a judge under this title to conduct electronic surveillance involving communications and the judge grants such application, upon the request of the applicant, the judge shall also authorize the installation and use of pen registers and trap and trace devices, and direct the disclosure of the information set forth in section 402(d)(2).

USE OF INFORMATION

SEC. 106. [50 U.S.C. §1806]

(a) Information acquired from an electronic surveillance conducted pursuant to this title concerning any United States person may be used and disclosed by Federal officers and employees without the consent of the United States person only in accordance with the minimization procedures required by this title. No otherwise privileged communication obtained in accordance with, or in violation of, the provisions of this Act shall lose its privileged character. No information acquired from an electronic surveillance pursuant to this title may be used or disclosed by Federal officers or employees except for lawful purposes.

(b) No information acquired pursuant to this title shall be disclosed for law enforcement purposes unless such disclosure is accompanied by a statement that such information, or any information derived therefrom, may only be used in a criminal proceeding with the advance authorization of the Attorney General.

(c) Whenever the Government intends to enter into evidence or otherwise use or disclose in any trial, hearing, or other proceeding in or before any court, department, officer, agency, regulatory body, or other authority of the United States, against an aggrieved person, any information obtained or derived from an electronic surveillance of that aggrieved person pursuant to the authority of this Act, the Government shall, prior to the trial, hearing, or other proceeding or at a reasonable time prior to an effort to so disclose or so use that information or submit it in evidence, notify the aggrieved person and the court or other authority in which the information is to be disclosed or used that the Government intends to so disclose or so use such information.

(d) Whenever any State or political subdivision thereof intends to enter into evidence or otherwise use or disclose in any trial, hearing, or other proceeding in or before any court, department, officer, agency, regulatory body, or other authority of a State or a political subdivision thereof, against an aggrieved person any information obtained or derived from an electronic surveillance of that aggrieved person pursuant to the authority of this Act, the State or political subdivision thereof shall notify the aggrieved person, the court or other authority in which the information is to be disclosed or used, and the Attorney General that the State or political subdivision thereof intends to so disclose or so use such information.

(e) Any person against whom evidence obtained or derived from an electronic surveillance to which he is an aggrieved person is to be, or has been, introduced or otherwise used or disclosed in any trial, hearing, or other proceeding in or before any court, department, officer, agency, regulatory body, or other authority of the United States, a State, or a political subdivision thereof, may move to suppress the evidence obtained or derived from such electronic surveillance on the grounds that—

(1) the information was unlawfully acquired; or

(2) the surveillance was not made in conformity with an order of authorization or approval. Such a motion shall be made before the trial, hearing, or other proceeding unless there was no opportunity to make such a motion or the person was not aware of the grounds of the motion.

(f) [IN CAMERA AND EX PARTE REVIEW BY DISTRICT COURT.—] Whenever a court or other authority is notified pursuant to subsection (c) or (d), or whenever a motion is made pursuant to subsection (e), or whenever any motion or request is made by an aggrieved person pursuant to any other statute or rule of the United States or any State before any court or other authority of the United States or any State to discover or obtain applications or orders or other materials relating to electronic surveillance or to discover, obtain, or suppress evidence or information obtained or derived from electronic surveillance under this Act, the United States district court or, where the motion is made before another authority, the United States district court in the same district as the authority, shall, notwithstanding any other law, if the Attorney General files an affidavit under oath that disclosure or an adversary hearing would harm the national security of the United States, review in camera and ex parte the application, order, and such other materials relating to the surveillance as may be necessary to determine whether the surveillance of the aggrieved person was lawfully authorized and conducted. In making this determination, the court may disclose to the aggrieved person, under appropriate security procedures and protective orders, portions of the application, order, or other materials relating to the surveillance only where such disclosure is necessary to make an accurate determination of the legality of the surveillance.

(g) If the United States district court pursuant to subsection (f) determine that the surveillance was not lawfully authorized or conducted, it shall, in accordance with the requirements of law, suppress the evidence which was unlawfully obtained or derived from electronic surveillance of the aggrieved person or otherwise grant the motion of the aggrieved person. If the court determines that the surveillance was lawfully authorized and conducted, it shall deny the motion of the aggrieved person except to the extent that due process requires discovery or disclosure.

(h) Orders granting motions or requests under subsection (g), decisions under this section that electronic surveillance was not lawfully authorized or conducted, and orders of the United States district court requiring review or granting disclosure of applications, orders, or other materials relating to a surveillance shall be final orders and binding upon all courts of the United States and the several States except a United States court of appeals and the Supreme Court.

(i) In circumstances involving the unintentional acquisition by an electronic, mechanical, or other surveillance device of the contents of any communication, under circumstances in which a person has a reasonable expectation of privacy and a warrant would be required for law enforcement purposes, and if both the sender and all intended recipients are located within the United States, such contents shall be destroyed upon recognition, unless the Attorney General determines that the contents indicates a threat of death or serious bodily harm to any person.

(j) If an emergency employment of electronic surveillance is authorized under section 105(e) and a subsequent order approving the surveillance is not obtained, the judge shall cause to be served on any United States person named in the application and on such other United States persons subject to electronic surveillance as the judge may determine in his discretion it is in the interest of justice to serve, notice of—

(1) the fact of the application;

(2) the period of the surveillance; and

(3) the fact that during the period information was or was not obtained. On an ex parte showing of good cause to the judge the serving of the notice required by this subsection may be postponed or suspended for a period not to exceed ninety days. Thereafter, on a further ex parte showing of good cause, the court shall forego ordering the serving of the notice required under this subsection.

(k)(1) Federal officers who conduct electronic surveillance to acquire foreign intelligence information under this title may consult with Federal law enforcement officers or law enforcement personnel of a State or political subdivision of a State (including the chief executive officer of that State or political subdivision who has the authority to appoint or direct the chief law enforcement officer of that State or political subdivision) to coordinate efforts to investigate or protect against—

(A) actual or potential attack or other grave hostile acts of a foreign power or an agent of a foreign power;

(B) sabotage, international terrorism, or the international proliferation of weapons of mass destruction by a foreign power or an agent of a foreign power; or

(C) clandestine intelligence activities by an intelligence service or network of a foreign power or by an agent of a foreign power.

(2) Coordination authorized under paragraph (1) shall not preclude the certification required by section 104(a)(7)(B) or the entry of an order under section 105.

REPORT OF ELECTRONIC SURVEILLANCE

SEC. 107. [50 U.S.C. §1807] In April of each year, the Attorney General shall transmit to the Administrative Office of the United States Court and to Congress a report setting forth with respect to the preceding calendar year—

(a) the total number of applications made for orders and extensions of orders approving electronic surveillance under this title; and

(b) the total number of such orders and extensions either granted, modified, or denied.

CONGRESSIONAL OVERSIGHT

SEC. 108. [50 U.S.C. §1808]

(a)(1) On a semiannual basis the Attorney General shall fully inform the House Permanent Select Committee on Intelligence and the Senate Select Committees on Intelligence and the Committee on the Judiciary of the Senate concerning all electronic surveillance under this title. Nothing in this title shall be deemed to limit the authority and responsibility of the appropriate committees of each House of Congress to obtain such information as they may need to carry out their respective functions and duties.

(2) Each report under the first sentence of paragraph (1) shall include a description of—

(A) the total number of applications made for orders and extensions of orders approving electronic surveillance under this title where the nature and location of each facility or place at which the electronic surveillance will be directed is unknown;

(B) each criminal case in which information acquired under this Act has been authorized for use at trial during the period covered by such report; and

(C) the total number of emergency employments of electronic surveillance under section 105(e) and the total number of subsequent orders approving or denying such electronic surveillance.

(b) On or before one year after the effective date of this Act and on the same day each year for four years thereafter, the Permanent Select Committee on Intelligence and the Senate Select Committee on Intelligence shall report respectively to the House of Representatives and the Senate, concerning the implementation of this Act. Said reports shall include but not be limited to an analysis and recommendations concerning whether this Act should be (1) amended, (2) repealed, or (3) permitted to continue in effect without amendment.

PENALTIES

SEC. 109. [50 U.S.C. §1809]

(a) OFFENSE.—A person is guilty of an offense if he intentionally—

(1) engages in electronic surveillance under color of law except as authorized by this Act, chapter 119, 121, or 206 of title 18, United States Code, or any express statutory authorization that is an additional exclusive means for conducting electronic surveillance under section 112; or

(2) disclose or uses information obtained under color of law by electronic surveillance, knowing or having reason to known that the information was obtained through electronic surveillance not authorized by this Act, chapter 119, 121, or 206 of title 18, United States Code, or any express statutory authorization that is an additional exclusive means for conducting electronic surveillance under section 112.

(b) DEFENSE.—It is a defense to a prosecution under subsection (a) that the defendant was a law enforcement or investigative officer engaged in the course of his official duties and the electronic surveillance was authorized by and conducted pursuant to a search warrant or court order of a court of competent jurisdiction.

(c) PENALTY.—An offense in this section is punishable by a fine of not more than $10,000 or imprisonment for not more than five years, or both.

(d) JURISDICTION.—There is Federal jurisdiction over an offense under this section if the person committing the offense was an officer or employee of the United States at the time the offense was committed.

CIVIL LIABILITY

SEC. 110. [50 U.S.C. §1810] CIVIL ACTION.—An aggrieved person, other than a foreign power or an agent of a foreign power, as defined in section 101 (a) or (b)(1)(A), respectively, who has been subjected to an electronic surveillance or about whom information obtained by electronic surveillance of such person has been disclosed or used in violation of section 109 shall have a cause of action against any person who committed such violation and shall be entitled to recover—

(a) actual damages, but not less than liquidated damages of $1,000 or $100 per day for each day of violation, whichever is greater;

(b) punitive damages; and

(c) reasonable attorney's fees and other investigation and litigation costs reasonably incurred.

AUTHORIZATION DURING TIME OF WAR

SEC. 111. [50 U.S.C. §1811] Notwithstanding any other law, the President, through the Attorney General, may authorize electronic surveillance without a court order under this title to acquire foreign intelligence information for a period not to exceed fifteen calendar days following a declaration of war by the Congress.

STATEMENT OF EXCLUSIVE MEANS BY WHICH ELECTRONIC SURVEILLANCE AND INTERCEPTION OF CERTAIN COMMUNICATIONS MAY BE CONDUCTED
SEC. 112. [50 U.S.C. § 1812]

(a) Except as provided in subsection (b), the procedures of chapters 119, 121, and 206 of title 18, United States Code, and this Act shall be the exclusive means by which electronic surveillance and the interception of domestic wire, oral, or electronic communications may be conducted.

(b) Only an express statutory authorization for electronic surveillance or the interception of domestic wire, oral, or electronic communications, other than as an amendment to this Act or chapters 119, 121, or 206 of title 18, United States Code, shall constitute an additional exclusive means for the purpose of subsection (a).

TITLE II—CONFORMING AMENDMENTS

AMENDMENTS TO CHAPTER 119 OF TITLE 18, UNITED STATES CODE

SEC. 201. Chapter 119 of title 18, United States Code, is amended as follows:

(a) Section 2511(2)(a)(ii) is amended to read as follows:

> "(ii) Notwithstanding any other law, communication common carriers, their officers, employees, and agents, landlords, custodians, or other persons, are authorized to provide information, facilities, or technical assistance to persons authorized by law to intercept wire or oral communications or to conduct electronic surveillance, as defined in section 101 of the Foreign Intelligence Surveillance Act of 1978, if the common carrier, its officers, employees, or agent, landlord, custodian, or other specified person, has been provided with—

"(A) a court order directing such assistance signed by the authorizing judge, or "(B) a certification in writing by a person specified in section 2518(7) of title or the Attorney General of the United States that no warrant or court order is required by law, that all statutory requirements have been met, and that the specified assistance is required, setting forth the period of time during which the provision of the information, facilities, or technical assistance is authorized and specifying the information, facilities, or technical assistance required. No communications common carrier, officer, employee, or agent thereof, or landlord, custodian, or other specified person shall disclose the existence of any interception or surveillance or the device used to accomplish the interception or surveillance with respect to which the person has been furnished an order or certification under this subparagraph, except as may otherwise be required by legal process and then only after prior notification of the Attorney General or to the principal prosecuting attorney of a State or any political subdivision of a State, as may be appropriate. Any violation of this subparagraph by a communication common carrier or an officer, employee, or agent thereof, shall render the carrier liable for the civil damages provided for in section 2520. No cause of action shall lie in any court against any communication common carrier, its officers, employees, or agents, landlord, custodian, or other specified person for providing information, facilities, or assistance in accordance with the terms of an order or certification under this subparagraph.".

(b) Section 2511(2) is amended by adding at the end thereof the following new provisions:

> "(e) Notwithstanding any other provision of this Act or section 605 or 606 of the Communications Act of 1934, it shall not be unlawful for an officer, employee, or agent of the United States in the normal course of his official duty to conduct electronic surveillance, as defined in section 101 of the Foreign Intelligence Surveillance

Act of 1978, as authorized by that Act. "(f) Nothing contained in this chapter, or section 605 of the Communications Act of 1934, shall be deemed to affect the acquisition by the United States Government of foreign intelligence information from international or foreign communications by a means other than electronic surveillance as defined in section 101 of the Foreign Intelligence Surveillance Act of 1978, and procedures in this chapter and the Foreign Intelligence Surveillance Act of 1978 shall be the exclusive means by which electronic surveillance, as defined in section 101 of such Act, and the interception of domestic wire and oral communications may be conducted.".

(c) Section 2511(3) is repealed.

(d) Section 2518(1) is amended by inserting "under this chapter" after "communication".

(e) Section 2518(4) is amended by inserting "under this chapter" after both appearances of "wire or oral communication".

(f) Section 2518(9) is amended by striking out "intercepted" and inserting "intercepted pursuant to this chapter" after "communication".

(g) Section 2518(10) is amended by striking out "intercepted" and inserting "intercepted pursuant to this chapter" after the first appearance of "communication".

(h) Section 2519(3) is amended by inserting "pursuant to this chapter" after "wire or oral communications" and after "granted or denied".

TITLE III—PHYSICAL SEARCHES WITHIN THE UNITED STATES FOR FOREIGN INTELLIGENCE PURPOSES

DEFINITIONS

SEC. 301. [50 U.S.C. §1821] As used in this title:

(1) The terms "foreign power", "agent of a foreign power", "international terrorism", "sabotage", "foreign intelligence information", "Attorney General", "United States person", "United States", "person", weapon of mass destruction, and "State" shall have the same meanings as in section 101 of this Act, except as specifically provided by this title.

(2) "Aggrieved person" means a person whose premises, property, information, or material is the target of physical search or any other person whose premises, property, information, or material was subject to physical search.

(3) "Foreign Intelligence Surveillance Court" means the court established by section 103(a) of this Act.

(4) "Minimization procedures" with respect to physical search, means—

(A) specific procedures, which shall be adopted by the Attorney General, that are reasonably designed in light of the purposes and technique of the particular physical search, to minimize the acquisition and retention, and prohibit the dissemination, of nonpublicly available information concerning unconsenting United States persons consistent with the need of the United States to obtain, produce, and disseminate foreign intelligence information;

(B) procedures that require that nonpublicly available information, which is not foreign intelligence information, as defined in section 101(e)(1) of this Act, shall not be disseminated in a manner that identifies any United States person, without such person's consent, unless such person's identity is necessary to understand such foreign intelligence information or assess its importance;

(C) notwithstanding subparagraphs (A) and (B), procedures that allow for the retention and dissemination of information that is evidence of a crime which has been, is being, or is about to be committed and that is to be retained or disseminated for law enforcement purposes; and

(D) notwithstanding subparagraphs (A), (B), and (C), with respect to any physical search approved pursuant to section 302(a), procedures that require that no information, material, or property of a United States person shall be disclosed, disseminated, or used for any purpose or retained for longer than 72 hours unless a court order under section 304 is obtained or unless the Attorney General determines that the information indicates a threat of death or serious bodily harm to any person.

(5) "Physical search" means any physical intrusion within the United States into premises or property (including examination of the interior of property by technical means) that is intended to result in a seizure, reproduction, inspection, or alteration of information, material, or property, under circumstances in which a person has a reasonable expectation of privacy and a warrant would be required for law enforcement purposes, but does not include (A) "electronic surveillance", as defined in section 101(f) of this Act, or (B) the acquisition by the United States Government of foreign intelligence information from international or foreign communications, or foreign intelligence activities conducted in accordance with otherwise applicable Federal law involving a foreign electronic communications system, utilizing a means other than electronic surveillance as defined in section 101(f) of this Act.

AUTHORIZATION OF PHYSICAL SEARCHES FOR FOREIGN INTELLIGENCE PURPOSES

SEC. 302. [50 U.S.C. §1822]

(a)(1) Notwithstanding any other provision of law, the President, acting through the Attorney General, may authorize physical searches without a court order under this title to acquire foreign intelligence information for periods of up to one year if—

(A) the Attorney General certifies in writing under oath that—

(i) the physical search is solely directed at premises, information, material, or property used exclusively by, or under the open and exclusive control of, a foreign

power or powers (as defined in section 101(a) (1), (2), or (3));

(ii) there is no substantial likelihood that the physical search will involve the premises, information, material, or property of a United States person; and

(iii) the proposed minimization procedures with respect to such physical search meet the definition of minimization procedures under paragraphs (1) through (4) of section 301(4); and

(B) the Attorney General reports such minimization procedures and any changes thereto to the Permanent Select Committee on Intelligence of the House of Representatives and the Select Committee on Intelligence of the Senate at least 30 days before their effective date, unless the Attorney General determines that immediate action is required and notifies the committees immediately of such minimization procedures and the reason for their becoming effective immediately.

(2) A physical search authorized by this subsection may be conducted only in accordance with the certification and minimization procedures adopted by the Attorney General. The Attorney General shall assess compliance with such procedures and shall report such assessments to the Permanent Select Committee on Intelligence of the House of Representatives and the Select Committee on Intelligence of the Senate under the provisions of section 306.

(3) The Attorney General shall immediately transmit under seal to the Foreign Intelligence Surveillance Court a copy of the certification. Such certification shall be maintained under security measures established by the Chief Justice of the United States with the concurrence of the Attorney General, in consultation with the Director of National Intelligence, and shall remain sealed unless—

(A) an application for a court order with respect to the physical search is made under section 301(4) and section 303; or

(B) the certification is necessary to determine the legality of the physical search under section 305(g). (4)(A) With respect to physical searches authorized by this subsection, the Attorney General may direct a specified landlord, custodian, or other specified person to—

    (i) furnish all information, facilities, or assistance necessary to accomplish the physical search in such a manner as will protect its secrecy and produce a minimum of interference with the services that such landlord, custodian, or other person is providing the target of the physical search; and

    (ii) maintain under security procedures approved by the Attorney General and the Director of National Intelligence any records concerning the search or the aid furnished that such person wishes to retain.

(B) The Government shall compensate, at the prevailing rate, such landlord, custodian, or other person for furnishing such aid.

(b) Applications for a court order under this title are authorized if the President has, by written authorization, empowered the Attorney General to approve applications to the Foreign Intelligence Surveillance Court. Notwithstanding any other provision of law, a judge of the court to whom application is made may grant an order in accordance with section 304 approving a physical search in the United States of the premises, property, information, or material of a foreign power or an agent of a foreign power for the purpose of collecting foreign intelligence information.

(c) The Foreign Intelligence Surveillance Court shall have jurisdiction to hear applications for and grant orders approving a physical search for the purpose of obtaining foreign intelligence information anywhere within the United States under the procedures set forth in this title, except that no judge (except when sitting en banc) shall hear the same application which has been denied previously by another judge designated under section 103(a) of this Act. If any judge so designated denies an application for an order authorizing a physical search under this title, such judge shall provide immediately for the record a written statement of each reason for such decision and, on motion of the United States, the record shall be transmitted, under seal, to the court of review established under section 103(b).

(d) The court of review established under section 103(b) shall have jurisdiction to review the denial of any application made under this title. If such court determines that the application was properly denied, the court shall immediately provide for the record a written statement of each reason for its decision and, on petition of the United States for a writ of certiorari, the record shall be transmitted under seal to the Supreme Court, which shall have jurisdiction to review such decision.

(e) Judicial proceedings under this title shall be concluded as expeditiously as possible. The record of proceedings under this title, including applications made and orders granted, shall be maintained under security measures established by the Chief Justice of the United States in consultation with the Attorney General and the Director of National Intelligence.

APPLICATION FOR AN ORDER

SEC. 303. [50 U.S.C. §1823]

(a) Each application for an order approving a physical search under this title shall be made by a Federal officer in writing upon oath or affirmation to a judge of the Foreign Intelligence Surveillance Court. Each application shall require the approval of the Attorney General based upon the Attorney General's finding that it satisfies the criteria and requirements for such application as set forth in this title. Each application shall include—

(1) the identity of the Federal officer making the application;

(2) the identity, if known, or a description of the target of the search, and a description of the premises or property to be searched and of the information, material, or property to be seized, reproduced, or altered;

(3) a statement of the facts and circumstances relied upon by the applicant to justify the applicant's belief that—

> (A) the target of the physical search is a foreign power or an agent of a foreign power;
>
> (B) the premises or property to be searched contains foreign intelligence information; and
>
> (C) the premises or property to be searched is or is about to be owned, used, possessed by, or is in transit to or from a foreign power or an agent of a foreign power;

(4) a statement of the proposed minimization procedures;

(5) a statement of the nature of the foreign intelligence sought and the manner in which the physical search is to be conducted;

(6) a certification or certifications by the Assistant to the President for National Security Affairs, an executive branch official or officials designated by the President from among those executive branch officers employed in the area of national security or defense and appointed by the President, by and with the advice and consent of the Senate, or the Deputy Director of the Federal Bureau of Investigation, if designated by the President as a certifying official—

> (A) that the certifying official deems the information sought to be foreign intelligence information;
>
> (B) that a significant purpose of the search is to obtain foreign intelligence information;
>
> (C) that such information cannot reasonably be obtained by normal investigative techniques;
>
> (D) that designates the type of foreign intelligence information being sought according to the categories described in section 101(e); and
>
> (E) includes a statement explaining the basis for the certifications required by subparagraphs (C) and (D);

(7) where the physical search involves a search of the residence of a United States person, the Attorney General shall state what investigative techniques have previously been utilized to obtain the foreign intelligence information concerned and the degree to which these techniques resulted in acquiring such information; and

(8) a statement of the facts concerning all previous applications that have been made to any judge under this title involving any of the persons, premises, or property specified in the application, and the action taken on each previous application.

(b) The Attorney General may require any other affidavit or certification from any other officer in connection with the application.

(c) The judge may require the applicant to furnish such other information as may be necessary to make the determinations required by section 304.

(d)(1)(A) Upon written request of the Director of the Federal Bureau of Investigation, the Secretary of Defense, the Secretary of State, or the Director of National Intelligence, the Attorney General shall personally review under subsection (a) an application under that subsection for a target described in section 101(b)(2).

> (B) Except when disabled or otherwise unavailable to make a request referred to in subparagraph (A), an official referred to in that subparagraph may not delegate the authority to make a request referred to in that subparagraph.
>
> (C) Each official referred to in subparagraph (A) with authority to make a request under that subparagraph shall take appropriate actions in advance to ensure that

delegation of such authority is clearly established in the event such official is disabled or otherwise unavailable to make such request.

(2)(A) If as a result of a request under paragraph (1) the Attorney General determines not to approve an application under the second sentence of subsection (a) for purposes of making the application under this section, the Attorney General shall provide written notice of the determination to the official making the request for the review of the application under that paragraph. Except when disabled or otherwise unavailable to make a determination under the preceding sentence, the Attorney General may not delegate the responsibility to make a determination under that sentence. The Attorney General shall take appropriate actions in advance to ensure that delegation of such responsibility is clearly established in the event the Attorney General is disabled or otherwise unavailable to make such determination.

(B) Notice with respect to an application under subparagraph (A) shall set forth the modifications, if any, of the application that are necessary in order for the Attorney General to approve the application under the second sentence of subsection (a) for purposes of making the application under this section.

(C) Upon review of any modifications of an application set forth under subparagraph (B), the official notified of the modifications under this paragraph shall modify the application if such official determines that such modification is warranted. Such official shall supervise the making of any modification under this subparagraph. Except when disabled or otherwise unavailable to supervise the making of any modification under the preceding sentence, such official may not delegate the responsibility to supervise the making of any modification under that preceding sentence. Each such official shall take appropriate actions in advance to ensure that delegation of such responsibility is clearly established in the event such official is disabled or otherwise unavailable to supervise the making of such modification.

ISSUANCE OF AN ORDER

SEC. 304. [50 U.S.C. §§1824]

(a) Upon an application made pursuant to section 303, the judge shall enter an ex parte order as requested or as modified approving the physical search if the judge finds that—

(1) the application has been made by a Federal officer and approved by the Attorney General;

(2) on the basis of the facts submitted by the applicant there is probable cause to believe that—

(A) the target of the physical search is a foreign power or an agent of a foreign power, except that no United States person may be considered an agent of a foreign power solely upon the basis of activities protected by the first amendment to the Constitution of the United States; and

(B) the premises or property to be searched is or is about to be owned, used, possessed by, or is in transit to or from an agent of a foreign power or a foreign power;

(3) the proposed minimization procedures meet the definition of minimization contained in this title; and

(4) the application which has been filed contains all statements and certifications required by section 303, and, if the target is a United States person, the certification or certifications are not clearly erroneous on the basis of the statement made under section 303(a)(6)(E) and any other information furnished under section 303(c).

(b) In determining whether or not probable cause exists for purposes of an order under subsection (a)(3), a judge may consider past activities of the target, as well as facts and circumstances relating to current or future activities of the target.

(c) An order approving a physical search under this section shall—

    (1) specify—

        (A) the identity, if known, or a description of the target of the physical search;

        (B) the nature and location of each of the premises or property to be searched;

        (C) the type of information, material, or property to be seized, altered, or reproduced;

        (D) a statement of the manner in which the physical search is to be conducted and, whenever more than one physical search is authorized under the order, the authorized scope of each search and what minimization procedures shall apply to the information acquired by each search; and

        (E) the period of time during which physical searches are approved; and

    (2) direct—

        (A) that the minimization procedures be followed;

        (B) that, upon the request of the applicant, a specified landlord, custodian, or other specified person furnish the applicant forthwith all information, facilities, or assistance necessary to accomplish the physical search in such a manner as will protect its secrecy and produce a minimum of interference with the services that such landlord, custodian, or other person is providing the target of the physical search;

        (C) that such landlord, custodian, or other person maintain under security procedures approved by the Attorney General and the Director of National Intelligence any records concerning the search or the aid furnished that such person wishes to retain;

        (D) that the applicant compensate, at the prevailing rate, such landlord, custodian, or other person for furnishing such aid; and

        (E) that the Federal officer conducting the physical search promptly report to the court the circumstances and results of the physical search.

(d)(1) An order issued under this section may approve a physical search for the period necessary to achieve its purpose, or for 90 days, whichever is less, except that

        (A) an order under this section shall approve a physical search targeted against a foreign power, as defined in paragraph (1), (2), or (3) of section 101(a), for the period specified in the application or for one year, whichever is less, and

        (B) an order under this section for a physical search targeted against an agent of a foreign power who is not a United States person may be for the period specified in the application or for 120 days, whichever is less.

    (2) Extensions of an order issued under this title may be granted on the same basis as the original order upon an application for an extension and new findings made in the same manner as required for the original order, except that an extension of an order under this Act for a physical search targeted against a foreign power, as defined in paragraph (5), (6), or (7) of section 101(a), or against a foreign power, as defined in section 101(a)(4), that is not a United States person, or against an agent of a foreign power who is not a United States person, may be for a period not to exceed one year if the judge finds probable cause to believe that no property of any individual United States person will be acquired during the period.

    (3) At or before the end of the period of time for which a physical search is approved by an order or an extension, or at any time after a physical search is carried out, the judge may assess compliance with the minimization procedures by reviewing the circumstances under which information concerning United States persons was acquired, retained, or disseminated.

(e)(1) Notwithstanding any other provision of this title, the Attorney General may authorize the emergency employment of a physical search if the Attorney General—

        (A) reasonably determines that an emergency situation exists with respect to the employment of a physical search to obtain foreign intelligence information before an order authorizing such physical search can with due diligence be obtained;

(B) reasonably determines that the factual basis for issuance of an order under this title to approve such physical search exists;

(C) informs, either personally or through a designee, a judge of the Foreign Intelligence Surveillance Court at the time of such authorization that the decision has been made to employ an emergency physical search; and

(D) makes an application in accordance with this title to a judge of the Foreign Intelligence Surveillance Court as soon as practicable, but not more than 7 days after the Attorney General authorizes such physical search.

(2) If the Attorney General authorizes the emergency employment of a physical search under paragraph (1), the Attorney General shall require that the minimization procedures required by this title for the issuance of a judicial order be followed.

(3) In the absence of a judicial order approving such physical search, the physical search shall terminate when the information sought is obtained, when the application for the order is denied, or after the expiration of 7 days from the time of authorization by the Attorney General, whichever is earliest.

(4) A denial of the application made under this subsection may be reviewed as provided in section 103.

(5) In the event that such application for approval is denied, or in any other case where the physical search is terminated and no order is issued approving the physical search, no information obtained or evidence derived from such physical search shall be received in evidence or otherwise disclosed in any trial, hearing, or other proceeding in or before any court, grand jury, department, office, agency, regulatory body, legislative committee, or other authority of the United States, a State, or political subdivision thereof, and no information concerning any United States person acquired from such physical search shall subsequently be used or disclosed in any other manner by Federal officers or employees without the consent of such person, except with the approval of the Attorney General if the information indicates a threat of death or serious bodily harm to any person.

(6) The Attorney General shall assess compliance with the requirements of paragraph (5).

(f) Applications made and orders granted under this title shall be retained for a period of at least 10 years from the date of the application.

USE OF INFORMATION
SEC. 305. [50 U.S.C. §1825]

(a) Information acquired from a physical search conducted pursuant to this title concerning any United States person may be used and disclosed by Federal officers and employees without the consent of the United States person only in accordance with the minimization procedures required by this title. No information acquired from a physical search pursuant to this title may be used or disclosed by Federal officers or employees except for lawful purposes.

(b) Where a physical search authorized and conducted pursuant to section 304 involves the residence of a United States person, and, at any time after the search the Attorney General determines there is no national security interest in continuing to maintain the secrecy of the search, the Attorney General shall provide notice to the United States person whose residence was searched of the fact of the search conducted pursuant to this Act and shall identify any property of such person seized, altered, or reproduced during such search.

(c) No information acquired pursuant to this title shall be disclosed for law enforcement purposes unless such disclosure is accompanied by a statement that such information, or any information derived therefrom, may only be used in a criminal proceeding with the advance authorization of the Attorney General.

(d) Whenever the United States intends to enter into evidence or otherwise use or disclose in any trial, hearing, or other proceeding in or before any court, department, officer, agency, regulatory body, or other authority of the United States, against an aggrieved person, any information obtained or derived from a physical search pursuant to the authority of this Act, the United States shall, prior to the trial, hearing, or the other proceeding or at a reasonable time prior to an effort to so disclose or so use that information or submit it in evidence, notify the aggrieved person and the court or other authority in which the information is to be disclosed or used that the United States intends to so disclose or so use such information.

(e) Whenever any State or political subdivision thereof intends to enter into evidence or otherwise use or disclose in any trial, hearing, or other proceeding in or before any court, department, officer, agency, regulatory body, or other authority of a State or a political subdivision thereof against an aggrieved person any information obtained or derived from a physical search pursuant to the authority of this Act, the State or political subdivision thereof shall notify the aggrieved person, the court or other authority in which the information is to be disclosed or used, and the Attorney General that the State or political subdivision thereof intends to so disclose or so use such information.

(f)(1) Any person against whom evidence obtained or derived from a physical search to which he is an aggrieved person is to be, or has been, introduced or otherwise used or disclosed in any trial, hearing, or other proceeding in or before any court, department, officer, agency, regulatory body, or other authority of the United States, a State, or a political subdivision thereof, may move to suppress the evidence obtained or derived from such search on the grounds that—

> (A) the information was unlawfully acquired; or
> (B) the physical search was not made in conformity with an order of authorization or approval.

> (2) Such a motion shall be made before the trial, hearing, or other proceeding unless there was no opportunity to make such a motion or the person was not aware of the grounds of the motion.

(g) Whenever a court or other authority is notified pursuant to subsection (d) or (e), or whenever a motion is made pursuant to subsection (f), or whenever any motion or request is made by an aggrieved person pursuant to any other statute or rule of the United States or any State before any court or other authority of the United States or any State to discover or obtain applications or orders or other materials relating to a physical search authorized by this title or to discover, obtain, or suppress evidence or information obtained or derived from a physical search authorized by this title, the United States district court or, where the motion is made before another authority, the United States district court in the same district as the authority shall, notwithstanding any other provision of law, if the Attorney General files an affidavit under oath that disclosure or any adversary hearing would harm the national security of the United States, review in camera and ex parte the application, order, and such other materials relating to the physical search as may be necessary to determine whether the physical search of the aggrieved person was lawfully authorized and conducted. In making this determination, the court may disclose to the aggrieved person, under appropriate security procedures and protective orders, portions of the application, order, or other materials relating to the physical search, or may require the Attorney General to provide to the aggrieved person a summary of such materials, only where such disclosure is necessary to make an accurate determination of the legality of the physical search.

(h) If the United States district court pursuant to subsection (g) determines that the physical search was not lawfully authorized or conducted, it shall, in accordance with the requirements of law, suppress the evidence which was unlawfully obtained or derived from the physical search of the aggrieved person or otherwise grant the motion of the aggrieved person. If the court determines that the physical search was lawfully authorized or conducted, it shall deny the motion of the aggrieved person except to the extent that due process requires discovery or disclosure.

(i) Orders granting motions or requests under subsection (h), decisions under this section that a physical search was not lawfully authorized or conducted, and orders of the United States district court requiring review or granting disclosure of applications, orders, or other materials relating to the physical search shall be final orders and binding upon all courts of the United States and the several States except a United States Court of Appeals or the Supreme Court.

(j)(1) If an emergency execution of a physical search is authorized under section 304(d) and a subsequent order approving the search is not obtained, the judge shall cause to be served on any United States person named in the application and on such other United States persons subject to the search as the judge may determine in his discretion it is in the interests of justice to serve, notice of—

> (A) the fact of the application;
> (B) the period of the search; and
> (C) the fact that during the period information was or was not obtained.

(2) On an ex parte showing of good cause to the judge, the serving of the notice required by this subsection may be postponed or suspended for a period not to exceed 90 days. Thereafter, on a further ex parte showing of good cause, the court shall forego ordering the serving of the notice required under this subsection.

(k)(1) Federal officers who conduct physical searches to acquire foreign intelligence information under this title may consult with Federal law enforcement officers or law enforcement personnel of a State or political subdivision of a State (including the chief executive officer of that State or political subdivision who has the authority to appoint or direct the chief law enforcement officer of that State or political subdivision) to coordinate efforts to investigate or protect against—

> (A) actual or potential attack or other grave hostile acts of a foreign power or an agent of a foreign power;
> (B) sabotage, international terrorism, or the international proliferation of weapons of mass destruction by a foreign power or an agent of a foreign power; or
> (C) clandestine intelligence activities by an intelligence service or network of a foreign power or by an agent of a foreign power.

(2) Coordination authorized under paragraph (1) shall not preclude the certification required by section 303(a)(6) or the entry of an order under section 304.

CONGRESSIONAL OVERSIGHT

SEC. 306. [50 U.S.C. §1826] On a semiannual basis the Attorney General shall fully inform the Permanent Select Committee on Intelligence of the House of Representatives and the Select Committee on Intelligence of the Senate and the Committee on the Judiciary of the Senate concerning all physical searches conducted pursuant to this title. On a semiannual basis the Attorney General shall also provide to those committees and the Committee on the Judiciary of the House of Representatives a report setting forth with respect to the preceding six-month period—

> (1) the total number of applications made for orders approving physical searches under this title;
> (2) the total number of such orders either granted, modified, or denied;
> (3) the number of physical searches which involved searches of the residences, offices, or personal property of United States persons, and the number of occasions, if any, where the Attorney General provided notice pursuant to section 305(b); and

(4) the total number of emergency physical searches authorized by the Attorney General under section 304(e) and the total number of subsequent orders approving or denying such physical searches.

PENALTIES

SEC. 307. [50 U.S.C. §1827]

(a) A person is guilty of an offense if he intentionally—

(1) under color of law for the purpose of obtaining foreign intelligence information, executes a physical search within the United States except as authorized by statute; or

(2) discloses or uses information obtained under color of law by physical search within the United States, knowing or having reason to know that the information was obtained through physical search not authorized by statute, for the purpose of obtaining intelligence information.

(b) It is a defense to a prosecution under subsection (a) that the defendant was a law enforcement or investigative officer engaged in the course of his official duties and the physical search was authorized by and conducted pursuant to a search warrant or court order of a court of competent jurisdiction.

(c) An offense described in this section is punishable by a fine of not more than $10,000 or imprisonment for not more than five years, or both.

(d) There is Federal jurisdiction over an offense under this section if the person committing the offense was an officer or employee of the United States at the time the offense was committed.

CIVIL LIABILITY

SEC. 308. [50 U.S.C. §1828] An aggrieved person, other than a foreign power or an agent of a foreign power, as defined in section 101 (a) or (b)(1)(A), respectively, of this Act, whose premises, property, information, or material has been subjected to a physical search within the United States or about whom information obtained by such a physical search has been disclosed or used in violation of section 307 shall have a cause of action against any person who committed such violation and shall be entitled to recover—

(1) actual damages, but not less than liquidated damages of $1,000 or $100 per day for each day of violation, whichever is greater;

(2) punitive damages; and

(3) reasonable attorney's fees and other investigative and litigation costs reasonably incurred.

AUTHORIZATION DURING TIME OF WAR

SEC. 309. [50 U.S.C. §1829]

Notwithstanding any other provision of law, the President, through the Attorney General, may authorize physical searches without a court order under this title to acquire foreign intelligence information for a period not to exceed 15 calendar days following a declaration of war by the Congress.

TITLE IV—PEN REGISTERS AND TRAP AND TRACE DEVICES FOR FOREIGN INTELLIGENCE PURPOSES

DEFINITIONS

SEC. 401. [50 U.S.C. §1841] As used in this title:

(1) The terms "foreign power", "agent of a foreign power", "international terrorism", "foreign intelligence information", "Attorney General", "United States person", "United States", "person", and "State" shall have the same meanings as in section 101 of this Act.

(2) The terms "pen register" and "trap and trace device" have the meanings given such terms in section 3127 of title 18, United States Code.

(3) The term "aggrieved person" means any person—

(A) whose telephone line was subject to the installation or use of a pen register or trap and trace device authorized by this title; or

(B) whose communication instrument or device was subject to the use of a pen register or trap and trace device authorized by this title to capture incoming electronic or other communications impulses.

PEN REGISTERS AND TRAP AND TRACE DEVICES FOR FOREIGN INTELLIGENCE AND INTERNATIONAL TERRORISM INVESTIGATIONS

SEC. 402. [50 U.S.C. §1842]

(a)(1) Notwithstanding any other provision of law, the Attorney General or a designated attorney for the Government may make an application for an order or an extension of an order authorizing or approving the installation and use of a pen register or trap and trace device for any investigation to obtain foreign intelligence information not concerning a United States person or to protect against international terrorism or clandestine intelligence activities, provided that such investigation of a United States person is not conducted solely upon the basis of activities protected by the first amendment to the Constitution which is being conducted by the Federal Bureau of Investigation under such guidelines as the Attorney General approves pursuant to Executive Order No. 12333, or a successor order.

(2) The authority under paragraph (1) is in addition to the authority under title I of this Act to conduct the electronic surveillance referred to in that paragraph.

(b) Each application under this section shall be in writing under oath or affirmation to—

(1) a judge of the court established by section 103(a) of this Act; or

(2) a United States Magistrate Judge under chapter 43 of title 28, United States Code, who is publicly designated by the Chief Justice of the United States to have the power to hear applications for and grant orders approving the installation and use of a pen register or trap and trace device on behalf of a judge of that court.

(c) Each application under this section shall require the approval of the Attorney General, or a designated attorney for the Government, and shall include—

(1) the identity of the Federal officer seeking to use the pen register or trap and trace device covered by the application; and

(2) a certification by the applicant that the information likely to be obtained is foreign intelligence information not concerning a United States person or is relevant to an ongoing investigation to protect against international terrorism or clandestine intelligence activities, provided that such investigation of a United States person is not conducted solely upon the basis of activities protected by the first amendment to the Constitution.

(d)(1) Upon an application made pursuant to this section, the judge shall enter an ex parte order as requested, or as modified, approving the installation and use of a pen register or trap and trace device if the judge finds that the application satisfies the requirements of this section.

(2) An order issued under this section—

(A) shall specify—

(i) the identity, if known, of the person who is the subject of the investigation;

(ii) the identity, if known, of the person to whom is leased or in whose name is listed the telephone line or other facility to which the pen register or trap and trace device is to be attached or applied;

(iii) the attributes of the communications to which the order applies, such as the number or other identifier, and, if known, the location of the telephone line or other facility to which the pen register or trap and trace device is to be attached or applied and, in the case of a trap and trace device, the geographic limits of the trap and trace order;

(B) shall direct that—

(i) upon request of the applicant, the provider of a wire or electronic communication service, landlord, custodian, or other person shall furnish any information, facilities, or technical assistance necessary to accomplish the installation and operation of the pen register or trap and trace device in such a manner as will protect its secrecy and produce a minimum amount of interference with the services that such provider, landlord, custodian, or other person is providing the person concerned;

(ii) such provider, landlord, custodian, or other person—

(I) shall not disclose the existence of the investigation or of the pen register or trap and trace device to any person unless or until ordered by the court; and

(II) shall maintain, under security procedures approved by the Attorney General and the Director of National Intelligence pursuant to section 105(b)(2)(C) of this Act, any records concerning the pen register or trap and trace device or the aid furnished; and

(iii) the applicant shall compensate such provider, landlord, custodian, or other person for reasonable expenses incurred by such provider, landlord, custodian, or other person in providing such information, facilities, or technical assistance; and

(C) shall direct that, upon the request of the applicant, the provider of a wire or electronic communication service shall disclose to the Federal officer using the pen register or trap and trace device covered by the order—

(i) in the case of the customer or subscriber using the service covered by the order (for the period specified by the order)—

(I) the name of the customer or subscriber;

(II) the address of the customer or subscriber;

(III) the telephone or instrument number, or other subscriber number or identifier, of the customer or subscriber, including any temporarily assigned network address or associated routing or transmission information;

(IV) the length of the provision of service by such provider to the customer or subscriber and the types of services utilized by the customer or subscriber;

(V) in the case of a provider of local or long distance telephone service, any local or long distance telephone records of the customer or subscriber;

(VI) if applicable, any records reflecting period of usage (or sessions) by the customer or subscriber; and

(VII) any mechanisms and sources of payment for such service, including the number of any credit card or bank account utilized for payment for such service; and

(ii) if available, with respect to any customer or subscriber of incoming or outgoing communications to or from the service covered by the order—

(I) the name of such customer or subscriber;

(II) the address of such customer or subscriber;

(III) the telephone or instrument number, or other subscriber number or identifier, of such customer or subscriber, including any temporarily assigned network address or associated routing or transmission information; and

(IV) the length of the provision of service by such provider to such customer or subscriber and the types of services utilized by such customer or subscriber.

(e)(1) Except as provided in paragraph (2), an order issued under this section shall authorize the installation and use of a pen register or trap and trace device for a period not to exceed 90 days. Extensions of such an order may be granted, but only upon an application for an order under this section and upon the judicial finding required by subsection (d). The period of extension shall be for a period not to exceed 90 days.

(2) In the case of an application under subsection (c) where the applicant has certified that the information likely to be obtained is foreign intelligence information not concerning a United States person, an order, or an extension of an order, under the section may be for a period not to exceed one year.

(f) No cause of action shall lie in any court against any provider of a wire or electronic communication service, landlord, custodian, or other person (including any officer, employee, agent, or other specified person thereof) that furnishes any information, facilities, or technical assistance under subsection (d) in accordance with the terms of an order issued under this section.

(g) Unless otherwise ordered by the judge, the results of a pen register or trap and trace device shall be furnished at reasonable intervals during regular business hours for the duration of the order to the authorized Government official or officials.

AUTHORIZATION DURING EMERGENCIES
SEC. 403. [50 U.S.C. §1843]

(a) Notwithstanding any other provision of this Act, when the Attorney General makes a determination described in subsection (b), the Attorney General may authorize the installation and use of a pen register or trap and trace device on an emergency basis to gather foreign intelligence information not concerning a United States person or information to protect against international terrorism or clandestine intelligence activities, provided that such investigation of a United States person is not conducted solely upon the basis of activities protected by the first amendment to the Constitution if—

(1) a judge referred to in section 402(b) of this Act is informed by the Attorney General or his designee at the time of such authorization that the decision has been made to install and use the pen register or trap and trace device, as the case may be, on an emergency basis; and

(2) an application in accordance with section 402 of this Act is made to such judge as soon as practicable, but not more than 7 days, after the Attorney General authorizes the installation and use of the pen register or trap and trace device, as the case may be, under this section.

(b) A determination under this subsection is a reasonable determination by the Attorney General that—

(1) an emergency requires the installation and use of a pen register or trap and trace device to obtain foreign intelligence information not concerning a United States person or information to protect against international terrorism or clandestine intelligence activities, provided that such investigation of a United States person is not conducted solely upon the basis of activities protected by the first amendment to the Constitution before an order authorizing the installation and use of the pen register or trap and trace device, as the case may be, can with due diligence be obtained under section 402 of this Act; and

(2) the factual basis for issuance of an order under such section 402 to approve the installation and use of the pen register or trap and trace device, as the case may be, exists.

(c)(1) In the absence of an order applied for under subsection (a)(2) approving the installation and use of a pen register or trap and trace device authorized under this section, the installation and use of the pen register or trap and trace device, as the case may be, shall terminate at the earlier of—

    (A) when the information sought is obtained;

    (B) when the application for the order is denied under section 402 of this Act; or

    (C) 7 days after the time of the authorization by the Attorney General.

(2) In the event that an application for an order applied for under subsection (a)(2) is denied, or in any other case where the installation and use of a pen register or trap and trace device under this section is terminated and no order under section 402 of this Act is issued approving the installation and use of the pen register or trap and trace device, as the case may be, no information obtained or evidence derived from the use of the pen register or trap and trace device, as the case may be, shall be received in evidence or otherwise disclosed in any trial, hearing, or other proceeding in or before any court, grand jury, department, office, agency, regulatory body, legislative committee, or other authority of the United States, a State, or political subdivision thereof, and no information concerning any United States person acquired from the use of the pen register or trap and trace device, as the case may be, shall subsequently be used or disclosed in any other manner by Federal officers or employees without the consent of such person, except with the approval of the Attorney General if the information indicates a threat of death or serious bodily harm to any person.

AUTHORIZATION DURING TIME OF WAR

SEC. 404. [50 U.S.C. §1844] Notwithstanding any other provision of law, the President, through the Attorney General, may authorize the use of a pen register or trap and trace device without a court order under this title to acquire foreign intelligence information for a period not to exceed 15 calendar days following a declaration of war by Congress.

USE OF INFORMATION

SEC. 405. [50 U.S.C. §1845]

(a)(1) Information acquired from the use of a pen register or trap and trace device installed pursuant to this title concerning any United States person may be used and disclosed by Federal officers and employees without the consent of the United States person only in accordance with the provisions of this section.

    (2) No information acquired from a pen register or trap and trace device installed and used pursuant to this title may be used or disclosed by Federal officers or employees except for lawful purposes.

(b) No information acquired pursuant to this title shall be disclosed for law enforcement purposes unless such disclosure is accompanied by a statement that such information, or any information derived therefrom, may only be used in a criminal proceeding with the advance authorization of the Attorney General.

(c) Whenever the United States intends to enter into evidence or otherwise use or disclose in any trial, hearing, or other proceeding in or before any court, department, officer, agency, regulatory body, or other authority of the United States against an aggrieved person any information obtained or derived from the use of a pen register or trap and trace device pursuant to this title, the United States shall, before the trial, hearing, or the other proceeding or at a reasonable time before an effort to so disclose or so use that information or submit it in evidence, notify the aggrieved person and the court or other authority in which the information is to be disclosed or used that the United States intends to so disclose or so use such information.

(d) Whenever any State or political subdivision thereof intends to enter into evidence or otherwise use or disclose in any trial, hearing, or other proceeding in or before any court, department, officer, agency, regulatory body, or other authority of the State or political subdivision thereof against an aggrieved person any information obtained or derived from the use of a pen register or trap and trace device pursuant to this title, the State or political subdivision thereof shall notify the aggrieved person, the court or other authority in which the information is to be disclosed or used, and the Attorney General that the State or political subdivision thereof intends to so disclose or so use such information.

(e)(1) Any aggrieved person against whom evidence obtained or derived from the use of a pen register or trap and trace device is to be, or has been, introduced or otherwise used or disclosed in any trial, hearing, or other proceeding in or before any court, department, officer, agency, regulatory body, or other authority of the United States, or a State or political subdivision thereof, may move to suppress the evidence obtained or derived from the use of the pen register or trap and trace device, as the case may be, on the grounds that—

    (A) the information was unlawfully acquired; or

    (B) the use of the pen register or trap and trace device, as the case may be, was not made in conformity with an order of authorization or approval under this title.

  (2) A motion under paragraph (1) shall be made before the trial, hearing, or other proceeding unless there was no opportunity to make such a motion or the aggrieved person concerned was not aware of the grounds of the motion.

(f)(1) Whenever a court or other authority is notified pursuant to subsection (c) or (d), whenever a motion is made pursuant to subsection (e), or whenever any motion or request is made by an aggrieved person pursuant to any other statute or rule of the United States or any State before any court or other authority of the United States or any State to discover or obtain applications or orders or other materials relating to the use of a pen register or trap and trace device authorized by this title or to discover, obtain, or suppress evidence or information obtained or derived from the use of a pen register or trap and trace device authorized by this title, the United States district court or, where the motion is made before another authority, the United States district court in the same district as the authority shall, notwithstanding any other provision of law and if the Attorney General files an affidavit under oath that disclosure or any adversary hearing would harm the national security of the United States, review in camera and ex parte the application, order, and such other materials relating to the use of the pen register or trap and trace device, as the case may be, as may be necessary to determine whether the use of the pen register or trap and trace device, as the case may be, was lawfully authorized and conducted.

  (2) In making a determination under paragraph (1), the court may disclose to the aggrieved person, under appropriate security procedures and protective orders, portions of the application, order, or other materials relating to the use of the pen register or trap and trace device, as the case may be, or may require the Attorney General to provide to the aggrieved person a summary of such materials, only where such disclosure is necessary to make an accurate determination of the legality of the use of the pen register or trap and trace device, as the case may be.

(g)(1) If the United States district court determines pursuant to subsection (f) that the use of a pen register or trap and trace device was not lawfully authorized or conducted, the court may, in accordance with the requirements of law, suppress the evidence which was unlawfully obtained or derived from the use of the pen register or trap and trace device, as the case may be, or otherwise grant the motion of the aggrieved person.

  (2) If the court determines that the use of the pen register or trap and trace device, as the case may be, was lawfully authorized or conducted, it may deny the motion of the aggrieved person except to the extent that due process requires discovery or disclosure.

(h) Orders granting motions or requests under subsection (g), decisions under this section that the use of a pen register or trap and trace device was not lawfully authorized or conducted, and orders of the United States district court requiring review or granting disclosure of applications, orders, or other materials relating to the installation and use of a pen register or trap and trace device shall be final orders and binding upon all courts of the United States and the several States except a United States Court of Appeals or the Supreme Court.

CONGRESSIONAL OVERSIGHT
SEC. 406. [50 U.S.C. §1846]
(a) On a semiannual basis, the Attorney General shall fully inform the Permanent Select Committee on Intelligence of the House of Representatives and the Select Committee on Intelligence of the Senate and the Committee on the Judiciary of the House of Representatives and the Committee on the Judiciary of the Senate concerning all uses of pen registers and trap and trace devices pursuant to this title.

(b) On a semiannual basis, the Attorney General shall also provide to the committees referred to in subsection (a) and to the Committees on the Judiciary of the House of Representatives and the Senate a report setting forth with respect to the preceding 6-month period—

(1) the total number of applications made for orders approving the use of pen registers or trap and trace devices under this title;

(2) the total number of such orders either granted, modified, or denied; and

(3) the total number of pen registers and trap and trace devices whose installation and use was authorized by the Attorney General on an emergency basis under section 403, and the total number of subsequent orders approving or denying the installation and use of such pen registers and trap and trace devices.

TITLE V—ACCESS TO CERTAIN BUSINESS RECORDS FOR FOREIGN INTELLIGENCE PURPOSES

ACCESS TO CERTAIN BUSINESS RECORDS FOR FOREIGN INTELLIGENCE AND INTERNATIONAL TERRORISM INVESTIGATIONS
SEC. 501. [50 U.S.C. §1861]
(a)(1) Subject to paragraph (3), the Director of the Federal Bureau of Investigation or a designee of the Director (whose rank shall be no lower than Assistant Special Agent in Charge) may make an application for an order requiring the production of any tangible things (including books, records, papers, documents, and other items) for an investigation to obtain foreign intelligence information not concerning a United States person or to protect against international terrorism or clandestine intelligence activities, provided that such investigation of a United States person is not conducted solely upon the basis of activities protected by the first amendment to the Constitution.

(2) An investigation conducted under this section shall

(A) be conducted under guidelines approved by the Attorney General under Executive Order 12333 (or a successor order); and

(B) not be conducted of a United States person solely upon the basis of activities protected by the first amendment to the Constitution of the United States.

(3) In the case of an application for an order requiring the production of library circulation records, library patron lists, book sales records, book customer lists, firearms sales records, tax return records, educational records, or medical records containing information that would identify a person, the Director of the Federal Bureau of Investigation may delegate the authority to make such application to either the Deputy Director of the Federal Bureau of Investigation or the Executive Assistant Director for National Security (or any successor

position). The Deputy Director or the Executive Assistant Director may not further delegate such authority.

(b) Each application under this section

    (1) shall be made to—

        (A) a judge of the court established by section 103(a) of this Act; or

        (B) a United States Magistrate Judge under chapter 43 of Title 28, who is publicly designated by the Chief Justice of the United States to have the power to hear applications and grant orders for the production of tangible things under this section on behalf of a judge of that court; and

    (2) shall include—

        (A) a statement of facts showing that there are reasonable grounds to believe that the tangible things sought are relevant to an authorized investigation (other than a threat assessment) conducted in accordance with subsection (a)(2) of this section to obtain foreign intelligence information not concerning a United States person or to protect against international terrorism or clandestine intelligence activities, such things being presumptively relevant to an authorized investigation if the applicant shows in the statement of the facts that they pertain to—

            (i) a foreign power or an agent of a foreign power;

            (ii) the activities of a suspected agent of a foreign power who is the subject of such authorized investigation; or

            (iii) an individual in contact with, or known to, a suspected agent of a foreign power who is the subject of such authorized investigation; and

        (B) an enumeration of the minimization procedures adopted by the Attorney General under subsection (g) of this section that are applicable to the retention and dissemination by the Federal Bureau of Investigation of any tangible things to be made available to the Federal Bureau of Investigation based on the order requested in such application.

(c)(1) Upon an application made pursuant to this section, if the judge finds that the application meets the requirements of subsections (a) and (b) of this section, the judge shall enter an ex parte order as requested, or as modified, approving the release of tangible things. Such order shall direct that minimization procedures adopted pursuant to subsection (g) of this section be followed.

    (2) An order under this subsection—

        (A) shall describe the tangible things that are ordered to be produced with sufficient particularity to permit them to be fairly identified;

        (B) shall include the date on which the tangible things must be provided, which shall allow a reasonable period of time within which the tangible things can be assembled and made available;

        (C) shall provide clear and conspicuous notice of the principles and procedures described in subsection (d) of this section;

        (D) may only require the production of a tangible thing if such thing can be obtained with a subpoena duces tecum issued by a court of the United States in aid of a grand jury investigation or with any other order issued by a court of the United States directing the production of records or tangible things; and

        (E) shall not disclose that such order is issued for purposes of an investigation described in subsection (a) of this section.

(d)(1) No person shall disclose to any other person that the Federal bureau of investigation has sought or obtained tangible things pursuant to an order under this section, other than to

        (A) those persons to whom disclosure is necessary to comply with such order;

(B) an attorney to obtain legal advice or assistance with respect to the production of things in response to the order; or

(C) other persons as permitted by the Director of the Federal Bureau of Investigation or the designee of the Director.

(2)(A) A person to whom disclosure is made pursuant to paragraph (1) shall be subject to the nondisclosure requirements applicable to a person to whom an order is directed under this section in the same manner as such person.

(B) Any person who discloses to a person described in subparagraph (A), (B), or (C) of paragraph (1) that the Federal Bureau of Investigation has sought or obtained tangible things pursuant to an order under this section shall notify such person of the nondisclosure requirements of this subsection.

(C) At the request of the Director of the Federal Bureau of Investigation or the designee of the Director, any person making or intending to make a disclosure under subparagraph (A) or (C) of paragraph (1) shall identify to the Director or such designee the person to whom such disclosure will be made or to whom such disclosure was made prior to the request.

(e) A person who, in good faith, produces tangible things under an order pursuant to this section shall not be liable to any other person for such production. Such production shall not be deemed to constitute a waiver of any privilege in any other proceeding or context.

(f) [JUDICIAL REVIEW OF FISA ORDERS .—]

(1) In this subsection—

(A) the term "production order" means an order to produce any tangible thing under this section; and

(B) the term "nondisclosure order" means an order imposed under subsection (d) of this section.

(2)(A)(i) A person receiving a production order may challenge the legality of that order by filing a petition with the pool established by section 103(e)(1) of this Act. Not less than 1 year after the date of the issuance of the production order, the recipient of a production order may challenge the nondisclosure order imposed in connection with such production order by filing a petition to modify or set aside such nondisclosure order, consistent with the requirements of subparagraph (C), with the pool established by 103(e)(1) of this Act.

(ii) The presiding judge shall immediately assign a petition under clause (i) to 1 of the judges serving in the pool established by 103(e)(1) of this Act. Not later than 72 hours after the assignment of such petition, the assigned judge shall conduct an initial review of the petition. If the assigned judge determines that the petition is frivolous, the assigned judge shall immediately deny the petition and affirm the production order or nondisclosure order. If the assigned judge determines the petition is not frivolous, the assigned judge shall promptly consider the petition in accordance with the procedures established under 103(e)(2) of this Act.

(iii) The assigned judge shall promptly provide a written statement for the record of the reasons for any determination under this subsection. Upon the request of the Government, any order setting aside a nondisclosure order shall be stayed pending review pursuant to paragraph (3).

(B) A judge considering a petition to modify or set aside a production order may grant such petition only if the judge finds that such order does not meet the requirements of this section or is otherwise unlawful. If the judge does not modify or set aside the production order, the judge shall immediately affirm such order, and order the recipient to comply therewith.

(C)(i) A judge considering a petition to modify or set aside a nondisclosure order may grant such petition only if the judge finds that there is no reason to believe that disclosure may endanger the national security of the United States, interfere with a criminal, counterterrorism, or counterintelligence investigation, interfere with diplomatic relations, or endanger the life or physical safety of any person.

(ii) If, upon filing of such a petition, the Attorney General, Deputy Attorney General, an Assistant Attorney General, or the Director of the Federal Bureau of Investigation certifies that disclosure may endanger the national security of the United States or interfere with diplomatic relations, such certification shall be treated as conclusive, unless the judge finds that the certification was made in bad faith.

(iii) If the judge denies a petition to modify or set aside a nondisclosure order, the recipient of such order shall be precluded for a period of 1 year from filing another such petition with respect to such nondisclosure order.

(D) Any production or nondisclosure order not explicitly modified or set aside consistent with this subsection shall remain in full effect.

(3) A petition for review of a decision under paragraph (2) to affirm, modify, or set aside an order by the Government or any person receiving such order shall be made to the court of review established under 103(b) of this Act, which shall have jurisdiction to consider such petitions. The court of review shall provide for the record a written statement of the reasons for its decision and, on petition by the Government or any person receiving such order for writ of certiorari, the record shall be transmitted under seal to the Supreme Court of the United States, which shall have jurisdiction to review such decision.

(4) Judicial proceedings under this subsection shall be concluded as expeditiously as possible. The record of proceedings, including petitions filed, orders granted, and statements of reasons for decision, shall be maintained under security measures established by the Chief Justice of the United States, in consultation with the Attorney General and the Director of National Intelligence.

(5) All petitions under this subsection shall be filed under seal. In any proceedings under this subsection, the court shall, upon request of the Government, review ex parte and in camera any Government submission, or portions thereof, which may include classified information.

(g) MINIMIZATION PROCEDURES.—

(1) IN GENERAL.—Not later than 180 days after March 9, 2006, the Attorney General shall adopt specific minimization procedures governing the retention and dissemination by the Federal Bureau of Investigation of any tangible things, or information therein, received by the Federal Bureau of Investigation in response to an order under this subchapter.

(2) DEFINED.—In this section, the term "minimization procedures" means—

(A) specific procedures that are reasonably designed in light of the purpose and technique of an order for the production of tangible things, to minimize the retention, and prohibit the dissemination, of nonpublicly available information concerning unconsenting United States persons consistent with the need of the United States to obtain, produce, and disseminate foreign intelligence information;

(B) procedures that require that nonpublicly available information, which is not foreign intelligence information, as defined in 103(e)(1) of this Act, shall not be disseminated in a manner that identifies any United States person, without such person's consent, unless such person's identity is necessary to understand foreign intelligence information or assess its importance; and

(C) notwithstanding subparagraphs (A) and (B), procedures that allow for the retention and dissemination of information that is evidence of a crime which has been, is
being, or is about to be committed and that is to be retained or disseminated for law
enforcement purposes.

(h) USE OF INFORMATION.—Information acquired from tangible things received by the
Federal Bureau of Investigation in response to an order under this subchapter concerning any
United States person may be used and disclosed by Federal officers and employees without the
consent of the United States person only in accordance with the minimization procedures
adopted pursuant to subsection (g) of this section. No otherwise privileged information acquired from tangible things received by the Federal Bureau of Investigation in accordance
with the provisions of this subchapter shall lose its privileged character. No information acquired from tangible things received by the Federal Bureau of Investigation in response to an
order under this subchapter may be used or disclosed by Federal officers or employees except
for lawful purposes.

CONGRESSIONAL OVERSIGHT
SEC. 502. [50 U.S.C. §1862]
(a) On an annual basis, the Attorney General shall fully inform the Permanent Select Committee on Intelligence of the House of Representatives and the Select Committee on Intelligence
and the Committee on the Judiciary of the Senate concerning all requests for the production of
tangible things under section 501 of this Act.

(b) In April of each year, the Attorney General shall submit to the House and Senate Committees
on the Judiciary and the House Permanent Select Committee on Intelligence and the Senate
Select Committee on Intelligence a report setting forth with respect to the preceding calendar
year—

   (1) the total number of applications made for orders approving requests for the production
   of tangible things under section 501 of this Act;

   (2) the total number of such orders either granted, modified, or denied; and

   (3) the number of such orders either granted, modified, or denied for the production of
   each of the following:

      (A) Library circulation records, library patron lists, book sales records, or book cus-
      tomer lists.

      (B) Firearms sales records.

      (C) Tax return records.

      (D) Educational records.

      (E) Medical records containing information that would identify a person.

(c)(1) In April of each year, the Attorney General shall submit to Congress a report setting forth
with respect to the preceding year—

      (A) the total number of applications made for orders approving requests for the pro-
      duction of tangible things under section 501 of this Act; and

      (B) the total number of such orders either granted, modified, or denied.

   (2) Each report under this subsection shall be submitted in unclassified form.

TITLE VI—REPORTING REQUIREMENT

SEMIANNUAL REPORT OF THE ATTORNEY GENERAL
SEC. 601. [50 U.S.C. §1871]
(a) REPORT.—On a semiannual basis, the Attorney General shall submit to the Permanent
Select Committee on Intelligence of the House of Representatives, the Select Committee on

Intelligence of the Senate, and the Committees on the Judiciary of the House of Representatives and the Senate, in a manner consistent with the protection of the national security, a report setting forth with respect to the preceding 6-month period—

(1) the aggregate number of persons targeted for orders issued under this Act, including a breakdown of those targeted for—

(A) electronic surveillance under section 105;

(B) physical searches under section 304;

(C) pen registers under section 402;

(D) access to records under section 501;

(E) acquisitions under section 703; and

(F) acquisitions under section 704;

(2) the number of individuals covered by an order issued pursuant to section 101(b)(1)(C);

(3) the number of times that the Attorney General has authorized that information obtained under this Act may be used in a criminal proceeding or any information derived therefrom may be used in a criminal proceeding;

(4) a summary of significant legal interpretations of this Act involving matters before the Foreign Intelligence Surveillance Court or the Foreign Intelligence Surveillance Court of Review, including interpretations presented in applications or pleadings filed with the Foreign Intelligence Surveillance Court or the Foreign Intelligence Surveillance Court of Review by the Department of Justice; and

(5) copies of all decisions, orders, or opinions of the Foreign Intelligence Surveillance Court or Foreign Intelligence Surveillance Court of Review that include significant construction or interpretation of the provisions of this Act.

(b) FREQUENCY.—The first report under this section shall be submitted not later than 6 months after the date of enactment of this section. Subsequent reports under this section shall be submitted semi-annually thereafter.

(c) SUBMISSIONS TO CONGRESS.— The Attorney General shall submit to the committees of Congress referred to in subsection (a)—

(1) a copy of any decision, order, or opinion issued by the Foreign Intelligence Surveillance Court or the Foreign Intelligence Surveillance Court of Review that includes significant construction or interpretation of any provision of this Act, and any pleadings, applications, or memoranda of law associated with such decision, order, or opinion, not later than 45 days after such decision, order, or opinion is issued; and

(2) a copy of each such decision, order, or opinion, and any pleadings, applications, or memoranda of law associated with such decision, order, or opinion, that was issued during the 5-year period ending on the date of the enactment of the FISA Amendments Act of 2008 and not previously submitted in a report under subsection (a).

(d) PROTECTION OF NATIONAL SECURITY.— The Attorney General, in consultation with the Director of National Intelligence, may authorize redactions of materials described in subsection (c) that are provided to the committees of Congress referred to in subsection (a), if such redactions are necessary to protect the national security of the United States and are limited to sensitive sources and methods information or the identities of targets.

(e) DEFINITIONS.— In this section:

(1) FOREIGN INTELLIGENCE SURVEILLANCE COURT.— The term 'Foreign Intelligence Surveillance Court' means the court established under section 103(a).

(2) FOREIGN INTELLIGENCE SURVEILLANCE COURT OF REVIEW.— The term 'Foreign Intelligence Surveillance Court of Review' means the court established under section 103(b).

TITLE VII—ADDITIONAL PROCEDURES REGARDING CERTAIN PERSONS OUTSIDE THE UNITED STATES

DEFINITIONS

SEC. 701. [50 U.S.C. §1881]

(a) IN GENERAL.— The terms 'agent of a foreign power', 'Attorney General', 'contents', 'electronic surveillance', 'foreign intelligence information', 'foreign power', 'person', 'United States', and 'United States person' have the meanings given such terms in section 101, except as specifically provided in this title.

(b) ADDITIONAL DEFINITIONS.—

(1) CONGRESSIONAL INTELLIGENCE COMMITTEES.— The term 'congressional intelligence committees' means—

(A) the Select Committee on Intelligence of the Senate; and

(B) the Permanent Select Committee on Intelligence of the House of Representatives.

(2) FOREIGN INTELLIGENCE SURVEILLANCE COURT.— The terms 'Foreign Intelligence Surveillance Court' and 'Court' mean the court established under section 103(a).

(3) FOREIGN INTELLIGENCE SURVEILLANCE COURT OF REVIEW; COURT OF REVIEW.— The terms 'Foreign Intelligence Surveillance Court of Review' and 'Court of Review' mean the court established under section 103(b).

(4) ELECTRONIC COMMUNICATION SERVICE PROVIDER.— The term 'electronic communication service provider' means—

(A) a telecommunications carrier, as that term is defined in section 3 of the Communications Act of 1934 (47 U.S.C. 153);

(B) a provider of electronic communication service, as that term is defined in section 2510 of title 18, United States Code;

(C) a provider of a remote computing service, as that term is defined in section 2711 of title 18, United States Code;

(D) any other communication service provider who has access to wire or electronic communications either as such communications are transmitted or as such communications are stored; or

(E) an officer, employee, or agent of an entity described in subparagraph (A), (B), (C), or (D).

(5) INTELLIGENCE COMMUNITY.— The term 'intelligence community' has the meaning given the term in section 3(4) of the National Security Act of 1947 (50 U.S.C. 401a(4)).

PROCEDURES FOR TARGETING CERTAIN PERSONS OUTSIDE THE UNITED STATES OTHER THAN UNITED STATES PERSONS

SEC. 702. [50 U.S.C. §1881a]

(a) AUTHORIZATION.— Notwithstanding any other provision of law, upon the issuance of an order in accordance with subsection (i)(3) or a determination under subsection (c)(2), the Attorney General and the Director of National Intelligence may authorize jointly, for a period of up to 1 year from the effective date of the authorization, the targeting of persons reasonably believed to be located outside the United States to acquire foreign intelligence information.

(b) LIMITATIONS.— An acquisition authorized under subsection (a)—

(1) may not intentionally target any person known at the time of acquisition to be located in the United States;

(2) may not intentionally target a person reasonably believed to be located outside the United States if the purpose of such acquisition is to target a particular, known person reasonably believed to be in the United States;

(3) may not intentionally target a United States person reasonably believed to be located outside the United States;

(4) may not intentionally acquire any communication as to which the sender and all intended recipients are known at the time of the acquisition to be located in the United States; and

(5) shall be conducted in a manner consistent with the fourth amendment to the Constitution of the United States.

(c) CONDUCT OF ACQUISITION.—

(1) IN GENERAL.—An acquisition authorized under subsection (a) shall be conducted only in accordance with—

(A) the targeting and minimization procedures adopted in accordance with subsections (d) and (e); and

(B) upon submission of a certification in accordance with subsection (g), such certification.

(2) DETERMINATION.— A determination under this paragraph and for purposes of subsection (a) is a determination by the Attorney General and the Director of National Intelligence that exigent circumstances exist because, without immediate implementation of an authorization under subsection (a), intelligence important to the national security of the United States may be lost or not timely acquired and time does not permit the issuance of an order pursuant to subsection (i)(3) prior to the implementation of such authorization.

(3) TIMING OF DETERMINATION.— The Attorney General and the Director of National Intelligence may make the determination under paragraph (2)—

(A) before the submission of a certification in accordance with subsection (g); or

(B) by amending a certification pursuant to subsection (i)(1)(C) at any time during which judicial review under subsection (i) of such certification is pending.

(4) CONSTRUCTION.— Nothing in title I shall be construed to require an application for a court order under such title for an acquisition that is targeted in accordance with this section at a person reasonably believed to be located outside the United States.

(d) TARGETING PROCEDURES.—

(1) REQUIREMENT TO ADOPT.— The Attorney General, in consultation with the Director of National Intelligence, shall adopt targeting procedures that are reasonably designed to—

(A) ensure that any acquisition authorized under subsection (a) is limited to targeting persons reasonably believed to be located outside the United States; and

(B) prevent the intentional acquisition of any communication as to which the sender and all intended recipients are known at the time of the acquisition to be located in the United States.

(2) JUDICIAL REVIEW.— The procedures adopted in accordance with paragraph (1) shall be subject to judicial review pursuant to subsection (i).

(e) MINIMIZATION PROCEDURES.—

(1) REQUIREMENT TO ADOPT.— The Attorney General, in consultation with the Director of National Intelligence, shall adopt minimization procedures that meet the definition of minimization procedures under section 101(h) or 301(4), as appropriate, for acquisitions authorized under subsection (a).

(2) JUDICIAL REVIEW.— The minimization procedures adopted in accordance with paragraph (1) shall be subject to judicial review pursuant to subsection (i).

(f) GUIDELINES FOR COMPLIANCE WITH LIMITATIONS.—

(1) REQUIREMENT TO ADOPT.— The Attorney General, in consultation with the Director of National Intelligence, shall adopt guidelines to ensure—

(A) compliance with the limitations in subsection (b); and

(B) that an application for a court order is filed as required by this Act.

(2) SUBMISSION OF GUIDELINES.— The Attorney General shall provide the guidelines adopted in accordance with paragraph (1) to—

(A) the congressional intelligence committees;

(B) the Committees on the Judiciary of the Senate and the House of Representatives; and

(C) the Foreign Intelligence Surveillance Court.

(g) CERTIFICATION.—

(1) IN GENERAL.—

(A) REQUIREMENT.— Subject to subparagraph (B), prior to the implementation of an authorization under subsection (a), the Attorney General and the Director of National Intelligence shall provide to the Foreign Intelligence Surveillance Court a written certification and any supporting affidavit, under oath and under seal, in accordance with this subsection.

(B) EXCEPTION.— If the Attorney General and the Director of National Intelligence make a determination under subsection (c)(2) and time does not permit the submission of a certification under this subsection prior to the implementation of an authorization under subsection (a), the Attorney General and the Director of National Intelligence shall submit to the Court a certification for such authorization as soon as practicable but in no event later than 7 days after such determination is made.

(2) REQUIREMENTS.— A certification made under this subsection shall—

(A) attest that—

(i) there are procedures in place that have been approved, have been submitted for approval, or will be submitted with the certification for approval by the Foreign Intelligence Surveillance Court that are reasonably designed to—

(I) ensure that an acquisition authorized under subsection (a) is limited to targeting persons reasonably believed to be located outside the United States; and

(II) prevent the intentional acquisition of any communication as to which the sender and all intended recipients are known at the time of the acquisition to be located in the United States;

(ii) the minimization procedures to be used with respect to such acquisition—

(I) meet the definition of minimization procedures under section 101(h) or 301(4), as appropriate; and

(II) have been approved, have been submitted for approval, or will be submitted with the certification for approval by the Foreign Intelligence Surveillance Court;

(iii) guidelines have been adopted in accordance with subsection (f) to ensure compliance with the limitations in subsection (b) and to ensure that an application for a court order is filed as required by this Act;

(iv) the procedures and guidelines referred to in clauses (i), (ii), and (iii) are consistent with the requirements of the fourth amendment to the Constitution of the United States;

(v) a significant purpose of the acquisition is to obtain foreign intelligence information;

(vi) the acquisition involves obtaining foreign intelligence information from or with the assistance of an electronic communication service provider; and

(vii) the acquisition complies with the limitations in subsection (b);

(B) include the procedures adopted in accordance with subsections (d) and (e);

(C) be supported, as appropriate, by the affidavit of any appropriate official in the area of national security who is—

(i) appointed by the President, by and with the advice and consent of the Senate; or

(ii) the head of an element of the intelligence community;

(D) include—

(i) an effective date for the authorization that is at least 30 days after the submission of the written certification to the court; or

(ii) if the acquisition has begun or the effective date is less than 30 days after the submission of the written certification to the court, the date the acquisition began or the effective date for the acquisition; and

(E) if the Attorney General and the Director of National Intelligence make a determination under subsection (c)(2), include a statement that such determination has been made.

(3) CHANGE IN EFFECTIVE DATE.— The Attorney General and the Director of National Intelligence may advance or delay the effective date referred to in paragraph (2)(D) by submitting an amended certification in accordance with subsection (i)(1)(C) to the Foreign Intelligence Surveillance Court for review pursuant to subsection (i).

(4) LIMITATION.— A certification made under this subsection is not required to identify the specific facilities, places, premises, or property at which an acquisition authorized under subsection (a) will be directed or conducted.

(5) MAINTENANCE OF CERTIFICATION.— The Attorney General or a designee of the Attorney General shall maintain a copy of a certification made under this subsection.

(6) REVIEW.— A certification submitted in accordance with this subsection shall be subject to judicial review pursuant to subsection (i).

(h) DIRECTIVES AND JUDICIAL REVIEW OF DIRECTIVES-

(1) AUTHORITY.— With respect to an acquisition authorized under subsection (a), the Attorney General and the Director of National Intelligence may direct, in writing, an electronic communication service provider to—

(A) immediately provide the Government with all information, facilities, or assistance necessary to accomplish the acquisition in a manner that will protect the secrecy of the acquisition and produce a minimum of interference with the services that such electronic communication service provider is providing to the target of the acquisition; and

(B) maintain under security procedures approved by the Attorney General and the Director of National Intelligence any records concerning the acquisition or the aid furnished that such electronic communication service provider wishes to maintain.

(2) COMPENSATION.— The Government shall compensate, at the prevailing rate, an electronic communication service provider for providing information, facilities, or assistance in accordance with a directive issued pursuant to paragraph (1).

(3) RELEASE FROM LIABILITY.— No cause of action shall lie in any court against any electronic communication service provider for providing any information, facilities, or assistance in accordance with a directive issued pursuant to paragraph (1).

(4) CHALLENGING OF DIRECTIVES.—

(A) AUTHORITY TO CHALLENGE.— An electronic communication service provider receiving a directive issued pursuant to paragraph (1) may file a petition to modify or set aside such directive with the Foreign Intelligence Surveillance Court, which shall have jurisdiction to review such petition.

(B) ASSIGNMENT.— The presiding judge of the Court shall assign a petition filed under subparagraph (A) to 1 of the judges serving in the pool established under section 103(e)(1) not later than 24 hours after the filing of such petition.

(C) STANDARDS FOR REVIEW.— A judge considering a petition filed under subparagraph (A) may grant such petition only if the judge finds that the directive does not meet the requirements of this section, or is otherwise unlawful.

(D) PROCEDURES FOR INITIAL REVIEW.— A judge shall conduct an initial review of a petition filed under subparagraph (A) not later than 5 days after being assigned such petition. If the judge determines that such petition does not consist of claims, defenses, or other legal contentions that are warranted by existing law or by a nonfrivolous argument for extending, modifying, or reversing existing law or for establishing new law, the judge shall immediately deny such petition and affirm the directive or any part of the directive that is the subject of such petition and order the recipient to comply with the directive or any part of it. Upon making a determination under this subparagraph or promptly thereafter, the judge shall provide a written statement for the record of the reasons for such determination.

(E) PROCEDURES FOR PLENARY REVIEW.— If a judge determines that a petition filed under subparagraph (A) requires plenary review, the judge shall affirm, modify, or set aside the directive that is the subject of such petition not later than 30 days after being assigned such petition. If the judge does not set aside the directive, the judge shall immediately affirm or affirm with modifications the directive, and order the recipient to comply with the directive in its entirety or as modified. The judge shall provide a written statement for the record of the reasons for a determination under this subparagraph.

(F) CONTINUED EFFECT.— Any directive not explicitly modified or set aside under this paragraph shall remain in full effect.

(G) CONTEMPT OF COURT.— Failure to obey an order issued under this paragraph may be punished by the Court as contempt of court.

(5) ENFORCEMENT OF DIRECTIVES.—

(A) ORDER TO COMPEL.— If an electronic communication service provider fails to comply with a directive issued pursuant to paragraph (1), the Attorney General may file a petition for an order to compel the electronic communication service provider to comply with the directive with the Foreign Intelligence Surveillance Court, which shall have jurisdiction to review such petition.

(B) ASSIGNMENT.— The presiding judge of the Court shall assign a petition filed under subparagraph (A) to 1 of the judges serving in the pool established under section 103(e)(1) not later than 24 hours after the filing of such petition.

(C) PROCEDURES FOR REVIEW.— A judge considering a petition filed under subparagraph (A) shall, not later than 30 days after being assigned such petition, issue an order requiring the electronic communication service provider to comply with the directive or any part of it, as issued or as modified, if the judge finds that the directive meets the requirements of this section and is otherwise lawful. The judge shall provide a written statement for the record of the reasons for a determination under this paragraph.

(D) CONTEMPT OF COURT.— Failure to obey an order issued under this paragraph may be punished by the Court as contempt of court.

(E) PROCESS.— Any process under this paragraph may be served in any judicial district in which the electronic communication service provider may be found.

(6) APPEAL.—

(A) APPEAL TO THE COURT OF REVIEW.— The Government or an electronic communication service provider receiving a directive issued pursuant to paragraph (1) may file a petition with the Foreign Intelligence Surveillance Court of Review for review of a decision issued pursuant to paragraph (4) or (5). The Court of Review shall have jurisdiction to consider such petition and shall provide a written statement for the record of the reasons for a decision under this subparagraph.

(B) CERTIORARI TO THE SUPREME COURT.— The Government or an electronic communication service provider receiving a directive issued pursuant to paragraph (1) may file a petition for a writ of certiorari for review of a decision of the Court of Review issued under subparagraph (A). The record for such review shall be transmitted under seal to the Supreme Court of the United States, which shall have jurisdiction to review such decision.

(i) JUDICIAL REVIEW OF CERTIFICATIONS AND PROCEDURES.—

(1) IN GENERAL.—

(A) REVIEW BY THE FOREIGN INTELLIGENCE SURVEILLANCE COURT.— The Foreign Intelligence Surveillance Court shall have jurisdiction to review a certification submitted in accordance with subsection (g) and the targeting and minimization procedures adopted in accordance with subsections (d) and (e), and amendments to such certification or such procedures.

(B) TIME PERIOD FOR REVIEW.— The Court shall review a certification submitted in accordance with subsection (g) and the targeting and minimization procedures adopted in accordance with subsections (d) and (e) and shall complete such review and issue an order under paragraph (3) not later than 30 days after the date on which such certification and such procedures are submitted.

(C) AMENDMENTS.— The Attorney General and the Director of National Intelligence may amend a certification submitted in accordance with subsection (g) or the targeting and minimization procedures adopted in accordance with subsections (d) and (e) as necessary at any time, including if the Court is conducting or has completed review of such certification or such procedures, and shall submit the amended certification or amended procedures to the Court not later than 7 days after amending such certification or such procedures. The Court shall review any amendment under this subparagraph under the procedures set forth in this subsection. The Attorney General and the Director of National Intelligence may authorize the use of an amended certification or amended procedures pending the Court's review of such amended certification or amended procedures.

(2) REVIEW.— The Court shall review the following:

(A) CERTIFICATION.— A certification submitted in accordance with subsection (g) to determine whether the certification contains all the required elements.

(B) TARGETING PROCEDURES.— The targeting procedures adopted in accordance with subsection (d) to assess whether the procedures are reasonably designed to-

(i) ensure that an acquisition authorized under subsection (a) is limited to targeting persons reasonably believed to be located outside the United States; and

(ii) prevent the intentional acquisition of any communication as to which the sender and all intended recipients are known at the time of the acquisition to be located in the United States.

(C) MINIMIZATION PROCEDURES.— The minimization procedures adopted in accordance with subsection (e) to assess whether such procedures meet the definition of minimization procedures under section 101(h) or section 301(4), as appropriate.

(3) ORDERS.—

(A) APPROVAL.— If the Court finds that a certification submitted in accordance with subsection (g) contains all the required elements and that the targeting and minimization procedures adopted in accordance with subsections (d) and (e) are consistent with the requirements of those subsections and with the fourth amendment to the Constitution of the United States, the Court shall enter an order approving the certification and the use, or continued use in the case of an acquisition authorized pursuant to a determination under subsection (c)(2), of the procedures for the acquisition.

(B) CORRECTION OF DEFICIENCIES.— If the Court finds that a certification submitted in accordance with subsection (g) does not contain all the required elements, or that the procedures adopted in accordance with subsections (d) and (e) are not consistent with the requirements of those subsections or the fourth amendment to the Constitution of the United States, the Court shall issue an order directing the Government to, at the Government's election and to the extent required by the Court's order—

(i) correct any deficiency identified by the Court's order not later than 30 days after the date on which the Court issues the order; or

(ii) cease, or not begin, the implementation of the authorization for which such certification was submitted.

(C) REQUIREMENT FOR WRITTEN STATEMENT.— In support of an order under this subsection, the Court shall provide, simultaneously with the order, for the record a written statement of the reasons for the order.

(4) APPEAL.—

(A) APPEAL TO THE COURT OF REVIEW.— The Government may file a petition with the Foreign Intelligence Surveillance Court of Review for review of an order under this subsection. The Court of Review shall have jurisdiction to consider such petition. For any decision under this subparagraph affirming, reversing, or modifying an order of the Foreign Intelligence Surveillance Court, the Court of Review shall provide for the record a written statement of the reasons for the decision.

(B) CONTINUATION OF ACQUISITION PENDING REHEARING OR APPEAL.—Any acquisition affected by an order under paragraph (3)(B) may continue—

(i) during the pendency of any rehearing of the order by the Court en banc; and

(ii) if the Government files a petition for review of an order under this section, until the Court of Review enters an order under subparagraph (C).

(C) IMPLEMENTATION PENDING APPEAL.— Not later than 60 days after the filing of a petition for review of an order under paragraph (3)(B) directing the correction of a deficiency, the Court of Review shall determine, and enter a corresponding order regarding, whether all or any part of the correction order, as issued or modified, shall be implemented during the pendency of the review.

(D) CERTIORARI TO THE SUPREME COURT.— The Government may file a petition for a writ of certiorari for review of a decision of the Court of Review issued under subparagraph (A). The record for such review shall be transmitted under seal to the Supreme Court of the United States, which shall have jurisdiction to review such decision.

(5) SCHEDULE.—

(A) REAUTHORIZATION OF AUTHORIZATIONS IN EFFECT.— If the Attorney General and the Director of National Intelligence seek to reauthorize or replace an authorization issued under subsection (a), the Attorney General and the Director of National Intelligence shall, to the extent practicable, submit to the Court the certification prepared in accordance with subsection (g) and the procedures adopted in accordance with subsections (d) and (e) at least 30 days prior to the expiration of such authorization.

(B) REAUTHORIZATION OF ORDERS, AUTHORIZATIONS, AND DIRECTIVES.— If the Attorney General and the Director of National Intelligence seek to reauthorize or replace an authorization issued under subsection (a) by filing a certification pursuant to subparagraph (A), that authorization, and any directives issued thereunder and any order related thereto, shall remain in effect, notwithstanding the expiration provided for in subsection (a), until the Court issues an order with respect to such certification under paragraph (3) at which time the provisions of that paragraph and paragraph (4) shall apply with respect to such certification.

(j) JUDICIAL PROCEEDINGS.—

(1) EXPEDITED JUDICIAL PROCEEDINGS.— Judicial proceedings under this section shall be conducted as expeditiously as possible.

(2) TIME LIMITS.— A time limit for a judicial decision in this section shall apply unless the Court, the Court of Review, or any judge of either the Court or the Court of Review, by order for reasons stated, extends that time as necessary for good cause in a manner consistent with national security.

(k) MAINTENANCE AND SECURITY OF RECORDS AND PROCEEDINGS.—

(1) STANDARDS.— The Foreign Intelligence Surveillance Court shall maintain a record of a proceeding under this section, including petitions, appeals, orders, and statements of reasons for a decision, under security measures adopted by the Chief Justice of the United States, in consultation with the Attorney General and the Director of National Intelligence.

(2) FILING AND REVIEW.— All petitions under this section shall be filed under seal. In any proceedings under this section, the Court shall, upon request of the Government, review ex parte and in camera any Government submission, or portions of a submission, which may include classified information.

(3) RETENTION OF RECORDS.— The Attorney General and the Director of National Intelligence shall retain a directive or an order issued under this section for a period of not less than 10 years from the date on which such directive or such order is issued.

(l) ASSESSMENTS AND REVIEWS.—

(1) SEMIANNUAL ASSESSMENT.— Not less frequently than once every 6 months, the Attorney General and Director of National Intelligence shall assess compliance with the targeting and minimization procedures adopted in accordance with subsections (d) and (e) and the guidelines adopted in accordance with subsection (f) and shall submit each assessment to—

(A) the Foreign Intelligence Surveillance Court; and

(B) consistent with the Rules of the House of Representatives, the Standing Rules of the Senate, and Senate Resolution 400 of the 94th Congress or any successor Senate resolution—

(i) the congressional intelligence committees; and

(ii) the Committees on the Judiciary of the House of Representatives and the Senate.

(2) AGENCY ASSESSMENT.— The Inspector General of the Department of Justice and the Inspector General of each element of the intelligence community authorized to acquire foreign intelligence information under subsection (a), with respect to the department or element of such Inspector General—

(A) are authorized to review compliance with the targeting and minimization procedures adopted in accordance with subsections

(d) and (e) and the guidelines adopted in accordance with subsection (f);

(B) with respect to acquisitions authorized under subsection (a), shall review the number of disseminated intelligence reports containing a reference to a United States-person identity and the number of United States-person identities subsequently disseminated by the element concerned in response to requests for identities that were not referred to by name or title in the original reporting;

(C) with respect to acquisitions authorized under subsection (a), shall review the number of targets that were later determined to be located in the United States and, to the extent possible, whether communications of such targets were reviewed; and

(D) shall provide each such review to—

    (i) the Attorney General;

    (ii) the Director of National Intelligence; and

    (iii) consistent with the Rules of the House of Representatives, the Standing Rules of the Senate, and Senate Resolution 400 of the 94th Congress or any successor Senate resolution—

        (I) the congressional intelligence committees; and

        (II) the Committees on the Judiciary of the House of Representatives and the Senate.

(3) ANNUAL REVIEW.—

(A) REQUIREMENT TO CONDUCT.— The head of each element of the intelligence community conducting an acquisition authorized under subsection (a) shall conduct an annual review to determine whether there is reason to believe that foreign intelligence information has been or will be obtained from the acquisition. The annual review shall provide, with respect to acquisitions authorized under subsection (a)—

    (i) an accounting of the number of disseminated intelligence reports containing a reference to a United States-person identity;

    (ii) an accounting of the number of United States-person identities subsequently disseminated by that element in response to requests for identities that were not referred to by name or title in the original reporting;

    (iii) the number of targets that were later determined to be located in the United States and, to the extent possible, whether communications of such targets were reviewed; and

    (iv) a description of any procedures developed by the head of such element of the intelligence community and approved by the Director of National Intelligence to assess, in a manner consistent with national security, operational requirements and the privacy interests of United States persons, the extent to which the acquisitions authorized under subsection (a) acquire the communications of United States persons, and the results of any such assessment.

(B) USE OF REVIEW.— The head of each element of the intelligence community that conducts an annual review under subparagraph (A) shall use each such review to evaluate the adequacy of the minimization procedures utilized by such element and, as appropriate, the application of the minimization procedures to a particular acquisition authorized under subsection (a).

(C) PROVISION OF REVIEW.— The head of each element of the intelligence community that conducts an annual review under subparagraph (A) shall provide such review to—

    (i) the Foreign Intelligence Surveillance Court;

    (ii) the Attorney General;

    (iii) the Director of National Intelligence; and

    (iv) consistent with the Rules of the House of Representatives, the Standing Rules of the Senate, and Senate Resolution 400 of the 94th Congress or any successor Senate resolution—

(I) the congressional intelligence committees; and

(II) the Committees on the Judiciary of the House of Representatives and the Senate.

CERTAIN ACQUISITIONS INSIDE THE UNITED STATES TARGETING UNITED STATES PERSONS OUTSIDE THE UNITED STATES

SEC. 703. [50 U.S.C. §1881b]

(a) JURISDICTION OF THE FOREIGN INTELLIGENCE SURVEILLANCE COURT.—

(1) IN GENERAL.— The Foreign Intelligence Surveillance Court shall have jurisdiction to review an application and to enter an order approving the targeting of a United States person reasonably believed to be located outside the United States to acquire foreign intelligence information, if the acquisition constitutes electronic surveillance or the acquisition of stored electronic communications or stored electronic data that requires an order under this Act, and such acquisition is conducted within the United States.

(2) LIMITATION.— If a United States person targeted under this subsection is reasonably believed to be located in the United States during the effective period of an order issued pursuant to subsection (c), an acquisition targeting such United States person under this section shall cease unless the targeted United States person is again reasonably believed to be located outside the United States while an order issued pursuant to subsection (c) is in effect. Nothing in this section shall be construed to limit the authority of the Government to seek an order or authorization under, or otherwise engage in any activity that is authorized under, any other title of this Act.

(b) APPLICATION.—

(1) IN GENERAL.— Each application for an order under this section shall be made by a Federal officer in writing upon oath or affirmation to a judge having jurisdiction under subsection (a)(1). Each application shall require the approval of the Attorney General based upon the Attorney General's finding that it satisfies the criteria and requirements of such application, as set forth in this section, and shall include—

(A) the identity of the Federal officer making the application;

(B) the identity, if known, or a description of the United States person who is the target of the acquisition;

(C) a statement of the facts and circumstances relied upon to justify the applicant's belief that the United States person who is the target of the acquisition is—

(i) a person reasonably believed to be located outside the United States; and

(ii) a foreign power, an agent of a foreign power, or an officer or employee of a foreign power;

(D) a statement of proposed minimization procedures that meet the definition of minimization procedures under section 101(h) or 301(4), as appropriate;

(E) a description of the nature of the information sought and the type of communications or activities to be subjected to acquisition;

(F) a certification made by the Attorney General or an official specified in section 104(a)(6) that—

(i) the certifying official deems the information sought to be foreign intelligence information;

(ii) a significant purpose of the acquisition is to obtain foreign intelligence information;

(iii) such information cannot reasonably be obtained by normal investigative techniques;

(iv) designates the type of foreign intelligence information being sought according to the categories described in section 101(e); and

        (v) includes a statement of the basis for the certification that—

           (I) the information sought is the type of foreign intelligence information designated; and

           (II) such information cannot reasonably be obtained by normal investigative techniques;

    (G) a summary statement of the means by which the acquisition will be conducted and whether physical entry is required to effect the acquisition;

    (H) the identity of any electronic communication service provider necessary to effect the acquisition, provided that the application is not required to identify the specific facilities, places, premises, or property at which the acquisition authorized under this section will be directed or conducted;

    (I) a statement of the facts concerning any previous applications that have been made to any judge of the Foreign Intelligence Surveillance Court involving the United States person specified in the application and the action taken on each previous application; and

    (J) a statement of the period of time for which the acquisition is required to be maintained, provided that such period of time shall not exceed 90 days per application.

(2) OTHER REQUIREMENTS OF THE ATTORNEY GENERAL.— The Attorney General may require any other affidavit or certification from any other officer in connection with the application.

(3) OTHER REQUIREMENTS OF THE JUDGE.— The judge may require the applicant to furnish such other information as may be necessary to make the findings required by subsection (c)(1).

(c) ORDER.—

    (1) FINDINGS.— Upon an application made pursuant to subsection (b), the Foreign Intelligence Surveillance Court shall enter an ex parte order as requested or as modified by the Court approving the acquisition if the Court finds that—

        (A) the application has been made by a Federal officer and approved by the Attorney General;

        (B) on the basis of the facts submitted by the applicant, for the United States person who is the target of the acquisition, there is probable cause to believe that the target is—

           (i) a person reasonably believed to be located outside the United States; and

           (ii) a foreign power, an agent of a foreign power, or an officer or employee of a foreign power;

        (C) the proposed minimization procedures meet the definition of minimization procedures under section 101(h) or 301(4), as appropriate; and

        (D) the application that has been filed contains all statements and certifications required by subsection (b) and the certification or certifications are not clearly erroneous on the basis of the statement made under subsection (b)(1)(F)(v) and any other information furnished under subsection (b)(3).

    (2) PROBABLE CAUSE.— In determining whether or not probable cause exists for purposes of paragraph (1)(B), a judge having jurisdiction under subsection (a)(1) may consider past activities of the target and facts and circumstances relating to current or future activities of the target. No United States person may be considered a foreign power, agent of a foreign power, or officer or employee of a foreign power solely upon the basis of activities protected by the first amendment to the Constitution of the United States.

    (3) REVIEW.—

        (A) LIMITATION ON REVIEW.— Review by a judge having jurisdiction under subsection (a)(1) shall be limited to that required to make the findings described in paragraph (1).

(B) REVIEW OF PROBABLE CAUSE.— If the judge determines that the facts submitted under subsection (b) are insufficient to establish probable cause under paragraph (1)(B), the judge shall enter an order so stating and provide a written statement for the record of the reasons for the determination. The Government may appeal an order under this subparagraph pursuant to subsection (f).

(C) REVIEW OF MINIMIZATION PROCEDURES.— If the judge determines that the proposed minimization procedures referred to in paragraph (1)(C) do not meet the definition of minimization procedures under section 101(h) or 301(4), as appropriate, the judge shall enter an order so stating and provide a written statement for the record of the reasons for the determination. The Government may appeal an order under this subparagraph pursuant to subsection (f).

(D) REVIEW OF CERTIFICATION.— If the judge determines that an application pursuant to subsection (b) does not contain all of the required elements, or that the certification or certifications are clearly erroneous on the basis of the statement made under subsection (b)(1)(F)(v) and any other information furnished under subsection (b)(3), the judge shall enter an order so stating and provide a written statement for the record of the reasons for the determination. The Government may appeal an order under this subparagraph pursuant to subsection (f).

(4) SPECIFICATIONS.— An order approving an acquisition under this subsection shall specify—

(A) the identity, if known, or a description of the United States person who is the target of the acquisition identified or described in the application pursuant to subsection (b)(1)(B);

(B) if provided in the application pursuant to subsection (b)(1)(H), the nature and location of each of the facilities or places at which the acquisition will be directed;

(C) the nature of the information sought to be acquired and the type of communications or activities to be subjected to acquisition;

(D) a summary of the means by which the acquisition will be conducted and whether physical entry is required to effect the acquisition; and

(E) the period of time during which the acquisition is approved.

(5) DIRECTIVES.— An order approving an acquisition under this subsection shall direct—

(A) that the minimization procedures referred to in paragraph (1)(C), as approved or modified by the Court, be followed;

(B) if applicable, an electronic communication service provider to provide to the Government forthwith all information, facilities, or assistance necessary to accomplish the acquisition authorized under such order in a manner that will protect the secrecy of the acquisition and produce a minimum of interference with the services that such electronic communication service provider is providing to the target of the acquisition;

(C) if applicable, an electronic communication service provider to maintain under security procedures approved by the Attorney General any records concerning the acquisition or the aid furnished that such electronic communication service provider wishes to maintain; and

(D) if applicable, that the Government compensate, at the prevailing rate, such electronic communication service provider for providing such information, facilities, or assistance.

(6) DURATION.— An order approved under this subsection shall be effective for a period not to exceed 90 days and such order may be renewed for additional 90-day periods upon submission of renewal applications meeting the requirements of subsection (b).

(7) COMPLIANCE.— At or prior to the end of the period of time for which an acquisition is approved by an order or extension under this section, the judge may assess compliance with the minimization procedures referred to in paragraph (1)(C) by reviewing the circumstances under which information concerning United States persons was acquired, retained, or disseminated.

(d) EMERGENCY AUTHORIZATION.—

(1) AUTHORITY FOR EMERGENCY AUTHORIZATION.— Notwithstanding any other provision of this Act, if the Attorney General reasonably determines that—

(A) an emergency situation exists with respect to the acquisition of foreign intelligence information for which an order may be obtained under subsection (c) before an order authorizing such acquisition can with due diligence be obtained, and

(B) the factual basis for issuance of an order under this subsection to approve such acquisition exists, the Attorney General may authorize such acquisition if a judge having jurisdiction under subsection (a)(1) is informed by the Attorney General, or a designee of the Attorney General, at the time of such authorization that the decision has been made to conduct such acquisition and if an application in accordance with this section is made to a judge of the Foreign Intelligence Surveillance Court as soon as practicable, but not more than 7 days after the Attorney General authorizes such acquisition.

(2) MINIMIZATION PROCEDURES.— If the Attorney General authorizes an acquisition under paragraph (1), the Attorney General shall require that the minimization procedures referred to in subsection (c)(1)(C) for the issuance of a judicial order be followed.

(3) TERMINATION OF EMERGENCY AUTHORIZATION.— In the absence of a judicial order approving an acquisition under paragraph (1), such acquisition shall terminate when the information sought is obtained, when the application for the order is denied, or after the expiration of 7 days from the time of authorization by the Attorney General, whichever is earliest.

(4) USE OF INFORMATION.— If an application for approval submitted pursuant to paragraph (1) is denied, or in any other case where the acquisition is terminated and no order is issued approving the acquisition, no information obtained or evidence derived from such acquisition, except under circumstances in which the target of the acquisition is determined not to be a United States person, shall be received in evidence or otherwise disclosed in any trial, hearing, or other proceeding in or before any court, grand jury, department, office, agency, regulatory body, legislative committee, or other authority of the United States, a State, or political subdivision thereof, and no information concerning any United States person acquired from such acquisition shall subsequently be used or disclosed in any other manner by Federal officers or employees without the consent of such person, except with the approval of the Attorney General if the information indicates a threat of death or serious bodily harm to any person.

(e) RELEASE FROM LIABILITY.— No cause of action shall lie in any court against any electronic communication service provider for providing any information, facilities, or assistance in accordance with an order or request for emergency assistance issued pursuant to subsection (c) or (d), respectively.

(f) APPEAL.—

(1) APPEAL TO THE FOREIGN INTELLIGENCE SURVEILLANCE COURT OF REVIEW.— The Government may file a petition with the Foreign Intelligence Surveillance

Court of Review for review of an order issued pursuant to subsection (c). The Court of Review shall have jurisdiction to consider such petition and shall provide a written statement for the record of the reasons for a decision under this paragraph.

(2) CERIORARI TO THE SUPREME COURT.— The Government may file a petition for a writ of certiorari for review of a decision of the Court of Review issued under paragraph (1). The record for such review shall be transmitted under seal to the Supreme Court of the United States, which shall have jurisdiction to review such decision.

(g) CONSTRUCTION.— Except as provided in this section, nothing in this Act shall be construed to require an application for a court order for an acquisition that is targeted in accordance with this section at a United States person reasonably believed to be located outside the United States.

OTHER ACQUISITIONS TARGETING UNITED STATES PERSONS OUTSIDE THE UNITED STATES

SEC. 704. [50 U.S.C. §1881c]

(a) JURISDICTION AND SCOPE.—

(1) JURISDICTION.— The Foreign Intelligence Surveillance Court shall have jurisdiction to enter an order pursuant to subsection (c).

(2) SCOPE.— No element of the intelligence community may intentionally target, for the purpose of acquiring foreign intelligence information, a United States person reasonably believed to be located outside the United States under circumstances in which the targeted United States person has a reasonable expectation of privacy and a warrant would be required if the acquisition were conducted inside the United States for law enforcement purposes, unless a judge of the Foreign Intelligence Surveillance Court has entered an order with respect to such targeted United States person or the Attorney General has authorized an emergency acquisition pursuant to subsection (c) or (d), respectively, or any other provision of this Act.

(3) LIMITATIONS.—

(A) MOVING OR MISIDENTIFIED TARGETS.— If a United States person targeted under this subsection is reasonably believed to be located in the United States during the effective period of an order issued pursuant to subsection (c), an acquisition targeting such United States person under this section shall cease unless the targeted United States person is again reasonably believed to be located outside the United States during the effective period of such order.

(B) APPLICABILITY.— If an acquisition for foreign intelligence purposes is to be conducted inside the United States and could be authorized under section 703, the acquisition may only be conducted if authorized under section 703 or in accordance with another provision of this Act other than this section.

(C) CONSTRUCTION.— Nothing in this paragraph shall be construed to limit the authority of the Government to seek an order or authorization under, or otherwise engage in any activity that is authorized under, any other title of this Act.

(b) APPLICATION.— Each application for an order under this section shall be made by a Federal officer in writing upon oath or affirmation to a judge having jurisdiction under subsection (a)(1). Each application shall require the approval of the Attorney General based upon the Attorney General's finding that it satisfies the criteria and requirements of such application as set forth in this section and shall include—

(1) the identity of the Federal officer making the application;

(2) the identity, if known, or a description of the specific United States person who is the target of the acquisition;

(3) a statement of the facts and circumstances relied upon to justify the applicant's belief that the United States person who is the target of the acquisition is—

(A) a person reasonably believed to be located outside the United States; and

(B) a foreign power, an agent of a foreign power, or an officer or employee of a foreign power;

(4) a statement of proposed minimization procedures that meet the definition of minimization procedures under section 101(h) or 301(4), as appropriate;

(5) a certification made by the Attorney General, an official specified in section 104(a)(6), or the head of an element of the intelligence community that—

(A) the certifying official deems the information sought to be foreign intelligence information; and

(B) a significant purpose of the acquisition is to obtain foreign intelligence information;

(6) a statement of the facts concerning any previous applications that have been made to any judge of the Foreign Intelligence Surveillance Court involving the United States person specified in the application and the action taken on each previous application; and

(7) a statement of the period of time for which the acquisition is required to be maintained, provided that such period of time shall not exceed 90 days per application.

(c) ORDER.—

(1) FINDINGS.— Upon an application made pursuant to subsection (b), the Foreign Intelligence Surveillance Court shall enter an ex parte order as requested or as modified by the Court if the Court finds that—

(A) the application has been made by a Federal officer and approved by the Attorney General;

(B) on the basis of the facts submitted by the applicant, for the United States person who is the target of the acquisition, there is probable cause to believe that the target is—

(i) a person reasonably believed to be located outside the United States; and

(ii) a foreign power, an agent of a foreign power, or an officer or employee of a foreign power;

(C) the proposed minimization procedures, with respect to their dissemination provisions, meet the definition of minimization procedures under section 101(h) or 301(4), as appropriate; and

(D) the application that has been filed contains all statements and certifications required by subsection (b) and the certification provided under subsection (b)(5) is not clearly erroneous on the basis of the information furnished under subsection (b).

(2) PROBABLE CAUSE.— In determining whether or not probable cause exists for purposes of paragraph (1)(B), a judge having jurisdiction under subsection (a)(1) may consider past activities of the target and facts and circumstances relating to current or future activities of the target. No United States person may be considered a foreign power, agent of a foreign power, or officer or employee of a foreign power solely upon the basis of activities protected by the first amendment to the Constitution of the United States.

(3) REVIEW.—

(A) LIMITATIONS ON REVIEW.— Review by a judge having jurisdiction under subsection (a)(1) shall be limited to that required to make the findings described in paragraph (1). The judge shall not have jurisdiction to review the means by which an acquisition under this section may be conducted.

(B) REVIEW OF PROBABLE CAUSE.— If the judge determines that the facts submitted under subsection (b) are insufficient to establish probable cause to issue an order under this subsection, the judge shall enter an order so stating and provide a written statement for the record of the reasons for such determination. The Government may appeal an order under this subparagraph pursuant to subsection (e).

(C) REVIEW OF MINIMIZATION PROCEDURES.— If the judge determines that the minimization procedures applicable to dissemination of information obtained through an acquisition under this subsection do not meet the definition of minimization procedures under section 101(h) or 301(4), as appropriate, the judge shall enter an order so stating and provide a written statement for the record of the reasons for such determination. The Government may appeal an order under this subparagraph pursuant to subsection (e).

(D) SCOPE OF REVIEW OF CERTIFICATION.— If the judge determines that an application under subsection (b) does not contain all the required elements, or that the certification provided under subsection (b)(5) is clearly erroneous on the basis of the information furnished under subsection (b), the judge shall enter an order so stating and provide a written statement for the record of the reasons for such determination. The Government may appeal an order under this subparagraph pursuant to subsection (e).

(4) DURATION.— An order under this paragraph shall be effective for a period not to exceed 90 days and such order may be renewed for additional 90-day periods upon submission of renewal applications meeting the requirements of subsection (b).

(5) COMPLIANCE.— At or prior to the end of the period of time for which an order or extension is granted under this section, the judge may assess compliance with the minimization procedures referred to in paragraph (1)(C) by reviewing the circumstances under which information concerning United States persons was disseminated, provided that the judge may not inquire into the circumstances relating to the conduct of the acquisition.

(d) EMERGENCY AUTHORIZATION.—

(1) AUTHORITY FOR EMERGENCY AUTHORIZATION.— Notwithstanding any other provision of this section, if the Attorney General reasonably determines that—

(A) an emergency situation exists with respect to the acquisition of foreign intelligence information for which an order may be obtained under subsection (c) before an order under that subsection can, with due diligence, be obtained, and

(B) the factual basis for the issuance of an order under this section exists, the Attorney General may authorize the emergency acquisition if a judge having jurisdiction under subsection (a)(1) is informed by the Attorney General or a designee of the Attorney General at the time of such authorization that the decision has been made to conduct such acquisition and if an application in accordance with this section is made to a judge of the Foreign Intelligence Surveillance Court as soon as practicable, but not more than 7 days after the Attorney General authorizes such acquisition.

(2) MINIMIZATION PROCEDURES.— If the Attorney General authorizes an emergency acquisition under paragraph (1), the Attorney General shall require that the minimization procedures referred to in subsection (c)(1)(C) be followed.

(3) TERMINATION OF EMERGENCY AUTHORIZATION.— In the absence of an order under subsection (c), an emergency acquisition under paragraph

(1) shall terminate when the information sought is obtained, if the application for the order is denied, or after the expiration of 7 days from the time of authorization by the Attorney General, whichever is earliest.

(4) USE OF INFORMATION.— If an application submitted to the Court pursuant to paragraph (1) is denied, or in any other case where the acquisition is terminated and no order with respect to the target of the acquisition is issued under subsection (c), no infor-

mation obtained or evidence derived from such acquisition, except under circumstances in which the target of the acquisition is determined not to be a United States person, shall be received in evidence or otherwise disclosed in any trial, hearing, or other proceeding in or before any court, grand jury, department, office, agency, regulatory body, legislative committee, or other authority of the United States, a State, or political subdivision thereof, and no information concerning any United States person acquired from such acquisition shall subsequently be used or disclosed in any other manner by Federal officers or employees without the consent of such person, except with the approval of the Attorney General if the information indicates a threat of death or serious bodily harm to any person.

(e) APPEAL.—

(1) APPEAL TO THE COURT OF REVIEW.— The Government may file a petition with the Foreign Intelligence Surveillance Court of Review for review of an order issued pursuant to subsection (c). The Court of Review shall have jurisdiction to consider such petition and shall provide a written statement for the record of the reasons for a decision under this paragraph.

(2) CERTIORARI TO THE SUPREME COURT.— The Government may file a petition for a writ of certiorari for review of a decision of the Court of Review issued under paragraph (1). The record for such review shall be transmitted under seal to the Supreme Court of the United States, which shall have jurisdiction to review such decision.

JOINT APPLICATIONS AND CONCURRENT AUTHORIZATIONS
SEC. 705. [50 U.S.C. §1881d]

(a) JOINT APPLICATIONS AND ORDERS.— If an acquisition targeting a United States person under section 703 or 704 is proposed to be conducted both inside and outside the United States, a judge having jurisdiction under section 703(a)(1) or 704(a)(1) may issue simultaneously, upon the request of the Government in a joint application complying with the requirements of sections 703(b) and 704(b), orders under sections 703(c) and 704(c), as appropriate.

(b) CONCURRENT AUTHORIZATION.— If an order authorizing electronic surveillance or physical search has been obtained under section 105 or 304, the Attorney General may authorize, for the effective period of that order, without an order under section 703 or 704, the targeting of that United States person for the purpose of acquiring foreign intelligence information while such person is reasonably believed to be located outside the United States.

USE OF INFORMATION ACQUIRED UNDER TITLE VII
SEC. 706. [50 U.S.C. §1881e]

(a) INFORMATION ACQUIRED UNDER SECTION 702.— Information acquired from an acquisition conducted under section 702 shall be deemed to be information acquired from an electronic surveillance pursuant to title I for purposes of section 106, except for the purposes of subsection (j) of such section.

(b) INFORMATION ACQUIRED UNDER SECTION 703.— Information acquired from an acquisition conducted under section 703 shall be deemed to be information acquired from an electronic surveillance pursuant to title I for purposes of section 106.

CONGRESSIONAL OVERSIGHT
SEC. 707. [50 U.S.C. §1881f]

(a) SEMIANNUAL REPORT.— Not less frequently than once every 6 months, the Attorney General shall fully inform, in a manner consistent with national security, the congressional intelligence committees and the Committees on the Judiciary of the Senate and the House of Representatives, consistent with the Rules of the House of Representatives, the Standing

Rules of the Senate, and Senate Resolution 400 of the 94th Congress or any successor Senate resolution, concerning the implementation of this title.

(b) CONTENT.— Each report under subsection (a) shall include—

(1) with respect to section 702—

(A) any certifications submitted in accordance with section 702(g) during the reporting period;

(B) with respect to each determination under section 702(c)(2), the reasons for exercising the authority under such section;

(C) any directives issued under section 702(h) during the reporting period;

(D) a description of the judicial review during the reporting period of such certifications and targeting and minimization procedures adopted in accordance with subsections (d) and (e) of section 702 and utilized with respect to an acquisition under such section, including a copy of an order or pleading in connection with such review that contains a significant legal interpretation of the provisions of section 702;

(E) any actions taken to challenge or enforce a directive under paragraph (4) or (5) of section 702(h);

(F) any compliance reviews conducted by the Attorney General or the Director of National Intelligence of acquisitions authorized under section 702(a);

(G) a description of any incidents of noncompliance-

(i) with a directive issued by the Attorney General and the Director of National Intelligence under section 702(h), including incidents of noncompliance by a specified person to whom the Attorney General and Director of National Intelligence issued a directive under section 702(h); and

(ii) by an element of the intelligence community with procedures and guidelines adopted in accordance with subsections (d), (e), and (f) of section 702; and

(H) any procedures implementing section 702;

(2) with respect to section 703—

(A) the total number of applications made for orders under section 703(b);

(B) the total number of such orders—

(i) granted;

(ii) modified; and

(iii) denied; and

(C) the total number of emergency acquisitions authorized by the Attorney General under section 703(d) and the total number of subsequent orders approving or denying such acquisitions; and

(3) with respect to section 704—

(A) the total number of applications made for orders under section 704(b);

(B) the total number of such orders—

(i) granted;

(ii) modified; and

(iii) denied; and

(C) the total number of emergency acquisitions authorized by the Attorney General under section 704(d) and the total number of subsequent orders approving or denying such applications.

SAVINGS PROVISION

SEC. 708. [50 U.S.C. §1881g] Nothing in this title shall be construed to limit the authority of the Government to seek an order or authorization under, or otherwise engage in any activity that is authorized under, any other title of this Act.

TITLE VIII—PROTECTION OF PERSONS ASSISTING
THE GOVERNMENT

DEFINITIONS

SEC. 801. [50 U.S.C. §1885] In this title:

(1) ASSISTANCE.— The term 'assistance' means the provision of, or the provision of access to, information (including communication contents, communications records, or other information relating to a customer or communication), facilities, or another form of assistance.

(2) CIVIL ACTION.— The term 'civil action' includes a covered civil action.

(3) CONGRESSIONAL INTELLIGENCE COMMITTEES.— The term 'congressional intelligence committees' means—

    (A) the Select Committee on Intelligence of the Senate; and

    (B) the Permanent Select Committee on Intelligence of the House of Representatives.

(4) CONTENTS.— The term 'contents' has the meaning given that term in section 101(n).

(5) COVERED CIVIL ACTION.— The term 'covered civil action' means a civil action filed in a Federal or State court that—

    (A) alleges that an electronic communication service provider furnished assistance to an element of the intelligence community; and

    (B) seeks monetary or other relief from the electronic communication service provider related to the provision of such assistance.

(6) ELECTRONIC COMMUNICATION SERVICE PROVIDER.— The term 'electronic communication service provider' means—

    (A) a telecommunications carrier, as that term is defined in section 3 of the Communications Act of 1934 (47 U.S.C. 153);

    (B) a provider of electronic communication service, as that term is defined in section 2510 of title 18, United States Code;

    (C) a provider of a remote computing service, as that term is defined in section 2711 of title 18, United States Code;

    (D) any other communication service provider who has access to wire or electronic communications either as such communications are transmitted or as such communications are stored;

    (E) a parent, subsidiary, affiliate, successor, or assignee of an entity described in subparagraph (A), (B), (C), or (D); or

    (F) an officer, employee, or agent of an entity described in subparagraph (A), (B), (C), (D), or (E).

(7) INTELLIGENCE COMMUNITY.— The term 'intelligence community' has the meaning given the term in section 3(4) of the National Security Act of 1947 (50 U.S.C. 401a(4)).

(8) PERSON.— The term 'person' means-

    (A) an electronic communication service provider; or

    (B) a landlord, custodian, or other person who may be authorized or required to furnish assistance pursuant to—

        (i) an order of the court established under section 103(a) directing such assistance;

        (ii) a certification in writing under section 2511(2)(a)(ii)(B) or 2709(b) of title 18, United States Code; or

        (iii) a directive under section 102(a)(4), 105B(e), as added by section 2 of the Protect America Act of 2007 (Public Law 110-55), or 702(h).

(9) STATE.—The term 'State' means any State, political subdivision of a State, the Com-

monwealth of Puerto Rico, the District of Columbia, and any territory or possession of the United States, and includes any officer, public utility commission, or other body authorized to regulate an electronic communication service provider.

PROCEDURES FOR IMPLEMENTING STATUTORY DEFENSES

SEC. 802. [50 U.S.C. §1885a]

(a) REQUIREMENT FOR CERTIFICATION.— Notwithstanding any other provision of law, a civil action may not lie or be maintained in a Federal or State court against any person for providing assistance to an element of the intelligence community, and shall be promptly dismissed, if the Attorney General certifies to the district court of the United States in which such action is pending that—

(1) any assistance by that person was provided pursuant to an order of the court established under section 103(a) directing such assistance;

(2) any assistance by that person was provided pursuant to a certification in writing under section 2511(2)(a)(ii)(B) or 2709(b) of title 18, United States Code;

(3) any assistance by that person was provided pursuant to a directive under section 102(a)(4), 105B(e), as added by section 2 of the Protect America Act of 2007 (Public Law 110-55), or 702(h) directing such assistance;

(4) in the case of a covered civil action, the assistance alleged to have been provided by the electronic communication service provider was—

(A) in connection with an intelligence activity involving communications that was—

(i) authorized by the President during the period beginning on September 11, 2001, and ending on January 17, 2007; and

(ii) designed to detect or prevent a terrorist attack, or activities in preparation for a terrorist attack, against the United States; and

(B) the subject of a written request or directive, or a series of written requests or directives, from the Attorney General or the head of an element of the intelligence community (or the deputy of such person) to the electronic communication service provider indicating that the activity was—

(i) authorized by the President; and

(ii) determined to be lawful; or

(5) the person did not provide the alleged assistance.

(b) JUDICIAL REVIEW.—

(1) REVIEW OF CERTIFICATIONS.— A certification under subsection (a) shall be given effect unless the court finds that such certification is not supported by substantial evidence provided to the court pursuant to this section.

(2) SUPPLEMENTAL MATERIALS.— In its review of a certification under subsection (a), the court may examine the court order, certification, written request, or directive described in subsection (a) and any relevant court order, certification, written request, or directive submitted pursuant to subsection (d).

(c) LIMITATIONS ON DISCLOSURE.— If the Attorney General files a declaration under section 1746 of title 28, United States Code, that disclosure of a certification made pursuant to subsection (a) or the supplemental materials provided pursuant to subsection (b) or (d) would harm the national security of the United States, the court shall—

(1) review such certification and the supplemental materials in camera and ex parte; and

(2) limit any public disclosure concerning such certification and the supplemental materials, including any public order following such in camera and ex parte review, to a statement as to whether the case is dismissed and a description of the legal standards that govern the order, without disclosing the paragraph of subsection (a) that is the basis for the certification.

(d) ROLE OF THE PARTIES.— Any plaintiff or defendant in a civil action may submit any relevant court order, certification, written request, or directive to the district court referred to in subsection (a) for review and shall be permitted to participate in the briefing or argument of any legal issue in a judicial proceeding conducted pursuant to this section, but only to the extent that such participation does not require the disclosure of classified information to such party. To the extent that classified information is relevant to the proceeding or would be revealed in the determination of an issue, the court shall review such information in camera and ex parte, and shall issue any part of the court's written order that would reveal classified information in camera and ex parte and maintain such part under seal.

(e) NONDELEGATION.— The authority and duties of the Attorney General under this section shall be performed by the Attorney General (or Acting Attorney General) or the Deputy Attorney General.

(f) APPEAL.— The courts of appeals shall have jurisdiction of appeals from interlocutory orders of the district courts of the United States granting or denying a motion to dismiss or for summary judgment under this section.

(g) REMOVAL.— A civil action against a person for providing assistance to an element of the intelligence community that is brought in a State court shall be deemed to arise under the Constitution and laws of the United States and shall be removable under section 1441 of title 28, United States Code.

(h) RELATIONSHIP TO OTHER LAWS.— Nothing in this section shall be construed to limit any otherwise available immunity, privilege, or defense under any other provision of law.

(i) APPLICABILITY.— This section shall apply to a civil action pending on or filed after the date of the enactment of the FISA Amendments Act of 2008.

PREEMPTION

SEC. 803. [50 U.S.C. §1885b]

(a) IN GENERAL.— No State shall have authority to—

> (1) conduct an investigation into an electronic communication service provider's alleged assistance to an element of the intelligence community;
> (2) require through regulation or any other means the disclosure of information about an electronic communication service provider's alleged assistance to an element of the intelligence community;
> (3) impose any administrative sanction on an electronic communication service provider for assistance to an element of the intelligence community; or
> (4) commence or maintain a civil action or other proceeding to enforce a requirement that an electronic communication service provider disclose information concerning alleged assistance to an element of the intelligence community.

(b) SUITS BY THE UNITED STATES.— The United States may bring suit to enforce the provisions of this section.

(c) JURISDICTION.— The district courts of the United States shall have jurisdiction over any civil action brought by the United States to enforce the provisions of this section.

(d) APPLICATION.— This section shall apply to any investigation, action, or proceeding that is pending on or commenced after the date of the enactment of the FISA Amendments Act of 2008.

REPORTING

SEC. 804. [50 U.S.C. §1885c]

(a) SEMIANNUAL REPORT.— Not less frequently than once every 6 months, the Attorney General shall, in a manner consistent with national security, the Rules of the House of Representatives, the Standing Rules of the Senate, and Senate Resolution 400 of the 94th Congress or any successor Senate resolution, fully inform the congressional intelligence committees, the Committee on the Judiciary of the Senate, and the Committee on the Judiciary of the House of Representatives concerning the implementation of this title.

(b) CONTENT.— Each report made under subsection (a) shall include—

(1) any certifications made under section 802;

(2) a description of the judicial review of the certifications made under section 802; and

(3) any actions taken to enforce the provisions of section 803.

SELECTED ADDITIONAL PROVISIONS OF THE FISA AMENDMENTS ACT OF 2008

REVIEW OF PREVIOUS ACTIONS

Sec. 301.

(a) DEFINITIONS.— In this section:

(1) APPROPRIATE COMMITTEES OF CONGRESS.— The term "appropriate committees of Congress" means—

(A) the Select Committee on Intelligence and the Committee on the Judiciary of the Senate; and

(B) the Permanent Select Committee on Intelligence and the Committee on the Judiciary of the House of Representatives.

(2) FOREIGN INTELLIGENCE SURVEILLANCE COURT.— The term "Foreign Intelligence Surveillance Court" means the court established under section 103(a) of the Foreign Intelligence Surveillance Act of 1978 (50 U.S.C. 1803(a)).

(3) PRESIDENT'S SURVEILLANCE PROGRAM AND PROGRAM.— The terms "President's Surveillance Program" and "Program" mean the intelligence activity involving communications that was authorized by the President during the period beginning on September 11, 2001, and ending on January 17, 2007, including the program referred to by the President in a radio address on December 17, 2005 (commonly known as the Terrorist Surveillance Program).

(b) REVIEWS.—

(1) REQUIREMENT TO CONDUCT.— The Inspectors General of the Department of Justice, the Office of the Director of National Intelligence, the National Security Agency, the Department of Defense, and any other element of the intelligence community that participated in the President's Surveillance Program, shall complete a comprehensive review of, with respect to the oversight authority and responsibility of each such Inspector General—

(A) all of the facts necessary to describe the establishment, implementation, product, and use of the product of the Program;

(B) access to legal reviews of the Program and access to information about the Program;

(C) communications with, and participation of, individuals and entities in the private sector related to the Program;

(D) interaction with the Foreign Intelligence Surveillance Court and transition to court orders related to the Program; and

(E) any other matters identified by any such Inspector General that would enable that Inspector General to complete a review of the Program, with respect to such Department or element.

(2) COOPERATION AND COORDINATION.—

(A) COOPERATION.— Each Inspector General required to conduct a review under paragraph (1) shall—

(i) work in conjunction, to the extent practicable, with any other Inspector General required to conduct such a review; and

(ii) utilize, to the extent practicable, and not unnecessarily duplicate or delay, such reviews or audits that have been completed or are being undertaken by any such Inspector General or by any other office of the Executive Branch related to the Program.

(B) INTEGRATION OF OTHER REVIEWS.—The Counsel of the Office of Professional Responsibility of the Department of Justice shall provide the report of any investigation conducted by such Office on matters relating to the Program, including any investigation of the process through which legal reviews of the Program were conducted and the substance of such reviews, to the Inspector General of the Department of Justice, who shall integrate the factual findings and conclusions of such investigation into its review.

(C) COORDINATION.—The Inspectors General shall designate one of the Inspectors General required to conduct a review under paragraph (1) that is appointed by the President, by and with the advice and consent of the Senate, to coordinate the conduct of the reviews and the preparation of the reports.

(c) REPORTS.—

(1) PRELIMINARY REPORTS.— Not later than 60 days after the date of the enactment of this Act, the Inspectors General of the Department of Justice, the Office of the Director of National Intelligence, the National Security Agency, the Department of Defense, and any other Inspector General required to conduct a review under subsection (b)(1), shall submit to the appropriate committees of Congress an interim report that describes the planned scope of such review.

(2) FINAL REPORT.— Not later than 1 year after the date of the enactment of this Act, the Inspectors General of the Department of Justice, the Office of the Director of National Intelligence, the National Security Agency, the Department of Defense, and any other Inspector General required to conduct a review under subsection (b)(1), shall submit to the appropriate committees of Congress, in a manner consistent with national security, a comprehensive report on such reviews that includes any recommendations of any such Inspectors General within the oversight authority and responsibility of any such Inspector General with respect to the reviews.

(3) FORM.— A report under this subsection shall be submitted in unclassified form, but may include a classified annex. The unclassified report shall not disclose the name or identity of any individual or entity of the private sector that participated in the Program or with whom there was communication about the Program, to the extent that information is classified.

(d) RESOURCES.—

(1) EXPEDITED SECURITY CLEARANCE.— The Director of National Intelligence shall ensure that the process for the investigation and adjudication of an application by an Inspector General or any appropriate staff of an Inspector General for a security clearance necessary for the conduct of the review under subsection (b)(1) is carried out as expeditiously as possible.

(2) ADDITIONAL PERSONNEL FOR THE INSPECTORS GENERAL.— An Inspector General required to conduct a review under subsection (b)(1) and submit a report under subsection (c) is authorized to hire such additional personnel as may be necessary to carry out such review and prepare such report in a prompt and timely manner. Personnel authorized to be hired under this paragraph—

(A) shall perform such duties relating to such a review as the relevant Inspector General shall direct; and

(B) are in addition to any other personnel authorized by law.

(3) TRANSFER OF PERSONNEL.— The Attorney General, the Secretary of Defense, the Director of National Intelligence, the Director of the National Security Agency, or the head of any other element of the intelligence community may transfer personnel to the relevant Office of the Inspector General required to conduct a review under subsection (b)(1) and

submit a report under subsection (c) and, in addition to any other personnel authorized by law, are authorized to fill any vacancy caused by such a transfer. Personnel transferred under this paragraph shall perform such duties relating to such review as the relevant Inspector General shall direct.

SEVERABILITY

SEC. 401 [50 U.S.C. 1801 note] If any provision of this Act, any amendment made by this Act, or the application thereof to any person or circumstances is held invalid, the validity of the remainder of the Act, of any such amendments, and of the application of such provisions to other persons and circumstances shall not be affected thereby.

REPEALS

SEC. 403.

(a) REPEAL OF PROTECT AMERICA ACT OF 2007 PROVISIONS.—

    (1) AMENDMENTS TO FISA.—

        (A) IN GENERAL.—Except as provided in section 404, sections 105A, 105B, and 105C of the Foreign Intelligence Surveillance Act of 1978 (50 U.S.C. 1805a, 1805b, and 1805c) are repealed.

        (B) TECHNICAL AND CONFORMING AMENDMENTS.—

            (i) TABLE OF CONTENTS.—The table of contents in the first section of the Foreign Intelligence Surveillance Act of 1978 (50 U.S.C. 1801 et seq.) is amended by striking the items relating to sections 105A, 105B, and 105C.

            (ii) CONFORMING AMENDMENTS.—Except as provided in section 404, section 103(e) of the Foreign Intelligence Surveillance Act of 1978 (50 U.S.C. 1803(e)) is amended—

                (I) in paragraph (1), by striking "105B(h) or 501(f)(1)" and inserting "501(f)(1) or 702(h)(4)"; and

                (II) in paragraph (2), by striking "105B(h) or 501(f)(1)" and inserting "501(f)(1) or 702(h)(4)".

    (2) REPORTING REQUIREMENTS.—Except as provided in section 404, section 4 of the Protect America Act of 2007 (Public Law 110-55; 121 Stat. 555) is repealed.

    (3) [50 USC 1803 note.] TRANSITION PROCEDURES.— Except as provided in section 404, subsection (b) of section 6 of the Protect America Act of 2007 (Public Law 110-55; 121 Stat. 556) is repealed.

(b) FISA AMENDMENTS ACT OF 2008.-

    (1) [50 USC 1881 note.] IN GENERAL.—Except as provided in section 404, effective December 31, 2012, title VII of the Foreign Intelligence Surveillance Act of 1978, [50 USC 1881-1881g.] as amended by section 101(a), is repealed.

    (2) [18 USC 2511 note.] TECHNICAL AND CONFORMING AMENDMENTS.-Effective December 31, 2012—

        (A) the table of contents in the first section of such Act (50 U.S.C. 1801 et seq.) is amended by striking the items related to title VII;

        437 FOREIGN INTELLIGENCE SURVEILLANCE ACT OF 1978

        (B) except as provided in section 404, section 601(a)(1) of such Act (50 U.S.C. 1871(a)(1)) is amended to read as such section read on the day before the date of the enactment of this Act; and

        (C) except as provided in section 404, section 2511(2)(a)(ii)(A) of title 18, United States Code, is amended by striking "or a court order pursuant to section 704 of the Foreign Intelligence Surveillance Act of 1978".

TRANSITION PROCEDURES

SEC. 404.

(a) TRANSITION PROCEDURES FOR PROTECT AMERICA ACT OF 2007 PROVISIONS.—

(1) CONTINUED EFFECT OF ORDERS, AUTHORIZATIONS, DIRECTIVES.—Except as provided in paragraph (7), notwithstanding any other provision of law, any order, authorization, or directive issued or made pursuant to section 105B of the Foreign Intelligence Surveillance Act of 1978, as added by section 2 of the Protect America Act of 2007 (Public Law 11055; 121 Stat. 552), shall continue in effect until the expiration of such order, authorization, or directive.

(2) APPLICABILITY OF PROTECT AMERICA ACT OF 2007 TO CONTINUED ORDERS, AUTHORIZATIONS, DIRECTIVES.— Notwithstanding any other provision of this Act, any amendment made by this Act, or the Foreign Intelligence Surveillance Act of 1978 (50 U.S.C. 1801 et seq.)—

(A) subject to paragraph (3), section 105A of such Act, as added by section 2 of the Protect America Act of 2007 (Public Law 110-55; 121 Stat. 552), shall continue to apply to any acquisition conducted pursuant to an order, authorization, or directive referred to in paragraph (1); and

(B) sections 105B and 105C of the Foreign Intelligence Surveillance Act of 1978, as added by sections 2 and 3, respectively, of the Protect America Act of 2007, shall continue to apply with respect to an order, authorization, or directive referred to in paragraph (1) until the later of—

(i) the expiration of such order, authorization, or directive; or

(ii) the date on which final judgment is entered for any petition or other litigation relating to such order, authorization, or directive.

(3) USE OF INFORMATION.—Information acquired from an acquisition conducted pursuant to an order, authorization, or directive referred to in paragraph (1) shall be deemed to be information acquired from an electronic surveillance pursuant to title I of the Foreign Intelligence Surveillance Act of 1978 (50 U.S.C. 1801 et seq.) for purposes of section 106 of such Act (50 U.S.C. 1806), except for purposes of subsection (j) of such section.

(4) PROTECTION FROM LIABILITY.— Subsection (l) of section 105B of the Foreign Intelligence Surveillance Act of 1978, as added by section 2 of the Protect America Act of 2007, shall continue to apply with respect to any directives issued pursuant to such section 105B.

(5) JURISDICTION OF FOREIGN INTELLIGENCE SURVEILLANCE COURT.—Notwithstanding any other provision of this Act or of the Foreign Intelligence Surveillance Act of 1978 (50 U.S.C. 1801 et seq.), section 103(e) of the Foreign Intelligence Surveillance Act (50 U.S.C. 1803(e)), as amended by section 5(a) of the Protect America Act of 2007 (Public Law 110-55; 121 Stat. 556), shall continue to apply with respect to a directive issued pursuant to section 105B of the Foreign Intelligence Surveillance Act of 1978, as added by section 2 of the Protect America Act of 2007, until the later of—

(A) the expiration of all orders, authorizations, or directives referred to in paragraph (1); or

(B) the date on which final judgment is entered for any petition or other litigation relating to such order, authorization, or directive.

(6) REPORTING REQUIREMENTS.—

(A) CONTINUED APPLICABILITY.— Notwithstanding any other provision of this Act, any amendment made by this Act, the Protect America Act of 2007 (Public Law 110-55), or the Foreign Intelligence Surveillance Act of 1978 (50 U.S.C. 1801 et seq.), section 4 of the Protect America Act of 2007 shall continue to apply until the date that the certification described in subparagraph (B) is submitted.

(B) CERTIFICATION.— The certification described in this subparagraph is a certification—

(i) made by the Attorney General;

(ii) submitted as part of a semi-annual report required by section 4 of the Protect America Act of 2007;

(iii) that states that there will be no further acquisitions carried out under section 105B of the Foreign Intelligence Surveillance Act of 1978, as added by section 2 of the Protect America Act of 2007, after the date of such certification; and

(iv) that states that the information required to be included under such section 4 relating to any acquisition conducted under such section 105B has been included in a semi-annual report required by such section 4.

(7) REPLACEMENT OF ORDERS, AUTHORIZATIONS, AND DIRECTIVES.—

(A) IN GENERAL.— If the Attorney General and the Director of National Intelligence seek to replace an authorization issued pursuant to section 105B of the Foreign Intelligence Surveillance Act of 1978, as added by section 2 of the Protect America Act of 2007 (Public Law 110-55), with an authorization under section 702 of the Foreign Intelligence Surveillance Act of 1978 (as added by section 101(a) of this Act), the Attorney General and the Director of National Intelligence shall, to the extent practicable, submit to the Foreign Intelligence Surveillance Court (as such term is defined in section 701(b)(2) of such Act (as so added)) a certification prepared in accordance with subsection

(g) of such section 702 and the procedures adopted in accordance with subsections (d) and (e) of such section 702 at least 30 days before the expiration of such authorization.

(B) CONTINUATION OF EXISTING ORDERS.— If the Attorney General and the Director of National Intelligence seek to replace an authorization made pursuant to section 105B of the Foreign Intelligence Surveillance Act of 1978, as added by section 2 of the Protect America Act of 2007 (Public Law 110-55; 121 Stat. 522), by filing a certification in accordance with subparagraph (A), that authorization, and any directives issued thereunder and any order related thereto, shall remain in effect, notwithstanding the expiration provided for in subsection (a) of such section 105B, until the Foreign Intelligence Surveillance Court (as such term is defined in section 701(b)(2) of the Foreign Intelligence Surveillance Act of 1978 (as so added)) issues an order with respect to that certification under section 702(i)(3) of such Act (as so added) at which time the provisions of that section and of section 702(i)(4) of such Act (as so added) shall apply.

(8) EFFECTIVE DATE.— Paragraphs (1) through (7) shall take effect as if enacted on August 5, 2007.

(b) TRANSITION PROCEDURES FOR FISA AMENDMENTS ACT OF 2008 PROVISIONS.—

(1) ORDERS IN EFFECT ON DECEMBER 31, 2012.— Notwithstanding any other provision of this Act, any amendment made by this Act, or the Foreign Intelligence Surveillance Act of 1978 (50 U.S.C. 1801 et seq.), any order, authorization, or directive issued or made under title VII of the Foreign Intelligence Surveillance Act of 1978, as amended by section 101(a), shall continue in effect until the date of the expiration of such order, authorization, or directive.

(2) APPLICABILITY OF TITLE VII OF FISA TO CONTINUED ORDERS, AUTHORIZATIONS, DIRECTIVES.— Notwithstanding any other provision of this Act, any amendment made by this Act, or the Foreign Intelligence Surveillance Act of 1978 (50 U.S.C. 1801 et seq.), with respect to any order, authorization, or directive referred to in paragraph (1), title VII of such Act, as amended by section 101(a), shall continue to apply until the later of—

(A) the expiration of such order, authorization, or directive; or

(B) the date on which final judgment is entered for any petition or other litigation relating to such order, authorization, or directive.

(3) CHALLENGE OF DIRECTIVES; PROTECTION FROM LIABILITY; USE OF INFORMATION.— Notwithstanding any other provision of this Act or of the Foreign Intelligence Surveillance Act of 1978 (50 U.S.C. 1801 et seq.)—

(A) section 103(e) of such Act, as amended by section 403(a)(1)(B)(ii), shall continue to apply with respect to any directive issued pursuant to section 702(h) of such Act, as added by section 101(a);

(B) section 702(h)(3) of such Act (as so added) shall continue to apply with respect to any directive issued pursuant to section 702(h) of such Act (as so added);

(C) section 703(e) of such Act (as so added) shall continue to apply with respect to an order or request for emergency assistance under that section;

(D) section 706 of such Act (as so added) shall continue to apply to an acquisition conducted under section 702 or 703 of such Act (as so added); and

(E) section 2511(2)(a)(ii)(A) of title 18, United States Code, as amended by section 101(c)(1), shall continue to apply to an order issued pursuant to section 704 of the Foreign Intelligence Surveillance Act of 1978, as added by section 101(a).

(4) REPORTING REQUIREMENTS.—

(A) CONTINUED APPLICABILITY.— Notwithstanding any other provision of this Act or of the Foreign Intelligence Surveillance Act of 1978 (50 U.S.C. 1801 et seq.), section 601(a) of such Act (50 U.S.C. 1871(a)), as amended by section 101(c)(2), and sections 702(l) and 707 of such Act, as added by section 101(a), shall continue to apply until the date that the certification described in subparagraph (B) is submitted.

(B) CERTIFICATION.— The certification described in this subparagraph is a certification—

(i) made by the Attorney General;

(ii) submitted to the Select Committee on Intelligence of the Senate, the Permanent Select Committee on Intelligence of the House of Representatives, and the Committees on the Judiciary of the Senate and the House of Representatives;

(iii) that states that there will be no further acquisitions carried out under title VII of the Foreign Intelligence Surveillance Act of 1978, as amended by section 101(a), after the date of such certification; and

(iv) that states that the information required to be included in a review, assessment, or report under section 601 of such Act, as amended by section 101(c), or section 702(l) or 707 of such Act, as added by section 101(a), relating to any acquisition conducted under title VII of such Act, as amended by section 101(a), has been included in a review, assessment, or report under such section 601, 702(l), or 707.

(5) TRANSITION PROCEDURES CONCERNING THE TARGETING OF UNITED STATES PERSONS OVERSEAS.— Any authorization in effect on the date of enactment of this Act under section 2.5 of Executive Order 12333 to intentionally target a United States person reasonably believed to be located outside the United States shall continue in effect, and shall constitute a sufficient basis for conducting such an acquisition targeting a United States person located outside the United States until the earlier of—

(A) the date that authorization expires; or

(B) the date that is 90 days after the date of the enactment of this Act.

Uniting and Strengthening America By Fulfilling Rights and Ensuring Effective Discipline Over Monitoring Act of 2015 (USA FREEDOM)

Pub. L. 13-23, 129 Stat. 268 (June 2, 2015)
Titles VII and VIII only

TITLE VII—ENHANCED NATIONAL SECURITY PROVISIONS

SEC. 701. EMERGENCIES INVOLVING NON-UNITED STATES PERSONS.

(a) IN GENERAL.—Section 105 (50 U.S.C. 1805) is amended—

(1) by redesignating subsections (f), (g), (h), and (i) as subsections (g), (h), (i), and (j), respectively; and

(2) by inserting after subsection (e) the following:

"(f)(1) Notwithstanding any other provision of this Act, the lawfully authorized targeting of a non-United States person previously believed to be located outside the United States for the acquisition of foreign intelligence information may continue for a period not to exceed 72 hours from the time that the non-United States person is reasonably believed to be located inside the United States and the acquisition is subject to this title or to title III of this Act, provided that the head of an element of the intelligence community—

"(A) reasonably determines that a lapse in the targeting of such non-United States person poses a threat of death or serious bodily harm to any person;

"(B) promptly notifies the Attorney General of a determination under subparagraph (A); and

"(C) requests, as soon as practicable, the employment of emergency electronic surveillance under subsection (e) or the employment of an emergency physical search pursuant to section 304(e), as warranted.

459

"(2) The authority under this subsection to continue the acquisition of foreign intelligence information is limited to a period not to exceed 72 hours and shall cease upon the earlier of the following:

"(A) The employment of emergency electronic surveillance under subsection (e) or the employment of an emergency physical search pursuant to section 304(e).

"(B) An issuance of a court order under this title or title III of this Act.

"(C) The Attorney General provides direction that the acquisition be terminated.

"(D) The head of the element of the intelligence community conducting the acquisition determines that a request under paragraph (1)(C) is not warranted.

"(E) When the threat of death or serious bodily harm to any person is no longer reasonably believed to exist.

"(3) Nonpublicly available information concerning unconsenting United States persons acquired under this subsection shall not be disseminated during the 72 hour time period under paragraph (1) unless necessary to investigate, reduce, or eliminate the threat of death or serious bodily harm to any person.

"(4) If the Attorney General declines to authorize the employment of emergency electronic surveillance under subsection (e) or the employment of an emergency physical search pursuant to section 304(e), or a court order is not obtained under this title or title III of this Act, information obtained during the 72 hour acquisition time period under paragraph (1) shall not be retained, except with the approval of the Attorney General if the information indicates a threat of death or serious bodily harm to any person.

"(5) Paragraphs (5) and (6) of subsection (e) shall apply to this subsection.".

(b) NOTIFICATION OF EMERGENCY EMPLOYMENT OF ELECTRONIC SURVEILLANCE.—Section 106(j) (50 U.S.C. 1806(j)) is amended by striking "section 105(e)" and inserting "subsection (e) or (f) of section 105".

(c) REPORT TO CONGRESS.—Section 108(a)(2) (50 U.S.C. 1808(a)(2)) is amended—

(1) in subparagraph (B), by striking "and" at the end;

(2) in subparagraph (C), by striking the period at the end and inserting "; and"; and

(3) by adding at the end the following:

"(D) the total number of authorizations under section 105(f) and the total number of subsequent emergency employments of electronic surveillance under section 105(e) or emergency physical searches pursuant to section 301(e).".

SEC. 702. PRESERVATION OF TREATMENT OF NON-UNITED STATES PERSONS TRAVELING OUTSIDE THE UNITED STATES AS AGENTS OF FOREIGN POWERS.

Section 101(b)(1) is amended—

(1) in subparagraph (A), by inserting before the semicolon at the end the following: ", irrespective of whether the person is inside the United States"; and

(2) in subparagraph (B)—

(A) by striking "of such person's presence in the United States"; and

(B) by striking "such activities in the United States" and inserting "such activities".

SEC. 703. IMPROVEMENT TO INVESTIGATIONS OF INTERNATIONAL PROLIFERATION OF WEAPONS OF MASS DESTRUCTION.

Section 101(b)(1) is further amended by striking subparagraph (E) and inserting the following new subparagraph (E):

"(E) engages in the international proliferation of weapons of mass destruction, or activities in preparation therefor, for or on behalf of a foreign power, or knowingly aids or abets any person in the conduct of such proliferation or activities in preparation therefor, or knowingly conspires with any person to engage in such proliferation or activities in preparation therefor; or''.

SEC. 704. INCREASE IN PENALTIES FOR MATERIAL SUPPORT OF FOREIGN TERRORIST ORGANIZATIONS.

Section 2339B(a)(1) of title 18, United States Code, is amended by striking ''15 years'' and inserting ''20 years''.

SEC. 705. SUNSETS.

(a) USA PATRIOT IMPROVEMENT AND REAUTHORIZATION ACT OF 2005.—Section 102(b)(1) of the USA PATRIOT Improvement and Reauthorization Act of 2005 (50 U.S.C. 1805 note) is amended by striking ''June 1, 2015'' and inserting ''December 15, 2019''.
(b) INTELLIGENCE REFORM AND TERRORISM PREVENTION ACT OF 2004.—Section 6001(b)(1) of the Intelligence Reform and Terrorism Prevention Act of 2004 (50 U.S.C. 1801 note) is amended by striking ''June 1, 2015'' and inserting ''December 15, 2019''.
(c) CONFORMING AMENDMENT.—Section 102(b)(1) of the USA PATRIOT Improvement and Reauthorization Act of 2005 (50 U.S.C. 1805 note), as amended by subsection (a), is further amended by striking ''sections 501, 502, and'' and inserting ''title V and section''.

TITLE VIII—SAFETY OF MARITIME NAVIGATION AND NUCLEAR TERRORISM CONVENTIONS IMPLEMENTATION
Subtitle A—Safety of Maritime Navigation

SEC. 801. AMENDMENT TO SECTION 2280 OF TITLE 18, UNITED STATES CODE.

Section 2280 of title 18, United States Code, is amended—
(1) in subsection (b)—
 (A) in paragraph (1)(A)(i), by striking ''a ship flying the flag of the United States'' and inserting ''a vessel of the United States or a vessel subject to the jurisdiction of the United States (as defined in section 70502 of title 46)'';
 (B) in paragraph (1)(A)(ii), by inserting '', including the territorial seas'' after ''in the United States''; and (C) in paragraph (1)(A)(iii), by inserting '', by a United States corporation or legal entity,'' after ''by a national of the United States'';
(2) in subsection (c), by striking ''section 2(c)'' and inserting ''section 13(c)'';
(3) by striking subsection (d);
(4) by striking subsection (e) and inserting after subsection (c) the following:
''(d) DEFINITIONS.—As used in this section, section 2280a, section 2281, and section 2281a, the term—
 ''(1) 'applicable treaty' means—
  ''(A) the Convention for the Suppression of Unlawful Seizure of Aircraft, done at The Hague on 16 December 1970;
  ''(B) the Convention for the Suppression of Unlawful Acts against the Safety of Civil Aviation, done at Montreal on 23 September 1971;
  ''(C) the Convention on the Prevention and Punishment of Crimes against Internationally Protected Persons, including Diplomatic Agents, adopted by the General Assembly of the United Nations on 14 December 1973;
  ''(D) International Convention against the Taking of Hostages, adopted by the General Assembly of the United Nations on 17 December 1979;

"(E) the Convention on the Physical Protection of Nuclear Material, done at Vienna on 26 October 1979;

"(F) the Protocol for the Suppression of Unlawful Acts of Violence at Airports Serving International Civil Aviation, supplementary to the Convention for the Suppression of Unlawful Acts against the Safety of Civil Aviation, done at Montreal on 24 February 1988;

"(G) the Protocol for the Suppression of Unlawful Acts against the Safety of Fixed Platforms Located on the Continental Shelf, done at Rome on 10 March 1988;

"(H) International Convention for the Suppression of Terrorist Bombings, adopted by the General Assembly of the United Nations on 15 December 1997; and

"(I) International Convention for the Suppression of the Financing of Terrorism, adopted by the General Assembly of the United Nations on 9 December 1999;

"(2) 'armed conflict' does not include internal disturbances and tensions, such as riots, isolated and sporadic acts of violence, and other acts of a similar nature;

"(3) 'biological weapon' means—

"(A) microbial or other biological agents, or toxins whatever their origin or method of production, of types and in quantities that have no justification for prophylactic, protective, or other peaceful purposes; or

"(B) weapons, equipment, or means of delivery designed to use such agents or toxins for hostile purposes or in armed conflict;

"(4) 'chemical weapon' means, together or separately—

"(A) toxic chemicals and their precursors, except where intended for—

"(i) industrial, agricultural, research, medical, pharmaceutical, or other peaceful purposes;

"(ii) protective purposes, namely those purposes directly related to protection against toxic chemicals and to protection against chemical weapons;

"(iii) military purposes not connected with the use of chemical weapons and not dependent on the use

of the toxic properties of chemicals as a method of warfare; or

"(iv) law enforcement including domestic riot control purposes, as long as the types and quantities are consistent with such purposes;

"(B) munitions and devices, specifically designed to cause death or other harm through the toxic properties of those toxic chemicals specified in subparagraph (A), which would be released as a result of the employment of such munitions and devices; and

"(C) any equipment specifically designed for use directly in connection with the employment of munitions and devices specified in subparagraph (B);

"(5) 'covered ship' means a ship that is navigating or is scheduled to navigate into, through or from waters beyond the outer limit of the territorial sea of a single country or a lateral limit of that country's territorial sea with an adjacent country;

"(6) 'explosive material' has the meaning given the term in section 841(c) and includes explosive as defined in section 844(j) of this title;

"(7) 'infrastructure facility' has the meaning given the term in section 2332f(e)(5) of this title;

"(8) 'international organization' has the meaning given the term in section 831(f)(3) of this title;

"(9) 'military forces of a state' means the armed forces of a state which are organized, trained, and equipped under its internal law for the primary purpose of national defense or security, and persons acting in support of those armed forces who are under their formal command, control, and responsibility;

"(10) 'national of the United States' has the meaning stated in section 101(a)(22) of the Immigration and Nationality Act (8 U.S.C. 1101(a)(22));

"(11) 'Non-Proliferation Treaty' means the Treaty on the Non-Proliferation of Nuclear Weapons, done at Washington, London, and Moscow on 1 July 1968;

"(12) 'Non-Proliferation Treaty State Party' means any State Party to the Non-Proliferation Treaty, to include Taiwan, which shall be considered to have the obligations under the Non-Proliferation Treaty of a party to that treaty other than a Nuclear Weapon State Party to the Non-Proliferation Treaty;

"(13) 'Nuclear Weapon State Party to the Non-Proliferation Treaty' means a State Party to the Non-Proliferation Treaty that is a nuclear-weapon State, as that term is defined in Article IX(3) of the Non-Proliferation Treaty;

"(14) 'place of public use' has the meaning given the term in section 2332f(e)(6) of this title;

"(15) 'precursor' has the meaning given the term in section 229F(6)(A) of this title;

"(16) 'public transport system' has the meaning given the term in section 2332f(e)(7) of this title;

"(17) 'serious injury or damage' means—

"(A) serious bodily injury,

"(B) extensive destruction of a place of public use, State or government facility, infrastructure facility, or public transportation system, resulting in major economic loss, or

"(C) substantial damage to the environment, including air, soil, water, fauna, or flora;

"(18) 'ship' means a vessel of any type whatsoever not permanently attached to the sea-bed, including dynamically supported craft, submersibles, or any other floating craft, but does not include a warship, a ship owned or operated by a government when being used as a naval auxiliary or for customs or police purposes, or a ship which has been withdrawn from navigation or laid up;

"(19) 'source material' has the meaning given that term in the International Atomic Energy Agency Statute, done at New York on 26 October 1956;

"(20) 'special fissionable material' has the meaning given that term in the International Atomic Energy Agency Statute, done at New York on 26 October 1956;

"(21) 'territorial sea of the United States' means all waters extending seaward to 12 nautical miles from the baselines of the United States determined in accordance with international law;

"(22) 'toxic chemical' has the meaning given the term in section 229F(8)(A) of this title;

"(23) 'transport' means to initiate, arrange or exercise effective control, including decisionmaking authority, over the movement of a person or item; and

"(24) 'United States', when used in a geographical sense, includes the Commonwealth of Puerto Rico, the Commonwealth of the Northern Mariana Islands, and all territories and possessions of the United States."; and

(5) by inserting after subsection (d) (as added by paragraph (4) of this section) the following:

"(e) EXCEPTIONS.—This section shall not apply to—

"(1) the activities of armed forces during an armed conflict, as those terms are understood under the law of war, which are governed by that law; or

"(2) activities undertaken by military forces of a state in the exercise of their official duties.

"(f) DELIVERY OF SUSPECTED OFFENDER.—The master of a covered ship flying the flag of the United States who has reasonable grounds to believe that there is on board that ship any person who has committed an offense under section 2280 or section 2280a may deliver such person to the authorities of a country that is a party to the Convention for the Suppression of Unlawful Acts against the Safety of Maritime Navigation. Before delivering such person to the authorities of another country, the master shall notify in an appropriate manner the Attorney General of the United States of the alleged offense and await instructions from the Attorney General as to what action to take. When delivering the person to a country which is a state party to the Convention, the master shall, whenever practicable, and if possible before entering the territorial sea of such country, notify the authorities of such country of the master's intention to deliver such person and the reasons therefor. If the master delivers such person, the master shall furnish to the authorities of such country the evidence in the master's possession that pertains to the alleged offense.

"(g)(1) CIVIL FORFEITURE.—Any real or personal property used or intended to be used to commit or to facilitate the commission of a violation of this section, the gross proceeds of such violation, and any real or personal property traceable to such property or proceeds, shall be subject to forfeiture.

"(2) APPLICABLE PROCEDURES.—Seizures and forfeitures under this section shall be governed by the provisions of chapter 46 of title 18, United States Code, relating to civil forfeitures, except that such duties as are imposed upon the Secretary of the Treasury under the customs laws described in section 981(d) shall be performed by such officers, agents, and other persons as may be designated for that purpose by the Secretary of Homeland Security, the Attorney General, or the Secretary of Defense.".

SEC. 802. NEW SECTION 2280A OF TITLE 18, UNITED STATES CODE.

(a) IN GENERAL.—Chapter 111 of title 18, United States Code, is amended by adding after section 2280 the following new section:

"§ 2280a. Violence against maritime navigation and maritime transport involving weapons of mass destruction

"(a) OFFENSES.—

"(1) IN GENERAL.—Subject to the exceptions in subsection (c), a person who unlawfully and intentionally—

"(A) when the purpose of the act, by its nature or context, is to intimidate a population, or to compel a government or an international organization to do or to abstain from doing any act—

"(i) uses against or on a ship or discharges from a ship any explosive or radioactive material, biological, chemical, or nuclear weapon or other nuclear explosive device in a manner that causes or is likely to cause death to any person or serious injury or damage;

"(ii) discharges from a ship oil, liquefied natural gas, or another hazardous or noxious substance that is not covered by clause (i), in such quantity or concentration that causes or is likely to cause death to any person or serious injury or damage; or

"(iii) uses a ship in a manner that causes death to any person or serious injury or damage;

"(B) transports on board a ship—

"(i) any explosive or radioactive material, knowing that it is intended to be used to cause, or in a threat to cause, death to any person or serious injury or damage for the purpose of intimidating a population, or compelling a government or an international organization to do or to abstain from doing any act;

"(ii) any biological, chemical, or nuclear weapon or other nuclear explosive device, knowing it to be

a biological, chemical, or nuclear weapon or other nuclear explosive device;

"(iii) any source material, special fissionable material, or equipment or material especially designed or prepared for the processing, use, or production of special fissionable material, knowing that it is intended to be used in a nuclear explosive activity or in any other nuclear activity not under safeguards pursuant to an International Atomic Energy Agency comprehensive safeguards agreement, except where—

"(I) such item is transported to or from the territory of, or otherwise under the control of, a Non-Proliferation Treaty State Party; and

"(II) the resulting transfer or receipt (including internal to a country) is not contrary to the obligations under the Non-Proliferation Treaty of the Non-Proliferation Treaty State Party from which, to the territory of which, or otherwise under the control of which such item is transferred;

"(iv) any equipment, materials, or software or related technology that significantly contributes to the design or manufacture of a nuclear weapon or other nuclear explosive device, with the intention that it will be used for such purpose, except where—

"(I) the country to the territory of which or under the control of which such item is transferred

is a Nuclear Weapon State Party to the Non-Proliferation Treaty; and

"(II) the resulting transfer or receipt (including internal to a country) is not contrary to the obligations under the Non-Proliferation Treaty of a Non-Proliferation Treaty State Party from which, to the territory of which, or otherwise under the control of which such item is transferred;

"(v) any equipment, materials, or software or related technology that significantly contributes to the delivery of a nuclear weapon or other nuclear explosive device, with the intention that it will be used for such purpose, except where—

"(I) such item is transported to or from the territory of, or otherwise under the control of, a

Non-Proliferation Treaty State Party; and

"(II) such item is intended for the delivery system of a nuclear weapon or other nuclear explosive

device of a Nuclear Weapon State Party to the Non-Proliferation Treaty; or

"(vi) any equipment, materials, or software or related technology that significantly contributes to the design, manufacture, or delivery of a biological or chemical weapon, with the intention that it will be

used for such purpose;

"(C) transports another person on board a ship knowing that the person has committed an act that constitutes an offense under section 2280 or subparagraph (A), (B), (D), or (E) of this section or an offense set forth in an applicable treaty, as specified in section 2280(d)(1), and intending to assist that person to evade criminal prosecution;

"(D) injures or kills any person in connection with the commission or the attempted commission of any of the offenses set forth in subparagraphs (A) through (C), or subsection (a)(2), to the extent that the subsection (a)(2) offense pertains to subparagraph (A); or

"(E) attempts to do any act prohibited under subparagraph (A), (B) or (D), or conspires to do any act prohibited by subparagraphs (A) through (E) or subsection (a)(2), shall be fined under this title, imprisoned not more than 20 years, or both; and if the death of any person results from conduct prohibited by this paragraph, shall be imprisoned for any term of years or for life.

"(2) THREATS.—A person who threatens, with apparent determination and will to carry the threat into execution, to do any act prohibited under paragraph (1)(A) shall be fined under this title, imprisoned not more than 5 years, or both.

"(b) JURISDICTION.—There is jurisdiction over the activity prohibited in subsection (a)—

"(1) in the case of a covered ship, if—

"(A) such activity is committed—

"(i) against or on board a vessel of the United States or a vessel subject to the jurisdiction of the

United States (as defined in section 70502 of title 46) at the time the prohibited activity is committed;

"(ii) in the United States, including the territorial seas; or

"(iii) by a national of the United States, by a United States corporation or legal entity, or by a stateless person whose habitual residence is in the United

States;

"(B) during the commission of such activity, a national of the United States is seized, threatened, injured, or killed; or

"(C) the offender is later found in the United States after such activity is committed;

"(2) in the case of a ship navigating or scheduled to navigate solely within the territorial sea or internal waters of a country other than the United States, if the offender is later found in the United States after such activity is committed; or

"(3) in the case of any vessel, if such activity is committed in an attempt to compel the United States to do or abstain from doing any act.

"(c) EXCEPTIONS.—This section shall not apply to—

"(1) the activities of armed forces during an armed conflict, as those terms are understood under the law of war, which are governed by that law; or

"(2) activities undertaken by military forces of a state in the exercise of their official duties.

"(d)(1) CIVIL FORFEITURE.—Any real or personal property used or intended to be used to commit or to facilitate the commission of a violation of this section, the gross proceeds of such violation, and any real or personal property traceable to such property or proceeds, shall be subject to forfeiture.

"(2) APPLICABLE PROCEDURES.—Seizures and forfeitures under this section shall be governed by the provisions of chapter 46 of title 18, United States Code, relating to civil forfeitures, except that such duties as are imposed upon the Secretary of the Treasury under the customs laws described in section 981(d) shall be performed by such officers, agents, and other persons as may be designated for that purpose by the Secretary of Homeland Security, the Attorney General, or the Secretary of Defense.".

(b) CONFORMING AMENDMENT.—The table of sections at the beginning of chapter 111 of title 18, United States Code, is amended by adding after the item relating to section 2280 the following
new item:

"2280a. Violence against maritime navigation and maritime transport involving weapons of mass destruction.".

SEC. 803. AMENDMENTS TO SECTION 2281 OF TITLE 18, UNITED STATES CODE.

Section 2281 of title 18, United States Code, is amended—

(1) in subsection (c), by striking "section 2(c)" and inserting "section 13(c)";

(2) in subsection (d), by striking the definitions of "national of the United States," "territorial sea of the United States," and "United States"; and

(3) by inserting after subsection (d) the following:

"(e) EXCEPTIONS.—This section does not apply to—

"(1) the activities of armed forces during an armed conflict, as those terms are understood under the law of war, which are governed by that law; or

"(2) activities undertaken by military forces of a state in the exercise of their official duties.".

SEC. 804. NEW SECTION 2281A OF TITLE 18, UNITED STATES CODE.

(a) IN GENERAL.—Chapter 111 of title 18, United States Code, is amended by adding after section 2281 the following new section:

"§ 2281a. Additional offenses against maritime fixed platforms

"(a) OFFENSES.—

"(1) IN GENERAL.—A person who unlawfully and intentionally—

"(A) when the purpose of the act, by its nature or context, is to intimidate a population, or to compel a government or an international organization to do or to abstain from doing any act—

"(i) uses against or on a fixed platform or discharges from a fixed platform any explosive or radioactive material, biological, chemical, or nuclear weapon in a manner that causes or is likely to cause death or serious injury or damage; or

"(ii) discharges from a fixed platform oil, liquefied natural gas, or another hazardous or noxious substance that is not covered by clause (i), in such quantity or concentration that causes or is likely to cause death or serious injury or damage;

"(B) injures or kills any person in connection with the commission or the attempted commission of any of the offenses set forth in subparagraph (A); or

"(C) attempts or conspires to do anything prohibited under subparagraph (A) or (B), shall be fined under this title, imprisoned not more than 20 years, or both; and if death results to any person from conduct prohibited by this paragraph, shall be imprisoned for any term of years or for life.

"(2) THREAT TO SAFETY.—A person who threatens, with apparent determination and will to carry the threat into execution, to do any act prohibited under paragraph (1)(A), shall be fined under this title, imprisoned not more than 5 years, or both.

"(b) JURISDICTION.—There is jurisdiction over the activity prohibited in subsection (a) if—

"(1) such activity is committed against or on board a fixed platform—

"(A) that is located on the continental shelf of the United States;

"(B) that is located on the continental shelf of another country, by a national of the United States or by a stateless person whose habitual residence is in the United States; or

"(C) in an attempt to compel the United States to do or abstain from doing any act;

"(2) during the commission of such activity against or on board a fixed platform located on a continental shelf, a national of the United States is seized, threatened, injured, or killed; or

"(3) such activity is committed against or on board a fixed platform located outside the United States and beyond the continental shelf of the United States and the offender is later found in the United States.

"(c) EXCEPTIONS.—This section does not apply to—

"(1) the activities of armed forces during an armed conflict, as those terms are understood under the law of war, which are governed by that law; or

"(2) activities undertaken by military forces of a state in the exercise of their official duties.

"(d) DEFINITIONS.—In this section—

"(1) 'continental shelf' means the sea-bed and subsoil of the submarine areas that extend beyond a country's territorial sea to the limits provided by customary international law as reflected in Article 76 of the 1982 Convention on the Law of the Sea; and

"(2) 'fixed platform' means an artificial island, installation, or structure permanently attached to the sea-bed for the purpose of exploration or exploitation of resources or for other economic purposes.".

(b) CONFORMING AMENDMENT.—The table of sections at the beginning of chapter 111 of title 18, United States Code, is amended by adding after the item relating to section 2281 the following
new item:

"2281a. Additional offenses against maritime fixed platforms.".

SEC. 805. ANCILLARY MEASURE.

Section 2332b(g)(5)(B) of title 18, United States Code, is amended by inserting "2280a (relating to maritime safety)," before "2281", and by striking "2281" and inserting "2281 through 2281a".

Subtitle B—Prevention of Nuclear Terrorism

SEC. 811. NEW SECTION 2332I OF TITLE 18, UNITED STATES CODE.

(a) IN GENERAL.—Chapter 113B of title 18, United States Code, is amended by adding after section 2332h the following:

"§ 2332i. Acts of nuclear terrorism

"(a) OFFENSES.—

"(1) IN GENERAL.—Whoever knowingly and unlawfully—

"(A) possesses radioactive material or makes or possesses a device—

"(i) with the intent to cause death or serious bodily injury; or

"(ii) with the intent to cause substantial damage to property or the environment; or

"(B) uses in any way radioactive material or a device, or uses or damages or interferes with the operation of a nuclear facility in a manner that causes the release of or increases the risk of the release of radioactive material, or causes radioactive contamination or exposure to radiation—

"(i) with the intent to cause death or serious bodily injury or with the knowledge that such act is likely to cause death or serious bodily injury;

"(ii) with the intent to cause substantial damage to property or the environment or with the knowledge that such act is likely to cause substantial damage to property or the environment; or

"(iii) with the intent to compel a person, an international organization or a country to do or refrain from doing an act, shall be punished as prescribed in subsection (c).

"(2) THREATS.—Whoever, under circumstances in which the threat may reasonably be believed, threatens to commit an offense under paragraph (1) shall be punished as prescribed in subsection (c). Whoever demands possession of or access to radioactive material, a device or a nuclear facility by threat or by use of force shall be punished as prescribed in subsection (c).

"(3) ATTEMPTS AND CONSPIRACIES.—Whoever attempts to commit an offense under paragraph (1) or conspires to commit an offense under paragraph (1) or (2) shall be punished as prescribed in subsection (c).

"(b) JURISDICTION.—Conduct prohibited by subsection (a) is within the jurisdiction of the United States if—

"(1) the prohibited conduct takes place in the United States or the special aircraft jurisdiction of the United States;

"(2) the prohibited conduct takes place outside of the United States and—

"(A) is committed by a national of the United States, a United States corporation or legal entity or a stateless person whose habitual residence is in the United States;

"(B) is committed on board a vessel of the United States or a vessel subject to the jurisdiction of the United States (as defined in section 70502 of title 46) or on board an aircraft that is registered under United States law, at the time the offense is committed; or

"(C) is committed in an attempt to compel the United States to do or abstain from doing any act, or constitutes a threat directed at the United States;

"(3) the prohibited conduct takes place outside of the United States and a victim or an intended victim is a national of the United States or a United States corporation or legal entity, or the offense is committed against any state or government facility of the United States; or

"(4) a perpetrator of the prohibited conduct is found in the United States.

"(c) PENALTIES.—Whoever violates this section shall be fined not more than $2,000,000 and shall be imprisoned for any term of years or for life.

"(d) NONAPPLICABILITY.—This section does not apply to— "(1) the activities of armed forces during an armed conflict, as those terms are understood under the law of war, which are governed by that law; or

"(2) activities undertaken by military forces of a state in the exercise of their official duties.

"(e) DEFINITIONS.—As used in this section, the term—

"(1) 'armed conflict' has the meaning given that term in section 2332f(e)(11) of this title;

"(2) 'device' means:

"(A) any nuclear explosive device; or

"(B) any radioactive material dispersal or radiation-emitting device that may, owing to its radiological properties, cause death, serious bodily injury or substantial damage to property or the environment;

"(3) 'international organization' has the meaning given that term in section 831(f)(3) of this title;

"(4) 'military forces of a state' means the armed forces of a country that are organized, trained and equipped under its internal law for the primary purpose of national defense or security and persons acting in support of those armed forces who are under their formal command, control and responsibility;

"(5) 'national of the United States' has the meaning given that term in section 101(a)(22) of the Immigration and Nationality Act (8 U.S.C. 1101(a)(22));

"(6) 'nuclear facility' means:

"(A) any nuclear reactor, including reactors on vessels, vehicles, aircraft or space objects for use as an energy source in order to propel such vessels, vehicles, aircraft or space objects or for any other purpose;

"(B) any plant or conveyance being used for the production, storage, processing or transport of radioactive material; or

"(C) a facility (including associated buildings and equipment) in which nuclear material is produced, processed, used, handled, stored or disposed of, if damage to or interference with such facility could lead to the release of significant amounts of radiation or radioactive material;

"(7) 'nuclear material' has the meaning given that term in section 831(f)(1) of this title;

"(8) 'radioactive material' means nuclear material and other radioactive substances that contain nuclides that undergo spontaneous disintegration (a process accompanied by emission of one or more types of ionizing radiation, such as alpha-, beta-, neutron particles and gamma rays) and that may, owing to their radiological or fissile properties, cause death, serious bodily injury or substantial damage to property or to the environment;

"(9) 'serious bodily injury' has the meaning given that term in section 831(f)(4) of this title;

"(10) 'state' has the same meaning as that term has under international law, and includes all political subdivisions thereof;

"(11) 'state or government facility' has the meaning given that term in section 2332f(e)(3) of this title;

"(12) 'United States corporation or legal entity' means any corporation or other

entity organized under the laws of the United States or any State, Commonwealth, territory, possession or district of the United States;

"(13) 'vessel' has the meaning given that term in section 1502(19) of title 33;
and

"(14) 'vessel of the United States' has the meaning given that term in section
70502 of title 46.".

(b) CLERICAL AMENDMENT.—The table of sections at the beginning of chapter 113B of
title 18, United States Code, is amended by inserting after the item relating to section 2332h
the following:

"2332i. Acts of nuclear terrorism.".

(c) DISCLAIMER.—Nothing contained in this section is intended to affect the applicability
of any other Federal or State law that might pertain to the underlying conduct.

(d) INCLUSION IN DEFINITION OF FEDERAL CRIMES OF TERRORISM.—Section
2332b(g)(5)(B) of title 18, United States Code, is amended by inserting "2332i (relating to
acts of nuclear terrorism)," before "2339 (relating to harboring terrorists)".

SEC. 812. AMENDMENT TO SECTION 831 OF TITLE 18, UNITED STATES CODE.

Section 831 of title 18, United States Code, is amended—

(a) in subsection (a)—

(1) by redesignating paragraphs (3) through (8) as paragraphs (4) through (9);

(2) by inserting after paragraph (2) the following:

"(3) without lawful authority, intentionally carries, sends or moves nuclear material
into or out of a country;";

(3) in paragraph (8), as redesignated, by striking "an offense under paragraph (1), (2), (3),
or (4)" and inserting "any act prohibited under paragraphs (1) through (5)"; and

(4) in paragraph (9), as redesignated, by striking "an offense under paragraph (1), (2), (3),
or (4)" and inserting "any act prohibited under paragraphs (1) through (7)";

(b) in subsection (b)—

(1) in paragraph (1), by striking "(7)" and inserting "(8)"; and

(2) in paragraph (2), by striking "(8)" and inserting "(9)";

(c) in subsection (c)—

(1) in subparagraph (2)(A), by adding after "United States" the following: "or a stateless
person whose habitual residence is in the United States";

(2) by striking paragraph (5);

(3) in paragraph (4), by striking "or" at the end; and

(4) by inserting after paragraph (4), the following:

"(5) the offense is committed on board a vessel of the United States or a vessel subject
to the jurisdiction of the United States (as defined in section 70502 of title 46) or on
board an aircraft that is registered under United States law, at the time the offense is
committed;

"(6) the offense is committed outside the United States and against any state or
government facility of the United States; or

"(7) the offense is committed in an attempt to compel the United States to do or
abstain from doing any act, or constitutes a threat directed at the United States.";

(d) by redesignating subsections (d) through (f) as (e) through (g), respectively;

(e) by inserting after subsection (c) the following:

"(d) NONAPPLICABILITY.—This section does not apply to—

"(1) the activities of armed forces during an armed conflict, as those terms are understood under the law of war, which are governed by that law; or

"(2) activities undertaken by military forces of a state in the exercise of their official duties."; and

(f) in subsection (g), as redesignated—

    (1) in paragraph (6), by striking "and" at the end;

    (2) in paragraph (7), by striking the period at the end and inserting a semicolon; and

    (3) by inserting after paragraph (7), the following:

"(8) the term 'armed conflict' has the meaning given that term in section 2332f(e)(11) of this title;

"(9) the term 'military forces of a state' means the armed forces of a country that are organized, trained and equipped under its internal law for the primary purpose of national defense or security and persons acting in support of those armed forces who are under their formal command, control
and responsibility;

"(10) the term 'state' has the same meaning as that term has under international law, and includes all political subdivisions thereof;

"(11) the term 'state or government facility' has the meaning given that term in section 2332f(e)(3) of this title; and

"(12) the term 'vessel of the United States' has the meaning given that term in section 70502 of title 46.".

Approved June 2, 2015.

Classified Information Procedures Act

(Pub. L. 96–456 of October 15, 1980; 94 Stat. 2025, as amended)

> AN ACT To provide certain pretrial, trial, and appellate procedures for crimi]nal cases involving classified information.

Be it enacted by the Senate and House of Representatives of the United States of America in Congress assembled,

DEFINITIONS

SEC. 1. [18 U.S.C. App. §1]
(a) ''Classified information'', as used in this Act, means any information or material that has been determined by the United States Government pursuant to an Executive order, statute, or regulation, to require protection against unauthorized disclosure for reasons of national security and any restricted data, as defined in paragraph r. of section 11 of the Atomic Energy Act of 1954 (42 U.S.C. 2014(y)).
(b) ''National security'', as used in this Act, means the national defense and foreign relations of the United States.

PRETRIAL CONFERENCE

SEC. 2. [18 U.S.C. App. §2] At any time after the filing of the indictment or information, any party may move for a pretrial conference to consider matters relating to classified information that may arise in connection with the prosecution. Following such motion, or on its own motion, the court shall promptly hold a pretrial conference to establish the timing of requests for discovery, the provision of notice required by section 5 of this Act, and the initiation of the procedure established by section 6 of this Act. In addition, at the pretrial conference the court may consider any matters which relate to classified information or which may promote a fair and expeditious trial. No admission made by the defendant or by any attorney for the defendant at such a conference may be used against the defendant unless the admission is in writing and is signed by the defendant and by the attorney for the defendant.

PROTECTIVE ORDERS

SEC. 3. [18 U.S.C. App. §3] Upon motion of the United States, the court shall issue an order to protect against the disclosure of any classified information disclosed by the United States to any defendant in any criminal case in a district court of the United States.

DISCOVERY OF CLASSIFIED INFORMATION BY DEFENDANTS

SEC. 4. [18 U.S.C. App. §4] The court, upon a sufficient showing, may authorize the United States to delete specified items of classified information from documents to be made available to the defendant through discovery under the Federal Rules of Criminal Procedure, to substitute a summary of the information for such classified documents, or to substitute a statement admitting relevant facts that the classified information would tend to prove. The court may permit the United States to make a request for such authorization in the form of a written statement to be inspected by the court alone. If the court enters an order granting relief following such an ex parte showing, the entire text of the statement of the United States shall be sealed and preserved in the records of the court to be made available to the appellate court in the event of an appeal.

NOTICE OF DEFENDANT'S INTENTION TO DISCLOSE
CLASSIFIED INFORMATION

SEC. 5. [18 U.S.C. App. §5]
(a) Notice by Defendant.—If a defendant reasonably expects to disclose or to cause the disclo-

sure of classified information in any manner in connection with any trial or pretrial proceeding involving the criminal prosecution of such defendant, the defendant shall, within the time specified by the court or, where no time is specified, within thirty days prior to trial, notify the attorney for the United States and the court in writing. Such notice shall include a brief description of the classified information. Whenever a defendant learns of additional classified information he reasonably expects to disclose at any such proceeding, he shall notify the attorney for the United States and the court in writing as soon as possible thereafter and shall include a brief description of the classified information. No defendant shall disclose any information known or believed to be classified in connection with a trial or pretrial proceeding until notice has been given under this subsection and until the United States has been afforded a reasonable opportunity to seek a determination pursuant to the procedure set forth in section 6 of this Act, and until the time for the United States to appeal such determination under section 7 has expired or any appeal under section 7 by the United States is decided.

(b) Failure to Comply.—If the defendant fails to comply with the requirements of subsection (a) the court may preclude disclosure of any classified information not made the subject of notification and may prohibit the examination by the defendant of any witness with respect to any such information.

PROCEDURE FOR CASES INVOLVING CLASSIFIED INFORMATION
SEC. 6. [18 U.S.C. App. §6]

(a) Motion for Hearing.—Within the time specified by the court for the filing of a motion under this section, the United States may request the court to conduct a hearing to make all determinations concerning the use, relevance, or admissibility of classified information that would otherwise be made during the trial or pretrial proceeding. Upon such a request, the court shall conduct such a hearing. Any hearing held pursuant to this subsection (or any portion of such hearing specified in the request of the Attorney General) shall be held in camera if the Attorney General certifies to the court in such petition that a public proceeding may result in the disclosure of classified information. As to each item of classified information, the court shall set forth in writing the basis for its determination. Where the United States' motion under this subsection is filed prior to the trial or pretrial proceeding, the court shall rule prior to the commencement of the relevant proceeding.

(b) Notice.—

(1) Before any hearing is conducted pursuant to a
request by the United States under subsection (a), the United States shall provide the defendant with notice of the classified information that is at issue. Such notice shall identify the specific classified information at issue whenever that information previously has been made available to the defendant by the United States. When the United States has not previously made the information available to the defendant in connection with the case, the information may be described by generic category, in such forms as the court may approve, rather than by identification of the specific information of concern to the United States.

(2) Whenever the United States requests a hearing under subsection (a), the court, upon request of the defendant, may order the United States to provide the defendant, prior to trial, such details as to the portion of the indictment or information at issue in the hearing as are needed to give the defendant fair notice to prepare for the hearing.

(c) Alternative Procedure for Disclosure of Classified Information.—

(1) Upon any determination by the court authorizing the disclosure of specific classified information under the procedures established by this section, the United States may move that, in lieu of the disclosure of such specific classified information, the court order—

(A) the substitution for such classified information of a statement admitting relevant facts that the specific classified information would tend to prove; or

(B) the substitution for such classified information of a summary of the specific classified information. The court shall grant such a motion of the United States if it finds that the statement or summary will provide the defendant with substantially the same ability to make his defense as would disclosure of the specific classified information. The court shall hold a hearing on any motion under this section. Any such hearing shall be held in camera at the request of the Attorney General.

(2) The United States may, in connection with a motion under paragraph (1), submit to the court an affidavit of the Attorney General certifying that disclosure of classified information would cause identifiable damage to the national security of the United States and explaining the basis for the classification of such information. If so requested by the United States, the court shall examine such affidavit in camera and ex parte.

(d) Sealing of Records of In Camera Hearings.—If at the close of an in camera hearing under this Act (or any portion of a hearing under this Act that is held in camera) the court determines that the classified information at issue may not be disclosed or elicited at the trial or pretrial proceeding, the record of such in camera hearing shall be sealed and preserved by the court for use in the event of an appeal. The defendant may seek reconsideration of the court's determination prior to or during trial.

(e) Prohibition on Disclosure of Classified Information by Defendant, Relief for Defendant When United States Opposes Disclosure.—

(1) Whenever the court denies a motion by the United States that it issue an order under subsection (c) and the United States files with the court an affidavit of the Attorney General objecting to disclosure of the classified information at issue, the court shall order that the defendant not disclose or cause the disclosure of such information.

(2) Whenever a defendant is prevented by an order under paragraph (1) from disclosing or causing the disclosure of classified information, the court shall dismiss the indictment or information; except that, when the court determines that the interests of justice would not be served by dismissal of the indictment or information, the court shall order such other action, in lieu of dismissing the indictment or information, as the court determines is appropriate. Such action may include, but need not be limited to—

(A) dismissing specified counts of the indictment or information;

(B) finding against the United States on any issue as to which the excluded classified information relates; or

(C) striking or precluding all or part of the testimony of a witness.

An order under this paragraph shall not take effect until the court has afforded the United States an opportunity to appeal such order under section 7, and thereafter to withdraw its objection to the disclosure of the classified information at issue.

(f) Reciprocity.—Whenever the court determines pursuant to subsection (a) that classified information may be disclosed in connection with a trial or pretrial proceeding, the court shall, unless the interests of fairness do not so require, order the United States to provide the defendant with the information it expects to use to rebut the classified information. The court may place the United States under a continuing duty to disclose such rebuttal information. If the United States fails to comply with its obligation under this subsection, the court may exclude any evidence not made the subject of a required disclosure and may prohibit the examination by the United States of any witness with respect to such information.

INTERLOCUTORY APPEAL

SEC. 7. [18 U.S.C. App. §7]

(a) An interlocutory appeal by the United States taken before or after the defendant has been placed in jeopardy shall lie to a court of appeals from a decision or order of a district court in a criminal case authorizing the disclosure of classified information, imposing sanctions for nondisclosure of classified information, or refusing a protective order sought by the United States to prevent the disclosure of classified information.

(b) An appeal taken pursuant to this section either before or during trial shall be expedited by the court of appeals. Prior to trial, an appeal shall be taken within ten days after the decision or order appealed from and the trial shall not commence until the appeal is resolved. If an appeal is taken during trial, the trial court shall adjourn the trial until the appeal is resolved and the court of appeals (1) shall hear argument on such appeal within four days of the adjournment of the trial, (2) may dispense with written briefs other than the supporting materials previously submitted to the trial court, (3) shall render its decision within four days of argument on appeal, and (4) may dispense with the issuance of a written opinion in rendering its decision. Such appeal and decision shall not affect the right of the defendant, in a subsequent appeal from a judgment of conviction, to claim as error reversal by the trial court on remand of a ruling appealed from during trial.

INTRODUCTION OF CLASSIFIED INFORMATION
SEC. 8. [18 U.S.C. App. §8]

(a) Classification Status.—Writings, recordings, and photographs containing classified information may be admitted into evidence without change in their classification status.

(b) Precautions by Court.—The court, in order to prevent unnecessary disclosure of classified information involved in any criminal proceeding, may order admission into evidence of only part of a writing, recording, or photograph, or may order admission into evidence of the whole writing, recording, or photograph with excision of some or all of the classified information contained therein, unless the whole ought in fairness be considered.

(c) Taking of Testimony.—During the examination of a witness in any criminal proceeding, the United States may object to any question or line of inquiry that may require the witness to disclose classified information not previously found to be admissible. Following such an objection, the court shall take such suitable action to determine whether the response is admissible as will safeguard against the compromise of any classified information. Such action may include requiring the United States to provide the court with a proffer of the witness' response to the question or line of inquiry and requiring the defendant to provide the court with a proffer of the nature of the information he seeks to elicit.

SECURITY PROCEDURES
SEC. 9. [18 U.S.C. App. §9]

(a) Within one hundred and twenty days of the date of the enactment of this Act, the Chief Justice of the United States, in consultation with the Attorney General, the Director of Central Intelligence, and the Secretary of Defense, shall prescribe rules establishing procedures for the protection against unauthorized disclosure of any classified information in the custody of the United States district courts, courts of appeal, or Supreme Court. Such rules, and any changes in such rules, shall be submitted to the appropriate committees of Congress and shall become effective forty-five days after such submission.

(b) Until such time as rules under subsection (a) first become effective, the Federal courts shall in each case involving classified information adapt procedures to protect against the unauthorized disclosure of such information.

IDENTIFICATION OF INFORMATION RELATED TO THE
NATIONAL DEFENSE

SEC. 10 [18 U.S.C. App. §10] In any prosecution in which the United States must establish that material relates to the national defense or constitutes classified information, the United States shall notify the defendant, within the time before trial specified by the court, of the portions of the material that it reasonably expects to rely upon to establish the national defense or classified information element of the offense.

AMENDMENTS TO THE ACT

SEC. 11 [18 U.S.C. App. §11] Sections 1 through 10 of this Act may be amended as provided in section 2076, title 28, United States Code.

ATTORNEY GENERAL GUIDELINES
SEC. 12 [18 U.S.C. App. §12]

(a) Within one hundred and eighty days of enactment of this Act, the Attorney General shall issue guidelines specifying the factors to be used by the Department of Justice in rendering a decision whether to prosecute a violation of Federal law in which, in the judgment of the Attorney General, there is a possibility that classified information will be revealed. Such guidelines shall be transmitted to the appropriate committees of Congress.

(b) When the Department of Justice decides not to prosecute a violation of Federal law pursuant to subsection (a), an appropriate official of the Department of Justice shall prepare written findings detailing the reasons for the decision not to prosecute. The findings shall include—

> (1) the intelligence information which the Department of Justice officials believe might be disclosed,
>
> (2) the purpose for which the information might be disclosed,
>
> (3) the probability that the information would be disclosed, and
>
> (4) the possible consequences such disclosure would have on the national security.

REPORTS TO CONGRESS

(a) Consistent with applicable authorities and duties, including those conferred by the Constitution upon the executive and legislative branches, the Attorney General shall report orally or in writing semiannually to the Permanent Select Committee on Intelligence of the United States House of Representatives, the Select Committee on Intelligence of the United States Senate, and the chairmen and ranking minority members of the Committees on the Judiciary of the Senate and House of Representatives on all cases where a decision not to prosecute a violation of Federal law pursuant to section 12(a) has been made.

(b) The Attorney General shall deliver to the appropriate committees of Congress a report concerning the operation and effectiveness of this Act and including suggested amendments to this Act. For the first three years this Act is in effect, there shall be a report each year. After three years, such reports shall be delivered as necessary.

FUNCTIONS OF ATTORNEY GENERAL MAY BE EXERCISED BY DEPUTY ATTORNEY GENERAL, THE ASSOCIATE ATTORNEY GENERAL, OR A DESIGNATED ASSISTANT ATTORNEY GENERAL

SEC. 14 [18 U.S.C. App. §14] The functions and duties of the Attorney General under this Act may be exercised by the Deputy Attorney General, the Associate Attorney General, or by an Assistant Attorney General designated by the Attorney General for such purpose and may not be delegated to any other official.

EFFECTIVE DATE

SEC. 15 [18 U.S.C. App. §15] The provisions of this Act shall become effective upon the date of the enactment of this Act, but shall not apply to any prosecution in which an indictment or information was filed before such date.

SHORT TITLE

SEC. 16 [18 U.S.C. App. §16] That this Act may be cited as the ''Classified Information Procedures Act''.

POSSE COMITATUS ACT

18 U.S.C. § 1385. Use of Army and Air Force as posse comitatus

Whoever, except in cases and under circumstances expressly authorized by the Constitution or Act of Congress, willfully uses any part of the Army or the Air Force as a posse comitatus or otherwise to execute the laws shall be fined under this title or imprisoned not more than two years, or both.

Freedom of Information Act

(Pub. L. No. 89-554, 80 Stat. 383, as amended (as reproduced by the ODNI Intelligence Community Legal Reference Book, 2012))

SECTION 552. PUBLIC INFORMATION; AGENCY RULES, OPINIONS, ORDERS, RECORDS, AND PROCEEDINGS.

(a) Each agency shall make available to the public information as follows:

(1) Each agency shall separately state and currently publish in the Federal Register for the guidance of the public—

(A) descriptions of its central and field organization and the established places at which, the employees (and in the case of a uniformed service, the members) from whom, and the methods whereby, the public may obtain information, make submittals or requests, or obtain decisions;

(B) statements of the general course and method by which its functions are channeled and determined, including the nature and requirements of all formal and informal procedures available;

(C) rules of procedure, descriptions of forms available or the places at which forms may be obtained, and instructions as to the scope and contents of all papers, reports, or examinations;

(D) substantive rules of general applicability adopted as authorized by law, and statements of general policy or interpretations of general applicability formulated and adopted by the agency; and

(E) each amendment, revision, or repeal of the foregoing. Except to the extent that a person has actual and timely notice of the terms thereof, a person may not in any manner be required to resort to, or be adversely affected by, a matter required to be published in the Federal Register and not so published. For the purpose of this paragraph, matter reasonably available to the class of persons affected thereby is deemed published in the Federal Register when incorporated by reference therein with the approval of the Director of the Federal Register.

(2) Each agency, in accordance with published rules, shall make available for public inspection and copying—

(A) final opinions, including concurring and dissenting opinions, as well as orders, made in the adjudication of cases;

(B) those statements of policy and interpretations which have been adopted by the agency and are not published in the Federal Register;

(C) administrative staff manuals and instructions to staff that affect a member of the public;

(D) copies of all records, regardless of form or format, which have been released to any person under paragraph (3) and which, because of the nature of their subject matter, the agency determines have become or are likely to become the subject of subsequent requests for substantially the same records; and

(E) a general index of the records referred to under subparagraph (D); unless the materials are promptly published and copies offered for sale. For records created on or after November 1, 1996, within one year after such date, each agency shall make such records available, including by computer telecommunications or, if computer telecommunications means have not been established by the agency, by other electronic means. To the extent required to prevent a clearly unwarranted invasion of personal privacy, an agency may delete identifying details when it makes available or publishes an opinion, statement of policy, interpretation, staff manual, instruction, or copies of records referred to in subparagraph (D). However, in each case the justification for the deletion shall be explained fully in writing, and the extent of such deletion shall be indicated on the portion of the record which is made available or published, unless including that indication would harm an interest protected by the exemption in subsection (b) under which the deletion is made. If technically feasible, the extent of the deletion shall be indicated at the place in the record where the deletion was made. Each agency shall also maintain and make available for public inspection and copying current indexes providing identifying information for the public as to any matter issued, adopted, or promulgated after July 4, 1967, and required by this paragraph to be made available or published. Each agency shall promptly publish, quarterly or more frequently, and distribute (by sale or otherwise) copies of each index or supplements thereto unless it determines by order published in the Federal Register that the publication would be unnecessary and impracticable, in which case the agency shall nonetheless provide copies of such index on request at a cost not to exceed the direct cost of duplication. Each agency shall make the index referred to in subparagraph (E) available by computer telecommunications by December 31, 1999. A final order, opinion, statement of policy, interpretation, or staff manual or instruction that affects a member of the public may be relied on, used, or cited as precedent by an agency against a party other than an agency only if—

    (i) it has been indexed and either made available or published as provided by this paragraph; or

    (ii) the party has actual and timely notice of the terms thereof.

(3) (A) Except with respect to the records made available under paragraphs (1) and (2) of this subsection, and except as provided in subparagraph (E), each agency, upon any request for records which

    (i) reasonably describes such records and

    (ii) is made in accordance with published rules stating the time, place, fees (if any), and procedures to be followed, shall make the records promptly available to any person.

(B) In making any record available to a person under this paragraph, an agency shall provide the record in any form or format requested by the person if the record is readily reproducible by the agency in that form or format. Each agency shall make reasonable efforts to maintain its records in forms or formats that are reproducible for purposes of this section.

(C) In responding under this paragraph to a request for records, an agency shall make reasonable efforts to search for the records in electronic form or format, except when such efforts would significantly interfere with the operation of the agency's automated information system.

(D) For purposes of this paragraph, the term "search" means to review, manually or by automated means, agency records for the purpose of locating those records which are responsive to a request.

(E) An agency, or part of an agency, that is an element of the intelligence community (as that term is defined in section 3(4) of the National Security Act of 1947 (50 U.S.C. §401a (4))) shall not make any record available under this paragraph to—

    (i) any government entity, other than a State, territory, commonwealth, or district of the United States, or any subdivision thereof; or

    (ii) a representative of a government entity described in clause (i).

(4) (A) (i) In order to carry out the provisions of this section, each agency shall promulgate

regulations, pursuant to notice and receipt of public comment, specifying the schedule of fees applicable to the processing of requests under this section and establishing procedures and guidelines for determining when such fees should be waived or reduced. Such schedule shall conform to the guidelines which shall be promulgated, pursuant to notice and receipt of public comment, by the Director of the Office of Management and Budget and which shall provide for a uniform schedule of fees for all agencies.

(ii) Such agency regulations shall provide that—

(I) fees shall be limited to reasonable standard charges for document search, duplication, and review, when records are requested for commercial use;

(II) fees shall be limited to reasonable standard charges for document duplication when records are not sought for commercial use and the request is made by an educational or noncommercial scientific institution, whose purpose is scholarly or scientific research; or a representative of the news media; and

(III) for any request not described in (I) or (II), fees shall be limited to reasonable standard charges for document search and duplication.

In this clause, the term 'a representative of the news media' means any person or entity that gathers information of potential interest to a segment of the public, uses its editorial skills to turn the raw materials into a distinct work, and distributes that work to an audience. In this clause, the term 'news' means information that is about current events or that would be of current interest to the public. Examples of news-media entities are television or radio stations broadcasting to the public at large and publishers of periodicals (but only if such entities qualify as disseminators of 'news') who make their products available for purchase by or subscription by or free distribution to the general public. These examples are not all-inclusive. Moreover, as methods of news delivery evolve (for example, the adoption of the electronic dissemination of newspapers through telecommunications services), such alternative media shall be considered to be news-media entities. A freelance journalist shall be regarded as working for a newsmedia entity if the journalist can demonstrate a solid basis for expecting publication through that entity, whether or not the journalist is actually employed by the entity. A publication contract would present a solid basis for such an expectation; the Government may also consider the past publication record of the requester in making such a determination.

(iii) Documents shall be furnished without any charge or at a charge reduced below the fees established under clause (ii) if disclosure of the information is in the public interest because it is likely to contribute significantly to public understanding of the operations or activities of the government and is not primarily in the commercial interest of the requester.

(iv) Fee schedules shall provide for the recovery of only the direct costs of search, duplication, or review. Review costs shall include only the direct costs incurred during the initial examination of a document for the purposes of determining whether the documents must be disclosed under this section and for the purposes of withholding any portions exempt from disclosure under this section. Review costs may not include any costs incurred in resolving issues of law or policy that may be raised in the course of processing a request under this section. No fee may be charged by any agency under this section—

(I) if the costs of routine collection and processing of the fee are likely to equal or exceed the amount of the fee; or

(II) for any request described in clause (ii) (II) or

(III) of this subparagraph for the first two hours of search time or for the first one hundred pages of duplication.

(v) No agency may require advance payment of any fee unless the requester has previously failed to pay fees in a timely fashion, or the agency has determined that the fee will exceed $250.

(vi) Nothing in this subparagraph shall supersede fees chargeable under a statute specifically providing for setting the level of fees for particular types of records.

(vii) In any action by a requester regarding the waiver of fees under this section, the court shall determine the matter de novo: Provided, That the court's review of the matter shall be limited to the record before the agency.

(viii) An agency shall not assess search fees (or in the case of a requester described under clause (ii)(II), duplication fees) under this subparagraph if the agency fails to comply with any time limit under paragraph (6), if no unusual or exceptional circumstances (as those terms are defined for purposes of paragraphs (6)(B) and (C), respectively) apply to the processing of the request.

(B) On complaint, the district court of the United States in the district in which the complainant resides, or has his principal place of business, or in which the agency records are situated, or in the District of Columbia, has jurisdiction to enjoin the agency from withholding agency records and to order the production of any agency records improperly withheld from the complainant. In such a case the court shall determine the matter de novo, and may examine the contents of such agency records in camera to determine whether such records or any part thereof shall be withheld under any of the exemptions set forth in subsection (b) of this section, and the burden is on the agency to sustain its action. In addition to any other matters to which a court accords substantial weight, a court shall accord substantial weight to an affidavit of an agency concerning the agency's determination as to technical feasibility under paragraph (2)(C) and subsection (b) and reproducibility under paragraph (3)(B).

(C) Notwithstanding any other provision of law, the defendant shall serve an answer or otherwise plead to any complaint made under this subsection within thirty days after service upon the defendant of the pleading in which such complaint is made, unless the court otherwise directs for good cause shown.

(D) Repealed. Pub. L. 98–620, title IV, §402(2), Nov. 8, 1984, 98 Stat. 3357.

(E) (i) The court may assess against the United States reasonable attorney fees and other litigation costs reasonably incurred in any case under this section in which the complainant has substantially prevailed.

(ii) For purposes of this subparagraph, a complainant has substantially prevailed if the complainant has obtained relief through either—

(I) a judicial order, or an enforceable written agreement or consent decree; or

(II) a voluntary or unilateral change in position by the agency, if the complainant's claim is not insubstantial.

(F) (i) Whenever the court orders the production of any agency records improperly withheld from the complainant and assesses against the United States reasonable attorney fees and other litigation costs, and the court additionally issues a written finding that the circumstances surrounding the withholding raise questions whether agency personnel acted arbitrarily or capriciously with respect to the withholding, the Special Counsel shall promptly initiate a proceeding to determine whether disciplinary action is warranted against the officer or employee who was primarily responsible for the withholding. The Special Counsel, after investigation and consideration of the evidence submitted, shall submit his findings and recommendations to the administrative authority of the agency concerned and shall send copies of the findings and recommendations to the officer or employee or his representative. The administrative authority shall take the corrective action that the Special Counsel recommends.

(ii) The Attorney General shall—

(I) notify the Special Counsel of each civil action described under the first sentence of clause (i); and

(II) annually submit a report to Congress on the number of such civil actions in the preceding year.

(iii) The Special Counsel shall annually submit a report to Congress on the actions taken by the Special Counsel under clause (i).

(G) In the event of noncompliance with the order of the court, the district court may punish for contempt the responsible employee, and in the case of a uniformed service, the responsible member.

(5) Each agency having more than one member shall maintain and make available for public inspection a record of the final votes of each member in every agency proceeding.

(6) (A) Each agency, upon any request for records made under paragraph (1), (2), or (3) of this subsection, shall—

(i) determine within 20 days (excepting Saturdays, Sundays, and legal public holidays) after the receipt of any such request whether to comply with such request and shall immediately notify the person making such request of such determination and the reasons therefor, and of the right of such person to appeal to the head of the agency any adverse determination; and

(ii) make a determination with respect to any appeal within twenty days (excepting Saturdays, Sundays, and legal public holidays) after the receipt of such appeal. If on appeal the denial of the request for records is in whole or in part upheld, the agency shall notify the person making such request of the provisions for judicial review of that determination under paragraph (4) of this subsection. The 20-day period under clause (i) shall commence on the date on which the request is first received by the appropriate component of the agency, but in any event not later than ten days after the request is first received by any component of the agency that is designated in the agency's regulations under this section to receive requests under this section. The 20-day period shall not be tolled by the agency except—

(I) that the agency may make one request to the requester for information and toll the 20-day period while it is awaiting such information that it has reasonably requested from the requester under this section; or

(II) if necessary to clarify with the requester issues regarding fee assessment. In either case, the agency's receipt of the requester's response to the agency's request for information or clarification ends the tolling period.

(B) (i) In unusual circumstances as specified in this subparagraph, the time limits prescribed in either clause (i) or clause (ii) of subparagraph (A) may be extended by written notice to the person making such request setting forth the unusual circumstances for such extension and the date on which a determination is expected to be dispatched. No such notice shall specify a date that would result in an extension for more than ten working days, except as provided in clause (ii) of this subparagraph.

(ii) With respect to a request for which a written notice under clause (i) extends the time limits prescribed under clause (i) of subparagraph (A), the agency shall notify the person making the request if the request cannot be processed within the time limit specified in that clause and shall provide the person an opportunity to limit the scope of the request so that it may be processed within that time limit or an opportunity to arrange with the agency an alternative time frame for processing the request or a modified request. To aid the requester, each agency shall make available its FOIA Public Liaison, who shall assist in the resolution of any disputes between the requester and the agency. Refusal by the person to reasonably modify the request or arrange such an alternative time frame shall be considered as a factor in determining whether exceptional circumstances exist for purposes of subparagraph (C).

(iii) As used in this subparagraph, "unusual circumstances" means, but only to the extent reasonably necessary to the proper processing of the particular requests—

(I) the need to search for and collect the requested records from field facilities or other establishments that are separate from the office processing the request;

(II) the need to search for, collect, and appropriately examine a voluminous amount of separate and distinct records which are demanded in a single request; or

(III) the need for consultation, which shall be conducted with all practicable speed, with another agency having a substantial interest in the determination of the request or among two or more components of the agency having substantial subject-matter interest therein.

(iv) Each agency may promulgate regulations, pursuant to notice and receipt of public comment, providing for the aggregation of certain requests by the same requestor, or by a group of requestors acting in concert, if the agency reasonably believes that such requests actually constitute a single request, which would otherwise satisfy the unusual circumstances specified in this subparagraph, and the requests involve clearly related matters. Multiple requests involving unrelated matters shall not be aggregated.

(C) (i) Any person making a request to any agency for records under paragraph (1), (2), or (3) of this subsection shall be deemed to have exhausted his administrative remedies with respect to such request if the agency fails to comply with the applicable time limit provisions of this paragraph. If the Government can show exceptional circumstances exist and that the agency is exercising due diligence in responding to the request, the court may retain jurisdiction and allow the agency additional time to complete its review of the records. Upon any determination by an agency to comply with a request for records, the records shall be made promptly available to such person making such request. Any notification of denial of any request for records under this subsection shall set forth the names and titles or positions of each person responsible for the denial of such request.

(ii) For purposes of this subparagraph, the term "exceptional circumstances" does not include a delay that results from a predictable agency workload of requests under this section, unless the agency demonstrates reasonable progress in reducing its backlog of pending requests.

(iii) Refusal by a person to reasonably modify the scope of a request or arrange an alternative time frame for processing a request (or a modified request) under clause (ii) after being given an opportunity to do so by the agency to whom the person made the request shall be considered as a factor in determining whether exceptional circumstances exist for purposes of this subparagraph.

(D) (i) Each agency may promulgate regulations, pursuant to notice and receipt of public comment, providing for multitrack processing of requests for records based on the amount of work or time (or both) involved in processing requests.

    (ii) Regulations under this subparagraph may provide a person making a request that does not qualify for the fastest multitrack processing an opportunity to limit the scope of the request in order to qualify for faster processing.

    (iii) This subparagraph shall not be considered to affect the requirement under subparagraph (C) to exercise due diligence.

(E) (i) Each agency shall promulgate regulations, pursuant to notice and receipt of public comment, providing for expedited processing of requests for records—

    (I) in cases in which the person requesting the records demonstrates a compelling need; and

    (II) in other cases determined by the agency.

    (ii) Notwithstanding clause (i), regulations under this subparagraph must ensure—

    (I) that a determination of whether to provide expedited processing shall be made, and notice of the determination shall be provided to the person making the request, within 10 days after the date of the request; and

    (II) expeditious consideration of administrative appeals of such determinations of whether to provide expedited processing.

    (iii) An agency shall process as soon as practicable any request for records to which the agency has granted expedited processing under this subparagraph. Agency action to deny or affirm denial of a request for expedited processing pursuant to this subparagraph, and failure by an agency to respond in a timely manner to such a request shall be subject to judicial review under paragraph (4), except that the judicial review shall be based on the record before the agency at the time of the determination.

    (iv) A district court of the United States shall not have jurisdiction to review an agency denial of expedited processing of a request for records after the agency has provided a complete response to the request.

    (v) For purposes of this subparagraph, the term "compelling need" means—

    (I) that a failure to obtain requested records on an expedited basis under this paragraph could reasonably be expected to pose an imminent threat to the life or physical safety of an individual; or

    (II) with respect to a request made by a person primarily engaged in disseminating information, urgency to inform the public concerning actual or alleged Federal Government activity.

    (vi) A demonstration of a compelling need by a person making a request for expedited processing shall be made by a statement certified by such person to be true and correct to the best of such person's knowledge and belief.

(F) In denying a request for records, in whole or in part, an agency shall make a reasonable effort to estimate the volume of any requested matter the provision of which is denied, and shall provide any such estimate to the person making the request, unless providing such estimate would harm an interest protected by the exemption in subsection (b) pursuant to which the denial is made.

(7) Each agency shall—

    (A) establish a system to assign an individualized tracking number for each request received that will take longer than ten days to process and provide to each person making a request the tracking number assigned to the request; and

(B) establish a telephone line or Internet service that provides information about the status of a request to the person making the request using the assigned tracking number, including—

    (i) the date on which the agency originally received the request; and

    (ii) an estimated date on which the agency will complete action on the request.

(b) This section does not apply to matters that are—

(1) (A) specifically authorized under criteria established by an Executive order to be kept secret in the interest of national defense or foreign policy and

    (B) are in fact properly classified pursuant to such Executive order;

(2) related solely to the internal personnel rules and practices of an agency;

(3) specifically exempted from disclosure by statute (other than section 552b of this title), provided that such statute

    (A) requires that the matters be withheld from the public in such a manner as to leave no discretion on the issue, or

    (B) establishes particular criteria for withholding or refers to particular types of matters to be withheld;

(4) trade secrets and commercial or financial information obtained from a person and privileged or confidential;

(5) inter-agency or intra-agency memorandums or letters which would not be available by law to a party other than an agency in litigation with the agency;

(6) personnel and medical files and similar files the disclosure of which would constitute a clearly unwarranted invasion of personal privacy;

(7) records or information compiled for law enforcement purposes, but only to the extent that the production of such law enforcement records or information

    (A) could reasonably be expected to interfere with enforcement proceedings,

    (B) would deprive a person of a right to a fair trial or an impartial adjudication,

    (C) could reasonably be expected to constitute an unwarranted invasion of personal privacy,

    (D) could reasonably be expected to disclose the identity of a confidential source, including a State, local, or foreign agency or authority or any private institution which furnished information on a confidential basis, and, in the case of a record or information compiled by criminal law enforcement authority in the course of a criminal investigation or by an agency conducting a lawful national security intelligence investigation, information furnished by a confidential source,

    (E) would disclose techniques and procedures for law enforcement investigations or prosecutions, or would disclose guidelines for law enforcement investigations or prosecutions if such disclosure could reasonably be expected to risk circumvention of the law, or

    (F) could reasonably be expected to endanger the life or physical safety of any individual;

(8) contained in or related to examination, operating, or condition reports prepared by, on behalf of, or for the use of an agency responsible for the regulation or supervision of financial institutions; or

(9) geological and geophysical information and data, including maps, concerning wells. Any reasonably segregable portion of a record shall be provided to any person requesting such record after deletion of the portions which are exempt under this subsection. The amount of information deleted, and the exemption under which the deletion is made, shall be indicated on the released portion of the record, unless including that indication would harm an interest protected by the exemption in this subsection under which the deletion is made. If technically feasible, the amount of the information deleted, and the exemption

under which the deletion is made, shall be indicated at the place in the record where such deletion is made.

(c) (1) Whenever a request is made which involves access to records described in subsection (b)(7)(A) and—

(A) the investigation or proceeding involves a possible violation of criminal law; and

(B) there is reason to believe that

(i) the subject of the investigation or proceeding is not aware of its pendency, and

(ii) disclosure of the existence of the records could reasonably be expected to interfere with enforcement proceedings, the agency may, during only such time as that circumstance continues, treat the records as not subject to the requirements of this section.

(2) Whenever informant records maintained by a criminal law enforcement agency under an informant's name or personal identifier are requested by a third party according to the informant's name or personal identifier, the agency may treat the records as not subject to the requirements of this section unless the informant's status as an informant has been officially confirmed.

(3) Whenever a request is made which involves access to records maintained by the Federal Bureau of Investigation pertaining to foreign intelligence or counterintelligence, or international terrorism, and the existence of the records is classified information as provided in subsection (b)(1), the Bureau may, as long as the existence of the records remains classified information, treat the records as not subject to the requirements of this section.

(d) This section does not authorize withholding of information or limit the availability of records to the public, except as specifically stated in this section. This section is not authority to withhold information from Congress.

(e) (1) On or before February 1 of each year, each agency shall submit to the Attorney General of the United States a report which shall cover the preceding fiscal year and which shall include—

(A) the number of determinations made by the agency not to comply with requests for records made to such agency under subsection (a) and the reasons for each such determination;

(B) (i) the number of appeals made by persons under subsection (a)(6), the result of such appeals, and the reason for the action upon each appeal that results in a denial of information; and

(ii) a complete list of all statutes that the agency relies upon to authorize the agency to withhold information under subsection (b)(3), the number of occasions on which each statute was relied upon, a description of whether a court has upheld the decision of the agency to withhold information under each such statute, and a concise description of the scope of any information withheld;

(C) the number of requests for records pending before the agency as of September 30 of the preceding year, and the median and average number of days that such requests had been pending before the agency as of that date;

(D) the number of requests for records received by the agency and the number of requests which the agency processed;

(E) the median number of days taken by the agency to process different types of requests, based on the date on which the requests were received by the agency;

(F) the average number of days for the agency to respond to a request beginning on the date on which the request was received by the agency, the median number of days for the agency to respond to such requests, and the range in number of days for the agency to respond to such requests;

(G) based on the number of business days that have elapsed since each request was originally received by the agency—

(i) the number of requests for records to which the agency has responded with a determination within a period up to and including 20 days, and in 20- day increments up to and including 200 days;

(ii) the number of requests for records to which the agency has responded with a determination within a period greater than 200 days and less than 301 days;

(iii) the number of requests for records to which the agency has responded with a determination within a period greater than 300 days and less than 401 days; and

(iv) the number of requests for records to which the agency has responded with a determination within a period greater than 400 days;

(H) the average number of days for the agency to provide the granted information beginning on the date on which the request was originally filed, the median number of days for the agency to provide the granted information, and the range in number of days for the agency to provide the granted information;

(I) the median and average number of days for the agency to respond to administrative appeals based on the date on which the appeals originally were received by the agency, the highest number of business days taken by the agency to respond to an administrative appeal, and the lowest number of business days taken by the agency to respond to an administrative appeal;

(J) data on the 10 active requests with the earliest filing dates pending at each agency, including the amount of time that has elapsed since each request was originally received by the agency;

(K) data on the 10 active administrative appeals with the earliest filing dates pending before the agency as of September 30 of the preceding year, including the number of business days that have elapsed since the requests were originally received by the agency;

(L) the number of expedited review requests that are granted and denied, the average and median number of days for adjudicating expedited review requests, and the number adjudicated within the required 10 days;

(M) the number of fee waiver requests that are granted and denied, and the average and median number of days for adjudicating fee waiver determinations;

(N) the total amount of fees collected by the agency for processing requests; and

(O) the number of full-time staff of the agency devoted to processing requests for records under this section, and the total amount expended by the agency for processing such requests.

(2) Information in each report submitted under paragraph (1) shall be expressed in terms of each principal component of the agency and for the agency overall.

(3) Each agency shall make each such report available to the public including by computer telecommunications, or if computer telecommunications means have not been established by the agency, by other electronic means. In addition, each agency shall make the raw statistical data used in its reports available electronically to the public upon request.

(4) The Attorney General of the United States shall make each report which has been made available by electronic means available at a single electronic access point. The Attorney General of the United States shall notify the Chairman and ranking minority member of the Committee on Government Reform and Oversight of the House of Representatives and the Chairman and ranking minority member of the Committees on Governmental Affairs and the Judiciary of the Senate, no later than April 1 of the year in which each such report is issued, that such reports are available by electronic means.

(5) The Attorney General of the United States, in consultation with the Director of the Office of Management and Budget, shall develop reporting and performance guidelines in connection with reports required by this subsection by October 1, 1997, and may establish additional requirements for such reports as the Attorney General determines may be useful.

(6) The Attorney General of the United States shall submit an annual report on or before April 1 of each calendar year which shall include for the prior calendar year a listing of the number of cases arising under this section, the exemption involved in each case, the disposition of such case, and the cost, fees, and penalties assessed under subparagraphs (E), (F), and (G) of subsection (a)(4). Such report shall also include a description of the efforts undertaken by the Department of Justice to encourage agency compliance with this section.

(f) For purposes of this section, the term—

(1) "agency" as defined in section 551 (1) of this title includes any executive department, military department, Government corporation, Government controlled corporation, or other establishment in the executive branch of the Government (including the Executive Office of the President), or any independent regulatory agency; and

(2) 'record' and any other term used in this section in reference to information includes—

(A) any information that would be an agency record subject to the requirements of this section when maintained by an agency in any format, including an electronic format; and

(B) any information described under subparagraph (A) that is maintained for an agency by an entity under Government contract, for the purposes of records management.

(g) The head of each agency shall prepare and make publicly available upon request, reference material or a guide for requesting records or information from the agency, subject to the exemptions in subsection (b), including—

(1) an index of all major information systems of the agency;

(2) a description of major information and record locator systems maintained by the agency; and

(3) a handbook for obtaining various types and categories of public information from the agency pursuant to chapter 35 of title 44, and under this section.

(h)(1) There is established the Office of Government Information Services within the National Archives and Records Administration.

(2) The Office of Government Information Services shall—

(A) review policies and procedures of administrative agencies under this section;

(B) review compliance with this section by administrative agencies; and

(C) recommend policy changes to Congress and the President to improve the administration of this section.

(3) The Office of Government Information Services shall offer mediation services to resolve disputes between persons making requests under this section and administrative agencies as a nonexclusive alternative to litigation and, at the discretion of the Office, may issue advisory opinions if mediation has not resolved the dispute.

(i) The Government Accountability Office shall conduct audits of administrative agencies on the implementation of this section and issue reports detailing the results of such audits.

(j) Each agency shall designate a Chief FOIA Officer who shall be a senior official of such agency (at the Assistant Secretary or equivalent level).

(k) The Chief FOIA Officer of each agency shall, subject to the authority of the head of the agency—

(1) have agency-wide responsibility for efficient and appropriate compliance with this section;

(2) monitor implementation of this section throughout the agency and keep the head of the agency, the chief legal officer of the agency, and the Attorney General appropriately informed of the agency's performance in implementing this section;

(3) recommend to the head of the agency such adjustments to agency practices, policies, personnel, and funding as may be necessary to improve its implementation of this section;

(4) review and report to the Attorney General, through the head of the agency, at such times and in such formats as the Attorney General may direct, on the agency's performance in implementing this section;

(5) facilitate public understanding of the purposes of the statutory exemptions of this section by including concise descriptions of the exemptions in both the agency's hand-book issued under subsection (g), and the agency's annual report on this section, and by providing an overview, where appropriate, of certain general categories of agency records to which those exemptions apply; and

(6) designate one or more FOIA Public Liaisons.

(l) FOIA Public Liaisons shall report to the agency Chief FOIA Officer and shall serve as supervisory officials to whom a requester under this section can raise concerns about the service the requester has received from the FOIA Requester Center, following an initial response from the FOIA Requester Center Staff. FOIA Public Liaisons shall be responsible for assisting in reducing delays, increasing transparency and understanding of the status of requests, and assisting in the resolution of disputes.

Department of Defense Title 10 Authorities

CHAPTER 4 OF TITLE 10, UNITED STATES CODE UNDER SECRETARY OF DEFENSE FOR INTELLIGENCE (10 U.S.C. § 137)

SEC. 137.

(a) There is an Under Secretary of Defense for Intelligence, appointed from civilian life by the President, by and with the advice and consent of the Senate.

(b) Subject to the authority, direction, and control of the Secretary of Defense, the Under Secretary of Defense for Intelligence shall perform such duties and exercise such powers as the Secretary of Defense may prescribe in the area of intelligence.

(c) The Under Secretary of Defense for Intelligence takes precedence in the Department of Defense after the Under Secretary of Defense for Personnel and Readiness.

CHAPTER 21 OF TITLE 10, UNITED STATES CODE

SEC. 421. FUNDS FOR FOREIGN CRYPTOLOGIC SUPPORT

(a) The Secretary of Defense may use appropriated funds available to the Department of Defense for intelligence and communications purposes to pay for the expenses of arrangements with foreign countries for cryptologic support.

(b) The Secretary of Defense may use funds other than appropriated funds to pay for the expenses of arrangements with foreign countries for cryptologic support without regard for the provisions of law relating to the expenditure of United States Government funds, except that—

(1) no such funds may be expended, in whole or in part, by or for the benefit of the Department of Defense for a purpose for which Congress had previously denied funds; and

(2) proceeds from the sale of cryptologic items may be used only to purchase replacement items similar to the items that are sold; and

(3) the authority provided by this subsection may not be used to acquire items or services for the principal benefit of the United States.

(c) Any funds expended under the authority of subsection (a) shall be reported to the Select Committee on Intelligence of the Senate and the Permanent Select Committee on Intelligence of the House of Representatives pursuant to the provisions of title V of the National Security Act of 1947 (50 U.S.C. §413 et seq.). Funds expended under the authority of subsection (b) shall be reported pursuant to procedures jointly agreed upon by such committees and the Secretary of Defense.

SEC. 422. USE OF FUNDS FOR CERTAIN INCIDENTAL PURPOSES

(a) COUNTERINTELLIGENCE OFFICIAL RECEPTION AND REPRESENTATION EXPENSES.—The Secretary of Defense may use funds available to the Department of Defense for counterintelligence programs to pay the expenses of hosting foreign officials in the United States under the auspices of the Department of Defense for consultation on counterintelligence matters.

(b) PROMOTIONAL ITEMS FOR RECRUITMENT PURPOSES.—The Secretary of Defense may use funds available for an intelligence element of the Department of Defense to purchase promotional items of nominal value for use in the recruitment of individuals for employment by that element.

SEC. 423. AUTHORITY TO USE PROCEEDS FROM COUNTERINTELLIGENCE OPERATIONS OF THE MILITARY DEPARTMENTS

(a) The Secretary of Defense may authorize, without regard to the provisions of section 3302 of title 31, use of proceeds from counterintelligence operations conducted by components of the military departments to offset necessary and reasonable expenses, not otherwise prohibited by law, incurred in such operations, and to make exceptional performance awards to personnel involved in such operations, if use of appropriated funds to meet such expenses or to make such awards would not be practicable.

(b) As soon as the net proceeds from such counterintelligence operations are no longer necessary for the conduct of those operations, such proceeds shall be deposited into the Treasury as miscellaneous receipts.

(c) The Secretary of Defense shall establish policies and procedures to govern acquisition, use, management, and disposition of proceeds from counterintelligence operations conducted by components of the military departments, including effective internal systems of accounting and administrative controls.

SEC. 424. DISCLOSURE OF ORGANIZATIONAL AND PERSONNEL INFORMATION: EXEMPTION FOR SPECIFIED INTELLIGENCE AGENCIES

(a) EXEMPTION FROM DISCLOSURE.—Except as required by the President or as provided in subsection (c), no provision of law shall be construed to require the disclosure of—

(1) the organization or any function of an organization of the Department of Defense named in subsection (b); or

(2) the number of persons employed by or assigned or detailed to any such organization or the name, official title, occupational series, grade, or salary of any such person.

(b) COVERED ORGANIZATIONS.—This section applies to the following organizations of the Department of Defense:

(1) The Defense Intelligence Agency.

(2) The National Reconnaissance Office.

(3) The National Geospatial-Intelligence Agency.

(c) PROVISION OF INFORMATION TO CONGRESS.—Subsection (a) does not apply with respect to the provision of information to Congress.

SEC. 425. PROHIBITION OF UNAUTHORIZED USE OF NAME, INITIALS, OR SEAL: SPECIFIED INTELLIGENCE AGENCIES

(a) PROHIBITION.—Except with the written permission of both the Secretary of Defense and the Director of Central Intelligence, no person may knowingly use, in connection with any merchandise, retail product, impersonation, solicitation, or commercial activity in a manner reasonably calculated to convey the impression that such use is approved, endorsed, or authorized by the Secretary and the Director, any of the following (or any colorable imitation thereof):

(1) The words "Defense Intelligence Agency", the initials "DIA", or the seal of the Defense Intelligence Agency.

(2) The words "National Reconnaissance Office", the initials "NRO", or the seal of the National Reconnaissance Office.

(3) The words "National Imagery and Mapping Agency", the initials "NIMA", or the seal of the National Imagery and Mapping Agency.

(4) The words "Defense Mapping Agency", the initials "DMA", or the seal of the Defense Mapping Agency.

(5) The words "National Geospatial-Intelligence Agency", the initials "NGA," or the seal of the National Geospatial-Intelligence Agency.

(b) AUTHORITY TO ENJOIN VIOLATIONS.—Whenever it appears to the Attorney General that any person is engaged or is about to engage in an act or practice which constitutes or will constitute conduct prohibited by subsection (a), the Attorney General may initiate a civil proceeding in a district court of the United States to enjoin such act or practice. Such court shall proceed as soon as practicable to the hearing and determination of such action and may, at any time before final determination, enter such restraining orders or prohibitions, or take such other actions as is warranted, to prevent injury to the United States or to any person or class of persons for whose protection the action is brought.

SEC. 426. INTEGRATION OF DEPARTMENT OF DEFENSE INTELLIGENCE, SURVEILLANCE, AND RECONNAISSANCE CAPABILITIES

(a) ISR INTEGRATION COUNCIL.—

(1) The Under Secretary of Defense for Intelligence shall establish an Intelligence, Surveillance, and Reconnaissance Integration Council—

(A) to assist the Under Secretary with respect to matters relating to the integration of intelligence, surveillance, and reconnaissance capabilities, and coordination of related developmental activities, of the military departments, intelligence agencies of the Department of Defense, and relevant combatant commands; and

(B) otherwise to provide a means to facilitate the integration of such capabilities and the coordination [1] of such developmental activities.

(2) The Council shall be composed of—

(A) the senior intelligence officers of the armed forces and the United States Special Operations Command;

(B) the Director of Operations of the Joint Staff; and

(C) the directors of the intelligence agencies of the Department of Defense.

(3) The Under Secretary of Defense for Intelligence shall invite the participation of the Director of Central Intelligence (or that Director's representative) in the proceedings of the Council.

(b) ISR INTEGRATION ROADMAP.—

(1) The Under Secretary of Defense for Intelligence shall develop a comprehensive plan, to be known as the "Defense Intelligence, Surveillance, and Reconnaissance Integration Roadmap", to guide the development and integration of the Department of Defense intelligence, surveillance, and reconnaissance capabilities for the 15-year period of fiscal years 2004 through 2018.

(2) The Under Secretary shall develop the Defense Intelligence, Surveillance, and Reconnaissance Integration Roadmap in consultation with the Intelligence, Surveillance, and Reconnaissance Integration Council and the Director of National Intelligence.

SEC. 427. INTELLIGENCE OVERSIGHT ACTIVITIES OF DEPARTMENT OF DEFENSE: ANNUAL REPORTS

(a) ANNUAL REPORTS REQUIRED.—

(1) Not later than March 1 of each year, the Secretary of Defense shall submit—

(A) to the congressional committees specified in subparagraph (A) of paragraph (2) a report on the intelligence oversight activities of the Department of Defense during the previous calendar year insofar as such oversight activities relate to tactical intelligence and intelligence-related activities of the Department; and

(B) to the congressional committees specified in subparagraph (B) of paragraph (2) a report on the intelligence oversight activities of the Department of Defense during the previous calendar year insofar as such oversight activities relate to intelligence and intelligence-related activities of the Department other than those specified in subparagraph (A).

(2)(A) The committees specified in this subparagraph are the following:

(i) The Committee on Armed Services and the Committee on Appropriations of the Senate.

(ii) The Permanent Select Committee on Intelligence, the Committee on Armed Services, and the Committee on Appropriations of the House of Representatives.

(B) The committees specified in this subparagraph are the following:

(i) The Select Committee on Intelligence, the Committee on Armed Services, and the Committee on Appropriations of the Senate.

(ii) The Permanent Select Committee on Intelligence and the Committee on Appropriations of the House of Representatives.

(b) ELEMENTS.—Each report under subsection (a) shall include, for the calendar year covered by such report and with respect to oversight activities subject to coverage in that report, the following:

(1) A description of any violation of law or of any Executive order or Presidential directive (including Executive Order No. 12333) that comes to the attention of any General Counsel or Inspector General within the Department of Defense, or the Under Secretary of Defense for Intelligence, and a description of the actions taken by such official with respect to such activity.

(2) A description of the results of intelligence oversight inspections under-taken by each of the following:

(A) The Office of the Secretary of Defense.

(B) Each military department.

(C) Each combat support agency.

(D) Each field operating agency.

(3) A description of any changes made in any program for the intelligence oversight activities of the Department of Defense, including any training pro-gram.

(4) A description of any changes made in any published directive or policy memoranda on the intelligence or intelligence-related activities of—

(A) any military department;

(B) any combat support agency; or

(C) any field operating agency.

(c) DEFINITIONS.—In this section:

(1) The term "intelligence oversight activities of the Department of Defense" refers to any activity undertaken by an agency, element, or component of the Department of Defense to ensure compliance with regard to requirements or instructions on the intelligence and intelligence-related activities of the De-partment under law or any Executive order or Presidential directive (includ-ing Executive Order No. 12333).

(2) The term "combat support agency" has the meaning given that term in section 193(f) of this title.

(3) The term "field operating agency" means a specialized subdivision of the Department of Defense that carries out activities under the operational con-trol of the Department.

SEC. 431. AUTHORITY TO ENGAGE IN COMMERCIAL ACTIVITIES AS SECURITY FOR INTELLIGENCE COLLECTION ACTIVITIES

(a) AUTHORITY.—The Secretary of Defense, subject to the provisions of this subchapter, may authorize the conduct of those commercial activities necessary to provide security for authorized intelligence collection activities abroad under-taken by the Department of Defense. No commercial activity may be initiated pursuant to this subchapter after December 31, 2006.

(b) INTERAGENCY COORDINATION AND SUPPORT.—Any such activity shall—

(1) be coordinated with, and (where appropriate) be supported by, the Direc-tor of Central Intelligence; and

(2) to the extent the activity takes place within the United States, be coordi-nated with, and (where appropriate) be supported by, the Director of the Fed-eral Bureau of Investigation.

(c) DEFINITIONS.—In this subchapter:

(1) The term "commercial activities" means activities that are conducted in a manner consistent with prevailing commercial practices and includes—

(A) the acquisition, use, sale, storage and disposal of goods and services;

(B) entering into employment contracts and leases and other agreements for real and personal property;

(C) depositing funds into and withdrawing funds from domestic and foreign commercial business or financial institutions;

(D) acquiring licenses, registrations, permits, and insurance; and

(E) establishing corporations, partnerships, and other legal entities.

(2) The term "intelligence collection activities" means the collection of foreign intelligence and counterintelligence information.

SEC. 432. USE, DISPOSITION, AND AUDITING OF FUNDS

(a) USE OF FUNDS.—Funds generated by a commercial activity authorized pursuant to this subchapter may be used to offset necessary and reasonable expenses arising from that activity. Use of such funds for that purpose shall be kept to the minimum necessary to conduct the activity concerned in a secure manner. Any funds generated by the activity in excess of those required for that purpose shall be deposited, as often as may be practicable, into the Treasury as miscellaneous receipts.

(b) AUDITS.—

(1) The Secretary of Defense shall assign an organization within the Department of Defense to have auditing responsibility with respect to activities authorized under this subchapter.

(2) That organization shall audit the use and disposition of funds generated by any commercial activity authorized under this subchapter not less often than annually. The results of all such audits shall be promptly reported to the intelligence committees (as defined in section 437 (d) of this title).

SEC. 433. RELATIONSHIP WITH OTHER FEDERAL LAWS

(a) IN GENERAL.—Except as provided by subsection (b), a commercial activity conducted pursuant to this subchapter shall be carried out in accordance with applicable Federal law.

(b) AUTHORIZATION OF WAIVERS WHEN NECESSARY TO MAINTAIN SECURITY.—

(1) If the Secretary of Defense determines, in connection with a commercial activity authorized pursuant to section 431 of this title, that compliance with certain Federal laws or regulations pertaining to the management and administration of Federal agencies would create an unacceptable risk of compromise of an authorized intelligence activity, the Secretary may, to the extent necessary to prevent such compromise, waive compliance with such laws or regulations.

(2) Any determination and waiver by the Secretary under paragraph (1) shall be made in writing and shall include a specification of the laws and regulations for which compliance by the commercial activity concerned is not required consistent with this section.

(3) The authority of the Secretary under paragraph (1) may be delegated only to the Deputy Secretary of Defense, an Under Secretary of Defense, an Assistant Secretary of Defense, or a Secretary of a military department.

(c) FEDERAL LAWS AND REGULATIONS.—For purposes of this section, Federal laws and regulations pertaining to the management and administration of Federal agencies are only those Federal laws and regulations pertaining to the following:

(1) The receipt and use of appropriated and nonappropriated funds.

(2) The acquisition or management of property or services.

(3) Information disclosure, retention, and management.

(4) The employment of personnel.

(5) Payments for travel and housing.

(6) The establishment of legal entities or government instrumentalities.

(7) Foreign trade or financial transaction restrictions that would reveal the commercial activity as an activity of the United States Government.

SEC. 434. RESERVATION OF DEFENSES AND IMMUNITIES.
The submission to judicial proceedings in a State or other legal jurisdiction, in connection with a commercial activity undertaken pursuant to this subchapter, shall not constitute a waiver of the defenses and immunities of the United States.

SEC. 435. LIMITATIONS
(a) LAWFUL ACTIVITIES.—Nothing in this subchapter authorizes the conduct of any intelligence activity that is not otherwise authorized by law or Executive order.

(b) DOMESTIC ACTIVITIES.—Personnel conducting commercial activity authorized by this subchapter may only engage in those activities in the United States to the extent necessary to support intelligence activities abroad.

(c) PROVIDING GOODS AND SERVICES TO THE DEPARTMENT OF DEFENSE.— Commercial activity may not be undertaken within the United States for the purpose of providing goods and services to the Department of Defense, other than as may be necessary to provide security for the activities subject to this subchapter.

(d) NOTICE TO UNITED STATES PERSONS.—

(1) In carrying out a commercial activity authorized under this subchapter, the Secretary of Defense may not permit an entity engaged in such activity to employ a United States person in an operational, managerial, or supervisory position, and may not assign or detail a United States person to perform operational, managerial, or supervisory duties for such an entity, unless that person is informed in advance of the intelligence security purpose of that activity.

(2) In this subsection, the term "United States person" means an individual who is a citizen of the United States or an alien lawfully admitted to the United States for permanent residence.

SEC. 436. REGULATIONS
The Secretary of Defense shall prescribe regulations to implement the authority provided in this subchapter. Such regulations shall be consistent with this subchapter and shall at a minimum—

(1) specify all elements of the Department of Defense who are authorized to engage in commercial activities pursuant to this subchapter;

(2) require the personal approval of the Secretary or Deputy Secretary of Defense for all sensitive activities to be authorized pursuant to this subchapter;

(3) specify all officials who are authorized to grant waivers of laws or regulations pursuant to section 433 (b) of this title, or to approve the establishment or conduct of commercial activities pursuant to this subchapter;

(4) designate a single office within the Defense Intelligence Agency to be responsible for the management and supervision of all activities authorized under this subchapter;

(5) require that each commercial activity proposed to be authorized under this subchapter be subject to appropriate legal review before the activity is authorized; and

(6) provide for appropriate internal audit controls and oversight for such activities.

SEC. 437. CONGRESSIONAL OVERSIGHT

(a) PROPOSED REGULATIONS.—Copies of regulations proposed to be prescribed under section 436 of this title (including any proposed revision to such regulations) shall be submitted to the intelligence committees not less than 30 days before they take effect.

(b) CURRENT INFORMATION.—Consistent with title V of the National Security Act of 1947 (50 U.S.C. §413 et seq.), the Secretary of Defense shall ensure that the intelligence committees are kept fully and currently informed of actions taken pursuant to this subchapter, including any significant anticipated activity to be authorized pursuant to this subchapter.

(c) ANNUAL REPORT.—Not later each year than the date provided in section 507 of the National Security Act of 1947 (50 U.S.C. §415b), the Secretary shall submit to the congressional intelligence committees (as defined in section 3 of that Act (50 U.S.C. §401a)) a report on all commercial activities authorized under this subchapter that were undertaken during the previous fiscal year. Such report shall include (with respect to the fiscal year covered by the report) the following:

(1) A description of any exercise of the authority provided by section 433 (b) of this title.

(2) A description of any expenditure of funds made pursuant to this subchapter (whether from appropriated or non-appropriated funds).

(3) A description of any actions taken with respect to audits conducted pursuant to section 432 of this title to implement recommendations or correct deficiencies identified in such audits.

(4) A description of each corporation, partnership, or other legal entity that was established.

Homeland Security Act of 2002, §§ 101-237

(Titles I and II) (Pub. L. No. 107-296, 116 Stat. 2135), as amended

TITLE I—DEPARTMENT OF HOMELAND SECURITY

Sec. 101. [6 U.S.C. 111] EXECUTIVE DEPARTMENT; MISSION.

(a) ESTABLISHMENT.—There is established a Department of Homeland Security, as an executive department of the United States within the meaning of title 5, United States Code.

(b) MISSION.—

(1) IN GENERAL.—The primary mission of the Department is to—

(A) prevent terrorist attacks within the United States;

(B) reduce the vulnerability of the United States to terrorism;

(C) minimize the damage, and assist in the recovery, from terrorist attacks that do occur within the United States;

(D) carry out all functions of entities transferred to the Department, including by acting as a focal point regarding natural and manmade crises and emergency planning;

(E) ensure that the functions of the agencies and subdivisions within the Department that are not related directly to securing the homeland are not diminished or neglected except by a specific explicit Act of Congress;

(F) ensure that the overall economic security of the United States is not diminished by efforts, activities, and programs aimed at securing the homeland;

(G) ensure that the civil rights and civil liberties of persons are not diminished by efforts, activities, and programs aimed at securing the homeland; and

(H) monitor connections between illegal drug trafficking and terrorism, coordinate efforts to sever such connections, and otherwise contribute to efforts to interdict illegal drug trafficking.

(2) RESPONSIBILITY FOR INVESTIGATING AND PROSECUTING TERRORISM.— Except as specifically provided by law with respect to entities transferred to the Department under this Act, primary responsibility for investigating and prosecuting acts of terrorism shall be vested not in the Department, but rather in Federal, State, and local law enforcement agencies with jurisdiction over the acts in question.

Sec. 102. [6 U.S.C. 112] SECRETARY; FUNCTIONS.

(a) SECRETARY.—

(1) IN GENERAL.—There is a Secretary of Homeland Security, appointed by the President, by and with the advice and consent of the Senate.

(2) HEAD OF DEPARTMENT.—The Secretary is the head of the Department and shall have direction, authority, and control over it.

(3) FUNCTIONS VESTED IN SECRETARY.—All functions of all officers, employees, and organizational units of the Department are vested in the Secretary.

(b) FUNCTIONS.—The Secretary—

(1) except as otherwise provided by this Act, may delegate any of the Secretary's functions to any officer, employee, or organizational unit of the Department;

(2) shall have the authority to make contracts, grants, and cooperative agreements, and to enter into agreements with other executive agencies, as may be necessary and proper to carry out the Secretary's responsibilities under this Act or otherwise provided by law; and

(3) shall take reasonable steps to ensure that information systems and databases of the Department are compatible with each other and with appropriate databases of other Departments.

(c) COORDINATION WITH NON-FEDERAL ENTITIES.—With respect to homeland security, the Secretary shall coordinate through the Office of State and Local Coordination (established under section 801) (including the provision of training and equipment) with State and local government personnel, agencies, and authorities, with the private sector, and with other entities, including by—

(1) coordinating with State and local government personnel, agencies, and authorities, and with the private sector, to ensure adequate planning, equipment, training, and exercise activities;

(2) coordinating and, as appropriate, consolidating, the Federal Government's communications and systems of communications relating to homeland security with State and local government personnel, agencies, and authorities, the private sector, other entities, and the public; and

(3) distributing or, as appropriate, coordinating the distribution of, warnings and information to State and local government personnel, agencies, and authorities and to the public.

(d) MEETINGS OF NATIONAL SECURITY COUNCIL.—The Secretary may, subject to the direction of the President, attend and participate in meetings of the National Security Council.

(e) ISSUANCE OF REGULATIONS.—The issuance of regulations by the Secretary shall be governed by the provisions of chapter 5 of title 5, United States Code, except as specifically provided in this Act, in laws granting regulatory authorities that are transferred by this Act, and in laws enacted after the date of enactment of this Act.

(f) SPECIAL ASSISTANT TO THE SECRETARY.—The Secretary shall appoint a Special Assistant to the Secretary who shall be responsible for—

(1) creating and fostering strategic communications with the private sector to enhance the primary mission of the Department to protect the American homeland;

(2) advising the Secretary on the impact of the Department's policies, regulations, processes, and actions on the private sector;

(3) interfacing with other relevant Federal agencies with homeland security missions to assess the impact of these agencies' actions on the private sector;

(4) creating and managing private sector advisory councils composed of representatives of industries and associations designated by the Secretary to—

(A) advise the Secretary on private sector products, applications, and solutions as they relate to homeland security challenges; and

(B) advise the Secretary on homeland security policies, regulations, processes, and actions that affect the participating industries and associations;

(5) working with Federal laboratories, federally funded research and development centers, other federally funded organizations, academia, and the private sector to develop innovative approaches to address homeland security challenges to produce and deploy the best available technologies for homeland security missions;

(6) promoting existing public-private partnerships and developing new public-private partnerships to provide for collaboration and mutual support to address homeland security challenges;

(7) assisting in the development and promotion of private sector best practices to secure critical infrastructure;

(8) coordinating industry efforts, with respect to functions of the Department of Homeland Security, to identify private sector resources and capabilities that could be effective in supplementing Federal, State, and local government agency efforts to prevent or respond to a terrorist attack;

(9) coordinating with the Directorate of Border and Transportation Security and the Assistant Secretary for Trade Development of the Department of Commerce on issues related to the travel and tourism industries; and

(10) consulting with the Office of State and Local Government Coordination and Preparedness on all matters of concern to the private sector, including the tourism industry.

(g) STANDARDS POLICY.—All standards activities of the Department shall be conducted in accordance with section 12(d) of the National Technology Transfer Advancement Act of 1995 (15 U.S.C. 272 note) and Office of Management and Budget Circular A–119.

Sec. 103. [6 U.S.C. 113] OTHER OFFICERS.

(a) DEPUTY SECRETARY; UNDER SECRETARIES.—There are the following officers, appointed by the President, by and with the advice and consent of the Senate:

(1) A Deputy Secretary of Homeland Security, who shall be the Secretary's first assistant for purposes of subchapter III of chapter 33 of title 5, United States Code.

(2) An Under Secretary for Science and Technology.

(3) An Under Secretary for Border and Transportation Security.

(4) An Administrator of the Federal Emergency Management Agency.

(5) A Director of the Bureau of Citizenship and Immigration Services.

(6) An Under Secretary for Management.

(7) A Director of the Office of Counternarcotics Enforcement.

(8) Not more than 12 Assistant Secretaries.

(9) A General Counsel, who shall be the chief legal officer of the Department.

(b) INSPECTOR GENERAL.—There shall be in the Department an Office of Inspector General and an Inspector General at the head of such office, as provided in the Inspector General Act of 1978 (5 U.S.C. App.).

(c) COMMANDANT OF THE COAST GUARD.—To assist the Secretary in the performance of the Secretary's functions, there is a Commandant of the Coast Guard, who shall be appointed as provided in section 44 of title 14, United States Code, and who shall report directly to the Secretary. In addition to such duties as may be provided in this Act and as assigned to the Commandant by the Secretary, the duties of the Commandant shall include those required by section 2 of title 14, United States Code.

(d) OTHER OFFICERS.—To assist the Secretary in the performance of the Secretary's functions, there are the following officers, appointed by the President:

(1) A Director of the Secret Service.

(2) A Chief Information Officer.

(3) A Chief Human Capital Officer.

(4) An Officer for Civil Rights and Civil Liberties.

(5) A Director for Domestic Nuclear Detection.

(f) PERFORMANCE OF SPECIFIC FUNCTIONS.—Subject to the provisions of this Act, every officer of the Department shall perform the functions specified by law for the official's office or prescribed by the Secretary.

(e) CHIEF FINANCIAL OFFICER.—There shall be in the Department a Chief Financial Officer, as provided in chapter 9 of title 31, United States Code.

TITLE II—INFORMATION ANALYSIS AND INFRASTRUCTURE PROTECTION

Subtitle A—Directorate for Information Analysis and Infrastructure Protection; Access to Information

Sec. 201. [6 U.S.C. 121] DIRECTORATE FOR INFORMATION ANALYSIS AND INFRASTRUCTURE PROTECTION.

(a) UNDER SECRETARY OF HOMELAND SECURITY FOR INFORMATION ANALYSIS AND INFRASTRUCTURE PROTECTION.—

(1) IN GENERAL.—There shall be in the Department a Directorate for Information Analysis and Infrastructure Protection headed by an Under Secretary for Information Analysis and Infrastructure Protection, who shall be appointed by the President, by and with the advice and consent of the Senate.

(2) RESPONSIBILITIES.—The Under Secretary shall assist the Secretary in discharging the responsibilities assigned by the Secretary.

(b) ASSISTANT SECRETARY FOR INFORMATION ANALYSIS; ASSISTANT SECRETARY FOR INFRASTRUCTURE PROTECTION.—

(1) ASSISTANT SECRETARY FOR INFORMATION ANALYSIS.— There shall be in the Department an Assistant Secretary for Information Analysis, who shall be appointed by the President.

(2) ASSISTANT SECRETARY FOR INFRASTRUCTURE PROTECTION.— There shall be in the Department an Assistant Secretary for Infrastructure Protection, who shall be appointed by the President.

(3) RESPONSIBILITIES.—The Assistant Secretary for Information Analysis and the Assistant Secretary for Infrastructure Protection shall assist the Under Secretary for Informa-

tion Analysis and Infrastructure Protection in discharging the responsibilities of the Under Secretary under this section.

(c) DISCHARGE OF INFORMATION ANALYSIS AND INFRASTRUCTURE PROTECTION.— The Secretary shall ensure that the responsibilities of the Department regarding information analysis and infrastructure protection are carried out through the Under Secretary for Information Analysis and Infrastructure Protection.

(d) RESPONSIBILITIES OF UNDER SECRETARY.—Subject to the direction and control of the Secretary, the responsibilities of the Under Secretary for Information Analysis and Infrastructure Protection shall be as follows:

(1) To access, receive, and analyze law enforcement information, intelligence information, and other information from agencies of the Federal Government, State and local government agencies (including law enforcement agencies), and private sector entities, and to integrate such information in order to—

(A) identify and assess the nature and scope of terrorist threats to the homeland;

(B) detect and identify threats of terrorism against the United States; and

(C) understand such threats in light of actual and potential vulnerabilities of the homeland.

(2) To carry out comprehensive assessments of the vulnerabilities of the key resources and critical infrastructure of the United States, including the performance of risk assessments to determine the risks posed by particular types of terrorist attacks within the United States (including an assessment of the probability of success of such attacks and the feasibility and potential efficacy of various countermeasures to such attacks).

(3) To integrate relevant information, analyses, and vulnerability assessments (whether such information, analyses, or assessments are provided or produced by the Department or others) in order to identify priorities for protective and support measures by the Department, other agencies of the Federal Government, State and local government agencies and authorities, the private sector, and other entities.

(4) To ensure, pursuant to section 202, the timely and efficient access by the Department to all information necessary to discharge the responsibilities under this section, including obtaining such information from other agencies of the Federal Government.

(5) To develop a comprehensive national plan for securing the key resources and critical infrastructure of the United States, including power production, generation, and distribution systems, information technology and telecommunications systems (including satellites), electronic financial and property record storage and transmission systems, emergency preparedness communications systems, and the physical and technological assets that support such systems.

(6) To recommend measures necessary to protect the key resources and critical infrastructure of the United States in coordination with other agencies of the Federal Government and in cooperation with State and local government agencies and authorities, the private sector, and other entities.

(7) To administer the Homeland Security Advisory System, including—

(A) exercising primary responsibility for public advisories related to threats to homeland security; and

(B) in coordination with other agencies of the Federal Government, providing specific warning information, and advice about appropriate protective measures and countermeasures, to State and local government agencies and authorities, the private sector, other entities, and the public.

(8) To review, analyze, and make recommendations for improvements in the policies and procedures governing the sharing of law enforcement information, intelligence information, intelligence-related information, and other information relating to homeland security within

the Federal Government and between the Federal Government and State and local government agencies and authorities.

(9) To disseminate, as appropriate, information analyzed by the Department within the Department, to other agencies of the Federal Government with responsibilities relating to homeland security, and to agencies of State and local governments and private sector entities with such responsibilities in order to assist in the deterrence, prevention, preemption of, or response to, terrorist attacks against the United States.

(10) To consult with the Director of Central Intelligence and other appropriate intelligence, law enforcement, or other elements of the Federal Government to establish collection priorities and strategies for information, including law enforcement- related information, relating to threats of terrorism against the United States through such means as the representation of the Department in discussions regarding requirements and priorities in the collection of such information.

(11) To consult with State and local governments and private sector entities to ensure appropriate exchanges of information, including law enforcement-related information, relating to threats of terrorism against the United States.

(12) To ensure that—

    (A) any material received pursuant to this Act is protected from unauthorized disclosure and handled and used only for the performance of official duties; and

    (B) any intelligence information under this Act is shared, retained, and disseminated consistent with the authority of the Director of Central Intelligence to protect intelligence sources and methods under the National Security Act of 1947 (50 U.S.C. 401 et seq.) and related procedures and, as appropriate, similar authorities of the Attorney General concerning sensitive law enforcement information.

(13) To request additional information from other agencies of the Federal Government, State and local government agencies, and the private sector relating to threats of terrorism in the United States, or relating to other areas of responsibility assigned by the Secretary, including the entry into cooperative agreements through the Secretary to obtain such information.

(14) To establish and utilize, in conjunction with the chief information officer of the Department, a secure communications and information technology infrastructure, including data-mining and other advanced analytical tools, in order to access, receive, and analyze data and information in furtherance of the responsibilities under this section, and to disseminate information acquired and analyzed by the Department, as appropriate.

(15) To ensure, in conjunction with the chief information officer of the Department, that any information databases and analytical tools developed or utilized by the Department—

    (A) are compatible with one another and with relevant information databases of other agencies of the Federal Government; and

    (B) treat information in such databases in a manner that complies with applicable Federal law on privacy.

(16) To coordinate training and other support to the elements and personnel of the Department, other agencies of the Federal Government, and State and local governments that provide information to the Department, or are consumers of information provided by the Department, in order to facilitate the identification and sharing of information revealed in their ordinary duties and the optimal utilization of information received from the Department.

(17) To coordinate with elements of the intelligence community and with Federal, State, and local law enforcement agencies, and the private sector, as appropriate.

(18) To provide intelligence and information analysis and support to other elements of the Department.

(19) To perform such other duties relating to such responsibilities as the Secretary may provide.

(e) STAFF.—

(1) IN GENERAL.—The Secretary shall provide the Directorate with a staff of analysts having appropriate expertise and experience to assist the Directorate in discharging responsibilities under this section.

(2) PRIVATE SECTOR ANALYSTS.—Analysts under this subsection may include analysts from the private sector.

(3) SECURITY CLEARANCES.—Analysts under this subsection shall possess security clearances appropriate for their work under this section.

(f) DETAIL OF PERSONNEL.—

(1) IN GENERAL.—In order to assist the Directorate in discharging responsibilities under this section, personnel of the agencies referred to in paragraph (2) may be detailed to the Department for the performance of analytic functions and related duties.

(2) COVERED AGENCIES.—The agencies referred to in this paragraph are as follows:

(A) The Department of State.

(B) The Central Intelligence Agency.

(C) The Federal Bureau of Investigation.

(D) The National Security Agency.

(E) The National Imagery and Mapping Agency.

(F) The Defense Intelligence Agency.

(G) Any other agency of the Federal Government that the President considers appropriate.

(3) COOPERATIVE AGREEMENTS.—The Secretary and the head of the agency concerned may enter into cooperative agreements for the purpose of detailing personnel under this subsection.

(4) BASIS.—The detail of personnel under this subsection may be on a reimbursable or nonreimbursable basis.

(g) FUNCTIONS TRANSFERRED.—In accordance with title XV, there shall be transferred to the Secretary, for assignment to the Under Secretary for Information Analysis and Infrastructure Protection under this section, the functions, personnel, assets, and liabilities of the following:

(1) The National Infrastructure Protection Center of the Federal Bureau of Investigation (other than the Computer Investigations and Operations Section), including the functions of the Attorney General relating thereto.

(2) The National Communications System of the Department of Defense, including the functions of the Secretary of Defense relating thereto.

(3) The Critical Infrastructure Assurance Office of the Department of Commerce, including the functions of the Secretary of Commerce relating thereto.

(4) The National Infrastructure Simulation and Analysis Center of the Department of Energy and the energy security and assurance program and activities of the Department, including the functions of the Secretary of Energy relating thereto.

(5) The Federal Computer Incident Response Center of the General Services Administration, including the functions of the Administrator of General Services relating thereto. * *
* * * * *

Sec. 202. [6 U.S.C. 122] ACCESS TO INFORMATION.

(a) IN GENERAL.—

(1) THREAT AND VULNERABILITY INFORMATION.—Except as otherwise directed by

the President, the Secretary shall have such access as the Secretary considers necessary to all information, including reports, assessments, analyses, and unevaluated intelligence relating to threats of terrorism against the United States and to other areas of responsibility assigned by the Secretary, and to all information concerning infrastructure or other vulnerabilities of the United States to terrorism, whether or not such information has been analyzed, that may be collected, possessed, or prepared by any agency of the Federal Government.

(2) OTHER INFORMATION.—The Secretary shall also have access to other information relating to matters under the responsibility of the Secretary that may be collected, possessed, or prepared by an agency of the Federal Government as the President may further provide.

(b) MANNER OF ACCESS.—Except as otherwise directed by the President, with respect to information to which the Secretary has access pursuant to this section—

(1) the Secretary may obtain such material upon request, and may enter into cooperative arrangements with other executive agencies to provide such material or provide Department officials with access to it on a regular or routine basis, including requests or arrangements involving broad categories of material, access to electronic databases, or both; and

(2) regardless of whether the Secretary has made any request or entered into any cooperative arrangement pursuant to paragraph (1), all agencies of the Federal Government shall promptly provide to the Secretary—

(A) all reports (including information reports containing intelligence which has not been fully evaluated), assessments, and analytical information relating to threats of terrorism against the United States and to other areas of responsibility assigned by the Secretary;

(B) all information concerning the vulnerability of the infrastructure of the United States, or other vulnerabilities of the United States, to terrorism, whether or not such information has been analyzed;

(C) all other information relating to significant and credible threats of terrorism against the United States, whether or not such information has been analyzed; and

(D) such other information or material as the President may direct.

(c) TREATMENT UNDER CERTAIN LAWS.—The Secretary shall be deemed to be a Federal law enforcement, intelligence, protective, national defense, immigration, or national security official, and shall be provided with all information from law enforcement agencies that is required to be given to the Director of Central Intelligence, under any provision of the following:

(1) The USA PATRIOT Act of 2001 (Public Law 107–56).

(2) Section 2517(6) of title 18, United States Code.

(3) Rule 6(e)(3)(C) of the Federal Rules of Criminal Procedure.

(d) ACCESS TO INTELLIGENCE AND OTHER INFORMATION.—

(1) ACCESS BY ELEMENTS OF FEDERAL GOVERNMENT.—Nothing in this title shall preclude any element of the intelligence community (as that term is defined in section 3(4) of the National Security Act of 1947 (50 U.S.C. 401a(4)), or any other element of the Federal Government with responsibility for analyzing terrorist threat information, from receiving any intelligence or other information relating to terrorism.

(2) SHARING OF INFORMATION.—The Secretary, in consultation with the Director of Central Intelligence, shall work to ensure that intelligence or other information relating to terrorism to which the Department has access is appropriately shared with the elements of the Federal Government referred to in paragraph (1), as well as with State and local governments, as appropriate.

Subtitle B—Critical Infrastructure Information

Sec. 211. [6 U.S.C. 101 note] SHORT TITLE.
This subtitle may be cited as the "Critical Infrastructure Information Act of 2002."

Sec. 212. [6 U.S.C. 131] DEFINITIONS.
In this subtitle:

(1) AGENCY.—The term "agency" has the meaning given it in section 551 of title 5, United States Code.

(2) COVERED FEDERAL AGENCY.—The term "covered Federal agency" means the Department of Homeland Security.

(3) CRITICAL INFRASTRUCTURE INFORMATION.—The term "critical infrastructure information" means information not customarily in the public domain and related to the security of critical infrastructure or protected systems—

(A) actual, potential, or threatened interference with, attack on, compromise of, or incapacitation of critical infrastructure or protected systems by either physical or computer-based attack or other similar conduct (including the misuse of or unauthorized access to all types of communications and data transmission systems) that violates Federal, State, or local law, harms interstate commerce of the United States, or threatens public health or safety;

(B) the ability of any critical infrastructure or protected system to resist such interference, compromise, or incapacitation, including any planned or past assessment, projection, or estimate of the vulnerability of critical infrastructure or a protected system, including security testing, risk evaluation thereto, risk management planning, or risk audit; or

(C) any planned or past operational problem or solution regarding critical infrastructure or protected systems, including repair, recovery, reconstruction, insurance, or continuity, to the extent it is related to such interference, compromise, or incapacitation.

(4) CRITICAL INFRASTRUCTURE PROTECTION PROGRAM.—The term "critical infrastructure protection program" means any component or bureau of a covered Federal agency that has been designated by the President or any agency head to receive critical infrastructure information.

(5) INFORMATION SHARING AND ANALYSIS ORGANIZATION.—The term "Information Sharing and Analysis Organization" means any formal or informal entity or collaboration created or employed by public or private sector organizations, for purposes of—

(A) gathering and analyzing critical infrastructure information in order to better understand security problems and interdependencies related to critical infrastructure and protected systems, so as to ensure the availability, integrity, and reliability thereof;

(B) communicating or disclosing critical infrastructure information to help prevent, detect, mitigate, or recover from the effects of a interference, compromise, or a incapacitation problem related to critical infrastructure or protected systems; and

(C) voluntarily disseminating critical infrastructure information to its members, State, local, and Federal Governments, or any other entities that may be of assistance in carrying out the purposes specified in subparagraphs (A) and (B).

(6) PROTECTED SYSTEM.—The term "protected system"—

(A) means any service, physical or computer-based system, process, or procedure that directly or indirectly affects the viability of a facility of critical infrastructure; and

(B) includes any physical or computer-based system, including a computer, computer system, computer or communications network, or any component hardware or element thereof, software program, processing instructions, or information or data in transmission or storage therein, irrespective of the medium of transmission or storage.

(7) VOLUNTARY.—

(A) IN GENERAL.—The term "voluntary", in the case of any submittal of critical infrastructure information to a covered Federal agency, means the submittal thereof in the absence of such agency's exercise of legal authority to compel access to or submission of such information and may be accomplished by a single entity or an Information Sharing and Analysis Organization on behalf of itself or its members.

(B) EXCLUSIONS.—The term "voluntary"—

(i) in the case of any action brought under the securities laws as is defined in section 3(a)(47) of the Securities Exchange Act of 1934 (15 U.S.C. 78c(a)(47))—

(I) does not include information or statements contained in any documents or materials filed with the Securities and Exchange Commission, or with Federal banking regulators, pursuant to section 12(i) of the Securities Exchange Act of 1934 (15 U.S.C. 78l(I)); and

(II) with respect to the submittal of critical infrastructure information, does not include any disclosure or writing that when made accompanied the solicitation of an offer or a sale of securities; and

(ii) does not include information or statements submitted or relied upon as a basis for making licensing or permitting determinations, or during regulatory proceedings.

Sec. 213. [6 U.S.C. 132] DESIGNATION OF CRITICAL INFRASTRUCTURE PROTECTION PROGRAM.

A critical infrastructure protection program may be designated as such by one of the following:

(1) The President.

(2) The Secretary of Homeland Security.

Sec. 214. [6 U.S.C. 123] PROTECTION OF VOLUNTARILY SHARED CRITICAL INFRASTRUCTURE INFORMATION.

(a) PROTECTION.—

(1) IN GENERAL.—Notwithstanding any other provision of law, critical infrastructure information (including the identity of the submitting person or entity) that is voluntarily submitted to a covered Federal agency for use by that agency regarding the security of critical infrastructure and protected systems, analysis, warning, interdependency study, recovery, reconstitution, or other informational purpose, when accompanied by an express statement specified in paragraph (2)—

(A) shall be exempt from disclosure under section 552 of title 5, United States Code (commonly referred to as the Freedom of Information Act);

(B) shall not be subject to any agency rules or judicial doctrine regarding ex parte communications with a decision making official;

(C) shall not, without the written consent of the person or entity submitting such information, be used directly by such agency, any other Federal, State, or local authority, or any third party, in any civil action arising under Federal or State law if such information is submitted in good faith;

(D) shall not, without the written consent of the person or entity submitting such information, be used or disclosed by any officer or employee of the United States for purposes other than the purposes of this subtitle, except—

(i) in furtherance of an investigation or the prosecution of a criminal act; or

(ii) when disclosure of the information would be—

(I) to either House of Congress, or to the extent of matter within its jurisdiction, any committee or subcommittee thereof, any joint committee thereof or subcommittee of any such joint committee; or

(II) to the Comptroller General, or any authorized representative of the Comptroller General, in the course of the performance of the duties of the General Accounting Office.

(E) shall not, if provided to a State or local government or government agency—

(i) be made available pursuant to any State or local law requiring disclosure of information or records;

(ii) otherwise be disclosed or distributed to any party by said State or local government or government agency without the written consent of the person or entity submitting such information; or

(iii) be used other than for the purpose of protecting critical infrastructure or protected systems, or in furtherance of an investigation or the prosecution of a criminal act; and

(F) does not constitute a waiver of any applicable privilege or protection provided under law, such as trade secret protection.

(2) EXPRESS STATEMENT.—For purposes of paragraph (1), the term "express statement", with respect to information or records, means—

(A) in the case of written information or records, a written marking on the information or records substantially similar to the following: "This information is voluntarily submitted to the Federal Government in expectation of protection from disclosure as provided by the provisions of the Critical Infrastructure Information Act of 2002."; or

(B) in the case of oral information, a similar written statement submitted within a reasonable period following the oral communication.

(b) LIMITATION.—No communication of critical infrastructure information to a covered Federal agency made pursuant to this subtitle shall be considered to be an action subject to the requirements of the Federal Advisory Committee Act (5 U.S.C. App. 2).

(c) INDEPENDENTLY OBTAINED INFORMATION.—Nothing in this section shall be construed to limit or otherwise affect the ability of a State, local, or Federal Government entity, agency, or authority, or any third party, under applicable law, to obtain critical infrastructure information in a manner not covered by subsection (a), including any information lawfully and properly disclosed generally or broadly to the public and to use such information in any manner permitted by law.

(d) TREATMENT OF VOLUNTARY SUBMITTAL OF INFORMATION.— The voluntary submittal to the Government of information or records that are protected from disclosure by this subtitle shall not be construed to constitute compliance with any requirement to submit such information to a Federal agency under any other provision of law.

(e) PROCEDURES.—

(1) IN GENERAL.—The Secretary of the Department of Homeland Security shall, in consultation with appropriate representatives of the National Security Council and the Office of Science and Technology Policy, establish uniform procedures for the receipt, care, and storage by Federal agencies of critical infrastructure information that is voluntarily submitted to the Government. The procedures shall be established not later than 90 days after the date of the enactment of this subtitle.

(2) ELEMENTS.—The procedures established under paragraph

(1) shall include mechanisms regarding—

(A) the acknowledgement of receipt by Federal agencies of critical infrastructure information that is voluntarily submitted to the Government;

(B) the maintenance of the identification of such information as voluntarily submitted to the Government for purposes of and subject to the provisions of this subtitle;

(C) the care and storage of such information; and

(D) the protection and maintenance of the confidentiality of such information so as to permit the sharing of such information within the Federal Government and with State and local governments, and the issuance of notices and warnings related to the protection of critical infrastructure and protected systems, in such manner as to protect from public disclosure the identity of the submitting person or entity, or information that is proprietary, business sensitive, relates specifically to the submitting person or entity, and is otherwise not appropriately in the public domain.

(f) PENALTIES.—Whoever, being an officer or employee of the United States or of any department or agency thereof, knowingly publishes, divulges, discloses, or makes known in any manner or to any extent not authorized by law, any critical infrastructure information protected from disclosure by this subtitle coming to him in the course of this employment or official duties or by reason of any examination or investigation made by, or return, report, or record made to or filed with, such department or agency or officer or employee thereof, shall be fined under title 18 of the United States Code, imprisoned not more than 1 year, or both, and shall be removed from office or employment.

(g) AUTHORITY TO ISSUE WARNINGS.—The Federal Government may provide advisories, alerts, and warnings to relevant companies, targeted sectors, other governmental entities, or the general public regarding potential threats to critical infrastructure as appropriate. In issuing a warning, the Federal Government shall take appropriate actions to protect from disclosure—

(1) the source of any voluntarily submitted critical infrastructure information that forms the basis for the warning; or

(2) information that is proprietary, business sensitive, relates specifically to the submitting person or entity, or is otherwise not appropriately in the public domain.

(h) AUTHORITY TO DELEGATE.—The President may delegate authority to a critical infrastructure protection program, designated under section 213, to enter into a voluntary agreement to promote critical infrastructure security, including with any Information Sharing and Analysis Organization, or a plan of action as otherwise defined in section 708 of the Defense Production Act of 1950 (50 U.S.C. App. 2158).

Sec. 215. [6 U.S.C. 134] NO PRIVATE RIGHT OF ACTION.

Nothing in this subtitle may be construed to create a private right of action for enforcement of any provision of this Act.

Subtitle C—Information Security

Sec. 221. [6 U.S.C. 141] PROCEDURES FOR SHARING INFORMATION.

The Secretary shall establish procedures on the use of information shared under this title that—

(1) limit the redissemination of such information to ensure that it is not used for an unauthorized purpose;

(2) ensure the security and confidentiality of such information;

(3) protect the constitutional and statutory rights of any individuals who are subjects of such information; and

(4) provide data integrity through the timely removal and destruction of obsolete or erroneous names and information.

Sec. 222. [6 U.S.C. 142] PRIVACY OFFICER.

The Secretary shall appoint a senior official in the Department, who shall report directly to the Secretary, to assume primary responsibility for privacy policy, including—

(1) assuring that the use of technologies sustain, and do not erode, privacy protections relating to the use, collection, and disclosure of personal information;

(2) assuring that personal information contained in Privacy Act systems of records is handled in full compliance with fair information practices as set out in the Privacy Act of 1974;

(3) evaluating legislative and regulatory proposals involving collection, use, and disclosure of personal information by the Federal Government;

(4) conducting a privacy impact assessment of proposed rules of the Department or that of the Department on the privacy of personal information, including the type of personal information collected and the number of people affected;

(5) coordinating with the Officer for Civil Rights and Civil Liberties to ensure that—

(A) programs, policies, and procedures involving civil rights, civil liberties, and privacy considerations are addressed in an integrated and comprehensive manner; and

(B) Congress receives appropriate reports on such programs, policies, and procedures; and

(6) preparing a report to Congress on an annual basis on activities of the Department that affect privacy, including complaints of privacy violations, implementation of the Privacy Act of 1974, internal controls, and other matters.

Sec. 223. [6 U.S.C. 143] ENHANCEMENT OF NON-FEDERAL CYBERSECURITY.

In carrying out the responsibilities under section 201, the Under Secretary for Information Analysis and Infrastructure Protection shall—

(1) as appropriate, provide to State and local government entities, and upon request to private entities that own or operate critical information systems—

(A) analysis and warnings related to threats to, and vulnerabilities of, critical information systems; and

(B) in coordination with the Under Secretary for Emergency Preparedness and Response, crisis management support in response to threats to, or attacks on, critical information systems; and

(2) as appropriate, provide technical assistance, upon request, to the private sector and other government entities, in coordination with the Under Secretary for Emergency Preparedness and Response, with respect to emergency recovery plans to respond to major failures of critical information systems.

Sec. 224. [6 U.S.C. 144] NET GUARD.

The Under Secretary for Information Analysis and Infrastructure Protection may establish a national technology guard, to be known as "NET Guard", comprised of local teams of volunteers with expertise in relevant areas of science and technology, to assist local communities to respond and recover from attacks on information systems and communications networks.

Sec. 225. [6 U.S.C. 145] CYBER SECURITY ENHANCEMENT ACT OF 2002.

(a) SHORT TITLE.—This section may be cited as the "Cyber Security Enhancement Act of 2002."

(b) AMENDMENT OF SENTENCING GUIDELINES RELATING TO CERTAIN COMPUTER CRIMES.—

(1) DIRECTIVE TO THE UNITED STATES SENTENCING COMMISSION.— Pursuant to its authority under section 994(p) of title 28, United States Code, and in accordance with this

subsection, the United States Sentencing Commission shall review and, if appropriate, amend its guidelines and its policy statements applicable to persons convicted of an offense under section 1030 of title 18, United States Code.

(2) REQUIREMENTS.—In carrying out this subsection, the Sentencing Commission shall—

(A) ensure that the sentencing guidelines and policy statements reflect the serious nature of the offenses described in paragraph (1), the growing incidence of such offenses, and the need for an effective deterrent and appropriate punishment to prevent such offenses;

(B) consider the following factors and the extent to which the guidelines may or may not account for them—

(i) the potential and actual loss resulting from the offense;

(ii) the level of sophistication and planning involved in the offense;

(iii) whether the offense was committed for purposes of commercial advantage or private financial benefit;

(iv) whether the defendant acted with malicious intent to cause harm in committing the offense;

(v) the extent to which the offense violated the privacy rights of individuals harmed;

(vi) whether the offense involved a computer used by the government in furtherance of national defense, national security, or the administration of justice;

(vii) whether the violation was intended to or had the effect of significantly interfering with or disrupting a critical infrastructure; and

(viii) whether the violation was intended to or had the effect of creating a threat to public health or safety, or injury to any person;

(C) assure reasonable consistency with other relevant directives and with other sentencing guidelines;

(D) account for any additional aggravating or mitigating circumstances that might justify exceptions to the generally applicable sentencing ranges;

(E) make any necessary conforming changes to the sentencing guidelines; and

(F) assure that the guidelines adequately meet the purposes of sentencing as set forth in section 3553(a)(2) of title 18, United States Code.

(c) STUDY AND REPORT ON COMPUTER CRIMES.—Not later than May 1, 2003, the United States Sentencing Commission shall submit a brief report to Congress that explains any actions taken by the Sentencing Commission in response to this section and includes any recommendations the Commission may have regarding statutory penalties for offenses under section 1030 of title 18, United States Code.

(d) EMERGENCY DISCLOSURE EXCEPTION.—

(1) * * * * * * * * * *

(2) REPORTING OF DISCLOSURES.—A government entity that receives a disclosure under section 2702(b) of title 18, United States Code, shall file, not later than 90 days after such disclosure, a report to the Attorney General stating the paragraph of that section under which the disclosure was made, the date of the disclosure, the entity to which the disclosure was made, the number of customers or subscribers to whom the information disclosed pertained, and the number of communications, if any, that were disclosed. The Attorney General shall publish all such reports into a single report to be submitted to Congress 1 year after the date of enactment of this Act.

Subtitle D—Office of Science and Technology

Sec. 231. [6 U.S.C. 161] ESTABLISHMENT OF OFFICE; DIRECTOR.

(a) ESTABLISHMENT.—

(1) IN GENERAL.—There is hereby established within the Department of Justice an Office of Science and Technology

(hereinafter in this title referred to as the "Office").

(2) AUTHORITY.—The Office shall be under the general authority of the Assistant Attorney General, Office of Justice Programs, and shall be established within the National Institute of Justice.

(b) DIRECTOR.—The Office shall be headed by a Director, who shall be an individual appointed based on approval by the Office of Personnel Management of the executive qualifications of the individual.

Sec. 232. [6 U.S.C. 162] MISSION OF OFFICE; DUTIES.

(a) MISSION.—The mission of the Office shall be—

(1) to serve as the national focal point for work on law enforcement technology; and

(2) to carry out programs that, through the provision of equipment, training, and technical assistance, improve the safety and effectiveness of law enforcement technology and improve access to such technology by Federal, State, and local law enforcement agencies.

(b) DUTIES.—In carrying out its mission, the Office shall have the following duties:

(1) To provide recommendations and advice to the Attorney General.

(2) To establish and maintain advisory groups (which shall be exempt from the provisions of the Federal Advisory Committee Act (5 U.S.C. App.)) to assess the law enforcement technology needs of Federal, State, and local law enforcement agencies.

(3) To establish and maintain performance standards in accordance with the National Technology Transfer and Advancement Act of 1995 (Public Law 104–113) for, and test and evaluate law enforcement technologies that may be used by, Federal, State, and local law enforcement agencies.

(4) To establish and maintain a program to certify, validate, and mark or otherwise recognize law enforcement technology products that conform to standards established and maintained by the Office in accordance with the National Technology Transfer and Advancement Act of 1995 (Public Law 104–113). The program may, at the discretion of the Office, allow for supplier's declaration of conformity with such standards.

(5) To work with other entities within the Department of Justice, other Federal agencies, and the executive office of the President to establish a coordinated Federal approach on issues related to law enforcement technology.

(6) To carry out research, development, testing, evaluation, and cost-benefit analyses in fields that would improve the safety, effectiveness, and efficiency of law enforcement technologies used by Federal, State, and local law enforcement agencies, including, but not limited to—

(A) weapons capable of preventing use by unauthorized persons, including personalized guns;

(B) protective apparel;

(C) bullet-resistant and explosion-resistant glass;

(D) monitoring systems and alarm systems capable of providing precise location information;

(E) wire and wireless interoperable communication technologies;

(F) tools and techniques that facilitate investigative and forensic work, including computer forensics;

(G) equipment for particular use in counterterrorism, including devices and technologies to disable terrorist devices;

(H) guides to assist State and local law enforcement agencies;

(I) DNA identification technologies; and

(J) tools and techniques that facilitate investigations of computer crime.

(7) To administer a program of research, development, testing, and demonstration to improve the interoperability of voice and data public safety communications.

(8) To serve on the Technical Support Working Group of the Department of Defense, and on other relevant interagency panels, as requested.

(9) To develop, and disseminate to State and local law enforcement agencies, technical assistance and training materials for law enforcement personnel, including prosecutors.

(10) To operate the regional National Law Enforcement and Corrections Technology Centers and, to the extent necessary, establish additional centers through a competitive process.

(11) To administer a program of acquisition, research, development, and dissemination of advanced investigative analysis and forensic tools to assist State and local law enforcement agencies in combating cybercrime.

(12) To support research fellowships in support of its mission.

(13) To serve as a clearinghouse for information on law enforcement technologies.

(14) To represent the United States and State and local law enforcement agencies, as requested, in international activities concerning law enforcement technology.

(15) To enter into contracts and cooperative agreements and provide grants, which may require in-kind or cash matches from the recipient, as necessary to carry out its mission.

(16) To carry out other duties assigned by the Attorney General to accomplish the mission of the Office.

(c) COMPETITION REQUIRED.—Except as otherwise expressly provided by law, all research and development carried out by or through the Office shall be carried out on a competitive basis.

(d) INFORMATION FROM FEDERAL AGENCIES.—Federal agencies shall, upon request from the Office and in accordance with Federal law, provide the Office with any data, reports, or other information requested, unless compliance with such request is otherwise prohibited by law.

(e) PUBLICATIONS.—Decisions concerning publications issued by the Office shall rest solely with the Director of the Office.

(f) TRANSFER OF FUNDS.—The Office may transfer funds to other Federal agencies or provide funding to non-Federal entities through grants, cooperative agreements, or contracts to carry out its duties under this section: Provided, That any such transfer or provision of funding shall be carried out in accordance with section 605 of Public Law 107–77.

(g) ANNUAL REPORT.—The Director of the Office shall include with the budget justification materials submitted to Congress in support of the Department of Justice budget for each fiscal year (as submitted with the budget of the President under section 1105(a) of title 31, United States Code) a report on the activities of the Office. Each such report shall include the following:

(1) For the period of 5 fiscal years beginning with the fiscal year for which the budget is submitted—

(A) the Director's assessment of the needs of Federal, State, and local law enforcement agencies for assistance with respect to law enforcement technology and other matters consistent with the mission of the Office; and

(B) a strategic plan for meeting such needs of such law enforcement agencies.

(2) For the fiscal year preceding the fiscal year for which such budget is submitted, a description of the activities carried out by the Office and an evaluation of the extent to which those activities successfully meet the needs assessed under paragraph (1)(A) in previous reports.

Sec. 233. [6 U.S.C. 163] DEFINITION OF LAW ENFORCEMENT TECHNOLOGY.

For the purposes of this title, the term "law enforcement technology" includes investigative and forensic technologies, corrections technologies, and technologies that support the judicial process.

Sec. 234. [6 U.S.C. 164] ABOLISHMENT OF OFFICE OF SCIENCE AND TECHNOLOGY OF NATIONAL INSTITUTE OF JUSTICE; TRANSFER OF FUNCTIONS.

(a) AUTHORITY TO TRANSFER FUNCTIONS.—The Attorney General may transfer to the Office any other program or activity of the Department of Justice that the Attorney General, in consultation with the Committee on the Judiciary of the Senate and the Committee on the Judiciary of the House of Representatives, determines to be consistent with the mission of the Office.

(b) TRANSFER OF PERSONNEL AND ASSETS.—With respect to any function, power, or duty, or any program or activity, that is established in the Office, those employees and assets of the element of the Department of Justice from which the transfer is made that the Attorney General determines are needed to perform that function, power, or duty, or for that program or activity, as the case may be, shall be transferred to the Office: Provided, That any such transfer shall be carried out in accordance with section 605 of Public Law 107–77.

(c) REPORT ON IMPLEMENTATION.—Not later than 1 year after the date of the enactment of this Act, the Attorney General shall submit to the Committee on the Judiciary of the Senate and the Committee on the Judiciary of the House of Representatives a report on the implementation of this title. The report shall—

(1) provide an accounting of the amounts and sources of funding available to the Office to carry out its mission under existing authorizations and appropriations, and set forth the future funding needs of the Office; and

(2) include such other information and recommendations as the Attorney General considers appropriate.

Sec. 235. [6 U.S.C. 165] NATIONAL LAW ENFORCEMENT AND CORRECTIONS TECHNOLOGY CENTERS.

(a) IN GENERAL.—The Director of the Office shall operate and support National Law Enforcement and Corrections Technology Centers (hereinafter in this section referred to as "Centers") and, to the extent necessary, establish new centers through a meritbased, competitive process.

(b) PURPOSE OF CENTERS.—The purpose of the Centers shall be to—

(1) support research and development of law enforcement technology;

(2) support the transfer and implementation of technology;

(3) assist in the development and dissemination of guidelines and technological standards; and

(4) provide technology assistance, information, and support for law enforcement, corrections, and criminal justice purposes.

(c) ANNUAL MEETING.—Each year, the Director shall convene a meeting of the Centers in order to foster collaboration and communication between Center participants.

(d) REPORT.—Not later than 12 months after the date of the enactment of this Act, the Director shall transmit to the Congress a report assessing the effectiveness of the existing system of Centers and identify the number of Centers necessary to meet the technology needs of Federal, State, and local law enforcement in the United States.

SEC. 236. COORDINATION WITH OTHER ENTITIES WITHIN DEPARTMENT OF JUSTICE.

Section 102 of the Omnibus Crime Control and Safe Streets Act of 1968 (42 U.S.C. 3712) is amended in subsection (a)(5) by inserting "coordinate and" before "provide".

SEC. 237. AMENDMENTS RELATING TO NATIONAL INSTITUTE OF JUSTICE.

Section 202(c) of the Omnibus Crime Control and Safe Streets Act of 1968 (42 U.S.C. 3722(c)) is amended—

(1) in paragraph (3) by inserting ", including cost effectiveness where practical," before "of projects"; and

(2) by striking "and" after the semicolon at the end of paragraph (8), striking the period at the end of paragraph

(9) and inserting "; and", and by adding at the end the following:

"(10) research and development of tools and technologies relating to prevention, detection, investigation, and prosecution of crime; and

"(11) support research, development, testing, training, and evaluation of tools and technology for Federal, State, and local law enforcement agencies."

Counterintelligence Enhancement Act of 2002

(Pub. L. 107-306, 116 Stat. 2432)

TITLE IX—COUNTERINTELLIGENCE ACTIVITIES

SEC. 901. SHORT TITLE; PURPOSE.

(a) SHORT TITLE.—This title may be cited as the "Counterintelligence Enhancement Act of 2002".

(b) PURPOSE.—The purpose of this title is to facilitate the note. enhancement of the counterintelligence activities of the United States Government by—

(1) enabling the counterintelligence community of the United States Government to fulfill better its mission of identifying, assessing, prioritizing, and countering the intelligence threats to the United States;

(2) ensuring that the counterintelligence community of the United States Government acts in an efficient and effective manner; and

(3) providing for the integration of all the counterintelligence activities of the United States Government.

SEC. 902. NATIONAL COUNTERINTELLIGENCE EXECUTIVE.

(a) ESTABLISHMENT.—

(1) There shall be a National Counterintelligence Executive, who shall be appointed by the President.

(2) It is the sense of Congress that the President should seek the views of the Attorney General, Secretary of Defense, and Director of Central Intelligence in selecting an individual for appointment as the Executive.

(b) MISSION.—The mission of the National Counterintelligence Executive shall be to serve as the head of national counterintelligence for the United States Government.

(c) DUTIES.—Subject to the direction and control of the President, the duties of the National Counterintelligence Executive are as follows:

(1) To carry out the mission referred to in subsection (b).

(2) To act as chairperson of the National Counterintel ligence Policy Board under section 811 of the Counterintelligence and Security Enhancements Act of 1994 (title VIII of Public Law 103–359; 50 U.S.C. 402a), as amended by section 903 of this Act.

(3) To act as head of the Office of the National Counterintelligence Executive under section 904.

(4) To participate as an observer on such boards, commit-tees, and entities of the executive branch as the President considers appropriate for the discharge of the mission and functions of the Executive and the Office of the National Counterintelligence Executive under section 904.

SEC. 903. NATIONAL COUNTERINTELLIGENCE POLICY BOARD.

(a) CHAIRPERSON.—Section 811 of the Counterintelligence and Security Enhancements Act of 1994 (title VII of Public Law 103– 359; 50 U.S.C. 402a), as amended by section 811(b)(5)(B) of this Act, is further amended—

(1) by striking subsection (b);

(2) by redesignating subsection (c) as subsection (e); and

(3) by inserting after subsection (a) the following new sub-section (b): "(b) CHAIRPER-SON.—The National Counterintelligence Executive under section 902 of the Counterintelligence Enhancement Act of 2002 shall serve as the chairperson of the Board."

(b) MEMBERSHIP.—That section is further amended by inserting after subsection (b), as amended by subsection (a)(3) of this section, the following new subsection (c):

"(c) MEMBERSHIP.—The membership of the National Counterintelligence Policy Board shall consist of the following:

"(1) The National Counterintelligence Executive.

"(2) Senior personnel of departments and elements of the United States Government, appointed by the head of the department or element concerned, as follows:

"(A) The Department of Justice, including the Federal Bureau of Investigation.

"(B) The Department of Defense, including the Joint Chiefs of Staff.

"(C) The Department of State.

"(D) The Department of Energy.

"(E) The Central Intelligence Agency.

"(F) Any other department, agency, or element of the United States Government specified by the President.".

(c) FUNCTIONS AND DISCHARGE OF FUNCTIONS.—That section is further amended by inserting after subsection (c), as amended by subsection (b) of this section, the following new subsection:

"(d) FUNCTIONS AND DISCHARGE OF FUNCTIONS.—

(1) The Board shall—

"(A) serve as the principal mechanism for—

"(i) developing policies and procedures for the approval of the President to govern the conduct of counterintelligence activities; and

"(ii) upon the direction of the President, resolving conflicts that arise between elements of the Government conducting such activities; and

"(B) act as an interagency working group to—

"(i) ensure the discussion and review of matters relating to the implementation of the Counterintelligence Enhancement Act of 2002; and

"(ii) provide advice to the National Counterintelligence Executive on priorities in the implementation of the National Counterintelligence Strategy produced by the Office of the National Counterintelligence Executive under section 904(e)(2) of that Act.

"(2) The Board may, for purposes of carrying out its functions under this section, establish such interagency boards and working groups as the Board considers appropriate.".

SEC. 904. OFFICE OF THE NATIONAL COUNTERINTELLIGENCE EXECUTIVE.

(a) ESTABLISHMENT.—There shall be an Office of the National Counterintelligence Executive.

(b) HEAD OF OFFICE.—The National Counterintelligence Executive shall be the head of the Office of the National Counterintelligence Executive.

(c) LOCATION OF OFFICE.—The Office of the National Counterintelligence Executive shall be located in the Office of the Director of Central Intelligence.

(d) GENERAL COUNSEL.—

(1) There shall be in the Office of the National Counterintelligence Executive a general counsel who shall serve as principal legal advisor to the National Counterintelligence Executive.

(2) The general counsel shall—

(A) provide legal advice and counsel to the Executive on matters relating to functions of the Office;

(B) ensure that the Office complies with all applicable laws, regulations, Executive orders, and guidelines; and

(C) carry out such other duties as the Executive may specify.

(e) FUNCTIONS.—Subject to the direction and control of the National Counterintelligence Executive, the functions of the Office of the National Counterintelligence Executive shall be as follows:

(1) NATIONAL THREAT IDENTIFICATION AND PRIORITIZATION ASSESSMENT.—Subject to subsection (f), in consultation with appropriate department and agencies of the United States Government, and private sector entities, to produce on an annual basis a strategic planning assessment of the counterintelligence requirements of the United States to be known as the National Threat Identification and Prioritization Assessment.

(2) NATIONAL COUNTERINTELLIGENCE STRATEGY.—Subject to subsection (f), in consultation with appropriate department and agencies of the United States Government, and private sector entities, and based on the most current National Threat Identification and Prioritization Assessment under paragraph (1), to produce on an annual basis a strategy for the counterintelligence programs and activities of the United States Government to be known as the National Counterintelligence Strategy.

(3) IMPLEMENTATION OF NATIONAL COUNTERINTELLIGENCE STRATEGY.—To evaluate on an ongoing basis the implementation of the National Counterintelligence Strategy and to submit to the President periodic reports on such evaluation, including a discussion of any shortfalls in the implementation of the Strategy and recommendations for remedies for such shortfalls.

(4) NATIONAL COUNTERINTELLIGENCE STRATEGIC ANAL-YSES.—As directed by the Director of Central Intelligence and in consultation with appropriate elements of the departments and agencies of the United States Government, to oversee and coordinate the production of strategic analyses of counterintelligence matters, including the production of counterintelligence damage assessments and assessments of lessons learned from counter-intelligence activities.

(5) NATIONAL COUNTERINTELLIGENCE PROGRAM BUDGET.—In consultation with the Director of Central Intelligence—

(A) to coordinate the development of budgets and resource allocation plans for the counterintelligence programs and activities of the Department of Defense, the Federal Bureau of Investigation, the Central Intelligence Agency, and other appropriate elements of the United States Government;

(B) to ensure that the budgets and resource allocation plans developed under subparagraph (A) address the objectives and priorities for counterintelligence under the National Counterintelligence Strategy; and

(C) to submit to the National Security Council periodic reports on the activities undertaken by the Office under subparagraphs (A) and (B).

(6) NATIONAL COUNTERINTELLIGENCE COLLECTION AND TARGETING CO-ORDINATION.—To develop priorities for counterintelligence investigations and operations, and for collection of counterintelligence, for purposes of the National Counterintelligence Strategy, except that the Office may not—

(A) carry out any counterintelligence investigations or operations; or

(B) establish its own contacts, or carry out its own activities, with foreign intelligence services.

(7) NATIONAL COUNTERINTELLIGENCE OUTREACH, WATCH, AND WARNING.—

(A) COUNTERINTELLIGENCE VULNERABILITY SURVEYS.—To carry out and coordinate surveys of the vulnerability of the United States Government, and the private sector, to intelligence threats in order to identify the areas, programs, and activities that require protection from such threats.

(B) OUTREACH.—To carry out and coordinate outreach programs and activities on counterintelligence to other elements of the United States Government, and the private sector, and to coordinate the dissemination to the public of warnings on intelligence threats to the United States.

(C) RESEARCH AND DEVELOPMENT.—To ensure that research and development programs and activities of the United States Government, and the private sector, direct attention to the needs of the counterintelligence community for technologies, products, and services.

(D) TRAINING AND PROFESSIONAL DEVELOPMENT.—To develop policies and standards for training and professional development of individuals engaged in counterintelligence activities and to manage the conduct of joint training exercises for such personnel.

(f) ADDITIONAL REQUIREMENTS REGARDING NATIONAL THREAT IDENTIFICATION AND PRIORITIZATION ASSESSMENT AND NATIONAL COUNTERINTELLIGENCE STRATEGY.—

(1) A National Threat Identification and Prioritization Assessment under subsection (e)(1), and any modification of such assessment, shall not go into effect until approved by the President.

(2) A National Counterintelligence Strategy under subsection(e)(2), and any modification of such strategy, shall not go into effect until approved by the President.

(3) The National Counterintelligence Executive shall submit to the congressional intelligence committees each National Threat Identification and Prioritization Assessment, or modification thereof, and each National Counterintelligence Strategy, or modification thereof, approved under this section.

(4) In this subsection, the term "congressional intelligence committees" means—

(A) the Select Committee on Intelligence of the Senate; and

(B) the Permanent Select Committee on Intelligence of the House of Representatives.

(g) PERSONNEL.—

(1) Personnel of the Office of the National Counterintelligence Executive may consist of personnel employed by the Office or personnel on detail from any other department, agency, or element of the Federal Government. Any such detail may be on a reimbursable or nonreimbursable basis, at the election of the head of the agency detailing such personnel.

(2) Notwithstanding section 104(d) or any other provision of law limiting the period of the detail of personnel on a nonreimbursable basis, the detail of an officer or employee of United States or a member of the Armed Forces under paragraph (1) on a nonreimbursable basis may be for any period in excess of one year that the National Counterintelligence Executive and the head of the department, agency, or element concerned consider appropriate.

(3) The employment of personnel by the Office, including the appointment, compensation and benefits, management, and separation of such personnel, shall be governed by the provisions of law on such matters with respect to the personnel of the Central Intelligence Agency, except that, for purposes of the applicability of such provisions of law to personnel of the Office, the National Counterintelligence Executive shall be treated as the head of the Office.

(4) Positions in the Office shall be excepted service positions for purposes of title 5, United States Code.

(h) SUPPORT.—

(1) The Attorney General, Secretary of Defense, and Director of Central Intelligence may

each provide the Office of the National Counterintelligence Executive such support as may be necessary to permit the Office to carry out its functions under this section.

(2) Subject to any terms and conditions specified by the Director of Central Intelligence, the Director may provide administrative and contract support to the Office as if the Office were an element of the Central Intelligence Agency.

(3) Support provided under this subsection may be provided on a reimbursable or nonreimbursable basis, at the election of the official providing such support.

(i) AVAILABILITY OF FUNDS FOR REIMBURSEMENT.—The National Counterintelligence Executive may, from amounts available for the Office, transfer to a department or agency detailing personnel under subsection (g), or providing support under subsection (h), on a reimbursable basis amounts appropriate to reimburse such department or agency for the detail of such personnel or the provision of such support, as the case may be.

(j) CONTRACTS.—

(1) Subject to paragraph (2), the National Counterintelligence Executive may enter into any contract, lease, cooperative agreement, or other transaction that the Executive considers appropriate to carry out the functions of the Office of the National Counterintelligence Executive under this section.

(2) The authority under paragraph (1) to enter into contracts, leases, cooperative agreements, and other transactions shall be subject to any terms, conditions, and limitations applicable to the Central Intelligence Agency under law with respect to similar contracts, leases, cooperative agreements, and other transactions.

(k) TREATMENT OF ACTIVITIES UNDER CERTAIN ADMINISTRATIVE LAWS.—The files of the Office shall be treated as operational files of the Central Intelligence Agency for purposes of section 701 of the National Security Act of 1947 (50 U.S.C. 431) to the extent such files meet criteria under subsection (b) of that section for treatment of files as operational files of an element of the Agency.

(l) OVERSIGHT BY CONGRESS.—The location of the Office of the National Counterintelligence Executive within the Office of the Director of Central Intelligence shall not be construed as affecting access by Congress, or any committee of Congress, to—

(1) any information, document, record, or paper in thepossession of the Office; or

(2) any personnel of the Office.

(m) CONSTRUCTION.—Nothing in this section shall be construed as affecting the authority of the Director of Central Intelligence, the Secretary of Defense, the Secretary of State, the Attorney General, or the Director of the Federal Bureau of Investigation as provided or specified under the National Security Act of 1947 or under other provisions of law.

TITLE X—NATIONAL COMMISSION FOR REVIEW OF RESEARCH AND DEVELOPMENT PROGRAMS OF THE UNITED STATES INTELLIGENCE COMMUNITY

SEC. 1001. FINDINGS.

Congress makes the following findings:

(1) Research and development efforts under the purview of the intelligence community are vitally important to the national security of the United States.

(2) The intelligence community must operate in a dynamic, highly-challenging environment, characterized by rapid technological growth, against a growing number of hostile, technically-sophisticated threats. Research and development programs under the purview of the intelligence community are critical to ensuring that intelligence agencies, and their personnel, are provided with important technological capabilities to detect, characterize, assess, and ultimately counter the full range of threats to the national security of the United States.

(3) There is a need to review the full range of current research and development programs under the purview of the intelligence community, evaluate such programs against the scientific and technological fields judged to be of most importance, and articulate program and resource priorities for future research and development activities to ensure a unified and coherent research and development program across the entire intelligence community.

SEC. 1002. NATIONAL COMMISSION FOR THE REVIEW OF THE RESEARCH AND DEVELOPMENT PROGRAMS OF THE UNITED STATES INTELLIGENCE COMMUNITY.

(a) ESTABLISHMENT.—There is established a commission to be known as the "National Commission for the Review of the Research and Development Programs of the United States Intelligence Community" (in this title referred to as the "Commission").

(b) COMPOSITION.—The Commission shall be composed of 12 members, as follows:

(1) The Deputy Director of Central Intelligence for Community Management.

(2) A senior intelligence official of the Office of the Secretary of Defense, as designated by the Secretary of Defense.

(3) Three members appointed by the majority leader of the Senate, in consultation with the Chairman of the Select Committee on Intelligence of the Senate, one from Members of the Senate and two from private life.

(4) Two members appointed by the minority leader of the Senate, in consultation with the Vice Chairman of the Select Committee on Intelligence of the Senate, one from Members of the Senate and one from private life.

(5) Three members appointed by the Speaker of the House of Representatives, in consultation with the Chairman of the Permanent Select Committee on Intelligence of the House of Representatives, one from Members of the House of Representatives and two from private life.

(6) Two members appointed by the minority leader of the House of Representatives, in consultation with the ranking member of the Permanent Select Committee on Intelligence of the House of Representatives, one from Members of the House of Representatives and one from private life.

(c) MEMBERSHIP.—

(1) The individuals appointed from private life as members of the Commission shall be individuals who are nationally recognized for expertise, knowledge, or experience in—

(A) research and development programs;

(B) technology discovery and insertion;

(C) use of intelligence information by national policy makers and military leaders; or

(D) the implementation, funding, or oversight of the national security policies of the United States.

(2) An official who appoints members of the Commission may not appoint an individual as a member of the Commission if, in the judgment of the official, such individual possesses any personal or financial interest in the discharge of any of the duties of the Commission.

(3) All members of the Commission appointed from private life shall possess an appropriate security clearance in accordance with applicable laws and regulations concerning the handling of classified information.

(d) CO-CHAIRS.—

(1) The Commission shall have two co-chairs, selected from among the members of the Commission.

(2) One co-chair of the Commission shall be a member of the Democratic Party, and one co-chair shall be a member of the Republican Party.

(3) The individuals who serve as the co-chairs of the Commission shall be jointly agreed upon by the President, the majority leader of the Senate, the minority leader of the Senate, the Speaker of the House of Representatives, and the minority leader of the House of Representatives.

(e) APPOINTMENT; INITIAL MEETING.—

(1) Members of the Commission shall be appointed not later than 45 days after the date of the enactment of this Act.

(2) The Commission shall hold its initial meeting on the date that is 60 days after the date of the enactment of this Act.

(f) MEETINGS; QUORUM; VACANCIES.—

(1) After its initial meeting, the Commission shall meet upon the call of the co-chairs of the Commission.

(2) Six members of the Commission shall constitute a quorum for purposes of conducting business, except that two members of the Commission shall constitute a quorum for purposes of receiving testimony.

(3) Any vacancy in the Commission shall not affect its powers, but shall be filled in the same manner in which the original appointment was made.

(4) If vacancies in the Commission occur on any day after45 days after the date of the enactment of this Act, a quorum shall consist of a majority of the members of the Commission as of such day.

(g) ACTIONS OF COMMISSION.—

(1) The Commission shall act by resolution agreed to by a majority of the members of the Commission voting and present.

(2) The Commission may establish panels composed of less than the full membership of the Commission for purposes of carrying out the duties of the Commission under this title. The actions of any such panel shall be subject to the review and control of the Commission. Any findings and determinations made by such a panel shall not be considered the findings and determinations of the Commission unless approved by the Commission.

(3) Any member, agent, or staff of the Commission may, if authorized by the co-chairs of the Commission, take any action which the Commission is authorized to take pursuant to this title.

(h) DUTIES.—The duties of the Commission shall be—

(1) to conduct, until not later than the date on whichthe Commission submits the report under section 1007(a), thereview described in subsection (i); and

(2) to submit to the congressional intelligence committees, the Director of Central Intelligence, and the Secretary of Defense a final report on the results of the review.

(i) REVIEW.—The Commission shall review the status of research and development programs and activities within the intelligence community, including—

(1) an assessment of the advisability of modifying the scope of research and development for purposes of such programs and activities;

(2) a review of the particular individual research and development activities under such programs;

(3) an evaluation of the current allocation of resourcesf or research and development, including whether the allocation of such resources for that purpose should be modified;

(4) an identification of the scientific and technological fields judged to be of most importance to the intelligence community;

(5) an evaluation of the relationship between the research and development programs and activities of the intelligence community and the research and development programs and activities of other departments and agencies of the Federal Government; and

(6) an evaluation of the relationship between the research and development programs and activities of the intelligence community and the research and development programs and activities of the private sector.

SEC. 1003. POWERS OF COMMISSION.

(a) IN GENERAL.—

(1) The Commission or, on the authorization of the Commission, any subcommittee or member thereof, may, for the purpose of carrying out the provisions of this title—

(A) hold such hearings and sit and act at such times and places, take such testimony, receive such evidence, and administer such oaths; and

(B) require, by subpoena or otherwise, the attendance and testimony of such witnesses and the production of such books, records, correspondence, memoranda, papers, and documents, as the Commission or such designated subcommittee or designated member considers necessary.

(2) Subpoenas may be issued under subparagraph (1)(B) under the signature of the co-chairs of the Commission, and may be served by any person designated by such co-chairs.

(3) The provisions of sections 102 through 104 of the Revised Statutes of the United States (2 U.S.C. 192–194) shall apply in the case of any failure of a witness to comply with any subpoena or to testify when summoned under authority of this section.

(b) CONTRACTING.—The Commission may, to such extent and in such amounts as are provided in advance in appropriation Acts, enter into contracts to enable the Commission to discharge its duties under this title.

(c) INFORMATION FROM FEDERAL AGENCIES.—The Commission may secure directly from any executive department, agency, bureau, board, commission, office, independent establishment, or instrumentality of the Government information, suggestions, estimates, and statistics for the purposes of this title. Each such department, agency, bureau, board, commission, office, establishment, or instrumentality shall, to the extent authorized by law, furnish such information, suggestions, estimates, and statistics directly to the Commission, upon request of the co-chairs of the Commission. The Commission shall handle and protect all classified information provided to it under this section in accordance with applicable statutes and regulations.

(d) ASSISTANCE FROM FEDERAL AGENCIES.—

(1) The Director of Central Intelligence shall provide to the Commission, on a nonreimbursable basis, such administrative services, funds, staff, facilities, and other support services as are necessary for the performance of the Commission's duties under this title.

(2) The Secretary of Defense may provide the Commission, on a nonreimbursable basis, with such administrative services, staff, and other support services as the Commission may request.

(3) In addition to the assistance set forth in paragraphs (1)and (2), other departments and agencies of the United States may provide the Commission such services, funds, facilities, staff, and other support as such departments and agencies consider advisable and as may be authorized by law.

(4) The Commission shall receive the full and timely cooperation of any official, department, or agency of the United States Government whose assistance is necessary for the fulfillment of the duties of the Commission under this title, including the provision of full and current briefings and analyses.

(e) PROHIBITION ON WITHHOLDING INFORMATION.—No department or agency of the Government may withhold information from the Commission on the grounds that providing the information to the Commission would constitute the unauthorized disclosure of classified information or information relating to intelligence sources or methods.

(f) POSTAL SERVICES.—The Commission may use the United States mails in the same manner and under the same conditions as the departments and agencies of the United States.

(g) GIFTS.—The Commission may accept, use, and dispose of gifts or donations of services or property in carrying out its duties under this title.

SEC. 1004. STAFF OF COMMISSION.

(a) IN GENERAL.—

(1) The co-chairs of the Commission, in accordance with rules agreed upon by the Commission, shall appoint and fix the compensation of a staff director and such other personnel as may be necessary to enable the Commission to carry out its duties, without regard to the provisions of title 5, United States Code, governing appointments in the competitive service, and without regard to the provisions of chapter 51 and subchapter III of chapter 53 of such title relating to classification and General Schedule pay rates, except that no rate of pay fixed under this subsection may exceed the equivalent of that payable to a person occupying a position at level V of the Executive Schedule under section 5316 of such title.

(2) Any Federal Government employee may be detailed to the Commission without reimbursement from the Commission, and such detailee shall retain the rights, status, and privileges of his or her regular employment without interruption.

(3) All staff of the Commission shall possess a security clearance in accordance with applicable laws and regulations concerning the handling of classified information.

(b) CONSULTANT SERVICES.—

(1) The Commission may procure the services of experts and consultants in accordance with section 3109 of title 5, United States Code, but at rates not to exceed the daily rate paid a person occupying a position at level IV of the Executive Schedule under section 5315 of such title.

(2) All experts and consultants employed by the Commission shall possess a security clearance in accordance with applicable laws and regulations concerning the handling of classified information.

SEC. 1005. COMPENSATION AND TRAVEL EXPENSES.

(a) COMPENSATION.—

(1) Except as provided in paragraph (2), each member of the Commission may be compensated at not to exceed the daily equivalent of the annual rate of basic pay in effect for a position at level IV of the Executive Schedule under section 5315 of title 5, United States Code, for each day during which that member is engaged in the actual performance of the duties of the Commission under this title.

(2) Members of the Commission who are officers or employees of the United States or Members of Congress shall receive no additional pay by reason of their service on the Commission.

(b) TRAVEL EXPENSES.—While away from their homes or regular places of business in the performance of services for the Commission, members of the Commission may be allowed travel expenses, including per diem in lieu of subsistence, in the same manner as persons employed intermittently in the Government service are allowed expenses under section 5703 of title 5, United States Code.

SEC. 1006. TREATMENT OF INFORMATION RELATING TO NATIONAL SECURITY.

(a) IN GENERAL.—

(1) The Director of Central Intelligence shall assume responsibility for the handling and disposition of any information related to the national security of the United States that is received, considered, or used by the Commission under this title.

(2) Any information related to the national security of the United States that is provided to the Commission by a congressional intelligence committee may not be further provided or released without the approval of the chairman of such committee.

(b) ACCESS AFTER TERMINATION OF COMMISSION.—Not with-standing any other provision of law, after the termination of the Commission under section 1007, only the Members and designated staff of the congressional intelligence committees, the Director of Central Intelligence (and the designees of the Director), and such other officials of the executive branch as the President may designate shall have access to information related to the national security of the United States that is received, considered, or used by the Commission.

SEC. 1007. FINAL REPORT; TERMINATION.

(a) FINAL REPORT.—Not later than September 1, 2003, the Commission shall submit to the congressional intelligence committees, the Director of Central Intelligence, and the Secretary of Defense a final report as required by section 1002(h)(2).

(b) TERMINATION.—

(1) The Commission, and all the authorities of this title, shall terminate at the end of the 120-day period beginning on the date on which the final report under subsection (a) is transmitted to the congressional intelligence committees.

(2) The Commission may use the 120-day period referred to in paragraph (1) for the purposes of concluding its activities, including providing testimony to Congress concerning the final report referred to in that paragraph and disseminating the report.

Sec. 1008. ASSESSMENTS OF FINAL REPORT.

Not later than 60 days after receipt of the final report under section 1007(a), the Director of Central Intelligence and the Secretary of Defense shall each submit to the congressional intelligence committees an assessment by the Director or the Secretary, as the case may be, of the final report. Each assessment shall include such comments on the findings and recommendations contained in the final report as the Director or Secretary, as the case may be, considers appropriate.

SEC. 1009. INAPPLICABILITY OF CERTAIN ADMINISTRATIVE PROVISIONS.

(a) FEDERAL ADVISORY COMMITTEE ACT.—The provisions of the Federal Advisory Committee Act (5 U.S.C. App.) shall not apply to the activities of the Commission under this title.

(b) FREEDOM OF INFORMATION ACT.—The provisions of section 552 of title 5, United States Code (commonly referred to as the Freedom of Information Act), shall not apply to the activities, records, and proceedings of the Commission under this title.

SEC. 1010. FUNDING.

(a) TRANSFER FROM THE COMMUNITY MANAGEMENT ACCOUNT.— Of the amounts authorized to be appropriated by this Act for the Intelligence Technology Innovation Center of the Community Management Account, the Deputy Director of Central Intelligence for Community Management shall transfer to the Director of Central Intelligence $2,000,000 for purposes of the activities of the Commission under this title.

(b) AVAILABILITY IN GENERAL.—The Director of Central Intelligence shall make available to the Commission, from the amount transferred to the Director under subsection (a), such amounts as the Commission may require for purposes of the activities of the Commission under this title.

(c) DURATION OF AVAILABILITY.—Amounts made available to the Commission under subsection (b) shall remain available until expended.

SEC. 1011. DEFINITIONS.

In this title:

(1) CONGRESSIONAL INTELLIGENCE COMMITTEES.—The term "congressional intelligence committees" means—

(A) the Select Committee on Intelligence of the Senate; and

(B) the Permanent Select Committee on Intelligence of the House of Representatives.

(2) INTELLIGENCE COMMUNITY.—The term "intelligence community" has the meaning given that term in section 3(4) of the National Security Act of 1947 (50 U.S.C. 401a(4)).

Cyberspace-Related Matters in the John S. McCain National Defense Authorization Act for Fiscal Year 2019

(Pub. L. 115-232, §§1631, et. seq.)

Subtitle C—Cyberspace-Related Matters

Subtitle C—Cyberspace-Related Matters
SEC. 1631. REORGANIZATION AND CONSOLIDATION OF CERTAIN CYBER PROVISIONS.

(a) IN GENERAL.—Part I of subtitle A of title 10, United States Code, is amended—

(1) by transferring sections 130g, 130j, and 130k to chapter 19 of such part to appear after section 393 of such chapter; and

(2) by redesignating such sections 130g, 130j, and 130k, as transferred by paragraph (1), as sections 394, 395, and 396, respectively.

(b) CONFORMING AMENDMENT.—Section 108(m) of the Cybersecurity Information Sharing Act of 2015 (6 U.S.C. 1507(m)) is amended by striking "under section 130g" and inserting "under section 394".

(c) CLERICAL AMENDMENTS.—(1) The table of sections at the beginning of chapter 3 of title 10, United States Code, is amended by striking the items relating to sections 130g, 130j, and 130k.

(2) The table of sections at the beginning of chapter 19 of such title is amended by adding at the end the following new items:

"394. Authorities concerning military cyber operations.

"395. Notification requirements for sensitive military cyber operations.

"396. Notification requirements for cyber weapons.".

SEC. 1632. AFFIRMING THE AUTHORITY OF THE SECRETARY OF DEFENSE TO CONDUCT MILITARY ACTIVITIES AND OPERATIONS IN CYBERSPACE.

Section 394 of title 10, United States Code (as transferred and redesignated pursuant to section 1631), is amended—

(1) by striking "The Secretary" and inserting the following: "(a) IN GENERAL.— The Secretary";

(2) in subsection (a), as designated by paragraph (1)—

(A) by striking "conduct, a military cyber operation in response" and inserting "conduct, military cyber activities or operations in cyberspace, including clandestine military activities or operations in cyberspace, to defend the United States and its allies, including in

(B) by striking "(as such terms are defined in section 101 of the Foreign Intelligence Surveillance Act of 1978 (50 U.S.C. 1801))"; and

(3) by adding at the end the following new subsections:

"(b) AFFIRMATION OF AUTHORITY.—Congress affirms that the activities or operations referred to in subsection (a), when appropriately authorized, include the conduct of military activities or operations in cyberspace short of hostilities (as such term is used in the War Powers Resolution (Public Law 93–148; 50 U.S.C. 1541 et seq.)) or in areas in which hostilities are not occurring, including for the purpose of preparation of the environment, information operations, force protection, and deterrence of hostilities, or counterterrorism operations involving the Armed Forces of the United States.

"(c) CLANDESTINE ACTIVITIES OR OPERATIONS.—A clandestine military activity or operation in cyberspace shall be considered a traditional military activity for the purposes of section 503(e)(2) of the National Security Act of 1947 (50 U.S.C. 3093(e)(2)).

"(d) CONGRESSIONAL OVERSIGHT.—The Secretary shall brief the congressional defense committees about any military activities or operations in cyberspace, including clandestine military activities or operations in cyberspace, occurring during the previous quarter during the quarterly briefing required by section 484 of this title.

"(e) RULE OF CONSTRUCTION.—Nothing in this section may be construed to limit the authority of the Secretary to conduct military activities or operations in cyberspace, including clandestine military activities or operations in cyberspace, to authorize specific military activities or operations, or to alter or otherwise affect the War Powers Resolution (50 U.S.C. 1541 et seq.), the Authorization for Use of Military Force (Public Law 107–40; 50 U.S.C. 1541 note), or reporting of sensitive military cyber activities or operations required by section 395 of this title.

"(f) DEFINITIONS.—In this section:

"(1) The term 'clandestine military activity or operation in cyberspace' means a military activity or military operation carried out in cyberspace, or associated preparatory actions, authorized by the President or the Secretary that—

"(A) is marked by, held in, or conducted with secrecy, where the intent is that the activity or operation will not be apparent or acknowledged publicly; and

"(B) is to be carried out—

"(i) as part of a military operation plan approved by the President or the Secretary in anticipation of hostilities or as directed by the President or the Secretary;

"(ii) to deter, safeguard, or defend against attacks or malicious cyber activities against the United States or Department of Defense information, networks, systems, installations, facilities, or other assets; or

"(iii) in support of information related capabilities.

"(2) The term 'foreign power' has the meaning given such term in section 101 of the Foreign Intelligence Surveillance Act of 1978 (50 U.S.C. 1801).

"(3) The term 'United States person' has the meaning given such term in such section.".

SEC. 1633. DEPARTMENT OF DEFENSE CYBER SCHOLARSHIP PROGRAM SCHOLARSHIPS AND GRANTS.

(a) ADDITIONAL CONSIDERATIONS.—Section 2200c of title 10, United States Code, is amended—

(1) by inserting before "In the selection" the following:

"(a) CENTERS OF ACADEMIC EXCELLENCE IN CYBER EDUCATION.—"; and

(2) by adding at the end the following new subsection:

"(b) CERTAIN INSTITUTIONS OF HIGHER EDUCATION.—In the selection of a recipient for the award of a scholarship or grant under this chapter, consideration shall be given to whether—

"(1) in the case of a scholarship, the institution of higher education at which the recipient pursues a degree is an institution described in section 371(a) of the Higher Education Act of 1965 (20 U.S.C. 1067q(a)); and

"(2) in the case of a grant, the recipient is an institution described in such section.".

(b) CLERICAL AMENDMENTS.—

(1) SECTION HEADING.—The heading of section 2200c of title 10, United States Code, is amended to read as follows:

"§ 2200c. Special considerations in awarding scholarships and grants".

(2) TABLE OF SECTIONS.—The table of sections at the beginning of chapter

112 of title 10, United States Code, is amended by striking the item relating to section 2200c and inserting the following new item:

"2200c. Special considerations in awarding scholarships and grants.".

SEC. 1634. AMENDMENTS TO PILOT PROGRAM REGARDING CYBER VULNERABILITIES OF DEPARTMENT OF DEFENSE CRITICAL INFRASTRUCTURE.

Subsection (b) of section 1650 of the National Defense Authorization Act for Fiscal Year 2017 (10 U.S.C. 2224 note) is amended—

(1) in paragraph (1), in the matter preceding subparagraph (A), by inserting "and the Defense Digital Service" after "covered research laboratory";

(2) in paragraph (4), in the matter preceding subparagraph (A), by striking "2019" and inserting "2020"; and

(3) in paragraph (5), by striking "2019" and inserting "2020".

SEC. 1635. MODIFICATION OF ACQUISITION AUTHORITY OF THE COMMANDER OF THE UNITED STATES CYBER COMMAND.

(a) MODIFICATION OF LIMITATION ON USE OF CYBER OPERATIONS PROCURE-MENT FUND.—Subsection (e) of section 807 of the National Defense Authorization Act for Fiscal Year 2016 (Public Law 114– 92; 10 U.S.C. 2224 note) is amended by striking "2021" and inserting "2025".

(b) EXTENSION ON SUNSET.—Subsection (i)(1) of such section is amended by striking "September 30, 2021" and inserting "September 30, 2025".

SEC. 1636. POLICY OF THE UNITED STATES ON CYBERSPACE, CYBERSECURITY, CYBER WARFARE, AND CYBER DETERRENCE.

(a) IN GENERAL.—It shall be the policy of the United States, with respect to matters pertaining to cyberspace, cybersecurity, and cyber warfare, that the United States should employ all instruments of national power, including the use of offensive cyber capabilities, to deter if possible, and respond to when necessary, all cyber attacks or other malicious cyber activities of foreign powers that target United States interests with the intent to—

(1) cause casualties among United States persons or persons of United States allies;

(2) significantly disrupt the normal functioning of United States democratic society or government (including attacks against critical infrastructure that could damage systems used to provide key services to the public or government);

(3) threaten the command and control of the Armed Forces, the freedom of maneuver of the Armed Forces, or the industrial base or other infrastructure on which the United States Armed Forces rely to defend United States interests and commitments; or

(4) achieve an effect, whether individually or in aggregate, comparable to an armed attack or imperil a vital interest of the United States.

(b) RESPONSE OPTIONS.—In carrying out the policy set forth in subsection (a), the United States shall plan, develop, and, when appropriate, demonstrate response options to address the full range of potential cyber attacks on United States interests that could be conducted by potential adversaries of the United States.

(c) DENIAL OPTIONS.—In carrying out the policy set forth in sub-section (a) through response options developed pursuant to subsection (b), the United States shall, to the greatest extent practicable, prioritize the defensibility and resiliency against cyber attacks and malicious cyber activities described in subsection (a) of infrastructure critical to the political integrity, economic security, and national security of the United States.

(d) COST-IMPOSITION OPTIONS.—In carrying out the policy set forth in subsection (a) through response options developed pursuant to subsection (b), the United States shall develop and, when appropriate, demonstrate, or otherwise make known to adversaries the existence of, cyber capabilities to impose costs on any foreign power targeting the United States or United States persons with a cyber attack or malicious cyber activity described in subsection (a).

(e) MULTI-PRONG RESPONSE.—In carrying out the policy set forth in subsection (a) through response options developed pursuant to subsection (b), the United States shall leverage all instruments of national power.

(f) UPDATE ON PRESIDENTIAL POLICY.—

(1) IN GENERAL.—Not later than 180 days after the date of the enactment of this Act, the President shall transmit, in unclassified and classified forms, as appropriate, to the appropriate congressional committees a report containing an update to the report provided to the Congress on the policy of the United States on cyberspace, cybersecurity, and cyber warfare pursuant to section 1633 of the National Defense Authorization Act for Fiscal Year 2018 (Public Law 115–91; 10 U.S.C. 130g note).

(2) CONTENTS.—The report required under paragraph (1) shall include the following:

(A) An assessment of the current posture in cyberspace, including assessments of—

(i) whether past responses to major cyber attacks have had the desired deterrent effect; and

(ii) how adversaries have responded to past United States responses.

(B) Updates on the Administration's efforts in the development of—

(i) cost imposition strategies;

(ii) varying levels of cyber incursion and steps taken to date to prepare for the imposition of the consequences referred to in clause (i); and

(iii) the Cyber Deterrence Initiative.

(C) Information relating to the Administration's plans, including specific planned actions, regulations, and legislative action required, for—

(i) advancing technologies in attribution, inherently secure technology, and artificial intelligence society-wide;

(ii) improving cybersecurity in and cooperation with the private sector;

(iii) improving international cybersecurity cooperation; and

(iv) implementing the policy referred to in paragraph (1), including any realignment of government or government responsibilities required, writ large.

(f) RULE OF CONSTRUCTION.—Nothing in this subsection may be construed to limit the authority of the President or Congress to authorize the use of military force.

(g) DEFINITIONS.—In this section:

(1) APPROPRIATE CONGRESSIONAL COMMITTEES.—The term "appropriate congressional committees" means—

(A) the congressional defense committees;

(B) the Permanent Select Committee on Intelligence of the House of Representatives;

(C) the Select Committee on Intelligence of the Senate;

(D) the Committee on Foreign Affairs, the Committee on Homeland Security, and the Committee on the Judiciary of the House of Representatives; and

(E) the Committee on Foreign Relations, the Committee on Homeland Security and Governmental Affairs, and the Committee on the Judiciary of the Senate.

(2) FOREIGN POWER.—The term "foreign power" has the meaning given such term in section 101 of the Foreign Intelligence Surveillance Act of 1978 (50 U.S.C. 1801).

SEC. 1637. BUDGET DISPLAY FOR CYBER VULNERABILITY EVALUATIONS AND MITIGATION ACTIVITIES FOR MAJOR WEAPON SYSTEMS OF THE DEPARTMENT OF DEFENSE.

(a) BUDGET REQUIRED.—Beginning in fiscal year 2021 and in each fiscal year thereafter, the Secretary of Defense shall submit to Congress, as a part of the documentation that supports the President's annual budget for the Department of Defense, a consolidated Cyber Vulnerability Evaluation and Mitigation budget justification display for each major weapons system of the Department of Defense that includes the following:

(1) CYBER VULNERABILITY EVALUATIONS.—

(A) STATUS.—Whether, in accordance with paragraph (1) of section 1647(a) of the National Defense Authorization Act for Fiscal Year 2016 (Public Law 114–92; 129 Stat. 1118), the cyber vulnerability evaluation for each such major weapon system is pending, in progress, complete, or, pursuant to paragraph (2) of such section, waived.

(B) FUNDING.—The funding required for the fiscal year with respect to which the budget is submitted and for at least the four succeeding fiscal years required to complete the pending or in progress cyber vulnerability evaluation of each such major weapon system.

(C) DESCRIPTION.—A description of the activities planned in the fiscal year with respect to which the budget is submitted and at least the four succeeding fiscal years to complete the required evaluation for each such major weapon system.

(D) RISK ANALYSIS.—A description of operational or security risks associated with cyber vulnerabilities identified as a result of such cyber vulnerability evaluations that require mitigation.

(2) MITIGATION ACTIVITIES.—

(A) STATUS.—Whether activities to address identified cyber vulnerabilities of such major weapon systems resulting in operational or security risks requiring mitigation are pending, in progress, or complete.

(B) FUNDING.—The funding required for the fiscal year with respect to which the budget is submitted and for at least the four succeeding fiscal years required to complete the pending or in progress mitigation activities referred to in subparagraph (A) related to such major weapon systems.

(C) DESCRIPTION.—A description of the activities planned in the fiscal year with respect to which the budget is submitted and at least the four succeeding fiscal years to complete any necessary mitigation.

(b) FORM.—The display required under subsection (a) should, to the extent practicable, be submitted in an unclassified form, and shall include a classified annex as required.

SEC. 1638. DETERMINATION OF RESPONSIBILITY FOR THE DEPARTMENT OF DEFENSE INFORMATION NETWORKS.

(a) IN GENERAL.—Not later than March 1, 2019, the Secretary of Defense shall submit to the congressional defense committees a report containing a determination regarding the roles, missions, and responsibilities of the Commander, Joint Force Headquarters– Department of Defense Information Networks (JFHQ–DODIN) of the Defense Information Support Agency.

(b) ELEMENTS.—The report required under subsection (a) shall include the following:

(1) An assessment of the current JFHQ-DODIN command and control structure, adequacy of the Defense Information Support Agency's institutional support for the JFHQ-DODIN mission, resource requirements, and mission effectiveness. (2)(A) A determination and justification regarding—

(i) a transfer to the Commander, United States Cyber Command, from the JFHQ-DODIN of some or all roles, missions, and responsibilities of the JFHQ-DODIN; or

(ii) retention in the JFHQ-DODIN of such roles, missions, and responsibilities.

(B) If a determination under subparagraph (A)(i) is made in the affirmative regarding a transfer to the Commander, United States Cyber Command, from the JFHQ-DODIN of some or all roles, missions, and responsibilities of the JFHQ-DODIN, such report shall include the following:

(i) An identification of roles, missions, and responsibilities to be transferred.

(ii) A timeline for any such transfers.

(iii) A strategy for mitigating risk and ensuring no mission degradation.

SEC. 1639. PROCEDURES AND REPORTING REQUIREMENT ON CYBERSECURITY BREACHES AND LOSS OF PERSONALLY IDENTIFIABLE INFORMATION AND CONTROLLED UNCLASSIFIED INFORMATION.

(a) IN GENERAL.—In the event of a significant loss of personally identifiable information of civilian or uniformed members of the Armed Forces, or a significant loss of controlled unclassified information by a cleared defense contractor, the Secretary of Defense shall promptly submit to the congressional defense committees notice in writing of such loss. Such notice may be submitted in classified or unclassified formats.

(b) PROCEDURES.—Not later than 180 days after the date of the enactment of this Act, the Secretary of Defense shall establish and submit to the congressional defense committees procedures for complying with the requirement of subsection (a). Such procedures shall be consistent with the national security of the United States, the protection of operational integrity, the protection of personally identifiable information of civilian and uniformed members of the Armed Forces, and the protection of controlled unclassified information.

(c) DEFINITIONS.—In this section:

(1) SIGNIFICANT LOSS OF CONTROLLED UNCLASSIFIED INFORMATION.—The term ''significant loss of controlled unclassified information'' means an intentional, accidental, or otherwise known theft, loss, or disclosure of Department of Defense programmatic or technical controlled unclassified information the loss of which would have significant impact or consequence to a program or mission of the Department of Defense, or the loss of which is of substantial volume.

(2) SIGNIFICANT LOSS OF PERSONALLY IDENTIFIABLE INFORMATION.—

The term "significant loss of personally identifiable information" means an intentional, accidental, or otherwise known disclosure of information that can be used to distinguish or trace an individual's identity, such as the name, Social Security number, date and place of birth, biometric records, home or other phone numbers, or other demographic, personnel, medical, or financial information, involving 250 or more civilian or uniformed members of the Armed Forces.

SEC. 1640. PROGRAM TO ESTABLISH CYBER INSTITUTES AT INSTITUTIONS OF HIGHER LEARNING.

(a) PROGRAM AUTHORIZED.—The Secretary of Defense may carry out a program to establish a Cyber Institute at institutions of higher learning selected under subsection (b) for purposes of accelerating and focusing the development of foundational expertise in critical cyber operational skills for future military and civilian leaders of the Armed Forces and the Department of Defense, including such leaders of the reserve components.

(b) SELECTED INSTITUTIONS OF HIGHER LEARNING.—

(1) IN GENERAL.—The Secretary of Defense shall select institutions of higher learning for purposes of the program established under subsection (a) from among institutions of higher learning that have a Reserve Officers' Training Corps program.

(2) CONSIDERATION OF SENIOR MILITARY COLLEGES.—In selecting institutions of higher learning under paragraph (1), the Secretary shall consider the senior military colleges with Reserve Officers' Training Corps programs.

(c) ELEMENTS.—Each institute established under the program authorized by subsection (a) shall include the following:

(1) Programs to provide future military and civilian leaders of the Armed Forces or the Department of Defense who possess cyber operational expertise from beginning through advanced skill levels. Such programs shall include instruction and practical experiences that lead to recognized certifications and degrees in the cyber field.

(2) Programs of targeted strategic foreign language proficiency training for such future leaders that—

(A) are designed to significantly enhance critical cyber operational capabilities; and

(B) are tailored to current and anticipated readiness requirements.

(3) Programs related to mathematical foundations of cryptography and courses in cryptographic theory and practice designed to complement and reinforce cyber education along with the strategic language programs critical to cyber operations.

(4) Programs related to data science and courses in data science theory and practice designed to complement and reinforce cyber education along with the strategic language programs critical to cyber operations.

(5) Programs designed to develop early interest and cyber talent through summer programs, dual enrollment opportunities for cyber, strategic language, data science, and cryptography related courses.

(6) Training and education programs to expand the pool of qualified cyber instructors necessary to support cyber education in regional school systems.

(d) PARTNERSHIPS WITH DEPARTMENT OF DEFENSE AND THE ARMED FORCES.—Any institute established under the program authorized by subsection (a) may enter into a partnership with one or more components of the Armed Forces, active or reserve, or any agency of the Department of Defense to facilitate the development of critical cyber skills for students who may pursue a military career.

(e) PARTNERSHIPS.—Any institute established under the program authorized by subsection (a) may enter into a partnership with one or more local educational agencies to facilitate the development of critical cyber skills.

(f) SENIOR MILITARY COLLEGES DEFINED.—The term "senior military colleges" has the meaning given such term in section 2111a(f) of title 10, United States Code.

SEC. 1641. MATTERS PERTAINING TO THE SHARKSEER CYBERSECURITY PROGRAM.

(a) TRANSFER OF PROGRAM.—Not later than March 1, 2019, the Secretary of Defense shall transfer the operations and maintenance for the Sharkseer cybersecurity program from the National Security Agency to the Defense Information Systems Agency, including all associated funding and, as the Secretary considers necessary, personnel.

(b) LIMITATION ON FUNDING FOR THE INFORMATION SYSTEMS SECURITY PROGRAM.—Of the funds authorized to be appropriated by this Act or otherwise made available for fiscal year 2019 or any subsequent fiscal year for research, development, test, and evaluation for the Information Systems Security Program for the National Security Agency, not more than 90 percent may be obligated or expended unless the Chief of Information Officer, in consultation with the Principal Cyber Advisor, certifies to the congressional defense committees that the operations and maintenance funding for the Sharkseer program for fiscal year 2019 and the subsequent fiscal years of the current Future Years Defense Program are available or programmed.

(c) REPORT.—Not later than 90 days after the date of the enactment of this Act, the Chief Information Officer shall provide to the congressional defense committees a report that assesses the transition of base operations of the SharkSeer program to the Defense Information Systems Agency, including with respect to staffing, acquisition, contracts, sensor management, and the ability to conduct cyber threat analyses and detect advanced malware. Such report shall also include a plan for continued capability development.

(d) SHARKSEER BREAK AND INSPECT CAPABILITY.—

(1) IN GENERAL.—The Secretary of Defense shall ensure that the decryption capability described in section 1636 of the Carl Levin and Howard P. "Buck" McKeon National Defense Authorization Act for Fiscal Year 2015 (Public Law 113–291) is provided by the break and inspect subsystem of the Sharkseer cybersecurity program, unless the Chief of Information Officer, in consultation with the Principal Cyber Advisor, notifies the congressional defense committees on or before the date that is 90 days after the date of the enactment of this Act that a superior enterprise solution will be operational before October 1, 2019.

(2) INTEGRATION OF CAPABILITY.—The Secretary shall take such actions as are necessary to integrate the break and inspect subsystem of the Sharkseer cybersecurity program with the Department of Defense public key infrastructure.

(e) VISIBILITY TO ENDPOINTS.—The Secretary shall take such actions as are necessary to enable, by October 1, 2020, the Sharkseer cybersecurity program and computer network defense service providers to instantly and automatically determine the specific identity and location of computer hosts and other endpoints that received or sent malware detected by the Sharkseer cybersecurity program or other network perimeter defenses.

(f) SANDBOX AS A SERVICE.—The Secretary shall use the Sharkseer cybersecurity program sandbox-as-a-service capability as an enterprise solution and terminate all other such projects, unless the Chief of Information Officer, in consultation with the Principal Cyber Advisor, notifies the congressional defense committees on or before the date that is 90 days after the date of the enactment of this Act that a superior enterprise solution will be operational before October 1, 2019.

SEC. 1642. ACTIVE DEFENSE AGAINST THE RUSSIAN FEDERATION, PEOPLE'S REPUBLIC OF CHINA, DEMOCRATIC PEOPLE'S REPUBLIC OF KOREA, AND ISLAMIC REPUBLIC OF IRAN ATTACKS IN CYBERSPACE.

(a) AUTHORITY TO DISRUPT, DEFEAT, AND DETER CYBER ATTACKS.—

(1) IN GENERAL.—In the event that the National Command Authority determines that the Russian Federation, People's Republic of China, Democratic People's Republic of Korea, or Islamic Republic of Iran is conducting an active, systematic, and ongoing campaign of attacks against the Government or people of the United States in cyberspace, including attempting to influence American elections and democratic political processes, the National Command Authority may authorize the Secretary of Defense, acting through the Commander of the United States Cyber Command, to take appropriate and proportional action in foreign cyberspace to disrupt, defeat, and deter such attacks under the authority and policy of the Secretary of Defense to conduct cyber operations and information operations as traditional military activities.

(2) NOTIFICATION AND REPORTING.—

(A) NOTIFICATION OF OPERATIONS.—In exercising the authority provided in paragraph (1), the Secretary shall provide notices to the congressional defense committees in accordance with section 395 of title 10, United States Code (as transferred and redesignated pursuant to section 1631).

(B) QUARTERLY REPORTS BY COMMANDER OF THE UNITED STATES CYBER COMMAND.—

(i) IN GENERAL.—In any fiscal year in which the Commander of the United States Cyber Command carries out an action under paragraph (1), the Secretary of Defense shall, not less frequently than quarterly, submit to the congressional defense committees a report on the actions of the Commander under such paragraph in such fiscal year.

(ii) MANNER OF REPORTING.—Reports submitted under clause (i) shall be submitted in a manner that is consistent with the recurring quarterly report required by section 484 of title 10, United States Code.

(b) PRIVATE SECTOR COOPERATION.—The Secretary may make arrangements with private sector entities, on a voluntary basis, to share threat information related to malicious cyber actors, and any associated false online personas or compromised infrastructure, associated with a determination under subsection (a)(1), consistent with the protection of sources and methods and classification guidelines, as necessary.

(c) ANNUAL REPORT.—Not less frequently than once each year, the Secretary shall submit to the congressional defense committees, the congressional intelligence committees (as defined in section 3 of the National Security Act of 1947 (50 U.S.C. 3003)), the Committee on Foreign Affairs of the House of Representatives, and the Committee on Foreign Relations of the Senate a report on—

(1) the scope and intensity of the information operations and attacks through cyberspace by the countries specified in subsection (a)(1) against the government or people of the United States observed by the cyber mission forces of the United States Cyber Command and the National Security Agency; and

(2) adjustments of the Department of Defense in the response directed or recommended by the Secretary with respect to such operations and attacks.

(d) RULE OF CONSTRUCTION.—Nothing in this section may be construed to—

(1) limit the authority of the Secretary to conduct military activities or operations in cyberspace, including clandestine activities or operations in cyberspace; or

(2) affect the War Powers Resolution (Public Law 93–148; 50 U.S.C. 1541 et seq.) or the Authorization for Use of Military Force (Public Law 107–40; 50 U.S.C. 1541 note).

SEC. 1643. DESIGNATION OF OFFICIAL FOR MATTERS RELATING TO INTEGRATING CYBERSECURITY AND INDUSTRIAL CONTROL SYSTEMS WITHIN THE DEPARTMENT OF DEFENSE.

(a) DESIGNATION OF INTEGRATING OFFICIAL.—Not later than 180 days after the date of the enactment of this Act, the Secretary of Defense shall designate one official to be responsible for matters relating to integrating cybersecurity and industrial control systems for the Department of Defense.

(b) RESPONSIBILITIES.—The official designated pursuant to sub-section (a) shall be responsible for matters described in such sub-section at all levels of command, from the Department's leadership to the facilities owned by or operated on behalf of the Department of Defense using industrial control systems, including developing Department-wide certification standards for integration of industrial control systems and taking into consideration frameworks set forth by the National Institute of Standards and Technology for the cybersecurity of such systems.

SEC. 1644. ASSISTANCE FOR SMALL MANUFACTURERS IN THE DEFENSE INDUSTRIAL SUPPLY CHAIN AND UNIVERSITIES ON MATTERS RELATING TO CYBERSECURITY.

(a) DISSEMINATION OF CYBERSECURITY RESOURCES.—

(1) IN GENERAL.—The Secretary of Defense, in consultation with the Director of the National Institute of Standards and Technology, shall take such actions as may be necessary to enhance awareness of cybersecurity threats among small manufacturers and universities working on Department of Defense programs and activities.

(2) PRIORITY.—The Secretary of Defense shall prioritize efforts to increase awareness to help reduce cybersecurity risks faced by small manufacturers and universities referred to in paragraph (1).

(3) SECTOR FOCUS.—The Secretary of Defense shall carry out this subsection with a focus on such small manufacturers and universities as the Secretary considers critical.

(4) OUTREACH EVENTS.—Under paragraph (1), the Secretary of Defense shall conduct outreach to support activities consistent with this section. Such outreach may include live events with a physical presence and outreach conducted through Internet websites. Such outreach may include training, including via courses and classes, to help small manufacturers and universities improve their cybersecurity.

(5) ROADMAPS AND ASSESSMENTS.—The Secretary of Defense shall ensure that cybersecurity for defense industrial base manufacturing is included in appropriate research and development roadmaps and threat assessments.

(b) VOLUNTARY CYBERSECURITY SELF-ASSESSMENTS.—The Secretary of Defense shall develop mechanisms to provide assistance to help small manufacturers and universities conduct voluntary self-assessments in order to understand operating environments, cybersecurity requirements, and existing vulnerabilities, including through the Mentor Proteǵé Program, small business programs, and engagements with defense laboratories and test ranges.

(c) TRANSFER OF RESEARCH FINDINGS AND EXPERTISE.—

(1) IN GENERAL.—The Secretary of Defense shall promote the transfer of appropriate technology, threat information, and cybersecurity techniques developed in the

Department of Defense to small manufacturers and universities throughout the United States to implement security measures that are adequate to protect covered defense information, including controlled unclassified information.

(2) COORDINATION WITH OTHER FEDERAL EXPERTISE AND CAPABILITIES.—The Secretary of Defense shall coordinate efforts, when appropriate, with the expertise and capabilities that exist in Federal agencies and federally sponsored laboratories.

(3) AGREEMENTS.—In carrying out this subsection, the Secretary of Defense may enter into agreements with private industry, institutes of higher education, or a State, United States territory, local, or tribal government to ensure breadth and depth of coverage to the United States defense industrial base and to leverage resources.

(d) DEFENSE ACQUISITION WORKFORCE CYBER TRAINING PROGRAM.—The Secretary of Defense shall establish a cyber counseling certification program, or approve a similar existing program, to certify small business professionals and other relevant acquisition staff within the Department of Defense to provide cyber planning assistance to small manufacturers and universities.

(e) ESTABLISHMENT OF CYBERSECURITY FOR DEFENSE INDUSTRIAL BASE MANUFACTURING ACTIVITY.—

(1) AUTHORITY.—The Secretary of Defense may establish an activity to assess and strengthen the cybersecurity resiliency of the defense industrial base, if the Secretary determines such is appropriate.

(2) DESIGNATION.—The activity described in paragraph (1), if established, shall be known as the "Cybersecurity for Defense Industrial Base Manufacturing Activity".

(3) SPECIFICATION.—The Cybersecurity for Defense Industrial Base Manufacturing Activity, if established, shall implement the requirements specified in subsections (a) through (c).

(f) AUTHORITIES.—In carrying out this section, the Secretary may use the following authorities:

(1) The Manufacturing Technology Program established under section 2521 of title 10, United States Code.

(2) The Centers for Science, Technology, and Engineering Partnership program under section 2368 of title 10, United States Code.

(3) The Manufacturing Engineering Education Program established under section 2196 of title 10, United States Code.

(4) The Small Business Innovation Research program.

(5) The mentor-prote´ge´ program.

(6) Other legal authorities as the Secretary determines necessary to effectively and efficiently carry out this section.

(g) DEFINITIONS.—In this section:

(1) RESOURCES.—The term "resources" means guidelines, tools, best practices, standards, methodologies, and other ways of providing information.

(2) SMALL BUSINESS CONCERN.—The term "small business concern" means a small business concern as that term is used in section 3 of the Small Business Act (15 U.S.C. 632).

(3) SMALL MANUFACTURER.—The term "small manufacturer" means a small business concern that is a manufacturer in the defense industrial supply chain.

(4) STATE.—The term "State" means each of the several States, Territories, and possessions of the United States, the District of Columbia, and the Commonwealth of Puerto Rico.

SEC. 1645. EMAIL AND INTERNET WEBSITE SECURITY AND AUTHENTICATION.

(a) IMPLEMENTATION OF PLAN REQUIRED.—Except as provided by subsection (b), the Secretary of Defense shall develop and implement the plan outlined in Binding Operational Directive 18–01, issued by the Secretary of Homeland Security on October 16, 2017, relating to email security and authentication and Internet website security, according to the schedule established by the Binding Operational Directive for the rest of the Executive Branch beginning with the date of enactment of this Act.

(b) WAIVER.—The Secretary may waive the requirements of subsection (a) if the Secretary submits to the congressional defense committees, the Committee on Oversight and Government Reform of the House of Representatives, and the Committee on Homeland Security and Government Affairs of the Senate a certification that existing or planned security measures for the Department of Defense either meet or exceed the information security requirements of Binding Operational Directive 18–01.

(c) FUTURE BINDING OPERATIONAL DIRECTIVES.—The Chief Information Officer of the Department of Defense shall notify the congressional defense committees, the Committee on Oversight and Government Reform of the House of Representatives, and the Committee on Homeland Security and Government Affairs of the Senate within 180 days of the issuance by the Secretary of Homeland Security after the date of the enactment of this Act of any Binding Operational Directive for cybersecurity whether the Department of Defense will comply with the Directive or how the Department of Defense plans to meet or exceed the security objectives of the Directive.

SEC. 1646. SECURITY PRODUCT INTEGRATION FRAMEWORK.

The Principal Cyber Adviser, the Chief Information Officer, and the Commander of the United States Cyber Command shall select a network or network segment and associated computer network defense service provider to conduct a demonstration and evaluation of one or more existing security product integration frameworks, including modifying network security systems to enable such systems to ingest, publish, subscribe, tip and cue, and request information or services from each other.

SEC. 1647. INFORMATION SECURITY CONTINUOUS MONITORING AND CYBERSECURITY SCORECARD.

(a) LIMITATION.—After October 1, 2019, no funds may be obligated or expended to prepare the cybersecurity scorecard for the Secretary of Defense unless the Department of Defense is implementing a funded capability to meet the requirements—

(1) established by the Chief Information Officer and the Commander of United States Cyber Command pursuant to section 1653 of the National Defense Authorization for Fiscal Year 2017 (Public Law 114–328; 10 U.S.C. 2224 note); and

(2) as set forth in the Department of Defense's policies on modernized, Department-wide automated information security continuous monitoring.

(b) REPORT.—Not later than January 10, 2019, the Director of Cost Assessment and Program Evaluation shall submit to the congressional defense committees a report—

(1) comparing the current capabilities of the Department of Defense to—

(A) the requirements described in subsection (a);

(B) the capabilities deployed by the Department of Homeland Security and the General Services Administration under the Continuous Diagnostics and Mitigation program across the non-Department of Defense departments and agencies of the Federal Government; and

(2) that contains a review and determination of whether the current requirements

and policies described in subsection (a) are adequate to address the current threat environment.

(c) RISK THRESHOLDS.—The Chief Information Officer of the Department of Defense, in coordination with the Principal Cyber Advisor, the Director of Operations of the Joint Staff, and the Commander of United States Cyber Command, shall establish risk thresholds for systems and network operations that, when exceeded, would trigger heightened security measures, such as enhanced monitoring and access policy changes.

(d) ENTERPRISE GOVERNANCE, RISK, AND COMPLIANCE PLAN.— Not later than 180 days after the date of the enactment of this Act, the Chief Information Officer and the Principal Cyber Advisor shall develop a plan to implement an enterprise governance, risk, and compliance platform and process to maintain current status of all information and operational technology assets, vulnerabilities, threats, and mitigations.

SEC. 1648. TIER 1 EXERCISE OF SUPPORT TO CIVIL AUTHORITIES FOR A CYBER INCIDENT.

(a) IN GENERAL.—The Commander of the United States Cyber Command, the Commander of United States Northern Command, and such other commands or components of the Department of Defense as the Secretary of Defense considers appropriate, shall, consistent with the recommendations made by the Comptroller General of the United States in the Government Accountability Office report GAO–16–574, conduct a tier 1 exercise of support to civil authorities for a cyber incident.

(b) ELEMENTS.—The exercise required by subsection (a) shall include the following:

(1) Department level leadership and decision-making for providing cyber support to civil authorities.

(2) Testing of the policy, guidance, doctrine and other elements in the Department of Defense Cyber Incident Coordinating Procedure.

(3) Operational planning and execution by the Joint Staff and supported and supporting combatant commands.

(4) Coordination with, and incorporation of, as appropriate, the Department of Homeland Security, the Federal Bureau of Investigation, and elements across Federal and State governments and the private sector.

SEC. 1649. PILOT PROGRAM ON MODELING AND SIMULATION IN SUPPORT OF MILITARY HOMELAND DEFENSE OPERATIONS IN CONNECTION WITH CYBER ATTACKS ON CRITICAL INFRASTRUCTURE.

(a) PILOT PROGRAM REQUIRED.—

(1) IN GENERAL.—The Assistant Secretary of Defense for Homeland Defense and Global Security shall carry out a pilot program to model cyber attacks on critical infrastructure in order to identify and develop means of improving Department of Defense responses to requests for defense support to civil authorities for such attacks.

(2) RESEARCH EXERCISES.—The pilot program shall source data from and include consideration of the "Jack Voltaic" research exercises conducted by the Army Cyber Institute, industry partners of the Institute, and the cities of New York, New York, and Houston, Texas.

(b) PURPOSE.—The purpose of the pilot program shall be to accomplish the following:

(1) The development and demonstration of risk analysis methodologies, and the application of commercial simulation and modeling capabilities, based on artificial intelligence and hyperscale cloud computing technologies, as applicable—

(A) to assess defense critical infrastructure vulnerabilities and interdependencies to improve military resiliency;

(B) to determine the likely effectiveness of attacks described in subsection (a)(1), and countermeasures, tactics, and tools supporting responsive military homeland defense operations;

(C) to train personnel in incident response;

(D) to conduct exercises and test scenarios;

(E) to foster collaboration and learning between and among departments and agencies of the Federal Government, State and local governments, and private entities responsible for critical infrastructure; and

(F) improve intra-agency and inter-agency coordination for consideration and approval of requests for defense support to civil authorities.

(2) The development and demonstration of the foundations for establishing and maintaining a program of record for a shared high-fidelity, interactive, affordable, cloud-based modeling and simulation of critical infrastructure systems and incident response capabilities that can simulate complex cyber and physical attacks and disruptions on individual and multiple sectors on national, regional, State, and local scales.

(c) REPORT.—

(1) IN GENERAL.—At the same time the budget of the President for fiscal year 2021 is submitted to Congress pursuant to section 1105(a) of title 31, United States Code, the Assistant Secretary shall, in consultation with the Secretary of Homeland Security, submit to the congressional defense committees a report on the pilot program.

(2) CONTENTS.—The report required by paragraph (1) shall include the following:

(A) A description of the results of the pilot program as of the date of the report.

(B) A description of the risk analysis methodologies and modeling and simulation capabilities developed and demonstrated pursuant to the pilot program, and an assessment of the potential for future growth of commercial technology in support of the homeland defense mission of the Department of Defense.

(C) Such recommendations as the Secretary considers appropriate regarding the establishment of a program of record for the Department on further development and sustainment of risk analysis methodologies and advanced, large-scale modeling and simulation on critical infrastructure and cyber warfare.

(D) Lessons learned from the use of novel risk analysis methodologies and large-scale modeling and simulation carried out under the pilot program regarding vulnerabilities, required capabilities, and reconfigured force structure, coordination practices, and policy.

(E) Planned steps for implementing the lessons described in subparagraph (D).

(F) Any other matters the Secretary determines appropriate.

SEC. 1650. PILOT PROGRAM AUTHORITY TO ENHANCE CYBERSECURITY AND RESILIENCY OF CRITICAL INFRASTRUCTURE.

(a) AUTHORITY.—The Secretary of Defense, in coordination with the Secretary of Homeland Security, is authorized to provide, detail, or assign technical personnel to the Department of Homeland Security on a non-reimbursable basis to enhance cybersecurity cooperation, collaboration, and unity of Government efforts.

(b) SCOPE OF ASSISTANCE.—The authority under subsection (a) shall be limited in any fiscal year to the provision of not more than 50 technical cybersecurity personnel from the Department of Defense to the Department of Homeland Security, including the national cybersecurity and communications integration center (NCCIC) of the Department, or other locations as agreed upon by the Secretary of Defense and the Secretary of Homeland Security.

(c) LIMITATION.—The authority under subsection (a) may not negatively impact the primary missions of the Department of Defense or the Department of Homeland Security.

(d) ESTABLISHMENT OF PROCEDURES.—

(1) IN GENERAL.—The Secretary of Defense and the Secretary of Homeland Security shall establish procedures to carry out subsection (a), including procedures relating to the protection of and safeguards for maintenance of information held by the NCCIC regarding United States persons.

(2) LIMITATION.—Nothing in this subsection may be construed as providing authority to the Secretary of Defense to establish procedures regarding the NCCIC with respect to any matter outside the scope of this section.

(e) NO EFFECT ON OTHER AUTHORITY TO PROVIDE SUPPORT.— Nothing in this section may be construed to limit the authority of an Executive department, military department, or independent establishment to provide any appropriate support, including cybersecurity support, or to provide, detail, or assign personnel, under any other law, rule, or regulation.

(f) DEFINITIONS.—In this section, each of the terms "Executive department", "military department", and "independent establishment", has the meaning given each of such terms, respectively, in chapter 1 of title 5, United States Code.

(g) TERMINATION OF AUTHORITY.—This section shall terminate on September 30, 2022.

SEC. 1651. PILOT PROGRAM ON REGIONAL CYBERSECURITY TRAINING CENTER FOR THE ARMY NATIONAL GUARD.

(a) PILOT PROGRAM.—The Secretary of the Army may carry out a pilot program under which the Secretary establishes a National Guard training center to provide collaborative interagency education and training for members of the Army National Guard.

(b) CENTER.—

(1) TRAINING AND COOPERATION.—If the Secretary carries out the pilot program under subsection (a), the Secretary should ensure that the training center established under such sub-section—

(A) educates and trains members of the Army National Guard quickly and efficiently by concurrently training cyber protection teams and cyber network defense teams on a common standard in order to defend—

(i) the information network of the Department of Defense in a State environment;

(ii) while acting under title 10, United States Code, the information networks of State governments; and

(iii) critical infrastructure;

(B) fosters interagency cooperation by—

(i) co-locating members of the Army National Guard with personnel of departments and agencies of the Federal Government and State governments; and

(ii) providing an environment to develop inter-agency relationship to coordinate responses and recovery efforts during and following a cyber attack;

(C) collaborates with academic institutions to develop and implement curriculum for interagency education and training within the classroom; and

(D) coordinates with the Persistent Cyber Training Environment of the Army Cyber Command in devising and implementing interagency education and training using physical and information technology infrastructure.

(2) LOCATIONS.—If the Secretary carries out the pilot program under subsection (a), the Secretary may select one National Guard facility at which to carry out the pilot program. The Secretary may select a facility that is located in an area that meets the following criteria:

(A) The location has a need for cyber training, as measured by both the number of members of the Army National Guard that would apply for such training and the number of units of the Army National Guard that verify the unit would apply for such training.

(B) The location has high capacity information and telecommunications infrastructure, including high speed fiber optic networks.

(C) The location has personnel, technology, laboratories, and facilities to support proposed activities and has the opportunity for ongoing training, education, and research.

(c) ACTIVITIES.—If the Secretary carries out the pilot program under subsection (a), the Secretary should ensure that the pilot program includes the following activities:

(1) Providing joint education and training and accelerating training certifications for working in a cyber range.

(2) Integrating education and training between the National Guard, law enforcement, and emergency medical and fire first responders.

(3) Providing a program to continuously train the cyber network defense teams to not only defend the information network of the Department of Defense, but to also provide education and training on how to use defense capabilities of the team in a State environment.

(4) Developing curriculum and educating the National Guard on the different missions carried out under titles 10 and 32, United States Code, in order to enhance interagency coordination and create a common operating picture.

(d) NOTIFICATION REQUIRED.—If the Secretary carries out the pilot program under subsection (a), the Secretary shall provide immediate notification to the congressional defense committees that includes information relating to the resources required to carry out such pilot program, identification of units to be trained, the location of such training, and a description of agreements with Federal, State, local, and private sector entities.

(e) SUNSET.—The authority provided under this section shall expire on the date that is two years after the date of the enactment of this Act.

SEC. 1652. CYBERSPACE SOLARIUM COMMISSION.

(a) ESTABLISHMENT.—

(1) IN GENERAL.—There is established a commission to develop a consensus on a strategic approach to defending the United States in cyberspace against cyber attacks of significant consequences.

(2) DESIGNATION.—The commission established under paragraph (1) shall be

known as the "Cyberspace Solarium Commission" (in this section the "Commission").

(b) MEMBERSHIP.—

(1) COMPOSITION.—(A) Subject to subparagraph (B), the Commission shall be composed of the following members:

(i) The Principal Deputy Director of National Intelligence.

(ii) The Deputy Secretary of Homeland Security.

(iii) The Deputy Secretary of Defense.

(iv) The Director of the Federal Bureau of Investigation.

(v) Three members appointed by the majority leader of the Senate, in consultation with the Chairman of the Committee on Armed Services of the Senate, one of whom shall be a member of the Senate and two of whom shall not be.

(vi) Two members appointed by the minority leader of the Senate, in consultation with the Ranking Member of the Committee on Armed Services of the Senate, one of whom shall be a member of the Senate and one of whom shall not be.

(vii) Three members appointed by the Speaker of the House of Representatives, in consultation with the Chairman of the Committee on Armed Services of the House of Representatives, one of whom shall be a member of the House of Representatives and two of whom shall not be.

(viii) Two members appointed by the minority leader of the House of Representatives, in consultation with the Ranking Member of the Committee on Armed Services of the House of Representatives, one of whom shall be a member of the House of Representatives and one of whom shall not be.

(B)(i) The members of the Commission who are not members of Congress and who are appointed under clauses (iv) through (vii) of subparagraph (A) shall be individuals who are nationally recognized for expertise, knowledge, or experience in—

(I) cyber strategy or national-level strategies to combat long-term adversaries;

(II) cyber technology and innovation;

(III) use of intelligence information by national policy-makers and military leaders; or

(IV) the implementation, funding, or oversight of the national security policies of the United States.

(ii) An official who appoints members of the Commission may not appoint an individual as a member of the Commission if such individual possesses any personal or financial interest in the discharge of any of the duties of the Commission.

(iii) All members of the Commission described in clause (i) shall possess an appropriate security clearance in accordance with applicable provisions of law concerning the handling of classified information.

(2) CO-CHAIRS.—(A) The Commission shall have two co-chairs, selected from among the members of the Commission.

(B) One co-chair of the Commission shall be a member of the Democratic Party, and one co-chair shall be a member of the Republican Party.

(C) The individuals who serve as the co-chairs of the Commission shall be jointly agreed upon by the President, the majority leader of the Senate, the minority leader of the Senate, the Speaker of the House of Representatives, and the minority leader of the House of Representatives.

(c) APPOINTMENT; INITIAL MEETING.—

(1) APPOINTMENT.—Members of the Commission shall be appointed not later than 45 days after the date of the enactment of this Act.

(2) INITIAL MEETING.—The Commission shall hold its initial meeting on or before the date that is 60 days after the date of the enactment of this Act.

(d) MEETINGS; QUORUM; VACANCIES.—

(1) IN GENERAL.—After its initial meeting, the Commission shall meet upon the call of the co-chairs of the Commission.

(2) QUORUM.—Seven members of the Commission shall constitute a quorum for purposes of conducting business, except that two members of the Commission shall constitute a quorum for purposes of receiving testimony.

(3) VACANCIES.—Any vacancy in the Commission shall not affect its powers, but shall be filled in the same manner in which the original appointment was made.

(4) QUORUM WITH VACANCIES.—If vacancies in the Commission occur on any day after 45 days after the date of the enactment of this Act, a quorum shall consist of a majority of the members of the Commission as of such day.

(e) ACTIONS OF COMMISSION.—

(1) IN GENERAL.—The Commission shall act by resolution agreed to by a majority of the members of the Commission voting and present.

(2) PANELS.—The Commission may establish panels composed of less than the full membership of the Commission for purposes of carrying out the duties of the Commission under this title. The actions of any such panel shall be subject to the review and control of the Commission. Any findings and determinations made by such a panel shall not be considered the findings and determinations of the Commission unless approved by the Commission.

(3) DELEGATION.—Any member, agent, or staff of the Commission may, if authorized by the co-chairs of the Commission, take any action which the Commission is authorized to take pursuant to this title.

(f) DUTIES.—The duties of the Commission are as follows:

(1) To define the core objectives and priorities of the strategy described in subsection (a)(1).

(2) To weigh the costs and benefits of various strategic options to defend the United States, including the political system of the United States, the national security industrial sector of the United States, and the innovation base of the United States. The options to be assessed should include deterrence, norms-based regimes, and active disruption of adversary attacks through persistent engagement.

(3) To evaluate whether the options described in paragraph (2) are exclusive or complementary, the best means for executing such options, and how the United States should incorporate and implement such options within its national strategy.

(4) To review and make determinations on the difficult choices present within such options, among them what norms-based regimes the United States should seek to establish, how the United States should enforce such norms, how much damage the United States should be willing to incur in a deterrence or persistent denial strategy, what attacks warrant response in a deterrence or persistent denial strategy, and how the United States can best execute these strategies.

(5) To review adversarial strategies and intentions, current programs for the de-

fense of the United States, and the capabilities of the Federal Government to understand if and how adversaries are currently being deterred or thwarted in their aims and ambitions in cyberspace.

(6) To evaluate the effectiveness of the current national cyber policy relating to cyberspace, cybersecurity, and cyber warfare to disrupt, defeat and deter cyber attacks.

(7) In weighing the options for defending the United States, to consider possible structures and authorities that need to be established, revised, or augmented within the Federal Government.

(g) POWERS OF COMMISSION.—

(1) IN GENERAL.—(A) The Commission or, on the authorization of the Commission, any subcommittee or member thereof, may, for the purpose of carrying out the provisions of this section—

(i) hold such hearings and sit and act at such times and places, take such testimony, receive such evidence, and administer such oaths; and

(ii) require, by subpoena or otherwise, the attendance and testimony of such witnesses and the production of such books, records, correspondence, memoranda, papers, and documents, as the Commission or such designated subcommittee or designated member considers necessary.

(B) Subpoenas may be issued under subparagraph (A)(ii) under the signature of the co-chairs of the Commission, and may be served by any person designated by such co-chairs.

(C) The provisions of sections 102 through 104 of the Revised Statutes of the United States (2 U.S.C. 192–194) shall apply in the case of any failure of a witness to comply with any subpoena or to testify when summoned under authority of this section.

(2) CONTRACTING.—The Commission may, to such extent and in such amounts as are provided in advance in appropriation Acts, enter into contracts to enable the Commission to discharge its duties under this title.

(3) INFORMATION FROM FEDERAL AGENCIES.—

(A) The Commission may secure directly from any executive department, agency, bureau, board, commission, office, independent establishment, or instrumentality of the Government information, suggestions, estimates, and statistics for the purposes of this title.

(B) Each such department, agency, bureau, board, commission, office, establishment, or instrumentality shall, to the extent authorized by law, furnish such information, suggestions, estimates, and statistics directly to the Commission, upon request of the co-chairs of the Commission.

(C) The Commission shall handle and protect all classified information provided to it under this section in accordance with applicable statutes and regulations.

(4) ASSISTANCE FROM FEDERAL AGENCIES.—

(A) The Secretary of Defense shall provide to the Commission, on a nonreimbursable basis, such administrative services, funds, staff, facilities, and other support services as are necessary for the performance of the Commission's duties under this title.

(B) The Director of National Intelligence may provide the Commission, on a nonreimbursable basis, with such administrative services, staff, and other support services as the Commission may request.

(C) In addition to the assistance set forth in paragraphs (1) and (2), other departments and agencies of the United States may provide the Commission such services, funds, facilities, staff, and other support as such departments and agencies consider advisable and as may be authorized by law.

(D) The Commission shall receive the full and timely cooperation of any official, department, or agency of the United States Government whose assistance is necessary, as jointly determined by the co-chairs selected under subsection (b)(2), for the fulfillment of the duties of the Commission, including the provision of full and current briefings and analyses.

(5) POSTAL SERVICES.—The Commission may use the United States postal services in the same manner and under the same conditions as the departments and agencies of the United States.

(6) GIFTS.—No member or staff of the Commission may receive a gift or benefit by reason of the service of such member or staff to the Commission.

(h) STAFF OF COMMISSION.—

(1) IN GENERAL.—

(A) The co-chairs of the Commission, in accordance with rules agreed upon by the Commission, shall appoint and fix the compensation of a staff director and such other personnel as may be necessary to enable the Commission to carry out its duties, without regard to the provisions of title 5, United States Code, governing appointments in the competitive service, and without regard to the provisions of chapter 51 and subchapter III of chapter 53 of such title relating to classification and General Schedule pay rates, except that no rate of pay fixed under this subsection may exceed the equivalent of that payable to a person occupying a position at level V of the Executive Schedule under section 5316 of such title.

(B) Any Federal Government employee may be detailed to the Commission without reimbursement from the Commission, and such detailee shall retain the rights, status, and privileges of his or her regular employment without interruption.

(C) All staff of the Commission shall possess a security clearance in accordance with applicable laws and regulations concerning the handling of classified information.

(2) CONSULTANT SERVICES.—(A) The Commission may procure the services of experts and consultants in accordance with section 3109 of title 5, United States Code, but at rates not to exceed the daily rate paid a person occupying a position at level IV of the Executive Schedule under section 5315 of such title.

(B) All experts and consultants employed by the Commission shall possess a security clearance in accordance with applicable laws and regulations concerning the handling of classified information.

(i) COMPENSATION AND TRAVEL EXPENSES.—

(1) COMPENSATION.—(A) Except as provided in paragraph (2), each member of the Commission may be compensated at not to exceed the daily equivalent of the annual rate of basic pay in effect for a position at level IV of the Executive Schedule under section 5315 of title 5, United States Code, for each day during which that member is engaged in the actual performance of the duties of the Commission under this title.

(B) Members of the Commission who are officers or employees of the United States or Members of Congress shall receive no additional pay by reason of their service on the Commission.

(2) TRAVEL EXPENSES.—While away from their homes or regular places of business in the performance of services for the Commission, members of the Commis-

sion may be allowed travel expenses, including per diem in lieu of subsistence, in the same manner as persons employed intermittently in the Government service are allowed expenses under section 5703 of title 5, United States Code.

(j) TREATMENT OF INFORMATION RELATING TO NATIONAL SECURITY.—

(1) IN GENERAL.—(A) The Director of National Intelligence shall assume responsibility for the handling and disposition of any information related to the national security of the United States that is received, considered, or used by the Commission under this title.

(B) Any information related to the national security of the United States that is provided to the Commission by a congressional intelligence committees or the congressional armed services committees may not be further provided or released without the approval of the chairman of such committees.

(2) ACCESS AFTER TERMINATION OF COMMISSION.—Notwithstanding any other provision of law, after the termination of the Commission under subsection (k)(2), only the members and designated staff of the congressional intelligence committees, the Director of National Intelligence (and the designees of the Director), and such other officials of the executive branch as the President may designate shall have access to information related to the national security of the United States that is received, considered, or used by the Commission.

(k) FINAL REPORT; TERMINATION.—

(1) FINAL REPORT.—Not later than September 1, 2019, the Commission shall submit to the congressional defense committees, the congressional intelligence committees, the Committee on Homeland Security of the House of Representatives, the Committee on Homeland Security and Governmental Affairs of the Senate, the Director of National Intelligence, and the Secretary of Defense, and the Secretary of Homeland Security a final report on the findings of the Commission.

(2) TERMINATION.—(A) The Commission, and all the authorities of this section, shall terminate at the end of the 120-day period beginning on the date on which the final report under paragraph (1) is submitted to the congressional defense and intelligence committees.

(B) The Commission may use the 120-day period referred to in paragraph (1) for the purposes of concluding its activities, including providing testimony to Congress concerning the final report referred to in that paragraph and disseminating the report.

(l) ASSESSMENTS OF FINAL REPORT.—Not later than 60 days after receipt of the final report under subsection (k)(1), the Director of National Intelligence, the Secretary of Defense, and the Secretary of Homeland Security shall each submit to the congressional intelligence committees and the congressional defense committees an assessment by the Director or the Secretary, as the case may be, of the final report. Each assessment shall include such comments on the findings and recommendations contained in the final report as the Director or Secretary, as the case may be, considers appropriate.

(m) INAPPLICABILITY OF CERTAIN ADMINISTRATIVE PROVISIONS.—

(1) FEDERAL ADVISORY COMMITTEE ACT.—The provisions of the Federal Advisory Committee Act (5 U.S.C. App.) shall not apply to the activities of the Commission under this section.

(2) FREEDOM OF INFORMATION ACT.—The provisions of section 552 of title 5, United States Code (commonly referred to as the Freedom of Information Act), shall not apply to the activities, records, and proceedings of the Commission under this section.

(n) FUNDING.—

(1) AUTHORIZATION OF APPROPRIATIONS.—Of the amount authorized to be appropriated for fiscal year 2019 by this Act, as specified in the funding tables in division D, $4,000,000 may be used to carry out this section.

(2) AVAILABILITY IN GENERAL.—Subject to paragraph (1), the Secretary of Defense shall make available to the Commission such amounts as the Commission may require for purposes of the activities of the Commission under this section.

(3) DURATION OF AVAILABILITY.—Amounts made available to the Commission under paragraph (2) shall remain available until expended.

(o) CONGRESSIONAL INTELLIGENCE COMMITTEES DEFINED.—In this section, the term "congressional intelligence committees" means—

(1) the Select Committee on Intelligence of the Senate; and

(2) the Permanent Select Committee on Intelligence of the House of Representatives.

SEC. 1653. STUDY AND REPORT ON RESERVE COMPONENT CYBER CIVIL SUPPORT TEAMS.

(a) STUDY REQUIRED.—The Secretaries concerned shall conduct a study on the feasibility and advisability of the establishment of reserve component cyber civil support teams for each State.

(b) ELEMENTS.—The study under subsection (a) shall include the following:

(1) An examination of the potential ability of the teams referred to in such subsection to respond to an attack, natural disaster, or other large-scale incident affecting computer networks, electronics, or cyber capabilities, including an analysis of the following:

(A) The command structure and lines of authority for such teams.

(B) The operational capabilities of such teams.

(C) The legal authorities available to and constraints placed on such teams.

(D) The amount of funding and other resources that would be required by the Department of Defense to organize, train, and equip such teams.

(2) An analysis of the current use of reserve and active duty components in the Department of Defense and an explanation of how the establishment of such teams may affect the ability of the Department of Defense to—

(A) organize, train, equip, and employ the Cyber Mission Force, and other organic cyber forces; and

(B) perform the national defense missions and defense support to civil authorities for cyber incident response.

(3) An explanation of how the establishment of such teams may affect the ability of the Department of Homeland Security to—

(A) organize, train, equip, and employ cyber incident response teams; and

(B) perform civilian cyber response missions.

(4) An explanation as to how the establishment of such teams would fit into the current missions of the Department of Defense and the Department of Homeland Security.

(5) An analysis of current and projected State civilian and private sector cyber response capabilities and services, including an identification of any gaps in such capabilities and services, and including an analysis of the following:

(A) Whether such teams would be, on a risk- and cost-adjusted basis, of use for each State.

(B) How the establishment of such teams may impact Federal, State, and private sector resourcing for State civilian and private sector cyber response capabilities and services.

(6) An identification of the potential role of such teams with respect to the principles and processes set forth in—

(A) Presidential Policy Directive 20 (United States Cyber Operations Policy);

(B) Presidential Policy Directive 21 (Critical Infrastructure Security and Resilience); and

(C) Presidential Policy Directive 41 (United States Cyber Incident Coordination).

(7) An explanation of how such teams may interact with other organizations and elements of the Federal Government that have responsibilities under the Presidential Policy Directives referred to in paragraph (6).

(8) Any effects on the privacy and civil liberties of United States persons that may result from the establishment of such teams.

(9) Any other considerations determined to be relevant by the Secretaries concerned.

(c) REPORT REQUIRED.—Not later than 180 days after the date of the enactment of this Act, the Secretaries concerned shall submit to the appropriate congressional committees a report that includes—

(1) the results of the study conducted under subsection (a), including an explanation of each element described in sub-section (b); and

(2) the final determination of the Secretaries with respect to the feasibility and advisability of establishing reserve component cyber civil support teams for each State.

(d) DEFINITIONS.—In this section:

(1) The term "appropriate congressional committees" means—

(A) the congressional defense committees;

(B) the Committee on Homeland Security of the House of Representatives; and

(C) the Committee on Homeland Security and Governmental Affairs of the Senate.

(2) The term "reserve component cyber civil support team" means a team that—

(A) is comprised of members of the reserve components;

(B) is organized, trained, equipped, and sustained by the Department of Defense for the purpose of assisting State authorities in preparing for and responding to cyber incidents, cyber emergencies, and cyber attacks; and

(C) operates principally under the command and control of the Chief Executive of the State in which the team is located.

(3) The term "Secretaries concerned" means the Secretary of Defense and the Secretary of Homeland Security acting jointly.

(4) The term "State" means each of the several States, the District of Columbia, the Commonwealth of Puerto Rico, and the United States Virgin Islands.

SEC. 1654. IDENTIFICATION OF COUNTRIES OF CONCERN REGARDING CYBERSECURITY.

(a) IDENTIFICATION OF COUNTRIES OF CONCERN.—Not later than 180 days after the date of the enactment of this Act, the Secretary of Defense shall create a list of countries that pose a risk to the cybersecurity of United States defense and national security systems and infrastructure. Such list shall reflect the level of threat posed by each country included on such list. In creating such list, the Secretary shall take in to account the following:

(1) A foreign government's activities that pose force protection or cybersecurity risk to the personnel, financial systems, critical infrastructure, or information systems of the United States or coalition forces.

(2) A foreign government's willingness and record of providing financing, logistics, training or intelligence to other persons, countries or entities posing a force protection or cybersecurity risk to the personnel, financial systems, critical infrastructure, or information systems of the United States or coalition forces.

(3) A foreign government's engagement in foreign intelligence activities against the United States for the purpose of undermining United States national security.

(4) A foreign government's knowing participation in transnational organized crime or criminal activity.

(5) A foreign government's cyber activities and operations to affect the supply chain of the United States Government.

(6) A foreign government's use of cyber means to unlawfully or inappropriately obtain intellectual property from the United States Government or United States persons.

(b) UPDATES.—The Secretary shall continuously update and maintain the list under subsection (a) to preempt obsolescence.

(c) REPORT TO CONGRESS.—Not later than one year after the date of the enactment of this Act, the Secretary shall submit to the appropriate committees of Congress the list created pursuant to subsection (a) and any accompanying analysis that contributed to the creation of the list.

SEC. 1655. MITIGATION OF RISKS TO NATIONAL SECURITY POSED BY PROVIDERS OF INFORMATION TECHNOLOGY PRODUCTS AND SERVICES WHO HAVE OBLIGATIONS TO FOREIGN GOVERNMENTS.

(a) DISCLOSURE REQUIRED.—Subject to the regulations issued under subsection (b), the Department of Defense may not use a product, service, or system procured or acquired after the date of the enactment of this Act relating to information or operational technology, cybersecurity, an industrial control system, or weapons system provided by a person unless that person discloses to the Secretary of Defense the following:

(1) Whether, and if so, when, within five years before or at any time after the date of the enactment of this Act, the person has allowed a foreign government to review the code of a noncommercial product, system, or service developed for the Department, or whether the person is under any obligation to allow a foreign person or government to review the code of a noncommercial product, system, or service developed for the Department as a condition of entering into an agreement for sale or other transaction with a foreign government or with a foreign person on behalf of such a government.

(2) Whether, and if so, when, within five years before or at any time after the date of the enactment of this Act, the person has allowed a foreign government listed in section 1654 to review the source code of a product, system, or service that the Department is using or intends to use, or is under any obligation to allow a foreign person or government to review the source code of a product, system, or service that the Department is using or intends to use as a condition of entering into an agreement for sale or other transaction with a foreign government or with a foreign person on behalf of such a government.

(3) Whether or not the person holds or has sought a license pursuant to the Export Administration Regulations under sub-chapter C of chapter VII of title 15, Code of Federal Regulations, the International Traffic in Arms Regulations under subchapter M of chapter I of title 22, Code of Federal Regulations, or successor regulations, for information technology products, components, software, or services that contain code custom-developed for the noncommercial product, system, or service the Department is using or intends to use.

(b) REGULATIONS.—

(1) IN GENERAL.—The Secretary of Defense shall issue regulations regarding the implementation of subsection (a).

(2) UNIFORM REVIEW PROCESS.—If information obtained from a person under subsection (a) or the contents of the registry under subsection (f) are the subject of a request under section 552 of title 5, United States Code (commonly referred to as the "Freedom of Information Act"), the Secretary of Defense shall conduct a uniform review process, without regard to the office holding the information, to determine if the information is exempt from disclosure under such section 552.

(c) PROCUREMENT.—Procurement contracts for covered products or systems shall include a clause requiring the information contained in subsection (a) be disclosed during the period of the contract if an entity becomes aware of information requiring disclosure required pursuant to such subsection, including any mitigation measures taken or anticipated.

(d) MITIGATION OF RISKS.—

(1) IN GENERAL.—If, after reviewing a disclosure made by a person under subsection (a), the Secretary determines that the disclosure relating to a product, system, or service entails a risk to the national security infrastructure or data of the United States, or any national security system under the control of the Department, the Secretary shall take such measures as the Secretary considers appropriate to mitigate such risks, including, as the Secretary considers appropriate, by conditioning any agreement for the use, procurement, or acquisition of the product, system, or service on the inclusion of enforceable conditions or requirements that would mitigate such risks.

(2) THIRD-PARTY TESTING STANDARD.—Not later than two years after the date of the enactment of this Act the Secretary shall develop such third-party testing standard as the Secretary considers acceptable for commercial off the shelf (COTS) products, systems, or services to use when dealing with foreign governments.

(e) EXEMPTION OF OPEN SOURCE SOFTWARE.—This section shall not apply to open source software.

(f) ESTABLISHMENT OF REGISTRY.—Not later than one year after the date of the enactment of this Act, the Secretary of Defense shall—

(1) establish within the operational capabilities of the Committee for National Security Systems (CNSS) or within such other agency as the Secretary considers appropriate a registry containing the information disclosed under subsection (a); and

(2) upon request, make such information available to any agency conducting a procurement pursuant to the Federal Acquisition Regulations or the Defense Federal Acquisition Regulations.

(g) ANNUAL REPORTS.—Not later than one year after the date of the enactment of this Act and not less frequently than once each year thereafter, the Secretary of Defense shall submit to the appropriate committees of Congress a report detailing the number, scope, product classifications, and mitigation agreements related to each product, system, and service for which a disclosure is made under subsection (a).

(h) DEFINITIONS.—In this section:

(1) APPROPRIATE COMMITTEES OF CONGRESS DEFINED.—The term "appropriate committees of Congress" means—

(A) the Committee on Armed Services, the Select Committee on Intelligence, and the Committee on Homeland Security and Governmental Affairs of the Senate; and

(B) the Committee on Armed Services, the Permanent Select Committee on Intelligence, the Committee on Homeland Security, and the Committee on Oversight and Government Reform of the House of Representatives.

(2) COMMERCIAL ITEM.—The term "commercial item" has the meaning given such term in section 103 of title 41, United States Code.

(3) INFORMATION TECHNOLOGY.—The term "information technology" has the meaning given such term in section 11101 of title 40, United States Code.

(4) NATIONAL SECURITY SYSTEM.—The term "national security system" has the meaning given such term in section 3552(b) of title 44, United States Code.

(5) NONCOMMERCIAL PRODUCT, SYSTEM, OR SERVICE.—The term "noncommercial product, system, or service" means a product, system, or service that does not meet the criteria of a commercial item.

(6) OPEN SOURCE SOFTWARE.—The term "open source software" means software for which the human-readable source code is available for use, study, re-use, modification, enhancement, and redistribution by the users of such software.

SEC. 1656. REPORT ON CYBERSECURITY APPRENTICE PROGRAM.

Not later than 240 days after the date of the enactment of this Act, the Secretary of Defense shall submit to the congressional defense committees a report on the feasibility of establishing a Cybersecurity Apprentice Program to support on-the-job training for certain cybersecurity positions and facilitate the acquisition of cybersecurity certifications.

SEC. 1657. REPORT ON ENHANCEMENT OF SOFTWARE SECURITY FOR CRITICAL SYSTEMS.

(a) REPORT REQUIRED.—Not later than March 1, 2019, the Principal Cyber Adviser to the Secretary of Defense, the Under Secretary of Defense for Research and Engineering, and the Chief Information Officer of the Department of Defense shall jointly submit to the congressional defense committees a report on a study, based on the authorities specified in subsection (b), on the costs, benefits, technical merits, and other merits of applying the technologies described in subsection (c) to the vulnerability assessment and remediation of the following systems:

(1) Nuclear systems and nuclear command and control.

(2) A critical subset of conventional power projection capabilities.

(3) Cyber command and control.

(4) Other defense critical infrastructure.

(b) BASIS FOR CONDUCT OF STUDY.—The study required for purposes of subsection (a) shall be conducted pursuant to the following:

(1) Section 1640 of the National Defense Authorization Act for Fiscal Year 2018 (Public Law 115–91).

(2) Section 1650 of the National Defense Authorization Act for Fiscal Year 2017 (10 U.S.C. 2224 note).

(3) Section 1647 of the National Defense Authorization Act for Fiscal Year 2016 (Public Law 114–92; 129 Stat. 1118).

(4) Section 937 of the National Defense Authorization Act for Fiscal Year 2014 (Public Law 113–66; 10 U.S.C. 2224 note).

(c) TECHNOLOGIES.—The technologies described in this sub-section include the following:

(1) Technology acquired, developed, and used by Combat Support Agencies of the Department of Defense to discover flaws and weaknesses in software code by inputting immense quantities of pseudo-random data (commonly referred to as "fuzz") to identify inputs that cause the software to fail or degrade.

(2) Cloud-based software fuzzing-as-a-service to continuously test the security of Department of Defense software repositories at large scale.

(3) Formal programming and protocol language for software code development and other methods and tools developed under various programs such as the High Assurance Cyber Military Systems program of the Defense Advanced Research Projects Agency.

(4) The binary analysis and symbolic execution software security tools developed under the Cyber Grand Challenge of the Defense Advanced Research Projects Agency.

(5) Any other advanced or immature technologies with respect to which the Department of Defense determines there is particular potential for application to the vulnerability assessment and remediation of the systems specified in subsection (a).

Subtitle D—Nuclear Forces
SEC. 1661. UNDER SECRETARY OF DEFENSE FOR RESEARCH AND ENGINEERING AND THE NUCLEAR WEAPONS COUNCIL.
Section 179(a) of title 10, United States Code, is amended—

(1) in paragraph (1), by striking ", Technology, and Logistics" and inserting "and Sustainment";

(2) by redesignating paragraphs (4) and (5) as paragraphs

(5) and (6), respectively; and

(3) by inserting after paragraph (3) the following new paragraph (4):
"(4) The Under Secretary of Defense for Research and Engineering.".

SEC. 1662. LONG-RANGE STANDOFF WEAPON REQUIREMENTS.
Subparagraphs (A) and (B) of section 217(a)(1) of the National Defense Authorization Act for Fiscal Year 2014 (Public Law 113– 66; 127 Stat. 706) are amended to read as follows:

Foreign Investment Risk Review Modernization Act of 2018

(Pub. L. 115-232, §§1701, et. seq.)

TITLE XVII—REVIEW OF FOREIGN INVESTMENT AND EXPORT CONTROLS

Subtitle A—Committee on Foreign Investment in the United States

SEC. 1701. SHORT TITLE: FOREIGN INVESTMENT RISK REVIEW MODERNIZATION ACT OF 2018.

This subtitle may be cited as the "Foreign Investment Risk Review Modernization Act of 2018".

SEC. 1702. FINDINGS; SENSE OF CONGRESS.

(a) FINDINGS.—Congress makes the following findings:

(1) According to a February 2016 report by the International Trade Administration of the Department of Commerce, 12,000,000 United States workers, equivalent to 8.5 percent of the labor force, have jobs resulting from foreign investment, including 3,500,000 jobs in the manufacturing sector alone.

(2) In 2016, new foreign direct investment in United States manufacturing totaled $129,400,000,000.

(3) The Bureau of Economic Analysis of the Department of Commerce concluded that, in 2015—

(A) foreign-owned affiliates in the United States—

(i) contributed $894,500,000,000 in value added to the United States economy;

(ii) exported goods valued at $352,800,000,000, accounting for nearly a quarter of total exports of goods from the United States; and

(iii) undertook $56,700,000,000 in research and development; and

(B) the 7 countries investing the most in the United States, all of which are United

States allies (the United Kingdom, Japan, Germany, France, Canada, Switzerland, and the Netherlands) accounted for 72.1 percent of the value added by foreign-owned affiliates in the United States and more than 80 percent of research and development expenditures by such entities.

(4) According to the Government Accountability Office, from 2011 to 2016, the number of transactions reviewed by the Committee on Foreign Investment in the United States (commonly referred to as "CFIUS") grew by 55 percent, while the staff of the Committees assigned to the reviews increased by 11 percent.

(5) According to a February 2018 report of the Government Accountability Office on the Committee on Foreign Investment in the United States (GAO–18–249): "Officials from Treasury and other member agencies are aware of pressures on their CFIUS staff given the current workload and have expressed concerns about possible workload increases.". The Government Accountability Office concluded: "Without attaining an understanding of the staffing levels needed to address the current and future CFIUS workload, particularly if legislative changes to CFIUS's authorities further expand its workload, CFIUS may be limited in its ability to fulfill its objectives and address threats to the national security of the United States.".

(6) On March 30, 1954, Dwight David Eisenhower—five-star general, Supreme Allied Commander, and 34th President of the United States—in his "Special Message to the Congress on Foreign Economic Policy", counseled: "Great mutual advantages to buyer and seller, to producer and consumer, to investor and to the community where investment is made, accrue from high levels of trade and investment.". President Eisenhower continued: "The internal strength of the American economy has evolved from such a system of mutual advantage. In the press of other problems and in the haste to meet emergencies, this nation—and many other nations of the free world—have all too often lost sight of this central fact.". President Eisenhower concluded: "If we fail in our trade policy, we may fail in all. Our domestic employment, our standard of living, our security, and the solidarity of the free world—all are involved.".

(b) SENSE OF CONGRESS.—It is the sense of Congress that—

(1) foreign investment provides substantial economic benefits to the United States, including the promotion of economic growth, productivity, competitiveness, and job creation, thereby enhancing national security;

(2) maintaining the commitment of the United States to an open investment policy encourages other countries to reciprocate and helps open new foreign markets for United States businesses;

(3) it should continue to be the policy of the United States to enthusiastically welcome and support foreign investment, consistent with the protection of national security;

(4) at the same time, the national security landscape has shifted in recent years, and so has the nature of the investments that pose the greatest potential risk to national security, which warrants an appropriate modernization of the processes and authorities of the Committee on Foreign Investment in the United States and of the United States export control system;

(5) the Committee on Foreign Investment in the United States plays a critical role in protecting the national security of the United States, and, therefore, it is essential that the member agencies of the Committee are adequately resourced and able to hire appropriately qualified individuals in a timely manner, and that those individuals' security clearances are processed as a high priority;

(6) the President should conduct a more robust international outreach effort to urge and help allies and partners of the United States to establish processes that are similar to

the Committee on Foreign Investment in the United States to screen foreign investments for national security risks and to facilitate coordination;

(7) the President should lead a collaborative effort with allies and partners of the United States to strengthen the multilateral export control regime;

(8) any penalties imposed by the United States Government with respect to an individual or entity pursuant to a determination that the individual or entity has violated sanctions imposed by the United States or the export control laws of the United States should not be reversed for reasons unrelated to the national security of the United States; and

(9) the Committee on Foreign Investment in the United States should continue to review transactions for the purpose of protecting national security and should not consider issues of national interest absent a national security nexus.

(c) SENSE OF CONGRESS ON CONSIDERATION OF COVERED TRANSACTIONS.—It is the sense of Congress that, when considering national security risks, the Committee on Foreign Investment in the United States may consider—

(1) whether a covered transaction involves a country of special concern that has a demonstrated or declared strategic goal of acquiring a type of critical technology or critical infrastructure that would affect United States leadership in areas related to national security;

(2) the potential national security-related effects of the cumulative control of, or pattern of recent transactions involving, any one type of critical infrastructure, energy asset, critical material, or critical technology by a foreign government or foreign person;

(3) whether any foreign person engaging in a covered transaction with a United States business has a history of complying with United States laws and regulations;

(4) the control of United States industries and commercial activity by foreign persons as it affects the capability and capacity of the United States to meet the requirements of national security, including the availability of human resources, products, technology, materials, and other supplies and services, and in considering "the availability of human resources", should construe that term to include potential losses of such availability resulting from reductions in the employment of United States persons whose knowledge or skills are critical to national security, including the continued production in the United States of items that are likely to be acquired by the Department of Defense or other Federal departments or agencies for the advancement of the national security of the United States;

(5) the extent to which a covered transaction is likely to expose, either directly or indirectly, personally identifiable information, genetic information, or other sensitive data of United States citizens to access by a foreign government or foreign person that may exploit that information in a manner that threatens national security; and

(6) whether a covered transaction is likely to have the effect of exacerbating or creating new cybersecurity vulnerabilities in the United States or is likely to result in a foreign government gaining a significant new capability to engage in malicious cyber-enabled activities against the United States, including such activities designed to affect the outcome of any election for Federal office.

SEC. 1703. DEFINITIONS.

Section 721(a) of the Defense Production Act of 1950 (50 U.S.C. 4565(a)) is amended to read as follows:

"(a) DEFINITIONS.—In this section:

"(1) CLARIFICATION.—The term 'national security' shall be construed so as to include those issues relating to 'homeland security', including its application to critical infrastructure.

"(2) COMMITTEE; CHAIRPERSON.—The terms 'Committee' and 'chairperson' mean the Committee on Foreign Investment in the United States and the chairperson thereof, respectively.

"(3) CONTROL.—The term 'control' means the power, direct or indirect, whether exercised or not exercised, to determine, direct, or decide important matters affecting an entity, subject to regulations prescribed by the Committee.

"(4) COVERED TRANSACTION.—

"(A) IN GENERAL.—Except as otherwise provided, the term 'covered transaction' means—

"(i) any transaction described in subparagraph (B)(i); and

"(ii) any transaction described in clauses (ii) through (v) of subparagraph (B) that is proposed, pending, or completed on or after the effective date set forth in section 1727 of the Foreign Investment Risk Review Modernization Act of 2018.

"(B) TRANSACTIONS DESCRIBED.—A transaction described in this subparagraph is any of the following:

"(i) Any merger, acquisition, or takeover that is proposed or pending after August 23, 1988, by or with any foreign person that could result in foreign control of any United States business, including such a merger, acquisition, or takeover carried out through a joint venture.

"(ii) Subject to subparagraphs (C) and (E), the purchase or lease by, or a concession to, a foreign person of private or public real estate that—

"(I) is located in the United States;

"(II)(aa) is, is located within, or will function as part of, an air or maritime port; or

"(bb)(AA) is in close proximity to a United States military installation or another facility or property of the United States Government that is sensitive for reasons relating to national security;

"(BB) could reasonably provide the foreign person the ability to collect intelligence on activities being conducted at such an installation, facility, or property; or

"(CC) could otherwise expose national security activities at such an installation, facility, or property to the risk of foreign surveillance; and

"(III) meets such other criteria as the Committee prescribes by regulation, except that such criteria may not expand the categories of real estate to which this clause applies beyond the categories described in subclause (II).

"(iii) Any other investment, subject to regulations prescribed under subparagraphs (D) and (E), by a foreign person in any unaffiliated United States business that—

"(I) owns, operates, manufactures, supplies, or services critical infrastructure;

"(II) produces, designs, tests, manufactures, fabricates, or develops one or more critical technologies; or

"(III) maintains or collects sensitive personal data of United States citizens that may be exploited in a manner that threatens national security.

"(iv) Any change in the rights that a foreign person has with respect to a United States business in which the foreign person has an investment, if that change could result in—

"(I) foreign control of the United States business; or

"(II) an investment described in clause (iii).

"(v) Any other transaction, transfer, agreement, or arrangement, the structure of which is designed or intended to evade or circumvent the application of this section, subject to regulations prescribed by the Committee.

"(C) REAL ESTATE TRANSACTIONS.—

"(i) EXCEPTION FOR CERTAIN REAL ESTATE TRANSACTIONS.—A real estate purchase, lease, or concession described in subparagraph (B)(ii) does not include a purchase, lease, or concession of—

"(I) a single 'housing unit', as defined by the Census Bureau; or

"(II) real estate in 'urbanized areas', as defined by the Census Bureau in the most recent census, except as otherwise prescribed by the Committee in regulations in consultation with the Secretary of Defense.

"(ii) DEFINITION OF CLOSE PROXIMITY.—With respect to a real estate purchase, lease, or concession described in subparagraph (B)(ii)(II)(bb)(AA), the Committee shall prescribe regulations to ensure that the term 'close proximity' refers only to a distance or distances within which the purchase, lease, or concession of real estate could pose a national security risk in connection with a United States military installation or another facility or property of the United States Government described in that subparagraph.

"(D) OTHER INVESTMENTS.—

"(i) OTHER INVESTMENT DEFINED.—For purposes of subparagraph (B)(iii), the term 'other investment' means an investment, direct or indirect, by a foreign person in a United States business described in that subparagraph that is not an investment described in subparagraph (B)(i) and that affords the foreign person—

"(I) access to any material nonpublic technical information in the possession of the United States business;

"(II) membership or observer rights on the board of directors or equivalent governing body of the United States business or the right to nominate an individual to a position on the board of directors or equivalent governing body; or

"(III) any involvement, other than through voting of shares, in substantive decision-making of the United States business regarding—

"(aa) the use, development, acquisition, safekeeping, or release of sensitive personal data of United States citizens maintained or collected by the United States business;

"(bb) the use, development acquisition, or release of critical technologies; or

"(cc) the management, operation, manufacture, or supply of critical infrastructure.

"(ii) MATERIAL NONPUBLIC TECHNICAL INFORMATION DEFINED.—

"(I) IN GENERAL.—For purposes of clause (i)(I), and subject to regulations prescribed by the Committee, the term 'material nonpublic technical information' means information that—

"(aa) provides knowledge, know-how, or understanding, not available in the public domain, of the design, location, or operation of critical infrastructure; or

"(bb) is not available in the public domain, and is necessary to design, fabricate, develop, test, produce, or manufacture critical technologies, including processes, techniques, or methods.

"(II) EXEMPTION FOR FINANCIAL INFORMATION.—Notwithstanding subclause (I), for purposes of this subparagraph, the term 'material nonpublic technical information' does not include financial information regarding the performance of a United States business.

"(iii) REGULATIONS.—

"(I) IN GENERAL.—The Committee shall prescribe regulations providing guidance on the types of transactions that the Committee considers to be 'other investment' for purposes of subparagraph (B)(iii).

"(II) UNITED STATES BUSINESSES THAT OWN, OPERATE, MANUFACTURE, SUPPLY, OR SERVICE CRITICAL INFRASTRUCTURE.—The regulations prescribed by the Committee with respect to an investment described in subparagraph (B)(iii)(I) shall—

"(aa) specify the critical infrastructure subject to that subparagraph based on criteria intended to limit application of that subparagraph to the subset of critical infrastructure that is likely to be of importance to the national security of the United States; and

"(bb) enumerate specific types and examples of such critical infrastructure.

"(iv) SPECIFIC CLARIFICATION FOR INVESTMENT FUNDS.—

"(I) TREATMENT OF CERTAIN INVESTMENT FUND INVESTMENTS.—Notwithstanding clause (i)(II) and subject to regulations prescribed by the Committee, an indirect investment by a foreign person in a United States business described in subparagraph (B)(iii) through an investment fund that affords the foreign person (or a designee of the foreign person) membership as a limited partner or equivalent on an advisory board or a committee of the fund shall not be considered an 'other investment' for purposes of subparagraph (B)(iii) if—

"(aa) the fund is managed exclusively by a general partner, a managing member, or an equivalent;

"(bb) the general partner, managing member, or equivalent is not a foreign person;

"(cc) the advisory board or committee does not have the ability to approve, disapprove, or otherwise control—

"(AA) investment decisions of the fund; or

"(BB) decisions made by the general partner, managing member, or equivalent related to entities in which the fund is invested;

"(dd) the foreign person does not otherwise have the ability to control the fund, including the authority—

"(AA) to approve, disapprove, or otherwise control investment decisions of the fund;

"(BB) to approve, disapprove, or otherwise control decisions made by the general partner, managing member, or equivalent related to entities in which the fund is invested; or

"(CC) to unilaterally dismiss, prevent the dismissal of, select, or determine the compensation of the general partner, managing member, or equivalent;

"(ee) the foreign person does not have access to material nonpublic technical information as a result of its participation on the advisory board or committee; and

"(ff) the investment otherwise meets the requirements of this subparagraph.

"(II) TREATMENT OF CERTAIN WAIVERS.—

"(aa) IN GENERAL.—For the purposes of items (cc) and (dd) of subclause (I) and except as provided in item (bb), a waiver of a potential conflict of interest, a waiver of an allocation limitation, or a similar activity, applicable to a transaction pursuant to the terms of an agreement governing an investment fund shall not be considered to constitute control of investment decisions of the fund or decisions relating to entities in which the fund is invested.

"(bb) EXCEPTION.—The Committee may prescribe regulations providing for exceptions to item (aa) for extraordinary circumstances.

"(v) EXCEPTION FOR AIR CARRIERS.—For purposes of subparagraph (B)(iii), the term 'other investment' does not include an investment involving an air carrier, as defined in section 40102(a)(2) of title 49, United States Code, that holds a certificate issued under section 41102 of that title.

"(vi) RULE OF CONSTRUCTION.—Any definition of 'critical infrastructure' established under any provision of law other than this section shall not be determinative for purposes of this section.

"(E) COUNTRY SPECIFICATION.—The Committee shall prescribe regulations that further define the term 'foreign person' for purposes of clauses (ii) and (iii) of subparagraph (B). In prescribing such regulations, the Committee shall specify criteria to limit the application of such clauses to the investments of certain categories of foreign persons. Such criteria shall take into consideration how a foreign person is connected to a foreign country or foreign government, and whether the connection may affect the national security of the United States.

"(F) TRANSFERS OF CERTAIN ASSETS PURSUANT TO BANKRUPTCY PROCEEDINGS OR OTHER DEFAULTS.—The Committee shall prescribe regulations to clarify that the term 'covered transaction' includes any transaction described in subparagraph (B) that arises pursuant to a bankruptcy proceeding or other form of default on debt.

"(5) CRITICAL INFRASTRUCTURE.—The term 'critical infrastructure' means, subject to regulations prescribed by the Committee, systems and assets, whether physical or virtual, so vital to the United States that the incapacity or destruction of such systems or assets would have a debilitating impact on national security.

"(6) CRITICAL TECHNOLOGIES.—

"(A) IN GENERAL.—The term 'critical technologies' means the following:

"(i) Defense articles or defense services included on the United States Munitions List set forth in the International Traffic in Arms Regulations under subchapter M of chapter I of title 22, Code of Federal Regulations.

"(ii) Items included on the Commerce Control List set forth in Supplement No. 1 to part 774 of the Export Administration Regulations under subchapter C of chapter VII of title 15, Code of Federal Regulations, and controlled—

"(I) pursuant to multilateral regimes, including for reasons relating to national security, chemical and biological weapons proliferation, nuclear nonproliferation, or missile technology; or

"(II) for reasons relating to regional stability or surreptitious listening.

"(iii) Specially designed and prepared nuclear equipment, parts and components, materials, software, and technology covered by part 810 of title 10, Code of Federal Regulations (relating to assistance to foreign atomic energy activities).

"(iv) Nuclear facilities, equipment, and material covered by part 110 of title 10, Code of Federal Regulations (relating to export and import of nuclear equipment and material).

"(v) Select agents and toxins covered by part 331 of title 7, Code of Federal Regulations, part 121 of title 9 of such Code, or part 73 of title 42 of such Code.

"(vi) Emerging and foundational technologies controlled pursuant to section 1758 of the Export Control Reform Act of 2018.

"(B) RECOMMENDATIONS.—

"(i) IN GENERAL.—The chairperson may recommend technologies for identification under the interagency process set forth in section 1758(a) of the Export Control Reform Act of 2018.

"(ii) MATTERS INFORMING RECOMMENDATIONS.— Recommendations by the chairperson under clause (i) shall draw upon information arising from reviews and investigations conducted under subsection (b), notices submitted under subsection (b)(1)(C)(i), declarations filed under subsection (b)(1)(C)(v), and non-notified and non-declared transactions identified under subsection (b)(1)(H).

"(7) FOREIGN GOVERNMENT-CONTROLLED TRANSACTION.— The term 'foreign government-controlled transaction' means any covered transaction that could result in the control of any United States business by a foreign government or an entity controlled by or acting on behalf of a foreign government.

"(8) INTELLIGENCE COMMUNITY.—The term 'intelligence community' has the meaning given that term in section 3(4) of the National Security Act of 1947 (50 U.S.C. 3003(4)).

"(9) INVESTMENT.—The term 'investment' means the acquisition of equity interest, including contingent equity interest, as further defined in regulations prescribed by the Committee.

"(10) LEAD AGENCY.—The term 'lead agency' means the agency or agencies designated as the lead agency or agencies pursuant to subsection (k)(5).

"(11) PARTY.—The term 'party' has the meaning given that term in regulations prescribed by the Committee.

"(12) UNITED STATES.—The term 'United States' means the several States, the District of Columbia, and any territory or possession of the United States.

"(13) UNITED STATES BUSINESS.—The term 'United States business' means a person engaged in interstate commerce in the United States.".

SEC. 1704. ACCEPTANCE OF WRITTEN NOTICES.

Section 721(b)(1)(C)(i) of the Defense Production Act of 1950 (50 U.S.C. 4565(b)(1)(C)(i)) is amended—

(1) by striking "Any party" and inserting the following:

"(I) IN GENERAL.—Any party"; and

(2) by adding at the end the following:

"(II) COMMENTS AND ACCEPTANCE.—

"(aa) IN GENERAL.—Subject to item (cc), the Committee shall provide comments on a draft or formal written notice or accept a formal written notice submitted under sub-clause (I) with respect to a covered transaction not later than the date that is 10 business days after the date of submission of the draft or formal written notice.

"(bb) COMPLETENESS.—If the Committee determines that a draft or formal written notice described in item (aa) is not complete, the Committee shall notify the party or parties to the transaction in writing that the notice is not complete and provide an explanation of all material respects in which the notice is incomplete.

"(cc) STIPULATIONS REQUIRED.—The timing requirement under item (aa) shall apply only in a case in which the parties stipulate under clause (vi) that the transaction is a covered transaction.".

SEC. 1705. INCLUSION OF PARTNERSHIP AND SIDE AGREEMENTS IN NOTICE.

Section 721(b)(1)(C) of the Defense Production Act of 1950
(50 U.S.C. 4565(b)(1)(C)) is amended by adding at the end the following:

"(iv) INCLUSION OF PARTNERSHIP AND SIDE AGREE-MENTS.—The Committee may require a written notice submitted under clause (i) to include a copy of any partnership agreements, integration agreements, or other side agreements relating to the transaction, as specified in regulations prescribed by the Committee.".

SEC. 1706. DECLARATIONS FOR CERTAIN COVERED TRANSACTIONS.

Section 721(b)(1)(C) of the Defense Production Act of 1950 (50 U.S.C. 4565(b)(1)(C)), as amended by section 1705, is further amended by adding at the end the following:

"(v) DECLARATIONS FOR CERTAIN COVERED TRANSACTIONS.—

"(I) IN GENERAL.—A party to any covered transaction may submit to the Committee a declaration with basic information regarding the transaction instead of a written notice under clause (i).

"(II) REGULATIONS.—The Committee shall prescribe regulations establishing requirements for declarations submitted under this clause. In prescribing such regulations, the Committee shall ensure that such declarations are submitted as abbreviated notifications that would not generally exceed 5 pages in length.

"(III) COMMITTEE RESPONSE TO DECLARATION.—

"(aa) IN GENERAL.—Upon receiving a declaration under this clause with respect to a covered transaction, the Committee may, at the discretion of the Committee—

"(AA) request that the parties to the transaction file a written notice under clause (i);

"(BB) inform the parties to the transaction that the Committee is not able to complete action under this section with respect to the transaction on the basis of the declaration and that the parties may file a written notice under clause (i) to seek written notification from the Committee that the Committee has completed all action under this section with respect to the transaction;

"(CC) initiate a unilateral review of the transaction under subparagraph (D); or

"(DD) notify the parties in writing that the Committee has completed all action under this section with respect to the transaction.

"(bb) TIMING.—The Committee shall take action under item (aa) not later than 30 days after receiving a declaration under this clause.

"(cc) RULE OF CONSTRUCTION.—Nothing in this subclause (other than item (aa)(CC)) shall be construed to affect the authority of the President or the

Committee to take any action authorized by this section with respect to a covered transaction.

"(IV) MANDATORY DECLARATIONS.—

"(aa) REGULATIONS.—The Committee shall prescribe regulations specifying the types of covered transactions for which the Committee requires a declaration under this subclause.

"(bb) CERTAIN COVERED TRANSACTIONS WITH FOREIGN GOVERNMENT INTERESTS.—

"(AA) IN GENERAL.—Except as provided in subitem (BB), the parties to a covered transaction shall submit a declaration described in subclause (I) with respect to the transaction if the transaction involves an investment that results in the acquisition, directly or indirectly, of a substantial interest in a United States business described in subsection (a)(4)(B)(iii) by a foreign person in which a foreign government has, directly or indirectly, a substantial interest.

"(BB) SUBSTANTIAL INTEREST DEFINED.—In this item, the term 'substantial interest' has the meaning given that term in regulations which the Committee shall prescribe. In developing those regulations, the Committee shall consider the means by which a foreign government could influence the actions of a foreign person, including through board membership, ownership interest, or shareholder rights. An interest that is excluded under subparagraph (D) of subsection (a)(4) from the term 'other investment' as used in subparagraph (B)(iii) of that subsection or that is less than a 10 percent voting interest shall not be considered a substantial interest.

"(CC) WAIVER.—The Committee may waive, with respect to a foreign person, the requirement under subitem (AA) for the submission of a declaration described in subclause (I) if the Committee determines that the foreign person demonstrates that the investments of the foreign person are not directed by a foreign government and the foreign person has a history of cooperation with the Committee.

"(cc) OTHER DECLARATIONS REQUIRED BY COMMITTEE.—The Committee may require the submission of a declaration described in sub-clause (I) with respect to any covered transaction identified under regulations prescribed by the Committee for purposes of this item, at the discretion of the Committee, that involves a United States business described in subsection (a)(4)(B)(iii)(II).

"(dd) EXCEPTION.—The submission of a declaration described in subclause (I) shall not be required pursuant to this subclause with respect to an investment by an investment fund if—

"(AA) the fund is managed exclusively by a general partner, a managing member, or an equivalent;

"(BB) the general partner, managing member, or equivalent is not a foreign person; and

"(CC) the investment fund satisfies, with respect to any foreign person with membership as a limited partner on an advisory board or a committee of the fund, the criteria specified in items (cc) and (dd) of subsection (a)(4)(D)(iv).

"(ee) SUBMISSION OF WRITTEN NOTICE AS AN ALTERNATIVE.—Parties to a covered transaction for which a declaration is required under this subclause may instead elect to submit a written notice under clause (i).

"(ff) TIMING AND REFILING OF SUBMISSION.—

"(AA) IN GENERAL.—In the regulations prescribed under item (aa), the Committee may not require a declaration to be submitted under this sub-clause with respect to a covered transaction more than 45 days before the completion of the transaction.

"(BB) REFILING OF DECLARATION.— The Committee may not re-quest or recommend that a declaration submitted under this subclause be withdrawn and refiled, except to permit parties to a covered transaction to correct material errors or omissions in the declaration submitted with respect to that transaction.

"(gg) PENALTIES.—The Committee may impose a penalty pursuant to sub-section (h)(3) with respect to a party that fails to comply with this subclause.".

SEC. 1707. STIPULATIONS REGARDING TRANSACTIONS. Section 721(b)(1)(C) of the Defense Production Act of 1950 (50 U.S.C. 4565(b)(1)(C)), as amended by section 1706, is further amended by adding at the end the following:

"(vi) STIPULATIONS REGARDING TRANSACTIONS.—

"(I) IN GENERAL.—In a written notice submitted under clause (i) or a declara-tion submitted under clause (v) with respect to a transaction, a party to the transaction may—

"(aa) stipulate that the transaction is a covered transaction; and

"(bb) if the party stipulates that the transaction is a covered transaction under item (aa), stipulate that the transaction is a foreign government-controlled transaction.

"(II) BASIS FOR STIPULATION.—A written notice submitted under clause (i) or a declaration submitted under clause (v) that includes a stipulation under subclause (I) shall include a description of the basis for the stipulation.".

SEC. 1708. AUTHORITY FOR UNILATERAL INITIATION OF REVIEWS.

Section 721(b)(1) of the Defense Production Act of 1950 (50 U.S.C. 4565(b)(1)) is amended—

(1) by redesignating subparagraphs (E) and (F) as sub-paragraphs (F) and (G), respec-tively;

(2) in subparagraph (D)—

(A) in the matter preceding clause (i), by striking "subparagraph (F)" and insert-ing "subparagraph (G)";

(B) in clause (i), by inserting

"(other than a covered transaction described in subparagraph (E))" after "any covered transaction";

(C) by striking clause (ii) and inserting the following:

"(ii) any covered transaction described in subparagraph (E), if any party to the transaction submitted false or misleading material information to the Com-mittee in connection with the Committee's consideration of the transaction or omitted material information, including material documents, from information submitted to the Committee; or"; and

(D) in clause (iii)—

(i) in the matter preceding subclause (I), by striking "any covered transaction that has previously been reviewed or investigated under this section," and insert-ing "any covered transaction described in subparagraph (E),";

(ii) in subclause (I), by striking "intentionally";

(iii) in subclause (II), by striking "an intentional" and inserting "a"; and

(iv) in subclause (III), by inserting "adequate and appropriate" before "remedies or enforcement tools"; and

(3) by inserting after subparagraph (D) the following:

"(E) COVERED TRANSACTIONS DESCRIBED.—A covered transaction is described in this subparagraph if—

"(i) the Committee has informed the parties to the transaction in writing that the Committee has completed all action under this section with respect to the transaction; or

"(ii) the President has announced a decision not to exercise the President's authority under subsection (d) with respect to the transaction.".

SEC. 1709. TIMING FOR REVIEWS AND INVESTIGATIONS.

Section 721(b) of the Defense Production Act of 1950 (50 U.S.C. 4565(b)), as amended by section 1708, is further amended—

(1) in paragraph (1)(F), by striking "30" and inserting "45";

(2) in paragraph (2), by striking subparagraph (C) and inserting the following:

"(C) TIMING.—

"(i) IN GENERAL.—Except as provided in clause (ii), any investigation under subparagraph (A) shall be completed before the end of the 45-day period beginning on the date on which the investigation commenced.

"(ii) EXTENSION FOR EXTRAORDINARY CIRCUMSTANCES.—

"(I) IN GENERAL.—In extraordinary circumstances (as defined by the Committee in regulations), the chairperson may, at the request of the head of the lead agency, extend an investigation under subparagraph (A) for one 15-day period.

"(II) NONDELEGATION.—The authority of the chairperson and the head of the lead agency referred to in subclause (I) may not be delegated to any person other than the Deputy Secretary of the Treasury or the deputy head (or equivalent thereof) of the lead agency, as the case may be.

"(III) NOTIFICATION TO PARTIES.—If the Committee extends the deadline under subclause (I) with respect to a covered transaction, the Committee shall notify the parties to the transaction of the extension."; and

(3) by adding at the end the following:

"(8) TOLLING OF DEADLINES DURING LAPSE IN APPROPRIA-TIONS.—Any deadline or time limitation under this subsection shall be tolled during a lapse in appropriations.".

SEC. 1710. IDENTIFICATION OF NON-NOTIFIED AND NON-DECLARED TRANSACTIONS.

Section 721(b)(1) of the Defense Production Act of 1950 (50 U.S.C. 4565(b)(1)), as amended by sections 1708 and 1709, is fu amended by adding at the end the following:

"(H) IDENTIFICATION OF NON-NOTIFIED AND NON-DECLARED TRANS-ACTIONS.—The Committee shall establish a process to identify covered transactions for which—

"(i) a notice under clause (i) of subparagraph (C) or a declaration under clause (v) of that subparagraph is not submitted to the Committee; and

"(ii) information is reasonably available.".

SEC. 1711. SUBMISSION OF CERTIFICATIONS TO CONGRESS.
Section 721(b)(3)(C) of the Defense Production Act of 1950 (50 U.S.C. 4565(b)(3)(C)) is amended—

(1) in clause (i), by striking subclause (II) and inserting the following:

"(II) a certification that all relevant national security factors have received full consideration.";

(2) in clause (iv), by striking subclause (II) and inserting the following:

"(II) DELEGATION OF CERTIFICATIONS.—

"(aa) IN GENERAL.—Subject to item (bb), the chairperson, in consultation with the Committee, may determine the level of official to whom the signature requirement under sub-clause (I) for the chairperson and the head of the lead agency may be delegated. The level of official to whom the signature requirement may be delegated may differ based on any factor relating to a transaction that the chairperson, in consultation with the Committee, deems appropriate, including the type or value of the transaction.

"(bb) LIMITATION ON DELEGATION WITH RESPECT TO CERTAIN TRANSACTIONS.—The signature requirement under subclause (I) may be delegated not below the level of the Assistant Secretary of the Treasury or an equivalent official of the lead agency."; and

(3) by adding at the end the following:

"(v) AUTHORITY TO CONSOLIDATE DOCUMENTS.— Instead of transmitting a separate certified notice or certified report under subparagraph (A) or (B) with respect to each covered transaction, the Committee may, on a monthly basis, transmit such notices and reports in a consolidated document to the Members of Congress specified in clause (iii).".

SEC. 1712. ANALYSIS BY DIRECTOR OF NATIONAL INTELLIGENCE.
Section 721(b)(4) of the Defense Production Act of 1950 (50 U.S.C. 4565(b)(4)) is amended—

(1) by striking subparagraph (A) and inserting the following:

"(A) ANALYSIS REQUIRED.—

"(i) IN GENERAL.—Except as provided in subparagraph (B), the Director of National Intelligence shall expeditiously carry out a thorough analysis of any threat to the national security of the United States posed by any covered transaction, which shall include the identification of any recognized gaps in the collection of intelligence relevant to the analysis.

"(ii) VIEWS OF INTELLIGENCE COMMUNITY.—The Director shall seek and incorporate into the analysis required by clause (i) the views of all affected or appropriate agencies of the intelligence community with respect to the transaction.

"(iii) UPDATES.—At the request of the lead agency, the Director shall update the analysis conducted under clause (i) with respect to a covered transaction with respect to which an agreement was entered into under subsection (l)(3)(A).

"(iv) INDEPENDENCE AND OBJECTIVITY.—The Committee shall ensure that its processes under this section preserve the ability of the Director to conduct analysis under clause (i) that is independent, objective, and consistent with all applicable directives, policies, and analytic tradecraft standards of the intelligence community.";

(2) by redesignating subparagraphs (B), (C), and (D) as subparagraphs (C), (D), and

(E), respectively;

(3) by inserting after subparagraph (A) the following:

"(B) BASIC THREAT INFORMATION.—

"(i) IN GENERAL.—The Director of National Intelligence may provide the Committee with basic information regarding any threat to the national security of the United States posed by a covered transaction described in clause (ii) instead of conducting the analysis required by subparagraph (A).

"(ii) COVERED TRANSACTION DESCRIBED.—A covered transaction is described in this clause if—

"(I) the transaction is described in subsection (a)(4)(B)(ii);

"(II) the Director of National Intelligence has completed an analysis pursuant to subparagraph (A) involving each foreign person that is a party to the transaction during the 12 months preceding the review or investigation of the transaction under this section; or

"(III) the transaction otherwise meets criteria agreed upon by the Committee and the Director for purposes of this subparagraph.";

(4) in subparagraph (C), as redesignated by paragraph (2), by striking "20" and inserting "30"; and

(5) by adding at the end the following:

"(F) ASSESSMENT OF OPERATIONAL IMPACT.—The Director may provide to the Committee an assessment, separate from the analyses under subparagraphs (A) and (B), of any operational impact of a covered transaction on the intelligence community and a description of any actions that have been or will be taken to mitigate any such impact.

"(G) SUBMISSION TO CONGRESS.—The Committee shall submit the analysis required by subparagraph (A) with respect to a covered transaction to the Select Committee on Intelligence of the Senate and the Permanent Select Committee on Intelligence of the House of Representatives upon the conclusion of action under this section (other than compliance plans under subsection (l)(6)) with respect to the transaction.".

SEC. 1713. INFORMATION SHARING.

Section 721(c) of the Defense Production Act of 1950 (50 U.S.C. 4565(c)) is amended—

(1) by striking "Any information" and inserting the following:

"(1) IN GENERAL.—Except as provided in paragraph (2), any information";

(2) by striking ", except as may be relevant" and all that follows and inserting a period; and

(3) by adding at the end the following:

"(2) EXCEPTIONS.—Paragraph (1) shall not prohibit the disclosure of the following:

"(A) Information relevant to any administrative or judicial action or proceeding.

"(B) Information to Congress or any duly authorized committee or subcommittee of Congress.

"(C) Information important to the national security analysis or actions of the Committee to any domestic governmental entity, or to any foreign governmental entity of a United States ally or partner, under the exclusive direction and authorization of the chairperson, only to the extent necessary for national security purposes, and subject to appropriate confidentiality and classification requirements.

"(D) Information that the parties have consented to be disclosed to third parties.

"(3) COOPERATION WITH ALLIES AND PARTNERS.—

"(A) IN GENERAL.—The chairperson, in consultation with other members of the Committee, should establish a formal process for the exchange of information under paragraph (2)(C) with governments of countries that are allies or partners of the United States, in the discretion of the chairperson, to protect the national security of the United States and those countries.

"(B) REQUIREMENTS.—The process established under subparagraph (A) should, in the discretion of the chairperson—

"(i) be designed to facilitate the harmonization of action with respect to trends in investment and technology that could pose risks to the national security of the United States and countries that are allies or partners of the United States;

"(ii) provide for the sharing of information with respect to specific technologies and entities acquiring such technologies as appropriate to ensure national security; and

"(iii) include consultations and meetings with representatives of the governments of such countries on a recurring basis.".

SEC. 1714. ACTION BY THE PRESIDENT.

Section 721(d)(2) of the Defense Production Act of 1950 (50 U.S.C. 4565(d)(2)) is amended by striking "not later than 15 days" and all that follows and inserting the following: "with respect to a covered transaction not later than 15 days after the earlier of—

"(A) the date on which the investigation of the transaction under subsection (b) is completed; or

"(B) the date on which the Committee otherwise refers the transaction to the President under subsection (l)(2).".

SEC. 1715. JUDICIAL REVIEW.

Section 721(e) of the Defense Production Act of 1950 (50 U.S.C. 4565(e)) is amended—

(1) by striking "The actions" and inserting the following:

"(1) IN GENERAL.—The actions"; and

(2) by adding at the end the following:

"(2) CIVIL ACTIONS.—A civil action challenging an action or finding under this section may be brought only in the United States Court of Appeals for the District of Columbia Circuit.

"(3) PROCEDURES FOR REVIEW OF PRIVILEGED INFORMA-TION.—If a civil action challenging an action or finding under this section is brought, and the court determines that protected information in the administrative record, including classified or other information subject to privilege or protections under any provision of law, is necessary to resolve the challenge, that information shall be submitted ex parte and in camera to the court and the court shall maintain that information under seal.

"(4) APPLICABILITY OF USE OF INFORMATION PROVISIONS.— The use of information provisions of sections 106, 305, 405, and 706 of the Foreign Intelligence Surveillance Act of 1978 (50 U.S.C. 1806, 1825, 1845, and 1881e) shall not apply in a civil action brought under this subsection.".

SEC. 1716. CONSIDERATIONS FOR REGULATIONS.
Section 721(h) of the Defense Production Act of 1950 (50 U.S.C. 4565(h)) is amended—
    (1) by striking paragraph (2);
    (2) by redesignating paragraph (3) as paragraph (2); and
    (3) in paragraph (2), as redesignated—
        (A) in subparagraph (A), by striking "including any mitigation" and all that follows through "subsection (l)" and inserting "including any mitigation agreement entered into, conditions imposed, or order issued pursuant to this section";
        (B) in subparagraph (B)(ii), by striking "and" at the end;
        (C) in subparagraph (C), by striking the period at the end and inserting "; and"; and
        (D) by adding at the end the following:
        "(D) provide that, in any review or investigation of a covered transaction conducted by the Committee under subsection (b), the Committee should—
            "(i) consider the factors specified in subsection (f); and
            "(ii) as appropriate, require parties to provide to the Committee the information necessary to consider such factors.".

SEC. 1717. MEMBERSHIP AND STAFF OF COMMITTEE.
(a) HIRING AUTHORITY.—Section 721(k) of the Defense Production Act of 1950 (50 U.S.C. 4565(k)) is amended by striking paragraph (4) and inserting the following:
    "(4) HIRING AUTHORITY.—
        "(A) SENIOR OFFICIALS.—
            "(i) IN GENERAL.—Each member of the Committee shall designate an Assistant Secretary, or an equivalent official, who is appointed by the President, by and with the advice and consent of the Senate, to carry out such duties related to the Committee as the member of the Committee may delegate.
            "(ii) DEPARTMENT OF THE TREASURY.—
                "(I) IN GENERAL.—There shall be established in the Office of International Affairs at the Department of the Treasury 2 additional positions of Assistant Secretary of the Treasury, who shall be appointed by the President, by and with the advice and consent of the Senate, to carry out such duties related to the Committee as the Secretary of the Treasury may delegate, consistent with this section.
                "(II) ASSISTANT SECRETARY FOR INVESTMENT SECURITY.—One of the positions of Assistant Secretary of the Treasury authorized under subclause (I) shall be the Assistant Secretary for Investment Security, whose duties shall be principally related to the Committee, as delegated by the Secretary of the Treasury under this section.
        "(B) SPECIAL HIRING AUTHORITY.—The heads of the departments and agencies represented on the Committee may appoint, without regard to the provisions of sections 3309 through 3318 of title 5, United States Code, candidates directly to positions in the competitive service (as defined in section 2102 of that title) in their respective departments and agencies. The primary responsibility of positions authorized under the preceding sentence shall be to administer this section.".
(b) PROCEDURES FOR RECUSAL OF MEMBERS OF COMMITTEE FOR CONFLICTS OF INTEREST.—Not later than 90 days after the date of the enactment of this Act, the Committee on Foreign Investment in the United States shall—
    (1) establish procedures for the recusal of any member of the Committee that has a conflict of interest with respect to a covered transaction (as defined in section 721(a) of the Defense Production Act of 1950, as amended by section 1703);

(2) submit to the Committee on Banking, Housing, and Urban Affairs of the Senate and the Committee on Financial Services of the House of Representatives a report describing those procedures; and

(3) brief the committees specified in paragraph (1) on the report required by paragraph (2).

SEC. 1718. ACTIONS BY THE COMMITTEE TO ADDRESS NATIONAL SECURITY RISKS.

Section 721(l) of the Defense Production Act of 1950 (50 U.S.C. 4565(l)) is amended—

(1) in the subsection heading, by striking "MITIGATION, TRACKING, AND POSTCONSUMMATION MONITORING AND ENFORCEMENT" and inserting "ACTIONS BY THE COMMITTEE TO ADDRESS NATIONAL SECURITY RISKS";

(2) by redesignating paragraphs (1), (2), and (3) as paragraphs (3), (5), and (6), respectively;

(3) by inserting before paragraph (3), as redesignated by paragraph (2), the following:

"(1) SUSPENSION OF TRANSACTIONS.—The Committee, acting through the chairperson, may suspend a proposed or pending covered transaction that may pose a risk to the national security of the United States for such time as the covered transaction is under review or investigation under subsection (b).

"(2) REFERRAL TO PRESIDENT.—The Committee may, at any time during the review or investigation of a covered transaction under subsection (b), complete the action of the Committee with respect to the transaction and refer the transaction to the President for action pursuant to subsection (d).";

(4) in paragraph (3), as redesignated by paragraph (2)—

(A) in subparagraph (A)—

(i) in the subparagraph heading, by striking "IN GENERAL" and inserting "AGREEMENTS AND CONDITIONS";

(ii) by striking "The Committee" and inserting the following:

"(i) IN GENERAL.—The Committee";

(iii) by striking "threat" and inserting "risk"; and

(iv) by adding at the end the following:

"(ii) ABANDONMENT OF TRANSACTIONS.—If a party to a covered transaction has voluntarily chosen to abandon the transaction, the Committee or lead agency, as the case may be, may negotiate, enter into or impose, and enforce any agreement or condition with any party to the covered transaction for purposes of effectuating such abandonment and mitigating any risk to the national security of the United States that arises as a result of the covered transaction.

"(iii) AGREEMENTS AND CONDITIONS RELATING TO COMPLETED TRANSACTIONS.—The Committee or lead agency, as the case may be, may negotiate, enter into or impose, and enforce any agreement or condition with any party to a completed covered transaction in order to mitigate any interim risk to the national security of the United States that may arise as a result of the covered transaction until such time that the Committee has completed action pursuant to subsection (b) or the President has taken action pursuant to subsection (d) with respect to the transaction."; and

(B) by striking subparagraph (B) and inserting the following:

"(B) TREATMENT OF OUTDATED AGREEMENTS OR CONDI-TIONS.— The chairperson and the head of the lead agency shall periodically review the appropriateness of an agreement or condition imposed under subparagraph (A) and terminate, phase out, or otherwise amend the agreement or condition if a threat no longer requires mitigation through the agreement or condition.

"(C) LIMITATIONS.—An agreement may not be entered into or condition imposed under subparagraph (A) with respect to a covered transaction unless the Committee determines that the agreement or condition resolves the national security concerns posed by the transaction, taking into consideration whether the agreement or condition is reasonably calculated to—

"(i) be effective;

"(ii) allow for compliance with the terms of the agreement or condition in an appropriately verifiable way; and

"(iii) enable effective monitoring of compliance with and enforcement of the terms of the agreement or condition.

"(D) JURISDICTION.—The provisions of section 706(b) shall apply to any mitigation agreement entered into or condition imposed under subparagraph (A).";

(5) by inserting after paragraph (3), as redesignated by paragraph (2), the following:

"(4) RISK-BASED ANALYSIS REQUIRED.—

"(A) IN GENERAL.—Any determination of the Committee to suspend a covered transaction under paragraph (1), to refer a covered transaction to the President under paragraph (2), or to negotiate, enter into or impose, or enforce any agreement or condition under paragraph (3)(A) with respect to a covered transaction, shall be based on a risk-based analysis, conducted by the Committee, of the effects on the national security of the United States of the covered transaction, which shall include an assessment of the threat, vulnerabilities, and consequences to national security related to the transaction.

"(B) ACTIONS OF MEMBERS OF THE COMMITTEE.—

"(i) IN GENERAL.—Any member of the Committee who concludes that a covered transaction poses an unresolved national security concern shall recommend to the Committee that the Committee suspend the transaction under paragraph (1), refer the transaction to the President under paragraph (2), or negotiate, enter into or impose, or enforce any agreement or condition under paragraph (3)(A) with respect to the transaction. In making that recommendation, the member shall propose or contribute to the risk-based analysis required by subparagraph (A).

"(ii) FAILURE TO REACH CONSENSUS.—If the Committee fails to reach consensus with respect to a recommendation under clause (i) regarding a covered transaction, the members of the Committee who support an alternative recommendation shall produce—

"(I) a written statement justifying the alternative recommendation; and

"(II) as appropriate, a risk-based analysis that supports the alternative recommendation.

"(C) DEFINITIONS.—For purposes of subparagraph (A), the terms 'threat', 'vulnerabilities', and 'consequences to national security' shall have the meanings given those terms by the Committee by regulation.";

(6) in paragraph (5)(B), as redesignated by paragraph (2), by striking "(as defined in the National Security Act of 1947)"; and

(7) in paragraph (6), as redesignated by paragraph (2)—

(A) in subparagraph (A)—

(i) by striking "paragraph (1)" and inserting "paragraph (3)"; and

(ii) by striking the second sentence and inserting the following: "The lead agency may, at its discretion, seek and receive the assistance of other departments or agencies in carrying out the purposes of this paragraph.";

(B) in subparagraph (B)—

(i) by striking "DESIGNATED AGENCY" and all that follows through "The lead agency in connection" and inserting "DESIGNATED AGENCY.—The lead agency in connection";

(ii) by striking clause (ii); and

(iii) by redesignating subclauses (I) and (II) as clauses (i) and (ii), respectively, and by moving such clauses, as so redesignated, 2 ems to the left; and

(C) by adding at the end the following:

"(C) COMPLIANCE PLANS.—

"(i) IN GENERAL.—In the case of a covered transaction with respect to which an agreement is entered into under paragraph (3)(A), the Committee or lead agency, as the case may be, shall formulate, adhere to, and keep updated a plan for monitoring compliance with the agreement.

"(ii) ELEMENTS.—Each plan required by clause (i) with respect to an agreement entered into under paragraph (3)(A) shall include an explanation of—

"(I) which member of the Committee will have primary responsibility for monitoring compliance with the agreement;

"(II) how compliance with the agreement will be monitored;

"(III) how frequently compliance reviews will be conducted;

"(IV) whether an independent entity will be utilized under subparagraph (E) to conduct compliance reviews; and

"(V) what actions will be taken if the parties fail to cooperate regarding monitoring compliance with the agreement.

"(D) EFFECT OF LACK OF COMPLIANCE.—If, at any time after a mitigation agreement or condition is entered into or imposed under paragraph (3)(A), the Committee or lead agency, as the case may be, determines that a party or parties to the agreement or condition are not in compliance with the terms of the agreement or condition, the Committee or lead agency may, in addition to the authority of the Committee to impose penalties pursuant to subsection (h)(3) and to unilaterally initiate a review of any covered transaction under subsection (b)(1)(D)(iii)—

"(i) negotiate a plan of action for the party or parties to remediate the lack of compliance, with failure to abide by the plan or otherwise remediate the lack of compliance serving as the basis for the Committee to find a material breach of the agreement or condition;

"(ii) require that the party or parties submit a written notice under clause (i) of subsection (b)(1)(C) or a declaration under clause (v) of that subsection with respect to a covered transaction initiated after the date of the determination of noncompliance and before the date that is 5 years after the date of the determination to the Committee to initiate a review of the transaction under subsection (b); or

"(iii) seek injunctive relief.

"(E) USE OF INDEPENDENT ENTITIES TO MONITOR COMPLIANCE.— If the parties to an agreement entered into under paragraph (3)(A) enter into a contract with an independent entity from outside the United States Government for the purpose of monitoring compliance with the agreement, the Committee shall take such action as is necessary to prevent a conflict of interest from arising by ensuring that the independent entity owes no fiduciary duty to the parties.

"(F) SUCCESSORS AND ASSIGNS.—Any agreement or condition entered into or imposed under paragraph (3)(A) shall be considered binding on all successors and assigns unless and until the agreement or condition terminates on its own terms or is otherwise terminated by the Committee in its sole discretion.

"(G) ADDITIONAL COMPLIANCE MEASURES.—Subject to subparagraphs (A) through (F), the Committee shall develop and agree upon methods for evaluating compliance with any agreement entered into or condition imposed with respect to a covered transaction that will allow the Committee to adequately ensure compliance without unnecessarily diverting Committee resources from assessing any new covered transaction for which a written notice under clause (i) of subsection (b)(1)(C) or declaration under clause (i) of that subsection has been filed, and if necessary, reaching a mitigation agreement with or imposing a condition on a party to such covered transaction or any covered transaction for which a review has been reopened for any reason.".

SEC. 1719. MODIFICATION OF ANNUAL REPORT AND OTHER REPORTING REQUIREMENTS.

(a) MODIFICATION OF ANNUAL REPORT.—Section 721(m) of the Defense Production Act of 1950 (50 U.S.C. 4565(m)) is amended—

(1) in paragraph (2)—

(A) by amending subparagraph (A) to read as follows:

"(A) A list of all notices filed and all reviews or investigations of covered transactions completed during the period, with—

"(i) a description of the outcome of each review or investigation, including whether an agreement was entered into or condition was imposed under subsection (l)(3)(A) with respect to the transaction being reviewed or investigated, and whether the President took any action under this section with respect to that transaction;

"(ii) basic information on each party to each such transaction;

"(iii) the nature of the business activities or products of the United States business with which the transaction was entered into or intended to be entered into; and

"(iv) information about any withdrawal from the process."; and

(B) by adding at the end the following:

"(G) Statistics on compliance plans conducted and actions taken by the Committee under subsection (l)(6), including subparagraph (D) of that subsection, during that period, a general assessment of the compliance of parties with agreements entered into and conditions imposed under subsection (l)(3)(A) that are in effect during that period, including a description of any actions taken by the Committee to impose penalties or initiate a unilateral review pursuant to subsection (b)(1)(D)(iii), and any recommendations for improving the enforcement of such agreements and conditions.

"(H) Cumulative and, as appropriate, trend information on the number of declarations filed under subsection (b)(1)(C)(v), the actions taken by the Committee in response to those declarations, the business sectors involved in those declarations, and the countries involved in those declarations.

"(I) A description of—

"(i) the methods used by the Committee to identify non-notified and non-declared transactions under sub-section (b)(1)(H);

"(ii) potential methods to improve such identification and the resources required to do so; and

"(iii) the number of transactions identified through the process established under that subsection during the reporting period and the number of such transactions flagged for further review.

"(J) A summary of the hiring practices and policies of the Committee pursuant to subsection (k)(4).

"(K) A list of the waivers granted by the Committee under subsection (b)(1)(C)(v)(IV)(bb)(CC).";

(2) in paragraph (3)—

(A) by striking "CRITICAL TECHNOLOGIES" and all that follows through "In order to assist" and inserting "CRITICAL TECHNOLOGIES.—In order to assist";

(B) by striking subparagraph (B);

(C) by redesignating clauses (i) and (ii) as sub-paragraphs (A) and (B), respectively, and by moving such sub-paragraphs, as so redesignated, 2 ems to the left;

(D) in subparagraph (A), as redesignated by subparagraph (C), by striking "; and" and inserting a semicolon;

(E) in subparagraph (B), as so redesignated, by striking the period and inserting "; and"; and

(F) by adding at the end the following:

"(C) a description of the technologies recommended by the chairperson under subsection (a)(6)(B) for identification under the interagency process set forth in section 1758(a) of the Export Control Reform Act of 2018.".

(3) by adding at the end the following:

"(4) FORM OF REPORT.—

"(A) IN GENERAL.—All appropriate portions of the annual report under paragraph (1) may be classified. An unclassified version of the report, as appropriate, consistent with safeguarding national security and privacy, shall be made available to the public.

"(B) INCLUSION IN CLASSIFIED VERSION.—If the Committee recommends that the President suspend or prohibit a covered transaction because the transaction threatens to impair the national security of the United States, the Committee shall, in the classified version of the report required under paragraph (1), notify Congress of the recommendation and, upon request, provide a classified briefing on the recommendation.

"(C) INCLUSIONS IN UNCLASSIFIED VERSION.—The unclassified version of the report required under paragraph (1) shall include, with respect to covered transactions for the reporting period—

"(i) the number of notices submitted under subsection (b)(1)(C)(i);

"(ii) the number of declarations submitted under subsection (b)(1)(C)(v) and the number of such declarations that were required under subclause (IV) of that subsection;

"(iii) the number of declarations submitted under subsection (b)(1)(C)(v) for which the Committee required resubmission as notices under subsection (b)(1)(C)(i);

"(iv) the average number of days that elapsed between submission of a declaration under subsection (b)(1)(C)(v) and the acceptance of the declaration by the Committee;

"(v) the median and average number of days that elapsed between acceptance of a declaration by the Committee and a response described in subsection (b)(1)(C)(v)(III);

"(vi) information on the time it took the Committee to provide comments on, or to accept, notices submitted under subsection (b)(1)(C)(i), including—

"(I) the average number of business days that elapsed between the date of submission of a draft notice and the date on which the Committee provided written comments on the draft notice;

"(II) the average number of business days that elapsed between the date of submission of a formal written notice and the date on which the Committee accepted or provided written comments on the formal written notice; and

"(III) if the average number of business days for a response by the Committee reported under subclause (I) or (II) exceeded 10 business days—

"(aa) an explanation of the causes of such delays, including whether such delays are caused by resource shortages, unusual fluctuations in the volume of notices, transaction characteristics, or other factors; and

"(bb) an explanation of the steps that the Committee anticipates taking to mitigate the causes of such delays and otherwise to improve the ability of the Committee to provide comments on, or to accept, notices within 10 business days;

"(vii) the number of reviews or investigations conducted under subsection (b);

"(viii) the number of investigations that were subject to an extension under subsection (b)(2)(C)(ii);

"(ix) information on the duration of those reviews and investigations, including the median and average number of days required to complete those reviews and investigations;

"(x) the number of notices submitted under subsection (b)(1)(C)(i) and declarations submitted under subsection (b)(1)(C)(v) that were rejected by the Committee;

"(xi) the number of such notices and declarations that were withdrawn by a party to the covered transaction;

"(xii) the number of such withdrawals that were followed by the submission of a subsequent such notice or declaration relating to a substantially similar covered transaction; and

"(xiii) such other specific, cumulative, or trend information that the Committee determines is advisable to provide for an assessment of the time required for reviews and investigations of covered transactions under this section.".

(b) REPORT ON CHINESE INVESTMENT.—

(1) IN GENERAL.—Not later than 2 years after the date of the enactment of this Act, and every 2 years thereafter through 2026, the Secretary of Commerce shall submit to Congress and the Committee on Foreign Investment in the United States a report on

foreign direct investment transactions made by entities of the People's Republic of China in the United States.

(2) ELEMENTS.—Each report required by paragraph (1) shall include the following:

(A) Total foreign direct investment from the People's Republic of China in the United States, including total foreign direct investment disaggregated by ultimate beneficial owner.

(B) A breakdown of investments from the People's Republic of China in the United States by value using the following categories:

(i) Less than $50,000,000.

(ii) Greater than or equal to $50,000,000 and less than $100,000,000.

(iii) Greater than or equal to $100,000,000 and less than $1,000,000,000.

(iv) Greater than or equal to $1,000,000,000 and less than $2,000,000,000.

(vi) Greater than or equal to $2,000,000,000 and less than $5,000,000,000.

(vii) Greater than or equal to $5,000,000,000.

(C) A breakdown of investments from the People's Republic of China in the United States by 2-digit North American Industry Classification System code.

(D) A breakdown of investments from the People's Republic of China in the United States by investment type, using the following categories:

(i) Businesses established.

(ii) Businesses acquired.

(E) A breakdown of investments from the People's Republic of China in the United States by government and non-government investments, including volume, sector, and type of investment within each category.

(F) A list of companies incorporated in the United States purchased through government investment by the People's Republic of China.

(G) The number of United States affiliates of entities under the jurisdiction of the People's Republic of China, the total employees at those affiliates, and the valuation for any publicly traded United States affiliate of such an entity.

(H) An analysis of patterns in the investments described in subparagraphs (A) through (F), including in volume, type, and sector, and the extent to which those patterns of investments align with the objectives outlined by the Government of the People's Republic of China in its Made in China 2025 plan, including a comparative analysis of investments from the People's Republic of China in the United States and all foreign direct investment in the United States.

(I) An identification of any limitations on the ability of the Secretary of Commerce to collect comprehensive information that is reasonably and lawfully available about foreign investment in the United States from the People's Republic of China on a timeline necessary to complete reports every 2 years as required by paragraph (1), including—

(i) an identification of any discrepancies between government and private sector estimates of investments from the People's Republic of China in the United States;

(ii) a description of the different methodologies or data collection methods, including by private sector entities, used to measure foreign investment that may result in different estimates; and

(iii) recommendations for enhancing the ability of the Secretary of Commerce to improve data collection of information about foreign investment in the United States from the People's Republic of China.

(3) EXTENSION OF DEADLINE.—If, as a result of a limitation identified under paragraph (2)(I), the Secretary of Commerce determines that the Secretary will be unable to submit a report at the time required by paragraph (1), the Secretary may request additional time to complete the report.

(c) REPORT ON CERTAIN RAIL INVESTMENTS BY STATE-OWNED OR STATE-CONTROLLED ENTITIES.—

(1) IN GENERAL.—Not later than one year after the date of the enactment of this Act, the Secretary of Homeland Security shall, in coordination with the appropriate members of the Committee on Foreign Investment in the United States, submit to Congress a report assessing—

(A) national security risks, if any, related to investments in the United States by state-owned or state-controlled entities in the manufacture or assembly of rolling stock or other assets for use in freight rail, public transportation rail systems, or intercity passenger rail systems; and

(B) how the number and types of such investments could affect any such risks.

(2) CONSULTATION.—The Secretary, in preparing the report required by paragraph (1), shall consult with the Secretary of Transportation and the head of any agency that is not represented on the Committee on Foreign Investment in the United States that has significant technical expertise related to the assessments required by that paragraph.

SEC. 1720. CERTIFICATION OF NOTICES AND INFORMATION.

Section 721(n) of the Defense Production Act of 1950 (50 U.S.C. 4565(n)) is amended—

(1) by redesignating paragraphs (1) and (2) as sub-paragraphs (A) and (B), respectively, and by moving such sub-paragraphs, as so redesignated, 2 ems to the right;

(2) by striking "Each notice" and inserting the following:

"(1) IN GENERAL.—Each notice";

(3) by striking "paragraph (3)(B)" and inserting "paragraph (6)(B)";

(4) by striking "paragraph (1)(A)" and inserting "paragraph (3)(A)";

(5) by adding at the end the following:

"(2) EFFECT OF FAILURE TO SUBMIT.—The Committee may not complete a review under this section of a covered transaction and may recommend to the President that the President suspend or prohibit the transaction under subsection (d) if the Committee determines that a party to the transaction has—

"(A) failed to submit a statement required by paragraph (1); or

"(B) included false or misleading information in a notice or information described in paragraph (1) or omitted material information from such notice or information.

"(3) APPLICABILITY OF LAW ON FRAUD AND FALSE STATEMENTS.—The Committee shall prescribe regulations expressly providing for the application of section 1001 of title 18, United States Code, to all information provided to the Committee under this section by any party to a covered transaction.".

SEC. 1721. IMPLEMENTATION PLANS.

(a) IN GENERAL.—Not later than 180 days after the date of the enactment of this Act, the chairperson of the Committee on Foreign Investment in the United States and the Secretary of Commerce shall, in consultation with the appropriate members of the Committee—

(1) develop plans to implement this subtitle; and

(2) submit to the appropriate congressional committees a report on the plans developed under paragraph (1), which shall include a description of—

(A) the timeline and process to implement the provisions of, and amendments made by, this subtitle;

(B) any additional staff necessary to implement the plans; and

(C) the resources required to effectively implement the plans.

(b) ANNUAL RESOURCE NEEDS OF CFIUS MEMBER AGENCIES.— Not later than one year after the submission of the report under subsection (a)(2), and annually thereafter for 7 years, each department or agency represented on the Committee on Foreign Investment in the United States shall submit to the appropriate congressional committees a detailed spending plan to expeditiously meet the requirements of section 721 of the Defense Production Act of 1950, as amended by this subtitle, including estimated expenditures and staffing levels for not less than the following fiscal year.

(c) TESTIMONY.—Section 721 of the Defense Production Act of 1950 (50 U.S.C. 4565) is amended by adding at the end the following:

"(o) TESTIMONY.—

"(1) IN GENERAL.—Not later than March 31 of each year, the chairperson, or the designee of the chairperson, shall appear before the Committee on Financial Services of the House of Representatives and the Committee on Banking, Housing, and Urban Affairs of the Senate to present testimony on—

"(A) anticipated resources necessary for operations of the Committee in the following fiscal year at each of the departments or agencies represented on the Committee;

"(B) the adequacy of appropriations for the Committee in the current and the previous fiscal year to—

"(i) ensure that thorough reviews and investigations are completed as expeditiously as possible;

"(ii) monitor and enforce mitigation agreements; and

"(iii) identify covered transactions for which a notice under clause (i) of subsection (b)(1)(C) or a declaration under clause (v) of that subsection was not submitted to the Committee;

"(C) management efforts to strengthen the ability of the Committee to meet the requirements of this section; and

"(D) activities of the Committee undertaken in order to—

"(i) educate the business community, with a particular focus on the technology sector and other sectors of importance to national security, on the goals and operations of the Committee;

"(ii) disseminate to the governments of countries that are allies or partners of the United States best practices of the Committee that—

"(I) strengthen national security reviews of relevant investment transactions; and

"(II) expedite such reviews when appropriate; and

"(iii) promote openness to foreign investment, consistent with national security considerations.

"(2) SUNSET.—This subsection shall have no force or effect on or after the date that is 7 years after the date of the enactment of the Foreign Investment Risk Review Modernization Act of 2018.".

(d) APPROPRIATE CONGRESSIONAL COMMITTEES DEFINED.—In this section, the term "appropriate congressional committees" means—

(1) the Committee on Banking, Housing, and Urban Affairs and the Committee on Appropriations of the Senate; and

(2) the Committee on Financial Services and the Committee on Appropriations of the House of Representatives.

SEC. 1722. ASSESSMENT OF NEED FOR ADDITIONAL RESOURCES FOR COMMITTEE.

The President shall—

(1) determine whether and to what extent the expansion of the responsibilities of the Committee on Foreign Investment in the United States pursuant to the amendments made by this subtitle necessitates additional resources for the Committee and the departments and agencies represented on the Committee to perform their functions under section 721 of the Defense Production Act of 1950, as amended by this subtitle; and

(2) if the President determines that additional resources are necessary, include in the budget of the President for fiscal year 2019 and each fiscal year thereafter submitted to Congress under section 1105(a) of title 31, United States Code, a request for such additional resources.

SEC. 1723. FUNDING.

Section 721 of the Defense Production Act of 1950 (50 U.S.C. 4565), as amended by section 1721, is further amended by adding at the end the following:

"(p) FUNDING.—

"(1) ESTABLISHMENT OF FUND.—There is established in the Treasury of the United States a fund, to be known as the 'Committee on Foreign Investment in the United States Fund' (in this subsection referred to as the 'Fund'), to be administered by the chairperson.

"(2) AUTHORIZATION OF APPROPRIATIONS FOR THE COM-MITTEE.—There are authorized to be appropriated to the Fund for each of fiscal years 2019 through 2023 $20,000,000 to perform the functions of the Committee.

"(3) FILING FEES.—

"(A) IN GENERAL.—The Committee may assess and collect a fee in an amount determined by the Committee in regulations, to the extent provided in advance in appropriations Acts, without regard to section 9701 of title 31, United States Code, and subject to subparagraph (B), with respect to each covered transaction for which a written notice is submitted to the Committee under subsection (b)(1)(C)(i). The total amount of fees collected under this paragraph may not exceed the costs of administering this section.

"(B) DETERMINATION OF AMOUNT OF FEE.—

"(i) IN GENERAL.—The amount of the fee to be assessed under subparagraph (A) with respect to a covered transaction—

"(I) may not exceed an amount equal to the lesser of—

"(aa) 1 percent of the value of the transaction; or

"(bb) $300,000, adjusted annually for inflation pursuant to regulations prescribed by the Committee; and

"(II) shall be based on the value of the transaction, taking into account—

"(aa) the effect of the fee on small business concerns (as defined in section 3 of the Small Business Act (15 U.S.C. 632));

"(bb) the expenses of the Committee associated with conducting activities under this section;

"(cc) the effect of the fee on foreign investment; and

"(dd) such other matters as the Committee considers appropriate.

"(ii) UPDATES.—The Committee shall periodically reconsider and adjust the amount of the fee to be assessed under subparagraph (A) with respect to a covered transaction to ensure that the amount of the fee does not exceed the costs of administering this section and otherwise remains appropriate.

"(C) DEPOSIT AND AVAILABILITY OF FEES.—Notwithstanding section 3302 of title 31, United States Code, fees collected under subparagraph (A) shall—

"(i) be deposited into the Fund solely for use in carrying out activities under this section;

"(ii) to the extent and in the amounts provided in advance in appropriations Acts, be available to the chairperson;

"(iii) remain available until expended; and

"(iv) be in addition to any appropriations made available to the members of the Committee.

"(D) STUDY ON PRIORITIZATION FEE.—

"(i) IN GENERAL.—Not later than 270 days after the date of the enactment of the Foreign Investment Risk Review Modernization Act of 2018, the chairperson, in consultation with the Committee, shall complete a study of the feasibility and merits of establishing a fee or fee scale to prioritize the timing of the response of the Committee to a draft or formal written notice during the period before the Committee accepts the formal written notice under subsection (b)(1)(C)(i), in the event that the Committee is unable to respond during the time required by subclause (II) of that subsection because of an unusually large influx of notices, or for other reasons.

"(ii) SUBMISSION TO CONGRESS.—After completing the study required by clause (i), the chairperson, or a designee of the chairperson, shall submit to the Committee on Banking, Housing, and Urban Affairs of the Senate and the Committee on Financial Services of the House of Representatives a report on the findings of the study.

"(4) TRANSFER OF FUNDS.—To the extent provided in advance in appropriations Acts, the chairperson may transfer any amounts in the Fund to any other department or agency represented on the Committee for the purpose of addressing emerging needs in carrying out activities under this section. Amounts so transferred shall be in addition to any other amounts available to that department or agency for that purpose.".

SEC. 1724. CENTRALIZATION OF CERTAIN COMMITTEE FUNCTIONS.

Section 721 of the Defense Production Act of 1950 (50 U.S.C. 4565), as amended by section 1723, is further amended by adding at the end the following:

"(q) CENTRALIZATION OF CERTAIN COMMITTEE FUNCTIONS.—

"(1) IN GENERAL.—The chairperson, in consultation with the Committee, may centralize certain functions of the Committee within the Department of the Treasury for the purpose

of enhancing interagency coordination and collaboration in carrying out the functions of the Committee under this section.

"(2) FUNCTIONS.—Functions that may be centralized under paragraph (1) include identifying non-notified and non-declared transactions pursuant to subsection (b)(1)(H), and other functions as determined by the chairperson and the Committee.

"(3) RULE OF CONSTRUCTION.—Nothing in this section shall be construed as limiting the authority of any department or agency represented on the Committee to represent its own interests before the Committee.".

SEC. 1725. CONFORMING AMENDMENTS.

Section 721 of the Defense Production Act of 1950 (50 U.S.C. 4565), as amended by this subtitle, is further amended—

    (1) in subsection (b)—

        (A) in paragraph (1)(D)(iii)(I), by striking "subsection (l)(1)(A)" and inserting "subsection (l)(3)(A)"; and

        (B) in paragraph (2)(B)(i)(I), by striking "that threat" and inserting "the risk";

    (2) in subsection (d)(4)(A), by striking "the foreign interest exercising control" and inserting "a foreign person that would acquire an interest in a United States business or its assets as a result of the covered transaction"; and

    (3) in subsection (j), by striking "merger, acquisition, or takeover" and inserting "transaction".

SEC. 1726. BRIEFING ON INFORMATION FROM TRANSACTIONS REVIEWED BY COMMITTEE ON FOREIGN INVESTMENT IN THE UNITED STATES RELATING TO FOREIGN EFFORTS TO INFLUENCE DEMOCRATIC INSTITUTIONS AND PROCESSES.

Not later than 60 days after the date of the enactment of this Act, the Secretary of the Treasury (or a designee of the Secretary) shall provide a briefing to the Committee on Banking, Housing, and Urban Affairs of the Senate and the Committee on Financial Services of the House of Representatives on—

    (1) transactions reviewed by the Committee on Foreign Investment in the United States during the 5-year period preceding the briefing that the Committee determined would have allowed foreign persons to inappropriately influence democratic institutions and processes within the United States and in other countries; and

    (2) the disposition of such reviews, including any steps taken by the Committee to address the risk of allowing foreign persons to influence such institutions and processes.

SEC. 1727. EFFECTIVE DATE.

(a) IMMEDIATE APPLICABILITY OF CERTAIN PROVISIONS.—The following shall take effect on the date of the enactment of this Act and, as applicable, apply with respect to any covered transaction the review or investigation of which is initiated under section 721 of the Defense Production Act of 1950 on or after such date of enactment:

    (1) Sections 1705, 1707, 1708, 1709, 1710, 1713, 1714, 1715, 1716, 1717, 1718, 1720, 1721, 1722, 1723, 1724, and 1725 and any amendments made by those sections.

    (2) Section 1712 and the amendments made by that section (except for clause (iii) of section 721(b)(4)(A) of the Defense Production Act of 1950, as added by section 1712).

    (3) Paragraphs (1), (2), (3), (4)(A)(i), (4)(B)(i), (4)(B)(iv)(I), (4)(B)(v), (4)(C)(v), (5), (6), (7), (8), (9), (10), (11), (12), and

    (13) of subsection (a) of section 721 of the Defense Production Act of 1950, as amended by section 1703.

    (4) Section 721(m)(4) of the Defense Production Act of 1950, as amended by section 1719 (except for clauses (ii), (iii), (iv), and (v) of subparagraph (B) of that section).

(b) DELAYED APPLICABILITY OF CERTAIN PROVISIONS.—

    (1) IN GENERAL.—Any provision of or amendment made by this subtitle not specified in subsection (a) shall—

        (A) take effect on the earlier of—

            (i) the date that is 18 months after the date of the enactment of this Act; or

            (ii) the date that is 30 days after publication in the Federal Register of a determination by the chairperson of the Committee on Foreign Investment in the

United States that the regulations, organizational structure, personnel, and other resources necessary to administer the new provisions are in place; and

(B) apply with respect to any covered transaction the review or investigation of which is initiated under section 721 of the Defense Production Act of 1950 on or after the date described in subparagraph (A).

(2) NONDELEGATION OF DETERMINATION.—The determination of the chairperson of the Committee on Foreign Investment in the United States under paragraph (1)(A) may not be delegated.

(c) AUTHORIZATION FOR PILOT PROGRAMS.—

(1) IN GENERAL.—Beginning on the date of the enactment of this Act and ending on the date that is 570 days thereafter, the Committee on Foreign Investment in the United States may, at its discretion, conduct one or more pilot programs to implement any authority provided pursuant to any provision of or amendment made by this subtitle not specified in subsection (a).

(2) PUBLICATION IN FEDERAL REGISTER.—A pilot program under paragraph (1) may not commence until the date that is 30 days after publication in the Federal Register of a determination by the chairperson of the Committee of the scope of and procedures for the pilot program. That determination may not be delegated.

SEC. 1728. SEVERABILITY.

If any provision of this subtitle or an amendment made by this subtitle, or the application of such a provision or amendment to any person or circumstance, is held to be invalid, the application of that provision or amendment to other persons or circumstances and the remainder of the provisions of this subtitle and the amendments made by this subtitle, shall not be affected thereby.

Export Control Reform Act of 2018 and Export Controls Act of 2018

(Pub. L. 115-232, §§1741-68)

> *To authorize the President to control the export, reexport, and transfer of commodities, software, and technology to protect the national security, and to promote the foreign policy, of the United States, and for other purposes.*

SECTION 1. Short title; table of contents.

(a) Short title.—This Act may be cited as the "Export Control Reform Act of 2018".

(b) Table of contents.—The table of contents of this Act is as follows:

SEC. 2. Definitions.

In this Act:

(1) CONTROLLED.—The term "controlled", with respect to an item, means the export, reexport, or transfer of the item is controlled under title I.

(2) DUAL-USE.—The term "dual-use", with respect to an item, means the item has civilian applications and military, terrorism, or weapons of mass destruction-related applications.

(3) EXPORT.—The term "export", with respect to an item subject to controls under title I, includes—

587

(A) the shipment or transmission of the item out of the United States, including the sending or taking of the item out of the United States, in any manner; and

(B) the release or transfer of technology or source code relating to the item to a foreign person in the United States.

(4) EXPORT ADMINISTRATION REGULATIONS.—The term "Export Administration Regulations" means—

(A) the Export Administration Regulations as promulgated, maintained, and amended under the authority of the International Emergency Economic Powers Act and codified, as of the date of the enactment of this Act, in subchapter C of chapter VII of title 15, Code of Federal Regulations; or

(B) regulations that are promulgated, maintained, and amended under the authority of title I on or after the date of the enactment of this Act.

(5) FOREIGN PERSON.—The term "foreign person" means a person that is not a United States person.

(6) ITEM.—The term "item" means a commodity, software, or technology.

(7) PERSON.—

(A) IN GENERAL.—The term "person" means—

(i) a natural person;

(ii) a corporation, business association, partnership, society, trust, financial institution, insurer, underwriter, guarantor, and any other business organization, any other nongovernmental entity, organization, or group, and any governmental entity operating as a business enterprise; and

(iii) any successor to any entity described in clause (ii).

(B) APPLICATION TO GOVERNMENTAL ENTITIES.—The term "person" does not include a government or governmental entity that is not operating as a business enterprise.

(8) REEXPORT.—The term "reexport", with respect to an item subject to controls under title I, includes—

(A) the shipment or transmission of the item from a foreign country to another foreign country, including the sending or taking of the item from the foreign country to the other foreign country, in any manner; and

(B) the release or transfer of technology or source code relating to the item to a foreign person outside the United States.

(9) TECHNOLOGY.—The term "technology"—

(A) includes—

(i) information necessary for the development, production, use, operation, installation, maintenance, repair, overhaul or refurbishing of an item; and

(ii) information at whatever stage of its creation, such as foundational information and know-how, as further defined by regulations; and

(B) does not include published information, including prerecorded records, printed books, pamphlets, miscellaneous publications, or other information, that—

(i) arises during, or results from, fundamental research and is intended to be published;

(ii) is released by instruction in a catalog course or associated teaching laboratory of an academic institution;

(iii) appears in patents or open (published) patent publications available from or at any patent office, unless covered by an invention secrecy order;

(iv) is non-proprietary system descriptions;

(v) is telemetry data; or

(vi) is any other category or type of information, as determined by the President for purposes of national security or foreign policy concerns.

(10) TRANSFER.—The term "transfer", with respect to an item subject to controls under title I, means a change in the end-use or end user of the item within the same foreign country.

(11) UNITED STATES.—The term "United States" means the several States, the District of Columbia, the Commonwealth of Puerto Rico, the Commonwealth of the Northern Mariana Islands, American Samoa, Guam, the United States Virgin Islands, and any other territory or possession of the United States.

(12) UNITED STATES PERSON.—The term "United States person" means—

(A) any individual who is a citizen or national of the United States or who is an individual described in subparagraph (B) of section 274B(a)(3) of the Immigration and Nationality Act (8 U.S.C. 1324b(a)(3)); and

(B) a corporation or other legal entity which is organized under the laws of the United States, any State or territory thereof, or the District of Columbia, if natural persons described in subparagraph (A) own, directly or indirectly, more than 50 percent of the outstanding capital stock or other beneficial interest in such legal entity.

(13) WEAPONS OF MASS DESTRUCTION.—The term "weapons of mass destruction" means nuclear, radiological, chemical, and biological weapons and delivery systems for such weapons.

TITLE I—Authority and administration of controls

SEC. 101. Short title.

This title may be cited as the "Export Controls Act of 2018".

SEC. 102. Statement of policy.

The following is the policy of the United States:

(1) The national security and foreign policy of the United States require that the export, reexport, and transfer of items, and specific activities of United States persons, wherever located, be controlled for the following purposes:

(A) To control the access to items for use in—

(i) the proliferation of weapons of mass destruction or of conventional weapons;

(ii) the acquisition of destabilizing numbers or types of conventional weapons;

(iii) acts of terrorism;

(iv) military programs that could pose a threat to the security of the United States or its allies; or

(v) activities undertaken specifically to cause significant interference with or disruption of critical infrastructure.

(B) To preserve the qualitative military superiority of the United States.

(C) To strengthen the United States industrial base.

(D) To carry out the foreign policy of the United States, including the protection of human rights and the promotion of democracy.

(E) To carry out obligations and commitments under international agreements and arrangements, including multilateral export control regimes.

(F) To facilitate military interoperability between the United States and its North Atlantic Treaty Organization (NATO) and other close allies.

(G) To ensure national security controls are tailored to focus on those core technologies and other items that are capable of being used to pose a serious national security threat to the United States.

(2) The national security of the United States requires that the United States maintain its leadership in the science, technology, engineering, and manufacturing sectors. Such leadership requires that United States persons are competitive in global markets. The impact of the implementation of this title on such leadership and competitiveness must be evaluated on an ongoing basis and applied in imposing controls under sections 103 and 104 to avoid negatively affecting such leadership.

(3) The national security and foreign policy of the United States require that the United States participate in multilateral organizations and agreements regarding export controls on items that are consistent with the policy of the United States, and take all the necessary steps to secure the adoption and consistent enforcement, by the governments of such countries, of export controls on items that are consistent with such policy.

(4) Export controls should be fully coordinated with the multilateral export control regimes. Export controls that are multilateral are most effective, and should be tailored to focus on those core technologies and other items that are capable of being used to pose a serious national security threat to the United States and its allies.

(5) Export controls applied unilaterally to items widely available from foreign sources generally are less effective in preventing end-users from acquiring those items.

(6) The effective administration of export controls requires a clear understanding both inside and outside the United States Government of which technologies and other items are controlled and an efficient process should be created to update the controls, such as by removing and adding technologies and other items.

(7) The export control system must ensure that it is transparent, predictable, and timely, has the flexibility to be adapted to address new threats in the future, and allows seamless access to and sharing of export control information among all relevant United States national security and foreign policy agencies.

(8) Implementation and enforcement of United States export controls require robust capabilities in monitoring, intelligence, and investigation, appropriate penalties for violations, and the ability to swiftly interdict unapproved transfers.

(9) Export controls should be balanced with United States counterterrorism, information security, and cyber-security policies to ensure the ability to export, reexport, and transfer technology and other items in support of counterterrorism, critical infrastructure, and other homeland security priorities, while effectively preventing malicious cyber terrorists from obtaining items that threaten the United States and its interests, including the protection of and safety of United States citizens abroad.

(10) Export controls complement and are a critical element of the national security policies underlying the laws and regulations governing foreign direct investment in the United States, including controlling the transfer of critical technologies to certain foreign persons. Thus, the President, in close coordination with the Department of Commerce, the Department of Defense, the Department of State, the Department of Energy, and other agencies responsible for export controls, should have a regular and robust process to identify the emerging and other types of critical technologies of concern, as defined in United States foreign direct investment laws, and regulate their release to foreign persons as warranted regardless of the nature of the underlying transaction. Such identification efforts should draw upon the resources and expertise of all relevant parts of the United States Government, industry, and academia. These efforts should be in addition to traditional efforts to modernize and update the lists of controlled items under the multilateral export control regimes.

(11) The authority under this title may be exercised only in furtherance of all of the objectives set forth in paragraphs (1) through (10).

SEC. 103. Authority of the President.

(a) Authority.—In order to carry out the policy set forth in paragraphs (1) through (10) of section 102, the President shall control—

(1) the export, reexport, and transfer of items, whether by United States persons, wherever located, or by foreign persons, wherever located; and

(2) the activities of United States persons, wherever located, relating to specific—

(A) nuclear explosive devices;

(B) missiles;

(C) chemical or biological weapons;

(D) whole plants for chemical weapons precursors;

(E) foreign maritime nuclear projects; and

(F) foreign intelligence services.

(b) Requirements.—In exercising authority under this title, the President shall impose controls to achieve the following objectives:

(1) To regulate the export, reexport, and transfer of items described in subsection (a)(1) of United States persons, wherever located, or foreign persons, wherever located.

(2) To regulate the activities described in subsection (a)(2) of United States persons, wherever located.

(3) To secure the cooperation of other governments and multilateral organizations to impose control systems that are consistent, to the extent possible, with the controls imposed under subsection (a).

(4) To maintain the leadership of the United States in science, engineering, technology research and development, and manufacturing.

(5) To enhance the viability of commercial firms, academic institutions, and research establishments, and maintain the skilled workforce of such firms, institutions, and establishments, that are necessary to preserving the leadership of the United States described in paragraph (4).

(6) To strengthen the United States industrial base, both with respect to current and future defense requirements.

(7) To enforce the controls through means such as regulations, requirements for compliance, lists of controlled items, lists of foreign persons who threaten the national security or foreign policy of the United States, and guidance in a form that facilitates compliance by United States persons and foreign persons, in particular academic institutions, scientific and research establishments, and small- and medium-sized businesses.

SEC. 104. Additional authorities.

(a) In general.—In carrying out this title, the President shall—

(1) establish and maintain lists published by the Secretary of Commerce of items that are controlled under this title;

(2) establish and maintain lists published by the Secretary of Commerce of foreign persons and end-uses that are determined to be a threat to the national security and foreign policy of the United States pursuant to the policy set forth in section 102(1)(A) and to whom exports, reexports, and transfers of items are controlled;

(3) prohibit unauthorized exports, reexports, and transfers of controlled items;

(4) restrict exports, reexports, and transfers of any controlled items to any foreign person or end-use listed under paragraph (2);

(5) require licenses or other authorizations, as appropriate, for exports, reexports, and transfers of controlled items, including imposing conditions or restrictions on United States persons and foreign persons with respect to such licenses or other authorizations;

(6) establish a process by which the Secretary of Commerce or a license applicant requests an assessment that a foreign item is comparable in quality to an item controlled under this title, and is available in sufficient quantities to render the United States export control of that item or the denial of a license ineffective;

(7) require measures for compliance with the export controls established under this title;

(8) require and obtain such information from United States persons and foreign persons as is necessary to carry out this title;

(9) require, as appropriate, advance notice before an item is exported, reexported, or transferred, as an alternative to requiring a license;

(10) require, to the extent feasible, identification of items subject to controls under this title in order to facilitate the enforcement of such controls;

(11) inspect, search, detain, seize, or impose temporary denial orders with respect to items, in any form, that are subject to controls under this title, or conveyances on which it is believed that there are items that have been, are being, or are about to be exported, reexported, or transferred in violation of this title;

(12) monitor shipments, or other means of transfer;

(13) keep the public fully apprised of changes in policy, regulations, and procedures established under this title;

(14) appoint technical advisory committees in accordance with the Federal Advisory Committee Act;

(15) create, as warranted, exceptions to licensing requirements in order to further the objectives of this title; and

(16) undertake any other action as is necessary to carry out this title and is not otherwise prohibited by law.

(b) Relationship to IEEPA.—The authority under this title may not be used to regulate or prohibit under this title the export, reexport, or transfer of any item that may not be regulated or prohibited under section 203(b) of the International Emergency Economic Powers Act (50 U.S.C. 1702(b)).

(c) Countries supporting international terrorism.—

  (1) LICENSE REQUIREMENT.—

    (A) IN GENERAL.—A license shall be required for the export, reexport, or transfer of items to a country if the Secretary of State has made the following determinations:

      (i) The government of such country has repeatedly provided support for acts of international terrorism.

      (ii) The export, reexport, or transfer of such items could make a significant contribution to the military potential of such country, including its military logistics capability, or could enhance the ability of such country to support acts of international terrorism.

    (B) DETERMINATION UNDER OTHER PROVISIONS OF LAW.—A determination of the Secretary of State under section 620A of the Foreign Assistance Act of 1961 (22 U.S.C. 2371), section 40 of the Arms Export Control Act (22 U.S.C. 2780), or any other provision of law that the government of a country described in subparagraph (A) has repeatedly provided support for acts of international terrorism shall be deemed to be a determination with respect to such government for purposes of clause (i) of subparagraph (A).

  (2) NOTIFICATION TO CONGRESS.—The Secretary of State and the Secretary of Commerce shall notify the Committee on Foreign Affairs of the House of Representatives and the Committee on Banking, Housing, and Urban Affairs and the Committee on Foreign Relations of the Senate at least 30 days before issuing any license required by paragraph (1).

(3) PUBLICATION IN FEDERAL REGISTER.—Each determination of the Secretary of State under paragraph (1)(A) shall be published in the Federal Register, except that the Secretary of State may exclude confidential information and trade secrets contained in such determination.

(4) RESCISSION OF DETERMINATION.—A determination of the Secretary of State under paragraph (1)(A) may not be rescinded unless the President submits to the Speaker of the House of Representatives, the chairman of the Committee on Foreign Affairs, and the chairman of the Committee on Banking, Housing, and Urban Affairs and the chairman of the Committee on Foreign Relations of the Senate—

> (A) before the proposed rescission would take effect, a report certifying that—
>> (i) there has been a fundamental change in the leadership and policies of the government of the country concerned;
>> (ii) that government is not supporting acts of international terrorism; and
>> (iii) that government has provided assurances that it will not support acts of international terrorism in the future; or
> (B) at least 90 days before the proposed rescission would take effect, a report justifying the rescission and certifying that—
>> (i) the government concerned has not provided any support for acts international terrorism during the preceding 24-month period; and
>> (ii) the government concerned has provided assurances that it will not support acts of international terrorism in the future.

(5) DISAPPROVAL OF RESCISSION.—No rescission under paragraph (4)(B) of a determination under paragraph (1)(A) with respect to the government of a country may be made if Congress, within 90 days after receipt of a report under paragraph (4)(B), enacts a joint resolution described in subsection (f)(2) of section 40 of the Arms Export Control Act with respect to a rescission under subsection (f)(1) of such section with respect to the government of such country.

(6) NOTIFICATION AND BRIEFING.—Not later than—

> (A) ten days after initiating a review of the activities of the government of the country concerned within the 24-month period referred to in paragraph (4)(B)(i), the Secretary of State shall notify the Committee on Foreign Affairs of the House of Representatives and the Committee on Foreign Relations of the Senate of such initiation; and
> (B) 20 days after the notification described in paragraph (1), the Secretary of State shall brief the congressional committees described in paragraph (1) on the status of such review.

(7) CONTENTS OF NOTIFICATION OF LICENSE.—The Secretary of State shall include in the notification required by paragraph (2)—

> (A) a detailed description of the items to be offered, including a brief description of the capabilities of any item for which a license to export, reexport, or transfer the items is sought;
> (B) the reasons why the foreign country, person, or entity to which the export, reexport, or transfer is proposed to be made has requested the items under the export, reexport, or transfer, and a description of the manner in which such country, person, or entity intends to use such items;
> (C) the reasons why the proposed export, reexport, or transfer is in the national interest of the United States;
> (D) an analysis of the impact of the proposed export, reexport, or transfer on the military capabilities of the foreign country, person, or entity to which such transfer would be made;

(E) an analysis of the manner in which the proposed export, reexport, or transfer would affect the relative military strengths of countries in the region to which the items that are the subject of such export, reexport, or transfer would be delivered and whether other countries in the region have comparable kinds and amounts of items; and

(F) an analysis of the impact of the proposed export, reexport, or transfer on the relations of the United States with the countries in the region to which the items that are the subject of such export, reexport, or transfer would be delivered.

(d) Enhanced proliferation controls.—

(1) IN GENERAL.—In furtherance of section 103(a) of this title, the President shall, except to the extent authorized by a statute or regulation administered by a Federal department or agency other than the Department of Commerce, require a United States person, wherever located, to apply for and receive a license from the Department of Commerce for the export, reexport, or transfer of items described in paragraph (2) or for the performance of services relating to such items.

(2) ITEMS DESCRIBED.—The items described in this paragraph are—

(A) nuclear explosive devices;

(B) missiles;

(C) chemical or biological weapons;

(D) whole plants for chemical weapons precursors; and

(E) foreign maritime nuclear projects that would pose a risk to the national security or foreign policy of the United States.

(e) Additional prohibitions.—The Secretary of Commerce may inform United States persons, either individually by specific notice or through amendment to any regulation or order issued under this title, that a license from the Bureau of Industry and Security of the Department of Commerce is required to engage in any activity if the activity involves the types of movement, service, or support described in subsection (d). The absence of any such notification does not excuse the United States person from compliance with the license requirements of subsection (d), or any regulation or order issued under this title.

(f) License review standards.—The Secretary of Commerce shall deny an application to engage in any activity that involves the types of movement, service, or support described in subsection (d) if the activity would make a material contribution to any of the items described in subsection (d)(2).

SEC. 105. Administration of export controls.

(a) In general.—The President shall delegate to the Secretary of Commerce, the Secretary of Defense, the Secretary of State and, as appropriate, the Director of National Intelligence and the heads of other appropriate Federal departments and agencies, the authority to carry out the purposes set forth in subsection (b).

(b) Purposes.—

(1) IN GENERAL.—The purpose of the delegations of authority pursuant to subsection (a) are—

(A) to advise the President with respect to—

(i) identifying specific threats to the national security and foreign policy that the authority of this title may be used to address; and

(ii) exercising the authority under this title to implement policies, regulations, procedures, and actions that are necessary to effectively counteract those threats;

(B) to review and approve—

(i) criteria for including items on, and removing such an item from, a list of controlled items established under this title;

(ii) an interagency procedure for compiling and amending any list described in clause (i);

(iii) criteria for including a person on a list of persons to whom exports, reexports, and transfers of items are prohibited or restricted under this title;

(iv) standards for compliance by persons subject to controls under this title; and

(v) policies and procedures for the end-use monitoring of exports, reexports, and transfers of items controlled under this title;

(C) to obtain independent evaluations, including from Inspectors General of the relevant departments or agencies, on a periodic basis on the effectiveness of the implementation of this title in carrying out the policy set forth in section 102; and

(D) to benefit from the inherent equities, experience, and capabilities of the Federal officials described in subsection (a), including—

(i) the views of the Department of Defense with respect to the national security implications of a particular control or decision;

(ii) the views of the Department of State with respect to the foreign policy implications of a particular control or decision;

(iii) the views of the Department of Energy with respect to the implications for nuclear proliferation of a particular control or decision; and

(iv) the views of the Department of Commerce with respect to the administration of an efficient, coherent, reliable, enforceable, and predictable export control system, and the resolution of competing views or policy objectives described in section 102.

(2) AUTHORITY TO SEEK INFORMATION.—The Federal officials described in subsection (a) may, in carrying out the purposes set forth in paragraph (1), seek information and advice from experts who are not officers or employees of the Federal Government.

(3) TRANSMITTAL AND IMPLEMENTATION OF EVALUATIONS.—The results of the independent evaluations conducted pursuant to paragraph (1)(D) shall be transmitted to the President and the Congress, in classified form if necessary. Subject to the delegation of authority by the President, the Federal officials described in subsection (a) shall determine, direct, and ensure that improvements recommended in the evaluations are implemented.

SEC. 106. Control lists.

The President shall, pursuant to the delegation of authority in section 105, ensure that—

(1) a process is established for regular interagency review of each list established under section 104(a)(1), that pursuant to such review the Secretary of Commerce regularly updates such lists to ensure that new items (including emerging critical technologies) are appropriately controlled, and that the level of control of items on the lists are adjusted as conditions change;

(2) information and expertise is obtained from officers and employees from relevant Federal departments, agencies, and offices and persons outside the Federal Government who have technical expertise, with respect to the characteristics of the items considered for each list established under section 104(a)(1) and the effect of controlling the items on addressing the policy set forth in section 102;

(3) each list established under section 104(a)(1) appropriately identifies each entry that has been included by virtue of the participation of the United States in a multilateral regime, organization, or group the purpose of which is consistent with and supports the policy of the United States under this title relating to the control of exports, reexports, and transfers of items; and

(4) each list established under section 104(a)(1) is published by the Secretary of Commerce in a form that facilitates compliance with it and related requirements, particularly by small- and medium-sized businesses, and academic institutions.

SEC. 107. Licensing.

(a) In general.—The President shall, pursuant to the delegation of authority in section 105, establish a procedure for the Department of Commerce to license or otherwise authorize the export, reexport, and transfer of items controlled under this title in order to carry out the policy set forth in section 102 and the requirements set forth in section 103(b). The procedure shall ensure that—

(1) license applications, other requests for authorization, and related dispute resolution procedures are considered and decisions made with the participation of appropriate departments, agencies, and offices that have delegated functions under this title; and

(2) licensing decisions are made in an expeditious manner, with transparency to applicants on the status of license and other authorization processing and the reason for denying any license or request for authorization.

(b) Sense of Congress.—It is the sense of Congress that the President should make best efforts to ensure that an accurate, consistent, and timely evaluation and processing of licenses or other requests for authorization to export, reexport, or transfer items controlled under this title is accomplished within 30 days from the date of such license request.

(c) Fees.—No fee may be charged in connection with the submission, processing, or consideration of any application for a license or other authorization or other request made in connection with any regulation in effect under the authority of this title.

SEC. 108. Compliance assistance.

(a) System for seeking assistance.—The President may establish a system to provide United States persons with assistance in complying with this title, which may include a mechanism for providing information, in classified form as appropriate, who are potential customers, suppliers, or business partners with respect to items controlled under this title, in order to further ensure the prevention of the export, reexport, or transfer of items that may pose a threat to the national security or foreign policy of the United States.

(b) Security clearances.—In order to carry out subsection (a), the President may issue appropriate security clearances to persons described in that subsection who are responsible for complying with this title.

(c) Assistance for certain businesses.—

(1) IN GENERAL.—Not later than 120 days after the date of the enactment of this Act, the President shall develop and submit to Congress a plan to assist small- and medium-sized United States in export licensing and other processes under this title.

(2) CONTENTS.—The plan shall include, among other things, arrangements for the Department of Commerce to provide counseling to businesses described in paragraph (1) on filing applications and identifying items controlled under this title, as well as proposals for seminars and conferences to educate such businesses on export controls, licensing procedures, and related obligations.

SEC. 109. Requirements to identify and control emerging critical technologies in export control regulations.

(a) In general.—The President shall, pursuant to the delegation of authority in section 105, establish and, in coordination with the Department of Commerce, the Department of Defense, the Department of State, the Department of Energy, and other departments determined to be necessary, lead a regular, ongoing interagency process to identify emerging critical technologies that are not identified in any list of items controlled for export under United States law or regulations, but that nonetheless could be essential for maintaining or increasing the technological advantage of the United States over countries that pose a significant threat to the national security of the United States with respect to national defense, intelligence, or other areas of national security, or gaining such an advantage over such countries in areas where such an advantage may not currently exist.

(b) Requirements.—The interagency process required under subsection (a) shall—

(1) draw upon the expertise, resources, and equities of all relevant United States Government agencies, industries, and academic institutions to identify and describe such emerging critical technologies;

(2) require the relevant export control authority to publish proposed regulations for public comment that would control heretofore unlisted emerging critical technologies identified pursuant to subsection (a) and control the release of each such technology to destinations, end uses, or end users as determined by the President;

(3) require the Secretary of Commerce, the Secretary of State, and the Secretary of Defense to propose to the relevant multilateral export control regimes in the following year that such emerging critical technologies be added to the list of technologies controlled by such regimes;

(4) determine whether national security concerns warrant continued unilateral export controls over technologies identified pursuant to subsection (a) if the relevant multilateral export control regime does not agree to list such technologies on its control list within three years; and

(5) require the agencies responsible for administering the export controls identified in subsection (a) to remove or revise, as appropriate, existing controls determined to warrant removal or revision as a result of insight or information obtained during efforts undertaken to comply with the requirements of this section.

SEC. 110. Penalties.

(a) Unlawful acts.—

(1) IN GENERAL.—It shall be unlawful for a person to violate, attempt to violate, conspire to violate, or cause a violation of this title or of any regulation, order, license, or other authorization issued under this title, including any of the unlawful acts described in paragraph (2).

(2) SPECIFIC UNLAWFUL ACTS.—The unlawful acts described in this paragraph are the following:

(A) No person may engage in any conduct prohibited by or contrary to, or refrain from engaging in any conduct required by this title, the Export Administration Regulations, or any order, license or authorization issued thereunder.

(B) No person may cause or aid, abet, counsel, command, induce, procure, or approve the doing of any act prohibited, or the omission of any act required by this title, the Export Administration Regulations, or any order, license or authorization issued thereunder.

(C) No person may solicit or attempt a violation of this Act, the Export Administration Regulations, or any order, license or authorization issued thereunder.

(D) No person may conspire or act in concert with one or more other persons in any manner or for any purpose to bring about or to do any act that constitutes a violation of this title, the Export Administration Regulations, or any order, license or authorization issued thereunder.

(E) No person may order, buy, remove, conceal, store, use, sell, loan, dispose of, transfer, transport, finance, forward, or otherwise service, in whole or in part, any item exported or to be exported from the United States, or that is otherwise subject to the Export Administration Regulations, with knowledge that a violation of this title, the Export Administration Regulations, or any order, license or authorization issued thereunder, has occurred, is about to occur, or is intended to occur in connection with the item unless valid authorization is obtained therefor.

(F) No person may make any false or misleading representation, statement, or certification, or falsify or conceal any material fact, either directly to the Department of Commerce, or an official of any other United States agency, or indirectly through any other person—

(i) in the course of an investigation or other action subject to the Export Administration Regulations;

(ii) in connection with the preparation, submission, issuance, use, or maintenance of any export control document or any report filed or required to be filed pursuant to the Export Administration Regulations; or

(iii) for the purpose of or in connection with effecting any export, reexport, or transfer of an item subject to the Export Administration Regulations or a service or other activity of a United States person described in section 104.

(G) No person may engage in any transaction or take any other action with intent to evade the provisions of this title, the Export Administration Regulations, or any order, license, or authorization issued thereunder.

(H) No person may fail or refuse to comply with any reporting or recordkeeping requirements of the Export Administration Regulations or of any order, license, or authorization issued thereunder.

(I) Except as specifically authorized in the Export Administration Regulations or in writing by the Department of Commerce, no person may alter any license, authorization, export control document, or order issued under the Export Administration Regulations.

(J) No person may take any action that is prohibited by a denial order issued by the Department of Commerce to prevent imminent violations of this title, the Export Administration Regulations, or any order, license or authorization issued thereunder.

(3) ADDITIONAL REQUIREMENTS.—For purposes of subparagraph (G), any representation, statement, or certification made by any person shall be deemed to be continuing in effect. Each person who has made a representation, statement, or certification to the Department of Commerce relating to any order, license, or other authorization issued under this title shall notify the Department of Commerce, in writing, of any change of any material fact or intention from that previously represented, stated, or certified, immediately upon receipt of any information that would lead a reasonably prudent person to know that a change of material fact or intention had occurred or may occur in the future.

(b) Criminal penalty.—

(1) KNOWING VIOLATIONS.—Except as provided in paragraph (2), a person who knowingly violates or conspires or attempts to violate subsection (a) shall be fined not more than 5 times the amount or value of the exports, reexports, or transfers involved, or $500,000, whichever is greater, and, in the case of an individual, imprisoned not more than 5 years, or both.

(2) WILLFUL VIOLATIONS.—A person who willfully violates or conspires to or attempts to violate any provision of subsection (a) shall be fined not more than 5 times the amount or value of the exports, reexports, or transfers involved, or $1,000,000, whichever is greater, and, in the case of an individual, shall be fined not more than $250,000, or imprisoned not more than 10 years, or both.

(c) Civil penalties.—

    (1) AUTHORITY.—The President may impose the following civil penalties on a person for each violation by that person of this title or any regulation, order, or license issued under this title, for each violation:

        (A) A fine of not more than $250,000 or an amount that is twice the value of the transaction that is the basis of the violation with respect to which the penalty is imposed, whichever is greater.

        (B) Revocation of a license issued under this title to the person.

        (C) A prohibition on the person's ability to export, reexport, or transfer any items, whether or not subject to controls under this title.

    (2) PROCEDURES.—Any civil penalty under this subsection may be imposed only after notice and opportunity for an agency hearing on the record in accordance with sections 554 through 557 of title 5, United States Code.

    (3) STANDARDS FOR LEVELS OF CIVIL PENALTY.—The President may by regulation provide standards for establishing levels of civil penalty under this subsection based upon factors such as the seriousness of the violation, the culpability of the violator, and such mitigating factors as the violator's record of cooperation with the Government in disclosing the violation.

(d) Criminal forfeiture of property interest and proceeds.—

    (1) FORFEITURE.—Any person who is convicted under subsection (b) of a violation of a control imposed under section 103 (or any regulation, order, or license issued with respect to such control) shall, in addition to any other penalty, forfeit to the United States—

        (A) any of that person's interest in, security of, claim against, or property or contractual rights of any kind in the tangible items that were the subject of the violation;

        (B) any of that person's interest in, security of, claim against, or property or contractual rights of any kind in tangible property that was used in the violation; and

        (C) any of that person's property constituting, or derived from, any proceeds obtained directly or indirectly as a result of the violation.

    (2) PROCEDURES.—The procedures in any forfeiture under this subsection, and the duties and authority of the courts of the United States and the Attorney General with respect to any forfeiture action under this subsection or with respect to any property that may be subject to forfeiture under this subsection, shall be governed by the provisions of section 1963 of title 18, United States Code.

(e) Prior convictions.—

    (1) LICENSE BAR.—

        (A) IN GENERAL.—The President may—

            (i) deny the eligibility of any person convicted of a criminal violation described in subparagraph (B) to export, reexport, or transfer outside the United States any item, whether or not subject to controls under this title, for a period of up to 10 years beginning on the date of the conviction; and

            (ii) revoke any license or other authorization to export, reexport, or transfer items that was issued under this title and in which such person has an interest at the time of the conviction.

        (B) VIOLATIONS.—The violations referred to in subparagraph (A) are any criminal violations of, or criminal attempt or conspiracy to violate—

            (i) this title (or any regulation, license, or order issued under this title);

            (ii) any regulation, license, or order issued under the International Emergency Economic Powers Act;

            (iii) section 793, 794, or 798 of title 18, United States Code;

            (iv) section 4(b) of the Internal Security Act of 1950 (50 U.S.C. 783(b)); or

(v) section 38 of the Arms Export Control Act (22 U.S.C. 2778).

(2) APPLICATION TO OTHER PARTIES.—The President may exercise the authority under paragraph (1) with respect to any person related, through affiliation, ownership, control, or position of responsibility, to any person convicted of any violation of law set forth in paragraph (1), upon a showing of such relationship with the convicted party, and subject to the procedures set forth in subsection (c)(2).

(f) Other authorities.—Nothing in subsection (c), (d), or (e) limits—

(1) the availability of other administrative or judicial remedies with respect to violations of this title, or any regulation, order, license or other authorization issued under this title;

(2) the authority to compromise and settle administrative proceedings brought with respect to violations of this title, or any regulation, order, license, or other authorization issued under this title; or

(3) the authority to compromise, remit or mitigate seizures and forfeitures pursuant to section 1(b) of title VI of the Act of June 15, 1917 (22 U.S.C. 401(b)).

SEC. 111. Enforcement.

(a) Authorities.—In order to enforce this title, the President may—

(1) issue regulations, orders, and guidelines;

(2) require, inspect, and obtain books, records, and any other information from any person subject to the provisions of this title;

(3) administer oaths or affirmations and by subpoena require any person to appear and testify or to appear and produce books, records, and other writings, or both;

(4) conduct investigations (including undercover) in the United States and in other countries, including intercepting any wire, oral, and electronic communications, conducting electronic surveillance, using pen registers and trap and trace devices, and carrying out acquisitions, to the extent authorized under chapters 119, 121, and 206 of title 18, United States Code, and other applicable laws of the United States;

(5) inspect, search, detain, seize, or issue temporary denial orders with respect to items, in any form, that are subject to controls under this title, or conveyances on which it is believed that there are items that have been, are being, or are about to be exported, reexported, or transferred in violation of this title, or any regulations, order, license, or other authorization issued thereunder;

(6) conduct prelicense inspections and post-shipment verifications; and

(7) execute warrants and make arrests.

(b) Enforcement of subpoenas.—In the case of contumacy by, or refusal to obey a subpoena issued to, any person under subsection (a)(3), a district court of the United States, after notice to such person and a hearing, shall have jurisdiction to issue an order requiring such person to appear and give testimony or to appear and produce books, records, and other writings, regardless of format, that are the subject of the subpoena. Any failure to obey such order of the court may be punished by such court as a contempt thereof.

(c) Best practice guidelines.—

(1) IN GENERAL.—The President, in consultation with the Secretary of Commerce and other Federal officials described in section 105(a), should publish and update "best practices" guidelines to assist persons in developing and implementing, on a voluntary basis, effective export control programs in compliance with the regulations issued under this title.

(2) EXPORT COMPLIANCE PROGRAM.—The implementation by a person of an effective export compliance program and a high quality overall export compliance effort by a person should ordinarily be given weight as mitigating factors in a civil penalty action against the person under this title.

(d) Reference to enforcement.—For purposes of this section, a reference to the enforcement of, or a violation of, this title includes a reference to the enforcement or a violation of any regulation, order, license or other authorization issued pursuant to this title.

(e) Immunity.—A person shall not be excused from complying with any requirements under this section because of the person's privilege against self-incrimination, but the immunity provisions of section 6002 of title 18, United States Code, shall apply with respect to any individual who specifically claims such privilege.

(f) Confidentiality of information.—

    (1) EXEMPTIONS FROM DISCLOSURE.—

        (A) IN GENERAL.—Information obtained under this title may be withheld from disclosure only to the extent permitted by statute, except that information described in subparagraph (B) shall be withheld from public disclosure and shall not be subject to disclosure under section 552(b)(3) of title 5, United States Code, unless the release of such information is determined by the President to be in the national interest.

        (B) INFORMATION DESCRIBED.—Information described in this subparagraph is information submitted or obtained in connection with an application for a license or other authorization to export, reexport, or transfer items, engage in other activities, a recordkeeping or reporting requirement, enforcement activity, or other operations under this title, including—

            (i) the license application, license, or other authorization itself;

            (ii) classification or advisory opinion requests, and the response thereto;

            (iii) license determinations, and information pertaining thereto;

            (iv) information or evidence obtained in the course of any investigation; and

            (v) information obtained or furnished in connection with any international agreement, treaty, or other obligation.

    (2) INFORMATION TO THE CONGRESS AND GAO.—

        (A) IN GENERAL.—Nothing in this section shall be construed as authorizing the withholding of information from the Congress or from the Government Accountability Office.

        (B) AVAILABILITY TO THE CONGRESS.—

            (i) IN GENERAL.—Any information obtained at any time under any provision of the Export Administration Act of 1979 (as in effect on the day before the date of the enactment of this Act and as continued in effect pursuant to the International Emergency Economic Powers Act), under the Export Administration Regulations, or under this title, including any report or license application required under any such provision, shall be made available to a committee or subcommittee of Congress of appropriate jurisdiction, upon the request of the chairman or ranking minority member of such committee or subcommittee.

            (ii) PROHIBITION ON FURTHER DISCLOSURE.—No such committee or subcommittee, or member thereof, may disclose any information made available under clause (i), that is submitted on a confidential basis unless the full committee determines that the withholding of that information is contrary to the national interest.

        (C) AVAILABILITY TO GAO.—

            (i) IN GENERAL.—Information described in clause (i) of subparagraph (B) shall be subject to the limitations contained in section 716 of title 31, United States Code.

            (ii) PROHIBITION ON FURTHER DISCLOSURE.—An officer or employee of the Government Accountability Office may not disclose, except to the Congress in accordance with this paragraph, any such information that is submitted on a confidential basis or from which any individual can be identified.

(3) INFORMATION SHARING.—

(A) IN GENERAL.—Any Federal official described in section 105(a) who obtains information that is relevant to the enforcement of this title, including information pertaining to any investigation, shall furnish such information to each appropriate department, agency, or office with enforcement responsibilities under this section to the extent consistent with the protection of intelligence, counterintelligence, and law enforcement sources, methods, and activities.

(B) EXCEPTIONS.—The provisions of this paragraph shall not apply to information subject to the restrictions set forth in section 9 of title 13, United States Code, and return information, as defined in subsection (b) of section 6103 of the Internal Revenue Code of 1986 (26 U.S.C. 6103(b)), may be disclosed only as authorized by that section.

(C) EXCHANGE OF INFORMATION.—The President shall ensure that the heads of departments, agencies, and offices with enforcement authorities under this title, consistent with protection of law enforcement and its sources and methods—

(i) exchange any licensing and enforcement information with one another that is necessary to facilitate enforcement efforts under this section; and

(ii) consult on a regular basis with one another and with the head of other departments, agencies, and offices that obtain information subject to this paragraph, in order to facilitate the exchange of such information.

(D) INFORMATION SHARING WITH FEDERAL AGENCIES.—Licensing or enforcement information obtained under this title may be shared with heads of departments, agencies, and offices that do not have enforcement authorities under this title on a case-by-case basis at the discretion of the President. Such information may be shared only when the President makes a determination that the sharing of this information is in the national interest.

(g) Reporting requirements.—In the administration of this section, reporting requirements shall be designed so as to reduce the cost of reporting, recordkeeping, and documentation to the extent consistent with effective enforcement and compilation of useful trade statistics. Reporting, recordkeeping, and documentation requirements shall be periodically reviewed and revised in the light of developments in the field of information technology.

(h) Civil forfeiture.—

(1) IN GENERAL.—Any tangible items seized under subsection (a) by designated officers or employees shall be subject to forfeiture to the United States in accordance with applicable law, except that property seized shall be returned if the property owner is not found guilty of a civil or criminal violation under section 109.

(2) PROCEDURES.—Any seizure or forfeiture under this subsection shall be carried out in accordance with the procedures set forth in section 981 of title 18, United States Code.

SEC. 112. Administrative procedure.

(a) In general.—The functions exercised under this title shall be subject to sections 551, 553 through 559, and 701 through 706 of title 5, United States Code.

(b) Amendments to regulations.—The President shall notify in advance the Committee on Banking, Housing, and Urban Affairs of the Senate and the Committee on Foreign Affairs of the House of Representatives of any proposed amendments to the Export Administration Regulations with an explanation of the intent and rationale of such amendments.

SEC. 113. Annual report to Congress.

(a) In general.—The President shall submit to Congress, by December 31 of each year, a report on the implementation of this title during the preceding fiscal year. The report shall include an analysis of—

(1) the effect of controls imposed under this title on exports, reexports, and transfers of items in addressing threats to the national security or foreign policy of the United States, including a description of licensing processing times;

(2) the impact of such controls on the scientific and technological leadership of the United States;

(3) the consistency with such controls of export controls imposed by other countries;

(4) efforts to provide exporters with compliance assistance, including specific actions to assist small- and medium-sized businesses;

(5) a summary of regulatory changes from the prior fiscal year;

(6) a summary of export enforcement actions, including of actions taken to implement end-use monitoring of dual-use, military, and other items subject to the Export Administration Regulations;

(7) a summary of approved license applications to proscribed persons; and

(8) efforts undertaken within the previous year to comply with the requirements of section 109, including any "critical technologies" identified under such section and how or whether such critical technologies were controlled for export.

(b) Form.—The report required under subsection (a) shall be submitted in unclassified form, but may contain a classified annex.

SEC. 114. Repeal.

(a) In general.—The Export Administration Act of 1979 (50 U.S.C. App. 2401 et seq.) (as continued in effect pursuant to the International Emergency Economic Powers Act) is repealed.

(b) Implementation.—The President shall implement the amendment made by subsection (a) by exercising the authorities of the President under the International Emergency Economic Powers Act (50 U.S.C. 1701 et seq.).

SEC. 115. Effect on other Acts.

(a) In general.—Except as otherwise provided in this title, nothing contained in this title shall be construed to modify, repeal, supersede, or otherwise affect the provisions of any other laws authorizing control over exports, reexports, or transfers of any item, or activities of United States persons subject to the Export Administration Regulations.

(b) Coordination of controls.—

(1) IN GENERAL.—The authority granted to the President under this title shall be exercised in such manner so as to achieve effective coordination with all export control and sanctions authorities exercised by Federal departments and agencies delegated with authority under this title, particularly the Department of State, the Department of the Treasury, and the Department of Energy.

(2) SENSE OF CONGRESS.—It is the sense of Congress that in order to achieve effective coordination described in paragraph (1), such Federal departments and agencies—

(A) should continuously work to create enforceable regulations with respect to the export, reexport, and transfer by United States and foreign persons of commodities, software, technology, and services to various end uses and end users for foreign policy and national security reasons;

(B) should regularly work to reduce complexity in the system, including complexity caused merely by the existence of structural, definitional, and other non-policy based differences between and among different export control and sanctions systems; and

(C) should coordinate controls on items exported, reexported, or transferred in connection with a foreign military sale under chapter 2 of the Arms Export Control Act or a commercial sale under section 38 of the Arms Export Control Act to reduce as much unnecessary administrative burden as possible that is a result of differences between the exercise of those two authorities.

(c) Nonproliferation controls.—Nothing in this title shall be construed to supersede the procedures published by the President pursuant to section 309(c) of the Nuclear Non-Proliferation Act of 1978.

SEC. 116. Transition provisions.

(a) In general.—All delegations, rules, regulations, orders, determinations, licenses, or other forms of administrative action that have been made, issued, conducted, or allowed to become effective under the Export Administration Act of 1979 (as in effect on the day before the date of the enactment of this Act and as continued in effect pursuant to the International Emergency Economic Powers Act), or the Export Administration Regulations, and are in effect as of the date of the enactment of this Act, shall continue in effect according to their terms until modified, superseded, set aside, or revoked under the authority of this title.

(b) Administrative and judicial proceedings.—This title shall not affect any administrative or judicial proceedings commenced, or any applications for licenses made, under the Export Administration Act of 1979 (as in effect on the day before the date of the enactment of this Act and as continued in effect pursuant to the International Emergency Economic Powers Act), or the Export Administration Regulations.

(c) Certain determinations and references.—

(1) STATE SPONSORS OF TERRORISM.—Any determination that was made under section 6(j) of the Export Administration Act of 1979 (as in effect on the day before the date of the enactment of this Act and as continued in effect pursuant to the International Emergency Economic Powers Act) shall continue in effect as if the determination had been made under section 104(c) of this Act.

(2) REFERENCE.—Any reference in any other provision of law to a country the government of which the Secretary of State has determined, for purposes of section 6(j) of the Export Administration Act of 1979 (as in effect on the day before the date of the enactment of this Act and as continued in effect pursuant to the International Emergency Economic Powers Act), is a government that has repeatedly provided support for acts of international terrorism shall be deemed to refer to a country the government of which the Secretary of State has determined, for purposes of section 104(c) of this Act, is a government that has repeatedly provided support for acts of international terrorism.

TITLE II—Anti-Boycott Act of 2018

SEC. 201. Short title.

This Act may be cited as the "Anti-Boycott Act of 2018".

SEC. 202. Statement of policy.

Congress declares it is the policy of the United States—

(1) to oppose restrictive trade practices or boycotts fostered or imposed by any foreign country, or requests to impose restrictive trade practices or boycotts by any foreign country, against other countries friendly to the United States or against any United States person;

(2) to encourage and, in specified cases, require United States persons engaged in the export of goods or technology or other information to refuse to take actions, including furnishing information or entering into or implementing agreements, which have the effect of further-

ing or supporting the restrictive trade practices or boycotts fostered or imposed by any foreign country, or requests to impose restrictive trade practices or boycotts by any foreign country against a country friendly to the United States or against any United States person; and

(3) to foster international cooperation and the development of international rules and institutions to assure reasonable access to world supplies.

SEC. 203. Foreign boycotts.

(a) Prohibitions and exceptions.—

(1) PROHIBITIONS.—For the purpose of implementing the policies set forth in section 202, the President shall issue regulations prohibiting any United States person, with respect to that person's activities in the interstate or foreign commerce of the United States, from taking or knowingly agreeing to take any of the following actions with intent to comply with, further, or support any boycott fostered or imposed by any foreign country, or request to impose any boycott by any foreign country, against a country which is friendly to the United States and which is not itself the object of any form of boycott pursuant to United States law or regulation:

(A) Refusing, or requiring any other person to refuse, to do business with or in the boycotted country, with any business concern organized under the laws of the boycotted country, with any national or resident of the boycotted country, or with any other person, pursuant to an agreement with, a requirement of, or a request from or on behalf of the boycotting country. The mere absence of a business relationship with or in the boycotted country with any business concern organized under the laws of the boycotted country, with any national or resident of the boycotted country, or with any other person, does not indicate the existence of the intent required to establish a violation of regulations issued to carry out this subparagraph.

(B) Refusing, or requiring any other person to refuse, to employ or otherwise discriminating against any United States person on the basis of race, religion, sex, or national origin of that person or of any owner, officer, director, or employee of such person.

(C) Furnishing information with respect to the race, religion, sex, or national origin of any United States person or of any owner, officer, director, or employee of such person.

(D) Furnishing information, or requesting the furnishing of information, about whether any person has, has had, or proposes to have any business relationship (including a relationship by way of sale, purchase, legal or commercial representation, shipping or other transport, insurance, investment, or supply) with or in the boycotted country, with any business concern organized under the laws of the boycotted country, with any national or resident of the boycotted country, or with any other person which is known or believed to be restricted from having any business relationship with or in the boycotting country. Nothing in this subparagraph shall prohibit the furnishing of normal business information in a commercial context as defined by the Secretary.

(E) Furnishing information about whether any person is a member of, has made contributions to, or is otherwise associated with or involved in the activities of any charitable or fraternal organization which supports the boycotted country.

(F) Paying, honoring, confirming, or otherwise implementing a letter of credit which contains any condition or requirement compliance with which is prohibited by regulations issued pursuant to this paragraph, and no United States person shall, as a result of the application of this paragraph, be obligated to pay or otherwise honor or implement such letter of credit.

(2) EXCEPTIONS.—Regulations issued pursuant to paragraph (1) shall provide exceptions for—

(A) complying or agreeing to comply with requirements—

(i) prohibiting the import of goods or services from the boycotted country or goods produced or services provided by any business concern organized under the laws of the boycotted country or by nationals or residents of the boycotted country; or

(ii) prohibiting the shipment of goods to the boycotting country on a carrier of the boycotted country, or by a route other than that prescribed by the boycotting country or the recipient of the shipment;

(B) complying or agreeing to comply with import and shipping document requirements with respect to the country of origin, the name of the carrier and route of shipment, the name of the supplier of the shipment or the name of the provider of other services, except that no information knowingly furnished or conveyed in response to such requirements may be stated in negative, blacklisting, or similar exclusionary terms, other than with respect to carriers or route of shipment as may be permitted by such regulations in order to comply with precautionary requirements protecting against war risks and confiscation;

(C) complying or agreeing to comply in the normal course of business with the unilateral and specific selection by a boycotting country, or national or resident thereof, of carriers, insurers, suppliers of services to be performed within the boycotting country or specific goods which, in the normal course of business, are identifiable by source when imported into the boycotting country;

(D) complying or agreeing to comply with export requirements of the boycotting country relating to shipments or transshipments of exports to the boycotted country, to any business concern of or organized under the laws of the boycotted country, or to any national or resident of the boycotted country;

(E) compliance by an individual or agreement by an individual to comply with the immigration or passport requirements of any country with respect to such individual or any member of such individual's family or with requests for information regarding requirements of employment of such individual within the boycotting country; and

(F) compliance by a United States person resident in a foreign country or agreement by such person to comply with the laws of that country with respect to his activities exclusively therein, and such regulations may contain exceptions for such resident complying with the laws or regulations of that foreign country governing imports into such country of trademarked, trade named, or similarly specifically identifiable products, or components of products for his own use, including the performance of contractual services within that country, as may be defined by such regulations.

(3) SPECIAL RULES.—Regulations issued pursuant to paragraphs (2)(C) and (2)(F) shall not provide exceptions from paragraphs (1)(B) and (1)(C).

(4) RULE OF CONSTRUCTION.—Nothing in this subsection may be construed to supersede or limit the operation of the antitrust or civil rights laws of the United States.

(5) APPLICATION.—This section shall apply to any transaction or activity undertaken, by or through a United States person or any other person, with intent to evade the provisions of this section as implemented by the regulations issued pursuant to this subsection, and such regulations shall expressly provide that the exceptions set forth in paragraph (2) shall not permit activities or agreements (expressed or implied by a course of conduct, including a pattern of responses) otherwise prohibited, which are not within the intent of such exceptions.

(b) Foreign policy controls.—

(1) IN GENERAL.—In addition to the regulations issued pursuant to subsection (a), regulations issued under title I of this Act to carry out the policies set forth in section 102(1)(D) shall implement the policies set forth in this section.

(2) REQUIREMENTS.—Such regulations shall require that any United States person receiving a request for the furnishing of information, the entering into or implementing of agreements, or the taking of any other action referred to in subsection (a) shall report that fact to the Secretary, together with such other information concerning such request as the Secretary may require for such action as the Secretary considers appropriate for carrying out the policies of that section. Such person shall also report to the Secretary whether such person intends to comply and whether such person has complied with such request. Any report filed pursuant to this paragraph shall be made available promptly for public inspection and copying, except that information regarding the quantity, description, and value of any goods or technology to which such report relates may be kept confidential if the Secretary determines that disclosure thereof would place the United States person involved at a competitive disadvantage. The Secretary shall periodically transmit summaries of the information contained in such reports to the Secretary of State for such action as the Secretary of State, in consultation with the Secretary, considers appropriate for carrying out the policies set forth in section 202.

(c) Preemption.—The provisions of this section and the regulations issued pursuant thereto shall preempt any law, rule, or regulation of any of the several States or the District of Columbia, or any of the territories or possessions of the United States, or of any governmental subdivision thereof, which law, rule, or regulation pertains to participation in, compliance with, implementation of, or the furnishing of information regarding restrictive trade practices or boycotts fostered or imposed by foreign countries, or requests to impose restrictive trade practices or boycotts by any foreign country, against other countries friendly to the United States.

SEC. 204. Enforcement.

(a) Civil penalties.—The President may impose the following civil penalties on a person who violates section 203 or any regulation issued under this title:

(1) A fine of not more than $250,000 or an amount that is twice the amount of the transaction that is the basis of the violation with respect to which the penalty is imposed.

(2) Revocation of a license issued under title I to the person.

(3) A prohibition on the person's ability to export, reexport, or transfer any items, whether or not subject to controls under this title.

(b) Procedures.—Any civil penalty under this section may be imposed only after notice and opportunity for an agency hearing on the record in accordance with sections 554 through 557 of title 5, United States Code, and shall be subject to judicial review in accordance with chapter 7 of such title.

(c) Standards for levels of civil penalty.—The President may by regulation provide standards for establishing levels of civil penalty under this section based upon factors such as the seriousness of the violation, the culpability of the violator, and the violator's record of cooperation with the Government in disclosing the violation.

TITLE III—Sanctions Regarding Missile Proliferation and Chemical and Biological Weapons Proliferation

SEC. 301. Missile proliferation control violations.

(a) Violations by United States persons.—

(1) SANCTIONS.—

(A) SANCTIONABLE ACTIVITY.—The President shall impose the applicable sanctions described in subparagraph (B) if the President determines that a United States person knowingly—

(i) exports, reexports, or transfers of any item on the MTCR Annex, in violation of the provisions of section 38 (22 U.S.C. 2778) or chapter 7 of the Arms Export Control Act, title I of this Act, or any regulations or orders issued under any such provisions; or

(ii) conspires to or attempts to engage in such export, reexport, or transfer.

(B) SANCTIONS.—The sanctions that apply to a United States person under subparagraph (A) are the following:

(i) If the item on the MTCR Annex involved in the export, reexport, or transfer is missile equipment or technology within category II of the MTCR Annex, then the President shall deny to such United States person, for a period of 2 years, licenses for the transfer of missile equipment or technology controlled under title I.

(ii) If the item on the MTCR Annex involved in the export, reexport, or transfer is missile equipment or technology within category I of the MTCR Annex, then the President shall deny to such United States person, for a period of not less than 2 years, all licenses for items the transfer of which is controlled under title I.

(2) DISCRETIONARY SANCTIONS.—In the case of any determination referred to in paragraph (1), the President may pursue any other appropriate penalties under section 109 of this Act.

(3) WAIVER.—The President may waive the imposition of sanctions under paragraph (1) on a person with respect to a product or service if the President certifies to the Congress that—

(A) the product or service is essential to the national security of the United States; and

(B) such person is a sole source supplier of the product or service, the product or service is not available from any alternative reliable supplier, and the need for the product or service cannot be met in a timely manner by improved manufacturing processes or technological developments.

(b) Transfers of missile equipment or technology by foreign persons.—

(1) SANCTIONS.—

(A) SANCTIONABLE ACTIVITY.—Subject to paragraphs (3) through (7), the President shall impose the applicable sanctions under subparagraph (B) on a foreign person if the President—

(i) determines that a foreign person knowingly—

(I) exports, reexports, or transfers any MTCR equipment or technology that contributes to the design, development, or production of missiles in a country that is not an MTCR adherent and would be, if it were United States-origin equipment or technology, subject to the jurisdiction of the United States under title I;

(II) conspires to or attempts to engage in such export, reexport, or transfer; or

(III) facilitates such export, reexport, or transfer by any other person; or

(ii) has made a determination with respect to the foreign person under section 73(a) of the Arms Export Control Act.

(B) SANCTIONS.—The sanctions that apply to a foreign person under subparagraph (A) are the following:

(i) If the item involved in the export, reexport, or transfer is within category II of the MTCR Annex, then the President shall deny, for a period of 2 years, licenses for the transfer to such foreign person of missile equipment or technology the transfer of which is controlled under title I.

(ii) If the item involved in the export, reexport, or transfer is within category I of the MTCR Annex, then the President shall deny, for a period of not less than 2 years, licenses for the transfer to such foreign person of items the transfer of which is controlled under title I.

(2) INAPPLICABILITY WITH RESPECT TO MTCR ADHERENTS.—Paragraph (1) does not apply with respect to—

(A) any export, reexport, or transfer that is authorized by the laws of an MTCR adherent, if such authorization is not obtained by misrepresentation or fraud; or

(B) any export, reexport, or transfer of an item to an end user in a country that is an MTCR adherent.

(3) EFFECT OF ENFORCEMENT ACTIONS BY MTCR ADHERENTS.—Sanctions set forth in paragraph (1) may not be imposed under this subsection on a person with respect to acts described in such paragraph or, if such sanctions are in effect against a person on account of such acts, such sanctions shall be terminated, if an MTCR adherent is taking judicial or other enforcement action against that person with respect to such acts, or that person has been found by the government of an MTCR adherent to be innocent of wrongdoing with respect to such acts.

(4) WAIVER AND REPORT TO CONGRESS.—

(A) WAIVER AUTHORITY.—The President may waive the application of paragraph (1) to a foreign person if the President determines that such waiver is essential to the national security of the United States.

(B) NOTIFICATION AND REPORT TO CONGRESS.—In the event that the President decides to apply the waiver described in subparagraph (A), the President shall so notify the appropriate congressional committees not less than 20 working days before issuing the waiver. Such notification shall include a report fully articulating the rationale and circumstances which led the President to apply the waiver.

(5) ADDITIONAL WAIVER.—The President may waive the imposition of sanctions under paragraph (1) on a person with respect to a product or service if the President certifies to the appropriate congressional committees that—

(A) the product or service is essential to the national security of the United States; and

(B) such person is a sole source supplier of the product or service, the product or service is not available from any alternative reliable supplier, and the need for the product or service cannot be met in a timely manner by improved manufacturing processes or technological developments.

(6) EXCEPTIONS.—The President shall not apply the sanction under this subsection prohibiting the importation of the products of a foreign person—

(A) in the case of procurement of defense articles or defense services—

(i) under existing contracts or subcontracts, including the exercise of options for production quantities to satisfy requirements essential to the national security of the United States;

(ii) if the President determines that the person to which the sanctions would be applied is a sole source supplier of the defense articles or defense services, that the defense articles or defense services are essential to the national security of the United States, and that alternative sources are not readily or reasonably available; or

(iii) if the President determines that such articles or services are essential to the national security of the United States under defense coproduction agreements or NATO Programs of Cooperation;

(B) to products or services provided under contracts entered into before the date on which the President publishes his intention to impose the sanctions; or

(C) to—

(i) spare parts;

(ii) component parts, but not finished products, essential to United States products or production;

(iii) routine services and maintenance of products, to the extent that alternative sources are not readily or reasonably available; or

(iv) information and technology essential to United States products or production.

(c) Definitions.—In this section:

(1) APPROPRIATE CONGRESSIONAL COMMITTEES.—The term "appropriate congressional committees" means—

(A) the Committee on Foreign Affairs of the House of Representatives; and

(B) the Committee on Foreign Relations and the Committee on Banking, Housing, and Urban Affairs of the Senate.

(2) DEFENSE ARTICLES; DEFENSE SERVICES.—The terms "defense articles" and "defense services" mean those items on the United States Munitions List as defined in section 47(7) of the Arms Export Control Act (22 U.S.C. 2794 note).

(3) MISSILE.—The term "missile" means a category I system as defined in the MTCR Annex.

(4) MISSILE TECHNOLOGY CONTROL REGIME; MTCR.—The term "Missile Technology Control Regime" or "MTCR" means the policy statement, between the United States, the United Kingdom, the Federal Republic of Germany, France, Italy, Canada, and Japan, announced on April 16, 1987, to restrict sensitive missile-relevant transfers based on the MTCR Annex, and any amendments thereto.

(5) MTCR ADHERENT.—The term "MTCR adherent" means a country that participates in the MTCR or that, pursuant to an international understanding to which the United States is a party, controls MTCR equipment or technology in accordance with the criteria and standards set forth in the MTCR.

(6) MTCR ANNEX.—The term "MTCR Annex" means the Guidelines and Equipment and Technology Annex of the MTCR, and any amendments thereto.

(7) MISSILE EQUIPMENT OR TECHNOLOGY; MTCR EQUIPMENT OR TECHNOLOGY.—The terms "missile equipment or technology" and "MTCR equipment or technology" mean those items listed in category I or category II of the MTCR Annex.

SEC. 302. Chemical and biological weapons proliferation sanctions.

(a) Imposition of sanctions.—

(1) DETERMINATION BY THE PRESIDENT.—Except as provided in subsection (b)(2), the President shall impose the sanction described in subsection (c) if the President determines that a foreign person has knowingly and materially contributed—

(A) through the export from the United States of any item that is subject to the jurisdiction of the United States under this title; or

(B) through the export from any other country of any item that would be, if they were United States goods or technology, subject to the jurisdiction of the United States under this title, to the efforts by any foreign country, project, or entity described in paragraph (2) to use, develop, produce, stockpile, or otherwise acquire chemical or biological weapons.

(2) COUNTRIES, PROJECTS, OR ENTITIES RECEIVING ASSISTANCE.—Paragraph (1) applies in the case of—

    (A) any foreign country that the President determines has, at any time after January 1, 1980—

        (i) used chemical or biological weapons in violation of international law;

        (ii) used lethal chemical or biological weapons against its own nationals; or

        (iii) made substantial preparations to engage in the activities described in clause (i) or (ii);

    (B) any foreign country whose government is determined for purposes of section 104(c) of this Act to be a government that has repeatedly provided support for acts of international terrorism; or

    (C) any other foreign country, project, or entity designated by the President for purposes of this section.

(3) PERSONS AGAINST WHICH SANCTIONS ARE TO BE IMPOSED.—A sanction shall be imposed pursuant to paragraph (1) on—

    (A) the foreign person with respect to which the President makes the determination described in that paragraph;

    (B) any successor entity to that foreign person; and

    (C) any foreign person that is a parent, subsidiary, or affiliate of that foreign person if that parent, subsidiary, or affiliate knowingly assisted in the activities which were the basis of that determination.

(b) Consultations with and actions by foreign government of jurisdiction.—

(1) CONSULTATIONS.—If the President makes the determinations described in subsection (a)(1) with respect to a foreign person, the Congress urges the President to initiate consultations immediately with the government with primary jurisdiction over that foreign person with respect to the imposition of a sanction pursuant to this section.

(2) ACTIONS BY GOVERNMENT OF JURISDICTION.—In order to pursue such consultations with that government, the President may delay imposition of a sanction pursuant to this section for a period of up to 90 days. Following such consultations, the President shall impose the sanction unless the President determines and certifies to the appropriate congressional committees that the Government has taken specific and effective actions, including appropriate penalties, to terminate the involvement of the foreign person in the activities described in subsection (a)(1). The President may delay imposition of the sanction for an additional period of up to 90 days if the President determines and certifies to the Congress that the government is in the process of taking the actions described in the preceding sentence.

(3) REPORT TO CONGRESS.—The President shall report to the appropriate congressional committees, not later than 90 days after making a determination under subsection (a)(1), on the status of consultations with the appropriate government under this subsection, and the basis for any determination under paragraph (2) of this subsection that such government has taken specific corrective actions.

(c) Sanction.—

(1) DESCRIPTION OF SANCTION.—The sanction to be imposed pursuant to subsection (a)(1) is, except as provided that the United States Government shall not procure, or enter into any contract for the procurement of, any goods or services from any person described in subsection (a)(3).

(2) EXCEPTIONS.—The President shall not be required to apply or maintain a sanction under this section—

    (A) in the case of procurement of defense articles or defense services—

(i) under existing contracts or subcontracts, including the exercise of options for production quantities to satisfy United States operational military requirements;

(ii) if the President determines that the person or other entity to which the sanctions would otherwise be applied is a sole source supplier of the defense articles or defense services, that the defense articles or defense services are essential, and that alternative sources are not readily or reasonably available; or

(iii) if the President determines that such articles or services are essential to the national security under defense coproduction agreements;

(B) to products or services provided under contracts entered into before the date on which the President publishes his intention to impose sanctions;

(C) to—

(i) spare parts;

(ii) component parts, but not finished products, essential to United States products or production; or

(iii) routine servicing and maintenance of products, to the extent that alternative sources are not readily or reasonably available;

(D) to information and technology essential to United States products or production; or

(E) to medical or other humanitarian items.

(d) Termination of sanctions.—A sanction imposed pursuant to this section shall apply for a period of at least 12 months following the imposition of one sanction and shall cease to apply thereafter only if the President determines and certifies to the appropriate congressional committees that reliable information indicates that the foreign person with respect to which the determination was made under subsection (a)(1) has ceased to aid or abet any foreign government, project, or entity in its efforts to acquire chemical or biological weapons capability as described in that subsection.

(e) Waiver.—

(1) CRITERION FOR WAIVER.—The President may waive the application of any sanction imposed on any person pursuant to this section, after the end of the 12-month period beginning on the date on which that sanction was imposed on that person, if the President determines and certifies to the appropriate congressional committees that such waiver is important to the national security interests of the United States.

(2) NOTIFICATION OF AND REPORT TO CONGRESS.—If the President decides to exercise the waiver authority provided in paragraph (1), the President shall so notify the appropriate congressional committees not less than 20 days before the waiver takes effect. Such notification shall include a report fully articulating the rationale and circumstances which led the President to exercise the waiver authority.

(f) Definitions.—In this section:

(1) APPROPRIATE CONGRESSIONAL COMMITTEES.—The term "appropriate congressional committees" means—

(A) the Committee on Foreign Affairs of the House of Representatives; and

(B) the Committee on Foreign Relations and the Committee on Banking, Housing, and Urban Affairs of the Senate.

(2) DEFENSE ARTICLES; DEFENSE SERVICES.—The terms "defense articles" and "defense services" mean those items on the United States Munitions List or are otherwise controlled under the Arms Export Control Act.

ANNUAL INTELLIGENCE AUTHORIZATION ACT

Intelligence Authorization Act for Fiscal Year 2017

115th CONG. U.S. HR 244 (May 5, 2017)

To authorize appropriations for fiscal year 2017 for intelligence and intelligence-related activities of the United States Government, the Community Management Account, and the Central Intelligence Agency Retirement and Disability System, and for other purposes.

SECTION 1. Short title; table of contents.

(a) Short title.—This Act may be cited as the "Intelligence Authorization Act for Fiscal Year 2017".

(b) Table of contents.—The table of contents for this Act is as follows:

SEC. 2. Definitions.

In this Act:

(1) CONGRESSIONAL INTELLIGENCE COMMITTEES.—The term "congressional intelligence committees" means—

(A) the Select Committee on Intelligence of the Senate; and

(B) the Permanent Select Committee on Intelligence of the House of Representatives.

(2) INTELLIGENCE COMMUNITY.—The term "intelligence community" has the meaning given that term in section 3(4) of the National Security Act of 1947 (50 U.S.C. 3003(4)).

TITLE I—Intelligence Activities

SEC. 101. Authorization of appropriations.

Funds are hereby authorized to be appropriated for fiscal year 2017 for the conduct of the intelligence and intelligence-related activities of the following elements of the United States Government:

(1) The Office of the Director of National Intelligence.

(2) The Central Intelligence Agency.

(3) The Department of Defense.

(4) The Defense Intelligence Agency.

(5) The National Security Agency.

(6) The Department of the Army, the Department of the Navy, and the Department of the Air Force.

(7) The Coast Guard.

(8) The Department of State.

(9) The Department of the Treasury.

(10) The Department of Energy.

(11) The Department of Justice.

(12) The Federal Bureau of Investigation.

(13) The Drug Enforcement Administration.

(14) The National Reconnaissance Office.

(15) The National Geospatial-Intelligence Agency.

(16) The Department of Homeland Security.

(a) Specifications of amounts and personnel levels.—The amounts authorized to be appropriated under section 101 and, subject to section 103, the authorized personnel ceilings as of September 30, 2017, for the conduct of the intelligence activities of the elements listed in paragraphs (1) through (16) of section 101, are those specified in the classified Schedule of Authorizations prepared to accompany this Act.

(b) Availability of classified schedule of authorizations.—

(1) AVAILABILITY.—The classified Schedule of Authorizations referred to in subsection (a) shall be made available to the Committee on Appropriations of the Senate, the Committee on Appropriations of the House of Representatives, and to the President.

(2) DISTRIBUTION BY THE PRESIDENT.—Subject to paragraph (3), the President shall provide for suitable distribution of the classified Schedule of Authorizations, or of appropriate portions of the Schedule, within the executive branch.

(3) LIMITS ON DISCLOSURE.—The President shall not publicly disclose the classified Schedule of Authorizations or any portion of such Schedule except—

(A) as provided in section 601(a) of the Implementing Recommendations of the 9/11 Commission Act of 2007 (50 U.S.C. 3306(a));

(B) to the extent necessary to implement the budget; or

(C) as otherwise required by law.

SEC. 103. Personnel ceiling adjustments.

(a) Authority for increases.—The Director of National Intelligence may authorize employment of civilian personnel in excess of the number authorized for fiscal year 2017 by the classified Schedule of Authorizations referred to in section 102(a) if the Director of National Intelligence determines that such action is necessary to the performance of important intelligence functions, except that the number of personnel employed in excess of the number authorized under such section may not, for any element of the intelligence community, exceed 3 percent of the number of civilian personnel authorized under such schedule for such element.

(b) Treatment of certain personnel.—The Director of National Intelligence shall establish guidelines that govern, for each element of the intelligence community, the treatment under the personnel levels authorized under section 102(a), including any exemption from such personnel levels, of employment or assignment in—

(1) a student program, trainee program, or similar program;

(2) a reserve corps or as a reemployed annuitant; or

(3) details, joint duty, or long-term, full-time training.

(c) Notice to congressional intelligence committees.—The Director of National Intelligence shall notify the congressional intelligence committees in writing at least 15 days prior to each exercise of an authority described in subsection (a).

SEC. 104. Intelligence Community Management Account.

(a) Authorization of appropriations.—There is authorized to be appropriated for the Intelligence Community Management Account of the Director of National Intelligence for fiscal year 2017 the sum of $518,596,000. Within such amount, funds identified in the classified Schedule of Authorizations referred to in section 102(a) for advanced research and development shall remain available until September 30, 2018.

(b) Authorized personnel levels.—The elements within the Intelligence Community Management Account of the Director of National Intelligence are authorized 787 positions as of September 30, 2017. Personnel serving in such elements may be permanent employees of the Office of the Director of National Intelligence or personnel detailed from other elements of the United States Government.

(c) Classified authorizations.—

(1) AUTHORIZATION OF APPROPRIATIONS.—In addition to amounts authorized to be appropriated for the Intelligence Community Management Account by subsection (a), there are authorized to be appropriated for the Community Management Account for fiscal year 2017 such additional amounts as are specified in the classified Schedule of Authorizations referred to in section 102(a). Such additional amounts for advanced research and development shall remain available until September 30, 2018.

(2) AUTHORIZATION OF PERSONNEL.—In addition to the personnel authorized by subsection (b) for elements of the Intelligence Community Management Account as of September 30, 2017, there are authorized such additional personnel for the Community Management Account as of that date as are specified in the classified Schedule of Authorizations referred to in section 102(a).

TITLE II—Central Intelligence Agency Retirement and Disability System

SEC. 201. Authorization of appropriations.

There is authorized to be appropriated for the Central Intelligence Agency Retirement and Disability Fund for fiscal year 2017 the sum of $514,000,000.

TITLE III—General provisions

SEC. 301. Increase in employee compensation and benefits authorized by law.

Appropriations authorized by this Act for salary, pay, retirement, and other benefits for Federal employees may be increased by such additional or supplemental amounts as may be necessary for increases in such compensation or benefits authorized by law.

SEC. 302. Restriction on conduct of intelligence activities.

The authorization of appropriations by this Act shall not be deemed to constitute authority for the conduct of any intelligence activity which is not otherwise authorized by the Constitution or the laws of the United States.

SEC. 303. Authorization of appropriations for Privacy and Civil Liberties Oversight Board.

(a) Requirement for authorizations.—Subsection (m) of section 1061 of the Intelligence

Reform and Terrorism Prevention Act of 2004 (42 U.S.C. 2000ee(m)) is amended to read as follows:

"(m) Funding.—

"(1) SPECIFIC AUTHORIZATION REQUIRED.—Appropriated funds available to the Board may be obligated or expended to carry out activities under this section only if such funds were specifically authorized by Congress for use for such activities for such fiscal year.

"(2) DEFINITION.—In this subsection, the term 'specifically authorized by Congress' has the meaning given that term in section 504(e) of the National Security Act of 1947 (50 U.S.C. 3094(e)).".

(b) Authorization of appropriations.—There is authorized to be appropriated to the Privacy and Civil Liberties Oversight Board for fiscal year 2017 the sum of $10,081,000 to carry out the activities of the Board under section 1061 of the Intelligence Reform and Terrorism Prevention Act of 2004 (42 U.S.C. 2000ee(m)).

SEC. 304. Modification of certain whistleblowing procedures.

(a) Clarification of whistleblowing procedures available to certain personnel.—Subsection (a)(1)(A) of section 8H of the Inspector General Act of 1978 (5 U.S.C. App.) is amended by inserting after "Security Agency," the following: "including any such employee who is assigned or detailed to a combatant command or other element of the Federal Government,".

(b) Central Intelligence Agency.—

(1) ROLE OF DIRECTOR.—Section 17(d)(5) of the Central Intelligence Agency Act of 1949 (50 U.S.C. 3517(d)(5)) is amended—

(A) in subparagraph (B)—

(i) by striking clause (ii);

(ii) by striking "(i) Not" and inserting "Not"; and

(iii) by striking "to the Director" and inserting "to the intelligence committees"; and

(B) in subparagraph (D)—

(i) in clause (i), by striking "the Director" and inserting "the intelligence committees"; and

(ii) in clause (ii)—

(I) in subclause (I), by striking "the Director, through the Inspector General," and inserting "the Inspector General"; and

(II) in subclause (II), by striking "the Director, through the Inspector General," and inserting "the Inspector General, in consultation with the Director,".

(2) CONFORMING AMENDMENTS.—

(A) Section 17(d)(5) of such Act is further amended—

(i) by striking subparagraph (C); and

(ii) by redesignating subparagraphs (D) through (H) as subparagraphs (C) through (G), respectively.

(B) Section 3001(j)(1)(C)(ii) of the Intelligence Reform and Terrorism Prevention Act of 2004 (50 U.S.C. 3341(j)(1)(C)(ii)) is amended by striking "subparagraphs (A), (D), and (H)" and inserting "subparagraphs (A), (C), and (G)".

(c) Other elements of intelligence community.—

(1) ROLE OF HEADS.—Section 8H of the Inspector General Act of 1978 (5 U.S.C. App.) is amended—

  (A) in subsection (b)—

    (i) by striking paragraph (2);

    (ii) by striking "(1) Not" and inserting "Not"; and

    (iii) by striking "to the head of the establishment" and inserting "to the intelligence committees"; and

  (B) in subsection (d)—

    (i) in paragraph (1), by striking "the head of the establishment" and inserting "the intelligence committees"; and

    (ii) in paragraph (2)—

      (I) in subparagraph (A), by striking "the head of the establishment, through the Inspector General," and inserting "the Inspector General"; and

      (II) in subparagraph (B), by striking "the head of the establishment, through the Inspector General," and inserting "the Inspector General, in consultation with the head of the establishment,".

 (2) CONFORMING AMENDMENTS.—Section 8H of such Act is further amended—

  (A) by striking subsection (c);

  (B) by redesignating subsections (d) through (i) as subsections (c) through (h), respectively; and

  (C) in subsection (e), as so redesignated, by striking "subsections (a) through (e)" and inserting "subsections (a) through (d)".

(d) Office of the Director of National Intelligence.—

 (1) IN GENERAL.—Section 103H(k)(5) of the National Security Act of 1947 (50 U.S.C. 3033(k)(5)) is amended—

  (A) in subparagraph (B), by striking "to the Director" and inserting "to the congressional intelligence committees"; and

  (B) in subparagraph (D)—

    (i) in clause (i), by striking "the Director" and inserting "the congressional intelligence committees"; and

    (ii) in clause (ii)—

      (I) in subclause (I), by striking "the Director, through the Inspector General," and inserting "the Inspector General"; and

      (II) in subclause (II), by striking "the Director, through the Inspector General," and inserting "the Inspector General, in consultation with the Director,".

 (2) CONFORMING AMENDMENTS.—Section 103H(k)(5) of such Act is further amended—

  (A) by striking subparagraph (C); and

  (B) by redesignating subparagraphs (D) through (I) as subparagraphs (C) through (H), respectively.

(e) Rule of construction.—None of the amendments made by this section may be construed to prohibit or otherwise affect the authority of an Inspector General of an element of the intelligence community, the Inspector General of the Central Intelligence Agency, or the Inspector General of the Intelligence Community to notify the head of the element of the intelligence community, the Director of the Central Intelligence Agency, or the Director of National Intelligence, as the case may be, of a complaint or information otherwise authorized by law.

SEC. 305. Reports on major defense intelligence acquisition programs.

(a) In general.—The National Security Act of 1947 (50 U.S.C. 3001 et seq.) is amended by inserting after section 506J the following new section:

 "SEC. 506K. Reports on major defense intelligence acquisition programs at each milestone approval.

"(a) Report on milestone A.—Not later than 15 days after granting Milestone A or equivalent approval for a major defense intelligence acquisition program, the milestone decision authority for the program shall submit to the appropriate congressional committees a report containing a brief summary of the following:

"(1) The estimated cost and schedule for the program established by the military department concerned, including—

"(A) the dollar values estimated for the program acquisition unit cost and total life-cycle cost; and

"(B) the planned dates for each program milestone and initial operational capability.

"(2) The independent estimated cost for the program established pursuant to section 2334(a)(6) of title 10, United States Code, and any independent estimated schedule for the program, including—

"(A) the dollar values estimated for the program acquisition unit cost and total life-cycle cost; and

"(B) the planned dates for each program milestone and initial operational capability.

"(3) A summary of the technical risks, including cybersecurity risks and supply chain risks, associated with the program, as determined by the military department concerned, including identification of any critical technologies that need to be matured.

"(4) A summary of the sufficiency review conducted by the Director of Cost Assessment and Program Evaluation of the Department of Defense of the analysis of alternatives performed for the program (as referred to in section 2366a(b)(6) of such title).

"(5) Any other information the milestone decision authority considers relevant.

"(b) Report on milestone B.—Not later than 15 days after granting Milestone B or equivalent approval for a major defense intelligence acquisition program, the milestone decision authority for the program shall submit to the appropriate congressional committees a report containing a brief summary of the following:

"(1) The estimated cost and schedule for the program established by the military department concerned, including—

"(A) the dollar values estimated for the program acquisition unit cost, average procurement unit cost, and total life-cycle cost; and

"(B) the planned dates for each program milestone, initial operational test and evaluation, and initial operational capability.

"(2) The independent estimated cost for the program established pursuant to section 2334(a)(6) of title 10, United States Code, and any independent estimated schedule for the program, including—

"(A) the dollar values estimated for the program acquisition unit cost, average procurement unit cost, and total life-cycle cost; and

"(B) the planned dates for each program milestone, initial operational test and evaluation, and initial operational capability.

"(3) A summary of the technical risks, including cybersecurity risks and supply chain risks, associated with the program, as determined by the military department concerned, including identification of any critical technologies that have not been successfully demonstrated in a relevant environment.

"(4) A summary of the sufficiency review conducted by the Director of Cost Assessment and Program Evaluation of the analysis of alternatives performed for the program pursuant to section 2366a(b)(6) of such title.

"(5) A statement of whether the preliminary design review for the program described in section 2366b(a)(1) of such title has been completed.

"(6) Any other information the milestone decision authority considers relevant.

"(c) Report on milestone C.—Not later than 15 days after granting Milestone C or equivalent approval for a major defense intelligence acquisition program, the milestone decision authority for the program shall submit to the appropriate congressional committees a report containing a brief summary of the following:

"(1) The estimated cost and schedule for the program established by the military department concerned, including—

"(A) the dollar values estimated for the program acquisition unit cost, average procurement unit cost, and total life-cycle cost; and

"(B) the planned dates for initial operational test and evaluation and initial operational capability.

"(2) The independent estimated cost for the program established pursuant to section 2334(a)(6) of title 10, United States Code, and any independent estimated schedule for the program, including—

"(A) the dollar values estimated for the program acquisition unit cost, average procurement unit cost, and total life-cycle cost; and

"(B) the planned dates for initial operational test and evaluation and initial operational capability.

"(3) The cost and schedule estimates approved by the milestone decision authority for the program.

"(4) A summary of the production, manufacturing, and fielding risks, including cybersecurity risks and supply chain risks, associated with the program.

"(5) Any other information the milestone decision authority considers relevant.

"(d) Initial operating capability or full operating capability.—Not later than 15 days after a major defense intelligence acquisition program reaches initial operating capability or full operating capability, the milestone decision authority for the program shall notify the appropriate congressional committees of the program reaching such capability.

"(e) Additional information.—At the request of any of the appropriate congressional committees, the milestone decision authority shall submit to the appropriate congressional committees further information or underlying documentation for the information in a report submitted under subsection (a), (b), or (c), including the independent cost and schedule estimates and the independent technical risk assessments referred to in those subsections.

"(f) Nonduplication of effort.—If any information required under this section has been included in another report or assessment previously submitted to the congressional intelligence committees under sections 506A, 506C, or 506E, the milestone decision authority may provide a list of such reports and assessments at the time of submitting a report required under this section instead of including such information in such report.

"(g) Definitions.—In this section:

"(1) The term 'appropriate congressional committees' means the congressional intelligence committees and the congressional defense committees (as defined in section 101(a)(16) of title 10, United States Code).

"(2) The term 'major defense intelligence acquisition program' means a major defense acquisition program (as defined in section 2430 of title 10, United States Code) that relates to intelligence or intelligence-related activities.

"(3) The term 'Milestone A approval' has the meaning given that term in section 2366a(d) of title 10, United States Code.

"(4) The terms 'Milestone B approval' and 'Milestone C approval' have the meaning given those terms in section 2366(e) of such title.

"(5) The term 'milestone decision authority' has the meaning given that term in section 2366a(d) of such title.".

(b) Clerical amendment.—The table of contents in the first section of the National Security Act of 1947 is amended by inserting after the item relating to section 506J the following new item:

"Sec. 506K. Reports on major defense intelligence acquisition programs at each milestone approval.".

SEC. 306. Modifications to certain requirements for construction of facilities.

(a) Inclusion in budget requests of certain projects.—Section 8131 of the Department of Defense Appropriations Act, 1995 (Public Law 103–335; 50 U.S.C. 3303) is repealed.

(b) Notification.—Section 602(a)(2) of the Intelligence Authorization Act for Fiscal Year 1995 (Public Law 103–359; 50 U.S.C. 3304(a)(2)) is amended by striking "improvement project to" and inserting "project for the improvement, repair, or modification of".

SEC. 307. Information on activities of Privacy and Civil Liberties Oversight Board.

Section 1061(d) of the Intelligence Reform and Terrorism Prevention Act of 2004 (42 U.S.C. 2000ee(d)) is further amended by adding at the end the following new paragraph:

"(5) INFORMATION.—

"(A) ACTIVITIES.—In addition to the reports submitted to Congress under subsection (e)(1)(B), the Board shall ensure that each official and congressional committee specified in subparagraph (B) is kept fully and currently informed of the activities of the Board, including any significant anticipated activities.

"(B) OFFICIALS AND CONGRESSIONAL COMMITTEES SPECIFIED.—The officials and congressional committees specified in this subparagraph are the following:

"(i) The Director of National Intelligence.

"(ii) The head of any element of the intelligence community (as defined in section 3(4) of the National Security Act of 1947 (50 U.S.C. 3003(4)) the activities of which are, or are anticipated to be, the subject of the review or advice of the Board.

"(iii) The Permanent Select Committee on Intelligence of the House of Representatives and the Select Committee on Intelligence of the Senate.".

SEC. 308. Clarification of authorization of certain activities of the Department of Energy.

Funds appropriated for fiscal year 2016 for intelligence and intelligence-related activities of the Department of Energy shall be deemed to be authorized to be appropriated for such activities, including for purposes of section 504 of the National Security Act of 1947 (50 U.S.C. 3094).

SEC. 309. Technical correction to Executive Schedule.

Section 5313 of title 5, United States Code, is amended by striking the item relating to "Director of the National Counter Proliferation Center.".

SEC. 310. Maximum amount charged for declassification reviews.

In reviewing and processing a request by a person for the mandatory declassification of information pursuant to Executive Order No. 13526, a successor Executive order, or any other provision of law, the head of an element of the intelligence community—

(1) may not charge the person reproduction fees in excess of the amount of fees that the

head would charge the person for reproduction required in the course of processing a request for information under section 552 of title 5, United States Code (commonly referred to as the "Freedom of Information Act"); and

(2) may waive or reduce any processing fees in the same manner as the head waives or reduces fees under such section 552.

TITLE IV—Matters relating to elements of the Intelligence Community
Subtitle A—Office of the Director of National Intelligence

SEC. 401. Analyses and impact statements by Director of National Intelligence regarding actions by Committee on Foreign Investment in the United States.

Section 721(b)(4) of the Defense Production Act of 1950 (50 U.S.C. 4565) is amended by adding at the end the following new subparagraphs:

"(E) SUBMISSION TO CONGRESSIONAL INTELLIGENCE COMMITTEES.—Not later than 5 days after the completion of a review or an investigation of a covered transaction under this subsection that concludes action under this section, the Director shall submit to the Permanent Select Committee on Intelligence of the House of Representatives and the Select Committee on Intelligence of the Senate an analysis under subparagraph (A) relating to such covered transaction previously provided to the Committee, including any supplements or amendments to such analysis made by the Director.

"(F) IMPACT STATEMENTS.—Not later than 60 days after the completion of a review or an investigation of a covered transaction under this subsection that concludes action under this section, the Director shall determine whether the covered transaction will have an operational impact on the intelligence community, and, if so, shall submit a report on such impact to the Permanent Select Committee on Intelligence of the House of Representatives and the Select Committee on Intelligence of the Senate. Each such report shall—

"(i) describe the operational impact of the covered transaction on the intelligence community; and

"(ii) describe any actions that have been or will be taken to mitigate such impact.".

SEC. 402. National Counterintelligence and Security Center.

(a) Redesignation of Office of National Counterintelligence Executive.—Section 904 of the Counterintelligence Enhancement Act of 2002 (50 U.S.C. 3383) is amended—

(1) by striking "Office of the National Counterintelligence Executive" each place it appears (including in the section heading) and inserting "National Counterintelligence and Security Center";

(2) by striking "National Counterintelligence Executive" each place it appears and inserting "Director of the National Counterintelligence and Security Center";

(3) in the headings of subsections (b) and (c), by striking "of Office" both places it appears and inserting "Center";

(4) in subsection (d)—

(A) in paragraph (5)(C), by striking "by the Office" and inserting "by the Center"; and

(B) in paragraph (6), by striking "that the Office" and inserting "that the Center";

(5) in subsection (f)(1), by striking "by the Office" and inserting "by the Center";

(6) in subsection (g), by striking "of the Office" and inserting "of the Center"; and

(7) in subsection (h), by striking "of the Office" each place it appears and inserting "of the Center".

(b) Redesignation of National Counterintelligence Executive.—Section 902 of such Act (50 U.S.C. 3382) is amended—

(1) by striking subsection (a) and inserting the following new subsection:

"(a) Establishment.—There shall be a Director of the National Counterintelligence and Security Center (referred to in this section as 'the Director'), who shall be appointed by the President, by and with the advice and consent of the Senate.";

(2) by striking "National Counterintelligence Executive" each place it appears (including the section heading) and inserting "Director of the National Counterintelligence and Security Center"; and

(3) by striking "Office of the National Counterintelligence Executive" each place it appears and inserting "National Counterintelligence and Security Center".

(c) Conforming amendments.—

(1) NATIONAL SECURITY ACT OF 1947.—The National Security Act of 1947 (50 U.S.C. 3001 et seq.) is amended—

(A) in section 102A(f)(2), by inserting after "Counterterrorism Center" the following: ", the National Counterproliferation Center, and the National Counterintelligence and Security Center,";

(B) in section 103(c)(8), by striking "National Counterintelligence Executive (including the Office of the National Counterintelligence Executive)" and inserting "Director of the National Counterintelligence and Security Center"; and

(C) in section 103F, by striking "National Counterintelligence Executive" each place it appears (including in the headings) and inserting "Director of the National Counterintelligence and Security Center".

(2) INTELLIGENCE AUTHORIZATION ACT FOR FISCAL YEAR 1995.—Section 811 of the Counterintelligence and Security Enhancements Act of 1994 (title VIII of Public Law 103–359; 50 U.S.C. 3381) is amended—

(A) in subsections (b) and (c)(1), by striking "The National Counterintelligence Executive" and inserting "The Director of the National Counterintelligence and Security Center"; and

(B) in subsection (d)(1)(B)(ii)—

(i) by striking "to the National Counterintelligence Executive" and inserting "to the Director of the National Counterintelligence and Security Center"; and

(ii) by striking "Office of the National Counterintelligence Executive" and inserting "National Counterintelligence and Security Center".

(3) INTELLIGENCE AUTHORIZATION ACT FOR FISCAL YEAR 2004.—Section 341(b) of the Intelligence Authorization Act for Fiscal Year 2004 (Public Law 108–177; 28 U.S.C. 519 note) is amended by striking "Office of the National Counterintelligence Executive" and inserting "National Counterintelligence and Security Center".

(d) Clerical amendment.—The table of sections in the first section of the National Security Act of 1947 is amended by striking the item relating to section 103F and inserting the following:

"Sec. 103F. Director of the National Counterintelligence and Security Center.".

(e) Conforming style.—Any new language inserted or added to a provision of law by the amendments made by this section shall conform to the typeface and typestyle of the matter in which the language is so inserted or added.

(f) Technical effective date.—The amendment made by subsection (a) of section 401 of the Intelligence Authorization Act for Fiscal Year 2016 (division M of Public Law 114–113) shall not take effect, or, if the date of the enactment of this Act is on or after the effective date specified in subsection (b) of such section, such amendment shall be deemed to not have taken effect.

SEC. 403. Assistance for governmental entities and private entities in recognizing online violent extremist content.

(a) Assistance To recognize online violent extremist content.—Not later than 180 days after the date of the enactment of this Act, the Director of National Intelligence shall publish on a publicly available Internet website a list of all logos, symbols, insignia, and other markings commonly associated with, or adopted by, an organization designated by the Secretary of State as a foreign terrorist organization under section 219(a) of the Immigration and Nationality Act (8 U.S.C. 1189(a)).

(b) Updates.—The Director shall update the list published under subsection (a) every 180 days or more frequently as needed.

Subtitle B—Central Intelligence Agency and other elements

SEC. 411. Enhanced death benefits for personnel of the Central Intelligence Agency.

Section 11 of the Central Intelligence Agency Act of 1949 (50 U.S.C. 3511) is amended to read as follows:

"Benefits available in event of the death of personnel

"Sec. 11. (a) Authority.—The Director may pay death benefits substantially similar to those authorized for members of the Foreign Service pursuant to the Foreign Service Act of 1980 (22 U.S.C. 3901 et seq.) or any other provision of law. The Director may adjust the eligibility for death benefits as necessary to meet the unique requirements of the mission of the Agency.

"(b) Regulations.—Regulations issued pursuant to this section shall be submitted to the Permanent Select Committee on Intelligence of the House of Representatives and the Select Committee on Intelligence of the Senate before such regulations take effect.".

SEC. 412. Pay and retirement authorities of the Inspector General of the Central Intelligence Agency.

(a) In general.—Section 17(e)(7) of the Central Intelligence Agency Act of 1949 (50 U.S.C. 3517(e)(7)) is amended by adding at the end the following new subparagraph:

"(C) (i) The Inspector General may designate an officer or employee appointed in accordance with subparagraph (A) as a law enforcement officer solely for purposes of subchapter III of chapter 83 or chapter 84 of title 5, United States Code, if such officer or employee is appointed to a position with responsibility for investigating suspected offenses against the criminal laws of the United States.

"(ii) In carrying out clause (i), the Inspector General shall ensure that any authority under such clause is exercised in a manner consistent with section 3307 of title 5, United States Code, as it relates to law enforcement officers.

"(iii) For purposes of applying sections 3307(d), 8335(b), and 8425(b) of title 5, United States Code, the Inspector General may exercise the functions, powers, and duties of an agency head or appointing authority with respect to the Office.".

(b) Rule of construction.—Subparagraph (C) of section 17(e)(7) of the Central Intelligence Agency Act of 1949 (50 U.S.C. 3517(e)(7)), as added by subsection (a), may not be construed to confer on the Inspector General of the Central Intelligence Agency, or any other officer or employee of the Agency, any police or law enforcement or internal security functions or authorities.

SEC. 413. Clarification of authority, direction, and control over the information assurance directorate of the National Security Agency.

Section 142(b)(1) of title 10, United States Code, is amended—

(1) in subparagraph (B), by striking the semicolon and inserting "; and";

(2) in subparagraph (C), by striking "; and" and inserting a period; and

(3) by striking subparagraph (D).

SEC. 414. Living quarters allowance for employees of the Defense Intelligence Agency.

(a) Prohibition.—Notwithstanding sections 1603 and 1605 of title 10, United States Code, and subchapter III of chapter 59 of title 5, a civilian employee of the Defense Intelligence Agency who is assigned to a directorate of a geographic combatant command that is headquartered outside of the United States may not receive a living quarters allowance.

(b) Application.—Subsection (a) shall apply with respect to a pay period beginning on or after the date that is 1 year after the date of the enactment of this Act.

SEC. 415. Plan on assumption of certain weather missions by the National Reconnaissance Office.

(a) Plan.—

(1) IN GENERAL.—The Director of the National Reconnaissance Office shall develop a plan for the National Reconnaissance Office to address how to carry out covered space-based environmental monitoring missions. Such plan shall include—

(A) a description of the related national security requirements for such missions;

(B) a description of the appropriate manner to meet such requirements; and

(C) the amount of funds that would be necessary to be transferred from the Air Force to the National Reconnaissance Office during fiscal years 2018 through 2022 to carry out such plan.

(2) ACTIVITIES.—In developing the plan under paragraph (1), the Director may conduct pre-acquisition activities, including with respect to requests for information, analyses of alternatives, study contracts, modeling and simulation, and other activities the Director determines necessary to develop such plan.

(3) SUBMISSION.—Not later than the date on which the President submits to Congress the budget for fiscal year 2018 under section 1105(a) of title 31, United States Code, the Director shall submit to the appropriate congressional committees the plan under paragraph (1).

(b) Independent cost estimate.—The Director of the Cost Assessment Improvement Group of the Office of the Director of National Intelligence, in coordination with the Director of Cost Assessment and Program Evaluation of the Department of Defense, shall certify to the appropriate congressional committees that the amounts of funds identified under subsection (a)(1)(C) as being necessary to transfer are appropriate and include funding for positions and personnel to support program office costs.

(c) Definitions.—In this section:

(1) The term "appropriate congressional committees" means—

(A) the congressional intelligence committees; and

(B) the congressional defense committees (as defined in section 101(a)(16) of title 10, United States Code).

(2) The term "covered space-based environmental monitoring missions" means the acquisition programs necessary to meet the national security requirements for cloud characterization and theater weather imagery.

SEC. 416. Modernization of security clearance information technology architecture.

(a) In general.—The Director of National Intelligence shall support the Director of the Office of Personnel Management and the Secretary of Defense in the efforts of the Secretary to develop and implement an information technology system (in this section referred to as the "System") to—

(1) modernize and sustain the security clearance information architecture of the National Background Investigations Bureau and the Department of Defense;

(2) support decisionmaking processes for the evaluation and granting of personnel security clearances;

(3) improve cybersecurity capabilities with respect to sensitive security clearance data and processes;

(4) reduce the complexity and cost of the security clearance process;

(5) provide information to managers on the financial and administrative costs of the security clearance process;

(6) strengthen the ties between counterintelligence and personnel security communities; and

(7) improve system standardization in the security clearance process.

(b) Guidance.—The Director of National Intelligence shall support the Director of the Office of Personnel Management and the Secretary of Defense in the efforts of the Director of the Office of Personnel Management and the Secretary to issue guidance establishing the respective roles, responsibilities, and obligations of the Director of the Office of Personnel Management, the Secretary, and the Director of National Intelligence, with respect to the development and implementation of the System.

TITLE V—Matters relating to United States Naval Station, Guantanamo Bay, Cuba

SEC. 501. Declassification of information on past terrorist activities of detainees transferred from United States Naval Station, Guantanamo Bay, Cuba, after signing of Executive Order No. 13492.

(a) In general.—Not later than 120 days after the date of the enactment of this Act, the Director of National Intelligence shall—

(1) in the manner described in the classified annex that accompanies this Act—

(A) complete a declassification review of intelligence reports prepared by the National Counterterrorism Center prior to Periodic Review Board sessions or detainee transfers on the past terrorist activities of individuals detained at United States Naval Station, Guantanamo Bay, Cuba, who were transferred or released from United States Naval Station, Guantanamo Bay, Cuba, after the signing of Executive Order No. 13492 (relating to the closure of the detention facility at United States Naval Station, Guantanamo Bay, Cuba); and

(B) make available to the public any information declassified as a result of the declassification review; and

(2) submit to the congressional intelligence committees a report setting forth—

(A) the results of the declassification review; and

(B) if any information covered by the declassification review was not declassified pursuant to the review, a justification for the determination not to declassify such information.

(b) Past terrorist activities.—For purposes of this section, the past terrorist activities of an individual shall include the terrorist activities conducted by the individual before the transfer of the individual to the detention facility at United States Naval Station, Guantanamo Bay, Cuba, including, at a minimum, the following:

(1) The terrorist organization, if any, with which affiliated.

(2) The terrorist training, if any, received.

(3) The role in past terrorist attacks against the interests or allies of the United States.

(4) The direct responsibility, if any, for the death of citizens of the United States or members of the Armed Forces.

(5) Any admission of any matter specified in paragraphs (1) through (4).

TITLE VI—Reports and other matters

SEC. 601. Report on intelligence community employees detailed to National Security Council.

Not later than 60 days after the date of the enactment of this Act, the Director of National Intelligence shall submit to the congressional intelligence committees a report listing, by year, the number of employees of an element of the intelligence community who have been detailed to the National Security Council during the 10-year period preceding the date of the report.

SEC. 602. Intelligence community reporting to Congress on foreign fighter flows.

(a) Reports required.—Not later than 60 days after the date of the enactment of this Act, and every 180 days thereafter, the Director of National Intelligence, consistent with the protection of intelligence sources and methods, shall submit to the appropriate congressional committees a report on foreign fighter flows to and from terrorist safe havens abroad.

(b) Contents.—Each report submitted under subsection (a) shall include, with respect to each terrorist safe haven, the following:

(1) The total number of foreign fighters who have traveled or are suspected of having traveled to the terrorist safe haven since 2011, including the countries of origin of such foreign fighters.

(2) The total number of United States citizens present in the terrorist safe haven.

(3) The total number of foreign fighters who have left the terrorist safe haven or whose whereabouts are unknown.

(c) Form.—The reports submitted under subsection (a) may be submitted in classified form. If such a report is submitted in classified form, such report shall also include an unclassified summary.

(d) Sunset.—The requirement to submit reports under subsection (a) shall terminate on the date that is two years after the date of the enactment of this Act.

(e) Appropriate congressional committees defined.—In this section, the term "appropriate congressional committees" means—

(1) in the Senate—

(A) the Committee on Armed Services;

(B) the Select Committee on Intelligence;

(C) the Committee on the Judiciary;

(D) the Committee on Homeland Security and Governmental Affairs;

(E) the Committee on Banking, Housing, and Urban Affairs;

(F) the Committee on Foreign Relations; and

(G) the Committee on Appropriations; and

(2) in the House of Representatives—

(A) the Committee on Armed Services;

(B) the Permanent Select Committee on Intelligence;

(C) the Committee on the Judiciary;

(D) the Committee on Homeland Security;

(E) the Committee on Financial Services;

(F) the Committee on Foreign Affairs; and

(G) the Committee on Appropriations.

SEC. 603. Report on information relating to academic programs, scholarships, fellowships, and internships sponsored, administered, or used by the intelligence community.

(a) Report.—Not later than 90 days after the date of the enactment of this Act, the Director of National Intelligence shall submit to Congress a report by the intelligence community regarding covered academic programs. Such report shall include—

(1) a description of the extent to which the Director and the heads of the elements of the intelligence community independently collect information on covered academic programs, including with respect to—

(A) the number of applicants for such programs;

(B) the number of individuals who have participated in such programs; and

(C) the number of individuals who have participated in such programs and were hired by an element of the intelligence community after completing such program;

(2) to the extent that the Director and the heads independently collect the information described in paragraph (1), a chart, table, or other compilation illustrating such information for each covered academic program and element of the intelligence community, as appropriate, during the 3-year period preceding the date of the report; and

(3) to the extent that the Director and the heads do not independently collect the information described in paragraph (1) as of the date of the report—

(A) whether the Director and the heads can begin collecting such information during fiscal year 2017; and

(B) the personnel, tools, and other resources required by the Director and the heads to independently collect such information.

(b) Covered academic programs defined.—In this section, the term "covered academic programs" means—

(1) the Federal Cyber Scholarship-for-Service Program under section 302 of the Cybersecurity Enhancement Act of 2014 (15 U.S.C. 7442);

(2) the National Security Education Program under the David L. Boren National Security Education Act of 1991 (50 U.S.C. 1901 et seq.);

(3) the Science, Mathematics, and Research for Transformation Defense Education Program under section 2192a of title 10, United States Code;

(4) the National Centers of Academic Excellence in Information Assurance and Cyber Defense of the National Security Agency and the Department of Homeland Security; and

(5) any other academic program, scholarship program, fellowship program, or internship program sponsored, administered, or used by an element of the intelligence community.

SEC. 604. Report on cybersecurity threats to seaports of the United States and maritime shipping.

(a) Report.—Not later than 180 days after the date of the enactment of this Act, the Under Secretary of Homeland Security for Intelligence and Analysis, in consultation with the Director of National Intelligence, and consistent with the protection of sources and methods, shall submit to the appropriate congressional committees a report on the cybersecurity threats to, and the cyber vulnerabilities within, the software, communications networks, computer networks, or other systems employed by—

(1) entities conducting significant operations at seaports in the United States;

(2) the maritime shipping concerns of the United States; and

(3) entities conducting significant operations at transshipment points in the United States.

(b) Matters included.—The report under subsection (a) shall include the following:

(1) A description of any recent and significant cyberattacks or cybersecurity threats directed against software, communications networks, computer networks, or other systems

employed by the entities and concerns described in paragraphs (1) through (3) of subsection (a).

(2) An assessment of—

    (A) any planned cyberattacks directed against such software, networks, and systems;

    (B) any significant vulnerabilities to such software, networks, and systems; and

    (C) how such entities and concerns are mitigating such vulnerabilities.

(3) An update on the status of the efforts of the Coast Guard to include cybersecurity concerns in the National Response Framework, Emergency Support Functions, or both, relating to the shipping or ports of the United States.

(c) Appropriate congressional committees defined.—In this section, the term "appropriate congressional committees" means—

    (1) the congressional intelligence committees; and

    (2) the Committee on Homeland Security of the House of Representatives and the Committee on Homeland Security and Governmental Affairs of the Senate.

SEC. 605. Report on counter-messaging activities.

(a) Report.—Not later than 60 days after the date of the enactment of this Act, the Under Secretary of Homeland Security for Intelligence and Analysis, consistent with the protection of sources and methods, shall submit to the appropriate congressional committees a report on the counter-messaging activities of the Department of Homeland Security with respect to the Islamic State and other extremist groups.

(b) Elements.—The report under subsection (a) shall include the following:

    (1) A description of whether, and to what extent, the Secretary of Homeland Security, in conducting counter-messaging activities with respect to the Islamic State and other extremist groups, consults or coordinates with the Secretary of State, regarding the counter-messaging activities undertaken by the Department of State with respect to the Islamic State and other extremist groups, including counter-messaging activities conducted by the Global Engagement Center of the Department of State.

    (2) Any criteria employed by the Secretary of Homeland Security for selecting, developing, promulgating, or changing the counter-messaging approach of the Department of Homeland Security, including any counter-messaging narratives, with respect to the Islamic State and other extremist groups.

(c) Appropriate congressional committees defined.—In this section, the term "appropriate congressional committees" means—

    (1) the congressional intelligence committees; and

    (2) the Committee on Homeland Security of the House of Representatives and the Committee on Homeland Security and Governmental Affairs of the Senate.

SEC. 606. Report on reprisals against contractors of the intelligence community.

(a) Report.—Not later than 180 days after the date of the enactment of this Act, the Inspector General of the Intelligence Community, consistent with the protection of sources and methods, shall submit to the appropriate congressional committees a report on reprisals made against covered contractor employees.

(b) Elements.—The report under subsection (a) shall include the following:

    (1) Identification of the number of known or suspected reprisals made against covered contractor employees during the 5-year period preceding the date of the report.

    (2) An evaluation of the usefulness of establishing in law a prohibition on reprisals against covered contractor employees as a means of encouraging such contractors to make protected disclosures.

(3) A description of any challenges associated with establishing in law such a prohibition, including with respect to the nature of the relationship between the Federal Government, the contractor, and the covered contractor employee.

(4) A description of any approaches taken by the Federal Government to account for reprisals against non-intelligence community contractors who make protected disclosures, including pursuant to section 2409 of title 10, United States Code, and sections 4705 and 4712 of title 41, United States Code.

(5) Any recommendations the Inspector General determines appropriate.

(c) Definitions.—In this section:

(1) The term "appropriate congressional committees" means—

(A) the congressional intelligence committees; and

(B) the Committee on Oversight and Government Reform of the House of Representatives and the Committee on Homeland Security and Governmental Affairs of the Senate.

(2) The term "covered contractor employee" means an employee of a contractor of an element of the intelligence community.

(3) The term "reprisal" means the discharge, demotion, or other discriminatory personnel action made against a covered contractor employee for making a disclosure of information that would be a disclosure protected by law if the contractor were an employee of the Federal Government.

Passed the House of Representatives May 24, 2016.

Executive Orders

Executive Order 12333—United States Intelligence Activities

As amended by Executive Orders 13284 (2003), 13355 (2004), and 13470 (2008)
46 Fed. Reg. 59,941 (Dec. 4, 1981)

Timely, accurate, and insightful information about the activities, capabilities, plans, and intentions of foreign powers, organizations, and persons, and their agents, is essential to the national security of the United States. All reasonable and lawful means must be used to ensure that the United States will receive the best intelligence possible. For that purpose, by virtue of the authority vested in me by the Constitution and the laws of the United States of America, including the National Security Act of 1947, as amended, (Act) and as President of the United States of America, in order to provide for the effective conduct of United States intelligence activities and the protection of constitutional rights, it is hereby ordered as follows:

PART 1 GOALS, DIRECTIONS, DUTIES, AND RESPONSIBILITIES WITH RESPECT TO UNITED STATES INTELLIGENCE EFFORTS

SECTION 1.1 GOALS. The United States intelligence effort shall provide the President, the National Security Council, and the Homeland Security Council with the necessary information on which to base decisions concerning the development and conduct of foreign, defense, and economic policies, and the protection of United States national interests from foreign security threats. All departments and agencies shall cooperate fully to fulfill this goal.

(a) All means, consistent with applicable Federal law and this order, and with full consideration of the rights of United States persons, shall be used to obtain reliable intelligence information to protect the United States and its interests.

(b) The United States Government has a solemn obligation, and shall continue in the conduct of intelligence activities under this order, to protect fully the legal rights of all United States persons, including freedoms, civil liberties, and privacy rights guaranteed by Federal law.

(c) Intelligence collection under this order should be guided by the need for information to respond to intelligence priorities set by the President.

(d) Special emphasis should be given to detecting and countering:

(1) Espionage and other threats and activities directed by foreign powers or their intelligence services against the United States and its interests;

(2) Threats to the United States and its interests from terrorism; and

(3) Threats to the United States and its interests from the development, possession, proliferation, or use of weapons of mass destruction.

(e) Special emphasis shall be given to the production of timely, accurate, and insightful reports, responsive to decisionmakers in the executive branch, that draw on all appropriate sources of information, including open source information, meet rigorous analytic standards, consider diverse analytic viewpoints, and accurately represent appropriate alternative views.

(f) State, local, and tribal governments are critical partners in securing and defending the United States from terrorism and other threats to the United States and its interests. Our national intelligence effort should take into account the responsibilities and requirements of State, local, and tribal governments and, as appropriate, private sector entities, when undertaking the collection and dissemination of information and intelligence to protect the United States.

(g) All departments and agencies have a responsibility to prepare and to provide intelligence in a manner that allows the full and free exchange of information, consistent with applicable law and presidential guidance.

SECTION 1.2 THE NATIONAL SECURITY COUNCIL.

(a) *Purpose*. The National Security Council (NSC) shall act as the highest ranking executive branch entity that provides support to the President for review of, guidance for, and direction to the conduct of all foreign intelligence, counterintelligence, and covert action, and attendant policies and programs.

(b) *Covert Action and Other Sensitive Intelligence Operations*. The NSC shall consider and submit to the President a policy recommendation, including all dissents, on each proposed covert action and conduct a periodic review of ongoing covert action activities, including an evaluation of the effectiveness and consistency with current national policy of such activities and consistency with applicable legal requirements. The NSC shall perform such other functions related to covert action as the President may direct, but shall not undertake the conduct of covert actions. The NSC shall also review proposals for other sensitive intelligence operations.

SECTION 1.3 DIRECTOR OF NATIONAL INTELLIGENCE. Subject to the authority, direction, and control of the President, the Director of National Intelligence (Director) shall serve as the head of the Intelligence Community, act as the principal adviser to the President, to the NSC, and to the Homeland Security Council for intelligence matters related to national security, and shall oversee and direct the implementation of the National Intelligence Program and execution of the National Intelligence Program budget. The Director will lead a unified, coordinated, and effective intelligence effort. In addition, the Director shall, in carrying out the duties and responsibilities under this section, take into account the views of the heads of departments containing an element of the Intelligence Community and of the Director of the Central Intelligence Agency.

(a) Except as otherwise directed by the President or prohibited by law, the Director shall have access to all information and intelligence described in section 1.5(a) of this order. For the purpose of access to and sharing of information and intelligence, the Director:

(1) Is hereby assigned the function under section 3(5) of the Act, to determine that intelligence, regardless of the source from which derived and including information gathered within or outside the United States, pertains to more than one United States Government agency; and

(2) Shall develop guidelines for how information or intelligence is provided to or accessed by the Intelligence Community in accordance with section 1.5(a) of this order, and for how the information or intelligence may be used and shared by the Intelligence Community. All guidelines developed in accordance with this section shall be approved by the Attorney General and, where applicable, shall be consistent with guidelines issued pursuant to section 1016 of the Intelligence Reform and Terrorism Protection Act of 2004 (Public Law 108-458) (IRTPA).

(b) In addition to fulfilling the obligations and responsibilities prescribed by the Act, the Director:

(1) Shall establish objectives, priorities, and guidance for the Intelligence Community to ensure timely and effective collection, processing, analysis, and dissemination of intelligence, of whatever nature and from whatever source derived;

(2) May designate, in consultation with affected heads of departments or Intelligence Community elements, one or more Intelligence Community elements to develop and to maintain services of common concern on behalf of the Intelligence Community if the Director determines such services can be more efficiently or effectively accomplished in a consolidated manner;

(3) Shall oversee and provide advice to the President and the NSC with respect to all ongoing and proposed covert action programs;

(4) In regard to the establishment and conduct of intelligence arrangements and agreements with foreign governments and international organizations:

(A) May enter into intelligence and counterintelligence arrangements and agreements with foreign governments and international organizations;

(B) Shall formulate policies concerning intelligence and counterintelligence arrangements and agreements with foreign governments and international organizations; and

(C) Shall align and synchronize intelligence and counterintelligence foreign relationships among the elements of the Intelligence Community to further United States national security, policy, and intelligence objectives;

(5) Shall participate in the development of procedures approved by the Attorney General governing criminal drug intelligence activities abroad to ensure that these activities are consistent with foreign intelligence programs;

(6) Shall establish common security and access standards for managing and handling intelligence systems, information, and products, with special emphasis on facilitating:

(A) The fullest and most prompt access to and dissemination of information and intelligence practicable, assigning the highest priority to detecting, preventing, preempting, and disrupting terrorist threats and activities against the United States, its interests, and allies; and

(B) The establishment of standards for an interoperable information sharing enterprise that facilitates the sharing of intelligence information among elements of the Intelligence Community;

(7) Shall ensure that appropriate departments and agencies have access to intelligence and receive the support needed to perform independent analysis;

(8) Shall protect, and ensure that programs are developed to protect, intelligence sources, methods, and activities from unauthorized disclosure;

(9) Shall, after consultation with the heads of affected departments and agencies, establish guidelines for Intelligence Community elements for:

(A) Classification and declassification of all intelligence and intelligence-related information classified under the authority of the Director or the authority of the head of a department or Intelligence Community element; and

(B) Access to and dissemination of all intelligence and intelligence-related information, both in its final form and in the form when initially gathered, to include intelligence originally classified by the head of a department or Intelligence Community element, except that access to and dissemination of information concerning United States persons shall be governed by procedures developed in accordance with Part 2 of this order;

(10) May, only with respect to Intelligence Community elements, and after consultation with the head of the originating Intelligence Community element or the head of the originating department, declassify, or direct the declassification of, information or intelligence relating to intelligence sources, methods, and activities. The Director may only delegate this authority to the Principal Deputy Director of National Intelligence;

(11) May establish, operate, and direct one or more national intelligence centers to address intelligence priorities;

(12) May establish Functional Managers and Mission Managers, and designate officers or employees of the United States to serve in these positions.

(A) Functional Managers shall report to the Director concerning the execution of their duties as Functional Managers, and may be charged with developing and implementing strategic guidance, policies, and procedures for activities related to a specific intelligence discipline or set of intelligence activities; set training and tradecraft standards; and ensure coordination within and across intelligence disciplines and Intelligence Community elements and with related nonintelligence activities. Functional Managers may also advise the Director on: the management of resources; policies and procedures; collection capabilities and gaps; processing and dissemination of intelligence; technical architectures; and other issues or activities determined by the Director.

(i) The Director of the National Security Agency is designated the Functional Manager for signals intelligence;

(ii) The Director of the Central Intelligence Agency is designated the Functional Manager for human intelligence; and

(iii) The Director of the National Geospatial-Intelligence Agency is designated the Functional Manager for geospatial intelligence.

(B) Mission Managers shall serve as principal substantive advisors on all or specified aspects of intelligence related to designated countries, regions, topics, or functional issues;

(13) Shall establish uniform criteria for the determination of relative priorities for the transmission of critical foreign intelligence, and advise the Secretary of Defense concerning the communications requirements of the Intelligence Community for the transmission of such communications;

(14) Shall have ultimate responsibility for production and dissemination of intelligence produced by the
Intelligence Community and authority to levy analytic tasks on intelligence production organizations within the Intelligence Community, in consultation with the heads of the Intelligence Community elements concerned;

(15) May establish advisory groups for the purpose of obtaining advice from within the Intelligence
Community to carry out the Director's responsibilities, to include Intelligence Community executive management committees composed of senior Intelligence Community leaders. Advisory groups shall consist of representatives from elements of the Intelligence Community, as designated by the Director, or other executive branch departments, agencies, and offices, as appropriate;

(16) Shall ensure the timely exploitation and dissemination of data gathered by national intelligence collection means, and ensure that the resulting intelligence is disseminated immediately to appropriate government elements, including military commands;

(17) Shall determine requirements and priorities for, and manage and direct the tasking, collection, analysis, production, and dissemination of, national intelligence by elements of the Intelligence Community, including approving requirements for collection and analysis and resolving conflicts in collection requirements and in the tasking of national collection assets of Intelligence Community elements (except when otherwise directed by the President or when the Secretary of Defense exercises collection tasking authority under plans and arrangements approved by the Secretary of Defense and the Director);

(18) May provide advisory tasking concerning collection and analysis of information or intelligence relevant to national intelligence or national security to departments, agencies, and establishments of the United States Government that are not elements of the Intelligence Community; and shall establish procedures, in consultation with affected heads of departments or agencies and subject to approval by the Attorney General, to implement this authority and to monitor or evaluate the responsiveness of United States Government departments, agencies, and other establishments;

(19) Shall fulfill the responsibilities in section 1.3(b)(17) and (18) of this order, consistent with applicable law and with full consideration of the rights of United States persons, whether information is to be collected inside or outside the United States;

(20) Shall ensure, through appropriate policies and procedures, the deconfliction, coordination, and integration of all intelligence activities conducted by an Intelligence Community element or funded by the National Intelligence Program. In accordance with these policies and procedures:

(A) The Director of the Federal Bureau of Investigation shall coordinate the clandestine collection of foreign intelligence collected through human sources or through human-enabled means and counterintelligence activities inside the United States;

(B) The Director of the Central Intelligence Agency shall coordinate the clandestine collection of foreign intelligence collected through human sources or through human-enabled means and counterintelligence activities outside the United States;

(C) All policies and procedures for the coordination of counterintelligence activities and the clandestine collection of foreign intelligence inside the United States shall be subject to the approval of the Attorney General; and

(D) All policies and procedures developed under this section shall be coordinated with the heads of affected departments and Intelligence Community elements;

(21) Shall, with the concurrence of the heads of affected departments and agencies, establish joint procedures to deconflict, coordinate, and synchronize intelligence activities conducted by an Intelligence
Community element or funded by the National Intelligence Program, with intelligence activities, activities that involve foreign intelligence and security services, or activities that involve the use of clandestine methods, conducted by other United States Government departments, agencies, and establishments;

(22) Shall, in coordination with the heads of departments containing elements of the Intelligence
Community, develop procedures to govern major system acquisitions funded in whole or in majority part by the National Intelligence Program;

(23) Shall seek advice from the Secretary of State to ensure that the foreign policy implications of proposed intelligence activities are considered, and shall ensure, through appropriate policies and procedures, that intelligence activities are conducted in a manner consistent with the responsibilities pursuant to law and presidential direction of Chiefs of United States Missions; and

(24) Shall facilitate the use of Intelligence Community products by the Congress in a secure manner.

(c) The Director's exercise of authorities in the Act and this order shall not abrogate the statutory or other responsibilities of the heads of departments of the United States Government or the Director of the Central Intelligence Agency. Directives issued and actions taken by the Director in the exercise of the Director's authorities and responsibilities to integrate, coordinate, and make the Intelligence Community more effective in providing intelligence related to national security shall be implemented by the elements of the Intelligence Community, provided that any department head whose department contains an element of the Intelligence Community and who believes that a directive or action of the Director violates the requirements of section 1018 of the IRTPA or this subsection shall bring the issue to the attention of the Director, the NSC, or the President for resolution in a manner that respects and does not abrogate the statutory responsibilities of the heads of the departments.

(d) Appointments to certain positions.

(1) The relevant department or bureau head shall provide recommendations and obtain the concurrence of the Director for the selection of: the Director of the National Security Agency, the Director of the National Reconnaissance Office, the Director of the National Geospatial-Intelligence Agency, the Under Secretary of Homeland Security for Intelligence and Analysis, the Assistant Secretary of State for Intelligence and Research, the Director of the Office of Intelligence and Counterintelligence of the Department of Energy, the Assistant Secretary for Intelligence and Analysis of the Department of the Treasury, and the Executive Assistant Director for the National Security Branch of the Federal Bureau of Investigation. If the Director does not concur in the recommendation, the department head may not fill the vacancy or make the recommendation to the President, as the case may be. If the department head and the Director do not reach an agreement on the selection or recommendation, the Director and the department head concerned may advise the President directly of the Director's intention to withhold concurrence.

(2) The relevant department head shall consult with the Director before appointing an individual to fill a vacancy or recommending to the President an individual be nominated to fill a vacancy in any of the following positions: the Under Secretary of Defense for Intelligence; the Director of the Defense Intelligence Agency; uniformed heads of the intelligence elements of the Army, the Navy, the Air Force, and the Marine Corps above the rank of Major General or Rear Admiral; the Assistant Commandant of the Coast Guard for Intelligence; and the Assistant Attorney General for National Security.

(e) Removal from certain positions.

(1) Except for the Director of the Central Intelligence Agency, whose removal the Director may recommend to the President, the Director and the relevant department head shall consult on the removal, or recommendation to the President for removal, as the case may be, of: the Director of the National Security Agency, the Director of the National Geospatial-Intelligence Agency, the Director of the Defense Intelligence Agency, the Under Secretary of Homeland Security for Intelligence and Analysis, the Assistant Secretary of State for Intelligence and Research, and the Assistant Secretary for Intelligence and Analysis of the Department of the Treasury. If the Director and the department head do not agree on removal, or recommendation for removal, either may make a recommendation to the President for the removal of the individual.

(2) The Director and the relevant department or bureau head shall consult on the removal of: the Executive Assistant Director for the National Security Branch of the Federal Bureau of Investigation, the Director of the Office of Intelligence and Counterintelligence of the Department of Energy, the Director of the National Reconnaissance Office, the Assistant Commandant of the Coast Guard for Intelligence, and the Under Secretary of Defense for Intelligence. With respect to an individual appointed by a department head, the department head may remove the individual upon the request of the Director; if the department head chooses not to remove the individual, either the Director or the department head may advise the President of the department head's intention to retain the individual. In the case of the Under Secretary of Defense for Intelligence, the Secretary of Defense may recommend to the President either the removal or the retention of the individual. For uniformed heads of the intelligence elements of the Army, the Navy, the Air Force, and the Marine Corps, the Director may make a recommendation for removal to the Secretary of Defense.

(3) Nothing in this subsection shall be construed to limit or otherwise affect the authority of the President to nominate, appoint, assign, or terminate the appointment or assignment of any individual, with or without a consultation, recommendation, or concurrence.

SECTION 1.4 THE INTELLIGENCE COMMUNITY. Consistent with applicable Federal law and with the other provisions of this order, and under the leadership of the Director, as specified in such law and this order, the Intelligence Community shall:

(a) Collect and provide information needed by the President and, in the performance of executive functions, the Vice President, the NSC, the Homeland Security Council, the Chairman of the Joint Chiefs of Staff, senior military commanders, and other executive branch officials and, as appropriate, the Congress of the United States;

(b) In accordance with priorities set by the President, collect information concerning, and conduct activities to protect against, international terrorism, proliferation of weapons of mass destruction, intelligence activities directed against the United States, international criminal drug activities, and other hostile activities directed against the United States by foreign powers, organizations, persons, and their agents;

(c) Analyze, produce, and disseminate intelligence;

(d) Conduct administrative, technical, and other support activities within the United States and abroad necessary for the performance of authorized activities, to include providing services of common concern for the Intelligence Community as designated by the Director in accordance with this order;

(e) Conduct research, development, and procurement of technical systems and devices relating to authorized functions and missions or the provision of services of common concern for the Intelligence Community;

(f) Protect the security of intelligence related activities, information, installations, property, and employees by appropriate means, including such investigations of applicants, employees, contractors, and other persons with similar associations with the Intelligence Community elements as are necessary;

(g) Take into account State, local, and tribal governments' and, as appropriate, private sector entities' information needs relating to national and homeland security;

(h) Deconflict, coordinate, and integrate all intelligence activities and other information gathering in accordance with section 1.3(b)(20) of this order; and

(i) Perform such other functions and duties related to intelligence activities as the President may direct.

SECTION 1.5 DUTIES AND RESPONSIBILITIES OF THE HEADS OF EXECUTIVE BRANCH DEPARTMENTS AND AGENCIES. The heads of all departments and agencies shall:

(a) Provide the Director access to all information and intelligence relevant to the national security or that otherwise is required for the performance of the Director's duties, to include administrative and other appropriate management information, except such information excluded by law, by the President, or by the Attorney General acting under this order at the direction of the President;

(b) Provide all programmatic and budgetary information necessary to support the Director in developing the National Intelligence Program;

(c) Coordinate development and implementation of intelligence systems and architectures and, as appropriate, operational systems and architectures of their departments, agencies, and other elements with the Director to respond to national intelligence requirements and all applicable information sharing and security guidelines, information privacy, and other legal requirements;

(d) Provide, to the maximum extent permitted by law, subject to the availability of appropriations and not inconsistent with the mission of the department or agency, such further support to the Director as the Director may request, after consultation with the head of the department or agency, for the performance of the Director's functions;

(e) Respond to advisory tasking from the Director under section 1.3(b)(18) of this order to the greatest extent possible, in accordance with applicable policies established by the head of the responding department or agency;

(f) Ensure that all elements within the department or agency comply with the provisions of Part 2 of this order, regardless of Intelligence Community affiliation, when performing foreign intelligence and counterintelligence functions;

(g) Deconflict, coordinate, and integrate all intelligence activities in accordance with section 1.3(b)(20), and intelligence and other activities in accordance with section 1.3(b)(21) of this order;

(h) Inform the Attorney General, either directly or through the Federal Bureau of Investigation, and the Director of clandestine collection of foreign intelligence and counterintelligence activities inside the United States not coordinated with the Federal Bureau of Investigation;

(i) Pursuant to arrangements developed by the head of the department or agency and the Director of the Central Intelligence Agency and approved by the Director, inform the Director and the Director of the Central Intelligence Agency, either directly or through his designee serving outside the United States, as appropriate, of clandestine collection of foreign intelligence collected through human sources or through human-enabled means outside the United States that has not been coordinated with the Central Intelligence Agency; and

(j) Inform the Secretary of Defense, either directly or through his designee, as appropriate, of clandestine collection of foreign intelligence outside the United States in a region of combat or contingency military operations designated by the Secretary of Defense, for purposes of this paragraph, after consultation with the Director of National Intelligence.

SECTION 1.6 HEADS OF ELEMENTS OF THE INTELLIGENCE COMMUNITY. The heads of elements of the Intelligence Community shall:

(a) Provide the Director access to all information and intelligence relevant to the national security or that otherwise is required for the performance of the Director's duties, to include administrative and other appropriate management information, except such information excluded by law, by the President, or by the Attorney General acting under this order at the direction of the President;

(b) Report to the Attorney General possible violations of Federal criminal laws by employees and of specified Federal criminal laws by any other person as provided in procedures agreed upon by the Attorney General and the head of the department, agency, or establishment concerned, in a manner consistent with the protection of intelligence sources and methods, as specified in those procedures;

(c) Report to the Intelligence Oversight Board, consistent with Executive Order 13462 of February 29, 2008, and provide copies of all such reports to the Director, concerning any intelligence activities of their elements that they have reason to believe may be unlawful or contrary to executive order or presidential directive;

(d) Protect intelligence and intelligence sources, methods, and activities from unauthorized disclosure in accordance with guidance from the Director;

(e) Facilitate, as appropriate, the sharing of information or intelligence, as directed by law or the President, to State, local, tribal, and private sector entities;

(f) Disseminate information or intelligence to foreign governments and international organizations under intelligence or counterintelligence arrangements or agreements established in accordance with section 1.3(b)(4) of this order;

(g) Participate in the development of procedures approved by the Attorney General governing production and dissemination of information or intelligence resulting from criminal drug intelligence activities abroad if they have intelligence responsibilities for foreign or domestic criminal drug production and trafficking; and

(h) Ensure that the inspectors general, general counsels, and agency officials responsible for privacy or civil liberties protection for their respective organizations have access to any information or intelligence necessary to perform their official duties.

SECTION 1.7 INTELLIGENCE COMMUNITY ELEMENTS. Each element of the Intelligence Community shall have the duties and responsibilities specified below, in addition to those specified by law or elsewhere in this order. Intelligence Community elements within executive departments shall serve the information and intelligence needs of their respective heads of departments and also shall operate as part of an integrated Intelligence Community, as provided in law or this order.

(a) THE CENTRAL INTELLIGENCE AGENCY. The Director of the Central Intelligence Agency shall:

(1) Collect (including through clandestine means), analyze, produce, and disseminate foreign intelligence and counterintelligence;

(2) Conduct counterintelligence activities without assuming or performing any internal security functions within the United States;

(3) Conduct administrative and technical support activities within and outside the United States as necessary for cover and proprietary arrangements;

(4) Conduct covert action activities approved by the President. No agency except the Central Intelligence Agency (or the Armed Forces of the United States in time of war declared by the Congress or during any period covered by a report from the President to the Congress consistent with the War Powers Resolution, Public Law 93-148) may conduct any covert action activity unless the President determines that another agency is more likely to achieve a particular objective;

(5) Conduct foreign intelligence liaison relationships with intelligence or security services of foreign governments or international organizations consistent with section 1.3(b)(4) of this order;

(6) Under the direction and guidance of the Director, and in accordance with section 1.3(b)(4) of this order, coordinate the implementation of intelligence and counterintelligence relationships between elements of the Intelligence Community and the intelligence or security services of foreign governments or international organizations; and

(7) Perform such other functions and duties related to intelligence as the Director may direct.

(b) THE DEFENSE INTELLIGENCE AGENCY. The Director of the Defense Intelligence Agency shall:

(1) Collect (including through clandestine means), analyze, produce, and disseminate foreign intelligence and counterintelligence to support national and departmental missions;

(2) Collect, analyze, produce, or, through tasking and coordination, provide defense and defense-related intelligence for the Secretary of Defense, the Chairman of the Joint Chiefs of Staff, combatant commanders, other Defense components, and non-Defense agencies;(3) Conduct counterintelligence activities;

(4) Conduct administrative and technical support activities within and outside the United States as necessary for cover and proprietary arrangements;

(5) Conduct foreign defense intelligence liaison relationships and defense intelligence exchange programs with foreign defense establishments, intelligence or security services

of foreign governments, and international organizations in accordance with sections 1.3(b)(4), 1.7(a)(6), and 1.10(i) of this order;

(6) Manage and coordinate all matters related to the Defense Attaché system; and

(7) Provide foreign intelligence and counterintelligence staff support as directed by the Secretary of Defense.

(c) THE NATIONAL SECURITY AGENCY. The Director of the National Security Agency shall:

(1) Collect (including through clandestine means), process, analyze, produce, and disseminate signals intelligence information and data for foreign intelligence and counterintelligence purposes to support national and departmental missions;

(2) Establish and operate an effective unified organization for signals intelligence activities, except for the delegation of operational control over certain operations that are conducted through other elements of the Intelligence Community. No other department or agency may engage in signals intelligence activities except pursuant to a delegation by the Secretary of Defense, after coordination with the Director;

(3) Control signals intelligence collection and processing activities, including assignment of resources to an appropriate agent for such periods and tasks as required for the direct support of military commanders;

(4) Conduct administrative and technical support activities within and outside the United States as necessary for cover arrangements;

(5) Provide signals intelligence support for national and departmental requirements and for the conduct of military operations;

(6) Act as the National Manager for National Security Systems as established in law and policy, and in this capacity be responsible to the Secretary of Defense and to the Director;

(7) Prescribe, consistent with section 102A(g) of the Act, within its field of authorized operations, security regulations covering operating practices, including the transmission, handling, and distribution of signals intelligence and communications security material within and among the elements under control of the Director of the National Security Agency, and exercise the necessary supervisory control to ensure compliance with the regulations; and

(8) Conduct foreign cryptologic liaison relationships in accordance with sections 1.3(b)(4), 1.7(a)(6), and 1.10(i) of this order.

(d) THE NATIONAL RECONNAISSANCE OFFICE. The Director of the National Reconnaissance Office shall:

(1) Be responsible for research and development, acquisition, launch, deployment, and operation of overhead systems and related data processing facilities to collect intelligence and information to support national and departmental missions and other United States Government needs; and

(2) Conduct foreign liaison relationships relating to the above missions, in accordance with sections 1.3(b)(4), 1.7(a)(6), and 1.10(i) of this order.

(e) THE NATIONAL GEOSPATIAL-INTELLIGENCE AGENCY. The Director of the National Geospatial-Intelligence Agency shall:

(1) Collect, process, analyze, produce, and disseminate geospatial intelligence information and data for foreign intelligence and counterintelligence purposes to support national and departmental missions;

(2) Provide geospatial intelligence support for national and departmental requirements and for the conduct of military operations;

(3) Conduct administrative and technical support activities within and outside the United States as necessary for cover arrangements; and

(4) Conduct foreign geospatial intelligence liaison relationships, in accordance with sections 1.3(b)(4), 1.7(a)(6), and 1.10(i) of this order.

(f) THE INTELLIGENCE AND COUNTERINTELLIGENCE ELEMENTS OF THE ARMY, NAVY, AIR FORCE, AND MARINE CORPS. The Commanders and heads of the intelligence and counterintelligence elements of the Army, Navy, Air Force, and Marine Corps shall:

> (1) Collect (including through clandestine means), produce, analyze, and disseminate defense and defense-related intelligence and counterintelligence to support departmental requirements, and, as appropriate, national requirements;

> (2) Conduct counterintelligence activities;

> (3) Monitor the development, procurement, and management of tactical intelligence systems and equipment and conduct related research, development, and test and evaluation activities; and

> (4) Conduct military intelligence liaison relationships and military intelligence exchange programs with selected cooperative foreign defense establishments and international organizations in accordance with sections 1.3(b)(4), 1.7(a)(6), and 1.10(i) of this order.

(g) INTELLIGENCE ELEMENTS OF THE FEDERAL BUREAU OF INVESTIGATION. Under the supervision of the Attorney General and pursuant to such regulations as the Attorney General may establish, the intelligence elements of the Federal Bureau of Investigation shall:

> (1) Collect (including through clandestine means), analyze, produce, and disseminate foreign intelligence and counterintelligence to support national and departmental missions, in accordance with procedural guidelines approved by the Attorney General, after consultation with the Director;

> (2) Conduct counterintelligence activities; and

> (3) Conduct foreign intelligence and counterintelligence liaison relationships with intelligence, security, and law enforcement services of foreign governments or international organizations in accordance with sections 1.3(b)(4) and 1.7(a)(6) of this order.

(h) THE INTELLIGENCE AND COUNTERINTELLIGENCE ELEMENTS OF THE COAST GUARD. The Commandant of the Coast Guard shall:

> (1) Collect (including through clandestine means), analyze, produce, and disseminate foreign intelligence and counterintelligence including defense and defense-related information and intelligence to support national and departmental missions;

> (2) Conduct counterintelligence activities;

> (3) Monitor the development, procurement, and management of tactical intelligence systems and equipment and conduct related research, development, and test and evaluation activities; and

> (4) Conduct foreign intelligence liaison relationships and intelligence exchange programs with foreign intelligence services, security services or international organizations in accordance with sections 1.3(b)(4), 1.7(a)(6), and, when operating as part of the Department of Defense, 1.10(i) of this order.

(i) THE BUREAU OF INTELLIGENCE AND RESEARCH, DEPARTMENT OF STATE; THE OFFICE OF INTELLIGENCE AND ANALYSIS, DEPARTMENT OF THE TREASURY; THE OFFICE OF NATIONAL SECURITY INTELLIGENCE, DRUG ENFORCEMENT ADMINISTRATION; THE OFFICE OF INTELLIGENCE AND ANALYSIS, DEPARTMENT OF HOMELAND SECURITY; AND THE OFFICE OF INTELLIGENCE AND COUNTERINTELLIGENCE, DEPARTMENT OF ENERGY. The heads of the Bureau of Intelligence and Research, Department of State; the Office of Intelligence and Analysis, Department of the Treasury; the Office of National Security Intelligence, Drug Enforcement Administration; the Office of Intelligence and Analysis, Department of Homeland Security; and the Office of Intelligence and Counterintelligence, Department of Energy shall:

(1) Collect (overtly or through publicly available sources), analyze, produce, and disseminate information, intelligence, and counterintelligence to support national and departmental missions; and

(2) Conduct and participate in analytic or information exchanges with foreign partners and international organizations in accordance with sections 1.3(b)(4) and 1.7(a)(6) of this order.

(j) THE OFFICE OF THE DIRECTOR OF NATIONAL INTELLIGENCE. The Director shall collect (overtly or through publicly available sources), analyze, produce, and disseminate information, intelligence, and counterintelligence to support the missions of the Office of the Director of National Intelligence, including the National Counterterrorism Center, and to support other national missions.

SECTION 1.8 THE DEPARTMENT OF STATE. In addition to the authorities exercised by the Bureau of Intelligence and Research under sections 1.4 and 1.7(i) of this order, the Secretary of State shall:

(a) Collect (overtly or through publicly available sources) information relevant to United States foreign policy and national security concerns;

(b) Disseminate, to the maximum extent possible, reports received from United States diplomatic and consular posts;

(c) Transmit reporting requirements and advisory taskings of the Intelligence Community to the Chiefs of
United States Missions abroad; and

(d) Support Chiefs of United States Missions in discharging their responsibilities pursuant to law and presidential direction.

SECTION 1.9 THE DEPARTMENT OF THE TREASURY. In addition to the authorities exercised by the Office of Intelligence and Analysis of the Department of the Treasury under sections 1.4 and 1.7(i) of this order the Secretary of the Treasury shall collect (overtly or through publicly available sources) foreign financial information and, in consultation with the Department of State, foreign economic information.

1.10 *The Department of Defense.* The Secretary of Defense shall:

(a) Collect (including through clandestine means), analyze, produce, and disseminate information and intelligence and be responsive to collection tasking and advisory tasking by the Director;

(b) Collect (including through clandestine means), analyze, produce, and disseminate defense and defense-related intelligence and counterintelligence, as required for execution of the Secretary's responsibilities;

(c) Conduct programs and missions necessary to fulfill national, departmental, and tactical intelligence requirements;

(d) Conduct counterintelligence activities in support of Department of Defense components and coordinate counterintelligence activities in accordance with section 1.3(b)(20) and (21) of this order;

(e) Act, in coordination with the Director, as the executive agent of the United States Government for signals intelligence activities;

(f) Provide for the timely transmission of critical intelligence, as defined by the Director, within the United
States Government;

(g) Carry out or contract for research, development, and procurement of technical systems and devices relating to authorized intelligence functions;

(h) Protect the security of Department of Defense installations, activities, information, property, and employees by appropriate means, including such investigations of applicants, employees, contractors, and other persons with similar associations with the Department of Defense as are necessary;

(i) Establish and maintain defense intelligence relationships and defense intelligence exchange programs with selected cooperative foreign defense establishments, intelligence or security services of foreign governments, and international organizations, and ensure that such relationships and programs are in accordance with sections 1.3(b)(4), 1.3(b)(21) and 1.7(a)(6) of this order;

(j) Conduct such administrative and technical support activities within and outside the United States as are necessary to provide for cover and proprietary arrangements, to perform the functions described in sections (a) though (i) above, and to support the Intelligence Community elements of the Department of Defense; and

(k) Use the Intelligence Community elements within the Department of Defense identified in section 1.7(b) through (f) and, when the Coast Guard is operating as part of the Department of Defense, (h) above to carry out the Secretary of Defense's responsibilities assigned in this section or other departments, agencies, or offices within the Department of Defense, as appropriate, to conduct the intelligence missions and responsibilities assigned to the Secretary of Defense.

SECTION 1.11 THE DEPARTMENT OF HOMELAND SECURITY. In addition to the authorities exercised by the Office of Intelligence and Analysis of the Department of Homeland Security under sections 1.4 and 1.7(i) of this order, the Secretary of Homeland Security shall conduct, through the United States Secret Service, activities to determine the existence and capability of surveillance equipment being used against the President or the Vice President of the United States, the Executive Office of the President, and, as authorized by the Secretary of Homeland Security or the President, other Secret Service protectees and United States officials. No information shall be acquired intentionally through such activities except to protect against use of such surveillance equipment, and those activities shall be conducted pursuant to procedures agreed upon by the Secretary of Homeland Security and the Attorney General.

SECTION 1.12 THE DEPARTMENT OF ENERGY. In addition to the authorities exercised by the Office of Intelligence and Counterintelligence of the Department of Energy under sections 1.4 and 1.7(i) of this order, the Secretary of Energy shall:

(a) Provide expert scientific, technical, analytic, and research capabilities to other agencies within the Intelligence Community, as appropriate;

(b) Participate in formulating intelligence collection and analysis requirements where the special expert capability of the Department can contribute; and

(c) Participate with the Department of State in overtly collecting information with respect to foreign energy matters.

SECTION 1.13 THE FEDERAL BUREAU OF INVESTIGATION. In addition to the authorities exercised by the intelligence elements of the Federal Bureau of Investigation of the Department of Justice under sections 1.4 and 1.7(g) of this order and under the supervision of the Attorney General and pursuant to such regulations as the Attorney General may establish, the Director of the Federal Bureau of Investigation shall provide technical assistance, within or outside the United States, to foreign intelligence and law enforcement services, consistent with section 1.3(b)(20) and (21) of this order, as may be necessary to support national or departmental missions.

PART 2 CONDUCT OF INTELLIGENCE ACTIVITIES

SECTION 2.1 NEED. Timely, accurate, and insightful information about the activities, capabilities, plans, and intentions of foreign powers, organizations, and persons, and their agents, is essential to informed decisionmaking in the areas of national security, national defense, and foreign relations. Collection of such information is a priority objective and will be pursued in a vigorous, innovative, and responsible manner that is consistent with the Constitution and applicable law and respectful of the principles upon which the United States was founded.

SECTION 2.2 PURPOSE. This Order is intended to enhance human and technical collection techniques, especially those undertaken abroad, and the acquisition of significant foreign intelligence, as well as the detection and countering of international terrorist activities, the spread of weapons of mass destruction, and espionage conducted by foreign powers. Set forth below are certain general principles that, in addition to and consistent with applicable laws, are intended to achieve the proper balance between the acquisition of essential information and protection of individual interests. Nothing in this Order shall be construed to apply to or interfere with any authorized civil or criminal law enforcement responsibility of any department or agency.

SECTION 2.3 COLLECTION OF INFORMATION. Elements of the Intelligence Community are authorized to collect, retain, or disseminate information concerning United States persons only in accordance with procedures established by the head of the Intelligence Community element concerned or by the head of a department containing such element and approved by the Attorney General, consistent with the authorities provided by Part 1 of this Order, after consultation with the Director. Those procedures shall permit collection, retention, and dissemination of the following types of information:

(a) Information that is publicly available or collected with the consent of the person concerned;

(b) Information constituting foreign intelligence or counterintelligence, including such information concerning corporations or other commercial organizations. Collection within the United States of foreign intelligence not otherwise obtainable shall be undertaken by the Federal Bureau of Investigation (FBI) or, when significant foreign intelligence is sought, by other authorized elements of the Intelligence Community, provided that no foreign intelligence collection by such elements may be undertaken for the purpose of acquiring information concerning the domestic activities of United States persons;

(c) Information obtained in the course of a lawful foreign intelligence, counterintelligence, international drug or international terrorism investigation;

(d) Information needed to protect the safety of any persons or organizations, including those who are targets, victims, or hostages of international terrorist organizations;

(e) Information needed to protect foreign intelligence or counterintelligence sources, methods, and activities from unauthorized disclosure. Collection within the United States shall be undertaken by the FBI except that other elements of the Intelligence Community may also collect such information concerning present or former employees, present or former intelligence element contractors or their present or former employees, or applicants for such employment or contracting;

(f) Information concerning persons who are reasonably believed to be potential sources or contacts for the purpose of determining their suitability or credibility;

(g) Information arising out of a lawful personnel, physical, or communications security investigation;

(h) Information acquired by overhead reconnaissance not directed at specific United States persons;

(i) Incidentally obtained information that may indicate involvement in activities that may violate Federal, state, local, or foreign laws; and

(j) Information necessary for administrative purposes.

In addition, elements of the Intelligence Community may disseminate information to each appropriate element within the Intelligence Community for purposes of allowing the recipient element to determine whether the information is relevant to its responsibilities and can be retained by it, except that information derived from signals intelligence may only be disseminated or made available to Intelligence Community elements in accordance with procedures established by the Director in coordination with the Secretary of Defense and approved by the Attorney General.

SECTION 2.4 COLLECTION TECHNIQUES. Elements of the Intelligence Community shall use the least intrusive collection techniques feasible within the United States or directed against United States persons abroad. Elements of the Intelligence Community are not authorized to use such techniques as electronic surveillance, unconsented physical searches, mail surveillance, physical surveillance, or monitoring devices unless they are in accordance with procedures established by the head of the Intelligence Community element concerned or the head of a department containing such element and approved by the Attorney General, after consultation with the Director. Such procedures shall protect constitutional and other legal rights and limit use of such information to lawful governmental purposes. These procedures shall not authorize:

(a) The Central Intelligence Agency (CIA) to engage in electronic surveillance within the United States except for the purpose of training, testing, or conducting countermeasures to hostile electronic surveillance;

(b) Unconsented physical searches in the United States by elements of the Intelligence Community other than the FBI, except for:

> (1) Searches by counterintelligence elements of the military services directed against military personnel within the United States or abroad for intelligence purposes, when authorized by a military commander empowered to approve physical searches for law enforcement purposes, based upon a finding of probable cause to believe that such persons are acting as agents of foreign powers; and

> (2) Searches by CIA of personal property of non-United States persons lawfully in its possession;

(c) Physical surveillance of a United States person in the United States by elements of the Intelligence
Community other than the FBI, except for:

> (1) Physical surveillance of present or former employees, present or former intelligence element contractors or their present or former employees, or applicants for any such employment or contracting; and

> (2) Physical surveillance of a military person employed by a non-intelligence element of a military service; and

(d) Physical surveillance of a United States person abroad to collect foreign intelligence, except to obtain significant information that cannot reasonably be acquired by other means.

SECTION 2.5 ATTORNEY GENERAL APPROVAL. The Attorney General hereby is delegated the power to approve the use for intelligence purposes, within the United States or against a United States person abroad, of any technique for which a warrant would be required if undertaken for law enforcement purposes, provided that such techniques shall not be undertaken unless the Attorney General has determined in each case that there is probable cause to believe that the technique is directed against a foreign power or an agent of a foreign power. The authority delegated pursuant to this paragraph, including the authority to approve the use of electronic surveillance as defined in the Foreign Intelligence Surveillance Act of 1978, as amended, shall be exercised in accordance with that Act.

SECTION 2.6 ASSISTANCE TO LAW ENFORCEMENT AND OTHER CIVIL AUTHORI-TIES. Elements of the Intelligence Community are authorized to:

(a) Cooperate with appropriate law enforcement agencies for the purpose of protecting the employees, information, property, and facilities of any element of the Intelligence Community;

(b) Unless otherwise precluded by law or this Order, participate in law enforcement activities to investigate or prevent clandestine intelligence activities by foreign powers, or international terrorist or narcotics activities;

(c) Provide specialized equipment, technical knowledge, or assistance of expert personnel for use by any department or agency, or when lives are endangered, to support local law enforcement agencies. Provision of assistance by expert personnel shall be approved in each case by the general counsel of the providing element or department; and

(d) Render any other assistance and cooperation to law enforcement or other civil authorities not precluded by applicable law.

SECTION 2.7 CONTRACTING. Elements of the Intelligence Community are authorized to enter into contracts or arrangements for the provision of goods or services with private companies or institutions in the United States and need not reveal the sponsorship of such contracts or arrangements for authorized intelligence purposes. Contracts or arrangements with academic institutions may be undertaken only with the consent of appropriate officials of the institution.

SECTION 2.8 CONSISTENCY WITH OTHER LAWS. Nothing in this Order shall be construed to authorize any activity in violation of the Constitution or statutes of the United States.

SECTION 2.9 UNDISCLOSED PARTICIPATION IN ORGANIZATIONS WITHIN THE UNITED STATES. No one acting on behalf of elements of the Intelligence Community may join or otherwise participate in any organization in the United States on behalf of any element of the Intelligence Community without disclosing such person's intelligence affiliation to appropriate officials of the organization, except in accordance with procedures established by the head of the Intelligence Community element concerned or the head of a department containing such element and approved by the Attorney General, after consultation with the Director. Such participation shall be authorized only if it is essential to achieving lawful purposes as determined by the Intelligence Community element head or designee. No such participation may be undertaken for the purpose of influencing the activity of the organization or its members except in cases where:

(a) The participation is undertaken on behalf of the FBI in the course of a lawful investigation; or

(b) The organization concerned is composed primarily of individuals who are not United States persons and is reasonably believed to be acting on behalf of a foreign power.

SECTION 2.10 HUMAN EXPERIMENTATION. No element of the Intelligence Community shall sponsor, contract for, or conduct research on human subjects except in accordance with guidelines issued by the Department of Health and Human Services. The subject's informed consent shall be documented as required by those guidelines.

SECTION 2.11 PROHIBITION ON ASSASSINATION. No person employed by or acting on behalf of the United States Government shall engage in or conspire to engage in assassination.

SECTION 2.12 INDIRECT PARTICIPATION. No element of the Intelligence Community shall participate in or request any person to undertake activities forbidden by this Order.

SECTION 2.13 LIMITATION ON COVERT ACTION. No covert action may be conducted which is intended to influence United States political processes, public opinion, policies, or media.

PART 3 GENERAL PROVISIONS

SECTION 3.1 CONGRESSIONAL OVERSIGHT. The duties and responsibilities of the Director and the heads of other departments, agencies, elements, and entities engaged in intelligence activities to cooperate with the Congress in the conduct of its responsibilities for oversight of intelligence activities shall be implemented in accordance with applicable law, including title V of the Act. The requirements of applicable law, including title V of the Act, shall apply to all covert action activities as defined in this Order.

SECTION 3.2 IMPLEMENTATION. The President, supported by the NSC, and the Director shall issue such appropriate directives, procedures, and guidance as are necessary to implement this order. Heads of elements within the Intelligence Community shall issue appropriate procedures and supplementary directives consistent with this order. No procedures to implement Part 2 of this order shall be issued without the Attorney General's approval, after consultation with the Director. The Attorney General shall provide a statement of reasons for not approving any procedures established by the head of an element in the Intelligence Community (or the head of the department containing such element) other than the FBI. In instances where the element head or department head and the Attorney General are unable to reach agreements on other than constitutional or other legal grounds, the Attorney General, the head of department concerned, or the Director shall refer the matter to the NSC.

SECTION 3.3 PROCEDURES. The activities herein authorized that require procedures shall be conducted in accordance with existing procedures or requirements established under Executive Order 12333. New procedures, as required by Executive Order 12333, as further amended, shall be established as expeditiously as possible. All new procedures promulgated pursuant to Executive Order 12333, as amended, shall be made available to the Select Committee on Intelligence of the Senate and the Permanent Select Committee on Intelligence of the House of Representatives.

SECTION 3.4 REFERENCES AND TRANSITION. References to "Senior Officials of the Intelligence Community" or "SOICs" in executive orders or other Presidential guidance, shall be deemed references to the heads of elements in the Intelligence Community, unless the President otherwise directs; references in Intelligence Community or Intelligence Community element policies or guidance, shall be deemed to be references to the heads of elements of the Intelligence Community, unless the President or the Director otherwise directs.

SECTION 3.5 DEFINITIONS. For the purposes of this Order, the following terms shall have these meanings:

(a) *Counterintelligence* means information gathered and activities conducted to identify, deceive, exploit, disrupt, or protect against espionage, other intelligence activities, sabotage, or assassinations conducted for or on behalf of foreign powers, organizations, or persons, or their agents, or international terrorist organizations or activities.

(b) *Covert action* means an activity or activities of the United States Government to influence political, economic, or military conditions abroad, where it is intended that the role of the United States Government will not be apparent or acknowledged publicly, but does not include:

(1) Activities the primary purpose of which is to acquire intelligence, traditional counterintelligence activities, traditional activities to improve or maintain the operational secu-

rity of United States Government programs, or administrative activities;

(2) Traditional diplomatic or military activities or routine support to such activities;

(3) Traditional law enforcement activities conducted by United States Government law enforcement agencies or routine support to such activities; or

(4) Activities to provide routine support to the overt activities (other than activities described in paragraph (1), (2), or (3)) of other United States Government agencies abroad.

(c) *Electronic surveillance* means acquisition of a nonpublic communication by electronic means without the consent of a person who is a party to an electronic communication or, in the case of a nonelectronic communication, without the consent of a person who is visibly present at the place of communication, but not including the use of radio direction-finding equipment solely to determine the location of a transmitter.

(d) *Employee* means a person employed by, assigned or detailed to, or acting for an element within the Intelligence Community.

(e) *Foreign intelligence* means information relating to the capabilities, intentions, or activities of foreign governments or elements thereof, foreign organizations, foreign persons, or international terrorists.

(f) *Intelligence* includes foreign intelligence and counterintelligence.

(g) *Intelligence activities* means all activities that elements of the Intelligence Community are authorized to conduct pursuant to this order.

(h) *Intelligence Community* and elements of the Intelligence Community refers to:

(1) The Office of the Director of National Intelligence;

(2) The Central Intelligence Agency;

(3) The National Security Agency;

(4) The Defense Intelligence Agency;

(5) The National Geospatial-Intelligence Agency;

(6) The National Reconnaissance Office;

(7) The other offices within the Department of Defense for the collection of specialized national foreign intelligence through reconnaissance programs;

(8) The intelligence and counterintelligence elements of the Army, the Navy, the Air Force, and the
Marine Corps;

(9) The intelligence elements of the Federal Bureau of Investigation;

(10) The Office of National Security Intelligence of the Drug Enforcement Administration;

(11) The Office of Intelligence and Counterintelligence of the Department of Energy;

(12) The Bureau of Intelligence and Research of the Department of State;

(13) The Office of Intelligence and Analysis of the Department of the Treasury;

(14) The Office of Intelligence and Analysis of the Department of Homeland Security;

(15) The intelligence and counterintelligence elements of the Coast Guard; and

(16) Such other elements of any department or agency as may be designated by the President, or designated jointly by the Director and the head of the department or agency concerned, as an element of the Intelligence Community.

(i) *National Intelligence and Intelligence Related to National Security* means all intelligence, regardless of the source from which derived and including information gathered within or outside the United States, that pertains, as determined consistent with any guidance issued by the President, or that is determined for the purpose of access to information by the Director in accordance with section 1.3(a)(1) of this order, to pertain to more than one United States Government agency; and that involves threats to the United States, its people, property, or interests; the development, proliferation, or use of weapons of mass destruction; or any other matter bearing on United States national or homeland security.

(j) *The National Intelligence Program* means all programs, projects, and activities of the Intelligence

Community, as well as any other programs of the Intelligence Community designated jointly by the Director and the head of a United States department or agency or by the President. Such term does not include programs, projects, or activities of the military departments to acquire intelligence solely for the planning and conduct of tactical military operations by United States Armed Forces.

(k) *United States person* means a United States citizen, an alien known by the intelligence element concerned to be a permanent resident alien, an unincorporated association substantially composed of

United States citizens or permanent resident aliens, or a corporation incorporated in the United States, except for a corporation directed and controlled by a foreign government or governments.

SECTION 3.6 REVOCATION. Executive Orders 13354 and 13355 of August 27, 2004, are revoked; and paragraphs 1.3(b)(9) Executive Order 12958, as amended, are inconsistent with this Order.

SECTION 3.7 GENERAL PROVISIONS.

(a) Consistent with section 1.3(c) of this order, nothing in this order shall be construed to impair or otherwise affect:

    (1) Authority granted by law to a department or agency, or the head thereof; or

    (2) Functions of the Director of the Office of Management and Budget relating to budget, administrative, or legislative proposals.

(b) This order shall be implemented consistent with applicable law and subject to the availability of appropriations.

(c) This order is intended only to improve the internal management of the executive branch and is not intended to, and does not, create any right or benefit, substantive or procedural, enforceable at law or in equity, by any party against the United States, its departments, agencies or entities, its officers, employees, or agents, or any other person.

Executive Order 12139—Exercise of Certain Authority Respecting Electronic Surveillance

Fed. Reg. 30,311 (May 23, 1979)

> By the authority vested in me as President by Sections 102 and 104 of the Foreign Intelligence Surveillance Act of 1978 (50 U.S.C. 1802 and 1804), in order to provide as set forth in that Act (this chapter) for the authorization of electronic surveillance for foreign intelligence purposes, it is hereby ordered as follows:

SECTION 1-101. Pursuant to Section 102(a)(1) of the Foreign Intelligence Surveillance Act of 1978 (50 U.S.C. 1802(a)), the Attorney General is authorized to approve electronic surveillance to acquire foreign intelligence information without a court order, but only if the Attorney General makes the certifications required by that Section.

SECTION 1-102. Pursuant to Section 102(b) of the Foreign Intelligence Act of 1978 (50 U.S.C. 1802(b)), the Attorney General is authorized to approve applications to the court having jurisdiction under Section 103 of that Act (50 U.S.C. 1803) to obtain orders for electronic surveillance for the purpose of obtaining foreign intelligence information.

SECTION 1-103. Pursuant to Section 104(a)(7) of the Foreign Intelligence Surveillance Act of 1978 (50 U.S.C. 1804(a)(7)), the following officials, each of whom is employed in the area of national security or defense, is designated to make the certifications required by Section 104(a)(7) of the Act in support of applications to conduct electronic surveillance:

  (a) Secretary of State.
  (b) Secretary of Defense.
  (c) Director of Central Intelligence.
  (d) Director of the Federal Bureau of Investigation.
  (e) Deputy Secretary of State.
  (f) Deputy Secretary of Defense.
  (g) Deputy Director of Central Intelligence.

None of the above officials, nor anyone officially acting in that capacity, may exercise the authority to make the above certifications, unless that official has been appointed by the President with the advice and consent of the Senate.

SECTION 1-104. Section 2-202 of Executive Order No. 12036 (set out under section 401 of this title) is amended by inserting the following at the end of that section: ''Any electronic surveillance, as defined in the Foreign Intelligence Surveillance Act of 1978, shall be conducted in accordance with that Act as well as this Order.''.

SECTION 1-105. Section 2-203 of Executive Order No. 12036 (set out under section 401 of this title) is amended by inserting the following at the end of that section: "Any monitoring which constitutes electronic surveillance as defined in the Foreign Intelligence Surveillance Act of 1978 shall be conducted in accordance with that Act as well as this Order.".

JIMMY CARTER

Executive Order 12949—Foreign Intelligence Physical Searches

60 Fed. Reg. 8,169 (Feb. 13, 1995))

By the authority vested in me as President by the Constitution and the laws of the United States, including sections 302 and 303 of the Foreign Intelligence Surveillance Act of 1978 ("Act") (50 U.S.C. 1801, *et seq.*), as amended by Public Law 103–359, and in order to provide for the authorization of physical searches for foreign intelligence purposes as set forth in the Act, it is hereby ordered as follows:

Section 1. Pursuant to section 302(a)(1) of the Act, the Attorney General is authorized to approve physical searches, without a court order, to acquire foreign intelligence information for periods of up to one year, if the Attorney General makes the certifications required by that section.

Sec. 2. Pursuant to section 302(b) of the Act, the Attorney General is authorized to approve applications to the Foreign Intelligence Surveillance Court under section 303 of the Act to obtain orders for physical searches for the purpose of collecting foreign intelligence information.

Sec. 3. Pursuant to section 303(a)(7) of the Act, the following officials, each of whom is employed in the area of national security or defense, is designated to make the certifications required by section 303(a)(7) of the Act in support of applications to conduct physical searches:
(a) Secretary of State;
(b) Secretary of Defense;
(c) Director of Central Intelligence;
(d) Director of the Federal Bureau of Investigation;
(e) Deputy Secretary of State;
(f) Deputy Secretary of Defense; and
(g) Deputy Director of Central Intelligence.

None of the above officials, nor anyone officially acting in that capacity, may exercise the authority to make the above certifications, unless that official has been appointed by the President, by and with the advice and consent of the Senate.

WILLIAM J. CLINTON

Executive Order 13462—President's Intelligence Advisory Board and Intelligence Oversight Board

73 Fed. Reg. 11,805 (Feb. 29, 2008)

By the authority vested in me as President by the Constitution and the laws of the United States of America, it is hereby ordered as follows:

SECTION 1. POLICY. It is the policy of the United States to ensure that the President and other officers of the United States with responsibility for the security of the Nation and the advancement of its interests have access to accurate, insightful, objective, and timely information concerning the capabilities, intentions, and activities of foreign powers.

SECTION 2. DEFINITIONS. As used in this order:

(a) "department concerned" means an executive department listed in section 101 of title 5, United States Code, that contains an organization listed in or designated pursuant to section 3(4) of the National Security Act of 1947, as amended (50 U.S.C. 401a(4));

(b) "intelligence activities" has the meaning specified in section 3.4 of Executive Order 12333 of December 4, 1981, as amended; and

(c) "intelligence community" means the organizations listed in or designated pursuant to section 3(4) of the National Security Act of 1947, as amended.

SECTION 3. ESTABLISHMENT OF THE PRESIDENT'S INTELLIGENCE ADVISORY BOARD.

(a) There is hereby established, within the Executive Office of the President and exclusively to advise and assist the President as set forth in this order, the President's Intelligence Advisory Board (PIAB).

(b) The PIAB shall consist of not more than 16 members appointed by the President from among individuals who are not employed by the Federal Government.

(c) The President shall designate a Chair from among the members of the PIAB, who shall convene and preside at meetings of the PIAB, determine its agenda, and direct its work.

(d) Members of the PIAB and the Intelligence Oversight Board (IOB) established in section 5 of this order:

> (i) shall serve without any compensation for their work on the PIAB or the IOB; and
>
> (ii) while engaged in the work of the PIAB or the IOB, may be allowed travel expenses, including per diem in lieu of subsistence, as authorized by law for persons serving intermittently in the Government (5 U.S.C. 5701-5707).

(e) The PIAB shall utilize such full-time professional and administrative staff as authorized by the Chair and approved by the President or the President's designee. Such staff shall be supervised by an Executive Director of the PIAB, appointed by the President, whom the President may designate to serve also as the Executive Director of the IOB.

SECTION 4. FUNCTIONS OF THE PIAB. Consistent with the policy set forth in section 1 of this order, the PIAB shall have the authority to, as the PIAB determines appropriate, or shall, when directed by the President:

(a) assess the quality, quantity, and adequacy of intelligence collection, of analysis and estimates, and of counterintelligence and other intelligence activities, assess the adequacy of management, personnel and organization in the intelligence community, and review the performance of all agencies of the Federal Government that are engaged in the collection, evaluation, or production of intelligence or the execution of intelligence policy and report the results of such assessments or reviews:

    (i) to the President, as necessary but not less than twice each year; and

    (ii) to the Director of National Intelligence (DNI) and the heads of departments concerned when the PIAB determines appropriate; and

(b) consider and make appropriate recommendations to the President, the DNI, or the head of the department concerned with respect to matters identified to the PIAB by the DNI or the head of a department concerned.

SECTION 5. ESTABLISHMENT OF INTELLIGENCE OVERSIGHT BOARD.

(a) There is hereby established a committee of the PIAB to be known as the Intelligence Oversight Board.

(b) The IOB shall consist of not more than five members of the PIAB who are designated by the President from among members of the PIAB to serve on the IOB. The IOB shall utilize such full-time professional and administrative staff as authorized by the Chair and approved by the President or the President's designee. Such staff shall be supervised by an Executive Director of the IOB, appointed by the President, whom the President may designate to serve also as the Executive Director of the PIAB.

(c) The President shall designate a Chair from among the members of the IOB, who shall convene and preside at meetings of the IOB, determine its agenda, and direct its work.

SECTION 6. FUNCTIONS OF THE IOB. Consistent with the policy set forth in section 1 of this order, the IOB shall:

(a) issue criteria on the thresholds for reporting matters to the IOB, to the extent consistent with section 1.7(d) of Executive Order 12333 or the corresponding provision of any successor order;

(b) inform the President of intelligence activities that the IOB believes:

    (i)(A) may be unlawful or contrary to Executive Order or presidential directive; and

      (B) are not being adequately addressed by the Attorney General, the DNI, or the head of the department concerned; or

    (ii) should be immediately reported to the President.

(c) review and assess the effectiveness, efficiency, and sufficiency of the processes by which the DNI and the heads of departments concerned perform their respective functions under this order and report thereon as necessary, together with any recommendations, to the President and, as appropriate, the DNI and the head of the department concerned;

(d) receive and review information submitted by the DNI under subsection 7(c) of this order and make recommendations thereon, including for any needed corrective action, with respect to such information, and the intelligence activities to which the information relates, as necessary, but not less than twice each year, to the President, the DNI, and the head of the department concerned; and

(e) conduct, or request that the DNI or the head of the department concerned, as appropriate, carry out and report to the IOB the results of, investigations of intelligence activities that the IOB determines are necessary to enable the IOB to carry out its functions under this order.

SECTION 7. FUNCTIONS OF THE DIRECTOR OF NATIONAL INTELLIGENCE. Consistent with the policy set forth in section 1 of this order, the DNI shall:

(a) with respect to guidelines applicable to organizations within the intelligence community that concern reporting of intelligence activities described in subsection 6(b)(i)(A) of this order:

    (i) review and ensure that such guidelines are consistent with section 1.7(d) of Executive Order 12333, or a corresponding provision of any successor order, and this order; and

(ii) issue for incorporation in such guidelines instructions relating to the format and schedule of such reporting as necessary to implement this order;

(b) with respect to intelligence activities described in subsection 6(b)(i)(A) of this order:

(i) receive reports submitted to the IOB pursuant to section 1.7(d) of Executive Order 12333, or a corresponding provision of any successor order;

(ii) forward to the Attorney General information in such reports relating to such intelligence activities to the extent that such activities involve possible violations of Federal criminal laws or implicate the authority of the Attorney General unless the DNI or the head of the department concerned has previously provided such information to the Attorney General; and

(iii) monitor the intelligence community to ensure that the head of the department concerned has directed needed corrective actions and that such actions have been taken and report to the IOB and the head of the department concerned, and as appropriate the President, when such actions have not been timely taken; and

(c) submit to the IOB as necessary and no less than twice each year:

(i) an analysis of the reports received under subsection (b)(i) of this section, including an assessment of the gravity, frequency, trends, and patterns of occurrences of intelligence activities described in subsection 6(b)(i)(A) of this order;

(ii) a summary of direction under subsection (b)(iii) of this section and any related recommendations; and

(iii) an assessment of the effectiveness of corrective action taken by the DNI or the head of the department concerned with respect to intelligence activities described in subsection 6(b)(i)(A) of this order.

SECTION 8. FUNCTIONS OF HEADS OF DEPARTMENTS CONCERNED AND ADDITIONAL FUNCTIONS OF THE DIRECTOR OF NATIONAL INTELLIGENCE.

(a) To the extent permitted by law, the DNI and the heads of departments concerned shall provide such information and assistance as the PIAB and the IOB may need to perform functions under this order.

(b) The heads of departments concerned shall:

(i) ensure that the DNI receives:

(A) copies of reports submitted to the IOB pursuant to section 1.7(d) of Executive Order 12333, or a corresponding provision of any successor order; and

(B) such information and assistance as the DNI may need to perform functions under this order; and

(ii) designate the offices within their respective organizations that shall submit reports to the IOB required by Executive Order and inform the DNI and the IOB of such designations; and

(iii) ensure that departments concerned comply with instructions issued by the DNI under subsection 7(a)(ii) of this order.

(c) The head of a department concerned who does not implement a recommendation to that head of department from the PIAB under subsection 4(b) of this order or from the IOB under subsections 6(c) or 6(d) of this order shall promptly report through the DNI to the Board that made the recommendation, or to the President, the reasons for not implementing the recommendation.

(d) The DNI shall ensure that the Director of the Central Intelligence Agency performs the functions with respect to the Central Intelligence Agency under this order that a head of a department concerned performs with respect to organizations within the intelligence community that are part of that department.

SECTION 9. REFERENCES AND TRANSITION.

(a) References in Executive Orders other than this order, or in any other presidential guidance, to the "President's Foreign Intelligence Advisory Board" shall be deemed to be references to the President's Intelligence Advisory Board established by this order.

(b) Individuals who are members of the President's Foreign Intelligence Advisory Board under Executive Order 12863 of September 13, 1993, as amended, immediately prior to the signing of this order shall be members of the President's Intelligence Advisory Board immediately upon the signing of this order, to serve as such consistent with this order until the date that is 15 months following the date of this order.

(c) Individuals who are members of the Intelligence Oversight Board under Executive Order 12863 immediately prior to the signing of this order shall be members of the Intelligence Oversight Board under this order, to serve as such consistent with this order until the date that is 15 months following the date of this order.

(d) The individual serving as Executive Director of the President's Foreign Intelligence Advisory Board immediately prior to the signing of this order shall serve as the Executive Director of the PIAB until such person resigns, dies, or is removed, or upon appointment of a successor under this order and shall serve as the Executive Director of the IOB until an Executive Director of the IOB is appointed or designated under this order.

SECTION 10. REVOCATION. Executive Order 12863 is revoked.

SECTION 11. GENERAL PROVISIONS.

(a) Nothing in this order shall be construed to impair or otherwise affect:

    (i) authority granted by law to a department or agency, or the head thereof; or

    (ii) functions of the Director of the Office of Management and Budget relating to budget, administrative, or legislative proposals.

(b) Any person who is a member of the PIAB or IOB, or who is granted access to classified national security information in relation to the activities of the PIAB or the IOB, as a condition of access to such information, shall sign and comply with the agreements to protect such information from unauthorized disclosure. This order shall be implemented in a manner consistent with Executive Order 12958 of April 17, 1995, as amended, and Executive Order 12968 of August 2, 1995, as amended.

(c) This order shall be implemented consistent with applicable law and subject to the availability of appropriations.

(d) This order is intended only to improve the internal management of the executive branch and is not intended to, and does not, create any right or benefit, substantive or procedural, enforceable at law or in equity, by any party against the United States, its departments, agencies or entities, its officers, employees, or agents, or any other person.

GEORGE W. BUSH

Executive Order 13526—
Classified National Security Information

75 Fed. Reg. 707 (Jan. 5, 2010); correction printed 75 Fed. Reg. 1,013 (Jan. 8, 2010)

By the authority vested in me as President by the Constitution and the laws of the United States of America, it is hereby ordered as follows:

PART 1 — ORIGINAL CLASSIFICATION

SECTION 1.1. CLASSIFICATION STANDARDS.

(a) Information may be originally classified under the terms of this order only if all of the following conditions are met:

(1) an original classification authority is classifying the information;

(2) the information is owned by, produced by or for, or is under the control of the United States Government;

(3) the information falls within one or more of the categories of information listed in section 1.4 of this order; and

(4) the original classification authority determines that the unauthorized disclosure of the information reasonably could be expected to result in damage to the national security, which includes defense against transnational terrorism, and the original classification authority is able to identify or describe the damage.

(b) If there is significant doubt about the need to classify information, it shall not be classified. This provision does not:

(1) amplify or modify the substantive criteria or procedures for classification; or

(2) create any substantive or procedural rights subject to judicial review.

(c) Classified information shall not be declassified automatically as a result of any unauthorized disclosure of identical or similar information.

(d) The unauthorized disclosure of foreign government information is presumed to cause damage to the national security.

SEC. 1.2. CLASSIFICATION LEVELS.

(a) Information may be classified at one of the following three levels:

(1) "Top Secret" shall be applied to information, the unauthorized disclosure of which reasonably could be expected to cause exceptionally grave damage to the national security that the original classification authority is able to identify or describe.

(2) "Secret" shall be applied to information, the unauthorized disclosure of which reasonably could be expected to cause serious damage to the national security that the original classification authority is able to identify or describe.

(3) "Confidential" shall be applied to information, the unauthorized disclosure of which reasonably could be expected to cause damage to the national security that the original classification authority is able to identify or describe.

(b) Except as otherwise provided by statute, no other terms shall be used to identify United States classified information.

(c) If there is significant doubt about the appropriate level of classification, it shall be classified at the lower level.

SECTION 1.3. CLASSIFICATION AUTHORITY.

(a) The authority to classify information originally may be exercised only by:

(1) the President and the Vice President;

(2) agency heads and officials designated by the President; and

(3) United States Government officials delegated this authority pursuant to paragraph (c) of this section.

(b) Officials authorized to classify information at a specified level are also authorized to classify information at a lower level.

(c) Delegation of original classification authority.

(1) Delegations of original classification authority shall be limited to the minimum required to administer this order. Agency heads are responsible for ensuring that designated subordinate officials have a demonstrable and continuing need to exercise this authority.

(2) "Top Secret" original classification authority may be delegated only by the President, the Vice President, or an agency head or official designated pursuant to paragraph (a)(2) of this section.

(3) "Secret" or "Confidential" original classification authority may be delegated only by the President, the Vice President, an agency head or official designated pursuant to paragraph (a)(2) of this section, or the senior agency official designated under section 5.4(d) of this order, provided that official has been delegated "Top Secret" original classification authority by the agency head.

(4) Each delegation of original classification authority shall be in writing and the authority shall not be redelegated except as provided in this order. Each delegation shall identify the official by name or position.

(5) Delegations of original classification authority shall be reported or made available by name or position to the Director of the Information Security Oversight Office.

(d) All original classification authorities must receive training in proper classification (including the avoidance of over-classification) and declassification as provided in this order and its implementing directives at least once a calendar year. Such training must include instruction on the proper safeguarding of classified information and on the sanctions in section 5.5 of this order that may be brought against an individual who fails to classify information properly or protect classified information from unauthorized disclosure. Original classification authorities who do not receive such mandatory training at least once within a calendar year shall have their classification authority suspended by the agency head or the senior agency official designated under section 5.4(d) of this order until such training has taken place. A waiver may be granted by the agency head, the deputy agency head, or the senior agency official if an individual is unable to receive such training due to unavoidable circumstances. Whenever a waiver is granted, the individual shall receive such training as soon as practicable.

(e) Exceptional cases. When an employee, government contractor, licensee, certificate holder, or grantee of an agency who does not have original classification authority originates information believed by that person to require classification, the information shall be protected in a manner consistent with this order and its implementing directives. The information shall be transmitted promptly as provided under this order or its implementing directives to the agency that has appropriate subject matter interest and classification authority with respect to this information. That agency shall decide within 30 days whether to classify this information.

SECTION 1.4. CLASSIFICATION CATEGORIES. Information shall not be considered for classification unless its unauthorized disclosure could reasonably be expected to cause identifiable or describable damage to the national security in accordance with section 1.2 of this order, and it pertains to one or more of the following:

(a) military plans, weapons systems, or operations;

(b) foreign government information;

(c) intelligence activities (including covert action), intelligence sources or methods, or cryptology;

(d) foreign relations or foreign activities of the United States, including confidential sources;

(e) scientific, technological, or economic matters relating to the national security;

(f) United States Government programs for safeguarding nuclear materials or facilities;

(g) vulnerabilities or capabilities of systems, installations, infrastructures, projects, plans, or protection services relating to the national security; or

(h) the development, production, or use of weapons of mass destruction.

SECTION 1.5. DURATION OF CLASSIFICATION.

(a) At the time of original classification, the original classification authority shall establish a specific date or event for declassification based on the duration of the national security sensitivity of the information. Upon reaching the date or event, the information shall be automatically declassified. Except for information that should clearly and demonstrably be expected to reveal the identity of a confidential human source or a human intelligence source or key design concepts of weapons of mass destruction, the date or event shall not exceed the time frame established in paragraph (b) of this section.

(b) If the original classification authority cannot determine an earlier specific date or event for declassification, information shall be marked for declassification 10 years from the date of the original decision, unless the original classification authority otherwise determines that the sensitivity of the information requires that it be marked for declassification for up to 25 years from the date of the original decision.

(c) An original classification authority may extend the duration of classification up to 25 years from the date of origin of the document, change the level of classification, or reclassify specific information only when the standards and procedures for classifying information under this order are followed.

(d) No information may remain classified indefinitely. Information marked for an indefinite duration of classification under predecessor orders, for example, marked as "Originating Agency's Determination Required," or classified information that contains incomplete declassification instructions or lacks declassification instructions shall be declassified in accordance with part 3 of this order.

SECTION 1.6. IDENTIFICATION AND MARKINGS.

(a) At the time of original classification, the following shall be indicated in a manner that is immediately apparent:

(1) one of the three classification levels defined in section 1.2 of this order;

(2) the identity, by name and position, or by personal identifier, of the original classification authority;

(3) the agency and office of origin, if not otherwise evident;

(4) declassification instructions, which shall indicate one of the following:

(A) the date or event for declassification, as prescribed in section 1.5(a);

(B) the date that is 10 years from the date of original classification, as prescribed in section 1.5(b);

(C) the date that is up to 25 years from the date of original classification, as prescribed in section 1.5(b); or

(D) in the case of information that should clearly and demonstrably be expected to reveal the identity of a confidential human source or a human intelligence source or key design concepts of weapons of mass destruction, the marking prescribed in implementing directives issued pursuant to this order; and

(5) a concise reason for classification that, at a minimum, cites the applicable classification categories in section 1.4 of this order.

(b) Specific information required in paragraph (a) of this section may be excluded if it would reveal additional classified information.

(c) With respect to each classified document, the agency originating the document shall, by marking or other means, indicate which portions are classified, with the applicable classification level, and which portions are unclassified. In accordance with standards prescribed in directives issued under this order, the Director of the Information Security Oversight Office may grant and revoke temporary waivers of this requirement. The Director shall revoke any waiver upon a finding of abuse.

(d) Markings or other indicia implementing the provisions of this order, including abbreviations and requirements to safeguard classified working papers, shall conform to the standards prescribed in implementing directives issued pursuant to this order.

(e) Foreign government information shall retain its original classification markings or shall be assigned a U.S. classification that provides a degree of protection at least equivalent to that required by the entity that furnished the information. Foreign government information retaining its original classification markings need not be assigned a U.S. classification marking provided that the responsible agency determines that the foreign government markings are adequate to meet the purposes served by U.S. classification markings.

(f) Information assigned a level of classification under this or predecessor orders shall be considered as classified at that level of classification despite the omission of other required markings. Whenever such information is used in the derivative classification process or is reviewed for possible declassification, holders of such information shall coordinate with an appropriate classification authority for the application of omitted markings.

(g) The classification authority shall, whenever practicable, use a classified addendum whenever classified information constitutes a small portion of an otherwise unclassified document or prepare a product to allow for dissemination at the lowest level of classification possible or in unclassified form.

(h) Prior to public release, all declassified records shall be appropriately marked to reflect their declassification.

SEC. 1.7. CLASSIFICATION PROHIBITIONS AND LIMITATIONS.

(a) In no case shall information be classified, continue to be maintained as classified, or fail to be declassified in order to:

    (1) conceal violations of law, inefficiency, or administrative error;

    (2) prevent embarrassment to a person, organization, or agency;

    (3) restrain competition; or

    (4) prevent or delay the release of information that does not require protection in the interest of the national security.

(b) Basic scientific research information not clearly related to the national security shall not be classified.

(c) Information may not be reclassified after declassification and release to the public under proper authority unless:

    (1) the reclassification is personally approved in writing by the agency head based on a document-by-document determination by the agency that reclassification is required to prevent significant and demonstrable damage to the national security;

    (2) the information may be reasonably recovered without bringing undue attention to the information;

    (3) the reclassification action is reported promptly to the Assistant to the President for National Security Affairs (National Security Advisor) and the Director of the Information Security Oversight Office; and

    (4) for documents in the physical and legal custody of the National Archives and Records Administration (National Archives) that have been available for public use, the agency head has, after making the determinations required by this paragraph, notified the Archi-

vist of the United States (Archivist), who shall suspend public access pending approval of the reclassification action by the Director of the Information Security Oversight Office. Any such decision by the Director may be appealed by the agency head to the President through the National Security Advisor. Public access shall remain suspended pending a prompt decision on the appeal.

(d) Information that has not previously been disclosed to the public under proper authority may be classified or reclassified after an agency has received a request for it under the Freedom of Information Act (5 U.S.C. 552), the Presidential Records Act, 44 U.S.C. 2204(c)(1), the Privacy Act of 1974 (5 U.S.C. 552a), or the mandatory review provisions of section 3.5 of this order only if such classification meets the requirements of this order and is accomplished on a document-by-document basis with the personal participation or under the direction of the agency head, the deputy agency head, or the senior agency official designated under section 5.4 of this order. The requirements in this paragraph also apply to those situations in which information has been declassified in accordance with a specific date or event determined by an original classification authority in accordance with section 1.5 of this order.

(e) Compilations of items of information that are individually unclassified may be classified if the compiled information reveals an additional association or relationship that: (1) meets the standards for classification under this order; and (2) is not otherwise revealed in the individual items of information.

SECTION 1.8. CLASSIFICATION CHALLENGES.

(a) Authorized holders of information who, in good faith, believe that its classification status is improper are encouraged and expected to challenge the classification status of the information in accordance with agency procedures established under paragraph (b) of this section.

(b) In accordance with implementing directives issued pursuant to this order, an agency head or senior agency official shall establish procedures under which authorized holders of information, including authorized holders outside the classifying agency, are encouraged and expected to challenge the classification of information that they believe is improperly classified or unclassified. These procedures shall ensure that:

(1) individuals are not subject to retribution for bringing such actions;

(2) an opportunity is provided for review by an impartial official or panel; and

(3) individuals are advised of their right to appeal agency decisions to the Interagency Security Classification Appeals Panel (Panel) established by section 5.3 of this order.

(c) Documents required to be submitted for prepublication review or other administrative process pursuant to an approved nondisclosure agreement are not covered by this section.

SECTION 1.9. FUNDAMENTAL CLASSIFICATION GUIDANCE REVIEW.

(a) Agency heads shall complete on a periodic basis a comprehensive review of the agency's classification guidance, particularly classification guides, to ensure the guidance reflects current circumstances and to identify classified information that no longer requires protection and can be declassified. The initial fundamental classification guidance review shall be completed within 2 years of the effective date of this order.

(b) The classification guidance review shall include an evaluation of classified information to determine if it meets the standards for classification under section 1.4 of this order, taking into account an up-to-date assessment of likely damage as described under section 1.2 of this order.

(c) The classification guidance review shall include original classification authorities and agency subject matter experts to ensure a broad range of perspectives.

(d) Agency heads shall provide a report summarizing the results of the classification guidance review to the Director of the Information Security Oversight Office and shall release an unclassified version of this report to the public.

PART 2 — DERIVATIVE CLASSIFICATION

SECTION 2.1. USE OF DERIVATIVE CLASSIFICATION.

(a) Persons who reproduce, extract, or summarize classified information, or who apply classification markings derived from source material or as directed by a classification guide, need not possess original classification authority.

(b) Persons who apply derivative classification markings shall:

(1) be identified by name and position, or by personal identifier, in a manner that is immediately apparent for each derivative classification action;

(2) observe and respect original classification decisions; and

(3) carry forward to any newly created documents the pertinent classification markings. For information derivatively classified based on multiple sources, the derivative classifier shall carry forward:

(A) the date or event for declassification that corresponds to the longest period of classification among the sources, or the marking established pursuant to section 1.6(a)(4)(D) of this order; and

(B) a listing of the source materials.

(c) Derivative classifiers shall, whenever practicable, use a classified addendum whenever classified information constitutes a small portion of an otherwise unclassified document or prepare a product to allow for dissemination at the lowest level of classification possible or in unclassified form.

(d) Persons who apply derivative classification markings shall receive training in the proper application of the derivative classification principles of the order, with an emphasis on avoiding over-classification, at least once every 2 years. Derivative classifiers who do not receive such training at least once every 2 years shall have their authority to apply derivative classification markings suspended until they have received such training. A waiver may be granted by the agency head, the deputy agency head, or the senior agency official if an individual is unable to receive such training due to unavoidable circumstances. Whenever a waiver is granted, the individual shall receive such training as soon as practicable.

SECTION 2.2. CLASSIFICATION GUIDES

(a) Agencies with original classification authority shall prepare classification guides to facilitate the proper and uniform derivative classification of information. These guides shall conform to standards contained in directives issued under this order.

(b) Each guide shall be approved personally and in writing by an official who:

(1) has program or supervisory responsibility over the information or is the senior agency official; and

(2) is authorized to classify information originally at the highest level of classification prescribed in the guide.

(c) Agencies shall establish procedures to ensure that classification guides are reviewed and updated as provided in directives issued under this order.

(d) Agencies shall incorporate original classification decisions into classification guides on a timely basis and in accordance with directives issued under this order.

(e) Agencies may incorporate exemptions from automatic declassification approved pursuant to section 3.3(j) of this order into classification guides, provided that the Panel is notified of the intent to take such action for specific information in advance of approval and the information remains in active use.

(f) The duration of classification of a document classified by a derivative classifier using a classification guide shall not exceed 25 years from the date of the origin of the document, except for:

(1) information that should clearly and demonstrably be expected to reveal the identity of a confidential human source or a human intelligence source or key design concepts of weapons of mass destruction; and

(2) specific information incorporated into classification guides in accordance with section 2.2(e) of this order.

PART 3 — DECLASSIFICATION AND DOWNGRADING

SECTION 3.1. AUTHORITY FOR DECLASSIFICATION.

(a) Information shall be declassified as soon as it no longer meets the standards for classification under this order.

(b) Information shall be declassified or downgraded by:

(1) the official who authorized the original classification, if that official is still serving in the same position and has original classification authority;

(2) the originator's current successor in function, if that individual has original classification authority;

(3) a supervisory official of either the originator or his or her successor in function, if the supervisory official has original classification authority; or

(4) officials delegated declassification authority in writing by the agency head or the senior agency official of the originating agency.

(c) The Director of National Intelligence (or, if delegated by the Director of National Intelligence, the Principal Deputy Director of National Intelligence) may, with respect to the Intelligence Community, after consultation with the head of the originating Intelligence Community element or department, declassify, downgrade, or direct the declassification or downgrading of information or intelligence relating to intelligence sources, methods, or activities.

(d) It is presumed that information that continues to meet the classification requirements under this order requires continued protection. In some exceptional cases, however, the need to protect such information may be outweighed by the public interest in disclosure of the information, and in these cases the information should be declassified. When such questions arise, they shall be referred to the agency head or the senior agency official. That official will determine, as an exercise of discretion, whether the public interest in disclosure outweighs the damage to the national security that might reasonably be expected from disclosure. This provision does not:

(1) amplify or modify the substantive criteria or procedures for classification; or

(2) create any substantive or procedural rights subject to judicial review.

(e) If the Director of the Information Security Oversight Office determines that information is classified in violation of this order, the Director may require the information to be declassified by the agency that originated the classification. Any such decision by the Director may be appealed to the President through the National Security Advisor. The information shall remain classified pending a prompt decision on the appeal.

(f) The provisions of this section shall also apply to agencies that, under the terms of this order, do not have original classification authority, but had such authority under predecessor orders.

(g) No information may be excluded from declassification under section 3.3 of this order based solely on the type of document or record in which it is found. Rather, the classified information must be considered on the basis of its content.

(h) Classified nonrecord materials, including artifacts, shall be declassified as soon as they no longer meet the standards for classification under this order.

(i) When making decisions under sections 3.3, 3.4, and 3.5 of this order, agencies shall consider the final decisions of the Panel.

SECTION 3.2. TRANSFERRED RECORDS.

(a) In the case of classified records transferred in conjunction with a transfer of functions, and not merely for storage purposes, the receiving agency shall be deemed to be the originating agency for purposes of this order.

(b) In the case of classified records that are not officially transferred as described in paragraph (a) of this section, but that originated in an agency that has ceased to exist and for which there is no successor agency, each agency in possession of such records shall be deemed to be the originating agency for purposes of this order. Such records may be declassified or downgraded by the agency in possession of the records after consultation with any other agency that has an interest in the subject matter of the records.

(c) Classified records accessioned into the National Archives shall be declassified or downgraded by the Archivist in accordance with this order, the directives issued pursuant to this order, agency declassification guides, and any existing procedural agreement between the Archivist and the relevant agency head.

(d) The originating agency shall take all reasonable steps to declassify classified information contained in records determined to have permanent historical value before they are accessioned into the National Archives. However, the Archivist may require that classified records be accessioned into the National Archives when necessary to comply with the provisions of the Federal Records Act. This provision does not apply to records transferred to the Archivist pursuant to section 2203 of title 44, United States Code, or records for which the National Archives serves as the custodian of the records of an agency or organization that has gone out of existence.

(e) To the extent practicable, agencies shall adopt a system of records management that will facilitate the public release of documents at the time such documents are declassified pursuant to the provisions for automatic declassification in section 3.3 of this order.

SECTION 3.3. AUTOMATIC DECLASSIFICATION.

(a) Subject to paragraphs (b)–(d) and (g)–(j) of this section, all classified records that (1) are more than 25 years old and (2) have been determined to have permanent historical value under title 44, United States Code, shall be automatically declassified whether or not the records have been reviewed. All classified records shall be automatically declassified on December 31 of the year that is 25 years from the date of origin, except as provided in paragraphs (b)–(d) and (g)–(i) of this section. If the date of origin of an individual record cannot be readily determined, the date of original classification shall be used instead.

(b) An agency head may exempt from automatic declassification under paragraph (a) of this section specific information, the release of which should clearly and demonstrably be expected to:

(1) reveal the identity of a confidential human source, a human intelligence source, a relationship with an intelligence or security service of a foreign government or international organization, or a nonhuman intelligence source; or impair the effectiveness of an intelligence method currently in use, available for use, or under development;

(2) reveal information that would assist in the development, production, or use of weapons of mass destruction;

(3) reveal information that would impair U.S. cryptologic systems or activities;

(4) reveal information that would impair the application of state-of-the-art technology within a U.S. weapon system;

(5) reveal formally named or numbered U.S. military war plans that remain in effect, or reveal operational or tactical elements of prior plans that are contained in such active plans;

(6) reveal information, including foreign government information, that would cause seri-

ous harm to relations between the United States and a foreign government, or to ongoing diplomatic activities of the United States;

(7) reveal information that would impair the current ability of United States Government officials to protect the President, Vice President, and other protectees for whom protection services, in the interest of the national security, are authorized;

(8) reveal information that would seriously impair current national security emergency preparedness plans or reveal current vulnerabilities of systems, installations, or infrastructures relating to the national security; or

(9) violate a statute, treaty, or international agreement that does not permit the automatic or unilateral declassification of information at 25 years.

(c)(1) An agency head shall notify the Panel of any specific file series of records for which a review or assessment has determined that the information within that file series almost invariably falls within one or more of the exemption categories listed in paragraph (b) of this section and that the agency proposes to exempt from automatic declassification at 25 years.

(2) The notification shall include:

(A) a description of the file series;

(B) an explanation of why the information within the file series is almost invariably exempt from automatic declassification and why the information must remain classified for a longer period of time; and

(C) except when the information within the file series almost invariably identifies a confidential human source or a human intelligence source or key design concepts of weapons of mass destruction, a specific date or event for declassification of the information, not to exceed December 31 of the year that is 50 years from the date of origin of the records.

(3) The Panel may direct the agency not to exempt a designated file series or to declassify the information within that series at an earlier date than recommended. The agency head may appeal such a decision to the President through the National Security Advisor.

(4) File series exemptions approved by the President prior to December 31, 2008, shall remain valid without any additional agency action pending Panel review by the later of December 31, 2010, or December 31 of the year that is 10 years from the date of previous approval.

(d) The following provisions shall apply to the onset of automatic declassification:

(1) Classified records within an integral file block, as defined in this order, that are otherwise subject to automatic declassification under this section shall not be automatically declassified until December 31 of the year that is 25 years from the date of the most recent record within the file block.

(2) After consultation with the Director of the National Declassification Center (the Center) established by section 3.7 of this order and before the records are subject to automatic declassification, an agency head or senior agency official may delay automatic declassification for up to five additional years for classified information contained in media that make a review for possible declassification exemptions more difficult or costly.

(3) Other than for records that are properly exempted from automatic declassification, records containing classified information that originated with other agencies or the disclosure of which would affect the interests or activities of other agencies with respect to the classified information and could reasonably be expected to fall under one or more of the exemptions in paragraph (b) of this section shall be identified prior to the onset of automatic declassification for later referral to those agencies.

(A) The information of concern shall be referred by the Center established by section 3.7 of this order, or by the centralized facilities referred to in section 3.7(e) of this order, in a prioritized and scheduled manner determined by the Center.

(B) If an agency fails to provide a final determination on a referral made by the Center within 1 year of referral, or by the centralized facilities referred to in section 3.7(e) of this order within 3 years of referral, its equities in the referred records shall be automatically declassified.

(C) If any disagreement arises between affected agencies and the Center regarding the referral review period, the Director of the Information Security Oversight Office shall determine the appropriate period of review of referred records.

(D) Referrals identified prior to the establishment of the Center by section 3.7 of this order shall be subject to automatic declassification only in accordance with subparagraphs (d)(3)(A)–(C) of this section.

(4) After consultation with the Director of the Information Security Oversight Office, an agency head may delay automatic declassification for up to 3 years from the date of discovery of classified records that were inadvertently not reviewed prior to the effective date of automatic declassification.

(e) Information exempted from automatic declassification under this section shall remain subject to the mandatory and systematic declassification review provisions of this order.

(f) The Secretary of State shall determine when the United States should commence negotiations with the appropriate officials of a foreign government or international organization of governments to modify any treaty or international agreement that requires the classification of information contained in records affected by this section for a period longer than 25 years from the date of its creation, unless the treaty or international agreement pertains to information that may otherwise remain classified beyond 25 years under this section.

(g) The Secretary of Energy shall determine when information concerning foreign nuclear programs that was removed from the Restricted Data category in order to carry out provisions of the National Security Act of 1947, as amended, may be declassified. Unless otherwise determined, such information shall be declassified when comparable information concerning the United States nuclear program is declassified.

(h) Not later than 3 years from the effective date of this order, all records exempted from automatic declassification under paragraphs (b) and (c) of this section shall be automatically declassified on December 31 of a year that is no more than 50 years from the date of origin, subject to the following:

(1) Records that contain information the release of which should clearly and demonstrably be expected to reveal the following are exempt from automatic declassification at 50 years:

(A) the identity of a confidential human source or a human intelligence source; or

(B) key design concepts of weapons of mass destruction.

(2) In extraordinary cases, agency heads may, within 5 years of the onset of automatic declassification, propose to exempt additional specific information from declassification at 50 years.

(3) Records exempted from automatic declassification under this paragraph shall be automatically declassified on December 31 of a year that is no more than 75 years from the date of origin unless an agency head, within 5 years of that date, proposes to exempt specific information from declassification at 75 years and the proposal is formally approved by the Panel.

(i) Specific records exempted from automatic declassification prior to the establishment of the Center described in section 3.7 of this order shall be subject to the provisions of paragraph (h) of this section in a scheduled and prioritized manner determined by the Center.

(j) At least 1 year before information is subject to automatic declassification under this section, an agency head or senior agency official shall notify the Director of the Information Security Oversight Office, serving as Executive Secretary of the Panel, of any specific information that the agency proposes to exempt from automatic declassification under paragraphs (b) and (h) of this section.

(1) The notification shall include:

(A) a detailed description of the information, either by reference to information in specific records or in the form of a declassification guide;

(B) an explanation of why the information should be exempt from automatic declassification and must remain classified for a longer period of time; and

(C) a specific date or a specific and independently verifiable event for automatic declassification of specific records that contain the information proposed for exemption.

(2) The Panel may direct the agency not to exempt the information or to declassify it at an earlier date than recommended. An agency head may appeal such a decision to the President through the National Security Advisor. The information will remain classified while such an appeal is pending.

(k) For information in a file series of records determined not to have permanent historical value, the duration of classification beyond 25 years shall be the same as the disposition (destruction) date of those records in each Agency Records Control Schedule or General Records Schedule, although the duration of classification shall be extended if the record has been retained for business reasons beyond the scheduled disposition date.

SECTION 3.4. SYSTEMATIC DECLASSIFICATION REVIEW.

(a) Each agency that has originated classified information under this order or its predecessors shall establish and conduct a program for systematic declassification review for records of permanent historical value exempted from automatic declassification under section 3.3 of this order. Agencies shall prioritize their review of such records in accordance with priorities established by the Center.

(b) The Archivist shall conduct a systematic declassification review program for classified records: (1) accessioned into the National Archives; (2) transferred to the Archivist pursuant to 44 U.S.C. 2203; and (3) for which the National Archives serves as the custodian for an agency or organization that has gone out of existence.

SECTION 3.5. MANDATORY DECLASSIFICATION REVIEW.

(a) Except as provided in paragraph (b) of this section, all information classified under this order or predecessor orders shall be subject to a review for declassification by the originating agency if:

(1) the request for a review describes the document or material containing the information with sufficient specificity to enable the agency to locate it with a reasonable amount of effort;

(2) the document or material containing the information responsive to the request is not contained within an operational file exempted from search and review, publication, and disclosure under 5 U.S.C. 552 in accordance with law; and

(3) the information is not the subject of pending litigation.

(b) Information originated by the incumbent President or the incumbent Vice President; the incumbent President's White House Staff or the incumbent Vice President's Staff; committees, commissions, or boards appointed by the incumbent President; or other entities within the Executive Office of the President that solely advise and assist the incumbent President is exempted from the provisions of paragraph (a) of this section. However, the Archivist shall have the authority to review, downgrade, and declassify papers or records of former Presidents and Vice Presidents under the control of the Archivist pursuant to 44 U.S.C. 2107, 2111, 2111 note, or 2203. Review procedures developed by the Archivist shall provide for consultation with agencies having primary subject matter interest and shall be consistent with the provisions of applicable laws or lawful agreements that pertain to the respective Presidential papers or records. Agencies with primary subject matter interest shall be notified promptly of the Archivist's decision. Any final decision by the Archivist may be appealed by the requester or an agency to the Panel. The information shall remain classified pending a prompt decision on the appeal.

(c) Agencies conducting a mandatory review for declassification shall declassify information that no longer meets the standards for classification under this order. They shall release this information unless withholding is otherwise authorized and warranted under applicable law.

(d) If an agency has reviewed the requested information for declassification within the past 2 years, the agency need not conduct another review and may instead inform the requester of this fact and the prior review decision and advise the requester of appeal rights provided under subsection (e) of this section.

(e) In accordance with directives issued pursuant to this order, agency heads shall develop procedures to process requests for the mandatory review of classified information. These procedures shall apply to information classified under this or predecessor orders. They also shall provide a means for administratively appealing a denial of a mandatory review request, and for notifying the requester of the right to appeal a final agency decision to the Panel.

(f) After consultation with affected agencies, the Secretary of Defense shall develop special procedures for the review of cryptologic information; the Director of National Intelligence shall develop special procedures for the review of information pertaining to intelligence sources, methods, and activities; and the Archivist shall develop special procedures for the review of information accessioned into the National Archives.

(g) Documents required to be submitted for prepublication review or other administrative process pursuant to an approved nondisclosure agreement are not covered by this section.

(h) This section shall not apply to any request for a review made to an element of the Intelligence Community that is made by a person other than an individual as that term is defined by 5 U.S.C. 552a(a)(2), or by a foreign government entity or any representative thereof.

SEC. 3.6. PROCESSING REQUESTS AND REVIEWS. Notwithstanding section 4.1(i) of this order, in response to a request for information under the Freedom of Information Act, the Presidential Records Act, the Privacy Act of 1974, or the mandatory review provisions of this order:

(a) An agency may refuse to confirm or deny the existence or nonexistence of requested records whenever the fact of their existence or nonexistence is itself classified under this order or its predecessors.

(b) When an agency receives any request for documents in its custody that contain classified information that originated with other agencies or the disclosure of which would affect the interests or activities of other agencies with respect to the classified information, or identifies such documents in the process of implementing sections 3.3 or 3.4 of this order, it shall refer copies of any request and the pertinent documents to the originating agency for processing and may, after consultation with the originating agency, inform any requester of the referral unless such association is itself classified under this order or its predecessors. In cases in which the originating agency determines in writing that a response under paragraph (a) of this section is required, the referring agency shall respond to the requester in accordance with that paragraph.

(c) Agencies may extend the classification of information in records determined not to have permanent historical value or nonrecord materials, including artifacts, beyond the time frames established in sections 1.5(b) and 2.2(f) of this order, provided:

> (1) the specific information has been approved pursuant to section 3.3(j) of this order for exemption from automatic declassification; and
>
> (2) the extension does not exceed the date established in section 3.3(j) of this order.

SEC. 3.7. NATIONAL DECLASSIFICATION CENTER
(a) There is established within the National Archives a National Declassification Center to streamline declassification processes, facilitate quality-assurance measures, and implement standardized training regarding the declassification of records determined to have permanent historical value. There shall be a Director of the Center who shall be appointed or removed by the Archivist in consultation with the Secretaries of State, Defense, Energy, and Homeland Security, the Attorney General, and the Director of National Intelligence.
(b) Under the administration of the Director, the Center shall coordinate:
(1) timely and appropriate processing of referrals in accordance with section 3.3(d)(3) of this order for accessioned Federal records and transferred presidential records.
(2) general interagency declassification activities necessary to fulfill the requirements of sections 3.3 and 3.4 of this order;
(3) the exchange among agencies of detailed declassification guidance to enable the referral of records in accordance with section 3.3(d)(3) of this order;
(4) the development of effective, transparent, and standard declassification work processes, training, and quality assurance measures;
(5) the development of solutions to declassification challenges posed by electronic records, special media, and emerging technologies;
(6) the linkage and effective utilization of existing agency databases and the use of new technologies to document and make public declassification review decisions and support declassification activities under the purview of the Center; and
(7) storage and related services, on a reimbursable basis, for Federal records containing classified national security information.
(c) Agency heads shall fully cooperate with the Archivist in the activities of the Center and shall:
(1) provide the Director with adequate and current declassification guidance to enable the referral of records in accordance with section 3.3(d)(3) of this order; and
(2) upon request of the Archivist, assign agency personnel to the Center who shall be delegated authority by the agency head to review and exempt or declassify information originated by their agency contained in records accessioned into the National Archives, after consultation with subject-matter experts as necessary.
(d) The Archivist, in consultation with representatives of the participants in the Center and after input from the general public, shall develop priorities for declassification activities under the purview of the Center that take into account the degree of researcher interest and the likelihood of declassification.
(e) Agency heads may establish such centralized facilities and internal operations to conduct internal declassification reviews as appropriate to achieve optimized records management and declassification business processes. Once established, all referral processing of accessioned records shall take place at the Center, and such agency facilities and operations shall be coordinated with the Center to ensure the maximum degree of consistency in policies and procedures that relate to records determined to have permanent historical value.
(f) Agency heads may exempt from automatic declassification or continue the classification of their own originally classified information under section 3.3(a) of this order except that in the case of the Director of National Intelligence, the Director shall also retain such authority with respect to the Intelligence Community.
(g) The Archivist shall, in consultation with the Secretaries of State, Defense, Energy, and Homeland Security, the Attorney General, the Director of National Intelligence, the Director of the Central Intelligence Agency, and the Director of the Information Security Oversight Office, provide the National Security Advisor with a detailed concept of operations for the Center and

a proposed implementing directive under section 5.1 of this order that reflects the coordinated views of the aforementioned agencies.

PART 4 — SAFEGUARDING

SECTION 4.1. GENERAL RESTRICTIONS ON ACCESS.

(a) A person may have access to classified information provided that:

(1) a favorable determination of eligibility for access has been made by an agency head or the agency head's designee;

(2) the person has signed an approved nondisclosure agreement; and

(3) the person has a need-to-know the information.

(b) Every person who has met the standards for access to classified information in paragraph (a) of this section shall receive contemporaneous training on the proper safeguarding of classified information and on the criminal, civil, and administrative sanctions that may be imposed on an individual who fails to protect classified information from unauthorized disclosure.

(c) An official or employee leaving agency service may not remove classified information from the agency's control or direct that information be declassified in order to remove it from agency control.

(d) Classified information may not be removed from official premises without proper authorization.

(e) Persons authorized to disseminate classified information outside the executive branch shall ensure the protection of the information in a manner equivalent to that provided within the executive branch.

(f) Consistent with law, executive orders, directives, and regulations, an agency head or senior agency official or, with respect to the Intelligence Community, the Director of National Intelligence, shall establish uniform procedures to ensure that automated information systems, including networks and telecommunications systems, that collect, create, communicate, compute, disseminate, process, or store classified information:

(1) prevent access by unauthorized persons;

(2) ensure the integrity of the information; and

(3) to the maximum extent practicable, use:

(A) common information technology standards, protocols, and interfaces that maximize the availability of, and access to, the information in a form and manner that facilitates its authorized use; and

(B) standardized electronic formats to maximize the accessibility of information to persons who meet the criteria set forth in section 4.1(a) of this order.

(g) Consistent with law, executive orders, directives, and regulations, each agency head or senior agency official, or with respect to the Intelligence Community, the Director of National Intelligence, shall establish controls to ensure that classified information is used, processed, stored, reproduced, transmitted, and destroyed under conditions that provide adequate protection and prevent access by unauthorized persons.

(h) Consistent with directives issued pursuant to this order, an agency shall safeguard foreign government information under standards that provide a degree of protection at least equivalent to that required by the government or international organization of governments that furnished the information. When adequate to achieve equivalency, these standards may be less restrictive than the safeguarding standards that ordinarily apply to U.S. "Confidential" information, including modified handling and transmission and allowing access to individuals with a need-to-know who have not otherwise been cleared for access to classified information or executed an approved nondisclosure agreement.

(i)(1) Classified information originating in one agency may be disseminated to another agency or U.S. entity by any agency to which it has been made available without the consent of the originating agency, as long as the criteria for access under section 4.1(a) of this order are met, unless the originating agency has determined that prior authorization is required for such dissemination and has marked or indicated such requirement on the medium containing the classified information in accordance with implementing directives issued pursuant to this order.

(2) Classified information originating in one agency may be disseminated by any other agency to which it has been made available to a foreign government in accordance with statute, this order, directives implementing this order, direction of the President, or with the consent of the originating agency. For the purposes of this section, "foreign government" includes any element of a foreign government, or an international organization of governments, or any element thereof.

(3) Documents created prior to the effective date of this order shall not be disseminated outside any other agency to which they have been made available without the consent of the originating agency. An agency head or senior agency official may waive this requirement for specific information that originated within that agency.

(4) For purposes of this section, the Department of Defense shall be considered one agency, except that any dissemination of information regarding intelligence sources, methods, or activities shall be consistent with directives issued pursuant to section 6.2(b) of this order.

(5) Prior consent of the originating agency is not required when referring records for declassification review that contain information originating in more than one agency.

SECTON 4.2. DISTRIBUTION CONTROLS.

(a) The head of each agency shall establish procedures in accordance with applicable law and consistent with directives issued pursuant to this order to ensure that classified information is accessible to the maximum extent possible by individuals who meet the criteria set forth in section 4.1(a) of this order.

(b) In an emergency, when necessary to respond to an imminent threat to life or in defense of the homeland, the agency head or any designee may authorize the disclosure of classified information (including information marked pursuant to section 4.1(i)(1) of this order) to an individual or individuals who are otherwise not eligible for access. Such actions shall be taken only in accordance with directives implementing this order and any procedure issued by agencies governing the classified information, which shall be designed to minimize the classified information that is disclosed under these circumstances and the number of individuals who receive it. Information disclosed under this provision or implementing directives and procedures shall not be deemed declassified as a result of such disclosure or subsequent use by a recipient. Such disclosures shall be reported promptly to the originator of the classified information. For purposes of this section, the Director of National Intelligence may issue an implementing directive governing the emergency disclosure of classified intelligence information.

(c) Each agency shall update, at least annually, the automatic, routine, or recurring distribution mechanism for classified information that it distributes. Recipients shall cooperate fully with distributors who are updating distribution lists and shall notify distributors whenever a relevant change in status occurs.

SECTION 4.3. SPECIAL ACCESS PROGRAMS.

(a) Establishment of special access programs. Unless otherwise authorized by the President, only the Secretaries of State, Defense, Energy, and Homeland Security, the Attorney General, and the Director of National Intelligence, or the principal deputy of each, may create a special access program. For special access programs pertaining to intelligence sources, methods, and activities (but not including military operational, strategic, and tactical programs), this function shall be exercised by the Director of National Intelligence. These officials shall keep the number of these programs at an absolute minimum, and shall establish them only when the program is required by statute or upon a specific finding that:

(1) the vulnerability of, or threat to, specific information is exceptional; and

(2) the normal criteria for determining eligibility for access applicable to information classified at the same level are not deemed sufficient to protect the information from unauthorized disclosure.

(b) Requirements and limitations.

(1) Special access programs shall be limited to programs in which the number of persons who ordinarily will have access will be reasonably small and commensurate with the objective of providing enhanced protection for the information involved.

(2) Each agency head shall establish and maintain a system of accounting for special access programs consistent with directives issued pursuant to this order.

(3) Special access programs shall be subject to the oversight program established under section 5.4(d) of this order. In addition, the Director of the Information Security Oversight Office shall be afforded access to these programs, in accordance with the security requirements of each program, in order to perform the functions assigned to the Information Security Oversight Office under this order. An agency head may limit access to a special access program to the Director of the Information Security Oversight Office and no more than one other employee of the Information Security Oversight Office or, for special access programs that are extraordinarily sensitive and vulnerable, to the Director only.

(4) The agency head or principal deputy shall review annually each special access program to determine whether it continues to meet the requirements of this order.

(5) Upon request, an agency head shall brief the National Security Advisor, or a designee, on any or all of the agency's special access programs.

(6) For the purposes of this section, the term "agency head" refers only to the Secretaries of State, Defense, Energy, and Homeland Security, the Attorney General, and the Director of National Intelligence, or the principal deputy of each.

(c) Nothing in this order shall supersede any requirement made by or under 10 U.S.C. 119.

SECTION 4.4. ACCESS BY HISTORICAL RESEARCHERS AND CERTAIN FORMER GOVERNMENT PERSONNEL.

(a) The requirement in section 4.1(a)(3) of this order that access to classified information may be granted only to individuals who have a need to-know the information may be waived for persons who:

(1) are engaged in historical research projects;

(2) previously have occupied senior policy-making positions to which they were appointed or designated by the President or the Vice President; or

(3) served as President or Vice President.

(b) Waivers under this section may be granted only if the agency head or senior agency official of the originating agency:

(1) determines in writing that access is consistent with the interest of the national security;

(2) takes appropriate steps to protect classified information from unauthorized disclosure or compromise, and ensures that the information is safeguarded in a manner consistent with this order; and

(3) limits the access granted to former Presidential appointees or designees and Vice Presidential appointees or designees to items that the person originated, reviewed, signed, or received while serving as a Presidential or Vice Presidential appointee or designee.

PART 5 — IMPLEMENTATION AND REVIEW

SECTION 5.1. PROGRAM DIRECTION.
(a) The Director of the Information Security Oversight Office, under the direction of the Archivist and in consultation with the National Security Advisor, shall issue such directives as are necessary to implement this order. These directives shall be binding on the agencies. Directives issued by the Director of the Information Security Oversight Office shall establish standards for:

    (1) classification, declassification, and marking principles;

    (2) safeguarding classified information, which shall pertain to the handling, storage, distribution, transmittal, and destruction of and accounting for classified information;

    (3) agency security education and training programs;

    (4) agency self-inspection programs; and

    (5) classification and declassification guides.

(b) The Archivist shall delegate the implementation and monitoring functions of this program to the Director of the Information Security Oversight Office.

(c) The Director of National Intelligence, after consultation with the heads of affected agencies and the Director of the Information Security Oversight Office, may issue directives to implement this order with respect to the protection of intelligence sources, methods, and activities. Such directives shall be consistent with this order and directives issued under paragraph (a) of this section.

SECTION 5.2. INFORMATION SECURITY OVERSIGHT OFFICE.
(a) There is established within the National Archives an Information Security Oversight Office. The Archivist shall appoint the Director of the Information Security Oversight Office, subject to the approval of the President.

(b) Under the direction of the Archivist, acting in consultation with the National Security Advisor, the Director of the Information Security Oversight Office shall:

    (1) develop directives for the implementation of this order;

    (2) oversee agency actions to ensure compliance with this order and its implementing directives;

    (3) review and approve agency implementing regulations prior to their issuance to ensure their consistency with this order and directives issued under section 5.1(a) of this order;

    (4) have the authority to conduct on-site reviews of each agency's program established under this order, and to require of each agency those reports and information and other cooperation that may be necessary to fulfill its responsibilities. If granting access to specific categories of classified information would pose an exceptional national security risk, the affected agency head or the senior agency official shall submit a written justification recommending the denial of access to the President through the National Security Advisor within 60 days of the request for access. Access shall be denied pending the response;

    (5) review requests for original classification authority from agencies or officials not granted original classification authority and, if deemed appropriate, recommend Presidential approval through the National Security Advisor;

    (6) consider and take action on complaints and suggestions from persons within or outside the Government with respect to the administration of the program established under this order;

    (7) have the authority to prescribe, after consultation with affected agencies, standardization of forms or procedures that will promote the implementation of the program established under this order;

    (8) report at least annually to the President on the implementation of this order; and

(9) convene and chair interagency meetings to discuss matters pertaining to the program established by this order.

SECTION 5.3. INTERAGENCY SECURITY CLASSIFICATION APPEALS PANEL.

(a) Establishment and administration.

(1) There is established an Interagency Security Classification Appeals Panel. The Departments of State, Defense, and Justice, the National Archives, the Office of the Director of National Intelligence, and the National Security Advisor shall each be represented by a senior-level representative who is a full-time or permanent part-time Federal officer or employee designated to serve as a member of the Panel by the respective agency head. The President shall designate a Chair from among the members of the Panel.

(2) Additionally, the Director of the Central Intelligence Agency may appoint a temporary representative who meets the criteria in paragraph (a)(1) of this section to participate as a voting member in all Panel deliberations and associated support activities concerning classified information originated by the Central Intelligence Agency.

(3) A vacancy on the Panel shall be filled as quickly as possible as provided in paragraph (a)(1) of this section.

(4) The Director of the Information Security Oversight Office shall serve as the Executive Secretary of the Panel. The staff of the Information Security Oversight Office shall provide program and administrative support for the Panel.

(5) The members and staff of the Panel shall be required to meet eligibility for access standards in order to fulfill the Panel's functions.

(6) The Panel shall meet at the call of the Chair. The Chair shall schedule meetings as may be necessary for the Panel to fulfill its functions in a timely manner.

(7) The Information Security Oversight Office shall include in its reports to the President a summary of the Panel's activities.

(b) Functions. The Panel shall:

(1) decide on appeals by persons who have filed classification challenges under section 1.8 of this order;

(2) approve, deny, or amend agency exemptions from automatic declassification as provided in section 3.3 of this order;

(3) decide on appeals by persons or entities who have filed requests for mandatory declassification review under section 3.5 of this order; and

(4) appropriately inform senior agency officials and the public of final Panel decisions on appeals under sections 1.8 and 3.5 of this order.

(c) Rules and procedures. The Panel shall issue bylaws, which shall be published in the Federal Register. The bylaws shall establish the rules and procedures that the Panel will follow in accepting, considering, and issuing decisions on appeals. The rules and procedures of the Panel shall provide that the Panel will consider appeals only on actions in which:

(1) the appellant has exhausted his or her administrative remedies within the responsible agency;

(2) there is no current action pending on the issue within the Federal courts; and

(3) the information has not been the subject of review by the Federal courts or the Panel within the past 2 years.

(d) Agency heads shall cooperate fully with the Panel so that it can fulfill its functions in a timely and fully informed manner. The Panel shall report to the President through the National Security Advisor any instance in which it believes that an agency head is not cooperating fully with the Panel.

(e) The Panel is established for the sole purpose of advising and assisting the President in the discharge of his constitutional and discretionary authority to protect the national security of the United States. Panel decisions are committed to the discretion of the Panel, unless changed by the President.

(f) An agency head may appeal a decision of the Panel to the President through the National Security Advisor. The information shall remain classified pending a decision on the appeal.

SECTION 5.4. GENERAL RESPONSIBILITIES. Heads of agencies that originate or handle classified information shall:

(a) demonstrate personal commitment and commit senior management to the successful implementation of the program established under this order;

(b) commit necessary resources to the effective implementation of the program established under this order;

(c) ensure that agency records systems are designed and maintained to optimize the appropriate sharing and safeguarding of classified information, and to facilitate its declassification under the terms of this order when it no longer meets the standards for continued classification; and

(d) designate a senior agency official to direct and administer the program, whose responsibilities shall include:

(1) overseeing the agency's program established under this order, provided an agency head may designate a separate official to oversee special access programs authorized under this order. This official shall provide a full accounting of the agency's special access programs at least annually;

(2) promulgating implementing regulations, which shall be published in the Federal Register to the extent that they affect members of the public;

(3) establishing and maintaining security education and training programs;

(4) establishing and maintaining an ongoing self inspection program, which shall include the regular reviews of representative samples of the agency's original and derivative classification actions, and shall authorize appropriate agency officials to correct misclassification actions not covered by sections 1.7(c) and 1.7(d) of this order; and reporting annually to the Director of the Information Security Oversight Office on the agency's self-inspection program;

(5) establishing procedures consistent with directives issued pursuant to this order to prevent unnecessary access to classified information, including procedures that:

(A) require that a need for access to classified information be established before initiating administrative clearance procedures; and

(B) ensure that the number of persons granted access to classified information meets the mission needs of the agency while also satisfying operational and security requirements and needs;

(6) developing special contingency plans for the safeguarding of classified information used in or near hostile or potentially hostile areas;

(7) ensuring that the performance contract or other system used to rate civilian or military personnel performance includes the designation and management of classified information as a critical element or item to be evaluated in the rating of:

(A) original classification authorities;

(B) security managers or security specialists; and

(C) all other personnel whose duties significantly involve the creation or handling of classified information, including personnel who regularly apply derivative classification markings;

(8) accounting for the costs associated with the implementation of this order, which shall be reported to the Director of the Information Security Oversight Office for publication;

(9) assigning in a prompt manner agency personnel to respond to any request, appeal,

challenge, complaint, or suggestion arising out of this order that pertains to classified information that originated in a component of the agency that no longer exists and for which there is no clear successor in function; and

(10) establishing a secure capability to receive information, allegations, or complaints regarding over-classification or incorrect classification within the agency and to provide guidance to personnel on proper classification as needed.

SECTION 5.5. SANCTIONS

(a) If the Director of the Information Security Oversight Office finds that a violation of this order or its implementing directives has occurred, the Director shall make a report to the head of the agency or to the senior agency official so that corrective steps, if appropriate, may be taken.

(b) Officers and employees of the United States Government, and its contractors, licensees, certificate holders, and grantees shall be subject to appropriate sanctions if they knowingly, willfully, or negligently:

(1) disclose to unauthorized persons information properly classified under this order or predecessor orders;

(2) classify or continue the classification of information in violation of this order or any implementing directive;

(3) create or continue a special access program contrary to the requirements of this order; or

(4) contravene any other provision of this order or its implementing directives.

(c) Sanctions may include reprimand, suspension without pay, removal, termination of classification authority, loss or denial of access to classified information, or other sanctions in accordance with applicable law and agency regulation.

(d) The agency head, senior agency official, or other supervisory official shall, at a minimum, promptly remove the classification authority of any individual who demonstrates reckless disregard or a pattern of error in applying the classification standards of this order.

(e) The agency head or senior agency official shall:

(1) take appropriate and prompt corrective action when a violation or infraction under paragraph (b) of this section occurs; and

(2) notify the Director of the Information Security Oversight Office when a violation under paragraph (b)(1), (2), or (3) of this section occurs.

PART 6 — GENERAL PROVISIONS

SEC. 6.1. DEFINITIONS. For purposes of this order:

(a) "Access" means the ability or opportunity to gain knowledge of classified information.

(b) "Agency" means any "Executive agency," as defined in 5 U.S.C. 105; any "Military department" as defined in 5 U.S.C. 102; and any other entity within the executive branch that comes into the possession of classified information.

(c) "Authorized holder" of classified information means anyone who satisfies the conditions for access stated in section 4.1(a) of this order.

(d) "Automated information system" means an assembly of computer hardware, software, or firmware configured to collect, create, communicate, compute, disseminate, process, store, or control data or information.

(e) "Automatic declassification" means the declassification of information based solely upon:

(1) the occurrence of a specific date or event as determined by the original classification authority; or

(2) the expiration of a maximum time frame for duration of classification established under this order.

(f) "Classification" means the act or process by which information is determined to be classified information.

(g) "Classification guidance" means any instruction or source that prescribes the classification of specific information.

(h) "Classification guide" means a documentary form of classification guidance issued by an original classification authority that identifies the elements of information regarding a specific subject that must be classified and establishes the level and duration of classification for each such element.

(i) "Classified national security information" or "classified information" means information that has been determined pursuant to this order or any predecessor order to require protection against unauthorized disclosure and is marked to indicate its classified status when in documentary form.

(j) "Compilation" means an aggregation of preexisting unclassified items of information.

(k) "Confidential source" means any individual or organization that has provided, or that may reasonably be expected to provide, information to the United States on matters pertaining to the national security with the expectation that the information or relationship, or both, are to be held in confidence.

(l) "Damage to the national security" means harm to the national defense or foreign relations of the United States from the unauthorized disclosure of information, taking into consideration such aspects of the information as the sensitivity, value, utility, and provenance of that information.

(m) "Declassification" means the authorized change in the status of information from classified information to unclassified information.

(n) "Declassification guide" means written instructions issued by a declassification authority that describes the elements of information regarding a specific subject that may be declassified and the elements that must remain classified.

(o) "Derivative classification" means the incorporating, paraphrasing, restating, or generating in new form information that is already classified, and marking the newly developed material consistent with the classification markings that apply to the source information. Derivative classification includes the classification of information based on classification guidance. The duplication or reproduction of existing classified information is not derivative classification.

(p) "Document" means any recorded information, regardless of the nature of the medium or the method or circumstances of recording.

(q) "Downgrading" means a determination by a declassification authority that information classified and safeguarded at a specified level shall be classified and safeguarded at a lower level.

(r) "File series" means file units or documents arranged according to a filing system or kept together because they relate to a particular subject or function, result from the same activity, document a specific kind of transaction, take a particular physical form, or have some other relationship arising out of their creation, receipt, or use, such as restrictions on access or use.

(s) "Foreign government information" means:

    (1) information provided to the United States Government by a foreign government or governments,

    an international organization of governments, or any element thereof, with the expectation that the information, the source of the information, or both, are to be held in confidence;

    (2) information produced by the United States Government pursuant to or as a result of a joint arrangement with a foreign government or governments, or an international organization of governments, or any element thereof, requiring that the information, the arrangement, or both, are to be held in confidence; or

(3) information received and treated as "foreign government information" under the terms of a predecessor order.

(t) "Information" means any knowledge that can be communicated or documentary material, regardless of its physical form or characteristics, that is owned by, is produced by or for, or is under the control of the United States Government.

(u) "Infraction" means any knowing, willful, or negligent action contrary to the requirements of this order or its implementing directives that does not constitute a "violation," as defined below.

(v) "Integral file block" means a distinct component of a file series, as defined in this section, that should be maintained as a separate unit in order to ensure the integrity of the records. An integral file block may consist of a set of records covering either a specific topic or a range of time, such as a Presidential administration or a 5-year retirement schedule within a specific file series that is retired from active use as a group. For purposes of automatic declassification, integral file blocks shall contain only records dated within 10 years of the oldest record in the file block.

(w) "Integrity" means the state that exists when information is unchanged from its source and has not been accidentally or intentionally modified, altered, or destroyed.

(x) "Intelligence" includes foreign intelligence and counterintelligence as defined by Executive Order 12333 of December 4, 1981, as amended, or by a successor order.

(y) "Intelligence activities" means all activities that elements of the Intelligence Community are authorized to conduct pursuant to law or Executive Order 12333, as amended, or a successor order.

(z) "Intelligence Community" means an element or agency of the U.S. Government identified in or designated pursuant to section 3(4) of the National Security Act of 1947, as amended, or section 3.5(h) of Executive Order 12333, as amended.

(aa) "Mandatory declassification review" means the review for declassification of classified information in response to a request for declassification that meets the requirements under section 3.5 of this order.

(bb) "Multiple sources" means two or more source documents, classification guides, or a combination of both.

(cc) "National security" means the national defense or foreign relations of the United States.

(dd) "Need-to-know" means a determination within the executive branch in accordance with directives issued pursuant to this order that a prospective recipient requires access to specific classified information in order to perform or assist in a lawful and authorized governmental function.

(ee) "Network" means a system of two or more computers that can exchange data or information.

(ff) "Original classification" means an initial determination that information requires, in the interest of the national security, protection against unauthorized disclosure.

(gg) "Original classification authority" means an individual authorized in writing, either by the President, the Vice President, or by agency heads or other officials designated by the President, to classify information in the first instance.

(hh) "Records" means the records of an agency and Presidential papers or Presidential records, as those terms are defined in title 44, United States Code, including those created or maintained by a government contractor, licensee, certificate holder, or grantee that are subject to the sponsoring agency's control under the terms of the contract, license, certificate, or grant.

(ii) "Records having permanent historical value" means Presidential papers or Presidential records and the records of an agency that the Archivist has determined should be maintained permanently in accordance with title 44, United States Code.

(jj) "Records management" means the planning, controlling, directing, organizing, training, promoting, and other managerial activities involved with respect to records creation, records maintenance and use, and records disposition in order to achieve adequate and proper documentation of the policies and transactions of the Federal Government and effective and economical management of agency operations.

(kk) "Safeguarding" means measures and controls that are prescribed to protect classified information.

(ll) "Self-inspection" means the internal review and evaluation of individual agency activities and the agency as a whole with respect to the implementation of the program established under this order and its implementing directives.

(mm) "Senior agency official" means the official designated by the agency head under section 5.4(d) of this order to direct and administer the agency's program under which information is classified, safeguarded, and declassified.

(nn) "Source document" means an existing document that contains classified information that is incorporated, paraphrased, restated, or generated in new form into a new document.

(oo) "Special access program" means a program established for a specific class of classified information that imposes safeguarding and access requirements that exceed those normally required for information at the same classification level.

(pp) "Systematic declassification review" means the review for declassification of classified information contained in records that have been determined by the Archivist to have permanent historical value in accordance with title 44, United States Code.

(qq) "Telecommunications" means the preparation, transmission, or communication of information by electronic means.

(rr) "Unauthorized disclosure" means a communication or physical transfer of classified information to an unauthorized recipient.

(ss) "U.S. entity" includes:

    (1) State, local, or tribal governments;

    (2) State, local, and tribal law enforcement and firefighting entities;

    (3) public health and medical entities;

    (4) regional, state, local, and tribal emergency management entities, including State Adjutants General and other appropriate public safety entities; or

    (5) private sector entities serving as part of the nation's Critical Infrastructure/Key Resources.

(tt) "Violation" means:

    (1) any knowing, willful, or negligent action that could reasonably be expected to result in an unauthorized disclosure of classified information;

    (2) any knowing, willful, or negligent action to classify or continue the classification of information contrary to the requirements of this order or its implementing directives; or

    (3) any knowing, willful, or negligent action to create or continue a special access program contrary to the requirements of this order.

(uu) "Weapons of mass destruction" means any weapon of mass destruction as defined in 50 U.S.C. 1801(p).

SECTION 6.2. GENERAL PROVISIONS.

(a) Nothing in this order shall supersede any requirement made by or under the Atomic Energy Act of 1954, as amended, or the National Security Act of 1947, as amended. "Restricted Data" and "Formerly Restricted Data" shall be handled, protected, classified, downgraded, and declassified in conformity with the provisions of the Atomic Energy Act of 1954, as amended, and regulations issued under that Act.

(b) The Director of National Intelligence may, with respect to the Intelligence Community and after consultation with the heads of affected departments and agencies, issue such policy directives and guidelines as the Director of National Intelligence deems necessary to implement this order with respect to the classification and declassification of all intelligence and intelligence-related information, and for access to and dissemination of all intelligence and intelligence-related information, both in its final form and in the form when initially gathered. Procedures or other guidance issued by Intelligence Community element heads shall be in accordance with such policy directives or guidelines issued by the Director of National Intelligence. Any such policy directives or guidelines issued by the Director of National Intelligence shall be in accordance with directives issued by the Director of the Information Security Oversight Office under section 5.1(a) of this order.

(c) The Attorney General, upon request by the head of an agency or the Director of the Information Security Oversight Office, shall render an interpretation of this order with respect to any question arising in the course of its administration.

(d) Nothing in this order limits the protection afforded any information by other provisions of law, including the Constitution, Freedom of Information Act exemptions, the Privacy Act of 1974, and the National Security Act of 1947, as amended. This order is not intended to and does not create any right or benefit, substantive or procedural, enforceable at law by a party against the United States, its departments, agencies, or entities, its officers, employees, or agents, or any other person. The foregoing is in addition to the specific provisos set forth in sections 1.1(b), 3.1(c) and 5.3(e) of this order.

(e) Nothing in this order shall be construed to obligate action or otherwise affect functions by the Director of the Office of Management and Budget relating to budgetary, administrative, or legislative proposals.

(f) This order shall be implemented subject to the availability of appropriations.

(g) Executive Order 12958 of April 17, 1995, and amendments thereto, including Executive Order 13292 of March 25, 2003, are hereby revoked as of the effective date of this order.

SECTION 6.3. EFFECTIVE DATE. This order is effective 180 days from the date of this order, except for sections 1.7, 3.3, and 3.7, which are effective immediately.

SECTION 6.4. PUBLICATION. The Archivist of the United States shall publish this Executive Order in the Federal Register.

BARACK OBAMA

Executive Order 13549—Classified National Security Information Program for State, Local, Tribal, and Private Sector Entities

75 Fed. Reg. 162 (Aug. 23, 2010)

By the authority vested in me as President by the Constitution and the laws of the United States of America, in order to ensure the proper safeguarding of information shared with State, local, tribal, and private sector entities, it is hereby ordered as follows:

Section 1. Establishment and Policy.

Sec. 1.1. There is established a Classified National Security Information Program (Program) designed to safeguard and govern access to classified national security information shared by the Federal Government with State,
local, tribal, and private sector (SLTPS) entities.

Sec. 1.2. The purpose of this order is to ensure that security standards governing access to and safeguarding of classified material are applied in accordance with Executive Order 13526 of December 29, 2009 ("Classified National Security Information"), Executive Order 12968 of August 2, 1995, as amended ("Access to Classified Information"), Executive Order 13467 of June 30, 2008 ("Reforming Processes Related to Suitability for Government Employment, Fitness for Contractor Employees, and Eligibility for Access to Classified National Security Information"), and Executive Order 12829 of January 6, 1993, as amended ("National Industrial Security Program"). Procedures for uniform implementation of these standards by SLTPS entities shall be set forth in an implementing directive to be issued by the Secretary of Homeland Security within 180 days of the date of this order, in consultation with affected executive departments and agencies (agencies), and with the concurrence of the Secretary of Defense, the Attorney General, the Director of National Intelligence, and the Director of the Information Security Oversight Office.

Sec. 1.3. Additional policy provisions for access to and safeguarding of classified information shared with SLTPS personnel include the following:

(a) Eligibility for access to classified information by SLTPS personnel shall be determined by a sponsoring agency. The level of access granted shall not exceed the Secret level, unless the sponsoring agency determines on a case-by-case basis that the applicant has a demonstrated and foreseeable need for access to Top Secret, Special Access Program, or Sensitive Compartmented Information.

(b) Upon the execution of a non-disclosure agreement prescribed by the Information Security Oversight Office or the Director of National Intelligence, and absent disqualifying conduct as determined by the clearance granting official, a duly elected or appointed Governor of a State or territory, or an official who has succeeded to that office under applicable law, may be granted access to classified information without a background investigation in accordance with the implementing directive for this order. This authorization of access may not be further delegated by the Governor to any other person.

(c) All clearances granted to SLTPS personnel, as well as accreditations granted to SLTPS facilities without a waiver, shall be accepted reciprocally by all agencies and SLTPS entities.

(d) Physical custody of classified information by State, local, and tribal (SLT) entities shall be limited to Secret information unless the location housing the information is under the full-time management, control, and operation of the Department of Homeland Security or another agency.

A standard security agreement, established by the Department of Homeland Security in consultation with the SLTPS Advisory Committee, shall be executed between the head of the SLT entity and the U.S. Government for those locations where the SLT entity will maintain physical custody of classified information.

(e) State, local, and tribal facilities where classified information is or will be used or stored shall be inspected, accredited, and monitored for compliance with established standards, in accordance with Executive Order 13526 and the implementing directive for this order, by the Department of Homeland Security or another agency that has entered into an agreement with the Department of Homeland Security to perform such inspection, accreditation, and monitoring.

(f) Private sector facilities where classified information is or will be used or stored shall be inspected, accredited, and monitored for compliance with standards established pursuant to Executive Order 12829, as amended, by the Department of Defense or the cognizant security agency under Executive Order 12829, as amended.

(g) Access to information systems that store, process, or transmit classified information shall be enforced by the rules established by the agency that controls the system and consistent with approved dissemination and handling

markings applied by originators, separate from and in addition to criteria for determining eligibility for access to classified information. Access to information within restricted portals shall be based on criteria applied by

the agency that controls the portal and consistent with approved dissemination and handling markings applied by originators.

(h) The National Industrial Security Program established in Executive Order 12829, as amended, shall govern the access to and safeguarding of classified information that is released to contractors, licensees, and grantees of SLT entities.

(i) All access eligibility determinations and facility security accreditations granted prior to the date of this order that do not meet the standards set forth in this order or its implementing directive shall be reconciled with those standards within a reasonable period.

(j) Pursuant to section 4.1(i)(3) of Executive Order 13526, documents created prior to the effective date of Executive Order 13526 shall not be redisseminated to other entities without the consent of the originating agency. An agency head or senior agency official may waive this requirement for specific information that originated within that agency.

Sec. 2. Policy Direction.

With policy guidance from the National Security Advisor and in consultation with the Director of the Information Security Oversight Office, the Director of the Office of Management and Budget, and the heads of affected agencies, the Secretary of Homeland Security shall serve as the Executive Agent for the Program. This order does not displace any authorities provided by law or Executive Order and the Executive Agent shall, to the extent practicable, make use of existing structures and authorities to preclude duplication and to ensure efficiency.

Sec. 3. SLTPS Policy Advisory Committee.

(a) There is established an SLTPS Policy Advisory Committee (Committee) to discuss Program-related policy issues in dispute in order to facilitate their resolution and to otherwise recommend changes to policies and procedures that are designed to remove undue impediments to the sharing of information under the Program. The Director of the Information Security Oversight Office shall serve as Chair of the Committee. An official designated by the Secretary of Homeland Security and a representative of SLTPS entities shall serve as Vice Chairs of the Committee. Members of the Committee shall include designees of the heads of the Departments of State, Defense, Justice, Transportation, and Energy, the Nuclear Regulatory Commission, the Office of the Director of National Intelligence, the Central Intelligence Agency, and the Federal Bureau of Investigation. Members shall also include employees of other agencies and representatives of

SLTPS entities, as nominated by any Committee member and approved by the Chair.

(b) Members of the Committee shall serve without compensation for their work on the Committee, except that any representatives of SLTPS entities may be allowed travel expenses, including per diem in lieu of subsistence, as authorized by law for persons serving intermittently in the Government service (5 U.S.C. 5701–5707).

(c) The Information Security Oversight Office shall provide staff support to the Committee.

(d) Insofar as the Federal Advisory Committee Act, as amended (5 App. U.S.C.)(the "Act") may apply to this order, any functions of the President under that Act, except that of reporting to the Congress, which are applicable to the Committee, shall be performed by the Administrator of General Services in accordance with guidelines and procedures established by the General Services Administration.

Sec. 4. Operations and Oversight.

(a) The Executive Agent for the Program shall perform the following responsibilities:

(1) overall program management and oversight;

(2) accreditation, periodic inspection, and monitoring of all facilities owned or operated by SLT entities that have access to classified information, except when another agency has entered into an agreement with the Department of Homeland Security to perform some or all of these functions;

(3) processing of security clearance applications by SLTPS personnel, when requested by a sponsoring agency, on a reimbursable basis unless otherwise determined by the Department of Homeland Security and the sponsoring agency;

(4) documenting and tracking the final status of security clearances for all SLTPS personnel in consultation with the Office of Personnel Management, the Department of Defense, and the Office of the Director of National Intelligence;

(5) developing and maintaining a security profile of SLT facilities that have access to classified information; and

(6) developing training, in consultation with the Committee, for all SLTPS personnel who have been determined eligible for access to classified information, which shall cover the proper safeguarding of classified information and sanctions for unauthorized disclosure of classified information.

(b) The Secretary of Defense, or the cognizant security agency under Executive Order 12829, as amended, shall provide program management, oversight, inspection, accreditation, and monitoring of all private sector facilities that have access to classified information.

(c) The Director of National Intelligence may inspect and monitor SLTPS programs and facilities that involve access to information regarding intelligence sources, methods, and activities.

(d) Heads of agencies that sponsor SLTPS personnel and facilities for access to and storage of classified information under section 1.3(a) of this order shall:

(1) ensure on a periodic basis that there is a demonstrated, foreseeable need for such access; and

(2) provide the Secretary of Homeland Security with information, as requested by the Secretary, about SLTPS personnel sponsored for security clearances and SLT facilities approved for use of classified information prior to and after the date of this order, except when the disclosure of the association of a specific individual with an intelligence or law enforcement agency must be protected in the interest of national security, as determined by the intelligence or law enforcement agency.

Sec. 5. Definitions.

For purposes of this order:

(a) "Access" means the ability or opportunity to gain knowledge of classified information.

(b) "Agency" means any "Executive agency" as defined in 5 U.S.C. 105; any military department as defined in 5 U.S.C. 102; and any other entity within the executive branch that comes into possession of classified information.

(c) "Classified National Security Information" or "classified information" means information that has been determined pursuant to Executive Order 13526, or any predecessor or successor order, to require protection against unauthorized disclosure, and is marked to indicate its classified status when in documentary form.

(d) "Information" means any knowledge that can be communicated or documentary material, regardless of its physical form or characteristics, that is owned by, produced by or for, or is under the control of the United States Government.

(e) "Intelligence activities" means all activities that elements of the Intelligence Community are authorized to conduct pursuant to law or Executive Order 12333, as amended, or a successor order.

(f) "Local" entities refers to "(A) a county, municipality, city, town, township, local public authority, school district, special district, intrastate district, council of governments (regardless of whether the council of governments is incorporated as a nonprofit corporation under State law), regional or interstate government entity, or agency or instrumentality of a local government; and (B) a rural community, unincorporated town or village, or other public entity" as defined in section 2 of the Homeland Security Act of 2002 (6 U.S.C. 101(11)).

(g) "Private sector" means persons outside government who are critically involved in ensuring that public and private preparedness and response efforts are integrated as part of the Nation's Critical Infrastructure or Key Resources (CIKR), including:

> (1) corporate owners and operators determined by the Secretary of Homeland Security to be part of the CIKR;
> (2) subject matter experts selected to assist the Federal or State CIKR;
> (3) personnel serving in specific leadership positions of CIKR coordination, operations, and oversight;
> (4) employees of corporate entities relating to the protection of CIKR; or
> (5) other persons not otherwise eligible for the granting of a personnel security clearance pursuant to Executive Order 12829, as amended, who are determined by the Secretary of Homeland Security to require a personnel security clearance.

(h) "Restricted portal" means a protected community of interest or similar area housed within an information system and to which access is controlled by a host agency different from the agency that controls the information system.

(i) "Sponsoring Agency" means an agency that recommends access to or possession of classified information by SLTPS personnel.

(j) "State" means any State of the United States, the District of Columbia, the Commonwealth of Puerto Rico, the Virgin Islands, Guam, American Samoa, the Commonwealth of the Northern Mariana Islands, and any possession of the United States, as defined in section 2 of the Homeland Security Act of 2002 (6 U.S.C. 101(15)).

(k) "State, local, and tribal personnel" means any of the following persons:

> (1) Governors, mayors, tribal leaders, and other elected or appointed officials of a State, local government, or tribe;
> (2) State, local, and tribal law enforcement personnel and firefighters;
> (3) public health, radiological health, and medical professionals of a State, local government, or tribe; and
> (4) regional, State, local, and tribal emergency management agency personnel, including State Adjutants General and other appropriate public safety personnel and those personnel providing support to a Federal CIKR mission.

(l) "Tribe" means any Indian or Alaska Native tribe, band, nation, pueblo, village, or community that the Secretary of the Interior acknowledges to exist as an Indian tribe as defined in the Federally Recognized Tribe List Act of 1994 (25 U.S.C. 479a(2)).

(m) "United States" when used in a geographic sense, means any State of the United States, the District of Columbia, the Commonwealth of Puerto Rico, the Virgin Islands, Guam, American Samoa, the Commonwealth of the Northern Mariana Islands, any possession of the United States and any waters within the territorial jurisdiction of the United States.

Sec. 6. *General Provisions.*

(a) This order does not change the requirements of Executive Orders 13526, 12968, 13467, or 12829, as amended, and their successor orders and directives.

(b) Nothing in this order shall be construed to supersede or change the authorities of the Secretary of Energy or the Nuclear Regulatory Commission under the Atomic Energy Act of 1954, as amended (42 U.S.C. 2011 *et seq.*); the Secretary of Defense under Executive Order 12829, as amended; the Director of the Information Security Oversight Office under Executive Order 13526 and Executive Order 12829, as amended; the Attorney General under title 18, United States Code, and the Foreign Intelligence Surveillance Act (50 U.S.C. 1801 *et seq.*); the Secretary of State under title 22, United States Code, and the Omnibus Diplomatic Security and Antiterrorism Act of 1986; or the Director of National Intelligence under the National Security Act of 1947, as amended, Executive Order 12333, as amended, Executive Order 12968, as amended, Executive Order 13467, and Executive Order 13526.

(c) Nothing in this order shall limit the authority of an agency head, or the agency head's designee, to authorize in an emergency and when necessary to respond to an imminent threat to life or in defense of the homeland, in accordance with section 4.2(b) of Executive Order 13526, the disclosure of classified information to an individual or individuals who are otherwise not eligible for access in accordance with the provisions of Executive Order 12968.

(d) Consistent with section 892(a)(4) of the Homeland Security Act of 2002 (6 U.S.C. 482(a)(4)), nothing in this order shall be interpreted as changing the requirements and authorities to protect sources and methods.

(e) Nothing in this order shall supersede measures established under the authority of law or Executive Order to protect the security and integrity of specific activities and associations that are in direct support of intelligence operations.

(f) Pursuant to section 892(e) of the Homeland Security Act of 2002 (6 U.S.C. 482(e)), all information provided to an SLTPS entity from an agency shall remain under the control of the Federal Government. Any State or local law authorizing or requiring disclosure shall not apply to such information.

(g) Nothing in this order limits the protection afforded any classified information by other provisions of law. This order is not intended to, and does not, create any right or benefit, substantive or procedural, enforceable at law or in equity by any party against the United States, its departments, agencies, or entities, its officers, employees, or agents, or any other person.

(h) Nothing in this order shall be construed to obligate action or otherwise affect functions by the Director of the Office of Management and Budget relating to budgetary, administrative, or legislative proposals.

(i) This order shall be implemented subject to the availability of appropriations and consistent with procedures approved by the Attorney General pursuant to Executive Order 12333, as amended.

Sec. 7. *Effective Date.* This order is effective 180 days from the date of this order with the exception of section 3, which is effective immediately.

BARACK OBAMA

Executive Order 13587—Structural Reforms to Improve the Security of Classified Networks and the Responsible Sharing and Safeguarding of Classified Information

76 Fed. Reg. 63,811 (Oct. 13, 2011)

By the authority vested in me as President by the Constitution and the laws of the United States of America and in order to ensure the responsible sharing and safeguarding of classified national security information (classified information) on computer networks, it is hereby ordered as follows:

Section 1. Policy.

Our Nation's security requires classified information to be shared immediately with authorized users around the world but also requires sophisticated and vigilant means to ensure it is shared securely. Computer networks have individual and common vulnerabilities that require coordinated decisions on risk management.

This order directs structural reforms to ensure responsible sharing and safeguarding of classified information on computer networks that shall be consistent with appropriate protections for privacy and civil liberties. Agencies bear the primary responsibility for meeting these twin goals. These structural reforms will ensure coordinated interagency development and reliable implementation of policies and minimum standards regarding information security, personnel security, and systems security; address both internal and external security threats and vulnerabilities; and provide policies and minimum standards for sharing classified information both within and outside the Federal Government. These policies and minimum standards will address all agencies that operate or access classified computer networks, all users of classified computer networks (including contractors and others who operate or access classified computer networks controlled by the Federal Government), and all classified information on those networks.

Sec. 2. General Responsibilities of Agencies.

Sec. 2.1. The heads of agencies that operate or access classified computer networks shall have responsibility for appropriately sharing and safeguarding classified information on computer networks. As part of this responsibility, they shall:

(a) designate a senior official to be charged with overseeing classified information sharing and safeguarding efforts for the agency;

(b) implement an insider threat detection and prevention program consistent with guidance and standards developed by the Insider Threat Task Force established in section 6 of this order;

(c) perform self-assessments of compliance with policies and standards issued pursuant to sections 3.3, 5.2, and 6.3 of this order, as well as other applicable policies and standards, the results of which shall be reported annually to the Senior Information Sharing and Safeguarding Steering Committee established in section 3 of this order;

(d) provide information and access, as warranted and consistent with law and section 7(d) of this order, to enable independent assessments by the Executive Agent for Safeguarding Classified Information on Computer Networks and the Insider Threat Task Force of compliance with relevant established policies and standards; and

(e) detail or assign staff as appropriate and necessary to the Classified Information Sharing and Safeguarding Office and the Insider Threat Task Force on an ongoing basis.

Sec. 3. Senior Information Sharing and Safeguarding Steering Committee.

Sec. 3.1. There is established a Senior Information Sharing and Safeguarding Steering Committee (Steering Committee) to exercise overall responsibility and ensure senior-level accountability for the coordinated interagency development and implementation of policies and standards regarding the sharing and safeguarding of classified information on computer networks.

Sec. 3.2. The Steering Committee shall be co-chaired by senior representatives of the Office of Management and Budget and the National Security Staff. Members of the committee shall be officers of the United States as designated by the heads of the Departments of State, Defense, Justice, Energy, and Homeland Security, the Office of the Director of National Intelligence, the Central Intelligence Agency, and the Information Security Oversight Office within the National Archives and Records Administration (ISOO), as well as such additional agencies as the co-chairs of the Steering Committee may designate.

Sec. 3.3. The responsibilities of the Steering Committee shall include:

(a) establishing Government-wide classified information sharing and safeguarding goals and annually reviewing executive branch successes and shortcomings in achieving those goals;

(b) preparing within 90 days of the date of this order and at least annually thereafter, a report for the President assessing the executive branch's successes and shortcomings in sharing and safeguarding classified information on computer networks and discussing potential future vulnerabilities;

(c) developing program and budget recommendations to achieve Government-wide classified information sharing and safeguarding goals;

(d) coordinating the interagency development and implementation of priorities, policies, and standards for sharing and safeguarding classified information on computer networks;

(e) recommending overarching policies, when appropriate, for promulgation by the Office of Management and Budget or the ISOO;

(f) coordinating efforts by agencies, the Executive Agent, and the Task Force to assess compliance with established policies and standards and recommending corrective actions needed to ensure compliance;

(g) providing overall mission guidance for the Program Manager-Information Sharing Environment (PM-ISE) with respect to the functions to be performed by the Classified Information Sharing and Safeguarding Office established in section 4 of this order; and

(h) referring policy and compliance issues that cannot be resolved by the Steering Committee to the Deputies Committee of the National Security Council in accordance with Presidential Policy Directive/PPD-1 of February 13, 2009 (Organization of the National Security Council System).

Sec. 4. Classified Information Sharing and Safeguarding Office.

Sec. 4.1. There shall be established a Classified Information Sharing and Safeguarding Office (CISSO) within and subordinate to the office of the PM-ISE to provide expert, fulltime, sustained focus on responsible sharing and safeguarding of classified information on computer networks. Staff of the CISSO shall include detailees, as needed and appropriate, from agencies represented on the Steering Committee.

Sec. 4.2. The responsibilities of CISSO shall include:

(a) providing staff support for the Steering Committee;

(b) advising the Executive Agent for Safeguarding Classified Information on Computer Networks and the Insider Threat Task Force on the development of an effective program to monitor compliance with established policies and standards needed to achieve classified information sharing and safeguarding goals; and

(c) consulting with the Departments of State, Defense, and Homeland Security, the ISOO, the Office of the Director of National Intelligence, and others, as appropriate, to ensure consistency with policies and standards under Executive Order 13526 of December 29, 2009, Executive Order 12829 of January 6, 1993, as amended, Executive Order 13549 of August 18, 2010, and Executive Order 13556 of November 4, 2010.

Sec. 5. Executive Agent for Safeguarding Classified Information on Computer Networks.
Sec. 5.1. The Secretary of Defense and the Director, National Security Agency, shall jointly act as the Executive Agent for Safeguarding Classified Information on Computer Networks (the "Executive Agent"), exercising the existing authorities of the Executive Agent and National Manager for national security systems, respectively, under National Security Directive/NSD-42 of July 5, 1990, as supplemented by and subject to this order.
Sec. 5.2. The Executive Agent's responsibilities, in addition to those specified by NSD-42, shall include the following:

(a) developing effective technical safeguarding policies and standards in coordination with the Committee on National Security Systems (CNSS), as re-designated by Executive Orders 13286 of February 28, 2003, and 13231 of October 16, 2001, that address the safeguarding of classified information within national security systems, as well as the safeguarding of national security systems themselves;

(b) referring to the Steering Committee for resolution any unresolved issues delaying the Executive Agent's timely development and issuance of technical policies and standards;

(c) reporting at least annually to the Steering Committee on the work of CNSS, including recommendations for any changes needed to improve the timeliness and effectiveness of that work; and

(d) conducting independent assessments of agency compliance with established safeguarding policies and standards, and reporting the results of such assessments to the Steering Committee.

Sec. 6. Insider Threat Task Force.
Sec. 6.1. There is established an interagency Insider Threat Task Force that shall develop a Government-wide program (insider threat program) for deterring, detecting, and mitigating insider threats, including the safeguarding of classified information from exploitation, compromise, or other unauthorized disclosure, taking into account risk levels, as well as the distinct needs, missions, and systems of individual agencies. This program shall include development of policies, objectives, and priorities for establishing and integrating security, counterintelligence, user audits and monitoring, and other safeguarding capabilities and practices within agencies.
Sec. 6.2. The Task Force shall be co-chaired by the Attorney General and the Director of National Intelligence, or their designees. Membership on the Task Force shall be composed of officers of the United States from, and designated by the heads of, the Departments of State, Defense, Justice, Energy, and Homeland Security, the Office of the Director of National Intelligence, the Central Intelligence Agency, and the ISOO, as well as such additional agencies as the co-chairs of the Task Force may designate. It shall be staffed by personnel from the Federal Bureau of Investigation and the Office of the National Counterintelligence Executive (ONCIX), and other agencies, as determined by the co-chairs for their respective agencies and to the extent permitted by law. Such personnel must be officers or full-time or permanent part-time employees of the United States. To the extent permitted by law, ONCIX shall provide an appropriate work site and administrative support for the Task Force.
Sec. 6.3. The Task Force's responsibilities shall include the following:

(a) developing, in coordination with the Executive Agent, a Government-wide policy for the deterrence, detection, and mitigation of insider threats, which shall be submitted to the Steering Committee for appropriate review;

(b) in coordination with appropriate agencies, developing minimum standards and guidance for implementation of the insider threat program's Government-wide policy and, within 1 year of the date of this order, issuing those minimum standards and guidance, which shall be binding on the executive branch;

(c) if sufficient appropriations or authorizations are obtained, continuing in coordination with appropriate agencies after 1 year from the date of this order to add to or modify those minimum standards and guidance, as appropriate;

(d) if sufficient appropriations or authorizations are not obtained, recommending for promulgation by the Office of Management and Budget or the ISOO any additional or modified minimum standards and guidance developed more than 1 year after the date of this order; (e) referring to the Steering Committee for resolution any unresolved issues delaying the timely development and issuance of minimum standards;

(f) conducting, in accordance with procedures to be developed by the Task Force, independent assessments of the adequacy of agency programs to implement established policies and minimum standards, and reporting the results of such assessments to the Steering Committee;

(g) providing assistance to agencies, as requested, including through the dissemination of best practices; and

(h) providing analysis of new and continuing insider threat challenges facing the United States Government.

Sec. 7. General Provisions.

(a) For the purposes of this order, the word "agencies" shall have the meaning set forth in section 6.1(b) of Executive Order 13526 of December 29, 2009.

(b) Nothing in this order shall be construed to change the requirements of Executive Orders 12333 of December 4, 1981, 12829 of January 6, 1993, 12968 of August 2, 1995, 13388 of October 25, 2005, 13467 of June 30, 2008, 13526 of December 29, 2009, 13549 of August 18, 2010, and their successor orders and directives.

(c) Nothing in this order shall be construed to supersede or change the authorities of the Secretary of Energy or the Nuclear Regulatory Commission under the Atomic Energy Act of 1954, as amended; the Secretary of Defense under Executive Order 12829, as amended; the Secretary of Homeland Security under Executive Order 13549; the Secretary of State under title 22, United States Code, and the Omnibus Diplomatic Security and Antiterrorism Act of 1986; the Director of ISOO under Executive Orders 13526 and 12829, as amended; the PM-ISE under Executive Order 13388 or the Intelligence Reform and Terrorism Prevention Act of 2004, as amended; the Director, Central Intelligence Agency under NSD-42 and Executive Order 13286, as amended; the National Counterintelligence Executive, under the Counterintelligence Enhancement Act of 2002; or the Director of National Intelligence under the National Security Act of 1947, as amended, the Intelligence Reform and Terrorism Prevention Act of 2004, as amended, NSD-42, and Executive Orders 12333, as amended, 12968, as amended, 13286, as amended, 13467, and 13526.

(d) Nothing in this order shall authorize the Steering Committee, CISSO, CNSS, or the Task Force to examine the facilities or systems of other agencies, without advance consultation with the head of such agency, nor to collect information for any purpose not provided herein.

(e) The entities created and the activities directed by this order shall not seek to deter, detect, or mitigate disclosures of information by Government employees or contractors that are lawful under and protected by the Intelligence Community Whistleblower Protection Act of 1998, Whistleblower Protection Act of 1989, Inspector General Act of 1978, or similar statutes, regulations, or policies.

(f) With respect to the Intelligence Community, the Director of National Intelligence, after consultation with the heads of affected agencies, may issue such policy directives and guidance as the Director of National Intelligence deems necessary to implement this order.

(g) Nothing in this order shall be construed to impair or otherwise affect:

(1) the authority granted by law to an agency, or the head thereof; or

(2) the functions of the Director of the Office of Management and Budget relating to budgetary, administrative, or legislative proposals

(h) This order shall be implemented consistent with applicable law and appropriate protections for privacy and civil liberties, and subject to the availability of appropriations.

(i) This order is not intended to, and does not, create any right or benefit, substantive or procedural, enforceable at law or in equity by any party against the United States, its departments, agencies, or entities, its officers, employees, or agents, or any other person.

BARACK OBAMA

Executive Order 13388—Further Strengthening the Sharing of Terrorism Information to Protect Americans

70 Fed. Reg. 62,023 (Oct. 27, 2005)

By the authority vested in me as President by the Constitution and the laws of the United States of America, including of the Intelligence Reform and Terrorism Prevention Act of 2004 (Public Law 108-458), and in order to further strengthen the effective conduct of United States counterterrorism activities and protect the territory, people, and interests of the United States of America, including against terrorist attacks, it is hereby ordered as follows:

Section 1. Policy.

To the maximum extent consistent with applicable law, agencies shall, in the design and use of information systems and in the dissemination of information among agencies:

(a) give the highest priority to (i) the detection, prevention, disruption, preemption, and mitigation of the effects of terrorist activities against the territory, people, and interests of the United States of America; (ii) the interchange of terrorism information among agencies; (iii) the interchange of terrorism information between agencies and appropriate authorities of State, local, and tribal governments, and between agencies and appropriate private sector entities; and (iv) the protection of the ability of agencies to acquire additional such information; and

(b) protect the freedom, information privacy, and other legal rights of Americans in the conduct of activities implementing subsection (a).

Sec. 2. Duties of Heads of Agencies Possessing or Acquiring Terrorism Information.

To implement the policy set forth in section 1 of this order, the head of each agency that possesses or acquires terrorism information:

(a) shall promptly give access to the terrorism information to the head of each other agency that has counterterrorism functions, and provide the terrorism information to each such agency, unless otherwise directed by the President, and consistent with (i) the statutory responsibilities of the agencies providing and receiving the information; (ii) any guidance issued by the Attorney General to fulfill the policy set forth in subsection 1(b) of this order; and (iii) other applicable law, including sections 102A(g) and (i) of the National Security Act of 1947, section 1016 of the Intelligence Reform and Terrorism Prevention Act of 2004 (including any policies, procedures, guidelines, rules, and standards issued pursuant thereto), sections 202 and 892 of the Homeland Security Act of 2002, Executive Order 12958 of April 17, 1995, as amended, and Executive Order 13311 of July 29, 2003; and

(b) shall cooperate in and facilitate production of reports based on terrorism information with contents and formats that permit dissemination that maximizes the utility of the information in protecting the territory, people, and interests of the United States.

Sec. 3. Preparing Terrorism Information for Maximum Distribution.

To assist in expeditious and effective implementation by agencies of the policy set forth in section 1 of this order, the common standards for the sharing of terrorism information established pursuant to section 3 of Executive Order 13356 of August 27, 2004, shall be used, as appropriate, in carrying out section 1016 of the Intelligence Reform and Terrorism Prevention Act of 2004.

Sec. 4. Requirements for Collection of Terrorism Information Inside the United States.

To assist in expeditious and effective implementation by agencies of the policy set forth in section 1 of this order, the recommendations regarding the establishment of executive branch-wide collection and sharing requirements, procedures, and guidelines for terrorism information collected within the United States made pursuant to section 4 of Executive Order 13356 shall be used, as appropriate, in carrying out section 1016 of the Intelligence Reform and Terrorism Prevention Act of 2004.

Sec. 5. Establishment and Functions of Information Sharing Council.

(a) Consistent with section 1016(g) of the Intelligence Reform and Terrorism Prevention Act of 2004, there is hereby established an Information Sharing Council (Council), chaired by the Program Manager to whom section 1016 of such Act refers, and composed exclusively of designees of: the Secretaries of State, the Treasury, Defense, Commerce, Energy, and Homeland Security; the Attorney General; the Director of National Intelligence; the Director of the Central Intelligence Agency; the Director of the Office of Management and Budget; the Director of the Federal Bureau of Investigation; the Director of the National Counterterrorism Center; and such other heads of departments or agencies as the Director of National Intelligence may designate.

(b) The mission of the Council is to (i) provide advice and information concerning the establishment of an interoperable terrorism information sharing environment to facilitate automated sharing of terrorism information among appropriate agencies to implement the policy set forth in section 1 of this order; and (ii) perform the duties set forth in section 1016(g) of the Intelligence Reform and Terrorism Prevention Act of 2004.

(c) To assist in expeditious and effective implementation by agencies of the policy set forth in section 1 of this order, the plan for establishment of a proposed interoperable terrorism information sharing environment reported under section 5(c) of Executive Order 13356 shall be used, as appropriate, in carrying out section 1016 of the Intelligence Reform and Terrorism Prevention Act of 2004.

Sec. 6. Definitions.

As used in this order:

(a) the term "agency" has the meaning set forth for the term "executive agency" in section 105 of title 5, United States Code, together with the Department of Homeland Security, but includes the Postal Rate Commission and the United States Postal Service and excludes the Government Accountability Office; and

(b) the term "terrorism information" has the meaning set forth for such term in section 1016(a)(4) of the Intelligence Reform and Terrorism Prevention Act of 2004.

Sec. 7. General Provisions.

(a) This order:

(i) shall be implemented in a manner consistent with applicable law, including Federal law protecting the information privacy and other legal rights of Americans, and subject to the availability of appropriations;

(ii) shall be implemented in a manner consistent with the authority of the principal officers of agencies as heads of their respective agencies, including under section 199 of the Revised Statutes (22 U.S.C. 2651), section 201 of the Department of Energy Organization

Act (42 U.S.C. 7131), section 103 of the National Security Act of 1947 (50 U.S.C. 403-3), section 102(a) of the Homeland Security Act of 2002 (6 U.S.C. 112(a)), and sections 301 of title 5, 113(b) and 162(b) of title 10, 1501 of title 15, 503 of title 28, and 301(b) of title 31, United States Code;

(iii) shall be implemented consistent with the Presidential Memorandum of June 2, 2005, on "Strengthening Information Sharing, Access, and Integration Organizational, Management, and Policy Development Structures for Creating the Terrorism Information Sharing Environment;"

(iv) shall not be construed to impair or otherwise affect the functions of the Director of the Office of Management and Budget relating to budget, administrative, and legislative proposals; and

(v) shall be implemented in a manner consistent with section 102A of the National Security Act of 1947.

(b) This order is intended only to improve the internal management of the Federal Government and is not intended to, and does not, create any rights or benefits, substantive or procedural, enforceable at law or in equity by a party against the United States, its departments, agencies, instrumentalities, or entities, its officers, employees, or agents, or any other person.

Sec. 8. Amendments and Revocation.

(a) Executive Order 13311 of July 29, 2003, is amended:

(i) by striking "Director of Central Intelligence" each place it appears and inserting in lieu thereof in each such place "Director of National Intelligence"; and

(ii) by striking "103(c)(7)" and inserting in lieu thereof "102A(i)(1)".

(b) Executive Order 13356 of August 27, 2004, is hereby revoked.

George W. Bush

Executive Order 13556—Controlled Unclassified Information

75 Fed. Reg. 68,675 (Nov. 4, 2010)

By the authority vested in me as President by the Constitution and the laws of the United States of America, it is hereby ordered as follows:

Section 1. Purpose.

This order establishes an open and uniform program for managing information that requires safeguarding or dissemination controls pursuant to and consistent with law, regulations, and Government-wide policies, excluding information that is classified under Executive Order 13526 of December 29, 2009, or the Atomic Energy Act, as amended.

At present, executive departments and agencies (agencies) employ ad hoc, agency-specific policies, procedures, and markings to safeguard and control this information, such as information that involves privacy, security, proprietary business interests, and law enforcement investigations. This inefficient, confusing patchwork has resulted in inconsistent marking and safeguarding of documents, led to unclear or unnecessarily restrictive dissemination policies, and created impediments to authorized information sharing. The fact that these agency-specific policies are often hidden from public view has only aggravated these issues.

To address these problems, this order establishes a program for managing this information, hereinafter described as Controlled Unclassified Information, that emphasizes the openness and uniformity of Government-wide practice.

Sec. 2. Controlled Unclassified Information (CUI).

(a) The CUI categories and subcategories shall serve as exclusive designations for identifying unclassified information throughout the executive branch that requires safeguarding or dissemination controls, pursuant to and consistent with applicable law, regulations, and Government-wide policies.

(b) The mere fact that information is designated as CUI shall not have a bearing on determinations pursuant to any law requiring the disclosure of information or permitting disclosure as a matter of discretion, including disclosures to the legislative or judicial branches.

(c) The National Archives and Records Administration shall serve as the Executive Agent to implement this order and oversee agency actions to ensure compliance with this order.

Sec. 3. Review of Current Designations.

(a) Each agency head shall, within 180 days of the date of this order:

(1) review all categories, subcategories, and markings used by the agency to designate unclassified information for safeguarding or dissemination controls; and

(2) submit to the Executive Agent a catalogue of proposed categories and subcategories of CUI, and proposed associated markings for information designated as CUI under section 2(a) of this order. This submission shall provide definitions for each proposed category and subcategory and identify the basis in law, regulation, or Government-wide policy for safeguarding or dissemination controls.

(b) If there is significant doubt about whether information should be designated as CUI, it shall not be so designated.

Sec. 4. Development of CUI Categories and Policies.

(a) On the basis of the submissions under section 3 of this order or future proposals, and in consultation with affected agencies, the Executive Agent shall, in a timely manner, approve categories and subcategories of CUI and associated markings to be applied uniformly through-out the executive branch and to become effective upon publication in the registry established under subsection (d) of this section. No unclassified information meeting the requirements of section 2(a) of this order shall be disapproved for inclusion as CUI, but the Executive Agent may resolve conflicts among categories and subcategories of CUI to achieve uniformity and may determine the markings to be used.

(b) The Executive Agent, in consultation with affected agencies, shall develop and issue such directives as are necessary to implement this order. Such directives shall be made available to the public and shall provide policies and procedures concerning marking, safeguarding, dis-semination, and decontrol of CUI that, to the extent practicable and permitted by law, regula-tion, and Government-wide policies, shall remain consistent across categories and subcatego-ries of CUI and throughout the executive branch. In developing such directives, appropriate consideration should be given to the report of the interagency Task Force on Controlled Unclassified Information published in August 2009. The Executive Agent shall issue initial directives for the implementation of this order within 180 days of the date of this order.

(c) The Executive Agent shall convene and chair interagency meetings to discuss matters pertaining to the program established by this order.

(d) Within 1 year of the date of this order, the Executive Agent shall establish and maintain a public CUI registry reflecting authorized CUI categories and subcategories, associated mark-ings, and applicable safeguarding, dissemination, and decontrol procedures.

(e) If the Executive Agent and an agency cannot reach agreement on an issue related to the implementation of this order, that issue may be appealed to the President through the Director of the Office of Management and Budget.

(f) In performing its functions under this order, the Executive Agent, in accordance with appli-cable law, shall consult with representatives of the public and State, local, tribal, and private sector partners on matters related to approving categories and subcategories of CUI and devel-oping implementing directives issued by the Executive Agent pursuant to this order.

Sec. 5. Implementation.

(a) Within 180 days of the issuance of initial policies and procedures by the Executive Agent in accordance with section 4(b) of this order, each agency that originates or handles CUI shall provide the Executive Agent with a proposed plan for compliance with the requirements of this order, including the establishment of interim target dates.

(b) After a review of agency plans, and in consultation with affected agencies and the Office of Management and Budget, the Executive Agent shall establish deadlines for phased implemen-tation by agencies.

(c) In each of the first 5 years following the date of this order and biennially thereafter, the Executive Agent shall publish a report on the status of agency implementation of this order.

Sec. 6. General Provisions.

(a) This order shall be implemented in a manner consistent with:
    (1) applicable law, including protections of confidentiality and privacy rights;
    (2) the statutory authority of the heads of agencies, including authorities related to the protection of information provided by the private sector to the Federal Government; and
    (3) applicable Government-wide standards and guidelines issued by the National Institute of Standards and Technology, and applicable policies established by the Office of Man-agement and Budget.

(b) The Director of National Intelligence (Director), with respect to the Intelligence Commu-nity and after consultation with the heads of affected agencies, may issue such policy directives and guidelines as the Director deems necessary to implement this order with respect to intelligence and intelligence-related information. Procedures or other guidance issued by Intelligence Community element heads shall be in accordance with such policy directives or guidelines issued by the Director. Any such policy directives or guidelines issued by the Director shall be in accordance with this order and directives issued by the Executive Agent.

(c) This order shall not be construed to impair or otherwise affect the functions of the Director of the Office of Management and Budget relating to budgetary, administrative, and legislative proposals.

(d) This order is not intended to, and does not, create any right or benefit, substantive or procedural, enforceable at law or in equity by any party against the United States, its departments, agencies, or entities, its officers, employees, or agents, or any other person.

(e) This order shall be implemented subject to the availability of appropriations.

(f) The Attorney General, upon request by the head of an agency or the Executive Agent, shall render an interpretation of this order with respect to any question arising in the course of its administration.

(g) The Presidential Memorandum of May 7, 2008, entitled "Designation and Sharing of Controlled Unclassified Information (CUI)" is hereby rescinded.

BARACK OBAMA

Executive Order 13629—Establishing the White House Homeland Security Partnership Council

77 Fed. Reg. 66,353 (Nov. 2, 2012)

By the authority vested in me as President by the Constitution and the laws of the United States of America, and in order to advance the Federal Government's use of local partnerships to address homeland security challenges, it is hereby ordered as follows:

Section 1. Policy.

The purpose of this order is to maximize the Federal Government's ability to develop local partnerships in the United States to support homeland security priorities. Partnerships are collaborative working relationships in which the goals, structure, and roles and responsibilities of the relationships are mutually determined. Collaboration enables the Federal Government and its partners to use resources more efficiently, build on one another's expertise, drive innovation, engage in collective action, broaden investments to achieve shared goals, and improve performance. Partnerships enhance our ability to address homeland security priorities, from responding to natural disasters to preventing terrorism, by utilizing diverse perspectives, skills, tools, and resources.

The National Security Strategy emphasizes the importance of partnerships, underscoring that to keep our Nation safe "we must tap the ingenuity outside government through strategic partnerships with the private sector, nongovernmental organizations, foundations, and community-based organizations. Such partnerships are critical to U.S. success at home and abroad, and we will support them through enhanced opportunities for engagement, coordination, transparency, and information sharing." This approach recognizes that, given the complexities and range of challenges, we must institutionalize an all-of-Nation effort to address the evolving threats to the United States.

Sec. 2. White House Homeland Security Partnership Council and Steering Committee.

(a) *White House Homeland Security Partnership Council.* There is established a White House Homeland Security Partnership Council (Council) to foster local partnerships— between the Federal Government and the private sector, nongovernmental organizations, foundations, community-based organizations, and State, local, tribal, and territorial government and law enforcement—to address homeland security challenges. The Council shall be chaired by the Assistant to the President for Homeland Security and Counterterrorism (Chair), or a designee from the National Security Staff.

(b) *Council Membership.*

(i) Pursuant to the nomination process established in subsection (b)(ii) of this section, the Council shall be composed of Federal officials who are from field offices of the executive departments, agencies, and bureaus (agencies) that are members of the Steering Committee established in subsection (c) of this section, and who have demonstrated an ability to develop, sustain, and institutionalize local partnerships to address policy priorities.

(ii) The nomination process and selection criteria for members of the Council shall be established by the Steering Committee. Based on those criteria, agency heads may select and present to the Steering Committee their nominee or nominees to represent them on the Council. The Steering Committee shall consider all of the nominees and decide by consensus which of the nominees shall participate on the Council. Each member agency on the Steering Committee, with the exception of the Office of the Director of National Intelligence, may have at least one representative on the Council.

(c) *Steering Committee.* There is also established a Steering Committee, chaired by the Chair of the Council, to provide guidance to the Council and perform other functions as set forth in this order. The Steering Committee shall include a representative at the Deputy agency head level, or that representative's designee, from the following agencies:

(i) Department of State;

(ii) Department of the Treasury;

(iii) Department of Defense;

(iv) Department of Justice;

(v) Department of the Interior;

(vi) Department of Agriculture;

(vii) Department of Commerce;

(viii) Department of Labor;

(ix) Department of Health and Human Services;

(x) Department of Housing and Urban Development;

(xi) Department of Transportation;

(xii) Department of Energy;

(xiii) Department of Education;

(xiv) Department of Veterans Affairs;

(xv) Department of Homeland Security;

(xvi) Office of the Director of National Intelligence;

(xvii) Environmental Protection Agency;

(xviii) Small Business Administration; and

(xix) Federal Bureau of Investigation.

At the invitation of the Chair, representatives of agencies not listed in subsection (c) of this section or other executive branch entities may attend and participate in Steering Committee meetings as appropriate.

(d) *Administration.* The Chair or a designee shall convene meetings of the Council and Steering Committee, determine their agendas, and coordinate their work. The Council may establish subgroups consisting exclusively of Council members or their designees, as appropriate.

Sec. 3. Mission and Function of the Council and Steering Committee.

(a) The Council shall, consistent with guidance from the Steering Committee:

(i) advise the Chair and Steering Committee members on priorities, challenges, and opportunities for local partnerships to support homeland security priorities, as well as regularly report to the Steering Committee on the Council's efforts;

(ii) promote homeland security priorities and opportunities for collaboration between Federal Government field offices and State, local, tribal, and territorial stakeholders;

(iii) advise and confer with State, local, tribal, and territorial stakeholders and agencies interested in expanding or building local homeland security partnerships;

(iv) raise awareness of local partnership best practices that can support homeland security priorities;

(v) as appropriate, conduct outreach to representatives of the private sector, nongovernmental organizations, foundations, community-based organizations, and State, local, tribal, and territorial government and law enforcement entities with relevant expertise for local homeland security partnerships, and collaborate with other Federal Government bodies; and

(vi) convene an annual meeting to exchange key findings, progress, and best practices.

(b) The Steering Committee shall:

(i) determine the scope of issue areas the Council will address and its operating protocols, in consultation with the Office of Management and Budget;

(ii) establish the nomination process and selection criteria for members of the Council as set forth in section 2(b)(ii) of this order;

(iii) provide guidance to the Council on the activities set forth in subsection (a) of this section; and

(iv) within 1 year of the selection of the Council members, and annually thereafter, provide a report on the work of the Council to the President through the Chair.

Sec. 4. General Provisions.

(a) The heads of agencies participating in the Steering Committee shall assist and provide information to the Council, consistent with applicable law, as may be necessary to implement this order. Each agency shall bear its own expense for participating in the Council.

(b) Nothing in this order shall be construed to impair or otherwise affect:

(i) the authority granted by law to an executive department, agency, or the head thereof;

(ii) the functions of the Director of the Office of Management and Budget relating to budgetary, administrative, or legislative proposals; or

(iii) the functions of the Overseas Security Advisory Council.

(c) This order shall be implemented consistent with applicable law and appropriate protections for privacy and civil liberties, and subject to the availability of appropriations.

(d) This order is not intended to, and does not, create any right or benefit, substantive or procedural, enforceable at law or in equity by any party against the United States, its departments, agencies, or entities, its officers, employees, or agents, or any other person.

BARACK OBAMA

Executive Order 13636—
Improving Critical Infrastructure Cybersecurity

78 Fed. Reg. 11,739 (Feb. 19, 2013)

By the authority vested in me as President by the Constitution and the laws of the United States of America, it is hereby ordered as follows:

Section 1. Policy.

Repeated cyber intrusions into critical infrastructure demonstrate the need for improved cybersecurity. The cyber threat to critical infrastructure continues to grow and represents one of the most serious national security challenges we must confront. The national and economic security of the United States depends on the reliable functioning of the Nation's critical infrastructure in the face of such threats. It is the policy of the United States to enhance the security and resilience of the Nation's critical infrastructure and to maintain a cyber environment that encourages efficiency, innovation, and economic prosperity while promoting safety, security, business confidentiality, privacy, and civil liberties. We can achieve these goals through a partnership with the owners and operators of critical infrastructure to improve cybersecurity information sharing and collaboratively develop and implement risk-based standards.

Sec. 2. Critical Infrastructure.

As used in this order, the term critical infrastructure means systems and assets, whether physical or virtual, so vital to the United States that the incapacity or destruction of such systems and assets would have a debilitating impact on security, national economic security, national public health or safety, or any combination of those matters.

Sec. 3. Policy Coordination.

Policy coordination, guidance, dispute resolution, and periodic in-progress reviews for the functions and programs described and assigned herein shall be provided through the interagency process established in Presidential Policy Directive-1 of February 13, 2009 (Organization of the National Security Council System), or any successor.

Sec. 4. Cybersecurity Information Sharing.

(a) It is the policy of the United States Government to increase the volume, timeliness, and quality of cyber threat information shared with U.S. private sector entities so that these entities may better protect and defend themselves against cyber threats. Within 120 days of the date of this order, the Attorney General, the Secretary of Homeland Security (the "Secretary"), and the Director of National Intelligence shall each issue instructions consistent with their authorities and with the requirements of section 12(c) of this order to ensure the timely production of unclassified reports of cyber threats to the U.S. homeland that identify a specific targeted entity. The instructions shall address the need to protect intelligence and law enforcement sources, methods, operations, and investigations.

(b) The Secretary and the Attorney General, in coordination with the Director of National Intelligence, shall establish a process that rapidly disseminates the reports produced pursuant to section 4(a) of this order to the targeted entity. Such process shall also, consistent with the need to protect national security information, include the dissemination of classified reports to critical infrastructure entities authorized to receive them. The Secretary and the Attorney General, in coordination with the Director of National Intelligence, shall establish a system for tracking the production, dissemination, and disposition of these reports.

(c) To assist the owners and operators of critical infrastructure in protecting their systems from unauthorized access, exploitation, or harm, the Secretary, consistent with 6 U.S.C. 143 and in collaboration with the Secretary of Defense, shall, within 120 days of the date of this order, establish procedures to expand the Enhanced Cybersecurity Services program to all critical infrastructure sectors. This voluntary information sharing program will provide classified cyber threat and technical information from the Government to eligible critical infrastructure companies or commercial service providers that offer security services to critical infrastructure.

(d) The Secretary, as the Executive Agent for the Classified National Security Information Program created under Executive Order 13549 of August 18, 2010 (Classified National Security Information Program for State, Local, Tribal, and Private Sector Entities), shall expedite the processing of security clearances to appropriate personnel employed by critical infrastructure owners and operators, prioritizing the critical infrastructure identified in section 9 of this order.

(e) In order to maximize the utility of cyber threat information sharing with the private sector, the Secretary shall expand the use of programs that bring private sector subject-matter experts into Federal service on a temporary basis. These subject matter experts should provide advice regarding the content, structure, and types of information most useful to critical infrastructure owners and operators in reducing and mitigating cyber risks.

Sec. 5. Privacy and Civil Liberties Protections.

(a) Agencies shall coordinate their activities under this order with their senior agency officials for privacy and civil liberties and ensure that privacy and civil liberties protections are incorporated into such activities. Such protections shall be based upon the Fair Information Practice Principles and other privacy and civil liberties policies, principles, and frameworks as they apply to each agency's activities.

(b) The Chief Privacy Officer and the Officer for Civil Rights and Civil Liberties of the Department of Homeland Security (DHS) shall assess the privacy and civil liberties risks of the functions and programs undertaken by DHS as called for in this order and shall recommend to the Secretary ways to minimize or mitigate such risks, in a publicly available report, to be released within 1 year of the date of this order. Senior agency privacy and civil liberties officials for other agencies engaged in activities under this order shall conduct assessments of their agency activities and provide those assessments to DHS for consideration and inclusion in the report. The report shall be reviewed on an annual basis and revised as necessary. The report may contain a classified annex if necessary. Assessments shall include evaluation of activities against the Fair Information Practice Principles and other applicable privacy and civil liberties policies, principles, and frameworks. Agencies shall consider the assessments and recommendations of the report in implementing privacy and civil liberties protections for agency activities.

(c) In producing the report required under subsection (b) of this section, the Chief Privacy Officer and the Officer for Civil Rights and Civil Liberties of DHS shall consult with the Privacy and Civil Liberties Oversight Board and coordinate with the Office of Management and Budget (OMB).

(d) Information submitted voluntarily in accordance with 6 U.S.C. 133 by private entities under this order shall be protected from disclosure to the fullest extent permitted by law.

Sec. 6. Consultative Process.

The Secretary shall establish a consultative process to coordinate improvements to the cybersecurity of critical infrastructure. As part of the consultative process, the Secretary shall engage and consider the advice, on matters set forth in this order, of the Critical Infrastructure Partnership Advisory Council; Sector Coordinating Councils; critical infrastructure owners and operators; Sector-Specific Agencies; other relevant agencies; independent regulatory agencies; State, local, territorial, and tribal governments; universities; and outside experts.

Sec. 7. Baseline Framework to Reduce Cyber Risk to Critical Infrastructure.

(a) The Secretary of Commerce shall direct the Director of the National Institute of Standards and Technology (the "Director") to lead the development of a framework to reduce cyber risks to critical infrastructure (the "Cybersecurity Framework"). The Cybersecurity Framework shall include a set of standards, methodologies, procedures, and processes that align policy, business, and technological approaches to address cyber risks. The Cybersecurity Framework shall incorporate voluntary consensus standards and industry best practices to the fullest extent possible. The Cybersecurity Framework shall be consistent with voluntary international standards when such international standards will advance the objectives of this order, and shall meet the requirements of the National Institute of Standards and Technology Act, as amended (15 U.S.C. 271 et seq.), the National Technology Transfer and Advancement Act of 1995 (Public Law 104-113), and OMB Circular A-119, as revised.

(b) The Cybersecurity Framework shall provide a prioritized, flexible, repeatable, performance-based, and cost-effective approach, including information security measures and controls, to help owners and operators of critical infrastructure identify, assess, and manage cyber risk. The Cybersecurity Framework shall focus on identifying cross-sector security standards and guidelines applicable to critical infrastructure. The Cybersecurity Framework will also identify areas for improvement that should be addressed through future collaboration with particular sectors and standards-developing organizations. To enable technical innovation and account for organizational differences, the Cybersecurity Framework will provide guidance that is technology neutral and that enables critical infrastructure sectors to benefit from a competitive market for products and services that meet the standards, methodologies, procedures, and processes developed to address cyber risks. The Cybersecurity Framework shall include guidance for measuring the performance of an entity in implementing the Cybersecurity Framework.

(c) The Cybersecurity Framework shall include methodologies to identify and mitigate impacts of the Cybersecurity Framework and associated information security measures or controls on business confidentiality, and to protect individual privacy and civil liberties.

(d) In developing the Cybersecurity Framework, the Director shall engage in an open public review and comment process. The Director shall also consult with the Secretary, the National Security Agency, Sector-Specific Agencies and other interested agencies including OMB, owners and operators of critical infrastructure, and other stakeholders through the consultative process established in section 6 of this order. The Secretary, the Director of National Intelligence, and the heads of other relevant agencies shall provide threat and vulnerability information and technical expertise to inform the development of the Cybersecurity Framework. The Secretary shall provide performance goals for the Cybersecurity Framework informed by work under section 9 of this order.

(e) Within 240 days of the date of this order, the Director shall publish a preliminary version of the Cybersecurity Framework (the "preliminary Framework"). Within 1 year of the date of this order, and after coordination with the Secretary to ensure suitability under section 8 of this order, the Director shall publish a final version of the Cybersecurity Framework (the "final Framework").

(f) Consistent with statutory responsibilities, the Director will ensure the Cybersecurity Framework and related guidance is reviewed and updated as necessary, taking into consideration

technological changes, changes in cyber risks, operational feedback from owners and operators of critical infrastructure, experience from the implementation of section 8 of this order,
and any other relevant factors.

Sec. 8. Voluntary Critical Infrastructure Cybersecurity Program.

(a) The Secretary, in coordination with Sector-Specific Agencies, shall establish a voluntary
program to support the adoption of the Cybersecurity Framework by owners and operators of
critical infrastructure and any other interested entities (the "Program").

(b) Sector-Specific Agencies, in consultation with the Secretary and other interested agencies,
shall coordinate with the Sector Coordinating Councils to review the Cybersecurity Framework and, if necessary, develop implementation guidance or supplemental materials to address sector-specific risks and operating environments.

(c) Sector-Specific Agencies shall report annually to the President, through the Secretary, on
the extent to which owners and operators notified under section 9 of this order are participating in the Program.

(d) The Secretary shall coordinate establishment of a set of incentives designed to promote
participation in the Program. Within 120 days of the date of this order, the Secretary and the
Secretaries of the Treasury and Commerce each shall make recommendations separately to the
President, through the Assistant to the President for Homeland Security and Counterterrorism
and the Assistant to the President for Economic Affairs, that shall include analysis of the
benefits and relative effectiveness of such incentives, and whether the incentives would require legislation or can be provided under existing law and authorities to participants in the
Program.

(e) Within 120 days of the date of this order, the Secretary of Defense and the Administrator of
General Services, in consultation with the Secretary and the Federal Acquisition Regulatory
Council, shall make recommendations to the President, through the Assistant to the President
for Homeland Security and Counterterrorism and the Assistant to the President for Economic
Affairs, on the feasibility, security benefits, and relative merits of incorporating security standards into acquisition planning and contract administration. The report shall address what
steps can be taken to harmonize and make consistent existing procurement requirements
related to cybersecurity.

Sec. 9. Identification of Critical Infrastructure at Greatest Risk.

(a) Within 150 days of the date of this order, the Secretary shall use a risk-based approach to
identify critical infrastructure where a cybersecurity incident could reasonably result in catastrophic regional or national effects on public health or safety, economic security, or national
security. In identifying critical infrastructure for this purpose, the Secretary shall use the
consultative process established in section 6 of this order and draw upon the expertise of
Sector-Specific Agencies. The Secretary shall apply consistent, objective criteria in identifying such critical infrastructure. The Secretary shall not identify any commercial information
technology products or consumer information technology services under this section. The
Secretary shall review and update the list of identified critical infrastructure under this section
on an annual basis, and provide such list to the President, through the Assistant to the President for Homeland Security and Counterterrorism and the Assistant to the President for Economic Affairs.

(b) Heads of Sector-Specific Agencies and other relevant agencies shall provide the Secretary
with information necessary to carry out the responsibilities under this section. The Secretary
shall develop a process for other relevant stakeholders to submit information to assist in
making the identifications required in subsection (a) of this section.

(c) The Secretary, in coordination with Sector-Specific Agencies, shall confidentially notify owners and operators of critical infrastructure identified under subsection (a) of this section that they have been so identified, and ensure identified owners and operators are provided the basis for the determination. The Secretary shall establish a process through which owners and operators of critical infrastructure may submit relevant information and request reconsideration of identifications under subsection (a) of this section.

Sec. 10. Adoption of Framework.

(a) Agencies with responsibility for regulating the security of critical infrastructure shall engage in a consultative process with DHS, OMB, and the National Security Staff to review the preliminary Cybersecurity Framework and determine if current cybersecurity regulatory requirements are sufficient given current and projected risks. In making such determination, these agencies shall consider the identification of critical infrastructure required under section 9 of this order. Within 90 days of the publication of the preliminary Framework, these agencies shall submit a report to the President, through the Assistant to the President for Homeland Security and Counterterrorism, the Director of OMB, and the Assistant to the President for Economic Affairs, that states whether or not the agency has clear authority to establish requirements based upon the Cybersecurity Framework to sufficiently address current and projected cyber risks to critical infrastructure, the existing authorities identified, and any additional authority required.

(b) If current regulatory requirements are deemed to be insufficient, within 90 days of publication of the final Framework, agencies identified in subsection (a) of this section shall propose prioritized, risk-based, efficient, and coordinated actions, consistent with Executive Order 12866 of September 30, 1993 (Regulatory Planning and Review), Executive Order 13563 of January 18, 2011 (Improving Regulation and Regulatory Review), and Executive Order 13609 of May 1, 2012 (Promoting International Regulatory Cooperation), to mitigate cyber risk.

(c) Within 2 years after publication of the final Framework, consistent with Executive Order 13563 and Executive Order 13610 of May 10, 2012 (Identifying and Reducing Regulatory Burdens), agencies identified in subsection (a) of this section shall, in consultation with owners and operators of critical infrastructure, report to OMB on any critical infrastructure subject to ineffective, conflicting, or excessively burdensome cybersecurity requirements. This report shall describe efforts made by agencies, and make recommendations for further actions, to minimize or eliminate such requirements.

(d) The Secretary shall coordinate the provision of technical assistance to agencies identified in subsection (a) of this section on the development of their cybersecurity workforce and programs.

(e) Independent regulatory agencies with responsibility for regulating the security of critical infrastructure are encouraged to engage in a consultative process with the Secretary, relevant Sector-Specific Agencies, and other affected parties to consider prioritized actions to mitigate cyber risks for critical infrastructure consistent with their authorities.

Sec. 11. Definitions.

(a) "Agency" means any authority of the United States that is an "agency" under 44 U.S.C. 3502(1), other than those considered to be independent regulatory agencies, as defined in 44 U.S.C. 3502(5).

(b) "Critical Infrastructure Partnership Advisory Council" means the council established by DHS under 6 U.S.C. 451 to facilitate effective interaction and coordination of critical infrastructure protection activities among the Federal Government; the private sector; and State, local, territorial, and tribal governments.

(c) "Fair Information Practice Principles" means the eight principles set forth in Appendix A of the National Strategy for Trusted Identities in Cyberspace.

(d) "Independent regulatory agency" has the meaning given the term in 44 U.S.C. 3502(5).

(e) "Sector Coordinating Council" means a private sector coordinating council composed of representatives of owners and operators within a particular sector of critical infrastructure established by the National Infrastructure Protection Plan or any successor.

(f) "Sector-Specific Agency" has the meaning given the term in Presidential Policy Directive-21 of February 12, 2013 (Critical Infrastructure Security and Resilience), or any successor.

Sec. 12. General Provisions.

(a) This order shall be implemented consistent with applicable law and subject to the availability of appropriations. Nothing in this order shall be construed to provide an agency with authority for regulating the security of critical infrastructure in addition to or to a greater extent than the authority the agency has under existing law. Nothing in this order shall be construed to alter or limit any authority or responsibility of an agency under existing law.

(b) Nothing in this order shall be construed to impair or otherwise affect the functions of the Director of OMB relating to budgetary, administrative, or legislative proposals.

(c) All actions taken pursuant to this order shall be consistent with requirements and authorities to protect intelligence and law enforcement sources and methods. Nothing in this order shall be interpreted to supersede measures established under authority of law to protect the security and integrity of specific activities and associations that are in direct support of intelligence and law enforcement operations.

(d) This order shall be implemented consistent with U.S. international obligations.

(e) This order is not intended to, and does not, create any right or benefit, substantive or procedural, enforceable at law or in equity by any party against the United States, its departments, agencies, or entities, its officers, employees, or agents, or any other person.

BARACK OBAMA

Executive Order 13694—Blocking the Property of Certain Persons Engaging in Significant Malicious Cyber-Enabled Activities

80 Fed. Reg. 18,077 (April 1, 2015)

By the authority vested in me as President by the Constitution and the laws of the United States of America, including the International Emergency Economic Powers Act (50 U.S.C. 1701 *et seq.*) (IEEPA), the National Emergencies Act (50 U.S.C. 1601 *et seq.*) (NEA), section 212(f) of the Immigration and Nationality Act of 1952 (8 U.S.C. 1182(f)), and section 301 of title 3, United States Code,

I, Barack Obama, President of the United States of America, find that the increasing prevalence and severity of malicious cyber-enabled activities originating from, or directed by persons located, in whole or in substantial part, outside the United States constitute an unusual and extraordinary threat to the national security, foreign policy, and economy of the United States. I hereby declare a national emergency to deal with this threat.

Accordingly, I hereby order:

Section 1.

(a) All property and interests in property that are in the United States, that hereafter come within the United States, or that are or hereafter come within the possession or control of any United States person of the following persons are blocked and may not be transferred, paid, exported, withdrawn, or otherwise dealt in:

(i) any person determined by the Secretary of the Treasury, in consultation with the Attorney General and the Secretary of State, to be responsible for or complicit in, or to have engaged in, directly or indirectly, cyber-enabled activities originating from, or directed by persons located, in whole or in substantial part, outside the United States that are reasonably likely to result in, or have materially contributed to, a significant threat to the national security, foreign policy, or economic health or financial stability of the United States and that have the purpose or effect of:

(A) harming, or otherwise significantly compromising the provision of services by, a computer or network of computers that support one or more entities in a critical infrastructure sector;

(B) significantly compromising the provision of services by one or more entities in a critical infrastructure sector;

(C) causing a significant disruption to the availability of a computer or network of computers; or

(D) causing a significant misappropriation of funds or economic resources, trade secrets, personal identifiers, or financial information for commercial or competitive advantage or private financial gain; or

(ii) any person determined by the Secretary of the Treasury, in consultation with the Attorney General and the Secretary of State:

(A) to be responsible for or complicit in, or to have engaged in, the receipt or use for commercial or competitive advantage or private financial gain, or by a commercial entity, outside the United States of trade secrets misappropriated through cyber-enabled means, knowing they have been misappropriated, where the misappropriation of such trade secrets is reasonably likely to result in, or has materially contributed to, a significant threat to the national security, foreign policy, or economic health or financial stability of the United States;

(B) to have materially assisted, sponsored, or provided financial, material, or technological support for, or goods or services in support of, any activity described in subsections (a)(i) or (a)(ii)(A) of this section or any person whose property and interests in property are blocked pursuant to this order;

(C) to be owned or controlled by, or to have acted or purported to act for or on behalf of, directly or indirectly, any person whose property and interests in property are blocked pursuant to this order; or

(D) to have attempted to engage in any of the activities described in subsections (a)(i) and (a)(ii)(A)-(C) of this section.

(b) The prohibitions in subsection (a) of this section apply except to the extent provided by statutes, or in regulations, orders, directives, or licenses that may be issued pursuant to this order, and notwithstanding any contract entered into or any license or permit granted prior to the effective date of this order.

Sec. 2.

I hereby determine that the making of donations of the type of articles specified in section 203(b)(2) of IEEPA (50 U.S.C. 1702(b)(2)) by, to, or for the benefit of any person whose property and interests in property are blocked pursuant to section 1 of this order would seriously impair my ability to deal with the national emergency declared in this order, and I hereby prohibit such donations as provided by section 1 of this order.

Sec. 3.

The prohibitions in section 1 of this order include but are not limited to:

(a) the making of any contribution or provision of funds, goods, or services by, to, or for the benefit of any person whose property and interests in property are blocked pursuant to this order; and

(b) the receipt of any contribution or provision of funds, goods, or services from any such person.

Sec. 4.

I hereby find that the unrestricted immigrant and nonimmigrant entry into the United States of aliens determined to meet one or more of the criteria in section 1(a) of this order would be detrimental to the interests of the United States, and I hereby suspend entry into the United States, as immigrants or nonimmigrants, of such persons. Such persons shall be treated as persons covered by section 1 of Proclamation 8693 of July 24, 2011 (Suspension of Entry of Aliens Subject to United Nations Security Council Travel Bans and International Emergency Economic Powers Act Sanctions).

Sec. 5.

(a) Any transaction that evades or avoids, has the purpose of evading or avoiding, causes a violation of, or attempts to violate any of the prohibitions set forth in this order is prohibited.

(b) Any conspiracy formed to violate any of the prohibitions set forth in this order is prohibited.

Sec. 6.

For the purposes of this order:

(a) the term "person" means an individual or entity; (b) the term "entity" means a partnership, association, trust, joint venture, corporation, group, subgroup, or other organization;

(c) the term "United States person" means any United States citizen, permanent resident alien, entity organized under the laws of the United States or any jurisdiction within the United States (including foreign branches), or any person in the United States;

(d) the term "critical infrastructure sector" means any of the designated critical infrastructure sectors identified in Presidential Policy Directive 21; and

(e) the term "misappropriation" includes any taking or obtaining by improper means, without permission or consent, or under false pretenses.

Sec. 7.

For those persons whose property and interests in property are blocked pursuant to this order who might have a constitutional presence in the United States, I find that because of the ability to transfer funds or other assets instantaneously, prior notice to such persons of measures to be taken pursuant to this order would render those measures ineffectual. I therefore determine that for these measures to be effective in addressing the national emergency declared in this order, there need be no prior notice of a listing or determination made pursuant to section 1 of this order.

Sec. 8.

The Secretary of the Treasury, in consultation with the Attorney General and the Secretary of State, is hereby authorized to take such actions, including the promulgation of rules and regulations, and to employ all powers granted to the President by IEEPA as may be necessary to carry out the purposes of this order. The Secretary of the Treasury may redelegate any of these functions to other officers and agencies of the United States Government consistent with applicable law. All agencies of the United States Government are hereby directed to take all appropriate measures within their authority to carry out the provisions of this order.

Sec. 9.

The Secretary of the Treasury, in consultation with the Attorney General and the Secretary of State, is hereby authorized to submit the recurring and final reports to the Congress on the national emergency declared in this order, consistent with section 401(c) of the NEA (50 U.S.C. 1641(c)) and section 204(c) of IEEPA (50 U.S.C. 1703(c)).

Sec. 10.

This order is not intended to, and does not, create any right or benefit, substantive or procedural, enforceable at law or in equity by any party against the United States, its departments, agencies, or entities, its officers, employees, or agents, or any other person.

BARACK OBAMA

Executive Order 13769—Protecting the Nation from Foreign Terrorist Entry into the United States

82 Fed. Reg. 8,977 (Jan. 27, 2017)

By the authority vested in me as President by the Constitution and laws of the United States of America, including the Immigration and Nationality Act (INA), 8 U.S.C. 1101 *et seq.*, and section 301 of title 3, United States Code, and to protect the American people from terrorist attacks by foreign nationals admitted to the United States, it is hereby ordered as follows:

Section 1. Purpose.

The visa-issuance process plays a crucial role in detecting individuals with terrorist ties and stopping them from entering the United States. Perhaps in no instance was that more apparent than the terrorist attacks of September 11, 2001, when State Department policy prevented consular officers from properly scrutinizing the visa applications of several of the 19 foreign nationals who went on to murder nearly 3,000 Americans. And while the visa-issuance process was reviewed and amended after the September 11 attacks to better detect would-be terrorists from receiving visas, these measures did not stop attacks by foreign nationals who were admitted to the United States.

Numerous foreign-born individuals have been convicted or implicated in terrorism-related crimes since September 11, 2001, including foreign nationals who entered the United States after receiving visitor, student, or employment visas, or who entered through the United States refugee resettlement program. Deteriorating conditions in certain countries due to war, strife, disaster, and civil unrest increase the likelihood that terrorists will use any means possible to enter the United States. The United States must be vigilant during the visa-issuance process to ensure that those approved for admission do not intend to harm Americans and that they have no ties to terrorism.

In order to protect Americans, the United States must ensure that those admitted to this country do not bear hostile attitudes toward it and its founding principles. The United States cannot, and should not, admit those who do not support the Constitution, or those who would place violent ideologies over American law. In addition, the United States should not admit those who engage in acts of bigotry or hatred (including "honor" killings, other forms of violence against women, or the persecution of those who practice religions different from their own) or those who would oppress Americans of any race, gender, or sexual orientation.

Sec. 2. Policy.

It is the policy of the United States to protect its citizens from foreign nationals who intend to commit terrorist attacks in the United States; and to prevent the admission of foreign nationals who intend to exploit United States immigration laws for malevolent purposes.

Sec. 3. Suspension of Issuance of Visas and Other Immigration Benefits to Nationals of Countries of Particular Concern.

(a) The Secretary of Homeland Security, in consultation with the Secretary of State and the Director of National Intelligence, shall immediately conduct a review to determine the information needed from any country to adjudicate any visa, admission, or other benefit under the INA (adjudications) in order to determine that the individual seeking the benefit is who the individual claims to be and is not a security or public-safety threat.

(b) The Secretary of Homeland Security, in consultation with the Secretary of State and the Director of National Intelligence, shall submit to the President Start Printed Page 8978a report on the results of the review described in subsection (a) of this section, including the Secretary of Homeland Security's determination of the information needed for adjudications and a list of countries that do not provide adequate information, within 30 days of the date of this order. The Secretary of Homeland Security shall provide a copy of the report to the Secretary of State and the Director of National Intelligence.

(c) To temporarily reduce investigative burdens on relevant agencies during the review period described in subsection (a) of this section, to ensure the proper review and maximum utilization of available resources for the screening of foreign nationals, and to ensure that adequate standards are established to prevent infiltration by foreign terrorists or criminals, pursuant to section 212(f) of the INA, 8 U.S.C. 1182(f), I hereby proclaim that the immigrant and nonimmigrant entry into the United States of aliens from countries referred to in section 217(a)(12) of the INA, 8 U.S.C. 1187(a)(12), would be detrimental to the interests of the United States, and I hereby suspend entry into the United States, as immigrants and nonimmigrants, of such persons for 90 days from the date of this order (excluding those foreign nationals traveling on diplomatic visas, North Atlantic Treaty Organization visas, C-2 visas for travel to the United Nations, and G-1, G-2, G-3, and G-4 visas).

(d) Immediately upon receipt of the report described in subsection (b) of this section regarding the information needed for adjudications, the Secretary of State shall request all foreign governments that do not supply such information to start providing such information regarding their nationals within 60 days of notification.

(e) After the 60-day period described in subsection (d) of this section expires, the Secretary of Homeland Security, in consultation with the Secretary of State, shall submit to the President a list of countries recommended for inclusion on a Presidential proclamation that would prohibit the entry of foreign nationals (excluding those foreign nationals traveling on diplomatic visas, North Atlantic Treaty Organization visas, C-2 visas for travel to the United Nations, and G-1, G-2, G-3, and G-4 visas) from countries that do not provide the information requested pursuant to subsection (d) of this section until compliance occurs.

(f) At any point after submitting the list described in subsection (e) of this section, the Secretary of State or the Secretary of Homeland Security may submit to the President the names of any additional countries recommended for similar treatment.

(g) Notwithstanding a suspension pursuant to subsection (c) of this section or pursuant to a Presidential proclamation described in subsection (e) of this section, the Secretaries of State and Homeland Security may, on a case-by-case basis, and when in the national interest, issue visas or other immigration benefits to nationals of countries for which visas and benefits are otherwise blocked.

(h) The Secretaries of State and Homeland Security shall submit to the President a joint report on the progress in implementing this order within 30 days of the date of this order, a second report within 60 days of the date of this order, a third report within 90 days of the date of this order, and a fourth report within 120 days of the date of this order.

Sec. 4. Implementing Uniform Screening Standards for All Immigration Programs.

(a) The Secretary of State, the Secretary of Homeland Security, the Director of National Intelligence, and the Director of the Federal Bureau of Investigation shall implement a program, as part of the adjudication process for immigration benefits, to identify individuals seeking to enter the United States on a fraudulent basis with the intent to cause harm, or who are at risk of causing harm subsequent to their admission. This program will include the development of a

uniform screening standard and procedure, such as in-person interviews; a database of identity documents proffered by applicants to ensure that duplicate documents are not Start Printed
Page 8979used by multiple applicants; amended application forms that include questions
aimed at identifying fraudulent answers and malicious intent; a mechanism to ensure that the
applicant is who the applicant claims to be; a process to evaluate the applicant's likelihood of
becoming a positively contributing member of society and the applicant's ability to make
contributions to the national interest; and a mechanism to assess whether or not the applicant
has the intent to commit criminal or terrorist acts after entering the United States.
(b) The Secretary of Homeland Security, in conjunction with the Secretary of State, the Director of National Intelligence, and the Director of the Federal Bureau of Investigation, shall
submit to the President an initial report on the progress of this directive within 60 days of the
date of this order, a second report within 100 days of the date of this order, and a third report
within 200 days of the date of this order.

Sec. 5. Realignment of the U.S. Refugee Admissions Program for Fiscal Year 2017.

(a) The Secretary of State shall suspend the U.S. Refugee Admissions Program (USRAP) for
120 days. During the 120-day period, the Secretary of State, in conjunction with the Secretary
of Homeland Security and in consultation with the Director of National Intelligence, shall
review the USRAP application and adjudication process to determine what additional procedures should be taken to ensure that those approved for refugee admission do not pose a threat
to the security and welfare of the United States, and shall implement such additional procedures. Refugee applicants who are already in the USRAP process may be admitted upon the
initiation and completion of these revised procedures. Upon the date that is 120 days after the
date of this order, the Secretary of State shall resume USRAP admissions only for nationals of
countries for which the Secretary of State, the Secretary of Homeland Security, and the Director of National Intelligence have jointly determined that such additional procedures are adequate to ensure the security and welfare of the United States.
(b) Upon the resumption of USRAP admissions, the Secretary of State, in consultation with the
Secretary of Homeland Security, is further directed to make changes, to the extent permitted
by law, to prioritize refugee claims made by individuals on the basis of religious-based persecution, provided that the religion of the individual is a minority religion in the individual's
country of nationality. Where necessary and appropriate, the Secretaries of State and Homeland Security shall recommend legislation to the President that would assist with such
prioritization.
(c) Pursuant to section 212(f) of the INA, 8 U.S.C. 1182(f), I hereby proclaim that the entry of
nationals of Syria as refugees is detrimental to the interests of the United States and thus
suspend any such entry until such time as I have determined that sufficient changes have been
made to the USRAP to ensure that admission of Syrian refugees is consistent with the national
interest.
(d) Pursuant to section 212(f) of the INA, 8 U.S.C. 1182(f), I hereby proclaim that the entry of
more than 50,000 refugees in fiscal year 2017 would be detrimental to the interests of the
United States, and thus suspend any such entry until such time as I determine that additional
admissions would be in the national interest.
(e) Notwithstanding the temporary suspension imposed pursuant to subsection (a) of this
section, the Secretaries of State and Homeland Security may jointly determine to admit individuals to the United States as refugees on a case-by-case basis, in their discretion, but only so
long as they determine that the admission of such individuals as refugees is in the national
interest—including when the person is a religious minority in his country of nationality
facing religious persecution, when admitting the person would enable the United States to

conform its conduct to a preexisting international agreement, or when the person is already in transit and denying admission would cause undue hardship—and it would not pose a risk to the security or welfare of the United States.Start Printed Page 8980

(f) The Secretary of State shall submit to the President an initial report on the progress of the directive in subsection (b) of this section regarding prioritization of claims made by individuals on the basis of religious-based persecution within 100 days of the date of this order and shall submit a second report within 200 days of the date of this order.

(g) It is the policy of the executive branch that, to the extent permitted by law and as practicable, State and local jurisdictions be granted a role in the process of determining the placement or settlement in their jurisdictions of aliens eligible to be admitted to the United States as refugees. To that end, the Secretary of Homeland Security shall examine existing law to determine the extent to which, consistent with applicable law, State and local jurisdictions may have greater involvement in the process of determining the placement or resettlement of refugees in their jurisdictions, and shall devise a proposal to lawfully promote such involvement.

Sec. 6. Rescission of Exercise of Authority Relating to the Terrorism Grounds of Inadmissibility.

The Secretaries of State and Homeland Security shall, in consultation with the Attorney General, consider rescinding the exercises of authority in section 212 of the INA, 8 U.S.C. 1182, relating to the terrorism grounds of inadmissibility, as well as any related implementing memoranda.

Sec. 7. Expedited Completion of the Biometric Entry-Exit Tracking System.

(a) The Secretary of Homeland Security shall expedite the completion and implementation of a biometric entry-exit tracking system for all travelers to the United States, as recommended by the National Commission on Terrorist Attacks Upon the United States.

(b) The Secretary of Homeland Security shall submit to the President periodic reports on the progress of the directive contained in subsection (a) of this section. The initial report shall be submitted within 100 days of the date of this order, a second report shall be submitted within 200 days of the date of this order, and a third report shall be submitted within 365 days of the date of this order. Further, the Secretary shall submit a report every 180 days thereafter until the system is fully deployed and operational.

Sec. 8. Visa Interview Security.

(a) The Secretary of State shall immediately suspend the Visa Interview Waiver Program and ensure compliance with section 222 of the INA, 8 U.S.C. 1202, which requires that all individuals seeking a nonimmigrant visa undergo an in-person interview, subject to specific statutory exceptions.

(b) To the extent permitted by law and subject to the availability of appropriations, the Secretary of State shall immediately expand the Consular Fellows Program, including by substantially increasing the number of Fellows, lengthening or making permanent the period of service, and making language training at the Foreign Service Institute available to Fellows for assignment to posts outside of their area of core linguistic ability, to ensure that non-immigrant visa-interview wait times are not unduly affected.

Sec. 9. Visa Validity Reciprocity.

The Secretary of State shall review all nonimmigrant visa reciprocity agreements to ensure that they are, with respect to each visa classification, truly reciprocal insofar as practicable with respect to validity period and fees, as required by sections 221(c) and 281 of the INA, 8 U.S.C. 1201(c) and 1351, and other treatment. If a country does not treat United States nationals seeking nonimmigrant visas in a reciprocal manner, the Secretary of State shall adjust the visa validity period, fee schedule, or other treatment to match the treatment of United States nationals by the foreign country, to the extent practicable.

Sec. 10. Transparency and Data Collection.

(a) To be more transparent with the American people, and to more effectively implement policies and practices that serve the national interest, the Secretary of Homeland Security, in consultation with the Attorney General, shall, consistent with applicable law and national security, collect and make publicly available within 180 days, and every 180 days thereafter:

    (i) information regarding the number of foreign nationals in the United States who have been charged with terrorism-related offenses while in the United States; convicted of terrorism-related offenses while in the United States; or removed from the United States based on terrorism-related activity, affiliation, or material support to a terrorism-related organization, or any other national security reasons since the date of this order or the last reporting period, whichever is later;

    (ii) information regarding the number of foreign nationals in the United States who have been radicalized after entry into the United States and engaged in terrorism-related acts, or who have provided material support to terrorism-related organizations in countries that pose a threat to the United States, since the date of this order or the last reporting period, whichever is later; and

    (iii) information regarding the number and types of acts of gender-based violence against women, including honor killings, in the United States by foreign nationals, since the date of this order or the last reporting period, whichever is later; and

    (iv) any other information relevant to public safety and security as determined by the Secretary of Homeland Security and the Attorney General, including information on the immigration status of foreign nationals charged with major offenses.

(b) The Secretary of State shall, within one year of the date of this order, provide a report on the estimated long-term costs of the USRAP at the Federal, State, and local levels.

Sec. 11. General Provisions.

(a) Nothing in this order shall be construed to impair or otherwise affect:

    (i) the authority granted by law to an executive department or agency, or the head thereof; or

    (ii) the functions of the Director of the Office of Management and Budget relating to budgetary, administrative, or legislative proposals.

(b) This order shall be implemented consistent with applicable law and subject to the availability of appropriations.Start Printed Page 8982

(c) This order is not intended to, and does not, create any right or benefit, substantive or procedural, enforceable at law or in equity by any party against the United States, its departments, agencies, or entities, its officers, employees, or agents, or any other person.

DONALD J. TRUMP

Executive Order 13780—Protecting the Nation from Foreign Terrorist Entry into the United States

82 Fed. Reg. 13,209 (Mar. 6, 2017)

By the authority vested in me as President by the Constitution and the laws of the United States of America, including the Immigration and Nationality Act (INA), 8 U.S.C. 1101 et seq., and section 301 of title 3, United States Code, and to protect the Nation from terrorist activities by foreign nationals admitted to the United States, it is hereby ordered as follows:

Section 1. Policy and Purpose.

(a) It is the policy of the United States to protect its citizens from terrorist attacks, including those committed by foreign nationals. The screening and vetting protocols and procedures associated with the visa-issuance process and the United States Refugee Admissions Program (USRAP) play a crucial role in detecting foreign nationals who may commit, aid, or support acts of terrorism and in preventing those individuals from entering the United States. It is therefore the policy of the United States to improve the screening and vetting protocols and procedures associated with the visa-issuance process and the USRAP.

(b) On January 27, 2017, to implement this policy, I issued Executive Order 13769 (Protecting the Nation from Foreign Terrorist Entry into the United States).

(i) Among other actions, Executive Order 13769 suspended for 90 days the entry of certain aliens from seven countries: Iran, Iraq, Libya, Somalia, Sudan, Syria, and Yemen. These are countries that had already been identified as presenting heightened concerns about terrorism and travel to the United States. Specifically, the suspension applied to countries referred to in, or designated under, section 217(a)(12) of the INA, 8 U.S.C. 1187(a)(12), in which Congress restricted use of the Visa Waiver Program for nationals of, and aliens recently present in, (A) Iraq or Syria, (B) any country designated by the Secretary of State as a state sponsor of terrorism (currently Iran, Syria, and Sudan), and (C) any other country designated as a country of concern by the Secretary of Homeland Security, in consultation with the Secretary of State and the Director of National Intelligence. In 2016, the Secretary of Homeland Security designated Libya, Somalia, and Yemen as additional countries of concern for travel purposes, based on consideration of three statutory factors related to terrorism and national security: "(I) whether the presence of an alien in the country or area increases the likelihood that the alien is a credible threat to the national security of the United States; (II) whether a foreign terrorist organization has a significant presence in the country or area; and (III) whether the country or area is a safe haven for terrorists." 8 U.S.C. 1187(a)(12)(D)(ii). Additionally, Members of Congress have expressed concerns about screening and vetting procedures following recent terrorist attacks in this country and in Europe.

(ii) In ordering the temporary suspension of entry described in subsection (b)(i) of this section, I exercised my authority under Article II of the Constitution and under section 212(f) of the INA, which provides in relevant part: "Whenever the President finds that the entry of any aliens or of any class of aliens into the United States would be detrimental to the interests of the United States, he may by proclamation, and for such period as he shall deem necessary, suspend the entry of all aliens or any class of aliens as immigrants or nonimmigrants, or impose on the entry of aliens any restrictions he may deem to be appropriate." 8 U.S.C. 1182(f). Under these authorities, I determined that, for a brief period of 90 days, while existing screening and vetting procedures were

713

under review, the entry into the United States of certain aliens from the seven identified countries — each afflicted by terrorism in a manner that compromised the ability of the United States to rely on normal decision-making procedures about travel to the United States — would be detrimental to the interests of the United States. Nonetheless, I permitted the Secretary of State and the Secretary of Homeland Security to grant case-by-case waivers when they determined that it was in the national interest to do so.

(iii) Executive Order 13769 also suspended the USRAP for 120 days. Terrorist groups have sought to infiltrate several nations through refugee programs. Accordingly, I temporarily suspended the USRAP pending a review of our procedures for screening and vetting refugees. Nonetheless, I permitted the Secretary of State and the Secretary of Homeland Security to jointly grant case-by-case waivers when they determined that it was in the national interest to do so.

(iv) Executive Order 13769 did not provide a basis for discriminating for or against members of any particular religion. While that order allowed for prioritization of refugee claims from members of persecuted religious minority groups, that priority applied to refugees from every nation, including those in which Islam is a minority religion, and it applied to minority sects within a religion. That order was not motivated by animus toward any religion, but was instead intended to protect the ability of religious minorities — whoever they are and wherever they reside — to avail themselves of the USRAP in light of their particular challenges and circumstances.

(c) The implementation of Executive Order 13769 has been delayed by litigation. Most significantly, enforcement of critical provisions of that order has been temporarily halted by court orders that apply nationwide and extend even to foreign nationals with no prior or substantial connection to the United States. On February 9, 2017, the United States Court of Appeals for the Ninth Circuit declined to stay or narrow one such order pending the outcome of further judicial proceedings, while noting that the "political branches are far better equipped to make appropriate distinctions" about who should be covered by a suspension of entry or of refugee admissions.

(d) Nationals from the countries previously identified under section 217(a)(12) of the INA warrant additional scrutiny in connection with our immigration policies because the conditions in these countries present heightened threats. Each of these countries is a state sponsor of terrorism, has been significantly compromised by terrorist organizations, or contains active conflict zones. Any of these circumstances diminishes the foreign government's willingness or ability to share or validate important information about individuals seeking to travel to the United States. Moreover, the significant presence in each of these countries of terrorist organizations, their members, and others exposed to those organizations increases the chance that conditions will be exploited to enable terrorist operatives or sympathizers to travel to the United States. Finally, once foreign nationals from these countries are admitted to the United States, it is often difficult to remove them, because many of these countries typically delay issuing, or refuse to issue, travel documents.

(e) The following are brief descriptions, taken in part from the Department of State's Country Reports on Terrorism 2015 (June 2016), of some of the conditions in six of the previously designated countries that demonstrate why their nationals continue to present heightened risks to the security of the United States:

(i) Iran. Iran has been designated as a state sponsor of terrorism since 1984 and continues to support various terrorist groups, including Hizballah, Hamas, and terrorist groups in Iraq. Iran has also been linked to support for al-Qa'ida and has permitted al-Qa'ida to transport funds and fighters through Iran to Syria and South Asia. Iran does not cooperate with the United States in counterterrorism efforts.

(ii) Libya. Libya is an active combat zone, with hostilities between the internationally recognized government and its rivals. In many parts of the country, security and law enforcement functions are provided by armed militias rather than state institutions. Violent extremist groups, including the Islamic State of Iraq and Syria (ISIS), have exploited these conditions to expand their presence in the country. The Libyan government provides some cooperation with the United States' counterterrorism efforts, but it is unable to secure thousands of miles of its land and maritime borders, enabling the illicit flow of weapons, migrants, and foreign terrorist fighters. The United States Embassy in Libya suspended its operations in 2014.

(iii) Somalia. Portions of Somalia have been terrorist safe havens. Al-Shabaab, an al-Qa'ida-affiliated terrorist group, has operated in the country for years and continues to plan and mount operations within Somalia and in neighboring countries. Somalia has porous borders, and most countries do not recognize Somali identity documents. The Somali government cooperates with the United States in some counterterrorism operations but does not have the capacity to sustain military pressure on or to investigate suspected terrorists.

(iv) Sudan. Sudan has been designated as a state sponsor of terrorism since 1993 because of its support for international terrorist groups, including Hizballah and Hamas. Historically, Sudan provided safe havens for al-Qa'ida and other terrorist groups to meet and train. Although Sudan's support to al-Qa'ida has ceased and it provides some cooperation with the United States' counterterrorism efforts, elements of core al-Qa'ida and ISIS-linked terrorist groups remain active in the country.

(v) Syria. Syria has been designated as a state sponsor of terrorism since 1979. The Syrian government is engaged in an ongoing military conflict against ISIS and others for control of portions of the country. At the same time, Syria continues to support other terrorist groups. It has allowed or encouraged extremists to pass through its territory to enter Iraq. ISIS continues to attract foreign fighters to Syria and to use its base in Syria to plot or encourage attacks around the globe, including in the United States. The United States Embassy in Syria suspended its operations in 2012. Syria does not cooperate with the United States' counterterrorism efforts.

(vi) Yemen. Yemen is the site of an ongoing conflict between the incumbent government and the Houthi-led opposition. Both ISIS and a second group, al-Qa'ida in the Arabian Peninsula (AQAP), have exploited this conflict to expand their presence in Yemen and to carry out hundreds of attacks. Weapons and other materials smuggled across Yemen's porous borders are used to finance AQAP and other terrorist activities. In 2015, the United States Embassy in Yemen suspended its operations, and embassy staff were relocated out of the country. Yemen has been supportive of, but has not been able to cooperate fully with, the United States in counterterrorism efforts.

(f) In light of the conditions in these six countries, until the assessment of current screening and vetting procedures required by section 2 of this order is completed, the risk of erroneously permitting entry of a national of one of these countries who intends to commit terrorist acts or otherwise harm the national security of the United States is unacceptably high. Accordingly, while that assessment is ongoing, I am imposing a temporary pause on the entry of nationals from Iran, Libya, Somalia, Sudan, Syria, and Yemen, subject to categorical exceptions and case-by-case waivers, as described in section 3 of this order.

(g) Iraq presents a special case. Portions of Iraq remain active combat zones. Since 2014, ISIS has had dominant influence over significant territory in northern and central Iraq. Although that influence has been significantly reduced due to the efforts and sacrifices of the Iraqi government and armed forces, working along with a United States-led coalition, the ongoing conflict has impacted the Iraqi government's capacity to secure its borders and to identify fraudulent travel documents. Nevertheless, the close cooperative relationship between the United States and the democratically elected Iraqi government, the strong United States diplomatic presence in Iraq, the significant presence of United States forces in Iraq, and Iraq's commitment to combat ISIS justify different treatment for Iraq. In particular, those Iraqi government forces that have fought to regain more than half of the territory previously dominated by ISIS have shown steadfast determination and earned enduring respect as they battle an armed group that is the common enemy of Iraq and the United States. In addition, since Executive Order 13769 was issued, the Iraqi government has expressly undertaken steps to enhance travel documentation, information sharing, and the return of Iraqi nationals subject to final orders of removal. Decisions about issuance of visas or granting admission to Iraqi nationals should be subjected to additional scrutiny to determine if applicants have connections with ISIS or other terrorist organizations, or otherwise pose a risk to either national security or public safety.

(h) Recent history shows that some of those who have entered the United States through our immigration system have proved to be threats to our national security. Since 2001, hundreds of persons born abroad have been convicted of terrorism-related crimes in the United States. They have included not just persons who came here legally on visas but also individuals who first entered the country as refugees. For example, in January 2013, two Iraqi nationals admitted to the United States as refugees in 2009 were sentenced to 40 years and to life in prison, respectively, for multiple terrorism-related offenses. And in October 2014, a native of Somalia who had been brought to the United States as a child refugee and later became a naturalized United States citizen was sentenced to 30 years in prison for attempting to use a weapon of mass destruction as part of a plot to detonate a bomb at a crowded Christmas-tree-lighting ceremony in Portland, Oregon. The Attorney General has reported to me that more than 300 persons who entered the United States as refugees are currently the subjects of counterterrorism investigations by the Federal Bureau of Investigation.

(i) Given the foregoing, the entry into the United States of foreign nationals who may commit, aid, or support acts of terrorism remains a matter of grave concern. In light of the Ninth Circuit's observation that the political branches are better suited to determine the appropriate scope of any suspensions than are the courts, and in order to avoid spending additional time pursuing litigation, I am revoking Executive Order 13769 and replacing it with this order, which expressly excludes from the suspensions categories of aliens that have prompted judicial concerns and which clarifies or refines the approach to certain other issues or categories of affected aliens.

Sec. 2. Temporary Suspension of Entry for Nationals of Countries of Particular Concern During Review Period.

(a) The Secretary of Homeland Security, in consultation with the Secretary of State and the Director of National Intelligence, shall conduct a worldwide review to identify whether, and if so what, additional information will be needed from each foreign country to adjudicate an application by a national of that country for a visa, admission, or other benefit under the INA (adjudications) in order to determine that the individual is not a security or public-safety threat. The Secretary of Homeland Security may conclude that certain information is needed from particular countries even if it is not needed from every country.

(b) The Secretary of Homeland Security, in consultation with the Secretary of State and the Director of National Intelligence, shall submit to the President a report on the results of the worldwide review described in subsection (a) of this section, including the Secretary of Homeland Security's determination of the information needed from each country for adjudications and a list of countries that do not provide adequate information, within 20 days of the effective date of this order. The Secretary of Homeland Security shall provide a copy of the report to the Secretary of State, the Attorney General, and the Director of National Intelligence.

(c) To temporarily reduce investigative burdens on relevant agencies during the review period described in subsection (a) of this section, to ensure the proper review and maximum utilization of available resources for the screening and vetting of foreign nationals, to ensure that adequate standards are established to prevent infiltration by foreign terrorists, and in light of the national security concerns referenced in section 1 of this order, I hereby proclaim, pursuant to sections 212(f) and 215(a) of the INA, 8 U.S.C. 1182(f) and 1185(a), that the unrestricted entry into the United States of nationals of Iran, Libya, Somalia, Sudan, Syria, and Yemen would be detrimental to the interests of the United States. I therefore direct that the entry into the United States of nationals of those six countries be suspended for 90 days from the effective date of this order, subject to the limitations, waivers, and exceptions set forth in sections 3 and 12 of this order.

(d) Upon submission of the report described in subsection (b) of this section regarding the information needed from each country for adjudications, the Secretary of State shall request that all foreign governments that do not supply such information regarding their nationals begin providing it within 50 days of notification.

(e) After the period described in subsection (d) of this section expires, the Secretary of Homeland Security, in consultation with the Secretary of State and the Attorney General, shall submit to the President a list of countries recommended for inclusion in a Presidential proclamation that would prohibit the entry of appropriate categories of foreign nationals of countries that have not provided the information requested until they do so or until the Secretary of Homeland Security certifies that the country has an adequate plan to do so, or has adequately shared information through other means. The Secretary of State, the Attorney General, or the Secretary of Homeland Security may also submit to the President the names of additional countries for which any of them recommends other lawful restrictions or limitations deemed necessary for the security or welfare of the United States.

(f) At any point after the submission of the list described in subsection (e) of this section, the Secretary of Homeland Security, in consultation with the Secretary of State and the Attorney General, may submit to the President the names of any additional countries recommended for similar treatment, as well as the names of any countries that they recommend should be removed from the scope of a proclamation described in subsection (e) of this section.

(g) The Secretary of State and the Secretary of Homeland Security shall submit to the President a joint report on the progress in implementing this order within 60 days of the effective date of this order, a second report within 90 days of the effective date of this order, a third report within 120 days of the effective date of this order, and a fourth report within 150 days of the effective date of this order.

Sec. 3. Scope and Implementation of Suspension.

(a) Scope. Subject to the exceptions set forth in subsection (b) of this section and any waiver under subsection (c) of this section, the suspension of entry pursuant to section 2 of this order shall apply only to foreign nationals of the designated countries who:

(i) are outside the United States on the effective date of this order;

(ii) did not have a valid visa at 5:00 p.m., eastern standard time on January 27, 2017; and

(iii) do not have a valid visa on the effective date of this order.

(b) Exceptions. The suspension of entry pursuant to section 2 of this order shall not apply to:

(i) any lawful permanent resident of the United States;

(ii) any foreign national who is admitted to or paroled into the United States on or after the effective date of this order;

(iii) any foreign national who has a document other than a visa, valid on the effective date of this order or issued on any date thereafter, that permits him or her to travel to the United States and seek entry or admission, such as an advance parole document;

(iv) any dual national of a country designated under section 2 of this order when the individual is traveling on a passport issued by a non-designated country;

(v) any foreign national traveling on a diplomatic or diplomatic-type visa, North Atlantic Treaty Organization visa, C-2 visa for travel to the United Nations, or G-1, G-2, G-3, or G-4 visa; or

(vi) any foreign national who has been granted asylum; any refugee who has already been admitted to the United States; or any individual who has been granted withholding of removal, advance parole, or protection under the Convention Against Torture.

(c) Waivers. Notwithstanding the suspension of entry pursuant to section 2 of this order, a consular officer, or, as appropriate, the Commissioner, U.S. Customs and Border Protection (CBP), or the Commissioner's delegee, may, in the consular officer's or the CBP official's discretion, decide on a case-by-case basis to authorize the issuance of a visa to, or to permit the entry of, a foreign national for whom entry is otherwise suspended if the foreign national has demonstrated to the officer's satisfaction that denying entry during the suspension period would cause undue hardship, and that his or her entry would not pose a threat to national security and would be in the national interest. Unless otherwise specified by the Secretary of Homeland Security, any waiver issued by a consular officer as part of the visa issuance process will be effective both for the issuance of a visa and any subsequent entry on that visa, but will leave all other requirements for admission or entry unchanged. Case-by-case waivers could be appropriate in circumstances such as the following:

(i) the foreign national has previously been admitted to the United States for a continuous period of work, study, or other long-term activity, is outside the United States on the effective date of this order, seeks to reenter the United States to resume that activity, and the denial of reentry during the suspension period would impair that activity;

(ii) the foreign national has previously established significant contacts with the United States but is outside the United States on the effective date of this order for work, study, or other lawful activity;

(iii) the foreign national seeks to enter the United States for significant business or professional obligations and the denial of entry during the suspension period would impair those obligations;

(iv) the foreign national seeks to enter the United States to visit or reside with a close family member (e.g., a spouse, child, or parent) who is a United States citizen, lawful permanent resident, or alien lawfully admitted on a valid nonimmigrant visa, and the denial of entry during the suspension period would cause undue hardship;

(v) the foreign national is an infant, a young child or adoptee, an individual needing urgent medical care, or someone whose entry is otherwise justified by the special circumstances of the case;

(vi) the foreign national has been employed by, or on behalf of, the United States Government (or is an eligible dependent of such an employee) and the employee can document that he or she has provided faithful and valuable service to the United States Government;

(vii) the foreign national is traveling for purposes related to an international organization designated under the International Organizations Immunities Act (IOIA), 22 U.S.C. 288 et seq., traveling for purposes of conducting meetings or business with the United States Government, or traveling to conduct business on behalf of an international organization not designated under the IOIA;

(viii) the foreign national is a landed Canadian immigrant who applies for a visa at a location within Canada; or

(ix) the foreign national is traveling as a United States Government-sponsored exchange visitor.

Sec. 4. Additional Inquiries Related to Nationals of Iraq.

An application by any Iraqi national for a visa, admission, or other immigration benefit should be subjected to thorough review, including, as appropriate, consultation with a designee of the Secretary of Defense and use of the additional information that has been obtained in the context of the close U.S.-Iraqi security partnership, since Executive Order 13769 was issued, concerning individuals suspected of ties to ISIS or other terrorist organizations and individuals coming from territories controlled or formerly controlled by ISIS. Such review shall include consideration of whether the applicant has connections with ISIS or other terrorist organizations or with territory that is or has been under the dominant influence of ISIS, as well as any other information bearing on whether the applicant may be a threat to commit acts of terrorism or otherwise threaten the national security or public safety of the United States.

Sec. 5. Implementing Uniform Screening and Vetting Standards for All Immigration Programs.

(a) The Secretary of State, the Attorney General, the Secretary of Homeland Security, and the Director of National Intelligence shall implement a program, as part of the process for adjudications, to identify individuals who seek to enter the United States on a fraudulent basis, who support terrorism, violent extremism, acts of violence toward any group or class of people within the United States, or who present a risk of causing harm subsequent to their entry. This program shall include the development of a uniform baseline for screening and vetting standards and procedures, such as in-person interviews; a database of identity documents proffered by applicants to ensure that duplicate documents are not used by multiple applicants; amended application forms that include questions aimed at identifying fraudulent answers and malicious intent; a mechanism to ensure that applicants are who they claim to be; a mechanism to assess whether applicants may commit, aid, or support any kind of violent, criminal, or terrorist acts after entering the United States; and any other appropriate means for ensuring the proper collection of all information necessary for a rigorous evaluation of all grounds of inadmissibility or grounds for the denial of other immigration benefits.

(b) The Secretary of Homeland Security, in conjunction with the Secretary of State, the Attorney General, and the Director of National Intelligence, shall submit to the President an initial report on the progress of the program described in subsection (a) of this section within 60 days of the effective date of this order, a second report within 100 days of the effective date of this order, and a third report within 200 days of the effective date of this order.

Sec. 6. Realignment of the U.S. Refugee Admissions Program for Fiscal Year 2017.

(a) The Secretary of State shall suspend travel of refugees into the United States under the USRAP, and the Secretary of Homeland Security shall suspend decisions on applications for refugee status, for 120 days after the effective date of this order, subject to waivers pursuant to subsection (c) of this section. During the 120-day period, the Secretary of State, in conjunction with the Secretary of Homeland Security and in consultation with the Director of National Intelligence, shall review the USRAP application and adjudication processes to determine what additional procedures should be used to ensure that individuals seeking admission as refugees do not pose a threat to the security and welfare of the United States, and shall implement such additional procedures. The suspension described in this subsection shall not apply to refugee applicants who, before the effective date of this order, have been formally scheduled for transit by the Department of State. The Secretary of State shall resume travel of refugees into the United States under the USRAP 120 days after the effective date of this order, and the Secretary of Homeland Security shall resume making decisions on applications for refugee status only for stateless persons and nationals of countries for which the Secretary of State, the Secretary of Homeland Security, and the Director of National Intelligence have jointly determined that the additional procedures implemented pursuant to this subsection are adequate to ensure the security and welfare of the United States.

(b) Pursuant to section 212(f) of the INA, I hereby proclaim that the entry of more than 50,000 refugees in fiscal year 2017 would be detrimental to the interests of the United States, and thus suspend any entries in excess of that number until such time as I determine that additional entries would be in the national interest.

(c) Notwithstanding the temporary suspension imposed pursuant to subsection (a) of this section, the Secretary of State and the Secretary of Homeland Security may jointly determine to admit individuals to the United States as refugees on a case-by-case basis, in their discretion, but only so long as they determine that the entry of such individuals as refugees is in the national interest and does not pose a threat to the security or welfare of the United States, including in circumstances such as the following: the individual's entry would enable the United States to conform its conduct to a preexisting international agreement or arrangement, or the denial of entry would cause undue hardship.

(d) It is the policy of the executive branch that, to the extent permitted by law and as practicable, State and local jurisdictions be granted a role in the process of determining the placement or settlement in their jurisdictions of aliens eligible to be admitted to the United States as refugees. To that end, the Secretary of State shall examine existing law to determine the extent to which, consistent with applicable law, State and local jurisdictions may have greater involvement in the process of determining the placement or resettlement of refugees in their jurisdictions, and shall devise a proposal to lawfully promote such involvement.

Sec. 7. Rescission of Exercise of Authority Relating to the Terrorism Grounds of Inadmissibility.

The Secretary of State and the Secretary of Homeland Security shall, in consultation with the Attorney General, consider rescinding the exercises of authority permitted by section 212(d)(3)(B) of the INA, 8 U.S.C. 1182(d)(3)(B), relating to the terrorism grounds of inadmissibility, as well as any related implementing directives or guidance.

Sec. 8. Expedited Completion of the Biometric Entry-Exit Tracking System.

(a) The Secretary of Homeland Security shall expedite the completion and implementation of a biometric entry exit tracking system for in-scope travelers to the United States, as recommended by the National Commission on Terrorist Attacks Upon the United States.

(b) The Secretary of Homeland Security shall submit to the President periodic reports on the progress of the directive set forth in subsection (a) of this section. The initial report shall be submitted within 100 days of the effective date of this order, a second report shall be submitted within 200 days of the effective date of this order, and a third report shall be submitted within 365 days of the effective date of this order. The Secretary of Homeland Security shall submit further reports every 180 days thereafter until the system is fully deployed and operational.

Sec. 9. Visa Interview Security.

(a) The Secretary of State shall immediately suspend the Visa Interview Waiver Program and ensure compliance with section 222 of the INA, 8 U.S.C. 1202, which requires that all individuals seeking a nonimmigrant visa undergo an in-person interview, subject to specific statutory exceptions. This suspension shall not apply to any foreign national traveling on a diplomatic or diplomatic-type visa, North Atlantic Treaty Organization visa, C-2 visa for travel to the United Nations, or G-1, G-2, G-3, or G-4 visa; traveling for purposes related to an international organization designated under the IOIA; or traveling for purposes of conducting meetings or business with the United States Government.

(b) To the extent permitted by law and subject to the availability of appropriations, the Secretary of State shall immediately expand the Consular Fellows Program, including by substantially increasing the number of Fellows, lengthening or making permanent the period of service, and making language training at the Foreign Service Institute available to Fellows for assignment to posts outside of their area of core linguistic ability, to ensure that nonimmigrant visa-interview wait times are not unduly affected.

Sec. 10. Visa Validity Reciprocity.

The Secretary of State shall review all nonimmigrant visa reciprocity agreements and arrangements to ensure that they are, with respect to each visa classification, truly reciprocal insofar as practicable with respect to validity period and fees, as required by sections 221(c) and 281 of the INA, 8 U.S.C. 1201(c) and 1351, and other treatment. If another country does not treat United States nationals seeking nonimmigrant visas in a truly reciprocal manner, the Secretary of State shall adjust the visa validity period, fee schedule, or other treatment to match the treatment of United States nationals by that foreign country, to the extent practicable.

Sec. 11. Transparency and Data Collection.

(a) To be more transparent with the American people and to implement more effectively policies and practices that serve the national interest, the Secretary of Homeland Security, in consultation with the Attorney General, shall, consistent with applicable law and national security, collect and make publicly available the following information:

(i) information regarding the number of foreign nationals in the United States who have been charged with terrorism-related offenses while in the United States; convicted of terrorism-related offenses while in the United States; or removed from the United States based on terrorism-related activity, affiliation with or provision of material support to a terrorism-related organization, or any other national-security-related reasons;

(ii) information regarding the number of foreign nationals in the United States who have been radicalized after entry into the United States and who have engaged in terrorism-related acts, or who have provided material support to terrorism-related organizations in countries that pose a threat to the United States;

(iii) information regarding the number and types of acts of gender-based violence against women, including so-called "honor killings," in the United States by foreign nationals; and

(iv) any other information relevant to public safety and security as determined by the Secretary of Homeland Security or the Attorney General, including information on the immigration status of foreign nationals charged with major offenses.

(b) The Secretary of Homeland Security shall release the initial report under subsection (a) of this section within 180 days of the effective date of this order and shall include information for the period from September 11, 2001, until the date of the initial report. Subsequent reports shall be issued every 180 days thereafter and reflect the period since the previous report.

Sec. 12. Enforcement.

(a) The Secretary of State and the Secretary of Homeland Security shall consult with appropriate domestic and international partners, including countries and organizations, to ensure efficient, effective, and appropriate implementation of the actions directed in this order.

(b) In implementing this order, the Secretary of State and the Secretary of Homeland Security shall comply with all applicable laws and regulations, including, as appropriate, those providing an opportunity for individuals to claim a fear of persecution or torture, such as the credible fear determination for aliens covered by section 235(b)(1)(A) of the INA, 8 U.S.C. 1225(b)(1)(A).

(c) No immigrant or nonimmigrant visa issued before the effective date of this order shall be revoked pursuant to this order.

(d) Any individual whose visa was marked revoked or marked canceled as a result of Executive Order 13769 shall be entitled to a travel document confirming that the individual is permitted to travel to the United States and seek entry. Any prior cancellation or revocation of a visa that was solely pursuant to Executive Order 13769 shall not be the basis of inadmissibility for any future determination about entry or admissibility.

(e) This order shall not apply to an individual who has been granted asylum, to a refugee who has already been admitted to the United States, or to an individual granted withholding of removal or protection under the Convention Against Torture. Nothing in this order shall be construed to limit the ability of an individual to seek asylum, withholding of removal, or protection under the Convention Against Torture, consistent with the laws of the United States.

Sec. 13. Revocation.

Executive Order 13769 of January 27, 2017, is revoked as of the effective date of this order.

Sec. 14. Effective Date.

This order is effective at 12:01 a.m., eastern daylight time on March 16, 2017.

Sec. 15. Severability.

(a) If any provision of this order, or the application of any provision to any person or circumstance, is held to be invalid, the remainder of this order and the application of its other provisions to any other persons or circumstances shall not be affected thereby.

(b) If any provision of this order, or the application of any provision to any person or circumstance, is held to be invalid because of the lack of certain procedural requirements, the relevant executive branch officials shall implement those procedural requirements.

Sec. 16. General Provisions.

(a) Nothing in this order shall be construed to impair or otherwise affect:

(i) the authority granted by law to an executive department or agency, or the head thereof; or

(ii) the functions of the Director of the Office of Management and Budget relating to budgetary, administrative, or legislative proposals.

(b) This order shall be implemented consistent with applicable law and subject to the availability of appropriations.

(c) This order is not intended to, and does not, create any right or benefit, substantive or procedural, enforceable at law or in equity by any party against the United States, its departments, agencies, or entities, its officers, employees, or agents, or any other person.

DONALD J. TRUMP

Executive Order 13800—Strengthening the Cybersecurity of Federal Networks and Critical Infrastructure

82 Fed. Reg. 22,391 (May 11, 2017)

By the authority vested in me as President by the Constitution and the laws of the United States of America, and to protect American innovation and values, it is hereby ordered as follows:

Section 1. Cybersecurity of Federal Networks.

(a) Policy. The executive branch operates its information technology (IT) on behalf of the American people. Its IT and data should be secured responsibly using all United States Government capabilities. The President will hold heads of executive departments and agencies (agency heads) accountable for managing cybersecurity risk to their enterprises. In addition, because risk management decisions made by agency heads can affect the risk to the executive branch as a whole, and to national security, it is also the policy of the United States to manage cybersecurity risk as an executive branch enterprise.

(b) Findings.

(i) Cybersecurity risk management comprises the full range of activities undertaken to protect IT and data from unauthorized access and other cyber threats, to maintain awareness of cyber threats, to detect anomalies and incidents adversely affecting IT and data, and to mitigate the impact of, respond to, and recover from incidents. Information sharing facilitates and supports all of these activities.

(ii) The executive branch has for too long accepted antiquated and difficult–to-defend IT.

(iii) Effective risk management involves more than just protecting IT and data currently in place. It also requires planning so that maintenance, improvements, and modernization occur in a coordinated way and with appropriate regularity.

(iv) Known but unmitigated vulnerabilities are among the highest cybersecurity risks faced by executive departments and agencies (agencies). Known vulnerabilities include using operating systems or hardware beyond the vendor's support lifecycle, declining to implement a vendor's security patch, or failing to execute security-specific configuration guidance.

(v) Effective risk management requires agency heads to lead integrated teams of senior executives with expertise in IT, security, budgeting, acquisition, law, privacy, and human resources.

(c) Risk Management.

(i) Agency heads will be held accountable by the President for implementing risk management measures commensurate with the risk and magnitude of the harm that would result from unauthorized access, use, disclosure, disruption, modification, or destruction of IT and data. They will also be held accountable by the President for ensuring that cybersecurity risk management processes are aligned with strategic, operational, and budgetary planning processes, in accordance with chapter 35, subchapter II of title 44, United States Code.

(ii) Effective immediately, each agency head shall use The Framework for Improving Critical Infrastructure Cybersecurity (the Framework) developed by the National Institute of Standards and Technology, or any successor document, to manage the agency's cybersecurity risk. Each agency head shall provide a risk management report to the Secretary of Homeland Security and the Director of the Office of Management and Budget (OMB) within 90 days of the date of this order. The risk management report shall:

(A) document the risk mitigation and acceptance choices made by each agency head as of the date of this order, including:

(1) the strategic, operational, and budgetary considerations that informed those choices; and

(2) any accepted risk, including from unmitigated vulnerabilities; and

(B) describe the agency's action plan to implement the Framework.

(iii) The Secretary of Homeland Security and the Director of OMB, consistent with chapter 35, subchapter II of title 44, United States Code, shall jointly assess each agency's risk management report to determine whether the risk mitigation and acceptance choices set forth in the reports are appropriate and sufficient to manage the cybersecurity risk to the executive branch enterprise in the aggregate (the determination).

(iv) The Director of OMB, in coordination with the Secretary of Homeland Security, with appropriate support from the Secretary of Commerce and the Administrator of General Services, and within 60 days of receipt of the agency risk management reports outlined in subsection (c)(ii) of this section, shall submit to the President, through the Assistant to the President for Homeland Security and Counterterrorism, the following:

(A) the determination; and

(B) a plan to:

(1) adequately protect the executive branch enterprise, should the determination identify insufficiencies;

(2) address immediate unmet budgetary needs necessary to manage risk to the executive branch enterprise;

(3) establish a regular process for reassessing and, if appropriate, reissuing the determination, and addressing future, recurring unmet budgetary needs necessary to manage risk to the executive branch enterprise;

(4) clarify, reconcile, and reissue, as necessary and to the extent permitted by law, all policies, standards, and guidelines issued by any agency in furtherance of chapter 35, subchapter II of title 44, United States Code, and, as necessary and to the extent permitted by law, issue policies, standards, and guidelines in furtherance of this order; and

(5) align these policies, standards, and guidelines with the Framework.

(v) The agency risk management reports described in subsection (c)(ii) of this section and the determination and plan described in subsections (c)(iii) and (iv) of this section may be classified in full or in part, as appropriate.

(vi) Effective immediately, it is the policy of the executive branch to build and maintain a modern, secure, and more resilient executive branch IT architecture.

(A) Agency heads shall show preference in their procurement for shared IT services, to the extent permitted by law, including email, cloud, and cybersecurity services.

(B) The Director of the American Technology Council shall coordinate a report to the President from the Secretary of Homeland Security, the Director of OMB, and the Administrator of General Services, in consultation with the Secretary of Commerce, as appropriate, regarding modernization of Federal IT. The report shall:

(1) be completed within 90 days of the date of this order; and

(2) describe the legal, policy, and budgetary considerations relevant to — as well as the technical feasibility and cost effectiveness, including timelines and milestones, of — transitioning all agencies, or a subset of agencies, to:

(aa) one or more consolidated network architectures; and

(bb) shared IT services, including email, cloud, and cybersecurity services.

(C) The report described in subsection (c)(vi)(B) of this section shall assess the effects of transitioning all agencies, or a subset of agencies, to shared IT services with respect to cybersecurity, including by making recommendations to ensure consistency with section 227 of the Homeland Security Act (6 U.S.C. 148) and compliance with policies and practices issued in accordance with section 3553 of title 44, United States Code. All agency heads shall supply such information concerning their current IT architectures and plans as is necessary to complete this report on time.

(vii) For any National Security System, as defined in section 3552(b)(6) of title 44, United States Code, the Secretary of Defense and the Director of National Intelligence, rather than the Secretary of Homeland Security and the Director of OMB, shall implement this order to the maximum extent feasible and appropriate. The Secretary of Defense and the Director of National Intelligence shall provide a report to the Assistant to the President for National Security Affairs and the Assistant to the President for Homeland Security and Counterterrorism describing their implementation of subsection (c) of this section within 150 days of the date of this order. The report described in this subsection shall include a justification for any deviation from the requirements of subsection (c), and may be classified in full or in part, as appropriate.

Sec. 2. Cybersecurity of Critical Infrastructure.

(a) Policy. It is the policy of the executive branch to use its authorities and capabilities to support the cybersecurity risk management efforts of the owners and operators of the Nation's critical infrastructure (as defined in section 5195c(e) of title 42, United States Code) (critical infrastructure entities), as appropriate.

(b) Support to Critical Infrastructure at Greatest Risk. The Secretary of Homeland Security, in coordination with the Secretary of Defense, the Attorney General, the Director of National Intelligence, the Director of the Federal Bureau of Investigation, the heads of appropriate sector-specific agencies, as defined in Presidential Policy Directive 21 of February 12, 2013 (Critical Infrastructure Security and Resilience) (sector-specific agencies), and all other appropriate agency heads, as identified by the Secretary of Homeland Security, shall:

(i) identify authorities and capabilities that agencies could employ to support the cybersecurity efforts of critical infrastructure entities identified pursuant to section 9 of Executive Order 13636 of February 12, 2013 (Improving Critical Infrastructure Cybersecurity), to be at greatest risk of attacks that could reasonably result in catastrophic regional or national effects on public health or safety, economic security, or national security (section 9 entities);

(ii) engage section 9 entities and solicit input as appropriate to evaluate whether and how the authorities and capabilities identified pursuant to subsection (b)(i) of this section might be employed to support cybersecurity risk management efforts and any obstacles to doing so;

(iii) provide a report to the President, which may be classified in full or in part, as appropriate, through the Assistant to the President for Homeland Security and

Counterterrorism, within 180 days of the date of this order, that includes the following:

> (A) the authorities and capabilities identified pursuant to subsection (b)(i) of this section;
>
> (B) the results of the engagement and determination required pursuant to subsection (b)(ii) of this section; and
>
> (C) findings and recommendations for better supporting the cybersecurity risk management efforts of section 9 entities; and

> (iv) provide an updated report to the President on an annual basis thereafter.

(c) Supporting Transparency in the Marketplace. The Secretary of Homeland Security, in coordination with the Secretary of Commerce, shall provide a report to the President, through the Assistant to the President for Homeland Security and Counterterrorism, that examines the sufficiency of existing Federal policies and practices to promote appropriate market transparency of cybersecurity risk management practices by critical infrastructure entities, with a focus on publicly traded critical infrastructure entities, within 90 days of the date of this order.

(d) Resilience Against Botnets and Other Automated, Distributed Threats. The Secretary of Commerce and the Secretary of Homeland Security shall jointly lead an open and transparent process to identify and promote action by appropriate stakeholders to improve the resilience of the internet and communications ecosystem and to encourage collaboration with the goal of dramatically reducing threats perpetrated by automated and distributed attacks (e.g., botnets). The Secretary of Commerce and the Secretary of Homeland Security shall consult with the Secretary of Defense, the Attorney General, the Director of the Federal Bureau of Investigation, the heads of sector-specific agencies, the Chairs of the Federal Communications Commission and Federal Trade Commission, other interested agency heads, and appropriate stakeholders in carrying out this subsection. Within 240 days of the date of this order, the Secretary of Commerce and the Secretary of Homeland Security shall make publicly available a preliminary report on this effort. Within 1 year of the date of this order, the Secretaries shall submit a final version of this report to the President.

(e) Assessment of Electricity Disruption Incident Response Capabilities. The Secretary of Energy and the Secretary of Homeland Security, in consultation with the Director of National Intelligence, with State, local, tribal, and territorial governments, and with others as appropriate, shall jointly assess:

> (i) the potential scope and duration of a prolonged power outage associated with a significant cyber incident, as defined in Presidential Policy Directive 41 of July 26, 2016 (United States Cyber Incident Coordination), against the United States electric subsector;
>
> (ii) the readiness of the United States to manage the consequences of such an incident; and
>
> (iii) any gaps or shortcomings in assets or capabilities required to mitigate the consequences of such an incident.

> The assessment shall be provided to the President, through the Assistant to the President for Homeland Security and Counterterrorism, within 90 days of the date of this order, and may be classified in full or in part, as appropriate.

(f) Department of Defense Warfighting Capabilities and Industrial Base. Within 90 days of the date of this order, the Secretary of Defense, the Secretary of Homeland Security, and the Director of the Federal Bureau of Investigation, in coordination with the Director of National Intelligence, shall provide a report to the President, through the Assistant to the President for National Security Affairs and the Assistant to the President for Homeland

Security and Counterterrorism, on cybersecurity risks facing the defense industrial base, including its supply chain, and United States military platforms, systems, networks, and capabilities, and recommendations for mitigating these risks. The report may be classified in full or in part, as appropriate.

Sec. 3. Cybersecurity for the Nation.

(a) Policy. To ensure that the internet remains valuable for future generations, it is the policy of the executive branch to promote an open, interoperable, reliable, and secure internet that fosters efficiency, innovation, communication, and economic prosperity, while respecting privacy and guarding against disruption, fraud, and theft. Further, the United States seeks to support the growth and sustainment of a workforce that is skilled in cybersecurity and related fields as the foundation for achieving our objectives in cyberspace.

(b) Deterrence and Protection. Within 90 days of the date of this order, the Secretary of State, the Secretary of the Treasury, the Secretary of Defense, the Attorney General, the Secretary of Commerce, the Secretary of Homeland Security, and the United States Trade Representative, in coordination with the Director of National Intelligence, shall jointly submit a report to the President, through the Assistant to the President for National Security Affairs and the Assistant to the President for Homeland Security and Counterterrorism, on the Nation's strategic options for deterring adversaries and better protecting the American people from cyber threats.

(c) International Cooperation. As a highly connected nation, the United States is especially dependent on a globally secure and resilient internet and must work with allies and other partners toward maintaining the policy set forth in this section. Within 45 days of the date of this order, the Secretary of State, the Secretary of the Treasury, the Secretary of Defense, the Secretary of Commerce, and the Secretary of Homeland Security, in coordination with the Attorney General and the Director of the Federal Bureau of Investigation, shall submit reports to the President on their international cybersecurity priorities, including those concerning investigation, attribution, cyber threat information sharing, response, capacity building, and cooperation. Within 90 days of the submission of the reports, and in coordination with the agency heads listed in this subsection, and any other agency heads as appropriate, the Secretary of State shall provide a report to the President, through the Assistant to the President for Homeland Security and Counterterrorism, documenting an engagement strategy for international cooperation in cybersecurity.

(d) Workforce Development. In order to ensure that the United States maintains a long-term cybersecurity advantage:

(i) The Secretary of Commerce and the Secretary of Homeland Security, in consultation with the Secretary of Defense, the Secretary of Labor, the Secretary of Education, the Director of the Office of Personnel Management, and other agencies identified jointly by the Secretary of Commerce and the Secretary of Homeland Security, shall:

(A) jointly assess the scope and sufficiency of efforts to educate and train the American cybersecurity workforce of the future, including cybersecurity-related education curricula, training, and apprenticeship programs, from primary through higher education; and

(B) within 120 days of the date of this order, provide a report to the President, through the Assistant to the President for Homeland Security and Counterterrorism, with findings and recommendations regarding how to support the growth and sustainment of the Nation's cybersecurity workforce in both the public and private sectors.

(ii) The Director of National Intelligence, in consultation with the heads of other agencies identified by the Director of National Intelligence, shall:

(A) review the workforce development efforts of potential foreign cyber peers in order to help identify foreign workforce development practices likely to affect long-term United States cybersecurity competitiveness; and

(B) within 60 days of the date of this order, provide a report to the President through the Assistant to the President for Homeland Security and Counterterrorism on the findings of the review carried out pursuant to subsection (d)(ii)(A) of this section.

(iii) The Secretary of Defense, in coordination with the Secretary of Commerce, the Secretary of Homeland Security, and the Director of National Intelligence, shall:

(A) assess the scope and sufficiency of United States efforts to ensure that the United States maintains or increases its advantage in national-security-related cyber capabilities; and

(B) within 150 days of the date of this order, provide a report to the President, through the Assistant to the President for Homeland Security and Counterterrorism, with findings and recommendations on the assessment carried out pursuant to subsection (d)(iii)(A) of this section.

(iv) The reports described in this subsection may be classified in full or in part, as appropriate.

Sec. 4. Definitions. For the purposes of this order:

(a) The term "appropriate stakeholders" means any non-executive-branch person or entity that elects to participate in an open and transparent process established by the Secretary of Commerce and the Secretary of Homeland Security under section 2(d) of this order.

(b) The term "information technology" (IT) has the meaning given to that term in section 11101(6) of title 40, United States Code, and further includes hardware and software systems of agencies that monitor and control physical equipment and processes.

(c) The term "IT architecture" refers to the integration and implementation of IT within an agency.

(d) The term "network architecture" refers to the elements of IT architecture that enable or facilitate communications between two or more IT assets.

Sec. 5. General Provisions. (a) Nothing in this order shall be construed to impair or otherwise affect:

(i) the authority granted by law to an executive department or agency, or the head thereof; or

(ii) the functions of the Director of OMB relating to budgetary, administrative, or legislative proposals.

(b) This order shall be implemented consistent with applicable law and subject to the availability of appropriations.

(c) All actions taken pursuant to this order shall be consistent with requirements and authorities to protect intelligence and law enforcement sources and methods. Nothing in this order shall be construed to supersede measures established under authority of law to protect the security and integrity of specific activities and associations that are in direct support of intelligence or law enforcement operations.

(d) This order is not intended to, and does not, create any right or benefit, substantive or procedural, enforceable at law or in equity by any party against the United States, its departments, agencies, or entities, its officers, employees, or agents, or any other person.

DONALD J. TRUMP

Executive Order 13808—Imposing Additional Sanctions with Respect to the Situation in Venezuela

82 Fed. Reg. 41,155 (Aug. 24, 2017)

By the authority vested in me as President by the Constitution and the laws of the United States of America, including the International Emergency Economic Powers Act (50 U.S.C. 1701 et seq.) (IEEPA), the National Emergencies Act (50 U.S.C. 1601 et seq.), and section 301 of title 3, United States Code,

I, DONALD J. TRUMP, President of the United States of America, in order to take additional steps with respect to the national emergency declared in Executive Order 13692 of March 8, 2015, and particularly in light of recent actions and policies of the Government of Venezuela, including serious abuses of human rights and fundamental freedoms; responsibility for the deepening humanitarian crisis in Venezuela; establishment of an illegitimate Constituent Assembly, which has usurped the power of the democratically elected National Assembly and other branches of the Government of Venezuela; rampant public corruption; and ongoing repression and persecution of, and violence toward, the political opposition, hereby order as follows:

Section 1.

(a) All transactions related to, provision of financing for, and other dealings in the following by a United States person or within the United States are prohibited:

(i) new debt with a maturity of greater than 90 days of Petroleos de Venezuela, S.A. (PdVSA);

(ii) new debt with a maturity of greater than 30 days, or new equity, of the Government of Venezuela, other than debt of PdVSA covered by subsection (a)(i) of this section;

(iii) bonds issued by the Government of Venezuela prior to the effective date of this order; or

(iv) dividend payments or other distributions of profits to the Government of Venezuela from any entity owned or controlled, directly or indirectly, by the Government of Venezuela.

(b) The purchase, directly or indirectly, by a United States person or within the United States, of securities from the Government of Venezuela, other than securities qualifying as new debt with a maturity of less than or equal to 90 or 30 days as covered by subsections (a)(i) or (a)(ii) of this section, respectively, is prohibited.

(c) The prohibitions in subsections (a) and (b) of this section apply except to the extent provided by statutes, or in regulations, orders, directives, or licenses that may be issued pursuant to this order, and notwithstanding any contract entered into or any license or permit granted before the effective date of this order.

Sec. 2.

(a) Any transaction that evades or avoids, has the purpose of evading or avoiding, causes a violation of, or attempts to violate any of the prohibitions set forth in this order is prohibited.

(b) Any conspiracy formed to violate any of the prohibitions set forth in this order is prohibited.

Sec. 3.

For the purposes of this order:

(a) the term "person" means an individual or entity;

(b) the term "entity" means a partnership, association, trust, joint venture, corporation, group, subgroup, or other organization;

(c) the term "United States person" means any United States citizen, permanent resident alien, entity organized under the laws of the United States or any jurisdiction within the United States (including foreign branches), or any person in the United States; and

(d) the term "Government of Venezuela" means the Government of Venezuela, any political subdivision, agency, or instrumentality thereof, including the Central Bank of Venezuela and PdVSA, and any person owned or controlled by, or acting for or on behalf of, the Government of Venezuela.

Sec. 4.

The Secretary of the Treasury, in consultation with the Secretary of State, is hereby authorized to take such actions, including promulgating rules and regulations, and to employ all powers granted to the President by IEEPA as may be necessary to implement this order. The Secretary of the Treasury may, consistent with applicable law, redelegate any of these functions to other officers and executive departments and agencies of the United States Government. All agencies of the United States Government shall take all appropriate measures within their authority to carry out the provisions of this order.

Sec. 5.

For those persons whose property or interests in property are affected by this order who might have a constitutional presence in the United States, I find that because of the ability to transfer funds or other assets instantaneously, prior notice to such persons of measures to be taken pursuant to this order would render those measures ineffectual. I therefore determine that for these measures to be effective in addressing the national emergency declared in Executive Order 13692, there need be no prior notice of a listing or determination made pursuant to this order.

Sec. 6.

This order is not intended to, and does not, create any right or benefit, substantive or procedural, enforceable at law or in equity by any party against the United States, its departments, agencies, or entities, its officers, employees, or agents, or any other person.

Sec. 7. This order is effective at 12:01 a.m. eastern daylight time on August 25, 2017.

DONALD J. TRUMP

Executive Order 13810—Imposing Additional Sanctions with Respect to North Korea

82 Fed. Reg. 44,705 (Sept. 20, 2017)

By the authority vested in me as President by the Constitution and the laws of the United States of America, including the International Emergency Economic Powers Act (50 U.S.C. 1701 et seq.) (IEEPA), the National Emergencies Act (50 U.S.C. 1601 et seq.), the United Nations Participation Act of 1945 (22 U.S.C. 287c) (UNPA), section 1 of title II of Public Law 65-24, ch. 30, June 15, 1917, as amended (50 U.S.C. 191), sections 212(f) and 215(a) of the Immigration and Nationality Act of 1952 (8 U.S.C. 1182(f) and 1185(a)), and section 301 of title 3, United States Code; and in view of United Nations Security Council Resolution (UNSCR) 2321 of November 30, 2016, UNSCR 2356 of June 2, 2017, UNSCR 2371 of August 5, 2017, and UNSCR 2375 of September 11, 2017, I, DONALD J. TRUMP, President of the United States of America, find that:

The provocative, destabilizing, and repressive actions and policies of the Government of North Korea, including its intercontinental ballistic missile launches of July 3 and July 28, 2017, and its nuclear test of September 2, 2017, each of which violated its obligations under numerous UNSCRs and contravened its commitments under the September 19, 2005, Joint Statement of the SixParty Talks; its commission of serious human rights abuses; and its use of funds generated through international trade to support its nuclear and missile programs and weapons proliferation, constitute a continuing threat to the national security, foreign policy, and economy of the United States, and a disturbance of the international relations of the United States.

In order to take further steps with respect to the national emergency declared in Executive Order 13466 of June 26, 2008, as modified in scope by and relied upon for additional steps in subsequent Executive Orders, I hereby find, determine, and order:

Section 1.

(a) All property and interests in property that are in the United States, that hereafter come within the United States, or that are or hereafter come within the possession or control of any United States person of the following persons are blocked and may not be transferred, paid, exported, withdrawn, or otherwise dealt in:

Any person determined by the Secretary of the Treasury, in consultation with the Secretary of State:

(i) to operate in the construction, energy, financial services, fishing, information technology, manufacturing, medical, mining, textiles, or transportation industries in North Korea;

(ii) to own, control, or operate any port in North Korea, including any seaport, airport, or land port of entry;

(iii) to have engaged in at least one significant importation from or exportation to North Korea of any goods, services, or technology;

(iv) to be a North Korean person, including a North Korean person that has engaged in commercial activity that generates revenue for the Government of North Korea or the Workers' Party of Korea;

731

(v) to have materially assisted, sponsored, or provided financial, material, or technological support for, or goods or services to or in support of, any person whose property and interests in property are blocked pursuant to this order; or

(vi) to be owned or controlled by, or to have acted or purported to act for or on behalf of, directly or indirectly, any person whose property and interests in property are blocked pursuant to this order.

(b) The prohibitions in subsection (a) of this section apply except to the extent provided by statutes, or in regulations, orders, directives, or licenses that may be issued pursuant to this order, and notwithstanding any contract entered into or any license or permit granted before the effective date of this order. The prohibitions in subsection (a) of this section are in addition to export control authorities implemented by the Department of Commerce.

(c) I hereby determine that the making of donations of the types of articles specified in section 203(b)(2) of IEEPA (50 U.S.C. 1702(b)(2)) by, to, or for the benefit of any person whose property and interests in property are blocked pursuant to subsection (a) of this section would seriously impair my ability to deal with the national emergency declared in Executive Order 13466, and I hereby prohibit such donations as provided by subsection (a) of this section.

(d) The prohibitions in subsection (a) of this section include:

(i) the making of any contribution or provision of funds, goods, or services by, to, or for the benefit of any person whose property and interests in property are blocked pursuant to subsection (a) of this section; and

(ii) the receipt of any contribution or provision of funds, goods, or services from any such person.

Sec. 2.

(a) No aircraft in which a foreign person has an interest that has landed at a place in North Korea may land at a place in the United States within 180 days after departure from North Korea.

(b) No vessel in which a foreign person has an interest that has called at a port in North Korea within the previous 180 days, and no vessel in which a foreign person has an interest that has engaged in a shiptoship transfer with such a vessel within the previous 180 days, may call at a port in the United States.

(c) The prohibitions in subsections (a) and (b) of this section apply except to the extent provided by statutes, or in regulations, orders, directives, or licenses that may be issued pursuant to this order, and notwithstanding any contract entered into or any license or permit granted before the effective date of this order.

Sec. 3.

(a) All funds that are in the United States, that hereafter come within the United States, or that are or hereafter come within the possession or control of any United States person and that originate from, are destined for, or pass through a foreign bank account that has been determined by the Secretary of the Treasury to be owned or controlled by a North Korean person, or to have been used to transfer funds in which any North Korean person has an interest, are blocked and may not be transferred, paid, exported, withdrawn, or otherwise dealt in.

(b) No United States person, wherever located, may approve, finance, facilitate, or guarantee a transaction by a foreign person where the transaction by that foreign person would be prohibited by subsection (a) of this section if performed by a United States person or within the United States.

(c) The prohibitions in subsections (a) and (b) of this section apply except to the extent provided by statutes, or in regulations, orders, directives, or licenses that may be issued pursuant to this order, and notwithstanding any contract entered into or any license or permit granted before the effective date of this order.

Sec. 4.

(a) The Secretary of the Treasury, in consultation with the Secretary of State, is hereby authorized to impose on a foreign financial institution the sanctions described in subsection (b) of this section upon determining that the foreign financial institution has, on or after the effective date of this order:

    (i) knowingly conducted or facilitated any significant transaction on behalf of any person whose property and interests in property are blocked pursuant to Executive Order 13551 of August 30, 2010, Executive Order 13687 of January 2, 2015, Executive Order 13722 of March 15, 2016, or this order, or of any person whose property and interests in property are blocked pursuant to Executive Order 13382 in connection with North Korea‑related activities; or

    (ii) knowingly conducted or facilitated any significant transaction in connection with trade with North Korea.

(b) With respect to any foreign financial institution determined by the Secretary of the Treasury, in consultation with the Secretary of State, in accordance with this section to meet the criteria set forth in subsection (a)(i) or (a)(ii) of this section, the Secretary of the Treasury may:

    (i) prohibit the opening and prohibit or impose strict conditions on the maintenance of correspondent accounts or payable‑through accounts in the United States; or

    (ii) block all property and interests in property that are in the United States, that hereafter come within the United States, or that are or hereafter come within the possession or control of any United States person of such foreign financial institution, and provide that such property and interests in property may not be transferred, paid, exported, withdrawn, or otherwise dealt in.

(c) The prohibitions in subsection (b) of this section apply except to the extent provided by statutes, or in regulations, orders, directives, or licenses that may be issued pursuant to this order, and notwithstanding any contract entered into or any license or permit granted before the effective date of this order.

(d) I hereby determine that the making of donations of the types of articles specified in section 203(b)(2) of IEEPA (50 U.S.C. 1702(b)(2)) by, to, or for the benefit of any person whose property and interests in property are blocked pursuant to subsection (b)(ii) of this section would seriously impair my ability to deal with the national emergency declared in Executive Order 13466, and I hereby prohibit such donations as provided by subsection (b)(ii) of this section.

(e) The prohibitions in subsection (b)(ii) of this section include:

    (i) the making of any contribution or provision of funds, goods, or services by, to, or for the benefit of any person whose property and interests in property are blocked pursuant to subsection (b)(ii) of this section; and

    (ii) the receipt of any contribution or provision of funds, goods, or services from any such person.

Sec. 5.

The unrestricted immigrant and nonimmigrant entry into the United States of aliens determined to meet one or more of the criteria in section 1(a) of this order would be detrimental to the interests of the United States, and the entry of such persons into the United States, as immigrants or nonimmigrants, is therefore hereby suspended. Such persons shall be treated as persons covered by section 1 of Proclamation 8693 of July 24, 2011 (Suspension of Entry of Aliens Subject to United Nations Security Council Travel Bans and International Emergency Economic Powers Act Sanctions).

Sec. 6.

(a) Any transaction that evades or avoids, has the purpose of evading or avoiding, causes a violation of, or attempts to violate any of the prohibitions set forth in this order is prohibited.

(b) Any conspiracy formed to violate any of the prohibitions set forth in this order is prohibited.

Sec. 7.

Nothing in this order shall prohibit transactions for the conduct of the official business of the Federal Government or the United Nations (including its specialized agencies, programmes, funds, and related organizations) by employees, grantees, or contractors thereof.

Sec. 8.

For the purposes of this order:

(a) the term "person" means an individual or entity;

(b) the term "entity" means a partnership, association, trust, joint venture, corporation, group, subgroup, or other organization;

(c) the term "United States person" means any United States citizen, permanent resident alien, entity organized under the laws of the United States or any jurisdiction within the United States (including foreign branches), or any person in the United States;

(d) the term "North Korean person" means any North Korean citizen, North Korean permanent resident alien, or entity organized under the laws of North Korea or any jurisdiction within North Korea (including foreign branches). For the purposes of section 1 of this order, the term "North Korean person" shall not include any United States citizen, any permanent resident alien of the United States, any alien lawfully admitted to the United States, or any alien holding a valid United States visa;

(e) the term "foreign financial institution" means any foreign entity that is engaged in the business of accepting deposits, making, granting, transferring, holding, or brokering loans or credits, or purchasing or selling foreign exchange, securities, commodity futures or options, or procuring purchasers and sellers thereof, as principal or agent. The term includes, among other entities, depository institutions; banks; savings banks; money service businesses; trust companies; securities brokers and dealers; commodity futures and options brokers and dealers; forward contract and foreign exchange merchants; securities and commodities exchanges; clearing corporations; investment companies; employee benefit plans; dealers in precious metals, stones, or jewels; and holding companies, affiliates, or subsidiaries of any of the foregoing. The term does not include the international financial institutions identified in 22 U.S.C. 262r(c)(2), the International Fund for Agricultural Development, the North American Development Bank, or any other international financial institution so notified by the Secretary of the Treasury; and

(f) the term "knowingly," with respect to conduct, a circumstance, or a result, means that a person has actual knowledge, or should have known, of the conduct, the circumstance, or the result.

Sec. 9.

For those persons whose property and interests in property are blocked pursuant to this order who might have a constitutional presence in the United States, I find that because of the ability to transfer funds or other assets instantaneously, prior notice to such persons of measures to be taken pursuant to this order would render those measures ineffectual. I therefore determine that for these measures to be effective in addressing the national emergency declared in Executive Order 13466, there need be no prior notice of a listing or determination made pursuant to this order.

Sec. 10.

The Secretary of the Treasury, in consultation with the Secretary of State, is hereby authorized to take such actions, including adopting rules and regulations, and to employ all powers granted to me by IEEPA and UNPA as may be necessary to implement this order. The Secretary of the Treasury may, consistent with applicable law, redelegate any of these functions to other officers and agencies of the United States. All agencies shall take all appropriate measures within their authority to implement this order.

Sec. 11.

This order is effective at 12:01 a.m., Eastern Daylight Time, September 21, 2017.

Sec. 12. This order is not intended to, and does not, create any right or benefit, substantive or procedural, enforceable at law or in equity by any party against the United States, its departments, agencies, or entities, its officers, employees, or agents, or any other person.

DONALD J. TRUMP

Executive Order 13818—Blocking the Property of Persons Involved in Serious Human Rights Abuse or Corruption

82 Fed. Reg. 60,839 (Dec. 20, 2017)

By the authority vested in me as President by the Constitution and the laws of the United States of America, including the International Emergency Economic Powers Act (50 U.S.C. 1701 et seq.) (IEEPA), the National Emergencies Act (50 U.S.C. 1601 et seq.) (NEA), the Global Magnitsky Human Rights Accountability Act (Public Law 114-328) (the "Act"), section 212(f) of the Immigration and Nationality Act of 1952 (8 U.S.C. 1182(f)) (INA), and section 301 of title 3, United States Code,

I, DONALD J. TRUMP, President of the United States of America, find that the prevalence and severity of human rights abuse and corruption that have their source, in whole or in substantial part, outside the United States, such as those committed or directed by persons listed in the Annex to this order, have reached such scope and gravity that they threaten the stability of international political and economic systems. Human rights abuse and corruption undermine the values that form an essential foundation of stable, secure, and functioning societies; have devastating impacts on individuals; weaken democratic institutions; degrade the rule of law; perpetuate violent conflicts; facilitate the activities of dangerous persons; and undermine economic markets. The United States seeks to impose tangible and significant consequences on those who commit serious human rights abuse or engage in corruption, as well as to protect the financial system of the United States from abuse by these same persons.

I therefore determine that serious human rights abuse and corruption around the world constitute an unusual and extraordinary threat to the national security, foreign policy, and economy of the United States, and I hereby declare a national emergency to deal with that threat.

I hereby determine and order:

Section 1.

(a) All property and interests in property that are in the United States, that hereafter come within the United States, or that are or hereafter come within the possession or control of any United States person of the following persons are blocked and may not be transferred, paid, exported, withdrawn, or otherwise dealt in:

(i) the persons listed in the Annex to this order;

(ii) any foreign person determined by the Secretary of the Treasury, in consultation with the Secretary of State and the Attorney General:

(A) to be responsible for or complicit in, or to have directly or indirectly engaged in, serious human rights abuse;

(B) to be a current or former government official, or a person acting for or on behalf of such an official, who is responsible for or complicit in, or has directly or indirectly engaged in:

(1) corruption, including the misappropriation of state assets, the expropriation of private assets for personal gain, corruption related to government contracts or the extraction of natural resources, or bribery; or

(2) the transfer or the facilitation of the transfer of the proceeds of corruption;

(C) to be or have been a leader or official of:

(1) an entity, including any government entity, that has engaged in, or whose members have engaged in, any of the activities described in subsections (ii)(A), (ii)(B)(1), or (ii)(B)(2) of this section relating to the leader's or official's tenure; or

(2) an entity whose property and interests in property are blocked pursuant to this order as a result of activities related to the leader's or official's tenure; or

(D) to have attempted to engage in any of the activities described in subsections (ii)(A), (ii)(B)(1), or (ii)(B)(2) of this section; and

(iii) any person determined by the Secretary of the Treasury, in consultation with the Secretary of State and the Attorney General:

(A) to have materially assisted, sponsored, or provided financial, material, or technological support for, or goods or services to or in support of:

(1) any activity described in subsections (ii)(A), (ii)(B)(1), or (ii)(B)(2) of this section that is conducted by a foreign person;

(2) any person whose property and interests in property are blocked pursuant to this order; or

(3) any entity, including any government entity, that has engaged in, or whose members have engaged in, any of the activities described in subsections (ii)(A), (ii)(B)(1), or (ii)(B)(2) of this section, where the activity is conducted by a foreign person;

(B) to be owned or controlled by, or to have acted or purported to act for or on behalf of, directly or indirectly, any person whose property and interests in property are blocked pursuant to this order; or

(C) to have attempted to engage in any of the activities described in subsections (iii)(A) or (B) of this section.

(b) The prohibitions in subsection (a) of this section apply except to the extent provided by statutes, or in regulations, orders, directives, or licenses that may be issued pursuant to this order, and notwithstanding any contract entered into or any license or permit granted before the effective date of this order.

Sec. 2.

The unrestricted immigrant and nonimmigrant entry into the United States of aliens determined to meet one or more of the criteria in section 1 of this order would be detrimental to the interests of the United States, and the entry of such persons into the United States, as immigrants or nonimmigrants, is hereby suspended. Such persons shall be treated as persons covered by section 1 of Proclamation 8693 of July 24, 2011 (Suspension of Entry of Aliens Subject to United Nations Security Council Travel Bans and International Emergency Economic Powers Act Sanctions).

Sec. 3.

I hereby determine that the making of donations of the types of articles specified in section 203(b)(2) of IEEPA (50 U.S.C. 1702(b)(2)) by, to, or for the benefit of any person whose property and interests in property are blocked pursuant to this order would seriously impair my ability to deal with the national emergency declared in this order, and I hereby prohibit such donations as provided by section 1 of this order.

Sec. 4.

The prohibitions in section 1 include:

(a) the making of any contribution or provision of funds, goods, or services by, to, or for the benefit of any person whose property and interests in property are blocked pursuant to this order; and

(b) the receipt of any contribution or provision of funds, goods, or services from any such person.

Sec. 5.

(a) Any transaction that evades or avoids, has the purpose of evading or avoiding, causes a violation of, or attempts to violate any of the prohibitions set forth in this order is prohibited.

(b) Any conspiracy formed to violate any of the prohibitions set forth in this order is prohibited.

Sec. 6.

For the purposes of this order:

(a) the term "person" means an individual or entity;

(b) the term "entity" means a partnership, association, trust, joint venture, corporation, group, subgroup, or other organization; and

(c) the term "United States person" means any United States citizen, permanent resident alien, entity organized under the laws of the United States or any jurisdiction within the United States (including foreign branches), or any person in the United States.

Sec. 7.

For those persons whose property and interests in property are blocked pursuant to this order who might have a constitutional presence in the United States, I find that because of the ability to transfer funds or other assets instantaneously, prior notice to such persons of measures to be taken pursuant to this order would render those measures ineffectual. I therefore determine that for these measures to be effective in addressing the national emergency declared in this order, there need be no prior notice of a listing or determination made pursuant to this order.

Sec. 8.

The Secretary of the Treasury, in consultation with the Secretary of State, is hereby authorized to take such actions, including adopting rules and regulations, and to employ all powers granted to me by IEEPA and the Act as may be necessary to implement this order and section 1263(a) of the Act with respect to the determinations provided for therein. The Secretary of the Treasury may, consistent with applicable law, redelegate any of these functions to other officers and agencies of the United States. All agencies shall take all appropriate measures within their authority to implement this order.

Sec. 9.

The Secretary of State is hereby authorized to take such actions, including adopting rules and regulations, and to employ all powers granted to me by IEEPA, the INA, and the Act as may be necessary to carry out section 2 of this order and, in consultation with the Secretary of the Treasury, the reporting requirement in section 1264(a) of the Act with respect to the reports provided for in section 1264(b)(2) of that Act. The Secretary of State may, consistent with applicable law, redelegate any of these functions to other officers and agencies of the United States consistent with applicable law.

Sec. 10.

The Secretary of the Treasury, in consultation with the Secretary of State and the Attorney General, is hereby authorized to determine that circumstances no longer warrant the blocking of the property and interests in property of a person listed in the Annex to this order, and to take necessary action to give effect to that determination.

Sec. 11.

The Secretary of the Treasury, in consultation with the Secretary of State, is hereby authorized to submit recurring and final reports to the Congress on the national emergency declared in this order, consistent with section 401(c) of the NEA (50 U.S.C. 1641(c)) and section 204(c) of IEEPA (50 U.S.C. 1703(c)).

Sec. 12.

This order is effective at 12:01 a.m., Eastern Standard Time, December 21, 2017.

Sec. 13.

This order is not intended to, and does not, create any right or benefit, substantive or procedural, enforceable at law or in equity by any party against the United States, its departments, agencies, or entities, its officers, employees, or agents, or any other person.

DONALD J. TRUMP

Executive Order 13823—
Protecting America Through Lawful Detention of Terrorists

83 Fed. Reg. 4,831 (Jan. 30, 2018)

By the authority vested in me as President by the Constitution and the laws of the United States of America, it is hereby ordered as follows:

Section 1. Findings.

(a) Consistent with long-standing law of war principles and applicable law, the United States may detain certain persons captured in connection with an armed conflict for the duration of the conflict.

(b) Following the terrorist attacks of September 11, 2001, the 2001 Authorization for Use of Military Force (AUMF) and other authorities authorized the United States to detain certain persons who were a part of or substantially supported al-Qa'ida, the Taliban, or associated forces engaged in hostilities against the United States or its coalition partners. Today, the United States remains engaged in an armed conflict with al-Qa'ida, the Taliban, and associated forces, including with the Islamic State of Iraq and Syria.

(c) The detention operations at the U.S. Naval Station Guantánamo Bay are legal, safe, humane, and conducted consistent with United States and international law.

(d) Those operations are continuing given that a number of the remaining individuals at the detention facility are being prosecuted in military commissions, while others must be detained to protect against continuing, significant threats to the security of the United States, as determined by periodic reviews.

(e) Given that some of the current detainee population represent the most difficult and dangerous cases from among those historically detained at the facility, there is significant reason for concern regarding their reengagement in hostilities should they have the opportunity.

Sec. 2. Status of Detention Facilities at U.S. Naval Station Guantánamo Bay.

(a) Section 3 of Executive Order 13492 of January 22, 2009 (Review and Disposition of Individuals Detained at the Guantánamo Bay Naval Base and Closure of Detention Facilities), ordering the closure of detention facilities at U.S. Naval Station Guantánamo Bay, is hereby revoked.

(b) Detention operations at U.S. Naval Station Guantánamo Bay shall continue to be conducted consistent with all applicable United States and international law, including the Detainee Treatment Act of 2005.

(c) In addition, the United States may transport additional detainees to U.S. Naval Station Guantánamo Bay when lawful and necessary to protect the Nation.

(d) Within 90 days of the date of this order, the Secretary of Defense shall, in consultation with the Secretary of State, the Attorney General, the Secretary of Homeland Security, the Director of National Intelligence, and the heads of any other appropriate executive departments and agencies as determined by the Secretary of Defense, recommend policies to the President regarding the disposition of individuals captured in connection with an armed conflict, including policies governing transfer of individuals to U.S. Naval Station Guantánamo Bay.

(e) Unless charged in or subject to a judgment of conviction by a military commission, any detainees transferred to U.S. Naval Station Guantánamo Bay after the date of this order shall be subject to the procedures for periodic review established in Executive Order 13567 of March 7, 2011 (Periodic Review of Individuals Detained at Guantánamo Bay Naval Station Start Printed Page 4832Pursuant to the Authorization for Use of Military Force), to determine whether continued law of war detention is necessary to protect against a significant threat to the security of the United States.

Sec. 3. Rules of Construction.

(a) Nothing in this order shall prevent the Secretary of Defense from transferring any individual away from the U.S. Naval Station Guantánamo Bay when appropriate, including to effectuate an order affecting the disposition of that individual issued by a court or competent tribunal of the United States having lawful jurisdiction.

(b) Nothing in this order shall be construed to affect existing law or authorities relating to the detention of United States citizens, lawful permanent residents of the United States, or any persons who are captured or arrested in the United States.

(c) Nothing in this order shall prevent the Attorney General from, as appropriate, investigating, detaining, and prosecuting a terrorist subject to the criminal laws and jurisdiction of the United States.

Sec. 4. General Provisions.

(a) Nothing in this order shall be construed to impair or otherwise affect:

> (i) the authority granted by law to an executive department or agency, or the head thereof; or
>
> (ii) the functions of the Director of the Office of Management and Budget relating to budgetary, administrative, or legislative proposals.

(b) This order shall be implemented consistent with applicable law and subject to the availability of appropriations.

(c) This order is not intended to, and does not, create any right or benefit, substantive or procedural, enforceable at law or in equity by any party against the United States, its departments, agencies, or entities, its officers, employees, or agents, or any other person.

Executive Order 13833—Enhancing the Effectiveness of Agency Chief Information Officers

83 Fed. Reg. 23,345 (May 15, 2018)

By the authority vested in me as President by the Constitution and the laws of the United States of America, it is hereby ordered as follows:

Section 1. Purpose.

The Federal Government spends more than $90 billion annually on information technology (IT). The vast majority of this sum is consumed in maintaining legacy IT infrastructure that is often ineffective and more costly than modern technologies. Modern IT systems would enable agencies to reduce costs, mitigate cybersecurity risks, and deliver improved services to the American people. While the recently enacted Modernizing Government Technology Act will provide needed financial resources to help transition agencies to more effective, efficient, and secure technologies, more can be done to improve management of IT resources. Department and agency (agency) Chief Information Officers (CIOs) generally do not have adequate visibility into, or control over, their agencies' IT resources, resulting in duplication, waste, and poor service delivery. Enhancing the effectiveness of agency CIOs will better position agencies to modernize their IT systems, execute IT programs more efficiently, reduce cybersecurity risks, and serve the American people well.

Sec. 2. Policy.

It is the policy of the executive branch to:

(a) empower agency CIOs to ensure that agency IT systems are secure, efficient, accessible, and effective, and that such systems enable agencies to accomplish their missions;

(b) modernize IT infrastructure within the executive branch and meaningfully improve the delivery of digital services; and(c) improve the management, acquisition, and oversight of Federal IT.

Sec. 3. Definitions.

For purposes of this order:

(a) the term "covered agency" means an agency listed in 31 U.S.C. 901(b), other than the Department of Defense or any agency considered to be an "independent regulatory agency" as defined in 44 U.S.C. 3502(5);

(b) the term "information technology" has the meaning given that term in 40 U.S.C. 11101(6);

(c) the term "Chief Information Officer" or "CIO" means the individual within a covered agency as described in 40 U.S.C. 11315;

d) the term "component Chief Information Officer" or "component CIO" means an individual in a covered agency, other than the CIO referred to in subsection (c) of this section, who has the title Chief Information Officer, or who functions in the capacity of a CIO, and has IT management authorities over a component of the agency similar to those the CIO has over the entire agency;

(e) the term "IT position" means a position within the job family standard for the Information Technology Management Series, GS-2210, as defined by the Office of Personnel

Management (OPM) in the Handbook of Occupational Groups and Families and related guidance.

Sec. 4. Emphasizing Chief Information Officer Duties and Responsibilities.

The head of each covered agency shall take all necessary and appropriate action to ensure that:

(a) consistent with 44 U.S.C. 3506(a)(2), the CIO of the covered agency reports directly to the agency head, such that the CIO has direct access to the agency head regarding all programs that include IT;

(b) consistent with 40 U.S.C. 11315(b), and to promote the effective, efficient, and secure use of IT to accomplish the agency's mission, the CIO serves as the primary strategic advisor to the agency head concerning the use of IT;

(c) consistent with 40 U.S.C. 11319(b)(1)(A), the CIO has a significant role, including, as appropriate, as lead advisor, in all annual and multi-year planning, programming, budgeting, and execution decisions, as well as in all management, governance, and oversight processes related to IT; and

(d) consistent with 40 U.S.C. 11319(b)(2) and other applicable law, the CIO of the covered agency approves the appointment of any component CIO in that agency.

Sec. 5. Agency-wide IT Consolidation.

Consistent with the purposes of Executive Order 13781 of March 13, 2017 (Comprehensive Plan for Reorganizing the Executive Branch), the head of each covered agency shall take all necessary and appropriate action to:

(a) eliminate unnecessary IT management functions;

(b) merge or reorganize agency IT functions to promote agency-wide consolidation of the agency's IT infrastructure, taking into account any recommendations of the relevant agency CIO; and

(c) increase use of industry best practices, such as the shared use of IT solutions within agencies and across the executive branch.

Sec. 6. Strengthening Cybersecurity.

Consistent with the purposes of Executive Order 13800 of May 11, 2017 (Strengthening the Cybersecurity of Federal Networks and Critical Infrastructure), the head of each covered agency shall take all necessary and appropriate action to ensure that:

(a) the CIO, as the principal advisor to the agency head for the management of IT resources, works closely with an integrated team of senior executives with expertise in IT, security, budgeting, acquisition, law, privacy, and human resources to implement appropriate risk management measures; and

(b) the agency prioritizes procurement of shared IT services, including modern email and other cloud-based services, where possible and to the extent permitted by law.

Sec. 7. Knowledge and Skill Standards for IT Personnel.

The head of each covered agency shall take all necessary and appropriate action to ensure that:

(a) consistent with 40 U.S.C. 11315(c)(3), the CIO assesses and advises the agency head regarding knowledge and skill standards established for agency IT personnel;

(b) the established knowledge and skill standards are included in the performance standards and reflected in the performance evaluations of all component CIOs, and that the CIO is responsible for that portion of the evaluation; and

(c) all component CIOs apply those standards within their own components.

Sec. 8. Chief Information Officer Role on IT Governance Boards.

Wherever appropriate and consistent with applicable law, the head of each covered agency shall ensure that the CIO shall be a member of any investment or related board of the agency with purview over IT, or any board responsible for setting agency-wide IT standards. The head of each covered agency shall also, as appropriate and consistent with applicable law, direct the CIO to chair any such board. To the extent any such board operates through member votes, the head of each covered agency shall also, as appropriate and consistent with applicable law, direct the CIO to fulfill the role of voting member.

Sec. 9. Chief Information Officer Hiring Authorities.

The Director of OPM (Director) shall publish a proposed rule delegating to the head of each covered agency authority to determine whether there is a severe shortage of candidates (or, with respect to the Department of Veterans Affairs, that there exists a severe shortage of highly qualified candidates), or that a critical hiring need exists, for IT positions at the covered agency pursuant to 5 U.S.C. 3304(a)(3), under criteria established by OPM.

(a) Such proposed rule shall provide that, upon an affirmative determination by the head of a covered agency that there is a severe shortage of candidates (or, with respect to the Department of Veterans Affairs, that there exists a severe shortage of highly qualified candidates), or that a critical hiring need exists for IT positions, under the criteria established by OPM, the Director shall, within 30 days, grant that agency direct hiring authority for IT positions.

(b) Such proposed rule shall further provide that employees hired using this authority may not be transferred to positions that are not IT positions; that the employees shall initially be given term appointments not to exceed 4 years; and that the terms of such employees may be extended up to 4 additional years at the discretion of the hiring agency.

(c) The Director shall submit the proposed rule for publication within 30 days of the date of this order.

Sec. 10. Guidance.

The Director of the Office of Management and Budget shall amend or replace relevant guidance, as appropriate, to agencies to reflect the requirements of this order.

Sec. 11. General Provisions.

(a) Nothing in this order shall be construed to impair or otherwise affect:

(i) the authority granted by law to an executive department or agency, or the head thereof; or

(ii) the functions of the Director of the Office of Management and Budget relating to budgetary, administrative, or legislative proposals.

(b) This order shall be implemented consistent with applicable law and subject to the availability of appropriations.

(c) This order is not intended to, and does not, create any right or benefit, substantive or procedural, enforceable at law or in equity by any party against the United States, its departments, agencies, or entities, its officers, employees, or agents, or any other person.

DONLD J. TRUMP

Executive Order 13846—Reimposing Certain Sanctions with Respect to Iran

83 Fed. Reg. 38,939 (Aug. 6, 2018)

By the authority vested in me as President by the Constitution and the laws of the United States of America, including the International Emergency Economic Powers Act (50 U.S.C. 1701 et seq.) (IEEPA), the National Emergencies Act (50 U.S.C. 1601 et seq.) (NEA), the Iran Sanctions Act of 1996 (Public Law 104-172) (50 U.S.C. 1701 note), as amended (ISA), the Comprehensive Iran Sanctions, Accountability, and Divestment Act of 2010 (Public Law 111-195) (22 U.S.C. 8501 et seq.), as amended (CISADA), the Iran Threat Reduction and Syria Human Rights Act of 2012 (Public Law 112-158) (TRA), the Iran Freedom and Counter-Proliferation Act of 2012 (subtitle D of title XII of Public Law 112-239) (22 U.S.C. 8801 et seq.) (IFCA), section 212(f) of the Immigration and Nationality Act of 1952 (8 U.S.C. 1182(f)), and section 301 of title 3, United States Code, in order to take additional steps with respect to the national emergency declared in Executive Order 12957 of March 15, 1995,

I, DONALD J. TRUMP, President of the United States of America, in light of my decision on May 8, 2018, to cease the participation of the United States in the Joint Comprehensive Plan of Action of July 14, 2015 (JCPOA), and to re-impose all sanctions lifted or waived in connection with the JCPOA as expeditiously as possible and in no case later than 180 days from May 8, 2018, as outlined in the National Security Presidential Memorandum-11 of May 8, 2018 (Ceasing United States Participation in the Joint Comprehensive Plan of Action and Taking Additional Action to Counter Iran's Malign Influence and Deny Iran All Paths to a Nuclear Weapon), and to advance the goal of applying financial pressure on the Iranian regime in pursuit of a comprehensive and lasting solution to the full range of the threats posed by Iran, including Iran's proliferation and development of missiles and other asymmetric and conventional weapons capabilities, its network and campaign of regional aggression, its support for terrorist groups, and the malign activities of the Islamic Revolutionary Guard Corps and its surrogates, hereby order as follows:

Section 1. Blocking Sanctions Relating to Support for the Government of Iran's Purchase or Acquisition of U.S. Bank Notes or Precious Metals; Certain Iranian Persons; and Iran's Energy, Shipping, and Shipbuilding Sectors and Port Operators.

(a) The Secretary of the Treasury, in consultation with the Secretary of State, is hereby authorized to impose on a person the measures described in subsection (b) of this section upon determining that:

(i) on or after August 7, 2018, the person has materially assisted, sponsored, or provided financial, material, or technological support for, or goods or services in support of, the purchase or acquisition of U.S. bank notes or precious metals by the Government of Iran;

(ii) on or after November 5, 2018, the person has materially assisted, sponsored, or provided financial, material, or technological support for, or goods or services in support of, the National Iranian Oil Company (NIOC), Naftiran Intertrade Company (NICO), or the Central Bank of Iran;

(iii) on or after November 5, 2018, the person has materially assisted, sponsored, or provided financial, material, or technological support for, or goods or services to or in support of:

   (A) any Iranian person included on the list of Specially Designated Nationals and Blocked Persons maintained by the Office of Foreign Assets Control (SDN List) (other than an Iranian depository institution whose property and interests in property are blocked solely pursuant to Executive Order 13599 of February 5, 2012); or

   (B) any other person included on the SDN List whose property and interests in property are blocked pursuant to subsection (a) of this section or Executive Order 13599 (other than an Iranian depository institution whose property and interests in property are blocked solely pursuant to Executive Order 13599); or

(iv) pursuant to authority delegated by the President and in accordance with the terms of such delegation, sanctions shall be imposed on such person pursuant to section 1244(c)(1)(A) of IFCA because the person:

   (A) is part of the energy, shipping, or shipbuilding sectors of Iran;

   (B) operates a port in Iran; or

   (C) knowingly provides significant financial, material, technological, or other support to, or goods or services in support of any activity or transaction on behalf of a person determined under section 1244(c)(2)(A) of IFCA to be a part of the energy, shipping, or shipbuilding sectors of Iran; a person determined under section 1244(c)(2)(B) of IFCA to operate a port in Iran; or an Iranian person included on the SDN List (other than a person described in section 1244(c)(3) of IFCA).

(b) With respect to any person determined by the Secretary of the Treasury in accordance with this section to meet any of the criteria set forth in subsections (a)(i)-(a)(iv) of this section, all property and interests in property that are in the United States, that hereafter come within the United States, or that are or hereafter come within the possession or control of any United States person of such person are blocked and may not be transferred, paid, exported, withdrawn, or otherwise dealt in.

(c) The prohibitions in subsection (b) of this section apply except to the extent provided by statutes, or in regulations, orders, directives, or licenses that may be issued pursuant to this order, and notwithstanding any contract entered into or any license or permit granted prior to the effective date of this order or, where specifically provided, the effective date of the prohibition.

Sec. 2. Correspondent and Payable-Through Account Sanctions Relating to Iran's Automotive Sector; Certain Iranian Persons; and Trade in Iranian Petroleum, Petroleum Products, and Petrochemical Products.

(a) The Secretary of the Treasury, in consultation with the Secretary of State, is hereby authorized to impose on a foreign financial institution the sanctions described in subsection (b) of this section upon determining that the foreign financial institution has knowingly conducted or facilitated any significant financial transaction:

   (i) on or after August 7, 2018, for the sale, supply, or transfer to Iran of significant goods or services used in connection with the automotive sector of Iran;

   (ii) on or after November 5, 2018, on behalf of any Iranian person included on the SDN List (other than an Iranian depository institution whose property and interests in property are blocked solely pursuant to Executive Order 13599) or any other person included on the SDN List whose property and interests in property are blocked pursuant to subsection 1(a) of this order or Executive Order 13599 (other than an Iranian depository institution whose property and interests in property are blocked solely pursuant to Executive Order 13599);

(iii) on or after November 5, 2018, with NIOC or NICO, except for a sale or provision to NIOC or NICO of the products described in section 5(a)(3)(A)(i) of ISA provided that the fair market value of such products is lower than the applicable dollar threshold specified in that provision;

(iv) on or after November 5, 2018, for the purchase, acquisition, sale, transport, or marketing of petroleum or petroleum products from Iran; or

(v) on or after November 5, 2018, for the purchase, acquisition, sale, transport, or marketing of petrochemical products from Iran.

(b) With respect to any foreign financial institution determined by the Secretary of the Treasury in accordance with this section to meet any of the criteria set forth in subsections (a)(i)-(a)(v) of this section, the Secretary of the Treasury may prohibit the opening, and prohibit or impose strict conditions on the maintaining, in the United States of a correspondent account or a payable-through account by such foreign financial institution.

(c) Subsections (a)(ii)-(a)(iv) of this section shall apply with respect to a significant financial transaction conducted or facilitated by a foreign financial institution for the purchase of petroleum or petroleum products from Iran only if:

(i) the President determines under subparagraphs (4)(B) and (C) of subsection 1245(d) of the National Defense Authorization Act for Fiscal Year 2012 (Public Law 112-81) (2012 NDAA) (22 U.S.C. 8513a) that there is a sufficient supply of petroleum and petroleum products from countries other than Iran to permit a significant reduction in the volume of petroleum and petroleum products purchased from Iran by or through foreign financial institutions; and

(ii) an exception under subparagraph 4(D) of subsection 1245(d) of the 2012 NDAA from the imposition of sanctions under paragraph (1) of that subsection does not apply.

(d) Subsection (a)(ii) of this section shall not apply with respect to a significant financial transaction conducted or facilitated by a foreign financial institution for the sale, supply, or transfer to or from Iran of natural gas only if the financial transaction is solely for trade between the country with primary jurisdiction over the foreign financial institution and Iran, and any funds owed to Iran as a result of such trade are credited to an account located in the country with primary jurisdiction over the foreign financial institution.

(e) Subsections (a)(ii)-(a)(v) of this section shall not apply with respect to any person for conducting or facilitating a transaction for the provision (including any sale) of agricultural commodities, food, medicine, or medical devices to Iran.

(f) The prohibitions in subsection (b) of this section apply except to the extent provided by statutes, or in regulations, orders, directives, or licenses that may be issued pursuant to this order, and notwithstanding any contract entered into or any license or permit granted prior to the effective date of this order or, where specifically provided, the effective date of the prohibition.

Sec. 3. "Menu-based" Sanctions Relating to Iran's Automotive Sector and Trade in Iranian Petroleum, Petroleum Products, and Petrochemical Products.

(a) The Secretary of State, in consultation with the Secretary of the Treasury, the Secretary of Commerce, the Secretary of Homeland Security, and the United States Trade Representative, and with the President of the Export-Import Bank, the Chairman of the Board of

Governors of the Federal Reserve System, and other agencies and officials as appropriate, is hereby authorized to impose on a person any of the sanctions described in section 4 or 5 of this order upon determining that the person:

(i) on or after August 7, 2018, knowingly engaged in a significant transaction for the sale, supply, or transfer to Iran of significant goods or services used in connection with the automotive sector of Iran;

(ii) on or after November 5, 2018, knowingly engaged in a significant transaction for the purchase, acquisition, sale, transport, or marketing of petroleum or petroleum products from Iran;

(iii) on or after November 5, 2018, knowingly engaged in a significant transaction for the purchase, acquisition, sale, transport, or marketing of petrochemical products from Iran;

(iv) is a successor entity to a person determined by the Secretary of State in accordance with this section to meet any of the criteria set forth in subsections (a)(i)-(a)(iii) of this section;

(v) owns or controls a person determined by the Secretary of State in accordance with this section to meet any of the criteria set forth in subsections (a)(i)-(a)(iii) of this section, and had knowledge that the person engaged in the activities referred to in those subsections; or

(vi) is owned or controlled by, or under common ownership or control with, a person determined by the Secretary of State in accordance with this section to meet any of the criteria set forth in subsections (a)(i)-(a)(iii) of this section, and knowingly participated in the activities referred to in those subsections.

(b) Subsection (a)(ii) of this section shall apply with respect to a person only if:

(i) the President determines under subparagraphs (4)(B) and (C) of subsection 1245(d) of the 2012 NDAA that there is a sufficient supply of petroleum and petroleum products from countries other than Iran to permit a significant reduction in the volume of petroleum and petroleum products purchased from Iran by or through foreign financial institutions; and

(ii) an exception under subparagraph 4(D) of subsection 1245(d) of the 2012 NDAA from the imposition of sanctions under paragraph (1) of that subsection does not apply.

Sec. 4. Agency Implementation Authorities for "Menu-based" Sanctions.

When the Secretary of State, in accordance with the terms of section 3 of this order, has determined that a person meets any of the criteria described in subsections (a)(i)-(a)(vi) of that section and has selected any of the sanctions set forth below to impose on that person, the heads of relevant agencies, in consultation with the Secretary of State, as appropriate, shall take the following actions where necessary to implement the sanctions imposed by the Secretary of State:

(a) the Board of Directors of the Export-Import Bank of the United States shall deny approval of the issuance of any guarantee, insurance, extension of credit, or participation in an extension of credit in connection with the export of any goods or services to the sanctioned person;

(b) agencies shall not issue any specific license or grant any other specific permission or authority under any statute or regulation that requires the prior review and approval of the United States Government as a condition for the export or reexport of goods or technology to the sanctioned person;

(c) with respect to a sanctioned person that is a financial institution:

(i) the Chairman of the Board of Governors of the Federal Reserve System and the President of the Federal Reserve Bank of New York shall take such actions as they deem appropriate, including denying designation, or terminating the continuation of any prior designation of, the sanctioned person as a primary dealer in United States Government debt instruments; or

(ii) agencies shall prevent the sanctioned person from serving as an agent of the United States Government or serving as a repository for United States Government funds;

(d) agencies shall not procure, or enter into a contract for the procurement of, any goods or services from the sanctioned person;

(e) the Secretary of State shall deny a visa to, and the Secretary of Homeland Security shall exclude from the United States, any alien that the Secretary of State determines is a corporate officer or principal of, or a shareholder with a controlling interest in, a sanctioned person; or

(f) the heads of the relevant agencies, as appropriate, shall impose on the principal executive officer or officers, or persons performing similar functions and with similar authorities, of a sanctioned person the sanctions described in subsections (a)-(e) of this section, as selected by the Secretary of State.

(g) The prohibitions in subsections (a)-(f) of this section apply except to the extent provided by statutes, or in regulations, orders, directives, or licenses that may be issued pursuant to this order, and notwithstanding any contract entered into or any license or permit granted prior to the effective date of this order or, where specifically provided, the effective date of the prohibition.

Sec. 5. Additional Implementation Authorities for "Menu-based" Sanctions.

(a) When the President, or the Secretary of State or the Secretary of the Treasury pursuant to authority delegated by the President and in accordance with the terms of such delegation, has determined that sanctions described in section 6(a) of ISA shall be imposed on a person pursuant to ISA, CISADA, TRA, or IFCA and has selected one or more of the sanctions set forth below to impose on that person or when the Secretary of State, in accordance with the terms of section 3 of this order, has determined that a person meets any of the criteria described in subsections (a)(i)-(a)(vi) of that section and has selected one or more of the sanctions set forth below to impose on that person, the Secretary of the Treasury, in consultation with the Secretary of State, shall take the following actions where necessary to implement the sanctions selected and maintained by the President, the Secretary of State, or the Secretary of the Treasury:

(i) prohibit any United States financial institution from making loans or providing credits to the sanctioned person totaling more than $10,000,000 in any 12-month period, unless such person is engaged in activities to relieve human suffering and the loans or credits are provided for such activities;

(ii) prohibit any transactions in foreign exchange that are subject to the jurisdiction of the United States and in which the sanctioned person has any interest;

(iii) prohibit any transfers of credit or payments between financial institutions or by, through, or to any financial institution, to the extent that such transfers or payments are subject to the jurisdiction of the United States and involve any interest of the sanctioned person;

(iv) block all property and interests in property that are in the United States, that hereafter come within the United States, or that are or hereafter come within the possession or control of any United States person of the sanctioned person, and provide that such property and interests in property may not be transferred, paid, exported, withdrawn, or otherwise dealt in;

(v) prohibit any United States person from investing in or purchasing significant amounts of equity or debt instruments of a sanctioned person;

(vi) restrict or prohibit imports of goods, technology, or services, directly or indirectly, into the United States from the sanctioned person; or

(vii) impose on the principal executive officer or officers, or persons performing similar functions and with similar authorities, of a sanctioned person the sanctions described in subsections (a)(i)-(a)(vi) of this section, as selected by the President or Secretary of State or the Secretary of the Treasury, as appropriate.

(b) The prohibitions in subsection (a) of this section apply except to the extent provided by statutes, or in regulations, orders, directives, or licenses that may be issued pursuant to this order, and notwithstanding any contract entered into or any license or permit granted prior to the effective date of this order or, where specifically provided, the effective date of the prohibition.

Sec. 6. Sanctions Relating to the Iranian Rial.

(a) The Secretary of the Treasury, in consultation with the Secretary of State, is hereby authorized to impose on a foreign financial institution the sanctions described in subsection (b) of this section upon determining that the foreign financial institution has, on or after August 7, 2018:

(i) knowingly conducted or facilitated any significant transaction related to the purchase or sale of Iranian rials or a derivative, swap, future, forward, or other similar contract whose value is based on the exchange rate of the Iranian rial; or

(ii) maintained significant funds or accounts outside the territory of Iran denominated in the Iranian rial.

(b) With respect to any foreign financial institution determined by the Secretary of the Treasury in accordance with this section to meet the criteria set forth in subsection (a)(i) or (a)(ii) of this section, the Secretary of the Treasury may:

(i) prohibit the opening, and prohibit or impose strict conditions on the maintaining, in the United States of a correspondent account or a payable through account by such foreign financial institution; or

(ii) block all property and interests in property that are in the United States, that hereafter come within the United States, or that are or hereafter come within the possession or control of any United States person of such foreign financial institution, and provide that such property and interests in property may not be transferred, paid, exported, withdrawn, or otherwise dealt in.

(c) The prohibitions in subsection (b) of this section apply except to the extent provided by statutes, or in regulations, orders, directives, or licenses that may be issued pursuant to this order, and notwithstanding any contract entered into or any license or permit granted prior to the effective date of this order or, where specifically provided, the effective date of the prohibition.

Sec. 7. Sanctions with Respect to the Diversion of Goods Intended for the People of Iran, the Transfer of Goods or Technologies to Iran that are Likely to be Used to Commit Human Rights Abuses, and Censorship.

(a) The Secretary of the Treasury, in consultation with or at the recommendation of the Secretary of State, is hereby authorized to impose on a person the measures described in subsection (b) of this section upon determining that the person:

(i) has engaged, on or after January 2, 2013, in corruption or other activities relating to the diversion of goods, including agricultural commodities, food, medicine, and medical devices, intended for the people of Iran;

(ii) has engaged, on or after January 2, 2013, in corruption or other activities relating to the misappropriation of proceeds from the sale or resale of goods described in subsection (a)(i) of this section;

(iii) has knowingly, on or after August 10, 2012, transferred, or facilitated the transfer of, goods or technologies to Iran, any entity organized under the laws of Iran or otherwise subject to the jurisdiction of the Government of Iran, or any national of Iran, for use in or with respect to Iran, that are likely to be used by the Government of Iran or any of its agencies or instrumentalities, or by any other person on behalf of the Government of Iran or any of such agencies or instrumentalities, to commit serious human rights abuses against the people of Iran;

(iv) has knowingly, on or after August 10, 2012, provided services, including services relating to hardware, software, or specialized information or professional consulting, engineering, or support services, with respect to goods or technologies that have been transferred to Iran and that are likely to be used by the Government of Iran or any of its agencies or instrumentalities, or by any other person on behalf of the Government of Iran or any of such agencies or instrumentalities, to commit serious human rights abuses against the people of Iran;

(v) has engaged in censorship or other activities with respect to Iran on or after June 12, 2009, that prohibit, limit, or penalize the exercise of freedom of expression or assembly by citizens of Iran, or that limit access to print or broadcast media, including the facilitation or support of intentional frequency manipulation by the Government of Iran or an entity owned or controlled by the Government of Iran that would jam or restrict an international signal;

(vi) has materially assisted, sponsored, or provided financial, material, or technological support for, or goods or services to or in support of, the activities described in subsections (a)(i)-(a)(v) of this section or any person whose property and interests in property are blocked pursuant to this section; or

(vii) is owned or controlled by, or has acted or purported to act for or on behalf of, directly or indirectly, any person whose property and interests in property are blocked pursuant to this section.

(b) With respect to any person determined by the Secretary of the Treasury in accordance with this section to meet any of the criteria set forth in subsections (a)(i)-(a)(vii) of this section, all property and interests in property that are in the United States, that hereafter come within the United States, or that are or hereafter come within the possession or control of any United States person of such person are blocked and may not be transferred, paid, exported, withdrawn, or otherwise dealt in.

(c) The prohibitions in subsection (b) of this section apply except to the extent provided by statutes, or in regulations, orders, directives, or licenses that may be issued pursuant to this order, and notwithstanding any contract entered into or any license or permit granted prior to the effective date of this order or, where specifically provided, the effective date of the prohibition.

Sec. 8. Entities Owned or Controlled by a United States Person and Established or Maintained Outside the United States.

(a) No entity owned or controlled by a United States person and established or maintained outside the United States may knowingly engage in any transaction, directly or indirectly, with the Government of Iran or any person subject to the jurisdiction of the Government of

Iran, if that transaction would be prohibited by Executive Order 12957, Executive Order 12959 of May 6, 1995, Executive Order 13059 of August 19, 1997, Executive Order 13599, or sections 1 or 15 of this order, or any regulation issued pursuant to the foregoing, if the transaction were engaged in by a United States person or in the United States.

(b) Penalties assessed for violations of the prohibition in subsection (a) of this section, and any related violations of section 15 of this order may be assessed against the United States person that owns or controls the entity that engaged in the prohibited transaction.

(c) The prohibitions in subsection (a) of this section apply, except to the extent provided by statutes, or in regulations, orders, directives, or licenses that may be issued pursuant to this order, and notwithstanding any contract entered into or any license or permit granted prior to the effective date of this order or, where specifically provided, the effective date of the prohibition, except to the extent provided in subsection 20(c) of this order.

Sec. 9. Revoking and Superseding Prior Executive Orders. The following Executive Orders are revoked and superseded:

(a) Executive Order 13628 of October 9, 2012 (Authorizing the Implementation of Certain Sanctions Set Forth in the Iran Threat Reduction and Syria Human Rights Act of 2012 and Additional Sanctions With Respect to Iran); and

(b) Executive Order 13716 of January 16, 2016 (Revocation of Executive Orders 13574, 13590, 13622, and 13645 With Respect to Iran, Amendment of Executive Order 13628 With Respect to Iran, and Provision of Implementation Authorities for Aspects of Certain Statutory Sanctions Outside the Scope of U.S. Commitments Under the Joint Comprehensive Plan of Action of July 14, 2015).

Sec. 10. Natural Gas Project Exception.

Subsections 1(a), 2(a)(ii)-(a)(v), 3(a)(ii)-(a)(iii), and, with respect to a person determined by the Secretary of State in accordance with section 3 to meet the criteria of 3(a)(ii)-(iii), 3(a)(iv)-(vi) of this order shall not apply with respect to any person for conducting or facilitating a transaction involving a project described in subsection (a) of section 603 of TRA to which the exception under that section applies.

Sec. 11. Donations.

I hereby determine that, to the extent section 203(b)(2) of IEEPA (50 U.S.C. 1702(b)(2)) may apply, the making of donations of the types of articles specified in such section by, to, or for the benefit of any person whose property and interests in property are blocked pursuant to this order would seriously impair my ability to deal with the national emergency declared in Executive Order 12957, and I hereby prohibit such donations as provided by subsections 1(b), 5(a)(iv), 6(b)(ii), and 7(b) of this order.

Sec. 12. Prohibitions.

The prohibitions in subsections 1(b), 5(a)(iv), 6(b)(ii), and 7(b) of this order include:

(a) the making of any contribution or provision of funds, goods, or services by, to, or for the benefit of any person whose property and interests in property are blocked pursuant to this order; and

(b) the receipt of any contribution or provision of funds, goods, or services from any such person.

Sec. 13. Entry into the United States.

The unrestricted immigrant and nonimmigrant entry into the United States of aliens determined to meet one or more of the criteria in subsections 1(a), 3(a), and 7(a) of this order would be detrimental to the interests of the United States, and the entry of such persons into the United States, as immigrants or nonimmigrants, is hereby suspended. Such persons shall be treated as persons covered by section 1 of Proclamation 8693 of July 24, 2011 (Suspension of Entry of Aliens Subject to United Nations Security Council Travel Bans and International Emergency Economic Powers Act Sanctions).

Sec. 14. General Authorities.

The Secretary of the Treasury, in consultation with the Secretary of State, is hereby authorized to take such actions, including adopting rules and regulations, to employ all powers granted to me by IEEPA and sections 6(a)(6), 6(a)(7), 6(a)(8), 6(a)(9), 6(a)(11), and 6(a)(12) of ISA, and to employ all powers granted to the United States Government by section 6(a)(3) of ISA, as may be necessary to carry out the purposes of this order, other than the purposes described in sections 3, 4, and 13 of this order. The Secretary of the Treasury may, consistent with applicable law, redelegate any of these functions within the Department of the Treasury. All agencies of the United States shall take all appropriate measures within their authority to implement this order.

Sec. 15. Evasion and Conspiracy.

(a) Any transaction that evades or avoids, has the purpose of evading or avoiding, causes a violation of, or attempts to violate any of the prohibitions set forth in this order or in Executive Order 12957, Executive Order 12959, Executive Order 13059, or Executive Order 13599 is prohibited.

(b) Any conspiracy formed to violate any of the prohibitions set forth in this order or in Executive Order 12957, Executive Order 12959, Executive Order 13059, or Executive Order 13599 is prohibited.

Sec. 16. Definitions.

For the purposes of this order:

(a) the term "automotive sector of Iran" means the manufacturing or assembling in Iran of light and heavy vehicles including passenger cars, trucks, buses, minibuses, pick-up trucks, and motorcycles, as well as original equipment manufacturing and after-market parts manufacturing relating to such vehicles;

(b) the term "entity" means a partnership, association, trust, joint venture, corporation, group, subgroup, or other organization;

(c) the term "financial institution" includes (i) a depository institution (as defined in section 3(c)(1) of the Federal Deposit Insurance Act) (12 U.S.C. 1813(c)(1)), including a branch or agency of a foreign bank (as defined in section 1(b)(7) of the International Banking Act of 1978) (12 U.S.C. 3101(7)); (ii) a credit union; (iii) a securities firm, including a broker or dealer; (iv) an insurance company, including an agency or underwriter; and (v) any other company that provides financial services;

(d) the term "foreign financial institution" means any foreign entity that is engaged in the business of accepting deposits, making, granting, transferring, holding, or brokering loans or credits, or purchasing or selling foreign exchange, securities, commodity futures or options, or procuring purchasers and sellers thereof, as principal or agent. It includes, but is not limited to, depository institutions, banks, savings banks, money service businesses, trust companies, securities brokers and dealers, commodity futures and options brokers and dealers, forward contract and foreign exchange merchants, securities and commodities exchanges, clearing corporations, investment companies, employee benefit plans, dealers in precious metals, stones, or jewels, and holding companies, affiliates, or subsidiaries of any of the foregoing. The term does not include the international financial institutions identified in 22 U.S.C. 262r(c)(2), the International Fund for Agricultural Development, the North American Development Bank, or any other international financial institution so notified by the Secretary of the Treasury;

(e) the term "Government of Iran" includes the Government of Iran, any political subdivision, agency, or instrumentality thereof, including the Central Bank of Iran, and any person owned or controlled by, or acting for or on behalf of, the Government of Iran;

(f) the term "Iran" means the Government of Iran and the territory of Iran and any other territory or marine area, including the exclusive economic zone and continental shelf, over which the Government of Iran claims sovereignty, sovereign rights, or jurisdiction, provided that the Government of Iran exercises partial or total de facto control over the area or derives a benefit from economic activity in the area pursuant to international arrangements;

(g) the term "Iranian depository institution" means any entity (including foreign branches), wherever located, organized under the laws of Iran or any jurisdiction within Iran, or owned or controlled by the Government of Iran, or in Iran, or owned or controlled by any of the foregoing, that is engaged primarily in the business of banking (for example, banks, savings banks, savings associations, credit unions, trust companies, and bank holding companies);

(h) the term "Iranian person" means an individual who is a citizen or national of Iran or an entity organized under the laws of Iran or otherwise subject to the jurisdiction of the Government of Iran;

(i) the terms "knowledge" and "knowingly," with respect to conduct, a circumstance, or a result, mean that a person has actual knowledge, or should have known, of the conduct, the circumstance, or the result;

(j) the terms "Naftiran Intertrade Company" and "NICO" mean the Naftiran Intertrade Company Ltd. and any entity owned or controlled by, or operating for or on behalf of, the Naftiran Intertrade Company Ltd.;

(k) the terms "National Iranian Oil Company" and "NIOC" mean the National Iranian Oil Company and any entity owned or controlled by, or operating for or on behalf of, the National Iranian Oil Company;

(l) the term "person" means an individual or entity;

(m) the term "petrochemical products" includes any aromatic, olefin, and synthesis gas, and any of their derivatives, including ethylene, propylene, butadiene, benzene, toluene, xylene, ammonia, methanol, and urea;

(n) the term "petroleum" (also known as crude oil) means a mixture of hydrocarbons that exists in liquid phase in natural underground reservoirs and remains liquid at atmospheric pressure after passing through surface separating facilities;

(o) the term "petroleum products" includes unfinished oils, liquefied petroleum gases, pentanes plus, aviation gasoline, motor gasoline, naphtha-type jet fuel, kerosene-type jet fuel, kerosene, distillate fuel oil, residual fuel oil, petrochemical feedstocks, special naphthas, lubricants, waxes, petroleum coke, asphalt, road oil, still gas, and miscellaneous products obtained from the processing of: crude oil (including lease condensate), natural gas, and other hydrocarbon compounds. The term does not include natural gas, liquefied natural gas, biofuels, methanol, and other non-petroleum fuels;

(p) the term "sanctioned person" means a person that the President, or the Secretary of State or the Secretary of the Treasury pursuant to authority delegated by the President and in accordance with the terms of such delegation, has determined is a person on whom sanctions described in section 6(a) of ISA shall be imposed pursuant to ISA, CISADA, TRA, or IFCA, and on whom the President, the Secretary of State, or the Secretary of the Treasury has imposed any of the sanctions in section 6(a) of ISA or a person on whom the Secretary of State, in accordance with the terms of section 3 of this order, has decided to impose sanctions pursuant to section 3 of this order;

(q) the term "subject to the jurisdiction of the Government of Iran" means a person organized under the laws of Iran or any jurisdiction within Iran, ordinarily resident in Iran, or in Iran, or owned or controlled by any of the foregoing;

(r) the term "United States financial institution" means a financial institution as defined in subsection (c) of this section (including its foreign branches) organized under the laws of the United States or any jurisdiction within the United States or located in the United States; and

(s) the term "United States person" means any United States citizen, permanent resident alien, entity organized under the laws of the United States or any jurisdiction within the United States (including foreign branches), or any person in the United States.

Sec. 17. Notice.

For those persons whose property and interests in property are blocked pursuant to this order who might have a constitutional presence in the United States, I find that because of the ability to transfer funds or other assets instantaneously, prior notice to such persons of measures to be taken pursuant to this order would render those measures ineffectual. I therefore determine that for these measures to be effective in addressing the national emergency declared in Executive Order 12957, there need be no prior notice of a listing or determination made pursuant to subsections 1(b), 5(a)(iv), 6(b)(ii), and 7(b) of this order.

Sec. 18. Delegation to Implement Section 104A of CISADA.

The Secretary of the Treasury, in consultation with the Secretary of State, is hereby authorized to take such actions, including adopting rules and regulations, and to employ all powers granted to me by IEEPA, as may be necessary to carry out section 104A of CISADA (22 U.S.C. 8513b). The Secretary of the Treasury may, consistent with applicable law, redelegate any of these functions within the Department of the Treasury.

Sec. 19. Rights.

This order is not intended to, and does not, create any right or benefit, substantive or procedural, enforceable at law or in equity by any party against the United States, its departments, agencies, or entities, its officers, employees, or agents, or any other person.

Sec. 20. Effect on Actions or Proceedings, Blocked Property, and Regulations, Orders, Directives, and Licenses.

(a) Pursuant to section 202 of the NEA (50 U.S.C. 1622), the revocation of Executive Orders 13716 and 13628 as set forth in section 9 of this order, shall not affect any action taken or proceeding pending not finally concluded or determined as of the effective date of this order, or any action or proceeding based on any act committed prior to the effective date of this order, or any rights or duties that matured or penalties that were incurred prior to the effective date of this order.

(b) Except to the extent provided in statutes or regulations, orders, directives, or licenses that may be issued pursuant to this order, and notwithstanding any contract entered into or any license or permit granted prior to the effective date of this order, the following are blocked and may not be transferred, paid, exported, withdrawn, or otherwise dealt in: all property and interests in property that were blocked pursuant to Executive Order 13628 and remained blocked immediately prior to the effective date of this order.

(c) Except to the extent provided in regulations, orders, directives, or licenses that may be issued pursuant to this order, all regulations, orders, directives, or licenses that were issued pursuant to Executive Order 13628 and remained in effect immediately prior to the effective date of this order are hereby authorized to remain in effect — subject to their existing terms and conditions — pursuant to this order, which continues in effect certain sanctions set forth in Executive Order 13628.

Sec. 21. Relationship to Algiers Accords.

The measures taken pursuant to this order are in response to actions of the Government of Iran occurring after the conclusion of the 1981 Algiers Accords, and are intended solely as a response to those later actions.

Sec. 22. Effective Date.

This order is effective 12:01 a.m. eastern daylight time on August 7, 2018.

DONALD J. TRUMP

Executive Order 13848—Imposing Certain Sanctions in the Event of Foreign Interference in a United States Election

83 Fed. Reg. 46,843 (Sept. 14, 2018)

By the authority vested in me as President by the Constitution and the laws of the United States of America, including the International Emergency Economic Powers Act (50 U.S.C. 1701 *et seq.*) (IEEPA), the National Emergencies Act (50 U.S.C. 1601 *et seq.*) (NEA), section 212(f) of the Immigration and Nationality Act of 1952 (8 U.S.C. 1182(f)), and section 301 of title 3, United States Code,

I, DONALD J. TRUMP, President of the United States of America, find that the ability of persons located, in whole or in substantial part, outside the United States to interfere in or undermine public confidence in United States elections, including through the unauthorized accessing of election and campaign infrastructure or the covert distribution of propaganda and disinformation, constitutes an unusual and extraordinary threat to the national security and foreign policy of the United States. Although there has been no evidence of a foreign power altering the outcome or vote tabulation in any United States election, foreign powers have historically sought to exploit America's free and open political system. In recent years, the proliferation of digital devices and internet-based communications has created significant vulnerabilities and magnified the scope and intensity of the threat of foreign interference, as illustrated in the 2017 Intelligence Community Assessment. I hereby declare a national emergency to deal with this threat.

Accordingly, I hereby order:

Section 1.

(a) Not later than 45 days after the conclusion of a United States election, the Director of National Intelligence, in consultation with the heads of any other appropriate executive departments and agencies (agencies), shall conduct an assessment of any information indicating that a foreign government, or any person acting as an agent of or on behalf of a foreign government, has acted with the intent or purpose of interfering in that election. The assessment shall identify, to the maximum extent ascertainable, the nature of any foreign interference and any methods employed to execute it, the persons involved, and the foreign government or governments that authorized, directed, sponsored, or supported it. The Director of National Intelligence shall deliver this assessment and appropriate supporting information to the President, the Secretary of State, the Secretary of the Treasury, the Secretary of Defense, the Attorney General, and the Secretary of Homeland Security.

(b) Within 45 days of receiving the assessment and information described in section 1(a) of this order, the Attorney General and the Secretary of Homeland Security, in consultation with the heads of any other appropriate agencies and, as appropriate, State and local officials, shall deliver to the President, the Secretary of State, the Secretary of the Treasury, and the Secretary of Defense a report evaluating, with respect to the United States election that is the subject of the assessment described in section 1(a):

(i) the extent to which any foreign interference that targeted election infrastructure materially affected the security or integrity of that infrastructure, the tabulation of votes, or the timely transmission of election results; and

(ii) if any foreign interference involved activities targeting the infrastructure of, or pertaining to, a political organization, campaign, or candidate, the Start Printed Page 46844extent to which such activities materially affected the security or integrity of that infrastructure, including by unauthorized access to, disclosure or threatened disclosure of, or alteration or falsification of, information or data.

The report shall identify any material issues of fact with respect to these matters that the Attorney General and the Secretary of Homeland Security are unable to evaluate or reach agreement on at the time the report is submitted. The report shall also include updates and recommendations, when appropriate, regarding remedial actions to be taken by the United States Government, other than the sanctions described in sections 2 and 3 of this order.

(c) Heads of all relevant agencies shall transmit to the Director of National Intelligence any information relevant to the execution of the Director's duties pursuant to this order, as appropriate and consistent with applicable law. If relevant information emerges after the submission of the report mandated by section 1(a) of this order, the Director, in consultation with the heads of any other appropriate agencies, shall amend the report, as appropriate, and the Attorney General and the Secretary of Homeland Security shall amend the report required by section 1(b), as appropriate.

(d) Nothing in this order shall prevent the head of any agency or any other appropriate official from tendering to the President, at any time through an appropriate channel, any analysis, information, assessment, or evaluation of foreign interference in a United States election.

(e) If information indicating that foreign interference in a State, tribal, or local election within the United States has occurred is identified, it may be included, as appropriate, in the assessment mandated by section 1(a) of this order or in the report mandated by section 1(b) of this order, or submitted to the President in an independent report.

(f) Not later than 30 days following the date of this order, the Secretary of State, the Secretary of the Treasury, the Attorney General, the Secretary of Homeland Security, and the Director of National Intelligence shall develop a framework for the process that will be used to carry out their respective responsibilities pursuant to this order. The framework, which may be classified in whole or in part, shall focus on ensuring that agencies fulfill their responsibilities pursuant to this order in a manner that maintains methodological consistency; protects law enforcement or other sensitive information and intelligence sources and methods; maintains an appropriate separation between intelligence functions and policy and legal judgments; ensures that efforts to protect electoral processes and institutions are insulated from political bias; and respects the principles of free speech and open debate.

Sec. 2.

(a) All property and interests in property that are in the United States, that hereafter come within the United States, or that are or hereafter come within the possession or control of any United States person of the following persons are blocked and may not be transferred, paid, exported, withdrawn, or otherwise dealt in: any foreign person determined by the Secretary of the Treasury, in consultation with the Secretary of State, the Attorney General, and the Secretary of Homeland Security:

(i) to have directly or indirectly engaged in, sponsored, concealed, or otherwise been complicit in foreign interference in a United States election;

(ii) to have materially assisted, sponsored, or provided financial, material, or technological support for, or goods or services to or in support of, any activity described in subsection (a)(i) of this section or any person whose property and interests in property are blocked pursuant to this order; or

(iii) to be owned or controlled by, or to have acted or purported to act for or on behalf of, directly or indirectly, any person whose property or interests in property are blocked pursuant to this order.

(b) Executive Order 13694 of April 1, 2015, as amended by Executive Order 13757 of December 28, 2016, remains in effect. This order is not Start Printed Page 46845intended to, and does not, serve to limit the Secretary of the Treasury's discretion to exercise the authorities provided in Executive Order 13694. Where appropriate, the Secretary of the Treasury, in consultation with the Attorney General and the Secretary of State, may exercise the authorities described in Executive Order 13694 or other authorities in conjunction with the Secretary of the Treasury's exercise of authorities provided in this order.

(c) The prohibitions in subsection (a) of this section apply except to the extent provided by statutes, or in regulations, orders, directives, or licenses that may be issued pursuant to this order, and notwithstanding any contract entered into or any license or permit granted prior to the date of this order.

Sec. 3.

Following the transmission of the assessment mandated by section 1(a) and the report mandated by section 1(b):

(a) the Secretary of the Treasury shall review the assessment mandated by section 1(a) and the report mandated by section 1(b), and, in consultation with the Secretary of State, the Attorney General, and the Secretary of Homeland Security, impose all appropriate sanctions pursuant to section 2(a) of this order and any appropriate sanctions described in section 2(b) of this order; and

(b) the Secretary of State and the Secretary of the Treasury, in consultation with the heads of other appropriate agencies, shall jointly prepare a recommendation for the President as to whether additional sanctions against foreign persons may be appropriate in response to the identified foreign interference and in light of the evaluation in the report mandated by section 1(b) of this order, including, as appropriate and consistent with applicable law, proposed sanctions with respect to the largest business entities licensed or domiciled in a country whose government authorized, directed, sponsored, or supported election interference, including at least one entity from each of the following sectors: financial services, defense, energy, technology, and transportation (or, if inapplicable to that country's largest business entities, sectors of comparable strategic significance to that foreign government). The recommendation shall include an assessment of the effect of the recommended sanctions on the economic and national security interests of the United States and its allies. Any recommended sanctions shall be appropriately calibrated to the scope of the foreign interference identified, and may include one or more of the following with respect to each targeted foreign person:

(i) blocking and prohibiting all transactions in a person's property and interests in property subject to United States jurisdiction;

(ii) export license restrictions under any statute or regulation that requires the prior review and approval of the United States Government as a condition for the export or re-export of goods or services;

(iii) prohibitions on United States financial institutions making loans or providing credit to a person;

(iv) restrictions on transactions in foreign exchange in which a person has any interest;

(v) prohibitions on transfers of credit or payments between financial institutions, or by, through, or to any financial institution, for the benefit of a person;

(vi) prohibitions on United States persons investing in or purchasing equity or debt of a person;

(vii) exclusion of a person's alien corporate officers from the United States;

(viii) imposition on a person's alien principal executive officers of any of the sanctions described in this section; or

(ix) any other measures authorized by law.

Sec. 4.

I hereby determine that the making of donations of the type of articles specified in section 203(b)(2) of IEEPA (50 U.S.C. 1702(b)(2)) by, Start Printed Page 46846to, or for the benefit of any person whose property and interests in property are blocked pursuant to this order would seriously impair my ability to deal with the national emergency declared in this order, and I hereby prohibit such donations as provided by section 2 of this order.

Sec. 5.

The prohibitions in section 2 of this order include the following:

(a) the making of any contribution or provision of funds, goods, or services by, to, or for the benefit of any person whose property and interests in property are blocked pursuant to this order; and

(b) the receipt of any contribution or provision of funds, goods, or services from any such person.

Sec. 6.

I hereby find that the unrestricted immigrant and nonimmigrant entry into the United States of aliens whose property and interests in property are blocked pursuant to this order would be detrimental to the interests of the United States, and I hereby suspend entry into the United States, as immigrants or nonimmigrants, of such persons. Such persons shall be treated as persons covered by section 1 of Proclamation 8693 of July 24, 2011 (Suspension of Entry of Aliens Subject to United Nations Security Council Travel Bans and International Emergency Economic Powers Act Sanctions).

Sec. 7.

(a) Any transaction that evades or avoids, has the purpose of evading or avoiding, causes a violation of, or attempts to violate any of the prohibitions set forth in this order is prohibited.

(b) Any conspiracy formed to violate any of the prohibitions set forth in this order is prohibited.

Sec. 8.

For the purposes of this order:

(a) the term "person" means an individual or entity;

(b) the term "entity" means a partnership, association, trust, joint venture, corporation, group, subgroup, or other organization;

(c) the term "United States person" means any United States citizen, permanent resident alien, entity organized under the laws of the United States or any jurisdiction within the United States (including foreign branches), or any person (including a foreign person) in the United States;

(d) the term "election infrastructure" means information and communications technology and systems used by or on behalf of the Federal Government or a State or local government in managing the election process, including voter registration databases, voting machines, voting tabulation equipment, and equipment for the secure transmission of election results;

(e) the term "United States election" means any election for Federal office held on, or after, the date of this order;

(f) the term "foreign interference," with respect to an election, includes any covert, fraudulent, deceptive, or unlawful actions or attempted actions of a foreign government, or of any person acting as an agent of or on behalf of a foreign government, undertaken with the purpose or effect of influencing, undermining confidence in, or altering the result or reported result of, the election, or undermining public confidence in election processes or institutions;

(g) the term "foreign government" means any national, state, provincial, or other governing authority, any political party, or any official of any governing authority or political party, in each case of a country other than the United States;

(h) the term "covert," with respect to an action or attempted action, means characterized by an intent or apparent intent that the role of a foreign government will not be apparent or acknowledged publicly; and

(i) the term "State" means the several States or any of the territories, dependencies, or possessions of the United States.

Sec. 9.

For those persons whose property and interests in property are blocked pursuant to this order who might have a constitutional presence Start Printed Page 46847in the United States, I find that because of the ability to transfer funds or other assets instantaneously, prior notice to such persons of measures to be taken pursuant to this order would render those measures ineffectual. I therefore determine that for these measures to be effective in addressing the national emergency declared in this order, there need be no prior notice of a listing or determination made pursuant to section 2 of this order.

Sec. 10.

Nothing in this order shall prohibit transactions for the conduct of the official business of the United States Government by employees, grantees, or contractors thereof.

Sec. 11.

The Secretary of the Treasury, in consultation with the Attorney General and the Secretary of State, is hereby authorized to take such actions, including the promulgation of rules and regulations, and to employ all powers granted to the President by IEEPA as may be necessary to carry out the purposes of this order. The Secretary of the Treasury may re-delegate any of these functions to other officers within the Department of the Treasury consistent with applicable law. All agencies of the United States Government are hereby directed to take all appropriate measures within their authority to carry out the provisions of this order.

Sec. 12.

The Secretary of the Treasury, in consultation with the Attorney General and the Secretary of State, is hereby authorized to submit the recurring and final reports to the Congress on the national emergency declared in this order, consistent with section 401(c) of the NEA (50 U.S.C. 1641(c)) and section 204(c) of IEEPA (50 U.S.C. 1703(c)).

Sec. 13.

This order shall be implemented consistent with 50 U.S.C. 1702(b)(1) and (3).

Sec. 14.

(a) Nothing in this order shall be construed to impair or otherwise affect:

(i) the authority granted by law to an executive department or agency, or the head thereof; or

(ii) the functions of the Director of the Office of Management and Budget relating to budgetary, administrative, or legislative proposals.

(b) This order shall be implemented consistent with applicable law and subject to the availability of appropriations.

(c) This order is not intended to, and does not, create any right or benefit, substantive or procedural, enforceable at law or in equity by any party against the United States, its departments, agencies, or entities, its officers, employees, or agents, or any other person.

DONALD J. TRUMP

Intelligence Community Strategy, Policy Directives and Guidance

National Counterterrorism Strategy, 2018

October 2018

THE WHITE HOUSE
WASHINGTON, DC

My fellow Americans:

I made a solemn promise to the American people to spare no effort to preserve the safety and security of the United States. This National Strategy for Counterterrorism helps keep that promise. We must defeat the terrorists who threaten America's safety, prevent future attacks, and protect our national interests. This requires a new approach to combatting and preventing terrorism.

In fulfilling my promise to renew America's strength and security, I have revitalized our military, and we are now, through action and leadership, prevailing against the terrorists aiming to harm us and our interests. We are using all available tools at our disposal to combat terrorist groups, starve them of support, and prevent them from recruiting new followers. We are also disrupting terrorist threats within our own borders, from individuals mobilized to violence by a range of domestic and foreign terrorist ideologies and who threaten our safety.

This has not been easy. My Administration inherited a world in which the terrorist threat had become more complex and widespread than ever before. We, the people of the United States, face global terrorist networks and their affiliates. We face terrorist organizations backed by state sponsors. And we face homegrown threats inspired by terrorist propaganda.

The National Strategy for Counterterrorism recognizes the full range of terrorist threats that the United States confronts within and beyond our borders, and emphasizes the use of all elements of national power to combat terrorism and terrorist ideologies. It enhances our emphasis on targeting terrorist networks that threaten the United States and our allies and on disrupting and denying their ability to mobilize, finance, travel, communicate, and inspire new followers. We will deny terrorists the freedom to travel and communicate across international borders, and we will take action to limit their ability to recruit and radicalize online. We will combat the violent, extreme, and twisted ideologies that purport to justify the murder of innocent victims. We will also ensure that America's critical infrastructure is protected, in order to deter and prevent attacks, and is resilient so that we can quickly recover should it come under attack.

This National Strategy for Counterterrorism sets forth a new approach. We will protect our homeland, our interests overseas, and our allies and partners. We will defeat radical Islamist terrorists such as ISIS and al-Qa'ida, expand our agile counterterrorism toolkit to prevent future terrorist threats, deter emerging threats, roll back Iran's global terrorist network, and ensure our country's continued safety. Now, and in the future, we will secure our Nation and prevail against terrorism.

Sincerely,

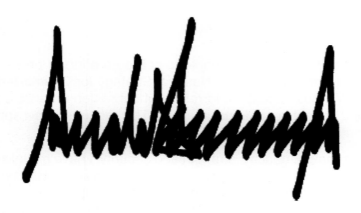

President Donald J. Trump

The White House
October 2018

Executive Summary

We Remain a Nation at War

Today's terrorist landscape is more fluid and complex than ever. For this reason, counterterrorism remains a top priority for this Administration. Our principal terrorist enemies are radical Islamist terrorist groups that seek to conduct attacks globally, violate our borders, and radicalize and recruit potential extremists within the United States and abroad. We continue to face threats from Iran, the most prominent state sponsor of terrorism, through its global network of operatives and its ongoing support to an array of terrorist groups. Terrorists motivated by other forms of extremism also use violence to threaten the homeland and challenge United States interests. These terrorist threats are different in many ways, but they all seek to use violence to undermine the United States and disrupt the American way of life.

Since September 11, 2001, we have learned that winning the war on terrorism requires our country to aggressively pursue terrorists. We have also learned, however, that we must do more than merely kill or capture terrorists. We must dismantle terrorists' networks and sever the sources of strength and support that sustain them, that allow them to regenerate, and that permit them to adapt. To secure a lasting victory, we must also maintain sufficient pressure on terrorist organizations to prevent them from reemerging.

This Administration has already taken significant steps to address the terrorist threat. Under the leadership of President Donald J. Trump, the United States has accelerated efforts to defeat those terrorists who pose a threat to the United States. For instance, working with coalition partners, we have

- This strategy uses all available instruments of United States power to counter terrorism. We will defeat our enemies with the full force of America's strengths.

- This strategy will protect the United States against all terrorists that threaten our country. We will not focus on a single organization but will counter all terrorists with the ability and the intent to harm the United States, our citizens, and our interests abroad.

- This strategy places America First and emphasizes protection of the homeland— building strong borders, strengthening security at all ports of entry into the United States, protecting its critical infrastructure, and facilitating preparedness.

- This strategy recognizes, however, that America First does not mean America alone. We will broaden our range of partners to combat radical Islamist terrorism, Iran-sponsored terrorism, and other forms of violent extremism; encourage capable partners to play a larger role in counterterrorism efforts; and assist other partners so that they can eventually address terrorist threats independently.

liberated nearly all of the territory once controlled by the self-declared Islamic State of Iraq and al-Sham (ISIS) in Iraq and Syria. While we have made much progress, additional challenges remain. We must continually work to stay ahead of an adaptive enemy.

This means that we must undertake additional efforts to prevent terrorists from acquiring or using weapons of mass destruction (WMD) and other advanced attack capabilities. We must prevent terrorists from exploiting new technologies in today's dynamic information environment, and we must counter terrorists' ability to recruit and radicalize online and through other means.

Likewise, experience has taught us that preparedness and prevention must be integral parts of our counterterrorism strategy. We must protect the homeland against the terrorist threat by building strong borders, securing United States infrastructure, and enhancing the preparedness of the American people.

Experience has also highlighted the importance of strong partnerships in sustaining our counterterrorism efforts. Whenever possible, the United States must develop more efficient approaches to achieve our security objectives, relying on our allies to degrade and maintain persistent pressure against terrorists.

This means collaborating so that foreign governments take the lead wherever possible, and working with others so that they can assume responsibility in the fight against terrorists. Domestically, we must empower our frontline defenders—our state and local law enforcement professionals—as well as many other government, civil society, and private sector partners to prevent and counter terrorism in the United States.

Building on the National Security Strategy and the Administration's progress to date, the National

Strategy for Counterterrorism outlines how the United States will combat terrorism at home and abroad and keep America safe. Acting in accordance with this strategy, we will defeat our enemies, just as we have defeated the purveyors of oppression, fascism, and totalitarianism in previous wars. We will always remember September 11, 2001, and the sacrifices made by so many brave patriots in defense of our country against the evil scourge of terrorism. With that same spirit of service and self-sacrifice, we will safeguard the homeland, protect our way of life, and eliminate our enemy's ability to threaten our country.

We are a nation at war—and it is a war that the United States will win.

Table of Contents

Introduction

The Path to Victory

The United States occupies a special role among nations as a vanguard of freedom, democracy, and constitutional governance. These luminous ideals must be assiduously defended in a world of increasing challenges and dangers from the forces that threaten America's people, our vital interests, and the security and prosperity of our allies and partners.

Terrorists seek to undermine American ideals and the United States Government by using violence and propaganda to advance their depraved goals. After seventeen years of armed conflict and significant costs in American blood and treasure, our efforts to prevent and counter terrorism have met with mixed success. While we have succeeded in disrupting large-scale attacks in the homeland since 2001, we have not sufficiently mitigated the overall threat that terrorists pose.

Today's terrorist threats have changed, and terrorist groups are now more geographically dispersed and their tactics more diversified. To address this evolving terrorist threat across the globe and within the homeland, our approach to counterterrorism must evolve. As President Donald J. Trump has stated, "America is committed to adjusting our strategies to meet evolving threats and new facts.

We will discard those strategies that have not worked—and will apply new approaches informed by experience and judgment." We must confront terrorists with the combined power of America's strengths—our strong military, our law enforcement and intelligence communities, our civilian government institutions, our vibrant private sector, our civil society, our international partnerships, and the firm resolve of the American people.

Harnessing our full potential, the spirit of innovation that has been key to our national greatness, and our tradition of working together toward our common goals, we will prevail and prevent terrorism from disrupting the American way of life.

Through the National Strategy for Counterterrorism, we will achieve the following end states to safeguard our homeland, way of life, and shared interests:

- The terrorist threat to the United States is eliminated;

- Our borders and all ports of entry into the United States are secure against terrorist threats;

- Terrorism, radical Islamist ideologies, and other violent extremist ideologies do not undermine the American way of life; and

- Foreign partners address terrorist threats so that these threats do not jeopardize the collective interests of the United States and our partners.

To achieve these aims, this strategy adopts an America First approach to counterterrorism—one that is guided by United States interests; shaped by realistic assessments of both our challenges and our capabilities; and attuned to the important roles of our allies and partners, both foreign and domestic, in our shared counterterrorism efforts.

This strategy differs from previous strategies in that it adopts a more agile and expansive approach that addresses the full spectrum of terrorist threats to the United States, including our enemies overseas and the people they seek to influence and mobilize to violence in the United States. We will also confront the threat of terrorists in the United States who seek to further their political or social aims through unlawful acts of violence without foreign direction or inspiration. In this pursuit, we will continue to protect American freedoms, and we will be unwavering in our commitment to defeat all those who turn to violence in an attempt to destroy, disrupt, or impair our society.

Importantly, this America First approach will harness the full span of United States power and use every available tool to combat terrorism at home, abroad, and in cyberspace. This includes military and intelligence operations overseas, law enforcement actions at home and abroad, diplomatic engagement, and the use of financial tools. We will modernize and integrate existing counterterrorism tools so we can secure our borders through, among other things, more rigorous scrutiny of entry applications. We will also deploy new technologies precisely where they are needed and protect critical infrastructure in the United States from terrorist attacks. Finally, we will incorporate two of the most potent tools in the information environment: cyber operations and strategic communications. These tools are an in-

tegral part of our counterterrorism activities, and we will continue to incorporate them when appropriate to maximize their effects.

In addition, this strategy prioritizes a broader range of non-military capabilities, such as our ability to prevent and intervene in terrorist recruitment, minimize the appeal of terrorist propaganda online, and build societal resilience to terrorism. This includes leveraging the skills and resources of civil society and non-traditional partners to diminish terrorists' efforts to radicalize and recruit people in the United States.

To defeat radical Islamist terrorism, we must also speak out forcefully against a hateful ideology that provides the breeding ground for violence and terrorism. We will expose the destructive, totalitarian nature of the ideology that fuels violent radical Islamist movements, such as ISIS and al-Qa'ida. We will reveal the way violent radical Islamist terrorists have killed, exploited, and betrayed Muslim communities, including women and children.

Through our efforts, we will thwart terrorists' ability to exploit the Internet for directing, enabling, or inspiring attacks.

We will not do this alone. This strategy recognizes that effective counterterrorism requires a wide range of public and private sector partners as well as foreign partnerships. As President Trump stated, "We must seek partners, not perfection—and to make allies of all who share our goals." Accordingly, from civil society and state, local, tribal, and territorial governments to private sector partners and foreign allies, the full range of our partnerships must be enhanced to effectively prevent and counter terrorist activity, particularly as tactics and actors can change quickly. We will expect more of our partners in this

Through this new approach, the United States will integrate our instruments of national power to achieve our end states through the following strategic objectives:

The capacity of terrorists to conduct attacks in the homeland and against vital United States interests overseas is sharply diminished;	✋
The sources of strength and support upon which terrorists rely are severed;	💵
Terrorists' ability to radicalize, recruit, and mobilize to violence in the homeland is diminished;	🚫
Americans are prepared and protected from terrorist attacks in the homeland, including through more exacting border security and law enforcement actions;	🛡
Terrorists are unable to acquire or use WMDs, including chemical, biological, radiological, and nuclear weapons, and other advanced weaponry; and	☣
Public sector partners, private sector partners, and foreign partners take a greater role in preventing and countering terrorism.	🤝

fight, but they will never doubt our resolute commitment to defending our shared interests. All the while, we will be pragmatic in our approach and mindful of the need to use our resources carefully.

This strategy, therefore, prioritizes United States counterterrorism efforts against those terrorists with the ability and intent to harm the United States and our vital national interests and limits United States efforts overseas to those that directly bolster our national security. Likewise, to maximize the effectiveness of our actions, we will continue to integrate United States Government counterterrorism efforts. Finally, we will continually review the efficacy of our approach through independent assessments (informed by research, intelligence, and analysis) to ensure that we are making measurable progress toward our strategic objectives. By rigorously monitoring our progress and measuring the impact of our activities, we can make informed adjustments when needed to advance our counterterrorism efforts.

Guided by this strategy, rooted in American principles, and harnessing our inherent strengths as a nation, we will eliminate terrorists' ability to threaten America, our interests, and our engagement in the world. The United States—forever the sentinel of democracy and freedom—will prevail over terrorism and preserve the American way of life. Through our triumph, we will demonstrate that American strength remains a lasting force for good in the world.

National Strategy for Counterterrorism at a Glance

The strategic objectives are critical to reaching the desired end states, and the lines of effort are the means for achieving them.

STRATEGIC OBJECTIVES

 The capacity of terrorists to conduct attacks in the homeland and against vital United States interests overseas is sharply diminished

 Americans are prepared and protected from terrorist attacks in the homeland, including through more exacting border security and law enforcement actions

 The sources of strength and support upon which terrorists rely are severed

 Terrorists are unable to acquire or use Weapons of Mass Destruction (WMD), including chemical, biological, radiological, and nuclear weapons, and other advanced weaponry

 Terrorists' ability to radicalize, recruit, and mobilize to violence in the homeland is diminished

 Public sector partners, private sector partners, and foreign partners take a greater role in preventing and countering terrorism

END STATES

End State	✋	💲	🚫	🛡	☣	🤝
The terrorist threat to the United States is eliminated	✋	💲	🚫	🛡	☣	🤝
Our borders and all ports of entry into the United States are secure against terrorist threats	✋	💲	🚫	🛡	☣	🤝
Terrorism, radical Islamist ideologies, and other violent extremist ideologies do not undermine the American way of life			🚫	🛡	☣	🤝
Foreign partners address terrorist threats so that these threats do not jeopardize the collective interests of the United States and our partners.	✋	💲	🚫		☣	🤝

LINES OF EFFORT

Line of Effort	✋	💲	🚫	🛡	☣	🤝
Pursue terrorist threats to their source	✋				☣	🤝
Isolate terrorists from financial, material, and logistical sources of support	✋	💲			☣	🤝
Modernize and integrate a broader set of United States tools and authorities to counter terrorism and protect the homeland	✋	💲	🚫		☣	🤝
Protect United States infrastructure and enhance preparedness	✋		🚫	🛡	☣	🤝
Counter terrorist radicalization and recruitment	✋		🚫			🤝
Strengthen the counterterrorism abilities of international partners	✋	💲			☣	🤝

The Terrorist Adversary

The United States and our allies face an increasingly complex terrorist landscape, populated by a diverse array of actors employing new technologies and tactics to advance their agendas. The terrorist threat to the United States is growing more dynamic and diffuse as an increasing number of groups, networks, and individuals exploit global trends, including the emergence of more secure modes of communications, the expansion of social and mass media, and persistent instability across several regions.

Radical Islamist terrorists remain the primary transnational terrorist threat to the United States and its vital national interests. Prominent terrorist organizations, particularly ISIS and al-Qa'ida, have repeatedly demonstrated the intent and capability to attack the homeland and United States interests and continue to plot new attacks and inspire susceptible people to commit acts of violence inside the United States.[1] These groups stoke and exploit weak governance, conflict, instability, and long-standing political and religious grievances to pursue their goal of eliminating Western influence in majority Muslim countries and remaking Islamic society. Radical Islamist terrorist groups have developed and used methods that have challenged United States counterterrorism efforts, including establishing state-like governing institutions within their safe havens, deploying sophisticated explosive devices to defeat aviation security measures, and using high-quality media products to recruit extremists in the West. Future radical Islamist terrorists and other terrorists will continually adapt these and other tactics to their circumstances and the technological advances of the age. It is, therefore, critical that the United States counterterrorism posture be agile enough to adapt as well. Radi-

cal Islamist terrorists have a violent extremist ideology that serves to create a common identity and sense of purpose for those susceptible to its core message. This vile ideology is used to indoctrinate new recruits to accept terrorist groups' goals and directives without question, and also allows these groups to maintain cohesion, ensure conformity, and justify the use of violence to meet the ideology's goals. It avails terrorists of a worldview that helps unify their efforts by fomenting conflict and attempts to legitimize terrorism by elevating the social status of group members and absolving individuals from culpability for their participation in violence. Because of this, we must ensure that our efforts will undermine the appeal of this ideology of hate. Its resilience, power, and appeal make it a grave danger to not just our own nation's security but also that of our allies across the globe. Without the appeal of this ideology, radical Islamist terrorism has no foundation.

ISIS remains the foremost radical Islamist terrorist group and the primary transnational terrorist threat to the United States, despite ongoing United States and coalition civilian

---

1. The intelligence and law enforcement communities refer to an individual in the United States radicalized and mobilized to violence by radical Islamist terrorist ideologies as a homegrown violent extremist (HVE).

and military efforts that have diminished the group's footprint in Iraq and Syria, killed thousands of its members, and curtailed its global expansion. ISIS retains the financial and material resources and expertise to launch external attacks—including against United States interests—and its senior leaders continue to call for attacks against the United States. The group's global reach remains robust, with eight official branches and more than two dozen networks regularly conducting terrorist and insurgent operations across Africa, Asia, Europe, and the Middle East. Despite many setbacks, ISIS maintains a sophisticated and durable media and online presence that allows it to encourage and enable sympathizers worldwide to conduct dozens of attacks within target countries, including the United States. The increase in attacks by persons mobilized to violence in the United States underscores the ability of ISIS to inspire terrorist attacks.

ISIS has been innovative and determined in its pursuit of attacks in the West. The group has exploited weaknesses in European border security to great effect by capitalizing on the migrant crisis to seed attack operatives into the region. For instance, two of the perpetrators of the 2015 ISIS attacks in Paris, France, infiltrated the country by posing as migrants. Further, ISIS is continuing its efforts to circumvent European efforts to shore up border security by identifying new routes. Europe's struggle to screen the people crossing its borders highlights the importance of ensuring strong United States borders so that terrorists cannot enter the United States.

In addition, the savagery of ISIS has caused a massive movement of millions of innocent refugees. Our battlefield successes, meanwhile, have given way to the flight of thousands of terrorists seeking to evade justice. As defeated fighters and their families disperse, the United States and our partners must remain vigilant to ensure that terrorists cannot evade our security measures to threaten our people and way of life.

Meanwhile, al-Qa'ida's global network remains resilient and poses an enduring threat to the homeland and United States interests around the world. Consistent United States-led counterterrorism pressure has removed many of its senior leaders and reduced the group's ability to operate in South Asia, but its affiliates continue to plan and carry out terrorist attacks against the United States and our allies, as well as raise funds from individual supporters through the international financial system. Affiliate resources are primarily focused on local and regional conflicts, but key operatives and elements within the network continue to seek out new opportunities to strike the homeland and United States interests and to inspire attacks inside the United States. Veteran al-Qa'ida leaders are working to consolidate and expand the group's presence in several regions, including in Syria, from which it aspires to launch new attacks against the United States and our allies.

Both ISIS and al-Qa'ida have inspired people susceptible to their malign influence to conduct terrorist attacks inside the United States. This will probably remain the most frequent form of radical Islamist terrorism in the United States for the next several years. Such attacks, motivated by a wide range of factors, will continue to be conducted primarily through the use of simple tactics against predominantly soft targets. ISIS is likely to remain the main inspiration for such attacks, particularly if the group can retain its prominence and use social and mainstream media coverage to promote its violent message.

In addition to ISIS and al-Qa'ida, dozens of other radical Islamist terrorist groups are working to advance more locally focused insurgent or terrorist campaigns, while still posing a threat to United States persons and interests overseas. These groups, including Boko Haram, Tehrik-e Taliban Pakistan, and Lashkar-e Tayyiba, employ a range of political and terrorist tactics to undermine local governments and conduct attacks. These organizations will probably prioritize regional goals over attacks against the homeland or United States interests because of resource constraints or political considerations. However, many of these groups are hostile to the United States, maintain networks of sympathizers around the world, and retain ties to ISIS or al-Qa'ida, underscoring their potential threat to United States interests.

Iran remains the most prominent state sponsor of terrorism, supporting militant and terrorist groups across the Middle East and cultivating a network of operatives that pose a threat in the United States and globally. These groups, most notably Lebanese Hizballah (Hizballah), use terrorism and other asymmetric means in partnership with Iran to expand their influence in Iraq, Lebanon, the Palestinian territories, Syria, and Yemen and to destabilize their rivals. Hizballah fields powerful military and intelligence elements, possesses large stocks of sophisticated arms, and maintains extensive networks of operatives and sympathizers overseas, including individuals in the homeland. Through the Islamic Revolutionary Guard Corps-Qods Force (IRGC-QF), Iran's primary terrorist support arm, the Government of Iran provides financial and material support, training, and guidance to Hizballah and other Shia militant groups operating in Bahrain, Iraq, Syria, and Yemen. It also supports HAMAS and other Palestinian terrorist groups. With operatives deployed around the world, the IRGC-QF has the capability to target United States interests and possibly the homeland.

There is also a broad range of revolutionary, nationalist, and separatist movements overseas whose use of violence and intent to destabilize societies often puts American lives at risk. For example, the Nordic Resistance Movement is a prominent transnational, self-described nationalist-socialist organization with anti-Western views that has conducted violent attacks against Muslims, left-wing groups, and others. The group has demonstrated against United States Government actions it perceives are supportive of Israel and has the potential to extend its targeting to United States interests. Similarly, the neo-Nazi National Action Group, a terrorist organization that was banned by the United Kingdom in 2016 for its promotion of violence against politicians and minorities, operates mainly in the United Kingdom but has engaged with like-minded groups in the United States, Estonia, France, Germany, Latvia, and Poland—expanding the potential influence of its violent ideology. Likewise, Babbar Khalsa International seeks, through violent means, to establish its own independent state in India and is responsible for significant terrorist attacks in India and elsewhere that have claimed the lives of innocent civilians. Such groups may avoid or deprioritize targeting United States interests for now to avoid detracting from their core goals but frequently conduct assassinations and bombings against major economic, political, and social targets, heightening the risk to United States personnel and interests overseas.

Lastly, the United States has long faced a persistent security threat from domestic terrorists who are not motivated by a radical Islamist ideology but are instead motivated by other forms of violent extremism, such as racially motivated extremism, animal rights extremism, environmental extremism, sovereign citizen extremism, and militia extremism. Such extremist groups attempt to advance their agendas through acts of force or violence. Notably, domestic terrorism in the United States is on the rise, with an increasing number of fatalities and violent nonlethal acts committed by domestic terrorists against people and property in the United States. The economic harm caused by domestic terrorists has also increased sharply as domestic terrorists have continued to destroy property, disrupt business, and perpetrate financial crimes that are designed to damage certain sectors of the United States economy.

Prioritization and Resourcing

As President Trump has noted, "America is a sovereign nation and our first priority is always the safety and security of our citizens." The United States must, therefore, relentlessly focus on countering terrorism that jeopardizes American citizens and interests. We will not dilute our counterterrorism efforts by attempting to be everywhere all the time, trying to eradicate all threats. We can and will, however, optimize and focus our resources to effectively prevent and counter those terrorists who pose a direct threat to the United States homeland and vital national interests.

To combat what has become a more complex and geographically dispersed terrorist threat, the United States will prioritize integrated actions and resources against those terrorists that have both the intent and capability to attack the United States and our interests abroad. As noted, radical Islamist terrorists present the most dangerous transnational terrorist threat to the United States and our vital national interests as defined in the National Security Strategy. At the same time, the United States also faces threats from Iran-backed terrorist groups and other transnational terrorist organizations. In the homeland, we will continue to confront the rising threat of attacks committed by persons inspired and mobilized to violence by both radical Islamist ideologies and domestic terrorist ideologies. Terrorists and the threats they pose, however, are not monolithic. The dangers posed by different terrorists vary by group and by region. The National Strategy for Counterterrorism, therefore, will guide the tools and approaches used for counterterrorism efforts and will generally defer to regional, functional, and group-specific strategies to prioritize terrorist groups based upon the threat they pose to our homeland and vital national interests. In addition, counterterrorism efforts must be properly balanced across all instruments of national power and include the efforts of traditional and non-traditional partners. While the United States must retain the ability to strike at terrorism around the globe, non-military tools—such as law enforcement, intelligence, diplomacy, financial measures, stabilization, development, prevention, and intervention and reintegration programs—are also required to prevent and counter terrorism. We must, therefore, increase our focus on developing domestic and foreign partners' non-military counterterrorism capabilities so they can act independently against terrorists. Finally, as we embark on this new approach, we must rigorously monitor and assess our effectiveness and adjust operations accordingly. Annual independent strategic assessments informed by research, intelligence, and analysis will ensure that we are making measurable progress toward our strategic objectives. These assessments will identify the impediments to our effectiveness and recommend adjustments to the strategy to outpace dynamic adversaries. They will also ensure that our progress is sustainable as we continue to address the full range of contemporary national security challenges.

Pursue Terrorist Threats to Their Source

Terrorists are difficult to disrupt because they are highly adaptive and use any means to achieve their ends. Within the United States, they exploit our open and free society to target civilians. They take advantage of technology, such as the Internet and encrypted communications, to promote their malicious goals and spread their violent ideologies. Overseas, they thrive in countries with weak governments and where disenfranchised populations are vulnerable to terrorists' destructive and misinformed narratives, and they are adaptive in the face of pressure from countries with strong governments. Some are sheltered and supported by foreign governments or even do their bidding.

In the past, when the United States and our partners have disrupted terrorist plots, some terrorists remained in hiding, only to reemerge when pressure subsided. Therefore, the United States must do more than disrupt individual plots—we must pursue the entirety of the network involved in terrorist plotting to prevent the remaining terrorists from reviving their operations. At home, law enforcement at all levels of government will continue to pursue known or suspected terrorists, integrating all sources of information available. Overseas, we will disrupt terrorist networks that pose a credible threat to United States interests by conducting military, intelligence, and law enforcement operations and employing financial measures against discrete targets—working by, with, and through partners where possible. We will also enhance intelligence-sharing arrangements, increasing the timeliness and quality of exchange to identify the entire network involved in terrorist activity and maintain pressure on key terrorists and terrorist organizations.

Priority Actions

TARGET KEY TERRORISTS AND TERRORIST GROUPS: Using both military and non-military capabilities, we will target the terrorists and terrorist groups who pose the greatest threat to American citizens and interests. This will include terrorist leaders, operational planners, and individuals deploying their expertise in areas such as WMD, explosives, cyber operations, and propaganda. We will apply persistent pressure through sustained United States and partner intelligence, law enforcement, economic and financial measures, and military action to disrupt, degrade, and prevent the reconstitution of terrorist networks.

ENHANCE REACH INTO DENIED AREAS OVERSEAS: Where we cannot establish a physical presence to protect our interests directly, we will develop innovative means and work with partners to expand our capability to identify and mitigate emerging threats before they can strike the United States and our national interests.

EFFECTIVELY USE LAW OF ARMED CONFLICT (LOAC) DETENTION AS A COUNTERTERRORISM TOOL: The detention of enemies under the LOAC permits the United States to humanely remove dangerous terrorists from the battlefield and enhances our ability to collect intelligence from captured terrorists. This capability, in certain circumstances, also permits detention of terrorists pending their transfer to the United States for criminal prosecution. We will, therefore, retain LOAC detention as a counterterrorism tool, preserve our ability to detain terrorists at the detention facilities at United States Naval Station Guantanamo Bay, Cuba, and explore ways to better integrate and maximize the utility of this capability where lawful and appropriate.

FURTHER INTEGRATE FEDERAL, STATE, AND LOCAL COUNTERTERRORISM INFORMATION-SHARING: We will improve the ability to share timely and sensitive information on threats and the individuals perpetrating them, whether motivated by domestic or foreign terrorist ideologies, across all levels of government. We will continue to ensure that law enforcement agencies across all levels of government have the information that they need to identify and act swiftly against terrorist activity.

AMPLIFY THE IMPACT OF COUNTERTERRORISM OPERATIONS WITH STRATEGIC COMMUNICATIONS: We will integrate our strategic communications capability across our efforts to send a clear message: those who threaten the United States will pay a serious price, and America stands in solidarity with the populations upon which terrorists prey. This message will aim to discredit terrorist narratives, dissuade potential terrorist supporters, and demonstrate that the effects of our counterterrorism operations are not limited solely to direct action.

Isolate Terrorists from Financial, Material, and Logistical Sources of Support

The technological advances of the past century have created an interconnected world in which it is easier than ever to quickly move people, funding, material, and information across the globe. The backbone of this interconnected system is information technology—largely created and facilitated by the United States Government and private industry—that is increasingly enabling faster transactions of all kinds across the world. Terrorists use these same publicly available technologies to command and control their organizations and to plot attacks, travel, and abuse the global financial system to raise funds and procure weapons, materiel, and basic necessities.

Terrorists cannot sustain their operations without these resources. The United States and our partners abroad and in the private sector must , therefore, prevent terrorists from using them while safeguarding these resources for legitimate use. To accomplish this, we will increase information-sharing with the private sector and will tear down existing barriers to information-sharing. Around the globe, we will promote effective enforcement of legislation and policies aimed at protecting the commerce, transportation, and communication industries. We will also identify policies that must change as terrorists adapt.

Priority Actions

ENHANCE DETECTION AND DISRUPTION OF TERRORIST TRAVEL: We will continue to collect and share relevant information on terrorist travel and identities, with a focus on providing information that the public and private sector can use to identify and disrupt the movement of terrorists. We will also continue to work closely with our partners to enhance travel security and border protection to prevent terrorists fleeing conflict zones from infiltrating civilian populations. By sharing identity information and exploiting publicly available information, such as social media, we will identify these terrorists and enable law enforcement action against them in their home countries. In these efforts, we will take appropriate steps to protect privacy, civil rights, and civil liberties.

COUNTER EXISTING AND EMERGING TERRORIST FUNDING METHODS: We will collaborate across the public and private sectors to enhance information-sharing regarding terrorists' financial data, transactions, and activities. We will use this information and our economic authorities, including financial sanctions and other financial measures, as well as law enforcement action, to deny terrorists the ability to raise funds, including by disrupting terrorist financing and dismantling terrorist support networks, to prevent terrorists from abusing the United States and global financial systems, and to dissuade people from providing funds or materiel to terrorists. We will also share this information and collaborate with foreign partners to support their own targeted actions against terrorist financing networks and promote the effective implementation of international standards to counter terrorist financing worldwide.

PREVENT DEVELOPMENT AND ACQUISITION OF ATTACK CAPABILITIES: We will prevent terrorists from developing or acquiring knowledge and material that enables the development of WMD and other advanced weapons, including the capability to perform large-scale cyber attacks. We will work with partner nations, international organizations, and commercial entities to improve their capacity to secure dangerous materials and ensure that terrorists cannot exploit the scientific and academic communities to acquire new capabilities.

EXPOSE AND COUNTER STATE SUPPORT TO TERRORISM: While some countries, such as Iran, continue to use terrorism as an overt tool of their foreign policy, most countries that provide support for terrorists do so clandestinely, exploiting legitimate commercial networks to conceal their support activity. The United States will continue to acquire evidence of these states' deceptive practices and work with allies and partners to identify and punish states that support terrorism.

Modernize and Integrate a Broader Set of United States Tools and Authorities to Counter Terrorism and Protect the Homeland

Terrorists are typically clandestine actors, banding in small groups or acting alone and hiding in plain sight. We must stay ahead of terrorist attacks by advancing our detection capabilities and capacity to share early indicators with those who can piece together plot information and take action.

We will, therefore, move toward seamless integration and analysis of all information available to the United States and our partners and develop technology to enable lawful and appropriate responses that rapidly identify and stop terrorist threats. As we continue to protect information appropriately, we will deny terrorists the ability to take advantage of our open society, and we will stop them before they can attack.

Priority Actions

SECURE OUR BORDERS FROM TERRORIST THREATS: We will integrate capabilities and authorities from across the United States Government and coordinate with our partners abroad to prevent terrorists from entering the homeland. Our efforts will begin overseas, where we will ensure that our partners share and use information, such as watchlists, biometric information, and travel data, to prevent terrorists and fleeing foreign fighters from traveling to the United States. We will also share technology that allows partners to screen cargo and baggage for threats, including WMD materials and precursors. At our borders, we will modernize our screening and identity intelligence capabilities to track terrorist travelers and prevent the entry of those who support terrorist ideologies and violence.

DEPLOY THE INTEGRATED FEDERAL COUNTERTERRORISM COMMUNITY AT LOCAL LEVELS: We will continue to appropriately staff and support joint terrorism task forces and interagency fusion centers with leaders and team members detailed from a variety of departments and agencies. This will ensure that the federal government is able to deploy our full range of expertise and authorities where it will most effectively support state and local law enforcement partners.

ADOPT TECHNOLOGIES TO PROCESS DATA: We will harness technologies that allow our counterterrorism efforts to keep pace with a dynamic environment and build holistic identities of terrorists. The technologies we develop will be usable and accessible across the agencies of the United States Government to ensure sharing and integration. We will also seek to enhance our ability to access terrorist communications, including by using technical tools and by law enforcement working with private industry to confront challenges posed by technological barriers.

BUILD A HOLISTIC PICTURE OF TERROR-ISTS' IDENTITIES: We will enhance the collection, discovery, and exploitation of identity information supporting the counterterrorism mission, particularly biometric data. We will also identify and use other categories of identity information, including publicly available information, financial intelligence, and captured enemy material. We will improve the interoperability among United States Government systems to enable more efficient sharing of this information, bolstering our analysis and screening capabilities.

INVESTIGATE AND INTEGRATE THREAT INFORMATION RELATING TO DOMESTIC TERRORISTS AND THEIR OVERSEAS COUNTERPARTS: Where lawful and appropriate, departments and agencies will investigate ties between domestic terrorists not motivated by radical Islamist ideologies and their overseas counterparts to more fully understand them. This investigation will include identifying indicators of mobilization to violence. Where applicable, we will better integrate domestic terrorism information into our analysis of homeland threats and continue information-sharing among our federal, state, local, and tribal law enforcement partners.

UPDATE COUNTERTERRORISM POLICIES: We will fully empower the national security and law enforcement communities to pursue terrorist threats to their source and prevent terrorist attacks while respecting Americans' rights. We will focus on policies that have not kept up with the evolving threat picture and technology environment. For example, we will allow agencies to more easily share identity intelligence about terrorists and use publicly available information to preempt emerging threats.

Protect United States Infrastructure and Enhance Preparedness

The critical infrastructure of the United States—much of which is privately owned—provides the essential goods and services that drive American prosperity. Coordinated efforts are, therefore, necessary to strengthen and maintain secure and resilient critical infrastructure and to prepare Americans to respond appropriately should an attack occur. By integrating and improving preparedness across all levels of government as well as the private and public sectors, we will stop terrorists from undermining our security and prosperity.

Critical infrastructure has long been subject to physical threats and is now increasingly exposed to the risk of attacks in cyberspace. Our infrastructure is also interconnected, meaning that damage or disruption of one infrastructure element can cause cascading effects impacting other forms of infrastructure. We will stop terrorists' attempts to break through our defenses by building strong partnerships and by implementing innovative methods for protecting our infrastructure from attack and disruption. In addition, working with a range of stakeholders, including those from the private sector and civil society, we will enhance preparedness and increase public awareness about national efforts and successes in confronting terrorism to increase public trust and confidence in America's strength.

Priority Actions

ENHANCE DEFENSIVE MEASURES FOR INFRASTRUCTURE AND SOFT TARGETS: As terrorists seek new ways to attack our infrastructure and soft targets— both at home and abroad—we will improve and innovate our layered defenses. We will ensure redundancy of our systems, including systems in cyberspace, and develop measures for rapid recovery for systems if an attack should occur, facilitating their quick return to normal operations.

BROADEN AWARENESS OF THE TERRORIST THREAT TO UNITED STATES CRITICAL INFRASTRUCTURE: We will ensure that key private sector and foreign partners are informed of the potential terrorist threat to their facilities. We will incorporate state and local law enforcement and emergency services personnel as well as critical infrastructure participants into national exercises featuring realistic terrorism scenarios.

ENHANCE PREPAREDNESS AND PROMOTE READINESS: Partnering with an expanded network of organizations, individuals, and all levels of government, we will ensure that our society is prepared to withstand and quickly recover from a terrorist attack, including the possibility of a WMD attack. We will do this by conducting public information campaigns, training emergency response personnel, and ensuring the viability of our emergency notification systems. Recognizing that past terrorist attacks often targeted the private sector and civilians, we will welcome their partnership in sharing best practices in stopping and recovering from terrorist attacks and related incidents.

DEVELOP A PUBLIC COMMUNICATIONS STRATEGY: Through a coordinated counterterrorism communications plan, we will educate the public on how to prepare for, respond during, and quickly recover after an attack. We will also train federal, state, and local interlocutors on interactions with the public that foster a culture of preparedness and resilience.

Counter Terrorist Radicalization and Recruitment

Over the past seventeen years, we have built a robust counterterrorism architecture to stop attacks and eliminate terrorists, but we have not developed a prevention architecture to thwart terrorist radicalization and recruitment. Unless we counter terrorist radicalization and recruitment, we will be fighting a never-ending battle against terrorism in the homeland, overseas, and online. Our strategy, therefore, will champion and institutionalize prevention and create a global prevention architecture with the help of civil society, private partners, and the technology industry.

Priority Actions

INSTITUTIONALIZE A PREVENTION ARCHITECTURE TO THWART TERRORISM: We will support local solutions and empower stakeholders, providing them with the knowledge and resources they need to address terrorist threats. Early warning systems, including bystander reporting, will be a critical component of this architecture. We will also work closely with foreign partners, the technology sector, religious leaders, local stakeholders, and international fora to identify and share best practices. We will also seek to promote voices of pluralism and tolerance. Through these efforts, we will prevent radicalization and mobilization to violence across all violent extremist ideologies.

COMBAT VIOLENT EXTREMIST IDEOLOGIES: We will undermine the ability of terrorist ideologies, particularly radical Islamist terrorist ideologies, to create a common identity and sense of purpose among potential recruits. We must combat the resilience of terrorist narratives by acknowledging that their ideologies contain elements that have enduring appeal among their audiences. To undercut terrorist recruiting, we will demonstrate that their claims are false and do not offer effective solutions. We will exploit doubts among potential recruits to reduce terrorists' ability to incite violence and recruit. We will also communicate alternatives and promote off ramps from violence to prevent individuals from becoming more committed to these ideologies and their violent means. Throughout this cycle of recruitment and mobilization, we will take advantage of our operational, diplomatic, and development successes to demonstrate the futility of terrorist violence.

INCREASE CIVIL SOCIETY'S ROLE IN TERRORISM PREVENTION: Through engagement, public communications, and diplomacy, we will strengthen and connect our partners in civil society who are eager to expand their limited terrorism prevention efforts. We will raise awareness of radicalization and recruitment dynamics, highlight successful prevention and intervention approaches domestically and overseas, and empower local partners through outreach, training, and international exchanges. We will also promote grassroots efforts to identify and address radicalization to insulate civilian populations from terrorist influence.

SUPPORT INTERVENTION, REINTEGRATION, AND COUNTER-RECIDIVISM EFFORTS: We will identify signs of violent radicalization and mobilization to focus real-world and online intervention efforts to prevent terrorist attacks. We will work to limit prison radicalization by training prison staff and supporting rehabilitation. We will also work with foreign partners to address the challenge of reintegrating returning foreign terrorist fighters, their families, and children into their communities.

COMBAT TERRORISTS' INFLUENCE ONLINE: We will combat terrorist use of cyberspace as a global stage to showcase their violent ideologies, to fundraise, and to radicalize, recruit, and mobilize individuals to violence. In concert with our partners, we will expand relationships with technology sector entities to empower them to combat violent extremism online and terrorists' abuse of their platforms. We will continue to expose and counter the flood of terrorist ideology online.

COUNTER RADICALIZATION THROUGH STRATEGIC COMMUNICATIONS: Within the United States Government, we will create a common operating picture of terrorists' propaganda activities to detect and combat terrorists' narratives and better understand the audiences that they try to influence. With coalition members and our partners in civil society and international media, we will explain our counterterrorism efforts, highlight examples of non-violent means to address grievances, amplify success stories of development and recovery, and promote positive narratives.

Strengthen the Counterterrorism Abilities of International Partners

While the United States will continue to lead and provide support to partners in the fight against terrorism, our country need not sustain the primary responsibility for counterterrorism activities around the world. To address this issue, we will work to increase our partners' awareness of terrorist threats and strengthen their capacity and willingness to address them.

Central to this approach is the adoption of proactive diplomatic engagement, development assistance, and security assistance to help our partners act independently and, ultimately, invest more of their own capital in bolstering counterterrorism efforts. We will call on our capable and well-resourced partners to increase their support to countries lacking resources and capabilities. Some partners have better access, expertise, resources, and relationships in particular geographic and thematic areas, and we will encourage them to employ and refine such tools to more effectively internationalize counterterrorism efforts while reducing reliance on United States assistance. We will also continue to work with our less resourced, non-traditional, or novel partners who may make unique contributions to help advance our shared counterterrorism efforts. Over time, this will result in a more balanced, equitable, and effective global approach to counterterrorism.

Priority Actions

ESTABLISH A BROADER RANGE OF COUNTERTERRORISM PARTNERSHIPS: Our increasingly interconnected world demands that we prioritize the partnerships that will lead to both actions and enduring efforts that diminish terrorism. The United States will, therefore, partner with governments and organizations, including allied nations, the technology sector, financial institutions, and civil society. We will use diplomatic engagement with partner governments and further mobilize existing coalitions and multilateral and international fora to increase the will of capable partners to act against threats while encouraging the implementation of international counterterrorism standards and the coordination of international burden-sharing efforts.

SUPPORT COUNTERTERRORISM CAPABILITIES OF KEY FOREIGN PARTNERS: We will continue to augment the capabilities of key foreign partners to conduct critical counterterrorism activities. We will help to professionalize the military, law enforcement, judicial, intelligence, and security services, as well as financial authorities, of key partners so that they are able to conduct counterterorrism operations effectively and justly. We will also work to ensure that partners meet their responsibilities in holding their citizens accountable for any acts of terrorism committed abroad. In addition, we will enhance the capabilities of key foreign partners to investigate and prosecute terrorism across borders through law enforcement cooperation, mutual legal assistance, and extradition.

EXPAND PARTNER INFORMATION-SHARING: To stay ahead of emerging terrorist trends and methods, we will prioritize the sharing of information, such as biometric and geolocational data and information about new threats, including terrorists' initial research into new attack capabilities. Building on solid partnerships and processes for sharing information, we will continue to improve the capacity for information-sharing and work with partners to allow them to more effectively act on shared information.

SUPPORT LOCALLY-DRIVEN TERRORISM PREVENTION: We will work with local stakeholders and civil society to mitigate the grievances that terrorists exploit. Internationally, where United States interests are at stake, we will seek and encourage locally driven solutions that target specific causes of terrorist radicalization and mobilization to violence. We will work with partners to encourage positive narratives that promote tolerance and security.

Conclusion

Projecting American Strength

This National Strategy for Counterterrorism marks a shift in America's approach to countering and preventing terrorism. We will lead with our principles and a clear-eyed understanding of a constantly changing operating environment. While this strategy was necessarily formulated against a backdrop of the threats we face today, it provides flexible guidance to enable an effective approach against an agile and adaptive terrorist threat.

This new approach to counterterrorism does not rest on the idealistic hope of an easy and unthreatening world. Terrorism will persist as a tactic of those who view our democracy as a threat to their tyrannical aspirations, but the United States will remain secure through our strength, innovation, and independence of action. We will stay ahead of our terrorist adversaries by ensuring that we have the infrastructure, tools, authorities, practices, people, and the political will to apply the full range of our strengths against their vulnerabilities. As fascists and communists did before them, terrorists seek to use our openness, tolerance, and freedoms against us. They will fail. We will relentlessly pursue those terrorists that seek to harm our country and remain vigilant and vigorous in our prevention of attacks. We will not yield to adversaries who attack us with bombs, bullets, or propaganda. We will rise to every challenge, face the enemy on every front, and ensure a future of peace, security, and prosperity for our country and the world. We will protect the American dream.

National Security Strategy, 2017

December 2017

THE WHITE HOUSE
WASHINGTON, DC

My fellow Americans:

The American people elected me to make America great again. I promised that my Administration would put the safety, interests, and well-being of our citizens first. I pledged that we would revitalize the American economy, rebuild our military, defend our borders, protect our sovereignty, and advance our values.

During my first year in office, you have witnessed my America First foreign policy in action. We are prioritizing the interests of our citizens and protecting our sovereign rights as a nation. America is leading again on the world stage. We are not hiding from the challenges we face. We are confronting them head-on and pursuing opportunities to promote the security and prosperity of all Americans.

The United States faces an extraordinarily dangerous world, filled with a wide range of threats that have intensified in recent years. When I came into office, rogue regimes were developing nuclear weapons and missiles to threaten the entire planet. Radical Islamist terror groups were flourishing. Terrorists had taken control of vast swaths of the Middle East. Rival powers were aggressively undermining American interests around the globe. At home, porous borders and unenforced immigration laws had created a host of vulnerabilities. Criminal cartels were bringing drugs and danger into our communities. Unfair trade practices had weakened our economy and exported our jobs overseas. Unfair burden-sharing with our allies and inadequate investment in our own defense had invited danger from those who wish us harm. Too many Americans had lost trust in our government, faith in our future, and confidence in our values.

Nearly one year later, although serious challenges remain, we are charting a new and very different course.

We are rallying the world against the rogue regime in North Korea and confronting the danger posed by the dictatorship in Iran, which those determined to pursue a flawed nuclear deal had neglected. We have renewed our friendships in the Middle East and partnered with regional leaders to help drive out terrorists and extremists, cut off their financing, and discredit their wicked ideology. We crushed Islamic State of Iraq and Syria (ISIS) terrorists on the battlefields of Syria and Iraq, and will continue pursuing them until they are destroyed. America's allies are now contributing more to our common defense, strengthening even our strongest alliances. We have also continued to make clear that the United States will no longer tolerate economic aggression or unfair trading practices.

At home, we have restored confidence in America's purpose. We have recommitted ourselves to our founding principles and to the values that have made our families, communities, and society so successful. Jobs are coming back and our economy is growing. We are making historic investments in the United States military. We are enforcing our borders, building trade relationships based on fairness and reciprocity, and defending America's sovereignty without apology.

The whole world is lifted by America's renewal and the reemergence of American leadership. After one year, the world knows that America is prosperous, America is secure, and America is strong. We will bring about the better future we seek for our people and the world, by confronting the challenges and dangers posed by those who seek to destabilize the world and threaten America's people and interests.

My Administration's National Security Strategy lays out a strategic vision for protecting the American people and preserving our way of life, promoting our prosperity, preserving peace through strength, and advancing American influence in the world. We will pursue this beautiful vision—a world of strong, sovereign, and independent nations, each with its own cultures and dreams, thriving side-by-side in prosperity, freedom, and peace—throughout the upcoming year.

In pursuit of that future, we will look at the world with clear eyes and fresh thinking. We will promote a balance of power that favors the United States, our allies, and our partners. We will never lose sight of our values and their capacity to inspire, uplift, and renew.

Most of all, we will serve the American people and uphold their right to a government that prioritizes their security, their prosperity, and their interests. This National Security Strategy puts America First.

President Donald J. Trump

The White House December 2017

Table of Contents

The Stratedy in a Regional Context
Indo-Pacific
Europe
Middle East
South and Central Asia
Western Hemisphere
Africa

Conclusion

INTRODUCTION

An America that is safe, prosperous, and free at home is an America with the strength, confidence, and will to lead abroad. It is an America that can preserve peace, uphold liberty, and create enduring advantages for the American people. Putting America first is the duty of our government and the foundation for U.S. leadership in the world.

A strong America is in the vital interests of not only the American people, but also those around the world who want to partner with the United States in pursuit of shared interests, values, and aspirations.

This National Security Strategy puts America first.

An America First National Security Strategy is based on American principles, a clear-eyed assessment of U.S. interests, and a determination to tackle the challenges that we face. It is a strategy of principled realism that is guided by outcomes, not ideology. It is based upon the view that peace, security, and prosperity depend on strong, sovereign nations that respect their citizens at home and cooperate to advance peace abroad. And it is grounded in the realization that American principles are a lasting force for good in the world.

"We the People" is America's source of strength.

The United States was born of a desire for life, liberty, and the pursuit of happiness—and a conviction that unaccountable political power is tyranny. For these reasons, our Founders crafted and ratified the Constitution, establishing the republican form of government we enjoy today. The Constitution grants our national government not only specified powers necessary to protect our God-given rights and liberties but also safeguards them by limiting the government's size and scope, separating Federal powers, and protecting the rights of individuals through the rule of law. All political power is ultimately delegated from, and accountable to, the people.

We protect American sovereignty by defending these institutions, traditions, and principles that have allowed us to live in freedom, to build the nation that we love. And we prize our national heritage, for the rare and fragile institutions of republican government can only endure if they are sustained by a culture that cherishes those institutions.

Liberty and independence have given us the flourishing society Americans enjoy today—a vibrant and confident Nation, welcoming of disagreement and differences, but united by the bonds of history, culture, beliefs, and principles that define who we are.

We are proud of our roots and honor the wisdom of the past. We are committed to protecting the rights and dignity of every citizen. And we are a nation of laws, because the rule of law is the shield that protects the individual from government corruption and abuse of power, allows families to live without fear, and permits markets to thrive.

Our founding principles have made the United States of America among the greatest forces for good in history. But we are also aware that we must protect and build upon our accomplishments, always conscious of the fact that the interests of the American people constitute our true North Star.

America's achievements and standing in the world were neither inevitable nor accidental. On many occasions, Americans have had to compete with adversarial forces to preserve and advance our security, prosperity, and the principles we hold dear. At home, we fought the Civil War to end slavery and preserve our Union in the long struggle to extend equal rights for all Americans. In the course of the bloodiest century in human history, millions of Americans fought, and hundreds of thousands lost their lives, to defend liberty in two World Wars and the Cold War. America, with our allies and partners, defeated fascism, imperialism, and Soviet communism and eliminated any doubts about the power and durability of republican democracy when it is sustained by a free, proud, and unified people.

The United States consolidated its military victories with political and economic triumphs built on market economies and fair trade, democratic principles, and shared security partnerships. American political, business, and military leaders worked together with their counterparts in Europe and Asia to shape the post-war order through the United Nations, the Marshall Plan, the North Atlantic Treaty Organization (NATO), and other institutions designed to advance our shared interests of security, freedom, and peace. We recognize the invaluable advantages that our strong relationships with allies and partners deliver.

Following the remarkable victory of free nations in the Cold War, America emerged as the lone superpower with enormous advantages and momentum in the world. Success, however, bred complacency. A belief emerged, among many, that American power would be unchallenged and self– sustaining. The United States began to drift. We experienced a crisis of confidence and surrendered our advantages in key areas. As we took our political, economic, and military advantages for granted, other actors steadily implemented their long-term plans to challenge America and to advance agendas opposed to the United States, our allies, and our partners.

We stood by while countries exploited the international institutions we helped to build. They subsidized their industries, forced technology transfers, and distorted markets. These and other actions challenged America's economic security. At home, excessive regulations and high taxes stymied growth and weakened free enterprise—history's greatest antidote to poverty. Each time government encroached on the productive activities of private commerce, it threatened not only our prosperity but also the spirit of creation and innovation that has been key to our national greatness.

A Competitive World

The United States will respond to the growing political, economic, and military competitions we face around the world.

China and Russia challenge American power, influence, and interests, attempting to erode American security and prosperity. They are determined to make economies less free and less fair, to grow their militaries, and to control information and data to repress their societies and expand their influence. At the same time, the dictatorships of the Democratic People's Republic of Korea and the Islamic Republic of Iran are determined to destabilize regions, threaten Americans and our allies, and brutalize their own people. Transnational threat groups, from jihadist terrorists to transnational criminal organizations, are actively trying to harm Americans. While these challenges differ in nature and magnitude, they are fundamentally contests between those who value human dignity and freedom and those who oppress individuals and enforce uniformity.

These competitions require the United States to rethink the policies of the past two decades—policies based on the assumption that engagement with rivals and their inclusion in international institutions and global commerce would turn them into benign actors and trustworthy partners. For the most part, this premise turned out to be false.

Rival actors use propaganda and other means to try to discredit democracy. They advance anti-Western views and spread false information to create divisions among ourselves, our allies, and our partners. In addition, jihadist terrorists such as ISIS and al-Qa'ida continue to spread a barbaric ideology that calls for the violent destruction of governments and innocents they consider to be apostates. These jihadist terrorists attempt to force those under their influence to submit to Sharia law.

America's military remains the strongest in the world. However, U.S. advantages are shrinking as rival states modernize and build up their conventional and nuclear forces. Many actors can now field a broad arsenal of advanced missiles, including variants that can reach the American homeland. Access to technology empowers and emboldens otherwise weak states. North Korea—a country that starves its own people—has spent hundreds of millions of dollars on nuclear, chemical, and biological weapons that could threaten our homeland. In addition, many actors have become skilled at operating below the threshold of military conflict—challenging the United States, our allies, and our partners with hostile actions cloaked in deniability. Our task is to ensure that American military superiority endures, and in combination with other elements of national power, is ready to protect Americans against sophisticated challenges to national security.

The contest over information accelerates these political, economic, and military competitions. Data, like energy, will shape U.S. economic prosperity and our future strategic position in the world. The ability to harness the power of data is fundamental to the continuing growth of America's economy, prevailing against hostile ideologies, and building and deploying the most effective military in the world.

We learned the difficult lesson that when America does not lead, malign actors fill the void to the disadvantage of the United States. When America does lead, however, from a position of strength and confidence and in accordance with our interests and values, all benefit.

Competition does not always mean hostility, nor does it inevitably lead to conflict—although none should doubt our commitment to defend our interests. An America that successfully competes is the best way to prevent conflict. Just as American weakness invites challenge, American strength and confidence deters war and promotes peace.

An America First National Security Strategy

The competitions and rivalries facing the United States are not passing trends or momentary problems. They are intertwined, long-term challenges that demand our sustained national attention and commitment.

America possesses unmatched political, economic, military, and technological advantages. But to maintain these advantages, build upon our strengths, and unleash the talents of the American people, we must protect four vital national interests in this competitive world.

First, our fundamental responsibility is to **protect the American people, the homeland, and**

the American way of life. We will strengthen control of our borders and reform our immigration system. We will protect our critical infrastructure and go after malicious cyber actors. A layered missile defense system will defend our homeland against missile attacks. And we will pursue threats to their source, so that jihadist terrorists are stopped before they ever reach our borders.

Second, we will **promote American prosperity**. We will rejuvenate the American economy for the benefit of American workers and companies. We will insist upon fair and reciprocal economic relationships to address trade imbalances. The United States must preserve our lead in research and technology and protect our economy from competitors who unfairly acquire our intellectual property. And we will embrace America's energy dominance because unleashing abundant energy resources stimulates our economy.

Third, we will **preserve peace through strength** by rebuilding our military so that it remains preeminent, deters our adversaries, and, if necessary, is able to fight and win. We will compete with all tools of national power to ensure that regions of the world are not dominated by one power. We will strengthen America's capabilities—including in space and cyberspace—and revitalize others that have been neglected. Allies and partners magnify our power. We expect them to shoulder a fair share of the burden of responsibility to protect against common threats.

Fourth, we will **advance American influence** because a world that supports American interests and reflects our values makes America more secure and prosperous. We will compete and lead in multilateral organizations so that American interests and principles are protected. America's commitment to liberty, democracy, and the rule of law serves as an inspiration for those living under tyranny. We can play a catalytic role in promoting private-sector-led economic growth, helping aspiring partners become future trading and security partners. And we will remain a generous nation, even as we expect others to share responsibility.

Strengthening our sovereignty—the first duty of a government is to serve the interests of its own people—is a necessary condition for protecting these four national interests. And as we strengthen our sovereignty we will renew confidence in ourselves as a nation. We are proud of our history, optimistic about America's future, and confident of the positive example the United States offers to the world. We are also realistic and understand that the American way of life cannot be imposed upon others, nor is it the inevitable culmination of progress. Together with our allies, partners, and aspiring partners, the United States will pursue cooperation with reciprocity. Cooperation means sharing responsibilities and burdens. In trade, fair and reciprocal relationships benefit all with equal levels of market access and opportunities for economic growth. An America First National Security Strategy appreciates that America will catalyze conditions to unleash economic success for America and the world.

In the United States, free men and women have created the most just and prosperous nation in history. Our generation of Americans is now charged with preserving and defending that precious inheritance. This National Security Strategy shows the way.

PILLAR I
PROTECT THE AMERICAN PEOPLE, THE HOMELAND, AND THE AMERICAN WAY OF LIFE

"We will defend our country, protect our communities, and put the safety of the American people first."

PRESIDENT DONALD J. TRUMP, JULY 2017

This National Security Strategy begins with the determination to protect the American people, the American way of life, and American interests. Americans have long recognized the benefits of an interconnected world, where information and commerce flow freely. Engaging with the world, however, does not mean the United States should abandon its rights and duties as a sovereign state or compromise its security. Openness also imposes costs, since adversaries exploit our free and democratic system to harm the United States.

North Korea seeks the capability to kill millions of Americans with nuclear weapons. Iran supports terrorist groups and openly calls for our destruction. Jihadist terrorist organizations such as ISIS and al-Qa'ida are determined to attack the United States and radicalize Americans with their hateful ideology. Non-state actors undermine social order through drug and human trafficking networks, which they use to commit violent crimes and kill thousands of American each year.

Adversaries target sources of American strength, including our democratic system and our economy. They steal and exploit our intellectual property and personal data, interfere in our political processes, target our aviation and maritime sectors, and hold our critical infrastructure at risk. All of these actions threaten the foundations of the American way of life. Reestablishing lawful control of our borders is a first step toward protecting the American homeland and strengthening American sovereignty.

We must prevent nuclear, chemical, radiological, and biological attacks, block terrorists from reaching our homeland, reduce drug and human trafficking, and protect our critical infrastructure. We must also deter, disrupt, and defeat potential threats before they reach the United States. We will target jihadist terrorists and transnational criminal organizations at their source and dismantle their networks of support.

We must also take steps to respond quickly to meet the needs of the American people in the event of natural disaster or attack on our homeland. We must build a culture of preparedness and resilience across our governmental functions, critical infrastructure, and economic and political systems.

Secure U.S. Borders and Territory

State and non-state actors place the safety of the American people and the Nation's economic vitality at risk by exploiting vulnerabilities across the land, air, maritime, space, and cyberspace domains. Adversaries constantly evolve their methods to threaten the United States and our citizens. We must be agile and adaptable.

Defend Against Weapons of Mass Destruction (WMD)

The danger from hostile state and non-state actors who are trying to acquire nuclear, chemical, radiological, and biological weapons is increasing. The Syrian regime's use of chemical weapons against its own citizens undermines international norms against these heinous weapons, which may encourage more actors to pursue and use them. ISIS has used chemical weapons in Iraq and Syria. Terrorist groups continue to pursue WMD-related materials. We would face grave danger if terrorists obtained inadequately secured nuclear, radiological, or biological material.

As missiles grow in numbers, types, and effectiveness, to include those with greater ranges, they are the most likely means for states like North Korea to use a nuclear weapon against the United States. North Korea is also pursuing chemical and biological weapons which could also be delivered by missile. China and Russia are developing advanced weapons and capabilities that could threaten our critical infrastructure and our command and control architecture.

Priority Actions

ENHANCE MISSILE DEFENSE: The United States is deploying a layered missile defense system focused on North Korea and Iran to defend our homeland against missile attacks. This system will include the ability to defeat missile threats prior to launch. Enhanced missile defense is not intended to undermine strategic stability or disrupt long-standing strategic relationships with Russia or China.

DETECT AND DISRUPT WEAPONS OF MASS DESTRUCTION: At our borders and within our territory, we will bolster efforts to detect nuclear, chemical, radiological, and biological agents and keep them from being used against us. We will also better integrate intelligence, law enforcement, and emergency management operations to ensure that frontline defenders have the right information and capabilities to respond to WMD threats from state and non-state actors.

ENHANCE COUNTERPROLIFERATION MEASURES: Building on decades of initiatives, we will augment measures to secure, eliminate, and prevent the spread of WMD and related materials, their delivery systems, technologies, and knowledge to reduce the chance that they might fall into the hands of hostile actors. We will hold state and non-state actors accountable for the use of WMD.

TARGET WMD TERRORISTS: We will direct counterterrorism operations against terrorist WMD specialists, financiers, administrators, and facilitators. We will work with allies and partners to detect and disrupt plots.

Combat Biothreats and Pandemics

Biological incidents have the potential to cause catastrophic loss of life. Biological threats to the U.S. homeland—whether as the result of deliberate attack, accident, or a natural outbreak—are growing and require actions to address them at their source.

Naturally emerging outbreaks of viruses such as Ebola and SARS, as well as the deliberate 2001 anthrax attacks in the United States, demonstrated the impact of biological threats on national security by taking lives, generating economic losses, and contributing to a loss of confidence in government institutions.

Advancements in life sciences that benefit our health, economy, and society also open up new avenues to actors who want to cause harm. Dedicated state actors are likely to develop more advanced bioweapons, and these capabilities may become available to malicious non-state actors as well.

Priority Actions

DETECT AND CONTAIN BIOTHREATS AT THEIR SOURCE: We will work with other countries to detect and mitigate outbreaks early to prevent the spread of disease. We will encourage other countries to invest in basic healthcare systems and to strengthen global health security across the intersection of human and animal health to prevent infectious disease outbreaks. And we will work with partners to ensure that laboratories that handle dangerous pathogens have in place safety and security measures.

SUPPORT BIOMEDICAL INNOVATION: We will protect and support advancements in biomedical innovation by strengthening the intellectual property system that is the foundation of the biomedical industry.

IMPROVE EMERGENCY RESPONSE: At home, we will strengthen our emergency response and unified coordination systems to rapidly characterize outbreaks, implement public health containment measures to limit the spread of disease, and provide surge medical care—including life-saving treatments.

Strengthen Border Control and Immigration Policy

Strengthening control over our borders and immigration system is central to national security, economic prosperity, and the rule of law. Terrorists, drug traffickers, and criminal cartels exploit porous borders and threaten U.S. security and public safety. These actors adapt quickly to outpace our defenses.

The United States affirms our sovereign right to determine who should enter our country and under what circumstances. The United States understands the contributions immigrants have made to our Nation throughout its history. Illegal immigration, however, burdens the economy, hurts American workers, presents public safety risks, and enriches smugglers and other criminals.

The United States recognizes that decisions about who to legally admit for residency, citizenship, or otherwise are among the most important a country has to make. The United States will continue to welcome lawful immigrants who do not pose a security threat and whose entry is consistent with the national interest, while at the same time enhancing the screening and vetting of travelers, closing dangerous loopholes, revising outdated laws, and eliminating easily exploited vulnerabilities. We will also reform our current immigration system, which, contrary to our national interest and national security, allows for randomized entry and extended-family chain migration. Residency and citizenship determinations should be based on individuals' merits and their ability to positively contribute to U.S. society, rather than chance or extended family connections.

Priority Actions

ENHANCE BORDER SECURITY: We will secure our borders through the construction of a border wall, the use of multilayered defenses and advanced technology, the employment of additional personnel, and other measures. The U.S. Government will work with foreign partners to deter, detect, and disrupt suspicious individuals well before they enter the United States.

ENHANCE VETTING: The U.S. Government will enhance vetting of prospective immigrants, refugees, and other foreign visitors to identify individuals who might pose a risk to national security or public safety. We will set higher security standards to ensure that we keep dangerous people out of the United States and enhance our information collection and analysis to identify those who may already be within our borders.

ENFORCE IMMIGRATION LAWS: We will enforce immigration laws, both at the border and in the interior, to provide an effective deterrent to illegal immigration. The apprehension and swift removal of illegal aliens at the border is critical to an effective border security strategy. We must also increase efforts to identify and counter fraud in the immigration process, which undermines the integrity of our immigration system, exploits vulnerable individuals, and creates national security risks.

BOLSTER TRANSPORTATION SECURITY: We will improve information sharing across our government and with foreign partners to enhance the security of the pathways through which people and goods enter the country. We will invest in technology to counter emerging threats to our aviation, surface, and maritime transportation sectors. We will also work with international and industry partners to raise security standards.

Pursue Threats to Their Source

There is no perfect defense against the range of threats facing our homeland. That is why America must, alongside allies and partners, stay on the offensive against those violent non-state groups that target the United States and our allies.

The primary transnational threats Americans face are from jihadist terrorists and transnational criminal organizations. Although their objectives differ, these actors pose some common challenges. First, they exploit our open society. Second, they often operate in loose confederations and adapt rapidly. Third, they rely on encrypted communication and the dark web to evade detection as they plot, recruit, finance, and execute their operations. Fourth, they thrive under conditions of state weakness and prey on the vulnerable as they accelerate the breakdown of rules to create havens from which to plan and launch attacks on the United States, our allies, and our partners. Fifth, some are sheltered and supported by states and do their bidding.

Defeat Jihadist Terrorists

Jihadist terrorist organizations present the most dangerous terrorist threat to the Nation. America, alongside our allies and partners, is fighting a long war against these fanatics who advance a totalitarian vision for a global Islamist caliphate that justifies murder and slavery, promotes repression, and seeks to undermine the American way of life. Jihadist terrorists use virtual and physical networks around the world to radicalize isolated individuals, exploit vulnerable populations, and inspire and direct plots.

Even after the territorial defeat of ISIS and al-Qa'ida in Syria and Iraq, the threat from jihadist terrorists will persist. They have used battlefields as test beds of terror and have exported tools and tactics to their followers. Many of these jihadist terrorists are likely to return to their home countries, from which they can continue to plot and launch attacks on the United States and our allies.

The United States also works with allies and partners to deter and disrupt other foreign terrorist groups that threaten the homeland—including Iranian-backed groups such as Lebanese Hizballah.

Priority Actions

DISRUPT TERROR PLOTS: We will enhance intelligence sharing domestically and with foreign partners. We will give our frontline defenders—including homeland security, law enforcement, and intelligence professionals—the tools, authorities, and resources to stop terrorist acts before they take place.

TAKE DIRECT ACTION: The U.S. military and other operating agencies will take direct action against terrorist networks and pursue terrorists who threaten the homeland and U.S. citizens regardless of where they are. The campaigns against ISIS and al-Qa'ida and their affiliates demonstrate that the United States will enable partners and sustain direct action campaigns to destroy terrorists and their sources of support, making it harder for them to plot against us.

ELIMINATE TERRORIST SAFE HAVENS: Time and territory allow jihadist terrorists to plot, so we will act against sanctuaries and prevent their reemergence, before they can threaten the U.S. homeland. We will go after their digital networks and work with private industry to confront the challenge of terrorists and criminals "going dark" and using secure platforms to evade detection.

SEVER SOURCES OF STRENGTH: We will disrupt the financial, materiel, and personnel supply chains of terrorist organizations. We will sever their financing and protect the U.S. and international financial systems from abuse. We will degrade their ability to message and attract potential recruits. This includes combating the evil ideology of jihadists by exposing its falsehoods, promoting counter-narratives, and amplifying credible voices.

SHARE RESPONSIBILITY: Our allies and partners, who are also targets of terrorism, will continue to share responsibility in fighting these barbaric groups. We will help our partners develop and responsibly employ the capacity to degrade and maintain persistent pressure against terrorists and will encourage partners to work independently of U.S. assistance.

COMBAT RADICALIZATION AND RECRUITMENT IN COMMUNITIES: The United States rejects bigotry and oppression and seeks a future built on our values as one American people. We will deny violent ideologies the space to take root by improving trust among law enforcement, the private sector, and American citizens. U.S. intelligence and homeland security experts will work with law enforcement and civic leaders on terrorism prevention and provide accurate and actionable information about radicalization in their communities.

Dismantle Transnational Criminal Organizations

The United States must devote greater resources to dismantle transnational criminal organizations (TCOs) and their subsidiary networks. Some have established global supply chains that are comparable to Fortune 500 corporations. Every day they deliver drugs to American communities, fuel gang violence, and engage in cybercrime. The illicit opioid epidemic, fed by drug cartels as well as Chinese fentanyl traffickers, kills tens of thousands of Americans each year. These organizations weaken our allies and partners too, by corrupting and undermining democratic institutions. TCOs are motivated by profit, power, and political influence. They exploit weak governance and enable other national security threats, including terrorist organizations. In addition, some state adversaries use TCOs as instruments of national power, offering them territorial sanctuary where they are free to conduct unattributable cyber intrusions, sabotage, theft, and political subversion.

Priority Actions

IMPROVE STRATEGIC PLANNING AND INTELLIGENCE: We will establish national-level strategic intelligence and planning capabilities to improve the ability of agencies to work together to combat TCOs at home and abroad.

DEFEND COMMUNITIES: We will deny TCOs the ability to harm Americans. We will support public health efforts to halt the growth of illicit drug use in the United States, expand national and community-based prevention efforts, increase access to evidenced-based treatment for addiction, improve prescription drug monitoring, and provide training on substance use disorders for medical personnel.

DEFEND IN DEPTH: U.S. agencies and foreign partners will target TCO leaders and their support infrastructure. We will assist countries, particularly in the Western Hemisphere, to break the power of these organizations and networks.

COUNTER CYBER CRIMINALS: We will use sophisticated investigative tools to disrupt the ability of criminals to use online marketplaces, cryptocurrencies, and other tools for illicit activities. The United States will hold countries accountable for harboring these criminals.

Keep America Safe in the Cyber Era

America's response to the challenges and opportunities of the cyber era will determine our future prosperity and security. For most of our history, the United States has been able to protect the homeland by controlling its land, air, space, and maritime domains. Today, cyberspace offers state and non-state actors the ability to wage campaigns against American political, economic, and security interests without ever physically crossing our borders. Cyberattacks offer adversaries low-cost and deniable opportunities to seriously damage or disrupt critical infrastructure, cripple American businesses, weaken our Federal networks, and attack the tools and devices that Americans use every day to communicate and conduct business.

Critical infrastructure keeps our food fresh, our houses warm, our trade flowing, and our citizens productive and safe. The vulnerability of U.S. critical infrastructure to cyber, physical, and electromagnetic attacks means that adversaries could disrupt military command and control, banking and financial operations, the electrical grid, and means of communication.

Federal networks also face threats. These networks allow government agencies to carry out vital functions and provide services to the American people. The government must do a better job of protecting data to safeguard information and the privacy of the American people. Our Federal networks must be modernized and updated.

In addition, the daily lives of most Americans rely on computer-driven and interconnected technologies. As our reliance on computers and connectivity increases, we become increasingly vulnerable to cyberattacks. Businesses and individuals must be able to operate securely in cyberspace.

Security was not a major consideration when the Internet was designed and launched. As it evolves, the government and private sector must design systems that incorporate prevention, protection, and resiliency from the start, not as an afterthought. We must do so in a way that respects free markets, private competition, and the limited but important role of government in enforcing the rule of law. As we build the next generation of digital infrastructure, we have an opportunity to put our experience into practice.

The Internet is an American invention, and it should reflect our values as it continues to transform the future for all nations and all generations. A strong, defensible cyber infrastructure fosters economic growth, protects our liberties, and advances our national security.

Priority Actions

IDENTIFY AND PRIORITIZE RISK: To improve the security and resilience of our critical infrastructure, we will assess risk across six key areas: national security, energy and power, banking and finance, health and safety, communications, and transportation. We will assess where cyberattacks could have catastrophic or cascading consequences and prioritize our protective efforts, capabilities, and defenses accordingly.

BUILD DEFENSIBLE GOVERNMENT NETWORKS: We will use the latest commercial capabilities, shared services, and best practices to modernize our Federal information technology. We will improve our ability to provide uninterrupted and secure communications and services under all conditions.

DETER AND DISRUPT MALICIOUS CYBER ACTORS: The Federal Government will ensure that those charged with securing critical infrastructure have the necessary authorities, information, and capabilities to prevent attacks before they affect or hold at risk U.S. critical infrastructure. The United States will impose swift and costly consequences on foreign governments, criminals, and other actors who undertake significant malicious cyber activities. We will work with allies and friends to expand our awareness of malicious activities. A stronger and more resilient critical infrastructure will strengthen deterrence by creating doubt in our adversaries that they can achieve their objectives.

IMPROVE INFORMATION SHARING AND SENSING: The U.S. Government will work with our critical infrastructure partners to assess their informational needs and to reduce the barriers to information sharing, such as speed and classification levels. We will also invest in capabilities that improve the ability of the United States to attribute cyberattacks. In accordance with the protection of civil liberties and privacy, the U.S. Government will expand collaboration with the private sector so that we can better detect and attribute attacks.

DEPLOY LAYERED DEFENSES: Since threats transit globally, passing through communications backbones without challenge, the U.S. Government will work with the private sector to remediate known bad activities at the network level to improve the security of all customers. Malicious activity must be defeated within a network and not be passed on to its destination whenever possible.

Promote American Resilience

Despite our best efforts, our government cannot prevent all dangers to the American people. We can, however, help Americans remain resilient in the face of adversity. Resilience includes the ability to withstand and recover rapidly from deliberate attacks, accidents, natural disasters, as well as unconventional stresses, shocks, and threats to our economy and democratic system. In the event of a disaster, Federal, state, and local agencies must perform essential functions and have plans in place to ensure the continuation of our constitutional form of government.

Reducing risk and building more resilient communities are the best ways to protect people, property, and taxpayer dollars from loss and disruption. Through risk-informed investments, we will build resilient communities and infrastructure to protect and benefit future generations.

Should tragedy strike, the U.S. Government will help communities recover and rebuild. Citizens must be confident in our government, but also recognize that response and recovery begins with individuals and local communities. In difficult times, the true character of the

American people emerges: their strength, their love, and their resolve. Our first responders selflessly run toward danger, and volunteers rally to the aid of neighbors when disaster strikes.

A democracy is only as resilient as its people. An informed and engaged citizenry is the fundamental requirement for a free and resilient nation. For generations, our society has protected free press, free speech, and free thought. Today, actors such as Russia are using information tools in an attempt to undermine the legitimacy of democracies. Adversaries target media, political processes, financial networks, and personal data. The American public and private sectors must recognize this and work together to defend our way of life. No external threat can be allowed to shake our shared commitment to our values, undermine our system of government, or divide our Nation.

Priority Actions

IMPROVE RISK MANAGEMENT: The United States will improve its ability to assess the threats and hazards that pose the greatest risks to Americans and will prioritize resources based on the highest risks.

BUILD A CULTURE OF PREPAREDNESS: This Administration will take steps to build a culture of preparedness, informing and empowering communities and individuals to obtain the skills and take the preparatory actions necessary to become more resilient against the threats and hazards that Americans face.

IMPROVE PLANNING: State and local governments must conduct realistic exercises that test existing plans to make sure that they are sound and can be executed. Agencies from all levels of government must coordinate better and apply lessons learned from exercises to pinpoint the areas and capabilities that require improvement.

INCENTIVIZE INFORMATION SHARING: To improve the coordination among the private sector and all levels of government that is needed to improve resilience, we must make a stronger commitment to protecting sensitive information so that all partners actively identify and share vulnerabilities and work collaboratively to reduce them.

PILLAR II
PROMOTE AMERICAN PROSPERITY

"Economic security is national security."

PRESIDENT DONALD J. TRUMP, NOVEMBER 2017

A strong economy protects the American people, supports our way of life, and sustains American power. American workers thrive when they are free to innovate, develop and access our abundant natural resources, and operate in markets free from excessive regulations and unfair foreign trade practices. A growing and innovative economy allows the United States to maintain the world's most powerful military and protect our homeland.

We must rebuild our economic strength and restore confidence in the American economic model. Over decades, American factories, companies, and jobs moved overseas. After the 2008 global financial crisis, doubt replaced confidence. Risk-aversion and regulations replaced investment and entrepreneurship. The recovery produced anemic growth in real earnings for American workers. The U.S. trade deficit grew as a result of several factors, including unfair trading practices.

For 70 years, the United States has embraced a strategy premised on the belief that leadership of a stable international economic system rooted in American principles of reciprocity, free markets, and free trade served our economic and security interests. Working with our allies and partners, the United States led the creation of a group of financial institutions and other economic forums that established equitable rules and built instruments to stabilize the international economy and remove the points of friction that had contributed to two world wars.

That economic system continues to serve our interests, but it must be reformed to help American workers prosper, protect our innovation, and reflect the principles upon which that system was founded. Trading partners and international institutions can do more to address trade imbalances and adhere to and enforce the rules of the order.

Today, American prosperity and security are challenged by an economic competition playing out in a broader strategic context. The United States helped expand the liberal economic trading system to countries that did not share our values, in the hopes that these states would liberalize their economic and political practices and provide commensurate benefits to the United States. Experience shows that these countries distorted and undermined key economic institutions without undertaking significant reform of their economies or politics. They espouse free trade rhetoric and exploit its benefits, but only adhere selectively to the rules and agreements.

We welcome all economic relationships rooted in fairness, reciprocity, and faithful adherence to the rules. Those who join this pursuit will be our closest economic partners. But the United States will no longer turn a blind eye to violations, cheating, or economic aggression. We must work with like-minded allies and partners to ensure our principles prevail and the rules are enforced so that our economies prosper.

The United States will pursue an economic strategy that rejuvenates the domestic economy, benefits the American worker, revitalizes the U.S. manufacturing base, creates middle-class jobs, encourages innovation, preserves technological advantage, safeguards the environment, and achieves energy dominance. Rebuilding economic strength at home and preserving a fair and reciprocal international economic system will enhance our security and advance prosperity and peace in the world.

Rejuvenate the Domestic Economy

Economic challenges at home demand that we understand economic prosperity as a pillar of national security. Despite low unemployment rates and stock market gains, overall economic growth has, until recently, been anemic since the 2008 recession. In the past five years, gross domestic product (GDP) growth hovered barely above two percent, and wages stagnated. Taxes increased, and health insurance and prescription drug costs continued to rise, albeit at a slower pace. Education costs climbed at rates far above inflation, increasing student debt. Productivity growth fell to levels not seen in decades.

Significant government intrusion in the economy slowed growth and job creation. Regulatory and corporate tax policies incentivized businesses to invest overseas and disadvantaged American companies against foreign competitors. Excessive regulations squelched new bank formation and caused hundreds of small banks to close. Regulation decreased credit availability to consumers and decreased product choice. Excessive environmental and infrastructure regulations impeded American energy trade and the development of new infrastructure projects.

Moreover, the poor state of our physical infrastructure stultified the economy, reduced the profitability of American small businesses, and slowed the productivity of American workers.

Americas digital infrastructure also fell behind. Improvements in bandwidth, better broadband connectivity, and protection from persistent cyberattacks are needed to support America's future growth. Economic and personal transactions are dependent upon the ".com world," and wealth creation depends on a reliable, secure Internet.

The Administration is dedicated to rejuvenating the U.S. economy, unleashing the potential of all Americans, and restoring confidence in our free market system. Promoting American prosperity makes America more secure and advances American influence in the world.

Priority Actions

REDUCE REGULATORY BURDENS: Departments and agencies will eliminate unnecessary regulations that stifle growth, drive up costs for American businesses, impede research and development, discourage hiring, and incentivize domestic businesses to move overseas. We will balance our reduction in regulations with adequate protections and oversight.

PROMOTE TAX REFORM: This Administration will work with the Congress to create a simpler, fairer, and pro-growth tax code that encourages the creation of higher wage jobs and gives middle-income families tax relief. Reduced business tax rates and a territorial system for foreign subsidiary earnings will improve the competitiveness of American companies and encourage their return to the United States.

IMPROVE AMERICAN INFRASTRUCTURE: Federal, state, and local governments will work together with private industry to improve our airports, seaports and waterways, roads and railways, transit systems, and telecommunications. The United States will use our strategic advantage as a leading natural gas producer to transform transportation and manufacturing. We will improve America's digital infrastructure by deploying a secure 5G Internet capability nationwide. These improvements will increase national competitiveness, benefit the environment, and improve our quality of life.

REDUCE THE DEBT THROUGH FISCAL RESPONSIBILITY: The national debt, now over $20 trillion, presents a grave threat to America's long-term prosperity and, by extension, our national security. By restraining Federal spending, making government more efficient, and by modernizing our tax system and making our businesses globally competitive, our economy will grow and make the existing debt more serviceable.

SUPPORT EDUCATION AND APPRENTICESHIP PROGRAMS: We will support apprenticeships and workforce development programs that prepare American workers for high-wage manufacturing and science, technology, engineering, and mathematics (STEM) jobs of the 21st century.

Promote Free, Fair, and Reciprocal Economic Relationships

For decades, the United States has allowed unfair trading practices to grow. Other countries have used dumping, discriminatory non-tariff barriers, forced technology transfers, non-economic capacity, industrial subsidies, and other support from governments and state-owned enterprises to gain economic advantages.

Today we must meet the challenge. We will address persistent trade imbalances, break down trade barriers, and provide Americans new opportunities to increase their exports. The United States will expand trade that is fairer so that U.S. workers and industries have more opportunities to compete for business. We oppose closed mercantilist trading blocks. By strengthening the international trading system and incentivizing other countries to embrace market-friendly policies, we can enhance our prosperity.

The United States distinguishes between economic competition with countries that follow fair and free market principles and competition with those that act with little regard for those principles. We will compete with like-minded states in the economic domain—particularly where trade imbalances exist—while recognizing that competition is healthy when nations share values and build fair and reciprocal relationships. The United States will pursue enforcement actions when countries violate the rules to gain unfair advantage. The United States will engage industrialized democracies and other like-minded states to defend against economic aggression, in all its forms, that threatens our common prosperity and security.

Priority Actions

ADOPT NEW TRADE AND INVESTMENT AGREEMENTS AND MODERNIZE EXISTING ONES: The United States will pursue bilateral trade and investment agreements with countries that commit to fair and reciprocal trade and will modernize existing agreements to ensure they are consistent with those principles. Agreements must adhere to high standards in intellectual property, digital trade, agriculture, labor, and the environment.

COUNTER UNFAIR TRADE PRACTICES: The United States will counter all unfair trade practices that distort markets using all appropriate means, from dialogue to enforcement tools.

COUNTER FOREIGN CORRUPTION: Using our economic and diplomatic tools, the United States will continue to target corrupt foreign officials and work with countries to improve their ability to fight corruption so U.S. companies can compete fairly in transparent business climates.

WORK WITH LIKE-MINDED PARTNERS: The United States will work with like-minded partners to preserve and modernize the rules of a fair and reciprocal economic order. Together we will emphasize fair trade enforcement actions when necessary, as well as multinational efforts to ensure transparency and adherence to international standards within trade and investment projects.

FACILITATE NEW MARKET OPPORTUNITIES: The United States will partner with countries as they build their export markets, promote free market competition, and incentivize private sector growth. We will expand U.S. trade and investment opportunities and increase the market base for U.S. goods and services.

Lead in Research, Technology, Invention, and Innovation

The United States will build on the ingenuity that has launched industries, created jobs, and improved the quality of life at home and abroad. To maintain our competitive advantage, the United States will prioritize emerging technologies critical to economic growth and security, such as data science, encryption, autonomous technologies, gene editing, new materials, nanotechnology, advanced computing technologies, and artificial intelligence. From self-driving cars to autonomous weapons, the field of artificial intelligence, in particular, is progressing rapidly.

The United States must continue to attract the innovative and the inventive, the brilliant and the bold. We will encourage scientists in government, academia, and the private sector to achieve advancements across the full spectrum of discovery, from incremental improvements to game-changing breakthroughs. We will nurture a healthy innovation economy that collaborates with allies and partners, improves STEM education, draws on an advanced technical workforce, and invests in early-stage research and development (R&D).

Priority Actions

UNDERSTAND WORLDWIDE SCIENCE AND TECHNOLOGY (S&T) TRENDS: To retain U.S. advantages over our competitors, U.S. Government agencies must improve their understanding of worldwide S&T trends and how they are likely to influence—or undermine—American strategies and programs.

ATTRACT AND RETAIN INVENTORS AND INNOVATORS: The U.S. Government must improve our collaboration with industry and academia and our recruitment of technical talent. We will remove barriers to the full use of talent across Federal agencies, and increase incentives for hiring and retaining Federal STEM employees. Initiatives will include rapid hiring, swift adjudication of national security clearances, and offers of competitive salaries. We must create easier paths for the flow of scientists, engineers, and technologists into and out of public service.

LEVERAGE PRIVATE CAPITAL AND EXPERTISE TO BUILD AND INNOVATE: The U.S. Government will use private sector technical expertise and R&D capabilities more effectively. Private industry owns many of the technologies that the government relies upon for critical national security missions. The Department of Defense and other agencies will establish strategic partnerships with U.S. companies to help align private sector R&D resources to priority national security applications.

RAPIDLY FIELD INVENTIONS AND INNOVATIONS: The United States must regain the element of surprise and field new technologies at the pace of modern industry. Government agencies must shift from an archaic R&D process to an approach that rewards rapid fielding and risk taking.

Promote and Protect the U.S. National Security Innovation Base

America's business climate and legal and regulatory systems encourage risk taking. We are a nation of people who work hard, dream big, and never give up. Not every country shares these characteristics. Some instead steal or illicitly acquire America's hard-earned intellectual property and proprietary information to compensate for their own systemic weaknesses.

Every year, competitors such as China steal U.S. intellectual property valued at hundreds of billions of dollars. Stealing proprietary technology and early-stage ideas allows competitors to unfairly tap into the innovation of free societies. Over the years, rivals have used sophisticated means to weaken our businesses and our economy as facets of cyber-enabled economic warfare and other malicious activities. In addition to these illegal means, some actors use largely legitimate, legal transfers and relationships to gain access to fields, experts, and trusted foundries that fill their capability gaps and erode America's long-term competitive advantages.

We must defend our National Security Innovation Base (NSIB) against competitors. The NSIB is the American network of knowledge, capabilities, and people—including academia, National Laboratories, and the private sector—that turns ideas into innovations, transforms discoveries into successful commercial products and companies, and protects and enhances the American way of life. The genius of creative Americans, and the free system that enables them, is critical to American security and prosperity.

Protecting the NSIB requires a domestic and international response beyond the scope of any individual company, industry, university, or government agency. The landscape of innovation does not divide neatly into sectors. Technologies that are part of most weapon systems often originate in diverse businesses as well as in universities and colleges. Losing our innovation and technological edge would have far-reaching negative implications for American prosperity and power.

Priority Actions

UNDERSTAND THE CHALLENGES: The U.S. Government will develop a capability to integrate, monitor, and better understand the national security implications of unfair industry trends and the actions of our rivals. We will explore new ways to share this information with the private sector and academia so they better understand their responsibilities in curtailing activities that undercut America's NSIB.

PROTECT INTELLECTUAL PROPERTY: The United States will reduce the illicit appropriation of U.S. public and private sector technology and technical knowledge by hostile foreign competitors. While maintaining an investor-friendly climate, this Administration will work with the Congress to strengthen the Committee on Foreign Investment in the United States (CFIUS) to ensure it addresses current and future national security risks. The United States will prioritize counterintelligence and law enforcement activities to curtail intellectual property theft by all sources and will explore new legal and regulatory mechanisms to prevent and prosecute violations.

TIGHTEN VI SA PROCEDURES: The United States will review visa procedures to reduce economic theft by non-traditional intelligence collectors. We will consider restrictions on foreign STEM students from designated countries to ensure that intellectual property is not transferred to our competitors, while acknowledging the importance of recruiting the most advanced technical workforce to the United States.

PROTECT DATA AND UNDERLYING INFRASTRUCTURE: The United States will expand our focus beyond protecting networks to protecting the data on those networks so that it remains secure—both at rest and in transit. To do this, the U.S. Government will encourage practices across companies and universities to defeat espionage and theft.

Embrace Energy Dominance

For the first time in generations, the United States will be an energy-dominant nation. Energy dominance—America's central position in the global energy system as a leading producer, consumer, and innovator—ensures that markets are free and U.S. infrastructure is resilient and secure. It ensures that access to energy is diversified, and recognizes the importance of environmental stewardship.

Access to domestic sources of clean, affordable, and reliable energy underpins a prosperous, secure, and powerful America for decades to come. Unleashing these abundant energy resources—coal, natural gas, petroleum, renewables, and nuclear—stimulates the economy and builds a foundation for future growth. Our Nation must take advantage of our wealth in domestic resources and energy efficiency to promote competitiveness across our industries.

The United States also anchors the North American energy system, which is one of the most highly integrated in the world. Our vibrant cross-border energy trade and investment are vital for a robust and resilient U.S. economy and energy market. We are committed to supporting energy initiatives that will attract investments, safeguard the environment, strengthen our energy security, and unlock the enormous potential of our shared region.

Climate policies will continue to shape the global energy system. U.S. leadership is indispensable to countering an anti-growth energy agenda that is detrimental to U.S. economic and energy security interests. Given future global energy demand, much of the developing world will require fossil fuels, as well as other forms of energy, to power their economies and lift their people out of poverty. The United States will continue to advance an approach that balances energy security, economic development, and environmental protection. The United States will remain a global leader in reducing traditional pollution, as well as greenhouse gases, while expanding our economy. This achievement, which can serve as a model to other countries, flows from innovation, technology breakthroughs, and energy efficiency gains, not from onerous regulation.

As a growing supplier of energy resources, technologies, and services around the world, the United States will help our allies and partners become more resilient against those that use energy to coerce. America's role as an energy exporter will also require an assessment of our vulnerabilities and a resilient American infrastructure.

Finally, the Nation's long-term energy security future rests with our people. We must invest in our future by supporting innovation and R&D, including through the National Laboratories.

Priority Actions

REDUCE BARRIERS: The United States will promote clean and safe development of our energy resources, while limiting regulatory burdens that encumber energy production and constrain economic growth. We will streamline the Federal regulatory approval processes for energy infrastructure, from pipeline and export terminals to container shipments and gathering lines, while also ensuring responsible environmental stewardship.

PROMOTE EXPORTS: The United States will promote exports of our energy resources, technologies, and services, which helps our allies and partners diversify their energy sources and brings economic gains back home. We will expand our export capacity through the continued support of private sector development of coastal terminals, allowing increased market access and a greater competitive edge for U.S. industries.

ENSURE ENERGY SECURITY: The United States will work with allies and partners to protect global energy infrastructure from cyber and physical threats. The United States will support the diversification of energy sources, supplies, and routes at home and abroad. We will modernize our strategic petroleum stocks and encourage other countries to develop their own—consistent with their national energy security needs.

ATTAIN UNIVERSAL ENERGY ACCESS: The United States will seek to ensure universal access to affordable, reliable energy, including highly efficient fossil fuels, nuclear, and renewables, to help reduce poverty, foster economic growth, and promote prosperity.

FURTHER AMERICA'S TECHNOLOGICAL EDGE: We will improve America's technological edge in energy, including nuclear technology, next-generation nuclear reactors, better batteries, advanced computing, carbon-capture technologies, and opportunities at the energy-water nexus. The United States will continue to lead in innovative and efficient energy technologies, recognizing the economic and environmental benefits to end users.

PILLAR III
Preserve Peace Through Strength

"As long as I am President, the servicemen and women who defend our Nation will have the equipment, the resources, and the funding they need to secure our homeland, to respond to our enemies quickly and decisively, and, when necessary, to fight, to overpower, and to always, always, always win."

PRESIDENT DONALD J. TRUMP, DECEMBER 2017

A central continuity in history is the contest for power. The present time period is no different. Three main sets of challengers—the revisionist powers of China and Russia, the rogue states of Iran and North Korea, and transnational threat organizations, particularly jihadist terrorist groups—are actively competing against the United States and our allies and partners. Although differing in nature and magnitude, these rivals compete across political, economic, and military arenas, and use technology and information to accelerate these contests in order to shift regional balances of power in their favor. These are fundamentally political contests between those who favor repressive systems and those who favor free societies.

China and Russia want to shape a world antithetical to U.S. values and interests. China seeks to displace the United States in the Indo-Pacific region, expand the reaches of its state-driven economic model, and reorder the region in its favor. Russia seeks to restore its great power status and establish spheres of influence near its borders. The intentions of both nations are not necessarily fixed. The United States stands ready to cooperate across areas of mutual interest with both countries.

For decades, U.S. policy was rooted in the belief that support for China's rise and for its integration into the post-war international order would liberalize China. Contrary to our hopes, China expanded its power at the expense of the sovereignty of others. China gathers and exploits data on an unrivaled scale and spreads features of its authoritarian system, including corruption and the use of surveillance. It is building the most capable and well-funded military in the world, after our own. Its nuclear arsenal is growing and diversifying. Part of China's military modernization and economic expansion is due to its access to the U.S. innovation economy, including America's world-class universities.

Russia aims to weaken U.S. influence in the world and divide us from our allies and partners. Russia views the North Atlantic Treaty Organization (NATO) and European Union (EU) as threats. Russia is investing in new military capabilities, including nuclear systems that remain the most significant existential threat to the United States, and in destabilizing cyber capabilities. Through modernized forms of subversive tactics, Russia interferes in the domestic political affairs of countries around the world. The combination of Russian ambition and growing military capabilities creates an unstable frontier in Eurasia, where the risk of conflict due to Russian miscalculation is growing.

The scourge of the world today is a small group of rogue regimes that violate all principles of free and civilized states. The Iranian regime sponsors terrorism around the world. It is developing more capable ballistic missiles and has the potential to resume its work on nuclear weapons that could threaten the United States and our partners. North Korea is ruled as a ruthless dictatorship without regard for human dignity. For more than 25 years, it has pursued nuclear weapons and ballistic missiles in defiance of every commitment it has made. Today, these missiles and weapons threaten the United States and our allies. The longer we ignore threats from countries determined to proliferate and develop weapons of mass destruction, the worse such threats become, and the fewer defensive options we have.

The United States continues to wage a long war against jihadist terrorist groups such as ISIS and al-Qa'ida. These groups are linked by a common radical Islamist ideology that encourages violence against the United States and our partners and produces misery for those under their control. Although the United States and our partners have inflicted defeats on ISIS and al-Qa'ida in Syria and Iraq, these organizations maintain global reach with established branches in strategic locations. The threat from jihadist terrorists will persist, even as we intensify efforts to prevent attacks on Americans, our allies, and our partners.

Protecting American interests requires that we compete continuously within and across these contests, which are being played out in regions around the world. The outcome of these contests will influence the political, economic, and military strength of the United States and our allies and partners.

To prevail, we must integrate all elements of America's national power—political, economic, and military. Our allies and partners must also contribute the capabilities, and demonstrate the will, to confront shared threats. Experience suggests that the willingness of rivals to abandon or forgo aggression depends on their perception of U.S. strength and the vitality of our alliances.

The United States will seek areas of cooperation with competitors from a position of strength, foremost by ensuring our military power is second to none and fully integrated with our allies and all of our instruments of power. A strong military ensures that our diplomats are able to operate from a position of strength. In this way we can, together with our allies and partners, deter and if necessary, defeat aggression against U.S. interests and increase the likelihood of managing competitions without violent conflict and preserving peace.

Renew America's Competitive Advantages

The United States must consider what is enduring about the problems we face, and what is new. The contests over influence are timeless. They have existed in varying degrees and levels of intensity, for millennia. Geopolitics is the interplay of these contests across the globe. But some conditions are new, and have changed how these competitions are unfolding. We face simultaneous threats from different actors across multiple arenas—all accelerated by technology. The United States must develop new concepts and capabilities to protect our homeland, advance our prosperity, and preserve peace.

Since the 1990s, the United States displayed a great degree of strategic complacency. We assumed that our military superiority was guaranteed and that a democratic peace was inevitable. We believed that liberal-democratic enlargement and inclusion would fundamentally alter the nature of international relations and that competition would give way to peaceful cooperation.

Instead of building military capacity, as threats to our national security increased, the United States dramatically cut the size of our military to the lowest levels since 1940. Instead of developing important capabilities, the Joint Force entered a nearly decade long "procurement holiday" during which the acquisition of new weapon systems was severely limited. The breakdown of the Nation's annual Federal budgeting process, exemplified by sequestration and repeated continuing resolutions, further contributed to the erosion of America's military dominance during a time of increasing threats.

Despite decades of efforts to reform the way that the United States develops and procures new weapons, our acquisition system remained sclerotic. The Joint Force did not keep pace with emerging threats or technologies. We got less for our defense dollars, shortchanging American taxpayers and warfighters.

We also incorrectly believed that technology could compensate for our reduced capacity—for the ability to field enough forces to prevail militarily, consolidate our gains, and achieve our desired political ends. We convinced ourselves that all wars would be fought and won quickly, from stand-off distances and with minimal casualties.

In addition, after being dismissed as a phenomenon of an earlier century, great power competition returned. China and Russia began to reassert their influence regionally and globally. Today, they are fielding military capabilities designed to deny America access in times of crisis and to contest our ability to operate freely in critical commercial zones during peacetime. In short, they are contesting our geopolitical advantages and trying to change the international order in their favor.

Moreover, deterrence today is significantly more complex to achieve than during the Cold War. Adversaries studied the American way of war and began investing in capabilities that targeted our strengths and sought to exploit perceived weaknesses. The spread of accurate and inexpensive weapons and the use of cyber tools have allowed state and non-state competitors to harm the United States across various domains. Such capabilities contest what was until recently U.S. dominance across the land, air, maritime, space, and cyberspace domains. They also enable adversaries to attempt strategic attacks against the United States—without resorting to nuclear weapons—in ways that could cripple our economy and our ability to deploy our military forces. Deterrence must be extended across all of these domains and must address all possible strategic attacks.

In addition, adversaries and competitors became adept at operating below the threshold of open military conflict and at the edges of international law. Repressive, closed states and organizations, although brittle in many ways, are often more agile and faster at integrating economic, military, and especially informational means to achieve their goals. They are unencumbered by truth, by the rules and protections of privacy inherent in democracies, and by the law of armed conflict. They employ sophisticated political, economic, and military campaigns that combine discrete actions. They are patient and content to accrue strategic gains over time—making it harder for the United States and our allies to respond. Such actions are calculated to achieve maximum effect without provoking a direct military response from the United States. And as these incremental gains are realized, over time, a new status quo emerges.

The United States must prepare for this type of competition. China, Russia, and other state and non-state actors recognize that the United States often views the world in binary terms, with states being either "at peace" or "at war," when it is actually an arena of continuous competition. Our adversaries will not fight us on our terms. We will raise our competitive game to meet that challenge, to protect American interests, and to advance our values.

Our diplomatic, intelligence, military, and economic agencies have not kept pace with the changes in the character of competition. America's military must be prepared to operate across a full spectrum of conflict, across multiple domains at once. To meet these challenges we must also upgrade our political and economic instruments to operate across these environments.

Bureaucratic inertia is powerful. But so is the talent, creativity, and dedication of Americans. By aligning our public and private sector efforts we can field a Joint Force that is unmatched. New advances in computing, autonomy, and manufacturing are already transforming the way we fight. When coupled with the strength of our allies and partners, this advantage grows. The future that we face is ours to win or lose. History suggests that Americans will rise to the occasion and that we can shift trends back in favor of the United States, our allies, and our partners.

Renew Capabilities

Given the new features of the geopolitical environment, the United States must renew key capabilities to address the challenges we face.

Military

U.S. military strength remains a vital component of the competition for influence. The Joint Force demonstrates U.S. resolve and commitment and provides us with the ability to fight and win across any plausible conflict that threatens U.S. vital interests.

The United States must retain overmatch—the combination of capabilities in sufficient scale to prevent enemy success and to ensure that America's sons and daughters will never be in a fair fight. Overmatch strengthens our diplomacy and permits us to shape the international environment to protect our interests. To retain military overmatch the United States must restore our ability to produce innovative capabilities, restore the readiness of our forces for major war, and grow the size of the force so that it is capable of operating at sufficient scale and for ample duration to win across a range of scenarios.

We must convince adversaries that we can and will defeat them—not just punish them if they attack the United States. We must ensure the ability to deter potential enemies by denial, convincing them that they cannot accomplish objectives through the use of force or other forms of aggression. We need our allies to do the same—to modernize, acquire necessary capabilities, improve readiness, expand the size of their forces, and affirm the political will to win.

Priority Actions

MODERNIZATION: Ensuring that the U.S. military can defeat our adversaries requires weapon systems that clearly overmatch theirs in lethality. Where possible, we must improve existing systems to maximize returns on prior investments. In other areas we should seek new capabilities that create clear advantages for our military while posing costly dilemmas for our adversaries. We must eliminate bureaucratic impediments to innovation and embrace less expensive and time-intensive commercial off-the-shelf solutions. Departments and agencies must work with industry to experiment, prototype, and rapidly field new capabilities that can be easily upgraded as new technologies come online.

ACQUISITION: The United States will pursue new approaches to acquisition to make better deals on behalf of the American people that avoid cost overruns, eliminate bloated bureaucracies, and stop unnecessary delays so that we can put the right equipment into the hands of our forces. We must harness innovative technologies that are being developed outside of the traditional defense industrial base.

CAPACITY: The size of our force matters. To deter conflict and, if deterrence fails, to win in war, the Nation must be able to field forces capable of operating in sufficient scale and for ample duration to defeat enemies, consolidate military gains, and achieve sustainable outcomes that protect the American people and our vital interests. The United States must reverse recent decisions to reduce the size of the Joint Force and grow the force while modernizing and ensuring readiness.

IMPROVE READINESS: The United States must retain a ready force that is capable of protecting the homeland while defending U.S. interests. Readiness requires a renewed focus on training, logistics, and maintenance. We must be able to get to a theater in time to shape events quickly. This will require a resilient forward posture and agile global mobility forces.

RETAIN A FULL-SPECTRUM FORCE: The Joint Force must remain capable of deterring and defeating the full range of threats to the United States. The Department of Defense must develop new operational concepts and capabilities to win without assured dominance in air, maritime, land, space, and cyberspace domains, including against those operating below the level of conventional military conflict. We must sustain our competence in irregular warfare, which requires planning for a long-term, rather than ad hoc, fight against terrorist networks and other irregular threats.

Defense Industrial Base

A healthy defense industrial base is a critical element of U.S. power and the National Security Innovation Base. The ability of the military to surge in response to an emergency depends on our Nation's ability to produce needed parts and systems, healthy and secure supply chains, and a skilled U.S. workforce. The erosion of American manufacturing over the last two decades, however, has had a negative impact on these capabilities and threatens to undermine the ability of U.S. manufacturers to meet national security requirements. Today, we rely on single domestic sources for some products and foreign supply chains for others, and we face the possibility of not being able to produce specialized components for the military at home. As America's manufacturing base has weakened, so too have critical workforce skills ranging from industrial welding, to high-technology skills for cybersecurity and aerospace. Support for a vibrant domestic manufacturing sector, a solid defense industrial base, and resilient supply chains is a national priority.

Priority Actions

UNDERSTAND THE PROBLEM: We will evaluate the strengths and weaknesses of our defense industrial base, including the identification of materials essential to national security, contingencies that could affect supply chains, and technologies that are likely to be critical for the future.

ENCOURAGE HOMELAND INVESTMENT: The United States will promote policies and incentives that return key national security industries to American shores. Where possible, the U.S. Government will work with industry partners to strengthen U.S. competitiveness in key technologies and manufacturing capabilities. In addition, we will reform regulations and processes to facilitate the export of U.S. military equipment.

PROTECT AND GROW CRITICAL SKILLS: The United States must maintain and develop skilled trades and high-technology skills through increased support for technical college and apprenticeship programs. We will support STEM efforts, at the Federal and state levels, and target national security technology areas.

Nuclear Forces

Nuclear weapons have served a vital purpose in America's National Security Strategy for the past 70 years. They are the foundation of our strategy to preserve peace and stability by deterring aggression against the United States, our allies, and our partners. While nuclear deterrence strategies cannot prevent all conflict, they are essential to prevent nuclear attack, non-nuclear strategic attacks, and large-scale conventional aggression. In addition, the extension of the U.S. nuclear deterrent to more than 30 allies and partners helps to assure their security, and reduces their need to possess their own nuclear capabilities.

Following the Cold War, the United States reduced investments in our nuclear enterprise and reduced the role of nuclear weapons in our strategy. Some parts of America's strategic nuclear Triad of bombers, sea-based missiles, and land-based missiles are over 30 years old, and much of our nuclear infrastructure dates to the World War II era. At the same time, however, nuclear-armed adversaries have expanded their arsenals and range of delivery systems. The United States must maintain the credible deterrence and assurance capabilities provided by our nuclear Triad and by U.S. theater nuclear capabilities deployed abroad. Significant investment is needed to maintain a U.S. nuclear arsenal and infrastructure that is able to meet national security threats over the coming decades.

Priority Actions

SUSTAIN U.S. NUCLEAR WEAPONS: The United States will sustain a nuclear force structure that meets our current needs and addresses unanticipated risks. The United States does not need to match the nuclear arsenals of other powers, but we must sustain a stockpile that can deter adversaries, assure allies and partners, and achieve U.S. objectives if deterrence fails.

MODERNIZE U.S. NUCLEAR FORCES AND INFRASTRUCTURE: We will modernize our nuclear enterprise to ensure that we have the scientific, engineering, and manufacturing capabilities necessary to retain an effective and safe nuclear Triad and respond to future national security threats. Modernization and sustainment require investing in our aging command and control system and maintaining and growing the highly skilled workforce needed to develop, manufacture, and deploy nuclear weapons.

MAINTAIN STABLE DETERRENCE: To avoid miscalculation, the United States will conduct discussions with other states to build predictable relationships and reduce nuclear risks. We will consider new arms control arrangements if they contribute to strategic stability and if they are verifiable. We will not allow adversaries to use threats of nuclear escalation or other irresponsible nuclear behaviors to coerce the United States, our allies, and our partners. Fear of escalation will not prevent the United States from defending our vital interests and those of our allies and partners.

Space

The United States must maintain our leadership and freedom of action in space. Communications and financial networks, military and intelligence systems, weather monitoring, navigation, and more have components in the space domain. As U.S. dependence on space has increased, other actors have gained access to space-based systems and information. Governments and private sector firms have the ability to launch satellites into space at increasingly lower costs. The fusion of data from imagery, communications, and geolocation services allows motivated actors to access previously unavailable information. This "democratization of space" has an impact on military operations and on America's ability to prevail in conflict.

Many countries are purchasing satellites to support their own strategic military activities. Others believe that the ability to attack space assets offers an asymmetric advantage and, as a result, are pursuing a range of anti-satellite (ASAT) weapons. The United States considers unfettered access to and freedom to operate in space to be a vital interest. Any harmful interference with or an attack upon critical components of our space architecture that directly affects this vital U.S. interest will be met with a deliberate response at a time, place, manner, and domain of our choosing.

Priority Actions

ADVANCE SPACE AS A PRIORITY DOMAIN: America's newly re-established National Space Council, chaired by the Vice President, will review America's long-range space goals and develop a strategy that integrates all space sectors to support innovation and American leadership in space.

PROMOTE SPACE COMMERCE: The United States will simplify and update regulations for commercial space activity to strengthen competitiveness. As the U.S. Government partners with U.S. commercial space capabilities to improve the resiliency of our space architecture, we will also consider extending national security protections to our private sector partners as needed.

MAINTAIN LEAD IN EXPLORATION: To enable human exploration across the solar system and to bring back to Earth new knowledge and opportunities, we will increase public-private partnerships and promote ventures beyond low Earth orbit with allies and friends.

Cyberspace

Malicious state and non-state actors use cyberattacks for extortion, information warfare, disinformation, and more. Such attacks have the capability to harm large numbers of people and institutions with comparatively minimal investment and a troubling degree of deniability. These attacks can undermine faith and confidence in democratic institutions and the global economic system.

Many countries now view cyber capabilities as tools for projecting influence, and some use cyber tools to protect and extend their autocratic regimes. Cyberattacks have become a key feature of modern conflict. The United States will deter, defend, and when necessary defeat malicious actors who use cyberspace capabilities against the United States. When faced with the opportunity to take action against malicious actors in cyberspace, the United States will be risk informed, but not risk averse, in considering our options.

Priority Actions

IMPROVE ATTRIBUTION, ACCOUNTABILITY, AND RESPONSE: We will invest in capabilities to support and improve our ability to attribute cyberattacks, to allow for rapid response.

ENHANCE CYBER TOOLS AND EXPERTISE: We will improve our cyber tools across the spectrum of conflict to protect U.S. Government assets and U.S. critical infrastructure, and to protect the integrity of data and information. U.S. departments and agencies will recruit, train, and retain a workforce capable of operating across this spectrum of activity.

IMPROVE INTEGRATION AND AGILITY: We will improve the integration of authorities and procedures across the U.S. Government so that cyber operations against adversaries can be conducted as required. We will work with the Congress to address the challenges that continue to hinder timely intelligence and information sharing, planning and operations, and the development of necessary cyber tools.

Intelligence

America's ability to identify and respond to geostrategic and regional shifts and their political, economic, military, and security implications requires that the U.S. Intelligence Community (IC) gather, analyze, discern, and operationalize information. In this information-dominant era, the IC must continuously pursue strategic intelligence to anticipate geostrategic shifts, as well as shorter-term intelligence so that the United States can respond to the actions and provocations of rivals.

The ability of the United States to modernize our military forces to overmatch our adversaries requires intelligence support. Intelligence is needed to understand and anticipate foreign doctrine and the intent of foreign leaders, prevent tactical and operational surprise, and ensure that U.S. capabilities are not compromised before they are fielded. In addition, virtually all modern weapon systems depend upon data derived from scientific and technical intelligence.

The IC, as well as the law enforcement community, offer unique abilities to defend against and mitigate threat actors operating below the threshold of open conflict. Both communities have exceptionally strong liaison relationships throughout the world, allowing the United States to cooperate with allies and partners to protect against adversaries.

Priority Actions

IMPROVE UNDERSTANDING: To prevent the theft of sensitive and proprietary information and maintain supply chain integrity, the United States must increase our understanding of the economic policy priorities of our adversaries and improve our ability to detect and defeat their attempts to commit economic espionage.

HARNESS ALL INFORMATION AT OUR DISPOSAL: The United States will, in concert with allies and partners, use the information-rich open-source environment to deny the ability of state and non-state actors to attack our citizens, conduct offensive intelligence activities, and degrade America's democratic institutions.

FUSE INFORMATION AND ANALYSIS: The United States will fuse our analysis of information derived from the diplomatic, information, military, and economic domains to compete more effectively on the geopolitical stage.

Diplomacy and Statecraft

Competitive Diplomacy

Across the competitive landscape, America's diplomats are our forward-deployed political capability, advancing and defending America's interests abroad. Diplomacy catalyzes the political, economic, and societal connections that create America's enduring alignments and that build positive networks of relationships with partners. Diplomacy sustains dialogue and fosters areas of cooperation with competitors. It reduces the risk of costly miscommunication.

Diplomacy is indispensable to identify and implement solutions to conflicts in unstable regions of the world short of military involvement. It helps to galvanize allies for action and marshal the collective resources of like-minded nations and organizations to address shared problems. Authoritarian states are eager to replace the United States where the United States withdraws our diplomats and closes our outposts.

We must upgrade our diplomatic capabilities to compete in the current environment and to embrace a competitive mindset. Effective diplomacy requires the efficient use of limited resources, a professional diplomatic corps, modern and safe facilities, and secure methods to communicate and engage with local populations.

Priority Actions

PRESERVE A FORWARD DIPLOMATIC PRESENCE: Our diplomats must be able to build and sustain relationships where U.S. interests are at stake. Face-to-face diplomacy cannot be replaced by technology. Relationships, developed over time, create trust and shared understanding that the United States calls upon when confronting security threats, responding to crises, and encouraging others to share the burden for tackling the world's challenges. We must enable forward-deployed field work beyond the confines of diplomatic facilities, including partnering with military colleagues in conflict-affected states.

ADVANCE AMERICAN INTERESTS: In the ongoing contests for power, our diplomats must build and lead coalitions that advance shared interests and articulate America's vision in international forums, in bilateral relationships, and at local levels within states. Our diplomats need additional flexibility to operate in complex conflict-affected areas.

CATALYZE OPPORTUNITIES: Diplomats must identify opportunities for commerce and cooperation, and facilitate the cultural, educational, and people-to-people exchanges that create the networks of current and future political, civil society, and educational leaders who will extend a free and prosperous world.

Tools of Economic Diplomacy Priority Actions

Retaining our position as the world's preeminent economic actor strengthens our ability to use the tools of economic diplomacy for the good of Americans and others. Maintaining America's central role in international financial forums enhances our security and prosperity by expanding a community of free market economies, defending against threats from state-led economies, and protecting the U.S. and international economy from abuse by illicit actors.

We want to create wealth for Americans and our allies and partners. Prosperous states are stronger security partners who are able to share the burden of confronting common threats. Fair and reciprocal trade, investments, and exchanges of knowledge deepen our alliances and partnerships, which are necessary to succeed in today's competitive geopolitical environment. Trade, export promotion, targeted use of foreign assistance, and modernized development finance tools can promote stability, prosperity, and political reform, and build new partnerships based on the principle of reciprocity.

Economic tools—including sanctions, anti-money-laundering and anti-corruption measures, and enforcement actions—can be important parts of broader strategies to deter, coerce, and constrain adversaries. We will work with like-minded partners to build support for tools of economic diplomacy against shared threats. Multilateral economic pressure is often more effective because it limits the ability of targeted states to circumvent measures and conveys united resolve.

REINFORCE ECONOMIC TIES WITH ALLIES AND PARTNERS: We will strengthen economic ties as a core aspect of our relationships with like-minded states and use our economic expertise, markets, and resources to bolster states threatened by our competitors.

DEPLOY ECONOMIC PRESSURE ON SECURITY THREATS: We will use existing and pursue new economic authorities and mobilize international actors to increase pressure on threats to peace and security in order to resolve confrontations short of military action.

SEVER SOURCES OF FUNDING: We will deny revenue to terrorists, WMD proliferators, and other illicit actors in order to constrain their ability to use and move funds to support hostile acts and operations.

Information Statecraft

America's competitors weaponize information to attack the values and institutions that underpin free societies, while shielding themselves from outside information. They exploit marketing techniques to target individuals based upon their activities, interests, opinions, and values. They disseminate misinformation and propaganda.

Risks to U.S. national security will grow as competitors integrate information derived from personal and commercial sources with intelligence collection and data analytic capabilities based on Artificial Intelligence (AI) and machine learning. Breaches of U.S. commercial and government organizations also provide adversaries with data and insights into their target audiences.

China, for example, combines data and the use of AI to rate the loyalty of its citizens to the state and uses these ratings to determine jobs and more. Jihadist terrorist groups continue to wage ideological information campaigns to establish and legitimize their narrative of hate, using sophisticated communications tools to attract recruits and encourage attacks against Americans and our partners.

Russia uses information operations as part of its offensive cyber efforts to influence public opinion across the globe. Its influence campaigns blend covert intelligence operations and false online personas with state-funded media, third-party intermediaries, and paid social media users or "trolls."

U.S. efforts to counter the exploitation of information by rivals have been tepid and fragmented. U.S. efforts have lacked a sustained focus and have been hampered by the lack of properly trained professionals. The American private sector has a direct interest in supporting and amplifying voices that stand for tolerance, openness, and freedom.

Priority Actions

PRIORITIZE THE COMPETITION: We will improve our understanding of how adversaries gain informational and psychological advantages across all policies. The United States must empower a true public diplomacy capability to compete effectively in this arena.

DRIVE EFFECTIVE COMMUNICATIONS: We will craft and direct coherent communications campaigns to advance American influence and counter challenges from the ideological threats that emanate from radical Islamist groups and competitor nations. These campaigns will adhere to American values and expose adversary propaganda and disinformation.

ACTIVATE LOCAL NETWORKS: Local voices are most compelling and effective in ideological competitions. We must amplify credible voices and partner with them to advance alternatives to violent and hateful messages. Since media and Internet companies are the platforms through which messages are transported, the private sector should lend its creativity and resources to promoting the values that inspire and grow a community of civilized groups and individuals.

SHARE RESPONSIBILITY: The United States will urge states where radicalism thrives to take greater responsibility for countering violent messaging and promoting tolerant and pluralistic worldviews.

UPGRADE, TAILOR, AND INNOVATE: We will reexamine legacy delivery platforms for communicating U.S. messages overseas. We must consider more cost-effective and efficient ways to deliver and evaluate content consistent with U.S. national security interests.

PILLAR IV
ADVANCE AMERICAN INFLUENCE

"Above all, we value the dignity of every human life, protect the rights of every person, and share the hope of every soul to live in freedom. That is who we are."

PRESIDENT DONALD J. TRUMP, JULY 2017

Our America First foreign policy celebrates America's influence in the world as a positive force that can help set the conditions for peace and prosperity and for developing successful societies.

There is no arc of history that ensures that America's free political and economic system will automatically prevail. Success or failure depends upon our actions. This Administration has the confidence to compete to protect our values and interests and the fundamental principles that underpin them.

During the Cold War, a totalitarian threat from the Soviet Union motivated the free world to create coalitions in defense of liberty. Today's challenges to free societies are just as serious, but more diverse. State and non-state actors project influence and advance their objectives by exploiting information, democratic media freedoms, and international institutions. Repressive leaders often collaborate to subvert free societies and corrupt multilateral organizations.

Around the world, nations and individuals admire what America stands for. We treat people equally and value and uphold the rule of law. We have a democratic system that allows the best ideas to flourish. We know how to grow economies so that individuals can achieve prosperity. These qualities have made America the richest country on earth—rich in culture, talent, opportunities, and material wealth.

The United States offers partnership to those who share our aspirations for freedom and prosperity. We lead by example. "The world has its eye upon America," Alexander Hamilton once observed. "The noble struggle we have made in the cause of liberty, has occasioned a kind of revolution in human sentiment. The influence of our example has penetrated the gloomy regions of despotism."

We are not going to impose our values on others. Our alliances, partnerships, and coalitions are built on free will and shared interests. When the United States partners with other states, we develop policies that enable us to achieve our goals while our partners achieve theirs.

Allies and partners are a great strength of the United States. They add directly to U.S. political, economic, military, intelligence, and other capabilities. Together, the United States and our allies and partners represent well over half of the global GDP. None of our adversaries have comparable coalitions.

We encourage those who want to join our community of like-minded democratic states and improve the condition of their peoples. By modernizing U.S. instruments of diplomacy and development, we will catalyze conditions to help them achieve that goal. These aspiring partners include states that are fragile, recovering from conflict, and seeking a path forward to sustainable security and economic growth. Stable, prosperous, and friendly states enhance American security and boost U.S. economic opportunities.

We will continue to champion American values and offer encouragement to those struggling for human dignity in their societies. There can be no moral equivalency between nations that uphold the rule of law, empower women, and respect individual rights and those that brutalize and suppress their people. Through our words and deeds, America demonstrates a positive alternative to political and religious despotism.

Encourage Aspiring Partners

Some of the greatest triumphs of American statecraft resulted from helping fragile and developing countries become successful societies. These successes, in turn, created profitable markets for American businesses, allies to help achieve favorable regional balances of power, and coalition partners to share burdens and address a variety of problems around the world. Over time, the United States has helped create a network of states that advance our common interests and values.

This historical record is unprecedented and exceptional. American support to aspiring partners enabled the recovery of the countries of Western Europe under the Marshall Plan, as well as the ongoing integration of Central and Eastern Europe into Western institutions after the Cold War. In Asia, the United States worked with South Korea and Japan, countries ravaged by war, to help them become successful democracies and among the most prosperous economies in the world.

These achievements were products of patient partnerships with those who aspired to build prosperous societies and join the community of democratic states. They resulted in mutually beneficial relationships in which the United States helped states mobilize their own resources to achieve transitions to growth and stability. Working with these countries made the United States wealthier and more competitive. This progress illustrates how effective foreign assistance programs should reach their natural endpoint.

Today, the United States must compete for positive relationships around the world. China and Russia target their investments in the developing world to expand influence and gain competitive advantages against the United States. China is investing billions of dollars in infrastructure across the globe. Russia, too, projects its influence economically, through the control of key energy and other infrastructure throughout parts of Europe and Central Asia. The United States provides an alternative to state-directed investments, which often leave developing countries worse off. The United States pursues economic ties not only for market access but also to create enduring relationships to advance common political and security interests.

The United States will promote a development model that partners with countries that want progress, consistent with their culture, based on free market principles, fair and reciprocal trade, private sector activity, and rule of law. The United States will shift away from a reliance on assistance based on grants to approaches that attract private capital and catalyze private sector activity. We will emphasize reforms that unlock the economic potential of citizens, such as the promotion of formal property rights, entrepreneurial reforms, and infrastructure improvements—projects that help people earn their livelihood and have the added benefit of helping U.S. businesses. By mobilizing both public and private resources, the United States can help maximize returns and outcomes and reduce the burden on U.S. Government resources. Unlike the state-directed mercantilism of some competitors that can disadvantage recipient nations and promote dependency, the purpose of U.S. foreign assistance should be to end the need for it. The United States seeks strong partners, not weak ones.

U.S. development assistance must support America's national interests. We will prioritize collaboration with aspiring partners that are aligned with U.S. interests. We will focus on development investments where we can have the most impact— where local reformers are committed to tackling their economic and political challenges.

Within this framework, the United States will also assist fragile states to prevent threats to the U.S. homeland. Transnational threat organizations, such as jihadist terrorists and organized crime, often operate freely from fragile states and undermine sovereign governments. Failing states can destabilize entire regions.

Across Africa, Latin America, and Asia, states are eager for investments and financing to develop their infrastructure and propel growth. The United States and its partners have opportunities to work with countries to help them realize their potential as prosperous and sovereign states that are accountable to their people. Such states can become trading partners that buy more American-made goods and create more predictable business environments that benefit American companies. American-led investments represent the most sustainable and responsible approach to development and offer a stark contrast to the corrupt, opaque, exploitive, and low-quality deals offered by authoritarian states.

Priority Actions: Developing Countries

MOBILIZE RESOURCES: The United States will modernize its development finance tools so that U.S. companies have incentives to capitalize on opportunities in developing countries. With these changes, the United States will not be left behind as other states use investment and project finance to extend their influence. In addition, the U.S. Government must not be an obstacle to U.S. companies that want to conduct business in the developing world.

CAPITALIZE ON NEW TECHNOLOGIES: We will incorporate innovative technologies in our diplomatic and development programs. For example, digital technologies enable millions to access financial services through their cell phones and can connect farmers to markets. Such technologies can reduce corruption, increase transparency, and help ensure that money reaches its intended destination.

INCENTIVIZE REFORMS: The United States will use diplomacy and assistance to encourage states to make choices that improve governance, rule of law, and sustainable development. We already do this through the Millennium Challenge Corporation, which selects countries that are committed to reform and then monitors and evaluates their projects.

Priority Actions: Fragile States

COMMIT SELECTIVELY: We will give priority to strengthening states where state weaknesses or failure would magnify threats to the American homeland. For instance, engagement in Afghanistan seeks to prevent the reemergence of terrorist safe havens.

WORK WITH REFORMERS: Political problems are at the root of most state fragility. The United States will prioritize programs that empower reform-minded governments, people, and civil society. As the United States designs its efforts, inputs from local actors improve the likelihood of enduring solutions, reduce costs, and increase accountability to the American taxpayer.

SYNCHRONIZE ACTIONS: The United States must use its diplomatic, economic, and military tools simultaneously when assisting aspiring partners. We will place a priority on economic support that achieves local and macroeconomic stability, helps build capable security forces, and strengthens the rule of law.

Achieve Better Outcomes in Multilateral Forums

The United States must lead and engage in the multinational arrangements that shape many of the rules that affect U.S. interests and values. A competition for influence exists in these institutions. As we participate in them, we must protect American sovereignty and advance American interests and values.

A range of international institutions establishes the rules for how states, businesses, and individuals interact with each other, across land and sea, the Arctic, outer space, and the digital realm. It is vital to U.S. prosperity and security that these institutions uphold the rules that help keep these common domains open and free. Free access to the seas remains a central principle of national security and economic prosperity, and exploration of sea and space provides opportunities for commercial gain and scientific breakthroughs. The flow of data and an open, interoperable Internet are inseparable from the success of the U.S. economy.

Authoritarian actors have long recognized the power of multilateral bodies and have used them to advance their interests and limit the freedom of their own citizens. If the United States cedes leadership of these bodies to adversaries, opportunities to shape developments that are positive for the United States will be lost. All institutions are not equal, however. The United States will prioritize its efforts in those organizations that serve American interests, to ensure that they are strengthened and supportive of the United States, our allies, and our partners. Where existing institutions and rules need modernizing, the United States will lead to update them. At the same time, it should be clear that the United States will not cede sovereignty to those that claim authority over American citizens and are in conflict with our constitutional framework.

Priority Actions

EXERCISE LEADERSHIP IN POLITICAL AND SECURITY BODIES: The United States will strive for outcomes in political and security forums that are consistent with U.S. interests and values—values which are shared by our allies and partners. The United Nations can help contribute to solving many of the complex problems in the world, but it must be reformed and recommit to its founding principles. We will require accountability and emphasize shared responsibility among members. If the United States is asked to provide a disproportionate level of support for an institution, we will expect a commensurate degree of influence over the direction and efforts of that institution.

SHAPE AND REFORM INTERNATIONAL FINANCIAL AND TRADE INSTITUTIONS: The United States will continue to play a leading role in institutions such as the International Monetary Fund (IMF), World Bank, and World Trade Organization (WTO), but will improve their performance through reforms. These reforms include encouraging multilateral development banks to invest in high-quality infrastructure projects that promote economic growth. We will press to make the WTO a more effective forum to adjudicate unfair trade practices.

ENSURE COMMON DOMAINS REMAIN FREE: The United States will provide leadership and technology to shape and govern common domains—space, cyberspace, air, and maritime—within the framework of international law. The United States supports the peaceful resolution of disputes under international law but will use all of its instruments of power to defend U.S. interests and to ensure common domains remain free.

PROTECT A FREE AND OPEN INTERNET: The United States will advocate for open, interoperable communications, with minimal barriers to the global exchange of information and services. The United States will promote the free flow of data and protect its interests through active engagement in key organizations, such as the Internet Corporation for Assigned Names and Numbers (ICANN), the Internet Governance Forum (IGF), the UN, and the International Telecommunication Union (ITU).

Champion American Values

The extraordinary trajectory of the United States from a group of colonies to a thriving, industrialized, sovereign republic—the world's lone superpower—is a testimony to the strength of the idea on which our Nation is founded, namely that each of our citizens is born free and equal under the law. America's core principles, enshrined in the Declaration of Independence, are secured by the Bill of Rights, which proclaims our respect for fundamental individual liberties beginning with the freedoms of religion, speech, the press, and assembly. Liberty, free enterprise, equal justice under the law, and the dignity of every human life are central to who we are as a people.

These principles form the foundation of our most enduring alliances, and the United States will continue to champion them. Governments that respect the rights of their citizens remain the best vehicle for prosperity, human happiness, and peace. In contrast, governments that routinely abuse the rights of their citizens do not play constructive roles in the world. For example, governments that fail to treat women equally do not allow their societies to reach their potential.

No nation can unilaterally alleviate all human suffering, but just because we cannot help everyone does not mean that we should stop trying to help anyone. For much of the world, America's liberties are inspirational, and the United States will always stand with those who seek freedom. We will remain a beacon of liberty and opportunity around the world.

The United States also remains committed to supporting and advancing religious freedom—America's first freedom. Our Founders understood religious freedom not as the state's creation, but as the gift of God to every person and a fundamental right for our flourishing society.

And it is part of our culture, as well as in America's interest, to help those in need and those trying to build a better future for their families. We aid others judiciously, aligning our means to our objectives, but with a firm belief that we can improve the lives of others while establishing conditions for a more secure and prosperous world.

Priority Actions

SUPPORT THE DIGNITY OF INDIVIDUALS: We support, with our words and actions, those who live under oppressive regimes and who seek freedom, individual dignity, and the rule of law. We are under no obligation to offer the benefits of our free and prosperous community to repressive regimes and human rights abusers. We may use diplomacy, sanctions, and other tools to isolate states and leaders who threaten our interests and whose actions run contrary to our values. We will not remain silent in the face of evil. We will hold perpetrators of genocide and mass atrocities accountable.

DEFEAT TRANSNATIONAL TERRORIST ORGANIZATIONS: There can be no greater action to advance the rights of individuals than to defeat jihadist terrorists and other groups that foment hatred and use violence to advance their supremacist Islamist ideologies. We will continue to join with other states to defeat this scourge of all civilized peoples.

EMPOWER WOMEN AND YOUTH: Societies that empower women to participate fully in civic and economic life are more prosperous and peaceful. We will support efforts to advance women's equality, protect the rights of women and girls, and promote women and youth empowerment programs.

PROTECT RELIGIOUS FREEDOM AND RELIGIOUS MINORITIES: We will advocate on behalf of religious freedom and threatened minorities. Religious minorities continue to be victims of violence. We will place a priority on protecting these groups and will continue working with regional partners to protect minority communities from attacks and to preserve their cultural heritage.

REDUCE HUMAN SUFFERING: The United States will continue to lead the world in humanitarian assistance. Even as we expect others to share responsibility, the United States will continue to catalyze international responses to man-made and natural disasters and provide our expertise and capabilities to those in need. We will support food security and health programs that save lives and address the root cause of hunger and disease. We will support displaced people close to their homes to help meet their needs until they can safely and voluntarily return home.

THE STRATEGY IN A REGIONAL CONTEXT

The United States must tailor our approaches to different regions of the world to protect U.S. national interests. We require integrated regional strategies that appreciate the nature and magnitude of threats, the intensity of competitions, and the promise of available opportunities, all in the context of local political, economic, social, and historical realities.

Changes in a regional balance of power can have global consequences and threaten U.S. interests. Markets, raw materials, lines of communication, and human capital are located within, or move among, key regions of the world. China and Russia aspire to project power worldwide, but they interact most with their neighbors. North Korea and Iran also pose the greatest menace to those closest to them. But, as destructive weapons proliferate and regions become more interconnected, threats become more difficult to contain. And regional balances that shift against the United States could combine to threaten our security.

The United States must marshal the will and capabilities to compete and prevent unfavorable shifts in the Indo-Pacific, Europe, and the Middle East. Sustaining favorable balances of power will require a strong commitment and close cooperation with allies and partners because allies and partners magnify U.S. power and extend U.S. influence. They share our interests and responsibility for resisting authoritarian trends, contesting radical ideologies, and deterring aggression.

In other regions of the world, instability and weak governance threaten U.S. interests. Some governments are unable to maintain security and meet the basic needs of their people, making their country and citizens vulnerable to predators. Terrorists and criminals thrive where governments are weak, corruption is rampant, and faith in government institutions is low. Strategic competitors often exploit rather than discourage corruption and state weakness to extract resources and exploit their populations.

Regions afflicted by instability and weak governments also offer opportunities to improve security, promote prosperity, and restore hope. Aspiring partner states across the developing world want to improve their societies, build transparent and effective governments, confront non-state threats, and strengthen their sovereignty. Many recognize the opportunities offered by market economies and political liberties and are eager for partnership with the United States and our allies. The United States will encourage aspiring partners as they undertake reforms and pursue their aspirations. States that prosper and nations that transition from recipients of development assistance to trading partners offer economic opportunities for American businesses. And stability reduces threats that target Americans at home.

Indo-Pacific

A geopolitical competition between free and repressive visions of world order is taking place in the Indo-Pacific region. The region, which stretches from the west coast of India to the western shores of the United States, represents the most populous and economically dynamic part of the world. The U.S. interest in a free and open Indo-Pacific extends back to the earliest days of our republic.

Although the United States seeks to continue to cooperate with China, China is using economic inducements and penalties, influence operations, and implied military threats to persuade other states to heed its political and security agenda. China's infrastructure investments and trade strategies reinforce its geopolitical aspirations. Its efforts to build and militarize outposts in the South China Sea endanger the free flow of trade, threaten the sovereignty of other nations, and undermine regional stability. China has mounted a rapid military modernization campaign designed to limit U.S. access to the region and provide China a freer hand there. China presents its ambitions as mutually beneficial, but Chinese dominance risks diminishing the sovereignty of many states in the Indo-Pacific. States throughout the region are calling for sustained U.S. leadership in a collective response that upholds a regional order respectful of sovereignty and independence.

In Northeast Asia, the North Korean regime is rapidly accelerating its cyber, nuclear, and ballistic missile programs. North Korea's pursuit of these weapons poses a global threat that requires a global response. Continued provocations by North Korea will prompt neighboring countries and the United States to further strengthen security bonds and take additional measures to protect themselves. And a nuclear-armed North Korea could lead to the proliferation of the world's most destructive weapons across the Indo-Pacific region and beyond.

U.S. allies are critical to responding to mutual threats, such as North Korea, and preserving our mutual interests in the Indo-Pacific region. Our alliance and friendship with South Korea, forged by the trials of history, is stronger than ever. We welcome and support the strong leadership role of our critical ally, Japan. Australia has fought alongside us in every significant conflict since World War I, and continues to reinforce economic and security arrangements that support our shared interests and safeguard democratic values across the region. New Zealand is a key U.S. partner contributing to peace and security across the region. We welcome India's emergence as a leading global power and stronger strategic and defense partner. We will seek to increase quadrilateral cooperation with Japan, Australia, and India.

In Southeast Asia, the Philippines and Thailand remain important allies and markets for Americans. Vietnam, Indonesia, Malaysia, and Singapore are growing security and economic partners of the United States. The Association of Southeast Asian Nations (ASEAN) and Asia-Pacific Economic Cooperation (APEC) remain centerpieces of the Indo-Pacific's regional architecture and platforms for promoting an order based on freedom.

Priority Actions

POLITICAL: Our vision for the Indo-Pacific excludes no nation. We will redouble our commitment to established alliances and partnerships, while expanding and deepening relationships with new partners that share respect for sovereignty, fair and reciprocal trade, and the rule of law. We will reinforce our commitment to freedom of the seas and the peaceful resolution of territorial and maritime disputes in accordance with international law. We will work with allies and partners to achieve complete, verifiable, and irreversible denuclearization on the Korean Peninsula and preserve the non-proliferation regime in Northeast Asia.

ECONOMIC: The United States will encourage regional cooperation to maintain free and open seaways, transparent infrastructure financing practices, unimpeded commerce, and the peaceful resolution of disputes. We will pursue bilateral trade agreements on a fair and reciprocal basis. We will seek equal and reliable access for American exports. We will work with partners to build a network of states dedicated to free markets and protected from forces that would subvert their sovereignty. We will strengthen cooperation with allies on high-quality infrastructure. Working with Australia and New Zealand, we will shore up fragile partner states in the Pacific Islands region to reduce their vulnerability to economic fluctuations and natural disasters.

MILITARY AND SECURITY: We will maintain a forward military presence capable of deterring and, if necessary, defeating any adversary. We will strengthen our long-standing military relationships and encourage the development of a strong defense network with our allies and partners. For example, we will cooperate on missile defense with Japan and South Korea to move toward an area defense capability. We remain ready to respond with overwhelming force to North Korean aggression and will improve options to compel denuclearization of the peninsula. We will improve law enforcement, defense, and intelligence cooperation with Southeast Asian partners to address the growing terrorist threat. We will maintain our strong ties with Taiwan in accordance with our "One China" policy, including our commitments under the Taiwan Relations Act to provide for Taiwan's legitimate defense needs and deter coercion. We will expand our defense and security cooperation with India, a Major Defense Partner of the United States, and support India's growing relationships throughout the region. We will re-energize our alliances with the Philippines and Thailand and strengthen our partnerships with Singapore, Vietnam, Indonesia, Malaysia, and others to help them become cooperative maritime partners.

Europe

A strong and free Europe is of vital importance to the United States. We are bound together by our shared commitment to the principles of democracy, individual liberty, and the rule of law. Together, we rebuilt Western Europe after World War II and created institutions that produced stability and wealth on both sides of the Atlantic. Today, Europe is one of the most prosperous regions in the world and our most significant trading partner.

Although the menace of Soviet communism is gone, new threats test our will. Russia is using subversive measures to weaken the credibility of America's commitment to Europe, undermine transatlantic unity, and weaken European institutions and governments. With its invasions of Georgia and Ukraine, Russia demonstrated its willingness to violate the sovereignty of states in the region. Russia continues to intimidate its neighbors with threatening behavior, such as nuclear posturing and the forward deployment of offensive capabilities.

China is gaining a strategic foothold in Europe by expanding its unfair trade practices and investing in key industries, sensitive technologies, and infrastructure. Europe also faces immediate threats from violent Islamist extremists. Attacks by ISIS and other jihadist groups in Spain, France, Germany, Belgium, the United Kingdom, and other countries show that our European partners continue to face serious threats. Instability in the Middle East and Africa has triggered the movement of millions of migrants and refugees into Europe, exacerbating instability and tensions in the region.

The United States is safer when Europe is prosperous and stable, and can help defend our shared interests and ideals. The United States remains firmly committed to our European allies and partners. The NATO alliance of free and sovereign states is one of our great advantages over our competitors, and the United States remains committed to Article V of the Washington Treaty.

European allies and partners increase our strategic reach and provide access to forward basing and overflight rights for global operations. Together we confront shared threats. European nations are contributing thousands of troops to help fight jihadist terrorists in Afghanistan, stabilize Iraq, and fight terrorist organizations across Africa and the greater Middle East.

The NATO alliance will become stronger when all members assume greater responsibility for and pay their fair share to protect our mutual interests, sovereignty, and values.

Priority Actions

POLITICAL: The United States will deepen collaboration with our European allies and partners to confront forces threatening to undermine our common values, security interests, and shared vision. The United States and Europe will work together to counter Russian subversion and aggression, and the threats posed by North Korea and Iran. We will continue to advance our shared principles and interests in international forums.

ECONOMIC: The United States will work with the European Union, and bilaterally with the United Kingdom and other states, to ensure fair and reciprocal trade practices and eliminate barriers to growth. We will encourage European foreign direct investment in the United States to create jobs. We will work with our allies and partners to diversify European energy sources to ensure the energy security of European countries. We will work with our partners to contest China's unfair trade and economic practices and restrict its acquisition of sensitive technologies.

MILITARY AND SECURITY: The United States fulfills our defense responsibilities and expects others to do the same. We expect our European allies to increase defense spending to 2 percent of gross domestic product by 2024, with 20 percent of this spending devoted to increasing military capabilities. On NATO's eastern flank we will continue to strengthen deterrence and defense, and catalyze frontline allies and partners' efforts to better defend themselves. We will work with NATO to improve its integrated air and missile defense capabilities to counter existing and projected ballistic and cruise missile threats, particularly from Iran. We will increase counterterrorism and cybersecurity cooperation.

Middle East

The United States seeks a Middle East that is not a safe haven or breeding ground for jihadist terrorists, not dominated by any power hostile to the United States, and that contributes to a stable global energy market.

For years, the interconnected problems of Iranian expansion, state collapse, jihadist ideology, socio-economic stagnation, and regional rivalries have convulsed the Middle East. The United States has learned that neither aspirations for democratic transformation nor disengagement can insulate us from the region's problems. We must be realistic about our expectations for the region without allowing pessimism to obscure our interests or vision for a modern Middle East.

The region remains home to the world's most dangerous terrorist organizations. ISIS and al-Qa'ida thrive on instability and export violent jihad. Iran, the world's leading state sponsor of terrorism, has taken advantage of instability to expand its influence through partners and proxies, weapon proliferation, and funding. It continues to develop more capable ballistic missiles and intelligence capabilities, and it undertakes malicious cyber activities. These activities have continued unabated since the 2015 nuclear deal. Iran continues to perpetuate the cycle of violence in the region, causing grievous harm to civilian populations. Rival states are filling vacuums created by state collapse and prolonged regional conflict.

Despite these challenges, there are emerging opportunities to advance American interests in the Middle East. Some of our partners are working together to reject radical ideologies, and key leaders are calling for a rejection of Islamist extremism and violence. Encouraging political stability and sustainable prosperity would contribute to dampening the conditions that fuel sectarian grievances.

For generations the conflict between Israel and the Palestinians has been understood as the prime irritant preventing peace and prosperity in the region. Today, the threats from jihadist terrorist organizations and the threat from Iran are creating the realization that Israel is not the cause of the region's problems. States have increasingly found common interests with Israel in confronting common threats.

Today, the United States has the opportunity to catalyze greater economic and political cooperation that will expand prosperity for those who want to partner with us. By revitalizing partnerships with reform-minded nations and encouraging cooperation among partners in the region, the United States can promote stability and a balance of power that favors U.S. interests.

Priority Actions

POLITICAL: We will strengthen partnerships, and form new ones, to help advance security through stability. Whenever possible, we will encourage gradual reforms. We will support efforts to counter violent ideologies and increase respect for the dignity of individuals. We remain committed to helping our partners achieve a stable and prosperous region, including through a strong and integrated Gulf Cooperation Council. We will strengthen our long-term strategic partnership with Iraq as an independent state. We will seek a settlement to the Syrian civil war that sets the conditions for refugees to return home and rebuild their lives in safety. We will work with partners to deny the Iranian regime all paths to a nuclear weapon and neutralize Iranian malign influence. We remain committed to helping facilitate a comprehensive peace agreement that is acceptable to both Israelis and Palestinians.

ECONOMIC: The United States will support the reforms underway that begin to address core inequities that jihadist terrorists exploit. We will encourage states in the region, including Egypt and Saudi Arabia, to continue modernizing their economies. We will play a role in catalyzing positive developments by engaging economically, supporting reformers, and championing the benefits of open markets and societies.

MILITARY AND SECURITY: We will retain the necessary American military presence in the region to protect the United States and our allies from terrorist attacks and preserve a favorable regional balance of power. We will assist regional partners in strengthening their institutions and capabilities, including in law enforcement, to conduct counterterrorism and counterinsurgency efforts. We will help partners procure interoperable missile defense and other capabilities to better defend against active missile threats. We will work with partners to neutralize Iran's malign activities in the region.

South and Central Asia

With over a quarter of the world's population, a fifth of all U.S.-designated terrorist groups, several fast-growing economies, and two nuclear-armed states, South and Central Asia present some of the most complicated national security challenges and opportunities. The region spans the terrorist threats emanating from the Middle East and the competition for power unfolding in Europe and the Indo-Pacific. The United States continues to face threats from transnational terrorists and militants operating from within Pakistan. The prospect for an Indo-Pakistani military conflict that could lead to a nuclear exchange remains a key concern requiring consistent diplomatic attention.

U.S. interests in the region include countering terrorist threats that impact the security of the U.S. homeland and our allies, preventing cross-border terrorism that raises the prospect of military and nuclear tensions, and preventing nuclear weapons, technology, and materials from falling into the hands of terrorists. We seek an American presence in the region proportionate to threats to the homeland and our allies. We seek a Pakistan that is not engaged in destabilizing behavior and a stable and self-reliant Afghanistan. And we seek Central Asian states that are resilient against domination by rival powers, are resistant to becoming jihadist safe havens, and prioritize reforms.

Priority Actions

POLITICAL: We will deepen our strategic partnership with India and support its leadership role in Indian Ocean security and throughout the broader region. We will press Pakistan to intensify its counterterrorism efforts, since no partnership can survive a country's support for militants and terrorists who target a partner's own service members and officials. The United States will also encourage Pakistan to continue demonstrating that it is a responsible steward of its nuclear assets. We will continue to partner with Afghanistan to promote peace and security in the region. We will continue to promote anti-corruption reform in Afghanistan to increase the legitimacy of its government and reduce the appeal of violent extremist organizations. We will help South Asian nations maintain their sovereignty as China increases its influence in the region.

ECONOMIC: We will encourage the economic integration of Central and South Asia to promote prosperity and economic linkages that will bolster connectivity and trade. And we will encourage India to increase its economic assistance in the region. In Pakistan, we will build trade and investment ties as security improves and as Pakistan demonstrates that it will assist the United States in our counter-terrorism goals.

MILITARY AND SECURITY: We are committed to supporting the Afghan government and security forces in their fight against the Taliban, al-Qa'ida, ISIS, and other terrorists. We will bolster the fighting strength of the Afghan security forces to convince the Taliban that they cannot win on the battlefield and to set the conditions for diplomatic efforts to achieve enduring peace. We will insist that Pakistan take decisive action against militant and terrorist groups operating from its soil. We will work with the Central Asian states to guarantee access to the region to support our counterterrorism efforts.

Western Hemisphere

Stable, friendly, and prosperous states in the Western Hemisphere enhance our security and benefit our economy. Democratic states connected by shared values and economic interests will reduce the violence, drug trafficking, and illegal immigration that threaten our common security, and will limit opportunities for adversaries to operate from areas of close proximity to us.

In the last half century, parts of this hemisphere were marred by dictatorships and insurgencies that killed tens of thousands of people. Today, this region stands on the cusp of prosperity and peace, built upon democracy and the rule of law.

U.S. trade in the region is thriving and market opportunities for American goods and services, energy and infrastructure projects, and foreign direct investment continue to expand.

Challenges remain, however. Transnational criminal organizations—including gangs and cartels— perpetuate violence and corruption, and threaten the stability of Central American states including Guatemala, Honduras, and El Salvador. In Venezuela and Cuba, governments cling to anachronistic leftist authoritarian models that continue to fail their people. Competitors have found operating space in the hemisphere.

China seeks to pull the region into its orbit through state-led investments and loans. Russia continues its failed politics of the Cold War by bolstering its radical Cuban allies as Cuba continues to repress its citizens. Both China and Russia support the dictatorship in Venezuela and are seeking to expand military linkages and arms sales across the region. The hemisphere's democratic states have a shared interest in confronting threats to their sovereignty.

Canada and the United States share a unique strategic and defense partnership. The United States also has important and deepening relations with key countries in the region. Together, we will build a stable and peaceful hemisphere that increases economic opportunities for all, improves governance, reduces the power of criminal organizations, and limits the malign influence of non-hemispheric forces.

Priority Actions

POLITICAL: We will catalyze regional efforts to build security and prosperity through strong diplomatic engagement. We will isolate governments that refuse to act as responsible partners in advancing hemispheric peace and prosperity. We look forward to the day when the people of Cuba and Venezuela can enjoy freedom and the benefits of shared prosperity, and we encourage other free states in the hemisphere to support this shared endeavor.

ECONOMIC: We will modernize our trade agreements and deepen our economic ties with the region and ensure that trade is fair and reciprocal. We will encourage further market-based economic reforms and encourage transparency to create conditions for sustained prosperity. We will ensure the U.S. financial system does not serve as a haven or transit point for criminal proceeds.

MILITARY AND SECURITY: We will build upon local efforts and encourage cultures of lawfulness to reduce crime and corruption, including by supporting local efforts to professionalize police and other security forces; strengthen the rule of law and undertake judicial reform; and improve information sharing to target criminals and corrupt leaders and disrupt illicit trafficking.

Africa

Africa remains a continent of promise and enduring challenges. Africa contains many of the world's fastest growing economies, which represent potential new markets for U.S. goods and services. Aspiring partners across the continent are eager to build market-based economies and enhance stability. The demand for quality American exports is high and will likely grow as Africa's population and prosperity increase. People across the continent are demanding government accountability and less corruption, and are opposing autocratic trends. The number of stable African nations has grown since the independence era as numerous countries have emerged from devastating conflicts and undergone democratic transitions.

Despite this progress, many states face political turbulence and instability that spills into other regions. Corruption and weak governance threaten to undermine the political benefits that should emerge from new economic opportunities. Many African states are battlegrounds for violent extremism and jihadist terrorists. ISIS, al-Qa'ida, and their affiliates operate on the continent and have increased the lethality of their attacks, expanded into new areas, and targeted U.S. citizens and interests.

African nations and regional organizations have demonstrated a commitment to confront the threat from jihadist terrorist organizations, but their security capabilities remain weak.

China is expanding its economic and military presence in Africa, growing from a small investor in the continent two decades ago into Africa's largest trading partner today. Some Chinese practices undermine Africa's long-term development by corrupting elites, dominating extractive industries, and locking countries into unsustainable and opaque debts and commitments.

The United States seeks sovereign African states that are integrated into the world economy, able to provide for their citizens' needs, and capable of managing threats to peace and security. Improved governance in these states supports economic development and opportunities, diminishes the attraction of illegal migration, and reduces vulnerability to extremists, thereby reducing instability.

Priority Actions

POLITICAL: The United States will partner with governments, civil society, and regional organizations to end long-running, violent conflicts. We will encourage reform, working with promising nations to promote effective governance, improve the rule of law, and develop institutions accountable and responsive to citizens. We will continue to respond to humanitarian needs while also working with committed governments and regional organizations to address the root causes of human suffering. If necessary, we are prepared to sanction government officials and institutions that prey on their citizens and commit atrocities. When there is no alternative, we will suspend aid rather than see it exploited by corrupt elites.

ECONOMIC: We will expand trade and commercial ties to create jobs and build wealth for Americans and Africans. We will work with reform-oriented governments to help establish conditions that can transform them into trading partners and improve their business environment. We will support economic integration among African states. We will work with nations that seek to move beyond assistance to partnerships that promote prosperity. We will offer American goods and services, both because it is profitable for us and because it serves as an alternative to China's often extractive economic footprint on the continent.

MILITARY AND SECURITY: We will continue to work with partners to improve the ability of their security services to counter terrorism, human trafficking, and the illegal trade in arms and natural resources. We will work with partners to defeat terrorist organizations and others who threaten U.S. citizens and the homeland.

CONCLUSION

This National Security Strategy sets a positive strategic direction for the United States that is meant to reassert America's advantages on the world stage and to build upon our country's great strengths. During the Trump Administration, the American people can be confident that their security and prosperity will always come first. A secure, prosperous, and free America will be strong and ready to lead abroad to protect our interests and our way of life.

America's renewed strategic confidence is anchored in our recommitment to the principles inscribed in our founding documents. The National Security Strategy celebrates and protects what we hold dear—individual liberty, the rule of law, a democratic system of government, tolerance, and opportunity for all. By knowing ourselves and what we stand for, we clarify what we must defend and we establish guiding principles for our actions.

This strategy is guided by principled realism. It is realist because it acknowledges the central role of power in international politics, affirms that sovereign states are the best hope for a peaceful world, and clearly defines our national interests. It is principled because it is grounded in the knowledge that advancing American principles spreads peace and prosperity around the globe. We are guided by our values and disciplined by our interests.

This Administration has a bright vision of America's future. America's values and influence, underwritten by American power, make the world more free, secure, and prosperous.

Our Nation derives its strength from the American people. Every American has a role to play in this grand, national effort to implement this America First National Security Strategy. Together, our task is to strengthen our families, to build up our communities, to serve our citizens, and to celebrate American greatness as a shining example to the world. We will leave our children and grandchildren a Nation that is stronger, better, freer, prouder, and greater than ever before.

National Intelligence Strategy 2014

Foreword

I've often said publicly that we are facing the most diverse set of threats I've seen in my 50 years in the intelligence business. That's true. It's also true, however, that we are better organized to face these threats than we were 13 years ago. We have strengthened and integrated our Intelligence Community (IC) in the decade since 9/11, supported by the *National Intelligence Strategy* (NIS).

This, the third iteration of the NIS, is our guide forward for the next four years to better serve the needs of our customers, to make informed decisions on national security issues, and ultimately, to make our nation more secure. We face significant changes in the domestic and global environment and must be ready to meet 21st century challenges and to recognize emerging opportunities. This guidance is designed to propel our mission and align our objectives with national strategies. The NIS provides an opportunity to communicate national priority objectives to our workforce, partners, and customers—from the policy maker, to the war-fighter, to the first responder, to our fellow citizens.

To navigate today's turbulent and complex strategic environment, we must: (1) Execute our mission smartly and identify ways to better leverage the substantive work of our partners and potential partners; (2) Continue to integrate, transform, and strengthen the IC's support to national security; (3) Protect privacy and civil liberties and adhere to the *Principles of Professional Ethics for the IC*; and (4) Adapt to changing needs and resources and innovate to provide unique anticipatory and strategic intelligence.

We have seen a great deal of success in integrating intelligence in the five years since our most recent NIS, with both high-profile operational achievements and significant enterprise improvements. Together, we must build on our successes and mitigate risks, guided by this updated strategy. We must continue to evolve as an integrated Community, advance our capabilities in technology and tradecraft, and push for improvements in both mission and enterprise management, through initiatives such as the IC Information Technology Enterprise.

We have crucial work before us. Senior policymakers depend on us to enable them to make wise national security decisions and Americans count on us to help protect the nation from attack, while increasing transparency and protecting their privacy and civil liberties. We must provide the best intelligence possible to support these objectives; doing so is a collective responsibility of all of our dedicated IC professionals and, together with our partners, we will realize our vision.

Thank you for your dedication to our mission and to the security of our fellow citizens as we continue this journey together.

James R. Clapper
Director of National Intelligence

Purpose

In support of the *National Security Strategy*, which sets forth national security priorities, the *National Intelligence Strategy* (NIS) provides the IC with the mission direction of the Director of National Intelligence (DNI) for the next four to five years. IC activities must be consistent with, and responsive to, national security priorities and must comply with the Constitution, applicable statutes, and Congressional oversight requirements. The NIS should be read along with the National Intelligence Priorities Framework and Unifying Intelligence Strategies to inform and guide mission, as well as planning, programming, and budgeting activities.

Organizational Framework

The NIS has four main components, described as follows:

(1) the *Strategic Environment* section portrays the global national security milieu;

(2) the *Mission Objective* section describes key mission priorities and expected outcomes;

(3) the *Enterprise Objective* section describes resource and capability outcomes needed to enable mission success; and

(4) the *Implementing the Strategy* section provides broad organizational guidance to meet the NIS's requirements.

Our success as a Community is measured as much by our defense of America's values as it is by the execution of our intelligence mission. What follows is a succinct depiction of the IC's Mission and Vision, which serves as the foundation for the Mission and Enterprise Objectives. Fundamental to all of these elements are the *Principles of Professional Ethics for the IC*.

IC Mission

Provide timely, insightful, objective, and relevant intelligence to inform decisions on national security issues and events.

IC Vision

A nation made more secure by a fully integrated, agile, resilient, and innovative Intelligence Community that exemplifies America's values.

Mission Objectives	Enterprise Objectives
Strategic Intelligence	Integrated Mission Management
Anticipatory Intelligence	Integrated Enterprise Management
Current Operations	Information Sharing and Safeguarding
Cyber Intelligence	Innovation
Counterterrorism	Our People
Counterproliferation	Our Partners
Counterintelligence	

Principles of Professional Ethics for the Intelligence Community

As members of the intelligence profession, we conduct ourselves in accordance with certain basic principles. These principles are stated below, and reflect the standard of ethical conduct expected of all Intelligence Community personnel, regardless of individual role or agency affiliation. Many of these principles are also reflected in other documents that we look to for guidance, such as statements of core values, and the *Code of Conduct: Principles of Ethical Conduct for Government Officers and Employees*; it is nonetheless important for the Intelligence Community to set forth in a single statement the fundamental ethical principles that unite us and distinguish us as intelligence professionals.

- **MISSION.** We serve the American people, and understand that our mission requires selfless dedication to the security of our nation.
- **TRUTH.** We seek the truth; speak truth to power; and obtain, analyze, and provide intelligence objectively.
- **LAWFULNESS.** We support and defend the Constitution, and comply with the laws of the United States, ensuring that we carry out our mission in a manner that respects privacy, civil liberties, and human rights obligations.
- **INTEGRITY.** We demonstrate integrity in our conduct, mindful that all our actions, whether public or not, should reflect positively on the Intelligence Community at large.
- **STEWARDSHIP.** We are responsible stewards of the public trust; we use intelligence authorities and resources prudently, protect intelligence sources and methods diligently, report wrongdoing through appropriate channels; and remain accountable to ourselves, our oversight institutions, and through those institutions, ultimately to the American people.
- **EXCELLENCE.** We seek to improve our performance and our craft continuously, share information responsibly, collaborate with our colleagues, and demonstrate innovation and agility when meeting new challenges.
- **DIVERSITY.** We embrace the diversity of our nation, promote diversity and inclusion in our workforce, and encourage diversity in our thinking.

Strategic Environment

The United States faces a complex and evolving security environment with extremely dangerous, pervasive, and elusive threats. The IC remains focused on the missions of cyber intelligence, counterterrorism, counterproliferation, counterintelligence, and on the threats posed by state and non-state actors challenging U.S. national security and interests worldwide.

Key nation states continue to pursue agendas that challenge U.S. interests. China has an interest in a stable East Asia, but remains opaque about its strategic intentions and is of concern due to its military modernization. Russia is likely to continue to reassert power and influence in ways that undermine U.S. interests, but may be willing to work with the United States on important high priority security issues, when interests converge. The IC spotlight remains on North Korea's pursuit of nuclear and ballistic missile capabilities and its international intransigence. Iran's nuclear efforts remain a key concern, in addition to its missile programs, support for terrorism, regime dynamics, and other developing military capabilities. The potential for greater instability in the Middle East and North Africa will require continued IC vigilance. Finally, continued IC vigilance will be required to maintain global coverage of conflicts as they arise and potentially threaten U.S. interests.

Violent extremist groups and transnational criminal networks threaten U.S. security and challenge the U.S. both in the homeland and abroad. Al-Qa'ida, its affiliates, and adherents, continue to plot against U.S. and Western interests, and seek to use weapons of mass destruction if possible. The actions of transnational criminal organizations have the potential to corrupt and destabilize governments, markets, and entire geographic regions. The IC will increasingly serve homeland security as well as military and foreign policy objectives.

Domestic Environment. The IC faces fiscal challenges as the U.S. Government operates under tightened budgets. We must meet our mission needs in innovative ways and sustain our core competencies with fewer resources. Likewise, our customers and partners will also grapple with resource challenges. While such constraints will require the IC to accept and balance risks, addressing these challenges presents additional opportunities to enhance partnerships, information sharing, and outreach.

The U.S. will continue to face threats of unauthorized disclosures from insiders and others that compromise intelligence sources, methods, capabilities, and activities, and may impact international and domestic political dynamics. These disclosures can degrade our ability to conduct intelligence missions and damage our national security.

Global Environment. Global power is becoming more diffuse. New alignments and informal networks—outside of traditional power blocs and national governments— will increasingly have significant impact in economic, social, and political affairs. Resolving complex security challenges will require the IC's attention to a broader array of actors. Private, public, governmental, commercial, and ideological players will become increasingly influential, both regionally and virtually. The projected rise of a global middle class and its growing expectations will fuel economic and political change. Some states and international institutions will be challenged to govern or operate effectively.

Many governments will face challenges to meet even the basic needs of their people as they confront demographic change, resource constraints, effects of climate change, and risks of global infectious disease outbreaks. These effects are threat multipliers that will aggravate stressors abroad such as poverty, environmental degradation, political instability, and social tensions—conditions that can enable terrorist activity and other forms of violence. The risk of conflict and mass atrocities may increase.

Small, local actions can have disproportionate and enduring effects. Groups can form, advocate, and achieve goals—for political, social, and economic change—all without central leadership. Identifying, understanding, and evaluating such movements will be both a continuing challenge and an opportunity for the IC.

Technology. Technology is constantly advancing, bringing benefits and challenges. Technological developments hold enormous potential for dramatic improvements in individual health, employment, labor productivity, global communications, and investment.

Technology will continue to be a catalyst for the rapid emergence of changes difficult to anticipate or prepare for; these forces can test the strength of governments and potentially jeopardize U.S. citizens and interests overseas. Technological advances also create the potential for increased systemic fragility as foreign governments and non-state actors attempt to leverage new and evolving technologies to press their interests.

Natural Resources. Competition for scarce resources, such as food, water, or energy, will likely increase tensions within and between states and could lead to more localized or regional conflicts, or exacerbate government instability. In contrast, prospective resource opportunities beyond U.S. borders and the potential for the U.S. to meet anticipated fossil fuel requirements through domestic production are likely to alter dramatically the global energy market and change the dynamics between the U.S. and other oil producing nations.

Introduction to Mission Objectives

The seven Mission Objectives broadly describe the priority outputs needed to deliver timely, insightful, objective, and relevant intelligence to our customers. Intelligence includes foreign intelligence and counterintelligence. The Mission Objectives are designed to address the totality of regional and functional issues facing the IC; their prioritization is communicated to the IC through the National Intelligence Priorities Framework.

IC Customers

- The President
- National Security Council
- Heads of Departments and Agencies of the Executive Branch
- Chairman of the Joint Chiefs of Staff and senior military commanders
- Congress
- Others as the DNI determines appropriate

Source: National Security Act of 1947, as amended

Three Mission Objectives refer to foundational intelligence missions the IC must accomplish, regardless of threat or topic:

- *Strategic Intelligence*—inform and enrich understanding of enduring national security issues;
- *Anticipatory Intelligence*—detect, identify, and warn of emerging issues and discontinuities;
- *Current Operations*—support ongoing actions and sensitive intelligence operations.

Four Mission Objectives identify the primary topical missions the IC must accomplish:

- *Cyber Intelligence*—provide intelligence on cyber threats;
- *Counterterrorism*—understand and counter those involved in terrorism and related activities;
- *Counterproliferation*—counter the threat and proliferation of weapons of mass destruction;
- *Counterintelligence*—thwart efforts of foreign intelligence entities.

1. Strategic Intelligence: Provide strategic intelligence on enduring issues to enrich understanding and enable decision advantage.

Strategic intelligence is the process and product of developing deep context, knowledge, and understanding to support national security decision-making.

The foundation for strategic intelligence is in understanding the histories, languages, and cultures of nations and non-state entities, their key leaders and opponents, their objectives and concerns, as well as natural resources, technology, and transnational issues. The IC masters vital national intelligence issues through research, knowledge development, outreach, and tradecraft in order to provide deep context for a wide variety of policy and strategy communities.

To meet this objective, the IC will:

- Deepen understanding of the strategic environment to enable IC customers to pursue national security, mission- and issue-specific goals;
- Access and assess foreign capabilities, activities, and intentions to provide IC customers with greater insight and certainty;
- Provide in-depth and contextual objective analysis and expertise to support U.S. national security policy and strategy.

2. Anticipatory Intelligence: Sense, anticipate, and warn of emerging conditions, trends, threats, and opportunities that may require a rapid shift in national security posture, priorities, or emphasis.

Anticipatory intelligence is the product of intelligence collection and analysis focused on trends, events, and changing conditions to identify and characterize potential or imminent discontinuities, significant events, substantial opportunities, or threats to U.S. national interests.

The complexity, scale, and pace of changes in the strategic environment will test the IC's ability to deliver insightful and actionable intelligence with the fidelity, scope, and speed required to mitigate threats and exploit opportunities. The IC will expand its use of quantitative analytic methods, while reinforcing long-standing qualitative methods, especially those that encourage new perspectives and challenge long-standing assumptions. With evolving intelligence requirements, anticipatory intelligence is critical for efficient IC resource allocation. The IC will improve its ability to foresee, forecast, and alert the analytic community of potential issues of concern and convey early warning to national security customers to provide them with the best possible opportunity for action.

To meet this objective, the IC will: . . . . •
Create capabilities for dynamic horizonscanning and discovery to assess changing and emerging conditions and issues that can affect U.S. national security; • Deepen understanding of conditions, issues, and trends to detect subtle shifts and assess their potential trajectories, and forecast the impact on U.S. national security thus generating opportunities to alert or warn; • Develop integrated capabilities to create alerts within the IC and to provide timely and relevant warning to our customers.

3. Current Operations: Provide timely intelligence support to achieve operational and national security goals.

Intelligence support to current operations, whether collection, analysis, counterintelligence, or intelligence operations, occurs in almost all IC organizations and cuts across almost every topic addressed by the IC. Intelligence support to current operations is characterized by the immediacy of the support provided. In addition to being responsive, this support also shapes future operations and investigations.

The IC will adapt to evolving operational requirements, maintain the robust support customers expect, and further enhance capabilities. As the IC facilitates whole-ofgovernment efforts to take action against terrorists and transnational organized crime, address cyber threats, and respond to emerging crises—from geo-political to humanitarian—it will also need to support policy imperatives such as the rebalance to the Asia-Pacific region and transition of the allied mission in Afghanistan. Faced with a wide spectrum of operations in support of military, diplomatic, and homeland security activities, the IC will prioritize its efforts and mitigate risk, operate in denied areas, balance forward presence with robust reach-back, and provide operational resiliency to more fully integrate intelligence with operations.

To meet this objective, the IC will:

- Provide actionable, timely, and agile intelligence support to achieve and maintain operational decision advantage;
- Integrate and collaborate with diverse partners to maximize the effectiveness and reach of intelligence capabilities in support of operations;
- Conduct sensitive intelligence operations to support effective national security action.

4. Cyber Intelligence: Detect and understand cyber threats to inform and enable national security decision making, cybersecurity, and cyber effects operations.

Cyber intelligence is the collection, processing, analysis, and dissemination of information from all sources of intelligence on foreign actors' cyber programs, intentions, capabilities, research and development, tactics, and operational activities and indicators; their impact or potential effects on national security, information systems, infrastructure, and data; and network characterization, or insight into the components, structures, use, and vulnerabilities of foreign information systems.

State and non-state actors use digital technologies to achieve economic and military advantage, foment instability, increase control over content in cyberspace, and achieve other strategic goals—often faster than our ability to understand the security implications and mitigate potential risks. To advance national objectives, customers increasingly rely upon the IC to provide timely, actionable intelligence and deeper insights into current and potential cyber threats and intentions. The IC also provides needed expertise to defend U.S.

Government networks along with other critical communications networks and national infrastructure. To be more effective, the IC will evolve its cyber capabilities, including our ability to attribute attacks. The IC will focus on identifying trends and providing the context to improve our customers' understanding of threats, vulnerabilities, and impact.

To meet this objective, the IC will:

- Increase our awareness and understanding of key foreign cyber threat actors— including their intentions, capabilities, and operations—to meet the growing number and complexity of cyber-related requirements;
- Expand tailored production and dissemination of actionable cyberintelligence to support the defense of vital information networks and critical infrastructure;
- Expand our ability to enable cyber effects operations to protect the nation and support U.S. national interests.

5. Counterterrorism: Identify, understand, monitor, and disrupt state and non-state actors engaged in terrorism-related activities that may harm the United States, its people, interests, and allies.

The dynamic and diverse nature of the terrorist threat will continue to challenge the U.S. and our interests and will require continued emphasis on targeting, collection, and analysis. The IC supports the national whole-of-government effort to protect the homeland from terrorist attack, disrupt and degrade terrorists who threaten U.S. interests abroad, counter the spread of violent extremist ideology that influences terrorist action, disrupt illicit financial and other support networks, and build counterterrorism capacity at home and overseas. Our government and our partners must anticipate, detect, deny, and disrupt terrorism wherever and however it manifests against U.S. interests. The IC will continue to monitor this threat to protect our nation, provide warning and assess the strategic factors that may enable future terror plots.

To meet this objective, the IC will:

- Conduct innovative analysis that supports disruption of terrorist actors posing threats to the U.S. and our interests;
- Provide insight to mitigate the spread of violent extremist ideology;
- Anticipate new and developing terrorist threats and explore opportunities to counter them;
- Bolster resiliency and build adaptive capability to counter terrorism at home and abroad.

6. Counterproliferation: Counter the threat and proliferation of weapons of mass destruction and their means of delivery by state and non-state actors.

The intelligence requirements and challenges related to countering the proliferation of weapons of mass destruction (WMD) are increasing. The IC will support objectives for countering the threat and proliferation of WMD and their means of delivery as well as WMD-related materials, technology, and expertise. The IC will work with partners inside and outside the U.S. Government to better understand, detect, and warn on foreign WMD capabilities, plans, and intentions; thwart WMD acquisition and employment; and inform U.S. policies and initiatives.

To meet this objective, the IC will:

- Develop capabilities and inform U.S. policies and efforts to dissuade or prevent states from acquiring WMD-related technologies, materials, or expertise or from reconstituting former programs;
- Advance our understanding of established state WMD programs to inform U.S. counterproliferation decisions, policies, and efforts to disrupt, roll back, and deter use;
- Support interagency efforts to secure global stockpiles of weapons of mass destruction and warn of and prevent the transfer of WMD-related materials, technology, and expertise to terrorists, extremists, or other non-state actors;
- Improve U.S. capabilities to anticipate and manage crises and support integrated U.S. Government responses to mitigate the consequences of WMD use or loss of state control.

7. Counterintelligence: Identify, understand, and mitigate the efforts of foreign intelligence entities to compromise U.S. economic and national security.

A foreign intelligence entity is any known or suspected foreign organization, person, or group (public, private, or government) that conducts intelligence activities to acquire U.S. information, block or impair U.S. intelligence collection, unlawfully influence U.S. policy, or disrupt U.S. systems and programs. The term includes foreign intelligence and security services and international terrorists.

The U.S. faces persistent and substantial challenges to its security and prosperity from the intelligence activities of traditional and non-traditional adversaries. Foreign intelligence entities relentlessly target the U.S. Government, the private sector, and academia to acquire national security information and to gain economic, diplomatic, military, or technological advantage.

IC elements will identify emerging technologies that can be leveraged by our adversaries to compromise classified information and assets, and develop and adopt robust mitigation strategies. Counterintelligence activities must be integrated into all steps of the intelligence process.

To meet this objective, the IC will:

- Understand, anticipate, and penetrate increasingly sophisticated foreign intelligence entity capabilities;
- Develop and implement capabilities to detect, deter, and mitigate insider threats;
- Stem the theft and exploitation of critical U.S. technologies, data, and information;
- Neutralize and/or mitigate adversarial attempts to exploit U.S. supply chain and acquisition vulnerabilities.

Introduction to Enterprise Objectives

Accomplishing the seven NIS Mission Objectives depends on achieving six Enterprise Objectives, which describe the resources and capabilities that are essential to fulfilling the Mission Objectives.

Two Enterprise Objectives focus on enterprise integration while optimizing resource management and decision making:

- *Integrated Mission Management*—optimize capabilities to achieve unity of effort;
- *Integrated Enterprise Management*—improve IC integration and interoperability.

Four Enterprise Objectives describe our strategy to build a solid foundation of key capabilities and capacity:

- *Information Sharing and Safeguarding*—improve collaboration while protecting information;
- *Innovation*—improve research and development, tradecraft, and processes;
- *Our People*—build a more agile, diverse, inclusive, and expert workforce;
- *Our Partners*—improve intelligence through partnership.

The Enterprise Objectives address both mission and enterprise integration and rest on the *Principles of Professional Ethics for the IC*.

1. Integrated Mission Management: Optimize collection, analysis, and counterintelligence capabilities and activities across the IC to achieve unity of effort and effect.

Integrated mission management is the strategic prioritization, coordination, and deconfliction of intelligence activities to align the interdependent disciplines of collection, analysis, and counterintelligence.

- Collection activities are responsive to and inform analytic requirements.
- Analytic activities produce intelligence judgments, identify intelligence gaps, and provide the basis for guidance to collectors.
- Counterintelligence activities complement collection and analytic activities and identify vulnerabilities of intelligence sources, methods, and activities.

Effective mission execution requires flexible, responsive, and resilient efforts to appropriately share knowledge, information, and capabilities across organizational boundaries. The IC will increase integration and collaboration across the Community to meet customer needs efficiently and effectively. In doing so, the IC will strike a balance between unity of effort and specialization within each discipline and function, using the best of each to meet mission requirements. Intelligence products will be appropriately tailored and classified at the lowest possible level.

Analytic, collection, and counterintelligence professionals, supported by coordinated governance, joint processes, and improved capabilities, will collaboratively work together to define and solve problems.

To meet this objective, the IC will:

- Leverage cross-IC, multi-disciplinary expertise and the full range of IC capabilities to jointly define and anticipate intelligence problems, develop options for action, and understand tradeoffs for implementing solutions;
- Strengthen and integrate governance bodies to optimize resources and manage risk;
- Foster joint IC planning, targeting, tasking, and assessment processes to coordinate intelligence activities and promote continuous improvement;
- Drive integrated investment decisions and the delivery of multi-disciplinary, integrated capabilities to provide optimal solutions for mission success.

2. Integrated Enterprise Management: Develop, implement, and manage IC-oriented approaches to improve integration and interoperability of IC enabling capabilities.

Integrated enterprise management is the strategic coordination of IC business practices to optimize resource management and enterprise business process decision making.

Effectively managing enterprise resources enables the IC to fully execute its mission efficiently. Specifically, the IC will seek solutions that increase efficiencies in areas such as continuity, security, acquisition and procurement, finance, facilities, and logistics. IC-wide performance evaluation and data-driven reviews—aligned to strategy and budgets—will strengthen performance, enhance oversight and compliance, and lead to unmodified audit opinions, improved results, and lower costs. The IC will promote information security, share timely intelligence with our partners, and educate customers on proper use and handling of classified information.

To meet this objective, the IC will:

- Advance a personnel security infrastructure that supports a one-Community approach through continuous evaluation and common practices and standards accepted across the IC;
- Pursue acquisition and procurement strategies and processes across the IC that enhance the cost-effectiveness and efficiency of procuring common-use products and services;
- Implement IC enterprise financial standards, processes, tools, and services that leverage both government and industry best practices;
- Mature strategy-based performance and evaluation across the IC to support proactive, balanced, and informed IC decision making;
- Leverage existing and future IC facilities and physical infrastructure to support joint-use functionality and improve energy efficiency;
- Adopt a risk management approach to continuity of operations efforts to provide an uninterrupted flow of national intelligence in all circumstances;
- Continue to implement approaches to provide appropriate transparency, protect privacy and civil liberties, and enhance oversight and compliance.

3. Information Sharing and Safeguarding: Enhance, integrate, and leverage IC capabilities to improve collaboration and the discovery, access, retrieval, retention, and safeguarding of information.

The Intelligence Community Information Technology Enterprise (IC ITE) transforms agency-centric information technology to a common enterprise platform where the IC can easily and securely share technology, information, and capabilities across the Community.

Mission success depends on the right people getting the right information at the right time. Improving our information sharing and safeguarding capabilities, as mutually reinforcing priorities, requires strengthening our people, processes, and technologies.

The IC will continue to identify and address information sharing gaps and coordinate efforts to reduce duplication across the IC Information Technology Enterprise to yield better results more efficiently.

In addition to recognizing the responsibility to provide intelligence and the growing demand to make information available across the IC, the IC will enhance safeguards to protect information and build trust among partners.

An integrated information sharing environment, dedicated to protecting privacy and civil liberties, allows the IC to carry out the mission, protect against external and insider threats, and maintain the public trust.

To meet this objective, the IC will:

- Consolidate existing and future information technology requirements into an effective and efficient IC information technology infrastructure to enable greater IC integration, information sharing, and safeguarding;

- Provide the IC workforce with discovery and access to information based on mission need to deliver timely, tailored, and actionable information;
- Integrate enterprise-wide information, as appropriate, to enhance discovery, improve correlation, and enable advanced analytics consistent with protection of privacy and civil liberties;
- Strengthen and synchronize security and data protection standards for new and existing intelligence information systems based on policy-driven interoperable approaches and attribute-based access to provide a trusted and secure IC-wide information environment;
- Promote a culture that embodies, supports, and furthers responsible information sharing respectful of privacy and civil liberties.

4.   Innovation: Find and deploy new scientific discoveries and technologies, nurture innovative thought, and improve tradecraft and processes to achieve mission advantage.

Innovation begins with a commitment to research and development as the seed for breakthroughs in science and technology. In order for innovation to provide results, the IC will further develop, support, and foster intellectual curiosity and creative problem solving. The IC must accept that initial failures may lead to successes and be willing to take calculated risks for high-value results when a rational basis for the risk is demonstrated.

The IC will leverage innovation wherever it is found, incorporating scientific breakthroughs and cutting-edge technologies for mission excellence. The IC will extend innovation to our daily work by embracing new processes and automation to streamline the business aspects of intelligence.

To meet this objective, the IC will:

- Conduct and leverage basic research and maintain core independent research in the most sensitive applied and social sciences, technologies, and mathematics arenas to achieve breakthrough results;
- Transition creative ideas and promising innovations to improve intelligence services and processes across the IC;
- Strengthen and unleash the innovative talents of the workforce to accept risk, improve tradecraft, and embrace new technologies and processes.

5.   Our People: Build a more agile, diverse, inclusive, and expert workforce.

Inclusion describes a culture that connects each employee to the organization; encourages collaboration, flexibility, and fairness; and leverages diversity of thought throughout the organization so all individuals can excel in their contributions to the IC mission.

Workforce planning is a framework addressing the total workforce balance (civilian, military, and core contract personnel) to ensure the IC has the right people with the right skills in the right place at the right time to accomplish the mission in high-performing teams and organizations.

Diversity considers, in a broad context and in relation to the mission, all aspects that make individuals unique and America strong— including race, color, ethnicity, national origin, gender, age, religion, language, disability, sexual orientation, gender identity, and heritage.

The IC workforce is united in protecting and preserving national security, which could not be accomplished without a talented workforce that embraces the IC's core values and *Principles of Professional Ethics for the IC*. To this end, the IC will continue to attract, develop, engage, and retain a workforce that possesses both the capabilities necessary to address current and evolving threats and a strong sense of integrity. Even with constrained budgets, the IC will make long-term strategic investments in the workforce to promote agility and mobility throughout employees' careers. Special emphasis is needed to recruit, retain, develop, and motivate employees with skills fundamental to the success of the intelligence mission, including foreign language, science, technology, engineering, and mathematics.

The IC needs effective tools for workforce planning, transformational learning programs, skills assessment and knowledge sharing, joint duty and other experiential assignment opportunities, and the resources to encourage and facilitate work-life balance.

All employees are accountable for cultivating a performance-driven culture that encourages collaboration, flexibility, and fairness without the fear of reprisal.

To meet this objective, the IC will:

- Shape a diverse and inclusive workforce with the skills and capabilities needed now and in the future;
- Provide continuous learning and development programs based on a mutual commitment between managers and employees to promote workforce competency, relevance, and agility;
- Nurture a culture of innovation and agility that advocates the sharing of ideas and resources adaptable to the changing environment, and promotes best practices across the IC;
- Provide a workplace free of discrimination, harassment, and the fear of reprisal, where all are treated with dignity and respect and afforded equal opportunity to contribute to their full potential.

6. Our Partners: Strengthen partnerships to enrich intelligence.

Partners consist of elements working to protect U.S. security interests, including U.S. military, our allies, foreign intelligence and security services, other federal departments and agencies, as well as state, local, tribal governments, and private sector entities.

The Community's partnerships are fundamental to our national security. Our partners are force multipliers, offering access, expertise, capabilities, and perspectives that enrich our intelligence capacity and help all of us succeed in our shared mission. The IC will deepen existing partnerships and forge new relationships to enhance intelligence and inform decisions.

Our approach to strengthening partnerships will align with broader national policy guidance and harmonize partner initiatives across the IC through policies, procedures, and practices that clearly delineate roles, responsibilities, and authorities. In working with the array of government, foreign, military, and private sector partners, the IC will remain cognizant of, and dedicated to, protecting privacy and civil liberties and maintaining the public trust.

To meet this objective, the IC will:

- Increase shared responsibility with and among, and incorporate insights from, all partners to advance intelligence;

- Develop an enterprise approach to partnership engagement to facilitate coordinated, integrated outreach;
- Deepen collaboration to enhance understanding of our partners and to effectively inform decisions and enable action.

Implementing the Strategy

The IC is an integrated intelligence enterprise working toward the common vision of a more secure nation. The NIS provides the overarching framework to accomplish the mission and achieve the vision. The IC will implement the NIS consistent with its statutory authorities under Congressional oversight.

The DNI and IC elements work together in an integrated fashion to execute the NIS. Functional managers monitor the health of important intelligence capabilities. Mission managers examine all facets of collection, analysis, and counterintelligence against specific areas of concern across missions. Program managers scrutinize how funds are executed. IC enterprise managers align support functions to enable each mission. The IC elements recruit, train, equip, and conduct intelligence missions. Inspectors General, legal counsel, and privacy and civil liberties officers ensure proper compliance and oversight.

The Office of the Director of National Intelligence provides the IC with overarching guidance and coordination. IC elements execute their missions consistent with their statutory authorities. Finally, it is the responsibility of all members of the IC workforce to understand how they contribute to the IC mission and execute their specific role to the best of their ability and consistent with the protection of privacy and civil liberties.

DNI

Serve as Principal Intelligence Advisor. As principal intelligence advisor to the President, the DNI must ensure intelligence addresses threats to national security. The DNI establishes the IC's strategic priorities and sets forth the enabling capabilities needed for mission success in the NIS.

Set Strategic Priorities for the IC. The NIS, in concert with the *National Security Strategy* and the National Intelligence Priorities Framework, represents the IC's mission priorities. The DNI informs Congress of significant priority realignment and activities.

Align the National Intelligence Program. The NIS serves as the DNI's mechanism to align the National Intelligence Program and guide the reporting of resource expenditures and performance to Congress. Additionally, the National Intelligence Program is coordinated with the Military Intelligence Program and the DNI's joint annual planning and programming guidance for the IC.

IC Elements

Align Strategies, Plans, and Actions. The mission and enterprise objectives in the NIS shall be incorporated and cascaded into IC element strategies and plans. IC elements and functional managers will facilitate an integrated approach to these objectives to achieve the IC's mission.

Inform Resource Allocation. The NIS will inform decisions about programs, budgets, policies, and acquisitions to develop and sustain capabilities. IC elements and program managers will reflect NIS objectives in their annual strategic program briefs and will articulate their intentions to mitigate risks in their annual planning and programming activities.

Measure Outcomes. The execution of the NIS objectives requires constant and consistent evaluation. IC elements will provide information through existing processes to clearly illustrate how they have performed against NIS objectives and the IC Priority Goals, which measure progress against enduring national security issues. Measuring progress against the NIS is crucial to improving overall IC performance.

Conclusion

The NIS supports intelligence integration and the IC's mission to provide timely, insightful, objective, and relevant intelligence to inform decisions on national security issues and events. The IC must fully reflect the NIS in agency strategic plans, annual budget requests, and justifications for the National Intelligence Program. The DNI will assess IC element proposals, projects, and programs against the objectives of the NIS to realize the IC's vision of a nation made more secure by a fully integrated, agile, resilient, and innovative Intelligence Community that exemplifies America's values.

> *"The Intelligence Community exists to provide political and military leaders with the greatest possible decision advantage.*
>
> *We understand, now more than ever, that the best way to accomplish our goal is thorough integration of all national intelligence capabilities."*

James R. Clapper, Director of National Intelligence

National Counterintelligence Strategy 2016

THE WHITE HOUSE

WASHINGTON

Today, the United States faces a daunting counterintelligence threat that seeks to undermine our economic strength, steal our most sensitive information, and weaken our defenses. As we have throughout history, we must rely on a strong counterintelligence regimen that detects, deters, and disrupts the threats of today while preparing for the challenges of tomorrow.

Foreign intelligence entities, as well as terrorist groups and non-state actors, use human and technical means, both overtly and covertly, to steal U.S. national security information. We know they are actively seeking to acquire data on a range of sensitive topics of vital importance to our security -- from advanced weapons systems and intelligence capabilities, to proprietary information from U.S. businesses and institutions in the fields of energy, finance, defense, and dual-use technology.

We also know that cyber tools and new technologies are giving our adversaries new ways to steal valuable data from the United States Government, academic institutions, and businesses -- oftentimes from the safety of a computer thousands of miles away. As the recent cyber intrusion against the Office of Personnel Management illustrated, even Federal agencies that hold sensitive but not classified data are at increased risk of being targeted by foreign adversaries. The expanding and interconnected nature of espionage threats demands a whole-of-government response to safeguard our most valuable security and economic information.

The *National Counterintelligence Strategy of the United States of America 2016* sets forth a coordinated plan to detect, deter, and disrupt foreign threats by strengthening bonds and information sharing among government, academic institutions, and the private sector. It elevates the focus on countering cyberespionage and provides guidance to U.S. entities to unify efforts at home and abroad against today's threats while preparing for those of tomorrow.

OFFICE OF THE DIRECTOR OF NATIONAL INTELLIGENCE
NATIONAL COUNTERINTELLIGENCE EXECUTIVE
WASHINGTON, DC 20511

This *National Counterintelligence Strategy of the United States of America 2016 (Strategy)* represents an evolution in our approach to a whole-of-government awareness of and response to foreign intelligence entity (FIE) threats. In recent decades, the United States Government has made extraordinary strides adapting to changing fiscal, technological, and cultural environments. However, the efforts to modernize and adapt have likewise provided opportunities for FIEs to expand their scope of collection and operations against the U.S. Government.

The United States remains vulnerable if it is only capable of recognizing the threat. Recognition must be followed by means to counter such threats. Fully integrating counterintelligence (CI) and security into our business practices—from information technology and acquisition to personnel decisions—is essential to preserving our national security. We must leverage the CI and security disciplines to create mission synergies and extend these synergies into the realm of cyberspace. We must work with our information assurance professionals to defend our networks from FIEs attempting to steal or compromise our sensitive data, information, and assets. We must bolster our collection and analytic efforts, improve targeting to disrupt the operations of FIEs, and foster widespread awareness and application of CI. By doing so, we will expand the reach and improve the effectiveness of CI across the U.S. Government.

My office is committed to working with leaders across the U.S. Government and private sector to drive reforms needed to protect our national security and mitigate the threats posed by FIEs. As leaders, it is our collective responsibility to be ahead of the threat. Each senior leader has the opportunity to be a change agent, to transform business practices and shape the workforce to support and protect our most sensitive information and assets. This *Strategy* is a roadmap to unify and modernize our efforts; through its implementation, we will leverage the talents of the entire U.S. Government to protect our nation's most sensitive information and assets.

William R. Evanina

Purpose

The *National Counterintelligence Strategy of the United States of A merica 2016 (Strategy)* was developed in accordance with the Counterintelligence Enhancement Act of 2002 (Pub.L. No. 107-306, 116 Stat. 2383 (as amended) codified at 50 U.S.C. sec. 3383(d)(2)). The *Strategy* sets forth how the United States (U.S.) Government will identify, detect, exploit, disrupt, and neutralize foreign intelligence entity (FIE) threats. It provides guidance for the counterintelligence (CI) programs and activities of the U.S. Government intended to mitigate such threats.

Each U.S. Government department and agency has a role in implementing this *Strategy* in the context of its own mission and through application of its unique responsibilities and authorities.

Nothing in this *Strategy* shall be construed as authorization of any department or agency to conduct CI activities not otherwise authorized under statute, executive order, or any other applicable law, policy, or regulation.

Strategic Environment

The United States is confronted with an array of diverse threats and challenges from FIE activities. Our adversaries include not only foreign intelligence services and their surrogates but also terrorists, cyber intruders, malicious insiders, transnational criminal organizations, and international industrial competitors with known or suspected ties to these entities. Many use sophisticated overt, covert, and clandestine methods to compromise our national security.

Just as the nature, scope, and volume of our protected information and other vulnerable assets have evolved, so too has the threat environment. Technological advances have enabled our adversaries to both broaden and tailor their approach to subvert our defensive measures, harm and penetrate our information systems, steal sensitive data, and otherwise degrade our instruments of national power.

Strategic Response

The current and emerging CI challenges facing the U.S. require an integrated, whole-ofgovernment response. Successfully countering threats from FIEs requires the U.S., both public and private sectors, to recognize the threat environment and implement appropriate countermeasures. The mission of countering FIEs is essential to preserving U.S. decisionmaking confidence and the critical information, technologies, infrastructure, and other assets that underpin our nation's security and prosperity. Understanding the threats and responding in an integrated fashion are imperative to the successful implementation of this *Strategy*.

This *Strategy* puts forth both mission and enabling objectives to address the full range of capabilities needed to counter the diverse threats to our nation's sensitive information and assets. The five mission objectives outline key activities required to identify, detect, exploit, disrupt, and neutralize FIE and insider threats and to safeguard our national assets, including cyberspace. The two enabling objectives provide the foundation for the mission objectives' success by highlighting the need for these activities to be undertaken as part of an effective, responsible, and collaborative effort. Implemented together, the mission and enabling objectives create a CI posture capable of meeting 21st century threats.

Force Multipliers

The unfailing application of proactive, effective security capabilities is crucial to protect sensitive U.S. information and assets from foreign adversaries. While the authorities that govern CI and security and the programs they drive are distinct, their respective actions must be synchronized and coordinated to achieve results. CI and security are interdependent and mutually supportive disciplines with shared objectives and responsibilities associated with the protection of sensitive information and assets. This Strategy acknowledges the critical role of security programs in contributing to the integrity of our CI efforts.

Moreover, defending the increasingly complex networks and technology that house and process our sensitive information against sophisticated 21st century threats requires a seamless and well-coordinated four-pronged defensive approach comprising CI, security, information assurance (IA), and cybersecurity professionals working together as a team. Essential to this Strategy is leveraging security and CI disciplines to create mission synergies and extending these synergies into the realm of cyberspace. CI, security, and IA combine in a multidisciplinary approach to provide a more stable network defense posture.

Mission Objective 1

Deepen our understanding of foreign intelligence entities' plans, intentions, capabilities, tradecraft, and operations targeting U.S. national interests and sensitive information and assets.

The United States faces enduring and emerging threats from FIEs that target our sensitive information and assets or otherwise jeopardize U.S. national interests. These threats continue to evolve in scope and complexity as FIE capabilities and activities become increasingly diverse and technically sophisticated. To meet this challenge, the U.S. Government must continue to evolve its CI programs and activities to improve our understanding of the full scope of current and emerging FIE threats, drive decision-making, and support U.S. national security goals.

In accordance with their existing authorities, mission, roles, and responsibilities, departments and agencies will:

- Conduct and support collection, investigative, and operational activities that yield intelligence on FIEs' strategic objectives and collection priorities;

- Conduct and support collection, investigative, and operational activities that yield intelligence on FIEs' plans, intentions, capabilities, and activities;
- Penetrate and pursue FIEs in order to holistically understand FIE threats;
- Produce timely, forward leaning all-source analytic products on FIE capabilities and intentions that provide warning and identify key changes, trends, and events;
- Disseminate CI-relevant information obtained during the course of investigations and operations;
- Pursue joint collection and analysis opportunities to expand and enrich reporting and production on priority FIE targets;
- Develop and implement efforts to anticipate, identify, and warn of emerging FIE threats; and
- Conduct and support collection, investigative, and operational activities that identify technical capabilities and threats.

Successful implementation of these actions will yield actionable intelligence on FIE threats to U.S. national security, including joint products that provide policymakers relevant, insightful, and credible intelligence to close the highest priority knowledge gaps. It will also provide warnings to U.S. Government departments and agencies and private sector partners of specific FIE threats to their information and assets.

Mission Objective 2

Disrupt foreign intelligence entities' capabilities, plans, and operations that threaten U.S. interests and sensitive information and assets.

FIEs pursue sophisticated measures to disrupt U.S. plans, policies, and processes and undermine U.S. national interests. All of these activities threaten the advancement of U.S. national security goals. The U.S. Government must employ coordinated offensive and defensive CI activities aligned to U.S. national security requirements to effectively disrupt FIE advances. By guarding against FIE threats while taking proactive steps to respond to them, we seek to counter, disrupt, and defeat activities inimical to the interests of the United States.

In accordance with their existing authorities, mission, roles, and responsibilities, departments and agencies will:

- Conduct and support, as appropriate, collection, investigative, and operational activities that identify and disrupt efforts to penetrate or influence the U.S. Government or otherwise harm U.S. interests;
- Conduct and support, as appropriate, CI operations that corrupt the integrity of foreign adversaries' intelligence cycles;
- Conduct and support, as appropriate, collection, investigative, and operational activities that counter, exploit, or otherwise defeat FIEs' activities; and

- Promote collaborative and integrated efforts to counter FIE threats in order to optimize government-wide capabilities and amplify individual lines of effort.

Successful implementation of these actions will result in disruptions of FIE intelligence activities. A measureable decline in the level of risk to sensitive information and assets, as determined and mitigated through periodic risk assessments, should occur. Information gleaned from these actions should form the basis of a coordinated, agile, and highly responsive process for identifying and prioritizing FIE threats and intelligence gaps. This process will provide greater fidelity in characterizing and countering FIE threats.

Mission Objective 3

Detect, deter, and mitigate threats from insiders with access to sensitive information and assets.

The U.S. Government continues to face threats from trusted insiders who compromise our intelligence sources and methods. These insiders range from those who are driven by personal ideology or directed by foreign governments to those whose unintentional actions jeopardize national security. Recent unauthorized public disclosures by trusted insiders have damaged international relationships, compromised intelligence sources, and prompted our adversaries to change their behavior, making it more difficult to understand their intentions.

The early detection of insider threats is essential to protecting our sensitive information and assets. Information and data gathered from multiple sources are integral components of a department's or agency's ability to detect and mitigate threats from malicious insiders. We must also recognize that the most effective safeguard against insider threats is a knowledgeable, trusted workforce which is confident that their privacy and civil liberties are respected.

Employees are the caretakers of our most sensitive information and resources, and they must be individually invested in the imperative to protect it.

In accordance with their existing authorities, mission, roles, and responsibilities, departments and agencies will:

- Integrate and analyze relevant CI data and work with enterprise insider threat programs to use a whole-person, whole-of -career concept to identify and continuously evaluate anomalous behavior;
- Review insider threat anomalies for FIE nexuses;
- Analyze FIE activities to discern patterns of behavior potentially indicative of an insider threat;
- Advocate for and influence the implementation of automated recordscheck methodologies to identify relevant CI information;

- Ensure CI equities are incorporated into a risk-based approach to insider threat detection techniques;
- Strengthen CI and insider threat awareness among the workforce to enhance and drive vigilance and consciousness across the U.S. Government;
- Enable network and system monitoring and ensure triggers are evaluated and cross-checked against other data sources to enhance detection and analysis of possible anomalous behavior; and
- Advocate for participation in enterprise audit programs to prevent unauthorized activity and facilitate a secure information infrastructure.

Successful implementation of these initiatives will best posture departments and agencies for early detection of anomalous behavior and improve the identification, prevention, and mitigation of uncharacteristic employee conduct or harmful insider threat activities. Enhanced insider threat and CI awareness across the U.S. Government will improve our ability to identify suspicious activities, identify FIE attempts to collect information or recruit employees, and instill a sense of urgency to report anomalous behaviors or activities to security and counterintelligence professionals. Better management of shared information will limit the availability of and access to classified and potentially sensitive information. Early detection and mitigation is critical for a successful insider threat program to minimize the damage caused by employees who intentionally or unintentionally compromise our information and systems, and, in more serious cases, to neutralize FIE attempts to recruit employees.

Mission Objective 4

Safeguard sensitive information and assets from foreign intelligence entities' theft, manipulation, or exploitation.

Foreign intelligence entities threaten U.S. national security as they relentlessly seek access to sensitive U.S. information and assets that will provide them with an economic, military, or technological edge. At the same time, vulnerabilities in global supply chains increase the potential for adversaries to exploit, deny, or damage U.S. assets and services. In the aggregate, such activities may undercut U.S. economic and military security and affect a wide variety of national security-related activities. The threat extends beyond the U.S. Government—U.S. companies and research establishments are target-rich environments for FIEs. To effectively protect our information and assets, the U.S. Government must engage stakeholders across the public and private sectors to ensure a common understanding of, and response to, FIE activities.

In accordance with their existing authorities, mission, roles, and responsibilities, departments and agencies will:

- Employ programs and activities to protect the integrity of the U.S. intelligence system and ensure the continuing performance of national essential functions;
- Use programs and activities to defend our critical infrastructure; critical and emerging technologies; and research, development, and acquisition programs from FIE collection or illicit acquisition;
- Implement programs and activities that facilitate secure information sharing and collaboration with foreign partners, vendors, researchers, and visitors while protecting sensitive information and assets from FIE theft, manipulation, or exploitation;
- Identify vulnerabilities and threats to private sector entities conducting sensitive U.S. Government-sponsored research, development, and acquisition programs;
- Integrate CI and security process into supply chain operations to secure the supply chain from exploitation and reduce its vulnerability to disruption;
- Expand partnerships with law enforcement agencies responsible for enforcing export control rules to identify unauthorized exports and take aggressive criminal and administrative enforcement actions against FIEs;
- Conduct risk assessments to identify and mitigate FIE threats to product development, acquisition, implementation, and maintenance cycles; and
- Coordinate efforts to safeguard sensitive information and assets across the U.S. Government.

Successful implementation of these actions will require an increase in U.S. Government and private sector partners sharing threat information; an increase in the education and awareness of employees on FIE interest in our sensitive information and assets; and an increase in the number of risk assessments conducted on organizations researching, manufacturing, or procuring sensitive technologies and assets. Other indicators of success include improvements in our application of protective measures countering FIE theft, manipulation, or exploitation throughout all phases of the supply chain.

Mission Objective 5

Identify and counter foreign intelligence entities' cyber activities that attempt to disrupt, exploit, or steal sensitive information, to include personally identifiable information, from U.S. networks.

FIEs continue to use computer network operations to exfiltrate sensitive data, information, and assets from the U.S. Government and the private sector, as observed in several recent data breaches. The loss of sensitive data, information, and assets through computer network operations conducted by or on behalf of FIEs has the potential to cause significant economic, technological, scientific, and national security harm and introduce counterintelligence and cybersecurity vulnerabilities. In addition to providing FIEs with sensitive U.S. information, network compromises may increase options for disrupting communications networks and critical infrastructure systems. Technological advances have accelerated the speed at which information moves, challenging our capability to protect sensitive information and assets. Because of these challenges, a robust capability to defend against adversarial computer network operations must be tightly woven into U.S. Government CI and security programs, including the expansion of outreach programs with private sector partners.

In accordance with their existing authorities, mission, roles, and responsibilities, and in response to recent cyberespionage breaches, departments and agencies will:

- Expand support to cyber effects operations;
- Pursue programs and activities that enhance understanding of FIE cyber intentions, capabilities, and operations affecting U.S. networks;
- Advance attribution capabilities to support disruption of cyber attacks and exploitation linked to FIEs;
- Enhance the relationship between CI elements, security, and IT to ensure personally identifiable information, and other sensitive information and assets of interests to FIEs is protected;
- Pursue programs and activities that counter FIE cyber operations directed against sensitive U.S. information; and
- Leverage expertise across the CI, security, and information technology mission sets to identify and assess stolen content, analyze and mitigate risks, and define protection requirements.

Successful implementation of these actions will enhance a department's or agency's ability to analyze incidents and attribute suspicious network behavior to FIE activities. Other indicators of success include a continued increase in threat informationsharing across all sectors and collaboration on mitigation strategies.

Enabling Objective 1

Strengthen secure collaboration, responsible information sharing and safeguarding, and effective partnerships.

FIEs target the U.S. Government and our private sector and international partners to obtain not only classified, but also sensitive information and assets. As a result, a persistent and growing need exists to collaborate and share FIE threat, warning, and awareness information across the entire U.S. Government and with the private sector and international partners. At the same time, we must ensure personnel engaged in these information discovery and retrieval efforts are mindful of the safeguards necessary to protect sensitive information and assets.

Secure collaboration, responsible information sharing, and effective partnerships are vital in detecting, identifying, exploiting, and neutralizing FIE efforts to compromise and degrade U.S. national and economic security.

In accordance with their existing authorities, mission, roles, and responsibilities, departments and agencies will:

- Drive responsible and secure information sharing to maximize unity of effort in identifying, exploiting, and neutralizing FIE threats and to inform decision making;
- Enhance synchronization of CI programs and activities, including the conduct of joint investigations and operations;
- Expand partnerships and share threat information across U.S. Government agencies and with key public and private sectors and international partners to establish a common understanding of FIE threats and promote coordinated mitigation approaches;
- Develop and deliver credible education and awareness programs that equip the U.S. Government workforce and public and private sector partners to identify threats and report CI concerns;
- Share information on FIE technical activities and capabilities across U.S. Government agencies and with key public and private sectors and international partners to address pervasive threats and vulnerabilities; and
- Share information on lessons learned and best practices with across U.S. Government agencies and with key public and private sectors and international partners to improve our processes for reporting, analyzing, investigating, and remediating incidents.

Successful implementation of these actions will yield an increase in information sharing to stem the damage caused by FIE activities. It should also improve the access of departments and agencies to reporting and production on common threats to U.S. national and economic security. In addition, it should result in an increase in CI training programs for U.S. Government personnel and in the percent of personnel trained.

Enabling Objective 2

Strengthen the nation's programs to counter threats from foreign intelligence entities.

The U.S. Government's CI programs vary significantly in breadth and are calibrated to the unique mission requirements and organizational capabilities of each department and agency. Regardless of individual program complexities and proficiencies, the U.S. Government must strengthen its CI programs and processes to adapt to the complexity of FIE and insider threats. U.S. Government departments and agencies must plan and fund programs and activities to ensure that CI practitioners have the proper tools and resources to execute their responsibilities.

At the same time, the tasks and activities that make up our CI programs must be continuously reviewed, renewed, and refined to ensure that the CI enterprise remains relevant, responsive, and effective.

In accordance with their existing authorities, mission, roles, and responsibilities, departments and agencies will:

- Promote well-reasoned and continuous integration of CI and FIE threat awareness into the execution of programs and activities across the U.S. Government;
- Provide continuous learning and professional development programs to increase professional skills and abilities in countering FIE;
- Develop strategies, policies, and oversight mechanisms to guide the execution of CI functions;
- Use risk assessment information to strengthen programs countering FIE threats; and
- Implement processes to track the effectiveness of CI efforts against stated national objectives and outcomes.

Successful implementation of these actions will result in an increase in the establishment, participation, and maturity of new and existing programs to counter FIE threats, as determined by formal evaluations. It should also result in greater awareness of and access to professional development opportunities to enhance the skills and proficiency of professionals responsible for protecting sensitive information and assets within departments and agencies. Additionally, it should result in an expanded use of existing and development, as needed, of new CI authorities, policies, and oversight mechanisms across the U.S. Government.

Conclusion

Countering FIE threats is a core obligation across the U.S. Government and should be reflected in the attitudes and daily behavior of the entire workforce. The U.S. Government must integrate CI principles and practices with business processes and workflows; mission-critical acquisitions; personnel, physical, and information security programs; and information assurance policies and procedures.

Our national security hinges on our ability to break down the wall separating CI from other core functions and transcend a paradigm that countering the FIE threats and protecting sensitive information and assets are the realm solely of CI and security professionals. While CI has traditionally operated as a stand-alone discipline, some U.S Government departments and agencies have made notable progress in recent years in integrating CI programs with security, insider threat, human resources, information assurance, budget, and other organizational functions. As the FIE threats facing us today continue to evolve, we must accelerate this integration and widen CI practices across the U.S. Government.

Achieving the mission and enabling objectives in this *National Counterintelligence Strategy of the United States of America 2016* is paramount to increasing our ability to counter FIE threats. Department and agency executives must become the change agents in implementing these mission and enabling objectives. Integrating our collective CI efforts and broadening their reach throughout the U.S. Government is vital to our success. By extending CI practices both across and within departments and agencies, we will exponentially strengthen the protection of the sensitive information and assets that underpin our national security.

Glossary

Terms not specifically cited were developed and defined in coordination with subject matter experts for use in this Strategy.

Acquisition – Acquiring by contract with appropriated funds of supplies or services (including construction) by and for the use of the Federal Government through purchase or lease, whether the supplies or services are already in existence or must be created, developed, demonstrated, and evaluated. Acquisition begins at the point when agency needs are established and includes the description of requirements to satisfy agency needs, solicitation and selection of sources, award of contract, contract financing, contract performance, contract administration, and those technical and management functions directly related to the process of fulfilling agency needs by contract. – *Federal A cquisition Regulations, as of 29 January 2013*

Counterintelligence – Information gathered and activities conducted to identify, deceive, exploit, disrupt, or protect against espionage, other intelligence activities, sabotage, or assassinations conducted for or on behalf of foreign powers, organizations, or persons, or their agents, or international terrorist organizations or activities. – *Executive Order 12333, as amended, United States Intelligence Activities*

Counterintelligence Programs – Capabilities and activities established within an organization for the purposes of identifying, deceiving, exploiting, disrupting, or protecting against espionage, other intelligence activities, sabotage, or assassinations conducted for or on behalf of foreign intelligence entities. – *Intelligence Community Directive 750, Counterintelligence Programs* **Counterintelligence Risk Assessment** – An assessment that examines threat information and identifies organizational vulnerabilities to make an informed determination about the likelihood and consequence of the loss or compromise of sensitive information and assets to foreign intelligence entities.

Cyber Effect – The manipulation, disruption, denial, degradation, or destruction of computers, information or communications systems, networks, physical or virtual infrastructure controlled by computers or information systems, or information resident thereon. – *Presidential Policy Directive/PPD-20, U.S. Cyber Operations*

Cyberspace – The interdependent network of information technology infrastructures, that includes the Internet, telecommunications networks, computer, information or communications systems, networks, and embedded processors and controllers. – *Presidential Policy Directive/ PPD-20, U.S. Cyber Operations Policy*

Espionage – Intelligence activity directed toward the acquisition of intelligence through clandestine methods. – *National Security Council Intelligence Directive No.5, U.S. Espionage and Counterintelligence Activities Abroad*

Foreign Intelligence Entity (FIE) – Known or suspected foreign state or non-state organizations or persons that conduct intelligence activities to acquire U.S. information, block or impair U.S. intelligence collection, influence U.S. policy, or disrupt U.S. systems and programs. The term includes foreign intelligence and security services and international terrorists. – *Intelligence Community Directive 750, Counterintelligence Programs*

Information Technology (IT) – Any equipment or interconnected system or subsystem of equipment that is used in the automatic acquisition, storage, manipulation, management, movement, control, display, switching, interchange, transmission, or reception of data or information by the executive agency. For purposes of the preceding sentence, equipment is used by an executive agency if the equipment is used by the executive agency directly or is used by a contractor under a contract with the executive agency which 1) requires the use of such equipment; or 2) requires the use, to a significant extent, of such equipment in the performance of a service or the furnishing of a product. The term information technology includes computers, ancillary equipment, software, firmware and similar procedures, services (including support services), and related resources. – *Committee on National Security S ystems Instruction No. 4009, National Information Assurance Glossary*

Insider – Any person with authorized access to any U.S. Government resource, to include personnel, facilities, information, equipment, networks, or systems. – *National Insider Threat Policy, 2012*

Insider Threat – The threat that an insider will use his/her authorized access, wittingly or unwittingly, to do harm to the security of the United States. This threat can include damage to the U.S. through espionage, terrorism, unauthorized disclosure of national security information, or through the loss or degradation of departmental resources or capabilities. – *National Insider Threat Policy, 2012*

Intelligence Community – The term "intelligence community" includes the following: (A) The Office of the Director of National Intelligence. (B) The Central Intelligence Agency. (C) The National Security Agency. (D) The Defense Intelligence Agency. (E) The National Geospatial-Intelligence Agency. (F) The National Reconnaissance Office. (G) Other offices within the Department of Defense for the collection of specialized national foreign intelligence through reconnaissance programs. (H) The intelligence and counterintelligence elements of the Army, the Navy, the Air Force, the Marine Corps, the Coast Guard, the Federal Bureau of Investigation, the Drug Enforcement Administration, and the Department of Energy. (I) The Bureau of Intelligence and Research of the Department of State. (J) The Office of Intelligence and Analysis of the Department of the Treasury. (K) The Office of Intelligence and Analysis of the Department of Homeland Security. (I) Such other elements of any department or agency as may be designated by the President, or designated jointly by the Director National Intelligence and the head of the department or agency concerned, as an element of the intelligence community. – *National Security A ct of 1947, 50 U.S.C. sec. 3003(4)*

Personally Identifiable Information (PII) – Information which can be used to distinguish or trace an individual's identity, such as their name, social security number, biometric records, etc. alone, or when combined with other personal or identifying information which is linked or linkable to a specific individual, such as date and place of birth, mother's maiden name, etc. – *Office of Management and Budget Memorandum 07-16 Safeguarding Against and Responding to the Breach of Personally Identifiable Information* **Private Sector** – For-profit businesses, non-profits, and non-governmental organizations (including but not limited to think tanks, business trade associations, and academia) not owned or operated by the government.

Public Sector – Federal, state, territorial, tribal, and local governments that provide basic goods and services that either are not or cannot be provided by the private sector.

Sensitive Information and Assets – Refers to: 1) Information classified pursuant to Executive Order 13526, Classified National Security Information, including such information provided to industry in accordance with EO 12829, National Industrial Security Program, and EO 13549, Classified National Security Information Programs for State, Local, Tribal, and Private Sector Entities; 2) Critical infrastructure, as defined in EO 13636, Improving Critical Infrastructure Cybersecurity, which includes systems and assets, whether physical or virtual, so vital to the U.S. that the incapacity or destruction of such systems and assets would have a debilitating impact on security, national economic security, national public health or safety, or any combination of those matters; and 3) Controlled unclassified information, as determined by department and agency heads in accordance with EO 13556, Controlled Unclassified Information.

Supply Chain – A system of organizations, people, activities, information, and resources, possibly international in scope, that provides products or services to customers. – *Committee on National Security Systems Instruction No. 4009, National Information Assura*

KEY INTELLIGENCE COMMUNITY DIRECTIVES

Intelligence Community Directive Number 101

Intelligence Community Policy System (Effective: January 16, 2009)

(Amended: June 12, 2009)

A. AUTHORITY: The National Security Act of 1947, as amended; Executive Order (EO) 12333, as amended; and other applicable provisions of law.

B. PURPOSE:

1. To effectively and efficiently promulgate Intelligence Community (lC) policy, this Intelligence Community Directive (lCD) establishes the IC Policy System which is comprised of a hierarchy of policy documents; processes for the development, coordination and evaluation of policy; and a governance structure to advise the Director of National Intelligence (DNI) or the DNI's designees regarding policy issues. This ICD also delegates decision authority for the promulgation of certain policies, and delineates the roles and responsibilities of the Office of the DNI (ODNI), IC elements, and Functional Managers, as designated by EO 12333 or the DNI, in the implementation of the IC Policy System.

2. This Directive rescinds Intelligence Community Policy Memorandum *2006-100-1, The Intelligence Community Policy Process* and supersedes all previous policies, memoranda, or portions thereof, regarding the IC policy process.

C. APPLICABILITY: This Directive applies to the Ie, as defined by the National Security Act of 1947, as amended; and such other elements of any other department or agency as may be designated by the President, or designated jointly by the DNI and the head of the department or agency concerned, as an element of the Ie.

D. POLICY:

1. The DNI shall establish IC policy to achieve a unified, integrated, effective and accountable IC postured to address and advance IC mission objectives to meet United States national security needs. The DNI shall establish IC policy consistent with applicable law, Exef.,:utive Order, National Security policy, and the DNI's strategic intent.

2. The IC Policy System shall be comprised of a hierarchy of policy instruments as defined in Section E.1. These interrelated IC directives, guidance, standards, or correspondence, herein referred to as policies, issued by the DNI, designated ODNI officials, Functional Managers, and other IC officials designated by the DNI are governed by this Directive and any subordinate policies.

3. Policies shall be:

    a. Developed in a collaborative manner to take into account the views of IC elements and others as appropriate;

    b. Deconflicted with any other applicable policies or regulations;

    c. Drafted in accordance with Section E.l, adhering to a common format and using common terms and definitions to the greatest extent possible;

    d. Formulated to be enforceable and implementable;

    e. Disseminated electronically and communicated broadly, except where restrictions are required by the classification of the document; and

    f. Evaluated for compliance, effectiveness and improvement.

E. FRAMEWORK

1. The IC Policy System shall establish policies applicable to the IC using the following instruments:

a. *Intelligence Community Directive (ICD).* ICDs may be based on statute, regulation, Executive Order, or other policy directives and establish policy and provide definitive direction to the Ie. ICDs may: defme activities, systems or missions; delegate authorities; establish roles and responsibilities; assign decision rights; establish governance structures; include evaluation criteria; or replace or modify previous policy, or provide other such guidance as the DNI deems appropriate. ICDs are developed and coordinated in accordance with ICPG 101.1, *Intelligence Community Directives and Policy Guidance* and are signed by the DNI or, in the DNI's absence, the Principal Deputy DNI (PDDNI).

b. *Intelligence Community Policy Guidance (ICPG).* ICPGs provide further guidance required for the implementation of ICDs. ICPGs are subsidiary to ICDs and may establish subordinate responsibilities, and define procedures, processes, or methodologies that enable ICDs to be implemented effectively. ICPGs shall be within the scope of and consistent with their associated ICDs. ICPGs are coordinated in accordance with ICPG 101.1 and are signed by the Deputy Director of National Intelligence for Policy, Plans, and Requirements (DDNIIPPR).

c. *Intelligence Community Standard (ICS).* ICSs are subordinate to ICDs and ICPGs, and are fully consistent with applicable ICDs and ICPGs. ICSs are policy instruments of the IC Policy System and provide specific procedures, sets of rules, conditions, guidelines, characteristics, or specifications for intelligence or intelligence-related products, processes, or activities in support of effective and uniform implementation of laws, Executive Orders, and IC policies. ICSs shall be developed, coordinated and approved pursuant to ICPG 101.2, *Intelligence Community Standards,* and are signed by officials designated in Section G.1.c.(2) or G.2 of this Directive.

d. *DNI Executive Correspondence (EC).* DNI EC focuses on issues or concerns of the DNI that impact the IC; communicates strategic policy intent, or preliminary approaches of the DNI; and may later culminate in, and contribute to, development of an ICD or ICPG. EC may also be used by the DNI to address emerging, immediate or urgent policy needs. The DNI or, in the DNI's absence, the PDDNI signs all EC.

2. Intelligence Community Policy Memoranda (ICPMs) will no longer be issued. All existing ICPMs will remain in effect until expressly rescinded by the DNI.

F. POLICY ADVISORY BODIES

1. The IC Policy System includes the following bodies, which serve an integral role in the process of developing and coordinating IC policy:

a. *Intelligence Community Policy Review Board (IC-PRB).* The IC-PRB is an advisory board comprised of deputy-level leaders from IC elements. The IC-PRB is chaired by the DDNIJPPR. The objective of the IC-PRB is to provide a forum for high-level issue discussion and resolution; to ensure that key stakeholders and constituencies have been appropriately engaged on individual policies; to align policies with DNI and IC strategic objectives and intent; and to further identify policy needs and priorities, as well as inconsistencies or gaps in current policy.

b. *Intelligence Policy Advisory Group (IPAG).* The IPAG is comprised of designated senior policy representatives from each IC element and is chaired by the Assistant Deputy DNI for Policy. The objective of the IPAG forum is to inform the development of policy and ensure an inclusive and collaborative process. The IPAG shall serve as the official channel of communication on policy matters, and each IC element is responsible for communicating its respective policy equities and interests and identifying members for working groups.

2. To facilitate the development and coordination of policy, the DDNIJPPR or his or her designee may establish IC policy working groups or consult other advisors, as appropriate, to inform decision making throughout the policy process.

G. ROLES AND RESPONSmILITIES

1. *Office ofthe Director ofNational Intelligence*

  a. The DNI or, in the DNI's absence, the PDDNI shall:

    (1) Establish, through signature, ICDs and EC;

    (2) Review and approve IC policies as required;

    (3) Establish or use advisory boards to inform or make decisions regarding policy issues as appropriate;

    (4) Ensure policies established under the IC Policy System are consistent with US law, Executive Orders, Presidential Directives, and other applicable provisions of law; and

    (5) In coordination with appropriate department or agency heads, establish joint agreements or procedures for issues which fall outside the scope of the IC Policy System, but which may be required for the conduct of the IC mission or activities related to national security.

  b. The DDNIJPPR shall serve as the DNI's designee for all matters pertaining to the IC Policy System and, in accordance with ICPG 101.1, shall:

    (1) Develop ICDs and ICPGs with Accountable Officials, as established in Section G.1.c.(2), and subject matter experts as appropriate;

    (2) Establish, through signature, ICPGs;

    (3) Make technical amendments to ICDs and ICPGs through memoranda;

    (4) Support ODNI officials, Functional Managers, and other IC officials designated by the DNI, in the development of ICSs where applicable;

    (5) Chair the IC-PRB;

    (6) Establish working groups to inform or develop specific policies as necessary;

    (7) Ensure IC policies are consistent with Section D.3;

    (8) Ensure IC policies are coordinated with department-level officials, when appropriate;

    (9) Oversee the implementation of this Directive; and

    (10) Serve as the office of record for all IC Policy System documents and maintain all comments, drafts and revisions as appropriate.

  c. ODNI elements shall:

    (1) Participate, as appropriate in the development, coordination and evaluation of IC policies, and provide subject matter expertise to the DNI designee; and

    (2) Establish ICSs in accordance with the requirements provided in ICPG 10 1.2.

(a) The Associate DNI (ADNI) and IC Chief Information Officer shall establish ICSs related to information technology, community-level data standards, information security, and information management issues.

(b) The ADNI and IC Chief Human Capital Officer shall establish ICSs related to human capital and the IC workforce.

(c) The ADNI and Chief Financial Officer shall establish ICSs related to the financial and resource management of National Intelligence Program.

(d) The DDNIIPPR shall establish ICSs related to IC security and classification marking.

(e) The National Counterintelligence Executive shall establish ICSs related to counterintelligence.

(f) Other ODNI officials as designated by the DNI or the DNI designee may establish ICSs.

2. Functional Managers and other officials designated by the DNI shall:

a. Establish ICSs applicable to their functional or other area, designated in accordance with ICPG 101.2;

b. Participate in the development, coordination and evaluation of IC policies, and provide subject matter expertise to the DNI designee as requested;

c. Ensure implementing standards are in accordance with IC policies; and

d. Inform the DNI designee when there is any IC element policy in conflict with IC policy.

3. Ie Elements shall:

a. Participate in the development, coordination and evaluation of IC policies, and provide subject matter expertise to the DNI designee as requested;

b. Develop internal implementing policies, standards, procedures, or processes applicable to their element, in accordance with IC policies;

c. Inform the DNI designee when there is any policy applicable to an IC element in conflict with IC policy; and

d. Designate representatives to the IC-PRB and IPAG at the level described in Section F.1.

H. EFFECTIVE DATE: This Directive becomes effective on the date of signature.

J. M. McConnell
Director of National Intelligence
16 January 2009

Intelligence Community Directive Number 102

Process for Developing Interpretive Principles and Proposing Amendments to Attorney General Guidelines Governing the Collection, Retention, and Dissemination of Information Regarding U.S. Persons

(Effective Date Remains: 19 November 2007)

NOTICE: RENUMBERING OF INTELLIGENCE COMMUNITY DIRECTIVE

A. REFERENCES: E/S 00558, Revision of the National Intelligence Policy System, dated 6 July 2007; PPR 00378, DNI Policy Taxonomy, dated 16 June 2008.

B. INTELLIGENCE COMMUNITY DIRECTIVE (ICD) RENUMBERING: Per references, ICD 153 Process for Developing Interpretive Principles and Proposing Amendments to Attorney General Guidelines Governing the Collection, Retention, and Dissemination of Information Regarding U.S. Persons is renumbered to ICD 102, effective 16 June 2008. The contents and page numbering of the ICD remain unchanged. This page is the coversheet for the existing ICD until its next revision.

Intelligence Community Directive Number 112

Congressional Notification

(Effective: November 16, 2011)

A. AUTHORITY: The National Security Act of 1947, as amended (hereinafter, National Security Act); Executive Order 12333, as amended; and other applicable provisions of law.

B. PURPOSE: This Directive establishes Intelligence Community (IC) policy to provide written notification to the Senate Select Committee on Intelligence and the House Permanent Select Committee on Intelligence (collectively the "Congressional intelligence committees") in order to keep them fully and currently informed of intelligence activities. This Directive replaces and rescinds Intelligence Community Policy Memorandum 2005-100-3, *Reporting of Intelligence Activities to Congress,* dated January 10,2006; *Timely Notification ofSignificant Intelligence Activities,* dated 24 March 2009; and *Follow-up to Reporting Intelligence Matters to Congress,* dated 15 October 2009.

C. APPLICABILITY

1.   This Directive applies to the IC, as defined by the National Security Act of 1947, and to elements of any other department or agency as may be designated by the President, or designated jointly by the Director of National Intelligence (DNI) and the head of the department or agency concerned, as an element of the IC.

2.   The Directive does not preclude or alter reporting responsibilities to the President's Intelligence Oversight Board as specified in Executive Order 13462 and any successor thereto.

3.   This Directive does not apply to reporting of covert actions to the Congressional intelligence committees, to statutory reporting requirements for IC Inspectors General, or to routine informational briefings.

D. POLICY

1. The IC is committed to full and current notification of all intelligence activities as required by the National Security Act, including significant anticipated intelligence actions, significant intelligence failures, and illegal intelligence activities.

2.   The provisions of this Directive shall be interpreted with a presumption of notification in fulfIllment of the statutory requirement to keep the Congressional intelligence committees fully and currently informed of all intelligence activities.

3. It is IC policy that IC elements shall, in a timely manner, keep the Congressional intelligence committees fully infonned, in writing, of all significant anticipated intelligence activities, significant intelligence failures, significant intelligence activities, and illegal activities.

4. IC element heads are responsible for determining whether an event is reportable under this Directive and are responsible for ensuring that Congress is notified of all intelligence activities in accordance with the provisions of this Directive.

5. Determining whether written notification should be provided of a particular intelligence activity is a judgment based on all the facts and circumstances known to the IC element, and on the nature and extent of previous notifications or briefings to Congress on the same matter. Not every intelligence activity warrants written notification. Facts and circumstances of intelligence

activities change over time; therefore, IC elements must continually assess whether there is an obligation to report a matter pursuant to the National Security Act and this Directive.

6. As required by the National Security Act, Congress must receive written notification of significant anticipated intelligence activities and significant intelligence failures. General guidelines for determining the types of intelligence activities that warrant written notification follow:

a. Significant anticipated intelligence activities include:

(1) intelligence activities that entail, with reasonable foreseeability, significant risk of exposure, compromise, and loss of human life;

(2) intelligence activities that are expected to have a major impact on important foreign policy or national security interests;

(3) an IC element's transfer, to a recipient outside that IC element, of defense articles, personnel services, or "controlled equipment" valued in excess of $1 million as provided in Section 505 of the National Security Act;

(4) extensive organizational changes in an IC element;

(5) deployment of new collection techniques that represent a significant departure from previous operations or activities or that result from evidence of significant foreign developments;

(6) significant activities undertaken pursuant to specific direction of the President or the National Security Council (this is not applicable to covert action, which is covered by Section 503 of the National Security Act); or

(7) significant acquisition, reprogramming, or non-routine budgetary actions that are of Congressional concern and that are not otherwise reportable under the National Intelligence Program Procedures for Reprogramming and Transfers.

b. Significant intelligence failures are failures that are extensive in scope, continuing in nature, or likely to have a serious impact on United States (US) national security interests and include:

(1) the loss or compromise of classified information on such a scale or over such an extended period as to indicate a systemic loss or compromise of classified intelligence infonnation that may pose a substantial risk to US national security interests;

(2) a significant unauthorized disclosure of classified intelligence infonnation that may pose a substantial risk to US national security interests;

(3) a potentially pervasive failure, interruption, or compromise of a collection capability or collection system; or

(4) a conclusion that an intelligence product is the result of foreign deception or denial activity, or othefVJise contains major errors in analysis, with a significant impact on US national security policies, programs, or activities.

7. As a matter of policy, IC elements shall provide Congress written notification of other significant intelligence activities and illegal activities. General guidelines for determining these types of intelligence activities warranting notification follow.

a. Significant intelligence activities include:

(1) substantial changes in the capabilities or known vulnerabilities of US intelligence operations or intelligence systems or resources;

(2) programmatic developments likely to be of Congressional interest, such as major cost overruns, a major modification of, or the termination of a significant contract;

(3) developments that affect intelligence programs, projects, or activities that are

likely to be of Congressional concern because of their substantial impact on national security or foreign policy;

(4) the loss of life in the perfonnance of an intelligence activity; or

(5) significant developments in, or the resolution of, a matter previously reported under these procedures.

b. illegal activities include:

(1) An intelligence activity believed to be in violation of US law, including any corrective action taken or planned in connection with such activity;

(2) Significant misconduct by an employee of an IC element or asset that is likely to seriously affect intelligence activities or othefVJise is of congressional concern, including human rights violations; or

(3) Other serious violations of US criminal law by an employee of an IC element or asset, which in the discretion of the head of an IC element warrants congressional notification.

8. Criteria described in Sections D.6 and D.7 above are not exhaustive. The absence of any of these criteria shall not be seen as determinative. Each potential determination shall be addressed on its particular merits. If it is unclear whether a notification is appropriate, IC elements should decide in favor of notification.

E. ROLES AND RESPONSIBILITIES:

To ensure full and current written notification of intelligence activities consistent with this Directive, each IC element head shall:

1. Designate as a point of contact a senior official who will have access to all relevant infonnation to assist the IC element head in identifying matters that should be reported and who will be responsible for ensuring that notifications are full and current.

2. Establish, in writing, internal processes that will ensure timely identification and full and current reporting of intelligence activities, consistent with this Directive.

3. Provide the Office of the Director of National Intelligence Office of Legislative Affairs (ODNIJOLA) with a point of contact pursuant to Section B.1 above and a copy of the procedures established pursu ant to section E.2 above.

4. Ensure that written notifications required under this Directive are provided promptly upon determination that the intelligence activity should be reported under this Directive and the National Security Act.

a. Within 14 days of final determination by an IC element head (or designee) that a significant activity should be reported, an IC element shall provide written notification. If a complete written notification is not possible at that time, an IC element may provide preliminary oral notification and a projected time for further or final notification.

b. Written notifications shall contain a concise statement of the pertinent facts, an explanation of the significance of the intelligence activity, and the role of all departments and agencies involved in the intelligence activity.

c. Oral notifications shall be followed by a written notification, which shall include, in addition to the information described in Section EA.b above, the date of the oral notification, the office responsible for the subject of the oral notification, and the Congressional members and staff orally notified.

d. Notification of routine administrative matters such as reprogrammings, facility lease arrangement and renewals, or contract awards should be made with reference to the element's established timeline for such issues and consistent with Congressional requirements and budget processes.

5. Coordinate, as appropriate, with any other department, agency, or other entity of the US Government involved in the intelligence activity to ensure that an intelligence activity is fully and currently reported to the Congressional intelligence committees.

6. Conduct annual training for element personnel involved in intelligence activities regarding the IC's obligation to provide information to Congress under the National Security Act and this Directive.

7. Provide the ODNIIOLA copies of all Congressional notifications at the time they are provided to Congress, and a summary of any oral notification.

F. COORDINATION WITH THE DEPARTMENT OF JUSTICE REGARDING CRIMINAL INVESTIGATIONS AND PROSECUTIONS: Where intelligence information subject to this Directive relates to criminal investigations and prosecutions or reasonably anticipated criminal investigations and prosecutions, the IC shall comply with the following procedures:

1. IC elements shall consult with the Attorney General's designee or designees prior to providing the information to Congressional committees, members, or staff. With respect to the Congressional intelligence committees, this coordination shall ensure that the IC meets its reporting obligations under the National Security Act in a manner consistent with the integrity and independence of criminal investigations and prosecutions.

2. Disagreements between an IC element and the Department of Justice regarding the application of this section will be referred for resolution to the Attorney General and the DNI.

G. LIMITATION: Nothing in this directive shall be construed to limit an IC element's obligation to report matters to other Congressional committees with oversight jurisdiction or appropriations responsibility for that IC element, subject to the principles identified above regarding criminal matters or potential criminal matters.

H. EFFECTIVE DATE: This Directive becomes effective on the date of signature.

James R, Clapper
Director of National Intelligence
November 16, 2011

Intelligence Community Directive Number 114

Comptroller General Access to Intelligence Community Information

(Effective: June 30, 2011)

A. AUTHORITY: The National Security Act of 1947, as amended; Executive Order (EO) 12333, as amended, and other applicable provisions of law.

B. PURPOSE

1. This Intelligence Community (IC) Directive addresses the requirement in the Intelligence Authorization Act of 2010 (Public Law 111-259, section 348) to establish policy for access to information in the possession of an IC element by the Comptroller General through the Government Accountability Office (GAO).

2. This Directive provides guidance to the IC elements that is consistent with both the National Security Act of 1947, which provides the oversight structure for intelligence activities, and Chapter 7 of Title 31, which provides GAO the jurisdiction and authority to conduct audits and reviews of government programs and activities.

C. APPLICABILITY

1. This Directive applies to the IC, as defined by the National Security Act of 1947, as amended, and to such other elements of any other department or agency as may be designated by the President, or designated jointly by the Director of National Intelligence (DNI) and the head of the department or agency concerned, as an element of the IC.

2. This Directive shall apply to requests by the Comptroller General for information in the possession of an IC element that is related to intelligence activities and programs. Nothing in this Directive is intended to diminish the scope of support that IC elements have provided to GAO. For IC elements within departments, this Directive complements departmental policies governing GAO access to departmental information to the greatest extent possible. Departmental policies shall have primacy except for requests for national intelligence information related to activities and programs funded wholly or in part by the National Intelligence Program (NIP).

3. Nothing in this Directive shall be construed to authorize the Comptroller General or GAO to audit or examine records and expenditures made under the authority of 22 U.S Code 2396(a)(8), 10 U.S Code 127, 7231, or 50 U.S Code 403j(b).

D. POLICY

1. It is IC policy to cooperate with the Comptroller General, through the GAO, to the fullest extent possible, and to provide timely responses to requests for information.

2. To the extent consistent with national security and the protection of intelligence sources and methods, IC elements shall provide GAO access to information that relates to matters that are the subject of announced GAO reviews.

3. IC element heads are responsible for decisions regarding GAO access to information consistent with the guidelines set forth in this Directive. Those decisions apply only to information or documents originated by that particular IC element.

4. IC elements shaH evaluate GAO requests for information on a case-by-case basis.

   a. Generally, IC elements shall cooperate with GAO audits or reviews and make information available to appropriately cleared GAO personnel. Finished, disseminated national intelligence information relevant to a GAO review, information relating to the administration of a

US government-wide program or activity, and publicly available information shall generally be provided to GAO.

b. Information that falls within the purview of the congressional intelligence oversight committees generally shall not be made available to GAO to support a GAO audit or review of core national intelligence capabilities and activities, which include intelligence collection operations, intelligence analyses and analytical techniques, counterintelligence operations, and intelligence funding. IC elements may on a case-by-case basis provide information in response to any GAO requests not related to GAO audits or reviews of core national intelligence capabilities and activities. Access determinations for all such requests shall be made in a manner consistent with this Directive and applicable Departmental directives.

c. When making access determinations, IC elements shall also consider whether the infonnation is subject to statutory restrictions or executive branch confidentiality interests. Information on intelligence sources and methods, and information related to covert action shall not be provided.

5. IC elements shall not categorically deny GAO access to information, nor shall they withhold information solely because the information relates to a program that is funded by the NIP.

a. IC elements shall carefully consider requests for information based on dialogue with GAO and in a manner consistent with this Directive.

b. IC elements shall work with GAO to explore alternative means to accommodate a request for access to specific information if it is determined that GAO should not have access to the specific information requested.

6. Information provided to GAO shall be made available in a manner consistent with the obligation to protect intelligence sources and methods. Access to information shall be tailored after discussion with GAO to address specific objectives of the particular review. Accordingly,

a. Access by GAO personnel to information held by IC elements shall be consistent with principles of eligibility for access to classified national security information and need-to-know as outlined in EOs 12968 and 13526;

b. Consistent with Section D above, GAO may be afforded access to classifled or other sensitive information only after GAO:

(1) Identifies the individuals who will have access to documents; and

(2) Verifies that: information and

(a) the individuals being granted access possess the appropriate security clearance, or have obtained a limited security approval and have signed an applicable nondisclosure agreement;

(b) if infonnation is to be retained by GAO it has secure facilities accredited to receive and store such information and holds such information, in accordance with classification, dissemination controls, and other special handling requirements;

(c) it has acknowledged and agreed to abide by the classification, dissemination controls, and other special handling requirements of any provided document or information; and

(d) its retention and dissemination of intelligence information shall comply with EO 12333, part 2, as it pertains to US persons information.

7. IC element responses to GAO products.

a. If GAO provides an IC element an opportunity to comment on a GAO product, the IC element is strongly encouraged to provide GAO with a timely response.

b. When a GAO report contains a recommendation concerning an IC element or intelligence activities, the concerned element shall submit a written statement addressing the recommendations within 60 calendar days of the date of the report to the appropriate House and Senate committees in the same manner as provided by 31 US Code 720. A copy of suchstatement shall also be provided to the ODNI Office of Legislative Affairs (OLA).

E. ROLES AND RESPONSIBILITIES: To ensure that this Directive is fully implemented, each IC element head shall:

1. Engage in dialogue with GAO, as appropriate;

2. Maintain or develop written procedures that detail the element's process for responding to GAO reviews. These procedures shall include at a minimum the following:

    a. A presumption of cooperation including a process for exploring alternative means of accommodating GAO requests, to the extent possible, and within a reasonable time;

    b. Designation of an appropriate initial point of contact in the element for coordinating GAO reviews. This point of contact shall be responsible for ensuring that GAO is informed of the classification and sensitivity of any infonnation provided as well a, any special handling instructions, as appropriate;

    c. A process to assess GAO requests for information that provides for access determinations to be made at the lowest possible level consistent with organizational needs;

    d. A requirement that the element respond to GAO requests for access to nformation within a reasonable timeframe to include notification to GAO of any delays;

    e. A review process whereby an access issue that is not resolved at the lowest possible level may be elevated within an Ie element in an attempt to facilitate resolution;

    f. A process for documenting formal denials of GAO requests for information; and, g. A method of alerting GAO to the confidentiality obligations and penalties at 31 US Code 716(e) and Section 348(b) of Public Law 111-259.

3. Provide the ODNI Office of Legislative Affairs (OLA) a copy of the procedures issued pursuant to Section E.2.

4. Promptly notify the ODNI OLA of GAO requests for engagement with an Ie element and subsequently of Ie element decisions on access. ODNI notification shall not delay Ie element responses to GAO requests.

5. Determine that information made available to GAO is responsive to the GAO review for which the information or record is requested and is supported by a written GAO request that clearly identifies the purpose of the request.

6. Upon receipt of any request for access to information that may affect the joint equities of other IC elements, coordinate responses with other affected offices and elements of the IC.

7. Ensure that any GAO request for access to another agency's information is referred to that agency or that information responsive to such a request is made available to GAO only after obtaining the documented consent of that agency.

8. If after following procedures developed pursuant to Section E.2, the IC element determines that a GAO request. for information cannot be accommodated, the IC element shall promptly advise GAO of the denial of a request for information with a written justification and provide a copy to the ODNI OLA.

F. EFFECTIVE DATE: This ICD becomes effective on June 30, 2011.

James R, Clapper
Director of National Intelligence
April 29, 2011

Intelligence Community Directive Number 116

Intelligence Planning, Programming, Budgeting, and Evaluation System

(Effective: September 14, 2011)

A. AUTHORITY: The National Security Act of '1947, as amended; Executive Order (EO) 12333, as amended; and other applicable provisions of law.

B. PURPOSE: This Intelligence Corrununity Directive (ICD) establishes overarching policy and a management framework relevant to the Director of National Intelligence (DNl) National Intelligence Program (NIP) development and budget execution authorities. This Directive also constitutes in part the procedures called for in EO 12333 Section 1.3(b)(20). This Directive rescinds lCD 106, *Intelligence Community Strategic Enterprise Management,* 20 November 2008.

C. APPLICABILITY: This Directive applies to the Intelligence Corrununity (IC) as defmed by the National Security Act of 1947, as amended; and such other elements of any other department or agencies as may be designated by the President, or designated jointly by the DNl and the head of the department or agency concerned, as an element of the lC.

D. POLICY

    1.   The Intelligence Planning, Programming, Budgeting, and Evaluation (IPPBE) system is designed to effectively shape and sustain intelligence capabilities through the development of the NIP and budget consistent with the National Intelligence Strategy (NlS) and other applicable National Strategies or Presidential Policy Directives. IPPBE ensures a predictable, transparent, and repeatable end-to-end process to collect and prioritize intelligence mission requirements in the context of the strategic objectives of the DNl and the Ie. In addition, IPPBE supports the DNl's participation in the development of the Military Intelligence Program (MIP).

    2. The IPPBE system comprises the interdependent phases of planning, programming, and budgeting that are informed by ongoing evaluation. Each phase is informed and guided by the products and decisions produced in other phases.

    a. **Planning:** The planning phase identifies IC strategic priorities and Major Issues to be addressed in the programming phase. Planning includes the following primary activities:

        (1) Analyzing impacts of sustaining current capabilities, long-term trends, and alternative future challenges;

        (2) Identifying and analyzing strategic issues and future customer needs; and

        (3) Identifying gaps and shortfalls by analyzing current IC capabilities.

    b. **Programming:** The programming phase provides options to frame DNI resource decisions through analysis of alternatives and studies that assess cost-performance benefits. Programming includes the following primary activities:

        (1) Conducting Major Issue Studies, which assess and analyze high impact crosscommunity issues and provide feasible alternatives;

        (2) Developing Independent Cost Estimates (ICE), which provide a total life-cycle cost estimate for Major System Acquisitions and other programs of interest;

        (3) Developing the Consolidated Intelligence Guidance (CIG), which documents IC strategic priorities and conveys DNI direction for building the United States intelligence program and budget;

(4) Deconflicting and integrating guidance for MIP-funded and joint NIPIMIPfunded activities into the CIG; and

(5) Managing the Strategic Program Briefings (SPB), which provide a strategic-level dialogue between the DNI and each Program Manager regarding incorporation of DNI priorities and other CIG direction into their program build.

c. **Budgeting:** Budgeting and execution activities addressed in IPPBE have the goal of produCing and implementing an annual consolidated NIP budget. Budgeting includes the following primary activities:

(1) Developing the Intelligence Program Budget Submission (IPBS) Procedural Guidance.

(2) Developing and issuing DNI Decision Documents to adjust NIP program resources.

(3) Developing the NIP portion of the President's Budget;

(4) Ensuring the budget submission is executable, aligned with the CIG, and reflects performance-based budget decisions;

(5) Presenting, justifying, and defending the NIP budget to the Office of Management and Budget (OMB) and Congress;

(6) Managing apportionment and reprogramming activities;

(7) Reviewing the execution of the NIP budget and participating in MIP execution reviews; and

(8) Developing supplemental appropriations requests.

d. **Evaluation:** Evaluation assesses the effectiveness of IC programs, activities, major initiatives, and investments in implementing DNI guidance in the context of their original objectives, measures of effectiveness, metrics, outcomes, benefits, shortfalls, and costs. The purpose is to provide insight to inform investment decisions and future guidance, to identify material and non-material solutions to IC challenges, and to identify best practices to improve IC effectiveness. The IPPBE evaluation process leverages existing reports to economize evaluation efforts across the Ie. Evaluation activities include:

(1) Strategic Evaluation Reports—Independent evaluations of prior major issue decisions and intelligence investments to assess their effectiveness relative to expected outcomes, success measures, prior investments, cost benefits, and potential utility;

(2 Budget and Performance Reports—Assessments of IC-wide budget, performance, and execution measures to enable performance-based budget decisions;

(3) NIS Progress Assessment—An assessment of IC progress towards achieving the goals and objectives of the NIS to inform decisions and products in each phase of the IPPBE System; and

(4) IC Strategic Assessment -An annual assessment of the implications for the IC of policy and strategy changes, long-term trends, and alternative future challenges to inform decisions and products in each phase of the IPPBE System.

E. ROLES AND RESPONSffiILITIES

1. The DNI provides guidance and:

a. Exercises final authority over NIP development and budget execution;

b. Approves the planning and programming priorities; and

c. Participates in the development of the MIP.

2. IC Element Heads:

a. Assess mission needs to identify intelligence gaps and shortfalls during the planning phase and identify requirements to the ODNI;

b. Recommend and participate in Major Issue Studies;

c. Develop and present SPBs to the DNI on implementation of the CIG;

d. Notify the *ADNIlCFO* and ADNIISRA when there is a major change from what was presented in the SPB;

e. Develop and submit an IPBS and Congressional Budget Justification Book;

f. Provide representation to staff-level fora for all phases of IPPBE;

g. Provide requested information to the DNI to support development and determination of a performance-based NIP budget;

h. Provide performance assessment information to the DNI detailing accomplishments and challenges in implementing NIS mission and enterprise objectives to support a comprehensive evaluation regime;

i. Manage and oversee the execution of appropriated programs, as applicable; and

j. Advise the DNI on reprogramming proposals required to address changing programs and emerging requirements.

3. ADNUSRA:

a. Manages the integration and synchronization of the IPPBE system;

b. Leads the planning and programming phases of IPPBE and publishes the CIG;

c. Develops the Major Issues List, which documents the Major Issue Studies to be completed in the programming phase;

d. Manages the SPBs;

e. Develops ICEs;

f. Manages the IC Capability Requirements process in accordance with DNI policy and guidance;

g. Produces Strategic Evaluation Reports; and

h. Consolidates and integrates evaluation findings for input to the IPPBE phases of planning, programming, and budgeting.

4. ADNUP&S:

a. Leads the development of the NIS;

b. Conducts NIS Progress Assessments; and

c. Manages the production of Strategic Assessments in consultation with the Deputy DNI for Intelligence Integration (DDNIJII).

5. ADNIJCFO:

a. Leads the budgeting phase;

b. Leads in-depth analysis of the IPBS and other budgets, as appropriate;

c. Leads IC budget and performance management by establishing, tracking, and reporting on goals, measures, and initiatives;

d. Develops and issues DNI Decision Documents;

e. Publishes the NIP portion of the President's Budget;

f. Develops, presents, justifies, and defends the NIP budget to OMB and Congress;

g. Develops Congressional appeal letters;

h. Develops and justifies supplemental appropriation requests;

i. Oversees budget execution by conducting NIP execution reviews and participating in the Office of the Under Secretary of Defense for Intelligence-led MIP execution reviews;

j. Manages financial reporting and analysis of NIP resources; to include apportionment and reprogramming of appropriated funds;

k. Maintains the DNI's budget and execution systems that support the NIP budget requests and historical program of record; and

1. Provides guidance on, and oversees all NIP-related fmancial management operations and reporting for the IC.

6. DDNIIll:

a. Leads the development, implementation, and assessment of the Unifying Intelligence Strategies;

b. Articulates, prioritizes, and conveys mission requirements identified by the Program Managers, IC Elements, and National Intelligence Mission Managers;

c. Participates in Major Issue Studies and other related studies; and

d. Coordinates, prioritizes, and optimizes intelligence integration capabilities and activities.

F. EFFECTIVE DATE: This Directive becomes effective on the date of signature.

James R, Clapper
Director of National Intelligence
September 14, 2011

Intelligence Community Directive Number 204

National Intelligence Priorities Framework

(Effective Jan. 2, 2015)

A. AUTHORITY

The National Security Act of 1947, as amended; the Intelligence Reform and Terrorism Prevention Act of 2004; Executive Order 12333, as amended; National Security Presidential Directive (NSPD)-26; and other applicable provisions of law.

B. PURPOSE

1. This Intelligence Community (IC) Directive (ICD) promulgates responsibilities within the Office of the Director of National Intelligence (ODNI) and IC elements for setting national intelligence priorities and translating them into action.

2. To establish objectives, priorities, and guidance for the IC to ensure timely and effective collection, processing, analysis, and dissemination of national intelligence.

3. The Director of National Intelligence (DNI) shall carry out responsibilities with regard to national intelligence priorities in accordance with NSPD-26.

4. This ICD rescinds Director of Central Intelligence Directive 2/3, *National Intelligence Priorities Framework,* dated 23 July 2003, and its accompanying Annex.

C. APPLICABILITY

1. This directive applies to the IC, as defined by the National Security Act of 1947, as amended, and other departments or agencies that may be designated by the President, or designated jointly by the DNI and the head of the department or agency concerned, as an element of the IC.

2. Nothing in this directive is intended to modify the authorities of the heads of executive departments and agencies to exercise, consistent with the DNI's authorities and responsibilities, their authorities to manage IC elements within their departments and agencies.

D. POLICY

1. The National Intelligence Priorities Framework (NIPF) is the DNI's sole mechanism for establishing national intelligence priorities.

2. Intelligence topics reviewed by the National Security Council (NC) Principals Committee (PC) and approved by the President semi-annually shall form the basis of the NIPF and the detailed priorities established by the DNI.

3. The NIPF consists of

   a. Intelligence topics approved by the President.

   b. A process for assigning priorities to countries and non-state actors relevant to the approved intelligence topics.

   c. A matrix showing those priorities.

4. The NIPF matrix reflects customers' priorities for intelligence support and ensures that long-term intelligence issues are addressed.

5. The NIPF matrix is updated semi-annually, and ad hoc adjustments may be made to reflect changes in world events and policy priorities.

6. The ODNI and IC elements shall use the NIPF in allocating collection and analytic resources.

E. RESPONSIBILITIES

1.　The DNI approves the NIPF and all aspects of the policies and processes for establishing national intelligence priorities.

2.　IC elements shall:

   a.　Allocate resources consistent with national intelligence priorities and with their missions.

   b.　Represent customer priorities in the DNI's NIPF process.

   c.　Report to the DNI on their coverage of NIPF priorities.

   d.　Associate intelligence collection requirements and analytic production with NIPF priorities.

3. The Deputy Director of National Intelligence for Analysis (DDNUA)

   a.　Oversee, on behalf of the DNI, the process for developing recommendations on national intelligence priorities.

   b.　Recommend to the DNI ad hoc changes to national intelligence priorities.

   c.　Issue guidance in coordination with DDNI for Collection (DDNI/C) to the analytic and collection communities on national intelligence priorities.

4. The Assistant Deputy Director of National Intelligence for Analytic Mission Management shall carry out all NIPF functions as directed by the DDNUA, including:

   a.　Preparing materials for the NSC PC's semi-annual review of intelligence topics.

   b.　Receiving inputs to and developing drafts of national intelligence priority recommendations.

   c.　Coordinating national intelligence priorities within the ODNI and IC and preparing the NIPF for the DNI's approval.

   d.　Assessing the analytic community's coverage of national intelligence priorities.

   e.　Recommending to the DDNUA any ad hoc changes to those priorities based on world events or changing policy priorities.

5. The National Intelligence Council (NIC) shall:

   a.　Provide written input to the DDNUA on customers' intelligence priorities based on the NIC's daily interactions with senior customers in support of NSC PC and Deputies Committee meetings.

b.   Identify long-term intelligence issues that need to be designated as national intelligence priorities.

c.   Recommend to the DDNUA ad hoc changes to national intelligence priorities based on world events or changes in policy priorities.

d.   Coordinate with Mission Managers on:

1)   Written input to the DDNI/A on customers' intelligence priorities in a mission manager area.

2)   Ad hoc changes to national intelligence priorities in a mission manager area.

6. The DDNUC shall:

a.   Direct IC collection elements to optimize collection against national intelligence priorities.

b.   Direct IC collection elements to develop collection capabilities to address national intelligence priorities.

c.   Coordinate on the draft NIPF prior to the DNI's approval.

d.   Assess the collection community's coverage of national intelligence priorities

7. The Deputy Director of National Intelligence for Policy, Plans, and Requirements shall:

a.   Gather information and provide written input to the DDNI/A on the priorities of senior-level military, policy, diplomatic, homeland security, law-enforcement, and other customers during semi-annual reviews of national intelligence priorities.

b.   Coordinate on the draft national intelligence priorities prior to the DNI's approval.

c.   Solicit feedback from military, policy, diplomatic, homeland security, law-enforcement, and other customers to gauge how the IC is addressing their priorities.

8. The DNI Chief Financial Officer shall:

a.   Ensure that national intelligence priorities are reflected in the planning, programming, and budgeting process.

b.   Coordinate with the DDNI/A and DDNI/C to translate national intelligence priorities into programmatic guidance for the IC.

c.   Depict and ensure how the National Intelligence Program is aligned to national intelligence priorities.

9. Mission Managers shall:

a.   Develop national intelligence priorities based on customers' needs in their respective mission areas.

b.   Provide written input to the DDNI/A on customers' priorities in their respective mission areas during semi-annual reviews of national intelligence priorities.

c.   Provide input to the DDNI/A and DDNI/C guidance to the analytic and collection communities.

d.   Focus analysis and collection in their respective mission areas on national intelligence priorities, in accordance with lCD 900.

e.   Assess the IC's analytic and collection coverage of national intelligence priorities in their respective mission areas.

f.   Recommend to the DDNI/A ad hoc changes to national intelligence priorities in their respective mission areas based on world events or changes in policy priorities.

10. The Assistant Deputy Director of National Intelligence for the President's Daily Brief shall assist the DDNI/A in developing national intelligence priorities during the semi-annual reviews.

F. EFFECTIVE DATE:

This ICD becomes effective on the date of signature.

James R, Clapper
Director of National Intelligence
Jan. 2, 2015

DEPARTMENT OF JUSTICE

The Attorney General's Guidelines
for Domestic FBI Operations

Sept. 29, 2008

PREAMBLE

These Guidelines are issued under the authority of the Attorney General as provided in sections 509, 510, 533, and 534 of title 28, United States Code, and Executive Order 12333. They apply to domestic investigative activities of the Federal Bureau of Investigation (FBI) and other activities as provided herein.

TABLE OF CONTENTS

INTRODUCTION

As the primary investigative agency of the federal government, the Federal Bureau of Investigation (FBI) has the authority and responsibility to investigate all violations of federal law that are not exclusively assigned to another federal agency. The FBI is further vested by law and by Presidential directives with the primary role in carrying out investigations within the United States of threats to the national security. This includes the lead domestic role in investigating international terrorist threats to the United States, and in conducting counterintelligence activities to meet foreign entities' espionage and intelligence efforts directed against the United States. The FBI is also vested with important hctions in collecting foreign intelligence as a member agency of the U.S. Intelligence Community. The FBI accordingly plays crucial roles in the enforcement of federal law and the proper administration of justice in the United States, in the protection of the national security, and in obtaining information needed by the United States for the conduct of its foreign affairs. These roles reflect the wide range of the FBI's current responsibilities and obligations, whch require the FBI to be both an agency that effectively detects, investigates, and prevents crimes, and an agency that effectively protects the national security and collects intelligence.

The general objective of these Guidelines is the full utilization of all authorities and investigative methods, consistent with the Constitution and laws of the United States, to protect the United States and its people from terrorism and other threats to the national security, to protect the United States and its people from victimization by all crimes in violation of federal law, and to further the foreign intelligence objectives of the United States. At the same time, it is axiomatic that the FBI must conduct its investigations and other activities in a lawful and reasonable manner that respects liberty and privacy and avoids unnecessary intrusions into the lives of law-abiding people. The purpose of these Guidelines, therefore, is to establish consistent policy in such matters. They will enable the FBI to perform its duties with effectiveness, certainty, and confidence, and will provide the American people with a firm assurance that the FBI is acting properly under the law.

The issuance of these Guidelines represents the culmination of the hstorical evolution of the FBI and the policies governing its domestic operations subsequent to the September 11,2001, terrorist attacks on the United States. Reflecting decisions and directives of the President and the Attorney General, inquiries and enactments of Congress, and the conclusions of national commissions, it was recognized that the FBI's hctions needed to be expanded and better integrated to meet contemporary realities:

> [Clontinuing coordination . . . is necessary to optimize the FBI's performance in both national security and criminal investigations . . . . [The] new reality requires first that the FBI and other agencies do a better job of gathering intelligence inside the United States, and second that we eliminate the remnants of the old "wall" between foreign intelligence and domestic law enforcement. Both tasks must be accomplished without sacrificing our domestic liberties and the rule of law, and both depend on building a very different FBI from the one we had on September 10,2001. (Report of the Commission on the Intelligence Capabilities of the United States Regarding Weapons of Mass Destruction 466,452 (2005).)

In line with these objectives, the FBI has reorganized and reoriented its programs and missions, and the guidelines issued by the Attorney General for FBI operations have been extensively revised over the past several years. Nevertheless, the principal directives of the Attorney General governing the FBI's conduct of criminal investigations, national security investigations, and foreign intelligence collection have persisted as separate documents involving different standards and procedures for comparable activities. These Guidelines effect a more complete integration and harmonization of standards, thereby providing the FBI and other affected Justice Department components with clearer, more consistent, and more accessible guidance for their activities, and making available to the public in a single document the basic body of rules for the FBI's domestic operations.

These Guidelines also incorporate effective oversight measures involving many Department of Justice and FBI components, which have been adopted to ensure that all FBI activities are conducted in a manner consistent with law and policy.

The broad operational areas addressed by these Guidelines are the FBI's conduct of investigative and intelligence gathering activities, including cooperation and coordination with other components and agencies in such activities, and the intelligence analysis and planning functions of the FBI.

A. FBI Responsibilities—Federal Crimes, Threats to The National Security, Foreign Intelligence

Part 11 of these Guidelines authorizes the FBI to carry out investigations to detect, obtain information about, or prevent or protect against federal crimes or threats to the national security or to collect foreign intelligence. The major subject areas of information gathering activities under these Guidelines—federal crimes, threats to the national security, and foreign intelligence—are not distinct, but rather overlap extensively. For example, an investigation relating to international terrorism will invariably crosscut these areas because international terrorism is included under these Guidelines' definition of "threat to the national security," because international terrorism subject to investigation within the United States usually involves criminal acts that violate federal law, and because information relating to international terrorism also falls within the definition of "foreign intelligence." Likewise, counterintelligence activities relating to espionage are likely to concern matters that constitute threats to the national security, that implicate violations or potential violations of federal espionage laws, and that involve information falling under the definition of "foreign intelligence."

While some distinctions in the requirements and procedures for investigations are necessary in different subject areas, the general design of these Guidelines is to take a uniform approach wherever possible, thereby promoting certainty and consistency regarding the applicable standards and facilitating compliance with those standards. Hence, these Guidelines do not require that the FBI's information gathering activities be differentially labeled as "criminal investigations," "national security investigations," or "foreign intelligence collections," or that the categories of FBI personnel who cany out investigations be segregated fiom each other based on the subject areas in which they operate. Rather, all of the FBI's legal authorities are available for deployment in all cases to which they apply to protect the public fiom crimes and threats to the national security and to further the United States' foreign intelligence objectives. In many cases, a single investigation will be supportable as an exercise of a number of these authorities -i.e., as an investigation of a federal crime or crimes, as an investigation of a threat to the national security, andlor as a collection of foreign intelligence.

1. Federal Crimes

The FBI has the authority to investigate all federal crimes that are not exclusively assigned to other agencies. In most ordinary criminal investigations, the immediate objectives include such matters as: determining whether a federal crime has occurred or is occurring, or if planning or preparation for such a crime is taking place; identifjmg, locating, and apprehending the perpetrators; and obtaining the evidence needed for prosecution. Hence, close cooperation and coordination with federal prosecutors in the United States Attorneys' Offices and the Justice Department litigating divisions are essential both to ensure that agents have the investigative tools and legal advice at their disposal for which prosecutorial assistance or approval is needed, and to ensure that investigations are conducted in a manner that will lead to successful prosecution. Provisions in many parts of these Guidelines establish procedures and requirements for such coordination.

2. Threats to the National Security

The FBI's authority to investigate threats to the national security derives from the executive order concerning U.S. intelligence activities, from delegations of functions by the Attorney General, and from various statutory sources. See, e.g., E.O. 12333; 50 U.S.C. 401 et seq.; 50 U.S.C. 1801 et seq. These Guidelines (Part VII.S) specifically define threats to the national security to mean: international terrorism; espionage and other intelligence activities, sabotage, and assassination, conducted by, for, or on behalf of foreign powers, organizations, or persons; foreign computer intrusion; and other matters determined by the Attorney General, consistent with Executive Order 12333 or any successor order.

Activities within the definition of "threat to the national security" that are subject to investigation under these Guidelines commonly involve violations (or potential violations) of federal criminal laws. Hence, investigations of such threats may constitute an exercise both of the FBI's criminal investigation authority and of the FBI's authority to investigate threats to the national security. As with criminal investigations generally, detecting and solving the crimes, and eventually arresting and prosecuting the perpetrators, are likely to be among the objectives of

investigations relating to threats to the national security. But these investigations also often serve important purposes outside the ambit of normal criminal investigation and prosecution, by providing the basis for, and informing decisions concerning, other measures needed to protect the national security. These measures may include, for example: excluding or removing persons involved in terrorism or espionage from the United States; recruitment of double agents; freezing assets of organizations that engage in or support terrorism; securing targets of terrorism or espionage; providing threat information and warnings to other federal, state, local, and private agencies and entities; diplomatic or military actions; and actions by other intelligence agencies to counter international terrorism or other national security threats.

In line with this broad range of purposes, investigations of threats to the national security present special needs to coordinate with other Justice Department components, including particularly the Justice Department's National Security Division, and to share information and cooperate with other agencies with national security responsibilities, including other agencies of the U.S. Intelligence Community, the Department of Homeland Security, and relevant White House (including National Security Council and Homeland Security Council) agencies and entities. Various provisions in these Guidelines establish procedures and requirements to facilitate such coordination.

3. Foreign Intelligence

As with the investigation of threats to the national security, the FBI's authority to collect foreign intelligence derives from a mixture of administrative and statutory sources. See, e.g., E.O. 12333; 50 U.S.C. 401 et seq.; 50 U.S.C. 1801 et seq.; 28 U.S.C. 532 note (incorporating P.L. 108-458 §§ 2001-2003). These Guidelines (Part VI1.E) define foreign intelligence to mean "information relating to the capabilities, intentions, or activities of foreign governments or elements thereof, foreign organizations or foreign persons, or international terrorists."

The FBI's foreign intelligence collection activities have been expanded by legislative and administrative reforms subsequent to the September 11, 2001, terrorist attacks, reflecting the FBI's role as the primary collector of foreign intelligence within the United States, and the recognized imperative that the United States' foreign intelligence collection activities become more flexible, more proactive, and more efficient in order to protect the homeland and adequately inform the United States' crucial decisions in its dealings with the rest of the world:

The collection of information is the foundation of everything that the Intelligence Community does. Wle successful collection cannot ensure a good analytical product, the failure to collect information . . . turns analysis into guesswork. And as our review demonstrates, the Intelligence Community's human and technical intelligence collection agencies have collected far too little information on many of the issues we care about most. (Report of the Commission on the Intelligence Capabilities of the United States Regafding Weapons of Mass Destruction 35 1 (2005).)

These Guidelines accordingly provide standards and procedures for the FBI's foreign intelligence collection activities that meet current needs and realities and optimize the FBI's ability to discharge its foreign intelligence collection functions.

The authority to collect foreign intelligence extends the sphere of the FBI's information gathering activities beyond federal crimes and threats to the national security, and permits the FBI to seek information regarding a broader range of matters relating to foreign powers, organizations, or persons that may be of interest to the conduct of the United States' foreign affairs. The FBI's role is central to the effective collection of foreign intelligence within the United States because the authorized domestic activities of other intelligence agencies are more constrained than those of the FBI under applicable statutes and Executive Order 12333. In collecting foreign intelligence, the FBI will generally be guided by nationally-determined intelligence requirements, including the National Intelligence Priorities Framework and the National HUMINT Collection Directives, or any successor directives issued under the authority of the Director of National Intelligence (DNI). As provided in Part VII.F of these Guidelines, foreign intelligence requirements may also be established by the President or Intelligence Community officials designated by the President, and by the Attorney General, the Deputy Attorney General, or an official designated by the Attorney General.

The general guidance of the FBI's foreign intelligence collection activities by DNI—authorized requirements does not, however, limit the FBI's authority to -conduct investigations supportable on the basis of its other authorities—to investigate federal crimes and threats to the national security -in areas in which the information sought also falls under the definition of foreign intelligence. The FBI conducts investigations of federal crimes and threats to the national security based on priorities and strategic objectives set by the Department of Justice and the FBI, independent of DNI-established foreign intelligence collection requirements.

Since the authority to collect foreign intelligence enables the FBI to obtain information pertinent to the United States' conduct of its foreign affairs, even if that information is not related to criminal activity or threats to the national security, the information so gathered may concern lawful activities. The FBI should accordingly operate openly and consensually with U.S. persons to the extent practicable when collecting foreign intelligence that does not concern criminal activities or threats to the national security.

B. The FBI as An Intelligence Agency

The FBI is an intelligence agency as well as a law enforcement agency. Its basic functions accordingly extend beyond limited investigations of discrete matters, and include broader analytic and planning functions. The FBI's responsibilities in this area derive fkom various administrative and statutory sources. See, e.g., E.O. 12333; 28 U.S.C. 532 note (incorporating P.L. 108-458 §§ 2001 -2003) and 534 note (incorporating P.L. 109-162 § 1107). Enhancement of the FBI's intelligence analysis capabilities and functions has consistently been recognized as a key priority in the legislative and administrative reform efforts following the September 1 1,2001, terrorist attacks:

[Counterterrorism] strategy should . . . encompass specific efforts to . . . enhance the depth and quality of domestic intelligence collection and analysis . . . . [Tlhe FBI should strengthen and improve its domestic [intelligence] capability as fully and expeditiously as possible by immediately instituting measures to . . . significantly improve strategic analytical capabilities . . . . (Joint Inquiry into Intelligence Community Activities Before and After the Terrorist Attacks of September 11,2001, S. Rep. No. 351 & H.R. Rep. No. 792, 107th Cong., 2d Sess. 4-7 (2002) (errata print).)

A "smart" government would *integrate* all sources of information to see the enemy as a whole. Integrated all-source analysis should also inform and shape strategies to collect more intelligence. . . . The importance of integrated, all-source analysis cannot be overstated. Without it, it is not possible to "connect the dots." (Final Report of the National Commission on Terrorist Attacks Upon the United States 401,408 (2004).)

Part IV of these Guidelines accordingly authorizes the FBI to engage in intelligence analysis and planning, drawing on all lawful sources of information. The functions authorized under that Part include: (i) development of overviews and analyses concerning threats to and vulnerabilities of the United States and its interests, (ii) research and analysis to produce reports and assessments concerning matters relevant to investigative activities or other authorized FBI activities, and (iii) the operation of intelligence systems that facilitate and support investigations through the compilation and analysis of data and information on an ongoing basis.

C. Oversight

The activities authorized by these Guidelines must be conducted in a manner consistent with all applicable laws, regulations, and policies, including those protecting privacy and civil liberties. The Justice Department's National Security Division and the FBI's Inspection Division, Office of General Counsel, and Office of Integrity and Compliance, along with other components, share the responsibility to ensure that the Department meets these goals with respect to national security and foreign intelligence matters. In particular, the National Security Division's Oversight Section, in conjunction with the FBI's Office of General Counsel, is responsible for conducting regular reviews of all aspects of FBI national security and foreign intelligence activities. These reviews, conducted at FBI field offices and headquarter units, broadly examine such activities for compliance with these Guidelines and other applicable requirements.

Various features of these Guidelines facilitate the National Security Division's oversight functions. Relevant requirements and provisions include:

(i) required notification by the FBI to the National Security Division concerning full investigations that involve foreign intelligence collection or investigation of United States persons in relation to threats of the national security,

(ii) annual reports by the FBI to the National Security Division concerning the FBI's foreign intelligence collection program, including information on the scope and nature of foreign intelligence collection activities in each FBI field office, and

(iii) access by the National Security Division to information obtained by the FBI through national security or foreign intelligence activities and general authority for the Assistant Attorney General for National Security to obtain reports from the FBI concerning these activities.

Pursuant to these Guidelines, other Attorney General guidelines, and institutional assignments of responsibility withn the Justice Department, additional Department components—including the Criminal Division, the United States Attorneys' Offices, and the Office of Privacy and Civil Liberties -are involved in the common endeavor with the FBI of ensuring that the activities of all Department components are lawful, appropriate, and ethxal as well as effective. Examples include the involvement of both FBI and prosecutorial personnel in the review of undercover operations involving sensitive circumstances, notice requirements for investigations involving sensitive investigative matters (as defined in Part VII.N of these Guidelines), and notice and oversight provisions for enterprise investigations, which may involve a broad examination of groups implicated in the gravest criminal and national security threats. These requirements and procedures help to ensure that the rule of law is respected in the Department's activities and that public confidence is maintained in these activities.

I. GENERAL AUTHORITIES AND PRINCIPLES

A. Scope

These Guidelines apply to investigative activities conducted by the FBI within the United States or outside the territories of all countries. They do not apply to investigative activities of the FBI in foreign countries, which are governed by the Attorney General's Guidelines for Extraterritorial FBI Operations.

B. General Authorities

The FBI is authorized to conduct investigations to detect, obtain information about, and prevent and protect against federal crimes and threats to the national security and to collect foreign intelligence, as provided in Part II of these Guidelines.

The FBI is authorized to provide investigative assistance to other federal agencies, state, local, or tribal agencies, and foreign agencies as provided in Part III of these Guidelines.

The FBI is authorized to conduct intelligence analysis and planning as provided in Part IV of these Guidelines.

The FBI is authorized to retain and share information obtained pursuant to these Guidelines as provided in Part VI of these Guidelines.

C. Use of Authorities and Methods

1. Protection of the United States and Its People

The FBI shall hlly utilize the authorities provided and the methods authorized by these Guidelines to protect the United States and its people from crimes in violation of federal law and threats to the national security, and to further the foreign intelligence objectives of the United States.

2. Choice of Methods

a. The conduct of investigations and other activities authorized by these Guidelines may present choices between the use of different investigative methods that are each operationally sound and effective, but that are more or less intrusive, considering such factors as the effect on the privacy and civil liberties of individuals and potential damage to reputation. The least intrusive method feasible is to be used in such situations. It is recognized, however, that the choice of methods is a matter of judgment. The FBI shall not hesitate to use any lawful method consistent with these Guidelines, even if intrusive, where the degree of intrusiveness is warranted in light of the seriousness of a criminal or national security threat or the strength of the information indicating its existence, or in light of the importance of foreign intelligence sought to the United States' interests. This point is to be particularly observed in investigations relating to terrorism.

b. United States persons shall be dealt with openly and consensually to the extent practicable when collecting foreign intelligence that does not concern criminal activities or threats to the national security.

3. Respect for Legal Rights

All activities under these Guidelines must have a valid purpose consistent with these Guidelines, and must be carried out in conformity with the Constitution and all applicable statutes, executive orders, Department of Justice regulations andpolicies, and Attorney General guidelines. These Guidelines do not authorize investigating or collecting or maintaining information on United States persons solely for the purpose of monitoring activities protected by the First Amendment or the lawful exercise of other rights secured by the Constitution or laws of the United States. These Guidelines also do not authorize any conduct prohibited by the Guidance Regarding the Use of Race by Federal Law Enforcement Agencies.

4. Undisclosed Participation in Organizations

Undisclosed participation in organizations in activities under these Guidelines shall be conducted in accordance with FBI policy approved by the Attorney General.

5. Maintenance of Records under the Privacy Act

The Privacy Act restricts the maintenance of records relating to certain activities of individuals who are United States persons, with exceptions for circumstances in which the collection of such information is pertinent to and within the scope of an authorized law enforcement activity or is otherwise authorized by statute. 5 U.S.C. 552a(e)(7). Activities authorized by these Guidelines are authorized law enforcement activities or activities for which there is otherwise statutory authority for purposes of the Privacy Act. These Guidelines, however, do not provide an exhaustive enumeration of authorized FBI law enforcement activities or FBI activities for which there is otherwise statutory authority, and no restriction is implied with respect to such activities carried out by the FBI pursuant to other authorities. Further questions about the application of the Privacy Act to authorized activities of the FBI should be addressed to the FBI Office of the General Counsel, the FBI Privacy and Civil Liberties Unit, or the Department of Justice Office of Privacy and Civil Liberties.

D. Nature and Application of the Guidelines

1. Repealers

These Guidelines supersede the following guidelines, which are hereby repealed:
a. The Attorney General's Guidelines on General Crimes, Racketeering Enterprise and Terrorism Enterprise Investigations (May 30,2002) and all predecessor guidelines thereto.
b. The Attorney General's Guidelines for FBI National Security Investigations and Foreign Intelligence Collection (October 3 1,2003) and all predecessor guidelines thereto.
c. The Attorney General's Supplemental Guidelines for Collection, Retention, and Dissemination of Foreign Intelligence (November 29, 2006).
d. The Attorney General Procedure for Reporting and Use of Information Concerning Violations of Law and Authorization for Participation in Otherwise Illegal Activity in FBI Foreign Intelligence, Counterintelligence or International Terrorism Intelligence Investigations (August 8, 1988).
e. The Attorney General's Guidelines for Reporting on Civil Disorders and Demonstrations Involving a Federal Interest (April 5, 1976).

2. Status as Internal Guidance

These Guidelines are set forth solely for the purpose of internal Department of Justice guidance. They are not intended to, do not, and may not be relied upon to create any rights, substantive or procedural, enforceable by law by any party in any matter, civil or criminal, nor do they place any limitation on otherwise lawful investigative and litigative prerogatives of the Department of Justice.

3. Departures from the Guidelines

Departures fiom these Guidelines must be approved by the Director of the FBI, by the Deputy Director of the FBI, or by an Executive Assistant Director designated 14 by the Director.

If a departure is necessary without such prior approval because of the immediacy or gravity of a threat to the safety of persons or property or to the national security, the Director, the Deputy Director, or a designated Executive Assistant Director shall be notified as soon thereafter as practicable. The FBI shall provide timely written notice of departures fiom these Guidelines to the Criminal Division and the National Security Division, and those divisions shall notify the Attorney General and the Deputy Attorney General. Notwithstanding this paragraph, all activities in all circumstances must be carried out in a manner consistent with the Constitution and laws of the United States.

4. Other Activities Not Limited

These Guidelines apply to FBI activities as provided herein and do not limit other authorized activities of the FBI, such as the FBI's responsibilities to conduct background checks and inquiries concerning applicants and employees under federal personnel security programs, the FBI's maintenance and operation of national criminal records systems and preparation of national crime statistics, and the forensic assistance and administration functions of the FBI Laboratory.

II. INVESTIGATIONS AND INTELLIGENCE GATHERING

This Part of the Guidelines authorizes the FBI to conduct investigations to detect, obtain information about, and prevent and protect against federal crimes and threats to the national security and to collect foreign intelligence.

When an authorized purpose exists, the focus of activities authorized by this Part may be whatever the circumstances warrant. The subject of such an activity may be, for example, a particular crime or threatened crime; conduct constituting a threat to the national security; an individual, group, or organization that may be involved in criminal or national security- threatening conduct; or a topical matter of foreign intelligence interest.

Investigations may also be undertaken for protective purposes in relation to individuals, groups, or other entities that may be targeted for criminal victimization or acquisition, or for terrorist attack or other depredations by the enemies of the United States. For example, the participation of the FBI in special events management, in relation to public events or other activities whose character may make them attractive targets for terrorist attack, is an authorized exercise of the authorities conveyed by these Guidelines. Likewise, FBI counterintelligence activities directed to identifying and securing facilities, personnel, or information that may be targeted for infiltration, recruitment, or acquisition by foreign intelligence services are authorized exercises of the authorities conveyed by these Guidelines.

The identification and recruitment of human sources -who may be able to provide or obtain information relating to criminal activities, information relating to terrorism, espionage, or other threats to the national security, or information relating to matters of foreign intelligence interest -is also critical to the effectiveness of the FBI's law enforcement, national security, and intelligence programs, and activities undertaken for this purpose are authorized and encouraged.

The scope of authorized activities under this Part is not limited to "investigation" in a narrow sense, such as solving particular cases or obtaining evidence for use in particular criminal prosecutions. Rather, these activities also provide critical information needed for broader analytic and intelligence purposes to facilitate the solution and prevention of crime, protect the national security, and further foreign intelligence objectives. These purposes include use of the information in intelligence analysis and planning under Part IV, and dissemination of the information to other law enforcement, Intelligence Community, and White House agencies under Part VI. Information obtained at all stages of investigative activity is accordingly to be retained and disseminated for these purposes as provided in these Guidelines, or in FBI policy consistent with these Guidelines, regardless of whether it furthers investigative objectives in a narrower or more immediate sense.

In the course of activities under these Guidelines, the FBI may incidentally obtain information relating to matters outside of its areas of primary investigative responsibility. For example, information relating to violations of state or local law or foreign law may be incidentally obtained in the course of investigating federal crimes or threats to the national security or in collecting foreign intelligence. These Guidelines do not bar the acquisition of such information in the course of authorized investigative activities, the retention of such information, or its dissemination as appropriate to the responsible authorities in other agencies or jurisdictions. Part VI of these Guidelines includes specific authorizations and requirements for sharing such information with relevant agencies and officials.

This Part authorizes different levels of information gathering activity, which afford the FBI flexibility, under appropriate standards and procedures, to adapt the methods utilized and the information sought to the nature of the matter under investigation and the character of the information supporting the need for investigation.

Assessments, authorized by Subpart A of this Part, require an authorized purpose but not any particular factual predication. For example, to carry out its central mission of preventing the commission of terrorist acts against the United States and its people, the FBI must proactively draw on available sources of information to identifl terrorist threats and activities. It cannot be content to wait for leads to come in through the actions of others, but rather must be vigilant in detecting terrorist activities to the full extent permitted by law, with an eye towards early intervention and prevention of acts of terrorism before they occur. Likewise, in the exercise of its protective functions, the FBI is not constrained to wait until information is received indicating that a particular event, activity, or facility has drawn the attention of those who would threaten the national security. Rather, the FBI must take the initiative to secure and protect activities and entities whose character may make them attractive targets for terrorism or espionage. The proactive investigative authority conveyed in assessments is designed for, and may be utilized by, the FBI in the discharge of these responsibilities. For example, assessments may be conducted as part of the FBI's special events management activities.

More broadly, detecting and interrupting criminal activities at their early stages, and preventing crimes from occurring in the first place, is preferable to allowing criminal plots and activities to come to fruition. Hence, assessments may be undertaken proactively with such objectives as detecting criminal activities; obtaining information on individuals, groups, or organizations of possible investigative interest, either because they may be involved in criminal or national security-threatening activities or because they may be targeted for attack or victimization by such activities; and identifying and assessing individuals who may have value as human sources. For example, assessment activities may involve proactively surfing the Internet to find publicly accessible websites and services through which recruitment by terrorist organizations and promotion of terrorist crimes is openly taking place; through which child pornography is advertised and traded; through which efforts are made by sexual predators to lure children for purposes of sexual abuse; or through which fraudulent schemes are perpetrated against the public. ,

The methods authorized in assessments are generally those of relatively low intrusiveness, such as obtaining publicly available information, checking government records, and requesting information fiom members of the public. These Guidelines do not impose supervisory approval requirements in assessments, given the types of techniques that are authorized at this stage (e.g., perusing the Internet for publicly available information). However, FBI policy will prescribe supervisory approval requirements for certain assessments, considering such matters as the purpose of the assessment and the methods being utilized.

Beyond the proactive information gathering functions described above, assessments may be used when allegations or other information concerning crimes or threats to the national security is received or obtained, and the matter can be checked out or resolved through the relatively non-intrusive methods authorized in assessments. The checking of investigative leads in this manner can avoid the need to proceed to more formal levels of investigative activity, if the results of an assessment indicate that further investigation is not warranted.

Subpart B of this Part authorizes a second level of investigative activity, predicated investigations. The purposes or objectives of predicated investigations are essentially the same as those of assessments, but predication as provided in these Guidelines is needed—generally, allegations, reports, facts or circumstances indicative of possible criminal or national security- threatening activity, or the potential for acquiring information responsive to foreign intelligence requirements -and supervisory approval must be obtained, to initiate predicated investigations. Corresponding to the stronger predication and approval requirements, all lawful methods may be used in predicated investigations. A classified directive provides further specification concerning circumstances supporting certain predicated investigations.

Predicated investigations that concern federal crimes or threats to the national security are subdivided into preliminary investigations and full investigations. Preliminary investigations may be initiated on the basis of any allegation or information indicative of possible criminal or national security-threatening activity, but more substantial factual predication is required for full investigations. Wle time limits are set for the completion of preliminary investigations, full investigations may be pursued without preset limits on their duration.

The final investigative category under this Part of the Guidelines is enterprise investigations, authorized by Subpart C, which permit a general examination of the structure, scope, and nature of certain groups and organizations. Enterprise investigations are a type of full investigations. Hence, they are subject to the purpose, approval, and predication requirements that apply to full investigations, and all lawful methods may be used in carrying them out. The distinctive characteristic of enterprise investigations is that they concern groups or organizations that may be involved in the most serious criminal or national security threats to the public -generally, patterns of racketeering activity, terrorism or other threats to the national security, or the commission of offenses characteristically involved in terrorism as described in 18 U.S.C. 2332b(g)(5)(B). A broad examination of the characteristics of groups satisfying these criteria is authorized in enterprise investigations, including any relationshp of the group to a foreign power, its size and composition, its geographic dimensions and finances, its past acts and goals, and its capacity for harm.

A. Assessments

1. Purposes

Assessments may be canied out to detect, obtain information about, or prevent or protect against federal crimes or threats to the national security or to collect foreign intelligence.

2. Approval

The conduct of assessments is subject to any supervisory approval requirements prescribed by FBI policy.

3. Authorized Activities

Activities that may be canied out for the purposes described in paragraph 1.in an assessment include:

   a. seeking information, proactively or in response to investigative leads, relating to:

    i. activities constituting violations of federal criminal law or threats to the national security,

    ..

ii. the involvement or role of individuals, groups, or organizations in such activities; or
. . .

iii. matters of foreign intelligence interest responsive to foreign intelligence requirements;

b. identifying and obtaining information about potential targets of or vulnerabilities to
criminal activities in violation of federal law or threats to the national security;

c. seeking information to identifl potential human sources, assess the suitability, credibility,
or value of individuals as human sources, validate human sources, or maintain the cover or
credibility of human sources, who may be able to provide or obtain information relating to
criminal activities in violation of federal law, threats to the national security, or matters of
foreign intelligence interest; and

d. obtaining information to inform or facilitate intelligence analysis and planning as described in Part IV of these Guidelines.

4. Authorized Methods

Only the following methods may be used in assessments:

a. Obtain publicly available information.

b. Access and examine FBI and other Department of Justice records, and obtain information
from any FBI or other Department of Justice personnel.

c. Access and examine records maintained by, and request information fkom, other federal,
state, local, or tribal, or foreign governmental entities or agencies.

d. Use online services and resources (whether nonprofit or commercial).

e. Use and recruit human sources in conformity with the Attorney General's Guidelines
Regarding the Use of FBI Confidential Human Sources.

f. Interview or request information from members of the public and private entities.

g. Accept information voluntarily provided by governmental or private entities.

h. Engage in observation or surveillance not requiring a court order.

i. Grand jury subpoenas for telephone or electronic mail subscriber information.

B. Predicated Investigations

1. Purposes

Predicated investigations may be carried out to detect, obtain information about, or prevent
or protect against federal crimes or threats to the national security or to collect foreign intelligence.

2. Approval

The initiation of a predicated investigation requires supervisory approval at a level or levels
specified by FBI policy. A predicated investigation based on paragraph 3.c. (relating to foreign
intelligence) must be approved by a Special Agent in Charge or by an FBI Headquarters official
as provided in such policy.

3. Circumstances Warranting Investigation

A predicated investigation may be initiated on the basis of any of the following circumstances:

a. An activity constituting a federal crime or a threat to the national security has or may have
occurred, is or may be occurring, or will or may occur and the investigation may obtain
information relating to the activity or the involvement or role of an individual, group, or
organization in such activity.

b. An individual, group, organization, entity, information, property, or activity is or may be
a target of attack, victimization, acquisition, infiltration, or recruitment in connection with

criminal activity in violation of federal law or a threat to the national security and the investigation may obtain information that would help to protect against such activity or threat.

c. The investigation may obtain foreign intelligence that is responsive to a foreign intelligence requirement.

4. Preliminary and Full Investigations

A predicated investigation relating to a federal crime or threat to the national security may be conducted as a preliminary investigation or a full investigation. A predicated investigation that is based solely on the authority to collect foreign intelligence may be conducted only as a full investigation.

a. Preliminary investigations

i. Predication Required for Preliminary Investigations. A preliminary investigation may be initiated on the basis of information or an allegation indicating the existence of a circumstance described in paragraph 3.a.-.b.

ii. Duration of Preliminary Investigations. A preliminary investigation must be concluded within six months of its initiation, which may be extended by up to six months by the Special Agent in Charge. Extensions of preliminary investigations beyond a year must be approved by FBI Headquarters.

iii. Methods Allowed in Preliminary Investigations. All lawful methods may be used in a preliminary investigation except for methods within the scope of Part V.A. 1 1 .-.13. of these Guidelines.

b. Full Investigations

i. Predication Required for Full Investigations. A full investigation may be initiated if there is an articulable factual basis for the investigation that reasonably indicates that a circumstance described in paragraph 3 .a.-.b. exists or if a circumstance described in paragraph 3 .c. exists.

ii. Methods Allowed in Full Investigations. All lawful methods may be used in a full investigation.

5. Notice Requirements

a. An FBI field office shall notify FBI Headquarters and the United States Attorney or other appropriate Department of Justice official of the initiation by the field office of a predicated investigation involving a sensitive investigative matter. If the investigation is initiated by FBI Headquarters, FBI Headquarters shall notify the United States Attorney or other appropriate Department of Justice official of the initiation of such an investigation. If the investigation concerns a threat to the national security, an official of the National Security Division must be notified. The notice shall identify all sensitive investigative matters involved in the investigation.

b. The FBI shall notify the National Security Division of:

i. the initiation of any full investigation of a United States person relating to a threat to the national security; and

. .

ii. the initiation of any full investigation that is based on paragraph 3.c. (relating to foreign intelligence).

c. The notifications under subparagraphs a. and b. shall be made as soon as practicable, but no later than 30 days after the initiation of an investigation.

d. The FBI shall notify the Deputy Attorney General if FBI Headquarters disapproves a field office's initiation of a predicated investigation relating to a threat to the national security on the ground that the predication for the investigation is insufficient.

C. Enterprise Investigations

1. Definition

A full investigation of a group or organization may be initiated as an enterprise investigation if there is an articulable factual basis for the investigation that reasonably indicates that the group or organization may have engaged or may be engaged in, or may have or may be engaged in planning or preparation or provision of support for:

a. a pattern of racketeering activity as defined in 18 U.-S.C. 1961 (5);

b. international terrorism or other threat to the national security;

c. domestic terrorism as defined in 18 U.S.C. 2331(5) involving a violation of federal criminal law;

d. futhering political or social goals wholly or in part through activities that involve force or violence and a violation of federal criminal law; or

e. an offense described in 18 U.S.C. 2332b(g)(5)(B) or 18 U.S.C. 43.

2. Scope

The information sought in an enterprise investigation may include a general examination of the structure, scope, and nature of the group or organization including: its relationship, if any, to a foreign power; the identity and relationship of its members, employees, or other persons who may be acting in furtherance of its objectives; its finances and resources; its geographical dimensions; and its past and future activities and goals.

3. Notice and Reporting Requirements

a. The responsible Department of Justice component for the purpose of notification and reports in enterprise investigations is the National Security Division, except that, for the purpose of notifications and reports in an enterprise investigation relating to a pattern of racketeering activity that does not involve an offense or offenses described in 18 U.S.C. 2332b(g)(5)(B), the responsible Department of Justice component is the Organized Crime and Racketeering Section of the Criminal Division.

b. An FBI field office shall notify FBI Headquarters of the initiation by the field office of an enterprise investigation.

c. The FBI shall notify the National Security Division or the Organized Crime and Racketeering Section of the initiation of an enterprise investigation, whether by a field office or by FBI Headquarters, and the component so notified shall notify the Attorney General and the Deputy Attorney General. The FBI shall also notify any relevant United States Attorney's Office, except that any investigation within the scope of Part V1.D.1.d of these Guidelines (relating to counterintelligence investigations) is to be treated as provided in that provision. Notifications by the FBI under this subparagraph shall be provided as soon as practicable, but no later than 30 days after the initiation of the investigation.

d. The Assistant Attorney General for National Security or the Chief of the Organized Crime and Racketeering Section, as appropriate, may at any time request the FBI to provide a report on the status of an enterprise investigation and the FBI will provide such reports as requested.

III. ASSISTANCE TO OTHER AGENCIES

The FBI is authorized to provide investigative assistance to other federal, state, local, or tribal, or foreign agencies as provided in ths Part.

The investigative assistance authorized by this Part is often concerned with the same objectives as those identified in Part II of these Guidelines—investigating federal crimes and threats to the national security, and collecting foreign intelligence. In some cases, however, investigative assistance to other agencies is legally authorized for purposes other than those identified in Part II, such as assistance in certain contexts to state or local agencies in the investigation of crimes under state or local law, see 28 U.S.C. 540, 540A, 540B, and assistance to foreign agencies in the investigation of foreign law violations pursuant to international agreements. Investigative assistance for such legally authorized purposes is permitted under this Part, even if it is not for purposes identified as grounds for investigation under Part II.

The authorities provided by this Part are cumulative to Part II and do not limit the FBI's investigative activities under Part II. For example, Subpart B.2 in this Part authorizes investigative activities by the FBI in certain circumstances to inform decisions by the President concerning the deployment of troops to deal with civil disorders, and Subpart B.3 authorizes investigative activities to facilitate demonstrations and related public health and safety measures. The requirements and limitations in these provisions for conducting investigations for the specified purposes do not limit the FBI's authority under Part II to investigate federal crimes or threats to the national security that occur in the context of or in connection with civil disorders or demonstrations.

A. The Intelligence Community

The FBI may provide investigative assistance (including operational support) to authorized intelligence activities of other Intelligence Community agencies.

B. Federal Agencies Generally

1. In General

The FBI may provide assistance to any federal agency in the investigation of federal crimes or threats to the national security or in the collection of foreign intelligence, and investigative assistance to any federal agency for any other purpose that may be legally authoized, including investigative assistance to the Secret Service in support of its protective responsibilities.

2. The President in Relation to Civil Disorders

a. At the direction of the Attorney General, the Deputy Attorney General, or the Assistant Attorney General for the Criminal Division, the FBI shall collect information relating to actual or threatened civil disorders to assist the President in determining (pursuant to the authority of the President under 10 U.S.C. 331-33) whether use of the armed forces or militia is required and how a decision to commit troops should be implemented. The information sought shall concern such matters as:

   i. The size of the actual or threatened disorder, both in number of people involved or affected and in geographic area.
   . .
   ii. The potential for violence.
   iii. The potential for expansion of the disorder in light of community conditions and underlying causes of the disorder.
   iv. The relationship of the actual or threatened disorder to the enforcement of federal law or court orders and the likelihood that state or local authorities will assist in enforcing those laws or orders.
   v. The extent of state or local resources available to handle the disorder.

b. Investigations under this paragraph will be authorized only for a period of 30 days, but the authorization may be renewed for subsequent 30 day periods.

c. Notwithstanding Subpart E.2 of this Part, the methods that may be used in an investigation under ths paragraph are those described in subparagraphs a.-.d., subparagraph f. (other than pretext interviews or requests), or subparagraph g. of Part II.A.4 of these Guidelines. The Attorney General, the Deputy Attorney General, or the Assistant Attorney General for the Criminal Division may also authorize the use of other methods described in Part II.A.4.

Public Health and Safety Authorities in Relation to Demonstrations

a. At the direction of the Attorney General, the Deputy Attorney General, or the Assistant Attorney General for the Criminal Division, the FBI shall collect information relating to demonstration activities that are likely to require the federal government to take action to facilitate the activities and provide public health and safety measures with respect to those activities. The information sought in such an investigation shall be that needed to facilitate an adequate federal response to ensure public health and safety and to protect the exercise of First Amendment rights, such as:

  i. The time, place, and type of activities planned.

  ..

  ii. The number of persons expected to participate.

  ...

  iii. The expected means and routes of travel for participants and expected time of arrival.

  iv. Any plans for lodging or housing of participants in connection with the demonstration.

b. Notwithstanding Subpart E.2 of this Part, the methods that may be used in an investigation under this paragraph are those described in subparagraphs a.-.d., subparagraph f. (other than pretext interviews or requests), or subparagraph g. of Part II.A.4 of these Guidelines. The Attorney General, the Deputy Attorney General, or the Assistant Attorney General for the Criminal Division may also authorize the use of other methods described in Part II.A.4.

C. State, Local, or Tribal Agencies

The FBI may provide investigative assistance to state, local, or tribal agencies in the investigation of matters that may involve federal crimes or threats to the national security, or for such other purposes as may be legally authorized.

D. Foreign Agencies

At the request of foreign law enforcement, intelligence, or security agencies, the FBI may conduct investigations or provide assistance to investigations by such agencies, consistent with the interests of the United States (including national security interests) and with due consideration of the effect on any United States person. Investigations or assistance under this paragraph must be approved as provided by FBI policy. The FBI shall notify the National Security Division concerning investigation or assistance under this paragraph where: (i) FBI Headquarters approval for the activity is required pursuant to the approval policy adopted by the FBI for purposes of this paragraph, and (ii) the activity relates to a threat to the national security. Notification to the National Security Division shall be made as soon as practicable but no later than 30 days after the approval. Provisions regarding notification to or coordination with the Central Intelligence Agency by the FBI in memoranda of understanding or agreements with the Central Intelligence Agency may also apply to activities under this paragraph.

The FBI may not provide assistance to foreign law enforcement, intelligence, or security officers conducting investigations within the United States unless such officers have provided prior notification to the Attorney General as required by 18 U.S.C. 951.

The FBI may conduct background inquiries concerning consenting individuals when requested by foreign government agencies.

The FBI may provide other material and technical assistance to foreign governments to the extent not otherwise prohibited by law.

E. Applicable Standards and Procedures

Authorized investigative assistance by the FBI to other agencies under this Part includes joint operations and activities with such agencies.

All lawful methods may be used in investigative assistance activities under this Part. 3. Where the methods used in investigative assistance activities under this Part go beyond the methods authorized in assessments under Part II.A.4 of these Guidelines, the following apply:

a. Supervisory approval must be obtained for the activity at a level or levels specified in FBI policy.

b. Notice must be provided concerning sensitive investigative matters in the manner described in Part II.B.5.

c. A database or records system must be maintained that permits, with respect to each such activity, the prompt retrieval of the status of the activity (open or closed), the dates of opening and closing, and the basis for the activity. This database or records system may be combined with the database or records system for predicated investigations required by Part VI.A.2.

IV. INTELLIGENCE ANALYSIS AND PLANNING

The FBI is authorized to engage in analysis and planning. The FBI's analytic activities enable the FBI to identify and understand trends, causes, and potential indicia of criminal activity and other threats to the United States that would not be apparent from the investigation of discrete matters alone. By means of intelligence analysis and strategic planning, the FBI can more effectively discover crimes, threats to the national security, and other matters of national intelligence interest and can provide the critical support needed for the effective discharge of its investigative responsibilities and other authorized activities. For example, analysis of threats in the context of special events management, concerning public events or activities that may be targeted for terrorist attack, is an authorized activity under this Part.

In carrying out its intelligence functions under this Part, the FBI is authorized to draw on all lawful sources of information, including but not limited to the results of investigative activities under these Guidelines. Investigative activities under these Guidelines and other legally authorized activities through which the FBI acquires information, data, or intelligence may properly be utilized, structured, and prioritized so as to support and effectuate the FBI's intelligence mission. The remainder of this Part provides further specification concerning activities and functions authorized as part of that mission.

A. Strategic Intelligence Analysis

The FBI is authorized to develop overviews and analyses of threats to and vulnerabilities of the United States and its interests in areas related to the FBI's responsibilities, including domestic and international criminal threats and activities; domestic and international activities, circumstances, and developments affecting the national security; and matters relevant to the conduct of the United States' foreign affairs. The overviews and analyses prepared under this Subpart may encompass present, emergent, and potential threats and vulnerabilities, their contexts and causes, and identification and analysis of means of responding to them.

B. Reports and Assessments Generally

The FBI is authorized to conduct research, analyze information, and prepare reports and assessments concerning matters relevant to authorized FBI activities, such as reports and assessments concerning: types of criminals or criminal activities; organized crime groups; terrorism, espionage, or other threats to the national security; foreign intelligence matters; or the scope and nature of criminal activity in particular geographic areas or sectors of the economy.

C. Intelligence Systems

The FBI is authorized to operate intelligence, identification, tracking, and information systems in support of authorized investigative activities, or for such other or additional purposes as may be legally authorized, such as intelligence and tracking systems relating to terrorists, gangs, or organized crime groups.

V. AUTHORIZED METHODS

A. Particular Methods

All lawful investigative methods may be used in activities under these Guidelines as authorized by these Guidelines. Authorized methods include, but are not limited to, those identified in the following list. The methods identified in the list are in some instances subject to special restrictions or review or approval requirements as noted:

1. The methods described in Part II.A.4 of these Guidelines.
2. Mail covers.
3. Physical searches of personal or real property where a warrant or court order is not legally required because there is no reasonable expectation of privacy (e.g., trash covers).
4. Consensual monitoring of communications, including consensual computer monitoring, subject to legal review by the Chief Division Counsel or the FBI Office of the General Counsel. Where a sensitive monitoring circumstance is involved, the monitoring must be approved by the Criminal Division or, if the investigation concerns a threat to the national security or foreign intelligence, by the National Security Division.
5. Use of closed-circuit television, direction finders, and other monitoring devices, subject to legal review by the Chief Division Counsel or the FBI Office of the General Counsel. (The methods described in this paragraph usually do not require court orders or warrants unless they involve physical trespass or non-consensual monitoring of communications, but legal review is necessary to ensure compliance with all applicable legal requirements.)
6. Polygraph examinations.
7. Undercover operations. In investigations relating to activities in violation of federal criminal law that do not concern threats to the national security or foreign intelligence, undercover operations must be carried out in conformity with the Attorney General's Guidelines on Federal Bureau of Investigation Undercover Operations. In investigations that are not subject to the preceding sentence because they concern threats to the national security or foreign intelligence, undercover operations involving religious or political organizations must be reviewed and approved by FBI Headquarters, with participation by the National Security Division in the review process.
8. Compulsory process as authorized by law, including grand jury subpoenas and other subpoenas, National Security Letters (1 5 U.S.C. 168 lu, 168 1v; 18 U.S.C. 2709; 12 U.S.C. 3414(a)(5)(A); 50 U.S.C. 436), and Foreign Intelligence Surveillance Act orders for the production of tangible things (50 U.S.C. 1861-63).
9. Accessing stored wire and electronic communications and transactional records in conformity with chapter 121 of title 18, United States Code (18 U.S.C. 2701- 2712).
10. Use of pen registers and trap and trace devices in conformity with chapter 206 of title 18, United States Code (18 U.S.C. 3121-3127), or the Foreign Intelligence Surveillance Act (50 U.S.C. 1841-1846).
12. Electronic surveillance in conformity with chapter 1 19 of title 18, United States Code (18 U.S.C. 2510-2522), the Foreign Intelligence Surveillance Act, or Executive Order 12333 5 2.5.
13. Physical searches, including mail openings, in conformity with Rule 41 of the Federal Rules of Criminal Procedure, the Foreign Intelligence Surveillance Act, or Executive

Order 12333 *5* 2.5. A classified directive provides additional limitation on certain searches.

14. Acquisition of foreign intelligence information in conformity with title VII of the Foreign Intelligence Surveillance Act.

B. Special Requirements

Beyond the limitations noted in the'list above relating to particular investigative methods, the following requirements are to be observed:

1. Contacts with Represented Persons

Contact with represented persons may implicate legal restrictions and affect the admissibility of resulting evidence. Hence, if an individual is known to be represented by counsel in a particular matter, the FBI will follow applicable law and Department procedure concerning contact with represented individuals in the absence of prior notice to counsel. The Special Agent in Charge and the United States Attorney or their designees shall consult periodically on applicable law and Department procedure. Where issues arise concerning the consistency of contacts with represented persons with applicable attorney conduct rules, the United States Attorney's Office should consult with the Professional Responsibility AdvisoryOffice.

2. Use of Classified Investigative Technologies

Inappropriate use of classified investigative technologies may risk the compromise of such technologies. Hence, in an investigation relating to activities in violation of federal criminal law that does not concern a threat to the national security or foreign intelligence, the use of such technologies must be in conformity with the Procedures for the Use of Classified Investigative Technologies in Criminal Cases.

C. Otherwise Illegal Activity

1. Otherwise illegal activity by an FBI agent or employee in an undercover operation relating to activity in violation of federal criminal law that does not concern a threat to the national security or foreign intelligence must be approved in conformity with the Attorney General's Guidelines on Federal Bureau of Investigation Undercover Operations. Approval of otherwise illegal activity in conformity with those guidelines is sufficient and satisfies any approval requirement that would otherwise apply under these Guidelines.

2. Otherwise illegal activity by a human source must be approved in conformity with the Attorney General's Guidelines Regarding the Use of FBI Confidential Human Sources.

3. Otherwise illegal activity by an FBI agent or employee that is not within the scope of paragraph 1.must be approved by a United States Attorney's Office or a Department of Justice Division, except that a Special Agent in Charge may authorize the following:

a. otherwise illegal activity that would not be a felony under federal, state, local, or tribal law;

b. consensual monitoring of communications, even if a crime under state, local, or tribal law;

c. the controlled purchase, receipt, delivery, or sale of drugs, stolen property, or other contraband;

d. the payment of bribes;

e. the making of false representations in concealment of personal identity or the true ownership of a proprietary; and

f. conducting a money laundering transaction or transactions involving an aggregate amount not exceeding $1 million.

However, in an investigation relating to a threat to the national security or foreign intelligence collection, a Special Agent in Charge may not authorize an activity that may constitute a violation of export control laws or laws that concern the proliferation of weapons of mass destruction. In such an investigation, a Special Agent in Charge may authorize an activity that may otherwise violate prohibitions of material support to terrorism only in accordance with standards established by the Director of the FBI and agreed to by the Assistant Attorney General for National Security.

4. The following activities may not be authorized:

a. Acts of violence.

b. Activities whose authorization is prohibited by law, including unlawful investigative methods, such as illegal electronic surveillance or illegal searches. Subparagraph a., however, does not limit the right of FBI agents or employees to engage in any lawful use of force, including the use of force in self-defense or defense of others or otherwise in the lawful discharge of their duties.

An agent or employee may engage in otherwise illegal activity that could be authorized under this Subpart without the authorization required by paragraph 3. if necessary to meet an immediate threat to the safety of persons or property or to the national security, or to prevent the compromise of an investigation or the loss of a significant investigative opportunity. In such a case, prior to engaging in the otherwise illegal activity, every effort should be made by the agent or employee to consult with the Special Agent in Charge, and by the Special Agent in Charge to consult with the United States Attorney's Office or appropriate Department of Justice Division where the authorization of that office or division would be required under paragraph 3., unless the circumstances preclude such consultation. Cases in which otherwise illegal activity occurs pursuant to this paragraph without the authorization required by paragraph 3. shall be reported as soon as possible to the Special Agent in Charge, and by the Special Agent in Charge to FBI Headquarters and to the United States Attorney's Office or appropriate Department of Justice Division.

In an investigation relating to a threat to the national security or foreign intelligence collection, the National Security Division is the approving component for otherwise illegal activity for which paragraph 3. requires approval beyond internal FBI approval. However, officials in other components may approve otherwise illegal activity in such investigations as authorized by the Assistant Attorney General for National Security.

VI. RETENTION AND SHARING OF INFORMATION

A. Retention of Information

The FBI shall retain records relating to activities under these Guidelines in accordance with a records retention plan approved by the National Archives and Records Administration.

The FBI shall maintain a database or records system that permits, with respect to each predicated investigation, the prompt retrieval of the status of the investigation (open or closed), the dates of opening and closing, and the basis for the investigation.

B. Information Sharing Generally

1. *Permissive Sharing*

Consistent with law and with any applicable agreements or understandings with other agencies concerning the dissemination 'of information they have provided, the FBI may disseminate information obtained or produced through activities under these Guidelines:

a. within the FBI and to other components of the Department of Justice;

b. to other federal, state, local, or tribal agencies if related to their responsibilities and, in relation to other Intelligence Community agencies, the determination whether the information is related to the recipient's responsibilities may be left to the recipient;

c. to congressional committees as authorized by the Department of Justice Office of Legislative Affairs;

d. to foreign agencies if the information is related to their responsibilities and the dissemination is consistent with the interests of the United States (including national security interests) and the FBI has considered the effect such dissemination may reasonably be expected to have on any identifiable United States person;

e. if the information is publicly available, does not identify United States persons, or is disseminated with the consent of the person whom it concerns;

f. if the dissemination is necessary to protect the safety or security of persons or property, to protect against or prevent a crime or threat to the national security, or to obtain information for the conduct of an authorized FBI investigation; or

g. if dissemination of the information is otherwise permitted by the Privacy Act (5 U.S.C. 552a).

2. Required Sharing

The FBI shall share and disseminate information as required by statutes, treaties, Executive Orders, Presidential directives, National Security Council directives, Homeland Security Council directives, and Attorney General-approved policies, memoranda of understanding, or agreements.

C. Information Relating to Criminal Matters

1. Coordination with Prosecutors

In an investigation relating to possible criminal activity in violation of federal law, the agent conducting the investigation shall maintain periodic written or oral contact with the appropriate federal prosecutor, as circumstances warrant and as requested by the prosecutor. When, during such an investigation, a matter appears arguably to warrant prosecution, the agent shall present the relevant facts to the appropriate federal prosecutor. Information on investigations that have been closed shall be available on request to a United States Attorney or his or her designee or an appropriate Department of Justice official.

2. Criminal Matters Outside FBI Jurisdiction

When credible information is received by an FBI field office concerning serious criminal activity not within the FBI's investigative jurisdiction, the field office shall promptly transmit the information or refer the complainant to a law enforcement agency having jurisdiction, except where disclosure would jeopardize an ongoing investigation, endanger the safety of an individual, disclose the identity of a human source, interfere with a human source's cooperation, or reveal legally privileged information. If full disclosure is not made for the reasons indicated, then, whenever feasible, the FBI field office shall make at least limited disclosure to a law enforcement agency or agencies having jurisdiction, and full disclosure shall be made as soon as the need for restricting disclosure is no longer present. Where full disclosure is not made to the appropriate law enforcement agencies within 180 days, the FBI field office shall promptly notify FBI Headquarters in writing of the facts and circumstances concerning the criminal activity. The FBI shall make periodic reports to the Deputy Attorney General on such nondisclosures and incomplete disclosures, in a form suitable to protect the identity of human sources.

3. Reporting of Criminal Activity

a. When it appears that an FBI agent or employee has engaged in criminal activity in the course of an investigation under these Guidelines, the FBI shall notify the United States Attorney's Office or an appropriate Department of Justice Division. When it appears that a human source has engaged in criminal activity in the course of an investigation under these

Guidelines, the FBI shall proceed as provided in the Attorney General's Guidelines Regarding the Use of FBI Confidential Human Sources. When information concerning possible criminal activity by any other person appears in the course of an investigation under these Guidelines, the FBI shall initiate an investigation of the criminal activity if warranted, and shall proceed as provided in paragraph 1. or 2.

b. The reporting requirements under this paragraph relating to criminal activity by FBI agents or employees or human sources do not apply to otherwise illegal activity that is authorized in conformity with these Guidelines or other Attorney General guidelines or to minor traffic offenses.

D. Information Relating to National Security and Foreign Intelligence Matters

The general principle reflected in current laws and policies is that there is a responsibility to provide information as consistently and fully as possible to agencies with relevant responsibilities to protect the United States and its people fiom terrorism and other threats to the national security, except as limited by specific constraints on such sharing. The FBI's responsibilities in this area include carrying out the requirements of the Memorandum of Understanding Between the Intelligence Community, Federal Law Enforcement Agencies, and the Department of Homeland Security Concerning, Information Sharing (March 4,2003), or any successor memorandum of understanding or agreement. Specific requirements also exist for internal coordination and consultation with other Department of Justice components, and for provision of national security and foreign intelligence information to White House agencies, as provided in the ensuing paragraphs.

1. Department of Justice

a. The National Security Division shall have access to all information obtained by the FBI through activities relating to threats to the national security or foreign intelligence. The Director of the FBI and the Assistant Attorney General for National Security shall consult concerning these activities whenever requested by either of them, and the FBI shall provide such reports and information concerning these activities as the Assistant Attorney General for National Security may request. In addition to any reports or information the Assistant Attorney General for National Security may specially request under this subparagraph, the FBI shall provide annual reports to the National Security Division concerning its foreign intelligence collection program, including information concerning the scope and nature of foreign intelligence collection activities in each FBI field office.

b. The FBI shall keep the National Security Division apprised of all information obtained through activities under these Guidelines that is necessary to the ability of the United States to investigate or protect against threats to the national security, which shall include regular consultations between the FBI and the National Security Division to exchange advice and information relevant to addressing such threats through criminal prosecution or other means.

c. Subject to subparagraphs d. and e., relevant United States Attorneys' Offices shall have access to and shall receive information from the FBI relating to threats to the national security, and may engage in consultations with the FBI relating to such threats, to the same extent as the National Security Division. The relevant United States Attorneys' Offices shall receive such access and information from the FBI field offices.

d. In a counterintelligence investigation—i.e., an investigation relating to a matter described in Part VII.S.2 of these Guidelines—the FBI's provision of information to and consultation with a United States Attorney's Office are subject to authorization by the National Security Division. In consultation with the Executive Office for United States Attorneys and the FBI, the National Security Division shall establish policies setting forth circumstances in which the FBI will consult with the National Security Division prior to informing relevant United

States Attorneys' Offices about such an investigation. The policies established by the National Security Division under this subparagraph shall (among other things) provide that:

    i. the National Security Division will, within 30 days, authorize the FBI to share with the United States Attorneys' Offices information relating to certain espionage investigations, as defined by the policies, unless such information is withheld because of substantial national security considerations; and

. .

    ii. the FBI may consult freely with United States Attorneys' Offices concerning investigations within the scope of this subparagraph during an emergency, so long as the National Security Division is notified of such consultation as soon as practical after the consultation.

e. Information shared with a United States Attorney's Office pursuant to subparagraph c. or d. shall be disclosed only to the United States Attorney or any Assistant United States Attorneys designated by the United States Attorney as points of contact to receive such information. The United States Attorneys and designated Assistant United States Attorneys shall have appropriate security clearances and shall receive training in the handling of classified information and information derived from the Foreign Intelligence Surveillance Act, including training concerning the secure handling and storage of such information and training concerning requirements and limitations relating to the use, retention, and dissemination of such information.

The disclosure and sharing of information by the FBI under ths paragraph is subject to any limitations required in orders issued by the Foreign Intelligence Surveillance Court, controls imposed by the originators of sensitive material, and restrictions established by the Attorney General or the Deputy Attorney General in particular cases. The disclosure and sharing of information by the FBI under hs paragraph that may disclose the identity of human sources is governed by the relevant provisions of the Attorney General's Guidelines Regarding the Use of FBI Confidential Human Sources.

2. White House

In order to carry out their responsibilities, the President, the Vice President, the Assistant to the President for National Security Affairs, the Assistant to the President for Homeland Security Affairs, the National Security Council and its

staff, the Homeland Security Council and its staff, and other White House officials and offices require information from all federal agencies, including foreign intelligence, and information relating to international terrorism and other threats to the national security. The FBI accordingly may disseminate to the mte House foreign intelligence and national security information obtained through activities under these Guidelines, subject to the following standards and procedures:

a. Requests to the FBI for such information fiom the White House shall be made through the National Security Council staff or Homeland Security Council staff including, but not limited to, the National Security Council Legal and Intelligence Directorates and Office of Combating Terrorism, or through the President's Intelligence Advisory Board or the Counsel to the President.

b. Compromising information concerning domestic officials or political organizations, or information concerning activities of United States persons intended to affect the political process in the United States, may be disseminated to the White House only with the approval of the Attorney General, based on a determination that such dissemination is needed for foreign intelligence purposes, for the purpose of protecting against international terrorism or other threats to the national security, or for the conduct of foreign affairs. However, such approval is not required for dissemination to the mte House of information concerning efforts of foreign intelligence services to penetrate the White House, or concerning contacts by White House personnel with foreign intelligence service personnel.

c. Examples of types of information that are suitable for dissemination to the mte House on a routine basis include, but are not limited to:

i. information concerning international terrorism;

. . .

ii. information concerning activities of foreign intelligence services in the United States;

. . .

iii. information indicative of imminent hostilities involving any foreign power;

iv. information concerning potential cyber threats to the United States or its allies;

v. information indicative of policy positions adopted by foreign officials, governments, or powers, or their reactions to United States foreign policy initiatives;

vi. information relating to possible changes in leadership positions of foreign governments, parties, factions, or powers;

vii. information concerning foreign economic or foreign political matters that might have national security ramifications; and

. . .

viii. information set forth in regularly published national intelligence requirements.

d. Communications by the FBI to the White House that relate to a national security matter and concern a litigation issue for a specific pending case must be made known to the Office of the Attorney General, the Office of the Deputy Attorney General, or the Office of the Associate Attorney General. White House policy may specially limit or prescribe the White House personnel who may request information concerning such issues fiom the FBI.

e. The limitations on dissemination of information by the FBI to the White House under these Guidelines do not apply to dissemination to the White House of information acquired in the course of an FBI investigation requested by the White House into the background of a potential employee or appointee, or responses to requests from the White House under Executive Order 10450.

3. **Special Statutory Requirements**

a. Dissemination of information acquired under the Foreign Intelligence Surveillance Act is, to the extent provided in that Act, subject to minimization procedures and other requirements specified in that Act.

b. Information obtained through the use of National Security Letters under 15 U.S.C. 1681v may be disseminated in conformity with the general standards of this Part. Information obtained through the use of National Security Letters under other statutes may be disseminated in conformity with the general standards of this Part, subject to any applicable limitations in their governing statutory provisions: 12 U.S.C. 3414(a)(5)(B); 15 U.S.C. 1681u(f); 18 U.S.C. 2709(d); 50 U.S.C. 436(e).

VII. DEFINITIONS

A. CONSENSUAL MONITORING: monitoring of communications for which a court order or warrant is not legally required because of the consent of a party to the communication.

B. EMPLOYEE: an FBI employee or an employee of another agency working under the direction and control of the FBI.

C. FOR OR ON BEHALF OF A FOREIGN POWER: the determination that activities are for or on behalf of a foreign power shall be based on consideration of the extent to which the foreign power is involved in:

control or policy direction;

financial or material support; or

leadership, assignments, or discipline.

D. FOREIGN COMPUTER INTRUSION: the use or attempted use of any cyber-activity or other means, by, for, or on behalf of a foreign power to scan, probe, or gain unauthorized access into one or more U.S.-based computers.

E. FOREIGN INTELLIGENCE: information relating to the capabilities, intentions, or activities of foreign governments or elements thereof, foreign organizations or foreign persons, or international terrorists.

F. FOREIGN INTELLIGENCE REQUIREMENTS: national intelligence requirements issued pursuant to authorization by the Director of National Intelligence, including the National Intelligence Priorities Framework and the National HUMINT Collection Directives, or any successor directives thereto; requests to collect foreign intelligence by the President or by Intelligence Community oficials designated by the President; and directions to collect foreign intelligence by the Attorney General, the Deputy Attorney General, or an official designated by the Attorney General.

G. FOREIGN POWER: a foreign government or any component thereof, whether or not recognized by the United States; a faction of a foreign nation or nations, not substantially composed of United States persons; an entity that is openly acknowledged by a foreign government or governments to be directed and controlled by such foreign government or governments; a group engaged in international terrorism or activities in preparation therefor; a foreign-based political organization, not substantially composed of United States persons; or an entity that is directed or controlled by a foreign government or governments.

H. HUMAN SOURCE: a Confidential Human Source as defined in the Attorney General's Guidelines Regarding the Use of FBI Confidential Human Sources.

I. INTELLIGENCE ACTIVITIES: any activity conducted for intelligence purposes or to affect political or governmental processes by, for, or on behalf of a foreign power.

J. INTERNATIONAL TERRORISM: Activities that: involve violent acts or acts dangerous to human life that violate federal, state, local, or tribal criminal law or would violate such law if committed within the United States or a state, local, or tribal jurisdiction; appear to be intended:

i. to intimidate or coerce a civilian population;

. . .

ii. to influence the policy of a government by intimidation or coercion; or

. . .

iii. to affect the conduct of a government by assassination or kidnapping; and

iv. occur totally outside the United States, or transcend national boundaries in terms of the means by which they are accomplished, the persons they appear to be intended to coerce or intimidate, or the locale in whch their perpetrators operate or seek asylum.

K. PROPRIETARY: a sole proprietorship, partnership, corporation, or other business entity operated on a commercial basis, which is owned, controlled, or operated wholly or in part on behalf of the FBI, and whose relationship with the FBI is concealed from thrd parties.

L. PUBLICLY AVAILABLE: information that has been published or broadcast for public consumption, is available on request to the public, is accessible on-line or otherwise to the public, is available to the public by subscription or purchase, could be seen or heard by any casual observer, is made available at a meeting open to the public, or is obtained by visiting any place or attending any event that is open to the public.

M. RECORDS: any records, databases, files, indices, information systems, or other retained information.

N. SENSITIVE INVESTIGATIVE MATTER: an investigative matter involving the activities of a domestic public official or political candidate (involving corruption or a threat to the national security), religious or political organization or individual prominent in such an organization, or news media, or any other matter which, in the judgment of the official authorizing an investigation, should be brought to the attention of FBI Headquarters and other Department of Justice officials.

O. SENSITIVE MONITORING CIRCUMSTANCE: investigation of a member of Congress, a federal judge, a member of the Executive Branch at Executive Level IV or above, or a person who has served in such capacity within the previous two years; investigation of the Governor, Lieutenant Governor, or Attorney General of any state or territory, or a judge or justice of the hghest court of any state or territory, concerning an offense involving bribery, conflict of interest, or extortion related to the performance of official duties; a party to the communication is in the custody of the Bureau of Prisons or the United States Marshals Service or is being or has been afforded protection in the Witness Security Program; or the Attorney General, the Deputy Attorney General, or an Assistant Attorney General has requested that the FBI obtain prior approval for the use of consensual monitoring in a specific investigation.

P. SPECIAL AGENT IN CHARGE: the Special Agent in Charge of an FBI field office (including an Acting Special Agent in Charge), except that the functions authorized for Special Agents in Charge by these Guidelines may also be exercised by the Assistant Director in Charge or by any Special Agent in Charge designated by the Assistant Director in Charge in an FBI field office headed by an Assistant Director, and by FBI Headquarters officials designated by the Director of the FBI.

Q. SPECIAL EVENTS MANAGEMENT: planning and conduct of public events or activities whose character may make them attractive targets for terrorist attack.

R. STATE, LOCAL, OR TRIBAL: any state or territory of the United States or political subdivision thereof, the District of Columbia, or Indian tribe.

S. THREAT TO THE NATIONAL SECURITY: international terrorism; espionage and other intelligence activities, sabotage, and assassination, conducted by, for, or on behalf of foreign powers, organizations, or persons; foreign computer intrusion; and other matters determined by the Attorney General, consistent with Executive Order 12333 or a successor order.

T. UNITED STATES: when used in a geographic sense, means all areas under the territorial sovereignty of the United States.

U. UNITED STATES PERSON: Any of the following, but not including any association or corporation that is a foreign power as defined in Subpart G.1.-.3.: an individual who is a United States citizen or an alien lawfully admitted for permanent residence; an unincorporated association substantially composed of individuals who are United States persons; or a corporation incorporated in the United States.

In applying paragraph 2., if a group or organization in the United States that is affiliated with a foreign-based international organization operates directly under the control of the international organization and has no independent program or activities in the United States, the membership of the entire international organization shall be considered in determining whether it is substantially composed of United States persons. If, however, the U.S.-based group or organization has programs or activities separate fiom, or in addition to, those directed by the international organization, only its membership in the United States shall be considered in determining whether it is substantially composed of United States persons. A classified directive provides firther guidance concerning the determination of United States person status.

V. USE: when used with respect to human sources, means obtaining information fiom, tasking, or otherwise operating such sources.

INFORMATION SHARING

Intelligence Community Policy Guidance 500.2

Attribute-Based Authorization and Access Management

(Effective: November 23, 2010)

A. AUTHORITY: The National Security Act of 1947, as amended; Executive Order 12333, as amended; and other applicable provisions of law.

B. PURPOSE: This Intelligence Community Policy Guidance establishes that attributes shall be used by Intelligence Community (IC) elements to authorize and manage access by personnel or processes to information resources in the information environment. This Guidance also addresses the management and protection of attributes.

C. APPLICABILITY: This Guidance applies to the IC, as defined by the National Security Act of 1947, as amended; and such other elements of any other department or agency as may be designated by the President, or designated jointly by the Director of National Intelligence and the head of the department or agency concerned, as an element of the IC.

D. DEFINITIONS

1. Information resources are defined as "information and related resources, such as personnel, equipment, funds, and information technology."[1]

2. Information environment is defined as the "aggregate of individuals, organizations, and/or systems that collect, process, or disseminate information, also included is the information itself."[2]

3. Attributes are distinct characteristics of an object or subject.

    a. An object is a "passive information system-related entity (e.g., devices, files, records, tables, processes, programs, domains) containing or receiving information. Access to an object implies access to the information it contains."[3]

    b. A subject is an active entity (generally an individual, process, or device) that causes information to flow among objects or changes the system state.[4]

E. POLICY

1. The Assistant Director of National Intelligence and Chief Information Officer (IC CIO) shall issue IC Standards) regarding the identification and maintenance of attributes.

2. IC elements shall implement and maintain attributes in accordance with IC Standards) issued by the ADNUIC CIO.

3. IC elements shall use attributes to authorize and manage access by personnel or processes to information resources in the information environment.

4. IC elements shall ensure attributes are:

---

1.   Committee on National Security Systems Instruction No. 4009, National Information Assurance Glossary

2.   *Ibid*

3.   *Ibid.*

4.   *Ibid.*

     a. Used by information resources to control access to information by personnel or processes;

     b. Attributable to a person or process;

     c. Derived from authoritative sources;

     d. Readily accessible;

     e. Maintained for accuracy and currency;

     f. Compatible with Department of Defense and other United States Government formats, to the maximum extent practicable;

     g. Managed via an integrated lifecycle approach; and

     h. Supportive of Che requirements of IC Directive 501, Discovery anti Dissemination or Retrieval of Information within the Intelligence Community.

    5. IC elements shall manage, audit, and protect information resources where attributes are collected, processed, developed, stored, maintained, or disseminated, in accordance with IC Standards) issued by the IC CIO.

E. EFFECTIVE DATE: This Guidance becomes effective on the date of signature.

Assistant Director of National Intelligence for Policy & Strategy
November 23, 2010

Intelligence Community Directive 501

Discovery and Dissemination or Retrieval of Information Within the Intelligence Community

(Effective: January 21, 2009)

A. AUTHORITY: The National Security Act of 1947, as amended; Executive Order (EO) 12333, as amended; and other applicable provisions of law.

B. PURPOSE:

1. This Intelligence Community Directive (ICD) establishes in part the Director of National Intelligence (DNI) guidelines called for in Section 1.3(b)(9)(B) of EO 12333, as amended, addresses mandates in the Intelligence Reform and Terrorism Prevention Act of 2004 to strengthen the sharing, integration, and management of information within the Intelligence Community (IC), and establishes policies for: (1) discovery; and (2) dissemination or retrieval of intelligence and intelligence-related information collected or analysis produced by the IC.

2. The overall objectives of this policy are to:

    a. Foster an enduring culture of responsible sharing and collaboration within an integrated IC;

    b. Provide an improved capacity to warn of and disrupt threats to the United States (U.S.) homeland, and U.S. persons and interests; and

    c. Provide more accurate, timely, and insightful analysis to inform decision making by the President, senior military commanders, national security advisers, and other executive branch officials.

3. This Directive rescinds Intelligence Community Policy Memorandum (ICPM) 2007-500-3, *Intelligence Information Sharing*, 22 December 2007. The following three Director of Central Intelligence Directive (DCID) 8 Series documents remain in effect: (1) Policy Memoranda 1, "Intelligence Community Implementation of Releasable by Information Disclosure Official (RELIDO) Dissemination Marking;" (2) Policy Memoranda 2, "Modification to Policy for NonICD 501 Title 50 Organizations' Access to Shared IC Services on TS/SCI Information Systems;" and (3) Implementation Issuance Number 1, "Guidelines for Tearline Reporting."

C. APPLICABILITY:

1. This Directive applies to the IC, as defined by the National Security Act of 1947, as amended; and such other elements of any other department or agency as may be designated by the President, or designated jointly by the Director of National Intelligence (DNI) and the head of the department or agency concerned, as an element of the IC.

2. This Directive does not apply to purely law enforcement information. When law enforcement information also contains intelligence or intelligence-related information, this Directive shall apply to the intelligence or intelligence-related information.

D. POLICY:

1. IC elements shall treat information collected and analysis produced as national assets and, as such, shall act as stewards of information who have a predominant "responsibility to provide." In addition, authorized IC personnel have a "responsibility to discover" informa-

tion believed to have the potential to contribute to their assigned mission need and a corresponding "responsibility to request" relevant information they have discovered.

2. *Responsibility to Provide.*

a. IC elements shall fulfill their "responsibility to provide" by making all intelligence and intelligence-related information (hereinafter referred to as "information") that IC elements are authorized to acquire, collect, hold, or obtain (hereinafter referred to as "information collected") or analysis an IC element is authorized to produce discoverable by automated means by "authorized IC personnel," in accordance with Section D, unless otherwise exempt in accordance with Intelligence Community Policy Guidance (ICPG) 501.1, *Exemption of Information from Discovery*. Authorized IC personnel are individuals identified by their element head and who have an appropriate security clearance and an assigned mission need for information collected or analysis produced. "Discovery," as defined in Appendix A, is the act of obtaining knowledge of the existence, but not necessarily the content, of information collected or analysis produced by any IC element.

b. "Stewards," as defined in Appendix A, shall fulfill their "responsibility to provide" by making all information collected and analysis produced by an IC element available for discovery by automated means by authorized IC personnel, unless otherwise determined by the DNI; by making as much information as possible available for automated retrieval upon discovery; and by presuming that authorized IC personnel who request information discovered possess a "need

to know," in accordance with Section F.

3. *Responsibility to Discover.* "Authorized IC personnel," as defined in Appendix A, have a "responsibility to discover" information believed to have the potential to contribute to their assigned mission need. The act of discovery does not itself constitute a request for receipt of the information collected or analysis produced.

4. *Responsibility to Request.*

a. Authorized IC personnel have a corresponding "responsibility to request" relevant information they have discovered that has the potential to contribute to an analytic judgment, to optimize collection, to inform collection strategies and priorities, or to otherwise advance the intelligence mission. Authorized IC personnel who have discovered information collected or analysis produced that is of possible relevance to their assigned mission shall meet in part their responsibility to request such information by taking affirmative steps to request such information collected or analysis produced from the appropriate steward in accordance with Section F if the content of the information is not already available.

b. Stewards shall determine whether authorized IC personnel who have discovered information collected or analysis produced, that may be relevant to an assigned mission need, and who have requested such information, may receive the information in accordance with procedures in Section F.

5. *Subsequent Use of Information.* Authorized IC personnel shall be responsible for the proper handling and use of information received from a steward. Use of information collected or analysis produced shall be in accordance with Section D.6. and ICPG 501.3, *Subsequent Use of* Information.

6. All IC personnel shall carry out their responsibilities under this Directive, including the discovery, dissemination, retrieval, and use of information collected or analysis produced, consistent with applicable law and in a manner that protects fully the privacy rights and civil liberties of all U.S. persons, as required by the Constitution, Federal statutes, Executive Orders, Presidential Directives, court orders, and Attorney General approved guidelines, including those regarding the dissemination of U.S. person information. In addition, the responsibilities under this Directive shall be carried out consistent with the Guidelines to Implement Informa-

tion Privacy Rights and Other Legal Protections in the Development and Use of the Information Sharing Environment.

7. To achieve the policy objectives in this Directive, the IC Information Sharing Executive (IC ISE) shall develop, in consultation with IC elements, integrated implementation plans that set forth required benchmarks each IC element head shall meet. Integrated implementation plans shall be subject to the approval of the DNI, after consultation with the Executive Committee (EXCOM).

    a. These benchmarks shall serve as a minimum baseline and shall not be construed as fulfilling each IC element head's overall obligation to achieve the policy objectives set forth in this Directive in full and as quickly as possible.

    b. At a minimum, stewards shall make disseminated analytic products discoverable by, and to the extent possible, available to authorized IC personnel by automated means as soon as possible, but no later than 1 June 2009.

8. Upon enactment of this Directive, IC elements shall ensure that new information technology (IT) systems or significant changes to existing IT systems provide the capability for discovery, dissemination, and retrieval of information collected or analysis produced through automated means. This requirement is not retroactive and shall be implemented in accordance with standards promulgated by the IC Chief Information Officer (IC CIO).

9. The Deputy Director of National Intelligence for Policy, Plans, and Requirements (DDNI/PPR), as the DNI's designee for policy, shall evaluate compliance with this policy as of 1 October 2009, and periodically thereafter, as determined by the DDNI/PPR or designee.Evaluation results shall be provided to the DNI and, at the DNI's discretion, to the EXCOM and others, as appropriate. An IC element that is unable to comply fully or is found to be in violation of this policy shall report in writing to the DNI the reasons for failing to meet the objectives of this policy and the steps that will be taken to come into compliance.

E. DISCOVERY OF INFORMATION COLLECTED OR ANALYSIS PRODUCED:

    1. *Collection Stewards and Analytic Production Stewards ("Stewards").*

        a. IC element heads shall appoint one or more "collection steward(s)" for each type of collection activity the IC element is authorized to conduct, and shall appoint one or more "analytic production steward(s)" for all analytic activity it is authorized to conduct. Stewards shall be senior IC element officials.

        b. Stewards shall make all information collected and all analysis produced by an IC element available for discovery by automated means by authorized IC personnel consistent with the requirements in Section D.6., including information collected through contracts, arrangements, agreements, or understandings. In some cases, this may mean that only standardized or limited metadata is made discoverable. In such cases, discovery requires that such information be described with sufficient detail to allow authorized IC personnel to make a reasonable determination regarding whether it is relevant to a mission need. In cases where content is not fully available, the steward shall provide instructions concerning how authorized IC personnel may request dissemination or retrieval of the content of the information collected or analysis produced.

        c. Should an IC element head determine that discovery of information collected or analysis produced, or the confirmation of the mere existence of such information or analysis, will jeopardize the protection of sources, methods, or activities; compromise a criminal or national security investigation; or be inconsistent with the requirements in Section D.6., the IC element head may exempt such information or analysis from discovery unless and until such time as the DNI makes an exemption decision in accordance with ICPG 501.1.

        d. IC elements that acquire or hold information provided by consent or by arrangement or agreement with federal departments; agencies; foreign nations or organizations; corporations; state, local, or tribal entities; or individuals outside the IC; shall seek to acquire or hold the information so as to authorize and provide discovery and dissemination or retrieval by authorized IC personnel, in a manner consistent with applicable Federal statutes, Executive Orders, Presidential Directives, court orders, and Attorney General approved guidelines.

2. *Authorized IC Personnel.*

a. Authorized IC personnel are U.S. persons employed by, assigned to, or acting on behalf of an IC element who, through the course of their duties and employment, have a mission need for information collected or analysis produced by an IC element, and who have an appropriate security clearance. Authorized IC personnel shall be identified by their IC element head.

b. Until such time as an attribute-based identity management capability that enables automated user authorization, discovery, retrieval, and auditing services for IC personnel is approved by the DNI and implemented throughout the IC, IC element heads shall identify authorized IC personnel within their IC element who have discovery rights to information collected and analysis produced by other IC elements.

c. The total number of authorized IC personnel approved by stewards to retrieve information collected or analysis produced may be subject to the IC's ability to adequately audit such activities. The IC ISE, in coordination with relevant stakeholders, shall include an auditing capability as part of an integrated implementation plan, pursuant to Section G.1.a. (1) and (2), and shall advise the DNI of constraints on retrieval, if any. The IC CIO shall promulgate IT system standards to govern audit practices.

F. DISSEMINATION OR RETRIEVAL OF INFORMATION COLLECTED OR ANALYSIS PRODUCED:

1. Dissemination or retrieval of information collected or analysis produced shall be made available to authorized IC personnel through automated means in accordance with Sections D.2. and D.6. Legacy information should be made available for dissemination or retrieval in accordance with Section D.6., to the greatest extent practicable.

2. Upon discovery of information collected or analysis produced that authorized IC personnel believe may fulfill an assigned mission need, authorized IC personnel shall request the information from the appropriate steward. Stewards may designate certain information as preapproved for automatic retrieval upon discovery. When seeking to obtain discovered information that the steward has not pre-approved for retrieval, authorized IC personnel shall provide the steward with information regarding their role, assigned mission need and when established, DNI approved identity attributes.

3. Stewards shall determine whether authorized IC personnel may retrieve or receive discovered information collected or analysis produced in accordance with this section.

4. Absent specific information to the contrary, stewards shall accept the information provided by authorized IC personnel, in accordance with Section F.2. above, as satisfying the "need-to-know" requirement. The steward may determine, based on specific, articulable facts, that the requestor's need for the information is significantly outweighed by the risks of providing it, using the risk management framework in Section F.5., or that providing the information would violate a statutory provision or a court order.

5. Stewards shall meet their responsibility to provide through a risk-managed approach when determining whether to permit the dissemination to or the retrieval by authorized IC personnel of the content of information collected or analysis produced. Stewards shall evaluate the risks associated with providing the content of information collected or analysis produced against the risks associated with denying the request and shall take special care to ensure determinations are made consistent with Section D.6.

a. Risks associated with providing information include, but are not limited to: risks to sources, methods, and activities; and risks of unauthorized or unintentional disclosure.

b. Risks associated with denying a request for information include, but are not limited to: risks to mission performance; and risks of incomplete or erroneous analytic judgments informing policy or other decisions.

6. In accordance with DNI guidelines, an IC element head may stipulate specific security and training requirements for authorized IC personnel to obtain the content of particularly sensitive discovered information. Such requirements shall be established as part of an integrated implementation plan developed and approved in accordance with Section D.7. and consistent with Section D.6.and IC policy. IC element heads may not stipulate specific security or training requirements that exceed those imposed on their authorized IC personnel.

7. Should a steward deny the request, or partially deny the request (such as providing "minimized" content), authorized IC personnel who are not satisfied with the steward's determination may initiate a formal review through his or her Sensitive Review Board (SRB) in accordance with ICPG 501.2, *Sensitive Review Board and Information Sharing Dispute Resolution Process*.

a. Stewards shall provide written justification for denial or partial denial of information to the requestor and appropriate SRBs, in accordance with ICPG 501.2.

b. The requestor's SRB and the steward's SRB shall attempt to resolve the dispute under the direction of the IC element heads. Disputes that cannot be resolved between SRBs shall be forwarded jointly by the affected SRBs to the DNI.

c. The DNI may resolve any risk management dispute that cannot be resolved at a lower level.

d. Disputes involving Attorney General approved guidelines, or court-ordered or statutory restrictions on the dissemination of information, such as dissemination of U.S. person information collected under the Foreign Intelligence Surveillance Act, shall be referred to the Attorney General if the dispute cannot be resolved by the DNI and affected IC element heads, in consultation with their General Counsels.

G. ROLES AND RESPONSIBILITIES:

1. The Office of the Director of National Intelligence (ODNI).

a. The IC ISE is the DNI's senior accountable official for the oversight and financial and program management of IC information integration efforts and shall:

(1) Develop a series of IC integrated implementation plans, in consultation with IC elements, and subject to DNI approval, that ensure all aspects of information sharing are addressed by the appropriate ODNI component or IC element, including but not limited to: IT architecture and standards; policies; human resource and cultural factors; business processes; information assurance; privacy; counterintelligence; risk management and security;

(2) Develop, in consultation with IC elements, a fully resourced, near-term, integrated implementation plan to achieve the policy objective in Section D.7.b.;

(3) Monitor implementation; identify, anticipate, and mitigate obstacles to implementation; and take appropriate steps to ensure any implementation plan developed pursuant to Section G.2.c. is appropriately resourced;

(4) Provide periodic progress reports to the DNI and the EXCOM;

(5) Provide subject matter expertise, as appropriate, to inform the development of IC policies in accordance with ICD 101, *IC Policy System*; ICPG 101.1, *IC Directives and Policy Guidance*; ICPG 101.2, *IC Standards*; and any other policy that may be promulgated pursuant to ICD 101;

(6) Implement, as appropriate, the dispute resolution process in accordance with ICPG 501.2;

(7) Assist the DDNI/PPR, as requested, in monitoring compliance and evaluating the effectiveness of this policy; and

(8) Create such committees, boards, or councils as the IC ISE deems necessary to carry out the responsibilities described herein.

b. The Chancellor of the National Intelligence University (NIU) shall, in coordination with IC elements, develop community-level information sharing training to promote understanding and individual responsibilities with respect to this Directive.

c. The IC CIO shall:

(1) Develop the IT architecture that supports this Directive;

(2) Develop and promulgate standards required to implement this Directive in accordance with ICPG 101.2, to include: documented procedures for the review and analysis of audit data to support security, counterintelligence, and intelligence oversight requirements; standards to allow information to be discoverable; and standards to define new or significant changes to existing IT systems in Section D.8.; and

(3) Maintain the list of designated stewards and authorized IC personnel.

d. The DDNI/PPR shall support policy requirements for implementation plans and shall evaluate and monitor compliance with this policy.

e. The IC Chief Human Capital Officer shall work with the Chancellor of the NIU to ensure information sharing education and training is mandatory for IC personnel and is linked to implementation of ICD 651, *Performance Management System Requirements for the IC Civilian Workforce*, and ICD 656, *Performance Management System Requirements for IC Senior Civilian* Officers.

f. The Deputy Director of National Intelligence for Collection and the Deputy Director of National Intelligence for Analysis shall work with stewards to develop a concept of operations to implement this Directive to inform the IT architecture and integrated implementation plans; and

g. The National Counterintelligence Executive shall provide a counterintelligence mission perspective to inform the IT architecture and any integrated implementation plans.

h. The Civil Liberties Protection Officer shall support IC elements in carrying out their responsibilities to implement this Directive in compliance with applicable requirements to protect privacy and civil liberties.

2. IC Element Heads shall:

a. Designate individuals in their IC element who are "authorized IC personnel." Until such time as an attribute-based identity management capability exists for the IC, provide the list of positions and names to the IC CIO;

b. Name collection steward(s) and analytic production steward(s), and provide the list of positions and names to the IC CIO;

c. Produce a strategy to implement this policy and provide it to the IC ISE, including a specific, appropriately resourced plan to meet the objectives of this Directive;

d. Seek a DNI exemption from discovery for information collected or analysis produced, in accordance with the procedures in ICPG 501.1, when appropriate;

e. Appoint appropriate personnel from their element to SRBs in accordance with Section G.3.;

f. Ensure that new information systems or significant enhancements to information systems comply with Section D.8. of this Directive;

g. Provide assistance, as requested, to the DDNI/PPR in evaluating implementation of this policy;

h. Incorporate mandatory education to collectors, analysts, and others who collect, process, retain, or use information regarding the importance of information sharing in accordance with curriculum developed by the Chancellor of the NIU. Initial training of all relevant IC personnel shall be accomplished within six months after the curriculum is developed;

i. Negotiate arrangements, agreements, understandings, or commercial contracts that shall, to the greatest extent possible, seek to obtain terms that permit discovery, and dissemination or retrieval by authorized IC personnel; and

j. Provide authorized IC personnel in all IC elements specific training recommended by an IC element that is part of an integrated implementation plan, in accordance with F.6.

3. SRBs shall:

a. In accordance with implementation procedures set forth in ICPG 501.2, serve as their respective IC element head's designated body to resolve dissemination and retrieval disputes; and take proactive measures to help ensure information is made available to authorized IC personnel, as appropriate;

b. Be established within the Office of the Director of National Intelligence (ODNI), the Central Intelligence Agency, the National Security Agency, the Defense Intelligence Agency (DIA), the National Geospatial-Intelligence Agency, and the Federal Bureau of Investigation, with limited membership.

(1) The DIA SRB shall include at least one member from the intelligence and counterintelligence elements of the Army, the Navy, the Air Force, and the Marine Corps, and represent the interests of the services;

(2) The ODNI SRB shall include a member from the National Reconnaissance Office; the Office of National Security Intelligence of the Drug Enforcement Administration; the Office of Intelligence and Counterintelligence of the Department of Energy; the Bureau of Intelligence and Research of the Department of State; the Office of Intelligence and Analysis of the Department of the Treasury; the Office of Intelligence and Analysis of the Department of Homeland Security; the intelligence and counterintelligence elements of the Coast Guard; and represent the interests of these elements, as well as those of the ODNI.

c. Consist of members cleared for access to all information, as determined by the DNI in consultation with IC element heads and in accordance with implementation procedures set forth in ICPG 501.2.

4. Stewards shall:

a. Make information collected and analysis produced available for discovery in accordance with this Directive; and

b. Make decisions with respect to information discovered and requested by authorized IC personnel in accordance with this Directive and pursue risk mitigation strategies to the greatest extent possible.

H. EFFECTIVE DATE: This ICD becomes effective on the date of signature.

J.M. McConnell
Director of National Intelligence Date
January 21, 2009

APPENDIX A - DEFINITIONS
ICD 501, DISCOVERY AND DISSEMINATION OR RETRIEVAL OF INFORMATION WITHIN THE INTELLIGENCE COMMUNITY
For the purposes of this Directive and all subordinate Policies and Standards, the terms below shall have the following meanings:

1. *Analysis Produced*: A disseminated or undisseminated product, assessment, study, estimate, compilation, or other report created and reviewed or validated by an IC element. It also includes databases comprised of information that may inform analysis. Databases become discoverable as part of a phased implementation plan in accordance with Section D.7.

2. *Authorized IC Personnel*: A U.S. person employed by, assigned to, or acting on behalf of an IC element who, through the course of their duties and employment, has a mission need and an appropriate security clearance. Authorized IC personnel shall be identified by their IC element head and shall have discovery rights to information collected and analysis produced by all elements of the IC. The term may include contractor personnel.

3. *Collected*: Any information, both in its final form and in the form when initially gathered, acquired, held, or obtained by an IC element that is potentially relevant to a mission need of any IC element. This includes information as it is obtained directly from its source, regardless of whether the information has been reviewed or processed.

4. *Discovery*: The act of obtaining knowledge of the existence, but not necessarily the content, of information collected or analysis produced by any IC element. Discovery, as it is applicable under this Directive, is not defined or intended to be interpreted as discovery under the Federal Rules of Civil Procedure, Federal Rules of Criminal Procedure, or other individual state discovery rules regarding non-privileged matter that is relevant to any party's claim or defense.

5. *Dissemination*: The act of a steward providing information collected or analysis produced by an IC element to authorized IC personnel, either through the ordinary course of business or in response to a request following discovery—(information "pushed" to authorized IC personnel).

6. *Information*: Intelligence and intelligence-related information. It does not include information pertaining to the internal administration or management of IC elements, such as IC personnel, medical, administrative, budget or security records.

7. *Intelligence*: As defined in EO 12333, as amended, includes foreign intelligence and counterintelligence.

8. *Mission Need*: A requirement for access to specific information to perform or assist in a lawful and authorized governmental function. Mission needs are determined by the mission and functions of an IC element or the roles and responsibilities of particular IC personnel in the course of their official duties.

9. *Retrieval:* The act of authorized IC personnel obtaining information collected or analysis produced by any IC element in response to a request following discovery through means other than dissemination.

10. *Steward (includes both Collection Steward and Analytic Production Steward):*

    a. *Collection Steward*: An appropriately cleared employee of an IC element, who is a senior official, designated by the head of that IC element to represent a collection activity that the IC element is authorized by law or executive order to conduct, and to make determinations regarding the dissemination to or the retrieval by authorized IC personnel of information collected by that activity.

    b. *Analytic Production Steward*: An appropriately cleared employee of an IC element, who is a senior official, designated by the head of that IC element to represent the analytic activity that the IC element is authorized by law or executive order to conduct, and to make determinations regarding the dissemination to or the retrieval by authorized IC personnel of analysis produced by that activity.

APPENDIX B – ACRONYM LIST
ICD 501, DISCOVERY AND DISSEMINATION OR RETRIEVAL OF INFORMATION WITHIN THE INTELLIGENCE COMMUNITY

CIO	Chief Information Officer
DCID	Director of Central Intelligence Directive
DDNI/PPR	Deputy Director of National Intelligence for Policy, Plans, and Requirements
DIA	Defense Intelligence Agency
DNI	Director of National Intelligence
EO	Executive Order
EXCOM	Executive Committee
IC	Intelligence Community
ICD	Intelligence Community Directive
IC ISE	Intelligence Community Information Sharing Executive
ICPG	Intelligence Community Policy Guidance
ICPM	Intelligence Community Policy Memorandum
IT	Information Technology
NIU	National Intelligence University
ODNI	Office of the Director of National Intelligence
RELIDO	Releasable by Information Disclosure Official
SRB	Sensitive Review Board
TS/SCI	TOP SECRET/Sensitive Compartmented Information

Intelligence Community Policy Guidance 501.1
Exemption of Information From Discovery

(Effective: May 26, 2009)

A. AUTHORITY: The National Security Act of 1947, as amended; Executive Order 12333, as amended; and other applicable provisions of law.

B. PURPOSE: This Intelligence Community Policy Guidance (ICPG) sets forth the implementing procedures for exemptions from discovery for information collected or analysis produced, as called for in Sections E. 1.c and G.2.d of Intelligence Community Directive (ICD) 501, Discovery and Dissemination or Retrieval of Information within the Intelligence Community.

C. APPLICABILITY

1. This guidance applies to the Intelligence Community (IC), as defined by the National Security Act of 1947, as amended; and such other elements of any other department or agency as may be designated by the President, or designated jointly by the Director of National Intelligence (DNI) and the head of the department or agency concerned, as an element of the IC.

2. This ICPG does not apply to purely law enforcement information. When law enforcement information also contains intelligence or intelligence-related information, this ICPG shall apply to the intelligence or intelligence-related information.

D. POLICY

1. In accordance with ICD 501, information may be exempt from discovery if it is determined that discovery, or the confirmation of the mere existence of such information, will jeopardize the protection of sources, methods, or activities; compromise a criminal or national security investigation; or be inconsistent with the requirements of Section D.6 of ICD 501. The term "information" in this ICPG constitutes "information collected or analysis produced" as used in ICD 501.

2. The definitions in Appendix A of ICD 501 apply to this ICPG.

E. PROCESS

1. Exemptions

    a. IC element heads shall submit recommendations to the DNI for the exemption of information from discovery in accordance with timelines established in IC integrated implementation plans. These timelines shall specify that exemption recommendations be submitted no later than 60 days prior to the information in question being made available for discovery, as called for in an IC integrated implementation plan. In recommending an exemption, IC element heads shall provide information in accordance with Section E.1.c.(1-6) of this ICPG.

    b. Should an IC element head deem it necessary to exempt information from discovery in advance of a DNI exemption decision, the IC element head shall provide information in accordance with Section E.1.c.(1-6) of this ICPG as soon as possible but no later than 10 business days after the IC element head's action to exempt the information. Information an IC element head has exempted from discovery shall not be discoverable unless and until the DNI makes an exemption decision.

    c. Exemptions shall:

        (1) Be addressed to the DNI in the form of Executive Correspondence;

        (2) Specifically identify and fully describe the information being exempted, to include scope and volume. Exemptions may be submitted for categories of information with common attributes or components, when appropriate;

        (3) Include an assessment of the risks to sources, methods, or activities, as well as an assessment of the risks of unauthorized or unintentional disclosure;

        (4) Include an assessment of the risks associated with exempting the information from discovery, to include risks to mission performance and risks of incomplete or erroneous analytic judgments informing national security decisions;

        (5) Specify the time period over which the exemption should endure; and

        (6) Provide any additional information or potential implications the IC element head believes the DNI should consider.

    d. Sensitive Review Boards (SRB) shall consist of members cleared for access to all information, as determined by the DNI in consultation with IC element heads. For efficiency, an IC element head may include, as part of a recommendation to exempt information from discovery by authorized IC personnel, a recommendation to restrict SRB member access in accordance with Section F.4 of ICPG 501.2, Sensitive Review Board and Information Sharing Dispute Resolution Process.

    2. DNI Decision

    a. The DNI may approve an exemption in whole or in part, or deny the exemption, and will provide a written copy of his decision to the IC element head who recommended the exemption, as well as inform the SRBs, as appropriate.

    b. Should the DNI deny an exemption in whole or in part, the relevant IC element head shall make the subject information discoverable immediately but no later than five business days after the relevant IC element head is notified of the DNI's decision, or in accordance with an approved IC integrated implementation plan, whichever is later.

    3. Information Handling

    a. IC element heads shall ensure that all information that is exempted from discovery is marked immediately with control markings unique for discovery exemptions, in accordance with the Controlled Access Program Coordination Office's (CAPCO) Authorized Classification and Control Markings Register.

    b. CAPCO shall establish control markings for exempted information in accordance with the IC integrated implementation plans.

    c. Information exempted from discovery shall adhere to IC metadata standards promulgated by the IC Chief Information Officer.

    4. The Senior Review Group of the Office of the Director of National Intelligence shall:

    a. Be chaired by the IC Information Sharing Executive and report to the DNI for matters pertaining to the exemption of information from discovery pursuant to this Guidance.

    b. Maintain records of all official communications between the DNI and an IC element head as specified in Section E, the disposition of exemptions, and the results of annual reviews; and

    c. Review by 1 June annually all exemptions.

F. EFFECTIVE DATE: This Guidance is effective on the date of signature.

May 26, 2009
Deputy Director of National Intelligence for Policy, Plans, and Requirements

Intelligence Community Policy Guidance 501.2

Sensitive Review Board and Information Sharing Dispute Resolution Process

(Effective: May 26, 2009)

A. AUTHORITY: The National Security Act of 1947, as amended; Executive Order 12333, as amended; and other applicable provisions of law.

B. PURPOSE

1. This Intelligence Community Policy Guidance (ICPG):

a. Further defines the process called for in Intelligence Community Directive (ICD) 501, Discovery and Dissemination or Retrieval of Information Within the Intelligence Community, to resolve disputes between authorized Intelligence Community (IC) personnel and stewards regarding the dissemination or retrieval of information discovered.

b. Sets forth the implementing procedures for access to information by Sensitive Review Board (SRB) members as required by Section G.3.c of ICD 501; and

c. Delineates specific roles and responsibilities of the Office of the Director of National Intelligence (ODNI), IC element heads, and SRBs.

C. APPLICABILITY

1. This guidance applies to the IC, as defined by the National Security Act of 1947, as amended; and such other elements of any other department or agency that may be designated by the President, or designated jointly by the Director of National Intelligence (DNI) and the head of the department or agency concerned, as an element of the IC.

2. This ICPG does not apply to purely law enforcement information. When law enforcement information also contains intelligence or intelligence-related information, this ICPG shall apply to the intelligence or intelligence-related information.

D. POLICY

1. Authorized IC personnel have a responsibility to request discovered information that has the potential to contribute to their assigned mission need. Discovery alone does not constitute a request for the content of the information. Stewards shall determine whether authorized IC personnel may receive the information, and shall make as much information as possible available for automated retrieval upon discovery. If a dispute arises regarding a request for information, authorized IC personnel, stewards, and their respective SRBs shall use the process in Section E of this ICPG to resolve the disputes.

2. This Guidance applies to authorized IC personnel seeking the content of information discovered with respect to information made discoverable as a result of an IC integrated implementation plan in accordance with Sections D.7 and G.1.a.(1) of ICD 501. This Guidance is in addition to and does not replace an IC employee's ability to seek information under other policies and procedures.

3. SRBs are comprised of members cleared for access to all information in accordance with Section F of this ICPG to facilitate their roles and responsibilities to resolve dissemination or retrieval disputes; and to take proactive measures to help ensure information is made available to authorized IC personnel, as appropriate.

4. An exemption of information from discovery made in accordance with ICPG 501.1, Exemption of Information from Discovery, does not apply to SRB members' access to said information, unless otherwise determined by the DNI. SRB members may, on behalf of specific personnel in their element, seek information regardless of whether the information has been made discoverable in accordance with an integrated implementation plan, and shall use the dispute resolution process in Section E of this ICPG, should a steward deny an SRB member's request.

5. The definitions in Appendix A of ICD 501 apply to this ICPG. The term "information" in this ICPG constitutes "information collected or analysis produced" as used in ICD 501.

E. INFORMATION SHARING DISPUTE RESOLUTION PROCESS

1. The process for resolving disputes regarding the dissemination or retrieval of IC information discovered and requested by authorized IC personnel shall include the following steps:

a. Authorized IC personnel ("requestor") shall make a written request to the steward to obtain the content of discovered information that has the potential to contribute to their mission need if the steward has not made the information available. The requestor shall provide the steward with information regarding their role, assigned mission need. and, when established, DN I approved identity attributes. Stewards shall accept the information provided by the requestor as satisfying the "need-to-know" requirement, absent specific information to the contrary. The requestor shall simultaneously provide a copy of the request to the steward, the requestor's SRB, and the steward's SRB.

b. In reviewing requests for the content of information discovered by authorized IC personnel, stewards shall apply the risk management principles of Section F.5 of ICD 501. In denying or partially denying requests, stewards shall provide written justification delineating specific, articulable facts that the requestor's mission need for the information is significantly outweighed by the risk of providing the information to the requestor, or that providing the information would violate Attorney General approved guidelines or court ordered or statutory restrictions in accordance with Section F.7.d of ICD 501.

c. The steward shall provide the original request and a written explanation of the rationale for a decision to deny or partially deny a request to the requestor's SRB and the steward's SRB within 10 business days of receiving the request. The requestor's SRB shall promptly notify the requestor of the steward's decision and, as appropriate, the rationale.

d. The requestor's SRB shall consult with the requester within five business days of receipt of the steward's justification for denial or partial denial of a request, and determine whether to dispute the steward's decision. The requestor's SRS shall provide written notice to the steward's SRB of the intent to dispute the steward's decision.

e. Under the direction of the relevant IC element heads, the requestor's SRB and the steward's SRB shall attempt to resolve the dispute by jointly and promptly reviewing the steward's decision to deny the request. SRBs are encouraged to consider multiple options for dispute resolution if providing the full content is not possible, such as providing partial, sanitized, or minimized content. SRBs may contact the requestor and steward for additional information, if needed. Within seven business days after the requestor's SRB initiates a dispute, the respective SRBs shall notify the affected requestor and steward of the outcome of the dispute, along with justification for the decision and disposition of the case.

f. If a dispute cannot be resolved between SRBs within seven business days, the dispute shall be forwarded jointly by the SRBs to the DNI within three business days. The SRBs involved in the dispute must each provide, as applicable, all necessary information to the DNI, through the ODNI Senior Review Group (SRG), including:

(1) Justifications for the request;

(2) Specific, articulable facts for the denial based on risk management principles in Section F.5 of ICD 501;

(3) Reasons for the dispute;

(4) Content of the information discovered and requested: and

(5) Any additional details or potential implications that the SRBs believe the DN I should consider.

g. The SRG shall ensure the information regarding the dispute is complete, and shall forward the dispute to the DNI within 15 business days of receipt.

h. The DNI will issue a written decision resolving the dispute. The SRG shall promptly convey the DNI's decision to the relevant SRBs, and oversee implementation of the decision.

2. At any time, the requestor's SRB may withdraw a dispute through written notification to the steward's SRB and the SRG, as applicable.

3. A requestor or requestor's SRB may request expedited review of the dispute based upon exigent circumstances, including the prevention of loss of life or serious bodily injury, significant threats to national security. informing time-critical intelligence collection or policy requirements, or significant input to a case under investigation or litigation. When an expedited request is submitted, SRBs or the DNI, as the case may be, shall make every effort to resolve the dispute as soon as possible.

4. For disputes involving Attorney General approved guidelines. or court-ordered or statutory restrictions on the dissemination of information, such as dissemination of U.S. persons information collected under the Foreign Intelligence Surveillance Act, SRBs shall consult with their respective General Counsel. In such cases, the SRBs shall have an additional 10 business days to obtain and integrate the response provided by their General Counsels. The DNI shall refer a dispute to the Attorney General if it cannot be resolved by the DNI and affected IC element heads, in consultation with their General Counsels.

5. SRB members are responsible for ensuring appropriate personnel within their IC element obtain information that is relevant to their assigned mission need, which may include information exempted by the DNI from discovery by authorized IC personnel. SRB members' access is not limited to infounation made discoverable as a result of an IC integrated implementation plan. SRB members may submit a request for information on behalf of specific personnel in their IC element to the appropriate steward for consideration, using procedures set forth in Section E.1 of this ICPG. If the SRB member is not satisfied with the steward's decision on the request, the SRB member and the steward's SRB shall use the dispute resolution procedures in Section E.1 of this ICPG to resolve the dispute.

F. SRB MEMBER ACCESS

1. SRB members shall be cleared for access to all information in accordance with instructions issued by the SRG. Appropriate security personnel in each IC element shall clear SRB members for access in accordance with SRG instructions within 15 business days of the SRB member's appointment to the position, and to any new controlled access program within 15 business days of establishment of the program, unless otherwise restricted by the DNI in accordance with this Section.

2. SRB member access to information is based on their assigned roles and responsibilities as SRB members. The SRG shall maintain a record of each IC element's SRB members, and their specific accesses. When an SRB member's assignment to an SRB ends, each IC element's SRB Chair is responsible for notifying the SRG to ensure unifoiin debriefing in accordance with applicable security procedures.

3. The DNI, in consultation with affected IC element heads, may restrict accesses of SRB

members. The DNI may approve a restriction in whole, approve a restriction with conditions, or deny a restriction.

4. IC element heads may recommend the DNI restrict SRB member access to information collected or analysis produced by their element.

a. Such recommendations shall:

(1) Be submitted to the DNI in the form of Executive Correspondence;

(2) Include a description of the access to be restricted;

(3) Provide a compelling justification, including an analysis of whether restricting access detracts from the objectives of the SRB in Section D.3 of this ICPG;

(4) Identify SRB member(s) subject to the recommended access restriction; and

(5) Include any additional details or potential implications the IC element head believes the DNI should consider.

b. As stated in Section E.1.d of ICPG 501.1, an IC element head may include, as part of a recommendation to exempt information from discovery by authorized IC personnel, a recommendation to restrict SRB member access to said information. in accordance with Section F.4.a.(1-5) of this ICPG.

c. The DNI will review the recommendation within 15 business days of receipt and will provide a written copy of his decision to the IC element head who submitted the recommendation.

G. ROLES AND RESPONSIBILITIES

1. Office of the Director of National Intelligence

a. The DNI will:

(1) Resolve disputes regarding dissemination or retrieval of information within the IC that cannot be resolved at a lower level, except that disputes described in Section E.4 of this ICPG shall be referred for resolution to the Attorney General, if necessary; and

(2) Make decisions regarding SRB member access restrictions.

b. The SRG shall:

(1) Be chaired by the IC Information Sharing Executive and report to the DNI for matters pertaining to information sharing dispute resolution and SRB member access pursuant to this Guidance;

(2) Maintain records of: all official communications between the DNI and IC element heads, and between the DNI and SRBs; disposition of disputes referred to the DNI for resolution; the names of SRB members and their specific accesses: and the disposition of recommendations to the DNI to restrict SRB member access to information;

(3) Review by 1 July annually SRB member access restrictions; and

(4) Evaluate, in collaboration with IC element SRBs, the effectiveness of the dispute resolution process established by this ICPG, including a review to identify best practices.

2. IC Element Heads shall:

a. Appoint a limited number of SRB members who:

(1) Are a General Schedule 15 or Band 5 officer. or higher: and are cleared for access to information in accordance with Section F of this ICPG: and

(2) Possess, either individually or collectively, a comprehensive understanding of their IC element's collection and analysis missions, as well as knowledge of collection and analysis missions of other IC elements.

b. Provide their SRB member names to the SRG, and keep their SRB membership roster current.

c. Ensure their respective SRB members are adequately informed, supported, and trained to perform their duties.

d. Ensure their SRB or their SRB member addresses disputes regarding dissemination or retrieval of information, and takes proactive measures to help ensure information is made available to appropriate authorized IC personnel.

e. Ensure any internal regulations established by their element for resolving disputes regarding dissemination or retrieval of information are consistent with the intent and objectives of ICD 501, this ICPG, and other policies as appropriate.

3. Sensitive Review Boards shall:

a. Attempt to resolve disputes regarding dissemination or retrieval of information with other SRBs in accordance with Section E of this ICPG;

b. Take proactive measures to help ensure information is made available to appropriate authorized IC personnel:

c. Assist the SRG in evaluating the effectiveness of the dispute resolution process in Section E of this ICPG;

d. Respond to SRG requests for information regarding dissemination or retrieval of information;

e. Provide quarterly reports as requested by the SRG, including information about disputes regarding dissemination or retrieval of information; and proactive actions taken by the SRB to ensure information is made available to appropriate authorized IC personnel. Reports should contain all relevant data, including the quantity, disposition. and timelines of all requests and disputes; and

f. Maintain records, including records of all requests raised by authorized IC personnel or the SRBs for dissemination or retrieval of information and the disposition thereof.

H. EFFECTIVE DATE: This Guidance is effective on the date of signature.

May 26, 2009
Deputy Director of National Intelligence for Policy, Plans, and Requirements

Intelligence Community Policy Guidance 501.3
Subsequent Use of Information

(Effective: May 20, 2010)

A. AUTHORITY: The National Security Act of 1947, as amended; Executive Order 12333, as amended; Executive Order 13526; and other applicable provisions of law.

B. PURPOSE: This Guidance addresses subsequent use, the proper handling and use of information collected or analysis produced that is received by authorized Intelligence Community personnel (AICP) to further a mission need ("received information"), pursuant to the provisions of Intelligence Community Directive (ICD) 501, Discovery and Dissemination or Retrieval of Information within the Intelligence Community. The definitions in Appendix A of ICD 501 apply to this Guidance.

C. APPLICABILITY

1. This Guidance applies to the Intelligence Community (IC), as defined by the National Security Act of 1947, as amended; and such other elements of any other department or agency as may be designated by the President, or designated jointly by the Director of National Intelligence and the head of the department or agency concerned, as an element of the IC.

2. This Guidance does not apply to purely law enforcement information. When law enforcement information also contains intelligence or intelligence-related information, this Guidance shall apply to the intelligence or intelligence-related information.

3. All IC personnel shall carry out their responsibilities under this Guidance consistent with applicable law and in a manner that protects fully the privacy rights and civil liberties of all U.S. persons, as required by the Constitution, Federal statutes, Executive Orders, Presidential Directives, court orders, and Attorney General approved guidelines, including those regarding the dissemination of U.S. person information.

D. POLICY

1. Received information may only be used in accordance with the mission need of the receiving AICP. All received information shall be handled in accordance with existing policy and procedures in the IC, including but not limited to bilateral agreements between IC elements, classification and control markings, retention, handling, destruction, and disclosure and release.

2. In determining possible uses of received information, AICPs are responsible for ascertaining to the best of their ability aspects of the information, including its quality and reliability, that would inform decisions on subsequent use by the receiving IC element. AICPs are encouraged to communicate with the originating IC steward in this regard. Similarly, IC stewards in the IC element that originated the information are responsible for fully and substantially assisting AICPs who communicate with them.

3. An IC element must determine if and how to use received information in its analytic products or for other purposes pursuant to its mission need. The receiving IC element shall bear the risks associated with the use of received information.

4. When using received information, AICPs shall cite sufficient details about the information to enable identification of the original information, and shall, to the extent possible, source the information in accordance with ICD 206, Sourcing Requirements for Disseminated Analytic Products.

E. EFFECTIVE DATE: This Guidance becomes effective on the date of signature.

May 20, 2010
Deputy Director of National Intelligence for Policy, Plans, and Requirements

INTELLIGENCE OVERSIGHT REPORTING CRITERIA

MEMORANDUM FOR   THE SECRETARY OF STATE
                            THE SECRETARY OF THE TREASURY
                            THE SECRETARY OF DEFENSE
                            THE ATTORNEY GENERAL
                            THE SECRETARY OF ENERGY
                            THE SECRETARY OF HOMELAND SECURITY
                            DIRECTOR, CENTRAL INTELLIGENCE AGENCY

SUBJECT: Intelligence Oversight Reporting Criteria

Executive Order (EO) 13462 tasks the Intelligence Oversight Board (IOB) with issuing criteria on the thresholds for reporting intelligence oversight matters to the IOB and to the Director of National Intelligence (DNI). It also tasks the DNI with issuing instructions relating to the format and scheduling of such reporting. The attached guidance provides those criteria and instructions.

EO 13462 and these criteria acknowledge the establishment of the DNI and seek to infuse a fresh awareness of the importance of intelligence oversight reporting. The criteria also provide guidance on what information the President and the DNI need to execute their respective duties to see that the laws are faithfully executed and that intelligence activities comply with the Constitution and laws of the United States.

To implement EO 13462, the DNI will execute day-to-day intelligence oversight responsibilities. Among other things, this will include reviewing the guidelines by which Intelligence Community (IC) components report intelligence activities to ensure they are consistent with Part I.7(d) of EO 12333 and with EO 13462, reviewing reports submitted to the IOB, and providing the IOB with a quarterly assessment of the content, quality, and timeliness of reporting by the IC.

The IOB continues to act as an independent entity appointed by the President to ensure that the Constitution and laws of the United States are respected and to report to the President in accordance with the functions assigned to the IOB by EO 13462. The IOB will audit, review, and assess the adequacy of the respective processes by which the DNI performs his oversight and review functions and the IC components perform their reporting functions under EO 13461. As necessary, the IOB may conduct its own investigations of intelligence activities. The IOB also will continue to receive and review reports of all matters that may be unlawful or contrary to executive order or presidential directive and to report to the President and the Attorney General concerning those matters.

In addition, a key element of intelligence oversight is the explicit direction that "significant or highly sensitive matters" must be reported immediately. "Significant or highly sensitive matters" are intelligence activities that may or may not be unlawful or contrary to executive order or presidential directive, that could impugn the reputation or integrity of the IC, or that could otherwise call into question the propriety of U.S. intelligence activities. These types of matters, initially articulated by Assistant to the President for National Security Affairs Stephen Hadley in his memorandum of April 17, 2007, are also captured in the accompanying criteria for reporting.

As a reminder, section 8(b)(ii) of EO 13462 provides that the heads of departments with organizations in the IC shall designate offices within their respective organizations that shall submit to the IOB the reports required by executive order and inform the IOB and the DNI of such designations.

Each component of the IC is responsible for reviewing its internal processes, guidelines, and training for reporting intelligence oversight matters to the IOB and DNI and updating them in accordance with EO 13462 and the criteria and instructions set forth in this memorandum. Please provide the IOB and the DNI with a progress report on your review by July 30, 2008.

J. M. McConnell
Director of National Intelligence

Stephen Friedman
Chairman, Intelligence Oversight Board

Attachment
Tab A Reporting Criteria

CRITERIA ON THRESHOLDS FOR REPORTING INTELLIGENCE OVERSIGHT MATTERS AND INSTRUCTIONS RELATING TO FORMATTING AND SCHEDULING

Intelligence oversight reporting serves as an early warning of intelligence activities of which the President should be informed, through either his Intelligence Oversight Board (IOB) or the Director of National Intelligence (DNI), or both, and provides a means by which the Executive Branch may timely identify and correct any deficiencies in the conduct of its intelligence activities. The following criteria on thresholds for reporting intelligence oversight matters to the Intelligence Oversight Board, and instructions on formatting and scheduling of reports, are issued under the authority of Executive Order 13462.

I. Criteria on Thresholds for Reporting. The heads of departments with organizations in the Intelligence Community (IC), or the beads of such organizations, or their designees, shall:

    A. Report to the IOB, with copies to the DNI, any intelligence activity with respect to which there is reason to believe may be unlawful or contrary to executive order (EO) or presidential directive (PD). The following guidance applies to determining whether a particular matter should he reported:

        1. "Intelligence activities" are defined in Part 34(e) of BC) 12333 and, for purposes of these criteria, include, but are not limited to, the acquisition, collection, retention, analysis, and dissemination of intelligence information,

        2. Intelligence activities are reportable if a reasonable person would believe they may he unlawful or contrary to EO or PD without waiting for substantiation, investigation, formal adjudication, or resolution of the issue of whether a particular matter is unlawful or contrary to EO or PD.

        3. Intelligence activities to be reported under EOs 13462 and 12333 are not limited to those that concern "United States persons," as defined in Part 3.4(i) of EO 12333 or in any successor EO.

4. "Executive order or presidential directive" means, for purposes of implementing these criteria, a document signed by the President of the United States that has the force of law for the Executive Branch or constitutes the exercise by the President of his Executive authority. Reports may include violations of procedures and guidelines that heads of departments or IC components have established to implement EO 12333, or a successor order, provided, however, that such matters are of potential presidential interest or deemed appropriate for the IOB's review, e.g., because they involve the apparent violation of substantive rights of individuals,

5. Reportable events include the initiation of, and significant developments in, investigations or other inquiries relating to the legality or propriety of intelligence activities.

6. Initial reports made on the basis of incomplete or inaccurate reporting are to be updated as additional information becomes available. Subsequent or updated reports should be identified in such a manner that they can be accurately related to the relevant initial reports.

7. Intelligence activities are reportable to the IOB if such activities are required to be reported or have been reported to the Attorney General as required by law or other directive, including the Memorandum of Understanding on Reporting of Information Concerning Federal Crimes (1995),

8. Any intelligence activity that is to be reported to any congressional committee or member of Congress because it is or may be unlawful or contrary to executive order or otherwise "significant or highly sensitive" (see paragraph B, below) shall also be reported to the IOB and DNI generally before such a congressional report is made, Any report concerning intelligence activities that is submitted to any committee or member of Congress shall also be submitted to the IOB and DNI if the commencement of the investigation or other inquiry regarding such activities was also reportable under these criteria.

B. Report to the DNI, and the IOB as appropriate, significant or highly sensitive matters, whether or not unlawful or contrary to EO or PD.

1. "Significant of highly sensitive matters" are developments or circumstances involving intelligence activities that could impugn the reputation or integrity of the IC, or otherwise call into question the propriety of intelligence activities.
2. Such matters might be manifested in or by:
   a. congressional inquiries or investigations;
   b. adverse media coverage;
   c. impact on foreign relations or foreign partners; or
   d. unauthorized disclosure of protected information.

II. Content of Reports. Intelligence oversight reports should include (to the extent practicable without compromising the timeliness of reporting) the following:

A. A narrative describing each intelligence activity in question.

B. Why the matter is being reported, i.e, it is:

1. a potential violation of law (cite the relevant law, if a judgment has been made);
2. potentially contrary to EO or PD (cite the relevant section or part of the EO or PD);

      3.   a potential violation of agency procedures implementing EO 12333 (cite the specific rule or procedure, if a judgment has been made);

      4.   "'significant' because. . ."; or

      5.   "'highly sensitive' because. . ."

   C.   An explanation and analysis of how or why the incident occurred.

   D.   An assessment of any impact of the incident on national security or international relations, as well as any mitigation efforts, including success and failures of such efforts,

   E.   Any remedial action the IC element has taken or is taking to prevent recurrence of the incident being reported.

   F.   An assessment of any impact the reported intelligence activity may have on civil liberties or protected privacy rights.

   G.   How the IC element concerned is addressing any information improperly acquired, handled, used, destroyed, etc., as a consequence of the matter being reported.

   H.   A summary of the gravity, frequency, trends, and patterns of matters reported for the quarter.

   I.   Any additional information that the reporting official considers relevant for purposes of fully and completely informing the IOB and the DNI on intelligence oversight matters.

III. Formatting of Reports. Reports may be formatted in accordance with departmental or agency policies, provided all the substantive information described above is included in each report.

IV. Schedule for Reporting.

   A.   Significant or highly sensitive matters must be reported immediately.

      1.   Significant of highly sensitive matters may be reported orally, if necessary, and followed up with a written report as soon as possible thereafter. The preference is for written reports.

      2.   Significant of highly sensitive matters that may be unlawful or contrary to EO or PD shall be reported to the DNI or IOB.

      3.   Significant of highly sensitive matters that are NOT unlawful or contrary to EO or PD shall be reported to the DNI.

   B.   Routine reports shall be submitted on a quarterly basis. The first report for the calendar years shall cover 1 January through 31 March, and so for each quarter of the year.

   C.   Quarterly reports are due the last day of the month following the end of the quarter. For example, a report for the first quarter of the calendar year is due 30 April.

   D.   All IC elements must submit reports at least quarterly, even if a component has not been made aware of any reportable matter during the reporting period.

Questions concerning the implementation of EO 13462, or intelligence oversight reporting in general, may be submitted to the IOB's General Counsel by calling 202-456-2352, or to the ODNI IOB Team by calling 703-482-6304 (ODNI/OIG) or 703-275-2523 (ODNI/OGC).

Signals Intelligence

Presidential Policy Directive 28, Signals Intelligence Activities

(January 17, 2014)

The United States, like other nations, has gathered intelligence throughout its history to ensure that national security and foreign policy decisionmakers have access to timely, accurate, and insightful information.

The collection of signals intelligence is necessary for the United States to advance its national security and foreign policy interests and to protect its citizens and the citizens of its allies and partners from harm. At the same time, signals intelligence activities and the possibility that such activities may be improperly disclosed to the public pose multiple risks. These include risks to: our relationships with other nations, including the cooperation we receive from other nations on law enforcement, counterterrorism, and other issues; our commercial, economic, and financial interests, including a potential loss of international trust in U.S. firms and the decreased willingness of other nations to participate in international data sharing, privacy, and regulatory regimes; the credibility of our commitment to an open, interoperable, and secure global Internet; and the protection of intelligence sources and methods.

In addition, our signals intelligence activities must take into account that all persons should be treated with dignity and respect, regardless of their nationality or wherever they might reside, and that all persons have legitimate privacy interests in the handling of their personal information.

In determining why, whether, when, and how the United States conducts signals intelligence activities, we must weigh all of these considerations in a context in which information and communications technologies are constantly changing. The evolution of technology has created a world where communications important to our national security and the communications all of us make as part of our daily lives are transmitted through the same channels. This presents new and diverse opportunities for, and challenges with respect to, the collection of intelligence – and especially signals intelligence. The United States Intelligence Community (IC) has achieved remarkable success in developing enhanced capabilities to perform its signals intelligence mission in this rapidly changing world, and these enhanced capabilities are a major reason we have been able to adapt to a dynamic and challenging security environment.[1]

The United States must preserve and continue to develop a robust and technologically advanced signals intelligence capability to protect our security and that of our partners and allies. Our signals intelligence capabilities must also be agile enough to enable us to focus on fleeting opportunities or emerging crises and to address not only the issues of today, but also the issues of tomorrow, which we may not be able to foresee.

---

1. For the purposes of this directive, the terms "Intelligence Community" and "elements of the Intelligence Community" shall have the same meaning as they do in Executive Order 12333 of December 4, 1981, as amended (Executive Order 12333).

Advanced technologies can increase risks, as well as opportunities, however, and we must consider these risks when deploying our signals intelligence capabilities. The IC conducts signals intelligence activities with care and precision to ensure that its collection, retention, use, and dissemination of signals intelligence account for these risks. In light of the evolving technological and geopolitical environment, we must continue to ensure that our signals intelligence policies and practices appropriately take into account our alliances and other partnerships; the leadership role that the United States plays in upholding democratic principles and universal human rights; the increased globalization of trade, investment, and information flows; our commitment to an open, interoperable and secure global Internet; and the legitimate privacy and civil liberties concerns of U.S. citizens and citizens of other nations.

Presidents have long directed the acquisition of foreign intelligence and counterintelligence[2] pursuant to their constitutional authority to conduct U.S. foreign relations and to fulfill their constitutional responsibilities as Commander in Chief and Chief Executive. They have also provided direction on the conduct of intelligence activities in furtherance of these authorities and responsibilities, as well as in execution of laws enacted by the Congress. Consistent with this historical practice, this directive articulates principles to guide why, whether, when, and how the United States conducts signals intelligence activities for authorized foreign intelligence and counterintelligence purposes.[3]

Section 1. Principles Governing the Collection of Signals Intelligence.

Signals intelligence collection shall be authorized and conducted consistent with the following principles:

(a) The collection of signals intelligence shall be authorized by statute or Executive Order, proclamation, or other Presidential directive, and undertaken in

(b) Privacy and civil liberties shall be integral considerations in the planning of U.S. signals intelligence activities. The United States shall not collect signals intelligence for the purpose of suppressing or burdening criticism or dissent, or for disadvantaging persons based on their ethnicity, race, gender, sexual orientation, or religion. Signals intelligence shall be collected exclusively where there is a foreign intelligence or counterintelligence purpose to support national and departmental missions and not for any other purposes.

(c) The collection of foreign private commercial information or trade secrets is authorized

---

2. For the purposes of this directive, the terms "foreign intelligence" and "counterintelligence" shall have the same meaning as they have in Executive Order 12333. Thus, "foreign intelligence" means "information relating to the capabilities, intentions, or activities of foreign governments or elements thereof, foreign organizations, foreign persons, or international terrorists," and "counterintelligence" means "information gathered and activities conducted to identify, deceive, exploit, disrupt, or protect against espionage, other intelligence activities, sabotage, or assassinations conducted for or on behalf of foreign powers, organizations, or persons, or their agents, or international terrorist organizations or activities." Executive Order 12333 further notes that "[i]ntelligence includes foreign intelligence and counterintelligence."

3. Unless otherwise specified, this directive shall apply to signals intelligence activities conducted in order to collect communications or information about communications, except that it shall not apply to signals intelligence activities undertaken to test or develop signals intelligence capabilities. accordance with the Constitution and applicable statutes, Executive Orders, proclamations, and Presidential directives.

only to protect the national security of the United States or its partners and allies. It is not an authorized foreign intelligence or counterintelligence purpose to collect such information to afford a competitive advantage[4] to U.S. companies and U.S. business sectors commercially.

(d) Signals intelligence activities shall be as tailored as feasible. In determining whether to collect signals intelligence, the United States shall consider the availability of other information, including from diplomatic and public sources. Such appropriate and feasible alternatives to signals intelligence should be prioritized.

Sec. 2. Limitations on the Use of Signals Intelligence Collected in Bulk.

Locating new or emerging threats and other vital national security information is difficult, as such information is often hidden within the large and complex system of modern global communications. The United States must consequently collect signals intelligence in bulk[5] in certain circumstances in order to identify these threats. Routine communications and communications of national security interest increasingly transit the same networks, however, and the collection of signals intelligence in bulk may consequently result in the collection of information about persons whose activities are not of foreign intelligence or counterintelligence value. The United States will therefore impose new limits on its use of signals intelligence collected in bulk. These limits are intended to protect the privacy and civil liberties of all persons, whatever their nationality and regardless of where they might reside.

In particular, when the United States collects nonpublicly available signals intelligence in bulk, it shall use that data The Assistant to the President and National Security Advisor (APNSA), in consultation with the Director of National Intelligence (DNI), shall coordinate, on at least an annual basis, a review of the permissible uses of signals intelligence collected in bulk through the National Security Council Principals and Deputies Committee system identified in PPD-1 or any successor document. At the end of this review, I will be presented with recommended additions to or removals from the list of the permissible uses of signals intelligence collected in bulk.

---

4.   Certain economic purposes, such as identifying trade or sanctions violations or government influence or direction, shall not constitute competitive advantage.

5.   The limitations contained in this section do not apply to signals intelligence data that is temporarily acquired to facilitate targeted collection. References to signals intelligence collected in "bulk" mean the authorized collection of large quantities of signals intelligence data which, due to technical or operational considerations, is acquired without the use of discriminants (e.g., specific identifiers, selection terms, etc.). only for the purposes of detecting and countering: (1) espionage and other threats and activities directed by foreign powers or their intelligence services against the United States and its interests; (2) threats to the United States and its interests from terrorism; (3) threats to the United States and its interests from the development, possession, proliferation, or use of weapons of mass destruction; (4) cybersecurity threats; (5) threats to U.S. or allied Armed Forces or other U.S or allied personnel; and (6) transnational criminal threats, including illicit finance and sanctions evasion related to the other purposes named in this section. In no event may signals intelligence collected in bulk be used for the purpose of suppressing or burdening criticism or dissent; disadvantaging persons based on their ethnicity, race, gender, sexual orientation, or religion; affording a competitive advantage to U.S. companies and U.S. business sectors commercially; or achieving any purpose other than those identified in this section.

The DNI shall maintain a list of the permissible uses of signals intelligence collected in bulk. This list shall be updated as necessary and made publicly available to the maximum extent feasible, consistent with the national security.

Sec. 3. Refining the Process for Collecting Signals Intelligence.

U.S. intelligence collection activities present the potential for national security damage if improperly disclosed. Signals intelligence collection raises special concerns, given the opportunities and risks created by the constantly evolving technological and geopolitical environment; the unique nature of such collection and the inherent concerns raised when signals intelligence can only be collected in bulk; and the risk of damage to our national security interests and our law enforcement, intelligence-sharing, and diplomatic relationships should our capabilities or activities be compromised. It is, therefore, essential that national security policymakers consider carefully the value of signals intelligence activities in light of the risks entailed in conducting these activities.

To enable this judgment, the heads of departments and agencies that participate in the policy processes for establishing signals intelligence priorities and requirements shall, on an annual basis, review any priorities or requirements identified by their departments or agencies and advise the DNI whether each should be maintained, with a copy of the advice provided to the APNSA.

Additionally, the classified Annex to this directive, which supplements the existing policy process for reviewing signals intelligence activities, affirms that determinations about whether and how to conduct signals intelligence activities must carefully evaluate the benefits to our national interests and the risks posed by those activities.[6]

Sec. 4. Safeguarding Personal Information Collected Through Signals Intelligence.

All persons should be treated with dignity and respect, regardless of their nationality or wherever they might reside, and all persons have legitimate privacy interests in the handling of their personal information.[7] U.S. signals intelligence activities must, therefore, include appropriate safeguards for the personal information of all individuals, regardless of the nationality of the individual to whom the information pertains or where that individual resides.[8]

---

6. Section 3 of this directive, and the directive's classified Annex, do not apply to (1) signals intelligence activities undertaken by or for the Federal Bureau of Investigation in support of predicated investigations other than those conducted solely for purposes of acquiring foreign intelligence; or (2) signals intelligence activities undertaken in support of military operations in an area of active hostilities, covert action, or human intelligence operations.

7. Departments and agencies shall apply the term "personal information" in a manner that is consistent for U.S. persons and non-U.S. persons. Accordingly, for the purposes of this directive, the term "personal information" shall cover the same types of information covered by "information concerning U.S. persons" under section 2.3 of Executive Order 12333.

8. The collection, retention, and dissemination of information concerning "United States persons" is governed by multiple legal and policy requirements, such as those required by the Foreign Intelligence Surveillance Act and Executive Order 12333. For the purposes of this directive, the term "United States person" shall have the same meaning as it does in Executive Order 12333.

(a) *Policies and Procedures*. The DNI, in consultation with the Attorney General, shall ensure that all elements of the IC establish policies and procedures that apply the following principles for safeguarding personal information collected from signals intelligence activities. To the maximum extent feasible consistent with the national security, these policies and procedures are to be applied equally to the personal information of all persons, regardless of nationality:[9]

> i. *Minimization.* The sharing of intelligence that contains personal information is necessary to protect our national security and advance our foreign policy interests, as it enables the United States to coordinate activities across our government. At the same time, however, by setting appropriate limits on such sharing, the United States takes legitimate privacy concerns into account and decreases the risks that personal information will be misused or mishandled. Relatedly, the significance to our national security of intelligence is not always apparent upon an initial review of information: intelligence must be retained for a sufficient period of time for the IC to understand its relevance and use it to meet our national security needs. However, long-term storage of personal information unnecessary to protect our national security is inefficient, unnecessary, and raises legitimate privacy concerns. Accordingly, IC elements shall establish policies and procedures reasonably designed to minimize the dissemination and retention of personal information collected from signals intelligence activities.

> • *Dissemination*: Personal information shall be disseminated only if the dissemination of comparable information concerning U.S. persons would be permitted under section 2.3 of Executive Order 12333.

> • *Retention*: Personal information shall be retained only if the retention of comparable information concerning U.S. persons would be permitted under section 2.3 of Executive Order 12333 and shall be subject to the same retention periods as applied to comparable information concerning U.S. persons. Information for which no such determination has been made shall not be retained for more than 5 years, unless the DNI expressly determines that continued retention is in the national security interests of the United States.

> Additionally, within 180 days of the date of this directive, the DNI, in coordination with the Attorney General, the heads of other elements of the IC, and the heads of departments and agencies containing other elements of the IC, shall prepare a report evaluating possible additional dissemination and retention safeguards for personal information collected through signals intelligence, consistent with technical capabilities and operational needs.

> ii. *Data Security and Access.* When our national security and foreign policy needs require us to retain certain intelligence, it is vital that the United States take appropri-

---

9. The policies and procedures of affected elements of the IC shall also be consistent with any additional IC policies, standards, procedures, and guidance the DNI, in coordination with the Attorney General, the heads of IC elements, and the heads of any other departments containing such elements, may issue to implement these principles. This directive is not intended to alter the rules applicable to U.S. persons in Executive Order 12333, the Foreign Intelligence Surveillance Act, or other applicable law.

ate steps to ensure that any personal information contained within that intelligence is secure. Accordingly, personal information shall be processed and stored under conditions that provide adequate protection and prevent access by unauthorized persons, consistent with the applicable safeguards for sensitive information contained in relevant Executive Orders, proclamations, Presidential directives, IC directives, and associated policies. Access to such personal information shall be limited to authorized personnel with a need to know the information to perform their mission, consistent with the personnel security requirements of relevant Executive Orders, IC directives, and associated policies. Such personnel will be provided appropriate and adequate training in the principles set forth in this directive. These persons may access and use the information consistent with applicable laws and Executive Orders and the principles of this directive; personal information for which no determination has been made that it can be permissibly disseminated or retained under section 4(a)(i) of this directive shall be accessed only in order to make such determinations (or to conduct authorized administrative, security, and oversight functions).

iii. *Data Quality*. IC elements strive to provide national security policymakers with timely, accurate, and insightful intelligence, and inaccurate records and reporting can not only undermine our national security interests, but also can result in the collection or analysis of information relating to persons whose activities are not of foreign intelligence or counterintelligence value. Accordingly, personal information shall be included in intelligence products only as consistent with applicable IC standards for accuracy and objectivity, as set forth in relevant IC directives. Moreover, while IC elements should apply the IC Analytic Standards as a whole, particular care should be taken to apply standards relating to the quality and reliability of the information, consideration of alternative sources of information and interpretations of data, and objectivity in performing analysis.

iv. *Oversight*. The IC has long recognized that effective oversight is necessary to ensure that we are protecting our national security in a manner consistent with our interests and values. Accordingly, the policies and procedures of IC elements, and departments and agencies containing IC elements, shall include appropriate measures to facilitate oversight over the implementation of safeguards protecting personal information, to include periodic auditing against the standards required by this section.

The policies and procedures shall also recognize and facilitate the performance of oversight by the Inspectors General of IC elements, and departments and agencies containing IC elements, and other relevant oversight entities, as appropriate and consistent with their responsibilities. When a significant compliance issue occurs involving personal information of any person, regardless of nationality, collected as a result of signals intelligence activities, the issue shall, in addition to any existing reporting requirements, be reported promptly to the DNI, who shall determine what, if any, corrective actions are necessary. If the issue involves a non-United States person, the DNI, in consultation with the Secretary of State and the head of the notifying department or agency, shall determine whether steps should be taken to notify the relevant foreign government, consistent with the protection of sources and methods and of U.S. personnel.

(b) *Update and Publication*. Within 1 year of the date of this directive, IC elements shall update or issue new policies and procedures as necessary to implement section 4 of this directive, in coordination with the DNI. To enhance public understanding of, and promote public trust in, the safeguards in place to protect personal information, these updated or newly issued policies and procedures shall be publicly released to the maximum extent possible, consistent with classification requirements.

(c) *Privacy and Civil Liberties Policy Official.* To help ensure that the legitimate privacy interests all people share related to the handling of their personal information are appropriately considered in light of the principles in this section, the APNSA, the Director of the Office of Management and Budget (OMB), and the Director of the Office of Science and Technology Policy (OSTP) shall identify one or more senior officials who will be responsible for working with the DNI, the Attorney General, the heads of other elements of the IC, and the heads of departments and agencies containing other elements of the IC, as appropriate, as they develop the policies and procedures called for in this section.

(d) *Coordinator for International Diplomacy.* The Secretary of State shall identify a senior official within the Department of State to coordinate with the responsible departments and agencies the United States Government's diplomatic and foreign policy efforts related to international information technology issues and to serve as a point of contact for foreign governments who wish to raise concerns regarding signals intelligence activities conducted by the United States.

Sec. 5. Reports.

(a) Within 180 days of the date of this directive, the DNI shall provide a status report that updates me on the progress of the IC's implementation of section 4 of this directive.

(b) The Privacy and Civil Liberties Oversight Board is encouraged to provide me with a report that assesses the implementation of any matters contained within this directive that fall within its mandate.

(c) Within 120 days of the date of this directive, the President's Intelligence Advisory Board shall provide me with a report identifying options for assessing the distinction between metadata and other types of information, and for replacing the "need-to-share" or "need-to-know" models for classified information sharing with a Work-Related Access model.

(d) Within 1 year of the date of this directive, the DNI, in coordination with the heads of relevant elements of the IC and OSTP, shall provide me with a report assessing the feasibility of creating software that would allow the IC more easily to conduct targeted information acquisition rather than bulk collection.

Sec. 6. General Provisions.

(a) Nothing in this directive shall be construed to prevent me from exercising my constitutional authority, including as Commander in Chief, Chief Executive, and in the conduct of foreign affairs, as well as my statutory authority. Consistent with this principle, a recipient of this directive may at any time recommend to me, through the APNSA, a change to the policies and procedures contained in this directive.

(b) Nothing in this directive shall be construed to impair or otherwise affect the authority or responsibility granted by law to a United States Government department or agency, or the head thereof, or the functions of the Director of OMB relating to budgetary, administrative, or legislative proposals. This directive is intended to supplement existing processes or procedures for reviewing foreign intelligence or counterintelligence activities and should not be read to supersede such processes and procedures unless explicitly stated.

(c) This directive shall be implemented consistent with applicable U.S. law and subject to the availability of appropriations.

(d) This directive is not intended to, and does not, create any right or benefit, substantive or procedural, enforceable at law or in equity by any party against the United States, its departments, agencies, or entities, its officers, employees, or agents, or any other person.

Presidential Policy Directive, FBI Policy and Procedures

(February 2, 2015)

I. Introduction

Presidential Policy Directive 28 regarding signals intelligence activities (hereinafter "PPD-28"), issued January 17, 2014, articulates principles to guide why, whether, when, and how the United States conducts signals intelligence activities for authorized foreign intelligence and counterintelligence purposes. Specifically, section 4 of PPD-28 sets forth principles for safeguarding personal information collected from signals intelligence activities and requires Intelligence Community ("IC") elements to establish policies and procedures to apply such principles, consistent with technical capabilities and operational needs.

As stated in PPD-28, all persons should be treated with dignity and respect, regardless of their nationality or wherever they might reside, and all persons have legitimate privacy interests in the handling of their personal information. Although the FBI does not conduct "signals intelligence activities," the FBI is applying the relevant provisions of PPD-28 to information it collects pursuant to FISA section 702 to further these principles.

Although the FBI does not conduct signals intelligence activities and does not have access to unevaluated, raw, or unminimized signals intelligence, it does receive from other IC elements engaged in such activities signals intelligence information that has been evaluated, minimized, or otherwise included in finished intelligence products. These policies and procedures also address the manner in which the FBI will handle signals intelligence information in these finished intelligence products.

II. General Provisions and Authorities

Pursuant to section 1.7(i) of Executive Order 12333, as amended, the FBI is authorized to:

(1) Collect (including through clandestine means), analyze, produce, and disseminate foreign intelligence and counterintelligence to support national and departmental missions, in accordance with procedural guidelines approved by the Attorney General, after consultation with the Director;

(2) Conduct counterintelligence activities; and

(3) Conduct foreign intelligence and counterintelligence liaison relationships with intelligence, security, and law enforcement services of foreign governments or international organizations in accordance with section 1.3(b)(4) and 1.7(a)(6) of E.O. 12333.

III. Safeguarding Personal Information Pursuant to PPD-28

(A) Collection Pursuant to Section 702 of FISA

The following policies and procedures apply to the FBI's safeguarding of personal information of non-U.S. persons collected pursuant to section 702 ofFISA.[1] The policies and procedures do not alter, but rather supplement, the protections that non-U.S. persons receive pursuant to FISA, the Attorney General's Guidelines for Domestic FBI Operations, or any other applicable law.[2]

(I) Minimization

Consistent with its need to retain intelligence for a sufficient period of time to understand its relevance and to disseminate intelligence as necessary to protect national security, the FBI shall apply the following protections to personal information concerning non-U.S. persons collected pursuant to section 702.

(a) Dissemination

The FBI will disseminate personal information of non-U.S. persons collected pursuant to Section 702 of FISA only if dissemination of comparable information concerning U.S. persons would be permitted under Section 2.3 of Executive Order 12333. The FBI will also disseminate personal information concerning a non-U.S. person collected pursuant to section 702 of FISA only if the information relates specifically to an activity authorized by the Attorney General or an intelligence requirement authorized by the Director of National Intelligence, and not solely because of the person's foreign status. The FBI will disseminate personal information concerning a non-U.S. person only if the information is relevant to the underlying purpose of the dissemination. When disseminating unevaluated personal information collected pursuant to section 702 of FISA, the FBI will inform the recipient that the disseminated information may contain personal information so that the recipient can take appropriate steps to protect that information.

The FBI shall not disseminate personal information concerning a non-U.S. person collected pursuant to section 702 of FISA that is foreign intelligence solely because of the person's foreign status or location. Thus, information about the routine activities of a foreign person would not meet this standard without some indication that the information is relevant to an intelligence requirement or an authorized law enforcement activity.

The FBI shall not disseminate personal information concerning any person, including non-U.S. persons, for the purpose of suppressing or burdening criticism or dissent, or for disadvantaging persons based on their ethnicity, race, gender, sexual orientation, or religion. The FBI shall not disseminate foreign private commercial information or trade secrets to afford a competitive advantage to U.S. companies or U.S. business sectors commercially.

Unless it possesses specific information to the contrary, the FBI will presume that any evaluated or minimized section 702 information it receives from other IC elements meets these standards. The FBI will further disseminate such information only in accordance with applicable FBI and IC policies and procedures.

(b) Retention

The FBI shall not retain unevaluated personal information concerning non-U.S. persons collected pursuant to section 702 of FISA for longer than five (5) years, unless retention of comparable information concerning U.S. persons would be permitted under section 2.3 of Executive Order 12333. The FBI will retain personal information concerning a non-U.S. person collected pursuant to section 702 of FISA that is foreign intelligence only if the information relates specifically to an activity authorized by the Attorney General or an intelligence requirement authorized by the Director of National Intelligence, and not solely because of the person's foreign status. Thus, information about the routine activities of a foreign person would not meet this standard without some indication that the information is relevant to an intelligence requirement or an authorized law enforcement activity.

Unless it possesses specific information to the contrary, the FBI will presume that any evaluated or minimized section 702 information it receives from other IC elements meets these standards. The FBI will retain such information in accordance with applicable record retention policies.

(c) Queries

When querying information collected pursuant to Section 702 of FISA, the FBI will structure queries or other search terms and techniques in order to identify information relevant to a valid intelligence requirement or an authorized law enforcement activity. The FBI will focus queries about persons, regardless of nationality, on the categories of intelligence information responsive to an intelligence requirement or an authorized law enforcement activity. The FBI will minimize the review of personal information not pertinent to an intelligence requirement or an authorized law enforcement activity.

(2) *Data Security and Access*

Access to all personal information collected pursuant to section 702 of FISA - irrespective of the nationality of the person whose information is collected - is restricted to those personnel who require access in order to perform their authorized duties in support of the FBI's mission or to assist in a lawful and authorized governmental function. Such information will be maintained in either electronic or physical form in secure facilities protected by physical and technological safeguards, and with access limited by appropriate security measures. Such information will be safeguarded in accordance with applicable laws, rules, and policies, including those of the FBI, the Department of Justice, and the Office of the Director of National Intelligence.

Classified information will be stored appropriately in a secured, certified, and accredited facility, in secured databases or containers, and in accordance with other applicable requirements. The FBI's electronic system in which such information may be stored will comply with applicable law, Executive Orders, and Office of the Director of National Intelligence and Department of Justice policies and procedures regarding information security, including with regard to access controls and monitoring.

(3) *Data Quality*

Personal information concerning any person, regardless of nationality, collected pursuant to section 702 of FISA shall be included in FBI intelligence products only as consistent with applicable IC standards of analytic tradecraft as set forth in relevant IC directives.

(4) *Oversight*

The FBI will include appropriate measures to facilitate oversight over the implementation of these safeguards protecting personal information collected pursuant to section 702 of FISA, to include periodic auditing. The results of periodic auditing will be reported to the Director, Deputy Director, Executive Assistant Director for the National Security Branch, the Executive Assistant Director for the Criminal, Cyber, Response, and

Services Branch, the Executive Assistant Director of the Intelligence Branch, the Assistant Director of the Office of Integrity and Compliance, and the General Counsel.

Instances of non-compliance with these policies and procedures shall be reported to the Assistant Director of the Inspection Division, the Assistant Director of the Office of Integrity and Compliance, the FBI's Privacy and Civil Liberties Officer, and the General Counsel, all of whom, shall determine what corrective actions are necessary, if any.

Significant instances of non-compliance with these policies and procedures involving the personal information of any person collected pursuant to section 702 of FISA shall be reported promptly to the Deputy Director, who in turn will report them to the DNI pursuant to section 4 ofPPD-28.

(5) *Training*

Training on these policies and procedures shall be required in order to gain access to unevaluated information concerning non-U.S. persons collected pursuant to section 702 of FISA.

(B) Signals Intelligence Collected by Other IC Elements The following policies and procedures apply to the FBI's safeguarding of personal information of non-U.S. persons collected pursuant to signals intelligence activities conducted by other IC elements.[3]

(I) *Minimization*

(a) Dissemination

The FBI will disseminate personal information of non-U.S. persons collected through signals intelligence activities only if dissemination of comparable information concerning U.S. persons would be permitted under section 2.3 of Executive Order 12333. The FBI will disseminate personal information concerning a non-U.S. person that is foreign intelligence only if the information relates specifically to an activity authorized by the Attorney General or an intelligence requirement authorized by the Director of National Intelligence, and not solely because of the person's foreign status. Unless it possesses specific information to the contrary, the FBI will presume that any evaluated or minimized signals intelligence information it receives from other IC elements meets these standards. The FBI will disseminate such information in accordance with applicable FBI and IC policies and procedures.

(b) Retention The FBI will retain personal information of non-U.S. persons collected through signals intelligence activities only if retention of comparable information concerning U.S. persons would be permitted under section 2.3 of Executive Order 12333. The FBI will retain personal information concerning a non-U.S. person that is foreign intelligence only if the information relates specifically to an activity authorized by the Attorney General or an intelligence requirement authorized by the Director of National Intelligence, and not solely because of the person's foreign status. Unless it possesses specific information to the contrary, the FBI will presume that any evaluated or minimized signals intelligence information it receives from other IC elements meets these standards. The FBI will retain such information in accordance with applicable record retention policies.

(2) *Data Security and Access*

Access to all personal information collected through signals intelligence activities - irrespective of the nationality of the person whose information is collected- is restricted to those personnel who require access in order to perform their authorized duties in support of the FBI's mission or to assist in a lawful and authorized governmental function. Such information will be maintained in either electronic or physical form in secure facilities protected by physical and technological safeguards, and with access limited by appropriate security measures. Such information will be safeguarded in accordance with applicable laws, rules, and policies, including those of the FBI, the Department of Justice, and the Office of the Director of National Intelligence.

Classified information will be stored appropriately in a secured, certified, and accredited facility, in secured databases or containers, and in accordance with other applicable requirements. The FBI's electronic system in which such information may be stored will comply with applicable law, Executive Orders, and the Office of the Director of National Intelligence and Department of Justice policies and procedures regarding information security, including with regard to access controls and monitoring.

(3) *Data Quality*

Personal information of both U.S. and non-U.S. persons collected through signals intelligence activities shall be included in FBI intelligence products only as consistent with applicable IC standards of analytic tradecraft as set forth in relevant IC directives.

(4) *Oversight*

The FBI will include appropriate measures to facilitate oversight over the implementation of these safeguards protecting personal information, to include periodic auditing. The results of periodic auditing will be reported to the Director, Deputy Director, the Executive Assistant Director for the National Security Branch, the Executive Assistant Director for the Criminal, Cyber, Response, and Services Branch, the Executive Assistant Director of the Intelligence Branch, the Assistant Director of the Office of Integrity and Compliance, and the General Counsel.

Instances of non-compliance with these policies and procedures shall be reported to the Assistant Director of the Inspection Division, the Assistant Director of the Office of Integrity and Compliance, the FBI's Privacy and Civil Liberties Officer, and the 6 General Counsel, all of whom shall determine what corrective actions are necessary, if any.

Significant instances of non-compliance with these policies and procedures involving the personal information of any person collected through signals intelligence activities shall be reported promptly to the Deputy Director, who in turn will report them to the DNI pursuant to section 4 of PPD-28.

IV. Departures from these Procedures

The Director, Deputy Director, or an Executive Assistant Director must approve in advance any departures from these procedures and provide notice to the Director of National Intelligence and the Attorney General. If there is not time for such advance approval and a departure from these procedures is necessary because of the immediacy or gravity of a threat to the safety of persons or property or to the national security, the departure must be reported to the Director, the Director of National Intelligence, and the Attorney General as soon as possible thereafter. Notwithstanding this paragraph, all activities in all circumstances must be carried out in a manner consistent with the Constitution and laws of the United States.

V. Conclusion

These procedures are set forth solely for internal guidance within the FBI. Questions on the applicability or interpretation of these procedures should be directed to the Office of the General Counsel, which shall determine such applicability or interpretation.

Approved:

Mark F. Giuliano
Deputy Director
Federal Bureau of Investigation

CIA Signals Intelligence Activities

(February 3, 2015)

While protecting our nation through the collection of signals intelligence (SIGINT) as authorized by law and policy, the Central Intelligence Agency (CIA), referred to herein as the "Agency," is committed to protecting the personal information of all people regardless of their nationality. This regulation establishes the principles that govern how the CIA conducts SIGINT activities and codifies into formal policy many existing practices which had not been previously put forth in a single regulatory issuance.

Definitions

- **Foreign person** - means a person who does not meet the definition of "United States person" in Executive Order 12333.

- **Intelligence** - has the same meaning as it does in the National Security Act of 1947.

- **Personal information** - covers the same types of information covered by "information concerning U.S. persons" under Section 2.3 of Executive Order 12333.

- **SIGINT collected in bulk** - means the authorized collection of large quantities of signals intelligence data which, due to technical or operations considerations, is acquired without the use of discriminants (e.g., specific identifiers, selection terms, etc.).

- **United States person** - has the same meaning as it does in Executive Order 12333.

General Policy

The Agency shall not collect SIGINT unless authorized to do so by statute or Executive Order, proclamation, or other Presidential directive, and such collection shall be undertaken in accordance with the Constitution and applicable statutes, Executive Orders, proclamations, Presidential directives, Agency regulatory issuances, and implementing guidance.

- Privacy and civil liberties shall be integral considerations in the planning of SIGINT activities. SIGINT shall be collected exclusively where there is a foreign intelligence or counterintelligence purpose to support national and CIA missions and not for any other purpose.

- The collection of foreign private commercial information or trade secrets is authorized only to protect the national security of the United States or its partners and allies. It is not an authorized foreign intelligence or counterintelligence purpose to collect such information to afford a competitive advantage to U.S. companies and U.S. business sectors commercially. Certain economic purposes, such as identifying trade or sanctions violations or government influence or direction, shall not constitute competitive advantage.

- SIGINT activities shall be as tailored as feasible. In determining whether to collect SIGINT, the Agency shall consider the availability of other information, including from diplomatic and public sources. Such appropriate and feasible alternatives to SIGINT shall be prioritized by means of the least intrusive technique required to obtain the intelligence of the nature, reliability, and timeliness required.

- The collection, use, retention, and dissemination of information concerning "United States persons" are governed by multiple legal and policy requirements, such as those required by the Foreign Intelligence Surveillance Act of 1978 (FISA), the Privacy Act of 1974, and Executive Order 12333. This regulation is not intended to alter the rules applicable to U.S. persons in FISA, the Privacy Act, Executive Order 12333, or other applicable law.

Collection

Refining the Process for Collecting Signals Intelligence: The Agency shall participate in the United States Government (USG) policy processes for establishing SIGINT collection priorities and requirements.

- PPD-28 provides that the Agency must collect bulk SIGINT in certain circumstances in order to identify new or emerging threats and other vital national security information which is often hidden within the large and complex system of modern global communications. It also recognizes the privacy and civil liberties concerns raised when bulk SIGINT is collected. PPD-28 directs the Intelligence Community (IC) to assess the feasibility of alternatives that would allow the IC to conduct targeted SIGINT collection rather than bulk SIGINT collection. Accordingly, when engaging in SIGINT collection, the Agency should conduct targeted SIGINT collection activities rather than bulk SIGINT collection activities when practicable. SIGINT collection activities should be directed against specific foreign intelligence targets or topics through the use of discriminants (e.g., specific facilities, identifiers, selection terms, etc.) when practicable.

- Agency components shall consult with the Privacy and Civil Liberties Officer (PCLO) and the Executive Director of the Central Intelligence Agency (EXDIR) or their designees on novel or unique SIGINT collection activities, and any significant changes to existing SIGINT collection activities, to ensure that there are appropriate safeguards to protect personal information.

- The Agency shall, on an annual basis, review SIGINT priorities and requirements identified by the Agency and advise the Director of National Intelligence (DNI) whether each should be maintained, with a copy of the advice provided to the Assistant to the President and National Security Advisor (APNSA).

Excluded Activities: The above does not apply to SIGINT activities undertaken by the

CIA in support of:

- human intelligence (HUMINT) operations;

- covert action;

- FBI predicated law enforcement investigations other than those conducted solely for purposes of acquiring foreign intelligence; or

- military operations in an area of active hostilities.

Use of SIGINT Collected in Bulk

The Agency shall use SIGINT collected in bulk only for the purposes of detecting or countering:

- espionage and other threats and activities directed by foreign powers or their intelligence services against the United States and its interests;

- threats to the United States and its interests from terrorism;

- threats to the United States and its interests from the development, possession, proliferation, or use of weapons of mass destruction;

- cybersecurity threats;

- threats to U.S. or allied Armed Forces or other U.S. or allied personnel;

- transnational criminal threats, including illicit finance and sanctions evasion related to the other purposes identified in the section on "Use of SIGINT Collection in Bulk"; and

- any threat to the national security determined to be a permissible use of SIGINT collected in bulk in the review process established by Section 2 of PPD-28, or for any other lawful purpose, when approved by the President.

The Agency shall not use SIGINT collected in bulk for the purpose of:

- suppressing or burdening criticism or dissent;

- disadvantaging persons based upon their ethnicity, race, gender, sexual orientation, or religion;

- affording a competitive advantage to U.S. companies and U.S. business sectors commercially; or

- achieving any other purpose than those identified above.

As provided in footnote 5 of PPD-28, the prohibitions noted immediately above on the use of SIGINT collected in bulk do not apply to SIGINT collected in bulk that is temporarily acquired to facilitate the acquisition of targeted collection.

The Agency shall participate in the policy processes for reviewing the permissible uses of SIGINT collected in bulk.

The Agency shall, on an annual basis, review the Agency's use of SIGINT collected in bulk and advise the DNI and APNSA on recommended additions to or removals from the list of permissible uses of SIGINT collected in bulk.

Systems containing SIGINT collected in bulk shall record sufficient details of queries to enable oversight and compliance with permissible uses of SIGINT collected in bulk, and to enable retention determinations.

Retention and Access

Retention of personal information concerning foreign persons acquired through SIGINT activities is authorized only if the Agency has lawfully collected or received the information in accordance with FISA or Part I of Executive Order 12333 and the processes established by PPD-28, and the retention of comparable information concerning U.S. persons would be permitted under Section 2.3 of Executive Order 12333. Such information shall be subject to the same retention periods as comparable information concerning U.S. persons. Information for which no permanent retention determination has been made shall not be retained for more than five (5) years, unless the DNI expressly determines that continued retention is in the national security interests of the United States. Information for which no permanent retention determination has been made may be retained for up to five (5) years, or the extended period approved by the DNI, to determine whether it falls within one of the following categories that meet the standard for permanent retention:

- information that is publicly available or collected with the consent of the person concerned;

- information constituting foreign intelligence or counterintelligence. If the Agency is permanently retaining personal information concerning a foreign person because it is foreign intelligence, the information must relate to an authorized intelligence requirement, and cannot be retained solely because of the person's foreign status.

Thus, for example, personal information about the routine activities of a foreign person may not be retained unless it relates to an authorized foreign intelligence requirement;

- information obtained in the course of a lawful foreign intelligence, counterintelligence, international drug or international terrorism investigation;

- information needed to protect the safety of any persons or organizations, including those who are targets, victims or hostages of international terrorist organizations;

- information needed to protect foreign intelligence or counterintelligence sources, methods and activities from unauthorized disclosure;

- information concerning persons who are reasonably believed to be potential sources or contacts for the purpose of determining their suitability or credibility;

- information arising out of a lawful personnel, physical or communications security investigation;

- information acquired by overhead reconnaissance not directed at specific U.S. persons;

- incidentally obtained information that may indicate involvement in activities that may violate Federal, state, local, or foreign laws; and

- information necessary for administrative purposes.

Personal information acquired through SIGINT activities for which no determination has been made that it can be permissibly disseminated or retained shall be accessed only in order to make such determinations (or to conduct authorized administrative, security, compliance, and oversight functions).

Adequate protections of personal information shall be provided to prevent unauthorized access, consistent with the applicable safeguards for sensitive information contained in relevant Executive Orders, proclamations, Presidential directives, Intelligence Community Directives (ICDs), and associated policies.

Access to personal information acquired through SIGINT activities shall be limited to authorized and trained personnel, such as personnel responsible for analyzing and processing the information who have a need to know the information in order to perform their mission, consistent with the personnel security requirements of relevant Executive Orders, ICDs, and associated policies.

Personnel will be provided appropriate and adequate training in the principles set forth in this regulation and any associated guidance before being authorized access to unevaluated and unminimized personal information acquired through SIGINT activities. Training is required for those personnel who engage in collection requirements, targeting, or other disciplines that deal with SIGINT collection. Further, administrators and other support personnel who require access to these collections also must be trained prior to being granted access. Failure to obtain or maintain training requirements will result in the loss of access until requirements are met.

Personnel querying databases containing information acquired through SIGINT activities shall structure query terms and techniques in a manner reasonably designed to identify intelligence relevant to an authorized intelligence requirement and minimize the review of personal information not relevant to an authorized intelligence requirement.

Systems containing SIGINT shall record sufficient details of purges to enable oversight and compliance with retention policies.

Dissemination

Dissemination of personal information concerning foreign persons acquired through SIGINT activities is authorized only if the Agency has lawfully collected or received the information in accordance with FISA or Part I of Executive Order 12333 and the processes established by PPD-28, and the dissemination of comparable information concerning U.S. persons would be permitted under Section 2.3 of Executive Order 12333, as listed in the Retention Section above. If the Agency is disseminating personal information concerning a foreign person because it is foreign intelligence, the information must relate to an authorized intelligence requirement, and cannot be disseminated solely because of the person's foreign status. Thus, for example, personal information about the routine activities of a foreign person may not be disseminated unless it relates to an authorized foreign intelligence requirement.

The Agency shall establish policies and procedures reasonably designed to minimize the retention and dissemination of personal information acquired through SIGINT activities.

The Agency shall include personal information in intelligence products and reports only as consistent with applicable IC standards for accuracy and objectivity, and as necessary to meet an analytic or operational purpose, as set forth in relevant IC directives.

When disseminating unevaluated SIGINT that may contain personal information, the Agency will inform the recipient that the dissemination may contain personal information so that the recipient can take appropriate steps to protect that information.

Dissemination of personal information acquired through SIGINT activities to a foreign government is authorized only if the dissemination meets the following criteria:

- the dissemination is in the interests of the United States; and

- the dissemination complies with applicable laws, Executive Orders, and IC policies.

Compliance

Agency policies and procedures shall include appropriate measures to facilitate compliance and oversight of the implementation of safeguards protecting personal information acquired through SIGINT activities, to include periodic auditing against the standards required by this regulation and implementing guidance, and training for personnel authorized to access such information.

Agency information systems will be designed to monitor activity in datasets involving personal information and facilitate the monitoring, recording, and auditing of queries of personal information.

The Agency shall notify personnel how they may securely report violations of law, regulation, or policy.

When a significant compliance issue occurs involving personal information of any person, regardless of nationality, collected as a result of SIGINT activities, the issue shall, in addition to any existing reporting requirements, be reported promptly to the PCLO, who shall determine what, if any, corrective actions are necessary. All significant compliance issues involving personal information shall be promptly reported to the DNI. If the issue involves a foreign person, the DNI, in consultation with the Secretary of State and the Director of the Central Intelligence Agency (D/CIA), shall determine whether steps should be taken to notify the relevant foreign government, consistent with the protection of sources and methods and of U.S. personnel.

Responsibilities

The Director of the Central Intelligence Agency (D/CIA) shall approve any exception to any provision of this regulation that is not required by the Constitution or a statute, Executive Order, proclamation, or Presidential directive, and notify, and if practicable consult in advance, the ODNI and the National Security Division (NSD) of the Department of Justice (DOJ).

The Deputy Director of Central Intelligence Agency (DD/CIA) or designee shall oversee the annual review of SIGINT priorities and requirements identified by the Agency and advise the D/CIA, for subsequent passage to the DNI and APNSA, on whether such activities should be maintained; manage the Agency's participation in the policy review process for reviewing SIGINT collection activities, to include sensitive SIGINT collection activities and the use of bulk SIGINT.

The Executive Director of the Central Intelligence Agency (EXDIR) or designee shall:

- Establish CIA policies, procedures, and guidance for the implementation of this regulation to include;

- Training;

- Limitations on the use of bulk SIGINT;

- Review of SIGINT collection activities;

- Procedures to minimize the retention and dissemination of personal information acquired through SIGINT activities; and

- Other issues, as required;

- In coordination with the Privacy and Civil Liberties Officer (PCLO),

- Coordinate on novel or unique collection activities, or significant changes to existing collection activities, to ensure that appropriate safeguards are in place to protect personal information acquired through such activities;

- Establish procedures to receive, evaluate, and report significant compliance incidents for this regulation to the DNI; and

- Review requests for extended retention of personal information concerning foreign persons acquired through SIGINT activities and advise the DD/CIA and the D/CIA whether they should be transmitted to the DNI;

- Monitor implementation and compliance with the established policies, procedures, and guidance for PPD-28.

The Inspector General shall as part of the IG's statutory responsibilities, conduct audits, inspections, and investigations of CIA programs and operations to determine compliance with applicable laws and regulations.

The PCLO shall:

- provide compliance advice and assistance regarding the requirements of PPD-28, this regulation, or any additional procedures or guidance for PPD-28;

- coordinate on novel or unique collection activities, or significant changes to existing collection activities, to ensure that appropriate safeguards are in place to protect personal information acquired through such activities;

- conduct periodic oversight and assessments of personal information acquired through SIGINT activities to ensure compliance with privacy and civil liberties;

- advise the D/CIA, the DD/CIA, the EXDIR or an appropriate designee and Heads of Directorates and Independent Offices on the development of:

- procedures to safeguard personal information acquired through SIGINT activities; and

- privacy and civil liberties training in support of PPD-28 principles;

- produce privacy and civil liberties reports, in coordination with the affected Directorates and Independent Offices;

- report significant compliance issues involving personal information acquired through SIGINT activities to the D/CIA and DNI; and

- coordinate on requests for extended retention of personal information concerning foreign persons acquired through SIGINT activities for privacy and civil liberties issues.

The Heads of CIA Directorates and Independent Offices shall:

- implement the policies, procedures, and guidance established by this regulation in coordination with the EXDIR or designee;

- provide training to personnel who require access in the performance of their duties to personal information acquired through SIGINT activities in the performance of their duties;

- initiate requests to the EXDIR or designee, in coordination with the PCLO, for extended retention of personal information of foreign persons acquired through SIGINT activities;

- on an annual basis, review SIGINT priorities and requirements identified by respective offices and advise the EXDIR or designee on whether these should be maintained;

- working with the EXDIR or designee, participate in the policy review process for SIGINT activities, to include sensitive SIGINT collection activities and permissible uses of bulk SIGINT;

- assist the EXDIR or designee, IG, and PCLO in conducting oversight and periodic assessments of SIGINT collection activities containing personal information; and

- consult with the EXDIR or designee and PCLO on novel or unique SIGINT collection activities and significant changes to existing SIGINT collection activities, to ensure that appropriate safeguards are in place to protect personal information acquired through such activities.

Agency personnel shall:

- comply with the principles, policies, and procedures of this regulation and any implementing guidance; and

- report compliance issues to the appropriate Head of Directorate or Independent Office and the PCLO.

National Security Agency
PPD-28 Section 4 Procedures

(Jan. 22, 2015)

Presidential Policy Directive 28 (PPD-28)[1] articulates principles to guide United States SIGINT activities for authorized foreign intelligence and counterintelligence purposes. In response to PPD-28 Section 4, NSA has developed Supplemental Procedures to United States Signals Intelligence Directive, USSID SP0018.[2] USSID SPOO18 implements the Attorney General-approved procedures contained in Department of Defense (DoD) Regulation 5240.1-R and its Classified Annex that govern NSA's SIGINT activities. USSID SP0018 prescribes specific minimization policies and procedures for U.S. Persons, and assigns responsibilities to assure that the missions and functions of the United States SIGINT System (USSS) are conducted in a manner that safeguards the constitutional rights of U.S. Persons. All personnel who are conducting E.O. 12333 SIGINT activities under the direction, authority, or control of the Director of the National Security Agency throughout the SIGINT lifecycle are responsible to protect the privacy of U.S. Persons,

PPD-28 Section 4 directs the Intelligence Community (IC) to establish policies and procedures for safeguarding personal information collected during signals intelligence activities. NSA's Supplemental Procedures are the guidance and procedures for implementing this direction from the President. Consistent with the requirements of Section 4.(a), NSA's Supplemental Procedures extend comparable safeguards currently provided for U.S. Persons to all persons, regardless of nationality, Section 4.(b) requires IC elements to issue procedures by 17 January 2015, one year after the President released PPD-28. As specified in section 4.(c), NSA worked with the White House in developing these policies and procedures to ensure the proper civil liberties and privacy safeguards are in place.

The new Supplemental Procedures are entitled "USSID SP0018 Supplemental Procedures for the Collection, Processing, Retention, and Dissemination of Signals Intelligence Information and Data Containing Personal Information of Non-United States Persons," and implement the privacy and civil liberties protections afforded to non-U.S. persons in a manner that is comparable, to the extent consistent with national security, to the privacy protections afforded to U.S. persons. These new Supplemental Procedures are written as a guide to SIGINT professionals. Wherever possible, language in the Supplemental Procedures mirrors the terminology and structure of parallel provisions in the USSID SP0018 and in PD-28.

---

1. http://www.whitehouse.govithe-press-office/2014/01/17ipresidential-policy-directive-signals-intelligence-activities Released by the White House on January 17, 2014, PPD-28 states that, "signals intelligence activities must take into account that all persons should be treated with dignity and respect, regardless of their nationality or wherever they might reside, and that all persons have legitimate privacy interests in the handling of their personal information."

2. https://www.dni.govifilesidocuments/1118/CLEANEDFinal%2OUSIID%20 SP0018. pdf USSID SPOO18 was approved for release by the National Security Agency on 13 November 2013.

(U) USSID SP0018 SUPPLEMENTAL PROCEDURES FOR THE COLLECTION, PROCESSING, RETENTION, AND DISSEMINATION OF SIGNALS INTELLIGENCE INFORMATION AND DATA CONTAINING PERSONAL INFORMATION OF NON-UNITED STATES PERSONS

ISSUE DATE

(U) USSID SP0018 Supplemental Procedures for the Collection, Processing, Retention and Dissemination of Signals Intelligence Information and Data Containing Personal Information of Non-United States Persons establishes guidance and procedures for implementing Presidential Policy Directive (PPD) – 28.

(U) This is the initial issuance of USSID SP0018 Supplemental Procedures for implementing PPD-28.

(U) OFFICE OF PRIMARY RESPONSIBILITY: NSA/CSS. Signals Intelligence Directorate, Signals Intelligence Policy and Corporate Issues Staff.

(U) The Executive Agent for this USSID is:

> Ron Moultrie
>
> Signals Intelligence Director
>
> 12 January 2015

(U) TABLE OF CONTENTS

(U) <u>Letter of Promulgation</u>

(U) Sections

(U) Refer to the <u>U.S. SIGNIT System Dictionary</u> for all signals intelligence (SIGINT) terms and definitions.

(U) USSID SP0018 SUPPLEMENTAL PROCEDURES FOR THE COLLECTION, PROCESSING, RETENTION, AND DISSEMINATION OF SIGNALS INTELLIGENCE INFORMATION AND DATA CONTAINING PERSONAL INFORMATION OF NON-UNITED STATES PERSONS

SECTION 1 – (U) PREFACE

(U) Purpose

1.1   (U) USSID SP0018 prescribes policies and procedures and assigns responsibilities to ensure that the missions and functions of the United States SIGINT System (USSS) are conducted in a manner that safeguards the constitutional rights of U.S. persons. These Supplemental Procedures implement the privacy and civil liberties protections afforded to non-U.S. persons, by Presidential Policy Directive No. 28 (PPD-28), "Signals Intelligence Activities," dated 17 January 2014.

(U) Scope

1.2   (U) Unless otherwise specified, these Supplemental Procedures shall apply to SIGINT activities conducted in order to acquire communications or information about communications, except that it shall not apply to SIGINT activities undertaken to test or develop SIGINT equipment or capabilities. The provisions of Annex D to USSID SP0018 govern SIGINT activities undertaken to test or develop SIGINT equipment or capabilities.

1.3   (U) For purposes of these Supplemental Procedures, the term "foreign intelligence" includes foreign intelligence and counterintelligence,

1.4   (U) Unless otherwise stated, these Supplemental Procedures use the same definitions contained in Section 9 of USSID 5P0018.

(U) Departures

1.5   (U) Generally. If, due to unanticipated or extraordinary circumstances, NSA determines that it must take action in apparent departure from these procedures to protect the national security of the United States, such action may be taken upon the approval of the NSA Director or a designee, following consultation with the Office of the Director of National Intelligence, the National Security Division of the Department of Justice, and the Office of the Secretary of Defense.

1.6   (U) Departures in Emergency Situations. If there is insufficient time for approval of a departure from these procedures in accordance with the preceding paragraph because of the immediacy or gravity of a threat to the safety of persons or property or to the national security, the NSA Director or the Director's senior representative present may approve a departure from these procedures. The General Counsel of NSA will be notified as soon thereafter as possible. The General Counsel of NSA will provide prompt written notice of any such departures to the Office of the Director of National Intelligence, to the National Security Division of the Department of Justice, and to the Office of the Secretary of Defense. Notwithstanding this paragraph, all activities in all circumstances must be carried out in a manner consistent with the Constitution and laws of the United States.

1.7   (U) Nothing in these procedures shall prohibit or restrict:

a. (U) The retention, processing, analysis or dissemination of information necessary to avoid unauthorized collection, retention, or dissemination; or to avoid the collection, retention, and dissemination of information that is not foreign intelligence information;

b. (U) The retention of information for data integrity backup purposes, provided that only personnel responsible for maintaining and administering such information have access to it. In the event that information retained for backup purposes must be restored, NSA shall apply these procedures to the restored information. Information will be retained for data backup purposes for such time as is reasonably necessary;

c. (U) NSA's ability to conduct vulnerability or network assessments in order to ensure that NSA systems are not or have not been compromised. Notwithstanding any other section in these procedures, information used by NSA to conduct vulnerability or network assessments may be retained for one year solely for that limited purpose. Any information retained for this purpose may be disseminated only in accordance with the applicable provisions of these procedures;

d. (U) The retention, processing, analysis or dissemination of information necessary to perform lawful oversight functions, including lawful oversight functions of the Congress of the United States, the Department of Justice, Office of the Director of National Intelligence, or the applicable Offices of the Inspectors General;

e. (U) The retention, processing, analysis or dissemination of information necessary to comply with law; an order of a federal court or the rules of such a court; or these procedures.

SECTION 2 - (U) REFERENCES

2.1   (U) The following documents are references to these Supplemental Procedures:

a.   (U) 50 U.S.C. 1801, et seq., Foreign Intelligence Surveillance Act (FISA) of 1978 as amended.

b.   (U) Executive Order 12333, "United States Intelligence Activities," as amended 30 July 2008.

c.   (U) Presidential Policy Directive No. 28, "Signals Intelligence Activities," dated 17 January 2014.

d.   (U) Department of Defense Directive 5100.20, "National Security Agency/Central Security Service (NSA/CSS)," dated 26 January 2010.

SECTION 3 - (U) POLICY

(U) Policy and the USSS Foreign Communications Mission

3.1   (U) The collection of SIGINT shall be authorized by statute or Executive Order, proclamation, or other Presidential directive and undertaken in accordance with the Constitution and applicable statutes, Executive Orders, proclamations, and Presidential directives.

3.2   (U) Privacy and civil liberties shall be integral considerations in the planning of USSS SIGINT activities. The USSS shall not collect SIGINT for the purpose of suppressing or burdening criticism or dissent, or for disadvantaging persons based on their ethnicity, race, color, gender, sexual orientation, or religion.

3.3   (U) The policy of the USSS is to TARGET or COLLECT only FOREIGN COMMUNICATIONS for foreign intelligence purposes to support national and departmental missions, including support for the conduct of military operations. If the USSS COLLECTS personal information of non-U.S. persons, it will process, analyze, disseminate, and retain such personal information only in accordance with these Supplemental Procedures. The USSS shall apply the term "personal information" in a manner that is consistent for U.S. persons and non-U.S. persons. Accordingly, for the purposes of these Supplemental Procedures, the term "personal information" shall cover the same types of information covered by "information concerning U.S. persons" under Section 2.3 of Executive Order 12333.

3.4   (U) The collection of foreign private commercial information or trade secrets is authorized only to protect the national security of the United States or its partners and allies. It is not an authorized foreign intelligence or counterintelligence purpose to collect such information to afford a competitive advantage to U.S. companies and U.S. business sectors commercially. Certain economic purposes, such as identifying trade or sanctions violations or government influence or direction, shall not constitute competitive advantage.

3.5   (U) SIGINT activities shall be as tailored as feasible. In determining whether to collect SIGINT, the USSS shall consider the availability of other information, including from diplomatic and public sources. Such appropriate and feasible alternatives to SIGINT should be prioritized.

SECTION 4 - (U) COLLECTION

4.1   (U) SIGINT activities that take place in response to foreign intelligence requirements, for example, those specified in the National Intelligence Priorities Framework, the National SIGINT Priorities Framework, and such follow-on direction or guidance that may be provided, as appropriate, by the President, the Director of National Intelligence, the Secretary of Defense, or DIRNSA/CHCSS as the SIGINT Functional Manager may result in the acquisition of communications that contain personal information of non-U.S. persons.

4.2   (U) Whenever practicable, collection will occur through the use of one or more SELECTION TERMS in order to focus the collection on specific foreign intelligence targets (e.g., a specific, known international terrorist or terrorist group) or specific foreign intelligence topics (e.g., the proliferation of weapons of mass destruction by a foreign power or its agents). In addition, if a collection method is regulated by FISA, the collection method will not be employed until the collection has been authorized in the manner prescribed by FISA. Collection acquired as the result of an authorization under FISA will be handled in accordance with these procedures and with any applicable minimization procedures adopted by the Attorney General and approved by the Foreign Intelligence Surveillance Court to govern the collection. For collection that is not regulated by FISA, the collection will be handled in accordance with these procedures and USSID SP0018, including its Annexes, as applicable.

SECTION 5 - (U) PROCESSING

(U) Intercepted Material

5.1   (U) Forwarding of Intercepted Material. FOREIGN COMMUNICATIONS collected by the USSS may be forwarded as intercepted to NSA/CSS, intermediate processing facilities, and collaborating centers for further processing and analysis to determine whether the communications contain foreign intelligence. 5.2 (U) Information from nonpublic communications acquired in bulk[1] that contain personal information to, from, or about non-U.S. persons may be used only for the purposes of detecting and countering:[2]

     a.   (U) Espionage and other threats and activities directed by foreign powers or their intelligence services against the United States and its interests;

     b.   (U) Threats to the United States and its interests from terrorism;

     c.   (U) Threats to the United States and its interests from the development, possession, proliferation, or use of weapons of mass destruction;

     d.   (U) Cybersecurity threats;

     e.   (U) Threats to U.S. or allied armed forces or other U.S or allied personnel; and

     f.   (U) Transnational criminal threats, including illicit finance and sanctions evasion related to the other purposes described above.

SECTION 6 - (U) RETENTION

(U) Retention of Communications

6.1   (U) Retention of Nonpublic Communications that Contain Personal Information of Non-U.S. Persons.

---

1.   (U) References to SIGINT collected in "bulk" mean the authorized collection of large quantities of SIGINT data that, because of technical or operational considerations, is acquired without the use of discriminants (e.g., without the use of specific identifiers or selection terms).

2.   (U) The limitations contained in this section do not apply to SIGINT data that is temporarily acquired to facilitate targeted collection, such as search and development activities permitted by Paragraph E1.2.a. of Annex E of USSID SP0018 or the processing of a signal that is necessary to select specific communications for forwarding for intelligence analysis. In contrast, intelligence analysis, such as communications metadata analysis, of SIGINT data collected in bulk that has not been limited through the use of one or more SELECTION TERMS (as described above in paragraph 4.2) will be subject to the limitations contained in this section.

a. (U) Nonpublic communications that are acquired by the USSS that contain personal information of non-U.S. persons may be retained in their original or transcribed form only as follows: for up to 5 years unless the Director of National Intelligence (DNI) or the DNI's designee has expressly determined in writing that continued retention is in the national security interests of the United States. Information that has not been processed into an intelligible form because of unknown communication methods, encryption, or other methods of concealing secret meaning is not subject to the foregoing retention limit; however, the up-to-5-year retention period for such information will begin when the information has been made intelligible.

b. (U) Communications that could be disseminated under Section 7, below (i.e., without elimination of references to specific non-U.S. persons or deletion of personal information of non-U.S. persons) may be retained in their original or transcribed form.

c. (U) Personal information of non-U.S. persons obtained during SIGINT operations shall be processed and stored under conditions that provide adequate protection and prevent access by unauthorized persons, consistent with the applicable safeguards for sensitive information contained in relevant Executive Orders, proclamations, Presidential Directives, Intelligence Community (IC) Directives, and associated policies. Access to such personal information of non-U.S. persons shall be limited to authorized personnel with a need to know the information to perform their mission, consistent with the personnel security requirements of relevant Executive Orders, IC Directives, and associated policies. Such personnel will be provided appropriate and adequate training concerning the requirements of these procedures.

SECTION 7 - (U) DISSEMINATION

(U) Focus of SIGINT Products and Services

7.1   (U) All SIGINT products and services will be written so as to focus solely on the provision of foreign intelligence to support national and departmental missions, including support for the conduct of military operations.

(U) Dissemination of Personal Information

7.2   (U) Personal information of non-U.S. persons obtained with the consent of the individual to whom it pertains may be disseminated in accordance with the terms of the consent. The USSS may also disseminate personal information, including personal information that specifically identifies or tends to identify one or more non-U.S. persons, if the personal information (i) is publicly available; (ii) is related to an authorized foreign intelligence requirement; (iii) is related to a crime that has been, is being, or is about to be committed; or (iv) indicates a possible threat to the safety of any person or organization. If the USSS is disseminating the personal information because it relates to a foreign intelligence requirement, it may not disseminate it solely because of the person's foreign status. Thus, for example, personal information about the routine activities of a non-U.S. person would not be disseminated without some indication that the personal information is related to an authorized foreign intelligence requirement,

(U) When disseminating unevaluated SIGINT that may contain personal information, the USSS should inform the recipient that the dissemination may contain personal information so that the recipient can take appropriate steps to protect that information.

(U) Improper Dissemination

7.3   (U) If personal information of a non-U.S. person is improperly disseminated, the incident must be reported to the SIGINT Directorate's (STD's) Information Sharing Services Group (S1S) and Oversight and Compliance Organization (SV) within 24 hours upon recognition of the error for remediation and follow-on reporting to the DNI in accordance with the provisions of PPD-28.

SECTION 8 - (U) RESPONSIBILITIES

(U) Inspector General

8.1   (U) The NSA/CSS Inspector General (IG) may perform general oversight of NSA/CSS

activities to ensure compliance with these Supplemental Procedures.

(U) General Counsel

8.2   (U) The NSA General Counsel (GC) shall provide legal advice and assistance to all elements of the USSS regarding the requirements of PPD-28 and the implementation guidance contained in these Supplemental Procedures.

(U) Civil Liberties and Privacy Director

8.3   (U) The NSA/CSS Civil Liberties and Privacy Director shall:

a.   (U) Provide civil liberties and privacy advice and assistance regarding the requirements of PPD-28 and the implementation guidance contained in these Supplemental Procedures.

b.   (U) Implement the guidance issued by the DNI for conducting SIGINT reviews and assessments from a civil liberties and privacy perspective, including assessments of the adequacy of safeguards to protect personal information that are either proposed or in place for new or unique SIGINT collection programs.

(U) Compliance Director

8.4   (U) The NSA/CSS Director of Compliance shall provide compliance advice and assistance regarding the requirements of PPD-28 and the implementation guidance contained in these procedures in coordination with SV.

(U) Enterprise Risk Management

8.5   (U) The NSA/CSS Enterprise Risk Management Officer shall provide advice and assistance regarding the requirements of PPD-28 and the implementation guidance contained in these procedures.

(U) Signals Intelligence Director

8.6   (U) The NSA/CSS Signals Intelligence Director shall:

a.   (U) Ensure that **all** SIGINT production personnel conducting SIGINT production activities under DIRNSA/CHCSS authorities understand and maintain a high degree of awareness and sensitivity to the requirements of these Supplemental Procedures.

b.   (U) Apply the provisions of these Supplemental Procedures to all SIGINT production activities governed by PPD-28 that are conducted under DIRNSA/CHCSS authorities. The SID staff focal point for USSID SP0018 matters is

c.   (U) Conduct necessary reviews of SIGINT production activities and practices governed by PPD-28 to ensure consistency with these Supplemental Procedures. These reviews will include periodic auditing against the standards required by these Supplemental Procedures.

d. (U) Ensure that all new major requirements levied on the USSS or internally generated activities are considered for review by the GC. All activities that raise questions of law or the proper interpretation of these Supplemental Procedures must be reviewed by the prior to acceptance or execution,

(U) All Elements of the USSS

8.7   (U) **All** elements of the USSS

a.   (U) Implement these Supplemental Procedures upon receipt.

b.   (U) Establish supplemental guidance, processes, and procedures or amend existing guidance, processes, and procedures as required to ensure adherence to these Supplemental Procedures. A copy of such shall be forwarded to NSA/CSS, Attn: SV.

c.   (U) Immediately inform the SIGINT Director of any tasking or instructions that appear to require actions at variance with these Supplemental Procedures.

d.   (U) In accordance with existing procedures, report to the NSA/CSS 1G and consult with the NSA GC on all activities that may raise a question of compliance with these Supplemental Procedures. When a significant compliance issue occurs involving personal information of any person, regardless of nationality, collected as a result of SIGINT activities, the issue **shall,** in addition to any existing reporting requirements, be reported promptly to the Director, for follow-on reporting to the DNI in accordance with PPD-28.